WORDS TO RHYME WITH

Books by Willard R. Espy

Bold New Program
The Game of Words
Omak Me Yours Tonight
Oysterville: Roads to Grandpa's Village
An Almanac of Words at Play
Another Almanac of Words at Play
A Children's Almanac of Words at Play
The Life and Works of Mr. Anonymous
O Thou Improper, Thou Uncommon Noun
Say It Me Way
Have a Word on Me
Espygrams
The Garden of Eloquence
Word Puzzles
Words to Rhyme With

WORDS TO RHYME WITH

WILLARD R. ESPY

AN OWL BOOK

HENRY HOLT AND COMPANY
NEW YORK

Copyright © 1986 by Willard R. Espy
All rights reserved, including the right to reproduce
this book or portions thereof in any form.
Published by Henry Holt and Company, Inc.,
115 West 18th Street, New York, New York 10011.
Published in Canada by Fitzhenry & Whiteside Limited,
195 Allstate Parkway, Markham, Ontario L3R 4T8.

Library of Congress Cataloging-in-Publication Data
Espy, Willard R.
Words to rhyme with.
"An Owl book."
Reprint. Originally published: New York : Facts
on File Publications, c1986.
Includes index.
1. English language—Rhyme—Dictionaries.
2. English language—Versification.   I. Title.
PE1519.E87 1988   423′.1   88-3259
ISBN 0-8050-0447-5 (pbk.)

First published in hardcover by Facts on File Publications
in 1986.
First Owl Book Edition—1988

Printed in the United States of America
10 9 8 7 6 5 4 3 2 1

ISBN 0-8050-0447-5

YOU'D BE A POET, BUT
YOU HEAR IT'S TOUGH?

You'd be a poet, but you hear it's tough?
  No problem. Just be strict about one rule:
No high-flown words, unless your aim is fluff;
  The hard thought needs the naked syllable.
For giggles, gauds like *pseudoantidis-*
  establishment fulfill the purpose well;
But when you go for guts, the big words miss:
  Trade *"pandemonic regions"* in for *"hell."*

. . . *Important* poems? Oh . . . excuse the snort . . .
  Sack scansion, then—and grammar, sense, and rhyme.
They only lie around to spoil the sport—
  They're potholes on the road to the sublime.

And poets with important things to say
Don't write Important Poems anyway.

Contents

Author's Note

It is not unusual for the writers of handbooks like this one to slip in few verses of their own making. I have gone a bit further than that. In this book I resurrect no moth-eaten old lines from such has-beens as Shakespeare or Milton. With the exception of one borrowed quatrain from the Latin and a contributed verse consisting of two one-letter words in two lines, *all* the verses are my own. Most of those in the early chapters have been published before (some appear here in slightly modified form); most of those in the rhyming list, and I think all those in the glossary, were written specially for this book.

Mind you, these are not POems. They are jingles—nominies—doggerel—amphigo-ries. They should serve to remind you that one need not be a Poet with a capital P to have a capital time putting rhymes together. They should also challenge you to prove that at least you can rhyme better than *that*.

W. R. E.

To Charles F. Dery: a Dedication

Some sleepers, myself included, occasionally dream in color; but of my acquaintance, only Charles F. Dery admits to dreaming regularly in puns. In the example he described most recently, a young woman turns down his offer of a canoe ride: "I hear," she explains, "that you are a big tipper."

That Charles, in his eighties, continues to pun even when asleep is itself enough to justify this dedication, but I have a defensive reason for it as well. He is a person of deadly critical faculties, sometimes loosely leashed; a few appreciative words written now may save me from having to read a twenty-page letter, with footnotes, listing just the more egregious errors he has uncovered in his first half-hour with WORDS TO RHYME WITH.

The preceding paragraph was a joke, Charles, I owe you this dedication because when it comes to choosing the right word for the occasion you are the quickest draw in the West. You are, moreover, the person who provided me with not one rhyme for "purple" but two, both from Scotland—first *hirple*, meaning "gimpy," and then the glorious *curple*, meaning "horse's ass." Language for you is both a mistress to embrace and a divinity to worship. I have found you a peerless guide to the magical world of words at play, and count you a dear friend to boot.

Thank you, Charles.

W.R.E.

Acknowledgments

WORDS TO RHYME WITH aches from every ill a rhyming guide produced by an amateur, more or less single-handedly, is heir to. Misspellings, missed rhymes, misplaced stresses and the like abound. I should have hired a crew.

Still, others were present, or almost so, at the creation, most of them without realizing it. I cannot think of a way to blame them for my errors, but at least they should share the credit for any redeeming features you find here.

Steven Wortman, for instance, turned over the first earth for this book back in 1981. I gave him as many different rhyming dictionaries as I could find in the bookstores, and he tirelessly and expertly collated the rhymes.

So the authors of those rhyming dictionaries are in some measure the authors of this one. I do not remember who they all were, but I do recall Burges Johnson, who wrote *New Rhyming Dictionary and Poet's Handbook* (1931), Clement Wood, author of *The Complete Rhyming Dictionary and Poet's Craft Book* (1934), and Frances Stillman, whose *The Poet's Manual and Rhyming Dictionary* appeared in England in 1966. More recently I found unexpected words in *The Penguin Rhyming Dictionary* (1985), by Rosalind Fergusson.

I next leafed through *The American Heritage Dictionary* (1969), a top-drawer reference at university level. From there I proceeded to four unabridged dictionaries: *The Encyclopaedic Dictionary* (1896), which is less comprehensive than today's mastodons, but lends comfort by its admirably simple phonetic system; *Webster's New International Dictionary*, Second Edition (1959); *Webster's Third New International Dictionary* (1961, with addenda in 1981); and *The Oxford English Dictionary* (1970, with supplements through SCZ).

I watched for additional words in the course of my general reading. Since many were too new on the scene to show up in my regular references, I checked their bona fides in *The Barnhart Dictionary of New English Words Since 1963* and *The Second Barnhart Dictionary of New English Words*, both by Clarence L. Barnhart, Sol Steinmetz, and Robert K. Reinhart; *The Morrow Book of New Words*, by N. H. and S. K. Mager; and Merriam-Webster's *9,000 Words*, a supplement to the Third.

Three teeming sources of outré terms were *Words*, by Paul Dickson; *Mrs. Byrne's Dictionary of Unusual, Obscure, and Preposterous Words*, by Josefa Heifetz Byrne; and *Hobble-de-hoy, The Word Game for Geniuses*, by Elizabeth Seymour. The extra words ending in -mancy in Appendix B are from *Words*. Those ending in -mania and -phobia (Appendices C and D) are from a remarkable collection, still unpublished as I write, by Rudy Ondrejka.

Richard E. Priest volunteered over drinks one day the elegant locution *sesquitricentennial*, meaning "four hundred and fiftieth." I owe to William Cole a persuasive rationale for taking all the trouble this book required. He pointed out that tens and tens of thousands of poets nowadays shun rhyme as if it were herpes. They will need *Words to Rhyme With* to know which words to avoid.

Jan McDonald typed the glossary. The speed of her word processor matches that of the space shuttle, and she appears incapable of hitting the wrong key. Recalcitrant words (*hippopotomonstrosesquipedalian* is a minor example) flowed flawlessly from her fingers, along with their phonetic equivalents (in this instance, *hip.o.pot'o.mons'tro.ses'kwi.pi.dāl'yun*).

I extend warm thanks to Steven Wortman; to Burges Johnson and Clement Wood (though they can scarcely be still alive); to Frances Stillman, Rosaline Fergusson, and Elizabeth Seymour; to the compilers of the rhyming dictionaries I have forgotten; to those responsible for the other standard dictionaries on my list; to Messrs. Barnhart, Steinmetz, Reinhart, and Mager (though I have only initials for the given names of the Magers; perhaps they are Madams or Mademoiselles); to Mrs. Byrne, Mr. Dickson, and Mr. Ondrejka; to Richard Priest; to Bill Cole; and to Jan McDonald.

And especially, to Louise. For better or worse, she once said. For better or worse, this book could not have been completed without her.

Espy Verses from Earlier Books

My thanks to the following publishers for permission to use the verses indicated:

Bramhall House, *The Game of Words:* A Dream of Couth; Applesauce; Drinking Song; Looking Glass Logic; New Words for an Old Saw; Noel, Noel; Oops! You Almost Picked Up the Check; On an Aging Prude; Passion's a Personal Perception; Singular Singulars, Peculiar Plurals; The Cry of a Cat's a Meow; Venereally Speaking; Words in Labor.

Doubleday & Company, *Say It My Way:* Although Informal Speech Is Free; Get That "Get;" Grammatical Usage for Stompers; Graveyard Square; I'd Say in Retrospect; My Idol, Your Idle; On a Distinguished Victorian Poet Who Never Pronounced His Name the Same Way Twice; On the Correct Use of Lie and Lay; Polonius to Laertes: a Grammatical Farewell; The Heaving of Her Maiden Breast; To a Young Lady Who Asked Me to "Do" Her in a Thumbnail Sketch.

Clarkson N. Potter, *An Almanac of Words at Play:* A Classical Education; A Mouse of My Acquaintance; A Positive Reaction; Bless These Sheep; E Pluribus Unum; Facsimile of a Love Song; Forecast, Chilly; Haikus Show IQ's; Identity Problem in the Mammoth Caves; I Love You to Infinity; In-Riddle; I Scarce Recall; Love's a Game; Macaulay Tells Us; My Amnesty to All; Never Emberlucock or Impurgalize Your Spirits With These Vain Thoughts and Idle Concepts; Pre-Parental Plaint; Some May Promise Riches; The Mrs. Kr. Mr.; There Are Numerous Locutions to Express the Idea of Never; The Susurrant Schwa; To a Praying Mantis; To a Young Poetess; Typesetting Tarradiddle; When Charon Ferries Me Across the Styx; Wild Boars and Lions Haul Admetus' Car.

Clarkson N. Potter, *Another Almanac of Words at Play:* A Pest Iamb, Anapest Rick Ballad Was; Brooklyn Love Song; Centripetal, Centrifugal; Charles Dickens and the Devil; Concede, My Own; Consider Now the Quark; Elegy for My Late Friend and Tailor, Canio Saluzzi: For Isaac Asimov; For Planets Forsaken; Grammar in Extremis; Had I Butt Nude; I Have a Little Philtrum; I Was a Stranger; I Was Prodigal with Time; Kitchy-koo; Larva, Pupa, Imago; Let Us Wonder, While We Loiter; Love Song; Manon? Mais Non; My Chinese Miss; Now, a Little While; Ode to an Elevator; On Joseph Brodsky's Contention; On the Hermit Crab; Our Love Will Never Dwindle, Being Never; Resquiescat in Pace; Round (a Roundelet); Scratch That Mudblower—One Love-Maiden to Go; The Active and the Passive Voice; There Ought to Be a Law; There's Seldom Been a Man I Knew; They Were As Fed Horses in the Morning; To God the Praise; Up-and-Down Counting Song.

Clarkson N. Potter, *A Children's Almanac of Words at Play:* The Pygmy Race Were Little Guys; Incident in a World's Series Game.

Harper & Row, *The Garden of Eloquence:* ''Alliteration's Artful Aid;'' Don't Tell Me No Grammatic Rules; If Love Be Fine, As Some Pretend; O Mangy Cat, O Scruffy Cat.

Simon & Schuster, *Have a Word on Me:* A Man in Our Town, Cal Y-clempt; A Certain Paris Avocat; Bactrian Camels Have Two Humps; Don Juan at College; Forgotten Words Are Mighty Hard to Rhyme; God Argues Constantly With Me; I Find It Curiositive; I Would I Were a Polyglot; Jogger, Jog; Veritas Mutatur.

Introduction

She warn't particular; she could write about anything you choose to give her to write about just so it was sadful. Every time a man died, or a woman died, or a child died, she would be on hand with her "tribute" before he was cold. She called them tributes. The neighbors said it was the doctor first, then Emmeline, then the undertaker—the undertaker never got in ahead of Emmeline but once, and then she hung fire on a rhyme for the dead person's name which was Whistler. She warn't ever the same after that; she never complained, but she kinder pined away and did not live long.

—MARK TWAIN

Mark Twain was a rigidly honest man, so beyond doubt Emmeline did indeed die of grief for want of a rhyme.

It is for addicts like Emmeline and me that one editor after another has cobbled together rhyming lists, generally preceded by a treatise on the craft (though not necessarily the art) of versification. But these lists can never be entirely satisfactory. Many words simply refuse to rhyme, even under torture; yet you would need a wheelbarrow to transport the hundreds of thousands that do have rhyming matches. So though I believe this book contains more rhyming words than any of its contemporaries, it does not pretend to be complete—not to mention that up to the last minute I was still thinking of obvious words I had missed, while you are bound to think of equally obvious words still missing.

Books of this genre often carry the rather showy word-pair "Rhyming Dictionary" in the title; but in the sense that I understand the term, they are not dictionaries at all. A distinguishing feature of a dictionary, as far as I am concerned, is that it defines its entries. Rhyming dictionaries never do. That is why my collection has to rest content with the humbler name *Words to Rhyme With*, even though it does introduce a glossary defining a smattering (sadly, that was all there turned out to be room for) of the more exotic specimens.

Checking on meanings was a process full of astonishments. Dictionary definitions are generally clear, and sometimes curt. Occasionally they labor, like a 1917 Ford climbing a steep hill. And once in awhile they thrill, like a fine line of poetry. But often they do become a bit prosy. The definition of *aubesic*, for instance, is likely to be on the order of "utilitarian; common in thought or taste; vocational; breadwinning." Yet one dictionary got to the heart of the matter in just four words: "Smacking of the workshop." Sheer genius!

Definitions repeatedly take me by surprise. *Pettitoes*, for instance, are the feet of a pig, often used as food, but they have no etymological connection with the toes of their last syllable at all; the word descends from two Middle French forebears meaning "little goose," and was first applied to goose giblets.

I know now that an *arter* is a worm that bores into wood; that *Aepyornis* is a genus of extinct birds that laid eggs thirteen inches long (the fabulous gillygaloo lays *square* eggs); that *storage* denotes instinctive parental affection; that the *arui* is an *aoudad*; and that the aoudad is a wild sheep of North Africa which may be the chamois mentioned in the Old Testament.

I even learned something about my own nickname, which is *Wede*. But before telling you the meaning, I must explain how I received the name.

Nearly seventy years ago, in my fifth or sixth year, I became for one matchless summer the worshipful slave of a ten-year-old boy whose family had just settled in our village.*

---

*Its name is Oysterville, and it is located in the southwestern corner of the state of Washington.

1

Not just his slave—his shadow. Day after day I trotted at his heels—through the marshes and woodlands; across the salt hay meadows; onto the mudflats at the edge of the bay; and, when the tide was low enough, out across the hard gray corduroyed sand.

The name of my idol was *Aquila,* pronounced a.*kwil'*a; and perhaps because of an echo between that and my own name, *Willard,* the neighbors began referring to us as if we were a monster with two joined bodies: ''Aquila-and-Willard.'' When Aquila announced that he preferred to be called *Quede* (I have no idea why), they immediately nicknamed me to match, and we became ''Quede-and-Wede.''

Nearly a lifetime later, as I was leafing through Webster's Second to confirm some rhyming word, my eye fell on my own name:

> wede (wēd), adj. Shriveled.

The description was accurate enough, but I turned to *The Oxford English Dictionary* in search of something kinder. Here is what I found:

> wede (wēd), v. intr. 1. To be or become mad.
> 2. To be wild with anger or desire; to rage.

As for quede, it too was waiting for me in both dictionaries. It means (or did, for, like wede, it is now obsolete) ''evil; also, an evil person; specif., the Devil.''

So now I know whose footsteps I began to walk in at the early age of five.

Even if you never have occasion to rhyme with words like *quede* and *wede* and *arter* and *Aepyornis* and *storge* and *arui* and *aoudad,* it is comforting to know that they are there, no less at your service than *love* and *dove* and *June* and *moon.*

Only God can make a poet, and for his own good reasons He makes one but seldom. If He has such a destiny in mind for you, I hope the pages ahead may provide a few shortcuts along the way. But do not expect me to be consistent. In the poem that opens this book, for instance, I plump for the use of simple words, and mean it. But if only a complicated word can express what is in your head and heart, you have no choice but to use it. In the trivia which is my own substitute for poetry the fact that a word is long and complicated may indeed be its only asset.

Since I have yet to experience Poetic Afflatus, I cannot possibly define it, much less communicate it. This book simply sets down certain basics of rhyme and metrics; demonstrates that even the noblest forms of poetry run risks when in hands that are mostly thumbs; and goes on and on listing rhyming words until you will find them coming out of your ears. If we are both lucky, some day the right ones will also start coming out of your pen, and you will find yourself saying something that the world needs to hear, in the one way in the world that it should be said.

Even if *Words to Rhyme With* had been around in time, though, it could not have saved Emmeline's life. There is no rhyme for Whistler.*

Rhythm and Meter

Rhythm is where poetry starts. Rhythm is older than speech; older than sound; older than the stars themselves. The Big Bang ushered it in. Rhythm is the heartbeat of the universe.

---

*I was wrong. There is *bristler;* and, as Charles F. Dery reminds me, there is George Harold Sisler, first baseman, a member of the Baseball Hall of Fame.

In prosody, which some dictionaries describe as the science of versification, rhythm is codified as *meter,* the regular beat of accent, or stress. Syllables are grouped in metrical units called feet, each a single accented syllable, generally combined with one or more that are unaccented. The way in which the feet are arranged determines the meter of a line. It is not intended that metrical rules should be slavishly followed—rocking-horse meter is widely scorned, though it may be tolerated for whistlers-in-rhyme such as I—but a good poet knows meter in his head and feels rhythm in his blood. If ever he violates their canons he does so deliberately, knowing exactly the purpose he is seeking to achieve. If he disobeys the king, it is only to serve him more faithfully.

The most widely used metric feet in our poetry are:

- The *iambic,* an unaccented (or unstressed, or short) syllable followed by an accented (or stressed, or long*) syllable. (. ' : De.*ny* him. *not.*)
- The *trochaic,* an accented followed by an unaccented syllable (' . : *Ho*.ly *Fa*.ther, *bless.* me).
- The *anapestic,* two unaccented syllables followed by an accented syllable (. . ' : Un.re.*tur*.ning is *Time*).
- The *dactylic,* an accented syllable followed by two unaccented syllables (' . . : *Al*.ice is *beau*.ti.ful).
- The *amphibrachic,* an accented syllable dividing two unaccented syllables (. ' . : Un.*cer*.tain.ly *walk*.ing).

Less usual are the *spondaic,* with two or more accented syllables in succession (' ' : *Fields, streams, skies I know; Death not yet*), and the *pyrrhic,* consisting of two or more unaccented syllables—so difficult to cut away from the attending stressed syllables that I cannot think offhand of an example that clearly makes the point. It is all but impossible to make a string of unstressed syllables; one of them will seize power. The merest hint of a shift in emphasis can alter the beat of a line. It can turn a trochee into an iamb (*fish*.wife into fish.*wife*) or an iamb into a trochee (in.*sult* into *in*.sult). And it frequently does.

Once formal meter is ingrained in you, it may be helpful at times not simply to change emphasis within a line, but even to add or drop part or all of a foot. But never take such a liberty by mistake. The rule is, master meter, *then* maneuver it.

ENJAMBMENT

(Enjambment, from Old French *enjamber,* "to straddle," is the run-on of a sentence or idea from one line or couplet of a poem to the next.)

Enjambment doesn't—say who may—
Start at mid-tide, either way
Flowing (as if poetry
First should lap about the knee;
Thence with climbing moon should rise,
Drowning inch by inch the thighs,
Navel, nipples, nape, and crown;
Then again come ebbing down,
All returning, till below
It at last reveals the toe)—

No—the problem is that it
Doesn't know the place to quit;
On and on it rushes, beckoned
From the first line to the second,
From the second to the third,
Shunning the concluding word,
Past the fourth line, fifth, and so on,
Always one more line to grow on,
Till, though ardor's undiminished,
It expires; enjambment's finished.

---

*The stressed part of a foot is sometimes also called the *thesis,* and the remainder the *arsis,* after corresponding Greek words that translate loosely as the heavier and the lighter part. But *arsis,* signifying literally "raising," was mistaken by some to apply to a raised or loudened voice, so the meaning of the two words is frequently reversed. You will avoid confusion by avoiding their use.

Rhyme

The beat of sound in poetry is always accounted as meter, but balance between sounds is not always accounted as rhyme. Rhyme as it is presently defined was unknown to the ancient Greeks, nor is there evidence of it in classic Latin poetry. It appeared in church Latin around 200 A.D., and took a thousand years to seep through Europe. Our Anglo-Saxon forebears preferred alliteration—the repetition of the opening sounds of accented syllables, as in Shakespeare's "Full fathoms five thy father lies." My home encyclopedia describes alliteration as the "jingle of like beginnings;" rhyme, in Milton's phrase, is "the jingling sound of like endings." His definition has a patronizing echo; though immortal poetry has been written in rhyme, there have been and continue to be poets who consider it beneath their dignity to employ it for serious business. If there must be any association at all between the sound of one word or another, they prefer that it be more oblique, as in assonance and consonance (see below).*

Blank verse—generally iambic pentameter—discards rhyme but not meter. Free verse, the favorite of many modern poets, drops them both. But neither is a threatened species. Writers will continue to produce some of our finest poetry in rhyme; and in the field of light verse it stands alone.

Types of Rhyme

Rhyme, says the dictionary, is

> The correspondence, in two or more words or verses, of terminal sounds beginning with an accented vowel, which, in modern English usage, must be preceded by different consonantal sounds, or by a consonant in one case and none in the other.

In traditional rhymed verse, the rhyme is carried by the last foot of the line. The briefest possible rhyming foot is a semi-iamb, a single stressed syllable, as in

> *Fly'*
> *High'!*

But the usual iambic (or single, or masculine) rhyming foot is made of two syllables, with the accent on the second:

> Don't *fly'*
> Too *high'*!†

A two-syllable rhyming foot with the accent on the first syllable is a trochaic (or double, or feminine) rhyme:

> *Pret'*ty
> *Kit'*ty'!

Even if the remainder of the line is iambic, or of some other beat, the final rhyming foot can be made trochaic by adding an unaccented syllable:

> His *moth'*er *said'*, "Son, *do'* not *wan'*der
> Out *yon'*der."

---

*A caution here. I have admitted words to this book that rhyme technically, but deplorably. You would have to be in desperate straits, for instance, to rhyme *tolerable* with *babble*. The result would probably not be tolerable, though it would be babble.

† Stressed syllables here are underlined and followed by ('). Unstressed syllables are not underlined.

A triple (or dactylic) rhyming foot has three syllables, with the accent on the first:

*Crick'*e.ty, *lick'*e.ty,
*Ma'*s are per.*snick'*e.ty.

The list of rhyming words in this book is divided into the foregoing three categories—single, double, and triple. The rhymes are traditional; that is, the accented vowels match exactly, and the unaccented syllables are similar enough not to jar the ear. Once conventional rhyming is second nature to you, you may wish to vary the position of the rhyming foot in the line or among lines to meet special needs. Here are some of the possibilities:

• *Random* rhyme, which goes beyond the common practice of alternating rhymed and unrhymed lines, instead mixing them irregularly;
• *Initial* rhyme, occurring at the beginning instead of the end of the line;
• *Interior* rhyme, occurring within the line;
• *Cross* rhyme, in which the rhyming sound at the end of one line is matched somewhere inside another.

Or, if you are acting deliberately and with full awareness of the risks, you may experiment with various sorts of *near*-rhyme, including the following:

• *Identicals*. These match the sound of the consonant as well as the vowel, though they are seldom simply repetitions of the same word:
   Praise, prays; bard, barred; coral, choral.
• *Consonance*. Here not the sound of the vowel in the stressed syllable but instead that of the opening and closing consonants makes the match:
   Tick, tack, tuck, tock; hit, hat, hot, hut.
• *Consonantal rhyme*. This matches only the sound that ends the syllable, whether accented or unaccented:
   Easy, busy; fast, waste; missing, bussing.
• *Assonance*. This simply echoes a vowel sound within a line:
   Old bones move slowly.
• *Vowel rhyme*. Here only the vowel sounds of the rhyming feet correspond:
   Age, rail, take; blue, move, flute.
• *Smothered (imperfect) rhyme*. The match is between an accented and an unaccented syllable:
   Bring, going; beaten, pen; hardly, foresee.
• *Unaccented rhyme*. The match is between the final unaccented syllables:
   Faster, mover, killer; happy, pretty, chummy.
• *Half-rhyme*. The rhyming foot ends in one or more unaccented syllables, but only the stressed syllable has a match:
   Differ, fifth; cavern, ravenous.
• *Spelling* (or *sight*) *rhyme*. The spellings but not the sound of the stressed vowels match:
   Woman, Roman; love, grove.

And if none of these ways of rhyming hits the mark for you, you can always make up your own rhyming words:

BACTRIAN CAMELS HAVE TWO HUMPS

I met on a tram in exotic Siam
   (Known as *tramela* out in Siamela)
Three Campbellite camels—a sire, dam, and lamb
   (In Siamese, *Camela famila*).

The sire was Ben-Amelel-Ben-Abraham,
A suitable name for a Bactrian cam
   (Which is Siamese shorthand for *camela*).
The femme of the cam was a well-trodden dam

Whom tram-trippers taunted as *Bactrian mam*
   On account of her uberous mammila.
The lamb of the Campbellite camels was Pam,
   Though sometimes she answered to Pamela.

And what has becam of that Camela fam
Since they traveled away on their Siamese tram?
I know not—and frankly, I don't give a damn,
   Or even a Siamese dammela.

To lengthen *tram* to *tramela* and *cam* to *camela*—to shorten *camel* to *cam*, *mammal* to *mam*, *family* to *fam*, *became* to *becam*—these are deliberate breaches of contract with the English language. As with the alteration of a metric beat, it is perfectly acceptable to abuse the language for effect—but only if you are fully aware of the abuse yourself, and are sure that the reader will recognize it as intentional.

There are two other ways to rhyme, one quite usual and the other rare except as sheer artifice. The usual way is called *mosaic* rhyme. It matches one word against two, or occasionally more:

       tiller, kill her; queenly, green lea; Ohio, I owe

Mosaic matches come readily to mind. Be sure, though, that the mosaic is a true rhyme. *Tiller* does not rhyme with *ill sir*; *queenly* does not rhyme with *green tea*; *Ohio* does not rhyme with *I know*.

The less common way is *Procrustean*, or *impossible*, rhyme, which may stretch words, chop them up, or squeeze several into one to make a match, as the mythical giant Procrustes rearranged the length of his victims to fit them to his bed.

You will find, beginning on page 37, verses built around these two rhyming tricks. But since such rhymes consist of either more than one word, or less than one, they are not included in the list of rhyming words.

Any sort of off-rhyme, if used with knowledge and sensitivity, increases the range and vocabulary of poetry. But so do the widely varying arrangements available in conventional rhyme schemes, as we are about to see.

I do not know if there is a name for spellings that change their sound, and so their rhyme, from one word to the next, but there should be. Among such perverse spellings, the syllable *-ough* has perhaps provided more grist than any other to versifiers. According to circumstance, it is pronounced at least five ways—as *uff, ow, oh, off,* or *oo:*

ON A DISTINGUISHED VICTORIAN POET WHO NEVER
PRONOUNCED HIS NAME THE SAME WAY TWICE

I seldom stretch beneath a bough
To browse on lines of Arthur Clough.
His work seems rather dated, though
Victorians loved Arthur Clough.
In fact, they could not get enough

Of poems penned by Arthur Clough;
While I—I groan, I snort, I cough
When forced to slog through Arthur Clough.
And I am glad that I am through
With this review of Arthur Clough.

(The ghost of Mr. Clough—who pronounced his name *cluf*—will forgive me for any apparent unkindness; the fact is that critics recall his works with respect. I did not mean to be mean; it was the fault of the rhyme.)

The Stanza

A stanza is a series of rhythmic lines that, put together, make up a poem. (*Stanza* and *verse* are sometimes used interchangeably, though verse may also mean either a complete poem or metric writing in general.) If the poem consists of two or more stanzas, they are divided by spaces. A stanza must contain at least two lines to make a rhymed unit; any greater number is permitted. The rhyme scheme, meter, and length of the line are up to the poet.

Couplet—Two Lines

A poem may consist of a single couplet:

INSPIRATION

The bard who Hippocrene* for gin gave up
Saw empty couplets gush from empty cup.

Couplets, not necessarily set apart as stanzas, can be building blocks for poems of any length. If two rhymed lines in iambic hexameter form a self-contained verse unit, expressing a complete thought, they are a *heroic couplet*. (The two lines above do not make a heroic couplet because they are written in pentameter—five syllables—instead of hexameter—six.)

I said earlier that the continuation of a sentence or idea from one couplet to the next is *enjambment*. The verse below starts to enjamb in the third stanza.

A PUP BY ANY OTHER NAME

Ah, Chloe, the animal kingdom's a-teem
With litters that turn out not quite what they seem:

For a cow has a *calf,* but the calf of a mare
Is a *foal,* and a *cub* is the foal of a bear;

A *fawn* is the cub of a deer, while the fawn
Of a beaver's a *kitten;* and, carrying on,

The kit of a sheep is a *lamb,* and the lamb
Of a wolf is a *whelp,* while the whelp of Madame

Is a *babe,* and the babe of a dog is a *pup,*
And I thought for a while this would wind the thing up,

But the pup of a goat is a *kid,* and—ah, Chloe—
What else is a kangaroo's kid but a *joey?*

Triplet (Tercet)—Three Lines

Except in *terza rima,* where they are strung together with a rhyme scheme of a b a, b c b, c d c, and so on, you can rhyme triplets any way you like. If a single triplet makes up a complete poem, you will have to rhyme it a a a, though, unless you are willing to leave one line unrhymed:

---

*Hippocrene, a legendary fountain on Mount Helicon, sprang up when Pegasus, the winged steed of the Muses, struck the earth with his hoof. The water from this fountain is said to provide inspiration for poets.

THE BRIEFER THE BETTER

For Jim's scant thought no style could be too terse;
A couplet were too long, a triplet worse;
Jim just might justify a one-line verse.

Quatrain—Four Lines

The quatrain is frequently a self-contained poem, though as often it is one stanza in a series. It may be written so that only the second and fourth lines rhyme: a b c b. Generally, though, it consists of two couplets (a a b b), called a *rubai*, or of lines rhyming a b a b, as in the two following examples:

THE HEAVING OF HER MAIDEN BREAST

The heaving of her maiden breast
  Had to be seen to be believed.
The boat lurched down another crest—
  And up she heaved.

ME VS. GOD

God holds a dialogue with me
  With which we both are growing fed up.
Says He to I, says I to He,
  "Oh, *shed*dup! *Shed*dup! *Shed*dup! *Shed*dup!"

Quintet—Five Lines

As the number of lines in a stanza increases, so does the potential number of rhyme schemes. The scheme here is a b a a b, and the subject is forgotten positives—words that reverse their meanings if you knock away their negative prefix.

A DREAM OF COUTH

I dreamt of a corrigible, nocuous youth,
  Gainly, gruntled, and kempt;
A mayed and a sidious fellow, forsooth—
Ordinate, effable, shevelled, and couth;
  A delible fellow I dreamt.

(If you play with forgotten positives, remember that the prefix *in-* does not always mean *not*. *Inflammable* means the same as *flammable*. *In-* may mean *in* or *into*, as in *innate, insert*. It may indicate intensive action, as in *inosculate*.)

Sextet—Six Lines

A sextet could run a a a b b b; or a b a b a b; or a b c a b c—oh, there is no need to bother listing all the possibilities. This one is a a b b c c.

Pygmy. One of a nation fabled to be only three spans high, and after long wars to have been destroyed by the cranes.—Johnson's Dictionary

Pygmies? Weren't they little guys,
Only three hand spans in size?
Yes—and they had pygmy brains
Not to know those giant cranes
Could beat them standing on one leg,
And still take time to lay an egg.

Septet—Seven Lines

There are too many possible rhyme variations in a seven-line stanza to bother listing them all. The verse that follows runs a b a a b a b.

THERE'S SELDOM BEEN A MAN I KNEW

There's seldom been a man I knew
   Who struck me as a pest.
Of women, there were quite a few.
Yet when I take the longer view,
   The women worked out best.
Those rare exceptions—one or two—
   Made up for all the rest.

Octave—Eight Lines

An octave can be rhymed as four couplets, or two quatrains, or two tercets and a couplet, or—well, here it has only three rhyming lines, a - a - a, and really consists of four lines split in two.

HOW MANY ANGELS CAN DANCE ON THE HEAD OF A PIN?
(Medieval Church argument)

If you're ab-
   le to spin
On the Head
   of a Pin,
You must be
   an An-
gel—or *ter-*
   ribly thin.

Nine-line Stanza

The rhyme scheme in this example is a b c c b B a B B.*

KITCHY-KOO

My dear's dear kitchy-koo am I,
   As she is my dear kitchy-koo.
What tears one kitchy-koo would shed
If t'other kitchy-koo were dead!
   And yet grief's freshets often do
   Wash up another kitchy-koo.
(I hear my kitchy-koo reply:
   "They do; they do,
   Kitchy-koo.")

Ten-line Stanza

The example consists of five rhyming couplets.

WILD BOARS AND LIONS

Wild boars and lions haul Admetus' car.
White horses seven pull the Morning Star.
Gold panthers lead bright Bacchus on his way;

---

*A capitalized letter represents a refrain line, or, as here, the repetition of part of a line.

Gemmed peacocks Juno's chariot convey.
By chastened lions Cybele is drawn,
And antlered stags tug fair Diana on.
Behind her wingèd dragons Ceres travels,
And flights of doves bear Venus to her revels.
Sea horses carry their thalassic lord.
    I drive a Ford.

The Metric Line

You have seen that the beat of iambic verse is da *da;* of trochaic, *da* da; of anapestic, da da *da;* of dactylic, *da* da da; of amphibrachic, da *da* da. I may also have suggested—if so, it is worth repeating—that lines in any meter will almost never scan perfectly when read aloud with normal emphasis. That is a good thing; an unaltering beat would be unbearably monotonous. Look at Elizabeth Barrett Browning's famous line:

How do I love thee? Let me count the ways.

That is iambic pentameter—in theory, five da *da* beats in a row. Forced into Procrustes's bed, it would come out like this:

How *do* I *love* thee? *Let* me *count* the *ways.*

But in fact that line is not iambic at all. It is lucky even to be a pentameter, with five feet, no more, no less; Mrs. Browning, like any other sensible poet, would not have hesitated to add or drop a syllable or so for the greater glory of the line. It begins, in my ear, with a dactyl, continues with three trochees, and concludes with a long iamb. The reader adjusts the stress automatically to the sense of the message, while allowing maximum sweetness to the flow of sound.

Yet it is considered an iambic line. So are Shakespeare's pentameters, any one of which co-opts the beat most suitable for the moment within the overall iambic framework.

The Beat and Length of Poetic Lines

A metric foot is a single beat of sound requiring a stressed syllable (except for those ridiculous pyrrhics, which don't count). It may have one, two, or more unstressed syllables, or it may have none.

A line of poetry comprising a single foot is a *monometer.* Two feet make a *dimeter;* three, a *trimeter;* four, a *tetrameter;* five, a *pentameter;* six, a *hexameter;* seven, a *heptameter.* And that is as far as there is any likely reason to go.

Lines come in all the metric beats that have been mentioned. Here are iambic, trochaic, anapestic, and dactylic examples:

Monometer:
Iambic:	A *gain* (or simply *gain*).
Trochaic:	*Ho'*ly.
Anapestic:	In the *night.*
Dactylic:	*Bear'*a.ble.

Dimeter:
Iambic:	They *fled* a.*way.*
Trochaic:	*Feet* that *stum'*ble.
Anapestic:	In a *song* that she *sang.*
Dactylic:	*El.*ea.nor *Roo'*se.velt.

Trimeter:
   Iambic: I *watched* a *sink'*ing *star.*
   Trochaic: *Fa'*ther, *call* the *doc'*tor.
   Anapestic: When the *dark* shall turn *bright* as the *day.*
   Dactylic: *Why* does the *teach'*er keep *shout'*ing so?

Tetrameter:
   Iambic: The *crows* have *fall'*en *si'*lent now.
   Trochaic: *In* the *ram'*age *of* the *elm* tree.
   Anapestic: And the *ech'*o now *fades* in the *streets;* he is *gone.*
   Dactylic: *Cor'*al sand *un'*der them, *pur'*ple sky *o'*ver them.

Pentameter:
   Iambic: I *know* one *won'*der *that* will *nev'*er *cease.*
   Trochaic: *Then* the *tel'*e.*phone'* will *cease* to *jin'*gle.
   Anapestic: Do not *speak* in that *voice;* it will *troub'*le the *wom'*en a.*sleep.*
   Dactylic: *No,* I'm a.*fraid* I'm not *read'*y to *give* to that *char'*i.ty.

Hexameter:
   Iambic: The *riv'*er *wat'*er *is* no *long'*er *run'*ning *clear.*
   Trochaic: *Sis'*ters, *let* us *raise* a *cup* to *ab'*sent *Ma.*ry.
   Anapestic: We were *walk'*ing on *cob'*bles; I *think* that my *feet* will be *ach*ing
                         to.*mor.*row.
   Dactylic: *Call* in the *preach'*er; I *sud'*den.ly *wish* to be *wed'*ded to *Jon'*a.than.

Heptameter:
   Iambic: Men *looked* at *him,* and *by* their *look* he *knew* he *neared* the *end.*
   Trochaic: *What* is *on* this *eve'*ning's *tel'*e.*vis'*ion *that's* worth *watch'*ing?
   Anapestic: Though I *find* it a *long* and un.*like'*ly ac.*count,* yet I *some*how be.*lieve*
                         it is *true.*
   Dactylic: *Out* of the *pas'*sion of *Le'*da, there's *on'*ly a *feath'*er re.*main'*ing
                         for *mem'*o.ry.

Not many poets have composed consistently graceful lines in dactylic heptameter. To try is excellent training, though, and you have as good a chance as anyone else of being the one who succeeds.

Shown below are verses in the four most common metric beats, ranging in length from one metric foot to seven.

Monometer: A One-Foot Line

Since a single metric foot is the shortest poetic line, while a one-syllable, one-letter word is the shortest metric foot, a matching pair of one-letter words is the shortest possible rhyming verse. Here is such a verse—though it must be admitted that for the sake of understanding I had to give it an unusually long title.

      A BRIEF AND SOMEWHAT UNGRACIOUS EXCHANGE BETWEEN
      THE BRITISH AMBASSADOR'S WIFE, WHO SPEAKS NO SPANISH,
      AND THE SPANISH AMBASSADOR'S WIFE, WHO SPEAKS NO
      ENGLISH, DURING A COURTESY CALL BY THE LATTER UPON
      THE FORMER: WRITTEN ON THE ASSUMPTION THAT MY
      READERS KNOW THE SOUND OF THE SPANISH WORD FOR "YES"

                                  "T?"
                                  "C."*

---

   *Charles F. Dery brought to my attention a similar summation in which a youth, gazing awed at the star-studded firmament and sensing his own insignificance, murmurs: "I . . .
                     Y?"*

A twelve-line verse in iambic monometer:

TO A YOUNG WOMAN WHO REFUSES TO DIET

No hu-
man eyes
Dare view
Your size

Lest day
And night
They stay
Shut tight

From hor-
ror at
Such store
Of fat.

These eighteen lines are in anapestic monometer:

WE CAN'T SEEM TO GET IT THROUGH OUR HEADS

If a boy
Understood,
He'd *enjoy*
Being good.
  The complaint
  Is, he ain't.

And the same,
It applies
Both to dames
And to guys:
  What a saint
  Is, they ain't.

Yes, if *I*
Understood,
I might try
Being good;
  But I don't,
  So I won't.

Eight lines of amphibrachic monometer:

EVENHANDEDNESS

On Sundays
You pray, in
Your quest for
Salvation.
On Mondays
You stray, in
Your zest for
Temptation.

Dimeter: A Two-Foot Line

This four-line dimeter is trochaic:

TO A SOAP OPERA ADDICT

> You there, watching
> Lights and shadows—
> Which are good-os?
> Which are bad-os?

Dimeters and monometers alternate in this iambic verse.

SLOWLY DIM THE SUNSET CLOUDS

> The fire, the ash
>   Take turn:
> Now flame and flash,
>   Now urn.
>
> What leagues we rose
>   We tell
> By counting those
>   We fell.

Trimeter: A Line of Three Metric Feet

Does a stalagmite build up from the floor of a damp cave and a stalactite build down from the roof, or is it the other way around? This twelve-line iambic trimeter (. ′ . ′ .′) was supposed to fix the distinction in my mind once and for all—but I still forget.

IDENTITY PROBLEM IN THE MAMMOTH CAVES

> O pendant stalactite,
>   Deposit crystalline,
> Insensate troglodyte
>   Shaped of accreted brine,
>
> Aspire you still to pierce
>   That upright stalagmite
> Who in a million years
>   Your love cannot requite?
>
> And if indeed your drip
>   With ardor one day fill her,
> And bring you lip to lip,
>   And make you two one pillar . . .
>
> Then how can you be sure,
>   O pendant stalactite,
> If you are you, or her—
>   Stalactite-stalagmite?

THERE ARE NUMEROUS LOCUTIONS TO EXPRESS THE NOTION OF 'NEVER'

> When all the world grows honest;
> When the Yellow River's clear;
> When Calais meets with Dover,
> Do you suppose, my dear,

I shall forget I've lost you? . . .
Not until St. Tib's eve,
Not for a year of Sundays
Shall I forbear to grieve—

Till noon strikes Narrowdale; till
Latter Lammas dawns;
Till Queen Dick reigns; till Fridays
Arrive in pairs like swans;

Till the Greek calends, and the
Conversion of the Jews.
I'll mourn you till the coming
Of the Cocqcigrues.

O SOME MAY PROMISE RICHES

O some may promise riches
And some may promise ease
But I will deck my darling
In suns and galaxies.

Upon her finger, Lyra's
Ring Nebula she'll wear;
Against her throat, the Cluster
In Berenice's Hair.

Rosette in Montesoros
Her bosom shall adorn,
And Veil of Cygnus hide her
Upon her wedding morn.

O some may promise riches
And some may promise ease
But I will deck my darling
In suns and galaxies.

The verse that follows is in trochaic trimeter (' . ' . ' .):

LARVA, PUPA, IMAGO

When I was a larva,
    Giddily I'd chortle,
"When I'm big I'll carve a
    Monument immortal."

When I was a pupa,
    Though more realistic,
Still I hoped to scoop a
    Funeral statistic.

Now, a worn imago,
    I do not declare
My advanced lumbago,
    Knowing none will care.

Tetrameter: A Line of Four Metric Feet

You may vary the number of feet in the lines of a verse according to any fixed pattern you choose. Four of the six trochaic lines below are tetrameter; two are trimeter.

NEIGH NEIGH, NEIGHBOR

They were as fed horses in the morning; every
one neighed after his neighbor's wife.—Jeremiah V:8.

After neighbors' wives you neigh?
   Neighbors' wives are fine—
Sorrel, chestnut, dapple gray,
Rolling neighing in the hay.
Neigh then, neighbor, neigh—but nay!—
   Neigh not after mine.

Overall, this tetrameter is anapestic, though some lines drop the last unstressed syllable.

I WOULD I WERE A POLYGLOT

I would that my palate were pat in
   Icelandic and Persian and Greek;
I would I were fluent in Latin,
   Instead of deplorably weak.

I'm sure it would help me to win you
   If polyglot hints I could spin
Of trading Herculean sinew
   For secret Lilithean sin.

Italian, Hungarian, Spanish,
   Might win me the right to caress you;
But English itself seems to vanish
   Whenever I try to address you.

   I barely can toast,
   "Hey, kid, you're the most!"

These time-honored similes arrive in dactylic tetrameter:

FACSIMILE OF A LOVE SONG

Mute as a mackerel, darling, I am;
You're fit as a fiddle, and gay as a lamb.
You're clean as a whistle; I'm ugly as sin.
I'm fat as a hog, you're as neat as a pin.
You're brave as a lion, I'm deaf as an adder;
You're brown as a berry, I'm mad as a hatter.

My ducky, my darling, the love of my life,
You're free as the wind, and as sharp as a knife.
I'm blind as a bat; you are sly as a fox.
You're pert as a sparrow; I'm dumb as an ox.
You're plump as a partridge, as sweet as a rose;
I'm flat as a flounder, and plain as my nose.

So come, let us marry, and dance in the lane
As merry as crickets, and righter than rain!
Our days will be brighter than rainbows are bright;
Our hearts will be lighter than feathers are light.
Our love will be surer than shooting is sure—
And we shall be poorer than churchmice are poor.

Each line of this amphibrachic tetrameter has an extra unaccented syllable:

FUNGIBLE: INTERCHANGEABLE, REPLACEABLE.

One fury alone has God found inexpungeable;
The wrath of a woman who finds herself fungible.

Iambic tetrameter:

OUR LOVE WILL NEVER DWINDLE, BEING NEVER

Our love will never dwindle, being never;
　　It could not be so dear if it could be.
The babe that never was is ours forever;
　　There is no need to set the wild deer free.

I know a country with nor dawn nor setting;
　　No summer there, nor winter; spring, nor fall;
No memories are there, and no forgetting;
　　The people there breathe barely, if at all.

Pentameter: A Line of Five Metric Feet

Iambic pentameter remains the most used line in English-language verse. Here are two examples of it:

TO A PRAYING MANTIS, STANDING IN THE NEED OF PRAYER

(The female mantis consumes her mate during copulation.)

The Male (or Lesser) Praying Mantis is
A victim of romantic fantasies.
He cries, ''My angel, let me prove
My insect life well lost for love!''
He takes her in his mantis arms;
He soothes her virginal alarms—
Pours all his love and longing in her,
While she is having him for dinner.
He reassures her that they'll wed;
Meanwhile, she's gnawing off his head.
He soothes her gastric pains with Borax
As she is gnawing at his thorax;
And when there's nothing left above,
Still doth the Lower Mantis love.

This system, as needs scarcely saying,
Breeds little Mantises . . . all praying.

Hexameter: A Line of Six Metric Feet

The most familiar hexameter is the Alexandrine, an iambic line which is a standard unit in French poetry, and usually deals with weightier subjects than the one considered below.

MY CHINESE MISS

My Chinese Miss is dainty as a Chinese fan;
The fare she serves is manna for the inner man.
Her breath is aromatic as her Chinese tea;
My Chinese Miss is won ton dumpling soup to me.

She dips into my heart as chopsticks dip in bowls;
Her lashes flutter when I praise her lobster rolls.
Her breasts are silken, tenderer than egg foo yong—
No Peking duck could match the savor of her tongue.

When I depart this feasting, sated is my need:
No dream remains of mooshi pork, or soup seaweed;
Of birdnest soup, or sweet and sour, or moo gai pen.
(How soon I'm starving for my Chinese Miss again!)

Heptameter: A Line of Seven Metric Feet

Iambic heptameter:

A MATTER OF ETIQUETTE

I've knocked her to the sidewalk and I've taken all she's got;
I can't make up my mind if I should stomp on her or not.
Such delicate decisions aggravate us muggers most—
There's not a word about them in my Emily Post.

Trochaic heptameter:

The following verse plays with *venereal nouns*—collective nouns, that is, covering groups of animals (in this case wildfowl) that men hunt for sport. The word venereal goes back to Venus, who was goddess of both love and the hunt.

VENEREALLY SPEAKING

Tarantara, tarantara, off the hunters ride,
Off to bag a nye of pheasants—failing that, a hide;
Stalking here a plump of wildfowl, there a spring of teal;
Seeking out a sord of mallards for their evening meal.

Tarantara, tarantara, home the hunters straggle,
With of choughs a chattering, and with of geese a gaggle;
Overhead, of geese a skein, a company of widgeons;
Underfoot, a trip of dotterel. On the sidewalk—pigeons.

You may venture to put a precise name to the meter of the following heptametric verse; I would rather not.

A MOUSE OF MY ACQUAINTANCE

A mouse of my acquaintance in seven days was fed
Twice twenty thousand swordfish, and *that mouse is dead.*
The mercury in swordfish is an enemy to dread;
He ate twice twenty thousand, and *that mouse is dead.*

His sister gnawed through pizzas (I am told one million four);
There's talk of botulism—and *that sister is no more.*
Their brother downed ten thousand turkeys lined with pesticide;
It took a week to kill him, but *that poor mouse died.*

So stay away from hormones, and from salmonella too;
Be impolite to cyclamates, and DDT eschew;
For additives and chemicals can kill you just like *that*—
Though (confidentially) those mice were done in by the cat.

Forms of Lyric Verse

Reading poetry has something in common with taking a Rohrschach test—what you bring out tells considerable about what you took in. But a poem also provides a glimpse of the poet, and perhaps not always what he thought he was showing you. The self-revelation may not be quite so evident when the work is epic, spreading heroic happenings over a huge canvas, or narrative, telling a more human story in a briefer compass, or dramatic, with characters speaking for themselves, or even satirical, jeering at human folly, as it is in the lyric poem, which deliberately opens to daylight very private feelings. Even if one wishes to, it is hard to lie successfully in a lyric poem—except perhaps to oneself. If a lie does convince the reader, it is probably because it reveals a truth by accident. And mawkishness and sentimentality show through like pentimento through overlaid painting.

The traditional verse forms that follow are generally associated with lyric poetry. It may seem in dubious taste to serve jug wine from such splendid bottles; but at least the bottles *are* splendid.

Most of the best-known lyric forms in English are imports, and most of the best-known imports are from Italy and France.

From Italy

Four Italian forms that have long been at home in English are the sonnet, ottava rima, terza rima, and the rhyming sestina.

The Sonnet

The sonnet is a fourteen-line poem in iambic pentameter, broken by stanzas and thought development into two movements—the octet, of eight lines, and the sestet, of six. But there may be only one movement, or there may be more than two; and the separations may be either sharp or blurred. The original rhyme scheme, still common, is a - b - b - a, a - b - b - a, c - d - e, c - d - e, with sometimes a shift in the sestet to c - d - c, d - c - d.

Milton used the Italian rhyme scheme for his sonnets, but not the arbitrary division of thoughts. The following verse is structured in the Miltonic fashion.

WHEN CHARON FERRIES ME ACROSS THE STYX

When Charon ferries me across the Styx,
   And Cerberus confines me with the dead,
     Pray, Boswell, carve some legend at my head.
Say that I sharpened Machiavelli's tricks;
Out-Croesused Croesus with my golden bricks;
     That tides obeyed me in Canute's bestead;
     That Casanova envied me in bed
As Newman paled beside me in the flicks.

Pray, Boswell, tell the waiting world that I
     Awhile to Joan was Darby, and awhile
To Damon, Pythias; and, pray, recall
There was the steel of Caesar in my eye,
     And Aristotle's wisdom in my smile.
What—can't you think of anything at all?

The Shakespearean Sonnet

The rhyme scheme of the sonnet form that carries Shakespeare's name is a - b - a - b, c - d - c - d, e - f - e - f, g - g. The thought may take a turn at the beginning of the sestet, but this is not required. The octet here enjambs into the sestet.

POLONIUS TO LAERTES: A GRAMMATICAL FAREWELL

Aboard, Laertes, and my blessing carry;
 And let these precepts in thy memory sit
When judging thy familiars. Be thou chary
 Of tongues that scuff in slipshod counterfeit,
With words all unproportioned to their thought;
 Ill-said is no less ill because intangible.
Give every man thy ear, but count him naught

 Who *friable* equates with *frangible;*
For *friable* is foreordained to crumble,
 While *frangible* is brittle, and must shatter.
From trope to trope do men, like drunkards, stumble,
 And make of synonyms identic matter.

Reserve thy love for the grammatic few.
I wouldn't count on more than one or two.

Ottava Rima

Ottava Rima has six lines rhyming a - b - a - b - a - b, followed by a rhyming couplet. Any meter will do. The example below is based on the conclusion of one of Chaucer's *Canterbury Tales,* in which a knight of King Arthur's court is condemned to die unless he can find an answer to the query, "What does a woman like best?" After hunting vainly far and near, he throws himself in desperation on the mercy of a stooped and withered crone:

HANDSOME IS AS HANDSOME DOES

He said, "Thou art ugly as e'er man did see;
 The bloom of thy nineties must seem long ago.
Yet rather than perish I'll marry with thee
 If thou halt my hanging by letting me know,
What is it a woman likes best?"
 Answered she,
"To have her own way."—And in answering, lo!
She threw her disguise off, and—son of a bitch!—
Proved beautiful, youthful, indulgent, and rich.

Terza Rima

Terza Rima is a series of three-line stanzas in chain rhyme: a - b - a, b - c - b, c - d - c, and so on. It may be as brief as two stanzas, or as long as Dante's *Divine Comedy.* The usual meter in English is iambic pentameter, and the final stanza is a quatrain instead of a triplet. The first line of the quatrain generally rhymes with the middle line of the preceding triplet as well as with the third line of the quatrain. The second and fourth lines rhyme with each other.

LOVE SONG (MULTO CON CORPORE)

THE WAYS
OF LOVE

How do I love thee? Let me count the ways:
 From top to toe, with torso in between.
Some days heels over head, and other days

THE GEOG-   Head over heels. No neck of land's as green
RAPHY OF   As your neck is; no arm of sea's as blue
LOVE   As your arm is; no hill's brow so serene

             As is your brow . . . Your headland's noble, too . . .
                 The widest river mouth is not so wide
             As your dear mouth . . .
THE COM-   Ah, men of mighty thew
PETITION   And jutting chin have wooed you—been denied!
THAT LOVE   Dare I, of lesser kidney, catch your ear?
ENGENDERS   Dare jellied backbone swim against such tide?

             I have no stomach for the fray, I fear;
                 I'm lily-livered, yellow-bellied, weak.
             I'd only put my foot in it, my dear,
THE PITY   By begging for your hand—I lack the cheek.
NEEDED   Yet let your bowels of compassion start!
FOR LOVE   Lend me a leg up! Quickly!—else I seek
                 A toehold in some softer, warmer heart.

The Rhyming Sestina

The sestina, a favorite form of Dante and Petrarch, comprises six six-line stanzas followed by a three-line envoy—thirty-nine lines in all. The last word of each stanza becomes the last word of the first line in the next, with a placement of end words throughout in a rigid pattern. Classically (though not in my example), the word repetition replaces rhyme. The end words are arranged in the following order:

                        Stanza 1. a - b - c - d - e - f
                        Stanza 2. f - a - e - b - d - c
                        Stanza 3. c - f - d - a - b - e
                        Stanza 4. e - c - b - f - a - d
                        Stanza 5. b - d - f - e - c - a

                        THE BANKRUPT'S SERENADE

                                    1.

            My television set is snowing snow;
                The snow is snowing television sets.
            The lambent moon is on the wane, and lo!
                The wane is on the moon. Wan parapets
            Have ceased to pet their paras, for they know
                Our debts repay us as we pay our debts.

                                    2.

            They said you only loved me for my debts;
                Yet flake on flake we snowed when we were snow
            Who now are mooning wanes and parapets
                And television sets. You murmured low,
            "Ah, sunsets, moonsets, hensets! Ah, the sets!"
                None know but nuns, and nuns will never know.

                                    3.

            But if a nun dun nuns, will I not know?
                Not I, for I am done with duns and debts,
            And done with parapetting in the snow.

Moon on, fair wane! Be petulant, dear pets!
My lows have cattled—let my cattle low;
My fortunes rise; my television sets.

4.

Dear love, you trounced me, matches, games, and sets.
You parapetted, but your eyes said no.
Behind my back you dallied with my debts,
While television sets were snowing snow;
You stroked the parapets of parapets
While on the moon the wanes crooned sweet and low.

5.

I hear the lambent moon start up below;
Above me soar the television sets;
The duns are nunning duns amid the snow;
You stroll in from the garden with my debts
To bring me tidings I am loath to know:
The paras have forsook their parapets.

6.

Alas, the paras! and alas! the pets!
The wane is on the moon and you, and lo!
The snow is snowing television sets.
The nuns are dunning all the nuns they know.
With lowered gaze you stand, distilling debts.
The television set is snowing snow.

ENVOY

White is the snow upon the parapets;
The television sets no more, for lo!
Tha pale nuns know that you have paid my debts.

From France

Represented below are ten examples of French verse forms, all with refrains and rigid rhyme schemes. Iambic pentameter is commonly used except in the triolet; but in most cases the poet may take his choice of meter.

The Ballade

The ballade, perhaps the earliest French form to win the English heart, consists of three eight-line stanzas followed by a four-line envoy—twenty-eight lines in all. The last line of the first stanza reappears as the last line of each succeeding stanza. The rhyme scheme is a - b - a - b - b - c - b - C for the principal stanzas, and b - c - b - C for the four-line envoy. The verse below is in iambic tetrameter.

MANON? MAIS NON*

HOW YOU TRICKED
ME INTO ATTENDING
AN OPERA WRITTEN
BY PUCCINI (OR
WAS IT MASSENET?)

Aida relish cymbal-smack,
  Horn-sweetness, shrill of piccolo
(To savor these, how Offenbach
To Bach and Offenbach I go!) . . .
  Or don't. I HATE *Manon Lescaut.*
(You said, "Lescaut to hear Manon.
  I've Boito tickets, second row . . .")
Manon Lescaut a mauvais ton.

Manon? Mais Non was prompted by a series of formidable puns which Boris Randolph contributed to *Word Ways,* the magazine of recreational linguistics.

HOW I DOZED AND	I go. Of Korsakov, and hack,
DREAMED OF MANON	As old men Lakme must; I blow
(OR WAS IT MANON	My nose, and doze. I'm in the sack
LESCAUT?)	From Faust plucked string to last *bravo*.
	I dream I'm Chopin up that shmo
	Puccini; *c'est un sal cochon*.
	Most art (Mozart, say) leaves a glow;
	Manon Lescaut a mauvais ton.

HOW I REFLECTED	Manon is Verdi vulgar pack
POSTLUDALLY ON	Hangs out. If Massenet should throw
THESE MATTERS . . .	A Mass in A, I'd lead the claque.
	(Giovanni hear Giovanni? So
	Do I. It's really *comme il faut*,
	Quite Gudenov.) *Alors, allons!*
	Indeed, I only hate one show:
	Manon Lescaut a mauvais ton.

ENVOY

AND THE MORAL	Prince, best of Gluck! . . .
I DREW.	One final *mot:*
	The opera is mostly *bon*.
	For Bizet folk, though, one's *de trop:*
	Manon Lescaut a mauvais ton.

Ballade with a Double Refrain

The ballade with a double refrain has three eight-line stanzas and a four-line envoy, like the ballad, but two refrain lines rather than one. The first appears in the fourth line of each stanza and the second line of the envoy, and the second in the final line of the stanzas and the envoy, thus: a - b - a - B - b - c - b - C, a - b - a - B - b - c - b - C, a - b - a - B - b - c -b - C, b - B - c - C. This specimen is in anapestic tetrameter.

WHEN THE WHOLE BLAMED CABOODLE HAS GONE UP THE SPOUT

When the whole blamed caboodle has gone up the spout;
    When you reckon you've fizzled, and flunked out, and so on;
When your hash has been settled, your string has run out,
    And you figure there's nothing much else left to go on;
When the coin of the realm is the coin that you're low on;
    When you look like a goner, a blooming galoot,
And your dishes are busted, save one to eat crow on—
    Let's clink glasses, my brother, and toss back a snoot.

You have kept your eyes skinned, you have gandered about,
    You have never said die, nor your row ceased to hoe on;
You have hefted your ax, you have tickled your trout,
    And you figure there's nothing much else left to go on;
You have taken life's wallops, and one more to grow on,
    And you've shut up, and buttoned your lip, and stayed mute.
Say, you're just the fellow I'll wager my dough on—
    Let's clink glasses, my buddy, and toss back a snoot.

So it's root, hog, or die—and you're sore in the snout?
    And it seems a coon's age since you last had a glow on?
And you're feeling knee-high to a skeeter, no doubt,
    And you figure there's nothing much else left to go on?

Well, I'll risk a simoleon, win, place, or show on
  My surmise you'll be dancing soon, playing your flute.
For you'll light a fire yet, pal; you've embers to blow on—
  Let's clink glasses, good buddy, and toss back a snoot.

ENVOY

Oh, you know you can't stop it; time's river will flow on,
And you figure there's nothing much else left to go on;
But I've got a prescription that chaws at the root:
Lesh clink glashes, ole buddy, an' tosh back a shnoot.

The Chant Royal

The chant royal, developed in medieval France, was popularized in English about a hundred years ago. It has five eleven-line stanzas and a five-line envoy, sixty lines in all. The stanzas are rhymed a - b - a - b - c - d - d - e - d - E, with the last line of each stanza as the refrain. The five-line envoy is rhymed d - d - e - d - E. The variant that follows has ten lines to a stanza, rhyming a - b - a - b - c - d - d - e - d - E, with the d - d - e - d - E envoy as before. The obsolete words are from *Poplollies and Bellibones*, by Susan Sperling.

FORGOTTEN WORDS ARE MIGHTY HARD TO RHYME

Quoth I to me, "A chant royal I'll dite,
  With much ado of words long laid away,
And make windsuckers of the bards who cite
  The sloomy phrases of the present day.
My song, though it encompass but a page,
  Will man illume from April bud till snow—
A song all merry-sorry, con and pro."
  (I would have pulled it off, too, given time,
Except for one small catch that didn't show:
  Forgotten words are mighty hard to rhyme.)

Ah, hadavist, in younghede, when from night
  There dawned abluscent some fair morn in May
(The word for dawning, 'sparrowfart,' won't quite
  Work in here)—hadavist, I say,
That I would ever by stoopgallant age
  Be shabbed, adushed, pitchkettled, suggiled so,
I'd not have been so redmod! Could I know?—
  One scantling piece of outwit's all that I'm
Still sure of, after all this catch-and-throw:
  Forgotten words are mighty hard to rhyme.

In younghede ne'er a thrip gave I for blight
  Of cark or ribble; I was ycore, gay;
I matched boonfellows hum for hum, each wight
  By eelpots aimcried, till we'd swerve and sway,
Turngiddy. Blashy ale could not assuage
  My thirst, nor kill-priest, even.
No Lothario

Could overpass me on Poplolly Row.
  A fairhead who eyebit me in my prime
Soon shared my donge. (The meaning's clear, although
  Forgotten words are mighty hard to rhyme.)

Fair draggle-tails once spurred my appetite;
    Then walking morts and drossels shared my play.
Bedswerver, smellsmock, housebreak was I hight—
    Poop-noddy at poop-noddy. Now I pray
That other fonkins reach safe anchorage—
    Find bellibone, straight-fingered, to bestow
True love, till truehead in their own hearts grow.
    Still, umbecasting friends who scrowward climb,
I'm swerked by mubblefubbles. Wit grows slow;
    Forgotten words are mighty hard to rhyme.

Dim on the wong at cockshut falls the light;
    Birds' sleepy croodles cease. Not long to stay . . .
Once nesh as open-tide, I now affright;
    I'm lennow, spittle-ready—samdead clay,
One clutched bell-penny left of all my wage.
    Acclumsied now, I dare no more the scrow,
But look downsteepy to the Pit below.
    Ah, hadavist! . . Yet silly is the chime;
Such squiddle is no longer apropos.
    Forgotten words are mighty hard to rhyme.

ENVOY

About me ghosts of old bawdreaminy blow;
    Eldnyng is gone, and flerd is long *de trop.*
Yet eaubruche pleased me well; I see no crime
In looking back with a "Bravissimo!"
    (Forgotten words are mighty hard to rhyme.)

Glossary of obsolete terms in "Forgotten Words Are Mighty Hard to Rhyme"

Windsucker. Covetous, envious person.
Sloomy. Lazy, dull, sleepy.
Merry-sorry. Part cheerful, part despondent.
Hadavist. Had I but known.
Younghede. Youth.
Abluscent. Cleansing, purifying.
Stoopgallant. That which humbles (the great).
Shab. To get rid of.
Adush. To cause to fall heavily.
Pitchkettle. Puzzle.
Suggil. To beat black and blue, defame.
Redmod. Hasty, rash.
Scantling. Scanty.
Outwit. Knowledge.
Thrip. A snap of the fingers.
Cark. Care, distress.
Ribble. Wrinkle, furrow.
Ycore. Chosen, elect.
Boonfellow. Warm companion.
Hum. A mixture of beer or ale and spirits.
Aimcry. Encourage.
Turngiddy. Drunk.
Blashy. Thin, weak.
Kill-priest. Port wine; any strong drink.
Fairhead. A beautiful woman.
Eyebite. To wink at.
Donge. Bed.
Draggle-tail. A wanton, a prostitute.

Mort. A harlot, a loose woman.
Drossel. A slut, hussy.
Bedswerver. An unfaithful husband.
Housebreak. A home wrecker.
Smellsmock. A licentious man.
Poop-noddy. A fool; also, the game of love.
Fonkin. A little fool.
Bellibone. A fair and good maiden.
Umbecast. To ponder.
Scrow. Sky.
Swerked. Troubled.
Mubblefubbles. Melancholy.
Wong. Moor.
Cockshut. Dusk.
Croodle. Cheeping.
Nesh. Fresh, young.
Open-tide. Spring.
Lennow. Flabby, limp.
Spittle. Hospital for indigents, lepers, etc.
Samdead. Half-dead.
Bell-penny. Money saved for one's funeral.
Acclumsied. Physically impaired, paralyzed.
Downsteepy. Precipitous.
Squiddle. Time-wasting chatter.
Bawdreaminy. Bawdry; unchastity; lewdness.
Eldnyng. Anxiety.
Flerd. Deceit, fraud.
Eaubruche. Adultery.

The Triolet

The triolet is an eight-line verse. Lines 7 and 8 repeat lines 1 and 2; line 1 is also repeated as line 4. The rhyme scheme is a - b - A - a - b - A - B; the metric system is iambic tetrameter.

ECHOING TRIOLET

O try, O try a triolet!—
   O try, O try! O try, O try
A triolet to win your pet!
O try, O try a triolet!—
What if the triolet's all wet?—
   The trial yet will catch her eye.
O try, O try a triolet!
   O try, O try! O try, O try!

IF LOVE BE FINE

If love be fine, as some contend,
   The lady's not for burning.
What blame is hers who love doth lend
If love be fine, as some contend?
The sin is when the kisses end—
   The fault in love is spurning.
If love be fine, as some pretend,
   The lady's not for burning.

The Rondel

The rondel, an outgrowth of the triolet, commonly nowadays has thirteen or fourteen lines, two rhymes, two stanzas, and a one- or two-line refrain. This is in iambic pentameter, rhyming A - B - b - a - a - b - A - B, a - b - b - a - A:

I WAS A STRANGER

"I was a stranger, and you took me in."
   So spake the Christ; and you seemed kind as He.
   When I was hungered, short of do-re-mi,
You offered introductions—credit—gin—
The shirt from off your back, come lose, come win;
   Your eyes were wet from selfless sympathy.
"I was a stranger, and you took me in."
   So spake the Christ; and you seemed kind as He.

I woke next morning, gulped down aspirin,
   And found you gone, and gone your charity . . .
   Also my wallet, credit cards, and key.
It's odd, in fact, that I still have my skin.
I was a stranger, and you took me in.

The Rondelet

The rondelet, a verse of seven lines, generally has a purport similar to a tickle on the inner elbow, or the dropped handkerchief of your great-great Aunt Jane. The rhyme scheme is A - b - A - a - b - b - A.

ROUND

> . . . then she from laving
> emerges fragrant misty and unkissed
>   then she from laving
> emerges and my heart is not behaving
> and how can I refrain or she resist
> and afterward anew the fragrant mist
>   then she from laving . . .

The Roundel

The roundel, an eleven-line verse derived from the rondel, was introduced into English verse in the nineteenth century by Algernon Swinburne. The usual rhyme scheme is a - b - a - B, b - a - b - a - b - a - B. The fourth and eleventh lines form the refrain, a repetition of the first two syllables of the opening line. Except for the refrain, the first of the roundels that follow is in iambic pentameter, and the second in iambic tetrameter.

TO A YOUNG LADY WHO ASKED ME
TO "DO" HER IN A THUMBNAIL SKETCH

> What? Do you in a thumbnail sketch? I may go
>   Too far, my dear; perhaps I'll kick your shin.
> Suppose I say you're often a virago?
>   What? Do you in?
>
>   Suppose I say how shamelessly you sin—
> How far from paths of virtue you agley go?—
>   How incoherent in your cups you've been—
> Your speech verbose, your logic a farrago?
>   All right, though, if you wish it . . . I'll begin.
> But . . . do you really *mean* it when you say "Go"?
>   What? Do you in?

The key word in the roundel below begged to be punned on, and I can't resist that sort of thing.

TO A CRITIC

> To die a critic will be tough;
>   Hell yawns for you, you shmo, you schnook.
> No ebony is black enough
>   To dye a critic.
>
> You brushed off my phonetics book—
>   Dismissed it as a bit of fluff.
> Look here, you nincompoop—it took
>   Me midnight oil to write that stuff;—
> To range from schwa and printer's hook
>   To circumflex; from macron gruff
>   To diacritic.

The Rondeau

There are thirteen rhyming lines in the rondeau, with part of the first line used twice as a refrain. My verse is in iambic tetrameter, but pentameter is more usual. The rhyme scheme is a - a - b - b - a - a - b - R; a - b - a - R.

HOW SAD, HOW SAD!

How sad, how sad that I must say
I shall not save the world today!
Just yesterday that wasn't true;
I knew exactly what to do
To end society's decay
And keep the atom bomb at bay
And make pollution fade away.
Today I fell in love with you.
        How sad, how sad!
Let victims weep, let villains prey!
Though all the earth's in disarray,
Let it go hang—who cares? We two
Will trade our kisses anyway.
        (How sad, how sad!)

The following version of the rondeau has seventeen rhyming lines in five stanzas, of which the last four conclude with a steadily shrinking refrain. The rhyme is a - a - b - b - a; a - a - b - R; a - a - b - R; a - a - b - R; a - a - b - R.

OOPS! YOU ALMOST PICKED UP THE CHECK!

"I'll pay for lunch this time," I hear you say,
"So join me in the best . . . What's good today?
Fresh *Escargots?* . . . *Saumon? Palourdes Farcies?* . . .
Coquille Saint-Jacques? . . . or *Jambon de Paris?* . . .
Bisque de Homard? Or *Soupe de Trois Filets?*

"*Délices de sole,* perhaps, for *entremets?* . . .
Quiche? Fruits de Mer? . . . or *Foie de Veau Sauté?*
Escallopines de Veau? . . . The treat's on me;
I'll pay for lunch this time." (I bet!)

"And then . . . *Filet mignon?* Or *Demi-Grain Grillé?* . . .
Chateaubriand? . . . *Paillard de Boeuf Vert-Pré?* . . .
With *Haut-Brion?* . . . Or *Haut-Lafitte?* Feel free:
I'll pay for lunch this time.

"We'll finish with . . . say *Mousse?* Or *Crêpes Flambées?*
And *Café Filtre,* after *Pousse-café?*"
(Again you murmur, reassuringly:
"I'll pay for lunch.")

But having lunched with you before, I'll stay
With toast and tea, and count my cash. The way
The record reads, it's sure as sure can be
I'll pay.

The Rondeau Redoublé

The rondeau redoublé has five quatrains of four iambic pentameter lines each, with a sixth of three iambic pentameter lines followed by an iambic dimeter. The first line of the first stanza recurs as the last line of the second; the second line of the first stanza as the last line of the third; the third line of the first stanza as the last line of the fourth; and the fourth line of the first stanza as the last line of the fifth. The last line of the sixth, concluding stanza repeats the opening of the first line of the first stanza. A bit complicated, but fun.

The following rondeau redoublé runs through several idiomatic uses of the word "get."

GET THAT "GET"!

Get gets around. *Get* also gets the air;
   Gets after; gets it in the neck; gets set.
Get gets off easy . . . back at . . . in my hair.
   Prince, marvel at all these: the get of *get!*

Get gets a wiggle on; gets off the ground; gets wet;
   Gets wise to; gets the gate; gets here; gets there;
Gets wind of . . . words in edgewise . . . even with. You bet,
   Get gets around! *Get* also gets the air.

Get gets a load of; gets ahead; gets square;
   Gets on the ball (I've hardly started yet).
Get gets the worst of; sometimes gets unfair;
   Gets after; gets it in the neck; gets set.

Get gets my number; gets me in a fret;
   Gets on my nerves . . . a move on . . . tells me where
I get off; gets a rise out of; gets met.
   Get gets off easy . . . back at . . . in my hair.

Get gets along; gets by; gets lost; gets rare;
   Gets better . . . down to cases . . . in a sweat . . .
The jump on . . . to first base . . . me down . . . a threat.
   Prince, marvel at all these: the get of *get!*

Get gets my back up; gets me into debt.
   Get gets the ax . . . the feel of . . . gets unbear-
Able . . . the picture . . . in a pet . . .
   Me off. *Get* even gets the clothes I wear.
      Get gets around.

The Villanelle

Villanelle is the diminutive of a Latin word for "rustic," and the form was first used for country songs. It is made up of five tercets and a final quatrain—a total of nineteen lines. Lines one and three of the first tercet are refrain lines, repeated alternately as the last lines of the succeeding stanzas. The final four-line stanza closes with the two refrain lines. The rhyme scheme is A^1 - b - A^2, a - b - A^1, a - b - A^2, a - b - A^1, a - b - A^2, a - b - A^1, A^2.

The first of the following villanelles is in trochaic tetrameter, the second in dactylic tetrameter.

GRAVEYARD SQUARE

None recalls that I am there,
So sedately do I lie
On the hill in Graveyard Square.

Tranquil is the mouse's lair
In the moss above my thigh;
None recalls that I am there.

Each intent on his affair,
Snake and mole and hare go by
On the hill in Graveyard Square.

Earth, diaphanous as air,
Opens heaven to my eye:
None recalls that I am there.

Cherubim raise wings in prayer,
Unsuspecting how I spy;
None recalls that I am there
On the hill in Graveyard Square.

WAS BACCHUS A BOIL VEXING JUPITER'S THIGH?

Never emberlucock or inpuregafize your spirits
with these vain thoughts and idle concepts.
—Rabelais

Was Bacchus a boil vexing Jupiter's thigh? . . .
Gargantua, wax formed in Gargamelle's ear?
(And where did we hail from ourselves, you and I?)

A heel burst its blister for Roquetaillade's cry;
From nurse's old slipper did Crocmosh appear.
(Was Bacchus a boil vexing Jupiter's thigh?)

When Castor and Pollux hatched, Leda clucked, "My!
Some gossips may hint that a swan has been here!"
(And where did we hail from ourselves, you and I?)

With myrrh bark the dad of Adonis did lie;
Minerva popped out of a migraine chimere.
(Was Bacchus a boil vexing Jupiter's thigh?)

Jehovah shaped Eve from the rib of her guy,
While Venus from foam undertook her career.
(And where did we hail from ourselves, you and I?)

We call for the Author, but hear no reply;
The future is mist, and the past is unclear.
Was Bacchus a boil vexing Jupiter's thigh?
And where did we hail from ourselves, you and I?

The Kyrielle

The kyrielle, which originated in medieval France, is from *kyrie eleison* (Greek, "Lord have mercy"), part of a short liturgy used especially at the beginning of the Mass in the Eastern and Roman churches. The words are repeated several times. Often used in hymns but by no means confined to them, the kyrielle consists of any number of four-line stanzas, the first three lines in iambic tetrameter and the fourth (which is unchanged throughout the verse) generally in iambic dimeter. The rhyme scheme is a - a - b - B.

TO GOD THE PRAISE

When I was keen and young as you,
I laid the world out to renew.
I laid it out, and there it lays—
To God the praise.

When I was new and young and dense,
My friends deplored my want of sense.
But, sense is silliness these days—
To God the praise.

Confounded by my flabby thighs,
They urged me on to exercise.
Their obsequies my spirits raise—
To God the praise.

No Jack more dearly loved his Jill
Than I loved mine. I love her still:
Love unrequited ne'er decays.
To God the praise.

My wife and I do well agree,
For she sees little hope for me;
And there is much in what she says.
To God the praise.

From Greece

The Ode

In ancient Greece, the ode, unrhymed, had a *strophe,* during which the chorus moved to the left side of the stage; an *antistrophe,* during which it moved back to the right; and an *epode,* or aftersong, during which it stood still. Today any dignified lyric may be styled an ode, providing there is constant progress in the stanzas toward a conclusion.

The following verse is not dignified; it is an ode simply because I chose to name it so.

ODE TO AN ELEVATOR

Capricious, upsy-downsy sweet,
    My patience with thy presence crown!
Pray, when thy rising I entreat,
No more, dear love, rush past my feet
    Down!

Behold, thy button burneth bright,
    A signal thou wilt be here soon—
If not today, if not tonight,
Anon—perhaps when clappers smite
    Noon.

I hear thee coming! Praise to thee,
    And praise to God, and praise to luck!—
(Though well I know that presently,
'Twixt Six and Seven, I shall be
    Stuck.)

Thy door slides open. Slightly squiffed,
    I sense too late the empty draft.
A lesser lover would be miffed
To step in lift, and find but lift
    Shaft.

No tears for me I pray thee shed;
    Drain not for me the hemlock cup.
But I adjure thee from the dead—
When next I press thy button, head
    Up.

The Sapphic

The verse form associated with the Greek poet Sappho, who flourished around 600 B.C., is a series of four-line stanzas. The first three lines are now variant trochaic pentameter (the third foot is a dactyl), while the fourth pairs a dactyl and a trochee. The form is traditionally without rhyme, so no example was needed in this book; but there was a specimen in my files, so here it is. There is nothing to prevent you from developing a rhyme scheme for your own sapphic.

SCRATCH THAT MUDBLOWER; ONE LOVE-MAIDEN TO GO

Research having demonstrated that diners will not order
fishes with ugly names, the National Marine Fisheries Service
is seeking to make the names more attractive.—The Wall Street Journal

Toadfish, croaker, hogsucker, safely swimming;
Harmless, care-free mudblower, spurned by humans—
Keep those names! they save you from being eaten—
    Flaunted on menus.

Ratfish, gag, grunt, viperfish, pray you never
Turn to ''lovefish, honeyfish, poached in parsley''!
Menus offer ''love-maiden'' just to render
    Mudblower tempting.

From Japan: the Haiku

The haiku is a Japanese verse form of seventeen syllables making three lines, with five syllables in the first, seven in the second, and five in the third. There is no rhyme. To the Japanese it is an allusive form, leaving much unsaid. Perhaps they do not use it in jest, as is done here:

HAIKUS SHOW I.Q.'S

Haikus show I. Q.'s:
High I. Q.'s try haikus. Low
I. Q.'s—no haikus.*

From the East Indies: The Pantoum

The pantoum is a Malay verse form popularized by Victor Hugo in the nineteenth century, and since widely imitated in both French and English. The stanzas are indefinite in number, rhyming a - b - a - b; the second and fourth lines of each stanza are repeated as the first and third of the next, and the fourth line of the final stanza is identical with the first line of the first.

This pantoum is in iambic tetrameter:

CONSIDER NOW THE QUARK

Consider now the Quark, which is
    A Concept sub-atomical.
No man alive has seen its phiz;
    Perhaps it isn't Is at all.

A Concept sub-atomical
    Too tenuous I find to prove.
Perhaps it isn't Is at all.
    This goes for Hate, and also Love.

Too tenuous I find to prove
    The Sun, the Shadow, and the Wind.
This goes for Hate, and also Love,
    And other matters of the kind.

The Sun, the Shadow, and the Wind—
    The Dream, the Doing, the Despair,

---

*Frank Johnson says I have it backward; *low* I. Q.'s write haikus.

And other matters of the kind
    I find are proven best in prayer.

The Dream, the Doing, the Despair,
    And other matters, being His,
I find are proven best in prayer.
    Consider now the Quark, which Is.

Local Products

The Ballad

Some English-language verse forms have kissing kin but no sure forebears in other languages. The ballad, for instance, may be related to the French ballade, but its temperament is Scottish. It is a fairly short poem, tending to four-line stanzas, which often tells a violent story. The meter and rhyme scheme are not fixed. The most popular line is iambic tetrameter, used in the sad and fictitious tale about Rick Ballad that follows.

When I first met the real Rick Ballad he was considerably overweight; the floor of his office was said to have required a series of reinforcements. But the last time I dined with him he had lost more than a hundred pounds and was still losing, as a result of restricting his ingestion to a mysterious white powder stirred in water. His entrees in this verse are all of prosodic origin.

A PEST IAMB, ANAPEST RICK BALLAD WAS

(Or, a Ballad in a Sad Cafe)

Rick Ballad (God him pity!)
    Set out one night to dine.
His menu was a Ditty
    In Galliambic line.

His soup was Virelaic;
    His cocktail, Dipodee;
His Spondee was Alcaic,
    His Distych, Ditrochee.

He took a pinch of Rhythm,
    Of Ode and Dithyramb,
And mixing Rondeaus with 'em
    He seasoned his Iamb.

He ordered baked Sestinas,
    And half-baked Doggerel;
He licked his Lyric clean as
    A Sapphic Kyrielle.

He flavored Terza Rima
    With Pastoral and Thesis,
And Chant Royal with cream—a
    Bucolic Diaeresis.

His Tercet was a salad
    Of Sonnet and Cinquain.
"Ballade too," ordered Ballad,
    "And Double the Refrain."

Verse Onomatopoeian,
    Szysigium to taste,
Enlarged unendingly an
    Enjambe-ment of waist.

Still Ballad gorged on Dactyl,
    While Trochee and Molossus
Still down his maw were packed till
    He out-colossed Colossus.

(Colossus fell, and wallowed.
    So, too, poor Ballad fell;
And, dying, left unswallowed
    His final Villanelle.)

The Venus and Adonis Stanza

Shakespeare wrote *Venus and Adonis* in a series of six-line stanzas rhyming a - b - a - b - c - c. Though the prototype was in iambic pentameter, Venus and Adonis stanzas now employ a variety of poetic lines.

I HAVE LONE AND LEVEL SANDS OF MY OWN, SHELLEY

Now may the heavens open up, and pour
    Into the desert of my mind, a rain
Of smarts . . . gray matter . . . "two and two make four"—
    A drench of brain!
What wit bloomed here before some early drought
    Parched it out!

The Spenserian Stanza

The Spenserian stanza, developed by the poet for the *Faerie Queen,* is made up of eight lines in iambic pentameter and a ninth in iambic hexameter, rhyming a - b - a - b - c - b - c - c.

The example below was inspired, if that is the word, by the Graeae sisters, three old sea deities of Greek mythology named Pephredo, Deino, and Enyo. Their hair was gray and straggly from birth, their shape was that of a swan, and they possessed among them but one eye and one tooth, which they passed back and forth.

You have probably read, as I have, poems that seem to suffer the ailments of the Graeaes: blindness the blacker by contrast with isolated flashes of vision; insights that might be meaty, if only a tooth were provided for chewing them.

A REFLECTION THAT BORROWS TROPES FROM CURRENT POEMS

The Graeaes' dreadful eye gets twenty-twenty
    On Aesculapius's chart.* That eye
Must serve for all three sisters, but sees plenty:
    Streaked-yellow urine dulling in the sky . . .
Robe like a door ajar . . . twigs stripped in rain . . .
    Legs under-tucked in grief . . . breasts brushing by . . .
Sees plenty, but cannot inform the brain—
The Graeaes shake dim heads, and pass it round again.

The Elegy

The elegy, first "a poem composed in elegiac couplets," is now any mournful poem, especially one lamenting the dead. Here the first, second, third, fifth, sixth, and seventh lines of the octet are iambic tetrameter; the fourth and eighth are iambic pentameter. The sestet alternates between iambic tetrameter and iambic trimeter.

---

*Aesculapius, son of Apollo, was the god of healing, and doubtless practiced ophthalmology among other specialties.

ELEGY FOR MY LATE FRIEND AND TAILOR, CANIO SALUZZI

As spread my waistful span (io),
You never failed, dear Canio,
To prove clothes make the man (io),
    However dropsical his lower part.
Your camouflaging suits (zi)
My ev'ry bulge confute (zi);
Saluto-te, Saluzzi,
Past master of the thread-and-needle art!

You're called aloft, to furbelow
    Our Lord Emmanuel.
Unhid henceforth must be my slow,
    Sure embonpointal swell.
Yet I am comforted to know
    That God is tailored well.

The Limerick

The limerick, though perhaps associated with a medieval Latin verse form, was popularized by Edward Lear in the nineteenth century; some speculate that the name corrupts Lear-ick. More often it is attributed to the refrain "Will you come up to Limerick" (an Irish county and city), said to have been sung between extemporized verses at convivial Irish gatherings. Limericks are judged by the elegance of their structure, the wittiness of their conceits, and often by their ribaldry. There are five lines, and the rhyme scheme is a - a - b - b - a. The first, second, and fifth lines have three feet each—an iamb and two anapests. The third and fourth have one iamb and one anapest each.

FOR ISAAC ASIMOV, WHO NEVER THOUGHT OF HIMSELF AS A COCKNEY

A Cockney named I. Asimov,
As 'is trousers 'e started to doff,
    Said, "My lydy friends yawn
    W'en I 'as 'em on,
But w'istle w'en I 'as 'em off."

ON JOSEPH BRODSKY'S CONTENTION THAT NINETY PERCENT OF THE BEST LYRIC POETRY IS WRITTEN FOLLOWING SEXUAL INTERCOURSE

A poetry writer named Brodsky
Came up with this theory oddsky:
    The best odes to sweetum
    Emerge post-coitum.
(From some folks. The rest of us nodsky.)

The Clerihew

The clerihew, created at the dawn of this century by the English journalist Edmund Clerihew Bentley, consists of two couplets of uneven length and scansion, the first line referring to some individual and the remainder reporting on him (or her). The intent is humorous, and the result often (but, as with the limerick, not always) funny.

DON JUAN AT COLLEGE

Don Juan
Carried on
Till they switched him from Biology
To Abnormal Psychology.

INCIDENT IN A WORLD SERIES GAME

Babe Ruth
Generally told the truth.
When he pointed over the wall
That's where he hit the ball.

The Double Dactyl

Perhaps half a century after the invention of the clerihew it was joined by another new verse form, the double dactyl. Anthony Hecht and Paul Pascal developed the device, and Mr. Hecht, with John Hollander, wrote the first examples. It has two stanzas of four lines each, each line a double dactyl, except that the last line of each stanza is truncated. Nonsense syllables make up the first line; a name, the second; a single word, the sixth. The third, fifth and seventh develop the theme, and the fourth and eighth are rhyme lines.

A DOUBLE DACTYL FOR HECHT, ECT.

Scribble a dribble a
Hecht on you Hollander
Pascal vobiscum you
Lyrical three!

Write me a poem in
Proceleusmaticus;*
Then I'll admit you are
Better than me.

LOOKING GLASS LOGIC

Tweedledum Tweedledee
Alice in Wonderland
First she was tiny and
Then she was tall;

Animal arguments
Anthropomorphical
Were not persuasive to
Alice at all.

Chain Verse

Chain (or *echoing*) verse repeats sounds in a fixed pattern. The following sonnet returns to the last sound of each preceding line in the first sound of the next.

I SCARCE RECALL

I scarce recall when first you said hello.
"Hello!" said I, too young to realize

---

*A poetic foot of four short syllables (pyrrhics), impractical in English.

Lies were your vade mecum. (Spiders so
  Sew webs, and lie in wait for hapless flies.)

Flies time so fast? Why is it I can know
  No more that lying lovelight in your eyes?
I scarce recall . . . it was so long ago . . .
  A golden time, before I grew too wise.

Why's wisdom executioner of youth?
  You thought I left because you lied. Not I!
I left when you began to tell the truth:
  Truth comes too dear for coinless youth to buy.

By lies I might regain you, after all.
Although . . . so long ago . . . I scarce recall.

The Epigram

An epigram is a pithy saying in either prose or verse. A translation from the Latin describes it this way:

The qualities rare in a bee that we meet
  In an epigram never should fail;
The body should always be little and sweet,
  And a sting should be left in its tail.

The epigrams below are intended not to instruct but to amuse.

TO A YOUNG POETESS

You're beautiful, you're sweet,
  But, God!—
How your iambic feet
  Plod!

LOVE'S A GAME

Love's a game
  Indeed, my pet;
I think its name
  Is Russian Roulette.

PAMPHLET FROM THE RIGHT TO LIFE FOUNDATION

To abort little Willy
Is silly.
That's what war
Is for.

MACAULAY TELLS US

Macaulay tells us Byron's rules of life
Were: Hate your neighbor; love your
  neighbor's wife.

ON AN AGING PRUDE

She who, when young and fair,
Would wink men up the stair,
Now, old and ugly, locks
The door where no man knocks.

Word Play In Rhyme

All poetry, even the most serious—not to say all literature, and indeed all verbal communication—requires word play for maximum effectiveness. Every rhetorical device, from metaphor to hyperbole to tmesis, is word play. When the purpose of the exercise is simply to amuse or divert, as is the case with most of the verses here, it is permissible to mispronounce, to split a word in two for a rhyme (Procrustean verse), to rhyme one word with two (mosaic verse), and to use any of the other devices that follow, along with many that I have not mentioned.

Procrustean (Impossible) Rhyme

There are no conventional rhymes for many words. As mentioned earlier, however, it is frequently possible to rhyme them by the method Procrustes used on his victims— stretching them if they were too short to fit his bed, and lopping something off if they were too long. Here the chopping process was used:

THE UNRHYMABLE WORD	THE RHYME
Month	It is unth- inkable to find A rhyme for month Except this special kind.
Orange	The four eng- ineers Wore orange Brassieres.*
Oblige	Love's lost its glow? No need to lie; j- ust tell me ''go!'' And I'll oblige.
Silver	If Pegasus Were but a bus That any man could board, I might distil Ver- ona's silver Beauty in a word.

Mosaic Rhyme

Mosaic rhyming, the match of one word with two or more, increases the rhyming potential of many words, and makes some available that otherwise would have no rhyme at all. With a few exceptions, however, my rhyming list does not include mosaics.

---

*This rhyme would not have worked before women began moving into jobs once reserved for men.

HOW ARIADNE BECAME DIFFERENTLY-ABLED

The dryad Ariadne used for play den
A cypress tree. When youths strolled by she'd note 'em,
And (quite unlike a proper blushing maiden)
Would downward swoop, and grab 'em by the scrotum.

They flocked to sample what that dryad's swoop meant;
She added lovers not as you and I add,
By ones or twos or threes, but by aggroupment;
She was the cypress grove's most active dryad

Until she pulled a tendon.
                                        Hence this sad ode.
Our discombobulated Ariadne
No longer swoops in love from bower shadowed;
She sits above and poultices her bad knee.

How sad for one who's wantoned from the cradle!
No more a light of love! No more a gay dish!
Below, youths pant galore, yet she must stay dull!
With all that fire inside, must act old-maidish!

(A dryad, being amorously matchless,
Needs quantity to show her what the French meant
By "Vive la difference!" When doomed to catch less,
She's very apt to die of the retrenchment.)

Anagram Verse

Anagrams are words which, by rearrangement of the letters, form other words. They can be the basis of puzzle verses:

DRINKING SONG

He **** for gold,
   As I for ale;
I've **** of this;
   Of that has he.
For me a kiss
   **** Holy Grail;
He'd go cuckold
   To **** a fee.
Yet, ****! I wist
   (And I'd **** bail)
He'd pay fourfold
   To be like me.

The anagrams: opts, pots, tops, spot, stop, post.

PRE-PARENTAL PLAINT

When I ******* to be a father,
You ******* my willingness to bother.
Now I *******, for I foresee
You'll leave the ******* to me.

The missing words: aspired, praised, despair, diapers.

The Doublet

Doublets are variants of anagram verse built around a series of missing words of which each differs from its predecessor by a single letter. The last word of the series contrasts in meaning with the first. Here is a nursery rhyme redone as a doublet:

SOLOMON GRUNDY

Solomon Grundy, Monday ****,
Tuesday orphaned, lone and ****,
Wednesday begged the **** relent,
Thursday 'neath his **** still bent,
Friday on the **** fell ill,
Saturday **** and signed his will.
Sunday final rites were said:
Solomon Grundy, he was ****.

The missing words: born, lorn, Lord, load, road, read, dead.

Ormonym

Verbatim, the language quarterly, defines "ormonym" as "a verbal pair of charade sentences, as 'some others I've seen' and 'some mothers I've seen.' " Here the verbal pair is a verbal quartet.

WANTED: AN UNDERSTANDING

Insinuate
That you, as I, impatient moan,
Nor longer can (so tumid grown
In breath, in blood, in pore, in pate,
In sinew) wait!

Vow you've nipped apples of your own
In sin! (You ate
Your share, I'm bound!) Admit it, mate!—
In sin you wait.

Homonym Couplet

Words that sound alike but have a different spelling and meaning are homonyms. You are supposed to guess the homonyms indicated by asterisks in the following couplets:

1.

Dammed be that beast who, as he ***** on others,
Gives ****** to God, and ***** all beasts be brothers.

2.

Say, **** man in thy ***** cot,
Art ****** pleased with thy lowly lot?

3.

I met a wise antelope, born in a zoo;
And I wish that I knew what that *** *** ****

1. Preys, praise, prays.
2. Holy, holey, wholly.
3. New, gnu, knew.

ESPYramids

In ESPYramids, another variant of the anagram verse, the first missing word consists of one letter. An added letter makes the next word in the sequence, and the accumulation continues throughout the verse, letters being rearranged as required to make each new word. Or the process may be reversed, going from a long word down. An ESPYramid:

JUST BRAGGING, REALLY

Though *, well gone ** ***, may ****,
"O tyrant Death, where is thy *****?"
The ****** of wicked things I've done
Makes ******* out my sins no fun.
There's but a ******** chance at best
That I will pass my final test.
For all my *********, I've mounting
Concern about that Last Accounting.

The missing words: I, in, gin, sing, sting, string, sorting, sporting, posturing. The verse in the clear:

Though I, well gone in gin, may sing,
"O tyrant Death, where is thy sting?"
The string of wicked things I've done
Makes sorting out my sins no fun.
There's but a sporting chance at best
That I will pass my final test.
For all my posturing, I've mounting
Concern about that Last Accounting.

TO AN IDIOT WHO SEES THE BEST IN EVERYTHING

Would * saw proof of God's restraint
** rank defects by Him deviced!—
In ***, saw gold!—in ****, saw *****!—
A ****, ** daub of mud and sand!—
** *****, a treasure underpriced!—
Plain ******, ** errant atoms!—and
* ******, ** every **********!

The missing words: I; in; tin; snit; saint; star; in; In trash; charts, in; A Christ, in; Antichrist. The verse in the clear:

Would *I* saw proof of God's restraint
In rank defects by Him deviced!—
In tin, saw gold!—in snit, saw saint!—
A star, in daub of mud and sand!—
In trash, a treasure underpriced!—
Plain charts, in errant atoms!—and
A Christ, in every Antichrist!

Pangrammic Couplet

A pangram is a passage containing all twenty-six letters of the alphabet with a minimum of repetitions. As the number of letters shrinks, it becomes increasingly difficult to create a sensible line, and there are few comprehensible pangrams of fewer than twenty-eight letters. "The quick brown fox jumps over the lazy dog," used as a touch-typing exercise, has thirty-five. It is almost impossible to create a sensible verse in that brief a compass. This pangram verse has seventy letters:

GOD BE HIS JUDGE

God be his judge: that passive, zealous Quaker
Who first yields Country, Kindred next; then Maker.

Univocalic Verse

A univocalic verse restricts itself to a single vowel, in this case *e:*

BLESS THESE SHEEP

Blessed Shepherd,
Bless these sheep;
Bless the shepherdess.
Gentle the bell-
wether keep;
Shelter send them,
Send them sleep;
Send them blessedness.

Lipogrammatic Verse

A lipogram bars entry to some one of the five vowels. But that does not mean, as you will see in three of the four verses below, that the *sound* of the vowel has to be forgone.

No A:

My weight, sir, you must not survey.
No, weigh me not—no weigh, no weigh.

No E:

Said Ann, ''Kiss not, sir—any
Would quickly turn to many.''
And all that happy night
I found that Ann was right.

No I:

Why doth the eyeless fellow cry? . . .
Would you not cry, had you no eye?

No U:

A needless vowel this—it's heard
E'en when not written in a word,
As in *eschew, kerchoo,* and *who;*
And *drew, anew,* and *interview.*
I now declare this vowel moot,
And ban it from the alphaboot.

Acrostic Verse

An acrostic verse is one in which certain letters, read in sequence, form a name, motto, or message. Though the acrostic letters are usually the first in each line, they may be anywhere in it, so long as the pattern is consistent. The acrostic below is a holiday greeting.

NOW, A LITTLE WHILE

Now, a little while,
    From the care and cark,
Something like a smile
    Shimmers in the dark.

Zephyr's scented art
   Dwindles rime and snow;
In a melted heart,
   Softly, flowers grow.

Joy, a moment now,
   Thumps old Sorrow's side;
Under festive bough
   Nemesis has died.

Brief, by iron laws,
   Though this magic be,
Unbeliever, pause:
   Pagan, bend your knee.

Zest as keen as this
   Pricks the sullen soul;
Vast polarities
   Blend in vaster whole.

Mark—the night is through.
Memory must do.

(You could waste a deal of time looking for the key here, but once you know it the message is simple to decipher. Simply replace the first letter of each line with the letter that precedes it in the alphabet, and read down; you have MERRY CHRISTMAS TO YOU ALL.)

Words, not letters, are the acrostic units in the verse below.

FORECAST: CHILLY

Time befriends
   For brief space—
Warm days sends;
   Clothes in grace

Man and maid.
   This I wot:
Looks must fade,
   Like or not.

One is not
   Long here, chums;
Cold from hot,
   Winter comes.

(If you take the first word of each line one after another, they read: TIME FOR WARM CLOTHES, MAN: THIS LOOKS LIKE ONE LONG COLD WINTER.)

Limerick with Palindrome

A palindrome is a passage that reads the same from left to right or right to left. Some fanatics have written palindromes pages long, generally conveying little except perhaps a mood. In this limerick, the palindrome takes up only the last line.

PASSION'S A PERSONAL PERCEPTION

Meg's fashion in passion, though warm, 'll
Strike some as a trifle too formal.
   In the midst of a bout
   She's been heard to cry out,
"La, Mr. O'Neill, lie normal!"

Abbreviation Verse

THE MRS. KR. MR. (A ROUND)

The Mrs. kr. Mr.
Then how her Mr. kr.!
He kr. kr. kr.
Until he raised a blr.
The blr. killed his Mrs.
Then how he mr. krs.!
He. mr. mr. mr.
Until he kr. sr.
He covered her with krs.
Till she became his Mrs.
The Mrs. kr. Mr.
(and so on and on)

Digital Verse

A digital verse replaces suitable words or syllables with digits:

UP-AND-DOWN COUNTING SONG

Up   Dear ewe, dear lamb, I've *1* thee; we
    Shall *2*tle through the fields together.
With *3*d and pipe we'll jubilee;
We'll gambol back and *4*th in glee;
If *5* thy heart, I'll bellow, ''Whee!''
    However *6* the weather.
In *7*th heaven I with thee
Shall culmin*8* our ecstasy;
Dear ewe be*9*, thou'rt tied to me,
    And *10*der is the tether.

Down   Yet I confess, I *10*d to see
    (When *9* no more am certain whether
This herb we *8* doth still agree—
Somehow it tastes less *7*ly)
That class*6* sense says thou shouldst flee
    (If *5* agreed) to new bellwether,
With him to *4*age. It may be,
From oath *3*leased, love grows more free—
Although (*2* change my simile)
    It's shrunk to *1* pin-feather.

Alphabetic verse

The first line of an alphabetical verse starts with A, the second with B, and so on through the twenty-six letters. The verses are often lists—of flowers, say, or beasts, rivers, countries—and in some of the more difficult examples several items are named to a line, each with the same opening letter. (In the example below, check the second word rather than the first in each indented line.)

THE ALPHABETIC CIRCUS WHERE THE BEASTS ALL SIT AND RHYME

I'll meet you at the circus where the beasts all sit and rhyme;
The keepers sing in sonnets, and admission is a dime.
    The *Addis*, a skink, can make lepers feel fine;
    The *Balisaur*, badger, is nosed like a swine;

The *Chil*, or the Indian kite, is a hawk;
The *Dikkop*'s a curlew with dikkopy squawk;
The *Essling*'s a salmon that isn't full-grown;
The *Fitchet*'s a polecat you don't want to own;
The *Gundi*'s a rodent as long as your hand;
The *Hassar*'s a catfish that walks on the land;
The *Inia*'s seven feet long—and a whale;
The *Jako's* a parrot, and gray beak to tail;
The *Koi* is a carp from a Japanese bay;
The *Lindo*'s a tanager, bright as the day;
The *Maha* is monkey and deer—two in one;
The *Naja*'s a serpent that kills just for fun;
Orignal's a moose, with great antlers like saws;
The *Pia*'s a rabbit-like creature that gnaws;
The *Quica*'s a possum that sighs in its sleep;
The *Rosella's* a parrakeet, also a sheep;
The *Simbil*'s a bronzy-backed stork with white belly;
The *Tua*'s a bird that eats honey and jelly;
The *Urva*'s a mongoose, the crab-eating kind;
The *Vison*'s a mink with fur coats on its mind;
The *Wou-wou*'s a gibbon that calls out ''Wow-wow;''
The *Xerus*, a squirrel, resides on a bough;
The *Yabu*'s a pony that's bred for hard wear;
Zyzzogeton, a leaf hopper, ends the affair.
I'll meet you at the circus where the beasts all sit and rhyme;
The keepers sing in sonnets, and admission is a dime.

Parthenogenetic Verse

Some words contain briefer near-equivalents within themselves, as in the instances that follow:

WORDS IN LABOR

I met some swollen words one day,
As full of roe as sturgeons;
For certain in a family way,
Yet innocent as virgins.

Parthenogenesis, they swore,
Had stocked their inner shelves,
And all those nascent words in store
Were carbons of themselves.

Lo! when at last their babies came,
They were indeed the spit
Of their mamás; each given name
Was ample proof of it:

For Aberrate did Err produce,
And Slithered mothered Slid,
And Utilize gave suck to Use,
And Cut was Curtail's kid.

The child of Jocularity
Was aptly christened Joy,
While Masculine's was instantly
Named Male, as fits a boy.

Transgression called her daughter *Sin,*
  And *Matches'* child was *Mates;*
Container's twins were *Can* and *Tin,*
  And *Prattles'* wee one, *Prates.*

So *Rascal*'s from *Rapscallion* born,
  So *Rules* from *Regulates;*
What babe, as *Rest* from *Respite*'s torn,
  Vacates Evacuates?

Now *Calumnies* is nursing *Lies;*
  Encourage, Urge doth hug;
Rage safe in arms of *Rampage* lies,
  And *Struggle* mothers *Tug.*

The letters of the shorter italicized words above are drawn from the longer ones, and appear in the same order. Below, letters from words are juggled to make shorter ones of different meaning.

EVE'S DREAM

In your demeanor there's a dream, dear friend,
  That leads to sorrow. Dreams hold something sad:
In dream, a part of Eden is Eden's end,
  And part of Adam is mad.

Demeanor—dream
Dreams—sad
Eden—end
Adam—mad

IN-RIDDLE

I was recently warned by a girl in Algeria
  There was peace in Hepaticae, war in Wisteria.
I put her in halter, that girl in Algeria;
  She wasn't insane, but she was in hysteria.

Algeria, girl
Hepaticae, peace
Wisteria, war
Halter, her
Hysteria, she

Symbols and Signs

Some signs and symbols are given exact equivalents in words. These can be fitted into verses easily enough, as you will see from the example below. Whether the effort is worthwhile is another question.

I LOVE YOU TO ∞ (±A°)

I am ♂ and you are ♀;
Amorous war shall rage between us—
War in which, as ♂, my *f*
Is to orbit toward ♀
While ℛ you pretend,
And ♂ to my end.
A ♀ knows dissatisfaction
A ⇄
Since (as always in these wars)

♀ → at last to ♂:
My Σ of love you'll give again
× eight or ten.

(Many dictionaries have lists of signs and symbols
with definitions. Just in case yours does not, here is the
above verse with the symbols translated.)

I LOVE YOU TO INFINITY (PLUS OR MINUS A DEGREE)

I am Mars and you are Venus;
Amorous war shall rage between us—
War in which, as male, my function
Is to orbit toward conjunction,
While reluctance you pretend,
And opposition tò my end.
A female knows dissatisfaction
A reversible reaction
Since (as always in these wars)
Venus yields at last to Mars;
My sum of love you'll give again
Multiplied by eight or ten.

TYPESETTING TARRADIDDLE

Friend John, whose (:) was removed,
When asked why he had lately proved
So free of caution and of fear,
Said, "I've no (*), my dear."

A schwa, indicated in dictionaries by ∂, is a vowel so unstressed that it loses its identity of sound:

THE SUSURRANT SCHWA

The ∂ on his diurn∂l rounds
Is min∂s all but min∂r sounds;
Yet may, phonet∂c∂sts ∂gree
Transmit a wide v∂ri∂ty
Of aud∂ble ph∂nom∂na:
　A∂, E∂, I∂, O∂ . . .
　　　U∂.

Acronyms in Verse

Many tantalizing acronyms (words formed of initial letters) can be matched in rhyme, but a sizable number cannot. It seems a shame that low poets cannot rhyme SNAFU (Situation Normal, All Fucked-Up); or SUBFU (Situation Unchanged, Still Fucked-Up); or TARFU (Things Are Really Fucked-Up); or SAPFU (Surpassing All Previous Fuck-Ups). Of the acronyms in the fuck-up team that have come to my attention, only FUBB (Fucked-Up Beyond Belief) lends itself to conventional rhyme:

The Lord said, "Stop complaining, bub;
Your situation's normal: FUBB."

Some acronyms were not eligible for my rhyming list because they match only mosaic rhymes. It takes two words, for instance, to rhyme POTUS (President of the United States):

> The opposition candidate
>   Reviles the current POTUS
> And calls the union's normal state
>   "The mess this POTUS got us."

But many acronyms do make standard rhymes—the Federal Register alone must contain scores of them. The fact is that I did not think of making a special search for acronyms until the book was almost ready to be set in type. I apologize.

Grammar Verse

Grammar, a subject larded with oddities and vagaries, offers fine resource material for light poetry (though perhaps one should avoid writing grammar verses when in a tense mood).

E PLURIBUS UNUM

The spelling of certain words ending in *s* does not change between singular and plural. For instance:

> The drunken Species homeward reels,
> Or reel; it sets the mind ajar
> That species is and Species are.
>
> A Congeries of conger eels
> Is either are or is a bunch;
> Are either is or are for lunch.
>
> A Shambles of new-slaughtered seals
> Is either are or is deplorable;
> Are either is or are abhorrable.
>
> No Kudos for this verse, one feels,
> Is either are or is in view;
> Nor is, are, it, he, she, they, due.

THE ACTIVE AND THE PASSIVE VOICE

> One acts, one's acted on. (I ment-
>   ion this re subjects of a sent-
> ence.) Subjects that commit an act
>   Are Male. This need not mean attract-
> ive (no!) but *prominent,*
>   With bulging Biceps; it's a fact
> That virile symbols make a dent
>   In ladies who enjoy a gent.
>   *Wherefore rejoice,*
> O Subjects of the Active Voice!
>
> Not so the subject of the Pass-
>   ive Voice; she is not corded round with mass-
> ive muscles, being of the lact-
>   ic or mammalian sort, well stacked,
> And virgin—till, like any lass,
>   She's acted on with her consent.
>   *Wherefore rejoice,*
> O Subjects of the Passive Voice!

SINGULAR SINGULARS, PECULIAR PLURALS

How singular some old words are!
I know two with *no* singular:
Agenda, marginalia, both
Are always plural, 'pon my oath.*

The opposite's the case to greet us
In *propaganda* and *coitus;*
Upon these never sets the sun,
And yet of each there's only one.
Phantasmagoria, likewise,
Pervades, yet never multiplies.

Strata pluralizes *stratum;*
Ultimata, ultimatum;
Why are *nostrums* then not *nostra?*
Why speak I not then from *rostra?*
Thus my *datum* grows to *data,*
My *erratum* to *errata.*

Child, put this on your next agenda:
Pudendum's half of two *pudenda.*

ALTHOUGH INFORMAL SPEECH IS FREE (A RONDEL)

Although informal speech is free,
    It isn't quite as free as air.
You *must* not say: "This here"; "That there";
    "I don't need nothing"; "Maybe me

And him can come"; "When we was three";
    "He don't." . . . You *must*n't! Don't you *dare!*—
Although informal speech is free,
    It isn't quite as free as air.

"Now you have did it!" *must* not be,
    And "irregardless" gets the air.
"He done"; "I seen"—another pair

To sweep away with the debris
(Although informal speech is free).

TRIOLET IN PRAISE OF AIN'T

My tongue can't handle 'amn't I'—
    I opt instead for 'ain't.'
Though 'am I not' is worth a try,
My tongue can't handle 'amn't I,'
And though I am a rugged guy,
    'Aren't I' makes me faint.
My tongue can't handle 'amn't I'—
    I opt instead for 'ain't.'

---

*But *agenda*, though plural in form, takes a singular verb.

ON THE CORRECT USE OF LIE AND LAY

Lie down once more where once we kissed,
  While I the laws of lie and lay
Lay down. Lie where we lay—and list,
  Here where you lay and lied, dear Kay;
Lie down once more where once we kissed.

Where with a hundred lads you'd lain,
  You swore to lie with me for aye.
You laid sweet ambush to my brain:
  You lay; lied; laid one more lad prey
Where with a hundred lads you'd lain.

GRAMMATICAL USAGE FOR STOMPERS

When stomping victims in a mugging,
  Attack the proper zone:
The belly if the victim's *supine,*
  The spine if he is *prone.*

GRAMMAR IN EXTREMIS

The vows that I exchanged with she
Were broken soon by both of we.
(The sacred love of you and I
May also wither by-and-by.)

  (The third line of the above verse is from a
prize-winning poem printed in the Pittsburgh
Press.)

Macaronic Verse

A macaronic is a verse, like this one, that stirs two or more languages together for the fun of it:

QUESTION DE FOI

An aging Paris *avocat*
  (An atheist, *bien entendu*),
  When asked about his point of view
On birthday number *soixante-trois,*
  Replied, "I find that *plus en plus*
    Je ne crois pas
      Que je ne crois pas."

Here is the simple English of it, with a rhyming change in the last three lines:

A QUESTION OF FAITH

An aging lawyer of Paree,
  To atheism long inclined,
  When asked if he had changed his mind
On reaching birthday sixty-three,
  Said, "I increasingly perceive
    That I don't believe
      That I don't believe."

This is not exactly a macaronic, but it contains the first words that used to be taught to students of Latin:

A CLASSICAL EDUCATION

The Latin teacher need not explicate
  Amo, amas
To Latin students who will conjugate
  After class.

Caution: Identicals Do Not Rhyme

In preparing *Words to Rhyme With*, I compared my word lists ad nauseam with those in comparable books, and am grateful for valuable entries that I might have missed otherwise. It was puzzling, however, to find that many rhyming dictionaries list identicals as if they were rhymes. Rhymes are not identicals; they are terminal sounds, beginning with an accented vowel, that are preceded by different consonantal sounds, or by a consonant in one case and none in the other. Hundreds of words end in *-phobia*, for instance, but they are included in this book only because of the existence of one rhyming word, *obeah*, meaning "a kind of voodoo religion once common in the British West Indies, or a priest of it." Scores of words end in *-lagnia*, which means erotic arousal, but they do not appear here because *-lagnia* has no rhyme.

One of my favorite handbooks for rhymesters points out that its list contains the following words that "have no rhyming mates." But it does not explain why, that being the case, the words are in the list at all:

aitch, H	fugue	swoln
bilge	gulf, engulf	sylph
bulb	month	torsk
coif	morgue	twelfth
culm	peart	plagued, unplagued
cusp	poulp	warmth
doth	scarce	wharves
film	spoilt	wolf
		wolves

(It is even more curious that this same list of unrhymables includes other words that in fact do rhyme—among them *avenge*, which rhymes with *Stonehenge; bourne*, which in one accepted pronunciation rhymes with *mourn* and in another with *horn; forge*, which rhymes with *gorge; lounge*, which rhymes with *scrounge; mauve*, which rhymes with *rove; porch*, which rhymes with *torch; pork*, which rhymes with *fork; rouge*, which rhymes with *gamboge;* and *sauce*, which rhymes with *toss.*

(A recent rhyming dictionary aimed especially at lyricists similarly lists legitimate rhyming words as unrhymables. Among them are *chaos*, which rhymes with *Laos; donkey*, which rhymes with *honky; obese*, which rhymes with *niece; torture*, which rhymes with *scorcher; roguish*, which rhymes with *voguish; chartreuse*, which rhymes with *Betelgeuse; consummate*, which rhymes with *grummet; coffin*, which rhymes with *dauphin* (and, according to dictionaries which treat the *i* as a schwa, with *often* and *soften* as well); *cuckold*, which rhymes with *chuckled; ogre*, which rhymes with *maugre* (archaic in some senses and obsolete in others, but absolutely valid); and even *moldy*, which must bring *golden oldy* to the mind of many lyricists.

(Many more unrhymables that in fact rhyme might be cited, but these suffice for my point: if you are doubtful, check. Remember that many words have more than one correct pronunciation, and that any pronunciation accepted by any standard dictionary is legitimate. If you find me saying a word has no legitimate rhyme, make me prove it.)

Back to identicals. Here are some from just one rhyming dictionary—and a superior dictionary, at that:

BAL′AN-SING	balancing, counterbalancing, overbalancing, unbalancing
BANGKMENT	bankment, embankment
BEZLER	bezzler, embezzler
DONA	belladonna, donna, Madonna, prima donna
DUKTIL	ductile, inductile, productile
DUK′TER-Ē	deductory, inductory, introductory, manuductory, reproductory
DŪSMENT	deducement, inducement, producement, superinducement
EM′I-NENS	eminence, preeminence, supereminence
ENTRANS	entrance, entrants
EPIK	epic, monoepic, orthoepic
ETHNIK	ethnic, holoethnic
FĀ′SED-LĒ	barefacedly, shamefacedly
FĀ′SI-ENT	facient, calefacient, liquefacient
FOOT′ED-NES	bigfootedness, duckfootedness, clubfootedness, splayfootedness
FURMANS	affirmance, disaffirmance, confirmance, reaffirmance
FUR′MA-TIV	affirmative, disaffirmative, confirmative, reaffirmative
GASTRIK	digastric, gastric, hypogastric, perigastric
GRĒ′A-BL	agreeable, disagreeable
HAR′TED-LĒ	bigheartedly, downheartedly, hardheartedly, kindheartedly, light-heartedly, lionheartedly, simpleheartedly
HAR′TED-NES	bigheartedness, downheartedness, hardheartedness, kindheartedness, lightheartedness, lionheartedness, simpleheartedness
HER′I-TANS	disinheritance, heritance, inheritance
HĒ′SIV-LĒ	adhesively, inhesively, cohesively
JEKTMENT	dejectment, ejectment, injectment, projectment, rejectment
JUJMENT	adjudgment, judgment, misjudgment, prejudgment, rejudgment
JUNGK′TIV-LĒ	adjunctively, disjunctively, conjunctively, subjunctively
KAL′I-BER	caliber, calibre, calabur, Excalibur
KARPAL	intercarpal, carpal, metacarpal
KLIV′I-TUS	acclivitous, declivitous, proclivitous
KON′SŪ-LAR	consular, non-consular, pro-consular, vice-consular
KOSTIK	caustic, costic
KRĒ′SHUN-AL	concretional, secretional
KUL′CHER-IST	agriculturalist, floriculturalist, horticulturalist, apiculturalist
KUM′BEN-SĒ	incumbency, decumbency, recumbency
KUMBENT	accument, decumbent, incumbent, procumbent, recumbent, super-incumbent
KUR′ENT-LĒ	concurrently, currently, recurrently
KWIZ′I-TIV	acquisitive, disquisitive, inquisitive, uninquisitive
LAB′O-RĀT	elaborate, collaborate
LAT′ER-AL	collateral, quadrilateral, lateral, multilateral, plurilateral, unilateral
LEKTRIK	analectric, dielectric, electric, idiolectric
LIS′I-TUS	felicitous, solicitous
MĒ′DI-ĀT	immediate, intermediate, mediate
MIS′I-BL	admissible, permissible

MORFĒ	geomorphy, metamorphy, zoomorphy
NACH'ER-AL	natural, preternatural, supernatural, unnatural
NIF'I-SENT	magnificent, munificent
NOUNS'MENT	announcement, denouncement, pronouncement, renouncement
PARTMENT	apartment, department, impartment, compartment
PASH'UN-IT	dispassionate, impassionate, incompassionate, compassionate, passionate
PET'A-LUS	apetalous, petalous, polypetalous
POS'I-TR	depositor, expositor, compositor, ovipositor, repositor, transpositor
PRAN'DI-AL	anteprandial, postprandial, prandial
PRĒ'SHI-ĀT	appreciate, depreciate
PRES'E-DEN-SĒ	antiprecedency, precedency (these words do *not* rhyme with hesitancy, presidency)
PUB'LI-KAN	publican, republican
PUGNANT	oppugnant, repugnant, unrepugnant
PUMIS	pomace, pumace, pumice
RAD'I-KAL	radical, sporadical, unradical
RĀ'DI-ĀT	erradiate, irradiate, radiate
RĒ'JEN-SĒ	regency, vice-regency
RĪPNES	deadripeness, overripeness, ripeness, underripeness
RUPSHUN	abruption, disruption, eruption, interruption, corruption
RUP'TIV-LĒ	disruptively, interruptively, corruptively
SEN'SHI-ENT	assentient, dissentient, insentient, consentient, presentient
SEP'SHUN-AL	exceptional, conceptional, unexceptional
SEP'TI-BL	acceptable, deceptible, perceptible, receptible, susceptible
SHAD'Ō-ING	foreshadowing, overshadowing, shadowing
SIK'LI-KAL	bicyclical, encyclical, cyclical
SIL'I-KA	basilica, silica
SIM'I-LĒ	dissimile, facsimile, simile
SIP'I-ENT	appercipient, desipient, incipient, insipient, percipient
SKRIP'SHUN-AL	inscriptional, conscriptional, transcriptional
SKRIPTIV	descriptive, prescriptive, circumscriptive
SKUCHUN	escutcheon, scutcheon, unscutcheon
SPIK'Ū-US	inconspicuous, conspicuous, perspicuous, transpicuous
SPONDENT	despondent, co-respondent, correspondent
STRUKCHER	constructure, structure, substructure, superstructure
TAG'O-NIZM	antagonism, protagonism
TEM'PO-RAL	atemporal, extemporal, supertemporal, temporal
TEN'Ū-ĀT	attenuate, extenuate, tenuate
THER'A-PĒ	autotherapy, balneotherapy, hydrotherapy, radiotherapy, psychotherapy, theotherapy
TŌ'TAL-ER	teetotaler, totaler
TRAN'SI-TIV	intransitive, transitive
TRENCHMENT	entrenchment, retrenchment, trenchment
VELUP	develop, envelop, underdevelop
VIN'SI-BL	evincible, invincible, convincible
VĪ'TA-LĪZ	devitalize, revitalize, vitalize
VUR'SI-TĒ	adversity, diversity, perversity, university
VUR'TIZ-MENT	advertisement, divertissement

You will find none of these identicals in my rhyming list. I hope, though I cannot guarantee, that you will find no others either.

How to Use the List of Rhyming Words

The Sets, Subsets, and Categories

The rhyming words ahead are divided into three sets: single, or masculine rhymes (accented on the last syllable); double, or feminine rhymes (accented on the syllable before the last); and triple, or dactylic, rhymes (accented usually on the syllable before the syllable before the last, but occasionally even on the one before that).

Each of the three sets is divided into five subsets, one for each vowel—A, E, I, O, and U.

The subsets are broken down into phonetically alphabetized categories, with headings. These category headings are the *mother rhymes*.

The Subcategories

Each mother rhyme broods over a clutch of subcategories. If the mother rhyme happens to be itself one of a rhyming set, it is relisted as the first of the subcategories, this way:

Ā

Ā   a, aye, DNA, dossier, habitué, Coué, couturier, roturier, roué

The other subcategories then follow in the alphabetical order of their opening sounds:

BĀ   bay, bey, Bombay, dapple bay, disobey, flambé, obey
BLĀ   criblé, seinsemblers
BRĀ   brae, bray

and so on.

Note: a mother rhyme that is also one of a rhyming set is always the first subcategory to be listed, whatever its opening sound:

UNDER

UNDER   down under, hereunder, thereunder, under
BLUNDER   blunder
BUNDER   bunder
DUNDER   dunder

and so on.

The Pronunciation and Order of Vowels

The usual sounds of stressed vowels are indicated as follows:

Ā	as in	*gate*
Â	as in	*air*
A	as in	*pat*
Ä	as in	*part, swaddle*
Ē	as in	*beet*

E	as in	*bet*
Ī	as in	*kite*
I	as in	*kit*
ÎR	as in	*ear*
Ō	as in	*coat*
Ô	as in	*caught*
O	as in	*hot*
ŌŌ	as in	*chew*
OO	as in	*foot*
OU	as in	*out*
Ū	as in	*cute*
U	as in	*cut, curt*

(A slightly different phonetic system is employed for the glossary. A guide to it appears there.)

Ū, ŌŌ

Ū in the rhyming syllables of some words has the sound of Ū, in other words the sound of ŌŌ, and in still other words either sound. Dictionaries disagree, moreover, on which words fit these categories. To add to the confusion, Ū is pronounced YŌŌ, and is so itself a rhyme for ŌŌ. Rather than give two listings for all the words which may be pronounced either way, I list each in the category which seems most appropriate to me (sometimes in both), and refer the reader from one category to the other.

The Order of Categories and Subcategories

Within each set of vowels—A, E, I, O, or U—the category headings, or mother rhymes, are listed in the alphabetical order of the *closing* consonant sound of the heading: Ā, ĀB, AB, ÄB, ABD, ACH, ACHT, etc. The order of the subcategory headings is determined by the *opening* sound of the rhyming syllable: BĀ, BLĀ, BRĀ, etc.

Headings Are Spelled Phonetically

Sound and spellings in the headings need not correspond. The word *precise*, for instance, is listed in the category ĪS and the subcategory SĪS, because though the rhyming syllable *-cise* begins with the *letter c*, it begins with the *sound s*. The word *colt* appears in the category ŌLT and the subcategory KŌLT; in this case, the *c* is pronounced like a *k*.

The Spelling of Consonants in the Headings of Categories and Subcategories

The phonetic spelling	The consonant	Sounded as in
B	b	*b*oy, am*b*ivalent
BL	bl	*bl*ack
BR	br	*br*and, am*br*osia
CH	ch	*ch*art, en*ch*ant
D	d	*d*ay, a*d*ore
F	f, ph	*f*amily, a*ph*asis
G	g	*g*ood, a*g*o
GL	gl	*gl*orious, a*gl*ey
GR	gr	*gr*eat, di*gr*ess
H	h	*h*appy, ab*h*or
HW	wh	*wh*ite, a*wh*ile

J	g, j	ingest, jest
K	c, ch, k	cat, alchemy, kitten
KL	chl, cl, kl	chlorine, clatter, klieg
KR	chr, cr, kr	Christian, crest, kraken
KW	qu	quit, requite
L	l	lengthy, allow
M	m	mayhem, admissible
N	GN, KN, MN, N	gnostic, knowledge, mnemonics, nothing
P	p	passage, repel
PL	pl	implacable, pleasant
PR	pr	prominent, improvident
R	r	raffish, meteorology
S	c, ps, s	receipt, psychology, song
SH	ch, s, sh	parachute, insure, shame
SK	sc, sk	scout, skirt
SKR	scr	scribe, subscription
SKW	squ	squiggle
SM	sm	smattering
SN	sn	sneer
SP	sp	spacious, inspissate
ST	st	still
STR	str	strong
T	pht, pt, t	phthisic, ptarmigan, toil
TH (as in thin)	th	thin, athirst
TH (as in then)	th	then, these
THR	thr	threaten
THW	thw	thwack
TR	tr	treasure, entreat
TW	tw	twaddle, between
V	v	various, invest
W	w	won, one
Y	y	young, unyielding
Z	z, s, ss, x	zeal, resolve, dissolve, exert
ZH	g	ingenue

Order of Words in a Subcategory

Since the rhyming element provides no guide for allocating words within any one subcategory—all the words being identical in that respect—their position is established instead by their opening sounds, as here:

> **BELĒ** belly, *gorbelly, whitebelly,* casus belli, *potbelly, redbelly, shadbelly, slowbelly,* tenterbelly, yellowbelly *

---

*Words in the rhyming list may be italicized if the vowel sound is not an exact match for others in the category. In the ÔRTH category, for instance, *fourth* is italicized because it would appear under ŌRTH if there were any other ŌRTH words. Under URV, *hors d'oeuvres* is italicized as an incorrect pronunciation. More commonly, words are italicized when the normal stress has been either advanced or put back by one or two syllables to force a match with others in the same category. The word snowdrift, for instance, is correctly accented on the penultimate, but may be made a single rhyme by pushing the accent forward:

> On winter evenings don't get squiffed:
> You may wind up in a *snowdrift.*

Make such metric liberties the exception rather than the rule.

I have used initial letters to facilitate the location of rhyming words when a subcategory runs over ten or so entries. It may be useful to give an example of how the system works:

> **FĀST** *A* angel-faced, apple-faced, *B* baby-faced, *baldfaced, barefaced, bold-faced, BR* brazen-faced, *D* defaced, dirty-faced, *dish-faced, doughfaced, E* ef-faced, *F* faced, furrow-faced, *FR* freckle-faced, *H hard-faced,* hatchet-faced, *horse-faced, HW whey-faced, J* Janus-faced, *KL clean-faced, L lean-faced,* lily-faced, *M* mottle-faced, *P pale-faced,* paper-faced, *pie-faced,* pickle-faced, pimple-faced, pippin-faced, pudding-faced, *pug-faced, PL* platter-faced, *plump-faced, R* refaced, *SH shame-faced, SM smooth-faced, smug-faced, T* tallow-faced, *two-faced, TR* triple-faced, *U* undefaced, unshamefaced, *V* vinegar-faced, *W* weasel-faced, wizen-faced

How to Locate Multi-Syllabled Words in a Subcategory

The rhyming element of a word establishes its category and subcategory, and its opening sound dictates its general position within the subcategory. But where a subcategory is a long one with long words, several of them may have the same opening sound. In that event, the specific position of a word depends on the overall sound of its non-rhyming part. Take these DĀSHUN words beginning with I:

> **I** infeudation, ingravidation, incommo-dation, intimidation, inundation, inval-idation

All six words begin with in- and end with -dation. Their sequence is determined by the opening sounds of the syllables in between: in*F*eudation, in*GR*avitation, in*K*ommodation, in*T*imidation, in*U*ndation, in*V*alidation.

Unstressed Vowels in the Phonetic Headings

A vowel that is unstressed but distinctly pronounced goes into the phonetic heading unchanged:

> **BRŌŌTISH**   brutish
> **DEDHED**   deadhead

Unstressed Vowels with Variant Pronunciations

When an unstressed vowel has a pronunciation not usually associated with it, the spelling of the heading changes accordingly:

> **ŪSIJ**   usage

Vowels That Substitute for Schwas

Many unaccented syllables are so lightly stressed that their vowel sound is indeterminate. The pronunciation of *mammary*, for instance, does not reveal whether the second vowel is an *a, e, i, o,* or *u*. Dictionaries indicate this vague sound by a schwa (∂). Instead of a schwa, a single handy vowel is used in each phonetic head or subhead of my rhyming list to represent that faint sound, even though it may be represented by different vowels in some of the words themselves. Suppose, for instance, that you are checking the word hobbit, and turn to OBIT. You will find

OBIT

(See **OBET**)

and under OBET there will be the subcategories

GOBET   gobbet
HOBET   hobbit

Similarly, if you look for *bodice* under ODIS, you will find

ODIS

(See **ODES**)

and, under ODES,

BODES   bodice
GODES   goddess

If a word ends in a faint vowel sound followed by -l, the vowel may be dropped from the phonetic listing altogether:

MODL

MODL   model
TODL   toddle

Plurals Formed by Adding -s or -es

The rhyming list seldom has categories confined to plurals formed by the addition of -s or -es, though such plurals appear as rhymes for other words.

Words Formed by the Addition of Suffixes

When words formed by adding the suffixes -ed, -er, -ful, -fully, -ing, -ish, -less, -let, -ment, or -ous to other words are not separately categorized, an entry directs the reader to the appropriate rhyme category to do his own suffixing.

Omission of Archaic -est and -eth as Suffixes

There are no separate listings of verbs with the archaic suffixes -est and -eth (runnest, runneth).

Other Omissions of Suffixed Words

With a few exceptions, there are no separate listings of words ending in the suffixes -like or -some, or of adjectives made superlative by the addition of -est.

A Passing Note on Pronunciation

Your dictionary on occasion gives several pronunciations for the same word; unless it adds a caveat, it accepts them all. The order in which they happen to appear is unimportant; after all, there is no way to avoid having one pronunciation or another come first. Some words therefore appear in more than one place in the rhyming list.

Unless italicized, all the rhyme sounds listed in this book are accepted by some standard dictionary.

Regional Accents

Pronunciation, especially in informal speech, varies from one locality to another. There are parts of the United States where any distinction between the sounds of *Mary, merry,* and *marry,* for instance, defies detection by the human ear. Such localisms are not included in this book; here, *Mary* rhymes with *airy, marry* with *tarry,* and *merry* with *very.* There is no reason not to use a local pronunciation as a rhyme, as long as you are aware of what you are doing; fine poets have done so. But you will generally be better off if you go by the dictionary.

Syllabification

In the list of single rhymes there is no need to divide category headings into syllables, since they have only one. Nor do I show the division between the two syllables in the headings of double rhymes, the emphasis being always on the first syllable; for rhyming purposes, the question of whether the second syllable happens to begin with a consonant or a vowel is irrelevant.

In the triple rhyme list, however, I do indicate syllabification; it would be confusing not to in, say, JELUSLĒ (jealously) or THROPIKAL (philanthropical). Here the rhyming emphasis is indicated by a (') following the accented syllable, and the other syllables are separated by (.): JEL'US.LĒ, THROP'I.KAL.

The words within categories are not syllabified or phoneticized; the rhyme has already been established, and to throw in phonetic markings would simply make the sledding harder for the reader.

Proper Names

I have used proper names sparingly as rhymes, and have tried (not altogether successfully) to confine myself to those of some historic, topical, or literary significance. I could not resist *Steven,* since it was the only rhyme for *even.* I also rhymed *Nilot* with *pilot* (a Nilot is a native of the Nile), and would have rhymed *hylism* with *Carlislism* if my wife had not put her foot down.

Italics

Imperfect rhymes are italicized in the list of rhyming words.

SINGLE RHYMES

(Words of one syllable, or words accented on the final syllable. Also called *iambic*, or *masculine*, rhymes.)

Ā

Ā	A, aye, DNA, dossier, habitué, Coué, couturier, plié, roturier, roué
BĀ	bay, bey, Bombay, bombé, dapple bay, disobey, flambé, obey
BLĀ	criblé, seinsemblers
BRĀ	brae, bray
DĀ	*A* alackaday, Ascension Day, *B* bidet, *birthday, D* D-day, day, démodé, *doomsday, E* everyday, *F* *firstday, FR Friday, G* good-day, *H half-day, heyday, high-day,* holiday, *I* intraday, *J* Judgment Day, *KR* Christmas Day, *KW* quarter day, *L* Labor Day, lackaday, Lord's day, *M* market day, *Mayday, midday, N noonday, P payday, PL playday, S* settling-day, seventh-day, *someday, sundae, Sunday, T* today, *Tuesday, TH Thursday, TR* trysting-day, *W* wedding day, *weekday,* welladay, *Wednesday, workaday, workday,* working day, *Y* yesterday
DRĀ	dray
DYĀ	boulevardier
FĀ	buffet, café, fay, fey, coryphée, ofay, au fait, auto-da-fé, parfait, pousse-café, rechauffé, Santa Fe
FLĀ	flay, soufflé
FRĀ	affray, defray, frae, fray
GĀ	assagai, distingué, gay, *margay, nosegay,* toujours gai
GLĀ	agley, gley
GRĀ	dapple-gray, emigré, gray, hodden-gray, iron-gray, *lean-gray,* silver-gray
GWĀ	ngwee
HĀ	hae, hay, hey, hey-hey
HWĀ	whey
JĀ	*deejay,* jay, popinjay
KĀ	*B* Biscay, bouquet, *D* decay, *K* cay, communiqué, *KR* croquet, *M* manqué, *O* okay, *P* parquet, piquet, *R* risqué, roquet, *S* sobriquet, *T* tokay, tourniquet
KLĀ	bouclé, bouclée, clay, fire clay, pipe clay, roman à clef
KYĀ	perruquier
LĀ	*A* allay, *B* belay, Beaujolais, Bordelais, *D* delay, *F* forelay, forlay, *H* haole, *I* inlay, interlay, *K* cabriolet, kantele, coulée *L* lai, lay, *M* Malay, Mandalay, melee, mislay, *O* olé, outlay, overlay, *P* parlay, Pelée, pis-aller, pourparler, *R* Rabelais, relay, reveillé, rissolé, rokelay, roundelay, *U* underlay, *unlay, uplay, V* virelay, *W waylay*
MĀ	dismay, entremets, gamay, gourmet, consommé, lamé, macramé, may, May, resumé, Salomé
NĀ	acharné, déraciné, estaminet, Hogmanay, cloisonné, matinée, nae, nay, née, neigh, Dubonnet, massinet, raisonné
PĀ	dead pay, épée, épopée, Gaspé, coupé, mortpay, overpay, pay, prepay, repay, strathspey, Taipei, toupée, toupet, underpay
PLĀ	*B* byplay, *D* display, *endplay, F* fair play, *foreplay,* photoplay, foul play, fun play, *H* horse play, *I* interplay, *M* misplay, *O* overplay, *P* Passion play, *PL* play, *R* replay, *S* satyr play, *SKR* screenplay, *ST* stage play, *U* underplay, *W wordplay*
PRĀ	bepray, pray, prey, repray, unpray
PYĀ	passepied
RĀ	*A* array, *B* beray, beret, bewray, *D* disarray, *F* foray, *G* green beret, *H* hip-hip-hooray, hooray, hurray, *M* Monterey, moray, *MW* moiré, *P* purée, *R* ray, re, *S* soirée, *ST* sting ray, *X* x-ray
SĀ	*A* assay, *D* déclassé, divorcé, divorcée, *E* essay, *F* fiancé, fiancée, foresay, *G* gainsay, *GL* glacé, *H hearsay, PL* plissé, *L* lycée, *M* matelassé, missay, *N* naysay, *P* passé, per se, *PL* plissé, *PR* presay, *R* retroussé, *S* say, *soothsay, U* undersay, unsay
SHĀ	attaché, brochet, cachet, cliché, couchée, crochet, papier-maché, recherché, ricochet, sachet, sashay, shay, touché
SKRĀ	scray
SLĀ	bob sleigh, slay, sleigh, sley
SPĀ	spay, strathspey
SPLĀ	splay
SPRĀ	auto-spray, bespray, featherspray, respray, spray
STĀ	astay, *backstay, bobstay, forestay, jackstay, mainstay, outstay,* overstay, stay, *upstay*
STRĀ	astray, distrait, estray, stray, windlestrae
SWĀ	sway, swing and sway
TĀ	tay, paté, volupté, velouté
THĀ	Cathay, they
TRĀ	*ashtray,* betray, distrait, distray, entrée, estray, outré, portray, tray, trey
TYĀ	métier
VĀ	inveigh, convey, corvée, névé, oy vay, pavé, purvey, resurvey, survey, chevet
WĀ	*A* airway, archway, aweigh, *B* beltway, byway, *BR* breakway, bridleway, Broadway, *D* doorway, *DR* driveway, *E* expressway, entryway, *F* fairway, footway, *FR* freeway, *G* Galloway, *Galway, gangway, gateway, getaway, guideway, H halfway, hatchway, headway, highway, K* cableway, *causeway, cogway,* cutaway, *KL clearway, KR* crossway, cruiseway, *L* leeway, *M* midway, *Midway,* Milky Way, motorway, *N Norway, O* overweigh, *outway,* outweigh, *P* passageway, *pathway, R railway, roadway,* runaway, *runway, S seaway,* cycle way, *someway, subway, SK* skidway, *SL slipway, SP* speedway, spillway, *ST stairway,* steerageway, *sternway,* stowaway, *STR* straightaway, *straightway, T* takeaway, *tideway,* towaway, *TH* that-a-way, thereaway, *THR throughway, TR* tramway,

	U underway, under way, underweigh, *W walkway,* waterway, way, wellaway, wey
YĀ	atelier, employé, employée, espalier, grandgoussier, métayer, Montgolfier, Olivier, Parmentier, plumassier, Récamier, roturier, soigné, sommelier, chevalier, yea
ZĀ	blasé, exposé, espasé, San José
ZHĀ	negligee, protegé

Ä

Ä	a, aa, ah
BÄ	aba, baa, baah, bah, bas, *Casbah, Poobah,* sis-boom-bah
BLÄ	blah
BRÄ	algebra, bra, chapeaubras, vertebra
CHÄ	cha-cha, cha-cha-cha
DÄ	andromeda, da, dada, *houdah, howdah, purdah*
DRÄ	clepsydra
FÄ	apocrypha, do re mi fa, fa
FRWÄ	sangfroid
FWÄ	paté de foie
GÄ	aga, budgereegah, Dégas, ga, *nougat*
GLÄ	verglas
GRÄ	paté de foie gras
HÄ	aha, ha, ha-ha, taiaha
HWÄ	Taniwha
KÄ	abaca, basilica, Jataka, majolica, ka, replica, sciatica, silica
KLÄ	éclat
KWÄ	qua, quaa
LÄ	*A* alala, *F* formula, *H* holla, *K* cabala, *qabbalah, cupola, L* la, lala, *N* nebula, *OO* oolala, *P* parabola, peninsula, pyrola, *R* ranula, *SP* spatula, sporabola, *T* tarantula, tarentola, *TR* tralala, *V* viola
MÄ	*amah,* anathema, Aceldama, grandmamma, ma, maa, mama, mamma, palama, Panama, cinema
MWÄ	moi
NÄ	alumina, phenomena, guarana, quadrumana, na, nah, padsamana, prolegomena, retina
PÄ	faux pas, n'est-ce-pas,

	oompah, pa, pah, papa, pas
PWÄ	petits pois
RÄ	*A* acara, *B* baccarat, *E* ephemera, et cetera, *H* Hegira, hurrah, *J* genera, *K* camera, carnivora, cholera, *L* last hurrah, *M* mandragora, *O* opera, *PL* plethora, *R* Ra, rah, rah-rah
SÄ	sah, yassah, yessah
SHÄ	padishah, *pasha,* shah
SHVÄ	schwa
SKÄ	ska
SPÄ	spa
SWÄ	peau de soie, soie
TÄ	Al Fatah, automata, incognita, coup d'état, taffeta, t'a, ta, taa, Ptah, ta-ta
THÄ	Golgotha
TRÄ	orchestra
TWÄ	patois
VÄ	baklava
WÄ	wa, waah, wah
YÄ	ja, Jah, yah, yaya, yeah
ZÄ	huzza
ZHWÄ	bourgeois, joie

ĀB

BĀB	babe, foster-babe, *scarebabe*
GRĀB	outgrabe
LĀB	astrolabe, cosmolabe

AB

AB	abb, Joab, Moab
BAB	bab, baobab
BLAB	blab
BRAB	brab
DAB	bedab, dab, dhabb
DRAB	drab
FAB	fab, confab, prefab
FRAB	frab
GAB	baffle-gab, gab
GRAB	grab
JAB	jab
KAB	cab, pedicab, taxicab
KRAB	crab
LAB	lab, *Skylab*
MAB	mab, Mab
NAB	knab, nab
RAB	rab
SHAB	shab
SKAB	scab
SLAB	slab
STAB	stab
TAB	*eartab,* tab

ÄB

BÄB	wooer-bab
LÄB	jelab
SKWÄB	squab
SWÄB	swab
WÄB	jawab

(See **OB**)

ÄBD

SWABD	swabbed

(See **OB**, add *-ed* where appropriate.)

ACH

BACH	bach, batch
BRACH	brach
HACH	hatch, *crosshatch, nuthatch*
KACH	catch, *seacatch*
KLACH	kaffeeklatsch, coffee klatch
KRACH	cratch
LACH	latch, *potlatch,* unlatch
MACH	match, mismatch, overmatch, rematch, shooting match, undermatch
NACH	natch
PACH	dispatch, *crosspatch,* patch, *tolpatch*
RACH	rach, ratch
SKACH	scatch
SKRACH	scratch
SLACH	slatch
SMACH	smatch
SNACH	snatch
TACH	attach, detach, tache
THACH	thatch

ÄCH

(See **OCH**)

ACHT

HACHT	hatched
TACHT	attached, detached, semi-detached

(See **ACH,** add *-ed* where appropriate.)

ĀD

ĀD	ade, aid, aide, co-aid, *Band-Aid,* first-aid, *hand-*

	aid, ginger-ade, lemonade, *limeade*, orangeade
BĀD	bade, bayed, forbade, gambade, obeyed
BLĀD	blade, Damascus blade, grass blade, *twayblade*
BRĀD	abrade, abraid, braid, brayed, unbraid, upbraid
DĀD	brandade
FĀD	fade
FLĀD	flayed, unflayed
FRĀD	afraid, defrayed, unafraid
GĀD	brigade, dragade, renegade
GLĀD	everglade, glade, *moonglade*
GRĀD	*A* aggrade, *B* Belgrade, *D* degrade, downgrade, *GR* grade, grayed, *P* palmigrade, *PL* plantigrade, *R* rectigrade, regrade, regrayed, retrograde, *S* Centigrade, *T* taligrade, tardigrade, *U* ungrayed
HĀD	hade
HWĀD	wheyed
JĀD	bejade, jade
KĀD	*A* alcaide, ambuscade, appliquéd, arcade, *B* barricade, *BL* blockade, *BR* brocade, *D* decade, decayed, *E* escalade, estacade, *F* falcade, *FR* frescade, *K* cade, cascade, cavalcade, cockade, Medicaid, *S* saccade, *ST* stockade
LĀD	*A* accolade, allayed, *D* *deep-laid*, defilade, delayed, *E* enfilade, escalade, *F* fusillade, *GR* grillade, *I* inlaid, interlaid, *L* lade, laid, *M* marmalade, *O* overlaid, *P* parlayed, pistolade, *R* relade, relaid, relayed, *U* underlaid, unlade, unlaid
MĀD	*B* barmaid, bondmaid, *BR* bridesmaid, *CH* chambermaid, *D* dairy maid, dismayed, *H* handmade, *handmaid,* homemade, *housemaid,* *M* made, maid, *mermaid,* meter maid, *milkmaid,* *N* newmade, nursemaid, *O* old maid, *P* pomade, *R* ready-made, remade, *S* sea maid, self-made, serving maid, *U* undismayed, unmade
NĀD	*B* bastinade, *DR* dragonnade, *E* esplanade,

	F fanfaronade, *FL* flanconnade, *G* gabionade, gasconade, *GR* grenade, *H* harlequinade, *K* cannonade, carbonade, carronade, cassonade, colonnade, cottonade, *L* lemonade, *M* marinade, *N* nayed, neighed, *P* panade, pasquinade, *PR* promenade, *S* serenade, citronade, *STR* strephonade
PĀD	*A* apaid, *E* escapade, estrapade, *G* gallopade, *KR* croupade, *O* overpaid, *P* paid, postpaid, *PR* prepaid, *R* repaid, *U* underpaid, unpaid, unrepaid, wellpaid
PLĀD	displayed, overplayed, plaid, played, underplayed, undisplayed, unplayed
PRĀD	prayed, preyed, unprayed, unpreyed
RĀD	*A* arrayed, *B* bewrayed, *D* disarrayed, *J* gingerade, *M* masquerade, *P* parade, *R* raid, rayed, *SH* charade, *T* tirade, *U* unarrayed, unrayed
SĀD	*A* ambassade, assayed, *E* essayed, *GL* glacéed, glissade, *H* harquebusade, *KR* crusade, *P* palisade, passade, pesade, *T* torsade, *U* unassayed, unessayed
SHĀD	crocheted, *eyeshade,* *nightshade,* overshade, ricocheted, *sunshade,* shade
SLĀD	slade, sleighed
SPĀD	spade, spayed, unspayed
SPLĀD	splayed
SPRĀD	besprayed, resprayed, sprayed, unsprayed
STĀD	overstayed, stade, staid, stayed, unstaid
STRĀD	balustrade, estrayed, strayed
SWĀD	dissuade, overpersuade, persuade, repersuade, suede, swayed, unswayed
TĀD	rodomontade, sautéed
THĀD	they'd
TRĀD	betrayed, fair trade, free trade, portrayed, retrad trade
VĀD	evade, invade, conveyed, pervade, purveyed, surveyed
WĀD	overweighed, reweighed, unweighed, wade, weighed

(See **Ā**, add *-ed* where appropriate.)

AD

AD	A ad, add, *D* dyad, Dunciad, *DR* dryad, *E* ennead, *G* Gilead, *GW* gwynniad, *H* hamadryad, *I* Iliad, *J jeremiad, K* chiliad, Columbiad, *L* Lusiad, *M* myriad, *N* Naiad, *O* ogdoad, Olympiad, oread, *R* re-add, superadd, *TR triad*
BAD	aubade, bad, bade, forbade, *Sinbad,* unforbade
BLAD	blad
BRAD	brad
CHAD	Chad
DAD	alidad, aoudad, Baghdad, bedad, dad, granddad, Trinidad
FAD	fad
GAD	begad, egad, gad
GLAD	glad
GRAD	grad, Leningrad, Petrograd, undergrad
HAD	Galahad, had
KAD	cad
KLAD	*E* y-clad, *H* heavy-clad, *I* ironclad, ivy-clad, *KL* clad, *M mail-clad, moss-clad, P pine-clad, U* unclad, *W* winter-clad
LAD	lad, reculade, cephalad
MAD	hebdomad, *nomad,* mad
PAD	*footpad,* helipad, *kneepad,* launching pad, pad, shoulder pad, tongue pad
PLAD	plaid
RAD	rad
SAD	*dorsad, hexad,* sad
SHAD	shad
SKAD	scad
TAD	*heptad, octad,* tad
TRAD	trad

ÄD

ÄD	ahed, ohed and ahed, oohed and ahed
BÄD	baaed, aubade
HÄD	jihad
KÄD	falcade
KWÄD	quad
LÄD	ballade, remolade, remoulade, roulade
MÄD	pomade, chamade
NÄD	esplanade, promenade
PÄD	gallopade
RÄD	hurrahed, kamerad, saraad
SÄD	façade, glissade, lancepesade

SHÄD	psha'd
SKWÄD	death squad, squad
TÄD	metad, rodomontade
TRÄD	estrade
VÄD	couvade
WÄD	wad
YÄD	noyade, oeillade
ZÄD	huzzahed

(See **Ä,** add *-ed* where appropriate; see also **OD.**)

ĀDZ

ĀDZ	aids, Aids

ADZ

(See **ĀD,** add *-s* where appropriate.)

ADZ	ads, adze, Lusiads
SKADZ	scads

(See **AD,** add *-s* where appropriate.)

ĀF

CHĀF	chafe, enchafe, rechafe
KĀF	kef
SĀF	*fail-safe, jail-safe,* safe, unsafe, vouchsafe
STRĀF	strafe
WĀF	waif

AF

AF	aff
BAF	baff
CHAF	chaff, chiff-chaff
DAF	daff
DRAF	draff
FAF	faff
GAF	gaff, gaffe, penny gaff, shandy-gaff
GRAF	*A* agraffe, actinograph, allograph, anagraph, areograph, *B* barograph, *D* diagraph, dictograph, *E* electrocardiograph, electograph, epigraph, *F* phonograph, photograph, *FR* phraseograph, *GR* graf, graph, *H* hagiograph, hectograph, heliograph, hydrograph, holograph, homograph, *I* ideograph, eidograph, *K* calligraph, cardiograph, caraunograph, kymograph, kindergraph, choreograph, coronograph, *KR* chronograph, cryptograph, *L* lithograph, logograph, *M* macrograph, mechanograph, melograph, mimeograph, myograph, myocardiograph, monograph, *N* nephograph, pneumograph, *O* oleograph, ondograph, opisthograph, autograph, autoradiograph, *P* paleograph, pantograph, paragraph, perigraph, pictograph, polygraph, *PL* pluviograph, *R* radiograph, rexograph, *S* serigraph, sillograph, seismograph, cinematograph, *SF* sphygmograph, *SH* shadowgraph, seismograph, *SP* spectrograph, spectroheliograph, spirograph, *ST* stathmograph, stenograph, stereograph, stylograph, *T* tachograph, telegraph, telephotograph, *TH* thermograph, *TR* trigraph, *Z* xylograph, zincograph
SKAF	bathyscaph
SKLAF	sclaff
STAF	*distaff, Falstaff, flagstaff,* half-staff, *gibstaff,* quarterstaff, overstaff, *pikestaff, plowstaff, tipstaff,* understaff
TAF	bibliotaph, epitaph, cenotaph
YAF	yaff

ÄF

HÄF	behalf, better half, half, half-and-half
KÄF	calf, Kaf, moon calf
KWÄF	quaff
LÄF	belly laugh, *horselaugh,* laugh
RÄF	giraffe, carafe, *riffraff*
STRÄF	strafe

ĀFT

CHĀFT	chafed
SĀFT	vouchsafed
STRĀFT	strafed

AFT

AFT	aft
BAFT	abaft, baffed
CHAFT	chaffed
DAFT	daft, daffed
DRAFT	draft, overdraft, redraft
GAFT	gaffed, ungaffed
GRAFT	allograft, engraft, photographed, graft, graphed, ingraft, lithographed, autographed, paragraphed, telegraphed
HAFT	haft
KRAFT	*A* aircraft, antiaircraft, *F* folkcraft, *H* handcraft, handicraft, hovercraft, *KR* Chriscraft, craft, *M* metalcraft, mooncraft, *N* needlecraft, *PR* priestcraft, *R* rivercraft, *S* seacraft, *ST* stagecraft, starcraft, *W* witchcraft, woodcraft
RAFT	raft
SHAFT	shaft
STAFT	overstaffed, restaffed, staffed, understaffed

(See **AF,** add *-ed* where appropriate.)

ÄFT

DRÄFT	draft, draught, overdraft. redraft
KWÄFT	quaffed
LÄFT	laughed
WÄFT	awaft, waft

ĀG

HĀG	Hague
NĀG	fainaigue
PLĀG	plague
PRĀG	Prague
VĀG	stravag, vague

AG

BAG	*B* bag, *beanbag,* *D* debag, *F* feedbag, *FL* fleabag, *H* handbag, *K* carpetbag, kitbag, *M* mailbag, moneybag, *N* nosebag, *P* postbag, *R* ragbag, ratbag, *S* saddlebag, *W* windbag, workbag
BRAG	brag, Fort Bragg
DAG	dag
DRAG	drag, wallydrag

FAG	fag, fish fag	**KĀJ**	discage, encage, cage,	**FLĀK**	flake, *cornflake, snowflake*
FLAG	battle flag, flag		uncage	**FRĀK**	frake
FRAG	frag	**MĀJ**	mage	**HĀK**	haik, hake
GAG	gag	**PĀJ**	*footpage,* op-ed page,	**JĀK**	jake
HAG	demihag, fag hag, hag,		page, rampage, repage	**KĀK**	*B* beefcake, *FR* friedcake,
	hellhag, night hag, old hag	**RĀJ**	enrage, outrage, rage		*fruitcake, GR* griddlecake,
JAG	*adjag,* jag	**SĀJ**	Osage, *presage,* sage,		*H* havercake, hoe cake,
KAG	cag		unsage		honey cake, *J* johnnycake,
KRAG	crag	**STĀJ**	backstage, downstage,		*K* cake, coffee cake,
KWAG	quag		forestage, center stage,		*cupcake, N* nutcake, *O*
LAG	jet lag, lag		stage, upstage		oatcake, *P* pancake, piece
MAG	mag	**SWĀJ**	assuage, swage		of cake, *S* seed cake, *SH*
NAG	Brobdignag, knag, nag	**WĀJ**	wage		*shortcake, T* tea cake, *W*
RAG	bullyrag, chew the rag, on				wedding cake
	the rag, rag, rowlyrag,	(See **IJ.**)		**KRĀK**	crake, water crake
	shag-rag			**KWĀK**	earthquake, *moonquake,*
SAG	sag				quake, *seaquake*
SHAG	abishag, shag	**AJ**		**LĀK**	lake
SKAG	skag			**MĀK**	make, on the make,
SKRAG	scrag	**BAJ**	badge		remake, unmake
SLAG	slag	**FAJ**	fadge	**PĀK**	opaque, radiopaque
SNAG	snag	**HAJ**	hadj	**RĀK**	afterrake, *muckrake,* rake
SPRAG	sprag	**KAJ**	cadge	**SĀK**	forsake, *keepsake,*
STAG	stag				*namesake,* sake
SWAG	swag	**ÄJ**		**SHĀK**	*handshake,* shake, sheik
TAG	ragtag, tag	(See **ÄZH**)		**SLĀK**	aslake, slake
VAG	vag			**SNĀK**	*blacksnake,* garter snake,
WAG	*chinwag,* scalawag, wag,				coral snake, milk snake,
	wagwag, wigwag	**ĀJD**			rattlesnake, ribbon snake,
ZAG	zag, *zigzag*				snake, water snake
		ĀJD	aged	**SPĀK**	forespake, spake
ÄG		**GĀJD**	disengaged, engaged,	**STĀK**	*beefsteak, grubstake,*
			gauged		mistake, stake, steak,
BLÄG	blague	**KĀJD**	encaged, caged		*sweepstake, vealsteak*
PRÄG	Prague	**PĀJD**	paged, rampaged, repaged	**STRĀK**	strake
TÄG	*qualtagh*	**RĀJD**	enraged, outraged, raged	**TĀK**	betake, *intake,* mistake,
		STĀJD	restaged, staged, unstaged		overtake, partake, retake,
AGD		**SWĀJD**	assuaged		take, undertake, uptake,
		WĀJD	waged		wapentake
(See **AG,** add *-ed* where appropriate.)				**TRĀK**	traik
				VĀK	*thalweg*
ĀGZ		**ĀK**		**WĀK**	awake, kittiwake, rewake,
					robin-wake, wake
PLÄGZ	plagues	**ĀK**	ache, *backache,* bellyache,		
VÄGZ	gyrovagues		*earache, headache,*	**AK**	
			heartache, stomach-ache,		
			toothache	**AK**	*A* aphrodisiac, ack-ack,
ĀJ		**BĀK**	bake, *hardbake, clambake,*		ammoniac, amnesiac, *B*
			sunbake		bivouac, *D* demoniac,
ĀJ	age, mid-age, middle age,	**BRĀK**	*B* barley brake, *BR* brake,		dipsomaniac, *Dyak,*
	old age, over-age, under-		break, *D* daybreak, *F*		Dionysiac, *E* egomaniac,
	age		firebreak, *H* handbrake,		elegiac, *H* haemophiliac,
FĀJ	alliaphage, anthropophage,		heartbreak, *J* jailbreak, *K*		hypochondriac, *I* ileac,
	bacteriophage,		canebrake, coffee-break, *L*		iliac, insomniac, *K*
	paedophage, theophage,		lunch break, *O* outbreak, *P*		cardiac, Kodiak, *KL*
	xylophage		parabrake, *U* upbreak, *W*		kleptomaniac, *M* maniac,
FRĀJ	saxifrage		waterbreak, *windbreak,*		megalomaniac,
GĀJ	disengage, engage, gage,		*wordbreak*		monomaniac, *N*
	gauge, *greengage,*	**DRĀK**	drake, firedrake,		nymphomaniac, *O* oomiak,
	reengage, weather gauge		mandrake, sheldrake		*P* pyromaniac, Pontiac, *S*
		FĀK	fake		sacroiliac, sal ammoniac,

	coeliac, symposiac, *Z* zodiac
BAK	*A* aback, *B* bac, back, *bareback*, biofeedback, *D* diamondback, *dieback*, *DR* drawback, *F* feedback, fiddleback, *fullback*, *FL* flashback, *G* giveback, *GR* greenback, *H* hatchback, *halfback*, *hardback*, *horseback*, huckaback, *humpback*, *hunchback*, *K* kickback, comeback, *cutback*, *KW* quarterback, *quillback*, *L* laid-back, leaseback, leatherback, *M* mossback, *O* outback, *P* paperback, pickaback, piggyback, pickaback, *pinchback*, *puffback*, *R* razorback, *SPL* splashback, *ST* stickleback, *SW* switchback, *T* tieback, *tumbak*, *TH* throwback, *W* wetback, *Z* zweiback
BLAK	black, *boneblack*, *bootblack*, *lampblack*, shoeblack
BRAK	amphibrach, brach, bricabrac, ladybrac, tetrabrach
CHAK	chak
DAK	dak, *Kodak*, *sandak*
FLAK	*flicflac*, flack, flak
HAK	hack, hard hack, tacamahak
HWAK	*bullwhack*, *bushwhack*, paddy-whack, whack
JAK	*A* amberjack, applejack, *B* bootblack, *BL* blackjack, *FL* flapjack, *H* hijack, *HW* whipjack, *J* jack, *KR* crackerjack, *crossjack*, *L* leatherjack, lumberjack, *M* muntjac, *N* natterjack, *SK* skipjack, skyjack, *SL* slapjack, *SM* smokejack, *ST* steeplejack, *Y* yellowjack, Union Jack
KAK	ipecac, macaque
KLAK	clack, claque
KRAK	*jimcrack*, crack, thundercrack, *wisecrack*
KWAK	quack
LAK	alack, *kulak*, lac, lack, lakh, shellac
MAK	mac, mack, *sumac*, *Tarmac*, yashmak
NAK	almanac, coronach, knack, nievie-nievie-nick-nack, Pasternak, Sassenach

PAK	*backpack*, *daypack*, *gopak*, *calpac*, *mudpack*, naughty-pack, unpack, wool pack
PLAK	plack, plaque
RAK	anorak, hayrack, rack, rickrack, sea wrack, serac, *Shadrach*, tamarack, wrack
SAK	*D* doodlesack, *G* gunnysack, *GR* gripsack, *H* Hackensack, haversack, *hopsack*, *K* cul-de-sac, *M* mailsack, *N* knapsack, *O* ovisack, *R* ransack, *rucksack*, *S* sac, sack, *sadsack*, *W* woolsack
SHAK	shack
SLAK	forslack, slack
SMAK	smack
SNAK	snack
STAK	*haystack*, *smokestack*, stack
TAK	attack, hackmatack, hard tack, *thumbtack*, tack, ticktack
THRAK	thrack
THWAK	thwack
TRAK	*backtrack*, *racetrack*, *sidetrack*, track
VAK	*Czechoslovak*, *Slovak*
WAK	Sarawak, Waac, Wac, wack
YAK	cattle-yak, *coulibiac*, yack, yak, yakkity-yak
ZAK	*Anzac*, *Balzac*, *Muzak*, ziczac

ÄK

KÄK	macaque
LÄK	lac
RÄK	Iraq
TÄK	*chittak*, *qualtagh*
WÄK	Sarawak

(See **OK**)

AKS

AKS	ax, axe, battleax, battleaxe, coax, pickax, poleax
DAKS	*addaks*, Adirondacks
FAKS	facts, fax, Halifax
FLAKS	flacks, flax, *toadflax*
JAKS	*Ajax*
LAKS	Analax, lax, *smilax*, parallax, relax, unlax
MAKS	*anticlimax*, Betamax, Blue Max, *climax*, Lomax, minimax, *subclimax*

NAKS	*Fornax*
PAKS	packs, pax, repacks, unpacks
RAKS	*borax*, *hyrax*, *styrax*, *storax*, *thorax*
SAKS	sacks, sax, Tay-Sachs
SLAKS	slacks
TAKS	attacks, excise tax, income tax, overtax, sales tax, *syntax*, supertax, *surtax*, tacks, tax, undertax
THRAKS	*anthrax*, thrax
WAKS	*beeswax*, bewax, *earwax*, sealing wax, unwax, wax
ZAKS	zax

(See **AK**, add *-s* where appropriate.)

ĀKT

(See **ĀK**, add *-d* where appropriate.)

AKT

AKT	abreact, act, enact, entr'acte, coact, counteract, overact, overreact, react, reenact, retroact, underact, underreact
BAKT	backed, *humpbacked*, *hunchbacked*, rebacked, saddle-backed, *stoopbacked*, unbacked
BRAKT	bract
DAKT	redact, autodidact
FAKT	artifact, fact, in fact, matter-of-fact
FRAKT	defract, diffract, fract, infract, catophract, refract
HAKT	hacked, unhacked
PAKT	*epact*, impact, compact, pact
RAKT	cataract, racked, wracked, tesseract
SAKT	resacked, retransact, sacked, transact
STRAKT	abstract, reabstract
SWAKT	swacked
TAKT	attacked, intact, contact, reattacked, recontact, tact, unattacked
TRAKT	attract, detract, distract, extract, contract, protract, retract, subtract, tracked, tract, untracked
ZAKT	exact, inexact, transact

(See **AK**, add *-ed* where appropriate.)

ĀL

ĀL	ail, ale, ginger ale
BĀL	Baal, bail, bale
BRĀL	brail, Braille
DĀL	*Airedale*, Chippendale, dale, *quardeel*, merdaille
DRĀL	drail
DWĀL	dwale
FĀL	fail, *pass-fail*
FLĀL	flail
FRĀL	frail
GĀL	farthingale, gale, galingale, martingale, nightingale, regale
GRĀL	engrail, grail, Holy Grail
HĀL	all hail, exhale, hail, hale, ylahayll, inhale
HWĀL	whale, *narwhale*
JĀL	engaol, enjail, gaol, jail, ungaol, unjail
KĀL	kail, kale, percale
KWĀL	quail
LĀL	Hallel
MĀL	*blackmail*, camail, mail, male, remail
NĀL	*agnail*, fingernail, *hangnail, hobnail,* canaille, nail, tenaille, *thumbnail, toenail, treenail*
PĀL	bepale, dead pale, *deathpale*, empale, impale, pail, pale
RĀL	derail, *guardrail, handrail, cograil, landrail,* monorail, rail, serail, *taffrail*
SĀL	*A* a-sail, assail, *F* foresail, *H* headsail, wholesale, *L* lugsail, *M* mainsail, *O* outsail, *R* resail, *resale, S* sail, sale, *SK* skysail, *SP* spritsail, *ST* staysail, *T* topsail, *TR* trysail, tresaiel, *W* wassail
SHĀL	shale
SKĀL	enscale, in scale, scale, sliding scale
SKWĀL	squail
SNĀL	snail
SPĀL	spale
STĀL	stale
SWĀL	swale
TĀL	*A* aventail, *B* bangtail, betail, *boattail, bobtail, bucktail, BR* broadtail, *D* detail, disentail, *dovetail, DR* draggletail, *E* entail, *F* fairytale, *fantail, fishtail, forktail, foxtail, H* hairtail, hightail, *horntail, K* cat- tail, *coattail, cocktail,*

coontail, cottontail, curtail, *O* oxtail, *P* pigtail, *pintail*, ponytail, *R* retail, *S* scissor-tail, *swordtail, SH* shavetail, *sheartail, short- tail, SPR* sprittail, *SW* swallowtail, *T* tael, tail, taille, tale, tattletale, *telltale*, teetertail, *TH thorntail, TR* trundletail, *V* ventail, *W* wagtail

THĀL	they'll
THRĀL	thrail
TRĀL	entrail, *contrail*, off-trail, trail
VĀL	*A* avail, *E* envail, *I* intervale, inveil, *K* countervail, *O* overvail, *P* paravail, *PR* prevail, *TR* travail, *U* unveil, *V* vail, vale, veil
WĀL	bewail, wail, wale
YĀL	Yale
ZĀL	grisaille

AL

AL	*A* accentual, aerial, allodial, alluvial, amatorial, ambrosial, annual, antediluvial, arboreal, asexual, *B* baronial, bestial, bisexual, boreal, *D* dictatorial, diluvial, *E* effectual, empyreal, ethereal, eventual, expurgatorial, *F* phantasmagorial, ferial, fiducial, finial, funereal, *GR* gradual, *H* habitual, hernial, hymeneal, *I* immaterial, immemorial, imperial, incorporeal, individual, industrial, ineffectual, infusorial, initial, inquisitorial, intellectual, *J* genial, gerundial, jovial, *K* casual, collegial, colloquial, commercial, congenial, conjugial, connubial, consanguineal, consistorial, continual, conventual, cordial, corporeal, *KW* quadrennial, *M* magisterial, marsupial, memorial, menstrual, mercurial, microbial, ministerial, mutual, *N* nectareal, novendial, *P*

participial, patrimonial, pedestrial, perennial, perpetual, pictorial, post- prandial, punctual, purpureal, *PR* preceptorial, primordial, *R* remedial, residual, *S* sartorial, sensual, seigneurial, serial, sexual, sidereal, *SP* splenial, *T* textual, terrestrial, territorial, tertial, testimonial, *TR* transsexual, trivial, *U* uxorial, unusual, *V* ventriloquial, vestigial, vicarial, victorial, virtual, visual, *Y* usual

BAL	bal, Hannibal, cabal, cannibal
BRAL	cerebral, vertebral
DAL	antipodal, iridal, quadrupedal, pyramidal
FAL	apocryphal
GAL	agal, gal, conjugal, madrigal, Portugal, Senegal
GRAL	integral
KAL	*A* academical, acritical, alchemical, alexipharmical, alexiterical, alphabetical, algebraical, alkalimetrical, allegorical, analytical, analogical, anarchical, anatomical, angelical, antarctical, anthological, antithetical, apical, apologetical, apostolical, arithmetical, archaeological, arsenical, ascetical, astrological, atypical, atmospherical, asthmatical *B* Babylonical, bacchical, bacteriological, balsamical, barometrical, basilical, beatifical, biblical, bibliophilical, bibliographical, bibliomanical, biographical, biological, botanical, bureaucratical, *BR* Brahmanical, *CH* cherubical, *D* deistical, democratical, demoniacal, demonological, despotical, diabolical, diaphonical, diagraphical, diacritical, dialectical, dialogical, dialogistical, diametrical, didactical, dietetical, dynamical, diplomatical, dipsomaniacal, dogmatical,

dolorifical, dominical, *DR* dramatical, dropsical, Druidical, *E* egoistical, egotistical, eccentrical, exegetical, exoterical, exotical, extrinsical, ecumenical, equivocal, electrical, elegiacal, ellipitical, emblematical, emphatical, empirical, endemical, energetical, enigmatical, encomiastical, encyclical, encyclopedical, enthusiastical, epical, epidemical, epigrammatical, episodical, epithetical, erotical, esoterical, aesthetical, esthetical, ethical, ethnical, ethnological, etymological, evangelical, *F* fanatical, phantasmagorical, fantastical, Pharisaical, pharmaceutical, farcical, philanthropical, philological, philosophical, finical, physical, physiological, forensical, photographical, *FR* phrenological, *G* galvanical, *GR* graphical, grammatical, *H* harmonical, Hebraical, helical, hemispherical, heretical, hermitical, heroical, hierarchical, hygienical, historical, hyperbolical, hypercritical, hypochondriacal, hypocritical, hysterical, *HW* whimsical, *I* identical, idiotical, illogical, immechanical, inimical, ironical, *J* genealogical, generical, jesuitical, juridical, *K* cacophonical, Calvinistical, canonical, caracal, characteristical, cardical, cartographical, categorical, catholical, casuistical, chemical, chimerical, codical, coxcombical, conical, conventical, cortical, caustical, cosmetical, cosmical, cubical, *KL* classical, clerical, climactical, climatological, clinical, *KR* critical, cryptical, chronological, *KW* quizzical, *L*

lackadaisical, laical, lethargical, Levitical, lyrical, liturgical, logical, locale, *M* magnifical, majestical, magical, maniacal, mathematical, medical, mechanical, metaphysical, metaphorical, methodical, Methodistical, metical, metrical, microscopical, misanthropical, mystical, mythical, mythological, monarchical, musical, *N* nymphical, nonclassical, nonsensical, nautical, pneumatological, numerical, *O* oneirocritical, optical, oratorical, *P* parabolical, paradisiacal, parasitical, parenthetical, pathetical, pathological, patronymical, pedagogical, pedantical, penological, periphrastical, periodical, pietistical, pyramidical, piratical, pyrotechnical, poetical, polemical, political, pontifical, puritanical, *PL* platonical, *PR* pragmatical, practical, problematical, prophetical, *R* radical, rhapsodical, reciprocal, rhetorical, rhythmical, rheumatical, *S* sabbatical, satanical, satirical, scenical, centrical, seraphical, cervical, sybaritical, psychiatrical, psychical, cyclical, psychological, cylindrical, cynical, symbolical, symmetrical, synchronical, synodical, synonymical, synoptical, synthetical, systematical, schismatical, soritical, *SF* spherical, *SK* schismatical, *SP* spasmodical, sporadical, *ST* stoical, *STR* strategical, *T* tactical, technical, technicological, technological, typical, typographical, tyrannical, topical, topographical, *TH* theoretical, *TR* tragical, tropical, *U* umbilical, unethical, uncanonical, *V* vatical, veridical, vertical, vesical, vortical, *Y* euphemistical, euphonical,

Eucharistical, eulogistical, *Z* zodiacal, zoological

KWAL ventriloqual

MAL animal, decimal, hexidecimal, infinitesimal, quadragesimal, lachrymal, millesimal, minimal, shamal, synonymal

NAL *A* aboriginal, adhesional, affectional, antiphonal, arsenal, *B* bacchanal, banal, *D* decanal, denominational, descensional, destinal, devotional, diagonal, diaconal, digressional, discretional, divisional, doctrinal, duodecimal, *E* educational, echinal, expansional, exceptional, emotional, evolutional, *F* phenomenal, fictional, functional, *FR* fractional, *H* hexagonal, heptagonal, *I* imaginal, imitational, impersonal, indigenal, inguinal, inspirational, institutional, instructional, insurrectional, intentional, interjectional, international, intercessional, intestinal, *J* geminal, germinal, *K* cardinal, carcinal, communal, complexional, conditional, confessional, congressional, conclusional, constitutional, contradictional, conventional, conversational, convulsional, *KR* criminal, *L* longitudinal, *M* machinal, marginal, matinal, matronal, matutinal, medicinal, meridional, missional, *N* national, nominal, notional, *O* occasional, octagonal, optional, original, *P* partitional, passional, patronal, pentagonal, personal, polygonal, *PR* precautional, probational, professional, progressional, proportional, processional, provisional, *R* rational, rationale, regional, recessional, retinal, *S* sensational, seasonal,

	synchronal, circumlocutional, *ST* staminal, *T* terminal, tympanal, torsional, *TR* traditional, trigonal, *V* vaginal, viminal, virginal, visional, volitional, *Y* urinal
PAL	Episcopal, municipal, pal, principal
RAL	*A* admiral, agricultural, anchoral, arbocultural, architectural, *D* doctoral, *E* ephemeral, extemporal, *F* falderal, federal, femoral, funeral, *G* geyseral, guttural, *H* horticultural, *I* inaugural, *J* general, gestural, *K* cantoral, carnivoral, collateral, chorale, corral, *L* literal, littoral, *M* magistral, mayoral, mensural, mineral, morale, *N* natural, *P* pastoral, pastorale, pastural, peripheral, pictural, postural, *PR* preceptoral, *S* several, supernatural, sutural, *SH* chapparal, *SK* sculptural, *SKR* scriptural, *T* tellural, temporal, textural, *TR* tragicomipastoral, *V* vesperal, visceral
SAL	Provençale, sal, salle, quetzal
SHAL	seneschal, shall
TAL	*D* digital, *H* hospital, *K* capital, *M* marital, *N* nepotal, *O* orbital, *P* palatal, pedestal, pivotal, *SK* skeletal, *V* vegetal
VAL	festival, interval, carnival, travale

ÄL

BÄL	Baal
DÄL	dal
FÄL	rafale
HÄL	mahal, Taj Mahal
KÄL	jacal
KRÄL	kraal
MÄL	grand mal
RÄL	rale

ĀLD

ĀLD	ailed

(See **ĀL,** add -*d* or -*ed* where appropriate.)

ALD

BALD	caballed
PALD	palled
RALD	emerald, corralled

ALK

ALK	alk
FALK	catafalque
KALK	calk
TALK	talc

ALKS

FALKS	falx, catafalques
KALKS	calx

(See **ALK,** add -*s* where appropriate.)

ALP

ALP	alp
GALP	galp
PALP	palp
SKALP	auriscalp, scalp

ALPS

ALPS	Alps

(See **ALP,** add -*s* where appropriate.)

ALT

ALT	alt
SHALT	shalt

ALV

SALV	salve
VALV	bivalve, priming valve, safety valve, valve, univalve

ĀLZ

ĀLZ	ails
SĀLZ	Marseilles, sails, sales
WĀLZ	Wales

(See **ĀL,** add -*s* where appropriate.)

ĀM

ĀM	aim
BLĀM	blame
DĀM	dame
DRĀM	melodrame
FĀM	defame, disfame, fame
FLĀM	aflame, flame, inflame
FRĀM	*airframe, doorframe,* frame
GĀM	*endgame,* game, videogame, *war-game*
HĀM	hame
KĀM	became, came, kame, overcame
KLĀM	acclaim, declaim, disclaim, exclaim, claim, counterclaim, *quitclaim,* proclaim, reclaim
KRĀM	*crème de la crème*
LĀM	lame
MĀM	maim
NĀM	*byname, forename,* misname, name, *nickname,* rename, *surname,* unname
SĀM	same, self-same, Sejm
SHĀM	ashame, shame
TĀM	entame, tame, untame

AM

AM	ad nauseam, am, Iamb, choriamb, Kayam, Siam
BAM	Alabam', bam, wham-bam
CHAM	cham
DAM	Amsterdam, *beldam,* dam, damn, goddamn, *grandam,* grande dame, cofferdam, madame, *milldam,* Rotterdam
DRAM	drachm, dram, dramme
FLAM	flam, *flimflam,* oriflamme
FRAM	diaphragm
GAM	gam, gamb
GRAM	*A* anagram, aerogram, *B* barogram, *D* dactylogram, diagram, *E* echocardiogram, electrocardiogram, electroencephalogram, encephalogram, epigram, *F* phonogram, photogram, *FR* phraseogram, *GR* gram, gramme, *H* hexagram, hectogram, *H* hierogram, histogram, *I* ideogram, ichnogram, *K* cablegram, candygram, kilogram, *KR* cryptogram, chronogram, *L* lexigram, lipogram, logogram, *M* melogram, milligram, *N* nephogram, pneumencephalogram, *P* pangram, paragram, parallelogram,

	pelmatogram, *PR* program, *R* roentgenogram, *S* centigram, sonogram, *ST* stereogram, *T tangram*, telegram, tetragram
HAM	Abraham, Birmingham, ham, Nottingham
HWAM	wham, *whimwham*
JAM	demijambe, *doorjamb*, enjamb, jam, jamb, *jimjam*
KAM	cam
KLAM	hardshell clam, clam, littleneck clam, mud clam, razor clam, softshell clam, steamer clam
KRAM	cram
LAM	lam, lamb
MAM	ma'am, Mam
NAM	Vietnam
PAM	pam
PRAM	pram
RAM	battering ram, dithyramb, marjoram, ram, rhamn
SAM	Assam, cheong-sam, *Samsam*, Uncle Sam
SHAM	sham
SHRAM	shram
SKAM	scam
SKRAM	scram
SLAM	slam
SPAM	Spam
SWAM	swam
TAM	tam, *tamtam*
TRAM	tram
YAM	yam, Omar Khayyam
ZAM	alakazam, Nizam, shazam, zam

ÄM

ÄM	ame, ad nauseam
BÄM	balm, embalm
BRÄM	parabrahm
DÄM	Madame
GWÄM	Guam
KÄM	calm
KWÄM	qualm
LÄM	Islam, salaam
MÄM	hammam, imam, malm
NÄM	withernam
PÄM	impalm, palm
SÄM	psalm
WÄM	walm
YÄM	Omar Khayyam

AMB

AMB	iamb, choriamb
GAMB	gamb, gambe

JAMB	enjamb
RAMB	dithyramb

ĀMD

(See **ĀM**, add *-ed* or *-d* where appropriate.)

AMD

(See **AM**, add *-ed* where appropriate.)

AMP

AMP	amp
CHAMP	champ
DAMP	afterdamp, *blackdamp*, *chokedamp*, damp, *deathdamp*, *firedamp*, *whitedamp*, *minedamp*
GAMP	gamp, guimpe
KAMP	decamp, encamp, camp
KLAMP	clamp, unclamp
KRAMP	cramp
LAMP	*blowlamp*, Davy lamp, electric lamp, gas lamp, kerosene lamp, lamp, safety lamp, signal lamp
PAMP	*slampamp*
RAMP	ramp
SAMP	samp
SKAMP	scamp
STAMP	*backstamp*, enstamp, restamp, stamp
TAMP	tamp, retamp
TRAMP	tramp
VAMP	revamp, vamp
HWAMP	whamp
YAMP	yamp

ÄMP

PÄMP	*slampamp*
SWÄMP	swamp

(See **OMP**)

AMPT

DAMPT	damped

(See **AMP**, add *-ed* where appropriate.)

ÄMPT

SWÄMPT	swamped

(See **OMP**, add *-ed* where appropriate.)

ĀMZ

(See **ĀM**, add *-s* where appropriate.)

ÄMZ

AMZ	alms

(See **ÄM**, add *-s* where appropriate.)

ĀN

ĀN	ain, Aisne, ane, eigne, inane
BĀN	bane, *bugbane, fleabane, henbane, herbbane, inurbane, cowbane, ratsbane,* urbane, *wolfsbane*
BLĀN	blain, *chilblain*
BRĀN	brain, *endbrain, featherbrain, forebrain, hindbrain, lamebrain, membrane, midbrain,* scatterbrain
CHĀN	chain, enchain, interchain, rechain, unchain
DĀN	Dane, deign, demimondaine, disdain, foreordain, intermundane, kadein, coordain, mundane, ordain, preordain, reordain, transmundane
DRĀN	*braindrain*, drain, *subdrain*
FĀN	*A* allophane, aerophane, areophane, *D* diaphane, *F* fain, fane, feign, *H* hydrophane, *L* lithophane, *M* misfeign, *PR* profane, *S* cellophane, Sinn Fein
FRĀN	refrain
GĀN	again, gain, gaine, regain
GRĀN	against the grain, engrain, grain, *grosgrain*, ingrain, *crossgrain, migraine*
KĀN	arcane, Biscayne, Duquesne, hurricane, Cain, cane, cocaine, Cockaigne, chicane, procaine, cinquain, sugar cane
KRĀN	crane, water crane, Ukraine
LĀN	chamberlain, delaine, lain, laine, lane, porcelain, chatelain, chatelaine
MĀN	*A* amain, *CH* chow mein, *D* demesne, domain, *H* humane, *I* immane,

PĀN inhumane, *J* germane, *L* legerdemain, *M* main, Maine, mane, *mortmain, R* remain, romaine, *SH* Charlemagne, *T* ptomaine elecampane, frangipane, campaign, campane, counterpane, *marchpane,* pain, pane, *propane,* Champaign, champagne, windowpane

PLĀN *A* aeroplane, *airplane,* aquaplane, *B* biplane, *E* explain, emplane, *H* hydroplane, *J* gyroplane, *K* complain, *M* monoplane, multiplane, *P* peneplain, pursuit plane, *PL* plain, plane, *S* sailplane, seaplane, *SH* Champlain, *SK* skiplane, *T* taxiplane, *tailplane, TR* triplane, *V* volplane, *W* warplane

RĀN *A* arraign, acid rain, *B* Bahrain, borane, *BR* bridle rein, *CH* check-rein, *D* darrein, *F* forane, *I* interreign, *KW* quatrain, *L* Lorraine, *M* mediterrane, moraine, *R* rain, reign, rein, *S* souterrain, subterrane, suzerain, *T* terrain, terrane, *U* unrein, *V* viceraine

SĀN Hussein, insane, sain, sane, seine, Seine, *sixain*

SKĀN skein

SLĀN slain

SPĀN Spain

SPRĀN sprain

STĀN abstain, bestain, *bloodstain,* distain, *tearstain*

STRĀN Andromeda strain, *eyestrain,* constrain, overstrain, restrain, strain

TRĀN distrain

SWĀN boatswain, coxswain, swain

TĀN *A* appertain, ascertain, attain, *B* butane, *D* detain, *E* entertain, *K* contain, curtein, *M* maintain, *O* obtain, *octane, P* pertain, *R* retain, *S* sextain, soutane, sustain, *SH* chevrotain, *T* ta'en, tain, *U* ultramontane

THĀN bower thane, *ethane, methane,* thane, thegn

TRĀN detrain, distrain, down train, entrain, hovertrain,

pleasure train, Pontchartrain, quatrain, train, uptrain

TWĀN atwain, twain

VĀN paravane, vain, vane, vein, vervain, weather vane

WĀN Gawain, *cordwain,* wain, wane

ZĀN quatorzain, zain

AN

AN an, yuan, Yuan, abecedarian (see **UN** for additional words, ending in the final syllable -an, which normally carry the principal stress on the antepenult and a secondary stress on the final syllable. They become single rhymes if the principal stress is shifted to the final syllable: Acadian, guardian, Zoroastrian, etc.)

BAN ban, cabane, Caliban, corban

BRAN bran

CHAN chan

DAN echinidan, foo young dan, harridan, *Houdan,* Mohammedan, oppidan, Ramadan, randan, redan, Sedan, shandrydan, Sudan

FAN fan, turbofan

FLAN flan

GAN *Afghan,* began, hooligan, cardigan, larrigan, Michigan, mulligan, origan, suffragan, ptarmigan, tsigane, wanigan, yataghan

GRAN gran

HAN Han

KAN *A* African, American, Anglican, astrakhan, *B* balmacaan, barbican, barracan, basilican, billycan, *D* Dominican, *G* Gallican, *I* indican, *K* can, khan, *cancan, M* Mexican, *O* oil can, *P* pecan, pelican, pemmican, publican, *R* republican, Republican, rubican, *U* ugly American, *V* Vatican

KLAN clan, Klan

KRAN cran

LAN gamelan, castellan, Catalan, Milan, ortolan, *tolan, yulan*

MAN *A* adman, amman, aircraftsman, *airman,* almsman, artilleryman, *B* backwoodsman, *bailsman,* bandman, bandsman, bankman, bargeman, barman, batman, Bat Man, batsman, beadsman, bellman, best man, billman, birdman, boatman, bondman, bondsman, bookman, bowman, Bushman, *BR* brakeman, *CH* chantman, chapman, checkman, Chinaman, churchman, *D* dairyman, deliveryman, dirgeman, dolesman, dollyman, *dolman,* Dutchman, *DR* draftsman, dragman, dragoman, drayman, *F* ferryman, fireman, fisherman, foeman, footman, foremostman, fugleman, *FL* flagman, flyman, floorman, *FR* freeman, Frenchman, freshman, frontiersman, *G* gangsman, guardsman, gunman, *GR* groomsman, *H* hangman, headman, headsman, helmsman, henchman, herdsman, highwayman, hodman, horseman, huntsman, husbandman, *HW* wherryman, *I* Isle of Man, infantryman, Englishman, Irishman, *iceman, J* gentleman, *jibman,* jinrikiman, journeyman, juryman, *K* cabman, cageman, campman, carman, cayman, kibblerman, *kinsman,* coachman, cogman, Cornishman, cowman, countryman, *KL* clansman, *Klansman,* clergyman, clubman, *KR* craftsman, crewman, *KW* quarryman, quarterman, *L* lady's man, landsman, leadman, leadsman, lighterman, lineman, linesman, liveryman, *lockman,* longshoreman, *M* madman, man, *marksman,* meatman, medicine man, merchantman, *merman,* merryman, *messman,*

middleman, midshipman,
militiaman, *milkman*,
millman, minuteman,
Mussulman, *N* nobleman,
Norman, *Norseman*,
Northman, *O* alderman,
oarsman, odd man,
oddsman, *oilman*,
Orangeman, ottoman,
outman, overman, *P Pac-
man*, *packman*, *passman*,
pegman, *penman*,
peterman, *pitman*,
postman, *Pullman*, *PL*
playman, *plowman*, *PR*
pressman, *R ragman*,
ranchman, reman,
rifleman, *roadman*,
rodman, *Roman*, *S*
sailorman, *salesman*,
sandman, *seaman*,
selectman, signalman,
songman, swordman,
swordsman, subman,
superman, Superman, *SH*
sheepman, *shipman*,
shopman, *shoreman*,
shoresman, *showman*, *SK*
schoolman, Scotchman,
Scotsman, *SL*
slaughterman, *SP*
spearman, *spoilsman*,
spokesman, *sportsman*, *ST*
statesman, stockman, *SW*
swagman, *switchman*, *T*
talesman, talisman,
tallyman, *tapeman*,
tipman, *tollman*, toman,
top man, *townsman*,
tubman, *tugman*, *tupman*,
TR tradesman, *trainman*,
trencherman, *tribesman*, *U*
unman, *V vestryman*, *W*
wardman, *watchman*,
waterman, *wayman*,
Welchman, Welshman,
wireman, wise man,
woman, *woodman*,
woodsman, *workman*, *Y*
yachtsman, *yeggman*,
yeoman

NAN   Hainan, nan, Hunan, Tainan
PAN   *B bedpan*, *BR brainpan*, *D*
deadpan, *dustpan*, *FR*
frying pan, *H hardpan*, *J*
jampan, Japan, *K cocopan*,
KL claypan, *M marzipan*,
Matapan, *N kneepan*, *P*
pan, Pan, panne, *sampan*,
Saipan, sapan, *SH* Chopin,
T taipan, *TR tragopan*,
trepan, *W warming pan*

PLAN   plan, rataplan, replan
RAN   Aldeberan, also-ran,
foreran, furan, Iran,
catamaran, Koran,
Lutheran, outran, overran,
ran, Teheran, trimaran,
veteran
SKAN   *cat-scan*, scan
SKRAN   scran
SPAN   inspan, life span, outspan,
span, spick-and-span, *wing
span*
STAN   Afghanistan, Pakistan,
Turkestan
TAN   *B* Bataan, *F fantan*, *K
caftan*, cosmopolitan, *M*
metropolitan, *N*
Neapolitan, *O* orangutan,
P Powhatan, puritan,
Puritan, *R* rattan, rheotan,
S sacristan, Samaritan,
sumpitan, *suntan*, *SH*
charlatan, *T* tan,
topopolitan, *Y* Yucatan
THAN   than
VAN   divan, caravan, cordovan,
luggage van, pavan, prison
van, van
YAN   shintiyan
ZAN   artisan, bartizan, fusain,
courtesan, Lausanne,
partisan, nonpartisan,
Parmesan, ptisane, tisane

ÄN

ÄN   liane, t'ai chi ch'uan
BÄN   autobahn
CHÄN   machan
CHWÄN   t'ai chi ch'uan
DÄN   maidan
DWÄN   macedoine
GÄN   tzigane
KÄN   Genghis Khan, khan,
macan, pecan
MÄN   Oman, toman
RÄN   buran, Iran, Koran
STÄN   Turkestan
SWÄN   swan
TÄN   Bataan, caftan, soutane,
Wotan
VÄN   pavane
WÄN   wan
ZÄN   Parmesan, tisane

(See **ON**)

ANCH

BLANCH   blanch

BRANCH   anabranch, branch,
disbranch, rebranch
FLANCH   flanch
GANCH   ganch
LANCH   avalanche
RANCH   horse ranch, cattle ranch,
ranch
SCRANCH   scranch
STANCH   stanch

ÄNCH

BLÄNCH   carte blanche
HÄNCH   haunch
KRÄNCH   craunch
LÄNCH   launch
MÄNCH   manche
PÄNCH   paunch
STÄNCH   stanch, staunch

(See **ÔNCH**)

ÄNCHT

LÄNCHT   launched

(See **ÄNCH**, add *-ed* where appropriate.)

ĀND

BRĀND   *B bird-brained*, *BR
brained*, *F feather-brained*,
H hare-brained, *hot-
brained*, *M muddy-
brained*, *R rattle-brained*,
SH shatter-brained, *SK
scatter-brained*
STĀND   blood-stained, stained,
travel-stained

(See **ĀN**, add *-d* or *-ed* where
appropriate.)

AND

AND   and, Chateaubriand,
waniand
BAND   *A* aband, *armband*, *B*
band, banned, bellyband,
BR breastband, *browband*,
D disband, *H hatband*,
headband, *I* imband, *N*
neckband, noseband, *K*
contraband, *R rainband*,
wristband, *S* saraband, *SP*
spaceband, *SW sweatband*,
TR trainband, *W*
waistband, *waveband*

BLAND	bland
BRAND	brand, *firebrand*
DAND	dand, deodand
FAND	fanned, refanned
GLAND	gland, goat gland, monkey gland
GRAND	grand, integrand, Rio Grande
HAND	*A* afterhand, *B* backhand, behindhand, *BR* bridlehand, *E* even hand, *F* fine Italian hand, *forehand*, four-in-hand, *H* hand, *hothand*, *L* longhand, *M* master hand, minute hand, *O* offhand, overhand, *S* secondhand, second hand, *SH* shorthand, *ST* stagehand, *U* underhand, unhand, upperhand
KAND	canned, multiplicand, Samarkand
KLAND	clanned
LAND	*A* abbeyland, *B* borderland, *D* Disneyland, *DR* dreamland, *E* eland, *F* fairyland, *farmland*, fatherland, *GR grassland*, Greenland, *H* headland, *heartland*, hinterland, Holy Land, *homeland*, *I* inland, *KR* crownland, *KW* Queensland, *L* land, *Lapland*, lotus land, *lowland*, *M* mainland, midland, moorland, motherland, *N* never-never land, no man's land, *northland*, *O* overland, *R* Rhineland, *T* toyland, *U* upland, *W* wasteland, woodland
MAND	*D* demand, *F full-manned*, *H half-manned*, *I ill-manned*, *K* command, confirmand, countermand, *M* manned, *R* remand, reprimand, *S* self-command, summand, *U* unmanned
NAND	ordinand
PAND	expand, panned, repand
PLAND	planned
RAND	rand
SAND	ampersand, analysand, *greensand*, *quicksand*, sand
SKAND	rescanned, scanned, unscanned
SPAND	respanned, spanned, unspanned
STAND	*bandstand*, *bedstand*, *grandstand*, *handstand*,

	inkstand, *kickstand*, *lampstand*, *newsstand*, stablestand, stand, understand, *washstand*, withstand
STRAND	strand
TAND	retanned, tanned, untanned
VAND	revanned, vanned

ÄND

(See **OND**)

ANG

BANG	bang, bhang, Big Bang, gang bang, gobang, interrobang, probang, shebang
DANG	dang, yardang
FANG	defang, fang, unfang
GANG	gang, gangue, *holmgang*, *outgang*, *oxgang*, *sirgang*
HANG	hang, overhang, uphang
HWANG	whang
KANG	cangue
KLANG	clang, reclang
KYANG	kiang
LANG	lang
MANG	mang, siamang
NANG	Penang
PANG	pang, trepang
PRANG	prang
RANG	boomerang, harangue, meringue, rang, serang
SANG	pisang, resang, sang
SLANG	*boomslang*, slang
SPANG	spang
SPRANG	resprang, sprang
STANG	stang
SWANG	swang
TANG	*mustang*, orangutang, sea tang, tang
TWANG	twang
VANG	vang
WANG	burrawang
YANG	Pyongyang, yang

ÄNG

FÄNG	*yesterfang*
TSVÄNG	*zugzwang*

ANGD

FANGD	bi-fanged, defanged, fanged, unfanged

(See **ANG**, add *-ed* where appropriate.)

ANGK

ANGK	ankh
BANGK	banc, bank, data bank, embank, *claybank*, mountebank, river bank, *sandbank*, savings bank
BLANGK	blank, Mont Blanc, point-blank
BRANGK	brank
CHANGK	chank
DANGK	dank
DRANGK	drank, outdrank
FLANGK	flank, outflank
FRANGK	franc, frank, Frank
HANGK	hank
KLANGK	clank, reclank
KRANGK	crank, recrank
LANGK	lank
PANGK	hanky-pank
PLANGK	*gangplank*, plank
PRANGK	prank
RANGK	disrank, enrank, outrank, rank
SANGK	sank
SHANGK	*foreshank*, *greenshank*, *redshank*, shank, *sheepshank*, *scrimshank*
SHRANGK	reshrank, shrank
SLANGK	slank
SPANGK	spank
STANGK	outstank, stank
SWANGK	swank
TANGK	antitank, tank, water tank
THANGK	thank
TRANGK	trank
TWANGK	twank
YANGK	yank, Yank

ANGKS

BANGKS	*Fairbanks*
BRANGKS	branks
LANGKS	*phalanx*, lanx
MANGKS	Manx
SHANGKS	bonyshanks, *longshanks*, spindleshanks
THANGKS	thanks
YANGKS	yanks, Yanks

(See **ANGK**, add *-s* where appropriate.)

ANGKT

SANGKT	sacrosanct, sanct

(See **ANGK**, add *-ed* where appropriate.)

ÄNJ

CHÄNJ	change, exchange, interchange,

	counterchange, shortchange
GRĀNJ	grange
MĀNJ	mange
RĀNJ	arrange, derange, disarrange, enrange, prearrange, range, rearrange
STRĀNJ	estrange, strange

ANJ

FLANJ	flange
GANJ	gange
LANJ	phalange
RANJ	*orange,* sporange

ANS

ANS	*A* anse, *appliance, D* discontinuance, *I* insouciance, irradiance, issuance, *K* continuance, *KL clairvoyance, L* luxuriance, *P* permeance, perpetuance, *pursuance, R* radiance, *S* seance, suppliance, *V* variance
BANS	*disturbance*
BRANS	*encumbrance, remembrance*
CHANS	bechance, chance, mischance, perchance
DANS	*ascendance, avoidance,* barn dance, break dance, dance, death dance, folk dance, *impedance,* country dance, courting dance, mating dance, *misguidance,* square dance, tap dance, witch dance
FRANS	France
GANS	arrogance, elegance, extravagance, inelegance
GLANS	glance, side glance
HANS	enhance, hance, hanse
JANS	*allegiance*
KANS	askance, insignificance, significance
LANS	ambulance, demilance, fer-de-lance, jubilance, lance, nonchalance, petulance, sibilance, simulance, vigilance
MANS	manse, romance
NANS	*A* appurtenance, assonance, *D* discountenance, dissonance, dominance, *F*

	finance, *G* governance, *H* high finance, *I* inconsonance, *K* consonance, countenance, *M* maintenance, *N* nance, *O* ordinance, *PR* predominance, preordinance, provenance, *R repugnance,* resonance, *S* sustenance
PANS	expanse
PRANS	prance
RANS	*A aberrance, D* deliverance, *E* exuberance, *F* furtherance, *I* ignorance, intemperance, intolerance, *PR* preponderance, protuberance, *R* rance, *S* severance, sufferance, *T* temperance, tolerance, *U* utterance, *V* vociferance
SANS	impuissance, *complaisance,* conversance, puissance, reconnaisance
SKANS	askance
STANS	*inconstance,* circumstance, stance
TANS	*A acceptance, D* disinheritance, *E* exorbitance, *expectance, H* heritance, *I inductance,* inhabitance, inhabitants, inheritance, *K* concomitance, *conductance, O* oscitance, *PR* precipitance, *R reluctance, remonstrance, repentance*
TRANS	entrance, penetrance, recalcitrance, *remonstrance,* trance, outrance
VANS	advance, irrelevance, relevance
ZANS	*defeasance, complaisance, malfeasance, obeisance,* recognizance

(See **ANT,** add -*s* where appropriate.)

ÄNS

ÄNS	insouciance, nuance, seance
BLÄNS	vraisemblance
FRÄNS	France
LÄNS	fer-de-lance, lance, nonchalance
SÄNS	Renaissance
TRÄNS	outrance

ĀNT

ĀNT	ain't
DĀNT	daint
FĀNT	faint, feint
HĀNT	hain't
KWĀNT	acquaint, quaint
MĀNT	mayn't
PĀNT	bepaint, depaint, *greasepaint,* paint, repaint
PLĀNT	complaint, plaint
RĀNT	Geraint
SĀNT	besaint, ensaint, enceinte, saint, unsaint
STRĀNT	constraint, restraint, self-restraint, straint, unconstraint
TĀNT	attaint, taint, 'tain't
TRĀNT	distraint

ANT

ANT	*A* ant, aunt, attenuant, *D* depreciant, *FL* fluctuant, *G* grand-aunt, great-aunt (etc.), *I* insouciant, irradiant, issuant, *K* continuant, *L* luxuriant, *M* menstruant, miscreant, *O* officiant, otiant, *P* permeant, *PR* procreant, *R* recreant, renunciant, resiant, *V* variant
BANT	bant, Corybant
BRANT	brant, celebrant, *Rembrandt*
CHANT	chant, disenchant, enchant
DANT	commandant, confidant, confidante, consolidant
FANT	elephant, hierophant, oliphant, sycophant, *triumphant*
GANT	*A* arrogant, *E* elegant, extravagant, *I* inelegant, irrigant, *K* congregant, *L* litigant, *M* mitigant, *O* obligant, *S* suffragant, *T* termagant
GRANT	block grant, emigrant, grant, immigrant, integrant
KANT	*A* abdicant, albicant, applicant, askant, *D* decant, dedicant, dodecant, descant, desiccant, *E* exsiccant, *F* fabricant, formicant, *I* imprecant, indicant, insignificant, intoxicant, *K* can't, cant, Kant, communicant, *coruscant, L* lubricant, *M* mendicant, *R* radicant,

	recant, resiccant, *S* safricant, significant, supplicant, *T* toxicant, *V* vesicant
KWANT	quant
LANT	*A* ambulant, articulant, *FL* flagellant, *G* gallant, *GR* gratulant, *I* impetulant, *J* jubilant, *K* capitulant, coagulant, congratulant, cumulant, *L* lant, *M* matriculant, *N* nonchalant, *O* osculant, *P* periculant, petulant, postulant, *R* revelant, *S* sibilant, scintillant, circulant, circumvolant, *ST* stimulant, *STR* stridulant, *T* tintinnabulant, *TR* tremolant, *U* ululant, undulant, *V* vigilant
MANT	adamant, *informant*
NANT	*A* agglutinant, appurtenant, assonant, *D* determinant, discriminant, dissonant, dominant, *F* fulminant, *H* horrisonant, *I* illuminant, imaginant, inconsonant, *J* germinant, *K* conglutinant, consonant, culminant, covenant, *L* luminant, *O* ordinant, *PR* predominant, *R* revenant, resonant, ruminant
PANT	anticipant, pant, Sacripant
PLANT	deplant, *eggplant*, implant, *pieplant*, plant, replant, supplant, transplant
RANT	*A* adulterant, agglomerant, alterant, ameliorant, *D* decolorant, deodorant, discolorant, *E* expectorant, exuberant, *F* figurant, figurante, fulturant, *I* ignorant, intolerant, itinerant, *K* cormorant, corroborant, cauterant, colorant, courant, courante, *M* mensurant, *O* obscurant, odorant, *PR* preponderant, protuberant, *R* rant, refrigerant, reiterant, reverberant, *T* tolerant, *V* vociferant
SANT	enceinte, impuissant, *complaisant, conversant*, puissant, recusant
SHANT	shan't
SKANT	askant, scant
SLANT	aslant, slant
TANT	*A* adjutant, annuitant, *D* debutante, dilettante, *disputant, E* executant, exorbitant, extant, *H*

	habitant, hebetant, hesitant, *I important*, inhabitant, incogitant, *inconstant*, irritant, *K* combatant, comitant, concomitant, *KR* crepitant, *M* militant, ministrant, *O* oscitant, *PR* precipitant, Protestant, *R* regurgitant, registrant, resuscitant, *V* vegetant, visitant
TRANT	administrant, penetrant, recalcitrant, registrant
VANT	gallivant, innovant, irrelevant, levant, Levant, pickedevant, poursuivant, relevant
ZANT	bezant, incognizant, cognizant, *complaisant*, corposant

ÄNT

ÄNT	aunt, grand-aunt, great-aunt (etc.)
DÄNT	confidant, confidante
KÄNT	can't, Kant
KWÄNT	quant
LÄNT	gallant, nonchalant
NÄNT	revenant
RÄNT	courant, courante, rente
SHÄNT	shan't
TÄNT	debutant, debutante, detente, dilettant, dilettante
VÄNT	cidevant
WÄNT	want
YÄNT	ondoyant

(See **ONT**)

ÄNTS

SPRÄNTS	spraints

(See **ÄNT**, add *-s* where appropriate.)

ANTS

ANTS	ants
HANTS	Hants
PANTS	fancy-pants, pants

(See **ANS**; also **ANT**, add *-s* where appropriate.)

ÄNTS

KRÄNTS	Liederkrantz

(See **ÄNT**, add *-s* where appropriate.)

ANZ

BANZ	banns
KANZ	Louis Quinze

(See **AN**, add *-s* where appropriate.)

ĀP

ĀP	ape, naked ape
CHĀP	chape
DRĀP	bedrape, drape, undrape
GĀP	agape, gape
GRĀP	graip, grape
JĀP	jape
KĀP	escape, fire escape, cape, uncape
KRĀP	crape, crepe
NĀP	nape
PĀP	pape
RĀP	*broomrape*, rape
SHĀP	misshape, reshape, shape, *shipshape*, transshape, unshape
SKĀP	escape, *inscape, cloudscape, landscape, seascape*, scape, *skyscape, townscape*, waterscape
SKRĀP	rescrape, scrape
SWĀP	swape
TĀP	*nametape*, audiotape, red-tape, tape, untape, videotape
TRĀP	trape

AP

BAP	bap
CHAP	chap, old chap, young chap
DAP	dap
DRAP	drap
FLAP	*earflap*, flap, *flipflap*
FRAP	frap, unfrap
GAP	agape, gap, gape, stopgap
HAP	hap, mayhap, mishap
JAP	Jap
KAP	*ASCAP, BL blackcap, bluecap, F foolscap*, forage cap, *H* handicap, hubcap, *HW whitecap, I icecap, K* cap, *M madcap, mobcap, N kneecap, nightcap, P* percussion cap, *R redcap*, recap, *SK skullcap, SN snowcap, T toecap, U* uncap, *W* wishing cap
KLAP	afterclap, beclap, clap, thunderclap

KRAP	crap
LAP	*burlap, dewlap, halflap, catlap,* lap, Lapp, *overlap, semordnilap, unlap*
MAP	photomap, map
NAP	genapp, genappe, *horsenap, catnap, kidnap,* knap, nap, nappe, *surnap*
PAP	pap, genipap
RAP	enwrap, *giftwrap,* rap, wrap, unwrap
SAP	homo sap, sap, *winesap*
SKRAP	scrap
SLAP	*backslap,* reslap, slap
SNAP	resnap, snap, unsnap
STRAP	bestrap, *blackstrap, checkstrap, jockstrap,* restrap, shoulder strap, strap, unstrap, *watchstrap*
TAP	heel tap, retap, tap, water tap
TRAP	*D deathtrap, E entrap, F firetrap, FL fleatrap, flytrap, KL claptrap, M mantrap, mousetrap, R rat trap, rattletrap, S sun trap, TR trap, untrap*
YAP	lagniappe, yap, yapp
ZAP	zap

ĀP

(See **OP**)

ĀPS

NĀPS	jackanapes
TRĀPS	traipse

(See **AP**, add *-s* where appropriate.)

APS

APS	apse
CHAPS	chaps, pettichaps
HAPS	haps, perhaps
KRAPS	craps
LAPS	elapse, illapse, interlapse, collapse, lapse, *prolapse,* relapse
NAPS	*synapse*
SHNAPS	schnapps

(See **AP**, *add -s* where appropriate.)

ĀPT

(See **ĀP**, *add -d* where appropriate.)

APT

APT	apt, inapt, periapt
CHAPT	chapped, unchapped
DAPT	adapt, maladapt
KAPT	capped, *moss-capped, snow-capped*
RAPT	enrapt, rapt, wrapped
STRAPT	bestrapped, restrapped, strapped, unstrapped

(See **AP**, add *-ped* where appropriate.)

ÂR

ÂR	*A* air, Aire, Ayr, Eir, e'er, ere, eyre, heir, *H* howe'er, *HW* whate'er, whatsoe'er, whene'er, whensoe'er, where'er, wheresoe'er, *J* jardiniere, *K* co-heir, *M* mid-air, *P* portiere, *PL* plein-air, *PR* premiere, *V* vivandiere
BÂR	*B* bare, bear, *bugbear, F* forbear, *forebear, K* Camembert, *cudbear, M* misbear, *O* overbear, *THR* threadbare, *U* underbear, upbear
BLÂR	blare
CHÂR	*armchair,* chair, chare, *highchair, wheelchair, pushchair,* rocking chair, sedan chair,
DÂR	bedare, dare, Kildare, outdare
FÂR	*A* affair, *CH* chargé d'affaires, *F* fanfare, fair, fare, *fieldfare, funfare, K* county fair, *L* laissez-faire, *M* Mayfair, misfare, *S* savoir faire, *ST* state fair, *TH* thoroughfare, *U* unfair, *V* Vanity Fair, *W* warfare, welfare
FLÂR	flair, flare
FRÂR	*confrère*
GÂR	gair, gare
GLÂR	beglare, glair, glare
HÂR	hair, hare, *horsehair,* camelhair, maidenhair, *mohair,* unhair
HWÂR	*elsewhere,* anywhere, everywhere, where, *nowhere, somewhere,* otherwhere
KÂR	aftercare, devil-may-care, care, Medicare, natal care, prenatal care
KLÂR	declare, eclair, undeclare
KWÂR	quair
LÂR	capillaire, lair
MÂR	mal de mer, mare, mayor, *nightmare*
NÂR	*B* billionaire, *D* debonair, doctrinaire, *K* commissionaire, concessionaire, *KW* questionnaire, *M* millionaire, *N* ne'er, *TR* trillionaire, *V* vin ordinaire
NYÂR	jardiniere
PÂR	disrepair, impair, compare, au pair, pair, pare, pear, prickly pear, repair
PRÂR	prayer
RÂR	rare
SÂR	*corsair*
SHÂR	share, joint share, crop share, *plowshare,* porte-cochere, torchère
SKÂR	rescare, scare, unscare
SKWÂR	*foursquare, headsquare,* resquare, square, T square, unsquare
SNÂR	ensnare, resnare, snare, unsnare
SPÂR	despair, spare
STÂR	*backstair,* front stair, cocklestair, outstare, spiral stair, stare, upstare
SWÂR	forswear, outswear, sware, swear, unswear
TÂR	parterre, pied-à-terre, proletaire, solitaire, tare, tear, up-tear, Voltaire
THÂR	their, there
VÂR	revers, vair, vare
WÂR	*A* aware, *B* beware, *D* Delaware, *E* earthenware, *F* firmware, footwear, *GL* glassware, *H* hardware, hornware, *L* liveware, *M* menswear, *N* neckwear, nightwear, *O* outwear, overwear, *R* rainwear, redware, *S* silverware, software, *SP* sportswear, *ST* stemware, stoneware, *T* tableware, *tinware, TR* treenware, *U* unaware, underwear, *W* ware, wear
YÂR	Gruyère, tuyère, mamelière, meunière, yair, yare
ZÂR	misère
ZHÂR	étagère, fourragère

ÄR

ÄR	antiar, aar, are, foliar, gangliar, jaguar, caviar

BÄR	*A* axlebar, *B* bar, *busbar*,		vermicular, vernacular,
	D debar, disbar, *durbar*,		versicular, *Y* uvular
	DR drawbar, *E* embar, *H*	**LWÄR**	couloir, Loire
	handlebar, *I* isallobar,	**MÄR**	jacamar, maar, mar,
	isobar, *KR crossbar*,		Palomar, cymar, tintamarre
	crowbar, *M* Malabar,	**MWÄR**	aide memoire, armoire,
	millibar, *R rollbar*, *S*		memoir, moire
	saddlebar, centibar,	**NÄR**	dinar, canard, *columnar*,
	cinnabar, *SH* shacklebar, *T*		gnar, knar, narr, laminar,
	towbar, *U* unbar, upbar, *W*		seminar, *sonar, thenar*
	Wunderbar, *Z* Zanzibar	**NWÄR**	bête noire, Renoir, rouge
BWÄR	pourboire		et noire
CHÄR	char	**PÄR**	par, parr
DÄR	dar, deodar, havildar,	**SÄR**	commissar, *pulsar*
	haznadar, hospodar,	**SKÄR**	rescar, scar, unscar
	jemadar, calendar, objet	**SPÄR**	*feldspar*, spar, unspar
	d'art, *radar, sirdar*,	**STÄR**	daystar, earthstar, evening
	subahdar, tahsildar,		star, falling star, instar,
	zamindar		*lonestar, lodestar,* morning
DWÄR	boudoir		star, north star, pilot star,
FÄR	afar, far, insofar, so far,		*polestar,* star, sunstar,
	shophar		*Telstar*
GÄR	budgerigar, gar, segar,	**TÄR**	avatar, guitar, kantar,
	cigar, *Trafalgar*, vinegar		catarrh, katar, scimitar,
JÄR	ajar, jar, *nightjar*		sitar, tahr, tar
KÄR	*B* boxcar, *CH* chukar, *J*	**STRÄR**	registrar
	jaunting car, gyrocar, *K*	**TSÄR**	tsar
	car, *L* Lascar, *M* motorcar,	**TWÄR**	abattoir, escritoire,
	O autocar, *R* railway car, *S*		repertoire
	sidecar, sircar, SH shikar,	**VÄR**	bolivar, Bolivar,
	STR streetcar, *T* turbocar,		*boulevard,* cultivar,
	TR trocar, trolley car		*louvar,* Navarre, samovar
KWÄR	quar	**VWÄR**	devoir, au revoir, reservoir
LÄR	*A* angular, animalcular,	**WÄR**	peignoir
	acetabular, annular,	**YÄR**	boyar, sillar, Wanderjahr
	axillar, *B* binocular, *D*	**ZÄR**	bazaar, bizarre, hussar,
	dissimilar, *E* escolar, *F*		czar
	fabular, funicular, *FL*		
	flagellar, *GL* glandular,	**ÄRB**	
	globular, *I* incunabular,		
	insular, irregular, *J*	**ÄRB**	*coarb*
	jocular, jugular, *K*	**BÄRB**	barb, rhubarb
	capsular, consular,	**DÄRB**	darb
	cunabular, *KR* crepuscular,	**GÄRB**	garb
	KW quadrangular, *L*	**TÄRB**	pantarbe
	lamellar, M modular,	**YÄRB**	yarb
	molecular, monocular, *N*		
	nebular, *O* ocular, ovular,		
	P particular, perpendicular,	**ÄRBD**	
	popular, *R* regular, *S*		
	secular, similar, simular,	(See **ÄRB**, add *-ed* where appropriate.)	
	singular, circular,		
	somnambular, *SF*	**ÄRCH**	
	spherular, *SK* scapular,		
	schedular, *SP* spatular,	**ÄRCH**	arch, inarch, overarch
	spectacular, *ST* stellular, *T*	**LÄRCH**	larch
	tabernacular, tabular,	**MÄRCH**	dead march, *frogmarch,*
	tesselar, tintinnabular,		countermarch, march,
	titular, tonsilar, torcular,		outmarch, overmarch,
	tubular, tutelar, *TR*		remarch, route march
	triangular, *V* valvular,	**PÄRCH**	parch
	vascular, vehicular,	**STÄRCH**	*cornstarch,* starch

ÂRD	
ÂRD	aired, heired, co-heired, un-heired
BÂRD	bared, rebared, unbared
CHÂRD	chaired, rechaired, unchaired
DÂRD	dared, redared, undared
FÂRD	fared
FLÂRD	flared, reflared
HÂRD	*BL* black-haired, *blond-haired, F fair-haired, G* golden-haired, *GR gray-haired, K* curly-haired, *R* raven-haired, *red-haired, S* silver-haired, *ST straight-haired, T* Titian-haired
KÂRD	cared, uncared
KLÂRD	declared, redeclared, undeclared
LÂRD	laird, laired
PÂRD	impaired, paired, prepared, repaired, unimpaired, unpaired, unprepared, unrepaired
SHÂRD	reshared, shared, unshared
SNÂRD	ensnared, snared
SPÂRD	despaired, spared, unspared
STÂRD	stared, outstared

(See **ÂR,** add *-d* or *-ed* where appropriate.)

ÄRD	
ÄRD	milliard
BÄRD	bard, barred, bombard, debarred, close-barred
CHÄRD	chard, charred
FÄRD	fard
GÄRD	*A* afterguard, *Asgard,* avant-garde, *B* bodyguard, *BL blackguard, D* disregard, *E* enguard, *G* guard, *K* Kierkegaard, *L laggard, lifeguard, M mudguard, N* noseguard, *R* regard, *rearguard, S safeguard, V* vanguard
HÄRD	*blowhard, die-hard,* hard
JÄRD	jarred
KÄRD	birthday card, discard, file card, Jacquard, calling card, card, *placard,* postal card, *postcard, racecard,* report card, *scorecard, timecard,* wedding card
LÄRD	Abelard, foulard, interlard, lard, poulard
MÄRD	marred, remarred, unmarred

NÄRD canard, gnarred, communard, knarred, nard, Reynard, *spikenard*
PÄRD camelopard, pard
SÄRD *brassard, mansard,* sard
SHÄRD shard
SKÄRD rescarred, scarred, unscarred
STÄRD bestarred, evil-starred, ill-starred, starred
TÄRD dynamitard, petard, retard, retarred, tarred, untarred
VÄRD boulevard
YÄRD *B* backyard, barnyard, boneyard, *BR* brickyard, *CH* chickenyard, churchyard, *D* dockyard, dooryard, *F* foreyard, *FR* front yard, *GR* graveyard, *H* hopyard, *J* junkyard, *K* kaleyard, courtyard, *L* lumberyard, *M* milliard, Montagnard, *P* poultry yard, *S* Savoyard, *SH* shipyard, *ST* steelyard, stockyard, *T* tiltyard, timberyard, *V* vineyard, *Y* yard

(See **ÄR,** add -*ed* or -*red* where appropriate.)

ÄRF

ÄRF *headscarf,* arf, 'arf-and-'arf
BÄRF barf
LÄRF larf
SKÄRF scarf
ZÄRF zarf

ÄRJ

BÄRJ barge
CHÄRJ charge, discharge, encharge, countercharge, overcharge, recharge, supercharge, *surcharge,* uncharge, undercharge
LÄRJ enlarge, large, reënlarge
MÄRJ lithomarge, marge, sea marge
SÄRJ sarge
SPÄRJ sparge
TÄRJ targe
THÄRJ litharge

ÄRJD

LÄRJD unenlarged

(See **ÄRJ,** add -*d* where appropriate.)

ÄRK

ÄRK arc, ark, Asiarch, *diarch,* ecclesiarch, heresiarch, gymnasiarch, matriarch, Noah's ark, patriarch, symposiarch
BÄRK bark, barque, debark, disembark, embark, ironbark, paperbark, *shagbark, shellbark, snakebark, soapbark, tanbark*
DÄRK bedark, dark, endark
GÄRK oligarch
HÄRK hark
KÄRK cark
KLÄRK clerk
KWÄRK quark
LÄRK lark, meadowlark, *mudlark, sealark, skylark, titlark, woodlark*
MÄRK *B* birthmark, Bismarck, bookmark, *D* Denmark, *E* earmark, easy mark, *F* fingermark, Finnmark, footmark, *FL* floodmark, *H* hallmark, *K* countermark, *L* landmark, *M* marc, mark, marque, Monomark, *O* ostmark, *P* pockmark, postmark, *PL* platemark, *PR* pressmark, *R* remark, remarque, *Reichsmark, S* sitzmark, *T* telemark, tidemark, touchmark, *TH* thumbmark, *TR* trademark, *W* watermark
NÄRK *anarch, ethnarch, irenarch, monarch,* knark, narc, nark
PÄRK amusement park, ball park, dispark, *eparch, hipparch,* impark, park, repark, *toparch,* unpark
RÄRK hierarch, *Petrarch, tetrarch, xerarch*
SÄRK *exarch,* sark
SHÄRK blacktip shark, blue shark, bullhead shark, dog shark, dusky shark, hammerhead shark, white shark, *landshark,* leopard shark, porbeagle shark, shark, shovelhead shark
SPÄRK spark
STÄRK stark
VÄRK *aardvark*
YÄRK yark
ZÄRK *Ozark*

ÄRKS

ÄRKS Marx

(See **ÄRK,** add -*s* where appropriate.)

ÄRKT

(See **ÄRK,** add -*ed* where appropriate.)

ÄRL

FÄRL farl
HÄRL harl
JÄRL jarl
KÄRL *housecarl,* carl
MÄRL Albemarle, marl
NÄRL gnarl
PÄRL imparl
SNÄRL snarl, unsnarl

ÄRM

ÄRM *A* arm, axle arm, *D* disarm, *F firearm, forearm, I* inarm, *KR crossarm, O* overarm, *R* rearm, *S sidearm, U* unarm, underarm, *Y yardarm*
BÄRM barm
CHÄRM becharm, charm, decharm, disencharm, counter-charm, love charm, uncharm
DÄRM gendarme
FÄRM aquafarm, farm, county farm, poor farm
HÄRM harm, unharm
LÄRM alarm, false alarm
MÄRM marm, *schoolmarm*
SMÄRM smarm
THÄRM tharm
ZÄRM gisarme

ÂRN

BÂRN bairn
DÂRN moderne
KÂRN cairn, *Pitcairn*

ÄRN

BÄRN barn, imbarn
DÄRN darn, goldarn, goshdarn
KÄRN incarn, lucarne
LÄRN l'arn

MÄRN	Marne
SÄRN	consarn
TÄRN	tarn
YÄRN	yarn

ÄRND

(See **ÄRN**, add *-ed* where appropriate.)

ÄRP

HÄRP	harp, Irish harp, Jew's harp, claviharp
KÄRP	archicarp, endocarp, epicarp, escarp, carp, mesocarp, monocarp, pericarp, *syncarp,* cystocarp
SHÄRP	*cardsharp,* sharp
SKÄRP	escarp, counterscarp, scarp
TÄRP	tarp
ZÄRP	zarp

ÄRS

ÄRS	arse
FÄRS	farce
GÄRS	garce
KÄRS	carse
PÄRS	parse
SPÄRS	sparse

ÄRSH

HÄRSH	harsh
MÄRSH	démarche, marsh

ÄRT

ÄRT	art, modern art, op art, pop art, state-of-the-art, video art (etc.)
BÄRT	Bart
CHÄRT	chart, flip chart, rechart, unchart
DÄRT	dart, indart
FÄRT	fart, sparrowfart
HÄRT	*Bernhardt, faintheart, flintheart, greenheart,* hart, heart, lionheart, *stoutheart, sweetheart,* unheart
KÄRT	à la carte, cart, quarte, Descartes, *dogcart, dumpcart, gocart,* uncart, watercart
KLÄRT	clart
MÄRT	jumart, mart
PÄRT	apart, depart, dispart, *forepart,* impart, counterpart, *mouthpart,* part, *rampart,* repart
SÄRT	assart, Mozart, sart
SMÄRT	outsmart, smart
STÄRT	astart, head start, *kick start,* restart, *redstart,* upstart
TÄRT	apple tart, sugar tart, tart

ÄRTH

GÄRTH	*fishgarth,* garth, *Hogarth*
HÄRTH	hearth
SWÄRTH	swarth

ÄRTS

ÄRTS	arts
SMÄRTS	smarts, street-smarts

(See **ÄRT**, add -s where appropriate.)

ÄRV

KÄRV	carve
LÄRV	larve
STÄRV	starve
VÄRV	varve

ÂRZ

STÂRS	*backstairs, downstairs,* front stairs, stairs, *upstairs*
WÂRS	unawares, unbewares, unwares

(See **ÂR**, add -s where appropriate.)

ÄRZ

MÄRZ	Mars

(See **ÄR**, add *-s* where appropriate.)

ĀS

ĀS	*ambsace,* ace, casease, nuclease, protease, ribonuclease
BĀS	abase, base, bass, debase, free base, *wheelbase,* contrabass, octobass, *subbase, surbase*
BRĀS	brace, embrace, *mainbrace,* unbrace, underbrace, *vambrace*
CHĀS	chase, enchase, steeplechase
DĀS	dace, dais, oxidase, peptidase, *vendace*
FĀS	*A* aface, angel face, *B* baby face, *boldface,* boniface, *BL* blackface, *D* deface, *E* efface, *F* face, *FR* frogface, *HW* wheyface, *I* interface, *K* catface, *O* outface, *P* paleface, pigface, *PL* platterface, *R* reface, *typeface*
GRĀS	begrace, disgrace, grace, *scapegrace*
KĀS	*B* basket case, *bookcase, BR* briefcase, *E* endcase, encase, *K* cardcase, case, *KR* crankcase, *N* notecase, nut-case, *S* seedcase, *SH* showcase, *SL* slipcase, *SM* smearcase, *ST* staircase, *T* test case, *typecase, U* uncase, *W* watchcase, *Y* ukase
KLĀS	orthoclase, periclase
KRĀS	*sucrase*
LĀS	bootlace, enlace, interlace, catalase, Queen Anne's lace, lace, *Lovelace,* populace, relace, cellulase, *shoelace,* unlace
MĀS	grimace, mace, Mace
NĀS	*tenace*
PĀS	apace, *footpace,* carapace, quarterpace, *lipace,* outpace, pace
PLĀS	*birthplace,* displace, *fireplace,* hiding place, commonplace, marketplace, misplace, place, plaice, replace, resting place, *showplace,* trysting place
RĀS	*B* boat race, *CH* channel race, chariot race, *D* dog race, *DR* drag race, *E* erase, *F* foot race, *H* headrace, horse race, *I* in media res, *L* land race, *M* mile race, millrace, marathon race, *O* auto race, *R* race, res, rat race, *S* sack race, *T* tail race, *TH* three-legged race (etc.)
SĀS	*Alsace*
SPĀS	aerospace, *airspace, backspace,* breathing space, inner space, hyperspace, interspace, outer space, space
TĀS	anatase, phosphatase,

invertase, *lactase, maltase,*
pectase

THRĀS Samothrace, Thrace
TRĀS retrace, trace
VĀS transvase, vase

AS

AS alias, ass, Boreas, habeas,
jackass, paterfamilias,
pancreas, Pythias
BAS anabas, bass, contrabass,
octobass, rubasse
BRAS brass, brasse
FAS volte-face
FRAS frass, sassafras
GAS bagasse, degas, fougasse, gas,
megass, noble gas, *syngas*
GLAS *FL* flint glass, *G*
gallowglass, *GL* glass, *I*
isinglass, *eyeglass, L*
looking glass, *M*
magnifying glass, minute
glass, *O* object glass,
hourglass, SP spyglass, ST
stained glass, *W*
waterglass, weatherglass
GRAS aftergrass, *eelgrass,* grass,
coup de grace, *crabgrass,*
peppergrass, sparrowgrass
KAS *fracas*
KLAS declass, *first-class,* class,
middle class, outclass,
reclass, second-class,
third-class, underclass,
upperclass, working class
KRAS crass, hippocras
LAS alas, lass
MAS *A admass,* Allhallowmas,
amass, *B* biomass, *D*
damasse, *E* en masse, *GR*
groundmass, *H*
Hallowmas, *K camass,*
Candlemas, *KR Christmas,*
L land mass, *M*
Martinmas, mass, Mass,
Michaelmas, *R* remass
NAS vinasse
PAS impasse, Khyber Pass,
overpass, pass, repass,
surpass, *trespass,*
underpass, Eurailpass
RAS *arras,* harass, cuirass,
morass, wrasse, terrasse
SAS Alsace, sass
STRAS strass
TAS demitasse, tarantass, tass,
Tass, tasse
VAS kavass, crevasse, vas
YAS paillasse
ZAS rosace

ÄS

GRÄS coup de grace
KLÄS declass, *first-class,* class,
middle class, outclass,
reclass, second-class,
third-class, underclass,
upperclass, working class
KVÄS kvass
LÄS alas
PÄS Khyber Pass, overpass,
pass, repass, underpass,
Eurailpass
TÄS demitasse

ASH

ASH ash, mountain ash,
weeping ash
BASH abash, bash, *earbash,*
calabash, squabash,
Wabash
BLASH blash
BRASH brash
DASH balderdash, bedash,
interdash, pebble-dash,
rondache, *slapdash,*
spatterdash, splatterdash
FASH fash
FLASH photoflash, flash,
Syncroflash
GASH gash
HASH hache, rehash
KASH encache, encash, cache,
cash
KLASH clash
KRASH crash
LASH *backlash, frontlash,*
goulash, whiplash,
eyelash, calash, lash,
throatlash, unlash
MASH *quamash,* mash,
mishmash, shamash
NASH gnash, panache
PASH apache, Apache, calipash,
pash
PLASH plash
RASH rash
SASH sash
SLASH slash
SMASH smash
SNASH snash
SPLASH splash
STASH stash
TASH mustache, patache,
pistache, soutache,
sabretache, succotash, tash
THRASH thrash
TRASH trash
VASH *chichevache*

ASK

ASK ask
BASK bask, Basque
FLASK flask, hip flask, powder
flask
HASK hask
KASK cask, casque, watercask
MASK antimask, antimasque,
antic-mask, antic-masque,
bemask, mask, masque,
remask, unmask
TASK overtask, task

ÄSK

ÄSK ask
BÄSK bask
FLÄSK flask, hip flask, powder
flask
KÄSK cask, watercask
MÄSK antimask, antimasque,
antic-mask, antic-masque,
bemask, mask, masque,
remask, unmask
TÄSK overtask, task

ASKT

ASKT asked, unasked

(See **ASK,** add *-ed* where appropriate.)

ÄSKT

ÄSKT asked, unasked

(See **ÄSK,** add *-ed* where appropriate.)

ASP

ASP asp
GASP agasp, gasp
GRASP engrasp, grasp
HASP hasp, rehasp, unhasp
KLASP enclasp, *handclasp,* clasp,
reclasp, unclasp
RASP rasp

ASPT

(See **ASP,** add *-ed* where appropriate.)

ĀST

ĀST aced
BĀST abased, based, baste,
debased, lambaste, self-
abased

BRĀST braced, embraced, unbraced, unembraced

CHĀST chased, chaste, unchased, unchaste

FĀST *A* angel-faced, apple-faced, *B* baby-faced, *baldfaced, barefaced, bold-faced, BR* brazen-faced, *D* defaced, dirty-faced, *dish-faced, doughfaced,* double-faced, *E* effaced, *F* faced, furrow-faced, *FR* freckle-faced, *H hard-faced,* hatchet-faced, *horse-faced, HW whey-faced, J* Janus-faced, *KL* clean-faced, *L lean-faced,* lily-faced, *M* mottle-faced, *P pale-faced,* paper-faced, *pie-faced,* pickle-faced, pimple-faced, pippin-faced, pudding-faced, *pug-faced, PL* platter-faced, *plump-faced, R* refaced, *SH shamefaced, SM smooth-faced, smug-faced, T* tallow-faced, *two-faced, TR* triple-faced, *U* undefaced, *unshamefaced, V* vinegar-faced, *W* weasel-faced, wizen-faced

GRĀST disgraced, graced, undisgraced, ungraced, well-graced

HĀST haste, *posthaste*

KĀST encased, cased, uncased

LĀST enlaced, interlaced, laced, relaced, straitlaced, unlaced

MĀST grimaced

PĀST impaste, leaden-paced, outpaced, paced, paste, *slow-paced, snail-paced, toothpaste,* thorough-paced

PLĀST displaced, misplaced, placed, replaced, unplaced

SNĀST snaste

SPĀST interspaced, spaced, respaced, unspaced

TĀST after-taste, distaste, *foretaste,* taste

TRĀST retraced, traced, untraced

WĀST pantywaist, waist, waste

AST

AST bucoliast, ecdysiast, ecclesiast, elegiast, encomiast, enthusiast, gymnasiast, orgiast, scholiast, symposiast, cineast, *tight-assed*

BAST bast, *bombast*

BLAST blast, erythroblast, counterblast, lymphoblast, mesoblast, neuroblast, osteoblast, *sandblast, stormblast*

DAST dast

FAST *Belfast, breakfast,* emberfast, fast, *handfast, headfast, holdfast,* colorfast, *makefast, sitfast, sunfast, steadfast,* unfast

FNAST fnast

FRAST metaphrast, paraphrast

GAST aghast, flabbergast, gassed, gast

HAST hast

KAST *BR* broadcast, *D* dicast, *die-cast, downcast, F forecast, H half-caste, high-caste, K* cablecast, cast, caste, *L low-caste, M* miscast, *molecast, N* newscast, *O* opencast, outcast, overcast, *PR* precast, *R* recast, *rough-cast, S* simulcast, *SP* sportscast, *T* telecast, *typecast, U* undercast, under-caste, upcast, *W wormcast*

KLAST iconoclast, idoloclast, classed, osteoclast, outclassed, reclassed, theoclast, unclassed

LAST agelast, *ballast,* last, *oblast,* outlast, *portlast*

MAST *A* amassed, *D* dismast, *durmast, F* foremast, *H* half-mast, *J* jiggermast, jury mast, *M mainmast,* massed, mast, mizzen mast, *R* remassed, remast, *T* topmast, *U* unmassed, unmast

NAST dynast, gymnast, nast

PAST passed, past, repassed, repast, surpassed, *trispast,* unsurpassed

PLAST leucoplast, chloroplast, metaplast, protoplast

RAST harassed, pederast

SAST sassed, resassed

SNAST snast

SPAST antispast, *trispast*

TAST *fantast, phantast, peltast*

TRAST contrast

VAST avast, devast, vast

(See **AS,** add *-ed* where appropriate.)

ÄST

(See **OST**)

ĀT

ĀT *A* ate, ait, eight, eyot, abbreviate, absinthiate, affiliate, accentuate, actuate, aculeate, alleviate, ammoniate, ampliate, annunciate, appreciate, appropriate, asphyxiate, associate, attenuate, aviate, *B* benzoate, bifoliate, *BR* brachiate, *D* debulliate, defoliate, delineate, denunciate, depreciate, deviate, differentiate, dimidiate, disaffiliate, disambiguate, disassociate, discalceate, dissociate, *E* effectuate, exfodiate, exfoliate, excalceate, excruciate, expropriate, enucleate, enunciate, eradiate, evacuate, evaluate, eventuate, excoriate, expatiate, expatriate, expiate, extenuate, exuviate, *F* fasciate, figure-eight, filiate, foliate, *FL* floriate, fluctuate, *FR* free-associate, fructuate, *GL* gladiate, glaciate, *GR* graduate, *H* habituate, humiliate, *I* ideate, immateriate, impropriate, inchoate, increate, individuate, inebriate, infatuate, infuriate, ingratiate, initiate, insatiate, insinuate, instantiate, irradiate, *K* chalybeate, calumniate, caseate, cochleate, conciliate, consociate, *KR* create, *KW* quadrifoliate, *L* labiate, laciniate, lixiviate, lineolate, licentiate, luxuriate, *M* maleate, marsupiate, mediate, menstruate, miscreate, *N* negotiate, nauseate, novitiate, nucleate, *O* obganiate, obviate, officiate, oleate, opiate, aureate, overate, *P* palliate, permeate, perpetuate, pileate, poet

laureate, pogoniate,
potentiate, punctuate, *PR*
professoriate, procreate,
propitiate, provinciate, *R*
radiate, recreate,
remediate, renegotiate,
repatriate, repudiate,
retaliate, *S* sagaciate,
satiate, seriate, sinuate,
circumstantiate, situate,
substantiate, superannuate,
SP spoliate, *T* tenuate,
tertiate, toluate, *TR*
transsubstantiate, *U*
uncreate, *V* vacuate,
valuate, variate, vicariate,
vitiate

BĀT *A* abate, approbate,
acerbate, *B* bait, bate,
bilobate, *D* debate, *E*
exacerbate, *HW* whitebait,
I incubate, *K* cohobate,
conglobate, *KR* crowbait,
L lowbait, *M* makebate,
masturbate, *PR* probate,
rebate, reprobate, *S*
celibate, *ST* stereobate,
stylobate

BRĀT elucubrate, invertebrate,
calibrate, lucubrate,
obtenebrate, palpebrate,
celebrate, cerebrate,
vertebrate

DĀT *A* accommodate, afterdate,
antedate, *BL* blind date, *D*
date, *decaudate, denudate*,
depredate, dilapidate,
double date, Dutch date, *E*
exheredate, elucidate, *FL*
fluoridate, *GR gradate, I*
ingravidate, inlapidate,
interdate, intimidate,
inundate, invalidate, *K*
candidate, consolidate,
cuspidate, *KL* chlamydate,
L lapidate, liquidate, *M*
misdate, *O* oxidate,
outdate, *P* postdate, *PR*
predate, *R* redate,
rhipidate, *S* sedate, *V*
validate, vanadate

DRĀT *dehydrate*
FĀT fate, fete, caliphate
FLĀT deflate, efflate, inflate,
conflate, sufflate

FRĀT affreight, freight
GĀT *A* ablegate, abnegate,
abrogate, aggregate,
arrogate, *B* billingsgate, *D*
delegate, derogate,
desegregate, disgregate,
divagate, *E* expurgate,

extravagate, erugate, *F*
fumigate, fustigate, *FL*
floodgate, G gait, gate, *H*
homologate, *I* instigate,
interrogate, investigate,
irrigate, irrugate, *K*
castigate, colligate,
congregate, conjugate,
corrugate, *L* levigate,
litigate, *M* mitigate, *N*
navigate, negate, *O*
objurgate, obligate,
obrogate, *PR* promulgate,
propagate, *R* relegate,
religate, runagate, *S*
seagate, segregate,
sejugate, circumnavigate,
subjugate, subrogate,
suffumigate, supererogate,
T tailgate, *V* variegate,
vitiligate, *vulgate, W*
Watergate

GRĀT denigrate, disintegrate,
emigrate, grate, great,
immigrate, *ingrate*,
integrate, *migrate*,
redintegrate, regrate,
transmigrate

HĀT hate, *self-hate*
KĀT *A* abdicate, ablocate,
adjudicate, advocate,
allocate, altercate,
applicate, apricate, *B*
bifurcate, *bisulcate, D*
dedicate, defecate,
decorticate, delicate,
demarcate, deprecate,
desecate, desiccate,
detoxicate, diagnosticate,
dislocate, divaricate,
domesticate, duplicate, *E*
educate, excommunicate,
expiscate, explicate,
exsiccate, extricate,
equivocate, elasticate,
embrocate, eradicate, *F*
fabricate, *falcate,*
fimbricate, formicate,
fornicate, *H* hypothecate, *I*
imbricate, implicate,
imprecate, improlificate,
indicate, infuscate,
inculcate, intoxicate,
invocate, irradicate, *K*
Californicate, canonicate,
collocate, communicate,
complicate, confiscate,
conspurcate, corticate,
coruscate, *KW*
quadruplicate,
quintuplicate, *L* locate,
loricate, lubricate, *M*

masticate, medicate,
mendicate, metricate,
multiplicate, muricate, *N*
nidificate, nostrificate, *O*
obfuscate, authenticate, *P*
pontificate, *PL placate, PR*
predicate, prefabricate,
prevaricate, prognosticate,
R radicate, rededicate,
reduplicate, relocate,
resiccate, reciprocate,
revindicate, rubricate,
rusticate, *S* syllabicate,
syndicate, silicate,
sophisticate, suffocate,
sulcate, supplicate,
suricate, *SK* scholasticate,
SP spifflicate, *T* tunicate,
TR translocate, U urticate,
V vacate, vellicate,
vesicate, vindicate

KRĀT deconsecrate, desecrate,
execrate, consecrate,
obsecrate, crate, krait,
recrate, uncrate

KWĀT antiquate, equate, *liquate,*
torquate

LĀT *A* absquatulate, adulate,
accumulate, alveolate,
ambulate, angulate,
annihilate, annulate,
apostolate, articulate,
assibilate, acidulate,
assimilate, *B* barbellate,
belate, bimaculate,
binoculate, *D* de-escalate,
defloculate, *decollate*,
delate, depilate,
depopulate, depucelate,
desolate, dilate,
disarticulate,
discombobulate,
dissimilate, dissimulate, *E*
ejaculate, exoculate,
expostulate, exsibilate,
extrapolate, exungulate,
elate, emasculate, emulate,
encapsulate, epilate,
escalate, ethylate, etiolate,
F faveolate, fellate,
phenolate, foliolate,
formulate, funambulate,
FL flagellate, flocculate,
GR granulate, *I* immolate,
infibulate, incastellate,
inoculate, insolate,
insulate, interpolate,
interrelate, intumulate,
invigilate, inviolate,
isolate, *J* gesticulate,
jubilate, jugulate, *K*
calculate, campanulate,

cannulate, cancellate,
cantillate, capitulate,
capsulate, carboxylate,
cardinalate, coagulate,
collate, confabulate,
congratulate, constellate,
consulate, copulate,
corniculate, correlate,
cucullate, cumulate,
cupulate, *KR* crenellate,
crenulate, *L* lamellate,
lanceolate, late, legislate,
lingulate, lunulate, *M*
machicolate, mammilate,
manipulate, matriculate,
mentulate, miscalculate,
mistranslate, modulate,
morcellate, methylate,
mutilate, *N* nasillate,
nodulate, nucleolate, *O*
obambulate, oblate,
obnubilate, obvallate,
oxalate, oppilate, ocellate,
oscillate, osculate, ovulate,
P peculate, pendulate,
peninsulate, perambulate,
percolate, poculate,
populate, postulate,
pullulate, pustulate, *R*
regulate, recapitulate,
relate, repullulate,
reticulate, *S* salicylate,
sibilate, simulate,
scintillate,
circumambulate,
somnambulate, circulate,
sublate, substaquilate,
suggilate, succulate, *SF*
sphacelate, spherulate, *SK*
scutellate, *SKR*
scrobiculate, *SP* speculate,
sporulate, *ST* stellulate,
stimulate, stipulate, *STR*
strangulate, stridulate, *T*
tabulate, tasselate, titillate,
tubulate, tumulate, *TR*
translate, triangulate, *U*
ululate, undulate, ungulate,
ustulate, *V* vacillate,
vassalate, ventilate,
vermiculate, vinculate,
violate, virgulate

MĀT	*A* acclamate, acclimate,
amalgamate, animate,
approximate, *B bunkmate,
CH checkmate, D*
decimate, desquamate,
despumate, desublimate,
dichromate, diplomate, *E*
estimate, *F* first mate, *G*
guesstimate, *GL* glutamate,
H helpmate, hindermate, *I*

inanimate, infumate,
intimate, *K casemate,*
collimate, *comate,*
consummate, conformate,
KL classmate, KR cremate,
L legitimate, *M* mate,
messmate, metrobomate,
mismate, *O* optimate,
automate, *P* palamate,
palmate, penultimate,
perhiemate, *PL playmate,*
PR proximate, *S* second
mate, cyclamate,
sublimate, *SH shipmate,*
SK schoolmate, ST
stalemate, T tentmate, TH
third mate, *TR*
trenchermate, *U*
underestimate

NĀT	*A* abominate, agglutinate,
acuminate, alienate,
alternate, aluminate,
amirrate, ammonate,
arsenate, assassinate,
assonate, *B* bicarbonate,
bipinnate, D deaminate,
deglutinate, decaffeinate,
decarbonate,
decontaminate, declinate,
delaminate, denominate,
deracinate, desalinate,
designate, destinate,
detonate, devirginate,
discriminate, disseminate,
dominate, donate, *E*
echinate, explanate,
exsanguinate, exterminate,
extortionate, eliminate,
emanate, emarginate,
enate, evaginate, *F*
fascinate, foreordinate,
fulminate, functionate, *FL*
fluorinate, *FR* fractionate,
GL glutinate, *H*
hallucinate, hibernate,
hydrogenate, hyphenate, *I*
illuminate, immarginate,
impassionate, impersonate,
impregnate, indoctrinate,
ingeminate, ingerminate,
incatenate, incriminate,
inquinnate, innate,
inornate, inseminate,
interlaminate, interminate,
intonate, invaginate, *J*
gelatinate, geminate,
germinate, juvenate, *K*
cachinnate, cacuminate,
carbonate, carinate,
catenate, coadunate,
comminate, conditionate,
conglutinate, concatenate,

consternate, contaminate,
coordinate, coronate,
culminate, *KL* chlorinate,
KR criminate, *KW*
quaternate, *L* laminate,
lancinate, Latinate, *M*
machinate, marinate,
marginate, missionate, *N*
neonate, nominate, *O*
obsignate, oxygenate,
alternate, ordinate,
originate, ornate, *P*
paginate, patinate,
patronate, pectinate,
pepsinate, peregrinate,
perendinate,
permanganate, personate,
pollinate, pulvinate, *PR*
predestinate, predesignate,
predominate, procrastinate,
R raffinate, ratiocinate,
rejuvenate, reclinate,
recriminate, repristinate,
resinate, resonate,
ruminate, *S* saginate,
septenate, septentrionate,
cybernate, cincinnate,
circinate, succinate,
sultanate, supinate, *ST*
stellionate, *T* terminate,
tubicinate, turbinate, *TR*
trutinate, *U* uncinate, *V*
vaccinate, vaticinate,
vertiginate, *Y* urinate

PĀT	*A* adipate, anticipate, *D*
dissipate, dunderpate, *E*
exculpate, extirpate,
emancipate, episcopate, *K*
constipate, *M* mancipate, *P*
participate, pate, *R* rattle-
pate, *S* syncopate

PLĀT	*A* armorplate, *BR*
breastplate, D dial plate, *E*
electroplate, *F* fashion
plate, *K* contemplate,
copperplate, *N* nickelplate,
PL plait, plate, *S*
silverplate, *U* unplait

PRĀT	constuprate, prate
RĀT	*A* adulterate, advesperate,
aerate, agglomerate,
acculturate, accelerate,
alliterate, ameliorate,
annumerate, acerate,
aspirate, asseverate, *B*
berate, biforate, *birth-rate,*
D death rate, deblaterate,
decolorate, decorate,
degenerate, deliberate,
decelerate, decerebrate,
desiderate, deteriorate,
directorate, *E* edulcorate,

exaggerate, exasperate,
exenterate, exhilirate,
exaugurate, exonerate,
expectorate, equilibrate,
equiponderate, elaborate,
electorate, enumerate,
evaporate, eviscerate, *F*
federate, figurate, *firstrate,*
fulgurate, *H* hederate, *I*
immensurate, imperforate,
indurate, incarcerate,
incorporate, inaugurate,
incinerate, intenerate,
intenurate, invigorate,
irate, iterate, itinerate, *J*
generate, *K* camphorate,
chelicerate, collaborate,
commemorate,
commensurate,
commiserate, confederate,
conglomerate,
concelebrate, considerate,
contriturate, cooperate,
corporate, corroborate, *cut-
rate, KW* quatuorvirate, *L*
lacerate, levirate, liberate,
literate, *M* macerate,
micturate, moderate, *N*
narrate, numerate, *O*
obdurate, obliterate,
obturate, augurate,
operate, oppignorate,
orate, overrate, *P*
pastorate, perforate,
perorate, pignorate,
picrate, purpurate, *PR*
preponderate, presbyterate,
proliferate, prorate,
protectorate, protuberate, *R*
rate, redecorate,
refrigerate, reiterate,
regenerate, rectorate,
recuperate, remunerate,
reverberate, *S* saccharate,
saturate, second-rate,
scelerate, separate,
coelenterate, cicurate,
sororate, sulphurate,
suppurate, susurrate, *ST*
stearate, *T* tellurate,
tolerate, *TH* third-rate, *TR*
transliterate, triturate,
triumvirate, *U* ulcerate,
underrate, *V* venerate,
verberate, vituperate,
viscerate, vociferate, *W*
water rate

SĀT extravasate, improvisate,
inspissate, compensate,
condensate, marquisate,
pulsate, sate, *sensate,*
tergiversate

SKĀT *cheapskate,* roller skate,
skate
SLĀT slate
SPĀT spate
STĀT *D downstate, E* estate, *I*
instate, interstate, *M*
misstate, *O* overstate, *R*
reinstate, restate, *S* solid-
state, *ST* state, steady-
state, *U* understate,
unstate, *upstate*
STRĀT *D* defenestrate,
demonstrate, *F* fenestrate,
FR frustrate, I illustrate, *K
capistrate, M* magistrate,
O orchestrate, *PR
prostrate, R* registrate,
*remonstrate, S sequestrate,
STR* straight, strait
TĀT *A* acetate, acutate, agitate,
amputate, annotate,
apostate, B bidentate, *D*
debilitate, *degustate,*
decapitate, decrepitate,
*decurtate, delectate,
dentate,* devastate,
digitate, dictate, dissertate,
disorientate, *E edentate,*
excogitate, exorbitate,
eructate, estate, *F*
facilitate, felicitate, *G*
gurgitate, *GR* gravitate, *H*
habilitate, hebetate,
hesitate, *I* imitate,
ingurgitate, incapacitate,
interdigitate, *intestate,*
inusitate, irritate, *J gestate,*
K capacitate, capitate,
cogitate, commentate,
connotate, *costate, KR*
crepitate, *KW* quantitate, *L*
levitate, limitate, *M*
meditate, militate, *N*
necessitate, nictitate,
notate, O occultate,
orientate, oscitate,
auscultate, ostentate, *P*
palpitate, permutate,
potentate, *PR* premeditate,
precipitate, *prostate, R*
regurgitate, rehabilitate,
resuscitate, revegetate,
rotate, *S* sagittate, sanitate,
segmentate, subacetate,
supputate, *T testate,* tête-à-
tête, *TR tridentate,*
tridigitate, *V* vegetate
THWĀT thwaite
TRĀT *A* administrate, arbitrate, *D*
distrait, *I* impenetrate,
impetrate, infiltrate, *K*
concentrate, *M* magistrate,

O orchestrate, *P* penetrate,
perpetrate, portrait, *R*
recalcitrate, *S* citrate, *TR*
trait
VĀT *A* aggravate, activate, *D*
deactivate, depravate,
deprivate, derivate, *E*
excavate, elevate,
enervate, estivate, *I*
inactivate, *incurvate,*
innervate, innovate,
insalivate, *K* captivate,
coacervate, cultivate, *M*
motivate, *N nervate, R*
radioactivate, reactivate,
recaptivate, reclivate,
recurvate, renovate, *S*
salivate, *T* titivate
WĀT *A* await, *B* bantamweight,
D deadweight, F
featherweight, *H*
heavyweight,
hundredweight, *K*
counterweight, *L*
lightweight, M
middleweight, *O*
overweight, *P*
paperweight, pennyweight,
U underweight, *W* wait,
weight, welterweight

AT

AT *A* at, *D* Duat, *H* hereat,
HW whereat, *K* caveat,
commissariat, *KR* croat, *L*
lariat, *PR* proletariat, *S*
salariat, secretariat, *TH*
thereat
BAT *A* acrobat, *B* bat, *bullbat,
BR* brickbat, *D* dingbat, *E
esbat, FL* flitterbat, *FR
fruitbat, H* hurlbat, *K*
combat, *N* numbat, *S
sabbat, W* wombat
BLAT blat
BRAT brat, *firebrat*
CHAT *backchat,* chat, *chitchat,*
fallowchat, *furze-chat,
grasschat, whinchat,
stonechat, woodchat,*
waterchat, yellow-breasted
chat
DAT dis and dat, *concordat*
DRAT drat
FAT butterfat, fat, marrowfat
FLAT aflat, flat
FRAT frat
GAT begat, forgat, gat, *nougat*
HAT hat, high-hat, *sunhat,
tophat,* unhat

KAT	*B bearcat, bobcat, F fatcat, H hellcat, hepcat, K* cat, kat, kitty-cat, cool cat, *KR* Krazy Kat, *M* Magnificat, *meerkat, mudcat, muscat, P polecat,* pussycat, *R requiescat, S* civet cat, *T* tabby cat, *tipcat, tomcat, W wildcat*
KRAT	*A* aristocrat, *B* bureaucrat, *D* democrat, Democrat, *H* hierocrat, *I* isocrat, *J* gerontocrat, gynaeocrat, *M* meritocrat, monocrat, nomocrat, *O* ochiocrat, autocrat, *P* pantisocrat, pornocrat, *PL* plutocrat, *R* rheocrat, *T* technocrat, timocrat, ptochocrat, *TH* theocrat
LAT	lat, cervelat
MAT	anastigmat, diplomat, doormat, format, Laundromat, mat, matte, automat
NAT	assignat, gnat
PAT	bepat, cowpat, pat, patte, pit-a-pat
PLAT	plait, plat, Platte
PRAT	dandiprat, prat
RAT	Ararat, rat, *muskrat,* Surat, water rat, ziggurat
SAT	Intelsat, *comsat,* sat
SHAT	shat
SKAT	scat, skat
SLAT	slat
SPAT	spat
SPLAT	splat
SPRAT	sprat, Jack Spratt
STAT	*A* aerostat, *B* barostat, *F* photostat, *H* heliostat, haemostat, hydrostat, *K* chemostat, *KL* clinostat, *P* pyrostat, *R* rheostat, *TH* thermostat
TAT	aegrotat, habitat, ratatat, ratatattat, tit-for-tat, tat
VAT	cravat, savate, vat
ZAT	xat

ÄT

BÄT	*esbat*
BWÄT	boite
DÄT	iddat
GÄT	ghat
HWÄT	what
KWÄT	*cumquat, kumquat*
RÄT	ziarat
SKWÄT	resquat, squat
SWÄT	swat

| WÄT | Duat, giga-watt, kilowatt, megawatt, watt |
| YÄT | yacht, land yacht, motor yacht, Rubaiyat, sailing yacht, sand yacht, steam yacht |

(See OT)

ĀTH (as in bathe)

BĀTH	bathe
LĀTH	lathe
RĀTH	raith, rathe
SKĀTH	scathe
SNĀTH	snathe
SPĀTH	spathe
SWĀTH	swathe, unswathe

ĀTH (as in faith)

FĀTH	faith, i'faith, misfaith, unfaith
GRĀTH	graith
RĀTH	waterwraith, wraith

ATH

BATH	bath, Bath
GATH	Gath
HATH	hath
LATH	lath
MATH	aftermath, philomath, math, opsimath, polymath
NATH	chaetognath, plectognath
PATH	allopath, bridle path, *footpath,* physiopath, homeopath, naturopath, neuropath, osteopath, path, psychopath, sociopath
RATH	rath, wrath
SNATH	snath

ĀTS

| GĀTS | othergates |
| YĀTS | Yeats |

(See ĀT, add -*s* where appropriate.)

ATS

| KATS | dogs-and-cats |

(See AT, add -*s* where appropriate.)

ÄTS

| SÄTS | ersatz |

(See ÄT, add -*s* where appropriate.)

ĀV

BRĀV	brave, outbrave
GĀV	forgave, gave, misgave
GLĀV	glaive, *portglaive*
GRĀV	*burgrave,* engrave, photograve, grave, ingrave, *landgrave, margrave,* ungrave, *waldgrave*
HĀV	behave, misbehave
KĀV	biconcave, encave, concave, cave
KLĀV	angusticlave, *exclave, enclave, conclave,* autoclave
KRĀV	crave
KWĀV	quave
LĀV	belave, lave, unlave
NĀV	antenave, knave, nave
PĀV	impave, pave, repave, unpave
PRĀV	deprave
RĀV	rave
SĀV	save
SHĀV	aftershave, shave, *spokeshave*
SLĀV	beslave, enslave, galley slave, slave, wage slave
STĀV	stave
SWĀV	suave
THĀV	they've
THRĀV	thrave
TRĀV	architrave, trave
WĀV	microwave, *shortwave,* tidal wave, waive, wave

AV

HAV	halve, have
KAV	calve
LAV	lav
SAV	salve
SLAV	slav, Yugoslav

ÄV

HÄV	halve
KÄV	calve
SÄV	salve
SLÄV	Slav, Yugoslav
SWÄV	suave

ĀVD

(See ĀV, add -d where appropriate.)

AVD

(See AV, add -d where appropriate.)

ÄVD

(See ÄV, add -d where appropriate.)

ĀZ

ĀZ	liaise
BĀZ	baize, bays
BLĀZ	ablaze, beacon blaze, blaze, emblaze, outblaze, upblaze
BRĀZ	braise, braze
DĀZ	adaze, bedaze, days, daze, hollandaise, nowadays, oxidase, thenadays
DRĀZ	drays
FĀZ	anaphase, *diphase*, faze, phase, metaphase, polyphase, *prophase*, telephase
FLĀZ	flays, reflays
FRĀZ	fraise, phrase, metaphrase, paraphrase, rephrase, unphrase
GĀZ	gaze, ingaze, outgaze, *stargaze*, upgaze
GLĀZ	glaze, overglaze, underglaze, unglaze, reglaze
GRĀZ	graze
HĀZ	haze
JĀZ	jays
KĀZ	ukase
KLĀZ	clays
KRĀZ	craze, *sucrase*
LĀZ	Bordelaise, lase, lays, laze, malaise, Marseillaise
MĀZ	amaze, bemaze, maize, maze, *mizmaze*, wondermaze
NĀZ	béarnaise, lyonnaise, mayonnaise, naze, polonaise
PRĀZ	*A* appraise, *B* bepraise, *D* dispraise, *O* overpraise, *KR* chrysoprase, *PR* praise, prase, *R* reappraise, repraise, *S* self-praise, *U* underpraise, unpraise
RĀZ	*E* erase, x-rays, *G* gamma rays, *M* morays, mores, *R* raise, rase, rays, raze, reraise, rerase, reraze, *U* unraise, unrase, unraze, upraise
SĀZ	écossaise
SHĀZ	chaise
STĀZ	stays
VĀZ	vase
WĀZ	*edgeways, endways, lengthways, leastways, longways, always, sideways,* wase, ways
YĀZ	Marseillaise

(See Ā, add -s where appropriate.)

AZ

AZ	as, Boaz, whereas
HAZ	has
JAZ	jazz
PAZ	*topaz*
RAZ	razz
TAZ	razzmatazz
TRAZ	Alcatraz
ZAZ	bizzazz, pizzazz

ÄZ

ÄZ	ahs, ohs and ahs
BLÄZ	the blahs
MÄZ	mamas, mas
PÄZ	La Paz
SWÄZ	vichyssoise
VÄZ	vase

(See Ä, add -s where appropriate.)

ĀZD

(See ĀZ, add -ed where appropriate.)

AZD

(See AZ, add -ed where appropriate.)

ĀZH

BĀZH	beige
GRĀZH	greige
NĀZH	manège
TĀZH	cortege

ÄZH

ÄZH	*peage*
DÄZH	bavardage, sondage

FÄZH	staffage
FLÄZH	camouflage, marouflage, persiflage
KÄZH	bocage, carucage
LÄZH	fuselage, collage, moulage
NÄZH	badinage, espionage, griffonage, counterespionage, ménage
PÄZH	découpage
PLÄZH	plage
RÄZH	barrage, effleurage, entourage, garage, mirage, raj, swataj
SÄZH	corsage, massage, saj, vernissage
TÄZH	décolletage, photomontage, frottage, cabotage, curettage, matelotage, montage, potage, reportage, sabotage, taj
TRÄZH	arbitrage
VÄZH	esclavage, gavage, lavage
YÄZH	maquillage, torpillage

AZM

AZM	demoniasm, enthusiasm, chiliasm, miasm, orgiasm, schediasm
GAZM	orgasm
KAZM	chasm, sarcasm
KLAZM	biblioclasm, iconoclasm, cataclasm
NAZM	pleonasm
PAZM	empasm
PLAZM	bioplasm, ectoplasm, endoplasm, cataplasm, metaplasm, neoplasm, plasm, protoplasm, cytoplasm
SPAZM	blepharospasm, graphospasm, chirospasm, spasm
TAZM	phantasm

Ē

Ē	*A* advowee, amicus curiae, arrowy, *B* B and B, B and D, B and E, billowy, *D* Danae, diploë, *DR* drawee, *E* E, *F* facetiae, furrowy, *I* interviewee, *K* cooee, *M* meadowy, mildewy, minutiae, *P* payee, pillowy, *R* reliquiae, *S* sinewy, *SH* shadowy, *W* willowy

BĒ *A* A.B., Araby, *B* baby, B, be, bee, B and B, *bawbee*, bumblebee, *BR* bribee, *FR* Frisbee, *H* honeybee, humblebee, *J* jacoby, jambee, *K* Koochahbee, *KW* queen bee, *N* Niobe, R and B, *S* sassaby, cenoby, *SK* scarabee, *W* wallaby

BLĒ blea

BRĒ barleybree, bree, Brie, debris, vertebrae

CHĒ chee, *chee-chee*, chincherinchee, debauchee, *litchi*, vouchee

DĒ *A* accidie, *B* B.V.D., B and D, bastardy, Burgundy, *CH* Chaldee, chickadee, *D* D, Dee, D.D., dipody, dispondee, *F* fiddlededee, fundee, *GR* grandee, *H* hymnody, *J* jeopardy, *K* Chaldee, *killdee*, comedy, custodee, custody, *L* L.L.D., Lombardy, *M* M.D., malady, melody, monody, *N* Normandy, *O* organdy, *P* parody, perfidy, Ph. D., Picardy, *PR* prosody, *R* R and D, rhapsody, remedy, *S* psalmody, C.O.D., subsidy, *SP* spondee, *ST* standee, *TH* theody, *THR* threnody, *TR* tragedy, tripody, *TW* Tweedledee, *V* vendee

DRĒ dree, heraldry

FĒ *A* ach-y-fi, anaglyphy, antistrophe, apostrophe, atrophy, *B* biographee, biography, *D* dactylography, dystrophy, *E* ethnography, *F* fee, phi, feoffee, philosophy, photography, *H* hagiography, *J* geography, *K* catastrophe, coryphee, *KR* cryptography, *M* misophy, *P* paleography, pornography, *R* ratafee, *STR* strophe, *T* tachygraphy, telegraphy, topography, *TH* theosophy, *Y* uranography, *Z* xyloglyphy, xylography

FLĒ flea, flee

FRĒ duty-free, enfree, fancy-free, free, heart-free, *carefree*, unfree

GĒ ghee, whangee, muggee, Portugee, *thuggee*

GLĒ glee

GRĒ agree, degree, disagree, filigree, *grigri*, mistigris, pedigree, *puggree*, third degree

HĒ bohea, he, hehee, takahe, tehee

HWĒ whee

JĒ *A* agee, *algae*, allergy, analogy, anthropology, apogee, apology, astrology, *B* bacteriology, bargee, biology, *burgee*, *D* dactylology, demology, demonology, dermatology, dilogy, dyslogy, doxology, *E* effigy, ecology, elegy, embryology, endocrinology, energy, epistemology, ethnology, ethology, *F* physiology, *Fuji*, *G* galiongee, *J* G, gee, genealogy, geology, *K* cardiology, *KR* criminology, chronology, cryptology, *L* laryngology, lethargy, liturgy, *M* *metallurgy*, misology, mortgagee, morphology, mythology, *N* nomology, neurology, *O* obligee, ophthalmology, *ogee*, onycophagy, otology, *P* pathology, panurgy, perigee, pili, pongee, *PL* pledgee, *PR* prodigy, proctology, *R* refugee, *S* salvagee, psychology, psychurgy, sylloge, synergy, syzygy, sociology, *SH shoji*, *SKW* squeegee, *STR* strategy, *T* telenergy, telurgy, typology, *TH* theurgy, *TR* trilogy, *U* eulogy, *Z* zymurgy, zoology

KĒ *A* anarchy, *Bacchae*, *CH* Cherokee, *G* garlicky, *H* hillocky, hummocky, *K* cay, key, chi, colicky, *L* latchkey, *M* maquis, Manichee, marquee,

master key, monarchy, naumochy, *P* panicky, *passkey*, *R raki*, *S* synarchy, synecdoche, *T* turnkey, *TH* thelymachy, *TR trochee*, *W* Waikiki, *Z* xenodochy

KRĒ decree, Cree, cushlamochree

KWĒ *BL* blandiloquy, *BR* breviloquy, *D* dentiloquy, dulciloquy, *FL* flexiloquy, *G* gastriloquy, *I* inauiloquy, *K* colloquy, *M* multiloquy, *O* obloquy, *P* pectoroloquy, *PL* pleniloquy, *S* sanctiloquy, soliloquy, somniloquy, *ST* stultiloquy, *SW* suaviloquy, *T* tolutiloquy, *TR* tristiloquy, *V* vaniloquy, veritriloquy, veriloquy

LĒ *A* advisedly, alee, Annabel Lee, anomaly, appellee, *B* bailee, belee, *D* diastole, *E* enrollee, *F* facsimile, *FL* fleur-de-lis, *G* Galilee, *H* homily, hyperbole, *I* infulae, Italy, *J* jubilee, *L* lapis lazuli, lee, li, libelee, *M* *mallee*, *P* parolee, *S* Cybele, Sicily, simile, systole, *SH* shirallee, *SK* skillagalee, *TH* Thermopylae, Thessaly

[See also adverbs composed of a noun plus -ly (fatherly, motherly, etc.) or of an adjective plus -ly (absorbingly, abusively, etc.)]

MĒ *A* agronomy, academy, alchemy, anatomy, anthroponomy, antimony, appendectomy, astronomy, atomy, *B* balsamy, bigamy, bonhomie, *BL* blasphemy, blossomy, *D* dichotomy, dittamy, deuterogamy, Deuteronomy, *E* economy, endogamy, enemy, epitome, *F* physiognomy, *FL* phlebotomy, *I* infamy, *J* jessamy, *K* confirmee, *L*

lobotomy, *M* me, mi,
monogamy, *N*
neurotomy, *O* occamy,
autonomy, *P* polygamy,
S syntomy, sodomy, *T*
taxonomy, teknonymy,
Ptolemy, *TH thermae,*
TR trichotomy, *Z*
zootomy

NĒ *A* abandonee, aborigine,
Agapemone, agony,
accompany, Albany,
alienee, aknee, anemone,
Antigone, assignee, *B*
balcony, bargainee,
barony, Bimini, bouquet
garni, botany, *BR*
bryony, *CH* Chinee,
designee, destiny,
dysphony, distrainee,
dominie, donee, *E*
ebony, examinee,
epiphany, *F* felony, *G*
Gethsemane, *GL*
gluttony, *GW* guarani,
Guarani, *H* harmony,
hegemony, *I ignominy,*
irony, *J* Japanee,
Germany, jinni, *K*
cacophony, calumny,
kidney, kitcheny, *koine,*
colony, company,
consignee, cottony,
cushiony, *KR* crimsony,
L laryngophony, litany,
M macaroni, mahogany,
Melpomene, misogyny,
monotony, mutiny,
muttony, *N* knee,
Mnemosyne, nominee,
nominy, *O* optionee, *P*
pantemone, *patrimony,*
Persephone, petitionee,
pawnee, Pawnee, *PR*
progeny, *R rani,*
Romany, *S* Saxony,
symphony, simony, *SH*
Shawnee, *SKR* scrutiny,
ST stephane, *T* telegony,
tiffany, Tiffany, townee,
tyranny, Tuscany, *TR*
distrainee, trainee, *U*
oniony, *V* villainy, *Y*
euphony, Euphrosyne

PĒ *A* agape, allotropy,
apocope, *CH chick-pea,*
D diacope, *E* entropy,
epopee, escapee, *F*
philanthropy,
physianthropy, *H*
hydrotherapy, *J jalopy, K*
calipee, calliope, canopy,

cap-a-pie, *cowpea, M*
microscopy,
misanthropy, *P* P, pea,
pee, penotherapy, *R*
R.S.V.P., rapee, rappee,
recipe, rupee, *S*
psychotherapy, *SH*
charpie, T tapis, *tepee,*
teratoscopy, topee,
toupee, *TH*
thalassotherapy, therapy,
W wampee, *Y* yippee, *Z*
zomotherapy

PRĒ
RĒ belesprit, esprit
A adultery, alimentary,
anniversary, archery,
armory, artery, artillery,
B bain-marie, bakery,
Barbary, battery,
beggary, bijouterie,
boree, bottomry,
boundary, *BR* bravery,
bribery, brodery,
broidery, *CH* chancery,
chickaree, chicory, *D*
debauchery, delivery,
demonry, devilry, diary,
directory, discovery,
dissatisfactory,
dissuasory, dungaree, *DR*
drapery, drudgery, *E*
effrontery, equerry,
extempore, extrasensory,
elementary, elusory,
embroidery, enginery, *F*
factory, faerie, feathery,
fernery, fiery,
phylactery, phyllery,
finery, foppery, forestry,
forgery, *FL* flattery,
flowery, flummery, *FR*
frippery, *G* gallery,
gaucherie, *GR*
grivoiserie, H heathery,
heraldry, hickory,
history, hostelry,
husbandry, *I* ikary,
illusory, imagery,
infirmary, inlagary,
injury, in re, ivory, *J*
jamboree, gendarmery,
jigamaree, jewelry,
jugglery, *K* calorie,
Calvary, caravansari,
cartulary, cavalry,
kedgeree, commandery,
complementary,
complimentary,
compulsory, conferee,
contradictory, *contrary,*
corroboree, cautery,
causerie, *KW* quackery,

quandary, quaternary, *L*
library, lingerie, livery,
lottery, luxury, lusory, *M*
machinery, masonry,
mastery, memory,
mercury, minauderie,
mystery, misery,
mockery, mummery, *N*
knavery, notary, nursery,
O augury, honoree, *P*
palmary, parliamentary,
penury, peppery,
perfumery, perfunctory,
perjury, popery,
potagerie, potpourri,
puggree, PR precursory,
priory, professory,
prudery, *R* rotary,
raillery, rapparee,
recovery, rectory,
referee, refractory,
receptory, revelry,
reverie, ribaldry, rivalry,
robbery, roguery,
rockery, rookery, rosary,
rosemary, rotisserie,
rudimentary, *S* salary,
sangaree, satisfactory,
savagery, savory,
sectary, scenery,
seigniory, senary,
sensory, century,
serrurerie, silvery, sirree,
sorcery, summary,
summery, *SH* chicanery,
chivalry, charivari,
shivaree, shivery,
sugary, *SK* sculduddery,
skullduggery, *SL* slavery,
slippery, *SN* snuggery,
ST stingaree, *T* Tartary,
Terpsichore,
testamentary,
tomfoolery, *TH* theory,
thievery, thundery, *TR*
transferee, tracery,
treachery, trickery,
trumpery, *U* unsavory,
upholstery, *V vagary,*
vaccary, valedictory,
vapory, *W* waggery,
watery, wintery,
witchery, *Y* yessirree,
yeomanry, usury, *Z*
zephyry, zythepsary,
zoopery

SĒ *A* abbacy, abstinency,
adequacy, addressee,
advocacy, agency,
accountancy, acceptancy,
accuracy, apostasy,
ardency, argosy,

aristocracy, asea, assie, ascendancy, assessee, assis, *B* Baltic Sea, bankruptcy, belligerency, big C, buoyancy, *BL* blatancy, *BR* brilliancy, *CH* China Sea, *D* Debussy, delegacy, delicacy, delinquency, democracy, dependency, diplomacy, discordancy, discourtesy, discrepancy, divorcee, *E* effeminacy, efficiency, expectancy, expediency, excellency, ecstasy, embassy, emcee, emergency, endorsee, episcopacy, *F* fallacy, fantasy, Pharisee, pharmacy, farci, federacy, femcee, fervency, foresee, *FL* flagrancy, flatulency, flippancy, fluency, *FR* fragrancy, frequency, fricassee, *G* galaxy, *H* heresy, hesitancy, hypocrisy, Holy See, *I* idiocy, idiosyncrasy, illiteracy, immaculacy, immediacy, impendency, impenitency, impermanency, impertinacy, importunacy, impudency, inadequacy, inadvertency, inaccuracy, indelicacy, independency, indecency, inebriacy, inefficacy, infancy, inclemency, incompetency, inconsistency, incipiency, insufficiency, insurgency, intestacy, intimacy, intricacy, irradiancy, irrelevancy, irritancy, *J* jactancy, jealousy, *K* cadency, candidacy, captaincy, cogency, colonelcy, competency, compliancy, confederacy, conservancy, consistency, consonancy, conspiracy, constancy, constituency, conveniency, co-respondency, corpulency, courtesy, curacy, *KL* clemency, cliency, *KR*

Christmasy, *L* lambency, latency, legacy, legitimacy, leniency, leprosy, lessee, licensee, literacy, luxuriancy, lunacy, lucency, *M* magistracy, malignancy, minstrelsy, mordancy, *N* nascency, negligency, nomancy, normalcy, *O* obduracy, obstinacy, Odyssey, omnipotency, oscitancy, autopsy, oversea, oversee, *P* papacy, *Parsee,* peccancy, pendency, penitency, permanency, petulancy, piquancy, piracy, poesy, poignancy, policy, potency, pungency, pernancy, *PL* pleurisy, pliancy, *PR* pregnancy, prelacy, preponderancy, précis, primacy, privacy, promisee, prophecy, proficiency, profligacy, proliferacy, prominency, promisee, *R* regency, regeneracy, recadency, recalcitrancy, recumbency, releasee, relevancy, renascency, renitency, repellency, resplendency, romancy, *S* Sadducee, saliency, sans souci, C, sea, see, seducee, secrecy, celibacy, sycophancy, sycee, *sightsee,* solvency, sonancy, subsistency, sufficiency, succulency, supremacy, surfacy, sycee, surgeoncy, *ST* stagnancy, *T* tangency, tenancy, tendency, Tennessee, *TH* theocracy, *TR* truancy, truculency, *U* undersea, unforesee, urgency, *V* vagrancy, vacancy, valency, valiancy, verdancy, *Y* euphrasy

SHĒ

banshee, buckshee, debauchee, flourishy, garnishee, kamichi, rubbishy, she, shea, shee, ski, *chichi*

SHRĒ
sri

SKĒ
hydroski, ski

SKRĒ
scree

SMĒ
smee

SNĒ snee, snickersnee

SPRĒ esprit, joie d'esprit, jeu d'esprit, spree

STĒ mestee, mustee

TĒ *A* ability, absentee, absorptivity, absurdity, adaptability, adversity, advisability, affability, affinity, agility, acclivity, acridity, activity, actuality, alacrity, allottee, ambiguity, amenability, amenity, amiability, amicability, amity, amnesty, amputee, anxiety, animosity, anonymity, antiquity, annuity, applicability, appointee, aridity, acerbity, acidity, assiduity, asperity, attensity, atrocity, avidity, *B* barbarity, benignity, biggety, bootee, *BR* brevity, brutality, *CH* changeability, charity, chastity, *D* debility, dedicatee, deformity, deity, dexterity, dextrality, density, deportee, depravity, deputy, devotee, dignity, dimity, dynasty, dishonesty, disparity, dissimilarity, distributee, diversity, divinity, domesticity, docility, dubiety, duplicity, *DR* draftee, *E* extremity, equality, equanimity, equity, elasticity, electee, electricity, enmity, enormity, entity, eternity, E.T., *F* faculty, falsity, familiarity, facility, fatality, fatuity, fecundity, felicity, ferocity, fertility, festivity, fidelity, fidgety, fixity, formality, fortuity, futility, futurity, *FR* fragility, fraternity, frigidity, frivolity, frugality, *G* gaiety, garrulity, giftee, goatee, guarantee, guaranty, *GR* gratuity, gravity, *H* hatchety, heredity, high tea, hilarity, hospitality, hostility, humanity, humidity, humility, *I* identity, imbecility, immaturity, immensity, immodesty, immorality, immortality, immunity, imparity, impassivity, impecuniosity, impetuosity, impiety, importunity, impropriety, impunity, impurity, inability, indignity, individuality, inductee, inferiority, infinity, iniquity, incapacity, incomparability, incompatibility, incomprehensibility, incongruity, incredulity, intensity, *J* generosity, geniality, gentility, jollity, juvenility, *K* calamity, capability, capacity, captivity, carroty, cavity, casualty, coatee, collectivity, comity, *committee*, commodity, community, complexity, complicity, conformity, concavity, consanguinity, contiguity, *contrasty*, convexity, covenantee, cupidity, curiosity, Q.T., *KR* creativity, credulity, Christianity, crotchety, crudity, cruelty, *KW* quality, quantity, quiddity, quoddity, *L* laity, laxity, legality, legatee, lenity, levity, liberality, liberty, limpidity, lubricity, luminosity, lucidity, *M* magnanimity, maggoty, majesty, majority, manatee, mestee, modesty, moeity, morality, mortality, mustee, mutuality, *N* nativity, nebulosity, nicety, nonentity, normality, nudity, neutrality, *O* objectivity, audacity, ophelimity, omneity, austerity, authenticity, authority, *P* parity, parvanimity, passivity, patentee, permittee, personality, pertinacity, piety, picotee, polarity, poverty, puberty, pupilarity, *PR* pravity,

presentee, privity, probability, proclivity, prolixity, propensity, property, propinquity, propriety, prudibundity, *R* radioactivity, relativity, reliability, remittee, repartee, receptivity, russety, *S* sacristy, sanctiminity, sanctity, security, celebrity, celerity, sensibility, sensitivity, certainty, servility, settee, seventy, similarity, simultaneity, sincerity, synonymity, syntality, civility, sovereignty, subtlety, pseudonymity, surdity, suttee, *SHR* shrievalty, *SK* scarcity, *SN* snippety, *SP* sparsity, spigotty, spiralty, spontaneity, *T* T, tea, tee, temerity, tensity, typothetae, titi, torpidity, totality, tutee, *TR* trepidity, trinity, trinkety, triviality, trumpety, trustee, *U* uberty, unity, utility, *V* velleity, velvety, viraginity, virginity, *W* warrantee, warranty, witchety, *Y* unanimity *A* allopathy, antipathy, apathy, *D* dyspathy, *E* empathy, *H* homeopathy, *S* sympathy, *T* telepathy, timothy, *TH* the, thee, *Y* eupathy

THĒ three, twenty-three (etc.)
THRĒ *A* ancestry, apple tree
TRĒ (and other trees), artistry, axletree, *B* barratry, bigotry, bijouterie, *D* deviltry, doubletree, *E* errantry, *F* physiolatry, forestry, *G* gallantry, gallows tree, *gumtree*, *H* harlotry, harvestry, *HW* whiffletree, whippletree, *I* idolatry, industry, infantry, *J* geometry, *K* chemistry, coquetry, coventry, *KR* craniometry, Christmas tree, *M* mantletree, merchantry, ministry, *N* knight-errantry, *O* honesty, *P* pageantry, palmistry, pedantry,

peasantry, poetry, *PL* pleasantry, *S* saddletree, sequestree, psychiatry, psychometry, symmetry, sophistry, *SH shoetree*, *T* tapestry, telemetry, tenantry, *TH* thalassochemistry, *TR* tree, trestletree, *W* wapiti, weeping tree

TWĒ étui
VĒ anchovy, levee, lucivee, *maulvee, mulvee,* Muscovy, eau de vie, pont-levis, c'est la vie, TV, vee, vis-a-vis
WĒ *awiwi,* ennui, *peewee,* sallowy, yellowy
YĒ employee, fedayee, cuir-bouilli, payee, ye
ZĒ advisee, bourgeoisie, chimpanzee, DMZ, devisee, fusee, razee, recognizee, Z, Zuyder Zee
ZHĒ bougie

ĒB

DĒB dieb
FĒB ephebe
GLĒB glebe

BENTLEY CLERIHEW

Of Clerihew Bentley.
Speak reverently.
First name—a verse;
Second—a hearse.

GRĒB grebe
PLĒB plebe

EB

EB ebb
BEB *cubeb,* zibeb
BLEB bleb
DEB *ardeb,* deb, subdeb
KEB keb
NEB neb, *nebneb*
PLEB pleb
REB Johnny Reb, reb
WEB *cobweb,* web
YEB uayeb

EBD

EBD ebbed
NEBD nebbed
WEBD cobwebbed, webbed

ĒCH

ĒCH	each
BĒCH	beach, beech
BLĒCH	bleach, rebleach, unbleach
BRĒCH	breach, breech, *housebreach, spousebreach,* unbreech
FLĒCH	fleech
KĒCH	keach, keech
LĒCH	*horseleech,* leach, leech
MĒCH	meech
PĒCH	appeach, peach, impeach
PLĒCH	pleach
PRĒCH	preach, repreach
RĒCH	forereach, *headreach,* outreach, overreach, reach
SĒCH	beseech
SKRĒCH	screech
SLĒCH	sleech
SPĒCH	speech
TĒCH	teach, unteach

ECH

ECH	etch, photo-etch, re-etch
FECH	fetch
FLECH	fletch
KECH	ketch
KLECH	cletch
KVECH	kvetch
KWECH	quetch, quetsch
LECH	lech, letch
RECH	retch, wretch, reretch
SKECH	sketch
STRECH	outstretch, stretch, restretch
TECH	mistetch, tetch
VECH	bitter vetch, vetch

ĒCHT

BLĒCHT	bleached
RĒCHT	piobaireachd

(See **ĒCH,** add *-ed* where appropriate.)

ECHT

(See **ECH,** add *-ed* where appropriate.)

ĒD

BĒD	bead, Bede
BLĒD	bleed, *nosebleed*
BRĒD	brede, breed, *halfbreed,* inbreed, interbreed, *crossbreed,* outbreed, upbreed
DĒD	deed, indeed, Candide, misdeed
FĒD	feed, handfeed, off his feed, overfeed, spoonfeed, underfeed, unfeed, winterfeed, eutrophied
FLĒD	flead, fleaed, unfleaed
FRĒD	enfreed, freed, *Siegfried,* unfreed
GLĒD	glede, gleed
GRĒD	agreed, degreed, disagreed, filigreed, greed, pedigreed, undegreed, unpedigreed
HĒD	he'd, heed, *Lockheed*
KĒD	keyed, rekeyed, unkeyed
LĒD	*fairlead,* lead, mislead, Nibelungenlied, uplead
KWĒD	quede, Quede
MĒD	Ganymede, mead, Mede, meed, Runnymede
NĒD	ennead, knead, kneed, need, *knock-kneed*
PĒD	impede, capripede, millipede, peed, centipede, cirripede, stampede, velocipede
PLĒD	implead, interplead, misplead, plead
RĒD	bourride, jereed, copyread, *lip-read,* misread, *O* outread, overread, *PR* proofread, *R* read, rede, reed, refereed, reread, *S* sight-read, *SP* speed-read
SĒD	*A* accede, *axseed,* aniseed, antecede, *B* birdseed, *E* epicede, exceed, *FL flaxseed, H* hayseed, *I* intercede, *Jamshid, K* concede, cottonseed, *L* linseed, *M moonseed, O* allseed, *P* pumpkinseed, *PR* precede, proceed, *R rapeseed,* recede, reseed, retrocede, *S* secede, cede, seed, succeed, supersede, *ST stickseed, W wormseed*
SHĒD	Haroun al-Rashid, she'd
SKRĒD	screed
SNĒD	snead
SPĒD	*airspeed,* Godspeed, *groundspeed,* outspeed, speed
SPRĒD	spreed
STĒD	steed
SWĒD	Swede
TĒD	guaranteed, propertied, reguaranteed, reteed, tead, teaed, teed, unguaranteed, unteed
THRĒD	threed
TRĒD	treed, retreed, untreed
TWĒD	tweed
WĒD	*B* beggarweed, bugleweed, *CH chickweed, E* ennuied, *F fireweed, G* goutweed, *gulfweed, H* hogweed, *K* colicweed, cottonweed, *L* locoweed, *M mayweed, milkweed, musquashweed, N knapweed, knotweed, P pigweed, pickerelweed, pokeweed, pondweed, R ragweed, S* seaweed, silverweed, *ST stickweed, T tumbleweed, W* waterweed, we'd, wede, weed
YĒD	yede

(See **E,** add *-d* where appropriate.)

ED

ED	coed, continuèd, op-ed, sorrowèd, wearièd, winnowèd
BED	*A* abed, *B* bed, *CH childbed, D* deathbed, *E* embed, *F* featherbed, *FL* flowerbed, *H* hotbed, *I* imbed, *P* pissabed, *R* riverbed, *roadbed, S* seedbed, surbed, *SL* slugabed, *TR* trucklebed, trundlebed, *W* waterbed
BRED	*B* beebread, *BL blackbread, BR* bread, bred, *brownbread, H highbread,* homebred, wholewheat bread, *HW* white bread, *I* inbred, *J* gingerbread, *KR crispbread,* crossbred, *L lowbred, O* overbred, *P* pilot bread, pita bread, *purebred, R* raisin bread, *S* sourbread, *SH shortbread,* shortening bread, *shewbread, SW sweetbread, TH* thoroughbred, *TR*

	truebred, U unbred, underbred, *W* well-bred, *Y* yeast bread	**LED**	lead, led, misled, unlead, unled, jolie-laide	signeted, soft-spirited, *SP* spirited, *T* talented, ted, tenanted, turreted, *U*
DED	bediamonded, dead, diamonded, garlanded, heralded, jeoparded, shepherded	**MED** **PED**	med, pre-med *A* aliped, *B* biped, *BR* breviped, *F* fissiped, *K* cheliped, *KW* quadruped, *M* maxilliped, milliped,	unballasted, unbonneted, uninhabited, uninhibited, unlimited, unmerited, unprofited, unrespited, untenanted, unvisited, *V*
DRED **FED**	adread, dread fed, *fullfed, milkfed,* overfed, underfed, unfed, well-fed		*moped,* multiped, *O* octoped, *P* palmiped, paralleloped, ped, pinnatiped, pinniped, *PL*	visited, *W* weak-spirited
				THRED	*goldthread, packthread,* thread, rethread, unthread
FLED **HED**	fled *A* ahead, *airhead,* arrowhead, *B* behead, *bighead,* billethead, *bonehead, bowhead,*		planiped, plumiped, *R* remiped, *S* semiped, serriped, soliped, *T* taliped, *U* uniped	**TRED** **WED** **YED** **ZED**	retread, tread rewed, unwed, wed yed zed
	bufflehead, *bulkhead, bullhead,* bullethead, *BL blackhead, blockhead,* blunderhead, *CH*	**PLED** **RED**	pled Ethelred, boxy red, infrared, misread,	**ĒDZ**	
	chucklehead, *D deadhead, death's-head,* dunderhead, *DR dragonhead, drophead,*	**SED**	outread, read, red, redd, reread, unread *aforesaid, foresaid,* gainsaid, resaid, said,	**BĒDZ** (See **ĒD,** add | beads, worry beads *-s* where appropriate.)
	drumhead, E egghead, emptyhead, *F fathead,* featherhead, fiddlehead, figurehead, *forehead,* fountainhead, *FL*	**SHED** **SHRED**	unsaid *bloodshed,* shed, *snowshed,* watershed, *woodshed* shred	**ĒF**	
	flathead, G gilthead, go-ahead, *godhead, goodhead, GR greenhead, H*	**SLED** **SNED** **SPED** **SPRED**	*bobsled,* sled snead sped, unsped, well-sped *bedspread,* bespread,	**ĒF** **BĒF** **BRĒF** **CHĒF**	naïf beef brief, debrief chief, handkerchief, neckerchief
	hammerhead, *hardhead,* head, *hogshead,* Holyhead, *hophead, hothead, K cathead,*	**STED**	outspread, overspread, spread, underspread, *well-spread, widespread* bedstead, bestead,	**DĒF** **FĒF** **GRĒF** **LĒF**	deaf, deef, redif enfeoff, fief, feoff grief *B* bas-relief, belief, *BR*
	copperhead, *KR crosshead, L* letterhead, leatherhead, loggerhead, *M* maidenhead,	**TED**	*farmstead, homestead,* instead, *roadstead,* stead, *oersted A* attributed, *B* ballasted,		*broadleaf, D* demirelief, disbelief, *FL flyleaf, G goldleaf, I* interleaf, *KL* cloverleaf, *L* leaf, lief, *M*
	marblehead, *masthead, N* nailhead, niggerhead, knucklehead, *O* overhead, *P* pinhead, *poppyhead, pothead, R railhead, ramhead,*		barren-spirited, base-spirited, bigoted, bold-spirited, bonneted, *BR* breakfasted, *D* discomfited,	**NĒF** **RĒF**	misbelief, *O* overleaf, *R* relief, *TH thickleaf, U* unbelief, *V* velvetleaf hanif, neif, neife kharif, reef, reif, shereef, tashrif, Tenerife
	redhead, roundhead, rudderhead, *S sorehead, SH sheepshead,* shovelhead, *SK skinhead,*		discomforted, discredited, disinherited, disquieted, dispirited, distributed, *E* exhibited,	**SĒF** **SHĒF** **TĒF**	massif sheaf aperitif, leitmotif, motif, chetif
	SL sleepyhead, SP spearhead, springhead, ST stairhead, steelhead, T timberhead, *towhead, TH* thunderhead, *TR*		*F* faceted, fine-spirited, forfeited, *G* gay-spirited, *H* helmeted, high-spirited, *I* inhabited, inherited, inspirited, *K*	**THĒF**	infangthief, outfangthief, thief, utfangthief
	trundlehead, *U* unhead, *W* warhead, wellhead, woodenhead, woolly-head		carpeted, contributed, coveted, *KR* crescented, *KW* quieted, *L* light-spirited, limited, low-	**EF** **EF**	F, eff, ef, Kiev,
JED **KED**	ravagèd, jed ked, sheep-ked		spirited, *M* mean-spirited, merited, *P* patented, pirated, poor-spirited, public-spirited, *PR* profited, prohibited, *S*	**DEF** **FEF** **JEF** **KEF**	Prokofiev deaf enfeoff, feoff jeff kef

KLEF clef
LEF lev
NEF *Brezhnev,* nef
REF ref
SEF UNICEF
SHEF chef
TEF tef

EFT

EFT eft
DEFT deft
FEFT enfeoffed, feoffed, unfeoffed
HEFT heft
HWEFT wheft
JEFT jeffed
KLEFT cleft, klepht
LEFT aleft, left, New Left, ultraleft
REFT bereft, reft
THEFT theft
WEFT weft

ĒG

BRĒG brigue
GRĒG Grieg
KLĒG klieg
KRĒG *blitzkrieg, sitzkrieg*
LĒG league, *colleague*
NĒG banig, renege
PĒG peag
SKĒG skeeg
TĒG fatigue, squeteague
TRĒG intrigue
ZHĒG gigue

EG

EG boiled egg, duck egg, egg, goose egg (etc.)
BEG beg, filibeg
DREG dreg
GLEG gleg
KEG keg, *muskeg*
KLEG cleg, kleg
LEG *blackleg, bootleg, bowleg, dogleg, foreleg,* leg, *pegleg, proleg*
MEG *nutmeg*
NEG renege
PEG peg, repeg, unpeg, Winnipeg
REG reg
SEG seg
SKEG skeg
SNEG sneg
TEG teg
YEG yegg

ĒGD

NĒGD reneged

(See **ĒG**, add *-d* where appropriate.)

EGD

EGD egged
LEGD bow-legged
NEGD reneged

(See **EG**, add *-ed* or *-ged* where appropriate.)

EGZ

LEGZ legs, sea legs

(See **EG**, add *-s* where appropriate.)

ĒJ

LĒJ liege
SĒJ besiege, siege

EJ

EJ cutting edge, featheredge, edge, razor's edge, re-edge, *straightedge,* unedge
DREJ dredge
FLEJ fledge
HEJ enhedge, hedge
KEJ kedge
KLEJ cledge
LEJ allege, ledge, privilege, sacrilege, sortilege
PLEJ *frankpledge,* impledge, interpledge, pledge, repledge

PUZZLE FOR GRAMMARIANS AND MORALISTS

I find it curiositive
    My good intentionals despite,
That I am just as positive
    When I am wrong as when I'm right.

SEJ sedge
SKEJ skedge
SLEJ sledge
TEJ tedge
WEJ wedge

EJD

EJD edged, double-edged

(See **EJ**, add *-d* where appropriate.)

ĒK

ĒK eke, caique, saic
BĒK beak, beek, *grosbeak, halfbeak,* Mozambique, stickybeak
BLĒK bleak
CHĒK cheek, chic, radical chic
FĒK feak
FRĒK ecofreak, freak, Jesus freak
GĒK geek
GLĒK gleek
GRĒK fenugreek, Greek
KĒK keek
KLĒK cleek, clique
KRĒK creak, creek
LĒK aleak, Belleek, houseleek, leak, leek, oblique, relique, silique
MĒK comique, meak, meek
NĒK clinique, Martinique, technique, unique
PĒK *A* afterpeak, apeak, apeek, *CH* Chesapeake, *D* demipeak, *F* forepeak, *N* noddypeak, *P* peak, peek, Peke, pique, *R* repique, *W* widow's peak
RĒK areek, perique, wreak, reek
SĒK hide-and-seek, cacique, reseek, seek, Sikh
SHĒK radical chic, chic, sheik
SHRĒK shriek
SKRĒK screak
SKWĒK asqueak, bubble and squeak, *pipsqueak,* squeak
SLĒK sleek, unsleek
SNĒK sneak
SPĒK bespeak, forespeak, *newspeak,* speak, unspeak
STRĒK streak
TĒK *A* antique, *B* batik, boutique, *J* geopolitik, *KR* critique, *M* mystique, *N* novantique, *P* politique, *PL* plastique, *PR* pratique, *R* Realpolitik, *T* teak, *TR* triptyque
TWĒK tweak
WĒK Holy Week, *midweek,* Passion Week, weak, week, yesterweek

ZĒK
bezique, physique, cazique

EK

EK home-ec
BEK beck, Kennebec, *crombec*, Quebec, *pinchbeck, rebec, xebec*
BREK brek
CHEK blank check, bodycheck, check, cheque, Czech, *hatcheck, coatcheck,* countercheck, crosscheck, overcheck, recheck, *raincheck,* rubber check
DEK afterdeck, bedeck, deck, *foredeck,* quarterdeck, *sandek,* dreck, undeck
DREK dreck
FEK feck
FLEK fleck
GEK geck
HEK heck, by heck
KEK keck
KLEK cleck
LEK *cromlech,* lech, Lech, leck, lek
NEK *B* bottleneck, *BL blackneck, BR breakneck, KR crookneck,* crewneck, *L* leatherneck, *N* neck, nek, neck-and-neck, *R redneck,* rollneck, *roughneck,* rubberneck, *wryneck, SW* swanneck, *T* turtle-neck
PEK *henpeck, kopek,* OPEC, peck, repeck, sapek, Tehuantepec
REK bewreck, plane wreck, reck, *shipwreck, tenrec,* train wreck (etc.)
SEK *cusec, parsec,* sec
SHEK Chiang Kai-shek
SNEK sneck
SPEK *flyspeck,* spec, speck
TEK *Aztec,* discotheque, *conteck,* Mixtec, tec, tech, teck, *Toltec*
TREK Star Trek, trek
YEK yech, yecch

ĒKS

ĒKS eeks
BRĒKS breeks

LĒKS leeks
SĒKS maxixe, seeks

(See ĒK, add -s where appropriate.)

EKS

EKS ex, x
BEKS becks, *ibex, vibex*
DEKS bedecks, decks, *index, caudex, codex, subindex*
FEKS faex, pontifex, spinifex, tubifex
FLEKS *B biflex, D* deflects, deflex, *FL* flecks, flex, *I* inflects, inflex, *J* genuflects, genuflex, *R* reflects, *reflex,* retroflex, *S* circumflex
HEKS hex
KEKS kex
LEKS *ilex,* isolex, lex, *aulex, pollex, silex, scolex, telex*
MEKS Mex, *remex, cimex,* Tex-Mex
NEKS annex, disannex, *Kleenex,* connects, *connex*
PEKS *apex,* haruspex, *auspex*
PLEKS *D diplex,* duplex, *G* googolplex, *I* interrex, *K* complex, contraplex, *KW* quadruplex, *M* multiplex, *N* nulliplex, *P* perplex, *PL* plex, *S* simplex, *TR* triplex, *V* veniplex
PREKS prex
REKS *murex, Pyrex,* rex
SEKS desex, *Essex,* fair sex, homosex, intersex, Middlesex, sex, supersex, unisex, unsex, weaker sex
SPEKS *Perspex,* specs, spex
TEKS *dentex, cortex, latex, vertex, vortex*
THEKS *narthex*
VEKS biconvex, convex, vex, unvex
YEKS yex

(See EK, add -s where appropriate.)

EKST

FLEKST flexed, genuflexed
HEKST hexed
NEKST annexed, next
PLEKST perplexed, unperplexed

SEKST oversexed, sexed, sext, undersexed, unsexed
TEKST *context, pretext,* text
VEKST unvexed, vexed

ĒKT

ĒKT eked
CHĒKT apple-cheeked, cheeked, cherry-cheeked, *pale-cheeked, pink-cheeked, rosy-cheeked*
STRĒKT *ring-streaked,* streaked

(See ĒK, add -ed where appropriate.)

EKT

BEKT becked
CHEKT checked, unchecked
DEKT bedecked, decked, *pandect*
FEKT *A* affect, aftereffect, *D* defect, disaffect, disinfect, *E* effect, *F* photoelectric effect, *GR* greenhouse effect, *I* infect, *K* confect, *M* misaffect, *P* perfect, *PR* prefect, *R* refect, ripple effect
FLEKT deflect, flecked, flect, inflect, genuflect, reflect, circumflect
GLEKT benign neglect, neglect
JEKT *A* abject, adject, *D* deject, disject, *E* eject, *I* inject, interject, introject, *K* conject, *O* object, *PR* project, *R* reject, retroject, *S* subject, *TR* traject
LEKT *A* acrolect, analect, *B* basilect, *D* dialect, *E* elect, *I* idiolect, intellect, *K* collect, *N* non-elect, *PR* pre-elect, prelect, *R* re-elect, recollect, *S* select
NEKT disconnect, *goosenecked,* interconnect, connect, *crooknecked,* necked, reconnect
PEKT aspect, expect, *henpecked,* pecked, *prospect*
PLEKT complect
REKT *A* arrect, *D* direct, *E* erect, *I* indirect, incorrect, insurrect, *K*

	correct, *M* misdirect, *P* porrect, *R* wrecked, resurrect, rewrecked, *U* unwrecked
SEKT	bisect, dissect, exsect, *insect,* intersect, quadrisect, sect, transect, trisect, vivisect
SPEKT	*D* disrespect, *E* expect, *I* inspect, introspect, *R* respect, retrospect, *S* self-respect, circumspect, suspect, *SP* specked, spect, 'spect, *U* unspecked
TEKT	architect, detect, contect, obtect, overprotect, protect, underprotect, undetect, unprotect
TREKT	trekked

(See **EK,** add *-ed* where appropriate.)

ĒL

ĒL	eel, langue d'oïl
BĒL	*A* abeal, abele, *B* beal, beele, *D* deshabille, dishabille, *I* immobile, *L* locomobile, *M* mobile, Mobile, *O* automobile, *S* cebil, *SN* snowmobile, traymobile
DĒL	deal, deil, ideal, interdeal, misdeal, ordeal, redeal, misdeal, undeal, urodele
FĒL	feal, feel, feil, forefeel, Israfil, refeel
GWĒL	aiguille
HĒL	*allheal,* heal, heel, he'll, *clownheel,* Tarheel
HWĒL	*B* balance wheel, big wheel, *BR* breastwheel, *D* dial wheel, *DR* driving wheel, *FL* flywheel, *FR* freewheel, *G* gearwheel, *HW* wheal, wheel, *K* cartwheel, cogwheel, *M* millwheel, *P* paddlewheel, *pinwheel*
JĒL	jeel, jheel, jhil, congeal, recongeal, uncongeal
KRĒL	creel
LĒL	allele, leal, leel, Lille
MĒL	*B* barley meal, *F* fistmele, *H* havermele, *wholemeal, I inchmeal, K* Camille, camomile, *cornmeal, L landmil, M* meal, mil, *O* oatmeal, *P*

THE ELEVATOR OPERATOR-OPERATED ELEVATOR

When you sin, friend, know that later
You'll meet Charon, operator
Of an ancient elevator.
It goes down to Hades' crater;
It goes up to your Creator.
Charon sets the indicator.
Ponder well that antiquated
Manually operated
Elevator operator's
Elevator operator-
Operated elevator!

	piecemeal, SHL schlemiel, *ST stoundmeal, SW sweetmeal*
NĒL	anele, anneal, cochineal, manchineel, kneel, neele, chenille
PĒL	appeal, ylespil, peal, peel, repeal, repeel, thunderpeal
RĒL	baril, *newsreel,* real, reel, surreal, toril, unreal, unreel
SĒL	endocoele, enseal, goldenseal, imbecile, conceal, neurocoele, privy seal, ceil, seal, seel, cystocele, unseal
SHĒL	sheal, sheel, she'll
SKĒL	skeel
SKWĒL	squeal
SPĒL	*bonspiel,* festspiel, glockenspiel, *kriegspiel,* speel, spiel
STĒL	steal, steel, unsteel
SWĒL	sweal
TĒL	bastille, *datil,* infantile, genteel, castille, Castille, cockateel, manteel, pastille, shabby genteel, teal, teil, til
THĒL	thee'll
TWĒL	tweel, tuille
VĒL	bidonville, reveal, veal
WĒL	commonweal, weal, weel, we'll
ZĒL	cacozeal, zeal

EL

EL	A. W. O. L., el, ell, *L,* Emmanuel, Immanuel, materiel, Noel, ruelle, spirituel, vielle
BEL	*B* bar bell, bel, bell, belle, bonibel, bonnibell, *BL* bluebell, *D* decibel,

---

	deathbell, dinner bell, doorbell, dumbbell, *E* evening bell, *G* gabelle, *H* handbell, harebell, heatherbell, Isabel, *J* Jezebel, *K* Canterbury bell, *corbeil,* cowbell, *KL* claribel, *M* mirabelle, morning bell, *N* Nobel, *P* passing bell, *R* rebel, *S* sacring bell, sanctus bell, school bell, sunset bell, *V* vesper bell
DEL	*A* aludel, asphodel, *D* dell, *FR* fricandel, *H* hirondelle, *I* infidel, *K* cadelle, cordelle, *R* rondel, rondelle, *S* sardel, sardelle, citadel, *SH* chandelle, *Z* zinfandel
DWEL	dwell, indwell
FEL	Astrophel, befell, fell, refell
HEL	Hel, hell
JEL	aerogel, hydrogel, gel, jell, plasmagel
KEL	kell
KVEL	kvell
KWEL	quell
LEL	*hallel,* parallel
MEL	bechamel, oenomel, philomel, hydromel, jumel, calomel, caramel, Carmel, mel, mell, pall-mall, pell-mell
NEL	*F* fontanel, fustanel, *FR* fresnel, *J* jargonelle, *K* quenelle, Cornell, *KR* crenelle, *M* mangonel, *N* knell, *O* organelle, *P* parnel, Parnell, personnel, petronel, pimpernel, *PR* prunelle, *R* ritornel, *S* sentinel, *SP* spinel, *V* villanelle
PEL	appel, dispel, expel, impel, compel, lapel, pell, propel, rappel, repel, *scalpel*
REL	aquarelle, amerelle, doggerel, cockerel, jurel, mackerel, morel, nonpareil, pickerel, rel, Sacheverell, chanterelle
SEL	*E* excel, encell, *F* filoselle, ficelle, photocell, *H* hardsell, *HW* white cell, *I* involucel, *K* carousel, carrousel, *M* marcel, *N* nacelle, *O* outsell,

oversell, *P* pedicel,
pennoncelle, pucelle, *R*
radicel, red cell, resell, *S*
sarcel, sarcelle, cell, sell,
solar cell, *U* undersell,
unicell

SHEL   *bombshell, eggshell,*
cockleshell, nutshell,
seashell, shell, tortoise
shell, unshell

SMEL   smell
SNEL   snell
SPEL   love spell, misspell,
respell, spell, unspell

STREL   pipistrel
SWEL   *groundswell,* swell,
upswell

TEL   *A* artel, *B* bagatelle, *BR*
bretelle, brocatelle, *D*
dentelle, *F* foretell, *H*
hotel, *I* immortelle, *K*
cartel, *KL* clientele, *M*
maitre d'hotel,
moschatel, motel,
muscatel, *R* retell, *T* tell

VEL   divel, caravel, Ravel,
Tavel

WEL   *bridewell,* farewell,
inkwell, Cromwell,
speedwell, stairwell,
unwell, well

YEL   yell
ZEL   demoiselle, gazelle,
mademoiselle, Moselle

ELB

ELB   elb
SKELB   skelb

ELCH

BELCH   belch
KWELCH   quelch
SKWELCH   squelch
WELCH   welch, Welch

ĒLD

BĒLD   bield
FĒLD   *A* afield, *airfield, B*
battlefield, *CH*
chesterfield, *F* field, *H*
harvest field, *HW* wheat
field, *I* infield, *K*
canfield, coal field, corn
field, *L* left field, *M*
midfield, minifield, *O* oil
field, *outfield, R* right

field, *SH* sheffield, *SK*
Scofield, *SN* snowfield,
SPR Springfield, *U*
urnfield

HĒLD   heald, heeled, hield,
well-heeled

SHĒLD   enshield, shield,
windshield

WĒLD   weald, wield
YĒLD   yield

(See **EL**, add *-ed* where appropriate.)

ELD

ELD   eld
BELD   belled, rebelled, unbelled
FYELD   fjeld
GELD   *Danegeld,* geld
HELD   beheld, held, unbeheld,
upheld, withheld

KELD   keld
LELD   paralleled, unparalleled
MELD   meld
PELD   dispelled, expelled,
impelled, compelled,
misspelled, pelled,
propelled, repelled,
spelled

YELD   yeld, yelled

(See **EL**, add *-ed* where appropriate.)

ELF

ELF   elf
DELF   delf, *didelf*
GWELF   Guelph
PELF   pelf
SELF   herself, himself, itself,
myself, ourself, self,
thyself, oneself, yourself
SHELF   closet shelf, mantel shelf,
shelf, wall shelf (etc.)
SKELF   skelf

ELFT

DELFT   delft, Delft
PELFT   pelfed

ELK

ELK   elk
HWELK   whelk
YELK   yelk

ELM

ELM   elm, *wych-elm*
HELM   ahelm, dishelm, helm,
unhelm, weatherhelm,
Wilhelm
HWELM   whelm, overwhelm,
underwhelm
RELM   realm

ELP

HELP   help, self-help
HWELP   whelp, *yarwhelp*
KELP   kelp
SKELP   skelp
SWELP   swelp
YELP   yelp

ELT

BELT   belt, *blackbelt, borscht
belt,* rain belt, sun belt,
unbelt
DELT   dealt, misdealt, undealt
DWELT   dwelt, undwelt
FELT   felt, *heartfelt, homefelt,*
underfelt, unfelt, veldt
GELT   *Danegelt,* gelt, *Trinkgelt*
KELT   Celt, kelt, Kelt
MELT   melt, remelt
NELT   knelt
PELT   pelt
SELT   celt, Celt
SMELT   smelt
SPELT   misspelt, spelt, unspelt
SVELT   svelte
VELT   *backveld,* Roosevelt,
veld, veldt, *zuurveldt*
WELT   welt

ELTH

HELTH   health
STELTH   stealth
WELTH   commonwealth, wealth

ELTS

(See **ELT**, add *-s* where appropriate.)

ELV

DELV   delve
HELV   helve
SHELV   shelve
TWELV   twelve

ELZ

NELZ	Dardanelles
SHELZ	Seychelles

(See **EL,** add *-s* where appropriate.)

ĒM

ĒM	eme
BĒM	abeam, beam, embeam, *hornbeam, whitebeam, crossbeam, moonbeam, sunbeam*
BRĒM	bream
DĒM	addeem, adeem, academe, deem, deme, Hasidim, misdeem, redeem
DRĒM	*daydream,* dream
FĒM	blaspheme, *grapheme, morpheme,* telepheme
FLĒM	fleam
FRĒM	fream
GLĒM	agleam, gleam, weathergleam
HĒM	haem
KĒM	hakim, hyporcheme
KRĒM	cream, *icecream*
KWĒM	queme
LĒM	leam
MĒM	*sememe*
NĒM	*phoneme,* neem, *toneme*
PRĒM	supreme
RĒM	*bireme,* quinquereme, ream, reem, rheme, riem, reream, *spireme, trireme*
SĒM	beseem, berseem, enseam, *glosseme, lexeme, oxime, raceme,* seam, seem, unbeseem, unseam
SKĒM	rescheme, scheme
SKRĒM	escrime, scream
STĒM	disesteem, esteem, self-esteem, steam
STRĒM	*downstream, headstream, mainstream, midstream, millstream, slipstream,* stream, *upstream*
TĒM	eroteme, esteem, semanteme, *septime,* centime, team, teem
THĒM	anatheme, theme
TRĒM	extreme, monotreme
YĒM	yeme
ZHĒM	regime

EM

EM	em, 'em, m, requiem
BLEM	periblem
DEM	anadem, bediadem, diadem, condemn, *modem,* recondemn
FEM	feme, femme
FLEM	phlegm
HEM	ahem, Bethlehem, hem, *mayhem*
JEM	begem, Brummagem, gem, stratagem
KEM	Yquem, kemb
KLEM	clem
KREM	crème, crème de la crème
LEM	*golem, xylem*
MEM	mem
NEM	ad hominem
REM	ad rem, in rem, theorem
SEM	*semsem*
SHEM	Shem
STEM	*pipestem,* stem
TEM	contemn, pro tem
THEM	apothegm, apothem, them
WEM	wem

ĒMD

(See **ĒM,** add *-d* or *-ed* where appropriate.)

EMD

DEMD	diademed
FREMD	fremd

(See **EM,** add *-med* or *-ed* where appropriate.)

EMP

HEMP	hemp
KEMP	kemp
TEMP	temp

EMPT

EMPT	empt, coempt, preempt
DEMPT	adempt
DREMPT	adreamt, dreamt, undreamt
KEMPT	kempt, unkempt
REMPT	dirempt
TEMPT	attempt, contempt, self-contempt, tempt
ZEMPT	exempt

EMZ

TEMZ	temse, Thames

(See **EM,** add *-s* where appropriate.)

ĒN

ĒN	ean, e'en, goode'en, Hallowe'en, narceine, cysteine, toluene
BĒN	bean, been, *buckbean,* gombeen, *has-been,* jellybean, shebeen, terebene
CHĒN	Balanchine, Capuchin
DĒN	*A* Aberdeen, almandine, *BR* brigandine, *D* dean, dene, dudeen, *G* gabardine, gardeen, Gunga Din, *GR* gradine, grenadine, *I* indene, incarnadine, *K* codeine, *KR* crapaudine, *P* piperidine, *S* sardine, sourdine, undine
FĒN	dauphine, *phosphene, phosphine,* Josephine, caffeine, *morphine,* toxaphene, trephine
GĒN	*Begin,* Beguine, gean, carrageen
GLĒN	glean, reglean
GRĒN	*A* aquagreen, *B* bowling green, *E* evergreen, *G* gangrene, *GR* grassgreen, green, *L* long green, *M* mythogreen, *P* peagreen, peregrine, putting green, *S* sea-green, *SH* shagreen, chagrin, *W* wintergreen
HĒN	fellaheen
HWĒN	wheen
JĒN	*A* alpigene, *E* epigene, *F* phosgene, photogene, *G* gazogene, *H* heterogene, hygiene, hypogene, *I* indigene, *J* gene, jean, *KW* quadragene, *M* mutator gene, *O* aubergine, *P* polygene, porphyrogene, *S* sagene, seltzogene, supergene
KĒN	achene, buckeen, damaskene, keen, nankeen, palankeen, palanquin, sakeen, *takin,* Tolkien
KLĒN	clean, come clean, Mr. Clean, super-clean, ultraclean, unclean
KRĒN	Hippocrene
KWĒN	closet queen, *cuckquean,* quean, queen
LĒN	*A* anilene, *B* baleen, bandoline, *F* philhellene,

	G gasoline, Ghibelline, *H* Hellene, *K* choline, colleen, *KR* crinoline, *L* lean, lien, *M* magdalene, malines, moulleen, mousseline, *N* naphthalene, *O* opaline, *PR* praline, proline, *SK* scalene, *SKW* squalene, *T* tourmaline, *TH* phthalein, *U* uplean, *V* valine, vaseline
MĒN	ammine, bellarmine, *bromine*, bemean, dexemphetamine, demean, demesne, dopamine, physostigmene, gamine, imine, mean, mesne, mien, misdemean, spodumine
NĒN	Lenin, mavourneen, mezzanine, quinine, shoneen, cyanine, *strychnine*, torpinene
PĒN	alpeen, atropine, chopine, Philippine, pean, peen, reserpine, scalpeen, spalpeen, *terpene*
PRĒN	isoprene, preen
RĒN	*A* aquamarine, Algerine, anserine, *B* bismarine, butterine, dourine, *F* figurine, *FL* fluorine, *K* careen, kittereen, *KL* chlorine, *M* marine, margarine, mazarine, moreen, *N* Nazarene, nectarine, *O* oleomargarine, *P* Palmyrene, pelerine, pyrene, pistareen, *R* reen, rosmarine, *purine*, *S* serene, cismarine, submarine, subterrene, superterrene, *SKW* squidgereen, *SM* smithereen, *T* tambourine, tangerine, terrene, terrine, tureen, *TR* transmarine, *U* ultramarine, *W* wolverine
SĒN	*A* arsine, *D* damascene, *E* Eocene, epicene, Essene, *F* fantocine, fascine, foreseen, *GL* glassine, *K* kerosene, *M* Miocene, *N* Nicene, *O* obscene, overseen, *R* Racine, *S* scene, seen, psittacine, *U* unforeseen, unseen, *V* vaccine

SFĒN	sphene
SHĒN	arsheen, dasheen, Capuchin, machine, praying machine, sheen, voting machine
SKĒN	skean
SKRĒN	bescreen, multiscreen, rescreen, screen, split screen, unscreen, *windscreen*
SPLĒN	spleen
STĒN	mangosteen, stean, steen
TĒN	*A* Argentine, eighteen, *B* barkentine, Byzantine, bottine, *BR* brigantine, brilliantine, *D* dentine, duvetyn, *F* fifteen, fourteen, *FL* Florentine, *G* galantine, guillotine, *J* gelatine, *K* canteen, Constantine, costean, *KL* clementine, *KR* chryselephantine, *KW* quarantine, quarentene, *L* lateen, libertine, lovertine, *N* nicotine, nineteen, *O* Augustine, *P* patine, pentene, poteen, potheen, *PR* pre-teen, protein, pristine, *R* ratteen, ratine, routine, *S* sateen, serpentine, seventeen, sixteen, *Sistine, cystine*, subroutine, *T* teen, tontine, turbitteen, *TH* thirteen, *U* umpteen, *V* velveteen
THĒN	ornithene, polythene
THRĒN	threne
TRĒN	latrine, thestreen, treen, *vitrine*, yestreen
TWĒN	atween, between, go-between, therebetween, 'tween
VĒN	advene, intervene, contravene, convene, margravine, *nervine*, olivine, prevene, ravine, Slovene, subvene, supervene, visne
WĒN	overween, wean, ween
YĒN	yean
ZĒN	benzene, benzine, bombazine, chlorobenzene, cuisine, limousine, magazine, nitrobenzene, organzine

EN

EN	Darien, equestrienne, julienne, cayenne,

	comedienne, en, n, Parisienne, persienne, Cheyenne, Tyrolienne, tragedienne, Valenciennes
BEN	ben, *benben*, benn, Big Ben
CHEN	chen
DEN	Ardennes, den, quarenden
FEN	fen
GEN	again, born-again
GLEN	glen
HEN	*grayhen*, hen, *moorhen*, *peahen*, prairie hen, *sagehen*, turkeyhen, water hen
HWEN	when
JEN	endogen, exogen, estrogen, halogen, gen, carcinogen, kratogen, nitrogen, oxygen, pathogen, sagene
KEN	beken, ken
LEN	madeleine, madrilene, Magdalen
MEN	*A* aldermen, amen, *B* Bushmen, *H* horsemen, *I* Englishmen, *J* gentlemen, *M* men, *N* Norsemen, Northmen, *P* partimen, party men, *R* regimen, *S* seamen, semen, cyclamen, *SP* specimen, *T* tequmen
PEN	ballpoint pen, brevipen, *bullpen*, fountain pen, impen, *cowpen*, pen, *pigpen*, *playpen*, poison pen, unpen
REN	wren, viceraine
SEN	samisen, Saracen, sen, *sensen*, Sun Yat-sen
SHEN	Shen
SKEN	sken
STEN	Sten
TEN	ten
THEN	then
WEN	wen
VYEN	varsovieane
YEN	doyenne, Cayenne, yen
ZEN	denizen, citizen, Zen

ENCH

BENCH	bench, disbench, carpenter's bench, unbench, *workbench*
BLENCH	blench
DRENCH	bedrench, drench, redrench

FLENCH	flench	**REND**	rend, rerend, reverend
FRENCH	French, un-French	**SEND**	ascend, descend,

FLENCH flench
FRENCH French, un-French
KENCH kench
KLENCH clench, unclench
KWENCH quench, unquen .
MENCH mensch, Uebermensch, Untermensch
RENCH monkey wrench, wrench
SKWENCH squench
STENCH stench
TENCH tench
TRENCH entrench, intrench, retrench, trench
WENCH *oldwench,* wench

ENCHT

BENCHT benched

(See **ENCH,** add *-ed* where appropriate.)

ĒND

FĒND archfiend, fiend

(See **ĒN,** add *-ed* where appropriate.)

END

END end, gable end, Land's End, minuend, tag end, upend
BEND *backbend,* bend, *prebend,* rebend, South Bend, unbend
BLEND blend, blende, *hornblende,* interblend, *pitchblende*
DEND addend, dividend
FEND defend, fend, forfend, offend, weatherfend
FREND befriend, *boyfriend,* friend, *girlfriend,* ladyfriend
HEND apprehend, comprehend, misapprehend, miscomprehend, reprehend, subtrahend
KEND kenned, unkenned
LEND lend
MEND amend, emend, discommend, commend, mend, recommend, remend
PEND *A* append, *D* depend, *E* expend, *I* impend, *K* compend, *P* pend, penned, perpend, *PR* prepend, *ST* stipend, *U* unpenned, *V* vilipend

REND rend, rerend, reverend
SEND ascend, descend, *godsend,* condescend, scend, send, transcend, upsend
SHEND shend
SPEND expend, misspend, spend, suspend
STEND extend, coextend, ostend, Ostend
TEND *A* attend, *D* distend, *I* intend, *K* coextend, contend, *P* portend, *PR* pretend, *R* repetend, *S* subtend, superintend, *T* tend
TREND trend
VEND vend
WEND wend
ZEND Zend

(See **EN,** add *-ed* or *-ned* where appropriate.)

ENG

DRENG dreng, drengh
KRENG kreng
SHENG sheng

ENGTH

LENGTH length
STRENGTH strength

ENJ

HENJ *Stonehenge*
VENJ avenge, revenge

ENS

ENS *A* affluence, *D* disobedience, *E* ebullience, effluence, expedience, experience, ense, *I* inexpedience, inexperience, influence, incongruence, inconvenience, insipience, issuance, *K* confluence, congruence, continuance, convenience, *M* mellifluence, *N* nescience, *O* obedience, audience, omniscience, *P* percipience, *PR* prescience, prurience, *R* refluence, resilience, *S* salience, sapience, subservience

DENS *A* accidence, accidents, *D* dense, diffidence, dissidence, *E* evidence, *I* improvidence, impudence, incidence, *K* coincidence, condense, confidence, *N* nonresidence, nonresidents, *PR* providence, Providence, *R* recondense, residence, residents, *S* self-confidence, subsidence
FENS defense, fence, offense, self-defense
FLENS flense
HENS hence, herehence
HWENS whence
JENS diligence, exigence, indigence, intelligence, negligence
KWENS blandiloquence, breviloquence, eloquence, grandiloquence, inconsequence, consequence, magniloquence
LENS *B* benevolence, *E* equivalence, equivalents, excellence, *FL* flatulence, flocculence, *FR* fraudulence, *I* imprevalence, indolence, insolence, insomnolence, *K* condolence, corpulence, *KW* quantivalence, *L* lutulence, *M* malevolence, *O* opulence, *P* pestilence, purulence, *PR* prevalence, *R* redolence, *S* somnolence, succulence, *T* temulence, turbulence, *TR* truculence, *V* violence, virulence
MENS immense, commence, mense, recommence, vehemence
NENS *A* abstinence, *E* eminence, *I* immanence, imminence, impermanence, impertinence, incontinence, *K*

PENS
continence, *P* permanence, pertinence, *PR* preeminence, prominence, *S* supereminence dispense, expense, pence, prepense, propense, recompense, *sixpence, twopence, threepence*

RENS
B belligerence, *D* deference, difference, *I* indifference, inference, irreverence, *K* conference, *PR* preference, *R* reference, reverence, *S* circumference

SENS
B beneficence, *FR* frankincense, *I* incense, innocence, *K* commonsense, concupiscence, *M* magnificence, munificence, *N nonsense*, *R* reticence, *S* cense, sense

SPENS
spence, suspense

TENS
A appetence, *I* impenitence, impotence, inappetence, incompetence, incompetents, intense, intents, *K* competence, *O* omnipotence, *P* penitence, *PL* plenipotence, *PR* pretense, *S* subtense, *T* tense

THENS
thence

ENSH

(See ENCH)

ENST

ENST
experienced, inexperienced, influenced, uninfluenced

DENST
evidenced, condensed, recondensed, uncondensed

FENST fenced, unfenced
FLENST flensed, unflensed
GENST against, 'gainst
MENST commenced, recommenced
NENST anenst, fornenst
PENST dispensed, recompensed, unrecompensed

RENST
cross-referenced, referenced, reverenced, unreferenced, unreverenced

SENST
incensed, censed, sensed, unsensed

ENT

ENT
A affluent, accipient, ambient, aperient, *D* diffluent, diluent, disobedient, disorient, *E* effluent, expedient, emollient, esurient, *GR* gradient, *I* inexpedient, influent, ingredient, incongruent, inconvenient, insentient, incipient, interfluent, *K* confluent, congruent, constituent, convenient, *L* lenient, *M* mellifluent, *O* obedient, obstruent, audient, orient, *P* parturient, percipient, *PR* prescient, profluent, prurient, *R* recipient, refluent, resilient, *S* salient, sapient, sentient, circumambient, circumfluent, subservient, substituent

BENT bent, *hellbent*, unbent
BLENT blent, unblent
BRENT brent
DENT
A accident, *D* dent, diffident, dissident, *E* evident, *I* improvident, impudent, incident, incoincident, indent, *K* coincident, confident, *O* occident, *PR* precedent, president, provident, *R* resident, *S* subsident

FENT fent
GENT Ghent
HENT
attrahent, hent, contrahent, revehent
JENT
diligent, dirigent, exigent, gent, indigent, intelligent, intransigent, corrigent, negligent, transigent

KENT Kent
KWENT
acquent, eloquent, frequent, grandiloquent, inconsequent, consequent, magniloquent, subsequent

LENT
B benevolent, *E* excellent, equivalent, esculent, *FL* flatulent, flocculent, *FR* fraudulent, *I* indolent, insolent, *K* corpulent, *KW* querulent, *L* leant, lent, Lent, luculent, lutulent, *M* malevolent, muculent, *O* opulent, *P* pestilent, purulent, *PR* prevalent, *R* redolent, relent, *S* somnolent, succulent, *T* turbulent, *TR* truculent, *V* vinolent, violent, virulent

MENT
A abandonment, abolishment, admeasurement, admonishment, advertisement, affamishment, affranchisement, aggrandizement, acknowledgment, accomplishment, accouterment, aliment, ament, apportionment, arbitrament, argument, armament, astonishment, *B* babblement, banishment, battlement, bedevilment, bedizenment, beleaguerment, bemuddlement, betterment, bewilderment, botherment, BL blandishment, blazonment, blemishment, *BR* brabblement, *CH* chastisement, cherishment, *D* dazzlement, decrement, dement, demolishment, decipherment, detriment, development, devilment, diminishment, dimplement, disablement, disarmament, disfigurement, disfranchisement, discouragement, disparagement, dispiritment, distinguishment, divertissement, document, *E* excrement, experiment,

THE MÄDCHEN AND THE NAZI

A Mädchen met a Nazi,
  And said, "I will not heil.
It isn't hotsy-totsy,
  It's going out of style.
Today I'm feeling smoochy;
  I'm off to meet Il Duce;
We'll do the hoochy-koochy,
  And snuggle for awhile."

extinguishment, element, embarrassment, embattlement, embellishment, embezzlement, embitterment, emblazonment, embodiment, emolument, empanelment, enablement, endangerment, endeavorment, enfeeblement, enfranchisement, encompassment, encouragement, enlightenment, ennoblement, enravishment, entanglement, envelopment, environment, envisagement, establishment, *F* famishment, ferment, fibrocement, filament, firmament, foment, foremeant, fosterment, *FR* fragment, franchisement, *G* garnishment, government, *H* habiliment, harassment, hereditament, *I* impediment, imperilment, implement, impoverishment, imprisonment, increment, instrument, integument, inveiglement, *K* *comment*, complement, compliment, condiment, *L* lament, languishment, lavishment, ligament, lineament, liniment, *M* management, medicament, meant, merriment, measurement, monument, muniment, *N* nourishment, nutriment,

NENT

PENT
RENT

SENT

SKLENT
SPENT

SPRENT

STENT
TENT

O augment, ornament, *P* parliament, pediment, pesterment, punishment, *PR* prattlement, predicament, premonishment, presentiment, *R* ravishment, regiment, recrement, relinquishment, replenishment, revelment, rudiment, *S* sacrament, sediment, cement, sentiment, cerement, settlement, supplement, *T* tegument, temperament, tenement, testament, torment, tournament, *TR* tremblement, *U* unmeant, *V* vanishment, vanquishment, vehement, *W* wanderment, well-meant, wilderment, wonderment, worriment
A abstinent, anent, *E* eminent, *F* fornent, *I* immanent, imminent, impermanent, impertinent, incontinent, *K* continent, *P* permanent, pertinent, *PR* preeminent, prominent, *R* remanent, *S* supereminent, *TH* thereanent
pent, repent, unpent
afferent, belligerent, deferent, different, efferent, indifferent, irreverent, preferent, rent, reverent
A absent, accent, ascent, assent, *B* beneficent, *D* descent, dissent, docent, *H* heaven-sent, *I* innocent, *K* concent, consent, *M* magnificent, maleficent, missent, munificent, *P* percent, *R* re-sent, reticent, *S* cent, scent, sent, *U* unsent
sklent
forespent, misspent, overspent, spent, underspent, unspent, well-spent
besprent, sprent, unsprent
stent
A appetent, attent, *D* detent, discontent,

distent, *E* extent, *I* ignipotent, ill-content, impenitent, impotent, incompetent, intent, *K* competent, content, *M* malcontent, miscontent, *O* omnipotent, ostent, *P* penitent, *portent*, *PL* plenipotent, *T* tent, *U* untent, *W* well-content

VENT   *advent*, event, invent, non-event, prevent, circumvent, pseudo-event, *sirvente*, vent

WENT   overwent, underwent, went

ZENT   misrepresent, present, represent, resent

ĒNTH

GRĒNTH	greenth
TĒNTH	eighteenth, fifteenth, fourteenth (etc.)

ENTS

MENTS	accouterments
TENTS	contents, tents

(See **ENS**)

ĒNZ

GRĒNZ	greens
RĒNZ	smithereens
TĒNZ	teens

(See **ĒN,** add -*s* where appropriate.)

ENZ

ENZ	ens
BLENZ	*Coblenz*
JENZ	gens
LENZ	lens
SENZ	Vincennes

(See **EN,** add -*s* where appropriate.)

ĒP

BĒP	beep
BLĒP	bleep
CHĒP	cheap, cheep
DĒP	adeep, deep, down deep
GRĒP	la grippe

HĒP

HĒP	aheap, heap, *scrapheap*
JĒP	jeep
KĒP	keep, *upkeep*
KLĒP	clepe
KRĒP	creep
LĒP	leap, leep, outleap, overleap
NĒP	neap, neep
PĒP	Little Bopeep, peep
RĒP	cassareep, reap, rereap
SĒP	enseep, seep
SHĒP	sheep
SLĒP	asleep, beauty sleep, outsleep, oversleep, sleep, unasleep
SNĒP	sneap
STĒP	steep
SWĒP	chimneysweep, ensweep, clean sweep, *peesweep*, sweep, upsweep
TĒP	teap
THRĒP	threap, threep
TRĒP	estrepe
WĒP	beweep, outweep, *peesweep*, weep

EP

EP	Dieppe
HEP	hep, not hep
KEP	kep
PEP	pep
PREP	prep
REP	demirep, rep
SEP	cep
SHEP	shep
SHLEP	schlep
SKEP	skep
STEP	*D doorstep, F first step, footstep, giant step, I instep, K catstep, KW quickstep, M misstep, O overstep, S sidestep, ST stairstep, step, steppe, T two-step, W one-step*

EPS

SEPS	janiceps

(See **EP**, add -*s* where appropriate.)

ĒPT

BĒPT	beeped

(See **ĒP**, add -*ed* where appropriate.)

EPT

EPT	ept, inept
DEPT	adept
KEPT	kept, unkept
KLEPT	biblioklept, y-clept
KREPT	crept
LEPT	leapt, nympholept
NEPT	inept
PEPT	pepped
SEPT	accept, discept, except, incept, intercept, intussuscept, *concept, percept, precept, preconcept,* recept, sept, suscept, *transept*
SLEPT	slept
STEPT	stepped, unstepped
SWEPT	*backswept,* swept, unswept, *windswept*
THREPT	mammothrept
WEPT	wept, unwept

ĒR

(See ÎR)

ER

ER	err
HER	Herr
TER	parterre
YER	rivière, vivandière

(See ÂR)

ĒRD

(See ÎRD)

ĒRS

(See ÎRS)

ĒRZ

(See ÎRZ)

ĒS

ĒS	Thais
BĒS	obese
FLĒS	fleece
GĒS	geese
GRĒS	ambergris, degrease, grease, grece, Greece, verdigris
KRĒS	decrease, increase, crease, creese, kris, recrease, uncrease
LĒS	coulisse, lease, lis, pelisse, police, prelease, release, re-lease, sublease, valise
MĒS	semese
NĒS	nes, nese, Nice, niece
PĒS	*A* afterpiece, apiece, *B* battlepiece, *CH* chimneypiece, *E earpiece, endpiece, F fieldpiece,* fowling piece, *FR* frontispiece, *H hairpiece, I eyepiece, K codpiece,* cornerpiece, *KR crosspiece, crownpiece, M* mantelpiece, masterpiece, *mouthpiece, N* neckpiece, *O* altarpiece, *P* peace, piece, pocketpiece, *R* repiece, *S* centerpiece, *SH showpiece, T tailpiece, timepiece*
PRĒS	caprice
RĒS	cerise, reese
SĒS	decease, cassis, predecease, cease, surcease
TĒS	atis, métis
TRĒS	cantatrice

ES

(See also additional nouns made feminine by adding -*ess*, e.g., shepherdess, stewardess.)

ES	acquiesce, Es, s, SOS, quiesce
BES	bes, Bes, bouillabaisse
BLES	bless, noblesse, rebless, unbless
CHES	chess
DES	dess, frondesce, incandesce
DRES	*A* address, ambassadress, *D* diving dress, DR dress, *F* full dress, *G* gala dress, *H headdress, M* maladdress, *N nightdress, O* overdress, *R* readdress, redress, *sundress, U* underdress, undress
FES	fess, 'fess, fesse, confess, profess
GES	foreguess, guess, reguess
GRES	aggress, digress, *egress, ingress, congress,* regress, retrogress, transgress

HES	Hesse
JES	jess, largess, rejess, turgesce, unjess
KRES	accresce, cress, mustard cress, pennycress, water cress
KWES	deliquesce, liquesce
LES	coalesce, convalesce, less, nevertheless, nonetheless, obsolesce, opalesce, recalesce, reconvalesce, unless

(See appropriate nouns, add *-less:* e.g., blemishless, bodiless, etc.)

MES	intumesce, *kermes,* mess, tumesce
NES	baroness, Dungeness, evanesce, finesse, canoness, luminesce, nes, ness, Ness, pythoness, rejuvenesce

(See appropriate adjectives, add *-ness:* e.g. *fleetness, quickness,* beeriness, holiness, etc.)

PES	compesce, satrapess
PRES	decompress, depress, express, impress, compress, letterpress, oppress, press, recompress, repress, suppress, *winepress*
RES	archeress, duress, effloresce, fluoresce, phosphoresce, caress, manageress, votaress

(See also nouns ending in *r* made feminine by adding the suffix *-ess,* e.g., mayor*ess.*)

SES	*abscess, access,* assess, cess, excess, obsess, precess, *princess,* process, reassess, recess, sess, success
STRES	overstress, prestress, stress, understress
TES	giantess, poetess, politesse
TRES	ancestress, distress, editress, executress, idolatress, inheritress, comfortress, ministress, monitress, tress, *votress*
VES	effervesce
YES	yes
ZES	dispossess, possess, prepossess, repossess

ĒSH

BĒSH	babiche
FĒSH	affiche, fiche, microfiche, ultrafiche
KĒSH	quiche
LĒSH	leash, releash, unleash
MĒSH	miche
NĒSH	niche
RĒSH	nouveau riche
SNĒSH	sneesh
TĒSH	pastiche, postiche, potiche, *schottische*

ESH

BESH	bobêche, tête-bêche
FLESH	flesh, flèche, *horseflesh,* parfleche
FRESH	afresh, fresh, refresh, unfresh
KRESH	crèche
LESH	calèche
MESH	enmesh, mesh, syncromesh, unmesh
NESH	nesh
SESH	secesh
THRESH	rethresh, thresh

ESK

ESK	Junoesque, Kafkaesque, Rubensesque, statuesque
BESK	arabesque
DESK	desk, reading desk, writing desk
LESK	burlesque, naturalesque
NESK	Romanesque
RESK	barbaresque, humoresque, Moresque, picaresque, picturesque, plateresque, chivalresque, sculpturesque
TESK	blottesque, Dantesque, grotesque, gigantesque, soldatesque

ĒST

ĒST	east, northeast, southeast
BĒST	beast, hartebeest, wildebeest
DĒST	modiste
FĒST	*beanfeast,* feast, harvest feast, wedding feast
FLĒST	fleeced, unfleeced
GĒST	geest
GRĒST	greased, regreased, ungreased

JĒST	aubergiste
KĒST	keest
KRĒST	decreased, increased, recreased, uncreased
KWĒST	queest
LĒST	leased, least, overpoliced, policed, released, subleased, underpoliced, unleased
PĒST	pieced, piste, repieced
PRĒST	archpriest, priest, unpriest
SĒST	deceased, ceased
SNĒST	sneest
TĒST	artiste, batiste, teest
VĒST	arriviste
YĒST	yeast
ZHĒST	aubergiste

(See **ĒS,** add *-d* where appropriate.)

EST

EST	acquiesced, EST, SOS-ed, Trieste

(For the superlative degree of appropriate one- and two-syllable adjectives, add *-est,* e.g., *blackest,* prettiest.)

BEST	best, second-best
BLEST	blessed, blest, unblessed, unblest
BREST	abreast, *blackbreast,* breast, Brest, *redbreast,* unbreast
CHEST	chest
DEST	incandesced
DREST	addressed, dressed, overdressed, readdressed, redressed, underdressed, well-dressed, undressed, unredressed
FEST	disinfest, fessed, fest, *gabfest,* infest, confessed, counterfessed, manifest

GEST	guessed, guest, unguessed
GREST	digressed, progressed, regressed, retrogressed, transgressed
HEST	alkahest, behest, hest
JEST	almagest, beau geste, digest, egest, ingest, gest, geste, jest, congest, predigest, redigest, suggest
KREST	*firecrest, goldcrest,* increst, crest, undercrest
KWEST	acquest, bequest, deliquesced, *inquest,* quest, request
LEST	coalesced, convalesced, lest, molest, opalesced, recalesced, celeste
MEST	messed, unmessed
NEST	funeste, luminesced, nest
PEST	anapest, Budapest, impest, rinderpest, pest
PREST	*A* appressed, *D* depressed, *I* impressed, imprest, *K* compressed, *O* oppressed, *PR* pressed, *R* recompressed, repressed, *S* suppressed, *U* unimpressed, uncompressed, unpressed, unsuppressed
REST	*A armrest,* arrest, *B bookrest,* Bucharest, *D* disinterest, *E* effloresced, Everest, *F footrest,* phosphoresced, *FL* fluoresced, *H headrest, I* interest, *K* caressed, *N kniferest, O* au reste, *R* rest, wrest, *U* uninterested, uninterest, unrest
SEST	alceste, assessed, *incest,* obsessed, palimpsest, reassessed, recessed, cessed, unassessed
STREST	distressed, overstressed, prestressed, stressed, unstressed
TEST	attest, detest, contest, obtest, pretest, protest, retest, test
TREST	golden-tressed, raven-tressed, tressed, untressed
VEST	devest, divest, effervesced, invest, reinvest, revest, undervest, vest
WEST	Key West, midwest, northwest, southwest, west

YEST	yessed
ZEST	dispossessed, possessed, prepossessed, repossessed, self-possessed, unprepossessed, unpossessed, zest

(See **ES,** add *-d* or *-ed* where appropriate.)

ĒT

ĒT	eat, overeat, undereat
BĒT	beat, beet, *browbeat, deadbeat, downbeat, drumbeat, heartbeat, offbeat,* sugar beet, *upbeat*
BLĒT	bleat
CHĒT	cheat, cheet, escheat, recheat
FĒT	defeat, effete, feat, feet, Lafitte
FLĒT	fleet
FRĒT	afreet, freit
GLĒT	gleet
GRĒT	greet, congreet
HĒT	dead heat, heat, overheat, preheat, reheat, superheat, underheat, unheat
HWĒT	*buckwheat, wholewheat,* wheat
JĒT	exegete, munjeet, vegete
KĒT	keet, lorrikeet, mesquite, parakeet, polychaete, spirochete
KLĒT	cleat, cleete, paraclete
KRĒT	accrete, discreet, discrete, excrete, indiscreet, concrete, Crete, secrete
KWĒT	queet
LĒT	*athlete,* delete, elite, leat, leet, obsolete
MĒT	dead meat, *forcemeat,* fresh meat, gamete, *helpmeet,* meat, meet, mete, *mincemeat, pigmeat,* raw meat, *sweetmeat,* unmeet
NĒT	neat, proxenete
PĒT	compete, peat, repeat
PLĒT	deplete, incomplete, complete, pleat, replete, uncomplete
RĒT	afreet, marguerite, Masorete, terete
SĒT	*D* deceit, disseat, *I* inficete, *J* judgment seat,

	K catbird seat, conceit, county seat, country seat, *M* mercy seat, *PR* preconceit, *R* receipt, reseat, *S* cete, Cete, seat, self-deceit, self-conceit, *U* unseat
SHĒT	balance sheet, *broadsheet, dustsheet, foresheet, freesheet, groundsheet, clipsheet,* mainsheet, sheet, *slipsheet,* winding sheet
SKĒT	skeet, skete
SLĒT	sleet
STRĒT	*backstreet, bystreet, downstreet,* easy street, estreat, street, *upstreet*
SWĒT	bittersweet, bridal suite, honey-sweet, mansuete, meadowsweet, presidential suite, royal suite, sunnysweet, suite, sweet, unsweet
TĒT	petite, teat
THĒT	*aesthete,* thesmothete
TRĒT	Dutch treat, entreat, estreat, ill-treat, maltreat, mistreat, retreat, treat
TWĒT	tweet
VĒT	aquavit
WĒT	*peetweet,* weet
ZĒT	carte de visite

ET

ET	*A* ariette, *D* duet, *E* et, *H* historiette, *L* lariat, layette, *M* minuet, *O* oubliette, *P* pirouette, *S* serviette, silhouette, *ST* statuette, storiette, *W* winceyette
BET	abet, alphabet, barbette, bet, quodlibet, Tibet
BLET	blet
BRET	bret, soubrette, umbrette
DET	bidet, debt, indebt, judgment debt, cadet, muscadet, vedette
FET	estafette, fet, fète, mofette, *Tophet*
FLET	flet
FRET	fret, frett, frette, interfret
GET	baguet, baguette, beget, forget, get, misbeget, unget
GRET	aigrette, *egret,* regret, vinaigrette
HET	het
HWET	whet

JET	*fanjet,* jet, georgette, jumbo jet, *rainjet,* suffragette, turbojet	
KET	*B* banquette, *BL* blanquette, *BR* briquette, *D* diskette, *E* enquete, etiquette, *J* jockette, *K* casquette, ket, khet, coquet, coquette, *KR* croquette, *M* maquette, moquette, *P* paroket, piquet, *PL* plaquette, *R* Rockette, *SN* snackette, *T* tourniquet	
KWET	quet	
LET	*A* ailette, alette, amulet, *BR* briolette, *E* aiguillette, epaulet, *FL* flageolet, flannelette, *G* galette, *GL* globulet, *I* inlet, *K* cassolette, Colette, coverlet, *L* landaulet, let, Lett, *M* mantelet, *martlet,* medalet, *N* novelette, *O* omelet, oreillet, *outlet, R* rigolette, rivulet, rondolet, roulette, *S* sublet, *SK* squelette, *T* toilette, *TR* triolet, *V* violet, *Z* zonulet	
MET	allumette, fumette, calumet, *kismet,* met, Met, plumette, well-met	
NET	*A* alkanet, *B* ballonet, baronet, bassinet, bayonet, benet, bobbinet, burgonet, *BR* brunette, *D* dinette, *dragnet, F* falconet, *fishnet, H* hairnet, *J* genet, *K* canzonet, carcanet, castanet, kitchenette, cornet, coronet, *KL* clarinet, *L* lansquenet, lorgnette, luncheonette, lunette, *M* marionette, martinet, maisonette, midinette, mignonette, minionette, mosquito net, *N* net, nonet, *P* pianette, *R* remanet, *S* sarcenet, saxcornet, satinet, *SH* chansonette, *ST* stockinet, *T* tabinet, tournette, *V* vignette, villanette, *W* wagonette	
PET	parapet, pet, pipette, salopette	
PRET	mpret, pret	
RET	*A* amourette, anchoret, *B* bachelorette, banneret,	

	barrette, burette, *F* farmerette, formeret, *FL* fleurette, floweret, *I* imaret, *K* collaret, curet, curette, *L* lazaret, lenneret, leatherette, leveret, Launderette, *M* majorette, minaret, *P* Pierrette, pillaret, *R* ret, *S* cellaret, cigarette, solleret, *SH* chevrette, *SP* spinneret, *SW* swimmeret, *T* tabaret, taboret, *U* usherette	
SET	*A* anisette, *asset,* avocet, *B* backset, beset, *boneset, D* dancette, dead set, *deepset, F* facette, *farset,* film set, forset, fossette, photoset, *H* handset, headset, *I* illset, inset, interset, *K* cassette, *KR* crossette, crystal set, *KW* quickset, letterset, *M* marquisette, marmoset, *moonset,* musette, *O* offset, *onset, outset,* overset, *P* pincette, poussette, *R* reset, *S* salicet, set, sett, scilicet, somerset, Somerset, subset, *sunset, SH* sharp-set, chemisette, *SM* smart set, *T* typeset, *TH* thick-set, *U* underset, unset, upset, *V* videlicet	
SHET	brochette, flechette, fourchette, couchette, clochette, *planchet,* planchette, plushette, pochette, ricochet, shet, trebuchet	
SKET	sket	
STET	stet	
SWET	sweat	
TET	quartet, quintet, motet, octet, septet, sestet, sextet, tête-a-tête	
THET	epithet	
THRET	threat, triple threat	
TRET	tret	
VET	brevet, corvette, curvet, cuvette, minivet, olivet, revet, vet	
VYET	Viet	
WET	all wet, bewet, unwet, wet	
YET	lorgnette, nyet, oreillet, paillette, vignette, vilayet, yet, yette	
ZET	anisette, gazette, grisette, crepe suzette, marmoset,	

musette, noisette, rosette, chemisette

ĒTH

(th as in *with)*

ĒTH	ythe
HĒTH	heath
KWĒTH	bequeath
LĒTH	philalethe
NĒTH	beneath, neath, 'neath, underneath
SHĒTH	sheath
SNĒTH	sneath, sneeth
RĒTH	wreath
S̄HĒTH	sheath
TĒTH	*eyeteeth,* monteith, teeth

ĒTH

(th as in *this)*

BRĒTH	breathe, imbreathe, inbreathe, outbreathe
KWĒTH	bequeath, quethe
RĒTH	enwreathe, wreathe
SĒTH	seethe
SHĒTH	sheathe, ensheathe, unsheathe
SMĒTH	smeeth
TĒTH	teethe

ETH

(th as in *thin)*

ETH	eightieth, fiftieth, fortieth, ninetieth, seventieth, sixtieth, thirtieth, twentieth (etc.)
BETH	Macbeth
BRETH	breath
DETH	death, megadeath
LETH	shibboleth
PLETH	isopleth
SETH	saith, seth

(Archaic suffix *-eth* may be added to verbs.)

ĒTHD

BRĒTHD	breathed

(See **ĒTH,** add *-ed* where appropriate.)

ĒV

ĒV	eave, eve, Eve, Christmas Eve, naive,

	New Year's Eve, yestereve
BĒV	beeve
BRĒV	breve, semibreve
CHĒV	achieve, cheve, overachieve, underachieve
DĒV	deave, Khedive
GRĒV	aggrieve, greave, grieve, *Congreve*
HĒV	heave, upheave
KĒV	keeve
KLĒV	cleave, cleeve, cleve, uncleave
KWĒV	queeve
LĒV	believe, disbelieve, interleave, leave, lieve, make-believe, relieve, unbelieve
NĒV	nieve
PĒV	peeve
PRĒV	reprieve, unreprieve
RĒV	bereave, *portreeve*, reave, reeve, reve
SĒV	*A* apperceive, *D* deceive, *K* conceive, *M* misconceive, *P* perceive, *PR* preconceive, preperceive, *R* reconceive, reperceive, receive, *S* seave, *U* undeceive
SHĒV	sheave
SKRĒV	screeve
SLĒV	*shirtsleeve*, sleave, sleeve
STĒV	steeve
TĒV	recitative
THĒV	thieve
TRĒV	retrieve
VĒV	qui vive
WĒV	interweave, inweave, reweave, unweave, weave, we've

ĒVD

| CHĒVD | achieved |

(See **ĒV**, add *-d* where appropriate.)

ĒZ

ĒZ	ease, heartsease, unease
BĒZ	bise
BRĒZ	breeze, land breeze, sea breeze
CHĒZ	cheese, Big Cheese, head cheese, *nipcheese*, Swiss cheese (etc.)

DĒZ	antipodes, Atlantides, BVD's, galliardise, Hesperides, Caryatides, Maimonides, Pleiades, tiddledies, Eumenides
FĒZ	feaze, feeze
FLĒZ	fleas
FNĒZ	fnese
FRĒZ	antifreeze, enfreeze, freeze, frieze, nuclear freeze, cheval de frise, unfreeze
GĒZ	koksaghyz, Portuguese
GRĒZ	grease
HĒZ	heeze, he's
HWĒZ	wheeze
JĒZ	jeez
KĒZ	quais, keys, marquise
KLĒZ	Androcles, Damocles, Periclese
LĒZ	*B* Belize, Bengalese, *H* Hercules, *I* isosceles, *J* journalese, *K* cablese, *L* leas, lees, *M* Mephistopheles, *N* Nepalese, *S* Senegalese, Singhalese, *T* Tyrolese, *V* valise
MĒZ	acadamese, Annamese, Assamese, Burmese, demise, camise, mease, mise, remise, chemise, Siamese
NĒZ	*A* aborigines, Aragonese, *B* bee's knees, Bolognese, *CH* Chinese, *D* Diogenes, *H* Havanese, *J* Japanese, Javanese, *K* Cantonese, chersonese, *M* manganese, Milanese, *N* knees, neese, neeze, nese, *P* pekinese, Pekinese, Pyrenees, Polonese, *V* Veronese, Viennese
PĒZ	appease, peas, pease, trapeze
PLĒZ	displease, please
PRĒZ	imprese
RĒZ	computerese, congeries, Navarrese, reeze, cerise, suburbes
SĒZ	*A* analyses, antitheses, assise, *D* disseize, *H* hypothesese, *I* interstices, *P* periphrases, *R* reseize, *S* seas, sees, seize, syntheses, *V* vortices
SKWĒZ	squeeze
SLĒZ	sleaze

SNĒZ	sneeze
PLĒZ	displease, pleas, please
TĒZ	betise, D. T.'s, Maltese, tease, Socrates, sottise
THĒZ	these
TWĒZ	tweeze
VĒZ	Genevese
WĒZ	weeze
ZĒZ	disease

(See **Ē**, add *-s* where appropriate.)

EZ

EZ	Suez
FEZ	fez
MEZ	*kermes*
NEZ	knez
PREZ	prez
REZ	Juarez
SEZ	écossaise, says, sez
TEZ	Cortes
YEZ	yez

ĒZD

| LĒZD | lesed |

(See **ĒZ**, add *-d* where appropriate.)

EZH

BEZH	beige
NEZH	manège
REZH	barège
TEZH	cortege

Ī

| Ī | *B bigeye*, bindy-eye, *buckeye*, *BL* black eye, blind eye, *D* dead-eye, *E* eagle eye, evil eye, *F fish-eye*, *FR frog-eye*, *G* goldeneye, *goldeye*, *H* Helvetii, *I* ai, ay, aye, eye, I, aye-aye, *J* genii, *K* cat's eye, *cockeye*, *M* mooneye, *N* naked eye, nuclei, *O* oxeye, *P* peepeye, pink-eye, *PR* private eye, *R* radii, *red-eye*, *S sock-eye*, *SH* shiai, *sheep's-eye*, *shut-eye*, *T tiger's-eye*, *W* walleye, weather eye |
| BĪ | *A* alibi, *B* buy, by, bye, by-and-by, bye-bye, by-the-by, *F flyby*, forby, |

foreby, *G go-by*, goodbye, *H* hereby, hushaby, *HW* whereby, *I* incubi, *L* lullaby, *N* nearby, *O* overbuy, *P* passerby, *R rabbi*, rockaby, *S* syllabi, succubi, *ST standby*, stander-by, *TH* thereby, *U* underbuy

BLĪ bly

DĪ ao dai, bedye, die, dye, do-or-die, overdye, redye, sine die, undye

DRĪ adry, dry, high-and-dry

FĪ *A* acrify, alacrify, alkalify, acetify, acidify, amplify, angelify, Anglify, arefy, argufy, *B* basify, beatify, *BR* brutify, *CH* churchify, *D* daintify, damnify, dandify, defy, dehumanify, deify, declassify, demystify, demythify, demulsify, denazify, detoxify, diabolify, dignify, disqualify, dissatisfy, diversify, divinify, dulcify, duplify, *E* edify, exemplify, electrify, emulsify, esterify, *F* falsify, fie, fie-fie, phi, fortify, *FR* Frenchify, fructify, *G* gasify, *GL* glorify, *GR* gratify, *H hi-fi,* horrify, humanify, humidify, humify, *I* identify, indemnify, intensify, interstratify, *J* jellify, gentrify, jollify, justify, *K* calcify, carnify, casefy, codify, cockneyfy, chondrify, *KL* clarify, classify, *KR* crucify, *KW* qualify, quantify, *L* labefy, ladyfy, lapidify, lenify, lignify, liquefy, lubrify, *M* madefy, magnify, matrify, micrify, minify, mystify, mythify, modify, mollify, mortify, mummify, mundify, *N* Nazify, nidify, nigrify, nitrify, notify, nullify, *O* objectify, obstupefy, aurify, ossify, oversimplify, *P* pacify, personify, petrify, pinguefy, purify, putrefy, *PL* planefy, *PR* preachify, presignify, prettify, *R* ramify, rarefy, ratify, reify, regentrify, rectify,

remodify, reunify, revivify, rigidify, rubify, *S* saccharify, saxify, salify, salsify, sanctify, sanguify, sanify, saponify, satisfy, certify, sci-fi, signify, syllabify, simplify, citify, solemnify, solidify, subjectify, *SF* spherify, *SK* scarify, scorify, *SP* speechify, specify, *ST* steelify, stellify, stiltify, stultify, stupefy, *STR* stratify, *T* tabefy, tepefy, terrify, testify, typify, torpify, torrefy, tumefy, *TR* transmogrify, *U* uglify, *V* verify, versify, vilify, vitrify, vivify, *Y* unify

FLĪ *B* bobfly, botfly, butterfly, *BL* blackfly, blowfly, *D* damselfly, dobsonfly, *DR* dragonfly, *F* firefly, *FL* fly, *G* gadfly, gallfly, *GR* greenfly, *H* horsefly, housefly, *K* catchfly, *M* Mayfly, *O* outfly, overfly, *S* sandfly, *SH* shoofly, *U* underfly

FRĪ french fry, fry, small fry

GĪ assegai, fall guy, *gilgai, gilguy*, guy, *nilgei*, wise guy

GWĪ Paraguay, Uruguay

HĪ heigh, hi, hie, high, knee-high, on a high, riding high, shanghai, Shanghai, sky-high, ultrahigh

HWĪ why, kowhai

JĪ anthropophagi

KĪ akaakai, *bronchi, haikai,* chi, rocaille

KLĪ cly

KRĪ decry, descry, cry, outcry

LĪ *A* alkali, ally, antalkali, *B* belie, *D* disally, *F* forlie, *H* jai alai, *J* July, *K* quillai, *L* lapis lazuli, lazuli, lie, lye, Lorelei, *M* misally, mislie, *O* outlie, overlie, *R* re-ally, rely, *U* underlie, *V* vox populi

MĪ demi, demy, haeremai, my

NĪ *alumnae, alumni,* Anno Domini, decani, deny, Gemini, nigh, nye, redeny, termini

PĪ apple pie, blackberry pie, espy, humble pie, *magpie,* mince pie, *nanpie,* occupy, peach pie, pi, pie, *porkpie, potpie,* preoccupy, sea pie,

shoofly pie, umble pie (etc.)

PLĪ apply, imply, comply, misapply, multiply, oversupply, ply, reply, supply, undersupply

PRĪ pry, repry

RĪ awry, caravanserai, wry, rye, samurai, serai

SHĪ *cockshy,* shy, unshy, *workshy*

SĪ assai, prophesy, psi, scye, sigh, Versailles

SKĪ *bluesky,* blue sky, ensky, cloudy sky, sky, Skye

SKRĪ descry, scry

SLĪ sly

SNĪ sny, snye

SPĪ bespy, counterspy, spatrify, spy, weatherspy

SPRĪ spry, unspry

STĪ *pigsty,* sty

THĪ thigh, thy

SWĪ swy

TĪ *bowtie, hogtie, necktie,* tie, Thai, untie

TRĪ atry, retry, try

VĪ outvie, vie

WĪ wye, Y

ĪB

BĪB imbibe

BRĪB bribe

JĪB gibe, gybe, jibe

KĪB kibe

SKRĪB *A* ascribe, *D* describe, *E* escribe, *I* inscribe, interscribe, *K* conscribe, *P* perscribe, *PR* prescribe, proscribe, *S* circumscribe, subscribe, superscribe, *SKR* scribe, *TR* transcribe

TRĪB diatribe, tribe

VĪB vibe

IB

BIB bib, bibb

CHIB chib

DIB dib

DRIB drib

FIB fib

GIB gib

GLIB glib

JIB jib

KRIB *corncrib,* crib

KWIB quib

LIB ad lib, gay lib, lib, women's lib

NIB	nib
RIB	*midrib, sparerib,* rib
SIB	sib
SKWIB	squib
SNIB	snib

ĪBD

BĪBD	imbibed

(See **ĪB**, add *-d* where appropriate.)

IBD

RIBD	rock-ribbed

(See **IB**, add *-bed* where appropriate.)

ĪBZ

VĪBZ	vibes

(See **ĪB**, add *-s* where appropriate.)

IBZ

DIBZ	dibs, my dibs, your dibs
NIBZ	his nibs, nibs

(See **IB**, add *-s* where appropriate.)

ICH

ICH	itch
BICH	bitch, sonofabitch
BRICH	britch
DICH	ditch
FICH	fitch
FLICH	flitch
GLICH	glitch
HICH	hitch, unhitch
HWICH	which
KICH	kitsch
KWICH	quitch
LICH	lich
MICH	miche, mitch
NICH	niche
PICH	overpitch, pitch
RICH	enrich, rich, unrich
SICH	sich
SKICH	skitch
SKRICH	scritch
SMICH	smritch
SNICH	snitch
STICH	*backstitch, chainstitch,* featherstitch, *hemstitch,*

	whipstitch, catstitch, restitch, saddlestitch, *seamstitch,* stitch, unstitch
SWICH	switch, unswitch
TWICH	twitch
VICH	czarevitch
WICH	bewitch, witch

ICHT

ICHT	itched

(See **ICH**, add *-ed* where appropriate.)

ĪD

ĪD	*A* almond-eyed, Argus-eyed, *B* buck-eyed, *BL* black-eyed, blear-eyed, blue-eyed, *BR* bright-eyed, brown-eyed, *D* dioxide, *dove-eyed, dull-eyed, E* eagle-eyed, evil-eyed, *F full-eyed, G* goggle-eyed, *GR* green-eyed, *H* hazel-eyed, hawk-eyed, *I* eyed, I'd, ide, *K* calf-eyed, cat-eyed, cockeyed, *KL* clear-eyed, *KR* crosseyed, *L* lynx-eyed, *M* meek-eyed, misty-eyed, *monoxide, N* narrow-eyed, *O* ox-eyed, *oxide,* open-eyed, oroide, *owl-eyed, P* pale-eyed, peroxide, pie-eyed, pink-eyed, pop-eyed, *R* red-eyed, round-eyed, *S* soft-eyed, *SKW* squint-eyed, *SL* slant-eyed, sloe-eyed, *SN* snake-eyed, *W* wide-eyed, wall-eyed, *Y* yellow-eyed
BĪD	abide, bide, *carbide*
BRĪD	bride, child bride
CHĪD	chide
DĪD	died, dyed, double-dyed, iodide, redyed, *tie-dyed,* undyed
DRĪD	*anhydride,* dried, dryed, *hydride,* overdried, redried, underdried, undried
FĪD	*B* beatified, bona fide, beautified, *D* defied, deified, decalcified, dignified, dissatisfied, *disulfide,* diversified, dulcified, *E* edified, electrified, emulsified, *F* fortified, *phosfide, FR* fructified, *GL* glorified, *GR*

gratified, *I* identified, intensified, *J* justified, *K* confide, countrified, *KL* classified, *KR* crucified, *KW* qualified, *L* liquefied, *M* magnified, mystified, modified, mollified, mortified, *N* notified, nullified, *O* ossified, overqualified, *P* pacified, petrified, purified, putrefied, *R* rarefied, ratified, rectified, revivified, *S* sanctified, saponified, satisfied, self-satisfied, certified, citified, solidified, *sulphide, SK* scarified, scorified, *SP* specified, *ST* stultified, stupefied, *STR* stratified, *T* tepefied, terrified, testified, torrefied, tumefied, *TR trisulfide, U* (prefix *un* to obtain negative of appropriate words in the FĪD category—unbeatified, unbeautified, etc.), *V* versified, vitrified, vivified

FRĪD	fried, refried, unfried
GĪD	guide, guyed, misguide, *waveguide*
GLĪD	glide
GRĪD	gride
HĪD	aldehyde, acetaldehyde, benzaldehyde, formaldehyde, hide, hied, *horsehide, cowhide, oxhide, rawhide nuclide,* ophicleide
KLĪD	decried, cried
KRĪD	acetanilide, acetylide, allied, belied, *bolide,* elide, collide, lied, misallied, unallied, unbelied
LĪD	
MĪD	bromide, nicotinamide, polyamide, cyanimide, sodamide, sulphanilamide, sulphonamide, tolbutamide
NĪD	actinide, arsenide, denied, ferrocyanide, isocyanide, lanthanide, nide, platinocyanide, cyanide, uranide
PĪD	occupied, pied, preoccupied, unoccupied
PLĪD	applied, misapplied, multiplied, reapplied, replied, supplied, unapplied, unsupplied
PRĪD	pride, self-pride

RĪD   A arride, B boride, D deride, *dichloride, dioxide,* disaccharide, deuteride, *FL* fluoride, *H* hydrochloride, *KL* chloride, *M* monosaccharide, *N* night-ride, *nitride, O* outride, override, *R* ride, *S* saccharide, *T* telluride, *tetrachloride, TR* trichloride, trisaccharide, *Y* ureide

SĪD   A aborticide, acaricide, algicide, alongside, aside, *B backside,* bactericide, Barmecide, *bedside,* beside, biocide, *BL* blindside, blind side, *BR* broadside, brookside, D decide, deicide, dimethysulphoxide, *diopside,* dissatisfied, *downside, E* ecocide, excide, *epoxide, ethoxide, F* felicide, feticide, filicide, *fireside, foreside,* fungicide, *FL* flip side, *FR* fratricide, *GL* glycoside, glucoside, *H* herbicide, heroicide, herpicide, Heaviside, *hillside, hydroxide, hydrosulphide,* homicide, *I* infanticide, insecticide, inside, ironside, *J* genocide, germicide, giganticide, *K quayside,* coincide, countryside, *L* lakeside, lapicide, larvicide, liberticide, *M* magnicide, Merseyside, *methoxide,* miticide, *monoxide,* monstricide, mountainside, multicide, *N nearside,* nematocide, *nightside,* nucleoside, *O* oxide, oceanside, offside, onside, autocide, outside, override, *P* parasiticide, parenticide, parricide, patricide, *peroxide,* pesticide, piscicide, Port Said, *PR* prophesied, prolecide, *R* regicide, reprophesied, *ringside,* riverside, rodenticide, *S seaside,* cephalocide, side, silicide, silverside, sororicide, subside, cervicide, suicide, *superoxide, SL* slickenside, *SP* spermicide, *ST*

stateside, stillicide, *T* taeniacide, tyrannicide, *topside, TR* trioxide, uxoricide, underside, unprophesied, *upside, V* vaticide, verbicide, vermicide, vulpicide, *W* waterside, *wayside,* weatherside

SKRĪD   descried, escried, scride, scried, undescried

SLĪD   *backslide, landslide,* slide

SNĪD   snide

SPĪD   espied, spied, respied, unspied

STRĪD   astride, bestride, outstride, stride

TĪD   A Ascensciontide, B Bartholomewtide, betide, *D dispeptide, E* Eastertide, *ebbtide,* Embertide, eventide, *F* phosphatide, *FL* flood tide, *H* Hallowtide, high tide, *HW* Whitsuntide, *KR* Christmastide, *L* Lammastide, lee tide, low tide, *M mercaptide,* Michaelmastide, morning tide, *N* neap tide, noon tide, nucleotide, Allhallowtide, *P* Passiontide, *peptide,* polynucleotide, polypeptide, *R* retied, *riptide, SH* Shrovetide, *SP springtide, T* tide, tied, *TW* Twelfthtide, *U* unbetide, undertied, untied, *W* weathertide, *Y* Yuletide

TRĪD   *nitride,* tried, untried, well-tried

VĪD   divide, provide, redivide, reprovide, subdivide

WĪD   countrywide, nationwide, citywide, statewide, wide, worldwide

ZĪD   *azide,* chlorothiazide, preside, reside

(See **Ī,** change *-y* to *-ied* or add *-d* where appropriate.)

ID

ID   id
BID   bid, forbid, outbid, overbid, rebid, unbid, underbid, unforbid
BRID colubrid

CHID chid
DID   athodyd, did, katydid, outdid, overdid, pyralidid, undid
DRID Madrid
FID   *aphid, bifid,* fid, quadrifid, multifid, *trifid*
GID   gid
GRID grid
HID   hid, rehid, unhid
HWID whid
KID   kid
KWID quid, tertium quid
LID   annelid, invalid, *eyelid,* lid
MID   amid, mid, pyramid
NID   hominid, prehominid, serranid, cyprinid
PID   elapid
RID   rid
SID   Cid
SKID askid, skid, *tailskid*
SKWID squid
SLID slid
STRID strid
THRID thrid, unthrid
TID   hydatid, chromatid, spermatid, tid
TRID eupatrid
VID   *kid-vid*

ĪDZ

ĪDZ   Ides
SĪDZ besides, insides, Ironsides, slickensides, sobersides

(See **ĪD,** add *-s* where appropriate.)

ĪF

FĪF   fife
KĪF   kife
LĪF   afterlife, half-life, *highlife,* larger-than-life, *nightlife,* life, pro-life, *still-life, wildlife*
NĪF   bowie knife, *drawknife, jackknife, claspknife,* knife, paperknife, *penknife,* pocketknife, steak knife

---

NOEL, NOEL

Virgin Mary, meek and mum,
Dominus is in thy tum.
What a jolly *jeu d'ésprit*—
Christ beneath the Christmas tree!

RĪF	rife, *wakerife*
STRĪF	*loosestrife*, strife
WĪF	*alewife, fishwife, goodwife, housewife, lairwife, midwife, oldwife*, puddingwife, sweetiewife, wife

IF

IF	if
BIF	biff
CHIF	handkerchief, neckerchief
DIF	diff
FIF	pfiff
GLIF	anaglyph, gliff, glyph, hieroglyph, lithoglyph, petroglyph
GRIF	griff, griffe, griph, hippogriff, logogriph
HWIF	whiff
JIF	jiff
KIF	kif
KLIF	cliff, undercliff
KWIF	quiff
MIF	miff
NIF	niff
PIF	piff
RIF	eriff, *midriff*, Rif, riff, Tenerife
SIF	Sif
SKIF	skiff
SNIF	sniff
SPIF	spiff
STIF	bindle stiff, lucky stiff, stiff
TIF	positif, tiff
WIF	wiff
ZIF	ziff

IFS

ZIFS	ziffs

(See **IF,** add -s where appropriate.)

IFT

BIFT	biffed
DRIFT	adrift, drift, *snowdrift, spindrift, spoondrift*
GIFT	gift
HWIFT	whiffed
KLIFT	cliffed
LIFT	*airlift*, heli-lift, lift, ski lift, topping lift, uplift
MIFT	miffed
RIFT	rift
SHIFT	*gearshift, makeshift*, shift
SHRIFT	*festschrift*, short shrift, shrift, spiegelschrift
SIFT	resift, sift

SKWIFT	squiffed, unsquiffed
SNIFT	sniffed
SPIFFED	spiffed
SWIFT	chimney swift, swift, Tom Swift
TIFT	tift
THRIFT	*spendthrift*, thrift

(See **IF,** add -ed where appropriate.)

IG

BIG	big, bigg, Mr. Big
BRIG	brig, brigg
DIG	dig, infra dig, *shindig*
FIG	fig, honey fig, caprifig
FRIG	frig, Frigg
GIG	*fishgig, fizgig*, gig, whirligig
GRIG	grig
HWIG	whig, Whig
JIG	jig, majig, rejig, thingamajig
KRIG	crig
NIG	nig, renege
PIG	*bushpig*, guinea pig, male chauvinist pig, pig
PRIG	prig
RIG	outrig, rig, wrig, thimblerig, unrig
SIG	cig
SNIG	snig
SPIG	spig
SPRIG	sprig
SWIG	swig
THIG	thig
TIG	tig, tyg
TRIG	trig
TWIG	twig
WIG	bewig, *bigwig, earwig*, whirliwig, periwig, wig
ZIG	zig

IGD

RIGD	full-rigged, jury-rigged, square-rigged

(See **IG,** add -ged where appropriate.)

IGZ

DIGZ	digs

(See **IG,** add -s where appropriate.)

IJ

IJ	acreage, ferriage, foliage, *image*, lineage, verbiage, *voyage*

BRIJ	abridge, bridge, rebridge, unbridge
DIJ	brigandage
FIJ	fidge
FRIJ	saxifrage
LIJ	*D* diallage, *E* ensilage, *F* fortilage, *K* cartilage, curtilage, *M* mucilage, *P* pupilage, *PR* privilege, *S* sortilage, *T* tutelage, *V* vassalage
MIJ	*image*, midge, pilgrimage
NIJ	*A* alienage, appanage, *B* badinage, baronage, *E* espionage, *G* gallonage, *K* commonage, concubinage, *M* matronage, *N* nidge, *O* orphanage, *P* parsonage, patronage, peonage, personage, *S* siphonage, *V* villeinage, vicinage
PIJ	equipage
RIJ	*A* acreage, anchorage, average, *B* beverage, *BR* brokerage, *F* foliage, fosterage, *FL* flowerage, *H* harborage, hemorrhage, *K* Coleridge, cooperage, coverage, *KW* quarterage, *L* leverage, lineage, *O* overage, *P* pastorage, pasturage, pilferage, porterage, *PL* plunderage, *R* ridge, *S* cellarage, seigneurage, sewerage, *T* telpherage, tutorage, *U* upridge, *V* vicarage, *W* waterage
SIJ	surplusage
SKWIJ	squidge
SMIJ	smidge
TIJ	agiotage, armitage, heritage, hermitage, hospitage, clientage, parentage, pilotage
TRIJ	arbitrage

(Words in which a penultimate stressed syllable is followed by -age—*drayage* or *assemblage*, for instance—may be rhymed with -ij by shifting the accent to the last syllable, but in most instances the result is shameful. I have omitted such words here.)

ĪK

ĪK	Van Eyk
BĪK	bike, minibike, motorbike
DĪK	dike, dyke, *Klondike*, Vandyke, Vandyck
FĪK	fike, fyke

GRĪK	grike
HĪK	haik, Haikh, hike, *hitchhike*
KĪK	kike
LĪK	*A alike, antlike, apelike, B* belike, *beelike,* businesslike, *BR* brotherlike, *CH childlike,* *D deathlike,* dislike, *doglike, DR dreamlike, G* godlike, ghostlike, *GL* glasslike, *H hairlike,* homelike, husbandlike, *J* gemlike, *K catlike,* kinglike, *KR Christlike,* *KW queenlike, L ladylike,* lifelike, like, lookalike, *M* maidenlike, *manlike,* mislike, *P peasantlike,* piglike, *R ratlike, S* seedlike, swordlike, suchlike, susulike, *SH* sheeplike, *SN snakelike,* *SP sportsmanlike, ST* starlike, *SW swanlike, U* unalike, unlike, *W warlike,* wifelike, winglike, womanlike (etc.)
MĪK	mike
PĪK	boardingpike, *garpike,* pike, pyke, *turnpike*
RĪK	Reich
SHRĪK	shrike
SĪK	psych, sike
SPĪK	*handspike,* marlinspike, spike
STRĪK	strike, *ten-strike*
TĪK	tyke
TRĪK	trike

IK

IK	ich, ick, ik, ichthyic
BIK	Arabic, *iambic*
BRIK	*airbrick,* brick, *firebrick,* red-brick
CHIK	allocochick, chic, chick, *dabchick,* holluschick, *peachick*
DIK	benedick, Benedick, dick, *dik-dik, sandik*
FLIK	flick, *skin-flick*
HIK	hic, hick
KIK	kick, *sidekick, trochaic*
KLIK	click, click-click
KRIK	creek, crick
KWIK	doublequick, quick
LIK	*bootlick, dactylic,* Catholic, *cowlick,* lick, *relic*
MIK	*comic,* mick

NIK	arsenic, kinnikinnick, nick, *eugenic*
PIK	handpick, *nutpick,* pic, pick, *toothpick,* Waterpick
PRIK	pinprick, prick
RIK	*A archbishopric, B* bishopric, *H hayrick, K* choleric, *L limerick, M* maverick, *PL plethoric, R* rhetoric, rick, wrick, *SH* chivalric, *T tumeric,* turmeric
SHRIK	schrik
SHTIK	shtick, schtick
SIK	*A airsick, BR brainsick, H* heartsick, homesick, *K* carsick, *L landsick,* lovesick, *M moonsick, S* seasick, sic, sick, *SP* spacesick

---

LET US WONDER, WHILE WE LOITER

Let us wonder, while we loiter,
Which of us will die of goiter;
Which of stone or dysentery;
Which of rheum or beriberi;
Which of grippe or diarrhea,
Nettle rash, or pyorrhea;
Which of us turn turvy topsy,
Victim of paretic dropsy.
Be it pox or whooping cough,
Something's bound to bear us off.
All we know is, we're in trouble:
Barman, make my next one double.

SLIK	slick
SNIK	snick
SPIK	spick
STIK	*B bestick, BR broomstick, CH chapstick, chopstick, D* dipstick, *DR drumstick, F* fiddlestick, *GR greenstick, K candlestick, L lipstick, M matchstick, metestick, maulstick, monostich, N* knobstick, nonstick, *P* pentastich, *pigstick, S* singlestick, *swordstick, SL* slapstick, *ST stich,* stick, swizzle stick, *T telestich,* tetrastich, *U unstick, W* walkingstick, *Y yardstick*
STRIK	strick
THIK	thick
TIK	*anapestic,* arithmetic, heretic, impolitic, cosmopolitic, lunatic, politic, ricky-tick, tic, tick, *triptych*
TRIK	dirty trick, gastrotrich, *metric,* overtrick, trick, undertrick

VIK	Old Vic, Reykjavik
WIK	bailiwick, *Brunswick,* candlewick, *lampwick, Warwick,* wick

IKS

FIKS	*A adfix, affix, antefix, F* fix, *I infix, K confix, KR* crucifix, *KW quick fix, P* postfix, *PR prefix,* pre-fix, *R refix, S suffix,* superfix, *TR transfix*
LIKS	prolix
MIKS	admix, immix, intermix, commix, mix, overmix, undermix
NIKS	acronyx, nix, Nyx
PIKS	picks, pix, pyx
RIKS	apteryx, archaeopterics, rix, Vercingetorix
SIKS	eighty-six, six, ninety-six (etc.)
STIKS	*chopsticks,* fiddlesticks, Styx
TRIKS	*aviatrix,* dirty tricks, executrix, inheritrix, cicatrix

(See **IK**, add *-s* where appropriate.)

IKST

TWIKST	betwixt, 'twixt

(See **IKS**, add *-ed* where appropriate.)

IKT

DIKT	addict, benedict, *edict,* interdict, contradict, maledict, predict
FLIKT	afflict, inflict, conflict
LIKT	delict, derelict, *relict*
MIKT	apomict
PIKT	depict, Pict
STRIKT	astrict, derestrict, constrict, overstrict, restrict, strict, understrict
VIKT	evict, convict

(See **IK**, add *-ed* where appropriate.)

ĪL

ĪL	aisle, I'll, isle
BĪL	atrabile, bile
CHĪL	chile

DĪL   *aedile,* crocodile, merdaille

FĪL   *A* Anglophile, *B*
            bibliophile, *D* defile,
            demophile, discophile, *E*
            aelurophile, eosinnophile,
            ergophile, *F* file, photofile,
            FR Francophile, *G*
            Gallophile, gastrophile, *H*
            halophile, hippophile,
            homophile, *I* Italophile, *J*
            Japanophile,
            Germanophile,
            gynotikolobomassophile,
            M myrmecophile,
            mesophile, *N* nailfile,
            Negrophile, *O* audiophile,
            P paper file, paedophile,
            pyrophile, *PR profile, R*
            refile, rheophile,
            Russophile, *S* psychophile,
            psychrophile, cinephile,
            single file, *SL* Slavophile,
            SP spermophile, *T*
            typophile, Turkophile, *TH*
            theophile, thermophile, *Z*
            xenophile, Zionophile,
            zoophile

GĪL   beguile, guile, gyle

HĪL   heil

HWĪL   awhile, erewhile,
            erstwhile, meanwhile,
            otherwhile, somewhile,
            therewhile, while,
            worthwhile

KĪL   kyle

LĪL   Carlisle, lisle

MĪL   camomile, mile

NĪL   enisle, campanile,
            juvenile, Nile, *senile*

PĪL   aeolipile, micropyle,
            compile, pile, recompile,
            repile, *stockpile,*
            thermopile, unpile,
            woodpile, up-pile, voltaic
            pile

RĪL   puerile, rile

SĪL   domicile, ensile, exile,
            reconcile, sile

SMĪL   smile

SPĪL   spile

STĪL   *A* amphiprostyle, *D*
            decastyle, diastyle,
            dodecastyle, *E* epistyle, *FR*
            freestyle, H hairstyle,
            hypostyle, *L* life style, *M*
            menostyle, *P* pentastyle,
            peristyle, polystyle, *R*
            restyle, *S* cyclostyle, *ST*
            stile, style, *T turnstile, Y*
            urostyle

TĪL   *F fertile, futile, H hostile, I*
            infantile, *J gentile, M*

            mercantile, *P* pulsatile, *R*
            reptile, rutile, S saxatile,
            septile, T tile, *V* versatile,
            vibratile, volatile

TRĪL   acrylonitrile

VĪL   revile, vile

WĪL   weil, wile

ZĪL   *exile,* resile

(See ĪAL)

IL

IL   ill

BIL   *B* bill, *boatbill, BL*
            blackbill, bluebill, BR
            broadbill, brownbill, D
            deshabille, dishabille,
            dollar bill, *duckbill, H*
            handbill, hawksbill,
            hornbill, KR cranesbill,
            crossbill, PL playbill, R
            razorbill, *redbill, wrybill,*
            SH shoebill, *shortbill, SP*
            spoonbill, ST storksbill,
            TH thornbill, *TW* twibil, *W*
            waxbill, waybill, Y
            yellowbill

BRIL   brill

CHIL   chil, chill

DIL   daffodil, dill, cacodyl,
            piccadill, spadille

DRIL   drill, escadrille, espadrille,
            quadrille, *mandrill*

FIL   *A* Anglophil, *D* demophil,
            E eosinnophil, *F* fill,
            phytophil, fulfil, fulfill, *KL*
            cladophyll, chlorophyll,
            monophyll, *N* neutrophil,
            O overfill, *R* refill, *SKL*
            sclerophyll, *SP* sporophyll,
            U underfill, unfill, *Z*
            xanthophyll

FRIL   befrill, frill

GIL   gill, *bluegill, scrodgill*

GRIL   grill, grille

HIL   *anthill,* downhill, *dunghill,*
            foothill, hill, *molehill,*
            uphill

JIL   aspergill, gill, jill

KIL   kil, kill, kiln, limekiln,
            rekill, winterkill

KWIL   quill

LIL   li'l, lill

MIL   De Mille, *flourmill,*
            gristmill, mil, powdermill,
            cement mill, *sawmill,*
            steelmill, treadmill,
            watermill, *windmill*

NIL   juvenile, manille, nil,
            thionyl, uranyl

PIL   minipill, morning-after
            pill, pill

PRIL   prill

RIL   puerile, rill

SHIL   shill

SHRIL   shrill

SIL   domicile, *doorsill,*
            groundsill, headsill,
            imbecile, codicil, sill,
            verticil, windowsill

SKIL   skill

SKWIL   squill

SPIL   overspill, spill

STIL   bestill, instill, reinstill,
            standstill, still, stock-still

SWIL   *pigswill,* swill

THIL   thill

THRIL   enthrill, thrill

TIL   *A* acetyl, *D* distill, *I*
            infantile, intertill, *K* coutil,
            M mercantile, *O* overtill, *P*
            pastille, pulsatile, *R* retill,
            T 'til, till, tormentil, *TH*
            thereuntil, *U* until, untill,
            V versatile, vibratile,
            volatile

TRIL   trill

TWIL   'twill, twill

VIL   Amityville, *dullsville,*
            Evansville, Louisville,
            Oysterville, Seville (etc.),
            vill, ville, vaudeville

VRIL   vrille

WIL   free will, goodwill,
            whippoorwill, ill will,
            poorwill, self-will, will

ZIL   Brazil, frazil, zill

ILCH

FILCH   filch

MILCH   milch

PILCH   pilch

ZILCH   zilch

ĪLD

CHĪLD   brain child, child, childe,
            flower child, foster child,
            godchild, grandchild,
            lovechild, manchild,
            unchild

FĪLD   defiled, enfiled, filed,
            profiled, refiled, undefiled,
            unfiled

MĪLD   mild

WĪLD   hog wild, wild, Wilde

(See ĪL, add -*d* where appropriate.)

ILD

BILD	build, jerry-build, rebuild, unbilled, unbuild, upbuild
GILD	begild, gild, guild, octogild, regild, ungild, *wergild*
HILD	*Brunhild*
WILD	self-willed, strong-willed, unwilled, weak-willed, willed

(See **IL,** add *-ed* where appropriate.)

ILK

ILK	ilk
BILK	bilk
HWILK	whilk
MILK	milk
SILK	silk

ILS

GRILS	grilse

(See **ILT,** add *-s* where appropriate.)

ILT

BILT	built, frigate-built, jerry-built, clinker-built, clipper-built, rebuilt, unbuilt, Vanderbilt, well-built
GILT	begilt, gilt, guilt, regilt, ungilt
HILT	hilt
JILT	jilt, rejilt
KILT	kilt
KWILT	quilt, requilt
LILT	lilt
MILT	milt
SILT	silt, resilt, unsilt
SPILT	respilt, spilt, unspilt
STILT	stilt
TILT	retilt, tilt, untilt, uptilt
WILT	wilt

ILTH

ILTH	illth
FILTH	filth
SPILTH	spilth
TILTH	tilth

ĪLZ

HWĪLZ	erewhiles

(See **ĪL,** add *-s* where appropriate.)

ĪM

ĪM	I'm
BLĪM	sublime
CHĪM	chime, rechime
DĪM	dime, disme, nickel-and-dime, paradigm
GĪM	gime
GRĪM	begrime, grime
KĪM	isocheim, chyme, mesenchyme
KLĪM	climb, clime, upclimb
KRĪM	crime
LĪM	belime, *birdlime, brooklime, quicklime,* lime, Lyme
MĪM	mime, pantomime
PRĪM	overprime, prime, underprime
RĪM	berhyme, rhyme, rime
SĪM	cyme, sime
SLĪM	beslime, slime
TĪM	*A aforetime,* aftertime, *B bedtime,* betime, *BR breathing time, D daytime,* downtime, *E eaning time,* eating time, *F foretime, full-time, H halftime,* harvest time, haying time, *L lifetime, longtime, M maritime, meantime, midtime,* mistime, *N nighttime, noontime, O* overtime, *P pairing time, part-time, pastime, peacetime, PL playtime, PR prime time, R ragtime, S seedtime, sometime,* summertime, suppertime, *SP springtime, T thyme,* time, *two-time, U* undertime, *W wintertime, Y yeaning time*
ZĪM	*enzyme, co-enzyme,* lysozyme

IM

IM	Ephraim
BIM	bim, cherubim
BRIM	brim, *broadbrim*
CHIM	chimb
DIM	bedim, dim, Hasidim, paradigm
DRIM	Sanhedrim
FIM	seraphim
FRIM	frim
GLIM	glim
GRIM	grim, Grimm, grimme
HIM	him, hymn
HWIM	whim
JIM	gym
KRIM	crim
KWIM	quim
LIM	dislimb, dislimn, enlimn, *forelimb,* limb, limn, prelim
MIM	mim
NIM	*A* aconym, acronym, allonym, ananym, anonym, anthroponym, antonym, *E* eponym, exonym, *H* heteronym, homonym, *M* metonym, *N* nim, nimb, *O* ormonym, *S* synonym, pseudonym, *T* toponym, *U* undernim
PRIM	prim
RIM	borborygm, interim, *corymb,* rim
SHIM	shim
SKIM	skim
SKRIM	scrim
SLIM	slim
SWIM	swim
TIM	Tiny Tim
TRIM	betrim, retrim, trim, untrim
VIM	vim
ZIM	zimb

ĪMD

CHĪMD	chimed

(See **ĪM,** add *-d* where appropriate.)

IMD

BRIMD	brimmed

(See **IM,** add *-med* where appropriate.)

IMF

LIMF	endolymph, lymph
NIMF	nymph, paranymph, sea nymph, water nymph, wood nymph

IMP

IMP	imp
BLIMP	blimp
CHIMP	chimp
GIMP	gimp
GRIMP	grimp
JIMP	jimp
KRIMP	crimp

LIMP	limp
MIMP	mimp
PIMP	pimp
PLIMP	plimp
PRIMP	primp
SHRIMP	shrimp
SIMP	simp
SKIMP	skimp
SKRIMP	scrimp
TIMP	tymp
WIMP	wimp

IMPS

GLIMPS	glimpse

(See **IMP,** add -s where appropriate.)

ĪMZ

TĪMZ	betimes, oftentimes, *off-times,* oft-times, sometimes

(See **ĪM,** add -s where appropriate.)

ĪN

ĪN	eyn
BĪN	bine, cannabine, carabine, *carbine,* columbine, combine, concubine, *Sabine, turbine, woodbine*
BRĪN	brine, colubrine

PESSIMISM

(The mysterious celestial entities called quasars are receding at 90% of the speed of light.)

I saw quasars in the night
Leaving at the speed of light.
Why so hurried fared they?
Something must have scared they.

CHĪN	chine
DĪN	*A* alcidine, almandine, anodine, aerodyne, *D* dine, dyne, *H* heterodyne, *hirundine, I* indign, incarnadine, *K* kadein, condign, *M* muscadine, *N nundine, P* paludine, *S* celandine
FĪN	affine, define, fine, confine, refine, superfine, trephine
HWĪN	whine
JĪN	jine

KĪN	kine
KLĪN	decline, disincline, incline, monocline, recline
KRĪN	crine, volucrine
KWĪN	*equine*
LĪN	*A* align, *airline,* aquiline, alkaline, antalkaline, acervuline, *B baseline, beeline,* berylline, *byline, bowline,* borderline, bottom line, *D dateline, deadline,* dyaline, disalign, *F feline,* figuline, *fishline, FR* fringilline, *G guideline, H hairline, headline, hemline,* hyaline, *I* induline, inquiline, interline, *K* caballine, *carline, cauline,* coraline, *coastline, KL clothesline, KR crossline,* crystalline, *L lifeline,* limicoline, line, *loadline, M* malign, metalline, *moline,* musteline, *N neckline, O* opaline, *outline, P* penduline, petaline, *pipeline, R* realign, *red-line, S saline,* sepaline, sibyline, *sideline,* suilline, *SH shoreline, SK skyline, SN snowline, STR streamline, T tapeline,* timberline, *towline, touchline,* tump-line, tourmaline, *TR tramline, U* underline, unline, *V* vituline, *W waistline,* waterline, *Z* zibeline
MĪN	*D damine, G* gold mine, *I* intermine, *K* calamine, calcimine, *carmine,* countermine, *M* mine, *P* powdermine, *S* sycamine, *U* undermine
NĪN	*A* Apennine, asinine, *B* benign, *E* eburnine, *F* falconine, Fescennine, *K canine, KW quinine, L* leonine, *N* nine, *P* pavonine, *R ranine, S* saturnine, ciconine, *U* unbenign
PĪN	*A Alpine, E* elapine, *L lupine, O* opine, *P* pine, porcupine, *PR* Proserpine, *R* repine, resupine, *S* cisalpine, subalpine, supine, *U* unsupine, *V vespine, vulpine*
RĪN	*A* adulterine, anserine, azurine, *D* dirhine, *E*

---

	estuarine, extrauterine, *F ferine,* intrauterine, *K caprine,* catarrhine, *L* lemurine, leporine, *M* mesorhine, monorhine, *murrhine, P* passerine, piperine, *PL platyrrhine, R* Rhine, riverine, *S* saccharine, sapphirine, satyrine, sciurine, *cedrine,* turnverein, *V viperine,* viverrine, vulturine, *W* wolverine, *Y* uterine
SHĪN	ashine, beshine, Gegenschein, monkeyshine, *moonshine,* outshine, *sunshine,* shine, *shoeshine, starshine*
SHRĪN	enshrine, shrine
SĪN	*A* assign, *E* ensign, *F phocine, H* havercine, hystricine, *hircine, I* insigne, *K* calcine, consign, co-sign, *cosine,* countersign, *L* limacine, *O* auld lang syne, omphacine, *P piscine, porcine, R* reconsign, *S* sign, sine, syne, tsine, *sinsyne,* psittacine, soricine, subsign, *TH* thylacine, *U* undersign, *ursine*
SPĪN	spine
SPLĪN	spline
STĪN	*Einstein, Epstein,* Eisenstein, Frankenstein, Hammerstein, Liechtenstein, Rubinstein, stein, styan, Wittgenstein
STRĪN	strine
SWĪN	Gadarene swine, swine
THĪN	hyacinthine, labyrinthine, thine
TĪN	*A* adamantine, agatine, amethystine, anatine, argentine, Argentine, *B* Byzantine, *BR* brigantine, *D* diamantine, *E* eglantine, elephantine, *F* Philistine, *FL* Florentine, *I* infantine, *K* Constantine, *L* lacertine, Levantine, libertine, *M* matutine, *P* palatine, Palestine, *S* serotine, serpentine, *cisplatine, T* tine, Tyne, turpentine, *TR* transpontine, Tridentine, *V* valentine, vespertine
TRĪN	accipitrine, trine
TWĪN	disentwine, entwine, intertwine, overtwine, retwine, twine, untwine

VĪN   aberdevine, *bovine*, divine, *grapevine*, keelivine, *ovine*, provine, *cervine*, subdivine, vine

WĪN   apple wine, brandywine, cherry wine, dandelion wine, Essenwein, May wine, red wine, white wine, wine

ZĪN   design, Auld Lang Syne, lang syne, redesign, resign

IN

IN   Bedouin, benzoin, fibroin, heroin, heroine, herein, wherein, whipper-in, in, inn, genuine, caffeine, all-in, therein, within

BIN   *B* been, bin, *dustbin*, *GL* globin, *H hasbeen*, *hemoglobin*, *J* jacobin, Jacobin, *K* carabine, colobin

BRIN   brin, *fibrin*

CHIN   chin, tchin, Capuchin, matachin

DIN   *Aladdin*, almandine, amidin, din, *hirundine*, incarnadine, codeine, *morindin*, muscadine, *Odin*, paladin

DRIN   Benzedrine, ephedrin, Sanhedrin

FIN   *B bowfin*, *BL blackfin*, *D dauphin*, dolphin, *E elfin*, *F* fin, Finn, *M* Mickey Finn, *P paraffin*, *R ragamuffin*, *redfin*, *THR threadfin*

GIN   begin

GLIN   glin

GRIN   agrin, grin, Lohengrin, peregrine

HWIN   whin

JIN   *engine*, gin, gyn, jin, *margin*, origin, tchin, *virgin*, waringin

KIN   *A* akin, *B* baldachin, billikin, birdikin, bodikin, *bodkin*, baldachin, bootikin, *buskin*, *BL bloodkin*, *D dunnakin*, *F finikin*, *GR grimalkin*, *K* cannikin, *catkin*, kilderkin, kin, *L lambkin*, lambrequin, larrikin, *M* manikin, mannequin, minikin, *N napkin*, nipperkin, *P pannikin*, Pekin, *R* ramekin, *S sooterkin*, *SP spilikin*

KRIN   crin

KWIN   *Algonquin*, harlequin, quin, lambrequin

LIN   *A* adrenaline, aquiline, alkaline, amygdalin, analine, *B* bandoline, berlin, Berlin, botulin, *CH* chamberlain, *chaplain*, *DR drumlin*, *E* encephalin, *F* folliculin, formalin, *FR* francolin, *G* Ghibbeline, gobelin, Gobelin, *GL* globuline, *H* hyaline, *I* immunoglobulin, insulin, *J* javelin, *K caballine*, kaolin, capelin, capeline, *carline*, *cauline*, *colin*, *collin*, *colline*, coralline, cuculine, *KR* crinoline, crystalline, crotaline, *L* lanoline, lin, linn, lupulin, *M mafflin*, mandolin, *N* noradrenaline, *O* opaline, *P petaline*, porcelain, *R* ravelin, *S cephaline*, syballine, cipolin, *SH* chevaline, *T* ptyaline, tourmaline, *U* Ursuline, *V* vaseline, violin, *Z* zeppelin

MIN   *A albumin*, amphetamine, antihystamine, arsphenamine, *B* Benjamin, *H* Ho Chi Minh, *I illumine*, *J* jessamine, *M* maximin, Min, *PR* provitamin, *S* sycamine, *TH* thiamine, *V* Vietminh, vitamin

NIN   agglutinin, feminine, *legnine*, Lenin, melanin, mezzanine, pavonine, *rennin*, *tannin*

PIN   *A* atropine, *B* belaying pin, *breastpin*, *CH* chinkapin, chinquapin, *H hairpin*, *hatpin*, *I inchpin*, *K* calepin, *kingpin*, *KR crankpin*, *L lapin*, *linchpin*, *N* ninepin, *P* pin, *pippin*, *pushpin*, *R* repin, *S* safety pin, *SK* sculpin, *ST stickpin*, *T* tenpin, terrapin, *tiepin*, *TH* thoroughpin, *U* underpin, unpin, *W* wankapin

PLIN   discipline, indiscipline

RIN   *A* adulterine, alizarin, anserine, aspirin, aventurine, *B* bacterin, *E* elaterin, *F* fiorin, *G* gorgerin, *GL* glycerine, *H* heparin, *K* corinne,

coumarin, culverin, *L* luciferin, *M* mandarin, margarine, muscarine, *N* nectarine, nitroglycerin, *P* porphyrin, *S* sapphirine, saccharine, Sanhedrin, sovereign, suberin, *T* tamarin, tambourin, Turin, *V* viperine, vulturine, *W* warfarin

SHIN   Capuchin, shin

SIN   *D* damassin, *K* characin, kerasine, *KL* clavecin, *M* moccasin, mortal sin, *O* omphacine, *R* re-sin, *S* sin, *SP* spassadin, *T* tocsin, toxin, *U* unsin, *W* Wisconsin

SKIN   *B bearskin*, *buckskin*, *D deerskin*, *doeskin*, *foreskin*, *K calfskin*, *kidskin*, *L lambskin*, *M moleskin*, *O oilskin*, *P pigskin*, *R redskin*, reskin, *Rumpelstiltskin*, *S sealskin*, *SH sharkskin*, *sheepskin*, *SK scarfskin*, skin, *SN snakeskin*, *T tigerskin*, *U onionskin* (etc.)

SPIN   *backspin*, respin, *sidespin*, spin, *tailspin*, *topspin*

THIN   *absinthin*, *absinthine*, lecithin, sympathin, thick-and-thin, thin

TIN   *A agatine*, argentine, *asbestine*, astatine, *B* Byzantine, bulletin, *F* Philistine, *FL* Florentine, *I* infantine, *intestine*, *J* gelatin, *K* keratin, *KR* chromatin, *KW* quercitin, *L* libertine, *N* nicotine, *P* palmatin, *PR* precipitin, *R* Rasputin, *T* tin, *TR* travertine, *V* vespertine

TRIN   *alabastrine, alpestrine*

TWIN   twin

VIN   alevin, Angevin

WIN   win

YIN   yang and yin, yin

ZIN   *rosin*

INCH

INCH   half-inch, inch, quarter-inch

CHINCH   chinch

DINCH   dinch

FINCH   *bullfinch, chaffinch*, fallow finch, finch, *goldfinch*, *grassfinch, greatfinch*, greenfinch, hawfinch, redfinch

FLINCH	flinch
KINCH	kinch
KLINCH	clinch, unclinch
PINCH	bepinch, pinch
SINCH	recinch, cinch, uncinch
SKWINCH	squinch
WINCH	winch

ĪND

BĪND	bearbind, bind, inbind, cowbind, rebind, spellbind, unbind, underbind, upbind
BLĪND	blind, half-blind, color-blind, purblind, sandblind, snowblind, unblind
FĪND	affined, find, refind, refined, unrefined
GRĪND	greasy grind, grind, regrind
HĪND	ahind, behind, hind
KĪND	gavelkind, humankind, kind, mankind, unkind, womankind
KLĪND	enclined, inclined
LĪND	aligned, lined, nonaligned, realigned, relined, streamlined, unaligned, unlined
MĪND	mastermind, mind, remind
RĪND	rind, rynd
SĪND	re-signed, signed, undersigned, unsigned
TWĪND	intertwined, twined, untwined
WĪND	enwind, overwind, rewind, unwind, upwind, wind
ZĪND	resigned, unresigned

(See **ĪN,** add -d where appropriate.)

IND

IND	Ind
FIND	finned
KIND	wunderkind
LIND	lind, lynde
RIND	tamarind
SIND	abscind, exscind, prescind, rescind, sind
SKIND	reskinned, skinned, thick-skinned, thin-skinned, unskinned
TIND	retinned, tinned, untinned
WIND	downwind, east wind, forewind, headwind, whirlwind, crosswind, north wind, solar wind, south wind, stormwind, tailwind, upwind, west wind, woodwind, wind

(See **IN,** add -ed where appropriate.)

ING

ING	A arguing, B bandying, bellowing, bellringing, burying, billowing, busying, bullying, BL blarneying, CH churchgoing, D dallying, dairying, dishallowing, E echoing, elbowing, embodying, empitying, emptying, envying, F fancying, farrowing, following, falsifying, foregoing, foreshadowing, FL flurrying, H hallowing, harrowing, horseshoeing, HW whinnying, I ing, ingrowing, issuing, J jollying, journeying, K candying, carrying, continuing, copying, curtsying, KW querying, quarrying, quartering, L lazying, lobbying, M marrying, monkeying, mudslinging, N narrowing, O ongoing, outgoing, overshadowing, P parrying, partying, pitying, puttying, R rallying, rescuing, S sallying, seagoing, sightseeing, soothsaying, sorrowing, SH shadowing, SW swallowing, T tallying, tarrying, toadying, U undervaluing, unpitying, upbringing, V valuing, varying, volleying, W wearying, wellbeing, winnowing, worrying, Y yellowing (etc.)
BING	bing
BRING	bring
CHING	ching, Ching
DING	ding, forwarding, freestanding, garlanding, hazarding, heralding, jeoparding, outstanding, placarding, scaffolding, shepherding, smallholding, wingding
FING	triumphing
FLING	fling, refling

GING	ging
JING	CH challenging, D damaging, discouraging, disparaging, E encouraging, envisaging, F foraging, M managing, mismanaging, P pillaging, R ravaging, S savaging, SK scavenging, V voyaging
KING	A a la king, B barracking, beking, BR breathtaking, DR dressmaking, E earthshaking, F fairy king, finicking, H heartbreaking, housebreaking, K king, M mafficking, N Nanking, painstaking, pigsticking, sea king, sleepwalking, unking, trafficking
KLING	cling, recling
LING	A appareling, atheling, B barreling, bedeviling, bepummeling, beveling, bitterling, CH changeling, channeling, chiseling, chitterling, D daughterling, dialing, ding-a-ling, dueling, dukeling, DR driveling, E easterling, enameling, entrameling, F fingerling, fosterling, G gamboling, GR graveling, groveling, grueling, H hosteling, K canceling, caroling, caviling, cudgeling, KW quarreling, L labeling, leveling, libeling, ling, M marshaling, marveling, modeling, N naveling, O outrivaling, P paneling, pedaling, penciling, R reveling, rivaling, SN sniveling, SP spiraling, ST stenciling, STR stripling, T tasseling, tingaling, tinseling, toweling, tunneling, TR traveling, U underling, unraveling, unrivaling, wassailing
MING	daydreaming, Ming, slumming
NING	A abandoning, actioning, awakening, B bargaining, betokening, burdening, BL blackening, blazoning, BR broadening, CH chastening, D darkening, deadening, deafening, destining, determining, E examining, emblazoning, emboldening,

enheartening, envisaging, *evening*, F fashioning, fastening, fattening, foretokening, *FR* freshening, G gammoning, gardening, *GL* gladdening, *H* happening, hardening, heartening, hastening, *I* imagining, imprisoning, ironing, *K* cannoning, compassioning, conditioning, cautioning, *KR* christening, *KW* questioning, *L* lessening, ling, listening, livening, *M* maddening, mentioning, moistening, *O* auctioning, omening, opening, overburdening, *P* pardoning, passioning, pensioning, *PR* predestining, *R* rationing, ravening, reckoning, reasoning, roughening, *S* saddening, sanctioning, seasoning, sickening, softening, *SL* slackening, *SM* smartening, *ST* stationing, stiffening, *STR* strengthening, *SW* sweetening, *T* toughening, *TH* thickening, *THR* threatening, *U* unreasoning, *V* visioning, *W* wakening, wantoning, weakening, widening

PING bookkeeping, galloping, housekeeping, larruping, ping, Peiping, *piping*, showjumping, walloping, worshiping

RING *A* altering, angering, answering, armoring, ashlaring, *B* badgering, bantering, barbering, battering, beflattering, beggaring, belaboring, beleaguering, belecturing, bepowdering, bescattering, beslabbering, beslobbering, *besmearing*, bespattering, bewildering, bickering, bolstering, butchering, *bullring, BL* blathering, blistering, blithering, blubbering, blundering, blustering, *CH* chartering, chattering, cheeseparing, *D* deciphering, differing, dickering, disfavoring, dishonoring, displeasuring,

dissevering, doddering doctoring, dowering, *E* enamoring, enharboring, encumbering, enring, entering, *F* factoring, faltering, favoring, featuring, festering, feathering, *financing*, fingering, forgathering, *forgetting*, furnishing, furthering, *FL* flattering, flavoring, flickering, flittering, flowering, flustering, fluttering, *FR* fracturing, *G* gathering, guttering, *GL* glimmering, glittering, glowering, *H* hammering, hampering, hankering, harboring, hollering, hovering, humoring, hungering, *HW* whimpering, whispering, *I* indenturing, incumbering, *J* jabbering, gesturing, *K* cankering, cantering, capering, capturing, catering, cockering, coloring, conjecturing, conjuring, conquering, considering, covering, cowering, culturing, cumbering, *KL* clambering, clamoring, clattering, clustering, cluttering, *KW* quavering, quivering, quartering, *L* layering, laboring, lacquering, lathering, latticing, lecturing, lettering, liquoring, lingering, littering, long-suffering, lowering, lumbering, *M* manufacturing, martyring, meandering, measuring, mirroring, motoring, mouthwatering, murdering, murmuring, mustering, mothering, muttering, *N* neighboring, numbering, *O* offering, auguring, occasioning, opening, ordering, outnumbering, overmastering, overpowering, overtowering, *P* pampering, pandering, pattering, perishing, perjuring, pestering, picturing, pilfering, paltering, pondering, posturing, pottering,

powering, puttering, *PL* plastering, pleasuring, plundering, *PR* promising, prospering, *R* rapturing, recovering, remembering, rendering, ring, wring, roistering, rubbering, rupturing, *S* savoring, *seafaring*, seal ring, self-catering, centering, severing, ciphering, signet ring, silvering, simmering, simpering, sistering, soldering, solacing, soldiering, suffering, summering, sundering, *SH* shattering, sheepraising, sheepshearing, shimmering, shivering, shouldering, showering, shuddering, sugaring, shuttering, *SK* scampering, scattering, *SL* slandering, slobbering, slaughtering, slumbering, *SM* smattering, smoldering, *SP* spattering, *SPL* spluttering, *ST* staggering, stammering, stuttering, *SW* sweltering, *T* tampering, tapering, tempering, timbering, tittering, tottering, towering, *TH* thundering, *U* unflattering, unfaltering, unmurmuring, unremembering, unslumbering, unwandering, unwavering, upholstering, ushering, uttering, *V* vaporing, venturing, *W* wandering, wavering, weathering, westering, wintering, woolgathering, wondering, watering

SHING *A* admonishing accomplishing, astonishing, *B* banishing, burnishing, *BL* blandishing, blemishing, *BR* brandishing, brattishing, *D* diminishing, disestablishing, distinguishing, *E* embarrassing, embellishing, enravishing, establishing, *F* famishing, finishing, furnishing, *FL* flourishing, *G* garnishing, conveyancing, *L* languishing, lavishing, *N* nourishing, *P* perishing,

SING polishing, publishing, punishing, *R* ravishing, rubbishing, *T* tarnishing, *U* unperishing, *V* vanishing, vanquishing, varnishing *B* balancing, besing, buttressing, *E* embarrassing, *F* focussing, *H* harassing, *K* canvassing, conveyancing, *KL* climaxing, *KR* Christmasing, *L* latticing, *M* menacing, *O* outbalancing, overbalancing, *P* purchasing, purposing, *PR* practicing, promising, *S* sing, singh, Sing-Sing, *U* unpromising, *W* witnessing

SLING sling, unsling

SPRING *A* aspring, *dayspring*, *DR* driving spring, *H* *handspring*, *hairspring*, *headspring*, *L* *lifespring*, *M* *mainspring*, *O* *offspring*, *S* silent spring, *SPR* spring, *W* weeping spring, *watchspring*

STING afforesting, ballasting, breakfasting, foresting, harvesting, sting

STRING *bowstring*, string

SWING *beeswing*, full swing, swing

THING anything, everything, *plaything*

TING *B* balloting, bonneting, buffeting, *BL* blanketing, *BR* bracketing, *D* dieting, discrediting, dispiriting, disquieting, distributing, *E* exhibiting, *F* fagoting, fidgeting, forfeiting, *I* inhabiting, inheriting, inhibiting, inspiriting, *J* junketing, *K* carpeting, comforting, contributing, coveting, *KR* crediting, *KW* quieting, *L* limiting, *M* marketing, meriting, *O* auditing, *P* patenting, picketing, *PR* prohibiting, *R* racketing, riveting, *S* surfeiting, *SP* spiriting, spirketing, *T* ting, *U* unmeriting, *V* velveting, visiting

WING angel wing, *batwing*, bird wing, eagle wing, *forewing*, gull wing, hawk wing, *clearwing*, *lapwing*, *lacewing*, *redwing*, underwing, unwing, waxwing, wing

ZING stargazing, zing (and present participles of appropriate verbs ending in the sound of *z*)

(You may always add -*ing* to verbs ending in an unstressed syllable to make a masculine rhyme. If -*ing* is added to a verb ending in a stressed syllable, it is technically possible to make a masculine rhyme by shifting the stress to the -*ing*. Such forced rhymes should be italicized in this list, and are seldom felicitous.)

INGD

DINGD dinged
KINGD bekinged, kinged, unkinged
LINGD tingalinged
PINGD pinged
RINGD enringed, ringed, unringed
STRINGD restringed, stringed, unstringed
WINGD angel-winged, *bird-winged*, eagle-winged, *hawk-winged* (etc.), unwinged, winged
ZINGD zinged

INGK

INGK ink, Inc.
BLINGK blink, *iceblink*, *snowblink*
BRINGK brink
CHINGK chink
DINGK dink, rinky-dink
DRINGK drink, strong drink
FINGK fink, *ratfink*
GINGK gink
GLINGK glink
JINGK jink, perjink
KINGK kink
KLINGK clink
KWINGK quink
LINGK bobolink, enlink, interlink, link, Maeterlinck, relink, unlink
MINGK mink
PINGK meadowpink, pink, *pincpinc*, sea pink
PLINGK plink
PRINGK prink
RINGK oxyrhynch, rink
SHRINGK shrink
SINGK countersink, cinque, sink
SKINGK skink
SLINGK slink
SPINGK spink
STINGK stink
SWINGK swink
THINGK bethink, doublethink, forethink, outthink, rethink, think
TINGK tink
TRINGK trink
TWINGK twink
WINGK chewink, *hoodwink*, jinnywink, tiddlywink, wink
ZINGK zinc

INGKS

JINGKS high jinks, jinx
LINGKS links, lynx
MINGKS minx
PINGKS *salpinx*
SFINGKS androsphinx, hieracosphinx, criosphinx, sphinx
THINGKS methinks, thinks
WINGKS pilliwinks, tiddlywinks

(See **INGK,** add -*s* where appropriate.)

INGKT

INGKT inked, reinked, uninked
SINGKT discinct, *precinct*, succinct
STINGKT instinct
TINGKT distinct, extinct, indistinct, tinct

(See **INGK,** add -*ed* where appropriate.)

INGZ

STRINGZ apron strings, leading strings, strings

(See **ING,** add -*s* where appropriate.)

INJ

BINJ binge
DINJ dinge
FRINJ befringe, fringe, infringe
HINJ hinge, rehinge, unhinge
HWINJ whinge
KRINJ cringe
PINJ impinge
RINJ syringe
SINJ singe
SKRINJ scringe
SPRINJ springe

STRINJ	astringe, constringe, obstringe, perstringe
SWINJ	swinge
TINJ	attinge, tinge
TWINJ	atwinge, twinge

INJD

FRINJD	befringed

(See **INJ**, add -d where appropriate.)

INS

BLINS	blintz
CHINS	chinse, chintz
KWINS	quince
MINS	mince
PRINS	Black Prince, fairy prince, frog prince, merchant prince, prince, student prince, unprince
RINS	rinse, rerinse, unrinse
SINS	since
VINS	evince, convince
WINS	wince

(See **INT**, add -s where appropriate.)

ĪNT

HĪNT	ahint, behint
JĪNT	jint
PĪNT	half pint, cuckoopint, pint

INT

BINT	bint
DINT	dint
FLINT	flint, *gunflint, skinflint*
GLINT	glint
HINT	hint
JINT	septuagint
KWINT	quint
LINT	lint
MINT	*horsemint*, calamint, *catmint*, calamint, mint, peppermint, sodamint, *spearmint*
PRINT	*BL blueprint, F fingerprint, footprint, H hoofprint, I* imprint, *M microprint,* misprint, *N newsprint, O offprint, P* palm print, *S* surprint, *TH thumbprint, U* unprint, *V voiceprint, W woodprint*
SKWINT	asquint, squint

SPLINT	splint, resplint, unsplint
SPRINT	sprint, resprint
STINT	stint
SWINT	suint
TINT	aquatint, mezzotint, monotint, tint
VINT	vint

INTH

BINTH	terebinth
MINTH	*helminth*
PLINTH	plinth
RINTH	*Corinth*, labyrinth
SINTH	*absinthe*, hyacinth, colocynth

ĪNTS

HĪNTS	Heinz
JĪNTS	jints
PĪNTS	*halfpints*, pints

INTS

BLINTS	blintz
PRINTS	prince, prints

(See **INS**; see **INT**, add -s where appropriate.)

ĪNZ

NĪNZ	Apennines, baseball nines, nines

(See **ĪN**, add -s where appropriate.)

INZ

KINZ	ods bodikins, spoffokins
KWINZ	quinse
SHINZ	shins, widdershins, withershins
SKINZ	*buckskins, moleskins*
PINS	candlepins, *ninepins*, pins, *tenpins*
WINZ	winze

(See **IN**, add -s where appropriate.)

ĪP

BLĪP	blype
GRĪP	gripe
HĪP	hipe, hype

KĪP	kipe
KLĪP	clype
PĪP	*B bagpipe, BL blowpipe, D downpipe, DR drainpipe, H hornpipe, hawsepipe, I* Indian pipe, *L liripipe, P* Panpipe, pitchpipe, pipe, *ST standpipe, stovepipe, T* tailpipe, *W windpipe*

My mother used to encourage the young people of our village to continue their education. One paid her a visit years later to say thanks. "If it hadn't been for you," he told her, "I would never have known the importance of pronouncination."

PRONOUNCINATION SEPARATES THE HOMINID* FROM THE HOMINOID⁺

The hominid avoids
Saying 'woids'
When he means 'words.'
Saying 'woids' for 'words'
Is for the birds
(Not the 'boids'),
And for hominoids
(Not hominids—
Unless the hominids
Are on the skids.)

* Man.
⁺ Manlike, but not man.

RĪP	dead ripe, overripe, *rareripe*, ripe, underripe, unripe
SLĪP	slype
SNĪP	guttersnipe, *jacksnipe*, snipe
STĪP	stipe
STRĪP	pinstripe, restripe, stripe, unstripe
SWĪP	*sideswipe*, swipe
TĪP	*A antitype, archetype, B biotype, D daguerrotype, E ectype,* electrotype, *F* phenotype, phototype, *GR* graphotype, *H heliotype,* holotype, *J genotype, K* karyotype, collotype, countertype, *L* linotype, logotype, *M* megatype, monotype, *O autotype, PR* prototype, *R* retype, cyanotype, somatotype, *subtype, ST* stereotype, *T* teletype, *tintype,* type
TRĪP	tripe
WĪP	prewipe, rewipe, unwipe, wipe, wype

IP

BIP	bip
BLIP	blip

CHIP	chip
DIP	dip, redip
DRIP	adrip, drip
FLIP	flip, sherry flip
GIP	gip
GRIP	grip, grippe, *handgrip, hairgrip*
HIP	hip, hyp, *rosehip*
HWIP	*bullwhip, horsewhip, coachwhip*, whip
JIP	gip, gyp
KIP	kip
KLIP	clip, reclip, inclip, unclip
KWIP	equip, quip, reequip
LIP	fat lip, *harelip*, lip, underlip, upper lip
NIP	*catnip*, nip, pogonip
PIP	apple pip, pip
RIP	rip, unrip
SHIP	*A* administratorship, agentship, acquaintanceship, *amidship*, apprenticeship, *airship, heirship*, archonship, *B* babyship, bachelorship, battleship, *CH* chairmanship, championship, chancellorship, chaplainship, chieftainship, churchmanship, *D* deaconship, demonship, *DR* draughtsmanship, *E* eldership, electorship, emperorship, ensignship, *F* farmership, fathership, fellowship, *fireship, FL* flagship, *FR* friendship, *G* guardianship, good-fellowship, governorship, *H* hardship, headship, *J* generalship, jockeyship, *judgeship*, justiceship, *K* cardinalship, *kingship, kinship*, collectorship, commandership, companionship, comradeship, consortship, consulship, controllership, copartnership, *courtship*, cousinship, *KL clanship, KR* craftsmanship, creatorship, *KW queenship*, questorship, *L* ladyship, leadership, legislatorship, lectureship, librarianship, *lightship, longship, lordship, M* mayorship, marksmanship, marshalship, mastership, membership, Messiahship, *midship, N* neighborship,

noviceship, *O* aldermanship, authorship, ownership, *P* paintership, partisanship, partnership, pastorship, penmanship, *PR* praetorship, preachership, prelateship, probationship, professorship, proprietorship, *R* rajahship, wranglership, rangership, readership, regentship, recordership, rectorship, relationship, reship, *S* sailingship, *saintship*, secretaryship, sextonship, seamanship, censorship, *sibship*, citizenship, sizarship, swordsmanship, sultanship, sonship, survivorship, *SH* sheriffship, ship, surety-ship, *SK* scholarship, *SP* spaceship, speakership, sponsorship, sportsmanship, *ST* statesmanship, *steamship*, stewardship, studentship, *T* township, *TR* training ship, trans-ship, treasure ship, *troopship*, trusteeship, *U* umpireship, unship, upmanship, *V* viceroyship, virtuosoship, *W* wingmanship, wardenship, *wardship, warship*, watermanship, one-upmanship, workmanship, *worship*

SIP	sip
SKIP	skip
SKRIP	scrip
SLIP	*gymslip, cowslip, landslip, nonslip, sideslip*, slip, underslip
SNIP	snip
STRIP	*airstrip*, bumper strip, outstrip, strip, unstrip, weatherstrip
THRIP	thrip
TIP	tip
TRIP	atrip, business trip, head trip, *cantrip*, pleasure trip, trip
YIP	yip
ZIP	rezip, unzip, zip

ĪPS

KRĪPS	cripes
YĪPS	yipes

(See ĪP, add -*s* where appropriate.)

IPS

CHIPS	buffalo chips, chips, fish and chips, in the chips, potato chips
KLIPS	eclipse, partial eclipse, total eclipse
LIPS	Apocalypse, ellipse
SNIPS	resnips, snips, unsnips
SHIPS	*amidships, midships*, reships, ships, unships
THRIPS	thrips

(See IP, add -*s* where appropriate.)

ĪPT

GRIPY	griped

(See ĪP, add -*d* where appropriate.)

IPT

KRIPT	decrypt, encrypt, crypt, uncrypt
LIPT	apocalypt, *hare-lipped, close-lipped*, lipped, *pale-lipped, red-lipped, stiff-lipped*
SKRIPT	conscript, manuscript, nondescript, *postscript, prescript, proscript*, script, *subscript*, superscript, telescript, *typescript, transcript*

(See IP, add -*ped* where appropriate.)

ĪR

ĪR	ire
BĪR	byre
BRĪR	briar, brier
DĪR	dier, dire, dyer
FĪR	*A* afire, *B* backfire, beaconfire, bonfire, *BL* blackfire, *BR* brushfire, *D* death fire, *F* fire, *foxfire*, forest fire, *G* galley fire, *gunfire, GR* granophyre, *H* hellfire, *K* campfire, camphire, coal fire, *KR* crossfire, *L* lamprophyre, *M* melaphyre, misfire, *N* needfire, *P* peat fire, portfire, *R* retrofire, *S*

sapphire, signal fire, *SH shellfire, SP* spitfire, *SW* swamp fire, *W wildfire,* wood fire

FRĪR friar, fryer
HĪR hire, rehire
JĪR gyre
KWĪR acquire, antechoir, enquire, esquire, inquire, choir, quire, require, retrochoir
LĪR liar, lyre
MĪR admire, bemire, *quagmire,* mire, *pismire*
PĪR *empire,* pyr, pyre, *umpire*
PLĪR plier, plyer
PRĪR prior, pryer
SHĪR shire
SĪR *belsire, grandsire,* sire
SKWĪR squire, unsquire
SPĪR aspire, expire, inspire, conspire, perspire, respire, spire, suspire, transpire
TĪR attire, entire, flat tire, overtire, retire, *satire,* tire, Tyre
VĪR envire, vire
WĪR *barbwire,* barbed wire, *haywire,* rewire, *tripwire,* unwire, wire
ZĪR desire

(See **ĪER**)

ÎR

ÎR ear, ere, madrier, *wheatear,* rabbit's ear
BÎR beer, bier, gambier, ginger beer, light beer, near beer, shillibeer
BLÎR blear
CHÎR cheer, upcheer
DÎR *B* balladeer, bayadere, belvedere, bombardier, *BR* brigadier, *D* dear, deer, *E* endear, *F* fallow deer, *GR* grenadier, *H* halberdier, *K killdeer,* commandeer, *nadir, P* petardeer, petardier, *R reindeer, V* voir dire
DRÎR drear
FÎR fear, fere, interfere, isodiaphere
FLÎR fleer
GÎR bevel gear, *footgear,* friction gear, gear, gir, *headgear,* regear, running gear, ungear
HÎR adhere, hear, here, inhere, cohere, Mynheer, mishear, overhear
JÎR jeer, Tangier
KÎR fakir, kier
KLÎR chanticleer, clear, reclear, unclear
KWÎR queer, lequear, perqueer
LÎR *B* bandoleer, bandolier, *F* fusilier, *G* gaselier, gondolier, *K* camelier, cavalier, King Lear, *L* lavaliere, lear, Lear, leer, *P* pedalier, pistoleer, *SH* chandelier, chevalier
MÎR *A* actinomere, amir, antimere, *BL* blastomere, *E* emeer, emir, epimere, *K* kerseymere, *M* meer, mere, metamere, mir, *PR* premier, *S* centromere, *SH* chimere, *V* Vermeer
NÎR *A* anear, *B* bioengineer, buccaneer, *D* denier, domineer, *E* electioneer, engineer, *G* gonfalonier, *I* Indianeer, *J* jardiniere, *K* cannoneer, carabineer, carabinier, caravaneer, carbineer, *M* mountaineer, muffineer, mutineer, *N* near, neer, *O* auctioneer, *P* palfrenier, pioneer, pontonier, *S* souvenir, sermoneer, *SH* chiffonier, *SKR* scrutineer, *SL* sloganeer, *SP* specksioneer, *T* timoneer, *V* veneer
PÎR appear, diapir, disappear, compear, compeer, outpeer, peer, pier, pir, reappear
RÎR arrear, Fenrir, career, rear, uprear, vancourier
SFÎR *A* aerosphere, anthrosphere, atmosphere, *B* barysphere, bathysphere, biosphere, *E* ecosphere, exosphere, *F* photosphere, *H* hemisphere, hydrosphere, *I* insphere, *L* lithosphere, *M* magnetosphere, mesosphere, ionosphere, *P* perisphere, *PL* planisphere, *R* rhizosphere, *S* centrosphere, *SF* sphere, *STR* stratosphere, *TH* thermosphere, *TR* troposphere, *U* undersphere, unsphere
SHÎR cashier, shear, sheer, tabasheer

SÎR *A* adiposere, agricere, Aesir, *E* ensear, *F* financier, *I* insincere, *K* caboceer, *KW* cuirassier, *L* Landseer, *PL* plancier, *S* sear, seer, cere, sincere, xerosere
SKÎR skeer
SKLÎR sclere
SMÎR asmear, besmear, resmear, smear, unsmear
SNÎR sneer
SPÎR *Shakespeare,* spear
STÎR austere, oversteer, steer, stere, understeer
THÎR dinothere, isothere, chalicothere, titanothere, uintathere
TÎR *CH* charioteer, *FR* frontier, *G* gadgeteer, garreteer, gazetteer, *H* haltere, *K* corsetier, *KR* crocheteer, *M muleteer,* musketeer, *P* pamphleteer, pulpiteer, puppeteer, *PR* privateer, profiteer, *R* racketeer, rocketeer, *S* circuiteer, sonneteer, *T* targeteer, tear, teer, tier, Tyr, *V* volunteer
VÎR brevier, Guinivere, clavier, persevere, revere, revers, severe, veer, vire
WÎR *wasteweir,* weir, we're
YÎR *leapyear, lightyear, midyear,* year, yesteryear
ZÎR brassiere, grand vizier, vizier

ĪRD

FĪRD *all-fired, backfired* (etc.)

(See **ĪR,** add *d* where appropriate.)

ÎRD

ÎRD eared, *flap-eared, flop-eared, lop-eared*
BÎRD beard, *Blackbeard, Bluebeard, goatsbeard, graybeard, redbeard, treebeard*
FÎRD afeard, feared, fyrd, much feared, unfeared
WÎRD weird

(See **ÎR,** add *-ed* where appropriate.)

ÎRS

FÎRS	fierce, unfierce
PÎRS	pierce, transpierce
TÎRS	tierce

ÎRZ

JÎRZ	Algiers, Tangiers
SHÎRZ	shears, sheers

(See ÎR, add *-s* where appropriate.)

ĪS

ĪS	black ice, choc-ice, de-ice, dry ice, ice, camphor ice
BĪS	bice
DĪS	dice, paradise
FĪS	fice, human sacrifice, sacrifice, self-sacrifice, suffice
GRĪS	grice
LĪS	beggar's lice, body lice, head lice, lice
MĪS	church mice, field mice, country mice, mice, city mice, *titmice*
NĪS	gneiss, nice, overnice
PĪS	pice
PRĪS	*half-price, off-price,* price, reprice, underprice, unprice
RĪS	rais, rice
SĪS	imprecise, concise, precise, sice, syce
SLĪS	slice
SPĪS	*allspice,* bespice, speiss, spice
SPLĪS	resplice, splice, unsplice
TĪS	entice, tice
THRĪS	thrice
TRĪS	trice
TWĪS	twice
VĪS	advice, device, intrauterine device, edelweiss, vice, vise

IS

BIS	abyss, bis, cannabis
BLIS	bliss
DIS	dis, Dis, diss, hendiadys, *Charybdis,* cowardice, magadis, prejudice
FIS	artifice, benefice, edifice, orifice, sacrifice
FRIS	dentifrice

GRIS	ambergris, mistigris, verdigris
HIS	dehisce, hiss
KIS	butterfly kiss, chocolate kiss, French kiss, Judas kiss, kiss, rekiss, soul kiss
KRIS	kris, Kriss
KWIS	cuisse, quis
LIS	*A* acropolis, Annapolis, *F* fortalice, *G* Gallipolis, *H* Heliopolis, *I* Indianapolis, *K* cosmopolis, *KR* chrysalis, *L* lis, liss, *M* megalopolis, metropolis, Minneapolis, *N* necropolis, *P* Persepolis, *S* syphilis
MIS	amiss, Artemis, dynamis, dismiss, epididymis, fideicommiss, miss, Miss, remiss, submiss
NIS	reminisce
PIS	piss, precipice
PRIS	priss
RIS	avarice, Phalaris, licorice, sui generis
SIS	*A* abiogenesis, adipogenesis, aphaeresis, aphesis, agenesis, amoebiasis, anabasis, analysis, anamorphosis, anthropogenesis, anthropomorphisis, antiphrasis, antithesis, apodosis, apophysis, apotheosis, ascariasis, atelectasis, *B* bacteriolysis, bilharziasis, biogenesis, biolysis, biosynthesis, *BR* bronchiectasis, *D* dialysis, diaeresis, diastysis, diathesis, dichastasis, *E* ectogenesis, elephantiasis, electroanalysis, electrodialysis, electrolysis, emesis, emphasis, entasis, epiphysis, *F* filariasis, photokinesis, photosynthesis, *GL* glycolisis, *H* haematiogenesis, haematemisis, haemodialysis, haemolysis, hypostasis, histogenesis, histolysis, hypothesis, holophrasis, *J* genesis, *K* catabasis, katabesis, catalysis, *KE* cryptanalysis, *L* leishmaniasis, lithiasis, *M* metabasis, metamorphosis, metastisis, metathesis, myasis, myariasis, microanalysis, morphogenesis, *N* nemesis, pneumatolysis, *O* osteogenesis, oogenesis, osteoclasis, autholysis, *P* parabasis, paragenesis, paralysis, parasynthesis, parathesis, parenthesis, parthenogenesis, pathogenesis, paedomorphosis, periphrasis, *S* satyriasis, psychoanalysis, psychogenesis, *psychokinesis,* synthesis, sis, siss, cytolysis, psoriasis, *SP* spermatogenesis, sporogenesis, *T* telekinesis, taeniasis, tycolisis, *TH* thermogenesis, thermolysis, phthiriasis, *TR* trichiasis, trypanosomiasis, *Y* urinalysis, *Z* xenogenesis
STIS	armistice, *interstice*
SWIS	Swiss
TIS	abatis, clematis
THIS	this
TRIS	cockatrice, cicatrice
VIS	vis
WIS	iwis, wis, y-wis
YIS	yisse

ISH

ISH	babyish, dowdyish, Cockneyish, ogreish, willowish, yellowish
BISH	bish
DISH	chafing dish, dish
FISH	*A* amberfish, angelfish, *B* barberfish, *batfish, BL* blackfish, blowfish, bluefish, *D* damselfish, devilfish, *dogfish, F* filefish, fish, *FL* flatfish, flying fish, *FR* frogfish, *G* garfish, goldfish, *GR* greenfish, *H* hogfish, *HW* whitefish, *J* jellyfish, jewfish, *K* catfish, killfish, killifish, *kingfish, codfish, cowfish,* cuttlefish, *KL* clingfish, *KR* crawfish, crayfish, *M* mayfish, monkfish, *O* oarfish, *P* pilotfish, *PL* plowfish, *R* ratfish, redfish, ribbonfish, rockfish, *S* sailfish,

	sawfish, saltfish, swordfish, silverfish, SH shellfish, ST starfish, stingfish, stockfish, T tilefish, TR trunkfish, W weakfish (etc.)
GISH	gish
GWISH	*anguish*
HWISH	whish
ISH	ish
JISH	orangeish
KISH	kish
LISH	devilish, lish
NISH	heathenish, kittenish, mammonish, knish, vixenish, womanish
PISH	pish
RISH	*B* bitterish, *F* feverish, *G* gibberish, *I* impoverish, *J* gibberish, *KL* cleverish, *KW* quakerish, *L* lickerish, *T* tigerish, *V* vaporish, viperish, vulturish, *W* waterish
SHISH	shish
SKWISH	squish
SLISH	slish
SWISH	swish
TISH	tish, *schottische, Scottish*
WISH	death wish, rewish, unwish, wish

(The suffix *-ish* may be added to any suitable noun or adjective, many not listed here, to make a rhyme.)

ISK

BISK	bisque
BRISK	brisk
DISK	disc, disk, floppy disk, condensed disk
FISK	fisc
FRISK	frisk
HWISK	whisk
LISK	basilisk, lisk, obelisk, odalisque
PISK	pisk
RISK	asterisk, risk, tamarisk
SISK	francisc
TISK	tisk

ISP

HWISP	whisp
KRISP	crisp
LISP	lisp
RISP	rerisp, risp
WISP	will-o'-the-wisp, wisp

ĪST

ĪST	iced, uniced
GĪST	poltergeist, *Weltgeist, Zeitgeist*
HĪST	heist
KRĪST	antichrist, Christ
LĪST	beliced, liced

(See **ĪS,** add *-d* where appropriate.)

IST

IST	*A* altruist, archaist, atheist, *B* banjoist, *E* egoist, essayist, *H* hobbyist, Hebraist, *I* ist, *J* jingoist, Judaist, *K* casuist, copyist, *L* lobbyist, *M* Maoist, *O* oboist, *PR* prosaist, *S* soloist, *SH* Shintoist, *T* Taoist, *TR* tritheist, *U* ultraist, *V* vacuist, *Y* euphuist
BIST	Arabist
BRIST	equilibrist
DIST	*B* balladist, *K* chiropodist, concordist, *M* melodist, Methodist, monodist, *P* parodist, *PR* prejudiced, *R* rhapsodist, *S* psalmodist, synodist, *T* Talmudist, *THR* threnodist, *U* unprejudiced
FIST	*B* beneficed, *F* philosophist, fist, fyst, photographist, *J* gymnosophist, *K* chirographist, *P* pacifist, *puckfist, SP* specifist, *ST* steganographist, stenographist, *T* telegraphist, typographist, topographist, *TH* theosophist
FRIST	frist
GLIST	glist
GRIST	grist
HIST	hissed, hist
HWIST	whist, bridge whist
JIST	*A* agist, allergist, apologist, archaeologist, *B* biologist, *D* demonologist, dialogist, *E* ecclesiologist, electrobiologist, elegist, entomologist, etymologist, *F* pharmacologist, philologist, physiologist, fossilologist, *FR* phrenologist, *GR* graphologist, *J*

genealogist, geologist, gynecologist, gist, jist, *K* campanologist, conchologist, *KR* chronologist, *L* litholologist, liturgist, *M* martyrologist, metallurgist, meteorologist, mineralogist, mythologist, *N* necrologist, neologist, pneumatologist, *O* ophthalmologist, ornithologist, *P* pathologist, penologist, petrologist, *R* radiologist, *S* psychologist, synergist, Sinologist, seismologist, sociologist, suffragist, *STR* strategist, *T* technologist, teleologist, toxicologist, tautologist, *TH* theologist, *Y* ufologist, eulogist, *Z* zoologist

KIST	anarchist, bekissed, catechist, kissed, cist, kist, masochist, monachist, monarchist, rekissed, Sinarquist, unkissed
KRIST	theomicrist
KWIST	quist, ventriloquist
LIST	*A* agricolist, agriculturalist, alist, analyst, animalculist, annalist, annualist, anticatalyst, aeralist, *B* bibliophilist, bibliopolist, bicyclist, bimetallist, biocatalyst, *D* dactylist, devotionalist, dialist, dualist, duelist, *E* educationalist, existentialist, experimentalist, externalist, enamelist, enlist, environmentalist, Aeolist, eternalist, evangelist, *F* fabulist, fatalist, federalist, philatelist, finalist, financialist, formalist, fossilist, feudalist, funambulist, futilist, *GL* glacialist, *H* herbalist, hyperbolist, *I* idealist, immaterialist, immoralist, immortalist, imperialist, individualist, industrialist, instrumentalist, intellectualist, internationalist, *J* generalist, journalist, *K* cabalist, capitalist, catalyst, commercialist,

congregationalist,
constitutionalist,
controversialist,
conventionalist,
conversationalist, choralist,
KL classicalist, *KW*
querulist, *L* libelist,
liberalist, list, Liszt,
literalist, loyalist, *M*
maximalist, managerialist,
martialist, materialist,
medalist, medievalist,
memorialist, metalist,
minimalist, ministerialist,
monopolist, moralist,
nationalist, naturalist,
nihilist, nominalist,
novelist, *O* oculist,
orientalist, *automobilist*, *P*
panelist, parabolist,
pedalist, populist, pugilist,
PL pluralist, *PR*
proverbialist, provincialist,
R racialist, rationalist,
realist, removalist,
revivalist, ritualist,
royalist, ruralist, *S*
sexualist, semifinalist,
sensationalist, sensualist,
sentimentalist, centralist,
sibylist, psychoanalyst,
cymbalist, symbolist,
somnambulist, socialist,
surrealist, *SKR*
scripturalist, *SP* specialist,
spiritualist, *T* textualist, *TR*
traditionalist,
transcendentalist, *V* violist,
vitalist, vocabulist,
vocalist, verbalist, *Y*
universalist, *Z* zoophilist

MIST *A* academist, alchemist,
anatomist, animist,
antinomist, atomist, *B*
bemist, bigamist, *D*
dismissed, dynamist,
deuterogamist, *E*
economist, epitomist, *F*
physiognomist, *FL*
phlebotomist, *L*
lachrymist, legitimist, *M*
misogamist, missed, mist,
monogamist, *O*
ophthalmist, optimist, *P*
pessimist, polygamist, *S*
ceremist, synonomist, *U*
undismissed, unmissed, *V*
volumist, *Z* zoötomist

NIST *A* abolitionist, abortionist,
agonist, accompanist,
actionist, alienist, Alpinist,
antagonist, *B* botanist,

Bourbonist, *BR*
Brahmanist, *D* Darwinist,
degenerationist,
delusionist, demonist,
destinist, destructionist,
determinist, devotionist,
Deuteragonist, *E*
educationist, exhibitionist,
exclusionist, excursionist,
expansionist,
Expressionist, extensionist,
elocutionist,
emancipationist,
evolutionist, *F* factionist,
feminist, phenomenist,
fictionist, Philhellenist, *G*
galvanist, *H* harmonist,
hedonist, Hellenist,
hygienist, humanist, *I*
illusionist, imitationist,
immersionist,
impressionist,
indeterminist,
inspirationist,
insurrectionist,
interventionist, *K*
Calvinist, canonist,
coalitionist, colonist,
columnist, communionist,
communist, Communist,
Confucionist,
conservationist,
constitutionist,
constructionist, loose
constructionist, strict
constructionist,
contortionist,
conversationalist,
conversationist, co-
religionist, corruptionist,
KR cremationist, *L*
Latinist, lutanist, *M*
Malthusianist, mammonist,
mechanist, miscellanist,
misogynist, modernist, *N*
Napoleonist, mnemonist,
Neo-expressionist,
Neoplatonist, notionist,
nutritionist, *O*
obstructionist, opinionist,
opportunist, oppositionist,
organist, Orleanist, *P* pan-
Hellenist, passionist,
pianist, perfectionist,
percussionist, pythonist,
post-impressionist, *PL*
platonist, *PR* precisionist,
progressionist,
prohibitionist,
projectionist, protagonist,
protectionist, *R* reactionist,
religionist, reminisced,

repudiationist, receptionist,
revelationist, revisionist,
revolutionist,
resurrectionist, Romanist,
S salvationist, satanist,
saturnist, segregationist,
secessionist, symphonist,
circumlocutionist,
Sorbonnist, *SH* Shamanist,
chauvinist, *T* telephonist,
terminist, timpanist,
tobacconist, *TR* trade
unionist, traditionist,
trombonist, *U* urbanist, *V*
vacationist, vaccinist,
Vaticanist, vivisectionist,
visionist, volumnist,
vulcanist, *Y* eudemonist,
unionist, *Z* Zionist

PIST *E* emancipist, *F*
philanthropist,
physiotherapist, *L*
landscapist, *M*
misanthropist, *P* pissed, *R*
radiotherapist, *S* syncopist,
TH theophilanthropist,
therapist, *Z* xenoepist

PRIST prissed
RIST *A* aphorist, agriculturist,
aquarist, allegorist,
amorist, aorist, apiarist,
arborist, arborculturist,
armorist, artillerist, *B*
behaviorist, *D* diarist,
disinterest, *E* Everest, *FL*
floriculturist, *GL*
glossarist, *H* horticulturist,
humorist, *I* interest, *K*
caricaturist, colorist,
culturist, *L* laborist,
Lazarist, lepidopterist, *M*
mannerist, mesmerist,
militarist, motorist, *N*
naturist, *O* augurist,
ocularist, *P* particularist,
posturist, *PL* plagiarist,
pleasurist, *PR* preterist, *R*
rapturist, rigorist, rist,
wrist, *S* satirist, secularist,
singularist, solarist,
summarist, *SK* Scripturist,
T terrorist, *TH* theorist, *V*
votarist, *Y* Eucharist

SHIST schist
SIST *A* Anglicist, assist, *B*
biblicist, *BL* blastocyst, *E*
exorcist, empiricist,
encyst, ethicist, *F*
pharmacist, physicist, *H*
hydrocyst, *I* insist, *J*
genetecist, *K* consist, *KL*
classicist, *L* lyricist, *M*

macrocyst, mythicist, mosaicist, *N* nematocyst, *P* persist, polemicist, publicist, *PR* progressist, *R* romanticist, *S* synthesist, cist, sissed, sist, cyst, solecist, solipsist, subsist, supremacist, *SP* sporocyst, *ST* statocyst, *T* technicist, *TR* trichocyst

THIST allopathist, amethyst, antipathist, apathist, sympathist, telepathist

TIST *A* Adventist, anagrammatist, anaesthetist, *apocalyptist,* *D* despotist, diplomatist, dogmatist, *DR* dramatist, *E* egotist, experimentist, enigmatist, epigrammatist, *F* phoneticist, phonetist, *H* hereditist, hypnotist, *KW* quietist, *M* magnetist, melodramatist, *N* narcotist, nepotist, numismatist, *O* *occultist,* automatist, *P* pietist, portraitist, *PR* pragmatist, prelatist, presentist, problematist, *S* Semitist, separatist, scientist, syncretist, systematist, *SH* schoenobatist, *SK* schematist, *ST* stigmatist, *Z* zealotist

TRIST hexametrist, optometrist, pedometrist, psychiatrist, symmetrist, tryst

TWIST atwist, entwist, intertwist, twist, untwist

VIST activist, archivist, Bolshevist, Menshevist, passivist, positivist, subjectivist

WIST wist

ZIST desist, exist, co-exist, pre-exist, resist, xyst

ĪT

ĪT Shiite, *troostite,* Trotskyite

BĪT *backbite,* bight, bite, byte, *fleabite,* Jacobite, kilo-byte, Moabite, Niobite, Rechabite, cenobite, *snakebite,* trilobite

BLĪT blight, blite

BRĪT bright, *eyebright*

DĪT *B* bedight, *D* dight, dite, *E* expedite, extradite, endite, erudite, *H* heulandite,

DRĪT

FĪT hermaphrodite, *I* indite, incondite, *K* condite, *cordite, L* lyddite, *M* meropodite, *P* pentlandite, *podite, R* recondite, *S* synodite, *TR* troglodyte *achondrite, alexandrite, archimandrite, dendrite* *A* aerophyte, *B* bullfight, BR bryophyte, *D* dermophyte, *dogfight, E* ectophyte, endophyte, entophyte, epiphyte, *F* *fistfight,* fight, fite, *G* *gunfight, GR* graphite, *H* hanifite, hydrophyte, *J* geophyte, *K* cockfight, *KR* cryophite, *L* lithophyte, *M* mesophyte, microphyte, *N* neophyte, *O* osteophyte, *ophite, PR* prizefight, *S* sea fight, sciophyte, *sulphite,* *STR* street fight, *T* turfite, *Z* zoophyte

FLĪT flight, flite, overflight

FRĪT affright, fright, night fright, stage fright

GĪT annabergite

HĪT Fahrenheit, height, hight

HWĪT *bobwhite,* Heppelwhite, *lintwhite, offwhite, snow-white,* white

JĪT anthropophagite, eclogite

KĪT Amalekite, box kite, *hellkite,* kite, malachite, omphalopsychite

KLĪT heteroclite

KRĪT krait

KWĪT quite, not quite, requite

LĪT *A* aerolite, acolyte, actinolite, alight, amphibolite, ampelite, apophyllite, argillite, *B* Baalite, *D* daylight, *deadlight,* delight, *DR* *droplight, E* electrolyte, entomolite, *F* fanlight, *phonolite, footlight, FL* *flashlight, floodlight, G* gaslight, gastrophilite, *go-light, GR* grapholite, granulite, graptolite, green light, *H* half-light, halite, haplite, harbor light, *headlight, highlight,* hyalite, *hoplite, I* ichnolite, impolite, Ishmaelite, Islamite, Israelite, *K* candlelight, Carmelite, chiastolite, killer satellite, kimberlite, coprolite, corallite, cosmopolite, *KR*

cryolite, chrysolite, crystallite, crocidolite, *KW* quarterlight, *L* lamplight, lazulite, lepidolite, limelight, light, lite, *M* *marlite,* menilite, metabolite, microlight, monophylite, *moonlight, N* natrolite, nephelite, *nightlight,* novaculite, nummulite, *O* oolite, *P* pyrophyllite, polite, *PR* pre-Raphaelite, prophylite, proselyte, *R* Raphaelite, *redlight,* red light, relight, rhyolite, *S* satellite, sea light, cellulite, siderolite, *searchlight, sidelight,* signal light, socialite, *sunlight, SF* spherulite, *SK* scapolite, skylight, *SP* spotlight, *ST* starlight, stylite, styolite, *stoplight, STR streetlight,* stromatolite, *T* tachylyte, *taillight,* tantalite, toxophilite, topazolite, *TH* theodolite, *TR* traffic light, *TW* twilight, *V* variolite, ventriculite, *Y* uralite, *Z* zeolite, zoolite

MĪT *A* Adamite, Adullamite, *B* bedlamite, Bethlehemite, *BR* bromite, *D* dynamite, dolomite, *E* Edomite, Elamite, eremite, *G* Gothamite, *H* Hamite, hellgrammite, Hiramite, *I* Islamite, Itacolumite, *K* calamite, catamite, *M* midshipmite, might, mite, Moslemite, *PR* pre-Adamite, *S* Semite, sodomite, *somite, ST* stalagmite, *T* termite, *W* widow's mite, wolframite

NĪT *A* Aaronite, aconite, alunite, Ammonite, amazonite, arenite, *B* Babylonite, belemnite, beknight, benight, bentonite, *bornite, birthnight,* day and night, disunite, *E* Ebionite, ebonite, *F* finite, fortnight, *G* gadolinite, good night, white knight, *I* ichnite, ignite, ilmenite, *K* Canaanite, kaolinite, *KR* crinite, *KW* quarternight, *L* lignite, limonite, *M* Mammonite, manganite,

	Maronite, melanite, Midianite, midnight, monzonite, morganite, *N* nephelinite, knight, night, *O* austenite, autunite, overnight, *R* re-ignite, retinite, reunite, rhodonite, *S* selenite, *sennight,* cyanite, syenite, sylvanite, suburbanite, *Sunnite, SM* smithsonite, *STR* strontionite, *T* taconite, tonight, *U* unknight, urbanite, *V* vulcanite, *Y* unite, uraninite, uranite, yesternight, *W* wulfenite
PLĪT	plight
RĪT	*A* anchorite, aright, azurite, alright, all right, *B* barite, birthright, bookwright, D dolerite, downright, E enwrite, erythrite, yperite, F forthright, phosphorite, G garnierite, geyserite, ghostwrite, GR grossularite, HW wheelwright, K cartwright, copyright, cordierite, L laborite, Labradorite, laterite, Lazarite, lazurite, M margarite, meteorite, millwright, Minorite, N Naderite, Nazarite, New Right, O outright, overright, overwrite, ozocerite, P pyrite, PL playwright, plowright, R radical right, right, rite, write, S sybarite, siderite, SH shipwright, T tenorite, typewrite, U underwrite, unright, unwrite, upright, W wainwright
SĪT	A Adamsite, accite, andesite, anorthosite, anthracite, B bombsight, boracite, D dyophysite, dissight, E excite, erythrocyte, F phagocyte, felsite, foresight, H haemocyte, hindsight, I incite, insight, eyesight, J jarosite, K chalcocite, calcyte, kamacite, KW quartzite, L lymphocyte, lewisite, leucocyte, M macrocyte, marcasite, martensite, microcyte, monophosyte, O on-site, oocyte, outasight, oversight, P parasite,

	pargasite, *PL* plebiscite, *R* recite, *S* second sight, cite, sight, site, *SK* scolecite, *SP* spermatocyte, *U* unsight, *V* variscite
SKĪT	blatherskite, skite
SLĪT	sleight, slight
SMĪT	smite, resmite
SNĪT	snite
SPĪT	despite, spite
SPRĪT	spright, sprite, watersprite
TĪT	*A airtight,* albertite, apatite, appetite, *B bipartite, G* goniatite, *GR* granitite, *H* hematite, *I* ilmenitite, *KL* clematite, *L latite, M* magnetite, *multipartite, P partite,* peridotite, *R ratite, S* celestite, *SK skintight, SP* spessartite, *ST* stalactite, *sticktight, T* tight, tite, *TR transvestite, tripartite, U uptight, W* watertight
TRĪT	attrite, contrite, trite
TWĪT	twite
VĪT	invite, *Levite,* moldavite, Muscovite, reinvite
WĪT	wight, Wight, wite

IT

IT	*A* appropriate, *B* baccalaureate, *I* immediate, inappropriate, intermediate, it, *J* Jesuit, *K collegiate, KW* quadrifoliate, *PR* professoriate, *R* roseate, *S* secretariat, *TR* trifoliate
BIT	bit, bitt, forebitt, giga-bit, kilo-bit, mega-bit, *tidbit, titbit,* unbit, wait-a-bit
BRIT	brit, Brit
CHIT	chit
DIT	dit, ditt
FIT	befit, benefit, fit, phit, *comfit,* counterfeit, misfit, outfit, palafitte, refit, retrofit, unfit
FLIT	flit
FRIT	frit
GIT	git, profligate
GRIT	grit
HIT	hit
HWIT	whit
KIT	delicate, indelicate, intricate, kit, contortuplicate, quadruplicate, quintuplicate, centuplicate,

	septemplicate, certificate, triplicate
KLIT	clit
KRIT	hypocrite
KWIT	adequate, acquit, inadequate, quit, *quitquit*
LIT	alit, bimaculate, chocolate, disconsolate, immaculate, inarticulate, inviolate, lit, *moonlit,* relit, *starlit, sunlit, twilit,* unlit
MIT	A admit, antepenultimate, approximate, D demit, E emit, I illegitimate, immit, intermit, intimate, intromit, K commit, compromit, L legitimate, M manumit, mit, mitt, O omit, P permit, PR pretermit, proximate, R recommit, remit, S submit, TR transmit, U ultimate
NIT	A affectionate, B beknit, D definite, determinate, diaconate, dispassionate, disproportionate, E effeminate, F fortunate, I impassionate, importunate, indeterminate, indiscriminate, infinite, incompassionate, inordinate, insubordinate, interknit, K compassionate, coordinate, KL close-knit, N knit, nit, O obstinate, alternate, P passionate, PR proportionate, R reknit, S subalternate, subordinate, T tight-knit, U unaffectionate, unfortunate, unknit
PIT	*armpit, ashpit, coalpit, cockpit,* pit, pitt, *pitpit,* rifle pit, *shilpit, tarpit*
PLIT	quadruplet, quintuplet
RIT	A accurate, D daywrit, degenerate, deliberate, desparate, disparate, doctorate, E elaborate, F favorite, I illiterate, immoderate, inaccurate, incommensurate, inconsiderate, intemperate, inveterate, K commensurate, considerate, corporate, PR preterite, R rewrit, rit, writ, S separate, T temperate, U unwrit
SIT	*insensate,* outsit, plebiscite, cit, sit
SHIT	beshit, *bullshit, horseshit* (etc.), shit

SKIT	skit
SKWIT	squit
SLIT	slit
SHMIT	Messerschmitt
SMIT	smit
SPIT	*lickspit*, spit, *turnspit*
SPLIT	lickety-split, split
SPRIT	*bowsprit*, sprit
TIT	*bluetit*, tit, precipitate, *tomtit*

EVE, FEAR NOT

Eve, fear not lest through my dissent
  Our Eden be attacked;
Your theory most diffident
  I take as given fact.
Your inclinations and aversions
  Are magnified in me;
Your laws are as the Medes' and Persians'
  (Until we disagree).

TWIT	twit
VIT	aquavit
WIT	afterwit, *dimwit, godwit, halfwit*, motherwit, nimblewit, *nitwit*, outwit, to wit, thimblewit, unwit, wit, *wantwit*
ZIT	apposite, exquisite, inapposite, composite, opposite, perquisite, prerequisite, requisite, unopposite, zit

(Unstressed *-ate, -et, -it* following a stressed syllable *(striate, magnet, exit)* may be rhymed with *it,* but with little satisfaction.)

ITH

(**TH** as in *then*)

BLĪTH	blithe
LĪTH	lithe
RĪTH	writhe
SĪTH	scythe, sithe
STĪTH	stythe
TĪTH	tithe
WĪTH	withe, wythe

ITH

(**TH** as in *thin*)

BRITH	B'nai B'rith
FRITH	frith
GRITH	grith
KITH	kith
KRITH	crith
LITH	*A* aerolith, acrolith,

anthropolith, *B* batholith, *E* eolith, *G* gastrolith, *GR* granolith, *K* cactolith, coccolith, *L* lactolith, lith, *M* megalith, microlith, monolith, *N* neolith, *P* paleolith, *R* regolith, *ST* statolith, *TR* trilith, *Y* urolith, *Z* xenolith

MITH	engastrimyth, epimyth, Grecian myth, myth, Nordic myth, Roman myth
PITH	pith
SITH	sith
SMITH	arrowsmith, *blacksmith, goldsmith, gunsmith, whitesmith,* coppersmith, *locksmith,* silversmith, smith, *tinsmith, tunesmith, wordsmith*
WITH	forthwith, herewith, wherewith, therewith, with, withe, wythe

ĪTS

BRĪTS	brights
HWĪTS	whites
LĪTS	*footlights,* lights
MĪTS	Dolomites
NĪTS	anights, nights
RĪTS	rights, wrights, to-rights
TĪTS	tights

(See **ĪT,** add *-s* where appropriate.)

ITS

BLITS	blitz
GLITS	glitz
GRITS	grits
KWITS	quits
PITS	pits, the pits
RITS	Ritz
SHNITS	schnitz
SITS	sits
SPITS	spits, spitz
VITS	slivovitz
WITS	Horowitz, wits

(See **IT,** add *-s* where appropriate.)

ĪV

ĪV	I've
CHĪV	chive
DĪV	dive, *endive,* high dive, *high-dive, nose-dive,* power dive, redive, swan dive

DRĪV	chain drive, drive, outdrive, overdrive
FĪV	five, spoil five
HĪV	*beehive,* hive, rehive, unhive
JĪV	gyve, jive, *ogive,* ungyve
KLĪV	clive
LĪV	alive, live, unalive
NĪV	connive
PRĪV	deprive, redeprive
RĪV	arrive, derive, rive, rearrive, rederive
SHĪV	shive
SHRĪV	shrive
SKĪV	skive
STĪV	stive
STRĪV	strive
SWĪV	swive
THRĪV	thrive
TRĪV	contrive
VĪV	convive, redivive, revive, survive
WĪV	wive

IV

CHIV	chiv
DIV	div, *gerundive*
FLIV	fliv
GIV	forgive, give, misgive
LIV	live, outlive, overlive, relive
SHIV	shiv
SIV	purposive, sieve
SPIV	spiv
TIV	*A* ablative, additive, admonitive, adversative, affirmative, affricative, agglutinative, accumulative, accusative, acquisitive, alliterative, alternative, amative, appellative, applicative, appreciative, argumentative, associative, attributive, *D* definitive, declarative, decorative, deliberative, demonstrative, denominative, denotative, depurative, derivative, derogative, desiderative, desiccative, determinative, diapositive, diminutive, dispensative, disputative, distributive, donative, dormative, durative, *E* educative, executive, exhibitive, exclamative, explicative, expletive,

elative, electropositive, evocative, *F* factitive, *facultative,* figurative, fixative, formative, photosensitive, fugitive, *FR* frequentative, fricative, *H* hypersensitive, *I* illustrative, imaginative, *imitative,* impeditive, imperative, imputative, inappreciative, indicative, infinitive, informative, initiative, incarnative, inchoative, inquisitive, inoperative, insensitive, intensative, interpretive, interrogative, intransitive, intuitive, irrelative, *J* genitive, judicative, *K* calculative, calmative, carminative, coagulative, coercitive, *cogitative,* combative, combinative, commemorative, communicative, commutative, comparative, compellative, compensative, competitive, complimentative, compulsative, conative, confirmative, consecutive, conservative, conciliative, consultative, contemplative, continuative, contributive, cooperative, corporative, correlative, causative, cumulative, curative, *KW* *qualitative, quantitative,* quidditive, quietive, *L* laxative, lenitive, laudative, locative, lucrative, *M* manipulative, *meditative,* mercative, *multiplicative, N* narrative, negative, neoconservative, nominative, noncooperative, normative, nutritive, *O* auditive, augmentative, *alterative,* operative, optative, *authoritative, P* partitive, pejorative, performative, portative, positive, postoperative, postpositive, pulsative, punitive, purgative, putative, *PR* premonitive, preparative, prepositive, prerogative, preteritive, preventative, preservative, primitive, privative, probative,

prohibitive, provocative, *R* radiosensitive, rebarbative, reformative, relative, remunerative, reparative, recitative, restorative, retributive, reverberative, rotative, *ruminative, S* sanative, sedative, secretive, semblative, sensitive, separative, significative, siccative, substantive, superlative, suppositive, suppurative, *SP* speculative, *T* talkative, tentative, *TR* transitive, *U* ulcerative, undemonstrative, uncommunicative, *V* *vegetative,* vetative, vibrative, vituperative, vocative, volative, *Y* unitive

.

ĪVD

LĪVD   long-lived, short-lived

(See **ĪV**, add *-d* where appropriate.)

ĪZ

ĪZ   angel eyes, archaize, asses' eyes, atheize, bright eyes, dandyize, eyes, Hebraize, Judaize, sheep's eyes, twaddleize, euphuize

CHĪZ   *disfranchise, enfranchise*
DĪZ   *A* aggrandize, anodize, *B* balladize, bastardize, *D* dastardize, deoxidize, faradize, *FL* fluidize, *G* gormandize, *H* hybridize, *I* iodize, iridize, *J* jeopardize, *KL* chloridize, *L* liquidize, *M* melodize, merchandise, methodize, *O* oxidize, *P* paradise, *PR* propagandize, *R* rhapsodize, ruggedize *S* psalmodize, subsidize, *SH* sherardize, *ST* standardize
FĪZ   *anthropomorphize,* apostrophize, philosophize, sacrifice, theosophize
GĪZ   disguise, guise
JĪZ   *A* analogize, anthologize, apologize, astrologize, *B* battologize, *D* demythologize, dialogize, doxologize, *E* elegize,

energize, entomologize, etymologize, *H* homologize, *J* genealogize, geologize, *L* lethargize, *M* mythologize, *N* neologize, *S* psychologize, syllogize, *T* tautologize, *TH* theologize, *Y* eulogize
KĪZ   catechize

> *MY AMNESTY TO ALL, EXCEPT*
>
> My amnesty to all
>   The poor, imperfect throng,
> Excepting just one pest:
>   The man who has the gall
> To say, when things go wrong,
>   "I meant it for the best."

KWĪZ   colloquize, soliloquize, ventriloquize
LĪZ   *A* actualize, alcoholize, alkalize, ambrosialize, analyze, annalize, animalize, arterialize, artificialize, *B* banalize, bestialize, *BR* breathalyze, brutalize, *CH* channelize, *D* dematerialize, demineralize, demobilize, demoralize, denationalize, denaturalize, departmentalize, depersonalize, desexualize, decentralize, decimalize, destabilize, devilize, devitalize, diabolize, dialyze, digitalize, dualize, *E* editorialize, experimentalize, externalize, equalize, electrolyze, etherealize, evangelize, *F* fabulize, fictionalize, finalize, focalize, formalize, formulize, fossilize, feudalize, *FR* fractionalize, fraternize, *G* gospelize, gutturalize, *H* hydrolyze, hyperbolize, hospitalize, *I* idealize, illegalize, immaterialize, immobilize, immortalize, imperialize, impersonalize, individualize, industrialize, initialize, institutionalize, intellectualize, internalize, internationalize, irrationalize, *J* generalize, journalize, *K* canalize, cannibalize, capitalize,

caramelize, cardinalize, catalyze, coalize, communalize, compartmentalize, conceptualize, conventionalize, *KR* crystallize, *KW* quintessentialize, *L* legalize, liberalize, localize, *M* martialize, materialize, memorialize, mercurialize, metabolize, metagrobolize, metallize, mineralize, mobilize, modelize, mongrelize, monopolize, moralize, mortalize, mutualize, *N* nationalize, naturalize, nasalize, normalize, novelize, neutralize, *O* obelize, occidentalize, opalize, orientalize, *P* palatalize, papalize, parabolize, parallelize, paralyze, participialize, patronize, penalize, personalize, potentialize, *PL* pluralize, *PR* professionalize, proverbialize, provincialize, *R* radicalize, racialize, rationalize, realize, recrystallize, revitalize, ritualize, royalize, ruralize, Russianize, *S* sectionalize, sexualize, sensualize, sentimentalize, centralize, sepulchralize, serialize, signalize, psychoanalyze, symbolize, synchronize, civilize, solubilize, socialize, substantialize, subtilize, *SK* scandalize, *SKR* scrupulize, *SP* specialize, spiritualize, *ST* stabilize, sterilize, *T* tantalize, territorialize, testimonialize, totalize, *TH* thermalize, *TR* tranquilize, trivialize, *V* vandalize, verbalize, vernalize, visualize, vitalize, vocalize, volatilize, *Y* universalize, utilize

MĪZ *A* alchemize, amalgamize, anatomize, astronomize, atomize, *BR* bromize, *D* demise, *E* economize, emblemize, epitomize, *F* physiognomize, *FL* phlebotomize, *I* infamize,

Islamize, itemize, *K* compromise, customize, *L* legitimize, lobotomize, *M* macadamize, maximize, manumize, minimize, *O* optimize, autotomize, *P* pessimize, pilgrimize, polygamize, *PR* premise, presurmise, *R* randomize, racemize, remise, *S* synonymize, surmise, *V* victimize, *Y* euphemize

NĪZ *A* adonize, Africanize, agonize, agrarianize, albumenize, aluminize, Americanize, androgenize, antagonize, attitudinize, *B* bituminize, Balkanize, botanize, *D* dehumanize, decarbonize, decolonize, demonize, deoxygenize, detonize, dichotomize, disillusionize, disorganize, *E* ebonize, Edenize, effeminize, economize, excursionize, *F* feminize, *FR* fractionize, fraternize, *G* galvanize, gorgonize, *GL* glutenize, gluttonize, *H* harmonize, heathenize, Hellenize, histrionize, homogenize, humanize, *I* impatronize, immunize, ionize, ironize, Italianize, *J* jargonize, gelatinize, Germanize, *K* canonize, caponize, carbonize, keratinize, kyanize, *cognize,* colonize, communize, cauponize, cosmopolitanize, *KR* Christianize, *L* Latinize, lionize, Londonize, *M* macadamize, mammonize, mangonize, matronize, mechanize, modernize, Mohammedanize, *N* nitrogenize, *O* oxygenize, opsonize, organize, Australianize, Austrianize, *P* paganize, patronize, pavonize, pedestrianize, peptonize, personize, pollenize, Puritanize, *PL* platinize, platitudinize, Platonize, plebeianize, *PR* preconize, *R* recognize, rejuvenize, reorganize, republicanize, revolutionize, resurrectionize, Romanize, *S* sectarianize, sermonize,

PĪZ

PRĪZ

RĪZ

symphonize, simonize, cinchonize, synchronize, Socinianize, solemnize, suburbanize, *SK* skeletonize, *SKR* scrutinize, *T* tetanize, Timonize, tyrannize, Teutonize, *TR* trichonize, *U* urbanize, *V* villainize, volcanize, vulcanize, *W* wantonize, westernize, womanize, *Y* euphonize, unionize, Europeanize philanthropize, philippize, misanthropize, penelopize, pize, sinapize, syncopize, euripize

apprise, emprise, enterprise, comprise, misprize, prise, prize, reprise, surprise, underprise

A aphorize, allegorize, arise, *B* barbarize, bowdlerize, burglarize, *D* decolorize, demilitarize, demonetarize, denuclearize, deodorize, depressurize, desulphurize, *E* extemporize, exteriorize, etherize, *F* factorize, familiarize, formularize, *FL* fletcherize, *GL* glamorize, *GR* grangerize, *H* heterize, *I* isomerize, *J* jennerize, *K* characterize, categorize, catheterize, chimerize, computerize, containerize, contemporize, cauterize, *M* marmarize, memorize, mercerize, mesmerize, militarize, miniaturize, moisturize, *moonrise,* motorize, *N* notarize, *O* augurize, authorize, *P* panegyrize, particularize, pasteurize, peculiarize, polarize, polymerize, pauperize, popularize, pulverize, *PL* plagiarize, *PR* pressurize, proctorize, *R* rapturize, regularize, rhetorize, revalorize, rise, rubberize, *S* saccharize, satirize, secularize, seigniorize, seniorize, silverize, singularize, circularize, slenderize, soberize, solarize, suberize, sulphurize, summarize, *sunrise, T* tabularize, temporize, tenderize, terrorize, *TH* theorize, transistorize, *U* uprise, *V* valorize, vaporize, vulgarize

SĪZ *A* Anglicize, apotheosize, assize, atticize, *D* depoliticize, domesticize, *E* excise, exercise, exorcise, ecstasize, emblematicize, emphasize, ethicize, *F* fanaticize, fantasize, photosynthesize, *G* Gallicize, Gothicize, *H* hypostasize, hypotheosize, *I* incise, italicize, *K* capsize, Catholicize, *KL* classicize, *KR* criticize, *L* laicize, *M* metastasize, metathesize, mythicize, *O* ostracize, *outsize*, oversize, *P* parenthesize, poeticize, politicize, publicize, *PL* plasticize, *R* resize, romanticize, *S* Sinicize, *synopsize*, synthesize, circumcise, size, *SK* skepticize, Scotticize, *T* Turkicize

SPĪZ despise

THĪZ empathize, sympathize, telepathize, thighs

TĪZ *A* advertise, agatize, acclimatize, achromatize, alphabetize, amortize, anagrammatize, anathematize, anesthetize, appetize, apostatize, aromatize, athetize, *B* baptize, bureaucratize, *CH* chastise, *D* dehypnotize, demagnetize, democratize, demonetize, denarcotize, deputize, desensitize, diatize, digitize, dogmatize, *DR* dramatize, *E* egotize, emblematize, enigmatize, epigrammatize, *F* photosensitize, *H* hypersensitize, hypnotize, hyposensitize, hypostatize, *K* concretize, concertize, *KL* climatize, *L* legitimatize, *M* magnetize, mediatize, mediocratize, melodramatize, monetize, *N* narcotize, *O* operatize, automatize, *P* parasitize, poetize, *PR* pragmatize, prelatize, prioritize, proselytize, Protestantize,

R remonetize, *S* sanitize, sensitize, syncretize, synthesize, systematize, schismatize, sonnetize, sovietize, *SK* schematize, *ST* stigmatize, *TR* traumatize

TRĪZ idolatrize, geometrize, cicatrize, retries, tries·

VĪZ advise, devise, improvise, collectivize, revise, supervise, televise

WĪZ *A* afterwise, *anticlockwise*, *B* bookwise, *E* edgewise, *endwise*, anywise, *K* contrariwise, copywise, cornerwise, counterclockwise, *KL* *clockwise*, *KR* crabwise, crescentwise, *crosswise*, *L* likewise, *M* moneywise, *N* nowise, *O* overwise, *P* pennywise, *S* sidewise, somewise, *SL* slantwise, *ST* stagewise, *TR* travelwise, *U* unwise, otherwise, *W* weatherwise, *widthwise*, wise, *Z* zigzagwise

(See **Ī**, add -*s* or change -*y* to -*ies* where appropriate.)

IZ

IZ	is
BIZ	biz, show biz
DIZ	Cadiz
FIZ	fizz, phiz, golden fizz, gin fizz, rum fizz, silver fizz
FRIZ	frizz
HIZ	his
HWIZ	gee whiz, whiz
JIZ	gizz
KWIZ	quiz
MIZ	Ms.
RIZ	riz
SIZ	sizz
SKWIZ	squiz
SWIZ	swizz
TIZ	'tis
VIZ	vis, viz
WIZ	wis, wiz
ZIZ	zizz

ĪZD

ĪZD dandyized

(See **ĪZ** add -*ed* where appropriate.)

IZD

FIZD fizzed

(See **IZ**, add -*ed* or -*zed* where appropriate.)

IZM

IZM *A* absenteeism, allotheism, altruism, archaism, asteism, atheism, *B* babyism, Bahaism, bitheism, bogeyism, boobyism, bowwowism, *BL* bluestockingism, *D* deism, Dadaism, dandyism, dichroism, ditheism, *E* egoism, egotheism, echoism, *F* fairyism, fideism, physitheism, fogeyism, *FL* flunkeyism, *G* Ghandiism, ghettoism, *H* Hebraism, henotheism, heraism, heroism, hylozoism, Hinduism, *I* Englishism, Irishism, ism, *J* jingoism, jockeyism, Judaism, *K* kathenotheism, Cockneyism, *L* ladyism, Lamaism, Lamarckism, locoism, *M* Maoism, Mazdaism, McCarthyism, *misoneism*, Mithraism, monotheism, Mosaism, monkeyism, *O* ogreism, *P* pantheism, polytheism, powwowism, puppyism, *PR* Prosaism, *R* rowdyism, *S* Sivaism, sutteeism, *SH* Shintoism, *T* Taoism, Titoism, Toryism, *TH* theism, *TR* trichroism, tritheism, Trotskyism, *truism*, *U* ultraism, untruism, *Y* Yankeeism, euphuism, *Z* xanthachroism, zanyism

BIZM abysm, *cubism*, syllabism

BRIZM tenebrism

DIZM abecedism, braggardism, hyperthyroidism, hypothyroidism, invalidism, iodism, Lollardism, Methodism, monadism

FIZM *A* anthropomorphism, *B* biomorphism, *DW* dwarfism, *E* endomorphism, *F*

philosophism, *M*
mechanomorphism,
metamorphism, O
Orphism, *P* pacifism,
polymorphism, S
sapphism, SK scaphism

JIZM *A* antilogism, *D* dialogism,
E energism, *I* imagism, *J*
geophagism, jism, *L*
liturgism, *M*
meconophagism, *N*
neologism, *P* paralogism,
portmontologism, *S*
savagism, psychologism,
syllogism, synergism, *Y*
eulogism

KIZM anarchism, catechism,
masochism, monarchism,
sadomasochism,
sinarquism, *tychism*

KLIZM cataclysm
KRIZM chrism
KWIZM grandiloquism,
somniloquism,
ventriloquism

LIZM *A* agriculturalism,
accidentalism, alcoholism,
anabolism, animalism,
anomalism, *B Baalism,*
behavioralism,
bibliophilism,
bibliopolism, bimetallism,
botulism, *BR* brutalism, *D*
denominationalism,
departmentalism, devilism,
diabolism, digitalism,
dualism, *E* ebullism,
existentialism,
experimentalism,
externalism, embolism,
emotionalism,
environmentalism,
etherealism,
ethnophaulism,
evangelism, *F* fatalism,
federalism,
phenomenalism, finalism,
physicalism, formalism,
formulism, fossilism,
feudalism,
fundamentalism,
functionalism, *FR*
frivolism, frugalism, *H*
hyperbolism, *I* idealism,
eidolism, immaterialism,
immobilism, imperialism,
individualism,
industrialism, infantilism,
institutionalism,
instrumentalism,
intellectualism,
internationalism, *J*

gentilism, journalism, *K*
cabalism, cannibalism,
capitalism, carnalism,
catabolism, colloquialism,
colonialism,
commercialism,
communalism,
congregationalism,
conceptualism,
constitutionalism,
controversialism,
conventionalism, *KL*
classicalism, clericalism,
chloralism, *L* legalism,
liberalism, literalism,
localism, loyalism, *M*
materialism, medievalism,
Mendelism, mentalism,
mercantilism,
mercurialism, metabolism,
myalism, mongolianism,
monometallism,
monopolism, moralism,
municipalism, *N*
nationalism, naturalism,
necrophilism, nihilism,
neutralism, *O*
occasionalism,
operationalism, *P*
papalism, parallelism,
paternalism, personalism,
petalism, pointillism,
puerilism, pugilism, *PL*
pluralism, *PR* pre-
Raphaelism, probabilism,
professionalism,
proverbialism,
provincialism, *R*
radicalism, racialism,
rationalism, realism,
reformism, regionalism,
representationalism,
revivalism, ritualism,
rhopalism, royalism,
ruralism, *S*
sacramentalism,
sacerdotalism,
sensationalism,
sensualism,
sentimentalism, centralism,
servilism, symetallism,
syndicalism, symbolism,
sciolism, somnambulism,
somnolism, socialism,
supernaturalism,
surrealism, *SK* scopelism,
scoundrelism, *SKR*
scripturalism, *SP*
specialism, spiritualism,
ST structuralism, *T*
textualism, territorialism,
ptyalism, *THR*

thromboembolism, *TR*
traditionalism,
transsexualism,
transcendentalism,
tribalism, *traulism,*
troilism, V vandalism,
vanillism, verbalism,
virilism, vitalism,
vocalism, *Y* universalism,
Z Zoilism, zoophilism

MIZM *A* academism, *alarmism,*
anatomism, animism,
atomism, *D* dynamism,
dysphemism, *I* Islamism,
K cacophemism, *L*
legitimism, *M* Muslimism,
O optimism, *P* pessimism,
T totemism, *TR*
transformism, *U*
euphemism

NIZM *A* abolitionism,
abstractionism,
Africanism, agonism,
agrarianism, actinism,
albinism, alienism,
alpinism, Americanism,
anachronism, Anglicanism,
Anglo-Saxonism,
antagonism,
antidisestablishmentarianism,
antifeminism,
antiquarianism, Arianism,
asynchronism,
associationism, *B*
bacchanalianism,
Bohemianism,
Bourbonism, Buckmanism,
BR Brahmanism, *D*
Daltonism, Darwinism,
demonianism, demonism,
destinism, deviationism,
determinism, divisionism,
E exhibitionism,
expansionism,
expressionism,
equestrianism, eonism,
epicureanism, Erastianism,
establishmentarianism,
evolutionism, *F*
Fabianism, feminism,
Fenianism, phenomenism,
philanthropinism,
philhellenism, philistinism,
foreignism, *G* Galenism,
Gallicanism, galvanism,
GR grobianism, *H*
hedonism, Hellenism,
hereditarianism,
heathenism, Hibernianism,
hyperinsulinism,
histrionism, hooliganism,
humanism,

humanitarianism, *I*
Ibsenism, illuminism,
illusionism, immersionism,
impressionism,
indeterminism,
inflationism,
infralapsarianism,
infusionism, isolationism,
Italianism, *J* Jansenism,
Germanism, *K* Calvinism,
Canadianism, cocainism,
communism,
Confucianism, *KL*
cledonism, *KR*
creationism, cretinism, *L*
laconism, Latinism,
latitudinarianism,
Leninism, lesbianism,
libertinism, lionism,
Londonism, *M*
Mahometanism,
mammonism, mancinism,
McLuhanism, mechanism,
microorganism,
millenarianism,
minimifidianism,
misotramontanism,
modernism,
Mohammedanism,
monogenism, Montanism,
morphinism, Mormonism,
multitudinism,
Munchausenism, *N*
Neoimpressionism,
Neoplatonism,
necessarianism,
necessitarianism,
Nestorianism, nicotinism,
nonunionism, *O* onanism,
opportunism, organism,
Australianism,
Austrianism, *P* paganism,
parachronism,
parliamentarianism,
patricianism, pianism,
pedestrianism,
Pelagianism, pelmanism,
peonism, perfectionism,
pythonism,
postimpressionism,
Puritanism, *PL* Platonism,
plebianism, *PR*
predestinarianism,
Presbyterianism,
precisionism,
presentationism,
prohibitionism,
prochronism,
proletarianism,
protectionism, *R*
rabbinism, religionism,
republicanism,

restorationism,
revisionism, revolutionism,
Romanism, ruffianism, *S*
sabbatarianism, Saint-
Simonism, Satanism,
Saturnism,
sacramentarianism,
secessionism,
servomechanism,
synchronism, Syrianism,
socianism,
pseudoantidisestablishmentarianism,
SH shamanism,
charlatanism, Shavianism,
chauvinism, *SP*
spadonism, *ST* Stalinism,
STR strychninism, *SW*
Swedenborgianism, *T*
Timonism, Titanism,
tokenism, Teutonism, *TR*
traducianism,
Tractarianism, *U*
ultraantidesestablishment-
  arianism,
ultramontanism,
undinism, *V* Vaticanism,
vegetarianism, volcanism,
W westernism, *Y*
eudemonism, euphuism,
uniformitarianism,
Unitarianism, unionism
uranism, utilitarianism,
utopianism, *Z* Zionism,
Zoroastrianism

PIZM

PRIZM
RIZM

escapism, malapropism,
priapism, sinapism
pentaprism, prism
A adiaphorism,
adventurism, aphorism,
algorism, allegorism,
allomerism,
altrigenderism,
amateurism, anachronism,
aneurism, Archie
Bunkerism, asterism, *B*
bachelorism, barbarism,
behaviorism, bowdlerism,
bovarysm, *BL* bloomerism,
E Epicurism, etherism, *F*
phalansterism, futurism, *G*
Gongorism, *H* hetaearism,
hypocorism, historism,
Hitlerism, humorism, *I*
incendiarism, isomerism,
K characterism,
consumerism,
counterterrorism, *KW*
Quakerism, *L* laborism,
Lutherism, *M* mannerism,
metamerism, mesmerism,
mycterism, militarism, *N*

naturism, *O* odonterism, *P*
particularism, pasteurism,
peculiarism, pismerism,
pauperism, *PL* plagiarism,
R rigorism, *S* secularism,
Caesarism, psithurism,
solarism, *SP* spoonerism, *T*
terrorism, tigerism,
tautomerism, *TH* theorism,
V vampirism, *verism,*
vernacularism, vulturism,
vulgarism, *Y* euhemerism

SHIZM fetishism, Englishism,
Irishism

SIZM *A* agnosticism,
academicism, Anglicism,
asceticism, Atticism,
athleticism, Asiaticism, *BR*
Briticism, *D* demoniacism,
dichromaticism, *E*
eclecticism, ecclesiastism,
exorcism, exoticism,
electicism, empiricism,
eroticism, esotericism,
aestheticism, *F* phallicism,
fanaticism, fantasticism,
philanthropicism,
physicism, *G* Gothicism,
GR grammaticism, *H*
Hibernicism,
hypercriticism,
hypochondriacism,
Hispanicism, historicism,
histrionicism, *I* Italicism,
K Catholicism,
Kukluxicism, *KL*
classicism, *KR* criticism,
KW quixoticism, *L*
laconicism, lyricism,
logicism, *M Marxism,*
merycism metacism,
metricism, mysticism,
mytacism, monasticism, *N*
narcissism, neoclassicism,
neoplasticism, Gnosticism,
neuroticism, *O* ostracism,
P paroxysm, peripaticism,
publicism, *R* romanticism,
S cynicism, Sinicism,
schism, solecism,
solipsism, *SK* skepticism,
scholasticism, Scotticism,
ST stoicism, *T*
Teutonicism, *V* vorticism,
W witticism

THIZM agathism, erethism

TIZM *A* absolutism, Adamitism,
achromatism,
anathematism, animatism,
anti-Semitism,
astigmatism, *B*
Bonapartism, *CH*

chartism, *D* democratism, despotism, diamagnetism, dicrotism, dilettantism, diplomatism, dogmatism, Docetism, *E* egotism, exquisitism, electromagnetism, ergotism, *F* favoritism, ferromagnetism, fortuitism, *GR* grammatism, *H* helotism, *H* hylactism, hypnotism, homoerotism, *I* idiotism, ignorantism, immanentism, indifferentism, ipsedixitism, *J* geomagnetism, Jesuitism, gigantism, *K* charientism, cataglottism, conservatism, corybantism, *KW* quietism, *M* maritodespotism, magnetism, mithradatism, monochromatism, *mutism,* *N* narcotism, nepotism, *O* obscurantism, *occultism,* automatism, *P* paramagnetism, parasigmatism, patriotism, pedantism, pietism, pyrrhotism, pithiatism, *PR* pragmatism, prelatism, Protestantism, *R* rheumatism, *S* sabbatism, Semitism, separatism, scientism, cynicism, syncretism, syntheratism, systematism, Sovietism, suprematism, *SK* schematism, *ST* stigmatism, *T* tarantism, teratism, *TR* traumatism, *U* uxorodespotism, ultimatism, ultramontism, *V* virvestitism, *W* wegotism

TRIZM *androcentrism, egocentrism, ethnocentrism, polycentrism*

VIZM *A* activism, atavism, *B* Bolshevism, *I* intensivism, *K* collectivism, constructivism, *M* Menshevism, *N* nativism, negativism, *O* objectivism, *P* passivism, perspectivism, positivism, *PR* primitivism, progressivism, *R* relativism, recidivism, *S* subjectivism

WIZM *Yahwism*
ZIZM *Spinozism*

Ō

Ō *A* adagio, A.F.L.–C.I.O., Antonio, arpeggio, *B* billy-o, bocaccio, Boccaccio, borachio, Borachio, Borneo, *BR* braggadocio, *CH* cheerio, *D* deario, *E* ex officio, embryo, etaerio, *F* fabliau, fellatio, folio, *H* histrio, *I* imbroglio, impresario, intaglio, *K* k.o., kayo, cameo, capriccio, *carabao,* curio, *L* Lothario, *M* Montevideo, mustachio, *N* nuncio, *O* O, oe, oh, owe, audio, oleo, olio, Ontario, oratorio, *P* patio, pistachio, Pinocchio, portfolio, punctilio, *PR* presidio, *R* radio, ratio, rodeo, Romeo, *S* scenario, seraglio, solfeggio, *SK* Scorpio, *ST* stereo, studio, *T* tetrao, *V* vibrio, video, vireo

BLŌ blow, *by-blow,* death blow, counterblow, *pueblo,* tableau

BŌ *B* beau, 'bo, 'boe, bow, *E* embow, *G* gazabo, gazebo, *J* jabot, jambeau, *KR* crossbow, *L* long bow, *O* oboe, oxbow, *R* rainbow, *S* sabot, saddlebow

CHŌ Chou, *gazpacho, honcho, macho, poncho, Sancho*

DŌ bandeau, Bordeaux, *dado, dido, Dido, dildo,* doe, doh, dough, do-si-do, rideau, rondeau, *rondo*

FŌ Defoe, foe, comme il faut, *Sappho*

FLŌ aflow, *airflow,* floe, flow, ice floe, *inflow, outflow,* overflow

FRŌ fro, froe, to-and-fro
GLŌ afterglow, aglow, alpenglow, *earthglow,* glow, counterglow, *moonglow, starglow, sunglow*

GŌ *A* ago, archipelago, *argot, E* escargot, *F* forgo, forego, *G* Galapago, go, *I* indigo, *L* long ago, *O* outgo, *T* touch-and-go, *U* undergo, *V* Van Gogh, vertigo, gigot

GRŌ grow, ingrow, intergrow, outgrow, overgrow, upgrow

HŌ *A* Arapaho, *H* heigh-ho, ho, hoe, *M* mahoe, *I* Idaho, *N* Navaho, Navajo, *O* oho, *S* Soho, *T* tallyho, tuckahoe, *W* westward ho

HWŌ whoa
JŌ adagio, *banjo,* G. I. Joe
KŌ *A* angelico, *B* bunko, *H* haricot, *J* Jericho, *K* calico, cantico, ko, Ko, coquelicot, *coco, cocoa, M* magnifico, medico, Mexico, *moko, moko-moko, P* persico, politico, portico, *R* rococo, *S* simpatico, *U* unco

KRŌ *cockcrow, cro, crow, escrow, Jim Crow, overcrow, pilcrow, scarecrow*

KWŌ in statu quo, quid pro quo, quo, status quo
KYŌ *Tokyo*
LŌ *A* alow, *B* below, bibelot, bombolo, buffalo, bummalo, bungalow, *BR* brigalow, *D* diabolo, *F* furbelow, *H* hallo, hello, hullo, *J* gigolo, *K* cachalot, cattalo, *L* lo, low, *M* matelot, Michelangelo, *P* pedalo, piccolo, pomelo, *R* rouleau, rumbelow, *S* cembalo, cymbalo, *T* tableau, tangelo, *TR* tremolo

MŌ *A* alamo, Alamo, altissimo, *B* bon mot *BR* bravissimo, *D* dynamo, dulcissimo, duodecimo, *E* Eskimo, *F* fortissimo, *H* half a mo', *haymow, homo, J* generalissimo, Geronimo, *K* kokomo, *M* mho, mo, mot, mow, *P* paramo, pianissimo, *PR* proximo, *S* centissimo, *TW* twelvemo', *U* ultimo

NŌ domino, foreknow, know, no, pompano, tonneau, unknow

PŌ apropos, *depot,* entrepot, gapo, kakapo, malapropos, po, Poe, chapeau

PRŌ pro, semipro
PYŌ papiopio

RŌ	*A* arow, *B* bureau, *D* Death Row, *H* hedgerow, hetero, *J* genro, *K* carot, *P* Pernod, Pierrot, *R* rho, ro, roe, row, Rotten Row, *S* serow, Cicero, *SK* Skid Row, *T* tarot, *W* windrow
SHMŌ	schmo, shmo
SHŌ	*D* dogshow, *F* fashion show, foreshow, *G* girlie show, *H* horseshow, *M* motion-picture show, *P* peepshow, *S* sideshow, *SH* shew, sho', show, *ST* styleshow
SKRŌ	scrow
SLŌ	sloe, slow
SNŌ	besnow, snow
SŌ	how so, Curacao, oversow, resew, resow, Rousseau, sew, so, so-and-so, *so-so*, sow, trousseau, Tussaud
STŌ	bestow, stow
STRŌ	bestrow, strow
THŌ	although, *litho*, though
THRŌ	death throe, *downthrow*, overthrow, rethrow, throe, throw, *upthrow*
TŌ	*A* atiptoe, *B* bateau, *G* gateau, *H* hammertoe, *I* incognito, *K* cabatoe, couteau, *M* manito, manteau, mistletoe, *P* paletot, *potato*, portmanteau, *PL* plateau, *SH* chateau, *T* tick-tack-toe, timbertoe, *tomato*, *'tiptoe*, toe, tow, *U* undertow, *W* Watteau
TRŌ	de trop, trow
WŌ	wo, woe
YŌ	imbroglio, intaglio, maillot, seraglio, *yoyo*
ZŌ	dzo

Ô

Ô	aw, awe, overawe
BÔ	usquebaugh
BRÔ	braw
CHÔ	chaw
DÔ	dauw, daw, *jackdaw*, *landau*
DRÔ	draw, overdraw, redraw, undraw, withdraw
FLÔ	flaw
FÔ	faugh, guffaw
GÔ	gaw, *gewgaw*
HÔ	heehaw, haw, hawhaw
JÔ	jaw, *flapjaw*, *crackjaw*, *lockjaw*, underjaw

KLÔ	*dew-claw*, clappermaclaw, claw, crab claw, lobster claw
KÔ	caw, macaw
KRÔ	craw
LÔ	*B* by-law, *BR* brother-in-law, *D* daughter-in-law, *F* father-in-law, *I* in-law, *L* law, *M* mother-in-law, *O* outlaw, *P* pilau, pilaw, *S* sister-in-law, son-in-law, *SK* scofflaw
MÔ	maw
NÔ	begnaw, mackinaw, gnaw, naw
PÔ	foxpaw, forepaw, papaw, paw, pawpaw, southpaw
RÔ	hurrah, raw
SHÔ	*kickshaw, cumshaw, rickshaw, pshaw, Shaw, scrimshaw, wappenschaw*
SKÔ	scaw
SKWÔ	squaw
SLÔ	cole slaw, overslaugh, slaw
SMÔ	sma'
SÔ	Arkansas, *bowsaw, bucksaw, buzz saw, chainsaw, chickasaw, Chickasaw, foresaw, hacksaw, handsaw, whipsaw, jigsaw, oversaw, saw, seesaw*
SPÔ	spa
STRÔ	*bedstraw*, windlestraw, straw
TÔ	tau, taw, Wichita
THÔ	thaw
THRÔ	thraw
WÔ	williwaw, waw
YÔ	yaw

ŌB

ŌB	aube
DŌB	daube
FŌB	Anglophobe, aerophobe (etc. See **FŌ′BI.A,** change ending to *-phobe* where appropriate.)
GLŌB	englobe, globe, conglobe, 'round the globe
JŌB	Job
KRŌB	*microbe*
LŌB	*earlobe*, lobe
PRŌB	probe, reprobe, unprobe
RŌB	aerobe, *bathrobe*, disrobe, enrobe, rerobe, robe, unrobe, *wardrobe*
STRŌB	strobe

ÔB

DÔB	bedaub, daub, redaub
GÔB	gaub
WÔB	nawab

OB

BLOB	blob
BOB	bob, earbob, cabob, nabob, shishkabob, skibob, thingumabob, thingumbob
BROB	brob
FOB	fob, *watchfob*
GLOB	glob
GOB	gob
HOB	hob
JOB	job
KOB	*kincob*, cob, kob, *corncob*
KWOB	quab
LOB	lob
MOB	demob, mob
NOB	hob-and-nob, *hobnob*, knob, nob
ROB	*carob*, rob
SKOB	scob
SKWOB	squab
SLOB	slob
SNOB	snob
SOB	sob
STOB	stob
SWOB	swab
THROB	athrob, *heartthrob*, throb
YOB	yob

OBZ

BOBZ	ods bobs
GLOBZ	globs
GOBZ	gobs
SKOBZ	scobs

(See **OB**, add *-s* where appropriate.)

ŌCH

BRŌCH	abroach, broach, brooch
KŌCH	encoach, coach, *mailcoach*, motorcoach, *slowcoach*, stagecoach
KRŌCH	encroach, croche
LŌCH	loach
PŌCH	poach
PRŌCH	approach, reproach, self-reproach
RŌCH	caroche, *cockroach*, roach
SNŌCH	snoach

ÔCH

BÔCH	debauch
NÔCH	nautch, pootly-nauch
WÔCH	anchor watch, *deathwatch, dogwatch,* harbor watch, larboard watch, night watch, outwatch, starboard watch, watch

OCH

BLOCH	blotch
BOCH	botch
GOCH	gotch
HOCH	hotch
KROCH	crotch
NOCH	notch, topnotch
POCH	*hotchpotch*
ROCH	rotch, rotche
SKOCH	*hopscotch,* scotch, Scotch
SPLOCH	splotch
SWOCH	swatch
WOCH	death watch, digital watch, *dogwatch, nightwatch,* overwatch, *wristwatch, stopwatch,* watch

ŌCHT

BRŌCHT	broached

(See **ŌCH,** add *-ed* where appropriate.)

ÔCHT

BÔCHT	debauched

(See **ÔCH,** add *-ed* where appropriate.)

OCHT

BLOTCHT	blotched

(See **OCH,** add *-ed* where appropriate.)

ŌD

ŌD	ode, ohed, owed, unowed
BŌD	abode, bode, forebode
GŌD	goad
HŌD	hoed
KŌD	area code, decode, encode, genetic code, code, Morse code, postal code, zip code
LŌD	*B boatload, FR freeload, WH whipload, K carload, L* load, lode, *O* overload, *P payload, R* reload, *SH shipload, TR truckload U* unload, *W workload*
MŌD	a la mode, alamode, discommode, incommode, commode, mode
NŌD	*anode,* antinode, internode, node, palinode, staminode
PLŌD	explode, implode
PŌD	antipode, *epode,* hemipode, lycopode, megapode
RŌD	*byroad,* bridle road, erode, high road, *highroad, inroad,* corrode, low road, middle-of-the-road, Nesselrode, *railroad,* road, rode
SHŌD	shoad, shode, showed
SŌD	episode, resewed, resowed, sewed, sowed
SPŌD	spode
STŌD	bestowed, stowed, rebestowed, restowed, unbestowed, unstowed
STRŌD	bestrode, strode
THŌD	hydathode
TŌD	horned toad, nematode, pigeon-toed, retoed, retowed, toad, toed, towed, trematode, untoed
WŌD	woad
ZŌD	episode

(See **Ō,** add *-d* or *-ed* where appropriate.)

ÔD

ÔD	awed, over-awed, unawed
BÔD	baud, bawd, kilobaud
BRÔD	abroad, broad
FRÔD	defraud, fraud
GÔD	gaud
JÔD	glass-jawed, iron-jawed, steel-jawed, water-jawed
LÔD	belaud, laud, relaud
MÔD	maud
PLÔD	applaud, reapplaud
RÔD	maraud
YÔD	yaud, yauld

(See **Ô,** add *-ed* where appropriate.)

OD

OD	Hesiod, od, Od, odd
BOD	bod, Ichabod
GOD	demigod, god, God, river god, sea god
HOD	hod
KLOD	clod
KOD	Cape Cod, cod, *lingcod,* ostracod, *tomcod*
KWOD	quod
MOD	mod
NOD	*nid-nod,* nod
PLOD	plod
POD	*A* amphipod, anglepod, anthropod, arthropod, *BR* brachiopod, branchiopod, *D* decapod, diplopod, *G* gastropod, *H* hexapod, *K* chenopod, cheetopod, chilopod, copepod, *L* landing pod, *M* megapod, *O* octopod, ornithopod, *P peapod,* pod, polypod, *PL* platypod, *R* rhizopod, *S* cephalopod, sauropod, pseudopod, *SK* scaphopod, *T* pteropod, tetrapod, tylopod, *TH* theropod, *Y* unipod
PROD	prod, reprod
ROD	Aaron's rod, divining rod, emerod, goldenrod, *hotrod,* curling rod, *Nimrod,* piston rod, *pushrod, ramrod,* rod
SHOD	dry-shod, reshod, roughshod, shod, *slipshod,* unshod
SKROD	scrod
SKWOD	squad
SNOD	snod
SOD	sod
TOD	tod
TROD	retrod, trod, untrod
VOD	eisteddfod
WOD	*tightwad,* wad, wod

ŌDZ

RŌDZ	Rhodes

(See **ŌD,** add *-s* where appropriate.)

ODZ

ODZ	emerods, odds

(See **OD,** add *-s* where appropriate.)

ŌF

ŌF	oaf
GŌF	goaf
KŌF	koph, qoph

ROYAL LAP-YAP

By Louis' side in royal tumbril,
   How woefully his lapdog wailed!—
Not for the King to be beheaded,
   But for the Dog to be curtailed.

LŌF	*breadloaf,* half a loaf, quarterloaf, loaf, sugarloaf
STRŌF	monostrophe
TŌF	toph
TRŌF	limitrophe

ÔF

CHÔF	Gorbachev, Khrushchev
KÔF	*chincough,* whooping cough, cough, Nabakov, Rimsky-Korsakov
MÔF	maugh
NÔF	Romanov
TÔF	Molotov
TRÔF	trough

OF

OF	*brush-off,* cast-off, *kick-off,* kick off, off, *rip-off,* rip off, *send-off, takeoff, wave-off*
DOF	doff
GLOF	glof
GOF	goff, golf
KOF	coff
KWOF	quaff
NOF	gnoff, Rachmaninoff, Stroganoff
PROF	prof
SHROF	shroff
SKOF	scoff
SOF	bibliosoph, philosoph, soph
TOF	toff

OFT

OFT	oft
KROFT	croft, undercroft
LOFT	aloft, *hayloft, cockloft,* loft

SOFT	soft
TOFT	toft

(See **OF**, add *-ed* where appropriate.)

ŌG

BŌG	bogue, disembogue
BRŌG	brogue
DRŌG	drogh, drogue
LŌG	collogue
RŌG	pirogue, prorogue, rogue
SHŌG	pishogue
THŌG	kitthoge
TŌG	togue
TRŌG	trogue
VŌG	vogue

ÔG

MÔG	maug
SHÔG	*pishaug*

OG

OG	Og
BOG	bog, embog
BROG	brog
CHOG	Patchogue
DOG	attack-dog, *bird-dog, bulldog,* dog, *fog-dog, fire-dog, hangdog,* hot dog, hound dog, coach dog, mad dog, police dog, prairie dog, *seadog,* sun dog, *sheepdog,* underdog, *watchdog* (etc.)
FLOG	flog, reflog
FOG	befog, defog, fog, megafog, peasoup fog, pettifog
FROG	*bullfrog,* frog, *leapfrog*
GLOG	glogg
GOG	*A* agog, *D* demagogue, *E* emmenagogue, *F* physagogue, *FL* phlegmagogue, *G* galactagogue, gog, Gog, Gog and Magog, Gogmagog, *goosegog, H* haemagogue, hydragogue, holagogue, *L* logogogue, *M Magog,* mystagogue, *O* osmagogue, *P* pedagogue, *S* sialagogue, synagogue, *Z* xenagogue
GROG	grog
HOG	*groundhog, hedgehog,* hog, *quahog,* road hog,

sandhog, seahog, shearhog, warthog

JOG	jog
KLOG	clog, reclog, unclog
KOG	cog, incog
KWOG	quag
LOG	*A* analogue, apologue, *B* backlog, *D* decalogue, dialogue, duologue, *E* eclogue, epilogue, *F* philologue, *GR* grammalogue, *H* homologue, horologue, *K* catalogue, *L* Lincoln log, log, *loglog, M* melologue, myriologue, *N* necrologue, *P putlog, PR prologue, S* sinologue, *T* Tagalog, *TH* theologue, *TR* travelogue, trialogue
MOG	mog
NOG	*eggnog, crannog,* nog
POG	pogge
PROG	prog
SHOG	shog
SKROG	scrog
SLOG	footslog, slog
SMOG	smog
SNOG	snog
SOG	sog
TOG	*tautog,* tog
TROG	trog
WOG	golliwog, polliwog, wog

OGD

BOGD	bogged

(See **OG**, add *-ged* where appropriate.)

OI

OI	oi, oy
BOI	*A* attaboy, altar boy, *B* batboy, boy, buoy, *bellboy, bellbuoy,* ball boy, *BR* breeches buoy, *CH* charity boy, *D dayboy, doughboy, footboy, H highboy, hautboy, hallboy, houseboy, HW* whistlebuoy, *K* carboy, callboy, cowboy, *KW* choirboy, *L liftboy, linkboy,* loblolly boy, *lowboy, M* maccaboy, mama's boy, *messboy, O hautboy,* oh boy, *P pageboy,* paperboy,

	postboy, potboy, PL	**GOID**	*algoid, fungoid,*
	playboy, plowboy, S		*spongoid, tringoid*
	sonobuoy, SK *schoolboy,*	**GROID**	*congroid, Negroid*
	ST *stableboy,* T *tallboy,*	**JOID**	enjoyed, joyed, overjoyed
	tomboy, Y *yellowboy*	**KLOID**	*epicycloid,* cloyed,
CHOI	bok choy, *pakchoi*		*cycloid,* uncloyed
FOY	foy	**KOID**	A *alopecoid, anthracoid,*
GOI	goi, goy		D *discoid,* F *fucoid,* H
HOI	ahoy, hobberdehoy,		*helicoid,* J *gynaecoid,* K
	hobble-de-hoy, hoy		*coracoid,* KR *cricoid,* L
JOI	enjoy, joy, *killjoy,*		*lumbricoid,* M *maskoid,*
	montjoy, overjoy		*mineralocorticoid,*
KLOI	cloy		*mycoid, mucoid, muscoid,*
KOI	decoy, coy, koi		O *autacoid,* P *percoid,*
KWOI	Iroquois		*pinacoid,* PL *placoid,* S
LOI	alloy, hoi polloi,		*sarcoid, cercopithecoid,*
	kumbaloi, loy, permalloy,		*cysticercoid,* T *toxicoid,*
	saveloy		TR *trichoid, trochoid,* V
MOI	moy		*viscoid*
NOI	annoy, Hanoi, Illinois	**KROID**	*cancroid, melanochroid,*
PLOI	deploy, employ, ploy,		*chancroid, xanthocroid*
	redeploy, reemploy	**KWOID**	*equoid*
POI	avoirdupois, charpoi, poi,	**LOID**	A *alkaloid, alloyed,*
	sepoy, teapoy		*amygdaloid, amyloid,* D
ROI	corduroy, Rob Roy,		*dactyloid,* E *encephaloid,*
	viceroy		*eripsyloid,* F *phylloid,* H
SOI	paduasoy, soy		*haloid, haploid, hyaloid,*
STOI	*Tolstoi*		*hyperboloid, hypsiloid,* K
STROI	destroy, search-and-		*keloid, colloid,*
	destroy, stroy		*condyloid, coralloid,*
TOI	toy		*cotyloid, cuculoid,* KR
TROI	troy, Troy		*crystalloid,* M *meloid,*
VOI	*envoy,* convoy, cunjevoi,		*metalloid, myeloid,*
	lenvoi, savoy, Savoy,		*myloid, mongoloid,* N
	travois, travoy		*nautiloid,* O *omphaloid,*
ZOI	*borzoi*		*opaloid,* P *paraboloid,*

OID

			petaloid, R *reptiloid,* S
			cephaloid, celluloid,
			sepaloid, sialoid, SK
OID	blennioid, gobioid,		*squaloid,* ST *styloid,* T
	histioid, *hyoid,* ichthyoid,		*tabloid, tentaculoid,*
	cardioid, ophioid, *ooid,*		*tuberculoid,* TR *triploid,*
	osteoid, *pyoid,* scorpioid,		U *unalloyed,* V *varioloid,*
	zooid		*varicelloid,* Z *xyloid*
BOID	amoeboid, buoyed,	**MOID**	*dermoid, desmoid,*
	globoid, cuboid,		*entomoid, ethmoid,*
	rebuoyed, *rhomboid,*		*comoid, prismoid, sigmoid,*
	scaraboid, *stromboid,*		*cymoid, sphygmoid*
	unbuoyed	**NOID**	A *adenoid, actinoid,*
BROID	*fibroid, lambroid,*		*albuminoid,* annoyed,
	scombroid		*arachnoid,* B *balanoid,*
DOID	*gadoid, lambdoid,*		*bioflavinoid,* BL *blennoid,*
	pyramidoid		DR *drepanoid,* E
DROID	*android, dendroid,*		*echinoid,* G *ganoid,* GL
	octahedroid, polyhedroid,		*glenoid,* H *hypnoid,*
	salamandroid, cylindroid,		*hominoid, humanoid,* J
	tetrahedroid		*gelatinoid,* K *carotinoid,*
FOID	*didelphoid, lymphoid,*		*catenoid, conoid,*
	paratyphoid, scaphoid,		*coronoid,* KL *clenoid,* KR
	typhoid, xiphoid		*crinoid,* L *lunoid,* M
FROID	Freud		*melanoid,* N *nanoid,* O
			ochinoid, P *paranoid,* PL

	platinoid, R *resinoid,* S
	salmonoid, cynoid,
	cyprinoid, solenoid, SF
	sphenoid, SK
	scorpaenoid, SP *spinoid,*
	T *ctenoid, tetanoid*
PLOID	deployed, *diploid,*
	employed, misemployed,
	ployed, redeployed,
	reemployed, underemployed,
	undeployed, unemployed,
	euploid
POID	anthropoid, *lipoid,*
	polypoid, *trappoid,*
	vespoid
ROID	A *acaroid, amberoid,*
	aneroid, ankyroid,
	antheroid, asteroid, B
	bacteroid, D *diphtheroid,*
	H *hemorrhoid,*
	hemispheroid, hysteroid,
	K *chorioid, choroid,*
	corticosteroid, L
	lamuroid, laroid,
	lemuroid, liparoid, M
	meteoroid, N *nephroid,* O
	ochroid, P *parathyroid,*
	polaroid, porphyroid, R
	rhinoceroid, roid, S
	saccharoid, sciuroid, SF
	spheroid, SK *scleroid,* SP
	spiroid, ST *steroid,* T
	pteroid, toroid, TH
	theroid, thyroid
SLOID	sloyd
SOID	*ellipsoid, emulsoid,*
	Caucasoid, sinusoid,
	cissoid, suspensoid,
	schizoid, toxoid, ursoid
STROID	destroyed, redestroyed,
	undestroyed
THOID	*acanthoid, lithoid,* ornithoid
TOID	A *allantoid, archtoid,* D
	deltoid, dentoid, E
	elephantoid, epileptoid,
	GR *granitoid,* H
	hematoid, herpetoid,
	histoid, K *keratoid,* L
	lacertoid, lentoid, M
	mastoid, N *nematoid,* O
	odontoid, P
	pachydermatoid, parotoid,
	PL *planetoid,* PR
	prismatoid, R *rheumatoid,*
	S *cestoid, cystoid,* T
	teratoid, toyed
TROID	*astroid, centroid*
VOID	avoid, devoid, convoyed,
	obovoid, *ovoid,* void
ZOID	*rhizoid,* trapezoid

(See **OI**, add *-ed* where appropriate.)

OIL

OIL	enoil, lubricating oil, oil, snake oil
BOIL	aboil, boil, *gumboil, hardboil, parboil*
BROIL	broil, disembroil, embroil, rebroil, reembroil
DOIL	langue d'oïl
FOIL	quatrefoil, counterfoil, multifoil, cinquefoil, silverfoil, tin foil, *trefoil*
GOIL	*gargoyle,* goyle
KOIL	accoil, coil, recoil, uncoil, upcoil
MOIL	moil, moyle, *turmoil*
NOIL	noil
POIL	poil
ROIL	roil
SOIL	assoil, soil, *subsoil, topsoil,* undersoil
SPOIL	despoil, spoil, unspoil
STROIL	stroil
TOIL	entoil, estoile, overtoil, toil, toile
VOIL	voile

OILD

OILD	oiled

(See **OIL**, add *-ed* where appropriate.)

OIN

FOIN	*sainfoin*
GOIN	Burgoyne
GROIN	groin, groyne
JOIN	*A* adjoin, *D* disjoin, *E* enjoin, *I* interjoin, *J* join, *K* conjoin, *M* misjoin, *R* rejoin, *S* sejoin, subjoin, surrejoin, unjoin
KOIN	coigne, coin, quoin, recoin
KWOIN	quoin
LOIN	eloign, loin, purloin, *sirloin,* tenderloin
MOIN	almoign, Des Moines, frankalmoigne
POIN	talapoin
SOIN	essoin

OIND

POIND	poind

(See **OIN**, add *-ed* where appropriate.)

OINT

OINT	adjoint, disjoint, dowel joint, hinge joint, hip joint, joint, conjoint, knee joint (etc.)
NOINT	anoint, reanoint
POINT	*B* ballpoint, *BL* bluepoint, *BR* breakpoint, brownie point, *CH* checkpoint, *D* disappoint, *DR* drypoint, *E* embonpoint, *G* gunpoint, *K* counterpoint, coverpoint, *M* midpoint, *N* needlepoint, *knickpoint, P* pinpoint, point, *pourpoint, R* reappoint, repoint, *S* silverpoint, *ST standpoint, V* viewpoint, *W* West Point

OINTS

JOINTS	disjoints, joints (etc.)

(See **OINT**, add *-s* where appropriate.)

OIS

CHOIS	choice, fielder's choice, first choice, Hobson's choice, last choice, pro-choice, second choice, *top-choice*
JOIS	James Joyce, rejoice
ROIS	Rolls-Royce
VOIS	*invoice,* outvoice, revoice, unvoice, voice

OIST

FOIST	foist, refoist
HOIST	hoist, rehoist
JOIST	joist, rejoiced, unrejoiced
MOIST	moist
VOIST	*loud-voiced, low-voiced, shrill-voiced,* unvoiced

OIT

DOIT	doit
DROIT	adroit, droit, maladroit
KOIT	dacoit, coit
KWOIT	quoit
MOIT	moit
PLOIT	exploit, reexploit
TOIT	hoity-toit, toit
TROIT	Detroit

OITS

KROITS	hakenkreuz
KWOITS	quoits

(See **OIT**, add *-s* where appropriate.)

OIZ

FROIZ	froise
NOIZ	erminois, noise
POIZ	avoirdupois, equipoise, counterpoise, poise

(See **OI**, add *-s* where appropriate.)

ŌJ

BŌJ	gamboge
DŌJ	doge
LŌJ	horologe, loge

OJ

BOJ	bodge
DOJ	dodge
HOJ	hodge
LOJ	dislodge, horologe, lodge, relodge, unlodge
MOJ	modge
PLOJ	plodge
POJ	*hodgepodge,* podge
SPLOJ	splodge
STOJ	stodge
WOJ	wodge

OJD

BOJD	bodged

(See **OJ**, add *-d* where appropriate.)

ŌK

ŌK	black oak, British oak, evergreen oak, holm oak, white oak, English oak, oak, oke, pickled oak, pin oak, post oak, red oak, scrub oak (etc.)
BLŌK	bloke
BRŌK	broke, dead broke, go for broke, outbroke, unbroke, upbroke
CHŌK	artichoke, choke
DŌK	doke, okeydoke
FŌK	folk, gentlefolk, *kinfolk, kinsfolk,* countryfolk,

	little folk, *menfolk, seafolk, townfolk, townsfolk, tradesfolk, womenfolk, workfolk*
HŌK	hoke
JŌK	joke
KLŌK	cloak, mourning cloak, recloak, uncloak
KŌK	decoke, coak, coke
KRŌK	croak
LŌK	loke
MŌK	moch, moke
NŌK	Roanoke
PŌK	mopoke, pig-in-a-poke, poke, *shitepoke, slowpoke*
RŌK	baroque, roque
SLŌK	sloke
SMŌK	smoke, besmoke, smoke
SŌK	asoak, soak, soke
SPŌK	bespoke, forespoke, forspoke, respoke, spoke, unspoke
STŌK	stoke
STRŌK	*B backstroke, BR breaststroke, D deathstroke, H handstroke, heartstroke, K keystroke,* counterstroke, *M* masterstroke, *O* overstroke, *S sidestroke, sunstroke, STR* stroke, *TH* thunderstroke, *U* understroke, upstroke
TŌK	toke, toque
TRŌK	troke
VŌK	equivoke, equivoque, evoke, invoke, convoke, provoke, revoke
WŌK	awoke, rewoke, woke
YŌK	reyoke, unyoke, yoke, yolk

ÔK

ÔK	auk, awk
BÔK	balk, baulk
CHÔK	chalk
DÔK	dawk
GÔK	gawk, Van Gogh
HÔK	fish hawk, *goshawk,* hawk, *Mohawk, newshawk, nighthawk,* sparrow hawk, winklehawk (etc.)
JÔK	jauk
KÔK	calk
KWÔK	quawk
LÔK	lawk
MÔK	maugh, mawk
PÔK	pawk

RÔK	baroque
SKWÔK	squawk
STÔK	*beanstalk, leafstalk, cornstalk,* stalk
TÔK	baby-talk, back talk, *black-talk, girl-talk,* crosss talk, *man-talk,* man-to-man talk, *shoptalk,* table-talk, talk, woman-talk
WÔK	*boardwalk, jaywalk, cakewalk, catwalk, crosswalk, outwalk, overwalk, ropewalk, sheepwalk, sidewalk, sleepwalk, spacewalk,* walk

OK

OK	Antioch, och
BLOK	auction block, bloc, block, *breechblock,* butcher block, chockablock, en bloc, *roadblock,* city block, stumbling block, unblock
BOK	*blesbok, blaubok,* bock, bontebok, *grysbok, gemsbok, klipbok, rhebok, sjambok, springbok, steinbok*
BROK	broch, brock
CHOK	chock, *forechock*
DOK	*burdock,* doc, dock, *langue d'oc,* Medoc, spatterdock, undock
FLOK	flock
FROK	defrock, frock, unfrock
GOK	Van Gogh
GROK	grok
HOK	ad hoc, *ham-hock,* hock, hollyhock, *Mohock*
JOK	jock
KLOK	eight-day clock, biological clock, body clock, clock
KOK	*A acock, angekok, B Bangkok, bibcock,* billy cock, ball cock, *BL blackcock, G gamecock,* gocock, *H half-cock,* haycock, *K* cock, *M moorcock, P peacock, petcock, pinchcock,* poppycock, *PR princock, S seacock, SH shittlecock,* shuttlecock, *SP spatchcock, spitchcock, ST stopcock, T turkeycock, turncock, W* weathercock, *woodcock*

KROK	crock
LOK	*A airlock, B belock, CH charlock, D daglock, deadlock, E elflock, F fetlock,* fetterlock, *firelock, forelock, FL flintlock, G gavelock, gunlock, H havelock, headlock, hemlock, I* interlock, *L loch, lock, lough, lovelock, M Moloch, O oarlock, P padlock,* percussion lock, *picklock, R relock, wristlock, rowlock, SH Sherlock, Shylock, U* unlock, *W wedlock, warlock*
MOK	amok, bemock, moch, mock
NOK	*monadnock,* knock, nock
PLOK	plock
POK	*kapok,* pock, yapok
ROK	*A acid rock, B bedrock, H* hard rock, *L lavarock,* Little Rock, *P* Painted Rock, punk rock, *R ragarock, rimrock,* roc, rock, *SH shamrock, TR traprock, W* weeping rock
SHLOK	schlock
SHOK	*foreshock,* shock
SMOK	smock
SOK	soc, sock, *windsock*
STOK	*A alpenstock, B bitstock, BL bloodstock, D diestock, DR drillstock, G* gapingstock, *HW* whisperstock, *L* laughingstock, *linstock, livestock, O* overstock, *P penstock, R* restock, *rootstock, ST* stock, *T tailstock, U* understock, unstock
TOK	tick-tock, tock, Vladivostok
WOK	jabberwock, wok
YOK	yock

ŌKS

HŌKS	hoax
KŌKS	coax

(See ÔK, add -*s* where appropriate.)

ÔKS

LÔKS	lawks

(See ÔK, add -*s* where appropriate.)

OKS

OKS	*musk-ox*, ox
BOKS	*A abox, B ballot box, bandbox,* box, *CH chatterbox, G gearbox, gogglebox, H hatbox, horsebox, I idiot box, icebox, J jukebox, KR Christmas box, L loosebox, M matchbox, mailbox, O honor box, P paddlebox, paintbox, pillbox,* pillar box, *postbox,* powder box, *S saltbox,* signal box, *soapbox, soundbox, SH* shooting box, *SN snuffbox, STR strongbox, T tinderbox, W workbox*
DOKS	*boondocks, philodox, heterodox, homodox, orthodox, paradox, redox, unorthodox*
FLOKS	phlox
FOKS	fox, outfox
GROKS	groks
KOKS	cox, *princox*
LOKS	bladderlocks, Goldilocks, locks, lox
NOKS	equinox, Fort Knox, hard knocks, knocks, Nox
POKS	chickenpox, *cowpox,* pox, *smallpox, swinepox*
SOKS	socks, sox
TOKS	detox
VOKS	vox

(See **OK**, add *-s* where appropriate.)

ŌKT

CHŌKT	choked

(See **ŌK**, add *-d* where appropriate.)

OKT

GROKT	grokked
KOKT	decoct, concoct, recoct

(See **OK**, add *-ed* where appropriate.)

ŌL

ŌL	*A apiole, ariole, arteriole, BR bronchiole, D dariole, F foliole, GL gloriole,* glory 'ole, *K cabriole,* capriole, cariole, *KR* creole, Creole, *O* ol', 'ole, aureole, oriole, ostiole, *P* petiole, *S* centriole, *SH* Sheol, *V* vacuole, variole
BŌL	*A amphibole, B bole,* boll, bowl, *E embowl, F fishbowl, K carambole,* Cotton Bowl, *O obole, P punchbowl, R rocambole,* Rose Bowl, *S* Super Bowl, *SH* Sugar Bowl (etc.), *SW swillbowl, W* wassail bowl
DŌL	dhole, dole, farandole, *indole,* girandole, condole
DRŌL	droll
FŌL	foal
GŌL	de Gaulle, goal, segol
HŌL	*A armhole, B borehole, bunghole,* buttonhole, *BL* black hole, *blowhole, F foxhole, FR frijol, GL* gloryhole, *H heart-whole, hell-whole,* hole, whole, eyehole, *K keyhole,* cubbyhole, *L loophole, M* manhole, Mohole, *N* kneehole, knothole, *O* augur hole, *P peephole,* personhole, pigeonhole, *pinhole, porthole, pothole, SK* scupperhole, *SW* swimminghole, *T tophole, U* unwhole
JŌL	cajole, jole
KŌL	arvicole, bricole, *charcoal,* caracole, *clearcole,* coal, cole, kohl, latebricole, pratincole
MŌL	mole, septimole
NŌL	jobbernowl, knoll, Seminole
NYŌL	guignol, carmagnole, croquignole
PŌL	*B bargepole, beanpole, bibliopole, E edipol, F* fishing pole, *FL flagpole, K catchpole, M Maypole,* metropole, *P* pole, Pole, poll, *R rantipole, ridgepole, T tadpole,* telephone pole
RŌL	*A azarole, B banderole, bankroll, barcarole, bedroll, E enroll,* escarole, *F fumarole,* furole, fusarole, *J* jellyroll, *K casserole, L logroll, M multirole, P* parole, *payroll,* PR profiterole, *R* reroll, rigamarole, rigmarole, rock-and-roll, role, roll, *SKW* squatarole, *U* unroll, uproll, *V* virole
SHŌL	shoal, shole
SKŌL	skoal
SKRŌL	enscroll, inscroll, scroll
SŌL	*A anisole, E ensoul, H half-sole, I insole,* insoul, *J girasole, K camisole,* console, *O oversoul, R* resole, rissole, *S* Seoul, sol, sole, soul, *T turnsole, U* unsole, unsoul
STŌL	stole
STRŌL	stroll
THŌL	thole
TŌL	extol, extoll, pistole, *sestole, citole, sotol,* tole, toll
TRŌL	decontrol, comptrol, control, patrol, recontrol, remote control, self-control, troll
VŌL	vole
YŌL	guignol, carmagnole, croquignole
ZŌL	thiazole

ÔL

ÔL	all, all-in-all, awl, *BR brad-awl, FR* free-for-all, *H hold-all, HW* • wherewithal, *K* catchall, carry-all, *M* Montreal, *O* overall, *TH* therewithal, *W* withal
BÔL	*B* ball, bawl, *baseball,* basketball, *BL blackball, E emery ball, F fireball, football,* foul ball, *H handball, hairball, highball, I eyeball, K* cannonball, *M masked ball, meatball, mothball, N netball, O oddball, P pinball, punchball, R* wrecking-ball, *SKR screwball, SN snowball, V* volleyball
BRÔL	brawl
DRÔL	drawl
FÔL	*B befall, D downfall, E evenfall, F* fall, *footfall, FR freefall, K catfall, L landfall, N nightfall, O* overfall, *P pitfall, PR pratfall, R rainfall, SH*

shortfall, SN snowfall, W waterfall, *windfall*

GÔL Bengal, glass gall, gall, Gaul, *nutgall, spurgall, windgall*

HÔL *A* alcohol, *B* banquet hall, *D* dance hall, *G* gasohol, *guildhall, H* hall, haul, *HW* Whitehall, *J* judgment hall, *K* keelhaul, *O* overhaul, *T* townhall

KÔL *birdcall, catcall,* call, caul, miscall, nudicaul, protocol, recall, trumpet call

KRÔL crawl, kraal
MÔL bemaul, mall, maul
PÔL appall, Nepal, pall, pawl, St. Paul
SHÔL shawl
SKÔL scall
SKRÔL scrawl
SKWÔL squall
SMÔL small
SÔL Saul, tattersall
SPÔL spall, spawl
SPRÔL sprawl, urban sprawl
STÔL *bookstall, boxstall,* fingerstall, *footstall,* forestall, install, reinstall, stall, *thumbstall*
THRÔL bethrall, disenthrall, enthrall, thrall
TÔL atoll, tall
TRÔL trawl
VÔL devall
WÔL Berlin wall, Chinese wall, Hadrian's wall, caterwaul, *Cornwall,* off the wall, sea wall, *stonewall,* wall
YÔL yawl

OL

OL vitriol
DOL baby doll, dol, doll, rag doll
GOL Bengal
HOL alcohol
KOL col, guaiacol, protocol
LOL loll, trolll
MOL gun moll, moll
NOL ethanol, mestranol, methanol, eugenol
POL Interpol, Nepal, pol, poll
ROL folderol
SOL aerosol, entresol, girasol, *consol,* creosol, lithosol, parasol, planosol, plasmasol, regosol, sol
TOL amatol, xylotol

ŌLD

ŌLD *age-old,* old
BŌLD bold, bowled, *kobold,* overbold, overbowled, semibold
FŌLD *A* eightfold, *B* bifold, billfold, *BL* blindfold, *E* enfold, *F* fivefold, foaled, fold, *fourfold, G* gatefold, *H* hundredfold, *I* infold, interfold, *M* manifold, multifold, *N* ninefold, *R* refoaled, refold, *S* centerfold, sevenfold, *sixfold, SH* sheepfold, *T* tenfold, twofold, *TH* thousandfold, *threefold* (etc.), *U* unfold
GŌLD Acapulco gold, fool's gold, gold, good as gold, marigold, spun gold
HŌLD *A* afterhold, ahold, anchor hold, *B* behold, *F* foothold, FR freehold, *H* handhold, hold, household, *K* copyhold, *L* leasehold, *O* on hold, *P* pigeonholed, *ST* stokehold, *STR* stranglehold, *stronghold, T* to have and to hold, toehold, *THR* threshold, *U* uphold, *W* withhold
JŌLD cajoled
KŌLD acold, ice cold, coaled, cold, stone cold
MŌLD bullet mold, butter mold, button mold, leaf mold, mold, mould, pudding mold, remold, remould, salad mold
PŌLD polled, repolled, unpolled
RŌLD paroled, reparoled, rolled, rerolled, unparoled, unrolled
SHŌLD shoaled
SKŌLD rescold, reskoaled, scold, skoaled
SŌLD *F* full-soled, *H* half-soled, high-souled, *KW* quarter-soled, *O* oversold, *S* sold, soled, souled, *U* undersouled, unsold, unsoled, unsouled
STŌLD sable-stoled, stoled
TŌLD foretold, retold, told, tolled, *twice-told,* untold, untolled
WŌLD wold

(See ŌL, add -d or -ed where appropriate.)

ÔLD

ÔLD auld
BÔLD bald, *kobold, piebald, skewballed*
HÔLD hauled, close-hauled, rehauled, unhauled
SKÔLD rescald, scald

(See ÔL, add -ed where appropriate.)

ÔLS

FÔLS defaults, false, faults
HÔLS halse, halts
VÔLS valse, envaults, vaults
SÔLS assaults, old salts, salts, somersaults
WÔLS waltz
ZÔLS exalts

ŌLT

BŌLT *B* bolt, *D* deadbolt, *F* fishbolt, *I* eyebolt, *K* kingbolt, *L* lightning bolt, *R* rebolt, *ringbolt, wringbolt, SH* shacklebolt, *TH* thunderbolt, *U* unbolt
DŌLT dolt
HŌLT holt
JŌLT jolt
KŌLT colt, Colt, wood colt
MŌLT molt, moult
PŌLT poult
SMŌLT smolt
VŌLT demivolt, lavolt, millivolt, revolt, teravolt, volt

ÔLT

BÔLT Balt, *cobalt*
FÔLT *asphalt,* default, fault, *no-fault*
GÔLT gault
HÔLT halt, *stringhalt*
MÔLT malt
SMÔLT smalt
SÔLT assault, *basalt,* oxysalt, old salt, salt, sea salt, somersault, pseudosalt
SPÔLT spalt
VÔLT envault, vault
ZÔLT exalt

ÔLTS

FÔLTS	false
VÔLTS	valse
WÔLTS	waltz

(See **ÔLT,** add *-s* where appropriate.)

OLV

SOLV	absolve, dissolve, resolve, solve, unsolve
VOLV	devolve, evolve, intervolve, involve, convolve, obvolve, revolve, circumvolve
ZOLV	absolve, dissolve, exolve, resolve

OLVD

(See **OLV,** add *-d* where appropriate.)

ŌM

ŌM	oam, ohm, om
BŌM	abohm, *Beerbohm*
BRŌM	brome
DŌM	astrodrome, dom, dome, endome, *radome*, semidome, Teapot Dome
DRŌM	aerodrome, acrodrome, aquadrome, hippodrome, cosmodrome, autodrome, palindrome, *syndrome*, velodrome
FŌM	afoam, befoam, foam, *seafoam*
GLŌM	gloam, glome
HŌM	animal home, at home, harvest home, heaume, holm, home, motor home, nobody home, tumblehome
KLŌM	clomb
KŌM	*backcomb*, honeycomb, catacomb, *cockscomb*, *coxcomb*, comb, currycomb
KRŌM	heliochrome, haemochrome, chrome, metallochrome, monochrome, polychrome, urochrome
LŌM	loam, Salome, shalom
MŌM	mome
NŌM	gastronome, genome, gnome, metronome, Nome

PŌM	pome
RŌM	roam, rom, Rome
SLŌM	sloam
SŌM	endosome, chromosome, leptosome, microsome, monosome, autosome, ribosome, centrosome, schistosome
STŌM	monostome, cyclostome
STRŌM	*brostrome*
TŌM	apotome, dermatome, hecatomb, macrotome, microtome, tome

ÔM

ÔM	aum
DÔM	prudhomme
GÔM	gaum
HÔM	haulm
MÔM	imaum, Maugham
SHÔM	shawm

OM

OM	axiom, om
BOM	atom bomb, bomb, *firebomb*, gas bomb, h-bomb, hydrogen bomb, car bomb, laser bomb, mail bomb, neutron bomb, time bomb
DOM	dom, domn
FROM	from, therefrom, wherefrom
GLOM	glom
GROM	pogrom
GWOM	Guam
HOM	hom
KOM	intercom, non-com, *syn-com, sit-com*
KWOM	qualm
LOM	coulomb
MOM	cardimom, mam, mom
PLOM	aplomb
POM	pom, *pompom*
PROM	prom
ROM	rhomb
STROM	*maelstrom*, stromb
WOM	*wigwam*

(See **ÄM**)

OMB

OMB	chiliomb
ROMB	rhomb
STROMB	stromb

ŌMD

DŌMD	domed, endomed
FŌMD	befoamed, enfoamed, foamed
KŌMD	combed, recombed, uncombed
RŌMD	roamed

OMD

BOMD	bombed
GLOMD	glommed

OMP

CHOMP	chomp
KLOMP	clomp
KOMP	comp
POMP	pomp
ROMP	romp
STOMP	stomp
SWOMP	swamp
TROMP	tromp, trompe

OMPT

KOMPT	compt
PROMPT	prompt
SWOMPT	swamped

(See **OMP,** add *ed* where appropriate.)

ŌN

ŌN	disown, own, reown
BLŌN	blown, *flyblown, fresh-blown, full-blown, outblown,* overblown, unblown, weatherblown, *windblown*
BŌN	*A aitchbone,* anklebone, *B backbone,* bellibone, Beaune, bone, *BR breastbone, CH cheekbone, F fishbone,* funnybone, *H herringbone, hipbone, HW whalebone, I icebone, J jawbone, K carbon, collarbone, cuttlebone, M marrowbone, N knucklebone, SH shinbone, TH thighbone, TR trombone, W wishbone*

DŌN	condone, methadone, recondone, uncondone		reshown, shone, shown, unshown		**FÔN**	faun, fawn, plafond
DRŌN	drone, ladrone, padrone	**SKŌN**	scone		**GÔN**	*bygone, foregone,* gone
FLŌN	flown, *high-flown,* reflown, unflown	**SŌN**	ecdysone, cortisone, prednisone, presew,		**KÔN**	leprechaun
FŌN	*A* allophone, Anglophone, *D* Dictaphone, *E*		presown, resewn, resown, sewn, sone, sown,		**LÔN**	lawn
	earphone, electrophone,		unsewn, unsown		**PÔN**	impawn, pawn, repawn
	F phone, *FR*	**STŌN**	*B* bilestone, birthstone,		**PRÔN**	prawn
	Francophone, *GR*		*BL* bloodstone, *BR*		**RÔN**	raun
	graphophone,		*brimstone, E* end stone, *F*		**THÔN**	omadhaun
	gramophone, *H*		philosopher's stone,		**SÔN**	sawn
	headphone, heckelphone,		foundation stone, *FL*		**THÔN**	omadhaun
	hydrophone, homophone,		*flagstone, FR* freestone, *G*		**TÔN**	quinton
	I interphone, *K*		*gallstone, GR* gravestone,		**YÔN**	yawn
	chordophone, *M*		grindstone, *H* hailstone,			
	megaphone, mellophone,		headstone, hearthstone,		**ON**	
	microphone, *O*		holystone, *HW* whetstone,			
	audiphone, *P* pyrophone,		*I* imposing stone, *J*		**ON**	*A* Albion, alluvion,
	polyphone, *R* radiophone,		*gemstone, K* keystone,			amphibion, Anacreon, *B*
	S saxophone, sousaphone,		cobblestone, *copestone,*			*bion, E* enchiridion,
	V vibraphone, vitaphone,		cornerstone, *curbstone,*			Endymion, *G* gabion,
	Y euphone, *Z* xylophone		*KL* clingstone, *L*			galleon, *H* halcyon,
GŌN	epigone		*limestone, loadstone,*			hanger-on, hangers-on,
GRŌN	begroan, *full-grown,*		*lodestone, M* milestone,			hereon, Hyperion, *HW*
	grass-grown, groan,		millstone, moonstone, *R*			whereon, *K* campion,
	grown, *half-grown,*		*rhinestone,* rottenstone, *S*			carry-on, carryings-on, *L*
	ingrown, moss-grown,		*sandstone, soapstone, ST*			Laocoön, *M* melodeon,
	overgrown, undergrown,		staddlestone, stone, *T*			melodion, *N* Napoleon, *O*
	ungrown		*tilestone, toadstone,*			oblivion, on, *P* pantheon,
HŌN	hone		*tombstone, touchstone,*			*TH* thereon, walker-on
KLŌN	*anticyclone,* clone,		*TH* thunderstone (etc.)		**BON**	Audubon, bon, *bonbon*
	cyclone	**THRŌN**	dethrone, enthrone,		**DON**	*B* boustrophedon, *D* don,
KŌN	cone, ochone, rincon,		overthrown, rethrone,			*GL* glyptodon, *I*
	silicone		rethrown, throne, thrown,			iguanodon, *K* Corydon, *M*
KRŌN	crone		unthrone, unthrown			Macedon, mastodon,
LŌN	alone, Boulogne,	**TŌN**	*A* acetone, atone, *B*			myrmidon, celadon, *SF*
	cologne, Cologne, colon,		barbitone, baritone,			sphenadon, *ST* stegedon,
	loan, lone, eau de		barytone, *D* dial tone,			*Y* Euroclydon
	cologne, prednisolone,		duotone, *E* ecotone, *F*		**FON**	antiphon, Bellerophon,
	reloan		phenobarbitone, *H*			phon, harmoniphon,
MŌN	bemoan, pheromone,		*halftone,* whole tone, *I*			colophon, *chiffon,*
	hormone, moan, mown,		intone, isotone, *KW*			*euphon,* Xenophon
	remown, unmown		quarter tone, *M*		**FRON**	Neophron
NŌN	butanone, foreknown,		monotone, *O* overtone, *P*		**GON**	*A* agone, *B* begone,
	Ionone, known, none,		*peptone, S* sacaton,			*bygone, D*
	rotenone, sine qua non,		semitone, *T* tone, *two-tone,*			*Dagon,* decagon,
	unbeknown,		*TR* tritone, *U* undertone			dodecagon, doggone, *E*
	unforeknown, unknown	**ZŌN**	*endzone, enzone, ozone,*			estragon, *F foregone, G*
PŌN	Abipon, depone, dispone,		zone			gone, *GL* glucagon, *H*
	interpone, Capone,					hexagon, heptagon, *I*
	cornpone, pone,					isogon, *M* martagon, *N*
	postpone, propone,	**ÔN**				nonagon, *O* octagon,
	repone					oxygon, Oregon, *P*
PRŌN	accident-prone,	**ÔN**	awn			paragon, parergon,
	dependency-prone, prone	**BÔN**	bawn			pentagon, Pentagon,
RŌN	aldosterone, androsterone,	**BRÔN**	brawn			perigon, polygon, *PR*
	coumarone, progesterone,	**DÔN**	dawn			protagon, *S* Saigon, *T*
	Rhone, roan, rone,	**DRÔN**	drawn, indrawn,			tarragon, tetragon,
	chaperon, cicerone,		overdrawn, redrawn,			trimetragon, *U* ucalegon,
	testosterone, Tyrone		underdrawn, undrawn,			undecagon, undergone, *W*
SHŌN	foreshown, outshone,		withdrawn			woebegone
					JON	demijohn, john, John,
						Littlejohn, Prester John

KON   *A archon, B* basilicon, *E* etymologicon, *H* harmonicon, helicon, Helicon, *I* idioticon, irenicon, *K* catholicon, con, khan, *L* lexicon, *M* melodicon, *O* onomasticon, opticon, orthicon, *P* panopticon, pantechnicon, *R* Rubicon, *S* sciopticon, silicon, synonymicon, *SH* chaconne, *ST* stereopticon, *T* technicon, *V* vidicon, *Y* Yukon

KRON   omicron, pentacron

LON   *A* Avalon, *B* Babylon, *CH* chillon, *E* echelon, encephalon, epsilon, etalon, *G* gonfalon, *I* eidolon, *K* carillon, *M* mamelon, mesencephalon *P* papillon, petalon, *S* salon, Ceylon, *U* upsilon

MON   etymon, hoot mon, kikumon, mon, Pergamon

NON   *A* anon, argenon, *D* dies non, *G* guenon, gonfanon, *N* ninon, noumenon, *O* olecranon, organon, *P* Parthenon, perispomenon, *PR* prolegomenon, *S* sine qua non, *T* tympanon, *TH* theologoumenon, trimenon

PON   hereupon, whereupon, jupon, coupon, put upon, thereupon, upon

RON   *A* Acheron, aileron, *D* diatesseron, *E* ephemeron, enteron, *F* fanfaron, *H* hapteron, hexameron, hyperon, *I* interferon, *M* megaron, mesenteron, *N* nychthemoron, *neuron, O* Oberon, operon, *P* Percheron, *PR* prolegeron, *Z* xeromyron

SHON   cabochon

SKON   scone

SON   Alençon, parison, Tucson, venison

SWON   swan

THON   marathon, omadhaun, ornithon, telethon, trilithon

TON   *A* abaton, *antiproton,* asyndeton, *B* baryton, baton, *F phaeton,* feuilleton, *H* hyperbaton,

K cacemphaton, Canton, *KR* cretonne, crouton, *M* magneton, megaton, *O* automaton, *P* polysyndeton, *PR proton, W* won ton

TRON   anatron, balatron, *electron,* elytron, phytotron, *neutron,* positron, cyclotron, tevatron

VON   elevon, von

WON   won

YON   boeuf Bourguignon, filet mignon, sabayon, yon

ZON   amazon, Amazon, Barbizon, benison, borazon, cabezon, liaison, Luzon, orison

(See also **ÄN**)

ÔNCH

FLÔNCH   flaunch
HÔNCH   haunch
KRÔNCH   craunch
LÔNCH   launch, relaunch, unlaunch
PÔNCH   paunch
RÔNCH   raunch
STÔNCH   staunch

ŌND

MŌND   beau monde, demimonde, haut monde, moaned, unmoaned

(See **ŌN**, add *-ed* where appropriate.)

ÔND

MÔND   maund

(See **ÔN**, add *-ed* where appropriate.)

OND

BLOND   blond, blonde
BOND   bond, James Bond, pair bond, vagabond
DOND   donned
FOND   fond, overfond, plafond, underfond, unfond
FROND   frond
GOND   paragoned, unparagoned
KOND   conned, seconde, unconned

MOND   beau monde, demimonde, Garamond, monde
POND   fish pond, *millpond,* pond, skating pond
ROND   rond, ronde
SKOND   abscond
SOND   dropsonde, radiosonde, sonde
SPOND   despond, correspond, respond
WOND   wand, *yardwand*
YOND   beyond
ZOND   zond

ONG

BONG   bong, billabong
CHONG   *souchong*
DONG   *dingdong,* dong, quandong
FLONG   flong
FONG   underfong
GONG   *bogong, dugong,* gong, wobbegong
JONG   kurrajong, mah-jong
KONG   Hong Kong, King Kong, Viet Cong
LONG   *A* all along, along, *B* belong, *D* daylong, *E* endlong, ere long, *F* furlong, *H* headlong, *K* kalong, kampong, *L* lifelong, livelong, long, *N* nightlong, *O* oblong, overlong, *PR* prolong, *S* sidelong, so long, *SH* chaise longue
NONG   nong, scuppernong
PONG   *pingpong,* pong
PRONG   prong
RONG   barong, binturong, wrong, sarong
SHONG   souchong
SONG   aftersong, battle song, drinking song, evensong, cradlesong, love song, morning song, *plainsong, singsong,* song, undersong
STRONG   *headstrong,* strong
THONG   *diphthong,* monophthong, thong, *triphthong*
THRONG   throng
TONG   paktong, tong
WONG   currawong, *morwong,* wong
YONG   foo yong

ONGD

BONGD   bonged

(See **ONG**, add *-ed* where appropriate.)

ONGK

BONGK	bonk
BRONGK	bronc
DONGK	zedonk
GONGK	gonk
HONGK	honk
KLONGK	clonk
KONGK	conch, conk, konk, *triconch*
KRONGK	cronk
KWONGK	quonk
PLONGK	plonk
SKWONGK	squonk
STONGK	stonk
TONGK	honky-tonk, tonk
ZONGK	zonk

ONGKS

BRONGKS	Bronx

(See **ONGK**, add -*s* where appropriate.)

ONGKT

ZONGKT	zonked

(See **ONGK**, add -*ed* where appropriate.)

ONS

BONS	bonce
FONS	fonts
NONS	nonce
PONS	ponce
SKONS	ensconce, sconce
SPONS	response

(See **ONT**, add -*s* where appropriate.)

ŌNT

DŌNT	don't
WŌNT	won't

ÔNT

DÔNT	daunt, undaunt
FLÔNT	flaunt, reflaunt
GÔNT	gaunt
HÔNT	haunt, rehaunt
JÔNT	jaunt
MÔNT	romaunt
TÔNT	ataunt, taunt
VÔNT	avaunt, vaunt
WÔNT	want

ONT

ONT	halobiont, symbiont
DONT	acrodont, mastodont, xanthodont
FONT	font
KWONT	quant
MONT	*Beaumont, Piedmont, Vermont*
PLONT	*diplont*
PONT	Hellespont, pont
WONT	want, wont
ZONT	*schizont*

ŌNZ

BŌNZ	bones, funnybones, *crossbones*, lazybones, rolling the bones, *sawbones*
JŌNZ	Davy Jones, jones
NŌNZ	nones

(See **ŌN**, add -*s* where appropriate.)

ONZ

BONZ	bonze
BRONZ	bronze
FONZ	fons
FRONZ	frons
GONZ	*bygones*
JONZ	St. John's, long johns
PONZ	pons

(See **ON**, add -*s* where appropriate.)

OŌ

OŌ	oo, ooh, *spreeuw*, toodle-oo
BLOŌ	blew, blue, *skyblue*, true-blue
BOŌ	*A* aboo, Abou, abu, *B* baboo, babu, bamboo, boo, *booboo*, bugaboo, *E* ynambu, *G* gamdeboo, *J* jigaboo, *K* caribou, *M* Malibu, marabou, *P* peekaboo, *T* taboo, tabu, *U* urabu, *Y* yabu, *Z zebu*
BROŌ	barley-broo, brew, broo, *Hebrew*, imbrue, witch's brew
CHOŌ	chew, *choo-choo*, eschew, catechu, kerchoo, *Manchu*
DOŌ	*A* ado, amadou, *B* billet-doux, CH chandoo, *D* derring-do, didgerydoo, do, *doo-doo*, fordo, *F* foredo, *H* hairdo, Hindu, howdy-do, *hoodoo*, honeydew, *hoodoo*, *J* jadu, *K* cockadoodledoo, kudu, *M* misdo, *O* outdo, overdo, *R* redo, residue, *SK* skiddoo, *T* teledu, toodledoo, to-do, twenty-three skidoo, *U* underdo, undo, *V* voodoo, *W* well-to-do
DROŌ	drew, withdrew
FLOŌ	flew, flu, flue
FOŌ	Dien Bien Phu, fou, phoo, *phoo-phoo*, Corfu, kung fu, mafoo, mafu, snafu, succes fou, *wamefu*, widdifow
FROŌ	*froufrou*
GLOŌ	glue, igloo, reglue, unglue
GOŌ	burgoo, goo, *goo-goo*, gout, ragout
GROŌ	grew, gru, grue, outgrew, overgrew
HOŌ	*A* ahoo, ahu, *B* ballyhoo, boo-hoo, *H* who, hoo-hoo, Who's Who, *T* to-whit-to-hoo, *W wahoo, Y yahoo*, yoo-hoo
HWOŌ	to-whit-to-whoo
JOŌ	acajou, ejoo, Ju, Jew, juju, kinkajou, sapajou
KLOŌ	clew, clue, unclue
KOŌ	*aku, baku*, bill and coo, bunraku, Daikoku, coo, coup, coochy-coo, *coocoo, cuckoo*, worricow
KROŌ	accrew, accrue, *aircrew*, ecru, crew, cru, motley crew, premier cru
LOŌ	*B baloo, G* gardyloo, gillygaloo, *H* halloo, *Honolulu*, hullabaloo, *I* igloo, *K* calalu, *L* lieu, loo, *looloo, lulu*, lulliloo, *O* ormolu, *P* pililoo, poilu, *S* skip to my Lou, *V* view halloo, *W* Waterloo, *Z Zulu*

NEW WORDS FOR AN OLD SAW

I love the girls who don't,
I love the girls who do;
But best, the girls who say, "I don't . . .
But maybe . . . just for you . . ."

MŌŌ — emu, imu, moo, moue, mu, *muumuu*, tinamou, *umu*

NŌŌ — *A* anew, *D* detinue, *E* entre nous, *F foreknew*, *H* hoochinoo, *I* ingenue, *J* genu, *K* canoe, *N* gnu, new, *P* parvenu, *R* revenue, *T* Tippecanoe, *V Vishnu*

PLŌŌ — plew

PŌŌ — *hoopoe, coypu,* cockapoo, napoo, poo, pooh, pooh-pooh, shampoo, shapoo

RŌŌ — *B* buckaroo, buroo, *G garoo,* gillaroo, guru, *J* jabiru, jackaroo, jackeroo, *K* kaberu, kangaroo, karroo, *L* loup-garou, *M* meadow rue, *Nehru, P* Peru, potoroo, *R* roo, roux, rue, *SW* switcheroo, *W* wallaroo, wanderoo

SHŌŌ — *F* fichu, *G gumshoe, H horseshoe, K* cachou, cashew, cashoo, *O* old shoe, overshoe, *SO softshoe, SH* chou, choux, shoe, shoo, *SN snowshoe, U* unshoe

SHRŌŌ — beshrew, shrew

SKRŌŌ — *airscrew, corkscrew,* screw, *thumbscrew,* unscrew, *woodscrew*

SLŌŌ — slew, sloo, slough, slue

SŌŌ — ensue, *jujitsu,* lasso, pursue, Sioux, sou, sue, *susu*

SPRŌŌ — sprew, sprue

STRŌŌ — bestrew, construe, misconstrue, overstrew, reconstrue, strew, strue, unconstrue

THRŌŌ — overthrew, see through, threw, through, wirrasthru

TŌŌ — *B Bantu,* battue, *E et tu, H* hereinto, *hereto,* hereunto, hitherto, *HW* whereinto, whereto, whereunto, *I impromptu, into,* in transitu, *J* Gentoo, *K* cockatoo, *L lean-to, M* manitou, *onto, P* passe partout, *S set-to,* surtout, *T* tattoo, Timbuctu, to, too, two, tutu, *TH* thereto, thereunto, thitherto, *U unto, V* virtu

TRŌŌ — true, untrue

VŌŌ — kivu, parlez-voo, rendezvous

WŌŌ — woo, woowoo, Wu

YŌŌ — bayou, *W,* gayyou, *IOU* Vayu, ewe, *U* yew, you

ZŌŌ — bazoo, Kalamazoo, cousu, kazoo, razoo, zoo, *zoozoo,* Zu

ZHŌŌ — bijou

(See Ū)

ŌŌB

BŌŌB — boob, haboob
DŌŌB — doob
JŌŌB — jube, *jujube*
LŌŌB — loob, lube
RŌŌB — hey Rube, rube

ŌŌCH

ŌŌCH — ooch
BRŌŌCH — brooch
HŌŌCH — hooch
KŌŌCH — hoochy-cooch
MŌŌCH — mooch, mouch, Scaramouch
PŌŌCH — pooch, putsch
SMŌŌCH — smooch

ŌŌD

BRŌŌD — abrood, brood
DŌŌD — dude, subdued
FŌŌD — food, *wholefood, seafood,* soul food
JŌŌD — St. Jude
KLŌŌD — exclude, include, conclude, occlude, preclude, seclude
KŌŌD — Likud
KRŌŌD — crude
LŌŌD — allude, delude, elude, illude, interlude, collude, Quaalude, 'lude
MŌŌD — almud, mood
NŌŌD — nude
PŌŌD — pood
PRŌŌD — prude
RŌŌD — rood, rude
SHŌŌD — shoed, shood
SHRŌŌD — shrewd
SLŌŌD — slewed
SNŌŌD — snood
SŌŌD — transude
TŌŌD — *A* altitude, amplitude, aptitude, asuetude, attitude, *B* beatitude, *D* decrepitude, definitude, desuetude, disquietude, dissimilitude, *E* exactitude, eptitude, *F* fortitude, *GR* gratitude, gravitude, *H* habitude, hebetude, *I* inaptitude, inexactitude, ineptitude, infinitude, ingratitude, inquietude, incertitude, insuetude, *K* consuetude, correctitude, *KR* crassitude, *KW* quietude, *L* lassitude, latitude, lentitude, lippitude, longitude, *M* magnitude, mansuetude, mollitude, multitude, *N* necessitude, nigritude, *O* omnitude, *P* pinguitude, pulchritude, *PL* platitude, plenitude, *PR* promptitude, *R* rectitude, *S* sanctitude, senectitude, serenitude, certitude, servitude, similitude, solicitude, solitude, *SP* spissitude, *ST* stewed, stude, *T* torpitude, turpitude, *V* vastitude, verisimilitude, vicissitude

TRŌŌD — detrude, extrude, intrude, obtrude, protrude, retrude, subtrude

WŌŌD — rewooed, unwooed, wooed

YŌŌD — you'd

ZŌŌD — exude

(See ŪD)

OOD

GOOD — good

HOOD — *A* adulthood, angelhood, *B* babyhood, *boyhood, BR* brotherhood, *D* deaconhood, *F* fatherhood, falsehood, foolhardihood, *G girlhood, godhood, H* hardihood, hood, *J* gentlemanhood, *K* kinglihood, kittenhood, *L* ladyhood, likelihood, livelihood, *M* maidenhood, *manhood,* matronhood, *monkhood, monkshood,* motherhood, *N* neighborhood, *knighthood, O* orphanhood, *P* parenthood, *PR*

	priesthood, R Robin Hood, *S sainthood, selfhood,* sisterhood, *SP* spinsterhood, *U* unhood, unlikelihood, *W* widowerhood, widowhood, womanhood		*F fireproof, foolproof, FL flameproof, K* counterproof, *M mothproof, PR* proof, *R rainproof,* reproof, *rustproof, S sunproof, SH* shatterproof, *shellproof, shockproof,* showerproof, *SK skidproof, ST stormproof, W* waterproof	**JOOK**	jouk, juke
KOOD	could			**KOOK**	kook
MOOD	*Talmud*			**LOOK**	Mameluke
SHOOD	should			**NOOK**	Nanook
STOOD	misunderstood, stood, understood, withstood	**ROOF**	gable roof, mansard roof, composition roof, reroof, roof, shingle roof, thatch roof, tile roof, unroof	**ROOK**	charuk, Farouk, peruke, seruke
WOOD	*A* applewood, *B baywood, beachwood, beechwood, bentwood,* bitterwood, *bogwood, boxwood,* buttonwood, *BL* blackwood, *BR* brushwood, *CH* cherrywood, *D* deadwood, dyewood, dogwood, *DR* driftwood, *E* eaglewood, *F firewood, G gumwood, H* hardwood, heartwood, Hollywood, *HW* whitewood, *I* ironwood, *K* candlewood, *kingwood,* cordwood, cottonwood, *L legwood,* leatherwood, *M* matchwood, milkwood, *O* orangewood, *P pearwood, peachwood,* peckerwood, *pulpwood,* purplewood, *PL* plastic wood, *plywood, R* redwood, ribbonwood, *rosewood, S* sandalwood, sappanwood, *sapwood,* satinwood, *softwood,* summerwood, southernwood, *SKR scrubwood, SPR springwood, T teakwood,* touch wood, *touchwood, U* underwood, *W Wedgwood, wildwood,* wood, would, *wormwood, Z* zebrawood (etc.)	**SPOOF**	spoof	**SHOOK**	sheugh
		TOOF	Tartuffe	**SNOOK**	snoek, snook
		WOOF	woof, woof-woof, wowf	**SOOK**	sook
				SPOOK	spook
				STOOK	stook
		OOF		**TOOK**	Heptateuch, Hexateuch, Octateuch, Pentateuch, tuque
		OOF	oof	**ZOOK**	bashibazouk
		HOOF	hoof, cloven-hoof		
		ROOF	gable roof, composition roof, mansard roof, reroof, roof, shingle roof, thatch roof, tile roof, unroof	(See **ŬK**)	
				OOK	
		WOOF	woof, woof-woof	**BOOK**	*A* account book, appointment book, *B bankbook, boobook,* book, *BL* bluebook, *CH chapbook, checkbook, D daybook, FL flybook, H* handbook, hymnbook, *K* commonplace book, *cookbook, copybook, L logbook, M* minute book, *N notebook, P* paperback book, paperbook, *passbook,* pocketbook, *PR* prayerbook, *S sambuk, songbook, SK sketchbook, SKR scrapbook, ST studbook,* storybook, *T textbook, W workbook*
		OOFT			
		(See **OOF,** add *-ed* where appropriate.)			
		OOG		**BROOK**	Beaverbrook, Bolingbroke, brook, donnybrook, running brook
		BOOG	boog	**DOOK**	*fonduk*
		(See **ŬG**)		**HOOK**	*billhook, boathook,* buttonhook, *fishhook,* grapplehook, hook, rehook, tenterhook, unhook
		OOJ			
		BOOJ	bouge, gamboge	**KOOK**	fancy cook, French cook, cook, cuck, overcook, pastry cook, plain cook, undercook
		LOOJ	luge		
		ROOJ	rouge		
		SKROOJ	Scrooge, scrouge		
		STOOJ	stooge	**KROOK**	crook
OOF				**LOOK**	look, *outlook,* overlook, uplook
OOF	oof, ouf, ouphe	(See **ŬJ, OOZH**)			
BOOF	boof, opera bouffe			**NOOK**	Chinook, inglenook, gerenuk, nook
DOOF	shadoof	**OOK**			
GOOF	goof			**PLOOK**	plook
GROOF	agroof	**BOOK**	bambuk, chibouk, rebuke	**POOK**	Volapuk
HOOF	behoof, hoof, cloven-hoof	**CHOOK**	caoutchouc		
KLOOF	kloof	**DOOK**	archduke, douc, duke		
LOOF	aloof, loof	**FLOOK**	fluke		
POOF	poof, pouf, whiffenpoof	**GOOK**	gobbledygook, gook	**ROOK**	rook
PROOF	*B* bulletproof, *D* disproof,				

SHNOOK	schnook
SHOOK	shook
SOOK	forsook, *nainsook*
TOOK	betook, mistook, overtook, partook, took, undertook

OOKS

ZOOKS	gadzooks, odzooks

(See OOK, add -s where appropriate.)

OOKT

SOOKT	witzelsucht

(See OOK, add -ed where appropriate.)

OOL

BOOL	babul, boule, boulle, Istambul, Stambul
BROOL	brool
DOOL	*chandul,* hierodule
DROOL	drool, *chondrule*
FOOL	April fool, befool, fool, nobody's fool, poor fool, *tomfool*
GOOL	ghoul, gool
HOOL	who'll
JOOL	jhool, joule
KOOL	jokul, cool, supercool
MOOL	mool
NOOL	gallinule
POOL	*ampoule,* charity pool, dirty pool, *whirlpool,* gene pool, car pool, Liverpool, office pool, pool, pul, *cesspool,* swimming pool
ROOL	*ferrule, ferule,* misrule, rule, *spherule*
SHOOL	shul
SKOOL	boarding school, charity school, grammar school, high school, kindergarten school, nursery school, *playschool, preschool,* primary school, sabbath school, summer school, Sunday school, school
SOOL	pasul
SPOOL	spool
STOOL	*barstool,* ducking stool, *footstool,* stool
TOOL	retool, tool, tulle
YOOL	Yule

OOL

BOOL	*A* abominable, achievable, adaptable, adjustable, admirable, admissible, adorable, advisable, affable, affordable, agreeable, acceptable, accessible, accountable, actionable, alienable, allowable, amenable, amiable, amicable, answerable, applicable, appreciable, approachable, arable, arrestable, arguable, attainable, attemptable, attributable, available, avoidable, *B* bailable, bankable, bearable, beddable, believable, beatable, biddable, biodegradable, buhl, bull, *bulbul, BR* brakable, breakable, *CH* changeable, chargeable, charitable, chasuble, *D* damnable, debatable, deductible, defensible, definable, degradable, delectable, demonstrable, deniable, dependable, deplorable, depreciable, describable, despicable, destructible, detachable, detectable, determinable, detestable, devisable, desirable, differentiable, digestible, dirigible, disagreeable, dislikable, dishonorable, disreputable, discernible, dissociable, dispensable, disposable, distinguishable, disputable, divisible, doable, dowable, dubitable, durable, dutiable, *DR* drinkable, *E* edible, educable, effable, effaceable, execrable, exigible, excusable, exhaustible, expandable, expansible, expectable, expendable, explainable, explicable, expressible, excitable, extendible, extensible, extinguishable, extraditable, extricable, equable, equitable, eligible, employable, endurable, enjoyable, enviable, eradicable, erasable, estimable, eatable, *F* fallible, fashionable, fathomable, favorable, feasible, finable, fordable, forgettable, forgivable, formidable, foreseeable, forcible, fusible, *FL* flammable, flexible, *FR* friable, *G* gullible, governable, *H* habitable, heritable, horrible, hospitable, *I* identifiable, illegible, imaginable, immensurable, immeasurable, immiscible, immovable, immutable, impalpable, impassable, impeachable, impeccable, impenetrable, imperishable, impermeable, impermissible, imperceptible, imperturbable, implacable, implausible, imponderable, impossible impracticable, impregnable, impressionable, improbable, improvable, imputable, inadmissible, inadvisable, inalienable, inaccessible, inapplicable, inappreciable, indelible, indemonstrable, indecipherable, indescribable, indestructible, indigestible, indiscernible, indispensable, indissoluble, indisputable, indistinguishable, indictable, indivisible, indomitable, indubitable, ineducable, ineffable, ineffaceable, inexcusable, inexorable, inexhaustible, inexpressible, inextinguishable, inextricable, inequitable, ineligible, ineluctable, ineradicable, inescapable, inestimable, inevitable, infallible, inflammable, inflatable, inflexible, infrangible, infusible, inhospitable, inimitable, incalculable, incapable,

inclinable, incoercible,
incombustible,
incommunicable,
incommutable,
incomparable,
incompatible,
incomprehensible,
incomputable,
inconceivable,
inconsiderable,
inconsolable,
incontestable,
incontrovertible,
inconvertible,
inconvincible,
incorrigible,
incorruptible, incredible,
inculpable, incurable,
inaudible, inalterable,
inoculable, inoperable,
insatiable, insensible,
innumerable, inseparable,
inscrutable, insoluble,
insufferable, insuperable,
insupportable,
insupposable,
insuppressible, insurable,
insurmountable,
intangible, intelligible,
interchangeable,
interminable, intolerable,
intractable, invaluable,
invariable, inviable,
invincible, inviolable,
invisible, irascible,
irredeemable, irreducible,
irrefrangible, irrefutable,
irreconcilable,
irrecoverable, irrecusable,
irreparable, irreplaceable,
irreproachable,
irresponsible,
irretrievable, irreversible,
irresistible, irresolvable,
irritable, *J* generable,
justifiable, justiciable, *K*
calculable, capable,
kissable, combustible,
comfortable,
commendable,
commensurable,
comestible,
communicable,
commutable, conceivable,
considerable, constable,
consumable,
contemptible, contestable,
controllable, conversable,
convertible, convincible,
corrigible, corruptible,
culpable, curable, *KL*
classifiable, *KR* credible,

creditable, crucible, *KW*
quantifiable, quenchable,
questionable, quotable, *L*
laughable, lamentable,
legible, leviable, liable,
liftable, likable, litigable,
laudable, lockable,
lovable, *M* magnifiable,
malleable, manageable,
maneuverable,
marketable, marriageable,
medicable, memorable,
mendable, mensurable,
merchantable,
measurable, miscible,
mistakable, mitigable,
miserable, modifiable,
monosyllable, movable,
mutable, *N* navigable,
negligible, negotiable,
knowledgeable,
nonflammable,
nonreturnable, notable,
notifiable, noticeable, *O*
objectionable, obtainable,
observable, audible,
alterable, omissible,
honorable, operable,
opposable, ostensible, *P*
payable, palatable,
palpable, parable,
pardonable, passable,
peccable, pensionable,
perishable, perfectible,
permissible, perceptible,
personable, peaceable,
pitiable, portable,
possible, potable,
punishable, purchasable,
permeable, *PL* playable,
placable, pleasurable,
pliable, plausible, *PR*
practicable, praisable,
predictable, preferable,
pregnable, preventable,
presentable, presumable,
printable, probable,
producible, profitable,
programmable,
procurable,
pronounceable, provable,
R rateable, reachable,
readable, realizable,
redeemable, redoubtable,
reducible, refillable,
refrangible, refundable,
regrettable, regulable,
recognizable,
recommendable,
reconcilable, recordable,
rectifiable, reliable,
remarkable, removable,

renewable, repairable,
reparable, repeatable,
replaceable,
reprehensible,
reproachable, reputable,
resaleable, rescissible,
resoluble, respectable,
responsible, retractable,
retrievable, returnable,
reversible, revocable,
rewardable, resistible,
reasonable, risible, *S*
salvageable, satiable,
saturable, semipermeable,
sensible, seasonable,
circumnavigable, syllable,
sinkable, Sitting Bull,
sizable, sociable, suable,
submersible, suggestible,
superable, supportable,
surmountable, certifiable,
serviceable, susceptible,
suitable, *SK* scalable, *SP*
sparable, specifiable, *ST*
stoppable, *STR*
stretchable, *T* taxable,
tangible, teachable,
tenable, tensible,
terminable, tearable,
terrible, tithable,
tolerable, touchable,
tunable, *TH* thinkable, *TR*
tractable, transferable,
traceable, triable, *U*
unaccountable,
unacceptable,
unanswerable,
unapproachable,
unassailable, unattainable,
unavailable, unavoidable,
unbearable, unbelievable,
unbendable, unbrakable,
unbreakable, undeniable,
understandable,
undesirable, undrinkable,
unexplainable,
unemployable,
unenviable,
unfathomable,
unfavorable,
unforgettable,
unforgivable,
unforeseeable,
ungovernable,
unimaginable,
unimpeachable,
unintelligible,
uncomfortable,
unconscionable,
uncontrollable,
unconvincible,
unquestionable,

unmatchable,
unmentionable,
unmistakable,
unknowable,
unobtainable,
unpredictable,
unpreventable,
unpresentable,
unprintable,
unpronounceable,
unreadable,
unrecognizable,
unreliable, unreasonable,
unseasonable,
unshakable, unsinkable,
unsociable, unstoppable,
unsuitable, untearable,
unteachable, untenable,
unthinkable, untouchable,
untranslatable,
unutterable, unweighable,
unwearable,
unwarrantable, *V*
valuable, variable,
vegetable, vendible,
venerable, verifiable,
veritable, viable, vincible,
visible, visual, vocable,
voluble, vulnerable, *W*
weighable, wearable,
willable, warrantable,
washable, workable

DOOL *chandul*
FOOL *A armful, artful, B
baneful, bashful, bellyful,
bodeful, bookful,
bountiful, bowlful,
boastful, bountiful,
beautiful, BL blameful,
blissful, BR brimful, CH
cheerful, D delightful,
deceitful, disgraceful,
disrespectful, distasteful,
distrustful, doleful,
doubtful, dutiful, DR
dreadful, E earful,
eventful, F fanciful,
fateful, faithful, fearful,
fitful, forgetful, forkful,
forceful, full, FL
flavorful, FR fretful,
frightful, fruitful, G
gainful, guileful, GL
gleeful, GR graceful,
grateful, H half-full,
handful, harmful, hateful,
heedful, helpful,
healthful, hopeful,
hurtful, I eyeful, J joyful,
K careful, cartful,
caseful, colorful, cupful,
KW quiverful, quarter-*

full, *L lawful, lustful, M
manful, masterful,*
meaningful, merciful,
*mindful, mouthful,
mournful, mirthful, N*
needful, needleful,
*neglectful, O awful, P
painful, peaceful, pitiful,*
pocketful, *potful,*
powerful, purposeful, *PL
playful, plateful,*
plentiful, *PR prayerful, R
wrathful, regardful,
regretful, remindful,
remorseful, reproachful,
respectful, revengeful,
resentful, resourceful,
roomful, ruthful, S
sackful, sinful, songful,
soulful, successful, SH
shameful, SK skilful,
skinful, scornful, SL
slothful, SP spiteful, ST
stealthful, STR stressful,
T tactful, tankful, tasteful,
tuneful, TH thankful,*
thimbleful, *thoughtful, TR
trustful, U uneventful,
unfaithful, ungrateful,
unlawful, unmerciful,
unmindful, W wakeful,
wasteful, weariful, wilful,
windful, wishful, woeful,*
wonderful, worshipful, *Y
useful*

KOOL *B barnacle, BR bricole, K*
canticle, coracle, *KR*
chronicle, *M miracle,*
monocle, *O obstacle,*
oracle, *P pinnacle, T*
testicle, *V vehicle, versicle*

POOL principal, principle, pull
WOOL abb wool, cotton wool,
lamb's wool, wool

OOM

OOM oom
BLOOM abloom, checkerbloom,
embloom, rebloom
BOOM baby boom, boom, jib
boom, kaboom, sonic
boom
BROOM broom, brougham,
whiskbroom
DOOM doom, doum, foredoom,
predoom, redoom
FLOOM flume
FOOM perfume
GLOOM begloom, engloom,
gloom, glume

GOOM ghoom, legume
GROOM *bridegroom,* groom,
ungroom
HOOM whom
JOOM joom
KOOM coom, coomb, cwm
LOOM *broadloom, heirloom,
illume,* loom, *powerloom,
reloom, relume*
MOOM simoom
NOOM neume
PLOOM beplume, deplume,
displume, filoplume, nom
de plume, plume,
unplume
ROOM *A anteroom, B ballroom,
barroom, bathroom,
bedroom, boardroom,
boxroom, D darkroom,*
dining room, *DR drawing
room,* dressing room, *E*
elbowroom, *G
guardroom, gunroom, GR
greenroom, grillroom, H
headroom, houseroom, K
coatroom,* coffeeroom,
*cookroom, courtroom, KL
classroom, cloakroom, L*
living room, lumber
room, *M* meeting room,
mushroom, PL playroom,
R reading room, rheum,
room, *S* salesroom,
searoom, sitting room,
sunroom, *SH showroom,
SP* spare room, *ST
stateroom, stockroom,
storeroom, STR
strongroom, T taproom,
tearoom, V varoom, W
wareroom,* withdrawing
room, *workroom, washroom*
SOOM assume, consume, soum,
subsume
SPOOM spume
TOOM disentomb, entomb,
hecatomb, Khartoum,
costume, pantoum, tomb,
toom, untomb, womb-to-
tomb
VROOM vroom
WOOM enwomb, womb, woom
ZOOM bazoom, presume,
resume, zoom

(See ŪM)

OOMD

(See OOM, ŪM, add *-ed,* where appropriate.)

O͞ON

O͞ON	triune
BLO͞ON	doubloon
BO͞ON	baboon, boon, Daniel Boone
BRO͞ON	gombroon
DO͞ON	bridoon, doon, dune, cardoon, rigadoon
DRO͞ON	gadroon, quadroon, spadroon
FO͞ON	buffoon, typhoon
GO͞ON	dragoon, goon, lagoon, Rangoon
HO͞ON	cohune
JO͞ON	jejune, June
KO͞ON	barracoon, cacoon, cocoon, coon, raccoon, rockoon, tycoon
KRO͞ON	croon
LO͞ON	apolune, balloon, demilune, galloon, loon, lune, pantaloon, perilune, saloon, shalloon, walloon, Walloon
MO͞ON	F full moon, G gibbous moon, H half moon, harvest moon, honeymoon, KW quarter moon, M moon, N new moon, O old moon, S sickle moon, simoon, W waxing moon, waning moon
NO͞ON	afternoon, forenoon, highnoon, midnoon, noon
PO͞ON	harpoon, lampoon, poon, tampoon
PRO͞ON	prune
RO͞ON	floroon, Cameroon, macaroon, maroon, octoroon, picaroon, rune, seroon, Scandaroon, vinegarroon
SHO͞ON	shoon
SKO͞ON	scoon
SO͞ON	bassoon, eftsoon, gossoon, matzoon, monsoon, oversoon, soon
SPO͞ON	dessert spoon, Great Horned Spoon, coffee spoon, runcible spoon, silver spoon, spoon, tablespoon, teaspoon
STRO͞ON	bestrewn, overstrewn, strewn
SWO͞ON	aswoon, reswoon, swoon
TO͞ON	A altun, F festoon, FR frigatoon, I inopportune, K cantoon, cartoon, coquetoon, M musketoon, O opportune, P pontoon,

	PL platoon, R ratoon, S saskatoon, Saskatoon, SP spittoon, spontoon, T testoon, toon
TRO͞ON	quintroon, patroon, poltroon
WO͞ON	woon
YO͞ON	picayune

(See Ū͞N.)

O͞OND

BO͞OND	Bund
HO͞OND	dachshund, Mahound
LO͞OND	Lund
WO͞OND	wound

(See O͞ON, Ū͞N, add -ed where appropriate.)

O͞ONZ

RO͞ONZ	Cameroons
SO͞ONZ	eftsoons

(See O͞ON, Ū͞N, add -s where appropriate.)

O͞OP

BLO͞OP	bloop
BO͞OP	Betty Boop, boop
DO͞OP	boop-boop-a-doop, dupe
DRO͞OP	adroop, droop, drupe
GO͞OP	goop
GRO͞OP	aggroup, group, regroup, subgroup
HO͞OP	cock-a-hoop, hoop, unhoop
HWO͞OP	whoop
KLO͞OP	cloop
KO͞OP	chicken coop, hen-coop, coop, coup, coupe, recoup
KRO͞OP	croup, Krupp
LO͞OP	Guadeloupe, cantaloupe, loop, loupe, loop-the-loop, saloop, unloop
PO͞OP	liripoop, nincompoop, poop, twiddlepoop
RO͞OP	roup
SKO͞OP	scoop
SKRO͞OP	scroop
SLO͞OP	sloop
SNO͞OP	snoop
SO͞OP	soup, soupe, supe
STO͞OP	stoep, stoop, stoup, stupe

SWO͞OP	downswoop, swoop, upswoop
TRO͞OP	troop, troupe
WO͞OP	Woop Woop

(See Ū͞P)

O͞OPS

O͞OPS	oops
HWO͞OPS	whoops
WO͞OPS	woops

(See O͞OP, Ū͞P, add -s where appropriate.)

OO͞R

MOO͞R	affaire, d'amour, amour
ZHOO͞R	plat du jour, toujours

OO͞R

BLOO͞R	doublure
BOO͞R	Boer, boor, tambour
CHOO͞R	abature, amateur, aperture, armature, BR briature, D discomfiture, divestiture, E expenditure, entablature, F forfeiture, furniture, G garmenture, garniture, I immature, investiture, J judicature, K calenture, camerature, candidature, caricature, comfiture, confiture, coverture, curvature, KL climature, KW quadrature, L ligature, literature, M mature, miniature, O overture, P portraiture, PR premature, primogeniture, S secundogeniture, sepulture, signature, T tablature, temperature, V vestiture
DOO͞R	dour, endure, perdure, perendure, pompadour, tandoor, troubadour
JOO͞R	abjure, adjure, conjure, injure
LOO͞R	allure, colure, condylure, lure, chevelure, velours, velure
KOO͞R	concours
MOO͞R	armure, blackamoor, Dartmoor, Exmoor,

	moor, Moor, paramour, unmoor
NOOR	Kohinhoor, manure
POOR	poor
ROOR	parure, Ruhr
SHOOR	assure, brochure, embouchure, ensure, hachure, insure, co-insure, cocksure, commissure, reassure, reinsure, cynosure, unsure
SKYOOR	clair-obscure, obscure
TOOR	detour, *contour*
TYOOR	(see CHOOR)
YOOR	voyeur, you're
ZHOOR	voyageur

OORD

CHOORD	caricatured
DOORD	endured, perdured, perendured
GOORD	gourd
JOORD	abjured, adjured, conjured, *injured*
LOORD	allured, lured
MOORD	moored, remoored, unmoored
SHOORD	assured, ensured, insured, reassured, reinsured
TOORD	detoured, *contoured*

(See URD)

ŌOS

BOOS	boose, caboose, calaboose, camboose
DOOS	adduce, deduce, educe, induce, conduce, douce, obduce, produce, traduce,
GOOS	golden goose, goose, mongoose, silly goose, wayzgoose
JOOS	juice, *verjuice*
KLOOS	occluse, recluse
KOOS	*couscous*
KROOS	crouse, cruse
LOOS	*footloose*, cut loose, let loose, loose, *sooloos*, Toulouse, unloose
MOOS	moose, mousse, vamoose
NOOS	burnoose, hangman's noose, hypotenuse, noose, nous, *slipnoose*
POOS	papoose, pouce
ROOS	ceruse, charlotte russe
SLOOS	sluice, unsluice
SPROOS	spruce
STROOS	abstruse

TOOS	obtuse, retuse
TROOS	truce
YOOS	cayuse
ZOOS	Zeus

(See ŪS)

ŌOSH

BOOSH	bouche, debouch, tarboosh
DOOSH	douche, kiddush
GOOSH	syagush
HWOOSH	whoosh
LOOSH	louche
MOOSH	gobe-mouche, mouche, Scaramouch
POOSH	capuche
ROOSH	barouche, farouche, ruche
TOOSH	cartouche
WOOSH	woosh
ZOOSH	zuche

OOSH

BOOSH	*A* ambush, *B* bushbush, bush, buttonbush, *BL* blackberry bush, blueberry bush, *BR* bramblebush, brittlebush, *D* dogbush, *F* fetterbush, *forebush*, *FL* flannelbush, *G* gallbush, goatbush, *H* hobblebush, hollybush, *horsebush*, *J* jewbush, *K* kinksbush, coffee bush, currant bush, *L* loganberry bush, *lotebush*, *M* maybush, *N* needlebush, *P* peabush, pepperbush, *pearlbush*, *pinbush*, *R* raspberry bush, *S* saltbush, soldierbush, *SH* shadbush, sugarbush, *SKW* squawbush, *SM* smokebush, *SP* spicebush, *TW* twinebush (etc.)
KOOSH	cush
POOSH	push
SHOOSH	shoosh
SWOOSH	swoosh

OOST

BOOST	boost, deboost
BROOST	browst
GOOST	langouste
JOOST	joust

PROOST	Proust
ROOST	roost, roust

(See ŌOS, add -*d* where appropriate.)

ŌOT

BOOT	boot, *freeboot, jackboot, marabout, overboot,* unboot
BROOT	bruit, brute, imbrute
DOOT	folie de doute
FLOOT	flute
FROOT	*breadfruit,* first fruit, forbidden fruit, fruit, gallows fruit, *grapefruit, jackfruit,* passion fruit
HOOT	hoot, cahoot, mahout
JOOT	jute
KLOOT	cloot, clute
KOOT	baldicoot, bandicoot, coot
KROOT	croute, recruit
LOOT	*A* absolute, *D* dilute, dissolute, *E* elute, *G* galoot, *I* involute, irresolute, *K* consolute, convolute, *L* loot, lute, *O* obvolute, *P* pollute, *R* resolute, revolute, *S* salute, solute, *V* volute
MOOT	*folkmoot,* Malamute, moot
NOOT	Canute, comminute
ROOT	*A* arrowroot, *B* Beirut, *beetroot, birthroot, BR* breadroot, briarroot, *CH* cheroot, *E* enroot, en route, *K* coralroot, crinkleroot, *M* musquashroot, *O* orrisroot, auto-route, *P* puttyroot, *R* redroot, root, route, *S* seroot, *SN* snakeroot, *T* taproot, unroot, uproot
SHOOT	bumbershoot, *offshoot,* outshoot, overshoot, parachute, chute, undershoot, upshoot
SKOOT	scoot
SLOOT	sloot, sluit
SMOOT	smoot
SNOOT	snoot
SOOT	*B* birthday suit, *H* hirsute, *L* lawsuit, *P* pantsuit, pursuit, *PL* playsuit, *S* soot, suit, *sunsuit, SP* spacesuit, *SW* swimsuit, *TR* tracksuit, *W* wetsuit, *Z* zootsuit
TOOT	astute, destitute, institute,

constitute, prostitute,
rooty-toot, substitute,
toot, toot-toot, tute

(See ŪT)

OOT

FOOT	A afoot, B barefoot, Bigfoot, BL Blackfoot, F fanfoot, finfoot, foalfoot, foot, FL flatfoot, forefoot, G goosefoot, H hotfoot, K cocksfoot, coltsfoot, KL clubfoot, KR crossfoot, crowfoot, L lobefoot, O autofoot, outfoot, P padfoot, pussyfoot, SP spadefoot, T tenderfoot, U underfoot, W webfoot
POOT	input, cajuput, kaput, autoput, output, put, throughput
SOOT	soot

OOTH

(TH as in "then")

SMOOTH	besmooth, resmooth, unsmooth
SOOTH	resoothe, soothe, unsoothe

OOTH

(TH as in "thin")

BOOTH	booth, polling booth, voting booth
KOOTH	couth, uncouth
KROOTH	crwth
LOOTH	Duluth, thuluth
MOOTH	vermouth
ROOTH	ruth, Ruth
SLOOTH	sleuth
SMOOTH	smeuth
SOOTH	forsooth, sooth
STROOTH	'strewth, 'struth
TOOTH	backtooth, bucktooth, dogtooth, eyetooth, tooth, wisdom tooth
TROOTH	truth, untruth
YOOTH	youth

OOTHD

(TH as in "then")

SMOOTHD	besmoothed, resmoothed, unsmoothed
SOOTHD	resoothed, soothed, unsoothed

OOTS

WOOTS	wootz

(See OOT, add -s where appropriate.)

OOTS

BOOTS	kibbutz
FOOTS	foots, hotfoots, pussyfoots
POOTS	puts
SOOTS	soots

OOV

GROOV	groove, ingroove, in-the-groove, microgroove
HOOV	behoove, who've
MOOV	amove, countermove, move, on-the-move, remove
PROOV	approve, disapprove, disprove, improve, prove, reprove
YOOV	you've

OOZ

OOZ	ooze
BLOOZ	blues, the blues
BOOZ	boos, booze, rambooze
BROOZ	bruise
CHOOZ	choose
DROOZ	druse, Druse
FLOOZ	flews, flues
HOOZ	who's, whose
JOOZ	Betelgeuse, Jews
KROOZ	crews, cruise, cruse, Santa Cruz, Vera Cruz
LOOZ	lose, relose, Toulouse
POOZ	pouze
ROOZ	peruse, roose, ruse
SHMOOZ	schmooze
SHOOZ	shoes, shoos, reshoes, reshoos, unshoes
SNOOZ	snooze
THOOZ	enthuse
TOOZ	tattoos
TROOZ	trews
YOOZ	use, youse

(See ŪZ; see OO, add -s where appropriate.)

OOZD

OOZD	oozed

(See OOZ, add -d where appropriate.)

OOZH

BOOZH	gamboge
BROOZH	Bruges
LOOZH	luge
ROOZH	rouge
VOOZH	vouge

ŌP

ŌP	myope, ope, reope
DŌP	dope, rope-a-dope
GRŌP	agrope, grope
HŌP	Cape of Good Hope, hope
KŌP	cope
LŌP	antelope, elope, envelope, interlope, cantaloupe, lope
MŌP	mope
NŌP	nope
PŌP	antipope, dispope, pope, protopope, unpope
RŌP	dragrope, phalarope, footrope, jumprope, manrope, pyrope, rope, roup, skiprope, tightrope, towrope
SKŌP	A amnioscope, astroscope, B bioscope, D dipleidoscope, E electroscope, episcope, G galvanoscope, H helioscope, hydroscope, horoscope, J gyroscope, L laparoscope, M microscope, P periscope, polariscope, polemoscope, PR proctoscope, R radarscope, S seismoscope, SK scope, SP spectroscope, ST stereoscope, stethoscope, T telescope, TH thermoscope, zoopraxiscope
SLŌP	aslope, slope
SŌP	sandsoap, soft-soap, soap, sope
STŌP	stope
THRŌP	philanthrope, lycanthrope, misanthrope
TŌP	isotope, metope, radioisotope, taupe, tope
TRŌP	allotrope, trope, zootrope

OP

OP	coin-op, co-op, op
BLOP	blop

BOP	bop, diddly-bop, diddy-bop, Cu-bop
CHOP	chop, chop-chop, karate-chop
DOP	dop
DROP	*airdrop*, bedrop, *dewdrop*, drop, *eardrop*, *eavesdrop*, *gumdrop*, paradrop, *raindrop*, *snowdrop*, *teardrop*
FLOP	*flipflop*, flippity-flop, flop
FOP	fop
GLOP	glop
GOP	gape, gop
HOP	*barhop*, *bellhop*, *hedgehop*, hippity-hop, hop, *carhop*, table-hop
HWOP	whop
KLOP	clip-clop, clop, clop-clop, clippety-clop
KOP	bull cop, cop, kop, motor cop, traffic cop
KROP	after-crop, bumper crop, intercrop, crop, *outcrop*, overcrop, riding crop, *sharecrop*, *stonecrop*
KWOP	quop
LOP	alop, lop, *orlop*
MOP	mop, remop, *rollmop*
NOP	knop
PLOP	plop
POP	gingerpop, *joypop*, lollipop, pop, soda pop
PROP	agitprop, prop, reprop, turboprop, underprop, unprop
SHOP	barbershop, *bookshop*, coffeeshop, *pawnshop*, shop, *sweatshop*, *sweetshop*, teashop, *workshop*
SKOP	scop
SLOP	*aslop*, *slipslop*, slop
SOP	asop, milksop, *sweetsop*
STOP	*backstop*, estop, *fullstop*, *nonstop*, *reststop*, *shortstop*, stop, unstop
STROP	strop
SWOP	swap
TOP	atop, big top, *blacktop*, *flat-top*, *foretop*, *hardtop*, *housetop*, carrot top, *maintop*, *mizzentop*, *netop*, overtop, *pop-top*, *redtop*, *tiptop*, top
WOP	wop

OPS

CHOPS	chops, *lambchops*, *porkchops*, slobber-chops, *vealchops*

KOPS	copse

(See **OP**, add -*s* where appropriate.)

ŌPT

(See **ŌP**, add -*d* where appropriate.)

OPT

(See **OP**, add -*ped* where appropriate.)

OPT

OPT	co-opt

(See **OP**, add -*ped* where appropriate.)

ŌR

BŌR	boar, Boer, *chokebore*, bore, forbore, forebore, hellebore, *smoothbore*
CHŌR	chore
DŌR	*A* adore, *B* backdoor, *bandore*, battledore, *D* death's door, door, dor, dumbledore, *E* Ecuador, *I* indoor, *K* commodore, corridor, cuspidor, *L* Labrador, louis d'or, *M* matador, mirador, mogadore, moidore, *O* open-door, *outdoor*, *P* picador, Polydore, *S* Salvador, *ST* stevedore, *T* toreador, *TR* trapdoor, troubador
DRŌR	drawer
FLŌR	first floor, fifth floor, floor, fourth floor, ground floor, second floor (etc.), underfloor, upper floor
FŌR	*A* afore, *B* before, *F* fore, for, four, *H* hereinbefore, heretofore, *HW* wherefor, *wherefore*, *M* metaphor, *P* petit four, pinafore, *S* semaphore, *T* two-by-four, *TH* therefor, *therefore*, theretofore
GŌR	gore, obligor
HŌR	abhor, hoar, whore, Lahore
KŌR	*A* albacore, apple core, *D* décor, *E* encore, *H* hardcore, *K* core, corps, manticore, *markhor*, *R* rotten to the core, *S* softcore, *T* terpsichore

KRŌR	crore
LŌR	*booklore*, *folklore*, galore, counsellor, lor, lore, vice chancellor
MŌR	Baltimore, evermore, furthermore, *claymore*, mohr, moire, more, mor, nevermore, paramour, sagamore, sycamore, sophomore
NŌR	assignor, ignore, nor, pundonor
PLŌR	deplore, explore, implore
PŌR	blastopore, *downpour*, madrepore, millepore, nullipore, outpour, pore, pour, rapport, Singapore
RŌR	furore, *outroar*, roar, *uproar*
SHŌR	alongshore, ashore, foreshore, inshore, lee shore, *longshore*, offshore, onshore, *seashore*, shore, weathershore
SKŌR	*fourscore*, overscore, score, *twoscore*, *threescore* (etc.), underscore
SNŌR	snore
SŌR	*B* bedsore, *F* footsore, *H* heartsore, *I* eyesore, *K* canker sore, *coldsore*, *L* lessor, *O* outsoar, *PR* promisor, soar, sore, upsoar
SPLŌR	splore
SPŌR	archespore, spore
STŌR	*drugstore*, candy store (etc.)
SWŌR	forswore, reswore, swore
TŌR	apparitor, guarantor, imperator, legator, patentor, tore, torr, warrantor
VŌR	frugivore, herbivore, insectivore, carnivore, omnivore
WŌR	outwore, rewore, wore
YŌR	yore
ZŌR	bezoar

ÔR

BÔR	Dukhobor
DÔR	corridor, cuspidor, louis d'or, matador, mirador, picador, Salvador, toreador, troubador
FÔR	for, metaphor, therefor, *therefore*

KÔR	décor, encore
LÔR	chancellor, councillor, counsellor, vice chancellor
NÔR	nor, pundonor
SKÔR	scaur
SÔR	balisaur, dinosaur, dolichosaur, hedrosaur, ichthyosaur, lessor, megalosaur, plesiosaur, teleosaur, tyrannosaur
THÔR	Thor
TÔR	apparitor, guarantor, legator, tor (see TUR for words ending in -tor but pronounced -ter)
VÔR	frugivore, herbivore, carnivore, omnivore
WÔR	man-of-war, outwore, *postwar*, prewar, rewore, tug-of-war, war, wore
YÔR	señor, yore, your
ZÔR	bezoar, recognizor

(See **UR** for words ending in -or but pronounced -ur.)

ÔRB

ÔRB	orb, disorb, inorb
FÔRB	forb
KÔRB	corbe
SÔRB	absorb, reabsorb, resorb, sorb

ÔRBD

ÔRBD	orbed, disorbed, inorbed
SÔRBD	absorbed, reabsorbed, resorbed, sorbed

ÔRCH

PÔRCH	back porch, front porch, porch
SKÔRCH	scorch
TÔRCH	torch

ÔRCHT

PÔRCHT	porched
SKÔRCHT	scorched
TÔRCHT	torched

ŌRD

ŌRD	oared, ord
BŌRD	*A* aboard, *B* beaverboard, Big Board, *billboard*, board, bord, *backboard*, *buckboard*, BL *blackboard*, blockboard, BR breadboard, CH chairman of the board, checkerboard, chessboard, *cheeseboard*, *chipboard*, *chalkboard*, D dartboard, dashboard, diving board, *duckboard*, DR draftboard, F fiberboard, fingerboard, *fireboard*, *footboard*, FL *flashboard*, *floorboard*, FR freeboard, H headboard, I inboard, ironing board, K cardboard, keyboard, corkboard, KL clapboard, clapperboard, *clipboard*, L leeboard, M matchboard, millboard, mortarboard, O outboard, overboard, P paperboard, *pasteboard*, pegboard, PL plasterboard, S seaboard, centerboard, *sideboard*, signboard, surfboard, SH shipboard, shuffleboard, SK skateboard, scaleboard, scoreboard, SKR scraperboard, SM smorgasbord, SPL splashboard, SPR springboard, STR stringboard, strawboard, SW switchboard, T tailboard, W weatherboard, ouija board, *wallboard*
DŌRD	adored, doored, *four-doored (etc.)*, *close-doored, open-doored*
FŌRD	afford, ford, Ford
GŌRD	gored, gourd, ungored
HŌRD	hoard, horde, whored, unhoard
KŌRD	cored
PLŌRD	deplored, explored, implored, undeplored, unexplored, unimplored
PŌRD	pored, poured
SHŌRD	shored
SKŌRD	scored, rescored, unscored
SNŌRD	snored
SŌRD	*broadsword*, sord, sword
TŌRD	toward, untoward

(See **ŌR**, add -ed where appropriate.)

ÔRD

HÔRD	abhorred
KÔRD	*A* accord, *D* disaccord, *discord*, *E* encored, *H* harmonichord, harpsichord, hexichord, *HW* whipcord, *K* concord, chord, cord, *KL* clavichord, *L* lyrichord, *M* masterchord, misericord, monochord, *N* needlecord,, notochord, *R* record, ripcord *T* tetrachord, *Y* urochord
LÔRD	belord, *landlord*, lord, milord, overlord, unlord, *warlord*
NYÔRD	Njord
SWÔRD	*greensward*, sward
WÔRD	award, reward, ward, warred

ÔRF

ÔRF	orf, orfe
DÔRF	Dusseldorf, *Waldorf*
DWÔRF	dwarf, white dwarf, red dwarf
HWÔRF	wharf
KÔRF	corf
MÔRF	*A* allomorph, *B* bimorph, *D* dimorph, *E* ephememorph, ectomorph, enantiomorph, endomorph, *H* hystricomorph, *I* isomorph, *J* gynandromorph, *M* mesamorph, morph, *P* paramorph, perimorph, polymorph, *R* rhizomorph, *S* pseudomorph, *TR* trimorph
SWÔRF	swarf

ŌRG

ŌRG	orgue
BÔRG	borg, Swedenborg
MÔRG	morgue

ÔRJ

FÔRJ	forge
GÔRJ	disengorge, disgorge, engorge, gorge, overgorge, regorge

JÔRJ	St. George
KÔRJ	corge

ÔRJD

(See **ÔRJ**, add *-d* where appropriate.)

ÔRK

ÔRK	orc
DÔRK	dork
FÔRK	fork, *hayfork, pitchfork,* tuning fork, weeding fork
GÔRK	gork
KÔRK	cork, corke, recork, uncork
KWÔRK	quark
NÔRK	nork
PÔRK	morepork, pork, roast pork, salt pork
SPÔRK	spork
STÔRK	stork
TÔRK	torque
YÔRK	New York, york, York

ÔRKT

(See **ÔRK**, add *-ed* where appropriate.)

ÔRL

ÔRL	orle
HWÔRL	whorl
KWÔRL	quarl
SHÔRL	schorl, shorl

ÔRM

DÔRM	dorm
FÔRM	*A* aeriform, aquiform, aliform, anguiform, anguilliform, acinaciform, aciniform, *B biform,* boculiform, bursiform, *BR* bromoform, *D* deform, deiform, dendriform, dentiform, digitiform, diversiform, dolabriform, *E* electroform, ensiform, eruciform, *F* falciform, fibriform, filiform, form, forme, fungiform, fusiform, *FL* floriform, *FR freeform, G* gasiform, *H* hamiform, harengiform, hederiform, hippocrepiform, *I* inform, iodoform, ypsilliform, *K*

cheliform, Cominform, conform, cordiform, coroniform, cubiform, cuculiform, cucumiform, cuneiform, *KL* chloroform, *KR* cribiform, cruciform, *L landform,* lentiform, ligniform, linguiform, *M* misform, misinform, moniliform, multiform, *N* napiform, nitrochloriform, *O* oriform, oviform, *P* panduriform, pediform, perform, piliform, pyriform, pisiform, poculiform, *PL platform,* plexiform, *R* ramiform, reform, remiform, reniform, *S* salverform, selliform, *SK* scobiform, scutiform, *SKR* scrotiform, *SKW* squaliform, *ST* stelliform, *STR* stromboliform, *T* tectiform, tauriform, turdiform, *TR* transform, *U* unform, uniform, unciform, *V* variform, vermiform, verruciform, vitriform, vulviform, *W waveform, Y* uniform

GÔRM	*cairngorm*
KÔRM	corm
NÔRM	norm
STÔRM	*B* barnstorm, bestorm, *BR* brainstorm, *F* firestorm, *H* hailstorm, *I* ice storm, *R* rainstorm, *S* sandstorm, *SL* sleetstorm, *SN* snowstorm, *ST* storm, *TH* thunderstorm, *W* windstorm
SWÔRM	aswarm, swarm, upswarm
WÔRM	*lukewarm,* rewarm, sunny warm, unwarm, warm

ÔRMD

(See **ÔRM**, add *-ed* where appropriate.)

ŌRN

MŌRN	mourn

(See **ÔRN**)

ÔRN

BÔRN	*A airborne, B* born, *CH chairborne, E earthborn,*

F first-born, forborne, *FR freeborn, H* heaven-born, heliborne, *high-born, I* inborn, *KL cloud-born, cloud-borne, L* lowborn, *N* newborn, night-born, *O* autumn-born, *R* reborn, *S sea-born, sea-borne,* suborn, summer-born, *SH shardborn, SPR* spring-born, *ST* stillborn, *TR true-born, U* unborn, *V* virgin-born, *W* winter-born, winterbourne, waterborne

DÔRN	adorn, disadorn, dorn, readorn, unadorn
HÔRN	*A* alpenhorn, *alphorn, althorn, D* dehorn, dishorn, *DR* drinking-horn, *F* foghorn, *FL* flugelhorn, *FR* French horn, *GR* greenhorn, *H* horn, hunting horn, *I* inkhorn, *K* Cape Horn, *cowhorn, KR crumhorn, L leghorn, longhorn, M* Matterhorn, *P* powderhorn, *PR* priming horn, *pronghorn, S* saxhorn, *SH* shoehorn, shorthorn, *ST* staghorn, stinkhorn, *T* tinhorn
KÔRN	*acorn,* barleycorn, *bicorn,* candycorn, Capricorn, cavicorn, clavicorn, corn, lamellicorn, longicorn, peppercorn, *popcorn, tricorn,* unicorn
LÔRN	forlorn, lorn, *lovelorn*
MÔRN	midmorn, morn, yestermorn
NÔRN	Norn
PÔRN	hard porn, kiddie porn, porn, soft porn
SHÔRN	shorn, reshorn, unshorn
SKÔRN	bescorn, scorn, self-scorn
SÔRN	sorn
SWÔRN	forsworn, sworn, unsworn
THÔRN	*blackthorn, buckthorn, hawthorn,* thorn
TÔRN	betorn, torn, untorn
WÔRN	*F* footworn, forewarn, *K careworn, O* outworn, *R* rewarn, *S seaworn, T timeworn, toilworn, W waveworn, wayworn,* weatherworn, warn, worn, waterworn

(See **ŌRN**)

ÔRND

(See ÔRN, add -ed where appropriate.)

ÔRP

DÔRP	dorp
GÔRP	gorp
LÔRP	australorp
THÔRP	thorp
TÔRP	torp
WÔRP	*moldwarp*, time warp, warp

ÔRPS

KÔRPS	corpse

(See ÔRP, add -s where appropriate.)

ŌRS

FŌRS	enforce, force, inforce, perforce, reinforce, tour de force
KŌRS	damp course, discourse, *forecourse*, intercourse, *concourse*, coarse, course, *racecourse*, recourse, water-course
SŌRS	resource, source
VŌRS	divorce

ÔRS

DÔRS	endorse, indorse
GÔRS	gorse
HÔRS	*CH* charley horse, *D* dead horse, *DR* drayhorse, *H* hobbyhorse, hoarse, horse, *K* carthorse, cockhorse, *KR* Crazy Horse, *P* packhorse, *R* racehorse, rocking horse, *S* seahorse, sawhorse, *ST* stalkinghorse, *studhorse*, *U* unhorse, *W* walkinghorse, warhorse, wooden horse, *workhorse*
KÔRS	discourse, *forecourse*, intercourse, *concourse*, coarse, corse, course, *race course*, recourse, water-course
MÔRS	Morse, premorse, remorse
NÔRS	Norse
SÔRS	resource, source
TÔRS	torse

TRÔRS	antrorse, dextrorse, extrorse, introrse, retrorse, sinistrorse
VÔRS	divorce
ZÔRS	resource

ŌRST

(See ŌRS, add -d where appropriate)

ÔRST

(See ÔRS, add -d where appropriate.)

ŌRT

FŌRT	forte, pianoforte
KŌRT	decourt, *forecourt*, county court, court

ÔRT

ÔRT	ort
BÔRT	abort, bort
DÔRT	kankedort
FÔRT	fort, *hillfort*
HÔRT	dehort
KÔRT	Agincourt, escort, *forecourt*, county court, court
KWÔRT	quart
MÔRT	amort, mort
PÔRT	*A* airport, aport, *D* davenport, deport, disport, *E* export, *H* heliport, hoverport, *I* import, *inport*, *J* jetport, *K* carport, comport, *L* life-support, *M* misreport, *N* nonsupport, *Newport*, *O* outport, *P* passport, port, purport, *R* rapport, re-export, reimport, report, *S* sally port, seaport, support, *SP* spaceport, *TR* transport
RÔRT	rort
SHÔRT	short, ultrashort
SNÔRT	snort
SÔRT	assort, consort, re-sort, sort, unsort
SPÔRT	*spoilsport*, sport
SWÔRT	swart
THWÔRT	athwart, thwart
TÔRT	distort, extort, intort, contort, retort, tort, torte
VÔRT	cavort
WÔRT	wart, worry wart
ZÔRT	exhort, resort

ÔRTH

FÔRTH	forth, *fourth*, henceforth, setter-forth, thenceforth
MÔRTH	morth
NÔRTH	north
SWÔRTH	swarth

ÔRTS

KWÔRTS	*biquartz*, quarts, quartz, rose quartz

(See ÔRT, add -s where appropriate.)

ŌRZ

DŌRZ	door, indoors, outdoors
FŌRZ	fours, all fours, plus fours
YŌRZ	all yours, yours

(See ŌR, add -s where appropriate.)

ÔRZ

DRÔRZ	drawers
TÔRZ	Louis Quatorze, quatorze
YÔRZ	all yours, yours
ZÔRZ	Azores

(See ÔR, add -s where appropriate.)

ŌS

ŌS	os, foliose, grandiose, caseose, otiose
BŌS	boce, *gibbose, globose, ribose*, thrombose, verbose
DŌS	dose, nodose, overdose, underdose
DYŌS	adios
GŌS	rugose, strigose
GRŌS	engross, gross
HŌS	*chaparajos*
KLŌS	close
KŌS	arkose, bellicose, *floccose, glucose*, jocose, cose, kos, metempsychose, varicose, ventricose, verrucose, *viscose*
KRŌS	necrose
LŌS	*A* alose, amylose, ankylose, annulose, *F* filose, *K* capillose, *N* nodulose, *P* pilose, *R*

ramose, ramulose,
rimose, rugulose, *S*
cymose, supulose,
surculose, *SKW*
squamulose, *ST*,
stimulose, stupulose, *TR*
tremellose

```
┌─────────────────────────────────┐
│         VERITAS MUTATUR          │
│                                  │
│   Of truths I knew,              │
│   Not one or two,                │
│   But quite a few                │
│      (In fact, a bunch)          │
│   Have proved untrue.            │
│      I have a hunch              │
│   The things I know              │
│   Today may go                   │
│   That road also;                │
│      Most folks must munch       │
│      Roast crow for lunch.       │
└─────────────────────────────────┘
```

MŌS	albumose, lachrymose, *mammose, osmose,* racemose
NŌS	anthracnose, diagnose, farinose, pruinose, raffinose, *spinose, venose*, uliqinose
PŌS	adipose
RŌS	aggerose, erose, morose, mulierose, operose, saccharose, *squarrose*, torose, *virose*
SHŌS	chausses
SŌS	soce
STŌS	stowce
TŌS	keratose, comatose, sarmentose, setose, tomentose

ÔS

HÔS	hawse
SÔS	applesauce, sauce

OS

OS	os
BOS	Bos, boss, emboss
DOS	doss
DROS	dross
FLOS	floss, candyfloss
FOS	fosse, *vanfoss*
GLOS	gloss, isogloss
GOS	mishbegoss
JOS	joss
KOS	cos, coss
KROS	*A* across, *D* doublecross, *F* fiery cross, *I* incross, intercross, *KR* crisscross, *christcross*, cross, crosse, *L* lacrosse, *M* motocross, *O* outcross, autocross, *R* rallycross, rosy cross, *U* uncross, *W* weeping cross
LOS	krobylos, loss
MOS	moss, sea moss
PROS	pross
ROS	kaross, rhinoceros, ross
SOS	soss
STOS	stoss
TOS	toss, Thanatos
TROS	albatross

ŌSH

ŌSH	brioche
BŌSH	Boche
FŌSH	Foch
GŌSH	gauche
KLŌSH	cloche
LŌSH	guilloche
RŌSH	caroche

OSH

OSH	brioche
BOSH	Boche, bosch, bosh, debosh, *kibosh*
FROSH	frosh
GOSH	gosh
HOSH	cohosh
JOSH	josh
KOSH	cosh
KWOSH	quash, *musquash*
LOSH	galosh, tikolosh
NOSH	nosh
POSH	posh
SKWOSH	squash
SLOSH	slosh
SOSH	sosh
SPLOSH	splosh
SWOSH	swash
TOSH	mackintosh, tosh
WOSH	*A* awash, *B* backwash, bellywash, bewash, Bosnywash, *BR* brainwash, *H* hogwash, *HW* whitewash, *I* eyewash, *M* mouthwash, *O* outwash, *R* rewash, *S* siwash, Siwash, *U* unwash, *W* wishwash, wash

OSHT

SKWOSHT	squashed

(See **OSH**, add *-ed* where appropriate.)

OSK

OSK	kiosk
BOSK	Bosc, bosk, imbosk
MOSK	abelmosk, mosque

OSP

NOSP	knosp
WOSP	galliwasp, wasp

ŌST

ŌST	oast
BŌST	boast
DŌST	dosed, redosed, undosed
GŌST	ghost
GRŌST	engrossed, grossed
HŌST	host, *no-host*
KŌST	Gold Coast, coast, *seacoast*
MŌST	*A* aftermost, almost, *B* backmost, bettermost, bottommost, *E* easternmost, *endmost, F* farthermost, *foremost*, furthermost, *H* headmost, hindermost, *hindmost*, hithermost, *I* inmost, innermost, *L* lowermost, *M* midmost, most, *N* nethermost, northernmost, northermost, *O* outermost, *R* rearmost, *S* centermost, southernmost, southermost, *T* topmost, *U* undermost, upmost, uppermost, utmost, uttermost, *W* westermost, westernmost
NŌST	diagnosed
PŌST	*B* bedpost, *D* doorpost, *F* fingerpost, *G* gatepost, guidepost, *H* hitchingpost, *HW* whipping-post, *I* impost, *K* compost, *L* lamppost, letterpost, *M* milepost, *O* outpost, *P* post, poste, *R* riposte, *S* signpost, soundpost
RŌST	*ribroast*, roast
TŌST	*milquetoast*, toast

(See **ŌS**, add *-d* where appropriate.)

ÔST

FÔST	faust, infaust

KÔST	hippocaust, hypocaust, holocaust	**KŌT**	*Ä* entrecote, *D* dovecote, *GR* greatcoat, *H* housecoat, *K* coat, cote, *O* overcoat, *P* petticoat, *R* raincoat, recoat, *redcoat*, *S* surcoat, *SH* sheepcote, *T* topcoat, turncoat, *U* undercoat, *W* waistcoat, wyliecoat
ZÔST	exhaust		

RÔT — inwrought, overwrought, rewrought, underwrought, unwrought, upwrought, wrought

OST

OST	teleost
BOST	bossed, cabossed, embossed, imbost
DOST	adossed, dossed
FOST	fossed
FROST	befrost, defrost, frost, *hoarfrost*, Jack Frost, permafrost
GLOST	glossed, reglossed, unglossed
JOST	jossed
KOST	accost, *alecost*, cost, Pentecost
KROST	double-crossed, *criss-crossed*, crossed, recrossed, uncrossed
LOST	lost, relost, unlost
MOST	enmossed, mossed
NOST	anagnost, bibliognost, geognost
SOST	sossed
TOST	betossed, *sea-tossed*, tempest-tossed, tossed, untossed
WOST	wast

KWŌT — bequote, misquote, overquote, quote, requote, underquote, unquote

LŌT — matelote, papillote, pardalote

MŌT — demote, emote, *folkmote*, gemot, commote, moat, mote, promote, remote, witenagemot

NŌT — denote, *footnote*, *gracenote, keynote*, connote, note, *woodnote*

PLŌT — ploat

PŌT — capote, *compote*, pote

RŌT — garrote, rewrote, rote, wrote, underwrote

SHŌT — shoat, shote

SKŌT — scote

SLŌT — slote

SMŌT — smote, resmote

SŌT — creosote

STŌT — stoat, stote

THRŌT — *bluethroat, whitethroat, cutthroat, starthroat,* throat

TŌT — *aptote,* asymptote, *diptote,* Thoth, tote, *triptote*

TRŌT — throat

VŌT — devote, outvote, redevote, revote, vote

SLÔT — *onslaught*

SÔT — besought, resought, sought, unbesought, unsought

THÔT — *aforethought,* afterthought, bethought, *forethought,* free thought, merrythought, methought, rethought, thought, unthought

TÔT — retaught, self-taught, taught, taut, untaught, untaut

TRÔT — distraut

ŌT

ŌT	oat, nesiote
BLŌT	bloat
BŌT	*B* banana boat, boat, *F* ferryboat, *G* gunboat, *H* houseboat, *HW* whaleboat, *L* lifeboat, *longboat, M* manbote, motorboat, *P* pilot boat, power boat, *R* riverboat, *rowboat, S* sailboat, sea boat, *SH* ship's boat, *showboat, SP* speedboat, *ST* steamboat, *SW* swingboat
DŌT	anecdote, antidote, dote, epidote, lepidote, table d'hôte
FLŌT	afloat, *bobfloat*, float, refloat
FŌT	telephote
GLŌT	gloat
GŌT	billygoat, goat, mountain goat, nanny goat, old goat, redingote, *scapegoat, zygote*
GRŌT	groat

ÔT

ÔT	aught, ought
BÔT	bought, *dear-bought*, rebought
BRÔT	brought, upbrought
FLÔT	flaught
FÔT	fought, *hard-fought*, refought, unfought
FRÔT	fraught, unfraught
GÔT	ghat, ghaut
KÔT	caught, recaught, uncaught, upcaught
NÔT	aeronaut, aquanaut, argonaut, Argonaut, astronaut, *dreadnought*, *fearnought*, hydronaut, juggernaut, cosmonaut, naught, nought

OT

OT	*CH* chariot, cheviot, *G* galiot, *H* heriot, *I* idiot, Iscariot, *K* compatriot, *P* patriot, *S* Sciot, *SH* cheviot
BLOT	blot, *inkblot, simblot*
BOT	*abbott,* bot, bott, *robot*
DOT	dot, microdot, peridot, polka-dot, Wyandotte
FOT	phot
GLOT	*diglot,* glot, heptaglot, hexaglot, microglot, monoglot, pentaglot, polyglot, tessaraglot
GOT	*A* argot, *B* begot, *E* ergot, *F* fagot, *faggot,* first-begot, forgot, *G* ghat, got, *H* hard-got, *I* ill-got, ingot, *L* larigot, last-begot, *M* misbegot, *SP* spigot, *U* unbegot, unforgot, ungot
GROT	grot
HOT	fiery hot, hot, white-hot, red-hot
HWOT	somewhat, what
JOT	jot
KLOT	*bloodclot,* clot
KOT	apricot, boycott, *dovecot,* haricot, carrycot, cocotte, cot, *mascot,* massicot, persicot, *plumcot*
KWOT	aliquot, *kumquat, loquot, Pequot*
LOT	*A* allot, *B* billot, *E* eschalot, *feedlot, H* Helot, *K* cachalot, calotte, Camelot, culotte, *L* Lancelot, lot, Lot, *M* matelotte, melilot, *O*

MOT ocelot, *S* sans-culotte, *SH* shallot, Shalotte, *T tillot,* *Z zealot* / bergamot, guillemot, mot, motte, *motmot,* witenagemot

NOT *B bowknot, F forget-me-not, G Gordian knot, GR granny knot, H Huguenot, HW whatnot, J juggernaut, K cannot, L loveknot, N knot, not, R reef knot, reknot, SH shoulderknot, SKW square knot, SL slipknot, T topknot, U unknot*

PLOT *grassplot, complot,* counterplot, plot, subplot, underplot

POT *CH chimneypot, D dashpot, despot, F firepot, fusspot, FL fleshpot,* flowerpot, *G galipot, gallipot, GL glue pot, H hotchpot, hotpot, I inkpot, J jackpot, K catchpot,* coffeepot, *KR crackpot, M monkeypot, N nelipot, P pot, pott, R repot, S sexpot, SK skilpot, ST stinkpot,* stockpot, *T talipot, teapot, tin-pot, tosspot, trampot*

ROT dry rot, *garrot,* garrote, *parrot,* rot, tommyrot

SHOT *B bowshot, buckshot, BL bloodshot, CH cheap shot, E earshot, F foreshot, G gunshot, GR grapeshot, H hipshot, I eyeshot, L longshot, M moonshot, O overshot, P potshot, S sighting shot, SH shot, shott, SL slapshot, slingshot, SN snapshot, U undershot, upshot*

SKOT Scot, Scott, *wainscot*

SKWOT asquat, squat, resquat

SLOT slot

SNOT snot

SOT besot, sot

SPOT beauty spot, forty-sport, heli-spot, hot spot, *nightspot,* plague spot, spot, *sunspot*

STOT stot

SWOT swat, swot

TOT Hottentot, tot

TROT *dogtrot, foxtrot, jogtrot,* trot, turkeytrot

VOT gavotte

WOT kilowatt, megawatt, terawatt, watt, wot

YOT yacht

ŌTH

(TH as in "then")

KLŌTH clothe, reclothe, unclothe

LŌTH loathe

TRŌTH betroth

ŌTH

(TH as in "thin")

ŌTH oath

BŌTH both

GRŌTH aftergrowth, growth, *ingrowth, outgrowth,* overgrowth, *regrowth,* undergrowth, zero growth

KWŌTH quoth

LŌTH loath

MŌTH behemoth

RŌTH wroth

SLŌTH sloth

THŌTH Thoth

TRŌTH betroth, troth, untroth

OTH

(TH as in "thin")

BROTH barley broth, broth

FROTH froth

GOTH Goth, Ostrogoth, Visigoth

KLOTH *B backcloth, breechcloth, BR broadcloth, CH cheesecloth, D dishcloth, H haircloth, KL cloth, L loincloth, N neckcloth, O oilcloth, P pilot cloth, S saddle cloth, sackcloth, sailcloth, cerecloth*

MOTH behemoth, moth

ROTH wroth

SWOTH swath

TROTH troth

OTS

HOTS hots, the hots

TROTS trots, the trots

(See **OT,** add -*s* where appropriate.)

OU

OU luau, meow, miaow, ow

BOU bough, bow, golden bough

BROU brow, *highbrow, eyebrow, lowbrow, middlebrow,* overbrow

CHOU chou, ciao, *chowchow,* Foochow, Soochow

DOU disendow, dhow, endow, *landau,* tou

FROU frau, frow, *hausfrau*

GOU *hoosegow*

HOU and how, anyhow, how, *knowhow, somehow*

JOU jhow

KOU brown cow, cow, Krakow

LOU allow, disallow, Lao, *lau-lau, pilau,* reallow

MOU *haymow,* Mau Mau, mow

NOU enow, erenow, how now, now, *unau*

PLOU plough, plow, *snowplough, snowplow,* upplough, upplow

POU pow

PROU prow

ROU row

SKOU scow

SLOU slough

SOU sough, sow

SWOU swow

THOU thou

TOU *kowtow,* tao, tau

VOU avow, disavow, reavow, vow

WOU bow-wow, *pow-wow,* wow

YOU snarleyyow, yow

OUCH

OUCH ouch

GROUCH grouch

KOUCH couch

KROUCH crouch

MOUCH Scaramouch

POUCH pouch

SLOUCH slouch

VOUCH avouch, vouch

OUCHT

GROUCHT grouched

(See **OUCH,** add -*ed* where appropriate.)

OUD

BOUD bowed, unbowed

DOUD dowd, endowed, well-endowed

FOUD foud

KLOUD becloud, encloud, intercloud, cloud, overcloud, recloud, thundercloud, uncloud
KROUD crowd, overcrowd
LOUD aloud, allowed, loud, reallowed
PROUD proud, *purseproud*
SHOUD showd
SHROUD beshroud, disenshroud, enshroud, reshroud, shroud, unshroud
SOUD Ibn-Saud
STROUD stroud
VOUD avowed, reavowed, revowed, vowed

(See **OU**, add -ed where appropriate.)

OUJ

GOUJ gouge
SKROUJ scrouge

OUL

OUL night owl, owl, screech owl
BOUL bowel, disembowel
DOUL *dowel*, dowl
FOUL afowl, befoul, foul, fowl, guinea fowl, *moorfowl, peafowl, seafowl, wildfowl*, waterfowl
GROUL growl
HOUL behowl, howl
JOUL jowl
KOUL encowl, cowl, cowle, uncowl
PROUL prowl
SKOUL scowl
YOUL yowl

(See **OUEL**)

OULD

(See **OUL, OUEL,** add-ed where appropriate.)

OUN

BROUN brown, embrown, *nutbrown*
DOUN *A* adown, *BR* breakdown, bring down, *D* down, *G* godown, goose-down, *H* hand-me-down, hoedown,

I eiderdown, *K* comedown, countdown, *L* lowdown, *M* markdown, meltdown, moondown, *P* Piltdown, putdown, *R* reach-me-down, rubdown, *S* sundown, *SH* shakedown, showdown, shutdown, *SL* slowdown, *SPL* splashdown, *SW* swan's-down, *T* touchdown, tumbledown, *TH* thistledown, *U* upside-down
DROUN drown
FROUN frown
GOUN evening gown, gown, *nightgown*, regown, town and gown, ungown
KLOUN clown
KROUN decrown, discrown, crown, recrown, uncrown
NOUN *adnoun*, noun, *pronoun*, renown
TOUN Chinatown, *downtown*, cabbagetown, *crosstown*, midtown, Motown, shantytown, town, *uptown*

OUND

BOUND *A* abound, *B* bound, *BR* brassbound, *E* earthbound, eastbound, *F* fogbound, *H* hellbound, heavenbound, *hidebound*, homebound, hoofbound, housebound, *I* inbound, ironbound, *icebound*, *K* casebound, *KL* clothbound, *N* northbound, *O* outbound, outward-bound, *R* rebound, *S* southbound, super-abound, *SN* snowbound, *SP* spellbound, *ST* stormbound, *STR* strikebound, *U* unbound, *W* westbound, windbound
DOUND redound
FOUND *dumbfound*, found, confound, profound, refound, unfound
GROUND *A* aboveground, aground, *B* background, burial ground, burying ground, *F* fairground, *fine-ground, GR* ground, *H* high ground, holy ground,

K coarse-ground, *L* lost ground, *M* medium-ground, middle ground, *O* overground, *PL* playground, pleasure ground, *R* reground, *SP* sportsground, *U* underground, unground, *V* vantage ground
HOUND *B* bearhound, boarhound, boozehound, *BL* bloodhound, *D* deerhound, *DR* draghound, *E* elkhound, *F* foxhound, *GR* grayhound, grewhound, *H* hellhound, horehound, hound, *M* Mahound, *SL* sleuth-hound, *SM* smut-hound, *ST* staghound, *W* wolfhound
KROUND crowned, wreath-crowned, recrowned, uncrowned
MOUND mound
NOUND renowned, unrenowned
POUND decompound, expound, impound, compound, *geepound*, pound, propound
ROUND around, merry-go-round, round, surround, wraparound
SOUND infrasound, re-sound, sound, ultrasound, unsound
STOUND astound, stound
SWOUND swound
WOUND rewound, series-wound, shunt-wound, unwound, wound
ZOUND resound

(See **OUN**, add -ed where appropriate.)

OUNDZ

HOUNDZ *wishhounds, yethhounds*
ZOUNDZ zounds

(See **OUND**, add -s where appropriate.)

OUNJ

LOUNJ lounge
SKROUNJ scrounge

OUNS

OUNS ounce
BOUNS bounce

FLOUNS	flounce
FROUNS	frounce
JOUNS	jounce
NOUNS	announce, denounce, enounce, mispronounce, pronounce, renounce
POUNS	pounce
ROUNS	rounce
TROUNS	trounce

(See **OUNT**, add -s.)

OUNT

FOUNT	fount
KOUNT	account, discount, count, miscount, recount, *viscount*, uncount
MOUNT	amount, demount, dismount, catamount, mount, paramount, remount, *seamount*, surmount, tantamount, unmount

OUNZ

(See **OUN**, add -s where appropriate.)

OUR

OUR	evil hour, lucky hour, hour, our, unlucky hour
BOUR	bower, embower
DOUR	dour, dower
FLOUR	deflower, flour, flower, gillyflower, cauliflower, *cornflower, mayflower, moonflower,* passionflower, reflower, *wallflower*
GOUR	gaur
HOUR	Eisenhower
KOUR	cower
LOUR	lour, *safflower*
POUR	empower, hydropower, *horsepower, manpower,* overpower, power, superpower, *willpower*
SHOUR	rain shower, summer shower, shower, thundershower
SKOUR	bescour, rescour, scour
SOUR	besour, resour, sour
STOUR	stour
TOUR	*churchtower*, tower, *watchtower*
VOUR	devour, redevour

(See **OU**, add -er for imperfect rhymes; also see **OUER**.)

OURD

(See **OUR**, add -ed where appropriate.)

OUS

BLOUS	blouse
BOUS	bouse
CHOUS	chiaus, chouse
DOUS	douse
GOUS	degauss, gauss
GROUS	grouse, *sandgrouse, woodgrouse*
HOUS	*A* alehouse, almshouse, *B* bakehouse, bathhouse, backhouse, birdhouse, bawdy house, *Bauhaus,* boathouse, bughouse, *CH* chapter house, charnel house, charterhouse, *D* dosshouse, doghouse, *F* farmhouse, *FR* frat house, *G* guardhouse, gatehouse, guesthouse, *GL* glasshouse, *GR* greenhouse, *H* halfway house, henhouse, *whorehouse, hothouse,* house, *J* jailhouse, *K* cathouse, cookhouse, countinghouse, *courthouse,* customhouse, *KL* clubhouse, *L* lighthouse, *M* madhouse, *O* outhouse, *P* penthouse, poorhouse, porterhouse, pothouse, powerhouse, public house, *PL* playhouse, pleasure house, *PR* prison house, *R* roadhouse, roundhouse, *S* safe house, summerhouse, *SK* schoolhouse, *SL* slaughterhouse, *SP* sporting house, *ST* steakhouse, statehouse, storehouse, *T* teahouse, tollhouse, *W* warehouse, Wodehouse, workhouse
LOUS	book louse, delouse, louse, wood louse
MOUS	*CH* churchmouse, *D* dormouse, *F* fieldmouse, *FL* Fliedermaus, flindermouse, flittermouse, *K* country mouse, *M* Mickey Mouse, mouse, *R* reremouse, *S* city mouse, *T* titmouse, town mouse

NOUS	nous
SHOUS	shouse
SKOUS	*lobscouse,* scouse
SOUS	souse
SPOUS	spouse
STROUS	Strauss

OUST

OUST	oust
BROUST	browst
FOUST	Faust
FROUST	frowst
JOUST	joust
ROUST	roust

(See **OUS**, add -d where appropriate.)

OUT

OUT	*BL* blackout, *BR* brownout, *D* diner-out, dugout, *DR* dropout, *F* fallout, *H* hangout, hereout, *holdout,* hole out, *HW* whereout, *I* in-and-out, *K* cookout, *L* lookout, lock-out, *N* knockout, *O* out, owt, out-and-out, *P* pig out, *R* rainout, *SH* shutout, *SP* spaced out, *ST* stakeout, *T* takeout, turnout, *TH* thereout, throughout, *TR* tryout, *W* walkout, without
BOUT	*A* about, *B* bout, *DR* drinking bout, *G* gadabout, *H* hereabout, *HW* whereabout, whirlabout, *N* knockabout, *R* rightabout, roundabout, roustabout, runabout, *ST* stirabout, *TH* thereabout
DOUT	doubt, misdoubt, redoubt
DROUT	drought
FLOUT	flout
GOUT	gout
GROUT	grout
HOUT	mahout
KLOUT	*breechclout,* clout
KROUT	kraut, sauerkraut
LOUT	*ablaut,* lout, *umlaut*
NOUT	knout, nowt
POUT	*eelpout,* pout
ROUT	derout, rout
SHOUT	beshout, shout
SKOUT	boy scout, girl scout, scout

SMOUT	smout
SNOUT	snout
SPOUT	bespout, *downspout*, spout, waterspout
SPROUT	sprout, resprout
STOUT	stout, stylish stout
TOUT	tout
TROUT	trout
VOUT	devout, undevout

OUTH

DROUTH	drouth
MOUTH	B bemouth, *badmouth*, *bigmouth*, BL blabbermouth, CH chiselmouth, FL *flutemouth*, FR *frogmouth*, H hand and mouth, hand to mouth, *hardmouth*, K cottonmouth, KL *closemouth*, L loudmouth, M mouth, SN *snakemouth*, warmouth
SOUTH	south

OUZ

BLOUZ	blouse
BOUZ	bouse
BROUZ	browse
DOUZ	douse, dowse
DROUZ	drowse
HOUZ	house, rehouse, unhouse
MOUZ	mouse
POUZ	disespouse, espouse
ROUZ	arouse, carouse, rouse, uprouse
SMOUZ	smouse
SOUZ	souse
SPOUZ	bespouse, disespouse, espouse, spouse
TOUZ	touse, towse
TROUZ	trouse

(See OU, add -s where appropriate.)

OUZD

| BOUZD | boused |

(See OUZ, add -d where appropriate.)

ŌV

| DŌV | dove |
| DRŌV | drove |

GRŌV	grove, *mangrove*
HŌV	behove, hove
JŌV	apojove, Jove, perijove
KLŌV	clove
KŌV	*alcove*, cove
MŌV	gemauve, mauve
RŌV	rove
SHRŌV	shrove, Shrove
STŌV	stove
STRŌV	strove
THRŌV	throve
TRŌV	treasure trove, trove
WŌV	interwove, inwove, rewove, wove

ŌVZ

| LŌVZ | loaves |

(See ŌV, add -s where appropriate.)

OY

(See OI)

ŌZ

BŌZ	beaux
BRŌZ	brose
CHŌZ	chose
DŌZ	*bulldoze*, doze
FŌZ	*metamorphose*
FRŌZ	froze, refroze, unfroze
GLŌZ	glose, glows, gloze
HŌZ	*half-hose*, hose, panty-hose
KLŌZ	disclose, enclose, foreclose, inclose, interclose, close, clothes, *parclose*, reclose, *smallclothes*, unclose
KŌZ	coze
KRŌZ	croze
MŌZ	anastomose
NŌZ	bladdernose, *bluenose*, bottlenose, diagnose, dominoes, *hooknose*, pug nose, shovelnose, snub nose
PŌZ	A appose, D decompose, depose, discompose, dispose, E expose, I impose, indispose, infrapose, interpose, J juxtapose, K compose, O oppose, overexpose, P pose, PR predispose, presuppose, propose, R recompose, repose, resuppose, S superpose, suppose, TR transpose, U underexpose

PRŌZ	prose
RŌZ	A arose, BR bramble rose, D damask rose, dog rose, G guelder-rose, I Irish rose, M moss rose, PR *primrose*, R rambling rose, *rockrose*, rose, SW sweetheart rose, T *tearose*, *tuberose*, W wild rose, York rose (etc.)
SHŌZ	quelquechose, shows
SKWŌZ	squoze
THŌZ	those
THRŌZ	throes, throws
TŌZ	pettitoes, toze

(See Ō, add -s, -es where appropriate.)

ÔZ

GÔZ	gauze, geegaws
HÔZ	hawse
JÔZ	jaws, lantern jaws
KLÔZ	clause, claws, Santa Claus
KÔZ	because, cause
PLÔZ	applause
PÔZ	aeropause, diapause, magnetopause, menopause, mesopause, pause, paws, stratopause
STRÔZ	*jackstraws*, straws
TÔZ	taws, tawse
VÔZ	vase
YÔZ	yaws

(See Ô, add -s where appropriate.)

OZ

BOZ	Boz
KOZ	cos
KWOZ	quoz
TWOZ	'twas
WOZ	was

ŌZD

(See ŌZ, add -d where appropriate.)

ŌZH

BŌZH	gamboge
LŌZH	éloge, loge
MŌZH	Limoges

Ū

| Ū | bayou, B.T.U., I.O.U., ewe, U, yew, you |

BŪ	imbue, reimbue
DŪ	*A* adieu, *B* bedew, bienentendu, bon dieu, *D* dew, *E* endew, endue, *F* fondue, *H* honeydew, *I* indew, *M* malentendu, mountain dew, *N* night dew, *O* overdue, *P* perdu, perdue, Purdue, *PR* prie-dieu, *R* residue, *S* sous-entendu, subdue, *sundew*, *U* undue, *V* vendue, *Z* Xanadu
FŪ	feu, feverfew, few, phew, *curfew*
HŪ	hew, hue, whew, clerihew, rough-hew
KŪ	curlicue, cue, queue, kyu, purlicue, ratamacue
LŪ	*curlew*, lieu, poilu, *purlieu*
MŪ	*emu*, immew, mew, sea mew, unmew
NŪ	*A* anew, avenue, *D* detinue, *E* enew, *F* foreknew, *K* continue, *N* gnu, knew, new, nu, *P* parvenu, *R* renew, retinue, revenue, *V* venue
PŪ	conspue, pew, pugh, rompu
SKŪ	askew, skew, unskew
SMŪ	smeu, smew
SPŪ	spew
STŪ	beef stew, Irish stew, stew
SŪ	ensue, resue, sue
THŪ	thew
TŪ	battue, tew, *virtue*
VŪ	bird's-eye view, interview, overview, *preview*, *purview*, review, view
YŪ	senryu

(See $\overline{OO}$)

HAD I BUTT NUDE

Had I butt nude,
Had I but seed,
Would I have dude
The dids I deed?

ŪB

TŪB	breathing tube, inner tube, tube

(See $\overline{OO}B$)

UB

BLUB	blub
BUB	Beelzebub, bub, *hubbub*, sillabub, syllabub, trillibub
CHUB	chub
DRUB	drub
DUB	dub, *flubdub*, rub-a-dub
FLUB	flub
FUB	fub
GLUB	glub, glub-glub
GRUB	grub
HUB	hub
KLUB	battle club, business club, Kiwanis club, country club, club, lunch club, men's club, *nightclub*, Rotary club, social club, war club, women's club
KUB	cub
NUB	knub, nub
PUB	pub
RUB	rub
SHRUB	shrub, *subshrub*
SKRUB	scrub
SLUB	slub
SNUB	snub
STUB	stub
SUB	sub
TUB	*bathtub*, tub, *washtub*

UBD

(See **UB**, add *-ed* where appropriate.)

ŪCH

(See $\overline{OO}CH$)

UCH

DUCH	Dutch
HUCH	hutch
KLUCH	clutch
KRUCH	crutch
KUCH	cutch
MUCH	forasmuch, inasmuch, insomuch, much, mutch, overmuch
RUCH	rutch
SKUCH	scutch
SMUCH	smutch
SUCH	*nonesuch*, such
TUCH	master touch, Midas touch, retouch, soft touch, touch, untouch

UCHT

(See **UCH**, add *-ed* where appropriate.)

ŪD

DŪD	dude
FŪD	feud
HŪD	many-hued, rainbow-hued, sombre-hued
LŪD	collude, interlude, lewd, *prelude, postlude*, unlewd
NŪD	denude, half nude, nude, renewed, unrenewed
STŪD	stewed, stude
SŪD	exude, transude
THŪD	thewed
TŪD	*A* altitude, amplitude, aptitude, asuetude, attitude, *B* beatitude, *D* decrepitude, definitude, desuetude, disquietude, dissimilitude, *E* eptitude, exactitude, *GR* gratitude, *H* habitude, hebetude, *I* inaptitude, inexactitude, ineptitude, infinitude, ingratitude, inquietude, incertitude, insuetude, *K* consuetude, correctitude, *KR* crassitude, *KW* quietude, *L* lassitude, latitude, lenitude, lentitude, lippitude, longitude, *M* magnitude, mansuetude, mollitude, multitude, *N* necessitude, negritude, nigritude, *O* omnitude, *P* pinguitude, pulchritude, *PL* platitude, plenitude, *PR* promptitude, *R* rectitude, *S* sanctitude, senectitude, serenitude, certitude, servitude, similitude, solicitude, solitude, *SP* spissitude, *T* torpitude, turpitude, *V* vastitude, verisimilitude, vicissitude
ZŪD	exude

(See $\overline{OO}D$; see Ū, add *-ed* or *-d* where appropriate.)

UD

BLUD	blood, *lifeblood, oxblood*, 'sblood
BUD	bud, disbud, *redbud, rosebud* (etc.)
DUD	dud, fuddydud
FLUD	flood, photoflood
FUD	fud
KRUD	crud

KUD	cud
LUD	lud, m' lud
MUD	mud
PUD	pud
RUD	rud, rudd
SHUD	shud
SKUD	scud
SPUD	spud
STUD	bestud, stud, unstud
SUD	sud, sudd
THUD	thud

ŪF

(See $\overline{OO}$F)

UF

BLUF	bluff, Council Bluff, Red Bluff
BUF	blindman's-buff, buff, counterbuff, rebuff
CHUF	chough, chuff
DRUF	*dandruff*
DUF	duff, Macduff, plum duff
FLUF	fluff
FUF	fuff
GRUF	gruff
GUF	guff
HUF	huff
HWUF	whuff
KLUF	clough
KUF	becuff, fisticuff, *handcuff,* handicuff, cuff, off-the-cuff, on the cuff, uncuff
LUF	luff
MUF	*earmuff,* muff
NUF	enough
PLUF	pluff
PUF	bepuff, *creampuff, wheatpuff,* powderpuff, puff
RUF	*crossruff,* rough, ruff, *woodruff*
SKRUF	scruff
SKUF	scuff
SLUF	slough, sluff
SNUF	besnuff, snuff
STUF	*breadstuff, dyestuff, foodstuff,* garden stuff, *greenstuff,* overstuff, stuff, unstuff
SUF	sough
TUF	tough, tuff

ŪFT

(See $\overline{OO}$F, add *-ed* where appropriate.)

UFT

SKUFT	scuffed, scuft
TUFT	candytuft, tuft

(See **UF**, add *-ed* where appropriate.)

ŪG

FŪG	fugue

(See $\overline{OO}$G)

UG

UG	ugh
BUG	*bedbug,* bug, debug, doodlebug, *firebug, humbug,* jitterbug, ladybug, litterbug, *redbug,* spittlebug, tumblebug
CHUG	chug
DRUG	drug
DUG	dug
FUG	fug
GLUG	glug
HUG	*bearhug,* bunny hug, hug
JUG	jug
LUG	lug
MUG	mug
PLUG	*earplug, noseplug,* plug, unplug
PUG	pug
RUG	rug
SHRUG	shrug
SLUG	forslug, slug
SMUG	smug
SNUG	snug
THUG	thug
TRUG	trug
TUG	tug
VUG	vug

UGD

(See **UG**, add *-ged* where appropriate.)

ŪJ

FŪJ	deonifuge, dolorifuge, febrifuge, insectifuge, calcifuge, centrifuge, subterfuge, taenifuge, *transfuge,* vermifuge
HŪJ	huge

(See $\overline{OO}$J)

UJ

BLUJ	bludge
BUJ	budge
DRUJ	drudge
FUJ	fudge
GRUJ	begrudge, grudge
JUJ	adjudge, forejudge, forjudge, judge, misjudge, prejudge, rejudge
MUJ	mudge
NUJ	nudge
PUJ	pudge
RUJ	rudge
SLUJ	sludge
SMUJ	smudge
TRUJ	trudge

UJD

JUJD	ill-judged, unjudged, well-judged

(See **UJ**, add *-d* where appropriate.)

ŪK

ŪK	uke, yeuk, yewk, yuke
BŪK	rebuke, sambuke
NŪK	antinuke, nuke, *pro-nuke*
PŪK	puke

GENESIS

It all just happened? No intent?
Then let us pray to Accident.

TŪK	Heptateuch, Hexateuch, Octateuch, Pentateuch, tuke

(See $\overline{OO}$K)

UK

BUK	*blackbuck,* buck, *bushbuck, jumbuck,* huckabuck, megabuck, *prongbuck, reedbuck, roebuck, sawbuck, springbuck,* waterbuck
CHUK	chuck, *woodchuck*
DUK	beduck, dead duck, Donald Duck, duck, lame duck, *shelduck*
FUK	fuck
GLUK	gluck
GUK	guck

HUK	huck
KLUK	dumb cluck, cluck
KRUK	cruck
KUK	cuck
LUK	beginner's luck, chuck-a-luck, dumb luck, ill-luck, Lady Luck, luck, misluck, *mukluk, potluck*
MUK	amuck, high muck-a-muck, muck
NUK	Canuck
PLUK	pluck
PUK	puck, Puck, Volapuk
RUK	laverock, ruck, rukh, sumbooruk
SHMUK	shmuck
SHUK	shuck
STRUK	*dumbstruck,* horror-struck, *moonstruck, awe-struck, stagestruck,* struck, *sunstruck,* terror-struck, thunderstruck, wonderstruck
STUK	stuck, unstuck
SUK	suck
TRUK	truck
TUK	Friar Tuck, nip and tuck, tuck
YUK	yuk

UKS

DUKS	dux, *redux*
FLUKS	flux, *influx*
KRUKS	crux
LUKS	de luxe, lux, Lux
MUKS	mucks, mux
SHUKS	shucks
TUKS	tux
YUKS	yucks

(See **UK,** add *-s* where appropriate.)

UKT

DUKT	*A* abduct, aqueduct, *D* deduct, duct, *E* educt, *F* fumiduct, *I* induct, *K* conduct, *M* misconduct, *O* obduct, oviduct, *PR* product, *R* reduct, *S* circumduct, subduct, *V* viaduct
FRUKT	usufruct
LUKT	reluct
PLUKT	plucked, unplucked, well-plucked
RUKT	eruct
STRUKT	destruct, instruct, construct, misconstruct, obstruct, reconstruct, self-destruct, substruct, superstruct

(See **UK,** add *-ed* where appropriate.)

ŪL

ŪL	Yule
BŬL	buhl, Istanbul, *jambul,* vestibule
DŬL	dual, duel, hierodule
GŬL	gule
KŬL	*macule,* molecule, reticule, ridicule, vermicule, verricule
MŪL	mewl, mule
NŪL	*newel, renewal*
PŪL	pule
SKŪL	*ulcuscule*

(See **ŌŌL, ŌŌEL, ŪAL.**)

UL

DUL	dull
GUL	gull, hooded gull, Mogul, *seagull*
HUL	ahull, dehull, hull, multihull
KUL	caracul, cull
LUL	lull
MUL	mull
NUL	annul, disannul, null
SKUL	*numskull,* scull, skull
STUL	stull
SUL	sull
TRUL	trull
WUL	wull

ULCH

GULCH	gulch
KULCH	culch, cultch
MULCH	mulch

ULD

(See **UL,** add *-ed* where appropriate.)

ULJ

BULJ	bulge
DULJ	indulge, overindulge, reindulge
FULJ	effulge
MULJ	promulge
VULJ	divulge

ULJD

(See **ULJ,** add *-d* where appropriate.)

ULK

BULK	bulk
HULK	hulk
MULK	mulk
SKULK	skulk
SULK	sulk

ULKT

MULKT	mulct

(See **ULK,** add *-ed* where appropriate.)

ULM

KULM	culm
MULM	mulm
STULM	stulm

ULP

GULP	gulp
KULP	culp
PULP	pulp
SKULP	sculp

ULPT

GULPT	gulped
PULPT	golden-pulped, *soft-pulped, sweet-pulped*
SKULPT	sculped, sculpt

ULS

BULS	bulse
DULS	dulce, dulse
MULS	mulse
PULS	appulse, expulse, *impulse,* pulse, repulse
SULS	insulse
VULS	avulse, convulse, revulse

(See **ULT,** add *-s* where appropriate.)

ULT

DULT	adult, indult, subadult, unadult
KULT	difficult, incult, cult, occult

NULT	antepenult, penult
PULT	catapult
SULT	insult, juriconsult, consult, reinsult, reconsult
ZULT	exult, result

ŪLZ

GŪLZ	gules

(See ŪL, OOL; add -*s* where appropriate.)

ULZ

(See UL, add -*s* where appropriate.)

ŪM

ŪM	Fiume
FŪM	fume, perfume
GŪM	legume
HŪM	exhume, inhume
LŪM	illume, reillume, relume
NŪM	neume
SPŪM	spume
SŪM	assume, consume, reassume, subsume
ZŪM	exhume, presume, resume

(See OOM)

UM

UM	*A* absinthium, agonium, Actium, allium, aluminum, alluvium, ammonium, ante meridium, anthurium, atrium, *B* Byzantium, *BR* brachium, *D* delphinium, dentalium, disequilibrium, decennium, deliquium, delirium, *E* effluvium, equilibrium, exordium, Elysium, emporium, encomium, epigastrium, epicardium, epithalamium, Eryngium, *F* fermium, *FR* francium, *G* gallium, *H* hafnium, harmonium, helium, hypogastrium, hypochondrium, holmium, horreum, *I* idiomindium, ischium, yttrium, *J* geranium, gymnasium, *K* cadmium, calcium, cambium, caputium, castoreum, colloquium, columbium, compendium, consortium, contagium, *KR* cranium, crematorium, chromium, *KW* quadrivium, quinquennium, *L* labium, lithium, linoleum, *M* martyrium, medium, menstruum, millennium, moratorium, mutuum, *N* nasturtium, natatorium, nephridium, *O* odeum, auditorium, odium, opium, opprobrium, opsonium, orpheum, osmium, ostium, otium, *P* palladium, pallium, pandemonium, pelargonium, pericardium, petroleum, podium, polonium, post meridiem, potassium, *PL* plutonium, *PR* premium, presidium, principium, proscenium, protium, *R* radium, residuum, *S* sanatorium, selenium, cerulium, coerulium, sestertium, silphium, symposium, sodium, *SK* scandium, *SP* sporangium, *ST* stadium, stibium, studium, *STR* stramonium, strontium, *T* tedium, tellurium, terrium, titanium, terbium, *TH* thallium, thulium, *TR* triennium, trillium, triodium, *U* um, um-um, euphonium, erbium, *V* vacuum, valium, vitium, vivarium, *Y* uranium, *Z* xenodochium
BRUM	cerebrum
BUM	bum, stumblebum
CHUM	chum
DRUM	bass drum, drum, *eardrum, humdrum, conundrum,* kettledrum, *panjandrum*
DUM	*A* heirdom, *B* Bumbledom, *D* dogdom, dukedom, dumb, *dumbdumb, dumdum, E* earldom, *FL* flunkeydom, *H* halidom, heathendom, *whoredom, K kingdom,* Cockneydom, *KR* Christendom, *M* martyrdom, *O* officialdom, oppidum, *PR prudhomme, R* rascaldom, rebeldom, *S* sardoodledum, Saxondom, solidum, *serfdom, TW* Tweedledum
FRUM	from, wherefrom, therefrom
FUM	fee-fi-fo-fum
GLUM	glum
GRUM	grum
GUM	begum, bubblegum, chewing gum, gum, *subgum*
HUM	ho-hum, hum
KRUM	crum, crumb
KUM	become, *income,* capsicum, misbecome, modicum, *outcome,* overcome, succumb, vaticum, viaticum, unicum
LUM	coagulum, curriculum, lum, pabulum, pendulum, seculum, septulum, scybalum, symbolum, cingulum, sertulum
MUM	chrysanthemum, *quadrimum,* maximum, minimum, mum, optimum
NUM	aluminum, benumb, labdanum, laudanum, molybdenum, numb, platinum, tympanum
PLUM	plum, plumb, replumb, sugar plum, unplumb
RUM	rhumb, rum, theorum
SKRUM	scrum
SKUM	scum
SLUM	slum
SNUM	snum
STRUM	strum
STUM	stum
SUM	*A* adventuresome, *B* bothersome, burdensome, *DR* drearisome, *F foursome, FR* frolicsome, *G* gamblesome, *GR gruesome, H* wholesome, horrorsome, humorsome, *I* intermeddlesome, *K* cuddlesome, cumbersome, *KW* quarrelsome, quietsome, *L* lonesome, *M* meddlesome, mettlesome, *N* nettlesome, *O* awesome, *R* wranglesome, *S* some, sum, *T* twosome, toothsome, *THR* threesome

(etc.), *TR* troublesome, *U*
ugglesome, *V*
venturesome, *W*
wearisome, worrisome, *Z*
zero sum

SWUM	swum
THRUM	thrum
THUM	green thumb, thumb
TUM	accubitum, acquisitum, ad libitum, adytum, debitum, cognitum, compitum, placitum, tum, *tum-tum,* zibetum
YUM	yum-yum, *Yum-Yum*
ZUM	zum

ŪMD

(See **ŪM, ŌŌM,** add *-d* or *-ed* where appropriate.)

UMD

(See **UM,** add *-ed* or *-med* where appropriate.)

UMF

UMF	umph
GRUMF	grumph
HUMF	humph

UMP

UMP	ump
BUMP	bump
CHUMP	chump
DUMP	dump
FLUMP	flump
FRUMP	frump
GLUMP	glump
GRUMP	grump
HUMP	hump
JUMP	*broadjump, highjump,* jump, *running jump, standing jump*
KLUMP	clump
KRUMP	crump
LUMP	lump
MUMP	mump
PLUMP	plump
PUMP	pump
RUMP	rump
SKRUMP	scrump
SLUMP	slump
STUMP	stump
SUMP	sump
THUMP	bethump, thump
TRUMP	*no-trump,* overtrump, trump, undertrump

TUMP	tump
WUMP	*mugwump,* wump
ZUMP	gazump

UMPS

BUMPS	*goosebumps*
MUMPS	mumps

(See **UMP,** add *-s* where appropriate.)

ŪN

ŪN	triune
BŪN	tribune
HŪN	hewn, rehewn, *rough-hewn,* unhewn
KŪN	lacune
LŪN	lune
MŪN	immune, intercommune, commune
PŪN	impugn, oppugn, repugn
TŪN	attune, entune, inopportune, importune, looney-tune, *Neptune,* opportune, retune, tune, untune
YŪN	picayune, triune

(See **ŌŌN**)

UN

UN   *A* abecedarian, Acadian, acanthropterygian, accordion, acromion, Alabamian, alabastrian, Albanian, Albion, Alexandrian, Algonquian, Algerian, alien, alluvian, amatorian, Amazonian, amoebian, Amerindian, amphibian, amphictyon, Amphitrion, amnion, Anatolian, Anglian, antediluvean, antemeridian, anthelion, anthemion, antiquarian, Appalachian, aphelion, apian, apiarian, Apollonian, apocynthion, Arian, Aristotelian, Arcadian, Archimedean, Armenian, artesian, Arthurian, ascidian, Atlantean, avian, *B* Babylonian, bacchanalian, Baconian, bactrian, Barbadian, barbarian, basion, bastian, bastion, batrachian, Bavarian, Belgian, Bezonian, Bohemian, Bulgarian, *BR* Brazilian, Briarean, *CH* champion, Czechoslovakian, Chaucerian, *D* Darien, Darwinian, Delphian, demibastion, Dickensian, diluvian, Dionysian, disciplinarian, Deucalion, durian, *DR* Dravidian, *E* Edwardian, equestrian, Elysian, *empyrean,* epilimnion, Episcopalian, Erachtheion, etesian, Ethiopian, Etonian, *F* Fallopian, favonian, Fenian, Fijian, fustian, *FR* Phrygian, Freudian, fruitarian, *G* gabion, galleon, gammadian, ganglion, guardian, gargantuan, Gideon, Gilbertian, gonion, Gordian, gorgonian, *GR* grammarian, Gratian, *H* Hadrian, halcyon, Haitian, Herculean, Hesperian, Hessian, Hibernian, historian, holothurian, humanitarian, *I* Icarian, Ilion, Indian, infralapsarian, inion, Iranian, *J* Georgian, Johnsonian, Jordanian, Jovian, *K* Caducean, Caledonian, callipygian, Cambrian, chameleon, camion, campion, Canadian, Cantabrigian, Caribbean, carnelian, Carolingian, carrion, Carpathian, Carthaginian, Carthusian, Caspian, Castilian, chelonian, Caucasian, collodeon, Columbian, Comanchean, comedian, commentarian, chorion, Corinthian, custodian, *KL* clarion, *KR* Christadelphian, crocodilian, criterion, Cromwellian, crossopterygian, *KW* quarrion, quaternion, Quintilion, quotidian, *L* labyrinthian, Lamarckian, lampion, Lancastrian, Lacedaemonian, lacertilian, latitudinarian,

Latvian, lesbian,
libertarian, librarian,
Libyan, limitarian,
Lithuanian, Liverpudian,
Lothian, Lucian, *M*
Machiavellian,
Maximillian,
malacopterygian,
Malaysian, Malthusian,
mammalian, Marxian,
Macedonian, median,
Mediterranean,
Melanesian, melodeon,
meridian, Merovingian,
metatherion, mezerion,
Midlothian, millenarian,
Mississippian,
mitochondrian, Mongolian,
Moravian, morion,
Morovingian, *N* Napoleon,
nasion, nectarean,
nemertean, Neptunian,
Nigerian, nickelodeon,
Noachian, nonagenarian,
Northumbrian, Nubian,
nullifidian, Newtonian, *O*
oblivion, obsidian,
Augustinian, Ogygian,
Oxonian, Octavian,
octogenarian, Olympian,
Aurelian, Orcadian,
ornithischian, Orwellian,
Ossian, Australian,
Austrian, authoritarian,
ovarian, *P* pagurian,
pampean, Panamerican,
pantheon, parhelion,
Parisian, Parthian,
pedestrian, Pelion,
Pennsylvanian, perihelion,
Peruvian, pericynthion,
Pierian, Pygmalion,
Pickwickian, Pythian,
Polynesian, Pomeranian,
pomeridian, postdiluvian,
postmeridian, *PL*
planarian, platitudinarian,
Plutonian, *PR*
predestinarian,
prehistorian, Presbyterian,
pretorian, proboscidian,
Procrustean, proletarian,
promethean, prosimian,
protean, prototherian, *R*
Rabelaisian, rampion,
riparian, Rhodesian,
Rhodian, Rotarian, ruffian,
Rumanian, Ruthenian, *S*
Sabbatarian, sabellian,
saffian, sacramentarian,
Salientian, samian,
Sardinian, selachian,

seminarian,
sesquipedalian, Siberian,
Cyclopean, centenarian,
Cimmerian, Cyprian,
Syrian, Circassian,
caecilian, Sicilian,
Sisyphean, solifidian,
saurian, Socinian,
subterranean, Sumerian,
supralapsarian, *SH*
Shakespearean, Shavian,
Shoshonean, *SK* Scandian,
scorpion, *SM* Smithsonian,
ST stentorian, steradian,
Stygian, *T* tallion,
tampion, Tasmanian,
tellurian, tellurion,
Tertullian, tinean,
Tyrrhenian, Tyrian,
Tocharion, turion, *TH*
theologian, thespian,
Thessalonian, *TR*
tragedian, Transylvanian,
U Umbrian, *V* Wagnerian,
Valentinian, valerian,
valetudinarian, Valkyrian,
vegetarian, Venusian,
Vespasian, veterinarian,
vesuvian, vaudevillian,
vulgarian, Vulcanian, *W*
Wagnerian, Wesleyan, *Y*
ubiquitarian, Yugoslavian,
Ukrainian, Jungian,
unitarian, Uranian,
eutherian, utilitarian,
utopian, *Z* Zyrian,
Zoroastrian (compare UN
with AN)

BUN	bonne, bun, honeybun, hotcross bun, raisin bun
DUN	*D* done, dun, *F* foredone, *I* ill-done, *KL* clarendon, *M* myrmidon, *O* outdone, overdone, *R* redone, *U* underdone, undone, *W* well-done
FUN	fun, colophon
GUN	*A* airgun, *B* BB gun, begun, *G* Gatling gun, gun, *H* handgun, *M* machine gun, minute gun, *P* paragon, percussion gun, *popgun, SH shotgun, U* unbegun
HUN	hon, Hun
KUN	helicon, Helicon, pantechnicon
LUN	gonfalon, Sally Lunn
MUN	cardamon, cinnamon
NUN	phenomenon, none, nun, Parthenon, prolegomenon, unnun
PUN	pun
RUN	Bull Run, forerun, *hard-run, millrun,* Oberon, outrun, overrun, rerun, run, underrun
SHUN	shun
SPUN	*finespun, homespun,* spun
STUN	stun
SUN	*F* foster son, *G* garrison, *GR* grandson, *HW* Whitsun, *J* jettison, *K* caparison, comparison, *O* orison, *S* son, sun, sunn, *ST* stepson, *T* Tennyson, *V* venison, *Y* unison
TUN	Chesterton, Galveston, kiloton, megaton, simpleton, singleton, skeleton, skimmington, ton, tonne, tun, Washington, Wellington
WUN	A-1, anyone, everyone, *hard-won,* number one, rewon, someone, unwon, one, won
ZUN	ʼamazon, Amazon, benison

UNCH

BRUNCH	brunch
BUNCH	bunch, honeybunch
HUNCH	hunch
KLUNCH	clunch
KRUNCH	crunch
LUNCH	box lunch, free lunch, heavy lunch, light lunch, lunch
MUNCH	munch
NUNCH	nunch
PUNCH	punch
RUNCH	runch
SKRUNCH	scrunch

ŪND

(See $\overline{OOND}$. See $\overline{OON}$, add -*ed* where appropriate. See ŬN, add -*d* where appropriate.)

UND

BUND	bund, bundh, errabund, cummerbund, moribund
FUND	fund, refund, re-fund, slush fund
KUND	rubicund, verecund
MUND	immund, mund
TUND	obrotund, obtund, orotund, retund, rotund

(See **UN,** add -*ned* where appropriate.)

UNG

BRUNG	brung
BUNG	bung
DUNG	dung
FLUNG	flung
HUNG	hung, overhung, underhung, unhung, well-hung
KLUNG	clung
LUNG	lung, *one-lung*
MUNG	among, hereamong, whereamong, mung, thereamong
PUNG	pung
RUNG	bewrung, rung, wrung, unrung, unwrung, wither-wrung
SLUNG	slung, underslung, unslung
SPRUNG	sprung, unsprung, upsprung
STRUNG	*hamstrung,* highly strung, *highstrung,* overstrung, strung, unstrung
STUNG	stung, unstung
SUNG	sung, unsung
SWUNG	swung, upswung
TUNG	betongue, *bluetongue,* mother tongue, *ox-tongue, shantung,* tongue
YUNG	young

UNGD

BUNGD	bunged
LUNGD	iron-lunged, leather-lunged, loud-lunged
TUNGD	*B* betongued, *bell-tongued, BL* black-tongued, *PL* pleasant-tongued, *S* silver-tongued, *soft-tongued, SH* sharp-tongued, *SHR* shrill-tongued, *T* tongued, *TH* thick-tongued, *TR* trumpet-tongued

UNGK

UNGK	unc, unk
BLUNGK	blunk
BUNGK	bunk, debunk
CHUNGK	chunk
DRUNGK	drunk
DUNGK	dunk
FLUNGK	flunk
FUNGK	duddyfunk, funk
GUNGK	gunk
HUNGK	hunk
JUNGK	junk
KLUNGK	kinclunk, clunk

LUNGK	lunk
MUNGK	*chipmunk,* monk
NUNGK	*quidnunc,* nunc
PLUNGK	kerplunk, plunk
PUNGK	punk
SHRUNGK	*preshrunk,* shrunk
SKUNGK	skunk
SLUNGK	slunk
SPUNGK	spunk
STUNGK	stunk
SUNGK	sunk
TRUNGK	steamer trunk, *treetrunk,* trunk
TUNGK	tunk

UNGKT

FUNGKT	defunct
JUNGKT	*adjunct,* disjunct, injunct, junked, conjunct
PUNGKT	compunct

(See **UNGK,** add *-ed* where appropriate.)

UNGST

MUNGST	amongst

(See verbs in **UNG,** add *-'st* for archaic usage.)

UNJ

BLUNJ	blunge
GRUNJ	grunge
GUNJ	gunge
LUNJ	allonge, longe, lunge, muskellunge
PLUNJ	plunge
PUNJ	expunge
SKUNJ	scunge
SPUNJ	sponge

UNJD

(See **UNJ,** add *-ed* where appropriate.)

UNS

BUNS	bunce
DUNS	dunce
WUNS	once

(See **UNT,** add *-s* where appropriate.)

PARADOX

Illogic I abhor;
And yet I have to own
That I've forgotten more
Than I have ever known.

UNT

UNT	exeunt
BLUNT	blunt
BRUNT	brunt
BUNT	bunt
DUNT	dunt
FRUNT	affront, afront, *bifront, breakfront, forefront,* front, confront, *seafront,* up front
GRUNT	grunt
HUNT	*deerhunt,* Easter egg hunt, *elkhunt,* pheasant hunt, *foxhunt,* hunt, *manhunt, staghunt, witchhunt* (etc.)
LUNT	lunt
KUNT	cunt
PUNT	punt
RUNT	runt
SHUNT	shunt
SPRUNT	sprunt
STUNT	stunt
WUNT	wont, wun't

ŪP

DŪP	dupe
STŪP	stupe

(See $\overline{OOP}$)

UP

UP	*B* backup, batter-up, *BL* blow-up, *BR* break-up, *CH* check-up, chin up, *F* fed up, *G* get-up, giddy-up, *H* hard-up, hiccup, *K* keyed-up, cock-up, *KL* closeup, *L* lash-up, let-up, lock-up, *M* makeup, *P* pick-up, pull-up, push-up, *R* rip-up, roundup, *S* setup, setter-up, sunup, *SL* slap up, *T* teacup, tip-up, toss-up, *U* up, up-and-up, *W* wickiup, wind-up
DUP	dup
GUP	gup
HUP	hup
KRUP	Krupp
KUP	buttercup, grace cup, *grease-cup,* hiccup, hiccough, *eyecup,* cup, loving cup, stirrup cup, *teacup,* wassail cup
PUP	pup
SKUP	scup
SUP	sup

TUP   tup
YUP   yup

UPT

RUPT   abrupt, *bankrupt*, disrupt, erupt, incorrupt, interrupt, irrupt, corrupt, uncorrupt

(See **UP**, add *-ped* where appropriate.)

ŪR

ŪR   ewer, inure, you're
DŪR   dure, endure, perdure, perendure
FŪR   coiffure
HŪR   hewer
KŪR   epicure, insecure, cure, manicure, pedicure, procure, secure, sinecure, water cure
LŪR   allure, chevelure, colure, condylure, lure, velure
MŪR   demure, immure, mure
NŪR   manure, revenuer, tournure
PŪR   guipure, impure, pure
SKŪR   obscure, skewer
VŪR   photogravure, gravure, autogravure, rotogravure

(See **OOR**; See **Ū**, add *-ēr* or *-r* where appropriate.)

UR

UR   *A* anterior, *B* borrower, burlier, *BL* blearier, *BR* breezier, brinier, *CH* cheerier, chillier, *D* dingier, dizzier, dowdier, doughtier, dustier, *DR* drearier, drowsier, *E* excelsior, exterior, emptier, er, 'er, err, Ur, earlier, eerier, easier, *F* filmier, filthier, foamier, funnier, fussier, *FL* fleecier, flimsier, flightier, *FR* friendlier, *G* giddier, guiltier, goutier, *GL* gloomier, glossier, *GR* greffier, grimier, *H* happier, hardanger, hardier, healthier, heavier, hillier, holier, homelier, huffier, hungrier, huskier, *HW* wheezier, *I* icier, inferior, inkier, interior, *J* jollier, journeyer, juicier,

K kindlier, kinglier, copier, costlier, cosier, curlier, *KL* cleanlier, *KR* creamier, creepier, *L* likelier, livelier, loftier, lowlier, lonelier, lovelier, *M* marrier, merrier, meteor, mightier, moldier, mossier, muskier, mustier, *N* narrower, knightlier, noisier, *P* pitier, portlier, posterior, pearlier, *PR* princelier, prosier, *R* rapier, rowdier, rosier, *S* seemlier, sightlier, sillier, soapier, sunnier, superior, surlier, *SH* shinier, shoddier, showier, *SK* skinnier, *SL* sleepier, slimier, *SP* spikier, spicier, spoonier, spongier, *SPR* springier, spritelier, *ST* steadier, stealthier, stingier, stormier, stuccoer, sturdier, *T* terrier, *TH* thirstier, thriftier, *TR* trustier, *U* ulterior, *V* valuer, *W* wealthier, wearier, widower, windier, wintrier
BLUR   blur
BRUR   br'er
BUR   birr, burr, butterbur, Excalibar, Excalibur, calaber, caliber, cocklebur, shillaber
CHUR   chirr, churr, calenture, *nightchurr*, ossiture, plicature
DUR   *A* ambassador, *H* highlander, horrider, *I* islander, *K* calendar, calender, colander, corridor, *L* lavender, lowlander, *PR* provender, *R* ruggeder, *S* cylinder, solider, *ST* stupider, *T* timider, *V* vivider
FLUR   fleur, persifleur, renifleur
FUR   *A* aquifer, artificer, *B* befur, bibliographer, biographer, *D* dapifer, defer, *F* philosopher, phonographer, photographer, fer, fir, fur, *furfur*, *FL* flammifer, *I* infer, *K* confer, conifer, *KR* chronopher, chronographer, crucifer, *L* lithographer, lucifer, Lucifer, *O* autobiographer, *P* pornographer, *PR* prefer,

R refer, rotifer, *SH* chauffeur, *ST* stenographer, *T* typographer, topographer, *TR* transfer
HUR   Ben Hur, her
HWUR   whir, whirr
JUR   *A* armiger, astrologer, *BR* breviger, *CH* challenger, *D* derringer, disparager, dowager, *E* encourager, *F* philologer, forager, *H* harbinger, *I* integer, *K* cottager, *KL* claviger, *M* manager, messenger, mortgagor, *O* onager, *P* passenger, pillager, porringer, *R* ravager, *SK* scavenger, *T* tanager, teenager, *V* villager, vintager, voltigeur, voyager
KLUR   chronicler
KUR   incur, claqueur, coniaker, concur, cur, liqueur, massacre, occur, recur, sepulchre
LUR   *B* bachelor, *CH* chancellor, cheerfuller, chiseler, *DR* driveler, *E* enameler, *H* hoveler, *J* jeweler, *KR* crueler, *KW* quarreler, *L* labeler, leveler, libeler, loyaler, *M* mitrailleur, modeler, mournfuler, *O* odaler, *R* reveler, *SH* shoveler, *SK* skilfuler, *TR* traveler, *V* victualer, *W* wassailer, *Y* yodeler
MUR   *A* astronomer, *D* demur, dulcimer, *G* gossamer, *K* *costumer,* customer, *L* lissomer, lithesomer, lonesomer, lorimer, *M* myrrh, *R* ransomer, *W* winsomer
NUR   *A* almoner, *B* bargainer, burdener, *BL* blazoner, *CH* chastener, cheapener, *D* deepener, determiner, *E* examiner, executioner, emblazoner, enlightener, enlivener, easterner, evener, *F* fastener, fashioner, foreigner, *FL* flaneur, *G* gardener, governor, *H* hardener, hastener, *I* imprisoner, ironer, *K* commissioner, commoner, confectioner, coparcener, coroner, cozener, *KW* questioner,

quickener, *L* lengthener, lessener, listener, Londoner, loosener, *M* mariner, milliner, moistener, *N* northerner, knur, *P* parishioner, parcener, petitioner, poisoner, *PR* practicioner, prisoner, probationer, *R* reasoner, reversioner, revisioner, *S* seasoner, sojourner, summoner, summerer, southerner, *SH* sharpener, shortener, *STR* strengthener, *SW* sweetener, *T* tobogganer, *THR* threatener, *W* wagoner, wakener, weakener, westerner

PUR *D* developer, diaper, *E* enveloper, *G* galloper, gossiper, *H* hanaper, *J* juniper, *K* caliper, *P* per, purr, *W* walloper, worshiper

RUR *A* adulterer, adventurer, answerer, armorer, *B* banterer, barterer, batterer, bickerer, botherer, *BL* blunderer, blusterer, *BR* broiderer, *CH* chafferer, chamferer, chatterer, *D* deliverer, discoverer, *E* embroiderer, emperor, endeavorer, engenderer, encounterer, *F* favorer, fosterer, furtherer, *FL* flatterer, flutterer, *FR* franc-tireur, *G* gatherer, *H* harborer, *HW* whimperer, whisperer, *J* jabberer, *K* capturer, caterer, cofferer, conjecturer, conjurer, conqueror, cornerer, coverer, *KL* clamorer, *KW* quaverer, *L* laborer, lecturer, lingerer, loiterer, *M* malingerer, maneuverer, manufacturer, measurer, murderer, murmurer, mutterer, *N* naperer, numberer, *O* offerer, *P* palaverer, panderer, pasturer, patterer, pepperer, perjurer, pesterer, pilferer, poulterer, posturer, pewterer, *PL* plasterer, plunderer, *PR* profferer, *R* roisterer, *S* saunterer, sorcerer, sufferer, succorer, *SH* shelterer, *SK*

scamperer, *SKW* squanderer, *SL* slanderer, slaughterer, slumberer, *SM* smatterer, *SPL* splatterer, splutterer, *ST* staggerer, stammerer, stutterer, *SW* swaggerer, *T* tamperer, torturer, totterer, *TH* thunderer, *TR* treasurer, *U* upholsterer, utterer, usurer, *V* verderer, *W* wagerer, wanderer, waverer, weatherer, wonderer

SHUR *A* admonisher, accoucheur, assure, *B* banisher, burnisher, *BL* blandisher, *BR* Britisher, *CH* cherisher, *D* demolisher, *E* embellisher, embouchure, ensure, establisher, *H* hachure, *I* insure, *K* cocksure, *L* languisher, *N* nourisher, *P* polisher, publisher, punisher, *R* ravisher, reassure, reinsure, relinquisher, *SH* shirr, sure, cynosure, *SK* skirmisher, *U* unsure, *V* vanquisher

SLUR slur
SMUR smur, smurr
SPUR *hotspur, Hotspur, larkspur,* spur
STUR *A* administer, apparitor, astir, *B* baluster, banister, bannister, barrister, bestir, *F* forester, *H* harvester, *K* canister, *M* maladminister, minister, *P* Pasteur, *R* restir, *ST* stir
SUR *A* affiancer, artificer, *F* farceur, *H* harnesser, *K* canvasser, connoisseur, *L* licenser, *M* masseur, *O* officer, *P* purchaser, *S* silencer, sir, susurr, *SH* chasseur, *TR* trespasser
TUR *A* accipiter, amateur, amphitheater, *ancestor,* arbiter, *archiater, B* banqueter, barometer, bucketer, *CH* chapiter, *chapter, D* depositor, deter, diameter, disinter, distributor, *E* editor, executor, expositor, *F* forfeiter, *FR frankfurter, G* guarantor, *H* harvester, hexameter, hauteur, *I* idolater, inheritor, inquisitor, inter, interlocutor, interpreter, *J*

janitor, Jupiter, *K* carpenter, carpeter, character, *colporteur,* competitor, comforter, compositor, conspirator, contributor, *KR* creditor, cricketer, *L* legator, litterateur, *M* magister, marketer, monitor, *O* auditor, orator, auteur, *P* pentameter, *PL* pleasanter, *PR* presbyter, primogenitor, progenitor, proprietor, *R* register, restaurateur, rioter, riveter, *S* senator, servitor, silenter, scimitar, sinister, solicitor, sophister, surfeiter, *SH* shamateur, *T* tetrameter, *TH* theater, theatre, thermometer, *TR* traiteur, tregetour, trumpeter, *V* visitor, *W* warranter

VUR Andover, aver, gilliver, Gulliver, caliver, miniver, Miniver, *passover,* Passover, sandiver
WUR were
ZUR friseur
ZHUR melangeur, voltageur, voyageur

(Add *-er* also to appropriate words not listed here.)

URB

URB	herb, urb
BLURB	blurb
BURB	*suburb*
HURB	herb, *cowherb, potherb,* willowherb
JURB	gerb, gerbe
KURB	curb, uncurb
PURB	superb
SLURB	slurb
SURB	acerb, Serb
TURB	disturb, perturb, undisturb, unperturb
VURB	*adverb, proverb,* reverb, verb

URBD

(See **URB**, add *-ed* where appropriate.)

URCH

BURCH	birch, white birch, weeping birch (etc.)

CHURCH	church, unchurch
LURCH	lurch
PURCH	perch, *pikeperch*, reperch, *surfperch*, unperch
SMURCH	besmirch, smirch
SURCH	research, search

URCHT

(See **URCH**, add -*ed* where appropriate.)

ŪRD

(See **ŪR**, add -*d* where appropriate.)

URD

URD	urd
BURD	*B* bird, bowerbird, butcherbird, *BL blackbird*, *bluebird*, *D diving bird*, dollarbird, *F firebird*, *FR friarbird*, frigate bird, *G gallows bird*, *H halberd*, *hedgebird*, hummingbird, *HW* whirlybird, *J jailbird*, *jarbird*, *K* cardinal bird, *L* ladybird, *lyrebird*, *lovebird*, *M* myna bird, mockingbird, *N nightbird*, *P* pilotbird, *puffbird*, *R rambird*, redbird, *S seabird*, songbird, sunbird, *SN snowbird*, *ST stormbird*, *T* tailorbird, *TH* thunderbird, *W* wattlebird, weaverbird (etc.)
FURD	ferd, furred, fyrd
GURD	begird, engird, gird, undergird, ungird
HURD	*goatherd*, heard, herd, *cowherd*, overheard, *shepherd*, *swanherd*, *swineherd*, unheard
KURD	curd, Kurd, sepulchred, unsepulchred
MURD	immerd, mird
NURD	nerd
SHURD	*potsherd*
SNURD	Mortimer Snerd
SURD	absurd, surd
THURD	third
TURD	deterred, disinterred, interred, turd, undeterred
VURD	verd
WURD	*A* afterward, afterword, *B byword*, *F foreword*, *I inward*, *K catchword*, *KR crossword*, *L leeward*, *N* nonce word, *O outward*, overword, *P password*, *R* reword, *SW swearword*, *W watchword*, *wayward*, word

(See **UR**, add -*red* where appropriate.)

URF

URF	urf
KURF	kerf
NURF	nerf
SKURF	scurf
SURF	hippocerf, serf, surf
TURF	surf and turf, turf

URG

URG	erg
BURG	*B* berg, burg, burgh, *BR* Brandenburg, *G* Gettysburg, *H Hamburg*, *Hapsburg*, Harrisburg, Heidelberg, *homburg*, iceberg, *J Johannesburg*, *L Lindbergh*, *N* Nuremberg, *P Pittsburgh*, *S* Saint Petersburg, *STR Strasbourg*, *W* Williamsburg (etc.)
ZURG	exergue

URJ

URJ	demiurge, Demiurge, unurge, urge
DURJ	dirge
GURJ	gurge, regurge
MURJ	emerge, immerge, merge, submerge
PURJ	asperge, purge
SKURJ	scourge
SNURJ	snurge
SPLURJ	splurge
SPURJ	spurge
SURJ	resurge, serge, surge
TURJ	deterge, dramaturge, thaumaturge
VURJ	diverge, converge, verge

URJD

(See **URJ**, add -*d* where appropriate.)

URK

URK	erk, irk
BURK	berk, burke, *hauberk*

DURK	dirk
FURK	firk
GURK	gurk
JURK	jerk, jerque, soda jerk
KURK	*Dunkirk*, kirk
KLURK	clerk
KWURK	quirk
LURK	lurk
MURK	murk
PURK	perk
SHURK	shirk
SMURK	smirk
STURK	stirk
SURK	cirque
TURK	Turk
WURK	*A* artwork, *B* beadwork, by-work, *BR* breastwork, brightwork, bridgework, brickwork, brushwork, *E* earthwork, *F* fancywork, farmwork, fieldwork, firework, falsework, footwork, *FR* framework, frostwork, *H* handiwork, housework, *K* casework, coachwork, *KL* clockwork, *KR* cribwork, *L* lattice work, *legwork*, *M* makework, masterwork, *N* needlework, *network*, *O* overwork, outwork, *P* patchwork, piecework, *PR* presswork, *R* roadwork, *SL* slopwork, *SP* spadework, *ST* stonework, *T* taskwork, teamwork, timework, *U* underwork, *W waxwork*, *wirework*, waterwork, *woodwork*, wonderwork, work
YURK	yerk

URKT

(See **URK**, add -*ed* where appropriate.)

URL

URL	earl
BURL	birl, burl
CHURL	churl
FURL	furl, refurl, unfurl
GURL	girl, gurl, *callgirl, cowgirl*, papergirl, *playgirl*, *showgirl, switchgirl*
HURL	herl, herle, hurl
HWIRL	upwhirl, whirl, whorl
KURL	becurl, curl, uncurl, upcurl
KWURL	querl, quirl
MURL	merle
NURL	knurl

PURL	bepearl, impearl, culture pearl, mother-of-pearl, pearl, pirl, purl, *seedpearl*
SKURL	skirl
SWURL	swirl, upswirl
THURL	thirl, thurl
TURL	tirl
TWURL	twirl

URLD

WURLD	afterworld, antiworld, new world, *old-world*, Third World, underworld, world

(See **URL**, add -*ed* where appropriate.)

URM

BURM	berm
CHURM	churm
DURM	blastoderm, derm, echtoderm, endoderm, phelloderm, mesoderm, pachyderm, periderm, xanthoderm
FURM	affirm, disaffirm, firm, infirm, confirm, reaffirm
JURM	germ
PURM	perm
SKWURM	squirm
SPURM	endosperm, gymnosperm, sperm, zoosperm
THURM	isotherm, therm
TURM	*midterm*, misterm, term
WURM	angleworm, *blindworm*, *bookworm*, *earthworm*, *flatworm*, *glowworm*, *grubworm*, *inchworm*, *silkworm*, *pinworm*, *ringworm*, *tapeworm*, *woodworm*, worm

URMD

(See **URM**, add *ed* where appropriate.)

URN

URN	earn, erne, inurn, lierne, urn
BURN	Berne, burn, *heartburn*, *Hepburn*, *ropeburn*, *sideburn*, *sunburn*, *Swinburne*, *windburn*
CHURN	churn
DURN	dern, durn
FURN	fern, foehn
GURN	girn, intergern

HURN	hern, herne
JURN	adjourn, sojourn
KURN	kern
KWURN	quern
LURN	learn, unlearn
PURN	epergne, pirn
SPURN	spurn
STURN	astern, stern
SURN	discern, concern, lucern, lucerne, secern, unconcern
TURN	*A* attorn, *E* externe, eterne, *G* gittern, *I* intern, interne, *N* nocturne, *O* overturn, *R* return, *S* Saturn, sempitern, *cistern*, *cittern*, *sauterne*, *subaltern*, *T* taciturn, tern, terne, turn, *U* upturn
VURN	Jules Verne
YURN	yearn, yirn
ZURN	discern

URND

(See **URN**, add -*ed* where appropriate.)

URNT

URNT	earnt
BURNT	burnt, *mowburnt*, *sunburnt*, unburnt, windburnt
LURNT	learnt, unlearnt
WURNT	weren't

URNZ

BURNZ	*sideburns*

(See **URN**, add -*s* where appropriate.)

URP

BURP	burp
CHURP	chirp
LURP	lirp
SLURP	slurp
SURP	discerp
TURP	terp, turp
TWURP	twerp, twirp
WURP	*Antwerp*
ZURP	usurp

URPS

(See **URP**, add -*s* where appropriate.)

URPT

SURPT	excerpt

(See **URP**, add -*ed* where appropriate.)

URS

URS	Erse, coerce
BURS	birse, burse, disburse, imburse, reimburse
HURS	hearse, herse, inhearse, rehearse
KURS	accurse, excurse, curse, precurse
MURS	immerse, merse, submerse
NURS	dry nurse, *dry-nurse*, foster nurse, nurse, practical nurse, registered nurse, wet nurse, *wet-nurse*
PURS	asperse, disperse, *cutpurse*, perse, purse
SPURS	intersperse
THURS	thyrse
TURS	*sesterce*, terce, terse
VURS	*A* adverse, averse, *D* diverse, *I* inverse, *K* converse, *O* obverse, *P* perverse, *R* reverse, *S* subverse, *TR* transverse, traverse, *V* verse, *Y* universe
WURS	worse

URST

URST	erst
BURST	*airburst*, burst, *cloudburst*, outburst, *starburst*, *sunburst*
DURST	durst
FURST	first, feetfirst, headfirst
HURST	hearsed, Hearst, hurst, rehearsed, unrehearsed
KURST	accursed, accurst, becursed, becurst, cursed, curst
THURST	athirst, thirst
VURST	reversed, unversed, versed, verst
WURST	*bratwurst*, liverwurst, *knackwurst*, wienerwurst, worst, wurst

(See **URS**, add -*d* where appropriate.)

URT

URT	inert
BLURT	blurt

CHURT	chert
DURT	dirt
FLURT	flirt
GURT	begirt, engirt, girt, gurt, *seagirt,* ungirt
HURT	hurt, unhurt
KURT	curt
KWURT	quirt
LURT	alert
NURT	inert
PURT	*expert, inexpert,* malapert, peart, pert
SHURT	*Blackshirt,* dress shirt, *nightshirt,* overshirt, *redshirt,* shirt, *T-shirt,* undershirt
SKURT	maxiskirt, midiskirt, microskirt, miniskirt, skirt
SKWURT	squirt
SPURT	spirt, spurt
SURT	assert, disconcert, exsert, insert, intersert, concert, navicert, *outsert,* preconcert, cert, syrt
VURT	*A* advert, ambivert, animadvert, avert, *D* divert, *E* extrovert, evert, *I* intervert, introvert, invert, *K* controvert, convert, *O* obvert, overt, *P* pervert, *R* reconvert, retrovert, revert, *S* subvert, *T* terreverte, *TR* transvert, *V* vert
WURT	*BL* bladderwort, *J* gipsywort, *L* liverwort, *lousewort, M milkwort,* moneywort, motherwort, *P* pennywort, *pipewort, R ragwort, SL* slipperwort, *ST* stonewort, *SW sweetwort, TH* thoroughwort, *W woundwort*
YURT	yurt
ZURT	desert, dessert, exert, indesert

URTS

ZURTS	xertz

(See **URT,** add -*s* where appropriate.)

URTH

URTH	earth, fuller's earth, inearth, mother earth, *night-earth,* unearth
BURTH	afterbirth, berth, birth, *childbirth,* rebirth, *stillbirth*

DURTH	dearth
FURTH	firth
GURTH	girth
MURTH	mirth
PURTH	Perth
WORTH	money's worth, pennyworth, unworth, worth

URV

DURV	derv, *hors d'oeuvre*
KURV	incurve, curve, *outcurve,* recurve
MURV	mirv
NURV	innerve, nerve, unnerve
PURV	perv
SURV	disserve, conserve, serve, subserve
SWURV	swerve
VURV	verve
ZURV	deserve, observe, preserve, reserve

URVD

ZURVD	ill-deserved, ill-preserved, preserved, undeserved, unpreserved, well-deserved, well-preserved

(See **URV,** add -*d* where appropriate.)

URVZ

DURVZ	*hors d'oeuvres*

(See **URV,** add -*s* where appropriate.)

URZ

URZ	rapiers
FURZ	furze

(See **UR,** add -*s* where appropriate.)

ŪS

ŪS	disuse, hard use, cayuse, misuse, use
BŪS	abuse, antabuse
DŪS	*A* adduce, *D* deduce, deuce, *E* educe, *I* induce, introduce, *K* conduce, *O* obduce, overproduce, *PR* produce, *R* reduce, reproduce, *S* seduce,

	superinduce, *TR* traduce, *U* underproduce
FŪS	diffuse, profuse
KŪS	excuse
LŪS	luce
PŪS	catapuce, *prepuce,* puce
TŪS	obtuse

(See $\overline{\text{OOS}}$)

US

US	*A* abstemious, acrimonious, aculeus, aqueous, alimonious, alias, alluvious, amatorious, ambiguous, amphibious, anfractuous, arboreous, arduous, assiduous, Asclepius, Asmodeus, *B* Belisarius, bifarious, bilious, Boreas, bounteous, burglarious, beauteous, *BR* Briareus, *D* deciduous, deleterious, delirious, denarius, deciduous, devious, dichroous, Dionysius, dipnoous, discontinuous, discourteous, disingenuous, dubious, dulcifluous, duteous, *E* exiguous, expurgatorious, extemporaneous, extraneous, equilibrious, envious, erroneous, Aesculapius, ethereous, *F* farinaceous, fastidious, fatuous, felonious, ferreous, furious, *FL* flexuous, *FR* fructuous, *G* gaseous, *GL* glorious, *GR* gramineous, gregarious, griseous, *H* halituous, harmonious, herbaceous, heterogeneous, hideous, hilarious, homogeneous, homoousious, *I* igneous, ignis fatuus, ignominious, ileus, illustrious, impecunious, imperious, impervious, impetuous, impious, indubious, industrious, inglorious, inharmonious, ingenious, ingenuous, injurious, incongruous, inconspicuous, incurious, innocuous, inquisitorious, incendious, insensuous, incestuous, insidious,

instantaneous, invidious, *J*
genius, *K* caduceus,
calcaneus, calcareous,
calumnious, carious,
carneous, caseous,
Cassius, coleus,
commodious,
compendious, congruous,
consanguineous,
conspicuous,
contemporaneous,
contemptuous, contiguous,
continuous, contrarious,
contumelious, copious,
corneous, cupreous,
curious, courteous,
cutaneous, *KL*
chlamydeous, *KR*
cretaceous, *L* laborious,
lacteous, lascivious,
ligneous, litigious,
lugubrious, Lucretius,
luxurious, luteous, *M*
malleus, mellifluous,
melodious, menstruous,
meritorious,
miscellaneous, mysterious,
multifarious, multivious, *N*
nacreous, nefarious,
nectareous, nimious,
niveous, nocuous,
nauplius, nauseous,
notorious, nucleus, *O*
oblivious, obsequious,
obvious, odious,
Odysseus, opprobrious,
Orpheus, osseous, *P*
pancreas, parsimonious,
penurious, perfidious,
percutaneous, perspicuous,
pervious, Petronius,
pileous, piteous, Polybius,
punctilious, *PL* plenteous,
plumbeous, pluvious, *PR*
precarious, previous,
presumptuous,
promiscuous, Proteus, *R*
radius, *S* salubrious,
sanguineous,
sanctimonious, sardius,
censorious, sensuous,
ceremonious, Cereus,
serious, cernuous,
Sibelius, simultaneous,
cinereous, symphonious,
sinuous, circumfluous,
Sirius, citreous,
subaqueous, subcutaneous,
subterraneous, sumptuous,
superfluous, supercilious,
SK scabious, scarious, *SP*
spiritous, spontaneous,

spurious, *SPL* splenius, *ST*
stentorious, stibious,
studious, *STR* Stradivarius,
strenuous, struthious, *T*
tautoousious, tedious,
temerarious, tempestuous,
tenuous, Tiberius,
tortuous, tumultuous, *TH*
Theseus, thybius, *TR*
transpicuous, trapezius, *U*
euphonious, uxorious,
unctuous, unceremonious,
uproarious, us, usurious, *V*
vagarious, vacuous,
valetudinarious,
vainglorious, various,
Vesuvius, viduous,
vicarious, victorious,
viminious, viparious,
virtuous, vitreous,
voluptuous, *Y* euphonious,
usurious

BRUS tenebrous
BUS *A* arquebus, *B* Barnabas,
bus, buss, *BL* blunderbuss,
E Erebus, *H* harquebus, *I*
incubus, *K* Colobus, *N*
kneeling bus, *O* omnibus,
autobus, *S* succubus,
syllabus, *Z* xerophobous
DUS hazardous, solidus
FUS fuss, Sisyphus
GUS *A* analagous,
androphagous, asparagus,
azygous, *E* esophagus, *G*
Galapagos, guss, *H*
heterologous, homologous,
homozygous, *I* isologous,
K carpophagous,
coprophagous, *KR*
creophagous, *M*
monophagous, *P*
pemphigus, polyphagous,
S saprophagous,
sarcophagus, *T*
tautologous, *TH*
theophagous, *Z*
xiphopagus, zoophagous
KRUS ludicrous
KUS abacus, discuss, excuss,
cuss, *khuskhus,* Leviticus,
oligotokous, percuss,
posticus, repercuss,
succuss
LUS *A* abaculus, agriculous,
alkalous, altocumulus,
alveolus, amphibolous,
anemophilous, angulous,
angelus, Angelus,
anomalous, annulus,
arenicolous, acephalous,
asepalous, acidulous,

astragalus, *B* bibulous,
bipetalous, bicephalous,
Bucephalus, *D* Daedalus,
discobolus, *E* edentulous,
emulous, *F* fabulous,
famulus, photipholous,
funiculus, *FL* flocculous,
flocculus, *FR* frivolous, *G*
garrulous, *GL* gladiolus,
globulous, *GR* granulous,
H hamulus,
hydrocephalous,
homunculus, *I* incredulous,
K calculus, calculus,
canaliculus, carolus,
convolvulous,
convolvulus, cautelous,
cumulous, cumulus, *KR*
crapulous, credulous,
crepusculous, *KW*
querulous, *L* libelous,
limicolous, limulus, *M*
malleolus, marvelous,
meticulous, miraculous,
modiolus, modulus,
monoculous, musculus, *N*
nebulous, nidicolous,
nodulous, noctambulous,
nautilus, nucleolus, *O*
obolus, *P* patulous, *P*
pendulous, periculous,
perilous, petalous,
populace, populous, *R*
ranunculus, regulus,
ridiculous, Romulus, *S*
sabulous, saxicolous,
sedulous, cellulous,
sibilous, sympetalous,
scintillous, cirrocumulus,
surculus, *SK* scandalous,
scurrilous, *SKR* scrofulous,
scrupulous, *ST*
stercoricolous, stimulus,
STR stratocumulus,
stridulous, *T* tantalus,
Tantalus, temulous,
terricolous, tintinnabulous,
tuberculous, tubulus,
tumulus, *TR* tremulous, *U*
undulous, unscrupulous, *V*
variolus, ventricolus,
verisimilous, vernaculous,
volvulous, *Z* xerophilous
MUS *A* animus, anonymous, *B*
bigamous, *BL*
blasphemous, *D*
diatomous, didymous,
didymus, didynamous, *E*
enormous, eponymous, *F*
physostomous, *H*
heteronymous,
hippopotamus,

hypothalamus, *I* infamous,
J ginglymus, *K* calamus,
catadromous, *M*
magnanimous, maximus,
minimus, mittimus,
monogamous,
mumpsimus, muss, *O*
onymous, autonymous,
autonomous, *P*
polygamous,
polyonymous,
posthumous,
pusillanimous, *S*
synonymous,
pseudonymous,
sumpsimus, *TR*
tridynamous, *TH* thalamus,
V venomous, *Y* unanimous,
euonymus, *Z* xylotomous
NUS *A* albuminous, aluminous,
amanous, androgenous,
androgynous, acinous,
acinus, athermanous, *B*
bimanous, bituminous, *D*
diaphanous, diginous,
dichronous,
diplostemonous, *E*
endogenous, epiphanous,
epigenous, erogenous, *F*
ferruginous, foraminous,
fortitudinous, phototonus,
fuliginous, *FL* fluminous,
G gangrenous, *GL*
glutenous, glutinous,
gluttonous, *H*
hydrogenous, hypogenous,
homophonous,
homogenous, hircinous, *I*
indigenous, *J* gelatinous, *K*
cavernous, cacophonous,
cartiliginous, consonous,
contaminous,
conterminous,
coterminous, *KR* cretinous,
criminous, *L* larcenous,
leguminous, lentitudinous,
libidinous, liminous,
luminous, misogynous, *M*
membranous, monotonous,
mountainous,
multitudinous,
mucilaginous, mutinous, *N*
nitrogenous, numinous, *O*
oleaginous, ominous,
autogenous,
autochthonous, *P*
pedimanous, perigynous,
poisonous, polygonous,
polygyonous, polygenous,
putredinous, *PL* platinous,
platitudinous, *R* ravenous,
resinous, rubiginous,

ruinous, *S* sanguinous,
synchronous, *SKR*
scrutinous, *T* tendinous,
terminus, terriginous,
tetanus, tyrannous,
torminous, *TR* treasonous,
trigeminous, trigeminus, *V*
valetudinous, velutinous,
verminous, vertiginous,
vicissitudinous, villainous,
voluminous, voraginous,
vortiginous, *Y* uranous,
urinous, urogenous, *Z*
xanthomelanous
PLUS nonplus, overplus,
PUS periplus, plus, *surplus*
Oedipus, octopus,
orthotropous,
pithecanthropus, platypus,
polypus, pus
RUS *A* adiaphorous, adulterous,
adventurous, acarus,
aliferous, aligerous,
amorous, anserous,
apiverous, apterous,
arborous, armigerous, *B*
balsamiferous, barbarous,
boisterous, bulbiferous, *BL*
blusterous, *D* dangerous,
decorous, dexterous,
dipterous, doloriferous,
dolorous, *E* ephemerous, *F*
fossiliferous, phosphorous,
phosphorus, fulgurous, *FL*
flavorous, *FR* frugivorous,
fructivorous, *GL*
glamorous, *GR*
graminivorous,
granivorous, *H*
herbivorous, Hesperus,
homopterous, horrorous,
humorous, humerus, *I*
Icarus, icterus,
imponderous, imposturous,
indecorous, inodorous,
insectivorous, isomerous, *J*
generous, *K* cadaverous,
calciferous, cankerous,
cancerous, coniferous,
cantankerous,
carboniferous, carnivorous,
KL clamorous, *L*
lactiferous, languorous,
Lazarus, lecherous, *M*
malodorous,
mammiferous, melliferous,
metalliferous,
monomerous, multiparous,
murderous, murmurous, *N*
nectarous, nidorous,
numerous, *O* obstreperous,
odoriferous, odorous,

augurous, omnivorous,
onerous, auriferous,
oviparous, *P* perjurous,
peripterous, pesterous,
pestiferous, piscivorous,
Pythagoras, polymerous,
ponderous, pulverous, *PR*
preposterous, prosperous,
R rancorous, rapturous,
rigorous, rhinoceros,
roisterous, rhus, Russ, *S*
sacchariferous, savorous,
seminiferous, Cerberus,
somniferous, sonorous,
sudoriferous, sulphurous,
susurrous, susurrus, SH
chivalrous, *SK* scutiferous,
SL slanderous,
slaughterous, slumberous,
ST stelliferous, stertorous,
T tartarous, Tartarus,
tetrapterous, timorous,
torturous, tuberous, *TH*
thunderous, *TR* traitorous,
treacherous, *U* ulcerous,
umbelliferous, ungenerous,
unchivalrous, *V* valorous,
vaporous, venturous,
verdurous, vermivorous,
vigorous, viperous,
viviparous, vociferous,
vulturous, *Y* uniparous,
uriniferous, uterus, *Z*
Zephyrus
STUS stuss
SUS Caucasus, Pegasus,
megalonisus, suss,
xeronisus
THUS antipathous, thus
TRUS idolatrous, sinistrous,
truss, untruss
TUS *A* aditus, acclivitous, *D*
Democritus, *E* edematous,
eczematous, exitus,
emeritus, *F* fatuitous,
felicitous, fortuitous, *FR*
fremitus, *GR* gratuitous, *H*
halitus, Herodotus,
Hypolitus, *I* impetus,
infelicitous, iniquitous, *K*
calamitous, covetous, *M*
microstomatous, *N*
necessitous, *P*
pachydermatous, *PR*
precipitous, propositous, *R*
riotous, *S* circuitous,
solicitous, *SKL*
sclerodermatous, *SP*
spiritous, *T* tuss, *TR*
transitus, trinitous, *V*
vagitous, velocitous, *Y*
ubiquitous

VUS	atavus, mischievous, tritavus

ŪSH

(See OOSH)

USH

BLUSH	blush, outblush, unblush
BRUSH	*airbrush*, bottlebrush, brush, *hairbrush*, *clothesbrush*, *nailbrush*, *paintbrush*, *toothbrush*, underbrush
FLUSH	flush, outflush, unflush
FRUSH	frush
GUSH	gush
HUSH	hush
KRUSH	crush
KUSH	Cush, namaycush
LUSH	lush
MUSH	mush
PLUSH	plush
RUSH	*bullrush*, bum's rush, *inrush*, outrush, rush, *uprush*, *woodrush*
SLUSH	slush
THRUSH	hermit thrush, missal thrush, thrush
TUSH	tush

USK

BRUSK	brusque
BUSK	busk
DUSK	adusk, dusk
FUSK	fusc, subfusc
HUSK	dehusk, husk, *cornhusk*
KUSK	cusk
LUSK	lusk, *mollusk*
MUSK	musk
RUSK	rusk
TUSK	tusk

ŪST

PŪST	puist

(See OOST; see OOS and ŪS, add *-d* where appropriate.)

UST

BUST	bust, combust, robust
DUST	adust, angel dust, bedust, dost, dust, gold dust, *sawdust, stardust*

FUST	fussed, fust
GUST	august, disgust, gust
JUST	adjust, just, coadjust, misadjust, readjust, unjust
KRUST	encrust, crust, mumblecrust, *piecrust*
KUST	discussed, cussed
LUST	lust, wanderlust
MUST	mussed, must
NUST	venust
PLUST	*nonplussed*
RUST	rust
THRUST	overthrust, thrust, underthrust, upthrust
TRUST	betrust, blind trust, distrust, entrust, mistrust, self-distrust, trust, untrust
TUST	vetust

ŪT

BŪT	attribute, beaut, butte, Butte
FŪT	confute, refute
GŪT	argute
KŪT	acute, execute, electrocute, cute, persecute, prosecute, sub-acute
MŪT	*deafmute*, emeute, commute, Malemute, meute, mute, permute, transmute
NŪT	Canute, comminute, cornute, minute, newt
PŪT	depute, dispute, disrepute, impute, compute, suppute
SKŪT	scute
STŪT	astute, destitute, institute, constitute, prostitute, substitute, tute

(See OOT)

UT

BUT	abut, *blackbutt*, but, butt, *hagbut, hackbut*, halibut, rebut, *sackbut*, scuttlebutt, surrebut, water butt
FUT	phut, go phut
GLUT	englut, glut
GUT	*foregut*, gut, *hindgut*, catgut, midgut, rotgut
HUT	hut
JUT	jut
KUT	*haircut, clean-cut, clear-cut, crosscut,* cut, linocut, uncut, uppercut, *woodcut*
MUT	mutt
NUT	*B beechnut,* betelnut,

	bitternut, butternut, *BL* bladdernut, *BR* Brazil nut, *CH chestnut, D doughnut, G gallnut, GR groundnut, H* hazelnut, hickory nut, *K* candlenut, cashew nut, *cobnut,* coconut, macadamia nut, *N* nut, *P peanut, W walnut*
PUT	Lilliput, occiput, putt, putt-putt, sinciput
RUT	rut
SHUT	half-shut, outshut, shut, unshut
SKUT	scut
SLUT	slut
SMUT	besmut, smut
STRUT	astrut, strut
TUT	King Tut, tut, tut-tut

UT

(as in *put*)

(See OOT)

ŪTH

SMŪTH	smeuth

(See OOTH)

UTH

DUTH	doth
MUTH	*bismuth*, azimuth

UTS

KLUTS	klutz
PUTS	putz
STUTS	Stutz

(See UT, add *-s* where appropriate.)

ŪV

(See OOV)

UV

UV	hereof, whereof, of, thereof
BUV	above
DUV	dove, mourning dove, *ringdove*, rock dove, turtledove

GLUV	*foxglove*, glove, unglove
GUV	gov
LUV	ladylove, light-o'love, love, puppy love, self-love, *truelove*
SHUV	shove

ŪVD

(See $\overline{OO}V$, add -*d* where appropriate.)

ŪZ

ŪZ	disuse, ill-use, misuse, use
BŪZ	abuse, disabuse
FŪZ	*BL* blow a fuse, *D* defuse, diffuse, *E* effuse, *F* fuse, *I* infuse, interfuse, *K* confuse, *P* percussion fuse, perfuse, *R* refuse, *S* suffuse, superinfuse, *TR* transfuse
GŪZ	guze
HŪZ	hues
KŪZ	accuse, excuse, incuse, Syracuse
MŪZ	amuse, bemuse, meuse, mews, muse
NŪZ	news
SŪZ	sues (*danseuse, masseuse* are near-rhymes)
THŪZ	thews
TŪZ	contuse

(See **Ū**, add -*s* where appropriate.)

UZ

UZ	Uz
BUZ	abuzz, buzz, *humbuzz*
DUZ	does, doz
FUZ	fuzz, *peachfuzz*
KUZ	coz

ŪZD

(See **ŪZ**, $\overline{OO}Z$, add -*d* where appropriate.)

ŪZH

(See $\overline{OO}ZH$)

DOUBLE RHYMES

(Words accented on the syllable before the last.
Also called *trochaic*, or *feminine*, rhymes.)

ĀA

FRĀA	Freya
HĀA	haya
LĀA	Himalaya
MĀA	Maya
ZĀA	Isaiah

ĀAL

BĀAL	Baal
FRĀAL	defrayal
GĀAL	gayal
TRĀAL	betrayal, portrayal
VĀAL	conveyal, purveyal, surveyal

ĀAM

FĀAM	faham
GRĀAM	graham

(See ĀEM)

ĀAN

GWĀAN	Paraguayan, Uruguayan
KĀAN	Biscayan
LĀAN	Malayan
MĀAN	Mayan
TĀAN	Altaian

ĀANS

BĀANS	abeyance
VĀANS	conveyance, purveyance, surveyance

ĀANT

BĀANT	abeyant
MĀANT	mayn't

ĀBA

FĀBA	faba
PĀBA	copaiba

ÄBA

ÄBA	aba
BÄBA	Addis Ababa, Ali Baba, baba, Cayubaba
DÄBA	indaba
KÄBA	kaaba, Kaaba
LÄBA	laaba
SÄBA	casaba, piassaba
TÄBA	aftaba

> *VISION SEEN THROUGH A HEADACHE*
>
> I love to watch the flocks
>   Of Aspirin at play
> On Rheumatism Rocks
>   Beside Placebo Bay.
> They frolic in the sun,
>   They race along the shore;
> I hear them shout as one,
>   "C O – H 8 – 0 4!"

ABARD

(See ABERD)

ĀBĒ

ĀBĒ	Abie
BĀBĒ	baby, big baby, bushbaby, crybaby
GĀBĒ	gaby
MĀBĒ	maybe

ABĒ

ABĒ	abbey
BABĒ	babby
BLABĒ	blabby
DABĒ	dabby
DRABĒ	drabby
FLABĒ	flabby
GABĒ	gabby
GRABĒ	grabby
KABĒ	cabby
KRABĒ	crabby
RABĒ	rabbi, kohlrabi
SABĒ	no sabe, sabe
SHABĒ	shabby
SKABĒ	scabby
SLABĒ	slabby
TABĒ	tabby
YABĒ	yabbi, yabby

ÄBĒ

DRÄBĒ	drabi
HÄBĒ	Wahabi
HWÄBĒ	whabby
JÄBĒ	Punjabi
RÄBĒ	rabi, kohlrabi
SKWÄBĒ	squabby
TÄBĒ	tabi
WÄBĒ	wabby, wabe

(See OBĒ)

ABED

(See ABID)

ĀBER

FABER	homo faber
GĀBER	Gheber
KĀBER	caber
LĀBER	belabor, labor
NĀBER	beggar-my-neighbor, good neighbor, neighbor
SĀBER	saber
TĀBER	tabor

ABER

BLABER	blabber
DABER	dabber
GABER	gabber
GRABER	grabber
JABER	jabber, gibber-jabber
KLABER	bonnyclabber, clabber
KRABER	crabber
NABER	knabber, nabber
SLABER	beslabber, slabber
STABER	stabber
YABER	yabber

ÄBER

(See OBER)

ĀBERD

(See ĀBER, add -ed where appropriate.)

ABERD

GABERD	gabbard
KLABERD	clapboard
SKABERD	scabbard
TABERD	tabard

(See ABER, add -ed where appropriate.)

ABET

(See ABIT)

ĀBEZ

BĀBEZ	babies
GĀBEZ	gabies
RĀBEZ	rabies
SKĀBEZ	scabies
TĀBEZ	tabes

ABID

KRABID	crabbed
RABID	rabid
TABID	tabid

ABIK

LABIK	asyllabic, bisyllabic, monosyllabic, multisyllabic, polysyllabic, trisyllabic
NABIK	cannabic
RABIK	rabik

ĀBIL

(See ĀBL)

ABIL

(See ABL)

ABIN

| KABIN | cabin |
| SABIN | sabin |

ABING

(See **AB,** add *-ing* where appropriate.)

ABIT

ABIT	abbot
BABIT	babbitt, Babbitt
DRABIT	drabbet
HABIT	habit, inhabit, cohabit
RABIT	jackrabbit, rabbet, rabbit
SABIT	sabot

ĀBL

ĀBL	able, Abel, disable, enable, unable
BĀBL	Babel
DWĀBL	dwaible
FĀBL	fable, fibble-fable
GĀBL	gable
JĀBL	jibble-jable
KĀBL	cable, pay cable
LĀBL	label, labile
NĀBL	nabel, nable
SĀBL	ensable, sable
STĀBL	stable, unstable

| TĀBL | retable, Round Table, table, timetable, turntable, water table, worktable |

ABL

(The adjective suffix *-able* in this category, when normally unstressed, provides only a forced and undesirable rhyme.)

ABL	*A* affiliable, amiable, *D* differentiable, dutiable, *E* expiable, enviable, *I* impermeable, imperviable, inexpiable, invaluable, invariable, irremediable, issuable, *J* justiciable, *L* leviable, *M* malleable, *P* permeable, perpetuable, pitiable, *R* remediable, renunciable, *S* semipermeable, *U* unenviable, *V* valuable, variable
BABL	babble, psychobabble
BRABL	brabble
DABL	bedabble, dabble, formidable, unformidable
DRABL	bedrabble, drabble
FABL	fibble-fabble
GABL	*G* gabble, gibble-gabble, *I* interrogable, irrigable, *M* mitigable, *N* navigable, *O* obligeable, *PR* propagable, *S* segregable, *U* unmitigable
GRABL	grabble
HABL	habile
JABL	acknowledgeable, challengeable, damageable, *dischargeable,* jabble, manageable, marriageable, knowledgeable, unchallengeable, unmanageable
KABL	*D* despicable, duplicable, *E*

educable, explicable, extricable, eradicable, *I* impracticable, inapplicable, inexplicable, *K* cabble, *M* manducable, masticable, *PR* practicable, prognosticable

KRABL	execrable
KWABL	*inequable*
LABL	incalculable, inoculable, inviolable, calculable, coagulable, regulable, violable
MABL	estimable, fathomable, inestimable, *reformable,* unfathomable
NABL	*D* disciplinable, *E* exceptionable, *F* fashionable, *I* imaginable, impassionable, impressionable, inalienable, interminable, *K* companionable, contaminable, *KW* questionable, *M* mentionable, *O* objectionable, *P* pardonable, pensionable, personable, poisonable, *PR* proportionable, *S* sanctionable, *U* unimaginable, unquestionable, unpardonable
PABL	developable, *exculpable,* undevelopable
RABL	*A* admirable, alterable, answerable, *D* deliverable, decipherable, dishonorable, discoverable, *E* exorable, *F* favorable, *I* immeasurable, immensurable, imponderable, inexorable, incommensurable, inconsiderable, innumerable, incensurable,

inseparable,
inseverable,
insufferable,
insuperable,
intolerable,
invulnerable,
irrecoverable, *K*
commemorable,
conquerable,
considerable, *M*
measurable,
memorable,
mensurable,
miserable, *N*
numerable, *O*
offerable, honorable,
P ponderable, *PL*
pleasurable, *PR*
preferable, *R* rabble,
recoverable,
rememberable,
renderable, ribble-
rabble, *S* censurable,
separable, cipherable,
sufferable, superable,
T temperable,
tolerable, *U*
undecipherable,
unalterable, *V*
venerable, vulnerable

SABL   balanceable,
                             disserviceable,
                             impassable,
                             noticeable,
                             purchasable,
                             serviceable,
                             unbalanceable,
                             unnoticeable,
                             unpurchasable,
                             unserviceable

SHABL   distinguishable,
                             extinguishable,
                             imperishable,
                             indistinguishable,
                             inextinguishable,
                             perishable,
                             publishable,
                             undistinguishable,
                             unextinguishable,
                             unpublishable

SKABL   scabble
SKRABL   scrabble, Scrabble
TABL   *A* attributable, *CH*
                             charitable, *D*
                             decapitable,
                             discreditable,
                             distributable,
                             dubitable, *E*
                             equitable, evitable, *F*
                             forgettable, H
                             habitable, heritable,
                             hospitable, *I*

illimitable,
indomitable,
indubitable,
inequitable,
inevitable,
inhabitable,
inhospitable,
inimitable,
interpretable,
irritable, *K*
comfortable,
covetable, *KR*
creditable, *L*
limitable, *PR*
precipitable,
profitable, *U*
uncharitable,
uncomfortable,
uninhabitable

TRABL   impenetrable
VABL   *unlivable, unlovable*

ÄBL

SKWÄBL   squabble
WÄBL   wabble, wobble

(See **OBL**)

ABLD

SMABLD   smabbled
SNABLD   snabbled

(See **ABL**, add *-d* where appropriate.)

ĀBLĒ

ĀBLĒ   ably
STĀBLĒ   stably

ABLĒ

BABLĒ   babbly
DABLĒ   dabbly
DRABLĒ   drably
GABLĒ   gabbly
SHABLĒ   Chablis
SKRABLĒ   scrabbly

ĀBLER

(See **ĀBL**, add *-r* where appropriate.)

ABLER

GABLER   gabbler, Hedda Gabler

(See **ABL**, add *-r* where appropriate.)

ABLET

KRABLET   crablet
TABLET   tablet

ABLISH

BABLISH   babblish
STABLISH   disestablish,
                  establish, reestablish,
                  stablish

ĀBŌ

VĀBŌ   lavabo
ZĀBŌ   gazabo, gazebo

ABŌ

ABŌ   babbo
SABŌ   sabot
ZHABŌ   jabot

ĀBOI

LĀBOI   layboy
PLĀBOI   playboy

ABOT

(See **ABIT**)

ÄBRA

ÄBRA   abra
DÄBRA   abracadabra
LÄBRA   candelabra

ĀBRAM

(See **ĀBRUM**)

ĀBRUM

ĀBRUM   Abram
FLĀBRUM   flabrum
LĀBRUM   labrum, candelabrum

ĀBRUS

ĀBRUS   Abrus
GLĀBRUS   glabrous
SKĀBRUS   scabrous

ACHĒ

BACHĒ	hibachi
KACHĒ	catchee, no catchee, seecatchie
MACHĒ	machi, matchy
PACHĒ	patchy
SKRACHĒ	scratchy
SNACHĒ	snatchy

ACHEL

HACHEL	hatchel
RACHEL	ratchel
SACHEL	satchel

ĀCHER

KĀCHER	*plicature*
KLĀCHER	nomenclature
LĀCHER	legislature
NĀCHER	denature, nature, unnature

ACHER

BACHER	bacher, batcher
KACHER	catcher, cony-catcher, *flycatcher,* birdcatcher, dogcatcher
SNACHER	bodysnatcher, snatcher

(See **ACH,** add *-er* where appropriate.)

ACHET

BRACHET	brachet
HACHET	hatchet
KRACHET	Bob Cratchet
LACHET	latchet
RACHET	ratchet
SMACHET	smatchet

ACHEZ

NACHEZ	Natchez

(See **ACH,** add *-es* where appropriate.)

ACHING

(See **ACH,** add *-ing* where appropriate.)

ACHLES

(See **ACH,** add *-less* where appropriate.)

ACHMENT

HACHMENT	hatchment
KACHMENT	catchment
PACHMENT	dispatchment
RACHMENT	ratchment
TACHMENT	attachment, detachment

ÄCHŌ

MÄCHŌ	macho
NÄCHŌ	nacho

ACHWERK

KACHWERK	catchwork
PACHWERK	patchwork

ĀDĀ

HĀDĀ	heyday
MĀDĀ	Mayday
PĀDĀ	payday
PLĀDĀ	playday

ĀDA

GRĀDA	digitigrada
KĀDA	cicada
MĀDA	armada
NĀDA	Granada, Grenada, panada
VĀDA	Veda

ADA

ADA	adda
DADA	dada
SADA	sadda

ÄDA

DÄDA	dada, Dada
GÄDA	Haggadah
KÄDA	cicada
LÄDA	big enchalada, enchalada, colada, mulada
MÄDA	armada
NÄDA	empanada, Granada, Grenada, journada, nada, panada
PÄDA	pratityasamutpada
SÄDA	pasada
SRÄDA	sraddha

STRÄDA	autostrada
TRÄDA	contrada
VÄDA	Nevada, Sierra Nevada
ZÄDA	shahzada

ĀDAL

TRĀDAL	tradal
VĀDAL	wedel

ADAM

ADAM	Adam
KADAM	macadam
MADAM	madam, queezmadam, prickmadam

ĀDANS

(See **ĀDENS**)

ĀDĒ

BRĀDĒ	braidy
FĀDĒ	fady
FRĀDĒ	'fraidy
GLĀDĒ	glady
JĀDĒ	jady
KĀDĒ	alcaide, cadi, cascady
LĀDĒ	bag lady, belady, charlady, forelady, cleaning lady, lady, landlady, milady
MĀDĒ	maidy
SHĀDĒ	shady
VĀDĒ	vade, vady

ADĒ

BADĒ	baddie, baddy
DADĒ	daddy, big daddy, sugar daddy
FADĒ	faddy
GADĒ	gaddi, Gaddi
GLADĒ	gladdie
HADĒ	haddie, finnan haddie
KADĒ	caddie, caddy
LADĒ	laddie, laddy
MADĒ	maddy
PADĒ	paddy
PLADĒ	plaidie

ÄDĒ

KÄDĒ	cadi, quadi
MÄDĒ	Mahdi

RĀDĒ   irade
SKWÄDĒ   squaddy
WÄDĒ   waddy, Wade, wadi

(See **ODĒ**)

ĀDED

(See **ĀD**, add -*ed* where appropriate.)

ADED

(see **AD**, add -*ed* where appropriate.)

ÄDED

(See **ÄD**, add-*ed* where appropriate.)

ĀDEN

ĀDEN   Aden
HĀDEN   menhaden
LĀDEN   heavy-laden, laden, overladen, underladen, unladen
MĀDEN   bower-maiden, dairy-maiden, flower-maiden, maiden, snow-maiden

ADEN

BADEN   Abaddon
GLADEN   engladden, gladden, regladden
MADEN   madden
SADEN   sadden

ĀDENS

ĀDENS   aidance
KĀDENS   cadence, decadence

ĀDENT

ĀDENT   abraidant, aidant
KĀDENT   cadent, decadent

ĀDER

NĀDER   nadir
SĀDER   Seder

(See **ĀD**, add -*er* where appropriate.)

ADER

ADER   adder
BADER   badder
BLADER   bladder
DADER   dadder
GADER   gadder
GLADER   gladder
LADER   ladder, stepladder
MADER   madder
NADER   nadder
SADER   sadr, sadder

(See **AD**, add -*er* where appropriate.)

ÄDER

SÄDER   sadr

(See **ÄD**, **OD**, add -*er* or -*der* where appropriate.)

ADEST

FADEST   faddist
GLADEST   gladdest
SADEST   saddest, sadist

ĀDĒZ

HĀDĒZ   Hades
KĀDĒZ   Cadiz
LĀDĒZ   ladies

ADĒZ

BADĒZ   baddies
DADĒZ   daddies
LADĒZ   laddies
PLADĒZ   plaidies

ADFUL

GLADFUL   gladful
MADFUL   madful
SADFUL   sadful

ADIK

ADIK   dyadic, triadic
GADIK   haggadic
KADIK   decadic, saccadic
KLADIK   Cycladic
LADIK   Helladic
MADIK   nomadic
NADIK   monadic, vanadic

RADIK   faradic, sporadic
TADIK   octadic, Sotadic
TRADIK   tetradic

ĀDING

(See **ĀD**, add -*ing* where appropriate.)

ADING

(See **AD**, add -*ing* where appropriate.)

ÄDING

(See **ÄD**, add -*ing*, **OD**, add -*ing*, where appropriate.)

ĀDISH

JĀDISH   jadish
MĀDISH   maidish, mermaidish, old-maidish
STĀDISH   staidish

ADISH

BADISH   baddish
FADISH   faddish
GLADISH   gladdish
KADISH   caddish, Kaddish
MADISH   maddish
PLADISH   plaidish
RADISH   horseradish, radish
SADISH   saddish

ADIST

(See **ADEST**)

ĀDL

DRĀDL   dreidel
GRĀDL   gradal
HĀDL   hadal
KRĀDL   encradle, cradle
TRĀDL   tradal
VĀDL   wedel

ADL

ADL   addle
DADL   daddle, skedaddle
FADL   faddle, fiddle-faddle
PADL   dogpaddle, paddle
RADL   raddle
SADL   packsaddle, saddle, sidesaddle, unsaddle, western saddle

SKADL	scaddle, skaddle
SPRADL	spraddle
STADL	staddle
STRADL	astraddle, bestraddle, straddle

ĀDL

KWÄDL	quaddle
SWÄDL	swaddle
TWÄDL	twaddle
WÄDL	waddle

(See ODL)

ĀDLD

KRĀDLD	encradled, cradled
WĀDLD	wedeled

ADLD

(See ADL, add -d where appropriate.)

ÄDLD

(See ÄDL, ODL, add -d where appropriate.)

ĀDLĒ

GRĀDLĒ	gradely, retrogradely
MĀDLĒ	dismayedly
STĀDLĒ	staidly

ADLĒ

BADLĒ	badly
GLADLĒ	gladly
MADLĒ	madly
SADLĒ	sadly

ÄDLĒ

TWÄDLĒ	twaddly
WÄDLĒ	waddly

(See ODLĒ)

ADLER

ADLER	Felix Adler, Mortimer Adler

(See ADL, add -r where appropriate.)

ÄDLER

(See ÄDL, ODL, add -r where appropriate.)

ĀDLES

ĀDLES	aidless

(See ĀD, add -less where appropriate.)

ĀDLING

KRĀDLING	encradling, cradling
MĀDLING	maidling
WĀDLING	wedeling

ADLING

(See ADL, add -ing where appropriate.)

ÄDLING

(See ÄDL, ODL, add -ing where appropriate.)

ĀDNES

FRĀDNES	afraidness, frayedness
STĀDNES	staidness, unstaidness

ADNES

BADNES	badness
GLADNES	gladness
MADNES	madness
PLADNES	plaidness
SADNES	sadness

ĀDŌ

BĀDŌ	gambado
DĀDŌ	dado
GĀDŌ	renegado
KĀDŌ	ambuscado, barricado, stoccado
KRĀDŌ	credo
LĀDŌ	scalado
MĀDŌ	fumado
NĀDŌ	bastinado, grenado, carbonado, tornado
PĀDŌ	strappado
RĀDŌ	desperado, Laredo
SĀDŌ	camisado, crusado
VĀDŌ	muscovado

ADŌ

RADŌ	Colorado
SHADŌ	foreshadow, overshadow, shadow

ÄDŌ

ÄDŌ	zapateado
DÄDŌ	dado
GÄDŌ	juzgado
KÄDŌ	avocado, imbrocado, incommunicado, Mikado, sticcado, stoccado
LÄDŌ	amontillado
MÄDŌ	quemado
NÄDŌ	aficionado, bastinado, carbonado
PÄDŌ	strappado
PRÄDŌ	Prado
RÄDŌ	amorado, desperado, dorado, El Dorado, Colorado
SÄDŌ	passado
TÄDŌ	pintado, remontado
VÄDŌ	bravado, muscovado

ÄDŌŌ

FÄDŌŌ	fado
SÄDOO	sadhu

ĀDŌS

BÄDŌS	Barbados
TRĀDŌS	extrados, intrados

ADSUM

GLADSUM	gladsome
MADSUM	madsome

ADUK

BADUK	baddock
HADUK	haddock
PADUK	paddock
SHADUK	shaddock

ĀDUS

GRĀDUS	gradus
KLĀDUS	cladus

ĀĒ

DĀĒ	Agnus Dei, Dei
HWĀĒ	wheyey
KLĀĒ	clayey
SPRĀĒ	sprayey

ÄĒ

BÄĒ	rubai
KÄĒ	kai, kai-kai
SÄĒ	sai
TÄĒ	Tai

ĀEM

ĀEM	A.M.
MĀEM	mayhem

(See ĀAM)

ĀER

DĀER	doomsdayer
MĀER	mayor, mormaor
PLĀER	player, record player, video player
SĀER	assayer, doomsayer, nay-sayer, sayer, yea-sayer
VĀER	conveyor, kurveyor, purveyor, surveyor

(See Ā, add -er when appropriate.)

ĀFĀR

MĀFĀR	Mayfair
PLĀFĀR	play fair, Playfair

AFĒ

BAFĒ	baffy
CHAFĒ	chaffy
DAFĒ	daffy
DRAFĒ	draffy
FAFĒ	faffy
TAFĒ	taffy

ĀFER

CHĀFER	chafer, cockchafer
SĀFER	safer, vouchsafer
STRĀFER	strafer
WĀFER	wafer

AFER

CHAFER	chaffer
GAFER	gaffer, ghaffir
GRAFER	graffer
KAFER	Kaffir
KWAFER	quaffer
LAFER	laugher
PYAFER	piaffer
ZAFER	zaffer

ÄFER

KWÄFER	quaffer
LÄFER	laugher

(See OFER)

AFIK

DAFIK	edaphic
GRAFIK	*A* analyptographic, *B* bibliographic, biographic, *D* dactylographic, demographic, diagraphic, *E* engraphic, epigraphic, ethneographic, ethnographic, *F* phonographic, photographic, *G* galvanographic, *GL* glyptographic, *GR* graphic, *H* heliographic, heterographic, hydrographic, hierographic, hyetographic, histographic, historiographic, holographic, homographic, homolographic, horologiographic, *I* ideographic, idiographic, ichnographic, isographic, *J* geographic, *K* cacographic, calligraphic, cartographic, chirographic, choreographic, chorographic, cosmographic, *KL* clinographic, *KR* cryptographic, crystallographic, chromographic, chronographic, *L* lexigraphic, lexicographic, logographic, *M* macrographic, melographic, micrographic, monographic, *N* noematachographic, neurographic, *O* oleographic, orographic, orthographic, autobiographic, autographic, *P* paleographic, pantographic, paragraphic, pasigraphic, petrographic, pyrographic, polygraphic, pornographic, *S* selenographic, scenographic, sciagraphic, siderographic, cinematographic, seismographic, *SF* sphenographic, *ST* stenographic, stylographic, *STR* stratigraphic, stratographic, *T* tachygraphic, telegraphic, typographic, topographic, *Y* uranographic, *Z* xylographic, zincographic, zoographic
MAFIK	maffick
SAFIK	Sapphic
RAFIK	seraphic
TAFIK	epitaphic
TRAFIK	traffic

ĀFING

(See ĀF, add -ing where appropriate.)

AFING

(See AF, add -ing where appropriate.)

ÄFING

(See ÄF, add -ing where appropriate.)

AFIZM

SAFIZM	sapphism
SKAFIZM	scaphism

AFL

BAFL	baffle
DAFL	daffle
GAFL	gaffle
HAFL	haffle
MAFL	maffle
RAFL	raffle
SKRAFL	scraffle
SNAFL	snaffle
TAFL	taffle
YAFL	yaffle

ÄFL

FÄFL	faffel
WÄFL	waffle

(See OFL)

AFLD

SKAFLD	scaffold

(See **AFL**, add -*d* where appropriate.)

ÄFLD

FÄFLD	faffled
WÄFLD	waffled

AFLER

BAFLER	baffler
HAFLER	haffler
RAFLER	raffler
SKRAFLER	scraffler

AFLING

BAFLING	baffling
HAFLING	halfling
KAFLING	calfling
RAFLING	raffling
SKRAFLING	scraffling
SNAFLING	snaffling

ÄFLING

HÄFLING	halfling

KÄFLING	calfling
WÄFLING	waffling

AFTĒ

DRAFTĒ	drafty
GRAFTĒ	grafty
KRAFTĒ	crafty
RAFTĒ	rafty
WAFTĒ	wafty

AFTER

DAFTER	dafter
DRAFTER	drafter
GRAFTER	grafter
HAFTER	hafter
LAFTER	laughter
RAFTER	rafter
WAFTER	wafter

ÄFTER

ÄFTER	after, hereafter, hereinafter, whereafter, thereafter
DRÄFTER	drafter, draughter
LÄFTER	laughter
WÄFTER	wafter

AFTIJ

DRAFTIJ	draftage, draughtage
GRAFTIJ	graftage
WAFTIJ	waftage

ÄFTIJ

DRÄFTIJ	draftage, draughtage
WÄFTIJ	waftage

AFTING

(See **AFT**, add -*ing* where appropriate.)

AFTLES

(See **AFT**, add -*less* where appropriate.)

AFTSMAN

DRAFTSMAN	draftsman
KRAFTSMAN	craftsman, handicraftsman
RAFTSMAN	raftsman

ÄFTSMAN

DRAFTSMAN	draftsman
KRAFTSMAN	craftsman, handicraftsman
RAFTSMAN	raftsman

ĀFUL

NĀFUL	nayful
PLĀFUL	playful, unplayful
TRĀFUL	trayful
YĀFUL	yeaful

ĀGA

BĀGA	rutabaga
DĀGA	bodega, Onondaga
MĀGA	omega
PLĀGA	plaga
SĀGA	saga
STRĀGA	strega
VĀGA	vega, Vega

ÄGA

ÄGA	aga, agha
GÄGA	gaga
KWÄGA	quagga
MÄGA	maga
SÄGA	saga

ĀGAL

(See **ĀGL**)

AĞAN

(See **ĀGEN**)

ÄGAR

(See **ÄGER**)

AGARD

(See **AGERD**)

AGART

(See **AGERT**)

AGAT

(See **AGUT**)

AGĒ

BAGĒ	baggie, baggy
BRAGĒ	braggy
DAGĒ	daggy
DRAGĒ	draggy
FAGĒ	faggy
FLAGĒ	flaggy
GAGĒ	gaggy
HAGĒ	haggy
JAGĒ	jaggy
KRAGĒ	craggy
KWAGĒ	quaggy
LAGĒ	laggy
NAGĒ	knaggy, naggy
RAGĒ	raggee, raggy, ragi
SAGĒ	saggy
SHAGĒ	shaggy
SKRAGĒ	scraggy
SLAGĒ	slaggy
SNAGĒ	snaggy
STAGĒ	staggy
SWAGĒ	swaggy
TAGĒ	taggy
WAGĒ	waggy

AGED

JAGED	jagged
KRAGED	cragged
RAGED	ragged
SKRAGED	scragged

ĀGEN

FĀGEN	fagin, Fagin
HĀGEN	Copenhagen
PĀGEN	pagan, upeygan
RĀGEN	Reagan
VĀGEN	Vegan

ĀGER

JĀGER	jager, jaeger
MĀGER	maigre
NĀGER	canaigre
PLĀGER	plaguer
VĀGER	vaguer
YĀGER	jaeger

AGER

AGER	agar, agar-agar
BAGER	bagger, carpetbagger, four-bagger, three-bagger, two-bagger, one-bagger

BRAGER	bragger
DAGER	dagger
DRAGER	dragger
FAGER	fagger
FLAGER	flagger
FRAGER	fragger
GAGER	gagger
JAGER	jagger
LAGER	lagger
MAGER	magger
NAGER	nagger
RAGER	ragger
SAGER	saggar, sagger
SHAGER	shagger
SNAGER	snagger
STAGER	stagger
SWAGER	swagger
TAGER	tagger
WAGER	wagger, wigwagger
ZAGER	zigzagger

ÄGER

ÄGER	agar, agar-agar
LÄGER	lager, laager

AGERD

BLAGERD	blackguard
BRAGERD	braggard
HAGERD	haggard
LAGERD	laggard
STAGERD	staggard, staggered
SWAGERD	swaggered

AGERT

BRAGERT	braggart
STAGERT	staggart

AGET

(See AGUT)

ĀGIN

(See ĀGEN)

AGING

FRAGING	fragging

(See AG, add -ing where appropriate.)

AGISH

BRAGISH	braggish
FLAGISH	flaggish

JAGISH	jaggish
LAGISH	laggish
NAGISH	naggish
WAGISH	waggish

ĀGL

BĀGL	bagel
HĀGL	Hegel
NĀGL	finagle
PĀGL	paigle
PLĀGL	plagal
VĀGL	vagal, inveigle

AGL

DAGL	bedaggle, daggle
DRAGL	bedraggle, draggle
GAGL	gaggle
HAGL	haggle
KWAGL	quaggle
PAGL	paggle
RAGL	raggle
STRAGL	straggle
TAGL	raggle-taggle
WAGL	waggel, waggle

ĀGLD

NĀGLD	finagled
VĀGLD	inveigled

AGLĒ

DRAGLĒ	draggly
HAGLĒ	haggly
STRAGLĒ	straggly
WAGLĒ	waggly

ĀGLER

NĀGLER	finagler
VĀGLER	inveigler

AGLER

DAGLER	daggler
DRAGLER	bedraggler, draggler
GAGLER	gaggler
HAGLER	haggler
STRAGLER	straggler
WAGLER	waggler

AGLING

DAGLING	boondaggling, daggling

(See AGL, add *-ing* where appropriate.)

AGMA

LAGMA	malagma
MAGMA	magma

AGMAN

BAGMAN	bagman
DRAGMAN	dragman
FLAGMAN	flagman
GAGMAN	gagman
RAGMAN	ragman

AGNĀT

AGNĀT	agnate
MAGNĀT	magnate
STAGNĀT	stagnate

AGNET

DRAGNET	dragnet
MAGNET	magnet

AGNUM

MAGNUM	magnum
SFAGNUM	sphagnum

AGNUS

MAGNUS	magnus
SFAGNUS	sphagnous

ĀGŌ

ĀGŌ	San Diego, pichiciago
BĀGŌ	lumbago, plumbago, sebago, Tobago
DĀGŌ	dago, solidago
FWĀGŌ	cacafuego, Tierra del Fuego
LĀGŌ	galago
MĀGŌ	archimago, imago
PĀGŌ	galapago
RĀGŌ	farrago, suffrago, virago, vorago
SĀGŌ	sago

ÄGŌ

ÄGŌ	Iago, Santiago
KÄGŌ	Chicago
LÄGŌ	salago
RÄGŌ	farrago

ĀGON

DĀGON	Dagon
SĀGON	Saigon

AGON

(See AGUN)

AGOT

(See AGUT)

ĀGRANS

FLĀGRANS	flagrance
FRĀGRANS	fragrance
VĀGRANS	vagrants

ĀGRANT

FLĀGRANT	flagrant
FRĀGRANT	fragrant, infragrant
VĀGRANT	vagrant

AGRIK

DAGRIK	podagric
RAGRIK	chiragric

AGUN

AGUN	agon
DRAGUN	dragon, pendragon, snapdragon
FLAGUN	flagon
WAGUN	chuckwagon, on the wagon, paddy wagon, wagon

ĀGUS

MĀGUS	archimagus, magus
PĀGUS	pagus
RĀGUS	choragus
TRĀGUS	tragus
VĀGUS	Las Vegas, vagus

AGUT

AGUT	agate
BAGUT	baggit
FAGUT	faggot, fagot
MAGUT	maggot, magot

ÄGWA

ÄGWA	agua
HÄGWA	majagua
JÄGWA	jagua
NÄGWA	Managua
RÄGWA	piragua
YÄGWA	yagua

AGZMAN

DRAGZMAN	dragsman
KRAGZMAN	cragsman
NAGZMAN	nagsman

ÄHA

ÄHA	aha, haha, taiaha
KÄHA	kaha
MÄHA	maha, maja
TÄHA	taha

ÄHOO

ÄHOO	Oahu
KÄHOO	kahu
MÄHOO	Mahu
SÄHOO	sahu
WÄHOO	wahoo
YÄHOO	yahoo, Yahoo

ĀIJ

DRĀIJ	drayage
PĀIJ	peage
WĀIJ	weighage

ĀIK

BRĀIK	algebraic, Alhambraic, Hebraic
DĀIK	Eddaic, Judaic, Chaldaic, sodaic, spondaic
KĀIK	Alcaic, archaic, Sadducaic, trochaic
LĀIK	formulaic, laic
MĀIK	Aramaic, Brahmaic, Romaic, Ptolemaic, stylagalmaic

NĀIK	Sinaic, Syrenaic
PĀIK	apotropaic, stenopaic
RĀIK	tesseraic
SĀIK	Pharisaic, Passaic
TĀIK	Altaic, deltaic, Jagataic, voltaic
ZĀIK	anti-Mosaic, mosaic, Mosaic, paradisaic, pre-Mosaic, prosaic, stanzaic

ĀIKS

TĀIKS	aretaics

(See ĀIK, add -s where appropriate.)

ĀIN

PRĀIN	pray-in
STĀIN	stay-in
WĀIN	weigh-in

ĀING

(See Ā, add -ing where appropriate.)

ĀIS

DĀIS	dais
LĀIS	Lais
NĀIS	nais
THĀIS	Thais

ĀISH

(See Ā, add -ish where appropriate.)

ĀIST

BRĀIST	algebraist
KĀIST	archaist
MĀIST	Ptolemaist
SĀIST	pharisaist
ZĀIST	prosaist

ĀIZM

DĀIZM	chaldaism
LĀIZM	Laism
ZĀIZM	Mosaism, prosaism

ĀJĒ

KĀJĒ	cagey
MĀJĒ	Meiji

RĀJĒ	ragy
SĀJĒ	sagy
STĀJĒ	stagy

AJĒ

HAJĒ	hadji
KAJĒ	cadgy
RAJĒ	karadji
WAJĒ	howadji

ĀJER

ĀJER	ager, golden-ager, teenager
GĀJER	disengager, engager, gager, gauger
KĀJER	cager
MĀJER	drum major, major, trumpet major
PĀJER	pager
RĀJER	enrager, rager
SĀJER	presager, sager
STĀJER	downstager, old-stager, stager, upstager
SWĀJER	assuager, swager
WĀJER	wager

AJER

AJER	agger
BAJER	badger
FAJER	fadger
KAJER	cadger

AJET

GAJET	gadget
WAJET	wadget

AJIK

FAJIK	androphagic, anthropophagic, lotophagic, omophagic, sarcophagic, theophagic
LAJIK	archipelagic, benthopelagic, ellagic, chimopelagic, pelagic
MAJIK	magic, theomagic
RAJIK	hemorrhagic, choragic
TRAJIK	antitragic, tragic

AJIL

AJIL	agile
FRAJIL	fragile

ĀJING

(See ĀJ, add -ing where appropriate.)

AJING

BAJING	badging
KAJING	cadging

ĀJLES

(See ĀJ, add -less where appropriate.)

ĀJMENT

GĀJMENT	disengagement, engagement, pre-engagement
KĀJMENT	encagement
RĀJMENT	enragement, curagement
SĀJMENT	presagement
SWĀJMENT	assuagement

ĀJUS

BĀJUS	ambagious
BRĀJUS	umbrageous
PĀJUS	rampageous
RĀJUS	harageous, courageous, oragious, outrageous
TĀJUS	advantageous, disadvantageous, contagious, noncontagious

ĀKA

ĀKA	cloaca, cueca
CHĀKA	Cheka
KĀKA	Macaca
LĀKA	kamalayka
MĀKA	Jamaica
RĀKA	bareca, raca
SHĀKA	abhiseka
WĀKA	weka

AKA

BAKA	bacca
DAKA	Dacca

FAKA	sifaka
LAKA	lacca, Malacca, polacca
PAKA	alpaca
RAKA	maraca

ÄKA

BÄKA	saltimbocca
DÄKA	medaca
HÄKA	Hakka
KÄKA	Titicaca, kaka
NÄKA	kanaka
PÄKA	paca
RÄKA	jararaca, karaka, raca
SÄKA	Osaka
TÄKA	pataca

AKAK

| AKAK | ack-ack |
| KAKAK | kakkak |

AKAL

(See AKL)

AKARD

| PAKARD | Packard |
| PLAKARD | placard |

ĀKĀT

PĀKĀT	opacate, pacate
PLĀKĀT	placate
VĀKĀT	vacate

AKĀT

BAKĀT	baccate
PLAKĀT	placate
SAKĀT	saccate

AKBRĀND

| KRAKBRĀND | crackbrained |
| SLAKBRĀND | slackbrained |

FORGETFULNESS

It was a lovely love affair . . .
  One of those.
But who, or why, or when, or where,
  God knows.

AKBUT

| HAKBUT | hackbut |
| SAKBUT | sackbut |

AKCHER

FAKCHER	facture, manufacture
FRAKCHER	fracture
PAKCHER	compacture
TRAKCHER	contracture

ĀKDOUN

| BRĀKDOUN | breakdown |
| SHĀKDOUN | shakedown |

AKDOUN

| BAKDOUN | backdown |
| KRAKDOUN | crackdown |

ĀKĒ

ĀKĒ	achy, headachy
BRĀKĒ	braky
FĀKĒ	faky
FLĀKĒ	flaky
KĀKĒ	caky
KWĀKĒ	quaky
LĀKĒ	laky
SHĀKĒ	shaky
SLĀKĒ	slaky
SNĀKĒ	snaky
TRĀKĒ	traiky

AKĒ

BLAKĒ	blackie, blacky
HAKĒ	hacky
HWAKĒ	whacky
KAKĒ	khaki
KRAKĒ	gimcracky, cracky
KWAKĒ	quacky
LAKĒ	lackey
MAKĒ	maki
NAKĒ	knacky
RAKĒ	raki
SAKĒ	Nagasaki, sake, saki
TAKĒ	tacky, ticky-tacky
WAKĒ	wacky

ÄKĒ

| KÄKĒ | kaki, khaki, cocky |
| MÄKĒ | *theomachy* |

RÄKĒ	Iraqi
SÄKĒ	Nagasaki, sake, saki
YÄKĒ	sukiyaki, teriyaki

(See **OK,** add *-y* where appropriate; also see **OKĒ**.)

ĀKEN

BĀKEN	bacon
KRĀKEN	kraken
MĀKEN	Jamaican, Macon
SĀKEN	forsaken, Godforsaken, unforsaken
SHĀKEN	shaken, unshaken, wind-shaken
TĀKEN	mistaken, overtaken, taken, undertaken, untaken, uptaken
WĀKEN	awaken, reawaken, rewaken, waken

AKEN

BLAKEN	blacken
BRAKEN	bracken
KRAKEN	kraken
SLAKEN	slacken

ÄKEN

ÄKEN	Aachen
KRÄKEN	kraken
LÄKEN	Interlaken

ĀKER

ĀKER	acher, acre, fiacre stavesacre, wiseacre
BĀKER	baker
BRĀKER	backbreaker, braker, breaker, heartbreaker, housebreaker, icebreaker, jawbreaker, law-breaker, Sabbath-breaker, strikebreaker, tiebreaker, trucebreaker
FĀKER	faker, fakir
FLĀKER	flaker
KWĀKER	Quaker
LĀKER	laker, simulacre
MĀKER	boilermaker, bookmaker, dressmaker,

	haymaker,
	clockmaker,
	lawmaker, maker,
	matchmaker,
	pacemaker,
	peacemaker,
	shoemaker,
	troublemaker,
	watchmaker
NĀKER	nacre, naker
RĀKER	moonraker, raker
SĀKER	forsaker, saker
SHĀKER	boneshaker, shaker, Shaker
STĀKER	grubstaker, mistaker, painstaker, staker
TĀKER	caretaker, partaker, taker, undertaker
WĀKER	awaker, waker

AKER

AKER	coniaker
BAKER	backer
BLAKER	blacker
CHAKER	whinchacker
HAKER	hacker
HWAKER	bushwhacker, whacker
JAKER	hijacker
KLAKER	clacker
KRAKER	firecracker, clamcracker, corncracker, cracker, nutcracker
KWAKER	quacker
LAKER	lacker, lacquer, polacre
NAKER	knacker
PAKER	packer
RAKER	racker
SAKER	ransacker, sacker
SLAKER	slacker
SMAKER	smacker
SNAKER	snacker
STAKER	stacker
TAKER	attacker, tacker
THWAKER	thwacker
TRAKER	tracker
YAKER	yacker, yakker

AKET

BRAKET	bracket
FLAKET	flacket
HAKET	hurley-hacket
JAKET	bluejacket, jacket, leatherjacket, lumberjacket, redjacket, straitjacket, yellowjacket

KRAKET	cracket
NAKET	nacket
PAKET	packet
PLAKET	placket
RAKET	racket, rackett, racquet
SAKET	sacket
TAKET	tacket

ĀKIJ

BRĀKIJ	brakage, breakage
FLĀKIJ	flakage

AKIJ

PAKIJ	package
RAKIJ	wrackage
SAKIJ	sackage
STAKIJ	stackage
TRAKIJ	trackage

AKIK

AKIK	Noachic
BAKIK	bacchic
MAKIK	stomachic
SKAKIK	scacchic

ĀKING

(See ĀK, add -ing where appropriate.)

AKING

(See AK, add -ing where appropriate.)

ĀKISH

ĀKISH	achish
RĀKISH	rakish
SNĀKISH	snakish

AKISH

BLAKISH	blackish
BRAKISH	brackish
KWAKISH	quackish
NAKISH	knackish
SLAKISH	slackish

AKKLOTH

PAKKLOTH	packcloth
SAKKLOTH	sackcloth

AKL

AKL	*piacle*
BAKL	debacle
BRAKL	brackle
GRAKL	grackle
HAKL	hackle
JAKL	jackal
KAKL	cackle
KRAKL	crackle
KWAKL	quackle
MAKL	mackle, macle
NAKL	hibernacle, tabernacle
SHAKL	hamshackle, ramshackle, shackle, unshackle
SPAKL	spackle, Spackle
TAKL	tackle, retackle, untackle

AKLD

KAKLD	cackled

(See AKL, add -d where appropriate.)

AKLĒ

BLAKLĒ	blackly
KAKLĒ	cackly
KRAKLĒ	crackly
SHAKLĒ	ramshackly, shackly
SLAKLĒ	slackly
TAKLĒ	tackly

AKLER

HAKLER	hackler
KAKLER	cackler
KRAKLER	crackler
SHAKLER	hamshackler, shackler
TAKLER	tackler

ĀKLES

(See ĀK, add -less where appropriate.)

AKLES

(See AK, add -less where appropriate.)

AKLING

HAKLING	hackling
KAKLING	cackling
KRAKLING	crackling
SHAKLING	hamshackling, shackling
TAKLING	tackling

AKLOG

BAKLOG	backlog
HAKLOG	hacklog

AKMA

CHAKMA	chacma
DRAKMA	drachma, tetradrachma

ĀKMAN

BRĀKMAN	brakeman
KĀKMAN	cakeman

AKMAN

BLAKMAN	blackman
JAKMAN	jackman
PAKMAN	pac-man, packman

AKMĒ

AKMĒ	acme
LAKMĒ	Lakme
NAKMĒ	menacme

AKNĒ

AKNĒ	acne
HAKNĒ	hackney

AKNES

BLAKNES	blackness
SLAKNES	slackness

ĀKŌ

DRĀKŌ	Draco
KĀKŌ	macaco
MĀKŌ	mako
SHĀKŌ	shako
WĀKŌ	Waco

AKŌ

BAKŌ	tobacco
HWAKŌ	whacko
JAKŌ	jako
KAKŌ	icaco
RAKŌ	goracco
SHAKŌ	shako
SKWAKŌ	squacko
WAKŌ	wacko

ÄKŌ

CHÄKO	cheechako
GWÄKŌ	guaco
MÄKŌ	mako, makomako
NÄKŌ	guanaco
PÄKŌ	paco
TÄKŌ	taco, mataco

ĀKOF

RĀKOF	rakeoff
TĀKOF	takeoff

ĀKON

(See ĀKEN)

ĀKOUT

BRĀKOUT	breakout
SHĀKOUT	shakeout
STĀKOUT	stakeout
TĀKOUT	takeout

AKPOT

JAKPOT	jackpot
KRAKPOT	crackpot

ĀKRON

ĀKRON	Akron
DĀKRON	Dacron
MĀKRON	macron

ĀKRUM

LĀKRUM	simulacrum
SĀKRUM	sacrum, synsacrum

AKSĒ

BRAKSĒ	braxy
DAKSĒ	tachydidaxy
FLAKSĒ	flaxy
MAKSĒ	maxi
TAKSĒ	ataky, biotaxy, heterotaxy, homotaxy, geotaxy, taxi, eutaxy
WAKSĒ	waxy

AKSEN

AKSEN	axon, diaxon
DRAKSEN	dendraxon
FLAKSEN	flaxen
KAKSEN	caxon
KLAKSEN	klaxon
SAKSEN	Anglo-Saxon, Saxon
WAKSEN	waxen

AKSHUN

AKSHUN	*A* abreaction, action, affirmative action, *E* enaction, *I* inaction, interaction, *K* coaction, counteraction, covert action, *R* reaction, retroaction, *S* subaction, *TR* transaction
DAKSHUN	redaction
FAKSHUN	*B* benefaction, *D* dissatisfaction, *E* expergefaction, *F* faction, *K* calefaction, *L* labefaction, liquefaction, lubrifaction, *M* madefaction, malefaction, *P* petrifaction, putrefaction, *R* rarefaction, rubefaction, *S* satisfaction, *ST* stupefaction, *T* tabefaction, tepefaction, torrefaction, tumefaction
FRAKSHUN	diffraction, fraction, infraction, refraction
PAKSHUN	compaction, paction
STRAKSHUN	abstraction
TAKSHUN	contaction, taction
TRAKSHUN	attraction, detraction, distraction, extraction, contraction, counterattraction, protraction, retraction, subtraction, traction
ZAKSHUN	exaction

AKSHUS

FAKSHUS	factious
FRAKSHUS	fractious

AKSIS

AKSIS	axis
DAKSIS	pseudaxis
LAKSIS	anaphylaxis, prophylaxis
NAKSIS	synaxis
PRAKSIS	ideopraxis, chiropraxis, parapraxis, praxis, radiopraxis
STAKSIS	epistaxis, staxis
TAKSIS	phototaxis, hypotaxis, geotaxis, parataxis, taxis, thermotaxis

AKSMAN

KRAKSMAN	cracksman
TAKSMAN	tacksman

AKSON

(See AKSEN)

AKSTĀ

BAKSTĀ	backstay
JAKSTĀ	jackstay

AKTA

AKTA	acta
FAKTA	facta

AKTĀT

LAKTĀT	ablactate, lactate
TRAKTĀT	tractate

AKTED

(See AKT, add -ed where appropriate.)

AKTER

AKTER	acter, actor, bad actor, enacter, reenacter, reactor, transactor
BAKTER	abactor
DAKTER	redactor
FAKTER	benefactor, factor, malefactor, calefactor, olfactor
FRAKTER	diffractor, infractor, refractor
LAKTER	pylacter
MAKTER	climacter
PAKTER	compacter
PRAKTER	chiropractor
RAKTER	varactor
STRAKTER	abstractor
TAKTER	contactor, tactor
TRAKTER	attractor, distracter, extracter, extractor, contracter, contractor, protractor, retractor, subtracter, tractor, subcontractor
ZAKTER	exacter, exactor

AKTIK

DAKTIK	didactic
FRAKTIK	emphractic
LAKTIK	anaphylactic, extragalactic, phylactic, galactic, hylactic, catallactic, lactic, malactic, parallactic, prophylactic, circumgalactic
MAKTIK	anticlimactic, climactic
NAKTIK	synactic
PRAKTIK	chiropractic, practic
RAKTIK	ataractic
TAKTIK	atactic, heliotactic, protactic, syntactic, tactic

AKTIL

DAKTIL	adactyl, dactyl, didactyl, syndactyl, pterodactyl
FRAKTIL	fractile
TAKTIL	tactile
TRAKTIL	contractile, protractile, tractile

AKTING

(See AKT, add -ing where appropriate.)

AKTIV

AKTIV	active, enactive, photoactive, hyperactive, inactive, interactive, coactive, counteractive, overactive, radioactive, reactive, retroactive
FAKTIV	factive, calefactive, olfactive, petrifactive, putrefactive, rarefactive, satisfactive, stupefactive
FRAKTIV	diffractive, refractive
STRAKTIV	abstractive
TRAKTIV	attractive, detractive, distractive, extractive, contractive, protractive, retractive, subtractive, tractive, unattractive

AKTLĒ

BAKTLĒ	humpbackedly, hunchbackedly, stoopbackedly
FAKTLĒ	matter-of-factly
PAKTLĒ	compactly
STRAKTLĒ	abstractly
TAKTLĒ	intactly
ZAKTLĒ	exactly

AKTRES

AKTRES	actress
FAKTRES	benefactress, malefactress
ZAKTRES	exactress

AKTUM

AKTUM	actum
FAKTUM	factum

AKTŪR

(See AKCHER)

AKTUS

AKTUS	actus
KAKTUS	cactus
TAKTUS	tactus

ĀKUP

BRĀKUP	breakup
MĀKUP	makeup
WĀKUP	wake-up

AKUP

BAKUP	back-up

HWAKUP	whack-up
KRAKUP	crack-up

AKUS

BAKUS	Bacchus
FLAKUS	Flaccus
JAKUS	jacchus

AKWĀ

BAKWĀ	backway
PAKWĀ	packway
TRAKWĀ	trackway

AKWA

AKWA	aqua
MAKWA	namaqua
NAKWA	anaqua

AKWERD

AKWERD	bass-ackward
BAKWERD	backward, ass-backward

ĀLA

ĀLA	ala, Venezuela
CHĀLA	chela
GĀLA	gala
LĀLA	shillalah, shillelagh
MĀLA	kamala, mala
NĀLA	panela
SĀLA	osela
ZWĀLA	zarzuela

ÄLA

ÄLA	Allah, koala
BÄLA	gaballa, cabala, kabala, quabbalah
GÄLA	fala
HÄLA	hala
KÄLA	kala
MÄLA	Guatemala, kamala
PÄLA	impala
SÄLA	Marsala
TÄLA	patala, tala
WÄLA	chuckwalla, owala, pozzy-wallah, wallah, walla-walla

ALAD

BALAD	ballad
KALAD	calid
PALAD	impallid, pallid
SALAD	salad
VALAD	invalid, valid

ALANS

(See ALENS)

ĀLANT

(See ĀLENT)

ALAS

(See ALUS)

ALBA

ALBA	alba
BALBA	xibalba
GALBA	galba

ALA

ALA	alla, Allah, boobyalla
BALA	cabala
GALA	emagalla, gala, Galla
HALA	Valhalla
KALA	calla
PALA	palla, pallah
SHALA	inshala, mashalla
VALA	cavalla

ÄLA

ÄLA	Allah, koala
BÄLA	gaballa, cabala, kabala, quabbalah
GÄLA	gala
HÄLA	hala
KÄLA	kala
MÄLA	Guatemala, kamala
PÄLA	impala
SÄLA	Marsala

ALĀT

KALĀT	cal'late
VALĀT	obvallate

ĀLĒ

ĀLĒ	aly
BĀLĒ	bailey, bailie, Bali, Old Bailey

CHĀLĒ	tjaele
DĀLĒ	daily
FRĀLĒ	frailly
GĀLĒ	gaily
GRĀLĒ	grayly
HĀLĒ	halely
KĀLĒ	cellidh
KWĀLĒ	quaily, quale
LĀLĒ	pasilaly, shillala, shillelagh, ukulele
PĀLĒ	palely, pali, paly
RĀLĒ	Disraeli, Israeli, jus naturalae
SHĀLĒ	shaly
SKĀLĒ	scaly
SNĀLĒ	snaily
STĀLĒ	stalely
TĀLĒ	taily
TRĀLĒ	traily
VĀLĒ	vale
WĀLĒ	waily
YĀLĒ	Yalie

ALĒ

ALĒ	alley, bially
BALĒ	Bali, bally
DALĒ	dally, dillydally
GALĒ	Bengali, galley, gally, Svengali
HALĒ	Halley
KALĒ	Kali, Mexicali, teocalli
LALĒ	soapolallie
MALĒ	tamale, tomalley
PALĒ	pally
RALĒ	rally
SALĒ	sallee, sally
SHALĒ	challis, chally, shilly-shally
TALĒ	tally
VALĒ	travale, trevally, valley
WALĒ	peelie-wally, wally

ÄLĒ

ÄLĒ	Ali
BÄLĒ	Bali, bally
DÄLĒ	Dali
GÄLĒ	Bengali, galee, gali, galley, gally, gregale
HÄLĒ	ahali, tahali
KÄLĒ	Kali, Mexicali, triticale
MÄLĒ	hot tamale, Somali, tamale
NÄLĒ	finale
PÄLĒ	pali, Pali
RÄLĒ	pastorale

TÄLĒ   tali
VÄLĒ   vali, Vali

(See **OLĒ**)

ALĒD

DALĒD   dallied, dillydallied
RALĒD   rallied
SALĒD   sallied
SHALĒD   shilly-shallied
TALĒD   tallied

ĀLENS

SĀLENS   assailance
VĀLENS   *ambivalence,*
bivalence,
polyvalence,
pronovalence,
stasivalence,
supinovalence,
surveillance,
trivalence,
uxoravalence,
uxorovalence, valence

ALENS

BALENS   balance,
counterbalance,
outbalance,
overbalance,
unbalance
VALENS   pronovalence,
stasivalence,
supinovalence,
uxoravalence,
uxorovalence, valance

ĀLENT

HĀLENT   exhalant, inhalant
KĀLENT   intranscalent,
transcalent
SĀLENT   assailant
VĀLENT   *ambivalent,* bivalent,
divalent, monovalent,
polyvalent,
pronovalent,
stasivalent,
supinovalent,
surveillant, trivalent,
uxoravalent,
uxorovalent, valent,
univalent

ALENT

GALENT   gallant, stoopgallant,
topgallant, ungallant
TALENT   talent
VALENT   polyvalent,
pronovalent,
stasivalent,
supinovalent,
uxoravalent,
uxorovalent

ĀLER

ĀLER   alar
BĀLER   bailer, bailor, baler
HĀLER   hailer, inhaler,
loud-hailer
HWĀLER   whaler
KĀLER   *intercalar*
MĀLER   mailer, Mailer, malar
SĀLER   wholesaler, sailor
SKĀLER   scalar, scaler
SKWĀLER   squalor
TĀLER   retailer, tailor, talar
TRĀLER   housetrailer, trailer
WĀLER   waler, Waler

(See **ĀL**, add *-er* where appropriate.)

ALER

PALER   pallor
VALER   potvalor, valor

ÄLER

DÄLER   daler
HÄLER   haler
SKÄLER   scalar
SKWÄLER   squalor
TÄLER   taler
THÄLER   thaler

(See **OLER**)

ĀLES

(See **Ā**, **ĀL**, add *-less* where appropriate.)

ALET

BALET   ballot
GALET   gallet
KALET   callet
MALET   mallet
PALET   palate, palette, pallet

SALET   sallet
TALET   tallet
VALET   valet

ÄLET

SWÄLET   swallet
WÄLET   wallet

ALĒZ

VALĒZ   sherryvallies

(See **ALĒ**, change *-y* or *-i* to *-ies* where appropriate.)

ALFA

ALFA   alfa, alpha
FALFA   alfalfa
TALFA   pentalpha

ĀLFUL

ĀLFUL   ailful
BĀLFUL   baleful
PĀLFUL   pailful, paleful
TĀLFUL   taleful
WĀLFUL   wailful

ALID

(See **ALAD**)

ĀLIF

ĀLIF   alef, aleph
BĀLIF   bailiff, bumbailiff
KĀLIF   calif, caliph

ĀLIJ

BĀLIJ   bailage
HĀLIJ   haylage
SĀLIJ   sailage
SKĀLIJ   scalage
TĀLIJ   entailage, curtailage,
retailage
TRĀLIJ   treillage

ĀLIK

GĀLIK   Gaelic
MĀLIK   malic
SĀLIK   salic

ALIK

ALIK	smart-alec, wise-alec
BALIK	cabalic
DALIK	medallic, vandalic
FALIK	A acrocephalic, BR brachistocephalic, D dolichocephalic, E encephalic, F phallic, I ithyphallic, M macrencephalic, macrocephalic, mesophalic, microcephalic, P pacycephalic, PL platycephalic, S cephalic, Y eurycephalic
GALIK	Gallic, misogallic
GRALIK	grallic
KALIK	alkalic, intervocalic, prevocalic, vocalic
MALIK	malic
PALIK	rhopalic
RALIK	Uralic
SALIK	oxalic, salic
TALIK	bimetallic, italic, genitalic, metallic, monometallic, nonmetallic, tantalic
THALIK	thallic
VALIK	intervallic

ĀLIKS

KĀLIKS	epicalyx, calix, calyx
SALIKS	salix

ĀLING

(See ĀL, add -ing where appropriate.)

ALING

BALING	caballing
PALING	palling

ALIS

ALIS	allice, Alice
CHALIS	chalice
MALIS	malice
PALIS	palace
TALIS	digitalis

(See ALUS)

ĀLISH

FRĀLISH	frailish

PĀLISH	palish
SHĀLISH	shalish
STĀLISH	stalish

ALJA

(See AL'JI.A)

ALJĒ

ALJĒ	algae
LALJĒ	cephalalgy
RALJĒ	neuralgy
TALJĒ	nostalgy, odontalgy

ALJIK

ALJIK	algic
FALJIK	cephalgic
RALJIK	neuralgic
TALJIK	antalgic, nostalgic, odontalgic
TRALJIK	gastralgic

ĀLKÄR

MĀLKÄR	mail-car
RĀLKÄR	rail-car

ALMA

ALMA	alma, Alma
GALMA	agalma
HALMA	halma

ĀLMENT

ĀLMENT	ailment
BĀLMENT	bailment
GĀLMENT	regalement
HĀLMENT	exhalement, inhalement
PĀLMENT	impalement
RĀLMENT	derailment
SĀLMENT	assailment
TĀLMENT	entailment, curtailment
VĀLMENT	availment, prevailment
WĀLMENT	bewailment

ALMUD

ALMUD	almud
TALMUD	Talmud

ĀLNES

FRĀLNES	frailness
MĀLNES	femaleness, maleness
PĀLNES	paleness
STĀLNES	staleness

ĀLŌ

HĀLŌ	halo
NĀLŌ	canelo, Canelo

ALŌ

ALŌ	aloe
FALŌ	fallow
GALŌ	gallow
HALŌ	Allhallow, dishallow, hallow, unhallow
KALŌ	callow, mackalow
MALŌ	mallow, marshmallow
SALŌ	sallow
SHALŌ	shallow
TALŌ	tallow, talo

ÄLŌ

KÄLŌ	calo
LÄLŌ	lalo
MÄLŌ	malo
PÄLŌ	palo
SWÄLŌ	swallow
TÄLŌ	talo
WÄLŌ	hogwallow, wallow

(See OLŌ)

ALON

(See ALUN)

ALOP

(See ALUP)

ALPIN

ALPIN	Alpine
SPALPIN	Spalpeen

ALPING

PALPING	palping
SKALPING	scalping

ALSA

| BALSA | balsa |
| SALSA | salsa |

ALTŌ

ALTŌ	alto, Rialto
PALTŌ	paletot
TRALTŌ	contralto

ALUM

ALUM	alum
RALUM	chloralum
TALUM	catallum
VALUM	vallum

ALUN

GALUN	gallon
KALUN	kalon
SALUN	salon
TALUN	talon

ALUP

GALUP	gallop, galop
JALUP	jalap
SALUP	salep
SHALUP	shallop
SKALUP	escallop, scallop

ALUS

BALUS	aryballus, balas
DALUS	Dallas
FALUS	phallus
KALUS	callous, callus
PALUS	palace, Pallas
THALUS	thallous, thallus

(See ALIS)

ĀLYA

DĀLYA	dahlia, vedalia
FĀLYA	Westphalia
GĀLYA	galea, regalia
KĀLYA	cacalia
LĀLYA	barbaralalia, barylalia, echolalia, embolalia, eschrolalia, glossolalia, idiolalia, coprolalia, tachylalia

MĀLYA	mammalia
NĀLYA	Bacchanalia, marginalia, paraphernalia, saturnalia, terminalia
RĀLYA	psoralia
TĀLYA	genitalia, castalia
TRĀLYA	Australia, Centralia, penetralia
ZĀLYA	azalea

ĀLYAN

ĀLYAN	alien, marsupalian
DĀLYAN	Daedalian, hippomonstrosesqui-edalian, septipedalian, sesquipedalian
GĀLYAN	Phigalian, regalian
KĀLYAN	Deucalion
MĀLYAN	phantasmalian, mammalian, Pygmalion, tatterdemalion
NĀLYAN	bacchanalian, saturnalian, tenaillon, tobacconalian
PĀLYAN	episcopalian, Episcopalian
RĀLYAN	paralian
SĀLYAN	Messalian, universalian
THĀLYAN	thalian
TRĀLYAN	Australian, Centralian

(See Ā'LI.AN)

ĀLYÄRD

| JĀLYÄRD | gaolyard, jailyard |
| KĀLYÄRD | kailyard |

ĀLYŌ

| RĀLYŌ | seraglio |
| TĀLYŌ | intaglio |

ÄLYŌ

BÄLYŌ	caballo
RÄLYŌ	seraglio
TÄLYŌ	intaglio

ĀLYUN

(See ĀLYAN, ĀL'LI.AN)

ALYUN

DALYUN	medallion
PALYUN	rampallion
SKALYUN	rapscallion, scallion
STALYUN	stallion
TALYUN	battalion, Italian, rantallion

ĀLZMAN

DĀLZMAN	dalesman
HWĀLZMAN	whalesman
SĀLZMAN	salesman
TĀLZMAN	talesman

ĀMA

BRĀMA	Brahma
DĀMA	Aceldama
FĀMA	Fama
HĀMA	Bahama
KRĀMA	krama
LĀMA	lama
SKWĀMA	squama

AMA

AMA	amma
BAMA	Alabama
CHAMA	chamma
DRAMA	drama, docudrama, duodrama, melodrama, monodrama, psychodrama
GAMA	digamma, gamma
JAMA	pajama, pyjama
RAMA	D diorama, J georama, K cosmorama, M myriorama, N neorama, P panorama, panstereorama, polyorama, R Rama, ramarama, S cyclorama, cinerama

ÄMA

ÄMA	ama, amah
BÄMA	Alabama
BRÄMA	Brahma
DRÄMA	drama, duodrama, melodrama, monodrama, psychodrama

GRÄMA	grama
HÄMA	Bahama, Yokohama
JÄMA	jama, pajama, pyjama
KÄMA	caama, kaama, Kama
LÄMA	Dalai Lama, lama, llama, palama
MÄMA	mama, mamma
RÄMA	*D* diorama, *J* georama, *K* cosmorama, *M* myriorama, *N* neorama, *P* panorama, panstereorama, polyorama, *R* Rama, ramarama, *S* cyclorama, cinerama
SHÄMA	shama
YÄMA	Fujiyama, pranayama, Yama

ĀMAN

DĀMAN	dayman
DRĀMAN	drayman
HĀMAN	Haman, hayman
KĀMAN	caiman, cayman
LĀMAN	layman
SHĀMAN	shaman
WĀMAN	highwayman, railwayman

(See ĀMEN)

AMAN

(See AMUN)

ÄMAN

ÄMAN	*Amen*
BRÄMAN	Brahman, Parabrahman
SÄMAN	saman, zaman
SHÄMAN	shaman

ĀMANT

(See ĀMENT)

ĀMĀT

DĀMĀT	daymate
HĀMĀT	hamate
KWĀMĀT	desquamate, esquamate
PLĀMĀT	playmate
RĀMĀT	ramate
SKWĀMĀT	esquamate, squamate

AMBA

RAMBA	caramba
SAMBA	samba

AMBER

AMBER	amber, grisamber, liquidamber
KAMBER	camber
KLAMBER	clamber
SAMBER	sambar
TAMBER	tambour

AMBIK

AMBIK	elegiambic, galliambic, iambic, choliambic, choriambic, pythiambic
RAMBIK	dithyrambic

AMBIST

AMBIST	iambist
GAMBIST	gambist
KAMBIST	cambist

AMBIT

AMBIT	ambit
GAMBIT	gambit

AMBL

AMBL	amble, preamble
BRAMBL	bramble
FAMBL	famble
GAMBL	gamble, gambol
HAMBL	hamble
RAMBL	ramble
SHAMBL	shamble
SKAMBL	scamble, skimble-skamble
SKRAMBL	scramble, scrimble-scramble, unscramble
WAMBL	wamble

AMBLER

AMBLER	ambler
GAMBLER	gambler
RAMBLER	rambler
SHAMBLER	shambler
SKRAMBLER	scrambler
WAMBLER	wambler

AMBŌ

AMBŌ	ambo
FLAMBŌ	flambeau
JAMBŌ	jambeau
KRAMBŌ	crambo
MAMBŌ	mambo
SAMBŌ	sambo
ZAMBŌ	zambo

AMBUS

AMBUS	iambus
RAMBUS	dithyrambus

ĀMĒ

FLĀMĒ	flamy
GĀMĒ	gamy
MĀMĒ	cockamamy, cockamamie
RĀMĒ	rami
SĀMĒ	zemi

AMĒ

AMĒ	Miami
DAMĒ	damme
GAMĒ	gammy
HAMĒ	hammy
HWAMĒ	double-whammy, whammy
JAMĒ	jammy
KLAMĒ	clammy
MAMĒ	mammy
NAMĒ	bonami
RAMĒ	ramie, rammy
SAMĒ	sammy
SHAMĒ	chamois, shammy
TAMĒ	tamis, tammy
TRAMĒ	trammie

ÄMĒ

BÄMĒ	balmy
GÄMĒ	krigami, origami
JÄMĒ	jami
KÄMĒ	calmy, kami
KWÄMĒ	qualmy
LÄMĒ	palame, salami
MÄMĒ	malmy
NÄMĒ	tsunami
PÄMĒ	pahmi, palmy

| SWÄMĒ | swami |
| TRÄMĒ | pastrami |

(See OMĒ)

AMEL

KAMEL	camel
MAMEL	mammal
NAMEL	enamel
SKAMEL	scamell, scammel
STAMEL	stammel
TAMEL	Tamil
TRAMEL	entrammel, trammel

AMELD

(See **AMEL,** add *-ed.*)

ĀMEN

ĀMEN	*amen*
BRĀMEN	Bremen
DĀMEN	daimen, daimon
FLĀMEN	flamen
LĀMEN	laymen, velamen
NĀMEN	clinamen
RĀMEN	duramen, foramen
STĀMEN	stamen
TĀMEN	putamen
VĀMEN	gravamen
ZĀMEN	examen

(See **ĀMAN**)

ÄMEN

(See **ĀMAN**)

ĀMENT

ĀMENT	ament
FRĀMENT	defrayment
HĀMENT	adhamant
KLĀMENT	claimant, clamant, reclaimant
LĀMENT	allayment
PĀMENT	pament, payment, repayment
RĀMENT	raiment
TRĀMENT	betrayment

ĀMER

ĀMER	aimer, amor
BLĀMER	blamer
FĀMER	defamer, disfamer
FLĀMER	inflamer
FRĀMER	framer
GĀMER	gamer
KLĀMER	acclaimer, declaimer, disclaimer, exclaimer, claimer, proclaimer, reclaimer
LĀMER	lamer
MĀMER	maimer
NĀMER	misnamer, namer, nicknamer
SHĀMER	shamer
TĀMER	horsetamer, liontamer, tamer, testamur

AMER

DAMER	dammar, dammer, damner
DRAMER	mellerdrammer
GAMER	gammer
GLAMER	glamor, glamour
GRAMER	grammar, grammer, programmer
HAMER	hammer, jackhammer, ninny-hammer, sledgehammer, yellowhammer
JAMER	jammer, windjammer
KLAMER	clamor
KRAMER	crammer
LAMER	lamber, lammer
NAMER	enamor
RAMER	rammer
SHAMER	shammer
SKRAMER	scrammer
SLAMER	slammer
STAMER	stammer
YAMER	yammer

ÄMER

BÄMER	balmer, embalmer
KÄMER	calmer
PÄMER	palmer

AMFER

| CHAMFER | chamfer |
| KAMFER | camphor |

AMIJ

| DAMIJ | damage |
| RAMIJ | ramage |

AMIK

DAMIK	Adamic, pre-Adamic
GAMIK	agamic, epigamic, phanerogamic, gamic, homogamic, isogamic, monogamic, polygamic, syngamic
GRAMIK	engrammic, cryptogrammic, monogrammic, parallelogrammic, telegrammic, trigrammic
HAMIK	Abrahamic
LAMIK	epithalamic, Islamic, olamic
NAMIK	adynamic, aerodynamic, biodynamic, dynamic, electrodynamic, hydrodynamic, hyperdynamic, isodynamic, autodynamic, cinnamic, thermodynamic
RAMIK	dioramic, cosmoramic, panoramic, ceramic, cycloramic
SAMIK	balsamic
TAMIK	potamic

AMIKS

| NAMIKS | zoodynamics |

(See **AMIK,** add *-s* where appropriate.)

AMIL

| AMIL | amyl |
| TAMIL | tamil |

AMIN

AMIN	amin, amine
FAMIN	famine
GAMIN	gamin
LAMIN	lamin, prolamine
STAMIN	stamin
ZAMIN	examine, cross-examine, reexamine

ĀMING

(See **ĀM,** add *-ing* where appropriate.)

AMING

(See **AM,** add *-ming* where appropriate.)

ÄMING

BÄMING	embalming
KÄMING	calming
PÄMING	palming
WÄMING	walming

AMIS

AMIS	amice
KLAMIS	chlamys
NAMIS	dynamis
TAMIS	tamis

ĀMISH

LĀMISH	lamish
SĀMISH	Samish, samish
TĀMISH	tamish

AMISH

AMISH	Amish
FAMISH	affamish, enfamish, famish
KLAMISH	clammish
LAMISH	lambish
RAMISH	rammish

ÄMIST

BÄMIST	embalmist
PÄMIST	palmist
SÄMIST	psalmist

AML

(See **AMEL**)

ĀMLĒ

GĀMLĒ	gamely
LĀMLĒ	lamely
NĀMLĒ	namely
SĀMLĒ	samely
TĀMLĒ	tamely

ĀMLES

(See **ĀM,** add *-less* where appropriate.)

AMLES

(See **AM,** add *-less* where appropriate.)

ÄMLES

(See **ÄM,** add *-less* where appropriate.)

AMLET

HAMLET	hamlet, Hamlet
KAMLET	camlet
SAMLET	samlet

ÄMMENT

BÄMMENT	embalmment
KÄMMENT	becalmment

ĀMNES

GĀMNES	gameness
LĀMNES	lameness
SĀMNES	sameness
TĀMNES	tameness

AMOK

(See **AMUK**)

AMON

(See **AMUN**)

AMPA

GRAMPA	grampa
PAMPA	pampa
TAMPA	Tampa

FOOTNOTE TO THE SINKING OF ATLANTIS

When the praying mantis
Learned that Atlantis
    Was about to go down,
Not waiting for scanties
Or even for panties
    She hopped out of town.

AMPAN

JAMPAN	jampan
SAMPAN	sampan
TAMPAN	tampan

AMPAS

LAMPAS	lampas
PAMPAS	pampas

(See **AMPUS**)

AMPĒ

DAMPĒ	dampy
KRAMPĒ	crampy
SKAMPĒ	scampi
VAMPĒ	vampy

ÄMPĒ

(See **OMPĒ**)

AMPER

CHAMPER	champer
DAMPER	damper
HAMPER	hamper
KAMPER	camper
KLAMPER	clamper
KRAMPER	cramper
PAMPER	pamper, pampre
RAMPER	ramper
SKAMPER	scamper
STAMPER	stamper
TAMPER	tamper
TRAMPER	tramper
VAMPER	vamper

AMPERD

HAMPERD	hampered, unhampered
PAMPERD	pampered, unpampered
TAMPERD	tampered

AMPING

(See **AMP,** add *-ing* where appropriate.)

AMPISH

(See **AMP,** add *-ish* where appropriate.)

AMPL

AMPL	ample
SAMPL	ensample, sample
TRAMPL	trample
ZAMPL	example

AMPLD

SAMPLD	sampled
TRAMPLD	trampled
ZAMPLD	exampled

AMPLĒ

AMPLĒ   amply
DAMPLĒ   damply

AMPLER

(See **AMPL**, add -r where appropriate.)

AMPLING

SAMPLING   ensampling, sampling
TRAMPLING   trampling
ZAMPLING   exampling

AMPUS

GRAMPUS   grampus
KAMPUS   hippocampus, campus

(See **AMPAS**)

ÄMPUS

(See **OMPUS**)

AMSEN

DAMSEN   damson
KAMSEN   khamsin
RAMSEN   ramson
SAMSEN   Samson

(See **AMZUN**)

AMUK

HAMUK   hammock
DRAMUK   drammock
KAMUK   cammock
MAMUK   mammock

AMUN

AMUN   Ammon
DAMUN   daman
GAMUN   backgammon,
               gammon
MAMUN   mammon
SAMUN   salmon
SHAMUN   shaman

ĀMUS

DĂMUS   mandamus
FĂMUS   famous

HĀMUS   hamus
RĀMUS   biramous, ignoramus,
              ramous, ramus,
              uniramous
SHĀMUS   shamus
SKWĂMUS   squamous

AMUT

GAMUT   gamut
MAMUT   Mammut

AMZEL

AMZEL   amsel
DAMZEL   damsel
MAMZEL   ma'mselle

AMZUN

DAMZUN   damson
RAMZUN   ramson

(See **AMSEN**)

ĀNA

ĀNA   ana, fistiana,
              Jeffersoniana,
              Johnsoniana (etc.)
              nicotiana, omniana,
              poinciana
GĀNA   Cartagena
KĀNA   Americana (etc.),
              arcana, Cana
LĀNA   cantilena, Magdalena
MĀNA   vox humana
NĀNA   anana
PĀNA   campana
PLĀNA   geoplana
RĀNA   rena
SHĀNA   scena
TĀNA   Curtana, lantana

ANA

ANA   A ana, anna, Anna, D
              Diana, dulciana, F
              fistiana, G Guiana,
              goanna, I Indiana,
              ipecacuanha, J
              Georgiana,
              Jeffersoniana,
              Johnsoniana, N
              nicotiana, L liana,
              Louisiana, O
              Australiana, P
              poinciana, Pollyanna,

              R ruana, T tertiana,
              SH Shakespeariana,
              Victoriana (etc.)
BANA   Urbana
DANA   bandana, bandanna
HANA   Susquehanna
KANA   Americana, canna,
              Texarkana
LANA   alannah
MANA   manna
NANA   banana, nanna
TANA   lantana, Montana,
              sultana
VANA   Havana, savanna,
              Savannah
ZANA   hosanna

ÄNA

ÄNA   damiana, dulciana,
              fistiana, Guiana,
              Jeffersoniana,
              Georgiana,
              Johnsoniana, liana,
              Australiana,
              Shakespeariana,
              Victoriana
BÄNA   bana, Bana, ikebana
BWÄNA   bwana
DÄNA   apadana
GÄNA   Ghana, hagana,
              hiragana, nagana
GWÄNA   iguana
HWÄNA   marijuana
KÄNA   Americana (etc.),
              gymkhana, kana,
              katakana
LÄNA   pozzuolana
MÄNA   mana, manna, vox
              humana
NÄNA   anana, banana,
              cassabanana, zenana
PRÄNA   prana
RÄNA   kerana, piranha,
              purana, rana
SHÄNA   Rosh Hashanah
TÄNA   Curtana, lantana,
              Montana, sultana,
              Tana, tramontana
THÄNA   thana
VÄNA   Nirvana
WÄNA   marijuana, Tia Juana,
              Tijuana
YÄNA   dhyana, Guyana,
              Hinayane, Mahayna,
              mañana

ĀNAL

ĀNAL   anal
BĀNAL   banal

KĂNAL	decanal
MĂNAL	bimanal, manal, septimanal
VĂNAL	interveinal, veinal

ĀNĀT

LĀNĀT	lanate
PĀNĀT	impanate

ANĀT

KANĀT	khanate
TANĀT	tannate

ANCHĒ

BRANCHĒ	branchy
MANCHĒ	Comanche
RANCHĒ	ranchy

ÄNCHĒ

(See ÔNCHĒ)

ANCHER

(See ANCH, add -er where appropriate.)

ÄNCHER

LÄNCHER	launcher
STÄNCHER	stancher, stauncher

ANCHET

MANCHET	manchet
PLANCHET	planchet

ANCHING

(See ANCH, add -ing where appropriate.)

ÄNCHING

LÄNCHING	launching
STÄNCHING	stanching, staunching

ANCHLES

(See ANCH, add -less where appropriate.)

ÄNCHLES

(See ÄNCH, add -less where appropriate.)

ANDA

GANDA	propaganda, Uganda
PANDA	panda
RANDA	jacaranda, memoranda, veranda
TANDA	notanda
VANDA	observanda, vanda, Vanda

ANDĀD

BANDĀD	Band-Aid
HANDĀD	hand-aid

ANDAL

(see ANDL)

ANDBAG

HANDBAG	handbag
SANDBAG	sandbag

ANDBOI

BANDBOI	bandboy
SANDBOI	sandboy

ANDBOKS

BANDBOKS	bandbox
SANDBOKS	sandbox

ANDĒ

BANDĒ	bandy, bandy-bandy, onus probandi
BRANDĒ	brandy
DANDĒ	dandy, handy-dandy, jack-a-dandy, jim-dandy
GANDĒ	Ghandi
GLANDĒ	glandy
GRANDĒ	Rio Grande
HANDĒ	handy, unhandy
KANDĒ	discandy, candy, sugar-candy
PANDĒ	pandy
RANDĒ	jaborandi, randy
SANDĒ	sandy, sandhi
SHANDĒ	shandy, Shandy

ÄNDĒ

GÄNDĒ	Ghandi
GRÄNDĒ	Rio Grande

ANDĒD

BRANDĒD	brandied
KANDĒD	discandied, candied

ANDED

KANDED	candid

(See AND, add -ed where appropriate.)

ANDENT

KANDENT	candent
SKANDENT	scandent

ĀNDER

MĀNDER	remainder
TĀNDER	attainder, detainder

ANDER

ANDER	coriander, Leander, meander, oleander
BANDER	bander, disbander
BLANDER	blander
BRANDER	brander
DANDER	dander
GANDER	gander, goosey-gander
GLANDER	glander
GRANDER	grander
HANDER	backhander, forehander, hander, left-hander, right-hander
KANDER	Africander, candor
KLANDER	esclandre
LANDER	philander, Greenlander, Icelander, inlander, lander, Newfoundlander, outlander, solander, Uitlander
MANDER	demander, germander, gerrymander, calamander, commander, pomander, remander, reprimander, salamander, scamander
PANDER	expander, pandar, pander
RANDER	rander

SANDER	Alexander, goosander, Isander, sander
SLANDER	slander
STANDER	bystander, outstander, stander, understander, withstander
STRANDER	strander
TANDER	dittander
ZANDER	Alexander, zander

ÄNDER

LÄNDER	Jutlander, uitlander
SKWÄNDER	squander
WÄNDER	wander

(See ONDER)

ANDERD

(See ANDER, add -ed where appropriate.)

ANDERZ

| FLANDERZ | Flanders |
| GLANDERZ | glanders |

(See ANDER, add -s where appropriate.)

ANDĒZ

| ANDĒZ | Andes |
| NANDĒZ | Hernandes |

(See ANDĒ, change -y to -ies where appropriate.)

ANDIJ

BANDIJ	bandage
GLANDIJ	glandage
STANDIJ	standage

ANDIK

GANDIK	propagandic
LANDIK	Icelandic
SANDIK	sandik

ANDING

| SPANDING | expanding, mind-expanding |
| STANDING | notwithstanding, withstanding |

(See AND, add -ing where appropriate.)

ANDISH

BLANDISH	blandish
BRANDISH	brandish
LANDISH	outlandish
STANDISH	standish

(See AND, add -ish where appropriate.)

ANDIST

| BANDIST | contrabandist |
| GANDIST | propagandist |

ANDIT

| BANDIT | bandit |
| PANDIT | Pandit |

ANDL

DANDL	dandle
HANDL	Handel, handle, manhandle, mishandle, panhandle
KANDL	candle
PANDL	pandal, pandle
SANDL	sandal
SKANDL	scandal, scandle
VANDL	vandal

ĀNDLĒ

| BRĀNDLĒ | bird-brainedly |
| STRĀNDLE | restrainedly |

(See ĀND, add -ly where appropriate.)

ANDLĒ

| BLANDLĒ | blandly |
| GRANDLĒ | grandly |

ANDLER

CHANDLER	chandler
DANDLER	dandler
HANDLER	handler, manhandler, panhandler
KANDLER	candler

ANDLES

(See AND, add -less where appropriate.)

ANDLING

BRANDLING	brandling
HANDLING	handling, manhandling, mishandling
KANDLING	candling

ANDMENT

| BANDMENT | disbandment |
| MANDMENT | commandment, remandment |

ANDNES

| BLANDNES | blandness |
| GRANDNES | grandness |

ANDŌ

BANDŌ	bandeau
LANDŌ	landau
MANDŌ	commando

ÄNDO

DÄNDŌ	ritardando
LÄNDŌ	calando
MÄNDŌ	declamando, lacrimando
TÄNDŌ	allentando, lentando, recitando, ritando
TSÄNDŌ	scherzando

ANDON

(See ANDUN)

ANDRA

| MANDRA | mandra |
| SANDRA | Cassandra |

ANDRĒ

ANDRĒ	polyandry
DANDRĒ	pseudandry
MANDRĒ	commandry
SHANDRĒ	shandry

ANDRIN

| MANDRIN | salamandrine |
| ZANDRIN | Alexandrine |

ANDSTAND

BANDSTAND	bandstand
GRANDSTAND	grandstand
HANDSTAND	handstand

ANDUM

LANDUM	manipulandum
MANDUM	mandom
RANDUM	memorandum, nil desperandum, random
TANDUM	notandum, tandem
VANDUM	observandum
ZANDUM	avizandum

ANDUN

BANDUN	abandon
LANDUN	Alf Landon

ANDZMAN

BANDZMAN	bandsman
LANDZMAN	landsman

ĀNĒ

BRĀNĒ	brainy
GĀNĒ	Allegheny
GRĀNĒ	grainy
KĀNĒ	cany
LĀNĒ	castellany, miscellany
MĀNĒ	Khomeini, meinie
RĀNĒ	Ranee, rainy
SĀNĒ	Dunsany
VĀNĒ	veiny
ZĀNĒ	zany

ANĒ

BRANĒ	branny
GANĒ	Afghani
GRANĒ	granny
KANĒ	canny, kokanee, uncanny
KLANĒ	clanny
KRANĒ	cranny
MANĒ	mannie
NANĒ	hootenanny, nanny
PANĒ	frangipanni, tin-panny
SHANĒ	shanny

ÄNĒ

ÄNĒ	ani
DÄNĒ	jamdani

PRÄNĒ	soprani
RÄNĒ	guarani, Guarani, Maharanee, Maharani, ranee, rani
STÄNĒ	Hindustani, Pakistani
SWÄNĒ	Suwanee, Swanee, swanny

(See **ONĒ**)

ANEL

ANEL	annal
BRANEL	branle
CHANEL	channel
FLANEL	flannel, outing flannel, winter flannel
KANEL	cannel
PANEL	empanel, impanel, panel, unpanel
SKRANEL	scrannel
STANEL	stannel

ĀNER

MĀNER	mainour

(See **ĀN**, add -er where appropriate.)

ANER

MANER	manner, manor
SKANER	photoscanner, scanner
VANER	caravanner

(See **AN**, add -er where appropriate.)

ANERD

BANER	banner
BANERD	bannered, unbannered
MANERD	ill-mannered, mannered, unmannered, well-mannered

ĀNES

DĀNES	everydayness

(See **Ā**, add -ness where appropriate.)

ANET

GANET	gannet
GRANET	granite, pomegranate

KANET	cannet
KWANET	quannet
MANET	manit
PLANET	planet
VANET	vannet

(See **ANIT**)

ĀNFUL

BĀNFUL	baneful
DĀNFUL	disdainful, undisdainful
GĀNFUL	gainful, ungainful
PĀNFUL	painful, unpainful
PLĀNFUL	complainful, uncomplainful

ANGĒ

BANGĒ	bangy
FANGĒ	fangy
HWANGĒ	whangy
KLANGĒ	clangy
SHANGĒ	collieshangie
SLANGĒ	slangy
TANGĒ	tangy
TWANGĒ	twangy

ANGER

BANGER	banger
FRANGER	franger
GANGER	doppelganger, ganger
HANGER	hangar, hanger, cliffhanger, paperhanger, straphanger
HWANGER	whanger, slang-whanger
KLANGER	clanger, clangor
LANGER	languor

ANGGER

ANGGER	anger, angor
BANGGER	Bangor
KLANGGER	clangor
LANGGER	languor

ANGGL

ANGGL	angle, leeangle, sexangle, triangle
BANGGL	bangle
BRANGGL	brangle, embrangle
DANGGL	dangle, fandangle

FANGGL	fangle, newfangle
GANGGL	gangle
JANGGL	interjangle, jangle, jingle-jangle
KRANGGL	cringle-crangle
LANGGL	phalangal
MANGGL	bemangle, mangle, mingle-mangle
RANGGL	quadrangle, wrangle
SPANGGL	bespangle, spangle
SPRANGGL	sprangle
STRANGGL	strangle
TANGGL	disentangle, entangle, intertangle, tangle, untangle, pentangle, rectangle, septangle
TWANGGL	twangle
WANGGL	wangle

ANGGLD

FANGGLD	newfangled

(See **ANGGL**, add -*d* where appropriate.)

ANGGLĒ

BANGGLĒ	bangly
DANGGLĒ	dangly
GANGGLĒ	gangly
JANGGLĒ	jangly
RANGGLĒ	wrangly
SPANGGLĒ	spangly
SPRANGGLĒ	sprangly
STRANGGLĒ	strangly
TANGGLĒ	tangly

ANGGLER

(See **ANGGL**, add -*r* where appropriate.)

ANGGLING

(See **ANGGL**, add -*ing* where appropriate.)

ANGGŌ

BANGGŌ	bango
DANGGŌ	fandango
KWANGGŌ	quango
MANGGŌ	mango
PANGGŌ	Pago Pago, Pango Pango
TANGGŌ	contango, tango

ANGGWIJ

LANGGWIJ	body language, language
SLANGGWIJ	slanguage

ANGGWIN

ANGGWIN	anguine
SANGGWIN	ensanguine, exsanguine, consanguine, sanguine, unsanguine

ANGGWISH

ANGGWISH	anguish
LANGGWISH	languish

ANGING

(See **ANG**, add -*ing* where appropriate.)

ANGKA

BLANGKA	Casablanca
FRANGKA	lingua franca
RANGKA	barranca
SANGKA	Sanka
TANGKA	tanka

ANGKĒ

ANGKĒ	ankee
BANGKĒ	banky
HANGKĒ	hankie
KLANGKĒ	clanky
KRANGKĒ	cranky
LANGKĒ	lanky
PANGKĒ	hanky-panky
PLANGKĒ	planky
PRANGKĒ	pranky
SWANGKĒ	swanky
TANGKĒ	tanky
THANGĒ	thank'ee
TRANGKĒ	tranky
YANGKĒ	Yankee

ANGKER

ANGKER	anchor, re-anchor, unanchor, up-anchor
BANGKER	banker
BLANGKER	blanker
DANGKER	danker
FLANGKER	flanker, outflanker
FRANGKER	franker
HANGKER	hanker
KANGKER	canker, encanker
KLANGKER	clanker
KRANGKER	cranker
LANGKER	lanker
PLANGKER	planker
RANGKER	rancor, ranker
SHANGKER	chancre, shanker
SPANGKER	spanker
TANGKER	tanker
THANGKER	thanker
YANGKER	yanker

ANGKERD

ANGKERD	anchored
BRANGKERD	brancard
TANGKERD	tankard

ANGKET

BANGKET	banket, *banquette*
BLANGKET	blanket

ANGKFUL

PRANGKFUL	prankful
TANGKFUL	tankful
THANGKFUL	thankful, unthankful

ANGKING

(See **ANGK**, add -*ing* where appropriate.)

ANGKISH

(See **ANGK**, add -*ish* where appropriate.)

ANGKL

ANGKL	ankle
HANGKL	hankle
KRANGKL	crankle
RANGKL	rankle
TANGKL	tankle

ANGKLĒ

BLANGKLĒ	blankly
DANGKLĒ	dankly
FRANGKLĒ	frankly
LANGKLĒ	lankly
RANGKLĒ	rankly

ANGKLER

(See **ANGKL**, add -*er* where appropriate.)

ANGKLES

(See **ANGK,** add -less where appropriate.)

ANGKLING

(See **ANGKL,** add -ing where appropriate.)

ANGKNES

(See **ANGK,** add -ness where appropriate.)

ANGKŌ

BANGKŌ	banco, saltimbanco, scaldabanco
MANGKŌ	calamanco

ANGKRUS

KANGKRUS	cancrous
SHANGKRUS	chancrous

ANGLES

(See **ANG,** add -less where appropriate.)

ANGMAN

GANGMAN	gangman
HANGMAN	hangman

ANGRAM

PANGRAM	pangram
TANGRAM	tangram

ANGSTER

ANGSTER	angster
BANGSTER	bangster
GANGSTER	gangster
HANGSTER	hangster
SLANGSTER	slangster

ANGUP

BANGUP	bang-up
HANGUP	hang-up

ĀNIJ

CHĀNIJ	chainage

DRĀNIJ	drainage
KRĀNIJ	cranage
TRĀNIJ	trainage

ANIJ

KRANIJ	crannage
MANIJ	manage, mismanage
PANIJ	pannage

ANIK

ANIK	F ferricyanic, H hydrocyanic, I interoceanic, M Messianic, N neanic, O opianic, oceanic, Ossianic, S cyanic, TR transoceanic, V valerianic
BANIK	Abanic
FANIK	Aristophanic, diaphanic, phanic, lexiphanic, theophanic
GANIK	exorganic, homorganic, inorganic, cosmorganic, organic, paganic
KANIK	aeromechanic, mechanic, automechanic, volcanic, vulcanic
LANIK	Magellanic, melanic
MANIK	Brahmanic, Germanic, Indo-Germanic, manic, Mussulmanic, aldermanic, Romanic, talismanic
PANIK	Hispanic, panic, tympanic
RANIK	Iranic, Koranic, ranic, transuranic, tyrannic, uranic
STANIK	stannic
TANIK	B botanic, BR Britannic, KW quercitannic, M montanic, P puritanic, S satanic, sultanic, SH charlatanic, SP Spartanic, T tannic, tetanic, titanic, Titanic
VANIK	galvanic

ANIKS

KANIKS	mechanics
MANIKS	humanics
PANIKS	panics

ĀNĪN

KĀNĪN	canine
RĀNĪN	ranine

ĀNING

(See **ĀN,** add -ing where appropriate.)

ANING

(See **AN,** add -ing where appropriate.)

ĀNISH

BĀNISH	urbanish
DĀNISH	Danish
SĀNISH	sanish
VĀNISH	vainish

ANISH

BANISH	banish
FANISH	fannish
KLANISH	clannish
MANISH	mannish, Mussulmanish
PLANISH	plannish
RANISH	Alcoranish
SPANISH	Spanish
VANISH	evanish, revanish, vanish

ÄNISH

SWÄNISH	swannish
WÄNISH	wannish

ANIST

ANIST	Orleanist, pianist
PRANIST	sopranist
RANIST	Alcoranist
TANIST	tanist

ANIT

(See **ANET**)

ĀNJĒ

MĀNJĒ	mangy
RĀNJĒ	rangy

ANJENT

FRANJENT	bifrangent, frangent, refrangent
PLANJENT	plangent
TANJENT	cotangent, subtangent, tangent

ĀNJER

DĀNJER	danger
MĀNJER	manger

(See ĀNJ, add -r where appropriate.)

ANJEZ

FLANJEZ	flanges
GANJEZ	Ganges
LANJEZ	phalanges
RANJEZ	*oranges*

ĀNJING

(See ĀNJ, add -ing where appropriate.)

ĀNJLES

(See ĀNJ, add -less where appropriate.)

ĀNJLING

CHĀNJLING	changeling
STRĀNJLING	strangeling

ĀNJMENT

CHĀNJMENT	changement, exchangement, interchangement
RĀNJMENT	arrangement, derangement, disarrangement, prearrangement, rearrangement
TRĀNJMENT	estrangement

ĀNLĒ

(See ĀN, add -ly where appropriate.)

ANLĒ

MANLĒ	gentlemanly, manly, unmanly
SPANLĒ	spick-and-spanly

ĀNLES

(See ĀN, add -less where appropriate.)

ANLES

(See AN, add -less where appropriate.)

ANLING

MANLING	manling
TANLING	tanling

ĀNMENT

CHĀNMENT	enchainment
DĀNMENT	ordainment, reordainment
GĀNMENT	regainment
RĀNMENT	arraignment
TĀNMENT	ascertainment, attainment, detainment, entertainment, containment, obtainment, retainment

ĀNNES

DĀNNES	mundaneness

(See ĀN, add -ness where appropriate.)

ĀNŌ

DRĀNŌ	Drano
KĀNŌ	hurricano, volcano
RĀNŌ	sereno
YĀNŌ	ripieno

ANŌ

ANŌ	melopiano, piano, player piano
PRANŌ	mezzo-soprano, soprano

ÄNŌ

ÄNŌ	anno, melopiano, piano, player piano, pudiano
GRÄNŌ	grano
GWÄNŌ	guano
KÄNŌ	Americano, Chicano, Meccano, Norte-Americano
LÄNŌ	solano
MÄNŌ	mano, Romano
PLÄNŌ	altiplano
PRÄNŌ	mezzo-soprano, soprano
RÄNŌ	marrano
SÄNŌ	Montesano
YÄNŌ	castellano, llano
ZÄNŌ	Cinzano

ANOK

(See ANUK)

ANON

ANON	Rhiannon
FANON	fanon
KANON	Buchanan, calecannon, cannon, canon, colcannon, water cannon
SHANON	Balleyshannon, Shannon

ANSĒ

ANSĒ	antsy, recreancy
CHANSĒ	chancy, mischancy, unchancy
DANSĒ	*accordancy*, dancy, *discordancy*, *mordancy*, *redundancy*, *verdancy*
FANSĒ	fancy, *infancy*, sycophancy, unfancy
GANSĒ	arrogancy, elegancy, extravagancy, termagancy
KANSĒ	insignificancy, mendicancy, significancy, supplicancy
LANSĒ	petulancy, sibilancy, vigilancy
MANSĒ	*A* aeromancy, axinomancy, aldermancy, alectromancy, alectryomancy, alphitomancy, aleuromancy, anthracomancy, anthropomancy, astragalomancy, *B* belomancy, bibliomancy, botanomancy, *D*

dactyliomancy,
diathermancy, *E*
oenomancy,
enoptromancy, *F*
phyllomancy, *FL*
floromancy, *G*
gastromancy, *H*
halomancy,
hieromancy,
hydromancy, *I*
ydromancy,
ichthyomancy, *J*
geomancy,
gyromancy, *K*
chalcomancy,
capnomancy,
captromancy,
chartomancy,
catoptromancy,
chiromancy,
coscinomancy, *KL*
cleromancy, *KR*
crithomancy,
crystallomancy, *L*
lampadomancy,
lecanomancy,
lithomancy,
logarithmancy,
logarithmomancy, *M*
mazomancy,
meteoromancy,
metopomancy,
myomancy,
molybdomancy, *N*
necromancy,
necyomancy,
knissomancy, *O*
ophiomancy,
onychomancy,
onymancy,
onomancy, oomancy,
ornithomancy,
austromancy, *P*
pedomancy,
pyromancy,
podomancy, *R*
rhabdomancy,
rhapsodomancy,
retromancy, *S*
cephalomancy,
psephomancy,
selenomancy,
ceromancy,
sideromancy,
psychomancy,
sycomancy,
sciomancy,
pseudomancy, *SK*
scapulomancy,
scatomancy, *SP*
spasmatomancy,
spatilomancy,

spatulamancy,
spodomancy, *ST*
stichomancy,
stiganomancy, *T*
tephromancy,
tyromancy,
topomancy, *TH*
theomancy,
theriomancy, *TR*
trochomancy, *U*
uromancy, *Z*
xenomancy,
zygomancy,
xylomancy

(For additional words ending in *-mancy,* see Appendix B)

NANSĒ   dissonancy,
            consonancy,
            lieutenancy,
            predominancy,
            pregnancy,
            stagnancy, tenancy
PANSĒ   *discrepancy,*
            occupancy
PRANSĒ prancy
RANSĒ   *errancy,* exuberancy,
            preponderancy
STANSĒ *inconstancy,*
            constancy
TANSĒ   *A* accountancy,
            assistancy, E
            exorbitancy,
            expectancy,
            exultancy, H
            habitancy, hesitancy,
            I inhabitancy,
            irritancy, *M*
            militancy, *O*
            oscitancy, *PR*
            precipitancy
TRANSĒ recalcitrancy
VANSĒ   irrelevancy, relevancy
YANSĒ   *brilliancy*

ANSEL

CHANSEL chancel
HANSEL   handsel, Hansel
KANSEL   cancel

ANSER

ANSER   answer
CHANSER chancer
DANSER ballet dancer, belly
           dancer, bubble
           dancer, dancer, exotic
           dancer, fan dancer,
           hula dancer, modern
           dancer, tap dancer
GANSER merganser
GLANSER glancer
HANSER enhancer
KANSER cancer
LANSER lancer
MANSER geomancer,
           chiromancer,
           necromancer, romancer
PRANSER prancer
RANSER rancer
TRANSER entrancer
VANSER advancer

ANSHAL

NANSHAL financial, ganancial
STANSHAL insubstantial,
            substantial,
            supersubstantial,
            circumstantial,
            transubstantial,
            unsubstantial

ANSHUN

MANSHUN mansion
PANSHUN expansion, panchion
SKANSHUN scansion
STANSHUN stanchion
ZANSHUN Byzantian

ANSING

(See **ANS,** add *-ing* where appropriate.)

ANSIV

HANSIV enhancive
PANSIV expansive,
           inexpansive
VANSIV advancive

ANSMENT

HANSMENT enhancement
TRANSMENT entrancement
VANSMENT advancement,
             nonadvancement

ANSUM

HANSOM   handsome, hansom,
            unhandsome
RANSOM   ransom
TRANSOM transom

ANTA

ANTA	anta
DANTA	danta, Vedanta
FANTA	Infanta
LANTA	Atlanta
MANTA	manta
PLANTA	planta
SANTA	Santa

ÄNTA

DÄNTA	danta
FÄNTA	Infanta

ANTAL

(See ANTL)

ANTAM

(See ANTUM)

ĀNTĒ

DĀNTĒ	dainty
FĀNTĒ	fainty, feinty
RĀNTĒ	suzerainty

ANTĒ

ANTĒ	ante, anti, auntie, aunty, Chianti
BANTĒ	banty
DANTĒ	andante, Dante
FANTĒ	infante
KANTĒ	bacchante, canty
LANTĒ	vigilante
MANTĒ	diamante
NANTĒ	Rosinante
PANTĒ	panty
RANTĒ	durante, ranty
SANTĒ	Santy
SHANTĒ	chanty, shanty
SKANTĒ	scanty
SLANTĒ	slanty
TANTĒ	dilettante, dilettanti, concertante, tanti
ZANTĒ	zante

ÄNTĒ

ÄNTĒ	aunty, Chianti
DÄNTĒ	andante, Dante

ĀNTED

(See ĀNT, add -ed where appropriate.)

ANTED

(See ANT, add -ed where appropriate.)

ANTEN

KANTEN	canton
PLANTEN	plantain
SANTEN	santon

ĀNTER

FĀNTER	fainter, feinter
KWĀNTER	acquainter, quainter
PĀNTER	painter
TĀNTER	attainter, tainter

ANTER

BANTER	banter, Brabanter
CHANTER	chanter, disenchanter, enchanter
GRANTER	granter, grantor
KANTER	almucantor, canter, cantor, decanter, descanter, recanter, trochanter
PANTER	panter
PLANTER	implanter, planter, supplanter, transplanter
RANTER	ranter
SKANTER	scanter
SLANTER	slanter
STANTER	instanter
VANTER	Levanter

ANTĒZ

ANTĒZ	antis, aunties
BANTĒZ	banties, corybantes
KANTĒZ	bacchantes
LANTĒZ	atlantes
PANTĒZ	panties
SHANTĒZ	chanties, shanties
SKANTĒZ	scanties
TANTĒZ	dilettantes

ANTHER

ANTHER	anther
PANTHER	panther

ANTHIK

NANTHIK	oenanthic
ZANTHIK	xanthic

ANTHIN

ANTHIN	anthine
KANTHIN	acanthin, acanthine, tragacanthin
MANTHIN	Rhadamanthine

ANTHUS

ANTHUS	amianthus, dianthus, helianthus, polyanthus, Strophanthus
KANTHUS	acanthous, acanthus, anacanthous, canthus, oxyacanthous
LANTHUS	ailanthus, galanthus
MANTHUS	haemanthus
NANTHUS	ananthous, monanthous, synanthous
PANTHUS	agapanthus, epanthous
RANTHUS	hysteranthous
SANTHUS	chrysanthous
ZANTHUS	xanthous

ANTIJ

PLANTIJ	plantage
SHANTIJ	chantage
VANTIJ	advantage, disadvantage, vantage

ANTIK

ANTIK	antic, antick, reboantic
BANTIK	corybantic
DANTIK	pedantic, Vedantic
FANTIK	elephantic, hierophantic, sycophantic
FRANTIK	frantic
GANTIK	gigantic
LANTIK	Atlantic, cisatlantic, transatlantic
MANTIK	*H* hydromantic, *J* geomantic, *K* chiromantic, *M* mantic, *N* necromantic, *O* onomantic, *P* pyromantic, *R* romantic, *S* semantic, *SP* spodomantic, *TH* theomantic
NANTIK	consonantic

ANTĬN

BANTĬN	Brabantine
FANTĬN	elephantine, chryselephantine
MANTĬN	adamantine
VANTĬN	Levantine
ZANTĬN	Byzantine

ĀNTING

FĀNTING	fainting, feinting
KWĀNTING	acquainting, reacquainting
PĀNTING	painting, repainting

ANTING

(See ANT, add -ing where appropriate.)

ANTIS

LANTIS	Atlantis
MANTIS	mantis, praying mantis

ĀNTISH

FĀNTISH	faintish
SĀNTISH	saintish

ANTIST

DANTIST	Vedantist
RANTIST	ignorantist, noncurantist
TANTIST	dilettantist

ÄNTIST

DÄNTIST	Vedantist
KÄNTIST	Kantist
RÄNTIST	Esperantist
TÄNTIST	dilettantist

ĀNTIV

PLĀNTIV	complaintive, plaintive
STRĀNTIV	constraintive

ANTIZM

KANTIZM	Kantism
RANTIZM	ignorantism, obscurantism, rantism
TANTIZM	dilettantism

ANTL

ANTL	antal
GANTL	gigantal
KANTL	cantle
LANTL	Atlantal
MANTL	dismantle, immantle, mantel, mantle, overmantle
NANTL	consonantal
RANTL	quadrantal

ANTLD

MANTLD	dismantled, mantled
SKANTLD	scantled

ĀNTLĒ

FĀNTLĒ	faintly, unfaintly
KWĀNTLĒ	quaintly, unquaintly
SĀNTLĒ	saintly, unsaintly

ANTLĒ

LANTLĒ	*gallantly*
SKANTLĒ	scantly
SLANTLĒ	aslantly, slantly

ANTLER

ANTLER	antler
MANTLER	dismantler, mantler
PANTLER	pantler

ANTLET

GANTLET	gantlet
KANTLET	cantlet
MANTLET	mantelet, mantlet
PLANTLET	plantlet

ANTLING

BANTLING	bantling
FRANTLING	frantling
MANTLING	mantling, dismantling
PLANTLING	plantling
SKANTLING	scantling

ĀNTNES

FĀNTNES	faintness
KWĀNTNES	quaintness

ANTŌ

KANTŌ	canto
MANTŌ	manteau, portmanteau
PANTŌ	panto
RANTŌ	Esperanto

ÄNTŌ

KÄNTŌ	canto
MÄNTŌ	portmanteau
RÄNTŌ	coranto, Esperanto
TÄNTŌ	allegro non tanto, pro tanto, tanto

ANTON

(See ANTEN)

ANTRĒ

CHANTRĒ	chantry
GANTRĒ	gantry
PANTRĒ	pantry

ANTRUM

ANTRUM	antrum
PANTRUM	hypantrum
TANTRUM	tantrum

ANTUM

ANTUM	Antum, adiantum
BANTUM	bantam
FANTUM	phantom

ĀNUM

KĀNUM	arcanum
LĀNUM	solanum

ANUK

BANUK	bannock
JANUK	jannock

ANUN

(See ANON)

ĀNUS

ĀNUS	anus
DĀNUS	pandanus

HĀNUS	heinous
JĀNUS	Janus
KĀNUS	incanous
LĀNUS	Coriolanus, parabolanus
MĀNUS	*bimanous, longimanous,* manus
VĀNUS	Silvanus, veinous

ĀNWURK

BRĀNWURK	brainwork
CHĀNWURK	chainwork
PLĀNWURK	plainwork

ANYAN

(See ANYUN)

ANYEL

DANYEL	Daniel
SPANYEL	field spaniel, spaniel, springer spaniel, toy spaniel, water spaniel

ANYERD

LANYERD	lanyard
SPANYERD	Spaniard

ANYUN

BANYUN	banian, banyan
FANYUN	fanion
FRANYUN	franion
KANYUN	cañon, canyon
PANYUN	companion

ANZA

ANZA	nyanza
GANZA	extravaganza, ganza, organza
GRANZA	granza
KWANZA	kwanza
NANZA	bonanza
STANZA	stanza
TANZA	matanza

ANZĒ

GANZĒ	ganzie
PANZĒ	chimpanzee, pansy
TANZĒ	tansy

ĀŌ

KĀŌ	cacao, K.O., kayo
MĀŌ	County Mayo, mayo
TRĀŌ	tetrao

ÄŌ

ÄŌ	ao
BÄŌ	carabao
DÄŌ	dao
KÄŌ	cacao, macao
LÄŌ	talao
NÄŌ	Mindanao
RÄŌ	karao, tarao
TÄŌ	tao

ĀON

KĀON	Lycaon
KRĀON	crayon
RĀON	rayon

ĀOR

(See ĀER)

ĀOS

KĀOS	chaos
LĀOS	Laos
NĀOS	epinaos, naos, pronaos
TĀOS	Taos

APA

KAPA	kappa, Kappa
LAPA	lappa

ÄPA

ÄPA	apa
HÄPA	jipijapa
KÄPA	capa, kapa, koppa
NÄPA	anapanapa
PÄPA	papa
TÄPA	tapa

APCHER

KAPCHER	capture, manucapture, recapture
RAPCHER	enrapture, rapture

ĀPĒ

GĀPĒ	gapy
KRĀPĒ	crapy, crepy
SKRĀPĒ	scrapy
TĀPĒ	red-tapy, tapy

APĒ

CHAPĒ	chappie, chappy
FLAPĒ	flappy
GAPĒ	gappy, gapy
HAPĒ	happy, slaphappy, unhappy
KAPĒ	cappy
KRAPĒ	crappie, crappy
MAPĒ	mappy
NAPĒ	knappy, nappy, shaganappi, shaganappy
PAPĒ	pappy
RAPĒ	serape
SAPĒ	sappy
SKRAPĒ	scrappy
SNAPĒ	snappy
TRAPĒ	trappy
YAPĒ	yappy

ÄPĒ

HÄPĒ	Hapi
KÄPĒ	okapi
RÄPĒ	serape

ĀPEN

SHĀPEN	misshapen, shapen, unshapen
TĀPEN	tapen

APEN

HAPEN	happen
LAPEN	lapin

ĀPER

ĀPER	aper
DRĀPER	draper, undraper
GĀPER	gaper
KĀPER	escaper, caper, nordcaper
PĀPER	endpaper, flypaper, newspaper, notepaper, paper, repaper, sandpaper, tarpaper, wallpaper

RĀPER

RĀPER	raper
SĀPER	sapor
SHĀPER	misshaper, reshaper, shaper
SKĀPER	landscaper
SKRĀPER	skyscraper, scraper
TĀPER	taper, tapir, red-taper
VĀPER	vapor

APER

CHAPER	chapper
DAPER	dapper, didapper
GAPER	gaper
KAPER	capper, handicapper
KLAPER	clapper, shoulderclapper
LAPER	lapper, overlapper
MAPER	mapper
NAPER	kidnapper, knapper, napper
RAPER	enwrapper, rapper, wrapper, unwrapper
SAPER	sapper
SKRAPER	scrapper
SLAPER	backslapper, slapper
SNAPER	whippersnapper, red snapper, snapper, snippersnapper
STRAPER	strapper, understrapper, unstrapper
TAPER	tapper, wiretapper
TRAPER	entrapper, trapper
YAPER	yapper
ZAPER	zapper

ÄPER

SWÄPER	swapper

(See OPER)

APET

LAPET	lappet
SKRAPET	scrappet
TAPET	tappet

APID

RAPID	rapid
SAPID	sapid
VAPID	vapid

APIJ

LAPIJ	lappage
RAPIJ	wrappage
SKRAPIJ	scrappage

APIN

(See APEN)

ĀPING

ĀPING	aping
DRĀPING	draping
GĀPING	gaping
KĀPING	escaping
PĀPING	Peiping
RĀPING	raping
SHĀPING	misshaping, reshaping, shaping
SKĀPING	landscaping
SKRĀPING	scraping, skyscraping
TĀPING	retaping, taping

ÄPING

(See OP, add -ing where appropriate.)

ĀPIS

ĀPIS	Apis, priapus
LĀPIS	lapis
NĀPIS	sinapis
TĀPIS	tapis

APIS

LAPIS	lapis
PAPIS	pappus
TAPIS	tapis
TRAPIS	trappous

ĀPISH

ĀPISH	apish
GĀPISH	gapish
PĀPISH	papish
TĀPISH	red-tapish, tapish

APISH

GAPISH	gappish
SNAPISH	snappish
YAPISH	yappish

ĀPIST

KĀPIST	escapist
PĀPIST	papist
RĀPIST	rapist
SKĀPIST	landscapist
TĀPIST	tapist, red-tapist

APIST

MAPIST	mappist
TRAPIST	Trappist

ĀPIZM

ĀPIZM	apism
KĀPIZM	escapism
PĀPIZM	papism
TĀPIZM	red-tapism

ĀPL

KĀPL	capel
MĀPL	maple
PĀPL	antipapal, nonpapal, papal, unpapal
STĀPL	staple, unstaple, woolstaple

APL

APL	apple, Big Apple, loveapple, crabapple, pineapple
CHAPL	antechapel, chapel, Whitechapel
DAPL	dapple
GRAPL	grapple
KAPL	capple
NAPL	knapple
SKAPL	scapple
SKRAPL	scrapple
THRAPL	thrapple

ĀPLES

(See ĀP, add -less where appropriate.)

APLES

(See AP, add -less where appropriate.)

ĀPLET

ĀPLET	apelet
GRĀPLET	grapelet
KĀPLET	capelet

APLET

CHAPLET	chaplet
STAPLET	staplet
STRAPLET	straplet
TAPLET	taplet

APLING

DAPLING	dappling
GRAPLING	grappling
LAPLING	lapling
SAPLING	sapling

ĀPLZ

MĀPLZ	maples
NĀPLZ	Naples
STĀPLZ	staples, woolstaples

APNEL

GRAPNEL	grapnel
SHRAPNEL	shrapnel

ÄPŌ

ÄPŌ	quiapo
GWÄPŌ	guapo
KÄPŌ	capo
SWÄPŌ	swapo

ĀPRUN

ĀPRUN	apron
NĀPRUN	napron

APSHUN

KAPSHUN	caption, manucaption, recaption, usucaption
LAPSHUN	elapsion, collapsion
TRAPSHUN	contraption

APTER

APTER	apter
CHAPTER	chapter
DAPTER	adapter
KAPTER	captor, manucaptor, recaptor
RAPTER	rapter, raptor

APTEST

APTEST	aptest, inaptest
BAPTEST	Anabaptist, Baptist

APTIV

DAPTIV	adaptive, unadaptive
KAPTIV	captive

APTLĒ

APTLĒ	aptly, inaptly
RAPTLĒ	raptly

APTNES

APTNES	aptness, inaptness, unaptness
RAPTNES	raptness

ĀPUS

(See ĀPIS)

APUS

(See APIS)

ÂRA

ÂRA	Eire
BÂRA	capybara
DÂRA	madeira, caldera
HÂRA	Sahara
KÂRA	cascara, mascara
MÂRA	dulcamara, Mara, samara
PÂRA	para
RÂRA	siserara
VÂRA	vara

ÄRĀ

KÄRĀ	ricercaré
SWÄRĀ	soireé

ARA

ARA	tiara
KARA	cascara, mascara
KLARA	Santa Clara
PARA	*nullipara, primipara*
TARA	tantara, tarantara

ÄRA

ÄRA	tiara, ziara
BÄRA	capybara
DWÄRA	gurdwara
GÄRA	fugara
HÄRA	Guadelajara, Sahara, vihara
KÄRA	cara, caracara, sakkara
KLÄRA	Santa Clara
MÄRA	Gemara, Mara

NÄRA (continued)

NÄRA	kanara, carbonara, marinara, narra, sayonara
PÄRA	apara
RÄRA	Ferrara
TÄRA	chitarra, solfatara, tantara, tarantara, tuatara
VÄRA	vara

ARAB

ARAB	Arab
SKARAB	scarab

ARAK

ARAK	arrack
BARAK	barrack
KARAK	carack, carrack

ÂRANS

(See ÂRENS)

ARANT

ARANT	arrant
PARANT	apparent, nontransparent, parent, step-parent, transparent, unapparent

ARAS

ARAS	arras
BARAS	barras, debarrass, disembarrass, embarrass
HARAS	harass
NARAS	naras
PARAS	nonparous, Paris, parous

ÂRBEL

HÂRBEL	harebell
PRÂRBEL	prayerbell

ÄRBEL

BÄRBEL	barbel, barbell
KÄRBEL	carbell

ÄRBER

ÄRBER	arbor, Ann Arbor
BÄRBER	barber
HÄRBER	enharbor, harbor, unharbor

ÄRBERD

ÄRBERD	arbored
HÄRBERD	harbored
JÄRBERD	jarbird
KÄRBERD	carboard
LÄRBERD	larboard
STÄRBERD	starboard

ÄRBL

GÄRBL	garble
JÄRBL	jarble
MÄRBL	enmarble, marble

ÄRBLER

GÄRBLER	garbler
MÄRBLER	marbler

ÄRBLING

GÄRBLING	garbling
MÄRBLING	marbling

ÄRBON

KÄRBON	hydrocarbon, carbon
SHÄRBON	charbon

ÄRBOR

(See ÄRBER)

ÄRBORD

(See ÄRBERD)

ÄRCHĒ

ÄRCHĒ	archy
LÄRCHĒ	larchy
STÄRCHĒ	starchy

ÄRCHER

ÄRCHER	archer
MÄRCHER	marcher

PÄRCHER	parcher
STÄRCHER	starcher

ÄRCHING

(See ÄRCH, add -ing where appropriate.)

ÄRCHMENT

ÄRCHMENT	archment
PÄRCHMENT	parchment

ÄRDANT

(See ÄRDENT)

ÄRDĒ

BÄRDĒ	bardy
FÄRDĒ	Sephardi
HÄRDĒ	foolhardy, hardy
LÄRDĒ	lardy
TÄRDĒ	tardy

ÄRDED

(See ÄRD, add -ed where appropriate.)

ÄRDEL

BÄRDEL	bardel
FÄRDEL	fardel
KÄRDEL	cardel
SÄRDEL	sardel, sardelle

ÄRDEN

BÄRDEN	bombardon
GÄRDEN	garden, flower garden, vegetable garden
HÄRDEN	enharden, harden, caseharden, weatherharden
PÄRDEN	pardon

ÄRDEND

(See ÄRDEN, add -ed where appropriate.)

ÄRDENT

ÄRDENT	ardent, unardent
GÄRDENT	gardant, guardant, regardant
TÄRDENT	retardant

ÄRDER

ÄRDER	ardor
BÄRDER	bombarder
GÄRDER	disregarder, guarder, regarder
HÄRDER	harder
KÄRDER	discarder, false-carder, carder, wool carder
LÄRDER	larder
TÄRDER	retarder

ÄRDIK

BÄRDIK	bardic, Lombardic
KÄRDIK	anacardic, pericardic

ÄRDING

(See ÄRD, add -ing where appropriate.)

ÄRDLES

GÄRDLES	guardless, regardless
KÄRDLES	cardless
LÄRDLES	lardless
YÄRDLES	yardless

ÄRDMENT

BÄRDMENT	bombardment
TÄRDMENT	retardment

ÄRDNER

GÄRDNER	gardener
HÄRDNER	hardener
PÄRDNER	pardner, pardoner

ÄRDNING

GÄRDNING	gardening
HÄRDNING	hardening
PÄRDNING	pardoning

ÄRDON

(See ARDEN)

ÄRDSHIP

GÄRDSHIP	guardship
HÄRDSHIP	hardship

ÂRDUM

ÂRDUM   heirdom
STÂRDUM   backstairdom

ÄRDUN

(See ÄRDEN)

ÂRĒ

ÂRĒ   *A* accidentiary,
actuary, aerie, airy,
ary, eyrie, *B*
beneficiary, *E*
estuary, *F* February,
fiduciary, *I*
incendiary,
intermediary, *J*
January, *KW*
questuary, *M*
mortuary, *N* natuary,
noctuary, nucleary, *O*
obituary, ossuary,
ostiary, *P* pecuniary,
R residuary, retiary,
ruptuary, *S* sanctuary,
silentiary, subsidiary,
sumptuary, *SKR*
scriniary, *ST* statuary,
stipendiary, *T*
tertiary, topiary,
tumultuary, *V*
voluptuary

BÂRĒ   columbary, syllabary
BLÂRĒ   blary
CHÂRĒ   chary, unchary
DÂRĒ   dairy, dromedary,
hebdomadary,
quandary, lapidary,
legendary,
prebendary,
secondary
FÂRĒ   airy-fairy, faerie,
fairy
FLÂRĒ   flary
GÂRĒ   vagary
GLÂRĒ   glairy, glary
HÂRĒ   hairy, unhairy
KÂRĒ   apothecary,
formicary,
hypothecary,
persicary
KLÂRĒ   clary
KWÂRĒ   antiquary, reliquary
LÂRĒ   *A* adminiculary,
axillary, ancillary, *B*
bacillary, *E*
epistolary, *F*
formulary, *K*
capillary,

MÂRĒ   constabulary,
corollary, *L* lairy, *M*
maxillary,
mammillary,
medullary, *O* obolary,
P patibulary, *SK*
scapulary, *T* titulary,
tumulary, tutelary, *V*
vocabulary
accustomary, Ave
Mary, calamary,
customary,
lachrymary, mary,
rosemary

NÂRĒ   *A* ablutionary,
abolitionary,
additionary, *B*
bicentenary, *D*
dictionary,
disciplinary,
discretionary,
divisionary,
doctrinary, *E*
extraordinary,
eleemosynary,
elocutionary,
evolutionary, *F*
functionary, *G*
ganglionary, *I*
imaginary,
insurrectionary, *K*
canary,
confectionary,
confectionery,
consuetudinary,
coparcenery,
coronary, cautionary,
culinary, *KW*
questionary, *L*
latitudinary,
legionary, luminary,
M mercenary,
millinary, millinery,
missionary,
multitudinary, *N*
nary, *O* ordinary, *P*
parcenary,
passionary,
pensionary,
petitionary, popinary,
pulmonary, *PR*
precautionary,
preliminary,
probationary,
prolegomenary,
provisionary, *R*
reactionary,
reversionary,
revisionary,
revolutionary, *S*
sanguinary,
seditionary, seminary,

centenary, sublunary,
ST stationary,
stationery, *T*
tutionary, *TR*
traditionary, *V*
valetudinary,
veterinary, vicenary,
vicissitudinary,
visionary

PRÂRĒ   prairie
RÂRĒ   extemporary,
itinerary, contemporary,
literary, honorary,
supernumerary,
temporary, Tipperary,
vulnerary
SÂRĒ   necessary, unnecessary
SKÂRĒ   scary
SNÂRĒ   snary
STÂRĒ   stary
TÂRĒ   *D* depositary, dietary,
dignitary,
distributary, *FR*
fragmentary, *H*
hereditary, *K*
commentary,
contributary, *M*
military, momentary,
monetary, *PL*
planetary, *PR*
proletary, proprietary,
prothonotary, *S*
salutary, sanitary,
sedentary, secretary,
circumplanetary,
solitary, *TR* tributary,
U ubiquitary, *V*
voluntary
TRÂRĒ   arbitrary, contrary
VÂRĒ   salivary, vairy, vary
WÂRĒ   cassowary, unwary,
wary

(See ERĒ)

ARĒ

GARĒ   gharry
HARĒ   harry
KARĒ   hari-kari, carry,
miscarry
MARĒ   intermarry, marry,
remarry, unmarry
PARĒ   pari, parry
TARĒ   tarry

ÄRĒ

BÄRĒ   Bari, Karharbari
CHÄRĒ   charry

HÄRĒ	mehari
KÄRĒ	harikari, uakari
LÄRĒ	lari
NÄRĒ	Carbonari
PÄRĒ	pari
RÄRĒ	curare
SÄRĒ	aracari
SKÄRĒ	scarry
STÄRĒ	starry
TÄRĒ	tarry
VÄRĒ	charivari

AREL

AREL	aril
BAREL	barrel, beer barrel, pork barrel
KAREL	carol, carrel
PAREL	apparel, disapparel, parral, parrel

ARELD

HARELD	Harold
BARELD	barreled, double-barreled

(See **AREL,** add -ed where appropriate.)

ÂREM

(See **ÂRUM**)

AREM

(See **ARUM**)

ÂRENS

BÂRENS	bearance, forbearance
PÂRENS	apparence, parents, transparence

ÂRENT

BÂRENT	forbearant
KLÂRENT	declarent
LÂRENT	celarent
PÂRENT	apparent, parent

ÂRER

ÂRER	airer
BÂRER	armor bearer, barer, bearer, forbearer, cupbearer, macebearer, overbearer, pallbearer, swordbearer, standard-bearer, tale-bearer
BLÂRER	blarer
DÂRER	darer, outdarer
FÂRER	fairer, farer, seafarer, unfairer, wayfarer
FLÂRER	flarer
KÂRER	carer, uncarer
KLÂRER	declarer
PÂRER	despairer, impairer, pairer, parer, preparer, repairer
RÂRER	rarer
SHÂRER	sharer
SKÂRER	scarer
SKWÂRER	squarer
SNÂRER	ensnarer, snarer
SPÂRER	sparer
STÂRER	starer
SWÂRER	swearer
TÂRER	tearer
WÂRER	awarer, wearer

(See **ERER**)

ARET

GARET	garret
KARET	carat, caret, carrot
KLARET	claret
PARET	parrot

ÂRĒZ

ÂRĒZ	Ares, Aries, Buenos Aires
KÂRĒZ	caries
LÂRĒZ	lares

(See **ÂRĒ,** add -s or change -y to -ies where appropriate.)

ÂRFĀST

BÂRFĀST	barefaced
FÂRFĀST	fair-faced

ÄRFISH

BÄRFISH	barfish
GÄRFISH	garfish, cigarfish
STÄRFISH	starfish
TÄRFISH	guitarfish

ÂRFUL

DÂRFUL	dareful
KÂRFUL	careful, uncareful
PÂRFUL	despairful
PRÂRFUL	prayerful, unprayerful

ÄRGL

ÄRGL	argal, argol, argle-bargle
GÄRGL	gargle

ÄRGŌ

ÄRGŌ	Argo, argot
BÄRGŌ	embargo
FÄRGŌ	Wells Fargo
KÄRGŌ	cargo, supercargo
LÄRGŌ	largo
PÄRGO	pargo
SÄRGO	sargo
TÄRGO	botargo

ÄRGON

ÄRGON	argon
JÄRGON	jargon

ARID

ARID	arid
LARID	Polarid

ARIF

HARIF	harif
TARIF	tariff

ARIJ

GARIJ	garage
KARIJ	carriage, miscarriage, undercarriage
MARIJ	intermarriage, marriage, remarriage
PARIJ	disparage

ARIK

ARIK	Balearic, stearic
BARIK	barbaric, baric, hyperbaric, isobaric, centrobaric, cinnabaric

DARIK   daric, Pindaric
GARIK   agaric, Bulgaric, margaric, Megaric
KARIK   saccharic
LARIK   polaric
MARIK   pimaric
TARIK   tartaric

ÂRING

(See **ÂR,** add -*ing* where appropriate.)

ÄRING

(See **ÄR,** add -*ing* where appropriate.)

ARINGKS

FARINGKS   pharynx
LARINGKS   larynx

ÂRIS

LÂRIS   polaris
NÂRIS   naris

ARIS

ARIS   arris
BARIS   baris
LARIS   phalaris, auricularis, polaris
PARIS   Paris

ÂRISH

BÂRISH   bearish
FÂRISH   fairish
GÂRISH   garish
MÂRISH   marish, nightmarish
PÂRISH   pairish
RÂRISH   rarish
SKWÂRISH   squarish

(See **ERISH**)

ÄRIST

TÄRIST   guitarist
TSÄRIST   tsarist
ZÄRIST   czarist

ÄRJENT

ÄRJENT   argent, minargent
MÄRJENT   margent
SÄRJENT   sergeant

ÄRJER

BÄRJER   barger
CHÄRJER   charger, discharger, turbocharger, overcharger, supercharger, surcharger, undercharger
LÄRJER   enlarger, larger
SPÄRJER   sparger

ÄRJIK

LÄRJIC   pelargic
THÄRJIK   lethargic

ÄRJING

(See **ÄRJ,** add -*ing* where appropriate.)

ÄRKA

CHÄRKA   charka, charkha
DÄRKA   bidarka
MÄRKA   markka
PÄRKA   parka
SÄRKA   anasarca

ÄRKAL

ÄRKAL   anarchal, matriarchal, patriarchal
GÄRKAL   oligarchal
NÄRKAL   monarchal
RÄRKAL   heterarchal, hierarchal, squirearchal

(See **ÄRKL**)

ÄRKĒ

ÄRKĒ   *anarchy,* arky, diarchy, hagiarchy, matriarchy, patriarchy, squirearchy, thearchy, triarchy
BÄRKĒ   barky
CHÄRKĒ   charqui
DÄRKĒ   bidarke, darky
GÄRKĒ   oligarchy
KÄRKĒ   carky
LÄRKĒ   larky, malarkey
MÄRKĒ   *nomarchy*
NÄRKĒ   *gynarchy,* menarche
PÄRKĒ   parky

RÄRKĒ   heterarchy, hetaerarchy, hierarchy
SHÄRKĒ   sharky
SPÄRKĒ   sparky
STÄRKĒ   starky
TÄRKĒ   *antarchy, heptarchy, cryptarchy, autarchy*

ÄRKEN

ÄRKEN   archon
BÄRKEN   barken
DÄRKEN   bedarken, darken, endarken
HÄRKEN   hearken
STÄRKEN   starken

ÄRKER

BÄRKER   barker, embarker
DÄRKER   darker
HÄRKER   harker
KÄRKER   carker
LÄRKER   larker, skylarker
MÄRKER   marker, markhor
PÄRKER   nosy-parker, parker
SHÄRKER   sharker
SPÄRKER   sparker
STÄRKER   starker

ÄRKERZ

STÄRKERZ   starkers

(See **ÄRKER,** add -*s*)

ÄRKĒZ

(See **ÄRKĒ,** change -*y* to -*ies* where appropriate.)

ÄRKIK

ÄRKIK   matriarchic, patriarchic
GÄRKIK   oligarchic
NÄRKIK   anarchic, antianarchic, monarchic, synarchic
RÄRKIK   hierarchic
TÄRKIK   heptarchic, climatarchic

I WAS PRODIGAL WITH TIME

I was prodigal with time—
   Spent it to my heart's content.
Now that I have passed my prime,
   Time remains, but I am spent.

ÄRKING

(See ÄRK, add -ing where appropriate.)

ÄRKISH

(See ÄRK, add -ish where appropriate.)

ÄRKIST

ÄRKIST	matriarchist, patriarchist
GÄRKIST	oligarchist
NÄRKIST	anarchist, antianarchist, monarchist, synarchist
RÄRKIST	hierarchist
TÄRKIST	heptarchist

ÄRKL

BÄRKL	barkle
DÄRKL	darkle
SÄRKL	sarcle
SPÄRKL	sparkle

(See ÄRKAL)

ÄRKLĒ

DÄRKLĒ	darkly
KLÄRKLĒ	clarkly, clerkly
STÄRKLĒ	starkly

ÄRKLET

PÄRKLET	parklet
SPÄRKLET	sparklet

ÄRKLING

DÄRKLING	darkling
LÄRKLING	larkling
SPÄRKLING	sparkling

ÄRKNER

DÄRKNER	darkener
HÄRKNER	hearkener

ÄRKNES

DÄRKNES	darkness
STÄRKNES	starkness

ÄRKTIK

ÄRKTIK	arctic, Arctic, Nearctic, Palearctic
BÄRKTIK	subarctic
LÄRKTIK	holarctic
TÄRKTIK	Antarctic

ÂRLĒ

BÂRLĒ	barely
FÂRLĒ	fairly, unfairly
NÂRLĒ	debonairly
RÂRLĒ	rarely
SKWÂRLĒ	squarely
WÂRLĒ	awarely
YÂRLĒ	yarely

ÄRLĒ

BÄRLĒ	barley
MÄRLĒ	marly
NÄRLĒ	gnarly
PÄRLĒ	parley
ZÄRLĒ	bizarrely

ÄRLER

JÄRLER	jarler
NÄRLER	gnarler
PÄRLER	parlor
SNÄRLER	snarler

ÂRLES

(See ÂR, add -less where appropriate.)

ÄRLES

PÄRLES	parlous

(See ÄR, add -less where appropriate.)

ÄRLET

HÄRLET	harlot
KÄRLET	carlet
MÄRLET	marlet
SKÄRLET	scarlet
STÄRLET	starlet
VÄRLET	varlet

ÄRLIK

GÄRLIK	garlic, pilgarlic
SÄRLIK	sarlyk

ÂRLĪN

ÂRLĪN	airline
HÂRLĪN	hairline

ÄRLIN

KÄRLIN	carlin, carline
MÄRLIN	marlin, marline

ÂRLĪND

HÂRLĪND	hairlined
KÂRLĪND	care-lined

ÄRLING

DÄRLING	darling
SNÄRLING	snarling
SPÄRLING	sparling
STÄRLING	starling

ÄRLĪT

KÄRLĪT	carlight
STÄRLĪT	starlight

ÄRLIT

FÄRLIT	farlit
KÄRLIT	carlit
STÄRLIT	starlit

ÄRLOK

CHÄRLOK	charlock
HÄRLOK	harlock
KÄRLOK	carlock
MÄRLOK	marlock

ÄRLOT

(See ÄRLET)

ÄRLOR

(See ÄRLER)

ÄRLUS

(See ARLES)

ÄRMA

DÄRMA	adharma, dharma
KÄRMA	karma

ÂRMAN

| ÂRMAN | airman |
| CHÂRMAN | chairman |

ÄRMĒ

ÄRMĒ	army
BÄRMĒ	barmy
FÄRMĒ	farmy
SMÄRMĒ	smarmy

ÄRMENT

BÄRMENT	debarment, disbarment
GÄRMENT	garment
SÄRMENT	sarment

ÄRMER

ÄRMER	armer, armor, disarmer, rearmer
CHÄRMER	charmer, snake-charmer
FÄRMER	dairy farmer, dirt farmer, farmer, subsistence farmer
HÄRMER	harmer
LÄRMER	alarmer

ÄRMFUL

ÄRMFUL	armful
CHÄRMFUL	charmful
HÄRMFUL	harmful, unharmful

ÄRMIK

| FÄRMIK | alexipharmic, pharmic, polypharmic |
| TÄRMIK | ptarmic |

ÄRMIN

| HÄRMIN | harmine |
| KÄRMIN | carmine, encarmine |

ÄRMING

(see ÄRM, add -ing where appropriate.)

ÄRMLES

(See ÄRM, add -less where appropriate.)

ÄRMLET

| ÄRMLET | armlet |
| CHÄRMLET | charmlet |

ÄRMOR

(see ARMER)

ÄRMOT

| KÄRMOT | carmot |
| MÄRMOT | marmot |

ÄRNA

ÄRNA	arna
DÄRNA	dharna
SÄRNA	sarna

ÄRNAL

(See ÄRNEL)

ÄRNARD

(see ÄRNERD)

ÄRNĒ

BÄRNĒ	barny
BLÄRNĒ	blarney
KÄRNĒ	carney, carny
LÄRNĒ	Killarney

ÄRNEL

CHÄRNEL	charnel
DÄRNEL	darnel
KÄRNEL	carnal, uncarnal

ÄRNER

DÄRNER	darner
GÄRNER	garner
YÄRNER	yarner

ÄRNERD

| BÄRNERD | Barnard |
| GÄRNERD | garnered |

ÂRNES

(See ÂR, add -ness where appropriate.)

ÄRNES

FÄRNES	farness
HÄRNES	harness, reharness, unharness
ZÄRNES	bizarreness

ÄRNING

DÄRNING	darning, goldarning, goshdarning
SÄRNING	consarning
YÄRNING	yarning

ÄRNISH

GÄRNISH	garnish
TÄRNISH	tarnish
VÄRNISH	varnish

ÄRNISHT

(See ÄRNISH, add -ed.)

ÂRŌ

FÂRŌ	faro
KÂRŌ	karo, Karo, vaquero
TÂRŌ	taro, tarot

(See ERŌ)

ARŌ

ARŌ	arrow
BARŌ	barrow, handbarrow, wheelbarrow
FARŌ	farrow
HARŌ	harrow, restharrow
KARŌ	carrow
MARŌ	marrow
NARŌ	narrow
SKARŌ	scarrow
SPARŌ	sparrow
TARŌ	tarot
YARŌ	yarrow

ÄRŌ

GÄRŌ	zingaro
GWÄRŌ	saguaro
JÄRŌ	Kilimanjaro
KÄRŌ	karo
KLÄRŌ	claro
NÄRŌ	denaro
SÄRŌ	Pissarro

TÄRŌ   cantaro, taro
ZÄRŌ   Pizarro

(See **ORŌ**)

AROL

(See **AREL**)

AROLD

(See **ARELD**)

ÂRON

HWÂRON   *whereon*
KÂRON   Charon
THÂRON   *thereon*

AROŌ

BAROŌ   baru
MAROŌ   maru

AROT

(See **ARET**)

ÄRPAL

(See **ÄRPL**)

ÄRPĒ

HÄRPĒ   harpy
KÄRPĒ   carpie, carpy
SHÄRPĒ   sharpie, sharpy

ÄRPER

HÄRPER   harper
KÄRPER   carper
SHÄRPER   cardsharper, sharper

ÄRPL

KÄRPL   carpal, intercarpal, metacarpal
PÄRPL   disparple

ÄRSEL

KÄRSEL   carcel
PÄRSEL   parcel
SÄRSEL   sarcel
TÄRSEL   metatarsal, tarsal

VÄRSEL   varsal
WÄRSEL   warsle

ÄRSER

KÄRSER   carcer
PÄRSER   parser
SÄRSER   Sarsar
SPÄRSER   sparser

ÄRSHA

GÄRSHA   Garcia
MÄRSHA   hamartia, Marcia

ÄRSHAL

MÄRSHAL   field marshal, immartial, marshal, martial, unmartial
PÄRSHAL   impartial, partial

ÄRSL

(See **ÄRSEL**)

ÄRSLĒ

PÄRSLĒ   parsley
SPÄRSLĒ   sparsely

ÄRSON

ÄRSON   arson
FÄRSON   mene mene tekel upharsin
PÄRSON   parson
SÄRSON   sarsen
SKWÄRSON   squarson

ÄRTA

KÄRTA   charta, Magna Charta
KWÄRTA   cuarta
SPÄRTA   Sparta

ÄRTAL

(See **ÄRTL**)

ÄRTAN

(See **ÄRTEN**)

ÄRTĒ

ÄRTĒ   arty
CHÄRTĒ   charty
DÄRTĒ   darty
HÄRTĒ   hearty
PÄRTĒ   ex parte, hen party, house party, nonparty, pajama party, party, stag party, tea party
SMÄRTĒ   smarty
STÄRTĒ   starty
TÄRTĒ   Astarte, tarty

ÄRTED

(See **ÄRT**, add *-ed* where appropriate.)

ÄRTEN

BÄRTEN   barton
GÄRTEN   kindergarten
HÄRTEN   dishearten, enhearten, hearten
KÄRTEN   carton
MÄRTEN   marten, martin
PÄRTEN   partan, parten
SMÄRTEN   smarten
SPÄRTEN   Spartan
TÄRTEN   tartan, tarten

ÄRTER

ÄRTER   arter
BÄRTER   barter
CHÄRTER   charter
DÄRTER   darter
GÄRTER   garter
MÄRTER   bemartyr, martyr, protomartyr, remartyr, unmartyr
PÄRTER   departer, imparter, parter
SÄRTER   sartor
SMÄRTER   smarter
STÄRTER   non-starter, restarter, self-starter, starter, upstarter
TÄRTER   cream-of-tartar, tartar, Tartar, tarter

ÄRTERD

(See **ÄRTER**, add *-ed* where appropriate.)

ÄRTING

(See **ÄRT**, add *-ing* where appropriate.)

ÄRTIST

ÄRTIST	artist
CHÄRTIST	chartist, Chartist
PÄRTIST	Bonapartist

ÄRTL

DÄRTL	dartle
HÄRTL	hartal
PÄRTL	partle
STÄRTL	startle

ÄRTLĒ

PÄRTLĒ	partly
SMÄRTLĒ	smartly
TÄRTLĒ	tartly

ÄRTLES

(See ÄRT, add -less where appropriate.)

ÄRTLET

ÄRTLET	artlet
BÄRTLET	Bartlett
HÄRTLET	heartlet
MÄRTLET	martlet
PÄRTLET	partlet
TÄRTLET	tartlet

ÄRTLING

DÄRTLING	dartling
SPÄRTLING	spartling
STÄRTLING	startling

ÄRTNES

| SMÄRTNES | smartness |
| TÄRTNES | tartness |

ÄRTŌ

| GÄRTŌ | lagarto |
| PÄRTŌ | esparto |

ÄRTON

(See ÄRTEN)

ÄRTRIJ

| KÄRTRIJ | cartridge |
| PÄRTRIJ | partridge |

ÄRTWÄ

| KÄRTWÄ | cartway |
| PÄRTWÄ | partway |

A coffeemaker underneath a wood cabinet will send steam bellowing up, damaging the cabinet.
—FROM A LETTER TO "DEAR HELOISE."

Doth steam from coffeemaker bellow?
Did Minotaur in cavern billow?
It's confusing to a fellow,
Or maybe I should say a fillow.

ÂRUM

ÂRUM	arum
GÂRUM	garum
HÂRUM	harem
MÂRUM	marum
SKÂRUM	harum-scarum

ARUM

GARUM	garum
HARUM	harem
KARUM	carom
LARUM	alarum, larum
MARUM	marum

ÄRVEL

ÄRVEL	arval, Arval
BÄRVEL	barvel
KÄRVEL	carval, carvel
LÄRVEL	larval
MÄRVEL	marvel

ÄRVER

KÄRVER	carver
MÄRVER	marver
STÄRVER	starver

ÄRVEST

HÄRVEST	harvest
KÄRVEST	carvest
STÄRVEST	starvest

ÄRVING

| KÄRVING | carving |
| STÄRVING | starving |

ÄRVL

(See ARVEL)

ÄRVLING

| MÄRVLING | marveling |
| STÄRVLING | starveling |

ÂRWORN

| KÂRWORN | careworn |
| PRÂRWORN | prayer-worn |

ASA

DASA	Hadassah
DRASA	madrasah
KASA	casa
KWASA	oquassa
MASA	massa
NASA	NASA

ĀSAL

ĀSAL	oasal
BĀSAL	basal
KĀSAL	casal
VĀSAL	vasal

ASĀT

| KASĀT | cassate |
| KRASĀT | incrassate |

ĀSĒ

JĀSĒ	jasey, Jaycee
LĀSĒ	lacy
MĀSĒ	contumacy
PĀSĒ	pace
PRĀSĒ	précis
RĀSĒ	racy
SPĀSĒ	spacy

ASĒ

BRASĒ	brassie, brassy
CHASĒ	chassis
DASĒ	dassie
GASĒ	gassy, Malagasy
GLASĒ	glacé, glassy
GRASĒ	grassy
HASĒ	Tallahassee
KLASĒ	classy
LASĒ	Haile Selassie, lassie

MASĒ	massy
RASĒ	morassy, rasse
SASĒ	sassy
TASĒ	tassie

ASEL

(See ASIL)

ĀSEN

BĀSEN	basin, washbasin
CHĀSEN	chasten, enchasten, unchasten
HĀSEN	hasten
JĀSEN	Jason
KĀSEN	caisson
MĀSEN	freemason, mason, meson, stonemason
SĀSEN	sasin, sasine

ASEN

DASEN	spadassin
FASEN	fasten
SASEN	assassin

ĀSENS

BĀSENS	abaisance, obeisance
JĀSENS	adjacence, interjacence
NĀSENS	connascence, renascence
PLĀSENS	complacence, complaisance, uncomplacence, uncomplaisance

ĀSENT

BĀSENT	obeisant
JĀSENT	adjacent, interjacent, jacent, circumjacent, subjacent, superjacent
NĀSENT	enascent, connascent, naissant, nascent, renaissant, renascent
PLĀSENT	complacent, complaisant, uncomplacent, uncomplaisant
RĀSENT	indurascent

ĀSER

ĀSER	acer
BĀSER	abaser, baser, debaser
BRĀSER	bracer, embracer
CHĀSER	chaser, steeplechaser
FĀSER	defacer, effacer, facer
GRĀSER	begracer, disgracer, gracer
KĀSER	encaser, caser
KWĀSER	quasar
LĀSER	belacer, interlacer, lacer, laser, unlacer
MĀSER	grimacer, macer
PĀSER	outpacer, pacer
PLĀSER	displacer, misplacer, placer, replacer
RĀSER	eraser, footracer, horseracer, racer
SPĀSER	spacer
TRĀSER	tracer

ASER

GASER	gasser
HASER	hassar
KASER	antimacassar, macassar
MASER	amasser, masser
PASER	passer, surpasser
PLASER	placer
RASER	harasser

ĀSET

PLĀSET	placet
TĀSET	tacet

ASET

ASET	asset
BASET	basset
BRASET	brasset
FASET	facet, fascet
PLASET	placet
TASET	tacet, tacit, tasset

ĀSEZ

ĀSEZ	oases

(See ĀS, add -s where appropriate.)

ASEZ

GLASEZ	field glasses, glasses, granny glasses, opera glasses
LASEZ	molasses

(See AS, add -es where appropriate.)

ĀSHA

ĀSHA	Asia, Croatia
GĀSHA	Geisha
GRĀSHA	ex gratia
KĀSHA	acacia
LĀSHA	osteomalacia
MĀSHA	Dalmatia
RĀSHA	Eurasia

(See ĀZHA)

ĀSHAL

BĀSHAL	abbatial, basial
FĀSHAL	facial, craniofacial, unifacial
GLĀSHAL	glacial, postglacial, preglacial, subglacial
LĀSHAL	palatial, prelatial
MĀSHAL	primatial
RĀSHAL	interracial, multiracial, racial
SPĀSHAL	interspatial, spatial
TĀSHAL	mystacial

(See Ā'SHI.AL)

ASHBORD

DASHBORD	dashboard
SPLASHBORD	splashboard

ASHĒ

ASHĒ	ashy
BASHĒ	bashy
BRASHĒ	brashy
DASHĒ	dashy
FLASHĒ	flashy
HASHĒ	hashy
KLASHĒ	clashy
MASHĒ	mashie, mashy
PLASHĒ	plashy
SLASHĒ	slashy
SPLASHĒ	splashy
TRASHĒ	trashy

ĀSHENS

FĀSHENS	facience
PĀSHENS	impatience, patience, patients, outpatients

ĀSHENT

FĀSHENT	abortifacient, facient, calefacient,

liquefacient,
parturifacient,
rubefacient, somnifacient,
sorbefacient,
stupefacient,
tumefacient

PĀSHENT   impatient, inpatient,
outpatient, patient

ASHER

BASHER	abasher, basher
BRASHER	brasher
DASHER	dasher, haberdasher
FLASHER	flasher
GASHER	gasher
HASHER	hasher, rehasher
KASHER	casher
KLASHER	clasher
KRASHER	gate-crasher, crasher
LASHER	lasher
MASHER	masher
NASHER	gnasher
PASHER	pasher
RASHER	rasher
SLASHER	slasher
SMASHER	smasher
SPLASHER	splasher
STASHER	stasher
TASHER	tasher
THRASHER	thrasher
TRASHER	trasher

ÄSHER

KWÄSHER	quasher
SKWÄSHER	squasher
SWÄSHER	swasher
WÄSHER	dishwasher, whitewasher, washer

(See **OSHER**)

ASHEZ

MASHEZ	gamashes

(See **ASH**, add -es where appropriate.)

ASHFUL

BASHFUL	bashful, unbashful
GASHFUL	gashful
RASHFUL	rashful

ASHING

(See **ASH, OSH,** add -ing where appropriate.)

ÄSHING

(See **ÄSH, OSH,** add -ing where appropriate.)

ASHLĒ

FLASHLĒ	flashly
GASHLĒ	gashly
RASHLĒ	rashly

ASHMAN

ASHMAN	ashman
TRASHMAN	trashman

ĀSHUN

ĀSHUN   *A* abbreviation, affiliation, accentuation, actuation, acupunctuation, alleviation, Alpha radiation, allineation, amelioration, ampliation, annunciation, appreciation, appropriation, arcuation, asphyxiation, Asian, association, attentuation, aviation, *B* Beta radiation, beneficiation, boation, *D* defoliation, delineation, denunciation, depreciation, despoliation, devaluation, deviation, differentiation, dimidiation, disaffiliation, discontinuation, dissociation, domiciliation, *E* effectuation, effoliation, exfoliation, excruciation, expatiation, expatriation, expiation, expoliation, expropriation,

extenuation, exuviation, emaciation, enunciation, evacuation, evaluation, *F* fasciation, februation, feriation, filiation, foliation, *FL* fluctuation, *FR* friation, fructuation, *GL* glaciation, gloriation, *GR* graduation, *H* habituation, humiliation, *I* ideation, illaqueation, inappreciation, individuation, inebriation, infatuation, infuriation, ingratiation, initiation, inchoation, insinuation, intercolumniation, interlineation, intermediation, invultuation, irradiation, *K* calumniation, caseation, columniation, confarreation, conciliation, consubstantiation, continuation, contumniation, creation, Croatian, *L* laniation, lixiviation, lineation, licentiation, laureation, luxuriation, *M* malleation, maleficiation, materiation, mediation, menstruation, misappropriation, mispronunciation, *N* negotiation, novitiation, nucleation, *O* obviation, officiation, otiation, *P* palliation, permeation, perpetuation, piation, punctuation, *PR* procreation, pronunciation, propitiation, *R* radiation,

reconciliation,
recreation,
remediation,
renunciation,
repatriation,
repudiation,
retaliation,
revaluation, *S*
satiation,
self-renunciation,
situation,
ciliation, sinuation,
circumstantiation,
sublineation,
substantiation,
superannuation, *SP*
spoliation, *STR*
striation, *SW*
suaviation, *T*
tumultuation, *TR*
trabeation,
transsubstantiation,
tripudiation, *V*
valuation, variation,
vindemiation,
vitiation

BĀSHUN   *A* accubation,
approbation, *D*
decubation,
dealbation,
disapprobation, *E*
exacerbation, *H*
humicubation, *I*
incubation,
intubation, *J* jobation,
K conurbation,
cubation, *L* libation,
limbation, *M*
masturbation, *O*
orbation, *P*
perturbation, *PR*
probation, *R*
recubation,
reprobation, *S*
cibation, *T* titubation

BRĀSHUN   *A* adumbration,
antilibration, *E*
equilibration, *K*
calibration, *L*
libration, lucubration,
P palpebration, *S*
celebration,
cerebration, *T*
terebration, *V*
vertebration, vibration

DĀSHUN   *A* aggradation,
accommodation, *B*
backwardation, *D*
defedation,
defraudation,
degradation,
denudation,

deoxidation,
depredation,
desudation,
dilapidation, *E*
exudation,
exundation,
elapidation,
elucidation,
emendation, *F*
fecundation,
foundation, *FL*
fluoridation, *FR*
frondation, *GR*
gradation,
gravidation, *I*
infeudation,
ingravidation,
incommodation,
intimidation,
inundation,
invalidation, *K*
commendation,
consolidation,
cuspidation, *L*
lapidation,
liquidation, laudation,
N nodation, nudation,
O oxidation, *PR*
predacean, predation,
R recommendation,
recordation,
retardation,
retrogradation, *S*
sedation, secundation,
sudation, *TR*
transudation,
trepidation,
trucidation, *V*
validation

DRĀSHUN   *D* dehydration, *H*
hydration

FĀSHUN   philosophation
FLĀSHUN   *A* afflation, *D*
deflation, *E* efflation,
exsufflation, *I*
inflation, insufflation,
K conflation, *P*
perflation, *R* reflation,
S sufflation, *SL*
slumpflation, *ST*
stagflation

GĀSHUN   *A* abnegation,
abrogation,
aggregation,
allegation, alligation,
arrogation, avigation,
D delegation,
deligation,
denegation,
derogation,
desegregation,
divagation,

divulgation, *E*
expurgation,
elongation, evagation,
F fumigation,
fustigation, *H*
homologation, *I*
instigation,
interrogation,
investigation,
irrigation, *J* jugation,
K castigation,
compurgation,
congregation,
conjugation,
corrugation, *L*
legation, levigation,
ligation, litigation, *M*
mitigation, *N*
navigation, negation,
noctivigation,
nugation, *O*
objurgation,
obligation, *P*
purgation,
pervulgation, *PR*
profligation,
prolongation,
promulgation,
propagation,
prorogation, *R*
relegation,
renegation, rigation,
rogation, *S*
segregation,
subjugation,
subligation,
subrogation,
supererogation,
circumnavigation,
surrogation, *V*
variegation

GRĀSHUN   *D* deflagration,
disintegration, *E*
emigration, *I*
immigration,
integration,
intermigration, *K*
conflagration, *M*
migration, *R*
redintegration,
reintegration,
remigration, *TR*
transmigration

HĀSHUN   Haitian
KĀSHUN   *A* abdication,
abjudication,
adjudication,
advocation,
albification,
albication,
alkalification,
allocation,

amplification,
Anglification,
application,
aerification,
acetification,
acidification,
asification,
averruncation,
avocation, *B*
basification,
beatification,
bifurcation,
beautification, *BR*
brutification, *D*
damnification,
dandification,
dedication,
defalcation,
defecation,
deification,
declassification,
deltafication,
demarcation,
demystification,
demulsification,
demarkation,
denazification,
deprecation,
desiccation,
detoxication,
detruncation,
dimication,
disbocation,
disembarkation,
disqualification,
dislocation,
divarication,
diversification,
domestication,
dulcinification,
duplication, *E*
edification, education,
exemplification,
excommunication,
explication,
exsiccation,
extrication,
equivocation,
electrification,
embarkation,
embourgeoisification,
embrocation,
emulsification,
emuscation,
eradication,
esterification,
evocation, *F*
fabrication, falcation,
falsification,
formication,
fornication,
fortification,

fossilification,
furcation, *FL*
floccinaucinihilipilification,
florification,
flossification, *FR*
franglification,
Frenchification,
frication,
fructification, *G*
gasification, *GL*
glorification, *GR*
granitification,
gratification, *H*
hypothecation,
horrification,
humidification, *I*
identification,
imbrication,
implication,
imprecation,
inapplication,
indemnification,
indication, infucation,
incarnification,
inculcation,
intensification,
intercommunication,
interlocation,
interlucation,
interstratification,
intoxication,
intrication,
invocation, *J*
jellification,
generification,
gentrification,
jollification,
justification, *K*
cacation,
calorification,
calcification,
carnification,
casefication,
codification,
cockneyfication,
collocation,
communication,
complication,
comprecation,
chondrification,
confiscation,
contraindication,
convocation,
cornification,
coruscation,
countrification, *KL*
clarification,
classification,
claudication, *KR*
crucification, *KW*
quadrification,
quadrifurcation,

quadruplication,
qualification,
quantification, *L*
ladyfication,
lactification,
liquefaction,
location, lorication,
lubrication,
ludification, *M*
magnification,
mastication,
matrification,
medification,
medication,
mendication,
metrification,
metrication, mication,
misapplication,
mystification,
modification,
mollification,
mortification,
multiplication,
mummification,
mundification, *N*
Nazification,
necation, nidification,
nigrification,
nimbification,
nitrification,
notification,
nudification,
nullification, *O*
obfuscation,
objectification,
occaecation,
altercation,
ossification,
authentication,
oversimplification,
ozonification, *P*
pacation, perfrication,
personification,
petrification,
piscation, publication,
purification,
putrefaction, *PL*
placation,
plebification,
plication, *PR*
preachification,
predication,
presignification,
prevarication,
prettification,
prognostication,
prolification,
provocation, *R*
radication,
ramification,
rarefaction,
ratification,

reduplication,
regentrification,
rectification,
renidification,
replication,
republication,
reciprocation,
rhetorication,
revivification,
revocation,
reunification,
rigidification,
rubefacation,
runcation, rustication,
S saccharification,
sacrification,
salification,
sanguification,
sanctification,
saponification,
certification,
sevocation,
signification,
siccation,
syllabification,
syllabication,
silication,
simplification,
citification,
sophistication,
solemnification,
solidification,
subjectification,
sublimification,
suffocation, sulcation,
supplication, *SK*
scarification,
scorification, *SP*
speechification,
specification,
spiflication, *ST*
stellification,
stultification,
stupefication, *STR*
stratification, *T*
telecommunication,
tepefication,
terrification,
testification,
typification,
toxication,
torrefication,
tumefication, *TH*
thurification, *TR*
translocation,
transmogrification,
triplication,
truncation, *U*
uglification, *V*
vacation, varication,
vellication,
verification,

versification,
vesication,
vilification,
vindication,
vinification,
vitrification,
vivification, vocation,
Y unification

KRĀSHUN *D* deconsecration,
desecration, *E*
execration, *K*
consecration, *O*
obsecration

KWĀSHUN adequation, equation,
inadequation,
inequation, liquation

LĀSHUN *A* ablation,
adosculation,
adulation,
accumulation, alation,
alkylation,
ambulation,
angulation,
annihilation,
annulation,
appelation,
articulation,
assimilation,
assimulation,
avolation, *B*
bombilation, *BL*
blood relation, *D* de-
escalation,
decollation, delation,
demodulation,
denticulation,
dentilation,
deoppilation,
depeculation,
depilation,
depopulation,
desolation, dilation,
disconsolation,
dissimulation,
distillation, *E*
ejaculation, ejulation,
exhalation,
expostulation,
extrapolation,
exungulation, elation,
emasculation,
emulation,
entortillation,
escalation, etiolation,
evolation, *F*
phallation,
fasciculation,
fibrillation,
formulation, *FL*
flabellation,
flagellation,
floccilation, *GL*

glandulation, *GR*
granulation,
graticulation,
gratulation, *H*
halation, hariolation,
hyperventilation,
horripilation, *I*
illation,
immaculation,
immolation,
inarticulation,
infibulation,
inhalation,
inoculation,
inosculation,
insolation,
installation,
instillation,
insulation,
intercalation,
interpellation,
interpolation,
interrelation,
intertessellation,
invigilation, isolation,
J jaculation, gelation,
gemmulation,
geniculation,
gesticulation,
jubilation, jugulation,
K calculation,
cancellation,
cantillation,
capitulation,
carbunculation,
castellation,
coagulation,
collation,
colliculation,
compellation,
compilation,
confabulation,
conglobulation,
congratulation,
congelation,
consolation,
constellation,
contravallation,
contumulation,
copulation,
correlation,
cumulation,
cupellation, *KR*
crenellation,
crenulation, *L*
lallation, lamellation,
legislation, *M*
machicolation,
maculation,
malassimilation,
manipulation,
matriculation,

miscalculation,
modulation,
mutilation, *N*
nidulation,
noctambulation,
nummulation, *O*
oblation,
obnubilation,
orbiculation,
oscillation,
osculation, ovulation,
P pabulation,
pandiculation,
peculation,
pendiculation,
perambulation,
percolation,
pestillation,
pixillation,
poculation,
population,
postillation,
postulation,
pullulation,
pustulation, *PR*
prolation, *R*
refocillation,
regelation, regulation,
recapitulation,
relation, repopulation,
reticulation,
retrocopulation,
revelation, *S*
serrulation, sibilation,
simulation,
scintillation,
circulation,
surculation,
circumambulation,
circumvallation,
somnambulation,
sublation, suggilation,
SK scutellation, *SP*
spallation,
speculation,
sporulation, *ST*
stellation,
stimulation,
stipulation, *STR*
strangulation,
stridulation,
strigilation,
strobilation, *T*
tabulation,
tessellation,
tintinnabulation,
titillation, tubulation,
turbination, *TR*
translation,
tremulation,
triangulation,
tribulation, *U*

MĀSHUN

ululation, undulation,
ustulation, *V*
vacuolation,
vallation, vapulation,
variolation,
vacillation,
vexillation, velation,
ventilation,
vermiculation,
vibratiunculation,
vigilation, violation,
vitriolation,
vocabulation,
volation, *Y* ululation
A affirmation,
acclamation,
acclimation,
amalgamation,
animation,
approximation, *D*
Dalmatian,
defamation,
deformation,
declamation,
deplumation,
decimation,
desquamation,
disinformation, *E*
exhumation,
exclamation,
estimation, *F*
formation, *I*
inanimation,
inflammation,
information,
inhumation,
incremation,
intimation,
irrumation, *J*
gemmation, *K*
collimation,
commation,
confirmation,
conformation,
consummation, *KR*
cremation,
chrismation, *L*
lachrymation,
lacrimation,
legitimation,
limation, *M*
malformation,
malconfirmation,
misinformation, *O*
automation,
overestimation, *PR*
preformation,
proclamation, *R*
racemation,
reaffirmation,
reformation,
reclamation, *S*

NĀSHUN

sigmation,
sublimation,
summation, *SKW*
squammation,
T tetragrammation,
TR transanimation,
transformation, *U*
underestimation, *V*
vigesimation
A abalienation,
abacination,
abomination,
adnation, adornation,
agglutination,
agnomination,
accrimination,
acumination,
alienation,
alternation,
assassination,
assignation, *D*
damnation,
declination,
decontamination,
denomination,
deoxygenation,
desalination,
destination,
designation,
determination,
detonation,
devirgination,
dissemination,
disinclination,
discrimination,
divination,
doctrination,
domination, donation,
E eburnation,
effemination,
examination,
exornation,
explanation,
expugnation,
extermination,
elimination,
emanation, enation, *F*
fascination,
ferrumination,
fibrination,
phonation,
foreordination,
fulmination, *FR*
fraternation, *G*
gunation, *GL*
glutination, *H*
hallucination,
hibernation,
hydrogenation,
hyphenation, *I*
illumination,
imagination,

immanation,
impanation,
impersonation,
impregnation,
indetermination,
indignation,
indiscrimination,
indoctrination,
ingannation,
ingemination,
incarnation,
inclination,
incoordination,
incrimination,
inordination,
insemination,
insubordination,
intonation,
invagination, *J*
gelatination,
gemination,
germination, *K*
cachinnation,
calcination,
carbonation,
carnation, catenation,
cognation,
combination,
commination,
conation,
condemnation,
condonation,
concatenation,
consarcination,
consternation,
contamination,
coordination,
coronation,
culmination, *KL*
chlorination, *KR*
crenation,
crimination, cross-
examination, *L*
lamination,
lancination,
lumination, lunation,
M machination,
miscegenation, *N*
nation, nomination, *O*
obsignation,
obstination,
oxygenation,
alternation,
oppugnation,
ordination,
origination,
ozonation, *P*
pagination,
pectination,
peregrination,
perfectionation,
personation,

pollination, *PR*
predestination,
predetermination,
predomination,
preordination,
profanation,
procrastination,
pronation,
propination,
propugnation, *R*
ratiocination,
reincarnation,
rejuvenation,
reclination,
recombination,
recrimination,
remanation,
resupination,
resignation, ruination,
rumination, *S*
salination, semination,
sermocination,
cybernation,
signation,
subordination,
subornation,
subsannation,
supination,
sermocination, *ST*
stagnation, *T*
tarnation, turbination,
termination, *TR*
trutination, *V*
vaccination,
vaticination,
venation, venenation,
vermination,
vernation, *Y*
urination, *Z* zonation

PĀSHUN

A anticipation, *D*
dissipation,
disculpation, *E*
exculpation,
extirpation,
emancipation, *F*
forcipation, *I*
increpation,
inculpation, *K*
constipation, *KR*
crispation, *N*
nuncupation, *O*
obstipation,
occupation, *P*
palpation,
participation, *PR*
preoccupation, *S*
syncopation,
suppalpation, *Y*
usurpation
contemplation

PLĀSHUN
PRĀSHUN
manustupration,
stupration

RĀSHUN

A aberration,
abjuration, adjuration,
admiration, adoration,
agglomeration,
aggeration,
acceleration,
alliteration,
amelioration,
annumeration,
aration, asperation,
aspiration,
asseveration, *B*
botheration, *BL*
blusteration, *D*
defeneration,
defloration,
degeneration,
declaration,
decoration,
deliberation,
deliration,
depauperation,
deploration,
depuration,
deceleration,
desideration,
desperation,
deterioration,
deterration,
disfiguration,
discoloration,
disoperation,
disseveration,
duration, *E*
edulcoration,
ejuration,
exaggeration,
exasperation,
exhiliration,
exoneration,
expectoration,
expiration,
exploration,
elaboration,
enumeration,
epuration,
evaporation,
eviration,
evisceration, *F*
federation, feneration,
figuration,
fissiparation,
fulguration,
furfuration, *FL*
flusteration, *GL*
glomeration, *H*
Horatian, *I*
immoderation,
imploration,
induration,
incameration,
incarceration,

inclination,
inconsideration,
incorporation,
inauguration,
inauration,
incineration,
inspiration,
instauration,
insussuration,
inteneration,
intoleration,
invigoration,
irroration, iteration, *J*
generation, gyration,
K carburation,
carceration,
collaboration,
coloration,
commemoration,
commensuration,
commiseration,
comploration,
confederation,
configuration,
conglomeration,
conjuration,
concameration,
consideration,
contesseration,
cooperation,
corporation,
corroboration,
culturation, curation,
L laceration,
liberation, libration,
liration, literation, *M*
marmoration,
maceration,
maturation,
melioration,
mensuration,
moderation,
moration,
murmuration, *N*
narration,
noncooperation,
numeration,
neuration, *O*
obduration,
objuration,
obliteration,
obscuration,
auguration, alteration,
oneration, operation,
oration, *P* pejoration,
perforation,
peroration,
perseveration,
perspiration,
pignoration,
ponderation, *PR*
prefiguration,

preparation,
preponderation,
procuration,
proliferation,
protuberation, *R*
ration, refrigeration,
reiteration,
regeneration,
reconsideration,
recuperation,
remuneration,
reparation,
respiration,
restoration,
reverberation,
roboration, *S*
saburration,
saturation, separation,
cerration, serration,
sideration, cineration,
circumgyration,
subarrhation,
sulphuration,
suppuration,
suspiration,
sussuration, *SF*
spheration, *T*
temeration,
titteration, toleration,
TR tractoration,
transfiguration,
transculturation,
transliteration,
transpiration,
trilateration,
trituration, *U*
ulceration, *V*
vaporation,
veneration,
verberation,
verbigeration,
vituperation,
vociferation, *Y*
Eurasian

SĀSHUN

A adversation,
affixation,
aftersensation,
Alsatian, annexation,
D decussation,
dispensation,
dispersation, *E*
extravasation,
elixation,
endorsation, *F*
fixation, *FL* fluxation,
I incrassation,
inspissation,
intensation,
intravasation, *K*
cassation, coaxation,
compensation,
condensation,

conspissation,
conversation, *KW*
quassation, *L*
laxation, luxation, *M*
malversation, *O*
overcompensation, *P*
pulsation, *PR*
prefixation,
presensation, *R*
relaxation, rixation, *S*
sarmassation, sation,
sensation, cessation,
suffixation,
succusation,
suspensation, *T*
taxation,
tergiversation,
undercompensation, *V*
vexation
outstation, station,
substation

STĀSHUN

TĀSHUN

A ablactation,
absentation,
adaptation,
adhortation,
affectation, agitation,
acceptation,
accreditation,
alimentation,
amputation,
annotation,
argumentation,
argentation,
arrestation,
assentation,
attestation,
attrectation, *D*
debilitation,
deforestation,
degustation,
dehortation,
decantation,
decapitation,
decrepitation,
dextrorotation,
delactation,
delectation,
delimitation,
dementation,
denotation, dentation,
deportation,
depositation,
deputation,
detestation,
devastation,
digitation, dictation,
dilatation,
disputation,
dissentation,
dissertation, ditation,
documentation,
dotation, dubitation,

E exagitation,
exaltation,
exercitation,
exhortation,
expectation,
experimentation,
exploitation,
exportation,
excitation, exultation,
equitation, enatation,
eructation, *F*
facilitation,
felicitation,
fermentation,
fetation, foetation,
fomentation,
forestation, *FL*
flagitation, flirtation,
flotation, *FR*
fragmentation,
frequentation,
frumentation, *G*
gurgitation, gustation,
guttation, *GR*
gravitation, *H*
habitation,
hebetation, hesitation,
hortation,
humectation, *I*
illutation, imitation,
immutation,
implantation,
implementation,
importation,
imputation,
inaffectation,
indentation,
infestation,
ingurgitation,
inhabitation,
incantation,
incapacitation,
incrustation,
incitation,
instrumentation,
insultation,
integumentation,
interdigitation,
intermutation,
interpretation,
intestation, invitation,
irritation, *J* jactation,
jactitation, gestation,
jotation, *K* cantation,
capacitation,
capitation, captation,
castrametation,
cavitation, coaptation,
cohabitation,
cogitation,
commentation,
commutation,

compotation,
computation,
confrontation,
confutation,
connotation,
concertation,
constatation,
consultation,
contestation,
contrectation,
cooptation,
cunctation, curtation,
KR crepitation,
crustacean,
crustation, *KW*
quartation, quotation,
L lactation,
lamentation,
levitation,
levorotation,
limitation, licitation,
luctation, *M*
manifestation,
meditation,
mentation, militation,
misinterpretation,
misquotation,
misrepresentation,
molestation,
mussitation,
mutation, *N* natation,
nepotation,
necessitation,
nictation, nictitation,
nobilitation, notation,
nutation, *O*
obequitation,
augmentation,
occultation,
orientation,
ornamentation,
oscitation,
auscultation,
ostentation, *P*
palpitation, peltation,
perfectation,
periclitation,
permutation,
pernoctation,
perscrutation,
pigmentation,
pollicitation, potation,
putation, *PL*
plantation,
placentation, *PR*
premeditation,
precipitation,
prestidigitation,
presentation,
protestation, *R*
reforestation,
refutation,

regurgitation,
rehabilitation,
regimentation,
recantation,
reluctation,
representation,
reptation, reputation,
recitation,
resuscitation,
retractation, rotation,
ructation, *S* saltation,
salutation, sanitation,
sedimentation,
segmentation,
cementation,
septation,
circumnutation,
cetacean, citation,
solicitation,
subhastation,
superalimentation,
supplantation,
supplementation,
supportation,
sustentation, *SK*
scortation, *SKR*
scrutation, *SP*
sputation, *ST*
sternutation, *T*
temptation, tentation,
testamentation,
testacean, testation,
TR tractation,
transmutation,
transplantation,
transportation, *V*
vegetation,
vectitation, velitation,
venditation,
visitation, volitation,
votation,
votation

THRĀSHUN Thracian
TRĀSHUN *A* administration,
arbitration, *D*
defenestration,
demonstration, *E*
engastration, *F*
fenestration,
filtration, *FR*
frustration, *I*
illustration,
impenetration,
impetration,
infiltration,
interfenestration,
interpenetration, *K*
castration,
concentration, *L*
lustration, *M*
maladministration,
ministration,
monstration, *N*

nitration, *O*
oblatration,
orchestration, *P*
penetration,
perlustration,
perpetration, *PR*
prostration, *R*
registration,
recalcitration,
remonstration, *S* self-
concentration,
sequestration, *T*
titration

VĀSHUN *A* aggravation,
activation, acervation,
D decurvation,
depravation,
deprivation,
derivation, *E*
excavation, elevation,
enervation, estivation,
I innervation,
innovation, *K*
captivation,
conservation,
cultivation, curvation,
L lavation, *M*
motivation, *N*
nervation, nivation,
novation, *O*
observation, ovation,
PR preservation,
privation, *R*
renovation,
reservation, *S*
salivation, salvation,
self-preservation,
servation, solvation,
ST starvation, *T*
titivation

ZĀSHUN *A* aggrandization,
acclimatization,
accusation,
actualization,
alphabetization,
alcoholization,
alkalization,
allegorization,
Americanization,
amortization,
analyzation,
anathematization,
anaesthetization,
Anglicization,
animalization,
antagonization,
arborization,
arithmetization,
aromatization,
atomization, *BR*
brutalization, *CH*
chattelization, *D*

decriminalization,
demobilization,
demonetization,
demoralization,
denaturalization,
denationalization,
denization,
denuclearization,
deodorization,
deoxydization,
depauperization,
desensitization,
decentralization,
decimalization,
desulfurization,
detonization,
devocalization,
disorganization, *DR*
dramatization, *E*
economization,
extemporization,
externalization,
equalization,
electrization,
epitomization,
eternization,
etherealization,
evangelization, *F*
familiarization,
fertilization,
Finlandization,
focalization,
phoneticization,
phosphorization,
fossilization,
feudalization, *FR*
fraternization, *G*
galvanization, *H*
harmonization,
Hellenization,
hepatization,
Hibernization,
hybridization,
humanization, *I*
idealization,
idolization,
immortalization,
improvisation,
individualization,
intellectualization,
internationalization,
ionization, iridization,
J gelatinization,
generalization,
Judaization, *K*
canalization,
canonization,
capitalization,
characterization,
caramelization,
carbonization,
categorization,

catechization,
colonization,
columnization,
commercialization,
cauterization,
causation, *KR*
crystallization,
Christianization, *L*
Latinization,
legalization,
legitimization,
liberalization,
literalization,
localization,
magnetization,
macadamization,
maximization,
martyrization,
materialization,
mediatization,
mercerization,
mesmerization,
metallization,
methodization,
militarization,
minimization,
mobilization,
modernization,
monetization,
monopolization,
mortalization, *N*
naturalization,
nationalization,
nasalization,
mnemonization,
neologization,
normalization,
neutralization, *O*
oxidization,
organization,
ostracization,
authorization,
ozonization, *P*
palatalization,
paralyzation,
pasteurization,
patronization,
penalization,
polarization,
pollenization,
polymerization,
popularization,
pauperization,
porphyrization,
pausation,
pulverization, *PL*
pluralization, *PR*
proctorization, *R*
racialization,
realization,
recognization,
recusation,

remonetization,
reorganization,
revitalization, *S*
secularization,
self-actualization,
sensitization,
sensualization,
centralization,
syllogization,
symbolization,
synchronization,
systematization,
civilization,
solarization,
solemnization,
solmization,
subtilization,
sulphurization,
summarization, *SK*
scandalization, *SP*
specialization,
spiritualization, *ST*
stabilization,
standardization,
sterilization,
stigmatization, *T*
tabularization,
tantalization,
tartarization,
temporization,
totalization, *TH*
theorization, *TR*
tranquilization,
trullization, *U*
urbanization, *V*
valorization,
vandalization,
vaporization,
verbalization,
victimization,
vitalization,
vitriolization,
visualization,
vocalization,
volcanization,
vulcanization, *Y*
universalization,
utilization

ASHUN

ASHUN	ashen
FASHUN	disfashion, fashion, prefashion, refashion
KASHUN	Circassian
NASHUN	Parnassian
PASHUN	dispassion, impassion, compassion, passion, satispassion
RASHUN	deration, ration, unration

ASHUND

FASHUND	fashioned, new-fashioned, old-fashioned

(See **ASHUN**, add *-ed* where appropriate.)

ĀSHUNZ

(See **ĀSHUN**, add *-s* where appropriate.)

ĀSHUS

ĀSHUS	alliaceous, foliaceous, hordeaceous, coriaceous, liliaceous, oleaceous, scoriaceous, tileaceous
BĀSHUS	bibacious, bulbaceous, fabaceous, herbaceous, sabaceous, sebaceous
DĀSHUS	amaryllidaceous, audacious, bodacious, edacious, glandaceous, hamamelidaceous, iridaceous, mendacious, mordacious, orchidaceous, predacious, rudaceous
DRĀSHUS	cylindraceous
FĀSHUS	tophaceous, torfaceous
GĀSHUS	fugacious, fungacious, sagacious, saxifragaceous
GRĀSHUS	disgracious, gracious, misgracious, ungracious
GWĀSHUS	linguacious
KĀSHUS	efficacious, ericaceous, inefficacious, micaceous, perspicacious, pervicacious, procacious, salicaceous, urticaceous
KRĀSHUS	execratious
KWĀSHUS	loquacious, sequacious, somniloquacious
LĀSHUS	*A* amylaceous, argillaceous, *F*

MĀSHUS	fallacious, ferulaceous, filaceous, *K* capillaceous, corallaceous, *L* lilaceous, *M* marlaceous, *P* palacious, perlaceous, polygalaceous, *R* ranunculaceous, *S* salacious, santalaceous, *SK* schorlaceous, *V* violaceous
NĀSHUS	fumacious, gemmaceous, contumacious, limaceous, palmaceous, pomaceous *A* acanaceous, arenaceous, *E* erinaceous, *F* farinaceous, *G* gallinaceous, *K* carbonaceous, *M* minacious, *P* papillonaceous, pectinaceous, pertinacious, pugnacious, *R* resinaceous, *S* sanguinaceous, saponaceous, solanaceous, *T* tenacious, *V* vinaceous
PĀSHUS	incapacious, capacious, lappaceous, rampacious, rapacious, cepaceous
RĀSHUS	arboraceous, feracious, furacious, furfuraceous, hederaceous, camphoraceous, piperaceous, porraceous, pulveraceous, ceraceous, stercoraceous, veracious, voracious
SĀSHUS	vexatious
SPĀSHUS	spacious, unspacious
TĀSHUS	*D* disputatious, *FL* flirtatious, *FR* frumentaceous, *K* cactaceous, chartaceous, *KR* cretaceous, crustaceous, *O*

ostentatious, *P*
pultaceous, *R*
rutaceous, *S*
cetaceous, setaceous,
psittaceous, *T*
testaceous, *TR*
truttaceous
THĀSHUS   acanthaceous
VĀSHUS   curvaceous,
olivaceous, vivacious
ZĀSHUS   quizzaceous,
rosaceous

ĀSĪD

BĀSĪD	bayside
BRĀSĪD	braeside
WĀSĪD	wayside

ASID

ASID	antacid, acid, monoacid, nucleic acid, oxyacid, triacid (etc.)
BASID	subacid
PLASID	placid
TASID	antacid

ASIJ

BRASIJ	brassage
PASIJ	passage

ĀSIK

BĀSIK	basic, bibasic, diabasic, polybasic, tribasic
FĀSIK	aphasic, monophasic, phasic
PĀSIK	carapasic
TĀSIK	diastasic

ASIK

ASIK	Liassic, Triassic
BASIK	sebacic
KLASIK	classic, neoclassic, postclassic, preclassic, pseudoclassic
LASIK	thalassic
RASIK	boracic, Jurassic, thoracic
TASIK	potassic

ASIL

(See ASL)

ĀSIN

(See ĀSEN)

ASIN

(See ASEN)

ĀSING

(See ĀS, add -*ing* where appropriate.)

ASING

(See AS, add -*ing* where appropriate.)

ĀSIS

ĀSIS	Acis, oasis
BĀSIS	basis
FĀSIS	phasis
FRĀSIS	holophrasis
GLĀSIS	glacis
KLĀSIS	cataclasis
KRĀSIS	crasis, krasis
STĀSIS	hemostasis, stasis

ASIS

ASIS	assis
CHASIS	chassis
FASIS	fascis
GLASIS	glacis
KASIS	*cassis*
NASIS	Jackie Onassis
RASIS	tarassis

ĀSIV

BRĀSIV	abrasive
SWĀSIV	assuasive, dissuasive, persuasive, suasive
VĀSIV	evasive, invasive, pervasive

ASIV

MASIV	massive
PASIV	impassive, passive

ASKA

BASKA	Athabasca
BRASKA	Nebraska
LASKA	Alaska
RASKA	burrasca, marasca

ASKAL

MASKL	mascle
PASKAL	antepaschal, Pascal, paschal
RASKAL	rascal
TASKAL	tascal

ASKER

ASKER	asker
BASKER	basker
FLASKER	flasker
GASKER	Madagascar
KASKER	casker, casquer, uncasker, uncasqer
LASKER	Lascar
MASKER	antimasker, antimasquer, masker, masquer, unmasker
TASKER	tasker

ASKET

BASKET	basket, breadbasket, flower basket
FLASKET	flasket
GASKET	gasket
KASKET	casket, casquet
LASKET	lasket
TASKET	taskit

ASKING

(See ASK, add -*ing* where appropriate.)

ASKL

(See ASKAL)

ASKŌ

ASKŌ	fiasco
BASKŌ	tabasco, verbasco
KASKŌ	casco
TASKŌ	tasco

ASKUS

ASKUS	ascus
MASKUS	Damascus

ASL

FASL	facile
GRASL	gracile
HASL	hassle
KASL	castle, forecastle, Newcastle
RASL	wrastle
TASL	entassel, tassel
VASL	envassal, vassal

ĀSLĒ

BĀSLĒ	basely
PLĀSLĒ	commonplacely

ĀSLES

(See **ĀS**, add -less where appropriate.)

ĀSLET

BRĀSLET	bracelet
HĀSLET	haslet
LĀSLET	lacelet

ASLET

HASLET	haslet
TASLET	taslet

ĀSLŌD

BĀSLŌD	baseload
KĀSLŌD	caseload

ASMAN

GASMAN	gasman
GLASMAN	glassman
GRASMAN	grassman
KLASMAN	classman, underclassman, upperclassman
PASMAN	passman

ĀSMENT

(See **ĀS**, add -ment where appropriate.)

ASMENT

MASMENT	amassment
RASMENT	harassment

ĀSNER

CHĀSNER	chastener
HĀSNER	hastener

ĀSŌ

PĀSŌ	peso
SĀSŌ	say-so

ASŌ

BASŌ	basso
GASŌ	Sargasso
LASŌ	lasso

ASOK

(See **ASUK**)

ĀSON

(See **ĀSEN**)

ASON

(See **ASEN**)

ASPER

ASPER	asper
GASPER	gasper
GRASPER	grasper
JASPER	jasper
KLASPER	enclasper, clasper, unclasper
RASPER	rasper

ASPING

(See **ASP**, add -ing where appropriate.)

ASTA

KASTA	shikasta
NASTA	canasta
SHASTA	Shasta
TASTA	catasta

ÄSTA

BÄSTA	basta
HÄSTA	hasta
PÄSTA	pasta

ASTARD

(See **ASTERD**)

ĀSTĒ

HĀSTĒ	hasty, unhasty
PĀSTĒ	pasty, unpasty
TĀSTĒ	tasty, untasty

ASTĒ

BLASTĒ	blasty
MASTĒ	masty
NASTĒ	photonasty, epinasty, hyponasty, nyctinasty, nasty
PLASTĒ	anaplasty, dermatoplasty, genioplasty, heteroplasty, keratoplasty, mammoplasty, neoplasty, autoplasty, rhinoplasty, cineplasty, zooplasty
RASTĒ	pederasty
TRASTĒ	contrasty
VASTĒ	vasty

ĀSTED

HĀSTED	hasted
PĀSTED	pasted
TĀSTED	distasted, foretasted, pretasted, tasted

ĀSTER

BĀSTER	baster
CHĀSTER	chaster
PĀSTER	paster
SLĀSTER	slaister
TĀSTER	foretaster, taster
WĀSTER	shirtwaister, waster

ASTER

ASTER	aster, China aster, geaster, oleaster, piaster, Zoroaster
BASTER	alabaster
BLASTER	blaster
DASTER	cadaster
FASTER	faster
GASTER	astrologaster, flabbergaster, gaster

KASTER	broadcaster, forecaster, grammaticaster, caster, castor, criticaster, medicaster	enthusiastic, chiastic, chiliastic, autoschediastic, orgiastic, parasceuastic, scholiastic, unenthusiastic	
LASTER	interpilaster, opulaster, pilaster, stylaster		
MASTER	*B* bandmaster, burgomaster, grandmaster, headmaster, housemaster, *K* concertmaster, cubmaster, *KW* choirmaster, quartermaster, *M* master, *O* overmaster, *P* past master, paymaster, postmaster, ringmaster, *SK* schoolmaster, scoutmaster, *ST* stationmaster, *T* taskmaster, toastmaster		

BASTIK bombastic
BLASTIK amphiblastic
BRASTIK Hudibrastic
DRASTIK drastic
FRASTIK antiphrastic, metaphrastic, paraphrastic, periphrastic
KASTIK dichastic, hesychastic, sarcastic, stochastic
KLASTIK anaclastic, anticlastic, iconoclastic, cataclastic, clastic, plagioclastic, synclastic
LASTIK agelastic, elastic, inelastic, interscholastic, gelastic, scholastic
MASTIK animastic, antonomastic, docimastic, gum mastic, mastic, onomastic, paronomastic
NASTIK dynastic, gymnastic, monastic, pleonastic
PLASTIK *A* anaplastic, aplastic, *B* bioplastic, *D* dentoplastic, *E* emplastic, esemplastic, *F* phelloplastic, *G* galvanoplastic, *N* neoplastic, *TH* thermoplastic, *THR* thromboplastic, *PL* plastic, *PR* proplastic, protoplastic, *S* ceroplastic, *Y* euplastic
RASTIK pederastic, peirastic, pornerastic, rastik
SASTIK doxastic
SPASTIK epispastic, spastic
TASTIK fantastic
TRASTIK tetrastich

NASTER	canaster, pinaster
PASTER	pastor
PLASTER	beplaster, court plaster, plaster, replaster, sticking plaster, unplaster
SASTER	disaster
TASTER	Latinitaster, poetaster
TRASTER	contraster
VASTER	vaster
ZASTER	disaster

ASTERD

BASTERD	bastard
DASTERD	dastard
LASTERD	pilastered
MASTERD	mastered, overmastered, unmastered
PLASTERD	beplastered, plastered, replastered, unplastered

ĀSTFUL

HĀSTFUL	hasteful
TĀSTFUL	distasteful, tasteful
WĀSTFUL	unwasteful, wasteful

ASTIK

ASTIK	ecclesiastic, encomiastic,

ĀSTING

(See **ĀST**, add *-ing* where appropriate.)

ASTING

KASTING	broadcasting
LASTING	everlasting

(See **AST**, add *-ing* where appropriate.)

ASTLĒ

FASTLĒ	*steadfastly*
GASTLĒ	ghastly
LASTLĒ	lastly
VASTLĒ	vastly

ASTMENT

BLASTMENT	blastment
TRASTMENT	contrastment

ASTNES

FASTNES	fastness, *steadfastness*
VASTNES	vastness

ASTON

GASTON	Gaston
SPASTON	trispaston

ASTOR

(See **ASTER**)

ASTRAL

ASTRAL	astral, subastral
DASTRAL	cadastral
KASTRAL	castral

ASTRON

PASTRON	apastron
PLASTRON	plastron

ASTRUM

ASTRUM	periastrum
BASTRUM	alabastrum
KASTRUM	castrum
PLASTRUM	plastrum

ASUK

HASUK	hassock
KASUK	cassock

ĀTA

ĀTA	eta
BĀTA	albata, beta
BRĀTA	invertebrata, vertebrata
DĀTA	data, caudata, chordata
LĀTA	postulata, relata
MĀTA	ultimata, squamata
RĀTA	desiderata, errata, pro rata, rata
SĀTA	peseta
STRĀTA	strata
TĀTA	dentata
THĀTA	theta
ZĀTA	zeta

ATA

ATA	atta
BATA	batta
GATA	regatta
MATA	matamata, paramatta
STRATA	strata

ÄTA

ÄTA	reata, riata
DÄTA	data
GÄTA	alpargata, regatta
HWÄTA	whata
KÄTA	imbrocata, stoccata, toccata
LÄTA	aballata
MÄTA	mata, matamata, paramatta
NÄTA	serenata, sonata
RÄTA	errata, inamorata, pro rata, rata
STRÄTA	strata
SÄTA	cassata
TÄTA	batata, cantata, patata

ĀTAL

DĀTAL	datal
FĀTAL	fatal
NĀTAL	antenatal, natal, neonatal, perinatal, postnatal, postneonatal, prenatal
RĀTAL	ratal, ratel
STĀTAL	statal
STRĀTAL	stratal, substratal

ĀTAN

(See ĀTEN)

ĀTANT

BLĀTANT	blatant
FLĀTANT	inflatant
LĀTANT	dilatant, latent
NĀTANT	natant, supernatant
PĀTANT	patent

ĀTĒ

ĀTĒ	Ate, eighty
HĀTĒ	Haiti, Hayti
LĀTĒ	Jubilate, Leyte
MĀTĒ	matey, maty
NĀTĒ	antenati
PLĀTĒ	platy
RĀTĒ	literati
SLĀTĒ	slaty
TĀTĒ	ex necessitate
WĀTĒ	weighty

ATĒ

BATĒ	batty
CHATĒ	chatty
FATĒ	fatty
KATĒ	catty
MATĒ	matty
NATĒ	gnatty, natty, Cincinnati
PATĒ	chapatty, patty
PLATĒ	platy
RATĒ	ratty
SKATĒ	scatty
TATĒ	tatty
YATĒ	yati

ÄTĒ

ÄTĒ	coati, piatti
LÄTĒ	Jubilate, oblati
MÄTĒ	Amati, mate
NÄTĒ	illuminati, Cincinnati
RÄTĒ	glitterati, karate, culturati, literati
SÄTĒ	Sati
SKWÄTĒ	squatty
SWÄTĒ	swatty
YÄTĒ	yachty
ZÄTĒ	zati

(See OTĒ)

ĀTED

ĀTED	superannuated
BĀTED	elumbated, surbated
KĀTED	indicated, contraindicated, spiflicated, vindicated
KWĀTED	torquated
LĀTED	etiolated, flammulated, mammilated, ocellated, stellated, tessellated
SĀTED	inspissated, spissated, sated, unsated

(See ĀT, add -ed where appropriate.)

ATED

ATED	caryatid

(See AT, add -ed.)

ĀTEN

DĀTEN	Dayton
PĀTEN	peyton
SĀTEN	Satan
STRĀTEN	straighten, straiten

ATEN

ATEN	Aten
BATEN	batten, Mountbatten
FATEN	fatten
FLATEN	flatten
GRATEN	au gratin, gratin, gratten
HATEN	Manhattan
LATEN	latten, Latin, pig Latin, Vulgar Latin
MATEN	*harmattan*, matin
PATEN	paten, patten, patin, patine
PLATEN	platan, platen
RATEN	rattan, ratten
SATEN	satin
STATEN	Staten

ĀTENT

(See ĀTANT)

ĀTER

ĀTER	*A* abbreviator, acutiator, annunciator, aviator, *D* delineator, *F* philiater, *GL* gladiator, *M* mediator, *N*

	negotiator, *K*	**NĀTER**	*B* buccinator, *D*	**MATER** antimatter, matter
	caveator, *R* rabiator,		denominator,	**NATER** natter
	radiator, *V* viator		detonator,	**PATER** patter, pitter-patter
BĀTER	abater, baiter, bater,		discriminator, *E*	**PLATER** platter
	debater, rebater		exterminator, *I*	**RATER** ratter
BLĀTER	ablator		impersonator, *J*	**SATER** satyr
BRĀTER	vibrator		jejunator, *K*	**SHATER** shatter
DĀTER	dater, laudator		coordinator, *O*	**SKATER** scatter
FRĀTER	frater, freighter,		alternator, *PR*	**SMATER** smatter
	confrater		propugnator, *S*	**SPATER** bespatter, spatter
GĀTER	alligator, gaiter,		supinator, *T*	**SPLATER** splatter
	'gater, interrogator,		terminator	**SPRATER** spratter
	investigator,	**PĀTER**	Dis Pater, pater	**TATER** tatter
	corrugator, navigator,	**PLĀTER**	plaiter, plater	**VATER** vatter
	negator, propagator	**PRĀTER**	prater	**YATER** yatter
GRĀTER	grater, greater	**RĀTER**	*A* accelerator,	
HĀTER	hater, manhater,		aspirator, *B* barrator,	
	womanhater		*D* decorator, *E*	**ÄTER**
KĀTER	*A* adjudicator,		elaborator, *I*	
	allocator, applicator,		incinerator, *J*	**MÄTER** alma mater, dura
	D desiccator,		generator, *K*	mater, mater, Stabat
	divaricator,		carburetor,	Mater
	duplicator, *E*		collaborator,	**PÄTER** Dis Pater, pater
	edificator, educator, *I*		corporator, *L*	**SKWÄTER** squatter
	indicator, *J* judicator,		liberator, literator, *M*	**SWÄTER** swatter
	K cater,		moderator, *N*	**YÄTER** yachter
	comiconomenclator,		numerator, *O*	
	KL classificator, *KW*		operator, *R*	(See **OTER**)
	qualificator, *L*		refrigerator,	
	lubricator, *M*		recuperator,	
	modificator,		respirator,	**ATERN**
	multiplicator, *N*		reverberator, *S*	
	nomenclator, *P*		separator, cinerator,	**PATERN** holding pattern,
	pacificator,		stellarator	pattern
	pontificator,	**SĀTER**	malaxator, sater, satyr	**SATERN** Saturn
	purificator, *PL*	**SKĀTER**	skater	**SLATERN** slattern
	placater, *S*	**TĀTER**	agitator, annotater,	
	significator, *SK*		illicitator, imitator,	
	scarificator, *TR*		mutator, resuscitator,	**ĀTĒZ**
	trafficator, *V* vacater,		spectator, 'tater	
	vinificator	**TRĀTER**	traitor	**ĀTĒZ** eighties
KRĀTER	crater	**VĀTER**	activator, elevator,	**DĀTĒZ** Mithridates
KWĀTER	equator, exequater		innovator,	**FRĀTĒZ** Euphrates
LĀTER	*A* ablator,		conservator,	**KĀTĒZ** Achates
	accumulator,		cultivator, levator	**MĀTĒZ** mateys
	articulator, *D*	**WĀTER**	dumbwaiter, waiter	**NĀTĒZ** lares and penates,
	defribillator, delator,			nates, penates
	dilator, *E* elater, *I*			**VĀTĒZ** vates
	insulator, invigilator,	**ATER**		
	K calculator, *L* later,			
	O oscillator, *P*	**ATER**	attar	**ATFOL**
	perambulator, pocket	**BATER**	batter	
	calculator, postulator,	**BLATER**	blatter	**KATFOL** catfall
	R regulator, relater,	**CHATER**	chatter	**PRATFOL** pratfall
	revelator, *S* simulator,	**FATER**	fatter	
	scintillator, *SP*	**FLATER**	flatter	
	speculator, *ST*	**HATER**	hatter, high-hatter,	**ĀTFUL**
	stimulator, *TR*		Mad Hatter	
	translator, *V* ventilator	**KATER**	catter, quatre,	**FĀTFUL** fateful
MĀTER	alma mater, dura		wildcatter	**GRĀTFUL** grateful, ungrateful
	mater, imprimatur,	**KLATER**	clatter, clitter-clatter	**HĀTFUL** hateful
	mater, Stabat Mater	**LATER**	latter	**PLĀTFUL** plateful

ATHED

FATHED	fathead
FLATHED	flathead

ĀTHER

(TH as in *then*)

BĀTHER	bather
LĀTHER	lather
SWĀTHER	swather

ATHER

(TH as in *then*)

BATHER	bather
BLATHER	blather
LATHER	lather

ÄTHER

(TH as in *then*)

FÄTHER	father
SWÄTHER	swather

(See OTHER)

ATHIK

(TH as in *thin*)

BATHIK	bathic, photobathic
MATHIK	philomathic, chrestomathic, polymathic
NATHIK	agnathic, gnathic, orthognathic, prognathic
PATHIK	*A* allopathic, antipathic, apathic, *E* electropathic, *H* heteropathic, hydropathic, homeopathic, *I* idiopathic, *K* cosmopathic, *N* naturopathic, neuropathic, *O* osteopathic, *P* pathic, *R* rectopathic, *S* psychopathic, *T* telepathic, *TH* theopathic
SPATHIK	feldspathic, spathic

ĀTHING

(TH as in *then*)

BĀTHING	bathing
LĀTHING	lathing
PLĀTHING	*plaything* (th as in thin)
SKĀTHING	scathing
SWĀTHING	swathing

ĀTHLES

(TH as in *thin*)

FĀTHLES	faithless
SKĀTHLES	scatheless

ATHLES

(TH as in *thin*)

BATHLES	bathless
MATHLES	mathless
PATHLES	pathless
RATHLES	wrathless

ATHLON

KATHLON	decathlon
TATHLON	pentathlon

ÄTHŌ

(th as in *then*)

(See ÄDŌ)

ĀTHOS

ĀTHŌS	Athos
BĀTHOS	bathos
NĀTHOS	*prognathous*
PĀTHOS	pathos

ATĪD

BATĪD	bat-eyed
KATĪD	cat-eyed
RATĪD	rat-eyed

ATIK

ATIK	*A* Adriatic, attic, Attic, aviatic, Asiatic, *D* diatic, *E* Eleatic, enneatic, *FL* fluviatic, *FR* phreatic, *H* halleluiatic, Hanseatic, *I* ischyatic, *K* caryatic, cuneatic, *KR* creatic, *M*

---

	mydriatic, muriatic, *O* opiatic, *P* pancreatic, *S* sciatic, *V* viatic
BATIK	acrobatic, adiabatic, anabatic, batic, ecbatic, hyperbatic, isodiabatic, catabatic, metabatic, sabbatic
FATIK	aliphatic, emphatic, phatic, phosphatic, lymphatic, sulphatic
KRATIK	*A* andocratic, aristocratic, arithmocratic, *B* bureaucratic, *D* democratic, Democratic, *F* pherecratic, physiocratic, *H* hagiocratic, harpocratic, Hippocratic, *I* idiocratic, idiosyncratic, isocratic, *J* gynocratic, *L* leuocecratic, *M* meritocratic, mesocratic, mobocratic, monocratic, *N* nomocratic, *O* ochlocratic, autocratic, *P* pancratic, pantisocratic, pornocratic, *PL* plutocratic, *S* Socratic, *SL* slavocratic, *SKW* squattocratic, *STR* stratocratic, *T* technocratic, timocratic, ptochocratic, *TH* theocratic
KWATIK	aquatic, subaquatic
LATIK	palatic, prelatic, villatic
MATIK	*A* aphorismatic, acousmatic, achromatic, acromonogrammatic, axiomatic, anagrammatic, anathematic, apophthegmatic, apochromatic, aposematic, aromatic, asymptomatic, astigmatic, athematic,

asthmatic, D
dalmatic,
diaphragmatic,
diagrammatic,
diastomatic,
dichromatic,
dilemmatic,
diplomatic, dogmatic,
DR dramatic, E
emblematic,
empyreumatic,
endermatic,
enigmatic,
epigrammatic,
episematic, F
phantomatic, FL
phlegmatic, GR
grammatic, gromatic,
H hematic,
hierogrammatic,
hypomnematic, I
idiomatic,
iconomatic,
isochromatic, J
judgmatic, K
charismatic,
categorematic,
cataclysmatic,
kinematic, komatik,
commatic, KL
climatic, KR
cryptogrammatic,
chromatic, L
lipogrammatic, M
magmatic,
macromatic,
mathematic,
melismatic,
melodramatic,
miasmatic,
micromatic,
monogrammatic,
monochromatic,
monomatic, N
noematic, pneumatic,
numismatic, O
onymatic, osmatic,
automatic, P
paradigmatic,
parallelogrammatic,
pathematic, pelmatic,
polygrammatic,
polychromatic,
porismatic, PL
plasmatic,
pleochromatic, PR
pragmatic, prismatic,
problematic,
programmatic,
proceleusmatic, R
rhematic, rheumatic,
S Sarmatic, sematic,

psychosomatic,
psymatic,
symptomatic,
synallagmatic,
cinematic, systematic,
schismatic, SK
schematic, ST
stigmatic, stomatic, T
termatic, TH
thematic,
theorematic, TR
traumatic,
trigrammatic,
trichromatic,
truismatic, U
unsystematic, Z
zygomatic, zeugmatic

NATIK — agnatic, aplanatic, enatic, fanatic, morganatic, venatic

PATIK — hepatic
PLATIK — platic
RATIK — biquadratic, erratic, hieratic, geratic, quadratic, operatic, piratic

STATIK — A anastatic, antistatic, apostatic, astatic, D diastatic, E ecstatic, electrostatic, F photostatic, H heliostatic, hemostatic, hydrostatic, hypostatic, I idiostatic, J geostatic, gyrostatic, K catastatic, M majestatic, metastatic, PR prostatic, ST static, TH thermostatic, Y eustatic

TATIK — protatic
TRATIK — magistratic
VATIK — lavatic, sylvatic, vatic

(Add -s for noun form or plural where appropriate.)

ÄTIK

KWÄTIK — aquatic
YÄTIK — halleluiatic

(See OTIK)

ĀTĪM

DĀTĪM — daytime
MĀTĪM — Maytime

PĀTĪM — paytime
PLĀTĪM — playtime

ĀTIM

ĀTIM — seriatim
BĀTIM — verbatim
DĀTIM — gradatim
RĀTIM — literatim
TĀTIM — guttatim

ATIN

(See ATEN)

ĀTING

(See ĀT, add -ing where appropriate.)

ATING

(See AT, add -ting where appropriate.)

ÄTING

SKWÄTING — squatting
SWÄTING — swatting
YÄTING — yachting

(See ÄT, OT, add -ing where appropriate.)

ATIS

BRATIS — brattice
GRATIS — gratis
LATIS — lattice

ĀTISH

LĀTISH — latish
SLĀTISH — slatish
STRĀTISH — straightish

ATISH

BATISH — battish
BRATISH — brattish
FATISH — fattish
FLATISH — flattish
KATISH — cattish
SKATISH — scattish
RATISH — rattish

ĀTIV

ĀTIV — A alleviative, annunciative,

appreciative,
appropriative,
associative, *D*
denunciative,
depreciative,
dissociative, *E*
enunciative, *I*
inappreciative,
initiative, insinuative,
K conciliative,
continuative, *KR*
creative, *M*
mediative, *P*
palliative,
punctuative, *PR*
procreative,
pronunciative, *R*
radiative, recreative,
renunciative, *U*
unappreciative,
uncreative, *V*
variative

THE HARTEBEEST IS ON THE ENDANGERED
LIST.—*News report*

The hartebeest grows beastly, and his heart starts
  beating fast,
Whene'er a hartebeestess wanders innocently past.
The hartebeestess quickly of his longing gains an
  inkling;
The beestess is as beastly as the beest is in a twinkling.
So fast they shift, those hartebeests, from he's and
  she's to he-she's,
I find it hard to think of them as an endangered species.

BĀTIV approbative,
  incubative,
  reprobative
DĀTIV accommodative,
  dative, elucidative,
  consolidative
GĀTIV abnegative,
  abrogative,
  aggregative,
  investigative,
  irrigative, mitigative,
  propagative,
  segregative
KĀTIV *A* adjudicative, *D*
  dedicative,
  deprecative,
  desiccative,
  duplicative, *E*
  educative,
  excommunicative,
  explicative,
  exsiccative,
  eradicative, *I*
  imbricative,
  implicative,

incommunicative,
invocative, *J*
judicative, *K*
communicative,
complicative, *KW*
qualificative, *M*
medificative,
medicative,
modificative,
multiplicative, *P*
purificative, *PR*
prognosticative, *R*
replicative, *S*
significative,
suffocative,
supplicative, *U*
uncommunicative, *V*
vellicative,
verificative,
vindicative,
vivificative
KLĀTIV nomenclative
KRĀTIV execrative,
  consecrative
LĀTIV *A* accumulative,
  assimilative, *D*
  dilative, *E*
  expostulative, elative,
  emulative, illative, *J*
  jaculative,
  gesticulative, *K*
  calculative,
  coagulative, collative,
  congratulative,
  copulative,
  cumulative, *L*
  legislative, *M*
  manipulative,
  modulative, *O*
  oscillative, *PR*
  prolative, *R*
  regulative,
  recapitulative, *S*
  simulative,
  circulative, *SP*
  speculative, *ST*
  stimulative, *TR*
  translative, *U*
  undulative, *V*
  ventilative, violative
MĀTIV animative,
  approximative,
  estimative
NĀTIV *A* agglutinative, *D*
  denominative,
  determinative,
  designative,
  discriminative,
  disseminative,
  dominative, *E*
  emanative, *GL*
  glutinative, *I*

illuminative,
imaginative,
indiscriminative, *J*
geminative,
germinative, *K*
carminative,
combinative,
contaminative,
concionative,
coordinative, *KR*
criminative, *N* native,
nominative, non-
native, *O* opionative,
originative, *PR*
predestinative, *R*
ratiocinative,
recriminative,
ruminative, *S*
subordinative, *T*
terminative, *U*
unimaginative
PĀTIV anticipative,
  participative
PLĀTIV contemplative
RĀTIV *A* agglomerative,
  accelerative,
  alliterative,
  ameliorative, *D*
  degenerative,
  decorative,
  deliberative,
  desiderative,
  deteriorative, *E*
  edulcorative,
  exaggerative,
  exhilarative,
  exonerative,
  elaborative,
  enumerative,
  evaporative, *F*
  federative, figurative,
  I incorporative,
  inoperative,
  invigorative, iterative,
  J generative, *K*
  commemorative,
  commiserative,
  confederative,
  cooperative,
  corporative,
  corroborative, *L*
  lacerative,
  noncooperative, *O*
  alterative, operative,
  P perforative,
  pignorative,
  postoperative, *R*
  refrigerative,
  reiterative,
  regenerative,
  remunerative,
  reverberative, *S*

separative,
suppurative, *U*
ulcerative,
unremunerative, *V*
vituperative,
vulnerative

TĀTIV *A* agitative, *F*
facultative, *GR*
gravitative, *H*
hesitative, *I* imitative,
inhabitative,
incognitative,
interpretative,
irritative, *K*
cogitative,
commutative,
consultative, *KW*
qualitative,
quantitative, *L*
limitative, *M*
meditative, *N*
necessitative, *O*
authoritative, *PR*
premeditative, *R*
resuscitative, *V*
vegetative

TRĀTIV administrative,
frustrative,
illustrative,
impenetrative,
ministrative,
penetrative

VĀTIV innovative

ĀTL

(See ĀTAL)

ATL

ATL	Quetzalcoatl, Seattle
BATL	battel, battle, embattle
BRATL	brattle
CHATL	chattel
PRATL	prattle
RATL	death rattle, rattle
TATL	tattle, tittle-tattle

ÄTL

(See OTL)

ATLAS

| ATLAS | atlas, Atlas |

(See **AT**, add *-less* for approximate rhyme.)

ĀTLĒ

DĀTLĒ	sedately
GRĀTLĒ	greatly
LĀTLĒ	lately, oblately, prolately
NĀTLĒ	innately, ornately
STRĀTLĒ	straightly, straitly
STĀTLĒ	stately, unstately
TĀTLĒ	*dentately,* precipitately

(For words ending in *-ately* with the primary accent on an earlier syllable, see **ITLĒ**.)

ATLĒ

| ATLĒ | atle |
| LATLĒ | philately |

(See **AT**, add *-ly* where appropriate.)

ATLER

BATLER	battler
PRATLER	prattler
RATLER	rattler
TATLER	tattler, Tatler

ĀTLES

(See **ĀT**, add *-less* where appropriate.)

ATLES

(See **AT**, add *-less* where appropriate.)

ATLING

BATLING	batling, battling
FATLING	fatling
GATLING	gatling
KATLING	catling
PRATLING	prattling
RATLING	rattling
TATLING	tattling

ĀTMENT

BĀTMENT	abatement, rebatement
FRĀTMENT	affreightment
STĀTMENT	instatement, overstatement, reinstatement, statement, understatement

ĀTNES

DĀTNES	sedateness
GRĀTNES	greatness
LĀTNES	lateness, oblateness
NĀTNES	innateness, ornateness
RĀTNES	irateness
STRĀTNES	straightness, straitness

ATNES

FATNES	fatness
FLATNES	flatness
PATNES	patness

ĀTŌ

BĀTŌ	cabatoe
KĀTŌ	Cato
MĀTŌ	pomato, tomato
NĀTŌ	NATO
PLĀTŌ	Plato
TĀTŌ	potato

ATŌ

BATŌ	*bateau*
GATŌ	*gateau*
LATŌ	mulatto
PLATŌ	plateau
SHATŌ	*chateau*

ÄTŌ

BÄTŌ	rebato, rubato
BRÄTŌ	vibrato
DÄTŌ	dato, datto
GÄTŌ	arigato, fugato, legato, obbligato, sfogato
KÄTŌ	marcato, pizzicato, spiccato, staccato
LÄTŌ	isolato
MÄTŌ	pomato, sfumato, tomato
NÄTO	annatto, appassionato, ostinato, passionato
RÄTŌ	barato, disperato, enamorato, inamorato, literato, moderato
TÄTŌ	allentato
TRÄTŌ	castrato, ritratto
SHÄTŌ	*chateau*

(See OTŌ)

ĀTON

(See ĀTEN)

ĀTOR

(See ĀTER)

ÄTRA

MÄTRA	matra
NÄTRA	Sinatra

ĀTRES

RĀTRES	*oratress*
TĀTRES	dictatress, imitatress, spectatress
TRĀTRES	traitress
WĀTRES	waitress

ATRES

LATRES	mulattress
MATRES	mattress

ATRIK

ATRIK	physiatric, hippiatric, iatric, geriatric, kinesiatric, pediatric, psychiatric, theatric
MATRIK	matric
PATRIK	allopatric, St. Patrick, sympatric

ĀTRIKS

ĀTRIKS	aviatrix, bariatrics, physiatrix, impropriatrix
DĀTRIKS	fundatrix
KĀTRIKS	indicatrix, cicatrix
LĀTRIKS	Bellatrix, legislatrix, osculatrix
MĀTRIKS	matrix
NĀTRIKS	gubernatrix, nominatrix
PĀTRIKS	patrix
RĀTRIKS	generatrics, quadratrix, separatrix
SĀTRIKS	rixatrix
TĀTRIKS	dictatrix, imitatrix, spectatrix, testatrix
TRĀTRIKS	administratrix

ATRIKS

ATRIKS	bariatrics, phoniatrics, geriatrics, mediatrics,

pediatrics, cyniatrics, theatrics, zoiatrics

MATRIKS	matrix
PATRIKS	St. Patrick's

ÄTSĒ

NÄTSĒ	Nazi
RÄTSĒ	paparazzi

(See OTSĒ)

ĀTRUN

MĀTRUN	matron
NĀTRUN	natron, salnatron
PĀTRUN	patron

ĀTUM

ĀTUM	seriatum
DĀTUM	datum
LĀTUM	mentholatum, petrolatum, postulatum, relatum
MĀTUM	pomatum, ultimatum
RĀTUM	ageratum, desideratum, erratum, quadratum
STRĀTUM	stratum, substratum, superstratum
TĀTUM	capitatum, testatum

ATUM

ATUM	atom
DATUM	datum
STRATUM	stratum

ĀTŪR

(See ĀCHER)

ĀTUS

ĀTUS	beatus, hiatus, meatus
FLĀTUS	afflatus, flatus, inflatus
LĀTUS	latus
NĀTUS	antenatus, conatus, postnatus, senatus
RĀTUS	apparatus, quadratus, literatus, saleratus
STĀTUS	status
STRĀTUS	altostratus, cumulostratus, nimbostratus,

cirrostratus, stratous, stratus

TĀTUS	comitatus

ĀTWÄ

GÄTWÄ	gateway
STÄTWÄ	stateway
STRÄTWÄ	straightway

ĀUN

(See ĀAN)

ÄVA

BRÄVA	brava
GWÄVA	guava
JÄVA	Java
KÄVA	kava, kavakava
KLÄVA	balaclava
LÄVA	lava, lava-lava
SÄVA	cassava, piassava
TÄVA	ottava

ĀVĒ

ĀVĒ	ave, Ave
DĀVĒ	affidavy, Mahadevi
GĀVĒ	agave
GRĀVĒ	gravy
KĀVĒ	cave, cavie, cavy, peccavi
NĀVĒ	navy
PĀVĒ	pavy
SLĀVĒ	slavy
WĀVĒ	wavy

AVĒ

NAVĒ	navvy
SAVĒ	savvy

ÄVĒ

ÄVĒ	Ave
GRÄVĒ	grave
HÄVĒ	Mojave
KÄVĒ	Kavi, peccavi
TÄVĒ	Rikki-tiki-tavi

ĀVEL

ĀVEL	aval
GĀVEL	gavel
NĀVEL	naval, navel
TĀVEL	octaval

AVEL

GAVEL	gavel
GRAVEL	gravel
KAVEL	cavil
RAVEL	ravel, unravel
TAVEL	tavell
TRAVEL	travel

AVELD

(See **AVEL**, add -ed where appropriate.)

ĀVEN

ĀVEN	Avon
GRĀVEN	engraven, graven
HĀVEN	haven, New Haven
KRĀVEN	craven
MĀVEN	maven, mavin
RĀVEN	raven
SHĀVEN	cleanshaven, shaven

AVEN

RAVEN	raven
SPAVEN	spavin

AVEND

RAVEND	ravened
SPAVEND	spavined

AVENZ

AVENZ	avens
RAVENZ	ravens

ĀVER

BRĀVER	braver
DĀVER	cadaver
FĀVER	disfavor, favor
FLĀVER	flavor, overflavor, underflavor
GRĀVER	engraver, graver
HĀVER	haver
KLĀVER	claver, clishmaclaver
KRĀVER	craver
KWĀVER	demiquaver, demisemiquaver, hemidemisemiquaver, quasihemidemisemiquaver, quaver, semiquaver
LĀVER	laver, lavor
PĀVER	paver

PRĀVER	depraver
RĀVER	raver
SĀVER	lifesaver, saver, savor, timesaver
SHĀVER	shaver
SLĀVER	enslaver, slaver
SWĀVER	suaver
WĀVER	waiver, waver

AVER

DAVER	cadaver
HAVER	haver
KLAVER	claver
LAVER	palaver
SLAVER	beslaver, slaver

ÄVER

HÄVER	halver
KÄVER	calver
LÄVER	palaver
SÄVER	salver
SWÄVER	suaver

ĀVERD

FĀVERD	favored, ill-favored, well-favored
FLĀVERD	flavored, unflavored
KWĀVERD	quavered
SĀVERD	savored
WĀVERD	wavered

AVERN

KAVERN	cavern
TAVERN	tavern

AVID

AVID	avid
GRAVID	gravid
PAVID	impavid, pavid

AVIJ

LAVIJ	lavage
RAVIJ	ravage
SAVIJ	savage
SKAVIJ	scavage

AVIK

GRAVIK	gravic

SLAVIK	Slavic, panslavic, Yugoslavic
TAVIK	atavic

AVIN

SAVIN	savin
SPAVIN	spavin

ĀVING

(See **ĀV**, add -ing where appropriate.)

ĀVING

ĀVING	halving
KĀVING	calving
SĀVING	salving

ĀVIS

ĀVIS	rara avis
KLĀVIS	clavis
PĀVIS	pavis

ĀVISH

BRĀVISH	bravish
NĀVISH	knavish
SLĀVISH	slavish

I HAVE A LITTLE PHILTRUM

(The philtrum is the vertical groove in the middle of the upper lip, running to the nose.)

I have a little philtrum
  Wherein my spilltrum flows
When I am feeling illtrum
  And runny at the nose.

AVISH

LAVISH	lavish
RAVISH	enravish, ravish
SLAVISH	Slavish

ĀVIT

DĀVIT	affidavit, davit
KĀVIT	indicavit
SĀVIT	cessavit
TĀVIT	devastavit

ĀVLĒ

BRĀVLĒ	bravely
GRĀVLĒ	gravely
NĀVLĒ	knavely
SWĀVLĒ	suavely

ĀVLES

(See ĀV, add -less where appropriate.)

AVLIN

JAVLIN	javelin
RAVLIN	ravelin

AVLOK

GAVLOK	gavelock
HAVLOK	havelock

ĀVMENT

GRĀVMENT	engravement
LĀVMENT	lavement
PĀVMENT	pavement
PRĀVMENT	depravement
SLĀVMENT	enslavement

ĀVNES

BRĀVNES	braveness
GRĀVNES	graveness
SWĀVNES	suaveness

ĀVOR

(See ĀVER)

ĀVYER

GRĀVYER	photogravure, gravure, autogravure, pyrogravure
HĀVYER	behavior, havier, havior
KLĀVYER	clavier, klavier
PĀVYER	pavior
SĀVYER	savior

ĀWERD

BĀWERD	bayward
HĀWERD	hayward
WĀWERD	wayward

ĀWŌRN

DĀWŌRN	day-worn
SPRĀWŌRN	spray-worn
WĀWŌRN	wayworn

ĀYA

GLĀYA	Aglaia
NĀYA	naia
SĀYA	calisaya
ZĀYA	Isaiah

ÄYA

BÄYA	kabaya, Surabaya
LÄYA	jambalaya
MÄYA	Maia, maya, Maya
PÄYA	papaya
RÄYA	raya
SÄYA	saya

ĀYŌ

BLĀŌ	bleo
KĀYŌ	cacao, kayo, K.O.
MĀYŌ	mayo, Mayo

ÄZA

ÄZA	piazza
GÄZA	Gaza
KÄZA	caza
PLÄZA	plaza
RÄZA	tabula rasa

AZARD

(See AZERD)

ĀZĒ

BLĀZĒ	blazy
DĀZĒ	daisy, lack-a-daisy, upsy-daisy
FRĀZĒ	paraphrasy, phrasy
HĀZĒ	hazy
KRĀZĒ	crazy
LĀZĒ	lazy
MĀZĒ	mazy
PĀZĒ	Bel Paese
SLĀZĒ	sleazy
TĀZĒ	patesi

ÄZĒ

GÄZĒ	Bengasi, Benghazi, ghazi
NÄZĒ	Ashkenazi
WÄZĒ	ghawazi

AZEM

(See single A, AZM)

ĀZEN

BLĀZEN	blazon, emblazon
BRĀZEN	brazen
GLĀZEN	glazen
MĀZEN	malmaison, mezon
PĀZEN	diapason
RĀZEN	raisin

ĀZER

BLĀZER	blazer, trailblazer
FRĀZER	phraser, paraphraser
GĀZER	gazer, geyser, stargazer
GLĀZER	glazer
GRĀZER	grazer
HĀZER	hazer
KWĀZER	quasar
LĀZER	laser, lazer
MĀZER	maser, mazer
PRĀZER	appraiser, disappraiser, dispraiser, praiser
RĀZER	raiser, raser, razer, razor, upraiser

HAZERD

HAZERD	haphazard, hazard
MAZERD	mazard, mazzard

ĀZHA

ĀZHA	Asia
BĀZHA	abasia
FĀZHA	aphasia
FRĀZHA	paraphrasia
GĀZHA	ergasia
KRĀZHA	acrasia
LĀZHA	Australasia
MĀZHA	paronomasia
NĀZHA	gymnasia
PLĀZHA	aplasia
RĀZHA	Eurasia

TĀZHA — Anastasia, astasia, fantasia

(See ĀSHA)

ĀZHAL
(See Ā'ZI.AL)

ĀZHER

ĀZHER — azure
BRĀZHER — brazier, embrasure
GLĀZHER — glazier
GRĀZHER — grazier
RĀZHER — erasure, razure

ĀZHING

FLĀZHING — camouflaging, persiflaging
RĀZHING — barraging, garaging

ĀZHUN

ĀZHUN — Asian
BRĀZHUN — abrasion
KĀZHUN — Caucasian, occasion
KWĀZHUN — equation
PĀZHUN — upasian
RĀZHUN — erasion, Eurasian
SWĀZHUN — dissuasion, persuasion, suasion
VĀZHUN — evasion, invasion, pervasion

(See Ā'ZI.AN)

ĀZING
(See ĀZ, add -ing where appropriate.)

AZING

JAZING — jazzing
RAZING — razzing
TAZING — razzmatazzing

ĀZL

FRĀZL — frazil
HĀZL — hazel
NĀZL — nasal
PRĀZL — appraisal, reappraisal
ZĀZL — Azazel

AZL

BAZL — basil
DAZL — bedazzle, dazzle, razzledazzle
FRAZL — frazzle
GAZL — gazel

ĀZIN
(See ĀZEN)

ĀZING
(See ĀZ, add -ing where appropriate.)

ĀZLES
(See ĀZ, add -less where appropriate.)

AZMA

AZMA — asthma, miasma
FAZMA — phasma
PLAZMA — plasma, protoplasma
TAZMA — phantasma

AZMAL

AZMAL — miasmal
KAZMAL — chasmal
PLAZMAL — protoplasmal
TAZMAL — phantasmal

ĀZMENT

MĀZMENT — amazement
PRĀZMENT — appraisement, praisement

AZMIK

AZMIK — miasmic
KAZMIK — chasmic
PLAZMIK — bioplasmic, plasmic, protoplasmic
RAZMIK — marasmic
SPAZMIK — spasmic
TAZMIK — phantasmic

ĀZON, ĀZUN
(See ĀZEN)

ĒA

ĒA — Aeaea
BĒA — dahabeah, obeah, rebia
CHĒA — Kampuchea
DĒA — badia, edea, idea, Judea, Chaldea, Medea
FĒA — kaffiyeh, ratafia
GRĒA — sangria
HĒA — Bahia, hia, ohia
JĒA — energia, Hygeia, eugea
KĒA — chia, quia-quia, latakia, pilikia
LĒA — abulia, dulia
MĒA — Crimea
NĒA — bromopnea, dyspnea, Dulcinea, eupnea hyperpnea
PĒA — pharmacopeia, Cassiopeia, melopoeia, onomatopoeia, pathopoeia, prosopopoeia, Tarpeia
RĒA — acoria, Ave Maria, diarrhea, galeria, gonorrhea, chorea, Korea, logorrhea, opisthoporeia, pyorrhea, rea, rhea, spirea, Spiraea
SĒA — Boadicea, Laodicea, panacea
TĒA — galatea, Galatea, callisteia, peripeteia, tortilla, zaptiah
THĒA — althea, barathea
TRĒA — aischrolatreia, Astraea
VĒA — tritavia, via
ZĒA — fantasia, Hosea, zea

ĒAL

DĒAL — beau ideal, ideal, unideal
FĒAL — feal, pheal
JĒAL — epigeal, pharyngeal, hypogeal, laryngeal, meningeal, perigeal
NĒAL — hymeneal
RĒAL — empyreal, correal, real, unreal

ĒAN

ĒAN — Aeaean, aeon, Behan, amoebean,

antipodean, Jacobean, Caribbean, Maccabean, Niobean, plebeian, Sabaean, scarabaean

BLĒAN Hyblaean
DĒAN Andean, antipodean, Archimedean, Assidean, Hebridean, Judean, Chaldean, Pandean, Shandean
FĒAN nymphean, Orphean, Sisyphean
JĒAN Aegean, amphigean, apogean, Argean, epigean, phalangean, pharyngean, Hygeian, Augean, perigean
KĒAN Achaean, ditrochean, Manichaean, trachean, trochean
KLĒAN Sophoclean
LĒAN Achillean, Antillean, Galilean, Herculean, leguleian, lien, mausolean, Mephistophelean, Ponce de Leon, spelean, Zoilean
MĒAN Anomoean, Cadmean, Crimean, Nemean
NĒAN Adonean, Etnean, Hasmonaean, hymenean, Linnaean, Pyrenean
PĒAN Indo-European, paean, pampean, Parthenopean, peon, priapean, cyclopean, tempean, European
PRĒAN Cyprean
RĒAN Berean, empyrean, epicurean, *Iberian*, Korean, Pythagorean, terpsichorean
SĒAN Pharisean, colossean, Laodicean, lyncean, Medicean, Odyssean, Sadducean, Circean, Tennesseean, theodicean
TĒAN adamantean, antaean, Dantean, Atlantean, gigantean, protean
THĒAN lethean, Pantheian, *pantheon*
TRĒAN astraean, Eritrean, petrean

(See ĒON)

ĒAS

(See ĒUS)

ĒBA

ĒBA	iba
MĒBA	amoeba, entamoeba
PĒBA	peba
RĒBA	tireba, zareba
SHĒBA	Bathsheba, Sheba

ĒBAN

MĒBAN	amoeban
SHĒBAN	Sheban
THĒBAN	Theban

ĒBĒ

FĒBĒ	Phoebe
FRĒBĒ	freebie
HĒBĒ	Hebe
JĒBĒ	heebie-jeebie
SĒBĒ	Seabee

EBĒ

BLEBĒ	blebby
DEBĒ	debby
PLEBĒ	plebby
TEBĒ	Entebbe
WEBĒ	cobwebby, webby

EBER

EBER	ebber
WEBER	cobwebber, webber

EBING

EBING	ebbing, unebbing
WEBING	cobwebbing, webbing

EBISH

DEBISH	debbish
NEBISH	nebbish

EBL

DEBL	debile
PEBL	pebble
REBL	arch-rebel, rebel
TREBL	treble

EBLĒ

PEBLĒ	pebbly
TREBLĒ	trebly

ĒBŌ

ĒBŌ	Ibo, eboe
NĒBŌ	Nebo
SĒBŌ	placebo
ZĒBŌ	gazebo

ĒBŌRD

FRĒBŌRD	freeboard
KĒBŌRD	keyboard
SĒBŌRD	seaboard

ĒBÔRN

FRĒBÔRN	freeborn
SĒBÔRN	sea-born, sea-borne

ĒBRA

LĒBRA	cuba libra, libra
ZĒBRA	zebra

ĒBRAL

FĒBRAL	antifebrile, febrile
RĒBRAL	acerebral, cerebral

ĒBUS

FĒBUS	ephebus, Phoebus
GLĒBUS	glebous
RĒBUS	rebus

ĒCHĒ

BĒCHĒ	beachy, beechy
BLĒCHĒ	bleachy, bleechy
BRĒCHĒ	breachy
KWĒCHĒ	queachy
LĒCHĒ	leachy, leechy, litchi
MĒCHĒ	meechy
PĒCHĒ	campeche, campeachy, peachy
PRĒCHĒ	preachy
RĒCHĒ	reachy, reechy

SKRĒCHĒ	screechy
SLĒCHĒ	sleechy
SPĒCHĒ	speechy
TĒCHĒ	teachy
YĒCHĒ	yeechy

ECHĒ

FECHĒ	fetchy
SKECHĒ	sketchy
STRECHĒ	stretchy
TECHĒ	tetchy
VECHĒ	vetchy

ĒCHER

BĒCHER	beacher
BLĒCHER	bleacher
FĒCHER	defeature, feature
KRĒCHER	creature
LĒCHER	leacher, leecher
MĒCHER	meecher
PĒCHER	impeacher, peacher
PRĒCHER	preacher
RĒCHER	forereacher, overreacher, reacher
SĒCHER	beseecher
SKRĒCHER	screecher
SPĒCHER	free speecher
TĒCHER	gym teacher, schoolteacher, teacher

ECHER

ECHER	etcher
FECHER	fetcher
FLECHER	fletcher
KWECHER	quetcher
LECHER	lecher
SKECHER	sketcher
STRECHER	stretcher

ĒCHING

(See ĒCH, add -ing where appropriate.)

ECHING

(See ECH, add -ing where appropriate.)

ĒCHLES

(See ĒCH, add -less where appropriate.)

ĒCHMENT

PĒCHMENT	appeachment, impeachment

PRĒCHMENT	preachment
SĒCHMENT	beseechment

ĒDĀ

BĒDĀ	bidet
DĒDĀ	D-day
FĒDĀ	fee-day
VĒDĀ	V-day

ĒDA

ĒDA	Aida, Ouida
DRĒDA	olla-podrida
LĒDA	Leda
MĒDA	alameda, Alameda, Meda
SĒDA	kasida, quasida, reseda
VĒDA	Veda, vida

ĒDAL

(See ĒDL)

ĒDĒ

BĒDĒ	beady, bidet
DĒDĒ	deedy, indeedy
GRĒDĒ	greedy
HĒDĒ	heedy, unheedy
KRĒDĒ	creedy
MĒDĒ	mide, *Midi*
NĒDĒ	needy, unneedy
PĒDĒ	orthopedy
RĒDĒ	reedy
SĒDĒ	C.D., cedi, seedy, sidi
SPĒDĒ	speedy, unspeedy
TWĒDĒ	tweedy, untweedy
WĒDĒ	seaweedy, weedy

EDĒ

EDĒ	eddy
BEDĒ	beddy
BREDĒ	bready
HEDĒ	heady
LEDĒ	leady
NEDĒ	neddy
REDĒ	already, ready, reddy, unready
SHREDĒ	shreddy
STEDĒ	steady, unsteady
TEDĒ	teddy
THREDĒ	thready

ĒDED

(See ĒD, add -ed where appropriate.)

EDED

LEDED	leaded, non-leaded, unleaded

(See ED, add -ed or -ded where appropriate.)

ĒDEN

ĒDEN	Eden
RĒDEN	reeden
SWĒDEN	Sweden

EDEN

DEDEN	deaden
GEDEN	Armageddon
LEDEN	leaden
REDEN	redden
THREDEN	threaden

ĒDENS

KRĒDENS	credence
KWĒDENS	outrecuidance
PĒDENS	impedance
SĒDENS	antecedence, antecedents, intercedence, concedence, precedence, recedence, retrocedence, supersedence

ĒDENT

(See ĒDNT)

ĒDĒP

NĒDĒP	kneedeep
SĒDĒP	seadeep

ĒDER

BĒDER	beader
BLĒDER	bleeder
BRĒDER	breeder, cattlebreeder, stockbreeder

LĒDER   bandleader, cheerleader, leader ringleader
PLĒDER   interpleader, pleader
RĒDER   lipreader, reader, proofreader, scripture-reader
SĒDER   cedar, ceder, seeder

(See ĒD, add -er where appropriate.)

EDER

EDER   edder
BEDER   bedder, embedder
CHEDER   cheddar
DEDER   deader
DREDER   dreader
HEDER   beheader, doubleheader, header, triple-header
NEDER   nedder
REDER   redder
SHEDER   shedder
SHREDER   shredder
SLEDER   sledder
SPREADER   spreader
STEDER   homesteader
TEDER   tedder
THREDER   threader, unthreader
TREDER   retreader, treader
WEDER   wedder

ĒDFUL

DĒDFUL   deedful
HĒDFUL   heedful, unheedful
MĒDFUL   meadful, meedful
NĒDFUL   needful, unneedful
SĒDFUL   seedful
SPĒDFUL   speedful

ĒDGRŌN

RĒDGRŌN   reedgrown
SĒDGRŌN   seedgrown
WĒDGRŌN   weedgrown

EDHED

DEDHED   deadhead
REDHED   redhead

EDHĒT

DEDHĒT   dead-heat
REDHĒT   red-heat

EDĪ

DEDĪ   dead-eye
REDĪ   red-eye

ĒDIK

ĒDIK   logaoedic
MĒDIK   comedic
PĒDIK   encyclopedic, orthopedic, cyclopedic, talipedic
VĒDIK   Vedic

ĒDING

(See ĒD, add -ing where appropriate.)

EDING

(See ED, add -ing or -ding where appropriate.)

EDISH

EDISH   eddish
BEDISH   beddish
BREDISH   breadish
DEDISH   deadish
REDISH   reddish

EDIT

EDIT   edit, re-edit, sub-edit
KREDIT   accredit, disaccredit, discredit, credit, miscredit, Eurocredit

ĒDL

BĒDL   beadle
DĒDL   daedal, dedal
HWĒDL   wheedle
KWĒDL   conquedle
NĒDL   needle
PĒDAL   equipedal, millipedal, centipedal, solipedal
TWĒDL   tweedle

EDL

HEDL   heddle
MEDL   intermeddle, medal, meddle
PEDL   bipedal, semipedal

REDL   reddle
TREDL   treadle
WEDL   wedel

EDLAND

HEDLAND   headland
ZEDLAND   zedland

EDLĒ

DEDLĒ   deadly
MEDLĒ   medley
REDLĒ   redly

ĒDLER

HWĒDLER   wheedler
NĒDLER   needler

EDLER

HEDLER   heddler
MEDLER   intermeddler, meddler, medlar
REDLER   reddler
TREDLER   treadler

ĒDLES

(See ĒD, add -less where appropriate.)

EDLES

(See ED, add -less where appropriate.)

EDLĪN

BREDLĪN   breadline
DEDLĪN   deadline
HEDLĪN   headline

ĒDLING

HWĒDLING   wheedling
NĒDLING   needling
RĒDLING   reedling
SĒDLING   seedling

EDLING

HEDLING   heddling
MEDLING   intermeddling, meddling
PEDLING   peddling

REDLING reddling
TREDLING treadling

EDLĪT

DEDLĪT deadlight
HEDLĪT headlight
REDLĪT redlight

EDLOK

DEDLOK deadlock
HEDLOK headlock
KEDLOK kedlock
WEDLOK wedlock

ĒDMAN

FRĒDMAN freedman
SĒDMAN seedman

EDMAN

DEDMAN deadman
HEDMAN headman
REDMAN redman

ĒDNT

KRĒDNT credent
NĒDNT needn't
SĒDNT antecedent, decedent, intercedent, precedent, recedent, cedent

ĒDŌ

ĒDŌ Aido, Ido
BĒDŌ albedo, libido
KRĒDŌ credo
LĒDŌ Lido, Toledo
PĒDŌ stampedo, torpedo
RĒDŌ Laredo, teredo
VĒDŌ gravedo

EDŌ

EDŌ eddo
MEDŌ meadow

EDON

DEDON dead-on
HEDON head-on

ĒDRA

SĒDRA exedra
THĒDRA ex cathedra, cathedra

ĒDRAL

HĒDRAL anhedral, decahedral, didocahedral, dihedral, hemihedral, orthotetrakaldekahedral, polyhedral, rhombohedral, rhombicosidodedecahedral, pseudorhombicuboctahedral, trihedral
THĒDRAL cathedral, procathedral

EDREST

BEDREST bedrest
HEDREST headrest

ĒDRIK

DĒDRIK diedric
HĒDRIK holohedric, polyhedric

ĒDRON

HĒDRON dihedron, orthotetrakaldekahedron, polyhedron, rhombohedron, rhombicosidodedecahedron, pseudorhombicuboctahedron, trihedron
SĒDRON cedron

ĒDTĪM

FĒDTĪM feedtime
SĒDTĪM seedtime

ĒDUM

FRĒDUM freedom
LĒDUM ledum
PĒDUM pedum

> *REFLECTION*
>
> The rich eat steak,
>   The poor eat umbles;
> That's the way
>   The cooky crumbles.

EDWOOD

DEDWOOD deadwood
REDWOOD redwood

ĒDZMAN

BĒDZMAN beadsman, bedesman
SĒDZMAN seedsman

ĒER

FĒER feer, fere
FLĒER fleer
FRĒER freer
GRĒER agreer, disagreer
KRĒER decreer
SĒER *foreseer,* overseer, seer, sightseer

(See ÎR)

ĒFDUM

CHĒFDUM chiefdom
FĒFDUM fiefdom

ĒFĒ

BĒFĒ beefy
LĒFĒ leafy
RĒFĒ reefy
SHĒFĒ sheafy

ĒFER

BĒFER beefer
BRĒFER briefer
CHĒFER chiefer
FĒFER feoffer
LĒFER leafer, liefer
RĒFER reefer

EFER

DEFER deafer
FEFER feoffer, hasenpfeffer
HEFER heifer
ZEFER zephyr

EFIK

LEFIK	malefic
NEFIK	benefic
SEFIK	isopsephic
STREFIK	peristrephic

ĒFLĒ

BRĒFLĒ	briefly
CHĒFLĒ	chiefly

ĒFLES

(See ĒF, add -less where appropriate.)

ĒFOUL

PĒFOUL	peafowl
SĒFOUL	seafowl

EFTĒ

HEFTĒ	hefty
KEFTĒ	Kefti
LEFTĒ	lefty

EFTLĒ

DEFTLĒ	deftly
REFTLĒ	bereftly

ĒGA

DĒGA	bodega
MĒGA	omega
RĒGA	Riga
VĒGA	Vega
ZĒGA	ziega

ĒGAL

(See ĒGL)

EGĒ

EGĒ	eggy
DREGĒ	dreggy
KEGĒ	keggy
LEGĒ	leggy
PEGĒ	peggy
REGĒ	reggae
SEGĒ	seggy

ĒGER

ĒGER	eager, eagre, overeager
LĒGER	beleaguer, big-leaguer, leaguer, little-leaguer, major-leaguer, minor-leaguer
MĒGER	meager, meagre
TĒGER	fatiguer
TRĒGER	intriguer
ZĒGER	zieger

EGER

EGER	egger
BEGER	beggar, begger
LEGER	booklegger, bootlegger, legger
PEGER	pegger
SEGER	seggar, segger
SKEGER	skegger

EGERZ

PREGERZ	preggers

(See EGER, add -s where appropriate.)

ĒGING

LĒGING	enleaguing, leaguing
TĒGING	fatiguing
TRĒGING	intriguing

EGING

LEGING	bootlegging, legging

(See EG, add -ging where appropriate.)

ĒGL

ĒGL	bald eagle, double eagle, eagle, golden eagle, harpy eagle, sea eagle
BĒGL	beagle, porbeagle
GRĒGL	gregal
KLĒGL	kleagle
LĒGL	illegal, legal, paralegal
RĒGL	regal, vice-regal
SĒGL	seagull
TĒGL	teagle
VĒGL	inveigle

ĒGLER

BĒGLER	beagler
VĒGLER	inveigler

EGMEN

LEGMEN	legmen
TEGMEN	tegmen

EGNANT

PREGNANT	impregnant, pregnant
REGNANT	queen-regnant, regnant

ĒGŌ

ĒGŌ	ego, alter ego, superego
GRĒGŌ	grego
JĒGO	gigot
MĒGŌ	amigo
WĒGŌ	Oswego

ĒGRĒN

PĒGRĒN	pea-green
SĒGRĒN	sea-green

ĒGRES

ĒGRES	egress
NĒGRES	Negress
RĒGRES	regress

ĒHĒ

HĒHĒ	heehee
RĒHĒ	bahuvrihi
TĒHĒ	teehee

ĒHŌL

KĒHŌL	keyhole
NĒHŌL	kneehole

ĒIK

ĒIK	caffeic, choreic
LĒIK	oleic
PĒIK	mythopoeic, onomatopoeic, tropeic

RĒIK	diarrheic
SĒIK	caseic
TĒIK	proteic,
	xanthroproteic

ĒIN

DĒIN	codein
FĒIN	caffeine
ZĒIN	zein

ĒING

BĒING	being, inbeing,
	nonbeing, well-being
SĒING	farseeing, foreseeing,
	clear-seeing,
	overseeing, seeing,
	sightseeing,
	unforeseeing,
	unseeing

(See Ē, add -ing where appropriate.)

ĒIST

DĒIST	deist, ideist
KĒIST	Manicheist
THĒIST	antitheist, hylotheist,
	monotheist,
	polytheist, theist
ZĒIST	zeist

ĒIZM

DĒIZM	deism
KĒIZM	Manicheism
SĒIZM	Phariseeism,
	Parseeism,
	Sadduceeism
TĒIZM	absenteeism,
	Sutteeism
THĒIZM	A antitheism,
	atheism, F
	philotheism, H
	henotheism,
	hylotheism, K
	cosmotheism, M
	McCarthyism,
	misotheism, O
	autotheism, P
	polytheism, S
	schiotheism, TH
	theism
WĒIZM	we-ism

EJBURD

| HEJBURD | hedgebird |
| SEJBURD | sedgebird |

ĒJĒ

FĒJĒ	Fiji
JĒJĒ	Gigi
SKWĒJĒ	squeegee

EJĒ

EJĒ	edgy
HEJĒ	hedgy
KLEJĒ	cledgy
LEJĒ	ledgy
SEJĒ	sedgy
WEJĒ	wedgy

EJER

EJER	edger
DREJER	dredger
HEJER	hedger
KEJER	kedger
LEJER	alleger, ledger, leger
PLEJER	pledger, repledger
SLEJER	sledger

ĒJIK

PĒJIK	bibliopegic
PLĒJIK	hemiplegic,
	quadriplegic,
	paraplegic, cycoplegic
TĒJIK	strategic

EJING

(See EJ, add -ing where appropriate.)

ĒJIT

| LĒJIT | college |
| MĒJIT | immediate |

EJLING

| FLEJLING | fledgling |
| HEJLING | hedgling |

EJŌ

| FEJŌ | solfeggio |
| PEJŌ | arpeggio |

ĒJOō

| ĒJOō | ejoo |
| BĒJOō | bijou |

ĒJUN

LĒJUN	collegian, legion
RĒJUN	region, subregion,
	underregion
WĒJUN	Glaswegian,
	Norwegian,
	Sou'wegian

(See Ē'JI.AN)

ĒJUS

ĒJUS	aegis, egis
GRĒJUS	egregious
LĒJUS	sacrilegious

ĒKA

BĒKA	sabeca
KĒKA	quica
NĒKA	Dominica
PĒKA	Topeka
PRĒKA	paprika
RĒKA	Costa Rica, eureka,
	Eureka
SĒKA	sika
SPĒKA	spica, Spica
THĒKA	bibliotheca,
	endotheca,
	glyptotheca,
	lipsanotheca,
	pinacotheca, theca
WĒKA	weka
YĒKA	Tanganyika

EKA

EKA	Ecca, ekka
BEKA	Rebecca
MEKA	Mecca

ĒKAL

FĒKAL	faecal, fecal
KĒKAL	caecal
THĒKAL	bibliothecal,
	intrathecal, thecal
TRĒKAL	treacle

EKANT

(See EKUNT)

EKCHER

FEKCHER	confecture
JEKCHER	dejecture, conjecture, projecture, subjecture
LEKCHER	belecture, lecture
TEKCHER	architecture

ĒKĒ

BĒKE	beaky
BLĒKĒ	bleaky
CHĒKĒ	cheeky, cheek-to-cheeky
FRĒKĒ	freaky
KLĒKĒ	cliquey
KRĒKĒ	creaky, creeky
LĒKĒ	cockaleeky, leaky, leeky
PĒKĒ	peaky, peeky
RĒKĒ	reeky
SĒKE	hide-and-seeky
SHĒKĒ	dashiki, sheiky
SHRĒKĒ	shrieky
SKWĒKĒ	squeaky
SLĒKĒ	sleeky
SNĒKE	sneaky
STRĒKĒ	streaky
TĒKĒ	batiky, teaky, tiki
VĒKĒ	Bolsheviki, Mensheviki
WĒKĒ	veni, vidi, vici

EKĒ

CHEKĒ	checky
FLEKĒ	flecky
KEKĒ	kecky
PEKĒ	pecky
REKĒ	wrecky, shipwrecky
SPEKĒ	specky

ĒKEN

BĒKEN	beacon
BLĒKEN	bleaken
DĒKEN	archdeacon, deacon
HĒKEN	Mohican
MĒKEN	meeken
SLĒKEN	sleeken
WĒKEN	weaken

EKEN

(See EKUN)

ĒKER

BĒKER	beaker
BLĒKER	bleaker
CHĒKER	cheeker
KRĒKER	creaker, krieker
LĒKER	leaker, obliquer
MĒKER	meeker
PĒKER	peeker
RĒKER	reeker
SĒKER	seeker, self-seeker
SHĒKER	chicer
SHRĒKER	shrieker
SKWĒKER	squeaker
SLĒKER	sleeker
SNĒKER	sneaker
SPĒKER	bespeaker, lipspeaker, speaker, stump-speaker
STRĒKER	streaker
TWĒKER	tweaker
WĒKER	weaker

EKER

CHEKER	checker, chequer, exchequer, rechecker
DEKER	bedecker, decker, double-decker, two-decker, three-decker
FLEKER	flecker
NEKER	necker, Dominecker
PEKER	henpecker, oxpecker, pecker, woodpecker
REKER	wrecker
SNEKER	snecker
TREKER	trekker, voortrekker

EKERD

CHEKERD	checkered
REKERD	record

EKERZ

CHEKERZ	checkers

(See EKER, add s where appropriate.)

ĒKĪD

LĒKĪD	oblique-eyed
MĒKĪD	meek-eyed
WĒKĪD	weak-eyed

ĒKING

(See ĒK, add -ing where appropriate.)

EKING

(See EK, add -ing where appropriate.)

ĒKISH

(See ĒK, add -ish where appropriate.)

ĒKL

(See ĒKAL)

EKL

DEKL	deckel, deckle
FREKL	befreckle, freckle
HEKL	heckle
JEKL	Jekyll
KEKL	keckle
SHEKL	shekel
SPEKL	bespeckle, kenspeckle, speckle

EKLD

(See EKL, add -ed where appropriate.)

ĒKLĒ

BLĒKLĒ	bleakly
LĒKLĒ	obliquely
MĒKLĒ	meekly
NĒKLĒ	uniquely
SLĒKLĒ	sleekly
TRĒKLĒ	treacly
WĒKLĒ	biweekly, semiweekly, triweekly, weakly, weekly

EKLĒ

FREKLĒ	freckly
SPEKLĒ	speckly

EKLER

FREKLER	freckler
HEKLER	heckler
SPEKLER	speckler

EKLES

(See EK, add -less where appropriate.)

EKLING

DEKLING	deckling
FREKLING	freckling

HEKLING	heckling	
KEKLING	keckling	
SPEKLING	speckling	

EKMĀT

CHEKMĀT	checkmate
DEKMĀT	deckmate

ĒKNES

PRĒKNES	Preakness

(See **ĒK,** add *-ness* where appropriate.)

ĒKŌ

CHĒKŌ	chico, Chico
FĒKŌ	beccafico, fico
KLĒKŌ	Cliquot
MĒKŌ	mico
NĒKŌ	Nikko
PĒKŌ	pekoe, picot, Tampico
RĒKŌ	Puerto Rico
SĒKŌ	zortzico
TĒKŌ	matico

EKŌ

EKŌ	echo, re-echo
BEKŌ	bekko
DEKŌ	art deco, dekko
GEKŌ	gecko
GREKŌ	El Greco
SEKŌ	secco

ĒKOK

MĒKOK	meacock
PĒKOK	peacock
SĒKOK	sea-cock

ĒKON

(See **ĒKEN**)

EKON

(See **EKUN**)

ĒKOUT

FRĒKOUT	freakout
SPĒKOUT	speak-out

ĒKRAB

PĒKRAB	pea-crab
SĒKRAB	sea-crab
TRĒKRAB	tree-crab

EKSAL

NEKSAL	adnexal, annexal, nexal
PLEKSAL	plexal

EKSĒ

KEKSĒ	kexy
LEKSĒ	kyriolexy
PLEKSĒ	apoplexy, cataplexy
PREKSĒ	prexy
REKSĒ	pyrexy
SEKSĒ	sexy, unsexy

EKSER

DEKSER	indexer
FLEKSER	dorsiflexer, flexer, flexor
NEKSER	annexer
PLEKSER	perplexer, plexor
SEKSER	unsexer, unisexer
VEKSER	vexer

EKSHER

FLEKSHER	deflexure, flexure, inflexure, contraflexure
PLEKSHER	plexure

EKSHUN

EKSHUN	ebriection
FEKSHUN	*A* affection, *D* defection, disaffection, disinfection, *E* effection, *I* imperfection, infection, *K* confection, *P* perfection, *PR* profection, *R* refection, reinfection
FLEKSHUN	deflection, dorsiflection, flection, flexion, inflection, genuflection, reflection, retroflexion, circumflexion
JEKSHUN	*A* abjection, adjection, *D* dejection, *E* ejection, *I* injection, insubjection, interjection, introjection, *O* objection, *PR* projection, *R* rejection, *S* subjection, *TR* trajection
LEKSHUN	by-election, bolection, *D* dilection, *E* election, *I* intellection, *K* collection, *L* lection, *PR* predilection, pre-election, prelection, *R* reelection, recollection, *S* selection
NEKSHUN	disconnection, connection, reconnection
PLEKSHUN	complexion
REKSHUN	direction, erection, indirection, incorrection, insurrection, correction, misdirection, piloerection, redirection, rection, resurrection
SEKSHUN	*B* bisection, *D* dissection, *E* exsection, *H* half-section, *I* insection, intersection, *KW* quarter-section, *M* midsection, *R* resection, *S* section, subsection, *TR* trisection, *V* venesection, vivisection
SPEKSHUN	inspection, introspection, prospection, retrospection, circumspection
TEKSHUN	detection, overprotection, protection, underprotection
VEKSHUN	advection, evection, convection, provection, circumvection, vection

EKSHUR

(See **EKSHER**)

EKSHUS

FEKSHUS	infectious
LEKSHUS	selectious

LEKSIK

LEKSIK	lexic
REKSIK	anorexic

EKSĪL

EKSĪL	exile
FLEKSĪL	flexile

EKSING

EKSING	X-ing

(See **EKS**, add -ing where appropriate.)

EKSIS

LEKSIS	catalexis, lexes, lexis
PLEKSIS	epiplexis
REKSIS	orexis
TEKSIS	lymacatexis, syntexis, Texas
THEKSIS	cathexis

(See **EKSUS**)

EKSLĒ

PLEKSLĒ	complexly
VEKSLĒ	convexly

EKSTANT

EKSTANT	extant
SEKSTANT	sextant

EKSTIL

SEXTIL	bissextile, sextile
TEKSTIL	textile

EKSTRIN

DEKSTRIN	dextrin, dextrine
TEKSTRIN	textrine

EKSTRUS

DEKSTRUS	ambidextrous, dextrous
SEKSTRUS	ambisextrous

EKSUS

NEKSUS	connexus, nexus
PLEKSUS	amplexus, complexus, plexus, solar plexus

(See **EKSIS**)

EKTAL

EKTAL	ectal
LEKTAL	dialectal
REKTAL	rectal
TEKTAL	tectal

EKTANT

FEKTANT	disinfectant, infectant
FLEKTANT	reflectant
MEKTANT	humectant
NEKTANT	annectant
PEKTANT	aspectant, expectant, inexpectant, respectant, suspectant, unexpectant
PLEKTANT	amplectant

EKTED

PLEKTED	dark-complected, complected, light-complected

(See **EKT**, add -ed where appropriate.)

EKTENT

(See **EKTANT**)

EKTER

FEKTER	affecter, defector, disaffecter, disinfecter, effecter, infecter, perfecter
FLEKTER	deflecter, flector, inflecter, genuflector, nonreflector
GLEKTER	neglecter
HEKTER	hector, Hector
JEKTER	ejecter, injecter, interjecter, objector, projector, rejecter, subjecter
LEKTER	dialector, elector, lector, collector, prelector, recollecter, selecter
NEKTER	connector, nectar
PEKTER	expecter, suspecter
REKTER	director, erector, corrector, misdirecter, rector, resurrecter
SEKTER	bisector, dissecter, prosector, vivisecter
SPEKTER	disrespecter, expecter, inspector, prospector, respecter, specter, spectre
TEKTER	detector, protector
VEKTER	bivector, convector, odorivector, vector

EKTERD

HEKTERD	hectored
SPEKTERD	spectered

EKTEST

REKTEST	directist

(See **EKT**, add -est where appropriate.)

EKTFUL

GLEKTFUL	neglectful
SPEKTFUL	disrespectful, respectful, suspectful, unrespectful, unsuspectful

EKTIK

FEKTIK	ephectic
HEKTIK	hectic
KEKTIK	cachectic
KLEKTIK	eclectic
LEKTIK	acatalectic, analectic, bracycatalectic, dialectic, dyslectic, hypercatalectic, catalectic
NEKTIK	synectic
PEKTIK	isopectic, pectic
PLEKTIK	apoplectic, epiplectic

REKTIK	orectic
SMEKTIK	smectic
TEKTIK	orthotectic, syntectic, eutectic
THEKTIK	cathectic

EKTIL

JEKTIL	projectile
LEKTIL	supellectile
REKTIL	erectile
SEKTIL	insectile, sectile

EKTING

(See **EKT,** add -ing where appropriate.)

EKTIV

FEKTIV	affective, defective, effective, imperfective, ineffective, infective, perfective, refective
FLEKTIV	deflective, inflective, irreflective, reflective
GLEKTIV	neglective
JEKTIV	ejective, injective, conjective, objective, projective, rejective, subjective, unobjective
LEKTIV	elective, intellective, collective, recollective, selective, unselective
MEKTIV	humective
NEKTIV	disconnective, connective
REKTIV	directive, erective, corrective
SEKTIV	sective
SPEKTIV	inspective, introspective, irrespective, perspective, prospective, respective, retrospective, circumspective
TEKTIV	detective, protective
VEKTIV	invective

EKTIZM

KLEKTIZM	eclectism
SEKTIZM	sectism

EKTL

(See **EKTIL**)

EKTLĒ

(See **EKT,** add -ly where appropriate.)

EKTNES

JEKTNES	abjectness
LEKTNES	selectness
REKTNES	directness, erectness, indirectness, incorrectness, correctness
SPEKTNES	circumspectness

EKTOR

(See **EKTER**)

EKTORD

(See **EKTERD**)

EKTRES

LEKTRES	electress, lectress
REKTRES	directress, rectress
SPEKTRES	inspectress
TEKTRES	protectress

EKTRIKS

REKTRIKS	directrix, rectrix
SEKTRIKS	bisectrics, trisectrics
TEKTRIKS	tectrix

EKTRUM

LEKTRUM	electrum
PLEKTRUM	plectrum
SPEKTRUM	spectrum

EKTUS

FEKTUS	prefectus
LEKTUS	delectus
PEKTUS	pectous, pectus
REKTUS	rectus
SPEKTUS	conspectus, prospectus

ĒKUM

MĒKUM	vade mecum
SĒKUM	caecum, cecum

EKUN

BEKUN	beckon
FLEKUN	flecken
REKUN	reckon
SHNEKEN	schnecken

EKUND

FEKUND	fecund
REKUND	reckoned
SEKUND	femtosecond, nanosecond, picosecond, second

(See **EKUN,** add -ed where appropriate.)

EKUNT

PEKUNT	impeccant, peccant
SEKUNT	femtosecond, nanosecond, picosecond, second

ĒKWAL

ĒKWAL	equal, inequal, coequal, unequal
PRĒKWAL	prequel
SĒKWEL	sequel

ĒKWENS

FRĒKWENS	frequence, infrequence
SĒKWENS	sequence

ĒKWENT

FRĒKWENT	frequent, infrequent
SĒKWENT	sequent

ĒLA

ĒLA	Venezuela
BĒLA	belah
DĒLA	candela
GĒLA	narghile, nargile, Weigela
HĒLA	Gila
JĒLA	Weigel
KĒLA	chela, tequila
KWĒLA	sequela
LĒLA	palila
MĒLA	Philomela

SĒLA

SĒLA	selah
STĒLA	stela, stele
TĒLA	tela

ELA

ELA	paella
BELA	glabella, Isabella, clarabella, mabela, rubella, tabella
BRELA	umbrella
DELA	padella, predella
FELA	fellah
GELA	Shigella
MELA	columella, lamella
NELA	fifinella, fustanella, gentianella, justanella, canella, pimpinella, prunella, salmonella, citronella, villanella
PELA	a cappella, cappella, Capella
RELA	chlorella, corella, lirella, mozzarella, Cinderella, tiarella
SELA	agacella, bonsela, doncella, micella, navicella, osella, rosella, cella, sella, varicella, vorticella
TELA	fenestella, panatella, patella, scutella, tarantella
VELA	favela, favella, novella
ZELA	rosella

ĒLAND

| ĒLAND | eland |
| ZĒLAND | New Zealand |

ELANT

JELANT	flagellant
PELANT	appellant, expellant, expellent, impellant, interpellant, propellant, repellant
VELANT	divellent, revellent

ELAR

(See ELER)

ELAS

(See ELUS)

ELĀT

BELĀT	debellate, flabellate
PELĀT	appellate, interpellate, pellate
PRELĀT	prelate
SELĀT	ocellate, cellate, varicellate
STELĀT	*constellate*, stellate
TELĀT	patellate, scutellate

ELBA

| ELBA | Elba |
| MELBA | peach melba |

ELBORN

| HELBORN | hell-born |
| WELBORN | well-born |

ELBOUND

| HELBOUND | hellbound |
| SPELBOUND | spellbound |

ELCHER

BELCHER	belcher
SKWELCHER	squelcher
WELCHER	welcher

ELCHING

BELCHING	belching
SKWELCHING	squelching
WELCHING	welching

ĒLDĒ

| WĒLDĒ | unwieldy, wieldy |
| YĒLDĒ | yieldy |

ĒLDED

(See ĒLD, add -ed where appropriate.)

ELDED

GELDED	gelded
MELDED	melded
WELDED	welded

ĒLDER

FĒLDER	fielder, infielder, outfielder
SHĒLDER	shielder
WĒLDER	wielder
YĒLDER	non-yielder, yielder

ELDER

ELDER	elder
GELDER	gelder
MELDER	melder
SKELDER	skelder
WELDER	welder

ELDEST

| ELDEST | eldest |

(See ELD, add -est where appropriate.)

ĒLDING

(See ĒLD, add -ing where appropriate.)

ELDING

GELDING	gelding
MELDING	melding
WELDING	welding

ELDUM

| SELDUM | seldom |
| SWELDUM | swelldom |

ĒLĒ

ĒLĒ	eely, Ely
DĒLĒ	dele
FĒLĒ	feally, feelie, feely
FRĒLĒ	freely
GRĒLĒ	Greeley
HĒLĒ	Swahili
HWĒLĒ	wheely
LĒLĒ	Lely
MĒLĒ	mealie, mealy
NĒLĒ	campanili
PĒLĒ	peele, peelee, peely, pili
SĒLĒ	seely
SKWĒLĒ	squealy
STĒLĒ	steely, stele
TĒLĒ	genteelly
VĒLĒ	jus civile, vealy

ELĒ

BELĒ	belly, gorbelly, whitebelly, casus belli, Leadbelly, potbelly, redbelly, shadbelly, slowbelly, sowbelly, tenterbelly, underbelly, yellowbelly
CHELĒ	Botticelli, vermicelli
DELĒ	deli, Delhi
FELĒ	felly
HELĒ	helly, rakehelly
JELĒ	jelly
KELĒ	kelly
MELĒ	melee
NELĒ	Nelly, nice Nelly
SELĒ	cancelli, vermicelli
SHELĒ	Shelley, shelly
SKELĒ	skelly
SMELĒ	smelly
TELĒ	tagliatelli, telly

ELĒD

BELĒD	bellied
JELĒD	*gelid*, jellied

ĒLER

ĒLER	eeler
DĒLER	dealer, double-dealer, interdealer, misdealer, New Dealer, wheeler-dealer
FĒLER	feeler
HĒLER	healer, heeler, ward heeler
HWĒLER	four-wheeler, sidewheeler, three-wheeler, two-wheeler, wheeler
JĒLER	congealer
KĒLER	keeler
NĒLER	annealer, kneeler
PĒLER	appealer, pealer, peeler, repealer
RĒLER	reeler
SĒLER	concealer, sealer, seeler
SKWĒLER	squealer
SPĒLER	spieler
STĒLER	stealer, steeler, stelar
VĒLER	revealer, vealer, velar

ELER

BELER	beller, glabellar, rebeller
DWELER	apartment dweller, dweller, house dweller, cave dweller, country dweller, city dweller
FELER	feller, Rockefeller
HELER	heller
KELER	bierkeller, Helen Keller
KWELER	queller
MELER	lamellar
NELER	kneller
PELER	*A* appellor, *D* dispeller, *E* expeller, *I* impeller, *K* compeller, *KL* cloud-compeller, *PR* propeller, propellor, *R* repeller, *SK* screw propeller, *TW* twin propeller
SELER	exceller, salt cellar, cellar, sellar, seller, underseller, wine cellar
SHELER	sheller
SMELER	smeller
SPELER	speller
STELER	interstellar, nonstellar, circumstellar, stellar
SWELER	sweller
TELER	foreteller, fortune-teller, patellar, story-teller, tale-teller, teller
WELER	weller
YELER	yeller

ELET

PELET	pellet

(See **ELĀT**)

ELFIK

DELFIK	Delphic, diadelphic, monodelphic
GELFIK	Guelphic

ELFIN

ELFIN	elfin
DELFIN	delphin, Delphin, delphine

ELFISH

ELFISH	elfish
PELFISH	pelfish
SELFISH	selfish, unselfish
SHELFISH	shellfish

ELFRĒ

BELFRĒ	belfry
PELFRĒ	pelfry

ĒLFUL

ĒLFUL	eelful
SĒLFUL	seelful
WĒLFUL	wealful
ZĒLFUL	zealful

ĒLIJ

HWĒLIJ	wheelage
KĒLIJ	keelage
STĒLIJ	stealage

ELIK

BELIK	bellic
DELIK	infidelic, psychedelic
FELIK	fellic
HELIK	parhelic
JELIK	angelic, archangelic, evangelic, superangelic, unangelic
KELIK	nickelic
MELIK	melic
PELIK	sapropelic, scalpelic
RELIK	relic
SKELIK	skelic
TELIK	Aristotelic, philatelic, heterotelic, autotelic, Pentelic, telic

ĒLĪN

BĒLĪN	beeline
FĒLĪN	feline
MĒLĪN	meline
SĒLĪN	sealine

ĒLING

SĒLING	ceiling
SHĒLING	shieling
SKĒLING	skeeling

(See **ĒL**, add -*ing* where appropriate.)

ELING

(See **EL**, add *-ing* where appropriate.)

ELISH

BELISH	embellish
HELISH	hellish
RELISH	disrelish, relish
SWELISH	swellish
WELISH	wellish

ELIST

CHELIST	cellist
TRELIST	trellist

ELIT

BELIT	flabellate
PELIT	appellate
PRELIT	prelate

ĒLMENT

JĒLMENT	congealment
PĒLMENT	repealment
SĒLMENT	concealment
VĒLMENT	revealment

ELMET

HELMET	helmet
PELMET	pelmet
WELMET	well-met

ELMING

HELMING	dishelming, helming, unhelming
HWELMING	overwhelming, underwhelming, whelming

ĒLNES

LĒLNES	lealness
TĒLNES	genteelness

ELNES

FELNES	fellness
SWELNES	swellness
WELNES	unwellness, wellness

ELŌ

ELŌ	Aello, duello, niello
BELŌ	bellow, sgabello
CHELŌ	cello, Monticello, violoncello
DELŌ	bordello, Sordello
FELŌ	bedfellow, felloe, fellow, good fellow, playfellow, yokefellow
HELŌ	*hello*
JELŌ	bargello, Jell-O
MELŌ	mellow, unmellow
NELŌ	prunello, Punchinello, ritornello
PELŌ	cobra de capello
RELŌ	albarello, morello, saltarello
SELŌ	choralcelo
TELŌ	brocatello, martello
THELŌ	Othello
VELŌ	scrivello
YELŌ	yellow

> ### *OBEAH AND PARENESIS CAN ASK THEIR OWN PRICE*
>
> The kind of sorcerer folks call an obeah
> Is not a man you'd want to hang around;
> A word from him may fill you with a phobia,
> Or cast a spell that lays you underground.
>
> He shakes his spear and utters his parenesis
> (A fancy way of saying 'exhortation').
> Avoid him, for his voodoos are the genesis
> Of babies' boils and dying men's damnation.
>
> (Words ending *-phobia* arrive in batches,
> With only *obeah* for rhyming mix;*
> There's no rhyme but *parenesis* that matches
> Words ending *-genesis*—some twenty-six.)

*Not true. There is also *cobia*, the sergeant fish.

ELŌD

BELŌD	bellowed
MELŌD	mellowed, unmellowed
YELŌD	yellowed

ELON

(See **ELUN**)

ELOT

HELOT	helot
ZELOT	zealot

ELPER

HELPER	helper, self-helper
HWELPER	whelper
KELPER	kelper
YELPER	yelper

ELPING

(See **ELP**, add *-ing* where appropriate.)

ELPLES

HELPLES	helpless
HWELPLES	whelpless
KELPLES	kelpless
YELPLES	yelpless

ĒLSKIN

ĒLSKIN	eelskin
SĒLSKIN	sealskin

ELTA

DELTA	delta
PELTA	pelta
SHELTA	shelta

ĒLTĒ

FĒLTĒ	fealty
RĒLTĒ	realty

ELTED

BELTED	belted
MELTED	melted
PELTED	pelted
SMELTED	smelted
WELTED	welted

ELTER

BELTER	belter
FELTER	felter
KELTER	kelter
MELTER	melter
PELTER	pelter
SHELTER	inshelter, shelter, tax shelter
SKELTER	helter-skelter, skelter
SMELTER	smelter
SPELTER	spelter
SWELTER	swelter
WELTER	welter

ELTERD

SHELTERED   sheltered

(See **ELTER,** add *-ed* where
appropriate.)

ELTHĒ

HELTHĒ   healthy, unhealthy
STELTHĒ   stealthy
WELTHĒ   unwealthy, wealthy

ELTING

(See **ELT,** add *-ing* where appropriate.)

ELTLES

(See **ELT,** add *-less* where appropriate.)

ELTRĒ

PELTRĒ   peltry
SWELTRĒ   sweltry

ELUM

BELUM   antebellum,
flabellum, cribellum,
labellum,
postbellum, pre-
bellum, cerebellum
FELUM   phellum
JELUM   flagellum
PELUM   pelham, Pelham
SELUM   sacellum
TELUM   haustellum,
clitellum, rostellum,
scutellum
VELUM   vellum

ELUN

FELUN   enfelon, felon
MELUN   melon, mushmelon,
muskmelon,
watermelon

ELUS

HELUS   Hellas
JELUS   jealous
PELUS   pellas
SELUS   marcellus, nucellus,
ocellus, procellas,
procellous

TELUS   entellus, vitellus
VELUS   vellus
ZELUS   overzealous, zealous

ELVER

(See **ELV,** add *-r* where appropriate.)

ELVING

DELVING   delving
HELVING   helving
SHELVING   shelving

ĒLYA

DĒLYLA   seguidilla
BĒLYA   lobelia
FĒLYA   alcoholophilia,
epistomophilia,
coprophilia,
chromatophilia,
melcryptovesti-
mentophilia,
ophelia, Ophelia,
scophophilia,
spasmophilia
KĒLYA   Barranquilla
MĒLYA   amelia, iatramelia,
camellia, cimelia

(See **Ē'LI.A**)

ĒLYUN

(See **Ē'LI.AN**)

ELYUN

ELYUN   perduellion
BELYUN   rebellion
HELYUN   hellion
KELYUN   kellion
SELYUN   selion
SKELYUN   tetraskelion

(See **EL'I.AN**)

ĒMA

ĒMA   empyema, seriema
BĒMA   bema, bimah
BLĒMA   emblema, epiblema
DĒMA   edema, myxedema
KĒMA   hyporchema

LĒMA   Lima
RĒMA   rhema, rima,
sclerema, sorema,
terza rima
SĒMA   emphysema
SHĒMA   Hiroshima
SKĒMA   schema
TĒMA   blastema, Fatima
THĒMA   enthema, erythema,
thema
TMĒMA   tmema
ZĒMA   eczema

EMA

JEMA   gemma
LEMA   analemma, dilemma,
lemma, neurilemma,
polylemma,
tetralemma, trilemma
NEMA   nema
REMA   maremma
STEMA   stemma
STREMA   stremma

ĒMAL

ĒMAL   hiemal
DĒMAL   demal
HĒMAL   hemal, pseudohemal
LĒMAL   lemel
TĒMAL   blastemel

ĒMAN

BĒMAN   beeman
DĒMAN   agathodemon,
demon, cacodemon,
endemon
FRĒMAN   freeman
JĒMAN   G-man
HĒMAN   he-man
LĒMAN   leman
SĒMAN   able seaman,
merchant seaman,
seaman, semen
TĒMAN   T-man, teaman

EMBER

EMBER   ember
MEMBER   dismember,
disremember,
member, nonmember,
remember
SEMBER   December
TEMBER   September
VEMBER   November

EMBL

SEMBL	assemble, disassemble, dissemble, reassemble, semble
TREMBL	atremble, tremble
ZEMBL	resemble

EMBLANS

SEMBLANS	assemblance, dissemblance, semblance
ZEMBLANS	resemblance

EMBLANT

SEMBLANT	semblant
ZEMBLANT	resemblant

EMBLD

(See **EMBL,** add -d where appropriate.)

EMBLĒ

SEMBLĒ	assembly, disassembly, dissembly
TREMBLĒ	trembly

EMBLER

SEMBLER	assembler, disassembler, dissembler, reassembler, sembler
TEMBLER	temblor
TREMBLER	trembler
ZEMBLER	resembler

EMBLING

(See **EMBL,** add -ing where appropriate.)

EMBRAL

MEMBRAL	bimembral, membral, trimembral
SEMBRAL	Decembral
TEMBRAL	Septembral
VEMBRAL	Novembral

ĒMĒ

BĒMĒ	beamy
DRĒMĒ	day-dreamy, dreamy
GLĒMĒ	gleamy
KRĒMĒ	creamy
NĒMĒ	mneme
PRĒMĒ	preemie
SĒMĒ	monosemy, polysemy, seamy
SKRĒMĒ	screamy
STĒMĒ	steamie, steamy
STRĒMĒ	streamy
TĒMĒ	teamy, teemy

EMĒ

DEMĒ	demi
FLEMĒ	phlegmy
HEMĒ	hemi
JEMĒ	gemmy, jemmy
SEMĒ	semi
TREMĒ	tremie
ZEMĒ	zemmi

ĒMEL

(See **ĒMAL**)

ĒMENT

GRĒMENT	agreement, disagreement
KRĒMENT	decreement

ĒMER

ĒMER	emir
BĒMER	beamer
DĒMER	deemer, redeemer
DRĒMER	daydreamer, dreamer
FĒMER	blasphemer, femur
KRĒMER	creamer
LĒMER	lemur
PRĒMER	supremer
RĒMER	reamer
SĒMER	seamer
SKĒMER	schemer
SKRĒMER	screamer
STĒMER	steamer
STRĒMER	streamer
TĒMER	teemer
TRĒMER	extremer, tremor

EMER

EMER	emmer
DEMER	condemner

HEMER	hemmer
JEMER	begemmer
STEMER	stemmer
TEMER	contemner
TREMER	tremor

ĒMFUL

BĒMFUL	beamful
DRĒMFUL	dreamful
KRĒMFUL	creamful
RĒMFUL	reamful
SKĒMFUL	schemeful
STRĒMFUL	streamful
TĒMFUL	teemful

ĒMIK

FĒMIK	phemic
HĒMIK	hemic, polyhemic
NĒMIK	anemic, phonemic
RĒMIK	eremic
SĒMIK	racemic, semic, septicemic
SKĒMIK	schemic

EMIK

DEMIK	academic, edemic, ecdemic, endemic, epidemic, pandemic, polydemic
HEMIK	hemic, polyhemic
JEMIK	stratagemic
KEMIK	alchemic, ischemic
LEMIK	philopolemic, misopolemic, Moslemic, polemic
NEMIK	phonemic
REMIK	eremic, theoremic
SEMIK	semic
TEMIK	systemic, totemic

EMIKS

EMIKS	noemics

(See **EMIK,** add -s where appropriate.)

ĒMING

(See **ĒM,** add -ing where appropriate.)

EMING

(See **EM,** add -ing or -ming where appropriate.)

ĒMISH

(See ĒM, add -ish where appropriate.)

EMISH

BLEMISH	blemish, unblemish
FLEMISH	flemish, Flemish

ĒMIST

FĒMIST	blasphemist
PRĒMIST	supremist
SKĒMIST	schemist
TRĒMIST	extremist

ĒMLĒ

PRĒMLĒ	supremely
SĒMLĒ	seemly, unseemly
TRĒMLĒ	extremely

ĒMLES

YĒMLES	yemeless

(See ĒM, add -less where appropriate.)

EMLIN

GREMLIN	gremlin
KREMLIN	Kremlin

ĒMŌ

NĒMŌ	Little Nemo, Nemo
PRĒMŌ	primo, supremo

ĒMON

(See ĒMAN)

EMPER

SEMPER	semper, sic semper
TEMPER	attemper, distemper, temper, untemper

EMPL

STEMPL	stemple
TEMPL	temple

EMPLER

TEMPLER	templar
ZEMPLER	exemplar

EMPSHUN

EMPSHUN	exemption, emption, coemption, preemption
DEMPSHUN	ademption, redemption
REMPSHUN	diremption
ZEMPSHUN	exemption

EMPSTER

DEMPSTER	dempster
SEMPSTER	sempster

EMPTED

(See EMPT, add -ed where appropriate.)

EMPTER

EMPTER	empter, caveat emptor, coemptor, preemptor
KEMPTER	unkempter
TEMPTER	attempter, tempter
ZEMPTER	exempter

EMPTING

(See EMPT, add -ing where appropriate.)

EMPTIV

EMPTIV	preemptive
DEMPTIV	redemptive

ĒMSONG

DRĒMSONG	dream-song
THĒMSONG	theme song

ĒMSTER

DĒMSTER	deemster
SĒMSTER	seamster
TĒMSTER	teamster

ĒNA

ĒNA	hyena
BĒNA	amphisbaena, anabaena, verbena
CHĒNA	kachina
DĒNA	modena
FĒNA	saphena
GLĒNA	Euglena
HĒNA	tahina
JĒNA	gena, Cartagena
KĒNA	coquina, marikina
LĒNA	dolina, cantilena, galena, Catalina, salina, semolina
PĒNA	philopena, subpoena
RĒNA	arena, ballerina, farina, marina, tsarina, czarina
SĒNA	dracaena, encina, cassena, Messina, piscina, scena
TĒNA	Argentina, phlyctena, flutina, cantina, catena, cavatena, concertina, poltina, sestina, scarlatina, sonatina
THĒNA	Athena
VĒNA	avena, novena, vina
ZĒNA	maizena

ENA

ENA	duenna, sienna, Vienna
BENA	bena
HENA	Gehenna, henna
JENA	jenna
SENA	senna
TENA	antenna
VENA	Ravenna

ĒNAL

DĒNAL	duodenal
PĒNAL	penal
PLĒNAL	plenal
RĒNAL	adrenal, marinal, renal
SHĒNAL	machinal
VĒNAL	venal
WĒNAL	weanel

ENANS

PENANS	penance
TENANS	tenants

ENANT

| PENANT | pennant |
| TENANT | lieutenant, sublieutenant, tenant, tenent |

ENANTS

(See ENANS)

ENAS

(See ENIS)

ĒNĀT

| ĒNĀT | enate |
| KRĒNĀT | crenate |

ENĀT

PENĀT	brevipennate, impennate, latipennate, longipennate, pennate, tripennate
RENĀT	perennate
TENĀT	antennate

ENCHANT

(See ENSHENT)

ENCHER

BENCHER	backbencher, bencher, debenture
BLENCHER	blencher
DENCHER	denture, indenture, rudenture
DRENCHER	bedrencher, drencher
FLENCHER	flencher
KLENCHER	clencher, unclencher
KWENCHER	quencher
RENCHER	wrencher
TENCHER	tenture
TRENCHER	intrencher, trencher
VENCHER	adventure, maladventure, misadventure, peradventure, reventure, venture
WENCHER	wencher

ENCHING

(See ENCH, add -ing where appropriate.)

ENCHLES

(See ENCH, add -less where appropriate.)

ENCHMAN

| FRENCHMAN | Frenchman |
| HENCHMAN | henchman |

ENDA

ENDA	hacienda
BENDA	benda
DENDA	addenda, denda, credenda
JENDA	agenda, corrigenda, legenda
LENDA	delenda
RENDA	merenda, referenda

ENDAL

(See ENDL)

ENDANS

(See ENDENS)

ENDANT

(See ENDENT)

ENDĒ

BENDĒ	bendy
FENDĒ	effendi, fendi, fendy
TRENDĒ	trendy
VENDĒ	modus vivendi

ENDED

(See END, add -ed where appropriate.)

ENDENS

PENDENS	dependence, impendence, independence, interdependence
SENDENS	ascendance, descendence, condescendence, transcendence
SPLENDENS	resplendence
TENDENS	attendance, attendants, intendance, superintendence, superintendents, tendance

ENDENT

FENDENT	defendant
PENDENT	appendant, dependant, dependent, equipendent, impendent, independent, interdependent, pendant, pendent
SENDENT	ascendant, descendant, transcendent
SPLENDENT	resplendent, splendent, transplendent
TENDENT	attendant, intendant, contendant, superintendent

ENDER

ENDER	ender, tail-ender, weekender
BENDER	bender, fender-bender, mind-bender
BLENDER	blender, interblender
FENDER	defender, fender, offender
FLENDER	flender
HENDER	apprehender, comprehender, reprehender
JENDER	engender, gender
LENDER	lender, moneylender
MENDER	amender, emender, commender, mender, recommender
PENDER	depender, expender, perpender, suspender
PRENDER	prender
RENDER	render, surrender
SENDER	ascender, descender, sender
SLENDER	slender
SPENDER	spender
SPLENDER	splendor
TENDER	attender, bartender, extender, intender, contender, pretender
TRENDER	trender
VENDER	vender, vendor
WENDER	wender

ENDERD

JENDERD	engendered, gendered
RENDERD	rendered, surrendered
SPLENDERD	many-splendored

ENDING

RENDING	heart-rending

(See END, add -ing where appropriate.)

ENDL

BENDL	prebendal
SENDL	sendal, sendle
TRENDL	trendle

ENDLES

ENDLES	endless
BENDLES	bendless
FRENDLES	friendless
MENDLES	mendless
TRENDLES	trendless

ENDMENT

FRENDMENT	befriendment
MENDMENT	amendment, commendment
TENDMENT	intendment

ENDŌ

ENDŌ	diminuendo, innuendo
KENDŌ	kendo
SHENDŌ	crescendo

ENDOR

(See ENDER)

ENDUM

ENDUM	definiendum
DENDUM	addendum, dedendum, credendum
JENDUM	agendum, corrigendum
RENDUM	referendum

ENDUS

DENDUS	pudendous
MENDUS	tremendous
PENDUS	stupendous
RENDUS	horrendous

ĒNĒ

ĒNĒ	eeny
BĒNĒ	beanie, beany
BLĒNĒ	blini
CHĒNĒ	fantoccini, fettuccini
DĒNĒ	Houdini
GRĒNĒ	greeny
GWĒNĒ	linguine, linguini
HĒNĒ	Tahine, wahine
JĒNĒ	genie
KĒNĒ	bikini, Bikini, monokini, zucchini
KRĒNĒ	hippocrene
LĒNĒ	galeeny, lene, Mussolini, Selene, tortellini
MĒNĒ	meanie, meany, eeny-meeny
NĒNĒ	campanini, Toscanini
PĒNĒ	scaloppini
PLĒNĒ	pleny
SĒNĒ	grissini, Messene
SHĒNĒ	sheeny
SKĒNĒ	skene
SPLĒNĒ	spleeny
SWĒNĒ	sweeny
TĒNĒ	martini, teeny
VĒNĒ	visne
WĒNĒ	teeny-weeny, weeny, wieny
ZĒNĒ	tetrazzini

ENĒ

ENĒ	any
BENĒ	beni, benne, benny
BLENĒ	blenny
FENĒ	fenny
HENĒ	henny
JENĒ	jenny, spinning jenny
KENĒ	Kilkenny
MENĒ	many
PENĒ	half-penny, ha'penny, Henny-Penny, catchpenny, passpenny, penny, pinchpenny, sixpenny, tuppenny, twopenny
TENĒ	tenney, tenny
WENĒ	wenny

ENEK

(See ENIK)

ENEL

BENEL	bennel
FENEL	fennel
KENEL	kennel, rekennel, unkennel
KRENEL	crenel
VENEL	vennel

ENEM

DENEM	denim
MENEM	mennom
VENEM	envenom, venom

ĒNER

BĒNER	shebeener
GLĒNER	gleaner
GRĒNER	greener
KĒNER	keener
KLĒNER	cleaner, uncleaner, vacuum cleaner, window cleaner (etc.)
LĒNER	leaner, lienor
MĒNER	demeaner, demeanor, meaner, mesner, misdemeanor
PRĒNER	preener
RĒNER	serener, submariner
SĒNER	obscener
SHĒNER	machiner
SKRĒNER	screener
TĒNER	routiner, teener
TWĒNER	go-betweener
VĒNER	advener, convener, contravener, intervenor, supervenor
WĒNER	weaner, wiener
ZĒNER	magaziner

ENER

KENER	kenner
MENER	menhir
PENER	penner
TENER	contratenor, countertenor, tenner, tenor
YENER	yenner

ĒNES

(See Ē, add -ness where appropriate.)

ENET

BENET	bennett
DENET	dennet
JENET	genet, jennet
RENET	rennet
SENET	senate, sennet
TENET	tenet

ENGTHĒ

LENGTHĒ	lengthy
STRENGTHĒ	strengthy

ENGTHEN

LENGTHEN	lengthen
STRENGTHEN	strengthen

ĒNĪ

GRĒNĪ	green-eye
MĒNĪ	mean-eye
SĒNĪ	Iceni

ĒNĪD

GRĒNĪD	green-eyed
KĒNĪD	keen-eyed
MĒNĪD	mean-eyed

ĒNIJ

GRĒNIJ	greenage
RĒNIJ	careenage
TĒNIJ	teenage

ĒNIK

FĒNIK	phenic
SĒNIK	scenic
SPLĒNIK	splenic

ENIK

DENIK	Edenic
FENIK	alphenic, fennec, phenic
FRENIK	phrenic, hebrephrenic, cacophrenic, paraphrenic, schizophrenic
JENIK	*A* agnogenic, allogenic, anthropogenic, *D* deuterogenic, Diogenic, diplogenic, dysgenic, *E* embryogenic, enteropathogenic, *F* phosphorogenic, photogenic, *GL* glycogenic, *H* hallucinogenic, hepatogenic, hysterogenic, *I* iatrogenic, *J* gelogenic, genic, *KR* cryogenic, crystallogenic, chronogenic, *M* mediagenic, metagenic, mythogenic, *N* nitrogenic, *O* oxygenic, organogenic, *P* paragenic, parthenogenic, pathogenic, pyrogenic, pythogenic, polygenic, *PR* protogenic, *S* saprogenic, suicidogenic, *T* telegenic, typhogenic, *TH* thermogenic, *Y* eugenic, *Z* zoogenic
KENIK	lichenic
LENIK	philhellenic, galenic, Hellenic, geoselenic, Panhellenic, selenic
MENIK	ecumenic, poimenic
RENIK	irenic, sirenic
SENIK	Saracenic, acenic
SFENIK	sphenic
SPLENIK	splenic
STENIK	tungstenic
STHENIK	sthenic
TENIK	neotenic
THENIK	asthenic, Demosthenic, calisthenic, neurasthenic, parthenic

ENIKS

JENIKS	oligogenics, eugenics
THENIKS	euthenics

(See **ENIK,** add -*s* where appropriate.)

ENIM

(See **ENEM**)

ENIN

LENIN	Lenin
RENIN	rennin
VENIN	antivenin, venin

ĒNING

ĒNING	eaning
BĒNING	shebeening
DĒNING	deaning
GLĒNING	gleaning
GRĒNING	greening
KĒNING	keening
KLĒNING	cleaning
KWĒNING	queening
LĒNING	leaning, upleaning, trampolining
MĒNING	demeaning, double meaning, ill-meaning, meaning, unmeaning, well-meaning
PRĒNING	preening
RĒNING	careening
SĒNING	damascening, scening
SHĒNING	machining
SKRĒNING	screening
TĒNING	costeaning, quarantining
VĒNING	advening, intervening, contravening, convening, subvening, supervening
WĒNING	overweening, weaning, weening
YĒNING	yeaning

ENING

KENING	kenning
PENING	penning

ĒNIS

(See **ĒNUS**)

ENIS

MENIS	menace
TENIS	tenace, tennis
VENIS	Venice

ĒNISH

BĒNISH	beanish
GRĒNISH	greenish
KĒNISH	keenish
KLĒNISH	cleanish
KWĒNISH	queenish
LĒNISH	leanish
MĒNISH	meanish
SPLĒNISH	spleenish

ENISH

HENISH	hennish
PLENISH	deplenish, displenish, plenish, replenish
RENISH	Rhenish
WENISH	wennish

ĒNIST

PLĒNIST	plenist
SHĒNIST	machinist
TĒNIST	routinist
ZĒNIST	magazinist

ENIT

JENIT	jennet
SENIT	senate, sennet, sennit, sennight

ĒNLĒ

GRĒNLĒ	greenly
KĒNLĒ	keenly
KLĒNLĒ	cleanly
KWĒNLĒ	queenly
LĒNLĒ	leanly
MĒNLĒ	meanly
RĒNLĒ	serenely
SĒNLĒ	obscenely

ENLĬK

DENLĬK	denlike
FENLĬK	fenlike
HENLĬK	henlike
PENLĬK	penlike
RENLĬK	wrenlike

ĒNLING

ĒNLING	eanling
KWĒNLING	queenling
WĒNLING	weanling
YĒNLING	yeanling

ENMAN

FENMAN	fenman
PENMAN	penman

ĒNNES

(See ĒN, add -ness where appropriate.)

ĒNŌ

BĒNŌ	albino, bambino, beano, sabino, wabeno
CHĒNŌ	cappuccino, chino
DĒNŌ	ladino, San Bernardino, tondino
FĒNŌ	fino
KĒNŌ	baldachino, keno, maraschino, zecchino
LĒNŌ	leno
MĒNŌ	amino, camino, comino, Mino, palomino
NĒNŌ	pianino, spranino
PĒNŌ	Filipino
RĒNŌ	whiskerino, merino, peacherino, peperino, Reno, San Marino, sereno, solferino, vetturino
SĒNŌ	casino
TĒNŌ	andantino, batino, festino, concertino, Latino, Valentino
TRĒNŌ	neutrino
VĒNŌ	vino

ENOM

(See ENEM)

ENON

(See ENUN)

ĒNOR

(See ĒNER)

ENOR

(See ENER)

ENSAL

MENSAL	bimensal, commensal, mensal
RENSAL	forensal

(See ENSIL)

ENSĀT

DENSĀT	condensate
PENSĀT	compensate
SENSĀT	insensate, sensate
TENSĀT	intensate

ENSEN

ENSEN	ensign
DENSEN	densen
SENSEN	Sensen

ENSER

DENSER	denser, condenser
FENSER	fencer
FLENSER	flenser
HENSER	prehenser
MENSER	commencer, menser
PENSER	dispenser, recompenser
SENSER	censer, censor, incensor, senser, sensor
SPENSER	spencer, Spencer, Spenser
TENSER	extensor, intenser, tenser, tensor

ENSĒZ

ENSĒZ	amanuenses
JENSĒZ	Albigenses
MENSĒZ	menses

ENSFORTH

HENSFORTH	henceforth
HWENSFORTH	whenceforth
THENSFORTH	thenceforth

ENSHAL

ENSHAL	expediential, experiential, influential,

DENSHAL	incruential, obediential, sapiential, sciential E evidential, J jurisprudential, K confidential, KR credential, PR precedential, presidential, providential, prudential, R residential, rodential
JENSHAL	agential, bigential, indulgential, intelligential, tangential
KWENSHAL	inconsequential, consequential, sequential, subsequential
LENSHAL	pestilential, querulential
NENSHAL	exponential
RENSHAL	D deferential, differential, I inferential, irreverential, K conferential, PR preferential, R referential, reverential, S circumferential, T torrential, TR transferential, U unreverential
SENSHAL	essential, inessential, coessential, concupiscential, quintessential, nonessential, reminiscential, super-essential, unessential
TENSHAL	equipotential, existential, penitential, potential, sentential
VENSHAL	Provencial
ZENSHAL	omnipresential

ENSHENT

PENSHENT	penchant
SENSHENT	assentient, dissentient, insentient, consentient, presentient, sentient
TRENSHENT	trenchant

ĒNSHIP

DĒNSHIP	deanship
KWĒNSHIP	queenship

ENSHUN

DENSHUN	indention
HENSHUN	apprehension, deprehension, inapprehension, incomprehension, comprehension, misapprehension, preapprehension, prehension, reprehension
JENSHUN	gentian
KLENSHUN	declension
MENSHUN	dimension, mention
PENSHUN	pension, propension, repension, suspension
SENSHUN	accension, ascension, descension, dissension, incension, condescension, consension, presention, reascension, recension, uncondescension
STENSHUN	abstention
TENSHUN	A attention, D detention, distention, E extension, H hypertension, hypotension, hortensian, I inattention, inextension, intention, K co-extension, contention, O obtention, ostension, P portention, PR pretension, R retention, T tension, TH thermotension
VENSHUN	intervention, invention, contravention, convention, nonintervention, obvention, prevention, circumvention, subvention, supervention
ZENSHUN	presention

ENSHUND

MENSHUND	ill-mentioned, mentioned, unmentioned, well-mentioned
TENSHUND	ill-intentioned, intentioned, unintentioned, well-intentioned

ENSHUS

ENSHUS	conscientious
DENSHUS	tendentious
LENSHUS	pestilentious, silentious
SENSHUS	dissentious, licentious
TENSHUS	contentious, pretentious, sententious, uncontentious, unpretentious

ENSIL

HENSIL	prehensile
PENSIL	pensel, pencil, pensile
SENSIL	sensile
STENSIL	stencil
TENSIL	extensile, tensile, utensil

(See **ENSAL**)

ENSILD

PENSILD	pencilled
STENSILD	stencilled

ENSING

DENSING	condensing, uncondensing, evidencing
FENSING	fencing
FLENSING	flensing
MENSING	commencing, recommencing
PENSING	dispensing, prepensing, propensing, recompensing
RENSING	referencing, reverencing
SENSING	censing, incensing, sensing
TENSING	pretensing, tensing

ENSIV

ENSIV	influencive
DENSIV	condensive
FENSIV	defensive, indefensive, inoffensive, counteroffensive, offensive, self-defensive
HENSIV	apprehensive, inapprehensive, incomprehensive, comprehensive, prehensive, reprehensive, unapprehensive
PENSIV	expensive, inexpensive, pensive, recompensive, suspensive
SENSIV	ascensive, descensive, incensive, condescensive
TENSIV	distensive, extensive, energy-intensive, inextensive, intensive, coextensive, labor-intensive, ostensive, protensive, tensive

ENSL

(See **ENSAL, ENSIL**)

ENSLĒ

DENSLĒ	densely
MENSLĒ	immensely
PENSLĒ	propensely
TENSLĒ	intensely, tensely

ENSLES

FENSLES	defenseless, fenceless, offenseless
PENSLES	expenseless, recompenseless, penceless
SENSLES	senseless

ENSMENT

MENSMENT	commencement
SENSMENT	incensement

ENSNES

DENSNES	denseness
MENSNES	immenseness
PENSNES	propenseness
TENSNES	intenseness, tenseness

ENSOR

(See **ENSER**)

ENSUM

PENSUM	pensum
SENSUM	sensum

ENTA

JENTA	magenta
LENTA	polenta
MENTA	impedimenta, pedimenta, pimenta, rejectamenta
MYENTA	pimienta
NENTA	nenta
SENTA	placenta
YENTA	yenta

ENTAD

ENTAD	ectoentad, entad
PENTAD	pentad

ENTAL

ENTAL	ental, oriental
DENTAL	*A* accidental, antecedental, *B* bidental, dental, dentil, dentile, *E* edental, *I* incidental, interdental, *K* coincidental, *L* labiodental, linguadental, *O* occidental, *P* postdental, *TR* transcendental, tridental
JENTAL	argental, gentle, ungentle
LENTAL	Lental, lentil
MENTAL	*D* departmental, detrimental, developmental, documental, *E* excremental, experimental, elemental, environmental, *F* firmamental, fundamental, *FR* fragmental, *G* governmental, *I* impedimental, incremental, instrumental, *K* compartmental, complemental, complimental, condimental, *L* ligamental, *M* medicamental, mental, momental, monumental, *N* nutrimental, *O* ornamental, *P* parliamental, pedimental, pigmental, *PR* predicamental, *R* regimental, recremental, rudimental, *S* sacramental, sedimental, segmental, sentimental, submental, supplemental, *T* tegmental, tegumental, temperamental, tenemental, testamental, tournamental
NENTAL	intercontinental, componental, continental, transcontinental
RENTAL	biparental, grandparental, parental, rental
SENTAL	percental, placental, cental
TRENTAL	trental

ENTANS

PENTANS	repentance, unrepentance
SENTANS	sentence

ENTANT

PENTANT	repentant, unrepentant
ZENTANT	representant

ENTĀT

DENTĀT	bidentate, dentate, edentate, quadridentate, tridentate
MENTĀT	dementate, testamentate
RENTĀT	parentate

ENTĒ

ENTĒ	Agua Caliente, aguardiente, dolce far niente, niente
DENTĒ	al dente, presidente
LENTĒ	dolente, festina lente
MENTĒ	lentamente, tormenty
PENTĒ	diapente
PLENTĒ	aplenty, plenty
SHENTĒ	cognoscente, cognoscenti
TWENTĒ	twenty

ENTED

(See **ENT**, add -ed where appropriate.)

ENTENS

(See **ENTANS**)

ENTER

ENTER	enter, reenter, scienter
DENTER	denter, indenter
KWENTER	frequenter
LENTER	lentor, relenter
MENTER	E experimenter, F fermenter, fermentor, fomenter, K commenter, L lamenter, M mentor, O augmenter, ornamenter, S cementer, supplementer, T tormenter
PENTER	repenter
RENTER	renter
SENTER	A accentor, assenter, B barycenter, bucentaur, D dissenter, E epicenter, H hypocenter, I incentor, K concenter, consenter, O orthocenter, PR precentor, S center, centaur, succentor
SHLENTER	schlenter
STENTER	stentor
TENTER	contenter, retentor, tenter
VENTER	inventor, preventer, circumventor, venter
ZENTER	misrepresenter, presenter, representer, resenter

ENTERD

ENTERD	entered
SENTERD	centered

ENTFUL

MENTFUL	lamentful
SENTFUL	scentful
TENTFUL	contentful
VENTFUL	eventful, inventful, uneventful, uninventful
ZENTFUL	resentful, unresentful

ENTIJ

SENTIJ	percentage
VENTIJ	ventage

ENTIK

DENTIK	identic
JENTIK	argentic
SENTIK	crescentic
THENTIK	authentic

ENTĪL

JENTĪL	Gentile
SENTĪL	percentile, centile

ENTIN

DENTIN	dentin, dentine, Tridentine
KWENTIN	San Quentin
RENTIN	torrentine

ENTING

(See **ENT**, add -ing where appropriate.)

ENTIS

MENTIS	non compos mentis
PENTIS	appentice, pentice
PRENTIS	apprentice, prentice

ENTIST

DENTIST	dentist, irredentist
PRENTIST	apprenticed, prenticed
VENTIST	Adventist, preventist, Seventh Day Adventist

ENTIV

DENTIV	pendentive
MENTIV	lamentive
SENTIV	assentive, incentive
TENTIV	attentive, disincentive, detentive, inattentive, irretentive, retentive, unretentive
VENTIV	adventive, interventive, inventive, circumventive, preventive
ZENTIV	presentive, resentive

ENTL

(See **ENTAL**)

ENTLĒ

DENTLĒ	evidently, confidently
JENTLĒ	gently, ungently
LENTLĒ	excellently, insolently
NENTLĒ	eminently
SENTLĒ	innocently
TENTLĒ	impotently, intently

ENTLES

(See **ENT**, add -less where appropriate.)

ENTMENT

LENTMENT	relentment
TENTMENT	discontentment, contentment
ZENTMENT	presentment, representment, resentment

ENTŌ

ENTŌ	à bientôt
CHENTŌ	cinquecento, quattrocento
LENTŌ	lento
MENTŌ	divertimento, fomento, memento, pentimento, pimento, portamento, pronunciamento, rifacimento, Risorgimento, Sacramento
MYENTŌ	pimiento, repartimiento
RENTŌ	Sorrento
SENTŌ	cento

ENTOR

(See ENTER)

ENTRAL

SENTRAL	metacentral, paracentral, precentral, central, subcentral
VENTRAL	biventral, dorsiventral, ventral

ENTRĒ

ENTRĒ	entry
DENTRĒ	den-tree
JENTRĒ	gentry
SENTRĒ	sentry

ENTRES

MENTRES	tormentress
VENTRES	inventress

ENTRIK

SENTRIK	*A* anthropocentric, acentric, *B* barycentric, *E* egocentric, eccentric, ethnocentric, *H* haliocentric, homocentric, *J* geocentric, gyneocentric, *K* concentric, *M* metacentric, *P* paracentric, *S*

	Saturnicentric selenocentric
VENTRIK	ventric

ENTUM

GWENTUM	unguentum
MENTUM	*A* amentum, *F* fermentum, fundamentum, *M* momentum, *P* paludamentum, *R* ramentum, *S* sacramentum, sarmentum, cementum, *T* tegumentum, testamentum, tormentum, *V* velamentum
SENTUM	percentum

ENTŪR

(See ENCHER)

ENTUS

GWENTUS	unguentous
MENTUS	filamentous, immomentous, jumentous, ligamentous, momentous, pigmentous, sarmentous
TENTUS	pedententous, portentous

ENŪ

MENŪ	menu
VENŪ	change of venue, venue
ZHENŪ	*ingenue*

ĒNUM

DĒNUM	duodenum
FRĒNUM	frenum
PLĒNUM	plenum

ENUM

(See ENEM)

ENUN

MENUN	mennon, trimenon
PENUN	pennon
TENUN	tenon

(See ENIN)

ĒNUS

FĒNUS	saphenous
JĒNUS	genus
LĒNUS	scalenus, Silenus
PĒNUS	hemipenis, penis
SĒNUS	Maecenas
VĒNUS	intravenous, venous, Venus

ĒNYAL

JĒNYAL	genial, congenial, primigenial, primogenial, uncongenial
MĒNYAL	menial
RĒNYAL	original

(See Ē'NI.AL)

ENYAL

(See EN'I.AL)

ĒNYENS

LĒNYENS	lenience
VĒNYENS	advenience, inconvenience, intervenience, introvenience, convenience, prevenience, supervenience

(See Ē'NI.ENS)

ĒNYENT

LĒNYENT	lenient, unlenient
VĒNYENT	advenient, inconvenient, intervenient, introvenient,

convenient,
prevenient,
supervenient

(See E'NI.ENT)

ĒNYER

SĒNYER   Senior, signor,
monsignor

(See Ē'NI.ER)

ĒNYUS

JĒNYUS   ingenious, genius

(See Ē'NI.US)

ENZA

ENZA   influenza, Spanish
influenza
DENZA   cadenza, credenza

ĒŌ

BRĒŌ   con brio
DĒŌ   deo
KLĒŌ   Clio
LĒŌ   Leo
NĒŌ   neo
PĒŌ   papiopio
RĒŌ   Rio, zorillo
TRĒŌ   trio

ĒŌL

KRĒŌL   Creole
SHĒŌL   Sheol

ĒON

ĒON   aeon
DĒON   odeon
KRĒON   Creon
LĒON   Ponce de Leon
NĒON   neon
PĒON   paeon, peon
PLĒON   pleon
THĒON   pantheon
THRĒON   thrion

(See ĒAN)

ĒPAL

(See ĒPL)

EPARD

(See EPERD)

ĒPĒ

CHĒPĒ   cheapy, cheepy
HĒPĒ   heapy
KĒPĒ   kepi
KRĒPĒ   creepy
LĒPĒ   Fra Lippo Lippi
PĒPĒ   pee-pee
SĒPĒ   seepy
SHĒPĒ   sheepy
SLĒPĒ   sleepy
STĒPĒ   steepy
TĒPĒ   tepee
WĒPĒ   weepy

EPĒ

KEPĒ   kepi
PEPĒ   Apepi, peppy
PREPĒ   preppy
STEPĒ   one-steppy, steppy,
three-steppy, two-
steppy
TEPĒ   tepee

ĒPEN

CHĒPEN   cheapen
DĒPEN   deepen
STĒPEN   steepen

ĒPER

ĒPER   Ypres
BĒPER   beeper
CHĒPER   cheaper, cheeper
DĒPER   deeper
HĒPER   heaper
KĒPER   barkeeper,
beekeeper,
bookkeeper,
doorkeeper,
gatekeeper,
goalkeeper, hedge-
keeper, housekeeper,
innkeeper, keeper,
shopkeeper,
storekeeper,
timekeeper, wicket-
keeper
KRĒPER   creeper
LĒPER   leaper
NĒPER   Dnieper
PĒPER   peeper
RĒPER   Grim Reaper, reaper

SĒPER   seeper
SLĒPER   sleeper
STĒPER   steeper
SWĒPER   carpetsweeper,
minesweeper,
sweeper
TĒPER   tepor
WĒPER   weeper

EPER

HEPER   hepper
LEPER   leper
PEPER   pepper
STEPER   high-stepper,
overstepper, stepper,
three-stepper, two-
stepper, one-stepper
STREPER   strepor
TEPER   tepor

EPERD

JEPERD   jeopard
LEPERD   leopard
PEPERD   peppered
SHEPERD   shepherd

EPID

LEPID   lepid
TEPID   tepid
TREPID   intrepid, trepid

ĒPIJ

SĒPIJ   seepage
SWĒPIJ   sweepage

EPIK

EPIK   epic, orthoepic
NEPIK   monepic

ĒPING

KĒPING   beekeeping,
bookkeeping,
housekeeping,
keeping,
safekeeping,
shopkeeping
SLĒPING   sleeping, unsleeping

(See ĒP, add -ing where appropriate.)

ĒPISH

CHĒPISH	cheapish
DĒPISH	deepish
SHĒPISH	sheepish
STĒPISH	steepish

ĒPL

ĒPL	ipil
HWĒPL	wheeple
PĒPL	boat people, flower people, country people, peepul, people, repeople, townspeople, unpeople
STĒPL	church steeple, steeple
TĒPL	tepal

ĒPLĒ

CHĒPLĒ	cheaply
DĒPLĒ	deeply
STĒPLĒ	steeply

ĒPLES

BĒPLES	beepless
JĒPLES	jeepless
SHĒPLES	sheepless
SLĒPLES	sleepless

ĒPNES

CHĒPNES	cheapness
DĒPNES	deepness
STĒPNES	steepness

ĒPŌ

CHĒPŌ	cheapo
DĒPŌ	depot
RĒPŌ	repo

ĒPOI

SĒPOI	Sepoy
TĒPOI	teapoy, tepoy

EPOR

(See EPER)

EPSĒ

LEPSĒ	epilepsy, catalepsy, narcolepsy, nympholepsy, prosolepsy
PEPSĒ	apepsy, dyspepsy, Pepsi, eupepsy

EPSHUN

REPSHUN	direption, ereption, correption, obreption, proreption, subreption, surreption
SEPSHUN	*A* apperception, *D* deception, *E* exception, *I* imperception, inception, interception, introsusception, intussusception, *K* conception, contraception, *M* misconception, *P* perception, preception, *PR* preconception, preperception, *R* reception, *S* self-deception, susception

EPSIS

KEPSIS	omphaloskepsis
LEPSIS	analepsis, epanalepsis, metalepsis, narcolepsis, prolepsis, syllepsis
SEPSIS	antisepsis, asepsis

EPTANT

REPTANT	reptant
SEPTANT	acceptant, exceptant

EPTER

DEPTER	adepter
SEPTER	accepter, beneceptor, excepter, inceptor, interceptor, preceptor, receptor, scepter, sceptre, susceptor

EPTIK

KLEPTIK	kleptic
LEPTIK	acataleptic, analeptic, epanaleptic, epileptic, iatraleptic, cataleptic, metaleptic, narcoleptic, nympholeptic, organoleptic, proleptic, sylleptic
PEPTIK	apeptic, bradypeptic, dyspeptic, peptic, eupeptic
SEPTIK	antiseptic, aseptic, septic
SKEPTIK	sceptic, skeptic
THREPTIK	threptic
TREPTIK	protreptic

EPTĪL

REPTĪL	reptile
SEPTĪL	septile

EPTIL

REPTIL	reptile
SEPTIL	septile

EPTLĒ

EPTLĒ	eptly, ineptly
DEPTLĒ	adeptly

EPTNES

EPTNES	eptness, ineptness
DEPTNES	adeptness, unadeptness

EPTOR

(See EPTER)

ĒPWÔK

SHĒPWÔK	sheepwalk
SLĒPWÔK	sleepwalk

ĒRA

(See ÎRA)

ERA

ERA	era, sierra
TERA	terra, Terra

ERAF

(See ERIF)

ĒRAL

(See ÎRAL)

ERALD

(See ERILD)

ĒRANS

(See ÎRANS)

ERAZ

ERAZ	eras, sierras
TERAZ	terras

ĒRĒ

(See ÎRĒ)

ERĒ

BERĒ	*B* bayberry, baneberry, barberry, beriberi, berry, bury, bilberry, bogberry, bumbleberry, burberry, *BL* blackberry, blueberry, *BR* brambleberry, breadberry, *CH* checkerberry, chinaberry, chokeberry, *D* dangleberry, dayberry, deerberry, dogberry, dewberry, *G* gooseberry, *GW* guavaberry, *H* hackberry, huckleberry, *HW* whortleberry, *I* inkberry, *J* Juneberry, *K* catberry, coffeeberry, *KR* cranberry, Christmasberry, crowberry, *L*

	loganberry, locustberry, lotusberry, *M* mossberry, mulberry, *N* naseberry, *O* orangeberry, *P* partridgeberry, pinkberry, *R* raspberry, redberry, rowanberry, *SH* shadberry, *SKW* squawberry, *SN* snowberry, *STR* strawberry, *T* tangleberry, *TH* thimbleberry, *W* wild strawberry, wineberry, winterberry, *U* unbury, *Y* youngberry
CHERĒ	cherry, chokecherry, Pondicherry
DERĒ	derry, Londonderry
FERĒ	ferry
FLERĒ	flerry
HWERĒ	wherry
JERĒ	jerry, Tom and Jerry
KERĒ	knobkerrie
KWERĒ	equerry
LERĒ	intercalary
MERĒ	mere, merry
NERĒ	matutinary, millinery, quatercentenary, stationary, stationery
PERĒ	perry
RERĒ	Miserere
SERĒ	lamasery, serry
SHERĒ	sherry
SKERĒ	skerry
TERĒ	phrontistery, lamastery, mesentery, monastery, presbytery, sedentary, cemetery, terry
VERĒ	very

(See ÂRĒ)

ĒRĒD

(See ÎRĒD)

ERĒD

BERĒD	berried, buried, reburied, unburied
CHERĒD	cherried

FERĒD	ferried
HWERĒD	wherried
SERĒD	serried, unserried

ĒRENS

(See ÎRENS)

ĒRENT

(See ÎRENT)

ĒRER

(See ÎRER)

ERER

ERER	error
TERER	terror

(See ÂRER)

ĒRES

(See ÎRES)

ERET

FERET	ferret
HERET	disherit, disinherit, inherit
HWERET	wherret
LERET	lerret
MERET	demerit, merit
SERET	serrate
TERET	terret

ĒRETH

(See ÎRETH)

ĒRĒZ

(See ÎRĒZ)

ERFOR

HWERFOR	*wherefor,* wherefore
THERFOR	*therefor,* therefore

ĒRĪD

(See ÎRĪD)

ERIF

ERIF	eriff

| SERIF | sanserif, cerif, seraph, serif |
| SHERIF | sheriff |

ĒRIJ

(See ÎRIJ)

ERIK

ERIK	eric, Eric
BERIK	suberic
DERIK	deric, derrick
FERIK	atmospheric, ferric, helispheric, hemispheric, chromospheric, peripheric, perispheric
KLERIK	cleric
LERIK	valeric
MERIK	alphanumeric, anisomeric, dimeric, Homeric, isomeric, chimeric, mesmeric, metameric, numeric, polymeric, poromeric
NERIK	dineric, generic
SERIK	ceric, glyceric
SFERIK	spheric
SKERIK	skerrick
STERIK	steric
TERIK	*A* alexiteric, amphoteric, *E* exoteric, ennaeteric, enteric, esoteric, *G* gastroenteric, *H* hysteric, *I* icteric, isoteric, *KL* climacteric, *N* neoteric, *P* penteteric, pteric, terek
THERIK	sciatheric

ERIKS

| SFERIKS | atmospherics, spherics |
| TERIKS | hysterics |

(See **ERIK,** add -*s* where appropriate.)

ERIL

BERIL	beryl, chrysoberyl
FERIL	ferrule, ferule
PERIL	imperil, peril
STERIL	sterile, unsterile

ERILD

| HERILD | herald |
| PERILD | imperilled, perilled |

ERIN

| ERIN | Erin, errhyne |
| SERIN | serin, serine |

ĒRING

(See ÎRING)

ERING

ERING	erring
BERING	Bering
HERING	herring

ERIS

DERIS	derris
FERIS	ferris
TERIS	terrace, terris

ERISH

| CHERISH | cherish |
| PERISH | perish |

(See ÂRISH)

ERIT

(See ERET)

ĒRLĒ

(See ÎRLĒ)

ĒRLES

(See ÎRLES)

ĒRLING

(See ÎRLING)

ĒRMENT

(See ÎRMENT)

ĒRNES

(See ÎRNES)

ĒRŌ

(See ÎRŌ)

ERŌ

BRERŌ	sombrero
CHERŌ	ranchero
DERŌ	escudero, hacendero, matadero
FERŌ	faro, Pharaoh
KERŌ	vaquero
LERŌ	bandalero, bolero, galero
MERŌ	primero
NERŌ	dinero, Rio de Janeiro, llanero
PERŌ	pampero
RERŌ	torero
TERŌ	montero, zapatero
YERŌ	banderillero, caballero
ZERŌ	cruzeiro

ĒRŌŌM

| SĒRŌŌM | searoom |
| TĒRŌŌM | tearoom |

EROR

(See ERER)

ERŌŌL

FERŌŌL	ferrule, ferule
PERŌŌL	perule
SFERŌŌL	spherule

ĒRSER

(See ÎRSER)

ĒRUS

(See ÎRUS)

ĒRZMAN

(See ÎRZMAN)

ESA

ESA	Duessa
DESA	Odessa
PESA	Marpessa
SESA	sessa

ESCHAL

BESCHAL	bestial
GRESCHAL	agrestial
LESCHAL	celestial, supercelestial

ESCHER

JESCHER	gesture
PRESCHER	purpresture
VESCHER	divesture, investure, revesture, vesture

ESCHUN

JESCHUN	digestion, indigestion, ingestion, congestion, suggestion
KWESCHUN	question, requestion

ESCHUND

JESCHUND	poorly digestioned, well-digestioned
KWESCHUND	questioned, requestioned, unquestioned

ĒSĒ

FLĒSĒ	fleecy
GRĒSĒ	greasy
KRĒSĒ	creasy
SĒSĒ	seesee

ESĒ

ESĒ	esse, esssse, in esse
DRESĒ	dressy, undressy
KRESĒ	Cressy
MESĒ	messy
TRESĒ	tressy

ĒSENS

BĒSENS	obeisance
DĒSENS	decence
RĒSENS	recence

ESENS

ESENS	acquiescence, essence, quiescence, nonacquiescence, requiescence
BESENS	albescence, erubescence, exacerbescence, contabescence, pubescence, rubescence, subescence
DESENS	frondescence, incandescence, iridescence, candescence, recrudescence, viridescence
GRESENS	nigrescence
JESENS	inturgescence, turgescence
KRESENS	accrescence, excrescence, concrescence, crescence, crescents, superexcrescence, supercrescence
KWESENS	deliquescence, liquescence
LESENS	*A* adolescence, *D* decalescence, *E* emollescence, *H* hyalescence, *I* incalescence, incoalescence, invalescence, *K* calescence, coalescence, convalescence, *M* mollescence, *O* obsolescence, opalescence, *R* recalescence, *SP* spinulescence, *V* virilescence
MESENS	detumescence, fremescence, intumescence, spumescence, tumescence
NESENS	evanescence, juvenescence, luminescence, rejuvenescence, senescence
PESENS	torpescence
RESENS	*A* arborescence, *D* deflorescence, *E* efflorescence, *F* phosphorescence, *FL* florescence, fluorescence, *I* inflorescence, *K* calorescence, *R* reflorescence, revirescence, *S* sonorescence, *V* vaporescence, virescence
SESENS	glaucescence
TESENS	delitescence, fructescence, frutescence, quintessence, lactescence, latescence, mutescence
TRESENS	petrescence, putrescence, vitrescence
VESENS	defervescence, effervescence, ineffervescence, ingravescence, noneffervescence

ĒSENT

BĒSENT	obeisant
DĒSENT	decent, indecent
RĒSENT	recent

ESENT

ESENT	acquiescent, quiescent, nonacquiescent, requiescent
BESENT	albescent, erubescent, herbescent, contabescent, pubescent, rubescent, tabescent
DESENT	frondescent, incandescent, iridescent, candescent, lapidescent, recrudescent, viridescent
FESENT	confessant, rufescent
GRESENT	nigrescent
GWESENT	languescent
JESENT	rigescent, surgescent, turgescent
KRESENT	accrescent, decrescent, excrescent, increscent, concrescent, crescent, superexcrescent, supercrescent
KWESENT	deliquescent, liquescent

LESENT   *A* adolescent, acaulescent, alkalescent, *D* decalescent, *E* emollescent, *I* incalescent, incoalescent, *K* calescent, coalescent, convalescent, *M* mollescent, *O* obsolescent, opalescent, *R* revalescent, *SP* spinulescent, *V* violescent, virilescent

MESENT   detumescent, fremescent, intumescent, spumescent, tumescent

NESENT   evanescent, gangrenescent, ignescent, juvenescent, canescent, luminescent, rejuvenescent, senescent, spinescent

PESENT   torpescent
PRESENT   antidepressant, depressant, compressant, oppressant, repressant, suppressant

RESENT   *A* arborescent, *D* deflorescent, *E* efflorescent, *FL* florescent, fluorescent, phosphorescent, *I* inflorescent, *K* calorescent, *M* maturescent, *S* cinerescent, sonorescent, *V* virescent

SESENT   acescent, glaucescent, incessant, marcescent, cessant

TESENT   delitescent, fructescent, frutescent, lactescent, latescent, lutescent, mutescent, obmutescent, suffrutescent

TRESENT   petrescent, putrescent, vitrescent
VESENT   effervescent, fervescent, flavescent, ineffervescent, ingravescent, uneffervescent

ĒSER

FLĒSER   fleecer
GRĒSER   greaser
KRĒSER   decreaser, increaser, creaser
LĒSER   leaser, releaser, subleaser
PĒSER   piecer

ESER

ESER   acquiescer, nonacquiescer
BLESER   blesser
DRESER   addresser, dresser, hairdresser, redresser, redressor, undresser
FESER   confessor, professor
GESER   guesser, second guesser
GRESER   aggressor, digressor, progressor, transgressor
LESER   lesser, lessor, sublessor
MESER   messer
PLESER   plesser
PRESER   depressor, impressor, clothes presser, oppressor, pants presser, presser, pressor, suit presser, suppressor
RESER   caresser
SESER   antecessor, assessor, intercessor, *microprocessor,* obsessor, predecessor, *processor,* cesser, successor, *word processor*
TRESER   distresser
ZESER   dispossesser, possessor

ĒSFUL

PĒSFUL   peaceful
PRĒSFUL   capriceful

ESFUL

SESFUL   nonsuccessful, successful, unsuccessful
TRESFUL   distressful, stressful, undistressful

ĒSHA

LĒSHA   silesia, Silesia
NĒSHA   magnesia, Polynesia
PĒSHA   alopecia
VĒSHA   Helvetia

(See **ĒZHA,** also **Ē'ZI.A.**)

ESHAL

(See **ESHL**)

ĒSHAN

(See **ĒSHUN**)

ĒSHĒ

MĒSHĒ   kamichi
SHĒSHĒ   chichi
VĒSHĒ   Vichy

ESHĒ

ESHĒ   esssse
FLESHĒ   fleshy
MESHĒ   meshy

ESHENS

(See **ESH'I.ENS**)

ESHENT

(See **ESH'I.ENT**)

ESHER

FLESHER   flesher
FRESHER   fresher, refresher
MESHER   mesher
PRESHER   high pressure, low pressure, nonpressure, pressure
THRESHER   grain-thresher, wheat-thresher, thresher
TRESHER   tressure

ESHING

FLESHING	fleshing
FRESHING	refreshing
MESHING	meshing
THRESHING	threshing

ESHL

DESHL	deasil
SPESHL	especial, special

ESHLĒ

FLESHLĒ	fleshly
FRESHLĒ	freshly

ESHMENT

FLESHMENT	enfleshment
FRESHMENT	refreshment
MESHMENT	enmeshment

ĒSHUN

GRĒSHUN	Grecian
KLĒSHUN	Diocletian
KRĒSHUN	accretion, excretion, incretion, concretion, secretion
LĒSHUN	deletion
NĒSHUN	internecion, magnesian, Polynesian, Venetian
PLĒSHUN	depletion, impletion, incompletion, completion, repletion
VĒSHUN	Helvetian

(See **Ē'SHI.AN**)

ESHUN

FESHUN	confession, profession
FRESHEN	enfreshen, freshen
GRESHUN	A aggression, D degression, digression, E egression, I ingression, introgression, K congression, N nonaggression, PR progression, R regression, retrogression, S subingression, TR transgression
HESHEN	Hessian
KRESHUN	discretion, indiscretion
PRESHUN	decompression, depression, expression, impression, intropression, compression, oppression, reimpression, repression, suppression
SESHUN	A accession, I insession, intercession, J jam session, K concession, O obsession, PR precession, procession, R recession, retrocession, S secession, cession, session, circumincession, succession, supersession
ZESHUN	dispossession, possession, prepossession, repossession, self-possession

ESHUNS

(See **ES'I.ENS**)

ĒSHUS

NĒSHUS	monoecious
SĒSHUS	facetious
SPĒSHUS	specious

ĒSĪD

KĒSĪD	quayside
LĒSĪD	leeside
SĒSĪD	seaside

ESIJ

MESIJ	message
PESIJ	pesage
PRESIJ	expressage, presage

ĒSIK

JĒSIK	algesic, analgesic
NĒSIK	gynesic, mnesic, polynesic

ESIK

DESIK	geodesic
NESIK	eugenesic
RESIK	xyresic

ESĪL

SESĪL	sessile
TRESĪL	tresayle

ESIL

(See **ESL**)

ĒSING

FLĒSING	fleecing
GRĒSING	greasing
KRĒSING	decreasing, increasing, creasing
LĒSING	leasing, policing, releasing
PĒSING	piecing
SĒSING	ceasing, surceasing, unceasing

ESING

ESING	acquiescing
BLESING	blessing, reblessing
DESING	dessing
DRESING	addressing, dressing, field dressing, readdressing, redressing, salad dressing, undressing, water dressing
FESING	fessing, confessing, professing
GESING	guessing
GRESING	digressing, progressing, regressing, retrogressing, transgressing
JESING	jessing, rejessing, unjessing
LESING	coalescing
MESING	messing
NESING	finessing

PRESING	depressing, expressing, impressing, compressing, oppressing, repressing, suppressing				
RESING	caressing				
SESING	assessing, excessing, processing, recessing				
STRESING	stressing, restressing				
TRESING	distressing, retressing, tressing, untressing				
YESING	yessing				
ZESING	dispossessing, possessing, prepossessing, repossessing, unprepossessing				

ESIV

DRESIV	redressive
GRESIV	aggressive, digressive, ingressive, congressive, progressive, regressive, retrogressive, transgressive, unprogressive
KRESIV	concrescive, crescive
PRESIV	*D* depressive, *E* expressive, *I* impressive, inexpressive, *K* compressive, *O* oppressive, *R* repressive, *S* suppressive, *U* unexpressive, unimpressive, unoppressive
RESIV	caressive
SESIV	accessive, excessive, concessive, obsessive, recessive, successive, unexcessive
ZESIV	possessive, unpossessive

ESKĒ

DESKĒ	desky, Tedeschi
MESKĒ	kromeski
NESKĒ	Neskhi
PESKĒ	pesky

ESKLĒ

ESKLĒ	statuesquely
RESKLĒ	picturesquely
TESKLĒ	blottesquely, grotesquely

ESKNES

ESKNES	statuesqueness
RESKNES	picturesqueness
TESKNES	grotesqueness

ESKŌ

DESKŌ	tedesco
FRESKŌ	al fresco, fresco

ĒSIS

ĒSIS	acyesis, deësis, diesis, hematopoiesis, noesis, poiesis, cyesis, pseudocyesis
JĒSIS	algesis, diegesis, exegesis, eisegesis, periegesis
KRĒSIS	antichresis, catachresis
LĒSIS	ochlesis
MĒSIS	koimesis, mimesis, necromimesis, neuromimesis, pathomimesis
NĒSIS	amnesis, anamnesis, phonesis, phronesis, kinesis
PĒSIS	aposiopesis
RĒSIS	aphaeresis, apocarteresis, diaphoresis, diaeresis, paresis, perichoresis, synderesis, synteresis
SĒSIS	amasesis, ascesis, execesis
SKĒSIS	schesis
TĒSIS	amniocentesis, erotesis, paracentesis, centesis
THĒSIS	anesthesis, anthesis, esthesis, hyperesthesis, mathesis, thesis
TMĒSIS	tmesis

ESKŪ

FESKŪ	fescue
RESKŪ	rescue

ESL

CHESL	chessel
DESL	deasil, decile, dessil
DRESL	redressal
KRESL	cresyl
NESL	nestle
PESL	pestle
RESL	wrestle
SESL	sessile
TRESL	trestle
VESL	vessel

ESLD

NESLD	nestled
PESLD	pestled
RESLD	wrestled

ESLER

NESLER	nestler
PESLER	pestler
RESLER	wrestler

ĒSLES

(See **ĒS**, add *-less* where appropriate.)

ESLING

ESLING	essling
NESLING	nestling
PESLING	pestling
RESLING	wrestling

ESMAN

CHESMAN	chessman
DESMAN	desman
PRESMAN	pressman
YESMAN	yes-man

ESMENT

DRESMENT	redressment
PRESMENT	impressment
SESMENT	assessment

ESOR

(See ESER)

ESPER

HESPER	Hesper
VESPER	vesper

ESTA

ESTA	fiesta, siesta
DESTA	podesta
JESTA	egesta, ingesta
KWESTA	cuesta
LESTA	celesta
SESTA	cesta
TESTA	testa
VESTA	Vesta, Zend-Avesta

ESTAL

FESTAL	festal
GRESTAL	agrestal
TESTAL	matripotestal, patripotestal
VESTAL	vestal

ESTANT

JESTANT	decongestant, digestant, gestant
RESTANT	restant
TESTANT	contestant

ĒSTĒ

BĒSTĒ	beastie, beasty, bheestie, bheesty
RĒSTĒ	reasty
SNĒSTĒ	sneasty
YĒSTĒ	yeasty

ESTĒ

CHESTĒ	chesty
FESTĒ	festy
KRESTĒ	cresty
PESTĒ	pesty
RESTĒ	resty
TESTĒ	teste, testy
WESTĒ	westy
ZESTĒ	zesty

ESTED

BESTED	bested
BRESTED	breasted, chicken-breasted, double-breasted, marble-breasted, pigeon-breasted, single-breasted, unbreasted
KRESTED	foam-crested, castle-crested, crested, uncrested

(See EST, add -ed where appropriate.)

ĒSTER

ĒSTER	down-easter, Easter, nor'easter, northeaster, sou'easter, southeaster
FĒSTER	feaster
KĒSTER	keister
NĒSTER	Dniester

ESTER

ESTER	ester
BESTER	bester
BRESTER	breaster, double-breaster, single-breaster
FESTER	fester, infester, manifester
JESTER	digester, jester, suggester
KWESTER	quaestor, quester, requester, sequester
LESTER	molester
MESTER	bimester, mid-semester, semester, trimester
NESTER	Dnester, nester, nestor, Nestor
PESTER	pester
PRESTER	prester
RESTER	arrester, rester, wrester
SESTER	ancestor
TESTER	attester, contester, protester, testar, tester
VESTER	divester, investor, vester
WESTER	far-wester, Midwester, nor'wester, sou'wester, wester
YESTER	yester
ZESTER	zester

ESTERD

FESTERD	festered
KWESTERD	sequestered, unsequestered
PESTERD	pestered

ESTERN

HESTERN	hestern
WESTERN	far-western, Midwestern, northwestern, southwestern, western
YESTERN	yestern

ESTFUL

BLESTFUL	blestful
JESTFUL	jestful
KWESTFUL	questful
RESTFUL	restful, unrestful
ZESTFUL	zestful

ESTIJ

PRESTIJ	prestige
VESTIJ	vestige

ESTIK

BESTIK	asbestic
GRESTIK	agrestic
HESTIK	alkahestic
JESTIK	gestic, majestic
KESTIK	orchestic
KRESTIK	catachrestic, polychrestic
LESTIK	telesic, telestich
MESTIK	domestic
NESTIK	amnestic, anamnestic
PESTIK	anapestic

ESTIN

BESTIN	asbestine
DESTIN	destine, clandestine, predestine
JESTIN	progestine
SESTIN	sestine
TESTIN	intestine

ĒSTING

ĒSTING	easting

BĒSTING	beasting, bee-sting
FĒSTING	feasting
KWĒSTING	queesting
YĒSTING	yeasting

ESTING

BESTING	besting
BREASTING	breasting
FESTING	infesting, manifesting
GESTING	guesting
JESTING	digesting, ingesting, jesting, congesting, predigesting, redigesting, suggesting, uncongesting
KRESTING	cresting
KWESTING	questing, requesting
LESTING	molesting
NESTING	nesting
RESTING	arresting, disinteresting, interesting, rearresting, resting, wresting, unarresting, uninteresting
TESTING	attesting, detesting, contesting, protesting, reattesting, reprotesting, retesting, unprotesting
VESTING	divesting, investing, reinvesting, vesting
WESTING	westing

ESTIS

(See **ESTUS**)

ESTIV

ESTIV	estive
FESTIV	festive, infestive, manifestive
JESTIV	digestive, congestive, suggestive
PESTIV	intempestive, tempestive
RESTIV	arrestive, restive
TESTIV	attestive

ĒSTLĒ

BĒSTLĒ	beastly
PRĒSTLĒ	priestly

ESTLES

(See **EST,** add *-less* where appropriate.)

ESTMENT

RESTMENT	arrestment
VESTMENT	divestment, investment, vestment

ESTŌ

FESTŌ	manifesto
PRESTŌ	presto

ĒSTŌN

FRĒSTŌN	freestone
KĒSTŌN	keystone

ESTRA

KESTRA	orchestra
LESTRA	palestra
NESTRA	fenestra

ESTRAL

KESTRAL	kestrel, orchestral
LESTRAL	palestral
MESTRAL	semestral, trimestral
NESTRAL	anoestral, fenestral
PESTRAL	campestral
SESTRAL	ancestral

ESTRĀT

KESTRĀT	*orchestrate*
KWESTRĀT	sequestrate
NESTRĀT	fenestrate

ESTRIK

KESTRIK	orchestric
LESTRIK	palestric

ESTŪR

(See **ESCHER**)

ESTUS

BESTUS	asbestos
RESTUS	restis
SESTUS	Alcestis, cestus

ĒSUS

(See **ĒSIS**)

ĒTA

ĒTA	eta, chaeta, paracoita
BĒTA	beta
CHĒTA	cheetah
DĒTA	dita, pandita
GĒTA	Bhagavad-Gita, geta
KĒTA	chiquita, keta, coquita
KRĒTA	excreta
LĒTA	Lolita, mulita, veleta
NĒTA	magneta, manzanita, planeta
PĒTA	pita
RĒTA	amorita, amrita, margarita, señorita
SĒTA	seta
TĒTA	partita, sortita
THĒTA	theta
VĒTA	chirivita, dolce vita, vita
WĒTA	vita
ZĒTA	granzita, zeta

ETA

ETA	arietta, comedietta
BETA	betta
BRETA	cabretta
DETA	codetta, vendetta
FETA	feta
LETA	burletta, caballetta, mantelletta, muleta, valetta, Valletta
META	animetta, lametta, meta
NETA	sinfonetta
RETA	biretta, moreta, operetta
VETA	anchovetta
ZETA	mozzetta, Rosetta

ĒTAL

(See **ĒTL**)

ĒTĒ

BĒTĒ	beety
FĒTĒ	graffiti
GLĒTĒ	gleety
JĒTĒ	jiti
MĒTĒ	meaty
PĒTĒ	peaty
RĒTĒ	pariti
SĒTĒ	spermaceti

SLĒTĒ	sleety
SWĒTĒ	sweety
TĒTĒ	titi
TRĒTĒ	entreaty, treaty

ETĒ

BETĒ	Betty, brown betty
BRETĒ	libretti
CHETĒ	chetty, concetti
DETĒ	vendetti
FETĒ	confetti
FRETĒ	fretty
GETĒ	spaghetti
JETĒ	jetty
NETĒ	netty
PETĒ	petit, petty
SETĒ	spermaceti
SHETĒ	machete
SWETĒ	sweaty
YETĒ	yeti
ZETĒ	Rossetti, Sacco-Vanzetti

ĒTED

FĒTED	fetid
LĒTED	deleted, expletive deleted

(See ĒT, add -ed where appropriate.)

ETED

FETED	feted, fetid

(See ET, add -ed where appropriate.)

ĒTEN

ĒTEN	eaten, Eton, moth-eaten, overeaten, uneaten, worm-eaten
BĒTEN	beaten, brow-beaten, storm-beaten, tempest-beaten, unbeaten, weather-beaten
HWĒTEN	wheaten
JĒTEN	zyzzogeton
KĒTEN	Buster Keaton
KRĒTEN	Cretan, cretin
PĒTEN	piton
SĒTEN	seton
SWĒTEN	sweeten, unsweeten
TĒTEN	Teton

ETEN

BRETEN	Breton
FRETEN	fretten
HWETEN	whetten
THRETEN	threaten

ĒTER

ĒTER	A ant-eater, B beef-eater, D dirt-eater, dung-eater, E eater, F fire-eater, FL flesh-eater, FR frog-eater, GR grass-eater, H hay-eater, humble-pie eater, honey-eater, K cake-eater, KL clay-eater, KR crow-eater, L lotus-eater, M man-eater, O overeater, SM smoke-eater, T toad-eater, U undereater, W woman-eater
BĒTER	beater, brow-beater, child-beater, drum-beater, eggbeater, goldbeater, jungle-beater, rug-beater, slave-beater, wife-beater
BLĒTER	bleater
CHĒTER	cheater, escheater, windcheater
FĒTER	defeater, fetor
GRĒTER	greeter
HĒTER	heater, overheater, superheater, water heater
KRĒTER	excreter, secreter
LĒTER	decaliter, half liter, hectoliter, milliliter, liter, litre
MĒTER	ammeter, Demeter, gas meter, kilometer, konimeter, meeter, meter, metre, nanometer, centimenter, taximeter, water meter

(See ETRIK, change -metric to -meter where appropriate.)

NĒTER	neater
PĒTER	competer, peter, repeater, St. Peter, saltpeter

PLĒTER	depleter, completer, pleater, repleter
PRĒTER	praetor, propraetor
RĒTER	rhetor, uretor
SĒTER	masseter, receiptor, saeter, seater, two-seater, three-seater, unseater, one-seater
SKĒTER	skeeter
SWĒTER	sweeter
TĒTER	teeter
TRĒTER	entreater, ill-treater, maltreater, mistreater, retreater, treater
TWĒTER	tweeter

ETER

BETER	abetter, better, bettor
DETER	debtor
FETER	enfetter, fetter, unfetter
FRETER	fretter
GETER	begetter, forgetter, getter, go-getter
GRETER	regretter
HWETER	whetter
JETER	jetter
LETER	black letter, dead letter, letter, newsletter, red letter, scarlet letter
NETER	netter
PETER	petter
RETER	carburetor, retter
SETER	besetter, bonesetter, Irish setter, jetsetter, pacesetter, setter, somersetter, typesetter, upsetter
SWETER	sweater, unsweater
TETER	tetter
VETER	curvetter
WETER	wetter

ETERD

FETERD	fettered, unfettered
LETERD	lettered, unlettered
SWETERD	sweatered, unsweatered

ĒTES

(See ĒTUS)

ETFUL

FRETFUL	fretful, unfretful
GETFUL	forgetful, unforgetful

GRETFUL	regretful, unregretful
NETFUL	netful

ĒTHAL
(**TH** as in *thin*)

ĒTHAL	ethal
KWĒTHAL	bequeathal
LĒTHAL	lethal

ĒTHĒ
(**TH** as in *thin*)

HĒTHĒ	heathy
LĒTHĒ	philalethe, Lethe, prosopolethy

ETHĒ
(**TH** as in *thin*)

BRETHĒ	breathy
DETHĒ	deathy

ETHEL
(**TH** as in *thin*)

ETHEL	ethal, ethel, Ethel, ethyl
BETHEL	Bethel
METHEL	methyl

ĒTHEN
(**TH** as in *then*)

HĒTHEN	heathen
RĒTHEN	wreathen

ĒTHER
(**TH** as in *then*)

ĒTHER	either
BRĒTHER	breather, lung-breather, mud-breather, water-breather
KWĒTHER	bequeather
NĒTHER	neither
RĒTHER	enwreather, wreather
SĒTHER	seether
SHĒTHER	sheather
TĒTHER	teether

ETHER
(**TH** as in *then*)

BLETHER	blether
FETHER	feather, white feather, pinfeather, tail-feather, unfeather
GETHER	altogether, together
HETHER	heather
HWETHER	whether
LETHER	boot-leather, hell-for-leather, whitleather, leather, patent leather, underspurleather
NETHER	nether
TETHER	tether, untether
WETHER	aweather, bellwether, weather, wether

ETHERD
(**TH** as in *then*)

BLETHERD	blethered
FETHERD	feathered, unfeathered
HETHERD	heathered
TETHERD	tethered, untethered
WETHERD	unweathered, weathered

ETHIL
(See **ETHEL**)

ĒTHING
(**TH** as in *then*)

BRĒTHING	breathing, inbreathing, incense-breathing, outbreathing
KWĒTHING	bequeathing
RĒTHING	enwreathing, wreathing
SĒTHING	seething
SHĒTHING	sheathing, ensheathing, unsheathing
SMĒTHING	smeething
TĒTHING	teething

ĒTHLES
(**TH** as in *thin*)

RĒTHLES	wreathless
SHĒTHLES	sheathless

ETHLES
(**TH** as in *thin*)

BRETHLES	breathless
DETHLES	deathless

ĒTHMENT
(**TH** as in *then*)

KWĒTHMENT	bequeathment
RĒTHMENT	enwreathment, wreathment
SHĒTHMENT	ensheathment

ĒTHRAL

PĒTHRAL	hypaethral
RĒTHRAL	urethral

ĒTIJ

ĒTIJ	eatage
CHĒTIJ	cheatage, escheatage
KLĒTIJ	cleatage
MĒTIJ	metage

ĒTIK

KRĒTIK	Cretic
RĒTIK	paretic
SĒTIK	acetic, cetic
THĒTIK	thetic

ETIK

ETIK	*A* abietic, aloetic, anoetic, *D* dianoetic, *G* galactopoietic, goetic, *H* hypnoetic, *M* mythopoetic, *N* noetic, nosopoetic, *O* onomatopoetic, *P* poetic, *R* robietic, *Z* zoetic
BETIK	alphabetic, diabetic, hebetic, quodlibetic, tabetic
DETIK	asyndetic, eidetic, geodetic, syndetic
FETIK	aphetic, Japhetic, prophetic
JETIK	*A* analgetic, apologetic, algetic, *E* energetic, exergetic, epexegetic, *G* Gangetic, *I* inergetic, *S* synergetic, syzygetic, *ST* strategetic

KETIK	catachetic
KRETIK	syncretic
LETIK	*A* amuletic, athletic, *B* balletic, *BR* brachycataletic, *F* phyletic, *H* homiletic, *K* colletic, *L* Lettic, *O* ochletic, auletic, *P* polyphyletic, *Y* uletic
METIK	arithmetic, Baphometic, emetic, epithymetic, gametic, hermetic, cosmetic, logarithmetic, metic, mimetic, seismetic
NETIK	*A* abiogenetic, agamogenetic, antimagnetic, *B* biogenetic, biomagnetic, *D* diamagnetic, dianoetic, *E* electromagnetic, epigenetic, *F* phylogenetic, phonetic, *FL* phlognetic, phlogogenetic, *FR* frenetic, *H* heterogenetic, histogenetic, homogenetic, *I* isomagnetic, *J* genetic, gyromagnetic, *K* kinetic, *L* limnetic, *M* magnetic, monogenetic, morphogenetic, *O* ontogenetic, oogenetic, autokinetic, *P* paleogenetic, palingenetic, pangenetic, parenetic, parthenogenetic, pathogenetic, pyrogenetic, polygenetic, *S* cybernetic, psychogenetic, *SP* splenetic, *T* telekinetic, tonetic, *TH* thermogenetic, thermomagnetic, *THR* threnetic, *Y* eugenetic
PETIK	flatulopetic
RETIK	*A* alexipyretic,

anchoretic, anoretic, antipyretic, apyretic, *D* diaphoretic, diuretic, *E* emporetic, *H* heuretic, *M* Masoretic, *P* paretic, pyretic, *PL* plethoretic, *TH* theoretic, *Y* uretic

SETIK	ascetic, dipsetic, Docetic, copacetic, quercetic, auxetic, Ossetic
TETIK	apatetic, dietetic, erotetic, peripatetic, synartetic, zetetic
THETIK	*A* allopathetic, anesthetic, antipathetic, antithetic, apathetic, *B* bathetic, *D* diathetic, *E* enthetic, epenthetic, epithetic, aesthetic, esthetic, *F* photosynthetic, *H* hyperesthetic, hypothetic, *I* idiopathetic, *K* cosmothetic, *L* ludicropathetic, *M* mesothetic, *N* nomothetic, *P* parathetic, parenthetic, pathetic, polysynthetic, *PR* prosthetic, prothetic, *S* sympathetic, synthetic, *TH* theopathetic
VETIK	Helvetic

ETIKS

ETIKS	poetics
JETIKS	apologetics, exegetics, energetics
LETIKS	athletics, homiletics, signaletics
NETIKS	aerodynetics phonetics, genetics, kinetics, magnetics, Mendelian genetics, molecular genetics, cybernetics
RETIKS	theoretics
TETIKS	dietetics
THETIKS	anaesthetics, aesthetics, esthetics, prosthetics, synthetics

(See **ETIK**, add *-s* where appropriate.)

ĒTING

ĒTING	*B* beef-eating, *D* dirt-eating, dung-eating, *E* eating, *F* fire-eating, *FL* flesh-eating, *FR* frog-eating, *GR* grass-eating, *H* hay-eating, *KL* clay-eating, *KR* crow-eating, *M* man-eating, *O* overeating, *P* pork-eating, *S* smoke-eating, *T* toad-eating, *U* undereating, *V* vegetable-eating (etc.)
BĒTING	beating, brow-beating, child-beating, slave-beating, wife-beating (etc.)

(See **ĒT**, add *-ing* where appropriate.)

ETING

NETING	fish-netting, mosquito netting

(See **ET**, add *-ting* where appropriate.)

ĒTIS

(See **ĒTUS**)

ETISH

FETISH	fetish
KETISH	coquettish, croquettish
LETISH	Lettish
PETISH	pettish
WETISH	wettish

ĒTIST

FĒTIST	defeatist
KRĒTIST	accretist, decretist
SWĒTIST	honey-sweetest, sweetest

ETIST

ETIST	duettist
BRETIST	librettist
NETIST	clarinetist, cornetist

TETIST motettist
YETIST vignettist

ĒTIV

KRĒTIV accretive, decretive, discretive, excretive, concretive, secretive
PLĒTIV depletive, completive, repletive

ETIZM

BETIZM alphabetism, analphabetism
SETIZM concettism

ĒTL

ĒTL hyetal
BĒTL beetle, betel
FĒTL fetal
HWĒTL wheetle
KRĒTL decretal
SĒTL acetyl, setal
WĒTL chalchihuitle

ETL

ETL ettle
BETL abettal
FETL fettle, fine fettle
KETL kettle
METL Babbitt metal, gunmetal, white metal, metal, mettle, Monel metal, nonmetal, type metal
NETL nettle, stinging nettle
PETL petal, Popocatapetl, *centripetal*
SETL resettle, settle, unsettle

ETLD

METLD high-mettled

(See **ETL**, add -d or -ed where appropriate.)

ĒTLĒ

FĒTLĒ featly
FLĒTLĒ fleetly

KRĒTLĒ discreetly, discretely, indiscreetly, concretely
LĒTLĒ obsoletely
MĒTLĒ meetly, unmeetly
NĒTLĒ neatly, unneatly
PLĒTLĒ incompletely, completely
SWĒTLĒ sweetly

ETLES

DETLES debtless
THRETLES threatless
WETLES wetless

ETLING

FETLING fettling
NETLING nettling
SETLING resettling, settling, unsettling

ĒTMENT

FĒTMENT defeatment
TRĒTMENT entreatment, ill-treatment, maltreatment, mistreatment, treatment

ETMENT

BETMENT abetment
DETMENT indebtment
SETMENT besetment
VETMENT brevetment, revetment

ĒTNES

(See **ĒT**, add -ness where appropriate.)

ETNES

SETNES setness
WETNES wetness

ĒTŌ

FĒTŌ graffito, sgraffito
KĒTŌ keto, Quito, coquito, mosquito
LĒTŌ angelito, Leto
NĒTŌ bonito, incognito, magneto, sanbenito

RĒTŌ burrito
TĒTŌ Tito
VĒTŌ veto

ETŌ

BRETŌ libretto
CHETŌ concetto
GETŌ ghetto
GRETŌ allegretto
KETŌ punquetto, zucchetto
LETŌ stiletto
METŌ palmetto
NETŌ giardinetto, sonnetto
PETŌ in petto, rispetto
RETŌ amaretto, amoretto, lazaretto, vaporetto
SETŌ falsetto
STRETŌ stretto
TRETŌ neutretto
VETŌ cavetto
ZETŌ terzetto

ĒTON

(See **ĒTEN**)

ĒTOP

NĒTOP netop
TRĒTOP treetop

ETRAD

RETRAD retrad
TETRAD tetrad

ETRAL

METRAL *diametral*
PETRAL petrel, stormy petrel

ETRIK

METRIK *A* accelerometric, actinometric, aerometric, algometric, alkalimetric, alcoholometric, allometric, altomometric, anisometric, anthropometric, astronometric, *B* barometric,

bathymetric,
bathometric,
biometric,
biosymmetric,
bolometric, *D*
densitometric,
decelerometric,
diametric,
dilatometric,
dimetric,
dynamometric, *E*
econometric,
electrometric, *F*
phonometric,
photometric, *FL*
fluorometric, *G*
galvanometric,
gasometric,
goniometric, *GR*
gravimetric, *H*
hexametric,
hydrometric,
hygrometric,
hypsometric, *I*
inclinometric,
interferometric,
iodometric,
isobarometric,
isometric, *J*
geometric, *K*
kilometric,
coulometric, *KL*
clinometric, *KR*
craniometric,
cryometric,
chronometric, *M*
magnetometric,
manometric, metric,
micrometric,
mileometric,
monometric, *N*
nitrometric, *O*
audiometric,
odometric,
optometric,
ozonometric, *P*
pedometric,
piezometric,
pycnometric,
pyrometric,
potentiometric, *PL*
planometric,
plastometric, *R*
radiometric,
refractometric,
rheometric, *S*
salinometric,
cephalometric,
sensitometric,
cyclometric,
psychometric,
sociometric, *SKL*

sclerometric, *SP*
speedometric,
spectrometric,
spirometric, *ST*
stereometric,
stoichiometric, *SW*
swingometric, *T*
tacheometric,
tachometric,
tellurometric,
tonometric, *TH*
thermometric, *TR*
trigonometric,
trimetric, *V*
viscometric,
volumetric, *Y*
eudiometric, *Z*
zoometric

TETRIK   obstetric

ETRIKS

METRIKS   econometrics,
                isometrics
STETRIKS   obstetrics

(See **ETRIK**, add -*s* where appropriate.)

ETSAL

KWETSAL   quetzal
PRETSAL   pretzel

ĒTUM

BĒTUM   zibetum
FRĒTUM   fretum
NĒTUM   pinetum
PĒTUM   tapetum
RĒTUM   arboretum
SĒTUM   acetum, Equisetum
SWĒTUM   sweetum

ĒTŪR

(See **ĒCHER**)

ĒTUS

ĒTUS   coitus, quietus,
                paracoitus
BĒTUS   diabetes
FĒTUS   fetus, foetus
KĒTUS   achaetous
LĒTUS   boletus
SĒTUS   acetóus, Cetus
TĒTUS   Epictetus
THĒTUS   Thetis
TRĒTUS   treatise

ETWERK

FRETWERK   fretwork
NETWERK   network

ĒUM

BĒUM   amoebaeum
DĒUM   odeum, stomodeum,
                te Deum
FĒUM   trophaeum
JĒUM   hypogeum, Geum
LĒUM   mausoleum,
                propylaeum
MĒUM   meum, tuum and
                meum
NĒUM   atheneum, perineum,
                peritoneum,
                prytaneum
SĒUM   gynaeceum,
                colosseum, lyceum,
                no-see'em
TĒUM   bronteum, notaeum
ZĒUM   museum

ĒUS

BĒUS   *plumbeous,*
                scarabaeus
FĒUS   coryphaeus
KĒUS   Manichaeus
MĒUS   Ptolemaeus
NĒUS   Aeneas
PĒUS   onomatopoeous
RĒUS   choreus, piraeus,
                reus, uraeus
TĒUS   aristaeus, gluteus

ĒVA

DĒVA   diva, khedive,
                Mahadeva
JĒVA   jivah
KĒVA   kiva
NĒVA   Geneva
SĒVA   Siva
SHĒVA   yeshiva
VĒVA   viva

ĒVAL

ĒVAL   evil, king's evil,
                coeval, medieval
HĒVAL   upheaval
JĒVAL   longeval
KWĒVAL   equaeval
MĒVAL   primeval
SHRĒVAL   shrieval

THĒVAL	thival
TRĒVAL	retrieval
WĒVAL	boll weevil, weevil

ĒVANS

CHĒVANS	achievance
GRĒVANS	grievance
SĒVANS	perceivance
TRĒVANS	retrievance

ĒVĒ

ĒVĒ	evoe
PĒVĒ	peavey, peevy
SWĒVĒ	Suevi
TĒVĒ	TV

EVĒ

EVĒ	evoe
BEVĒ	bevvy, bevy
CHEVĒ	chevy
HEVĒ	heart-heavy, heavy, top-heavy
KLEVĒ	clevy
LEVĒ	levee, levy
NEVĒ	nevvy
PLEVĒ	replevy
SHEVĒ	Chevvy, chevy

EVEL

BEVEL	bevel
DEVEL	bedevil, daredevil, devil, red devil
KEVEL	kevel
LEVEL	level, on the level, sea level, spirit level, split level, water level
NEVEL	nevel
REVEL	revel
SHEVEL	dishevel, shevel

EVEN

DEVEN	Devon
HEVEN	heaven, midheaven
LEVEN	eleven, leaven, levin
PLEVEN	plevin, replevin
SEVEN	seven
SWEVEN	sweven

EVENTH

| LEVENTH | eleventh |
| SEVENTH | seventh |

ĒVER

ĒVER	naiver
BĒVER	beaver
CHĒVER	achiever, overachiever, underachiever
DĒVER	Danny Deever
FĒVER	enfever, fever, hay fever, jungle fever, sea fever, scarlet fever, spring fever, typhoid fever, yellow fever
GRĒVER	aggriever, griever
HĒVER	ballast heaver, heaver, coal heaver, upheaver
KĒVER	keever
LĒVER	B believer, D disbeliever, I interleaver, K cantilever, L leaver, lever, liever, livre, M make-believer, R reliever, U unbeliever
PĒVER	peever
PRĒVER	repriever
RĒVER	bereaver, reaver, reever, riever
SĒVER	deceiver, conceiver, misconceiver, perceiver, preconceiver, receiver, transceiver, undeceiver
SHĒVER	sheaver
TRĒVER	retriever
WĒVER	interweaver, weaver, weever

APPLESAUCE

The Apple which the Snake supplied
Arrived complete, with Worm inside.
Child, shun the Sequence of the Snake:
First Fruit, then Worm, then Belly-ache.

EVER

EVER	E ever, F forever, H whoever, whomever, whomsoever, whosoever, however, howsoever, HW whatever, whatsoever, whencesoever, whenever, wherever, wheresoever, whichever, whichsoever, whithersoever
DEVER	endeavor
KLEVER	clever
LEVER	cantilever, lever
NEVER	never
SEVER	assever, dissever, sever, unsever

ĒVIJ

| KLĒVIJ | cleavage |
| LĒVIJ | leavage |

ĒVIL

(See ĒVAL)

EVIL

(See EVEL)

EVIN

(See EVEN)

ĒVING

(See ĒV, add -ing where appropriate.)

EVIS

BREVIS	brevis
CHEVIS	chevise
KLEVIS	clevis
KREVIS	crevis

ĒVISH

| PĒVISH | peevish |
| THĒVISH | thievish |

EVL

(See EVEL)

ĒVLES

(See ĒV, add -less where appropriate.)

ĒVMENT

CHĒVMENT	achievement
RĒVMENT	bereavement
TRĒVMENT	retrievement

ĒVUS

GRĒVUS	grievous
JĒVUS	longevous
MĒVUS	primevous
NĒVUS	nevus

ĒWĀ

FRĒWĀ	freeway
LĒWĀ	leeway
SĒWĀ	seaway

ĒWĒ

ĒWĒ	iiwi
KĒWĒ	kiwi
PĒWĒ	peewee
WĒWĒ	weewee

ĒWERD

LĒWERD	leeward
SĒWERD	seaward

ĒYA

(See ĒA)

ĒYAN

(See ĒAN)

ĒZA

LĒZA	Mona Lisa
PĒZA	Pisa, tower of Pisa
VĒZA	visa, reentry visa

EZANS

(See EZENS)

EZANT

(See EZENT)

ĒZĒ

ĒZĒ	easy, free-and-easy, speakeasy, uneasy
BĒZĒ	Zambezi
BRĒZĒ	breezy
CHĒZĒ	cheesy, pachisi, parcheesi
FRĒZĒ	freezy

GRĒZĒ	greasy
HWĒZĒ	wheezy
KWĒZĒ	queasy
RĒZĒ	reasy
SLĒZĒ	sleasy
SNĒZĒ	sneezy

ĒZEL

(See ĒZL)

ĒZELZ

(See ĒZLZ)

EZENS

PLEZENS	pleasance
PREZENS	omnipresence, presence

EZENT

BEZENT	bezant
FEZENT	pheasant
PEZENT	peasant
PLEZENT	pleasant, unpleasant
PREZENT	present, omnipresent

EZENTS

(See EZENT, add -s where appropriate.)

ĒZER

ĒZER	easer
BĒZER	beezer
CHĒZER	cheeser
FĒZER	misfeasor
FRĒZER	freezer, friezer
GĒZER	geezer, geyser
GRĒZER	greaser
HWĒZER	wheezer
LĒZER	leaser
NĒZER	ebenezer
PĒZER	appeaser
PLĒZER	displeaser, pleaser
SĒZER	Caesar, seizer, seizor, disseizor
SKWĒZER	squeezer
SNĒZER	sneezer
TĒZER	teaser
TWĒZER	tweezer

ĒZHA

BĒZHA	frambesia, Zambesia
DĒZHA	Rhodesia

FRĒZHA	freesia, oxyosphresia
JĒZHA	analgesia, hyperthemalgesia
KLĒZHA	ecclesia
LĒZHA	silesia, Silesia
NĒZHA	amnesia, ecmnesia, hyperkinesia, Indonesia, magnesia, neomnesia, paleomnesia, paramnesia, Polynesia, telamnesia
PĒZHA	trapesia
RĒZHA	parrhesia
THĒZHA	anesthesia, esthesia, hyperesthesia, hypesthesia, hyposthesia, kinesthesia, cryptesthesia, oxyesthesia, radiesthesia, synesthesia, telesthesia, thermanerthesia, thermesthesia, zonesthesia

(This is also pronounced as a triple rhyme, Ē'ZI.A.)

ĒZHER

LĒZHER	leisure
SĒZHER	seizure

EZHER

LEZHER	leisure
MEZHER	admeasure, comeasure, countermeasure, measure, outmeasure
PLEZHER	displeasure, pleasure
TREZHER	entreasure, treasure

EZHERD

MEZHERD	admeasured, comeasured, measured, outmeasured
TREZHERD	entreasured, treasured

ĒZHUN

FĒZHUN	Ephesian

HĒZHUN   adhesion, inadhesion, inhesion, cohesion
KLĒZHUN   ecclesian
LĒZHUN   lesion, Milesian, Silesian
NĒZHUN   magnesian, Polynesian
PĒZHUN   trapezian
TĒZHUN   artesian, etesian, Cartesian

ĒZIKS

JĒZIKS   analgesics
SKĒZIKS   Sheezix

ĒZING

(See ĒZ, add -ing where appropriate.)

ĒZL

ĒZL   easel
DĒZL   diesel
TĒZL   teasel
WĒZL   weasel

ĒZLD

FĒZLD   ramfeezled
TĒZLD   teaseled
WĒZLD   weaseled

ĒZLZ

MĒZLZ   measles

(See ĒZL, add -s where appropriate.)

ĒZMENT

ĒZMENT   easement
PĒZMENT   appeasement

ĒZN

MĒZN   mezon
RĒZN   reason, unreason
SĒZN   season, seisin, seizin, reseason, unseason
TRĒZN   treason

ĒZON

(See ĒZN)

ĪA

ĪA   ayah
DĪA   dia
FĪA   asaphia, St. Sophia
KRĬA   chria
LĬA   dulia, hyperdulia, Thalia
MĬA   Jeremiah
NĬA   asthenia, gorgoneia, sthenia
PĬA   pia
PRĬA   praya
RĬA   Ave Maria, Black Maria, pariah
SĪA   messiah
STRĬA   stria
TĬA   aristeia, callisteia
TRĬA   aischrolatreia, latria
VĬA   via
ZĪA   jeziah

ĪAD

DĬAD   dyad
DRĪAD   dryad, hamadryad
MĪAD   jeremiad
NĪAD   naiad
PLĪAD   Pleiad

ĪAK

DĪAK   Dayak, Dyak
GĪAK   guiac
JĪAK   elegiac
KĪAK   kayak, kyack, kyak
NĪAK   Nyack
ZĪAK   phrenesiac

ĪAL

DĪAL   dial, moon dial, redial, sundial
FĪAL   phial, defial
HĪAL   basihyal
KRĪAL   decrial, descrial
MĪAL   myall
NĪAL   denial, genial, self-denial
PĪAL   espial, intrapial, pial
PLĪAL   supplial
RĪAL   rial
SĪAL   sial
SPĪAL   spial
STRĪAL   interstrial
TRĪAL   mistrial, trial, retrial
VĪAL   bass viol, vial, viol

(See ĪL)

ĪAM

LĪAM   lyam
PRĪAM   Priam
SĪAM   Siam

ĪAN

ĪAN   ion, zwitterion
BĪAN   bion
LĪAN   antlion, dandelion, lion, sea lion, thalian
NĪAN   anion, genian
RĪAN   Arion, Orion
SĪAN   Ixion, scion
STĪAN   styan
TĪAN   altaian
WĪAN   Hawaiian
ZĪAN   Zion

ĪANS

FĪANS   affiance, affiants, defiance
JĪANS   giants, supergiants
KLĪANS   clients
LĪANS   alliance, misalliance, reliance, self-reliance
PLĪANS   appliance, incompliance, compliance, noncompliance, pliance, repliance, suppliance
SĪANS   science

ĪANT

FĪANT   affiant, defiant, calorifient
HĪANT   hiant
JĪANT   Green Giant, giant, red giant
KLĪANT   client
LĪANT   alliant, reliant, self-reliant
PLĪANT   appliant, compliant, pliant, repliant, uncompliant
RĪANT   riant

ĪANTS

(See ĪANS)

ĪAR

(See ĪER)

ĪAS

ĪAS	eyas
BĪAS	bias, unbias
DRĪAS	drias, hamadryas
KĪAS	antibacchius, bacchius
LĪAS	lias
NĪAS	Ananias
PĪAS	pious, Pius
PRĪAS	nisi prius, prius
RĪAS	Darius, Zacharias

ĪAT

(See ĪET)

ĪBAK

BĪBAK	buyback
DĪBAK	dieback
FLĪBAK	flyback
HĪBAK	high-back
TĪBAK	tieback
SWĪBAK	zwieback

ĪBAL

(See ĪBL)

IBALD

(See IBLD)

ĪBĒ

FRIBĒ	fribby
JIBĒ	gibby, gibby-jibby
LIBĒ	libbie, women's libbie
NIBĒ	nibby, nibby-jibby
TIBĒ	tibby

ĪBEKS

ĪBEKS	ibex
VĪBEKS	vibex

ĪBER

BĪBER	imbiber
BRĪBER	briber
FĪBER	fiber
JĪBER	giber, jiber
KĪBER	kiber
LĪBER	liber, Liber
SKRĪBER	ascriber, describer, inscriber, prescriber, proscriber, circumscriber, scriber, subscriber, transcriber
TĪBER	Tiber

IBER

BIBER	bibber, winebibber
DIBER	dibber
FIBER	fibber
GLIBER	glibber
JIBER	flibber-gibber, gibber, jibber
KRIBER	cribber
LIBER	ad libber, gay libber, libber, women's libber
NIBER	knibber, nibber
RIBER	ribber
SKWIBER	squibber

IBET

HIBET	adhibit, inhibit, cohibit, prohibit
JIBET	flibbertigibbet, gibbet
LIBET	*quodlibet*, libbet
RIBET	ribbit
ZIBET	exhibit, zibet

ĪBĪ

BĪBĪ	bye-bye
FLĪBĪ	flyby

ĪBING

BĪBING	imbibing
BRĪBING	bribing
JĪBING	gibing, jibing
KĪBING	kibing
SCRĪBING	ascribing, describing, inscribing, prescribing, proscribing, circumscribing, scribing, subscribing, transcribing

IBING

BIBING	bibbing, wine-bibbing
FIBING	fibbing
JIBING	jibbing
KRIBING	cribbing
LIBING	ad libbing
RIBING	ribbing
SKWIBING	squibbing

IBIT

(See IBET)

ĪBL

BĪBL	Bible
LĪBL	libel
SĪBL	postcibal, precibal
SKĪBL	skybal
SKRĪBL	scribal
TRĪBL	intertribal, tribal

IBL

BIBL	bibble, ishkabibble
DIBL	dibble
DRIBL	dribble
FRIBL	fribble
GIBL	gibel
GRIBL	gribble
KIBL	kibble
KRIBL	cribble
KWIBL	quibble
NIBL	nibble
RIBL	ribble
SIBL	sibyl, Sybil, cibol
SKRIBL	scribble, rescribble, transcribble
STIBL	stibble
THRIBL	thribble
TRIBL	tribble

IBLD

RIBLD	ribald

(See IBL, add -*d* where appropriate.)

ANIMAL NOISE

The cry of a cat's a meow,
And an oink is the meow of a hog;
And a moo is the oink of a cow,
And a bark is the moo of a dog;

And a neigh is the bark of a horse,
And a trumpet's an elephant's neigh;
And the trumpets of lions are roars,
And the roar of a donkey's a bray;

And the bray of a duck is a quack,
And the quack of a snake is a hiss;
And if that doesn't take you aback,
You may be confounded by this:

The hiss of a sheep is a baa,
And a hyena's baa is a laugh;
And the laugh of a babe is a waa,
And the waa of a . . . say a . . . giraffe
    Is so small
        It is nothing
            Nothing at all.

IBLĒ

DRIBLĒ	dribbly
GLIBLĒ	glibly
KWIBLĒ	quibbly
NIBLĒ	nibbly
SKRIBLĒ	scribbly
THRIBLĒ	thribbly
TRIBLĒ	tribbly

IBLER

DIBLER	dibbler
DRIBLER	dribbler
FRIBLER	fribbler
KIBLER	kibbler
KRIBLER	cribbler
KWIBLER	quibbler
NIBLER	nibbler
SKRIBLER	scribbler, transcribbler

IBLET

DRIBLET	driblet
GIBLET	giblet
RIBLET	riblet
TRIBLET	triblet

IBLIK

BIBLIK	Biblic, philobiblic
NIBLIK	mashie-niblick, niblick

IBLING

KIBLING	kibbling
SIBLING	sibling

(See IBL, add -ing where appropriate.)

ĪBLŌ

BĪBLŌ	byblow
FLĪBLŌ	flyblow

ĪBÔL

ĪBÔL	eyeball
FLĪBÔL	flyball
HĪBÔL	highball
SKĪBÔL	skyball

ĪBÔLD

ĪBÔLD	eyeballed

HĪBÔLD	highballed
PĪBÔLD	piebald

IBON

(See IBUN)

ĪBÔRN

HĪBÔRN	high-born
SKĪBÔRN	sky-born

ĪBRĀT

LĪBRĀT	equilibrate, librate
VĪBRĀT	vibrate

ĪBRID

HĪBRID	hybrid, polyhybrid
LĪBRID	Librid

ĪBROU

ĪBROU	eyebrow
HĪBROU	highbrow

IBUN

GIBUN	gibbon
RIBUN	blue ribbon, white ribbon, red ribbon, ribbon, yellow ribbon (etc.)

IBUNZ

BIBUNZ	bibbons

(See IBUN, add -s.)

IBYA

LIBYA	Libya

(See IB'I.A)

ICHĒ

ICHĒ	itchy
BICHĒ	bitchy
FICHĒ	fitchy
HICHĒ	hitchy
KICHĒ	kitschy

PICHĒ	pitchy
STICHĒ	stitchy
SWICHĒ	switchy
TWICHĒ	twitchy
WICHĒ	witchy

ICHER

(See ICH, add -er where appropriate.)

ICHET

FICHET	fitchet
WICHET	witchet

ICHEZ

BRICHEZ	breeches, britches

(See ICH, add -es where appropriate.)

ICHING

(See ICH, add -ing where appropriate.)

ICHKOK

HICHKOK	Alfred Hitchcock
PICHKOK	pitchcock

ICHLES

(See ICH, add -less where appropriate.)

ICHMENT

RICHMENT	enrichment
WICHMENT	bewitchment

ĪDAL

(See ĪDL)

ĪDANS

BĪDANS	abidance
GĪDANS	guidance, misguidance
SĪDANS	subsidence

IDANS

BIDANS	biddance, forbiddence
RIDANS	good riddance, riddance

ĪDANT

(See ĪDENT)

ĪDAS

MĪDAS	Midas
NĪDAS	nidus

ĪDĒ

DĪDĒ	didy
FĪDĒ	bona fide
FRĪDĒ	Friday
KĪDĒ	alcaide
SĪDĒ	sidy
TĪDĒ	tidy, untidy
VĪDĒ	vide

IDĒ

BIDĒ	biddy, chickabiddy
DIDĒ	diddy
GIDĒ	giddy
KIDĒ	kiddy
MIDĒ	middy, midi
SKIDĒ	skiddy
STIDĒ	stiddy
TIDĒ	tiddy
WIDĒ	widdy

ĪDED

SĪDED	decided, coincided, many-sided, presided, sided, slab-sided, subsided, undecided, one-sided

(See ĪD, add -d where appropriate.)

IDED

HWIDED	whidded
KIDED	kidded
RIDED	ridded
SKIDED	skidded
THRIDED	thridded

ĪDEN

DRĪDEN	Dryden
GĪDEN	guidon
LĪDEN	Leyden
SĪDEN	Poseidon
WĪDEN	widen

IDEN

BIDEN	bidden, forbidden, God-forbidden, unbidden, unforbidden
CHIDEN	chidden
HIDEN	hidden, unhidden
MIDEN	kitchen midden, midden, muckmidden
RIDEN	B bed-ridden, beridden, CH child-ridden, F fever-ridden, H hag-ridden, O overriden, PL plague-ridden, PR priest-ridden, R ridden, U unridden, W wife-ridden
SLIDEN	slidden
STRIDEN	stridden

ĪDENT

BĪDENT	bident
GĪDENT	guidant
RĪDENT	rident
SĪDENT	subsident
STRĪDENT	strident
TRĪDENT	trident
VĪDENT	dividant

ĪDER

ĪDER	eider
BĪDER	abider, bider
CHĪDER	chider
FĪDER	confider
GĪDER	guider, misguider
GLĪDER	glider, hang-glider
HĪDER	hider
LĪDER	elider, collider
NĪDER	nidor
RĪDER	horseback rider, joyrider, nightrider, outrider, rider, Rough Rider
SĪDER	D decider, E East-sider, I insider, K coincider, N North-sider, O outsider, S cider, sider, South-sider, subsider, W West-sider
SLĪDER	backslider, slider
SPĪDER	spider
STRĪDER	bestrider, strider, stridor
VĪDER	divider, provider, subdivider
WĪDER	wider
ZĪDER	presider

ĪDER

BIDER	bidder, forbidder, outbidder, overbidder, rebidder, underbidder
KIDER	kidder
RIDER	ridder
SIDER	consider, reconsider, sidder, siddur
SKIDER	skidder
SLIDER	slidder
WIDER	widder

ĪDIJ

GĪDIJ	guidage
HĪDIJ	hidage
SĪDIJ	sideage

IDIK

IDIK	druidic
BIDIK	rubidic
KIDIK	arachidic
MIDIK	pyramidic
RIDIK	iridic, juridic
SIDIK	acidic
TIDIK	fatidic

ĪDING

(See ĪD, add -ing where appropriate.)

IDING

(See ID, add -ding where appropriate.)

ĪDINGZ

RĪDINGZ	ridings
TĪDINGZ	tidings

(See ĪD, add -ings where appropriate.)

ĪDĪV

HĪDĪV	highdive
SKĪDĪV	skydive

ĪDL

ĪDL	idle, idol, idyll
BRĪDL	bridal, bridle, rebridle, unbridle
SĪDL	B biocidal, F fungicidal, FR fratricidal, H

	homicidal, *I* infanticidal, insecticidal, *L* liberticidal, *M* matricidal, *P* parricidal, patricidal, *R* regicidal, *S* septicidal, seidel, sidle, sororicidal, suicidal, *SP* spermicidal, *T* tyrannicidal, *U* uxoricidal, *V* vermicidal
TĪDL	cotidal, tidal

IDL

DIDL	diddle, flumdiddle, flummadiddle, hey-diddle-diddle, condiddle, paradiddle, taradiddle
FIDL	fiddle
GRIDL	griddle
KIDL	kiddle
KWIDL	quiddle
MIDL	middle
PIDL	piddle
RIDL	riddle, unriddle
TIDL	rumtumtiddle, tiddle
TWIDL	twiddle
WIDL	widdle

ĪDLD

ĪDLD	idled
BRĪDLD	bridled, rebridled, unbridled
SĪDLD	sidled

IDLD

(See **IDL**, add *-d* where appropriate.)

ĪDLĒ

ĪDLĒ	idly
BRĪDLĒ	bridely
SĪDLĒ	sidly
WĪDLĒ	widely

ĪDLER

ĪDLER	idler
BRĪDLER	bridler
SĪDLER	sidler

IDLER

DIDLER	diddler
FIDLER	fiddler
GRIDLER	griddler
PIDLER	piddler
RIDLER	riddler
TWIDLER	twiddler
WIDLER	widdler

ĪDLĪN

GĪDLĪN	guideline
SĪDLĪN	sideline

ĪDLING

(See **ĪDL**, add *-ing* where appropriate.)

IDLING

(See **IDL**, add *-ing* where appropriate.)

IDNA

DIDNA	didna
KIDNA	echidna

IDNAP

KIDNAP	kidnap
MIDNAP	mid-nap

ĪDNES

PĪDNES	piedness
SNĪDNES	snideness
WĪDNES	wideness

ĪDŌ

DĪDŌ	dido, Dido
FĪDŌ	Fido

IDŌ

KIDŌ	aikido, kiddo
WIDŌ	widow

ĪDON

(See **ĪDEN**)

ĪDUS

(See **ĪDAS**)

ĪENS

(See **ĪANS**)

ĪENT

(See **ĪANT**)

ĪER

ĪER	eyer, evil-eyer
BĪER	buyer
BRĪER	briar, brier, green brier, sweetbrier
DĪER	dier, dyer, never-say-dier
DRĪER	blow dryer, dryer, hair dryer
FĪER	amplifier, dehumidifier, disqualifier, humidifier, intensifier, qualifier, quantifier, magnifier, pacifier, preamplifier, purifier
FLĪER	flier, flyer, heli-flier, highflyer, kiteflyer
FRĪER	friar, fryer
GĪER	lammergeier
HĪER	higher
KRĪER	crier, town crier
LĪER	inlier, liar, lier, lyre, outlier
NĪER	nigher
PĪER	occupier
PLĪER	photomultiplier, multiplier, plier, plyer, supplier
PRĪER	prior, pryer
RĪER	wryer
SLĪER	slyer
SPĪER	spyer
SPRĪER	spryer
TRĪER	trier, trior

(See **Ī**, add *-er* where appropriate; also see **ĪR**.)

ĪET

ĪET	eyot
DĪET	diet
FĪET	fiat
KWĪET	disquiet, inquiet, quiet, unquiet
PĪET	piet, piot
RĪET	riot, ryot
SĪET	Sciot

IFĒ

IFĒ	iffy
BIFĒ	biffy
HWIFĒ	whiffy
JIFĒ	jiffy
KLIFĒ	cliffy
SKWIFĒ	squiffy
SNIFĒ	sniffy
SPIFĒ	spiffy

ĪFEN

HĪFEN	hyphen
SĪFEN	siphon

IFEN

IFEN	if'n
BIFEN	biffin
GRIFEN	griffin, griffon
SHIFEN	chiffon
STIFEN	stiffen
STRIFEN	striffen
TIFEN	tiffin

ĪFER

BĪFER	bifer
FĪFER	fifer
LĪFER	lifer
NĪFER	knifer
RĪFER	rifer
SĪFER	decipher, encipher, cipher, sypher

IFER

DIFER	differ
HWIFER	whiffer
NIFER	niffer
SKWIFER	squiffer
SNIFER	sniffer
STIFER	stiffer

IFIK

IFIK	deific
BIFIK	morbific, orbific, rubific, tabific
BRIFIK	febrific, tenebrific
DIFIK	acidific, grandific, lapidific
GLIFIK	anaglyphic, dactyloglyphic, diaglyphic, phytoglyphic, photoglyphic, glyphic, hieroglyphic, geoglyphic, lithoglyphic, petroglyphic, triglyphic
JIFIK	algific
LIFIK	mellific, prolific
NIFIK	damnific, finific, cornific, magnific, nific, omnific, somnific, vulnific
RIFIK	D dolorific, FR frigorific, H horrific, humorific, K calorific, colorific, M mirific, O honorific, aurific, S sacrific, saporific, sonorific, soporific, sudorific, T terrific, torporific, V vaporific
SIFIK	F felicific, K calcific, conspecific, KL classific, L lucific, M mucific, O ossific, P pacific, Pacific, pulsific, S sensific, SP specific, ST stereospecific, TR transpacific
TIFIK	beatific, incoherentific, lactific, pontific, scientific, unscientific
TRIFIK	petrific
VIFIK	salvific, vivific

IFIN

(See IFEN)

IFING

HWIFING	whiffing
MIFING	miffing
SKIFING	skiffing
SNIFING	sniffing
TIFING	tiffing

IFISH

MIFISH	miffish
SKWIFISH	squiffish
SNIFISH	sniffish
STIFISH	stiffish
TIFISH	tiffish

ĪFL

ĪFL	Eiffel
NĪFL	nifle

RĪFL

RĪFL	rifle
STĪFL	stifle
TRĪFL	trifle

IFL

HWIFL	whiffle
NIFL	nifle
PIFL	piffle
RIFL	riffle
SNIFL	sniffle

ĪFLĒ

RĪFLĒ	rifely
WĪFLĒ	wifely

IFLĒ

SNIFLĒ	sniffly
STIFLĒ	stiffly

ĪFLER

RĪFLER	rifler
STĪFLER	stifler
TRĪFLER	trifler

IFLER

HWIFLER	whiffler
PIFLER	piffler
RIFLER	riffler
SNIFLER	sniffler

ĪFLES

(See ĪF, add -less where appropriate.)

ĪFLING

RĪFLING	rifling
STĪFLING	stifling
TRĪFLING	trifling

IFLING

HWIFLING	whiffling
PIFLING	piffling
RIFLING	riffling
SKIFLING	skiffling
SNIFLING	sniffling

294

IFTĒ

DRIFTĒ	drifty
FIFTĒ	fifty, fifty-fifty
KLIFTĒ	clifty
NIFTĒ	nifty
RIFTĒ	rifty
SHIFTĒ	shifty
SNIFTĒ	snifty
THRIFTĒ	thrifty

IFTED

(See **IFT**, add -*ed* where appropriate.)

IFTER

DRIFTER	drifter
LIFTER	lifter, shoplifter, uplifter, weight lifter
RIFTER	rifter
SHIFTER	scene-shifter, shifter
SNIFTER	snifter
SWIFTER	swifter

IFTIJ

DRIFTIJ	driftage
SHIFTIJ	shiftage
SIFTIJ	siftage

IFTING

DRIFTING	drifting
LIFTING	lifting, shoplifting, uplifting
RIFTING	rifting
SHIFTING	sceneshifting, shifting
SIFTING	sifting

IFTLES

(See **IFT**, add -*less* where appropriate.)

IFTHONG

DIFTHONG	diphthong
TRIFTHONG	triphthong

IFTNES

DRIFTNES	adriftness
MIFTINES	miffedness
SKWIFTNES	squiffedness
SWIFTNES	swiftness

ĪGA

BĪGA	biga
RĪGA	quadriga
SĪGA	saiga
STRĪGA	striga
TĪGA	taiga

ĪGAL

PĪGAL	dasypygal, pygal
ZĪGAL	zygal

IGAN

BRIGAN	balbriggan
PIGAN	piggin
WIGAN	wigan

ĪGĀT

LĪGĀT	ligate
STRĪGĀT	strigate

IGĒ

BIGĒ	biggy
PIGĒ	piggy
SIGĒ	ciggie
SPRIGĒ	spriggy
TWIGĒ	twiggy
WIGĒ	piggy-wiggywiggy

ĪGER

GĪGER	geiger
LĪGER	liger
NĪGER	Niger
TĪGER	tiger

IGER

BIGER	bigger
CHIGER	chigger
DIGER	digger, gold-digger, grave-digger
FIGER	figger, figure
GIGER	gigger
JIGER	bejigger, jigger
LIGER	ligger
NIGER	nigger, reneger
PRIGER	prigger
RIGER	market rigger, outrigger, rigger, rigor, thimble-rigger
SNIGER	snigger
SPRIGER	sprigger
SWIGER	swigger
TRIGER	trigger
TWIGER	twigger
VIGER	vigor

IGERD

FIGERD	figgered
JIGERD	bejiggered, jiggered
NIGERD	niggard
SNIGERD	sniggered
TRIGERD	triggered

IGET

(See **IGOT**)

IGIN

(See **IGAN**)

IGING

THIGING	thigging

(See **IG**, add -*ing* where appropriate.)

IGISH

HWIGISH	whiggish
JIGISH	jiggish
PIGISH	piggish
PRIGISH	priggish
RIGISH	riggish
WIGISH	wiggish

IGL

FRIGL	friggle
GIGL	giggle
HIGL	higgle
JIGL	jiggle
NIGL	niggle
RIGL	wriggle
SIGL	sigil
SKWIGL	squiggle
SNIGL	sniggle
STRIGL	striggle
SWIGL	swiggle
WIGL	porwigle, wiggle

ĪGLAS

ĪGLAS	eyeglass
SPĪGLAS	spyglass

IGLD

(See IGL, add -d where appropriate.)

IGLĒ

GIGLĒ	giggly
RIGLĒ	wriggly
WIGLĒ	Piggly Wiggly, Uncle Wiggly, wiggly

(See IGL, add -y where appropriate.)

IGLER

(See IGL, add -r where appropriate.)

IGLET

GIGLET	giglet
PIGLET	piglet
WIGLET	wiglet

ĪGLIF

DĪGLIF	diglyph
TRĪGLIF	monotriglyph, triglyph

IGLING

(See IGL, add -ing where appropriate.)

IGMA

NIGMA	enigma
RIGMA	kerygma, sterigma
SIGMA	sigma
STIGMA	hypostigma, stigma

IGMĒ

PIGMĒ	pygmy
RIGMĒ	borborygmy
STIGMĒ	stigme

IGMENT

FIGMENT	figment
PIGMENT	pigment

IGNAL

RIGNAL	orignal
SIGNAL	signal

IGNANT

DIGNANT	indignant
LIGNANT	malignant
NIGNANT	benignant

IGNUM

LIGNUM	lignum
RIGNUM	rignum
SIGNUM	ecce signum
TIGNUM	tignum

ĪGŌ

BĪGŌ	by-go
LĪGŌ	caligo, fuligo
PĪGŌ	serpigo
RĪGŌ	prurigo
SLĪGŌ	Sligo
TĪGŌ	impetigo, lentigo, tentigo, vertigo
TRĪGŌ	intertrigo

ĪGON

BĪGON	bygone
TRĪGON	trigon

IGOT

BIGOT	bigot
FRIGOT	frigate
JIGOT	gigot
RIGOT	riggot
SPIGOT	spigot

IGYER

FIGYER	disfigure, figure, configure, prefigure, refigure, transfigure
LIGYER	ligure

ĪID

DRĪID	dry-eyed
PĪID	pie-eyed
SLĪID	sly-eyed

ĪING

(See Ī, add -ing where appropriate.)

ĪISH

DRĪISH	dryish
SHĪISH	shyish
SLĪISH	slyish

ĪJAK

HĪJAK	highjack, hi-jack
SKĪJAK	skyjack

IJĒ

GIJĒ	gidgee
SKWIJĒ	squidgy

IJER

BRIJER	abridger, bridger
RIJER	ridger

IJEST

BLIJEST	disobligest, obligest
DIJEST	digest

IJET

DIJET	digit, double-digit, triple-digit
FIJET	fidget
MIJET	midget
NIJET	nidget
WIJET	widget

IJID

FRIJID	frigid, unfrigid
RIJID	nonrigid, rigid, semirigid, unrigid

IJIL

SIJIL	sigil
STRIJIL	strigil
VIJIL	vigil

IJING

BRIJING	abridging, bridging
FIJING	fidging
NIJING	nidging
RIJING	ridging

IJIT

(See IJET)

IJUN

LIJUN	irreligion, religion
PIJUN	gyropigeon, pidgin, pigeon
SMIJUN	smidgen
WIJUN	widgeon

IJUS

DIJUS	prodigious
LIJUS	irreligious, religious, sacrilegious
TIJUS	litigious, prestigious

ĪKA

GĪKA	nagaika
LĪKA	balalaika, kamalayka, Leica
MĪKA	formica, hydromica, mica, Micah
PĪKA	pica, pika
PLĪKA	plica
RĪKA	lorica, Myrica
SPĪKA	spica
STĪKA	styka

IKA

LIKA	licca
SIKA	sicca
TIKA	ticca, tikka

ĪKAL

(See ĪKL)

ĪKĀT

| PLĪKĀT | plicate |
| SPĪKĀT | spicate |

IKCHER

| PIKCHER | depicture, impicture, picture, repicture, word picture |
| STRIKCHER | stricture |

ĪKĒ

ĪKĒ	ikey, Ikey
DĪKĒ	dikey
KRĪKĒ	crikey, by crikey
NĪKĒ	Nike
PĪKĒ	piky
SĪKĒ	photopsyche, psyche, Psyche
TĪKĒ	Tyche

IKĒ

IKĒ	icky
BRIKĒ	bricky
CHIKĒ	chicky
DIKĒ	dickey, dicky
HIKĒ	doohickey, hickey
KWIKĒ	quicky
PIKĒ	picky
PRIKĒ	pricky
RIKĒ	gin rickey, jinriki, rickey
SIKĒ	sicky
STIKĒ	sticky
TIKĒ	Rikki-Tikki
TRIKĒ	tricky

IKEN

CHIKEN	chicken
QUIKEN	quicken
SIKEN	sicken
SLIKEN	slicken
STRIKEN	horror-stricken, stricken, terror-stricken, wonder-stricken
THIKEN	thicken

IKENZ

| DIKENZ | dickens, Dickens |

(See IKEN, add -s where appropriate.)

ĪKER

ĪKER	ichor
BĪKER	biker
DĪKER	diker, duiker
HĪKER	hiker, hitchhiker
LĪKER	liker, obliquer
PĪKER	piker
SPĪKER	spiker
STRĪKER	striker

IKER

IKER	icker
BIKER	bicker
DIKER	dicker
FLIKER	flicker
HWIKER	whicker
KIKER	high-kicker, kicker
KLIKER	clicker
KWIKER	quicker
LIKER	bootlicker, licker, liquor
NIKER	dominicker, knicker, nicker
PIKER	berrypicker, cherrypicker, fruitpicker, cottonpicker, (ect.), picker
PRIKER	pricker
RIKER	ricker
SHIKER	shicker
SIKER	sicker
SLIKER	slicker
SMIKER	smicker
SNIKER	snicker
STIKER	bumper sticker, pigsticker, spitsticker, sticker
THIKER	thicker
TIKER	ticker, tikker
TRIKER	tricker
VIKER	vicar
WIKER	wicker

IKERZ

| NIKERZ | knickers |

(See IKER, add -s where appropriate.)

IKET

KLIKET	clicket
KRIKET	cricket
PIKET	picket
PRIKET	pricket
SMIKET	smicket
SNIKET	snicket
SPIKET	spicket
THIKET	thicket
TIKET	ticket
WIKET	sticky wicket, wicket

IKETS

| RIKETS | rickets |

(See IKET, add -s where appropriate.)

IKIN

KIKIN	kick-in
NIKIN	nikin
SIKIN	sick-in

ĪKING

DĪKING	diking
HĪKING	hiking, hitch-hiking
LĪKING	disliking, liking
PĪKING	piking
SPĪKING	spiking
STRĪKING	striking
VĪKING	viking, Viking

IKING

LIKING	bootlicking, finger-licking, licking
PIKING	berry-picking, cherry-picking, cotton-picking (etc.), picking

(See **IK**, add -ing where appropriate.)

IKISH

(See **IK**, add -ish where appropriate.)

ĪKL

PĪKL	pical
PLĪKL	plical
SĪKL	epicycle, gigacycle, hemicycle, motorcycle, recycle, psychal, cycle, unicycle

IKL

BRIKL	brickle, bricole
CHIKL	chicle
FIKL	fickle, unfickle
MIKL	mickle
NIKL	cupronickel, nickel, nickle, plugged nickel, pumpernickel, wooden nickel
PIKL	pickle, picul, pikle
PRIKL	prickle
SIKL	bicycle, sickle, tricycle
STIKL	stickle
STRIKL	strickle
TIKL	tickle
TRIKL	trickle

IKLĒ

(See **IK**, add -ly where appropriate.)

IKLER

FIKLER	fickler
PIKLER	pickler
PRIKLER	prickler
SIKLER	bicycler, sickler
STIKLER	stickler
STRIKLER	strickler
TIKLER	tickler
TRIKLER	trickler

IKLET

CHIKLET	Chiclet
TRIKLET	tricklet

IKLING

CHIKLING	chickling
PIKLING	pickling
PRIKLING	prickling
SIKLING	sickling
STIKLING	stickling
STRIKLING	strickling
TIKLING	tickling
TRIKLING	trickling

IKLISH

PRIKLISH	pricklish
TIKLISH	ticklish
TRIKLISH	tricklish

IKNES

SIKNES	lovesickness, sickness, sleeping sickness

(See **IK**, add -ness where appropriate.)

IKNIK

PIKNIK	isopycnic, isopyknic, picnic, pyknic
STRIKNIK	strychnic

IKNING

(See **IK'EN.ING.**)

IKSCHER

FIKSCHER	affixture, fixture, transfixture
MIKSCHER	admixture, immixture, incommixture, intermixture, commixture, mixture

IKSĒ

DIKSĒ	dixie, Dixie
JIKSĒ	jixie
MIKSĒ	mixy
NIKSĒ	nixie, water nixie
PIKSĒ	pixie, pyxie
TRIKSĒ	tricksy

IKSEN

BIKSEN	bixin
MIKSEN	mixen
VIKSEN	vixen

IKSER

FIKSER	affixer, fixer, *prefixer*, transfixer
LIKSER	elixir
MIKSER	admixer, intermixer, mixer
NIKSER	nixer

IKSET

KWIKSET	quickset
THIKSET	thickset

IKSHUN

DIKSHUN	A addiction, B benediction, D diction, I indiction, interdiction, J jurisdiction, K contradiction, M malediction, PR prediction, S satisdiction, V valediction
FIKSHUN	affixion, fiction, crucifixion, nonfiction, prefixion, suffixion, transfiction
FLIKSHUN	affliction, infliction, confliction
FRIKSHUN	affriction, friction

LIKSHUN	dereliction, reliction
PIKSHUN	depiction
STRIKSHUN	abstriction, derestriction, constriction, obstriction, restriction, striction
VIKSHUN	eviction, conviction, preconviction

IKSHUS

| DIKSHUS | contradictious |
| FIKSHUS | fictious |

IKSING

FIKSING	affixing, fixing, prefixing, refixing, suffixing, transfixing
MIKSING	admixing, intermixing, overmixing
NIKSING	nixing

IKSTŪR

(See IKSCHER)

IKTĀT

| DIKTĀT | dictate |
| NIKTĀT | nictate |

IKTED

(See IKT, add -ed where appropriate.)

IKTER

DIKTER	interdictor, contradictor, predictor
FIKTER	fictor
FLIKTER	afflicter, inflicter, conflicter
LIKTER	lictor
PIKTER	depicter, Pictor
STRIKTER	boa constrictor, constrictor, stricter, vasoconstrictor
VIKTER	evictor, convictor, victor

IKTIK

| IKTIK | ictic |

| DIKTIK | anapodictic, apodictic, dictic, endictic, epidictic |
| MIKTIK | amyctic |

IKTING

(See IKT, add -ing where appropriate.)

IKTIV

DIKTIV	addictive, apodictic, benedictive, indictive, interdictive, jurisdictive, contradictive, predictive, vindictive
FIKTIV	fictive
FLIKTIV	afflictive, inflictive, conflictive
PIKTIV	depictive
STRIKTIV	astrictive, constrictive, nonrestrictive, restrictive, unrestrictive
VIKTIV	evictive, convictive

IKTLĒ

| LIKTLĒ | derelictly |
| STRIKTLĒ | strictly |

IKTUM

| DIKTUM | dictum, obiter dictum |
| LIKTUM | delictum |

IKTŪR

(See IKCHER)

IKTUS

IKTUS	ictus
DIKTUS	Benedictus
NIKTUS	acronyctous
RIKTUS	rictus
VIKTUS	Invictus

IKUP

DIKUP	dikkop
HIKUP	hiccup
KIKUP	kickup
PIKUP	pickup
STIKUP	stickup

ĪKUS

FĪKUS	ficus
LĪKUS	umbilicus
PĪKUS	Picus
SPĪKUS	spicous
TĪKUS	anticous, anticus, posticous, posticus

ULTIMATUM TO MY CONGRESSMAN,
COMPOSED ON A MISERABLE DAY

Roads are muddy?
Make a study.

Day too warm?
Vote reform.

Feel a chill?
Draw a bill.

Morning raw?
Pass a law.

Snow and ice?
Pass it twice.

Storm and bluster?
Filibuster.

Though the weather's not affected,
This will get you re-elected.

ĪLA

ĪLA	Ila
BĪLA	strobila
HĪLA	hyla
LĪLA	Delilah
PĪLA	pyla

ILA

BILA	Sibylla
CHILA	chinchilla
DILA	granadilla, codilla, sabadilla, sapodilla, cedilla, seguidilla
GILA	megillah, Megillah
MILA	armilla, bismilla, camilla
NILA	anilla, granilla, manila, manilla, vanilla
RILA	barilla, gorilla, guerrilla, camarilla, cascarilla, sarsaparilla, sasparilla, spirilla, zorilla
SILA	axilla, maxilla, Scylla
SKWILA	squilla
TILA	flotilla, mantilla, scintilla
VILA	villa

ĪLAJ

(See ĪLIJ)

ĪLAKS

FĪLAKS	phylax
LĪLAKS	lilacs
SMĪLAKS	smilax

ĪLAN

(See ĪLIN)

ĪLAND

ĪLAND	island, Long Island, Rhode Island (etc.)
HĪLAND	highland
SKĪLAND	skyland
TĪLAND	Thailand

ĪLAR

(See ĪLER)

ĪLÄRK

FĪLÄRK	phylarch
SKĪLÄRK	skylark

ILCHER

FILCHER	filcher
MILCHER	milcher
PILCHER	pilcher

ILDA

HILDA	Brunhilde, Hilda
TILDA	tilde

ILDED

BILDED	builded
GILDED	begilded, gilded, guilded, unguilded

ĪLDER

MĪLDER	milder
WĪLDER	wilder

ILDER

BILDER	builder, home-builder, house-builder, castle-builder, rebuilder, shipbuilder, unbuilder
CHILDER	childer
GILDER	begilder, gilder, guilder
MILDER	milder
WILDER	bewilder, wilder

ĪLDING

CHĪLDING	childing
WĪLDING	wilding

ILDING

BILDING	building, housebuilding, homebuilding, castle-building, rebuilding, shipbuilding, unbuilding
GILDING	begilding, gilding, regilding, ungilding
HILDING	hilding

ILDISH

CHILDISH	childish
MILDISH	mildish
WILDISH	wildish

ĪLDLĒ

CHĪLDLĒ	childly
GĪLDLĒ	beguiledly
MĪLDLĒ	mildly
RĪLDLĒ	riledly
WĪLDLĒ	wildly

ĪLDLING

CHĪLDLING	childling
WĪLDLING	wildling

ĪLDNES

MĪLDNES	mildness
WĪLDNES	wildness

ĪLĒ

DĪLĒ	sedile
DRĪLĒ	drily
HĪLĒ	highly, hyle
KĪLĒ	kylie
RĪLĒ	wryly
SHĪLĒ	shyly
SĪLĒ	ancile
SLĪLĒ	slily, slyly
SMĪLĒ	smily
WĪLĒ	wily

ILĒ

ILĒ	illy
BILĒ	billy, Billy
CHILĒ	Chile, chili, chilly
DILĒ	daffy-down-dilly, daffodilly, dilly, Piccadilly
FILĒ	filly
FRILĒ	frilly
GILĒ	ghillie, gillie
GRILĒ	grilly
HILĒ	hilly
KILĒ	killy
KWILĒ	quilly
LILĒ	day lily, lily, meadow lily, piccalilli, pond lily, tiger lily, water lily, wood lily
NILĒ	willy-nilly
RILĒ	rilly
SHRILĒ	shrilly
SILĒ	silly
SKILĒ	skilly
STILĒ	stilly
THRILĒ	thrilly
TILĒ	tilly
TRILĒ	trilly
TWILĒ	twilly
WILĒ	nilly-willy, weary Willie, willy

ĪLEKS

ĪLEKS	ilex
SĪLEKS	silex

ĪLEM

(See ĪLUM)

ĪLER

ĪLER	defiler, filar, filer
GĪLER	beguiler
MĪLER	half-miler, quarter-miler, miler, two-miler (etc.)
PĪLER	compiler, pilar, piler, up-piler

RĪLER	riler
SĪLER	reconciler
SMĪLER	smiler
STĪLER	stylar, styler

ILER

ILER	iller
BILER	biller
CHILER	chiller
DILER	killer-diller
DRILER	driller
FILER	filler, fulfiller
FRILER	befriller, friller
GILER	giller
GRILER	griller
HILER	hiller
KILER	giant-killer, killer, lady-killer, man-killer, pain-killer, weed-killer (etc.)
KWILER	quiller
MILER	Joe Miller, miller
PILER	caterpillar, pillar
SHILER	schiller, shiller
SHRILER	shriller
SILER	maxillar, siller
SPILER	spiller
STILER	instiller, stiller
SWILER	swiller
THILER	thiller
THRILER	thriller
TILER	distiller, tiller
TRILER	pralltriller, triller
WILER	ill-willer, willer

ĪLES

ĪLES	eyeless

(See Ī, add -less where appropriate.)

ĪLET

ĪLET	eyelet, islet
PĪLET	co-pilot, Pilate, pilot, sky pilot
SMĪLET	smilet
STĪLET	stylet

ILET

BILET	billet
DRILET	drillet
FILET	fillet
KWILET	quillet
MILET	millet
PILET	pillet

RILET	rillet
SILET	penicillate, verticillate
SKILET	skillet
TILET	distillate
TRILET	trillet
WILET	pilwillet, willet

ILĒZ

KILĒZ	Achilles
WILĒZ	willies

(See ILĒ, add -s or change -y to -ies where appropriate.)

ĬLFUL

GĬLFUL	guileful
SMĬLFUL	smileful
WĬLFUL	wileful

ILFUL

SKILFUL	skillful
WILFUL	willful

ĪLIJ

MĪLIJ	mileage
SĪLIJ	silage
SMĪLIJ	smileage

ILIJ

GRILIJ	grillage
PILIJ	pillage
SPILIJ	spillage
STILIJ	stillage
TILIJ	tillage
VILIJ	global village, village

ILIK

DILIK	idyllic, odyllic
FILIK	A aelurophilic, Anglophilic, B bibliophilic, D discophilic, E ergophilic, FR Francophilic, G Gallophilic, gastrophilic, H halophilic, hemophilic, hydrophilic, I Italophilic, J Japanophilic, Germanophilic, KR cryophilic, L lyophilic, lipophilic, M mesophilic, N necrophilic, Negrophilic, P pyrophilic, R rheophilic, Russophilic, S psychrophilic, SL Slavophilic, T typophilic, Turkophilic, TH theophilic, thermophilic, Z Zionophilic, zoophilic
KILIK	killick, trochilic
KRILIK	acrylic
MILIK	amylic
NILIK	vanillic
RILIK	Cyrillic
SILIK	bacillic, basilic, exilic, imbecilic, cresylic, salicylic
THILIK	ethylic, methylic
TILIK	dactylic, holodactylic, macrodactylic, zygodactylic
ZILIK	exilic

ILIN

VILIN	archvillain, villain, villein
ZILIN	hoitzitzillin

ĪLING

(See ĪL, add -ing where appropriate.)

ILING

(See IL, add -ing where appropriate.)

ILIS

RILIS	amaryllis
SILIS	cilice

ĪLĪT

DRĪLĪT	dry light
HĪLĪT	highlight
SKĪLĪT	skylight
STĪLĪT	stylite
TWĪLĪT	twilight
ZĪLĪT	xylite

ĪLIT

SILIT	penicillate
TILIT	distillate

IFEN

BIFEN	biffin
GRIFEN	griffin, griffon
SHIFEN	chiffon
STIFEN	stiffen
STRIFEN	striffen
TIFEN	tiffin

ILKĒ

MILKĒ	milky
SILKĒ	silky
WILKĒ	Wendell Willkie

ILKEN

MILKEN	milken
SILKEN	silken

ILKER

BILKER	bilker
MILKER	milker
SILKER	silker

ILKING

(See **ILK,** add -ing where appropriate.)

ĪLLES

BĪLLES	bileless
FĪLLES	fileless
GĪLLES	guileless
STĪLLES	styleless
TĪLLES	tileless
TRĪLLES	trialless
WĪLLES	wileless

ILMAN

BILMAN	billman
GRILMAN	grillman
HILMAN	hillman
MILMAN	millman
PILMAN	pillman

ĪLMENT

FĪLMENT	defilement
GĪLMENT	beguilement
PĪLMENT	compilement
SĪLMENT	domicilement, exilement, irreconcilement, reconcilement, resilement
VĪLMENT	revilement
ZĪLMENT	exilement

ILMENT

FILMENT	fulfillment
STILMENT	distillment, instillment

ĪLNES

NĪLNES	juvenileness
VĪLNES	vileness

ILNES

ILNES	illness
CHILNES	chillness
SHRILNES	shrillness
STILNES	stillness

ĪLŌ

BĪLŌ	bye-low
HĪLŌ	high-low
MĪLŌ	milo
SHĪLŌ	Shiloh
SĪLŌ	silo
STĪLŌ	stylo

ILŌ

BILŌ	billow, embillow
DILŌ	armadillo, grenadillo, peccadillo, tabardillo
FILŌ	phyllo
GRILŌ	Negrillo
KILŌ	killow, kilo
PILŌ	lapillo, pillow, unpillow
RILŌ	Murillo, cigarillo
VILŌ	pulvillo
WILŌ	weeping willow, willow

ILŌD

BILŌD	billowed
PILŌD	empillowed, pillowed, unpillowed

ĪLOID

STĪLOID	styloid
ZĪLOID	xyloid

ILOK

(See **ILUK**)

ĪLON

FĪLON	phylon
NĪLON	nylon
PĪLON	pylon
TRĪLON	trylon

ĪLŌS

FĪLŌS	filose
PĪLŌS	pilose

ĪLOT

(See **ĪLET**)

ILRŌŌM

GRILRŌŌM	grillroom
STILRŌŌM	stillroom

ILSĪD

HILSĪD	hillside
RILSĪD	rillside

ILTĒ

GILTĒ	guilty
KILTĒ	kilty
KWILTĒ	quilty
LILTĒ	lilty
MILTĒ	milty
SILTĒ	silty
STILTĒ	stilty
TILTĒ	tilty
WILTĒ	wilty

ILTED

(See **ILT,** add -ed where appropriate.)

ILTER

FILTER	filter, philter, infilter, ultrafilter
JILTER	jilter
KILTER	kilter, out-of-kilter
KWILTER	quilter, crazy-quilter
LILTER	lilter
MILTER	milter
STILTER	stilter
TILTER	tilter
WILTER	wilter

ILTING

HILTING	hilting
JILTING	jilting
KILTING	kilting
KWILTING	quilting, crazy-quilting
LILTING	lilting
MILTING	milting
SILTING	silting
STILTING	stilting
TILTING	overtilting, tilting, tip-tilting, uptilting
WILTING	wilting

ILUK

FILUK	fillock
HILUK	hillock
SILUK	sillock

ĪLUM

FĪLUM	filum, phylum, subphylum
HĪLUM	hilum
HWĪLUM	whilom
SĪLUM	asylum
ZĪLUM	xylem

ILUM

FILUM	fillum
RILUM	spirillum

ĪLUS

HĪLUS	hilus
STĪLUS	monostylus, stylus

ILUS

BRILUS	*fibrillous*
FILUS	aphyllous, phyllous
GRILUS	grillos, gryllus, Grillus
JILUS	aspergillus, orgillous
KWILUS	quisquillous
MILUS	camillous
PILUS	lapillus
RILUS	arrilus
SILUS	bacillus
VILUS	favillous, pulvillus, villous, villus

ILYA

(See **IL'I.A**)

ILYAR

BILYAR	atrabiliar
MILYAR	familiar, overfamiliar, unfamiliar
SILYAR	domiciliar, conciliar
ZILYAR	auxiliar

(See **IL'I.AR**)

ILYARD

BILYARD	billiard
MILYARD	milliard

ILYARDZ

BILYARDZ	billiards
MILYARDZ	milliards

ILYENS

BRILYENS	brilliance
SILYENS	dissilience, consilience, transilience
ZILYENS	resilience

(See **IL'I.ENS**)

ILYENT

BRILYENT	brilliant
SILYENT	dissilient, consilient, transilient
ZILYENT	resilient

(See **IL'I.ENT**)

ILYUN

BILYUN	billion, tourbillion
DILYUN	mandillion, modillion
DRILYUN	drillion
JILYUN	gillion, jillion
KWILYUN	quisguillian
MILYUN	million, vermilion
NILYUN	nonillion, penillion
PILYUN	pillion
RILYUN	carillon, quadrillion
SILYUN	decillion
SKILYUN	skillion
STILYUN	stillion
TILYUN	dactylion, cotillion, quintillion, octillion, postillion, centillion, septillion, sextillion
TRILYUN	trillion
VILYUN	oyster villian, pavilion, civilian
ZILYUN	zillion

(See **IL'I.AN**)

ILYUS

BILYUS	atrabilious, bilious

(See **IL'I.US**)

ĪMA

FĪMA	phyma
LĪMA	lima, Lima, tellima
PĪMA	arapaima
RĪMA	rima
SĪMA	cyma, sima
TRĪMA	trima

IMAJ

(See **IMIJ**)

ĪMAKS

KLĪMAKS	climax
LĪMAKS	limax

ĪMAL

KĪMAL	isocheimal
KRĪMAL	isocrymal
PRĪMAL	primal
RĪMAL	rimal
SHTRĪMAL	shtreimel

IMAL

(See **IMEL**)

ĪMAN

(See **ĪMEN**)

ĪMĀT

(See ĪMIT)

IMBA

RIMBA	marimba
SIMBA	simba

IMBAL

(See IMBL)

IMBER

LIMBER	limber, unlimber
TIMBER	timber, timbre, retimber

IMBERD

LIMBERD	limbered, unlimbered
TIMBERD	timbered, untimbered

IMBL

BIMBL	bimbil
FIMBL	fimble
GIMBL	gimbal, gimble
NIMBL	nimble
SIMBL	cymbal, simbil, symbol, clavicymbal
THIMBL	thimble
THRIMBL	thrimble
TIMBL	tymbal, tymbale
WIMBL	wimble

IMBŌ

BIMBŌ	bimbo
KIMBŌ	akimbo, kimbo
LIMBŌ	limbo

IMBREL

HWIMBREL	whimbrel
TIMBREL	timbrel

IMBUS

LIMBUS	limbus, limbous
NIMBUS	nimbus, cumulo nimbus

ĪMĒ

BLĪMĒ	blimy, Gawblimy, cor blimy
GRĪMĒ	grimy
KRĪMĒ	crimy
LĪMĒ	limey, limy
PRĪMĒ	primy
RĪMĒ	rhymy, rimy
SLĪMĒ	beslimy, slimy
STĪMĒ	stymie
TĪMĒ	old-timey, thymy

IMĒ

IMĒ	immie
DIMĒ	dhimmie
GIMĒ	gimmie
HWIMĒ	whimmy
JIMĒ	jimmy
LIMĒ	limby
SHIMĒ	shimmy
SWIMĒ	swimmy
ZIMĒ	zimme, zimmy

ĪMEKS

SĪMEKS	cimex
TĪMEKS	Timex

ĪMEL

(See ĪMAL)

IMEL

GIMEL	gimel, gimmal
HIMEL	Himmel
KIMEL	kümmel

THE DANGEROUS YEARS

I'm aware a
Midlife crisis
Isn't rare a-
mong men's vices.
To defy a
Fading id-life
Some men try a
Mid-life mid-wife.

ĪMEN

HĪMEN	hymen, Hymen
LĪMEN	limen
SĪMEN	simple Simon
TĪMEN	timon, Timon

IMEN

SIMEN	persimmon
WIMEN	women

ĪMER

CHĪMER	chimer
DĪMER	dimer, nickel-and-dimer
GRĪMER	begrimer
KLĪMER	climber
LĪMER	sublimer, limer
MĪMER	mimer
PRĪMER	primer
RĪMER	rhymer, rimer
TĪMER	full-timer, old-timer, autotimer, part-timer, timer, timor, two-timer
TRĪMER	trimer

IMER

IMER	immer
BRIMER	brimmer
DIMER	dimmer
GIMER	gimmer
GLIMER	aglimmer, glimmer
GRIMER	grimmer
HIMER	hymner
KRIMER	krimmer
LIMER	limmer
NIMER	nimmer
PRIMER	primer, primmer
RIMER	rimmer
SHIMER	ashimmer, shimmer
SIMER	asimmer, simmer
SKIMER	hydroskimmer, skimmer
SLIMER	slimmer
SWIMER	nonswimmer, swimmer
TRIMER	trimmer

IMIJ

IMIJ	after-image, image
SKRIMIJ	scrimmage

ĪMIK

KĪMIK	isocheimic
RĪMIK	rhymic
THĪMIK	thymic
TĪMIK	hypothymic, catathymic, thymic
ZĪMIK	zymic

IMIK

BIMIK	cherubimic
GIMIK	gimmick
KIMIK	alchimic, cacochymic
MIMIK	mimic, pantomimic, zoömimic
NIMIK	acronymic, eponymic, homonymic, matronymic, metonymic, metronymic, patronymic, synonymic, pseudonymic, toponymic
THIMIK	lipothymic
TIMIK	etymic
ZIMIK	azymic, symic

IMIKS

(See **IMIK,** add -s where appropriate.)

ĪMING

CHĪMING	chiming
GRĪMING	begriming, griming
KLĪMING	climbing
MĪMING	miming
PRĪMING	priming, pump-priming
RĪMING	rhyming, riming
SLĪMING	sliming
TĪMING	timing, two-timing

IMING

BRIMING	brimming
DIMING	dimming
LIMING	limbing
SKIMING	skimming
SLIMING	slimming
SWIMING	swimming
TRIMING	retrimming, trimming

ĪMISH

CHĪMISH	chimish
RĪMISH	rhymish
TĪMISH	timish

IMISH

DIMISH	dimmish
GRIMISH	grimmish
PRIMISH	primmish
SLIMISH	slimmish
TRIMISH	trimmish

ĪMIST

RĪMIST	rhymist
TĪMIST	timist

(See **ĪM,** add -st where appropriate.)

ĪMIT

KLĪMIT	acclimate, climate
PRĪMIT	primate

ĪMLĒ

LĪMLĒ	sublimely
PRĪMLĒ	primely
TĪMLĒ	timely, untimely

IML

(See **IMEL.**)

IMLĒ

DIMLĒ	dimly
GRIMLĒ	grimly
PRIMLĒ	primly
SLIMLĒ	slimly
TRIMLĒ	trimly

ĪMLES

(See **ĪM,** add -less where appropriate.)

IMLES

(See **IM,** add -less where appropriate.)

IMNAL

HIMNAL	hymnal
SIMNAL	simnel

IMNER

HIMNER	hymner
LIMNER	limner

ĪMNES

LĪMNES	sublimeness
PRĪMNES	primeness

IMNES

DIMNES	dimness
GRIMNES	grimness
PRIMNES	primness
SLIMNES	slimness
TRIMNES	trimness

ĪMON

(See **ĪMAN**)

IMON

(See **IMEN**)

ĪMŌS

RIMŌS	rimose
SĪMŌS	cymose

IMPĒ

IMPĒ	impi, impy
KRIMPĒ	crimpy
SHRIMPĒ	shrimpy
SKIMPĒ	skimpy
SKRIMPĒ	scrimpy
WIMPĒ	wimpy, Wimpy

IMPER

GIMPER	gimper
HWIMPER	whimper
KRIMPER	crimper
LIMPER	limper
SHRIMPER	shrimper
SIMPER	simper
SKIMPER	skimper
SKRIMPER	scrimper

IMPING

(See **IMP,** add -ing where appropriate.)

IMPISH

(See **IMP,** add -ish where appropriate.)

ĪMPIT

LĪMPIT	limepit
SLĪMPIT	slimepit

IMPL

DIMPL	dimple
KRIMPL	crimple

PIMPL	pimple
RIMPL	rimple
SIMPL	simple
WIMPL	bewimple, wimple

IMPLĒ

DIMPLĒ	dimply
KRIMPLĒ	crimply
LIMPLĒ	limply
PIMPLĒ	pimply
RIMPLĒ	rimply
SIMPLĒ	simply

IMPLEKS

| IMPLEKS | implex |
| SIMPLEKS | simplex |

IMPLER

(See **IMPL**, add -*er* where appropriate.)

IMPLING

DIMPLING	dimpling
KRIMPLING	crimpling
PIMPLING	pimpling
RIMPLING	rimpling

ĪMUS

PRĪMUS	primus
RĪMUS	rimous
SĪMUS	cymous, simous
THĪMUS	thymus
TĪMUS	timeous, untimeous

IMZĒ

FLIMZĒ	flimsy
HWIMZĒ	whimsy
MIMZĒ	mimsey
SLIMZĒ	slimsy

ĪNA

CHĪNA	China, Indochina
JĪNA	angina, vagina
KĪNA	trichina
LĪNA	Carolina, Catalina, North Carolina, salina, South Carolina
MĪNA	mina, myna, mynah
RĪNA	farina, globigerina, Catarrhina, casuarina, Platyrrhina
SĪNA	glucina, piscina

INA

BINA	binna
MINA	meminna
PINA	pinna

ĪNAKS

| PĪNAKS | pinax |
| THRĪNAKS | Thrinax |

ĪNAL

BĪNAL	binal
FĪNAL	final, quarterfinal, semifinal
JĪNAL	vaginal
KLĪNAL	acclinal, anticlinal, declinal, isoclinal, cataclinal, periclinal, synclinal
KRĪNAL	endocrinal, crinal
KWĪNAL	equinal
NĪNAL	caninal
RĪNAL	prorhinal, rhinal
SĪNAL	officinal, piscinal, sinal
SPĪNAL	cerebrospinal, spinal
TĪNAL	matutinal
TRĪNAL	trinal
VĪNAL	vinal, vinyl

ĪNĀT

BĪNĀT	binate
KWĪNĀT	quinate
SPĪNĀT	spinate

INĀT

| INĀT | innate |
| PINĀT | pinnate |

INCHER

| PINCHER | penny-pincher, pincher |

(See **INCH**, add -*er* where appropriate.)

INCHING

INCHING	inching
FLINCHING	flinching, unflinching
KLINCHING	clinching
LYNCHING	lynching

| PINCHING | pinching, penny-pinching |
| SINCHING | cinching, uncinching |

INCHPIN

| LINCHPIN | linchpin |
| PINCHPIN | pinchpin |

INDĒ

PINDĒ	pindy
SHINDĒ	shindy
SINDĒ	Sindhi
WINDĒ	windy

ĪNDED

BLĪNDED	blinded, self-blinded, snow-blinded
MĪNDED	*A* alike-minded, *B* bloody-minded, *D* double-minded, *E* earthly-minded, earthy-minded, even-minded, evil-minded, *F* fair-minded, feebleminded, *FL* fleshly-minded, *FR* free-minded, *H* high-minded, *K* carnal-minded, *L* like-minded, light-minded, lofty-minded, low-minded, *M* minded, *N* narrow-minded, *P* public-minded, *R* reminded, *S* simple-minded, single-minded, sober-minded, *ST* strong-minded, *TR* travel-minded, *W* weak-minded, worldly-minded
RĪNDED	rinded
WĪNDED	winded

INDED

BRINDED	brinded
SINDED	abscinded, exscinded, interscinded, rescinded, scinded, sinded
WINDED	long-winded, short-winded, winded

ĪNDER

BĪNDER	binder, bookbinder, spellbinder
BLĪNDER	blinder
FĪNDER	faultfinder, finder, pathfinder, rangefinder, viewfinder, waterfinder
GRĪNDER	grinder, organ-grinder
HĪNDER	hinder
KĪNDER	kinder, unkinder
MĪNDER	minder, reminder
WĪNDER	rewinder, sidewinder, stem-winder, winder

INDER

DINDER	dinder
FLINDER	flinder
HINDER	hinder
LINDER	linder
PINDER	pinder, Pindar
SINDER	rescinder, cinder
TINDER	tinder
WINDER	winder

INDIK

INDIK	indic
SINDIK	syndic

ĪNDING

BĪNDING	binding, bookbinding, inbinding, unbinding, upbinding

(See ĪND, add -ing where appropriate.)

INDL

BINDL	bindle
BRINDL	brindle
DINDL	dindle
DWINDL	dwindle
FINDL	findal
KINDL	enkindle, kindle, rekindle
RINDL	rindle
SPINDL	spindle
SWINDL	swindle

INDLD

(See INDL, add -d where appropriate.)

ĪNDLĒ

BLĪNDLĒ	blindly, purblindly
KĪNDLĒ	kindly, unkindly

INDLER

BRINDLER	brindler
DWINDLER	dwindler
KINDLER	kindler
SPINDLER	spindler
SWINDLER	swindler

ĪNDLES

(See ĪND, add -less where appropriate.)

INDLING

(See INDL, add -ing where appropriate.)

ĪNDNES

BLĪNDNES	blindness, color blindness, night blindness, purblindness, sand-blindness, semiblindness, snow blindness
KĪNDNES	kindness, loving kindness, unkindness

INDŌ

LINDŌ	lindo
RINDŌ	tamarindo
WINDŌ	french window, shop window, window

INDRIFT

SPINDRIFT	spindrift
WINDRIFT	windrift

ĪNĒ

BRĪNĒ	briny
HĪNĒ	heinie
HWĪNĒ	whiney
LĪNĒ	liney, outliney
MĪNĒ	miny
PĪNĒ	piny
SHĪNĒ	moonshiny, shiny, sunshiny, starshiny
SĪNĒ	sine
SPĪNĒ	spiny
TĪNĒ	tiny
TWĪNĒ	twiny
VĪNĒ	viny
WĪNĒ	winy

INĒ

BLINĒ	blinny
BRINĒ	brinny
CHINĒ	chinny
FINĒ	finny
GINĒ	guinea, New Guinea
GRINĒ	grinny
HINĒ	hinny
HWINĒ	whinny
JINĒ	ginny, jinni
LINĒ	linhay
MINĒ	ignominy, mini
NINĒ	ninny, pickaninny
PINĒ	pinny
PLINĒ	Pliny
SHINĒ	shinny
SINĒ	cine
SKINĒ	skinny
SKWINĒ	squinny
SPINĒ	spinney
TINĒ	tinny
VINĒ	vinny

ĪNER

BĪNER	combiner
DĪNER	diner, condigner
FĪNER	definer, finer, confiner, refiner
HWĪNER	whiner
KLĪNER	incliner, recliner
LĪNER	A aquiliner, airliner, aligner, FR freightliner, H headliner, I eyeliner, J jetliner, L liner, M maligner, O outliner, P penny-a-liner, STR streamliner, Y underliner, W one-liner
MĪNER	miner, minor, underminer
NĪNER	benigner, forty-niner, saturniner
PĪNER	opiner, piner, repiner, supiner
SHĪNER	shiner
SHRĪNER	Shriner
SĪNER	assigner, designer, consigner, cosigner, countersigner, resigner, signer
TWĪNER	entwiner, twiner, intertwiner, untwiner
VĪNER	diviner, pulviner, viner
WĪNER	winer
ZĪNER	designer, resigner

INER

INER	inner
DINER	after-dinner, before-dinnner, dinner
FINER	finner
GINER	aginner, beginner
GRINER	grinner
JINER	ginner
PINER	pinner
SHINER	shinner
SINER	sinner
SKINER	muleskinner, skinner
SPINER	spinner
THINER	thinner
TINER	tinner
TWINER	twinner
WINER	breadwinner, winner

ĪNES

DRĪNES	dryness
FĪNES	finis
GĪNES	wise-guyness
HĪNES	highness
PĪNES	apple-pieness, humble-pieness
SHĪNES	shyness
SLĪNES	slyness
SPRĪNES	spryness

(See ĪNUS.)

INET

LINET	linnet
MINET	light-minute, minute
PINET	pinnet
SPINET	spinet

INFLIK

SINFLIK	sin-flick
SKINFLIK	skin-flick

INFUL

SINFUL	sinful
SKINFUL	skinful

INGBANG

BINGBANG	bingbang
JINGBANG	jingbang

INGBŌLT

KINGBŌLT	kingbolt
RINGBŌLT	ringbolt, wringbolt

INGĒ

BINGĒ	bingy
DINGĒ	dinghy
KLINGĒ	clinghy
PINGĒ	pingy
RINGĒ	ringy
SINGĒ	singy
SPRINGĒ	springy
STINGĒ	stingy
STRINGĒ	stringy
SWINGĒ	swingy
WINGĒ	wingy
ZINGĒ	zingy

INGER

BLINGER	blinger
BRINGER	bringer, fire bringer, news bringer
DINGER	dinger, humdinger
FLINGER	flinger
HWINGER	whinger
KLINGER	clinger
PINGER	pinger
RINGER	bell ringer, clothes-wringer, ringer, wringer
SINGER	ballad singer, blues singer, folksinger, jazz singer, choir singer, mastersinger, minnesinger, Meistersinger, opera singer, punk singer, rock singer, singer
SLINGER	gunslinger, hashslinger, ink-slinger, mudslinger, slinger, unslinger
SPRINGER	klipspringer, springer
STINGER	stinger
STRINGER	first-stringer, second-stringer, stringer
SWINGER	swinger
WINGER	left-winger, right-winger, winger
ZINGER	zinger

INGGA

HINGGA	anhinga
RINGGA	alcheringa, churinga
TINGGA	cotinga

INGGĒ

BINGGĒ	bingey, binghy, bingy
DINGGĒ	dinghy

INGGER

FINGGER	finger, fishfinger, forefinger, index finger, ladyfinger
LINGGER	linger, malinger

INGGERD

FINGGERD	fingered, light-fingered, rosy-fingered, web-fingered
LINGGERD	lingered, malingered

INGGL

INGGL	ingle
BINGGL	bingle
DINGGL	dingle, swing-dingle
JINGGL	jingal, jingle
KRINGGL	cringle, Kriss Kringle
LINGGL	lingel, lingle
MINGGL	immingle, intermingle, commingle, mingle
PINGGL	pingle
PRINGGL	pringle
SHINGGL	reshingle, shingle
SINGGL	single, surcingle
SPRINGGL	espringal, springal
SWINGGL	swingle
TINGGL	tingle
TRINGGL	tringle
TWINGGL	twingle

INGGLD

DINGGLD	dingled
JINGGLD	jingled
MINGGLD	immingled, intermingled, commingled, mingled
SHINGGLD	shingled
SINGGLD	singled
SWINGGLD	swingled
TINGGLD	tingled

INGGLĒ

DINGGLĒ	dingly
JINGGLĒ	jingly
MINGGLĒ	mingly

SHINGGLĒ	shingly
SINGGLĒ	singly
TINGGLĒ	tingly

INGGLER

JINGGLER	jingler
MINGGLER	intermingler, commingler, mingler
PINGGLER	pingler
SHINGGLER	shingler
TINGGLER	tingler

INGGLING

(See INGGL, drop -e and add -ing where appropriate.)

INGGLISH

INGGLISH	English
TINGGLISH	tinglish

INGGŌ

BINGGŌ	bingo
DINGGŌ	dingo, Mandingo
GRINGGŌ	gringo
JINGGŌ	jingo
LINGGŌ	lingo
MINGGŌ	flamingo, Santo Domingo
RINGGŌ	eryngo, Ringo
STINGGŌ	stingo

INGING

SINGING	singing, scat-singing

(See ING, add -ing where appropriate.)

INGKCHER

LINGKCHER	lincture, pollincture
SINGKCHER	encincture, cincture, uncincture
TINGKCHER	tincture, untincture

INGKCHERD

SINGKCHERD	encinctured, cinctured, uncinctured
TINGCHERD	tinctured, untinctured

INGKĒ

INGKĒ	inky
BLINGKĒ	blinky
CHINGKĒ	chinky
DINGKĒ	dinkey, dinky
KINGKĒ	kinky
LINGKĒ	linky
MINGKĒ	minky
PINGKĒ	pinky
SINGKĒ	Helsinki, sinky
SLINGKĒ	slinky
STINGKĒ	stinky
WINGKĒ	winky
ZINGKĒ	zinky

INGKER

INGKER	inker
BLINGKER	blinker
DRINGKER	drinker
KLINGKER	clinker
LINGKER	enlinker, linker
PINGKER	pinker
PRINGKER	prinker
RINGKER	rinker
SHRINGKER	headshrinker, shrinker
SINGKER	sinker
SKINGKER	skinker
SLINGKER	slinker
STINGKER	stinker
SWINGKER	swinker
THINGKER	bethinker, freethinker, thinker
TINGKER	tinker
WINGKER	hoodwinker, tiddledywinker, winker

INGKERD

BLINGKERD	blinkard, blinkered
TINGKERD	tinkered

INGKĪD

BLINGKĪD	blink-eyed
PINGKĪD	pink-eyed

INGKIJ

LINGKIJ	linkage
SHRINGKIJ	shrinkage

INGKING

(See INGK, add -ing where appropriate.)

INGKL

INGKL	inkle
KINGKL	kinkle
KRINGKL	crinkle
RINGKL	unwrinkle, wrinkle
SPRINGKL	besprinkle, sprinkle
STRINGKL	strinkle
TINGKL	tinkle
TWINGKL	twinkle
WINGKL	periwinkle, Rip Van Winkle, winkle

INGKLĒ

KRINGKLĒ	crinkly
PINGKLĒ	pinkly
RINGKLĒ	wrinkly
TINGKLĒ	tinkly
TWINGKLĒ	twinkly

INGKLER

INGKLER	inkler
RINGKLER	wrinkler
SPRINGKLER	sprinkler
STRINGKLER	strinkler
TINGKLER	tinkler
TWINGKLER	twinkler

CENTRIPETAL—CENTRIFUGAL

Centripetal force pulls an object toward the center of a circular path; centrifugal force pulls it away.

As planet gyres about its sun,
  Or cock about his hen,
'Round thee my revolutions run,
  And 'round and 'round again.

And yet as force centripetal
  Draws heart to waiting heart,
A counter-force centrifugal
  Keeps pulling us apart.

The push and pull go on and on,
  We never grasp the nettle.
I fear we two shall ne'er be one
  Centrifugalipetal.

INGKLING

(See INGKL, add -ing where appropriate.)

INGKŌ

CHINGKŌ	pachinko
GINGKŌ	gingko
PINGKŌ	pinko

INGTLĒ

SINGTLĒ	succinctly
TINGTLĒ	distinctly, indistinctly

INGKTNES

SINGTNES	succinctness
TINGTNES	distinctness, indistinctness

INGKTŪR

(See INGKCHER)

INGKTŪRD

(See INGKCHERD)

INGKUS

RINGKUS	Ornithorhynchus, ornithorhyncous, Oxyrhynchus, oxyrhyncous
SINGKUS	scincous
ZINGKUS	zincous

INGKWENS

LINGKWENS	delinquence, relinquence
PINGKWENS	propinquence

INGKWENT

LINGKWENT	delinquent, relinquent
PINGKWENT	propinquent

INGKWISH

LINGKWISH	relinquish
VINGKWISH	vinquish

INGLĒ

(See ING, add -ly where appropriate.)

INGLES

(See ING, add -less where appropriate.)

INGLET

DINGLET	dinglet
KINGLET	kinglet
RINGLET	ringlet
SPRINGLET	springlet
WINGLET	winglet

INGLING

KINGLING	kingling
RINGLING	Ringling
WINGLING	wingling

INGTĪM

RINGTĪM	ringtime
SPRINGTĪM	springtime

ĪNIK

KĪNIK	kinic
PĪNIK	pinic
TĪNIK	neoteinic
VĪNIK	vinic

INIK

BINIK	albinic, Jacobinic, rabbinic
DINIK	dinic, Odinic
FINIK	delphinic, finick, Finnic
KINIK	kinic
KLINIK	aclinic, apopemptoclinic, isoclinic, clinic, monoclinic, polyclinic, triclinic
KRINIK	endocrinic, encrinic
KWINIK	quinic
LINIK	pollinic, porcelainic
MINIK	Brahminic, fulminic, histaminic
PINIK	pinic
RINIK	mandarinic
SINIK	cynic, Sinic, succinic
TINIK	adiactinic, actinic, diactinic, hematinic, narcotinic, nicotinic, platinic
VINIK	vinic

ĪNING

(See ĪN, add -ing where appropriate.)

INING

WINING	breadwinning, winning

(See IN, add -ning where appropriate.)

INIS

FINIS	finis
PINIS	pinnace

INISH

FINISH	finish, Finnish, refinish
MINISH	diminish
THINISH	thinnish
TINISH	tinnish

INIST

BINIST	Jacobinist
LINIST	violinist, zeppelinist

(See IN, add -est or -ist where appropriate.)

ĪNĪT

FĪNĪT	finite
KRĪNĪT	crinite

INJĒ

DINJĒ	dingy
FRINJĒ	fringy
KRINJĒ	cringy
MINJĒ	mingy
STINJĒ	stingy
TWINJĒ	twingey

INJENS

PINJENS	impingence
STRINJENS	astringence, stringence
TINJENS	contingence

INJENT

FINJENT	fingent
FRINJENT	fringent, refringent
MINJENT	retromingent
PINJENT	impingent
RINJENT	ringent
STRINJENT	stringent
TINJENT	attingent, contingent, tingent
TRINJENT	astringent, constringent, restringent

INJER

INJER	injure
FRINJER	fringer, infringer
HINJER	hinger
JINJER	ginger
KRINJER	cringer
PINJER	impinger
SINJER	singer
SPRINJER	springer
SWINJER	swinger
TINJER	tinger
TWINJER	twinger

INJING

(See INJ, add -ing where appropriate.)

INJLES

(See INJ, add -less where appropriate.)

INJMENT

FRINGJMENT	infringement
HINJMENT	hingement, unhingement
PINJMENT	impingement
STRINJMENT	perstringement
TRINJMENT	astringement

ĪNKLAD

PĪNKLAD	pine-clad
VĪNKLAD	vine-clad

ĪNKROUND

PĪNKROUND	pine-crowned
VĪNKROUND	vine-crowned

INLAND

INLAND	inland
FINLAND	Finland

ĪNLĒ

DĬNLĒ	condignly
FĪNLĒ	finely, superfinely
LĪNLĒ	aquilinely, malignly
NĪNLĒ	benignly, caninely, saturninely, unbenignly
PĪNLĒ	supinely
VĪNLĒ	divinely

INLĒ

INLĒ	inly
THINLĒ	thinly
TWINLĒ	twinly

ĪNLES

(See ĪN, add -less where appropriate.)

INLES

(See IN, add -less where appropriate.)

ĪNMENT

FĪNMENT	confinement, refinement
LĪNMENT	alignment, interlinement, malignment, realignment
SHRĪNMENT	enshrinement
SĪNMENT	assignment, consignment
TWĪNMENT	entwinement, intertwinement
ZĪNMENT	designment, resignment

ĪNNES

DĬNNES	condignness
FĪNNES	fineness, superfineness
LĪNNES	salineness
NĪNNES	benignness
PĪNNES	*supineness*
VĪNNES	divineness

INNES

INNES	inness, genuineness
KINNES	akinness
LINNES	masculineness
NINNES	feminineness
THINNES	thinness, withinness
TWINNES	twinness

ĪNŌ

BĪNŌ	albino, sabino
FĪNŌ	damfino
RĪNŌ	rhino
WĪNŌ	wino

INŌ

MINŌ	minnow, top minnow
WINŌ	winnow

INSER

MINSER	mincer
PINSER	pincer
RINSER	rinser
VINSER	convincer
WINSER	wincer

INSING

(See INS, add -ing where appropriate.)

INSKĒ

LINSKĒ	kolinsky
MINSKĒ	Minsky

INSTER

MINSTER	minster, Axminster, Westminster
SPINSTER	spinster

INTAJ

(See INTIJ)

INTAL

(See INTL)

INTĒ

FLINTĒ	flinty
GLINTĒ	glinty
LINTĒ	lintie, linty
MINTĒ	minty
SHINTĒ	shinty
SINTĒ	teosinte
SKWINTĒ	squinty
SPLINTĒ	splinty
TINTĒ	tinty

INTED

TINTED	rainbow-tinted, rosy-tinted, tinted

(See INT, add -ed where appropriate.)

INTER

INTER	*inter*
DINTER	dinter
FLINTER	flinter
GLINTER	glinter
HINTER	hinter
LINTER	linter
MINTER	minter
PINTER	Pinter
PRINTER	printer, imprinter, teleprinter
SINTER	sinter
SKWINTER	squinter
SPLINTER	splinter
SPRINTER	sprinter
STINTER	stinter
TINTER	aquatinter, mezzotinter, tinter
TWINTER	twinter
VINTER	vinter
WINTER	midwinter, overwinter, winter

INTHIK

RINTHIK	labyrinthic
SINTHIK	absinthic

INTHIN

BINTHIN	terebinthine
RINTHIN	labyrinthine
SINTHIN	absinthine, hyacinthine

INTĪD

FLINTĪD	flint-eyed
SKWINTĪD	squint-eyed

INTIJ

MINTIJ	mintage
SPLINTIJ	splintage
TINTIJ	tintage
VINTIJ	vintage

INTING

(See **INT**, add *-ing* where appropriate.)

INTL

JINTL	triginal
KWINTAL	quintal
LINTL	lintel, lintle

PINTL	pintle
SINTL	scintle
SKINTL	skintle

INTŌ

PINTŌ	pinto
SHINTŌ	Shinto
TINTŌ	mezzotinto

INTRĒ

SPINTRĒ	spintry
VINTRĒ	vintry
WINTRĒ	wintry

(See **IN'TER.Ē**)

INŪ

FINŪ	finew
SINŪ	sinew, unsinew
TINŪ	discontinue, continue

INŪD

FINŪD	finewed
SINŪD	sinewed, unsinewed
TINŪD	discontinued, continued

ĪNUS

BĪNUS	binous
BRĪNUS	gambrinous
DĪNUS	dinus
FĪNUS	delphinus
KĪNUS	echinus, matroclinous, monoclinous
KLĪNUS	patroclinus
KWĪNUS	Aquinas
LĪNUS	botulinus, linous, salinous
MĪNUS	minus
PĪNUS	Pinus
RĪNUS	dirhinous, mesorhinous, platyrhinous
SĪNUS	sinus, incinus
SPĪNUS	spinous
TĪNUS	laurustinus
VĪNUS	pulvinus, vinous

(See **ĪNES**)

INYAL

	original

(See **IN'I.AL**)

INYUN

JINYUN	Virginian
MINYUN	dominion, mignon, minion, minyan
PINYUN	opinion, pignon, pinion, pinyon

(See **IN'I.AN**)

INYUND

MINYUND	dominioned, minioned
PINYUND	opinioned, pinioned, self-opinioned

INZĒ

KWINZĒ	quinsy
LINZĒ	linsey

ĬŌ

ĬŌ	Io
HĬŌ	*heigh-ho*, Ohio
KLĬŌ	Clio

ĬOL

(See **ĬAL**)

ĬON

(See **ĬAN**)

ĬOR

(See **ĬER**)

ĬOT

(See **ĬET**)

ĬOUT

BĬOUT	buy-out
TRĬOUT	tryout

ĪPA

NĪPA	nipa
PĪPA	pipa
RĪPA	ripa
STĪPA	Stipa

IPAJ

(See **IPIJ**)

ĪPAL

(See ĪPL)

IPANT

FLIPANT	flippant
TRIPANT	trippant

ĪPĒ

GRĪPĒ	gripy
PĪPĒ	pipy
STRĪPĒ	stripy
SWĪPĒ	swipy
TĪPĒ	antitypy, daguerreotypy, phonotypy, chromotypy, polytypy

IPĒ

CHIPĒ	chippy
DIPĒ	dippy
DRIPĒ	drippy
GRIPĒ	grippy
HIPĒ	hippie, hippy
KLIPĒ	klippe
LIPĒ	lippy
NIPĒ	nippy, Aganippe
PIPĒ	pippy
SHIPĒ	shippy
SIPĒ	Mississippi
SLIPĒ	slippy
SNIPĒ	snippy
THIPĒ	Xanthippe
TIPĒ	tippy, Xanthippe
YIPĒ	yippee, yippie, yippy
ZIPĒ	zippy

ĪPED

BĪPED	biped
PĪPED	parallelepiped
STRĪPED	striped

ĪPEND

RĪPEND	ripened
STĪPEND	stipend

ĪPER

GRĪPER	griper
HĪPER	hyper
PĪPER	bagpiper, piper, sandpiper
RĪPER	riper
SNĪPER	sniper
STRĪPER	striper
SWĪPER	sideswiper, swiper
TĪPER	daguerreotyper, electrotyper, linotyper, monotyper, stereotyper, typer
VĪPER	Russell's viper, viper
WĪPER	windshield wiper, wiper, Ypres

IPER

CHIPER	chipper
DIPER	Big Dipper, dipper, hipper-dipper
DRIPER	dripper
FLIPER	flipper
FRIPER	fripper
GIPER	gipper
GRIPER	gripper
HIPER	hipper
HWIPER	horsewhipper, whipper
JIPER	gypper
KIPER	kipper, Yom Kippur
KLIPER	clipper
KWIPER	quipper
LIPER	lipper
NIPER	gallinipper, nipper
RIPER	Jack the Ripper, ripper
SHIPER	shipper
SIPER	sipper
SKIPER	mudskipper, skipper
SLIPER	lady's-slipper, slipper
SNIPER	snipper
STRIPER	outstripper, stripper
SWIPER	swipper
TIPER	tipper
TRIPER	daytripper, tripper
YIPER	yipper
ZIPER	zipper

IPERD

KIPERD	kippered
SKIPERD	skippered
SLIPERD	slippered

IPET

HWIPET	whippet
LIPET	microlipet
PIPET	pipit
RIPET	rippet
SIPET	sippet
SKIPET	skippet
SNIPET	snippet
TIPET	tippet
TRIPET	trippet

IPIJ

CHIPIJ	chippage
KIPIJ	kippage
KWIPIJ	equipage
SKRIPIJ	scrippage
SLIPIJ	slippage
STRIPIJ	strippage

IPIK

DIPIK	adipic
HIPIK	hippic
LIPIK	philippic
TIPIK	A atypic, D daguerreotypic, E electrotypic, F phonotypic, H heterotypic, homeotypic, homotypic, I idiotypic, M monotypic, P polytypic, ST stenotypic, stereotypic, T typic

ĪPING

PĪPING	Peiping

(See ĪP, add -ing where appropriate.)

IPING

(See IP, add -ing where appropriate.)

IPISH

GRIPISH	grippish
HIPISH	hippish
KWIPISH	quippish
SNIPISH	snippish

IPJAK

HWIPJAK	whipjack
SKIPJAK	skipjack

ĪPL

RĪPL	ripal
SĪPL	disciple
STĪPL	stipel
TĪPL	archetypal, ectypal, typal

IPL

FIPL	fipple
GRIPL	gripple
KRIPL	becripple, cripple
NIPL	nipple
PIPL	pipple
RIPL	ripple
SIPL	participle, sipple
STIPL	stipple
SWIPL	swiple, swipple
THRIPL	thripple
TIPL	tipple
TRIPL	triple

IPLĒ

KRIPLĒ	cripply
RIPLĒ	ripply
STIPLĒ	stipply
TRIPLĒ	triply

IPLER

(See **IPL,** add -r where appropriate.)

ĪPLES

(See **ĪP,** add -less where appropriate.)

IPLES

(See **IP,** add -less where appropriate.)

IPLET

CHIPLET	chiplet
LIPLET	liplet
RIPLET	ripplet
SIPLET	siplet
STRIPLET	striplet
TIPLET	tiplet
TRIPLET	triplet

IPLING

KIPLING	Kipling

(See **IPL,** add -ing where appropriate.)

IPMENT

GRIPMENT	gripment
KWIPMENT	equipment
SHIPMENT	shipment, transshipment

ĪPŌ

HĬPŌ	hypo
TĬPŌ	typo

IPŌ

HIPŌ	hippo
JIPŌ	gippo
LIPŌ	filippo
SHIPŌ	*shippo*

IPOF

RIPOF	ripoff
TIPOF	tipoff

IPON

JIPON	gipon
NIPON	Nippon
SHIPON	shippon
SLIPON	slip-on

IPSĒ

IPSĒ	ipse
DIPSĒ	dipsey, dipsie, dipsy
HIPSĒ	hipsy
JIPSĒ	gypsy
KIPSĒ	Poughkeepsie
TIPSĒ	tipsy

IPSHUN

JIPSHUN	Egyptian
NIPSHUN	conniption
KRIPSHUN	*A* ascription, *D* description, *I* inscription, *K* conscription, *PR* prescription, proscription, *R* rescription, *S* circumscription, subscription, superscription, *SK* scription, *T* teletranscription, *TR* transcription

IPSIS

KRIPSIS	krypsis
LIPSIS	ellipsis
STIPSIS	stypsis
TRIPSIS	tripsis

IPSTER

HWIPSTER	whipster
KWIPSTER	quipster
TIPSTER	tipster

IPSTIK

DIPSTIK	dipstick
LIPSTIK	lipstick

IPTIK

DIPTIK	diptych
GLIPTIK	anaglyptic, glyptic
KLIPTIK	ecliptic
KRIPTIK	holocryptic, cryptic, procryptic
LIPTIK	apocalyptic, elliptic, iatroliptic, polyptych
STIPTIK	hypostyptic, styptic
TRIPTIK	triptych

IPUS

HIPUS	Eohippus, Epihippus, hippus, Protohippus, Proterohippus
LIPUS	philippus

ĪRA

ĪRA	eyra
BĪRA	beira
DĪRA	daira
JĪRA	hegira, spirogyra
LĪRA	Lyra
MĪRA	almirah, palmyra
TĪRA	hetaera, tayra

ÎRA

ÎRA	era
DÎRA	Madeira
GÎRA	gerah
HÎRA	Hera
LÎRA	galera, lira
MÎRA	chimera
PÎRA	lempira
SHÎRA	asherah
SÎRA	phylloxera, sera
SKLÎRA	sclera
TÎRA	hetaera, rangatira

(See **IRA**)

IRA

LĪRA	tirra-lira
SĪRA	sirrah
WĪRA	wirra

(See ÎRA)

ĪRAL

JĪRAL	gyral, polygyral
KĪRAL	allochiral, chiral
PĪRAL	papyral
SPĪRAL	spiral
STĪRAL	styryl
TĪRAL	retiral

ÎRAL

ÎRAL	eral
FÎRAL	feral, hemispheral
JÎRAL	vicegeral
SFÎRAL	spheral
SÎRAL	ceral
SKLÎRAL	scleral

ĪRANT

JĪRANT	gyrant
KWÎRANT	enquirent
PÎRANT	aspirant, expirant, conspirant, spirant
TĪRANT	archtyrant, tyrant
VĪRANT	sempivirent, virent

ĪRĀT

ĪRĀT	irate
JĪRĀT	agyrate, dextrogyrate, gyrate, sinistrogyrate, circumgyrate

ĪRĒ

ĪRĒ	eyrie, Dies Irae
DĪRĒ	dairi
KĪRĒ	kairi
KWĪRĒ	acquiry, enquiry, inquiry
MĪRĒ	miry
NĪRĒ	praemunire, venire
SKWĪRĒ	squiry
SPĪRĒ	expiree, expiry, perspiry, spiry
WĪRĒ	wiry

(See I'ER.Ē)

ÎRĒ

ÎRĒ	aerie, eerie, eery, Erie, eyrie
BÎRĒ	beery
BLÎRĒ	bleary
CHÎRĒ	cheery
DÎRĒ	dearie, deary
DRÎRĒ	dreary, Dundreary
JÎRĒ	jeery
KÎRĒ	bokmakierie, hara-kiri, keiri, kiri, kyrie
KWÎRĒ	query
LÎRĒ	whigmaleery, leary, leery
PÎRĒ	peri
RÎRĒ	miserere
SÎRĒ	seri, siri
SFÎRĒ	sphery
SMÎRĒ	smeary
SNÎRĒ	sneery
THÎRĒ	metatheory, theory
SPÎRĒ	speary
TÎRĒ	hetaerae, teary
VÎRĒ	veery
WÎRĒ	aweary, forweary, life-weary, overweary, weary, world-weary
YÎRĒ	cavaliere

ÎRĒD

KWÎRĒD	queried
WÎRĒD	unwearied, war-wearied, wearied, world-wearied

IREL

SKWIREL	squirrel
VIREL	virile

ÎRĒM

BÎRĒM	bireme
TRÎRĒM	trireme

ĪRĒN

ĪRĒN	irene, *Irene*
KĪRĒN	kairine, kyrine
PĪRĒN	pyrene
SKWĪRĒN	squireen
STĪRĒN	polystyrene, styrene

ĪREN

(See ĪRUN)

ÎRENS

FÎRENS	interference
HÎRENS	adherence, incoherence, inherence, coherence
KLÎRENS	clearance
PÎRENS	appearance, disappearance, non-appearance, reappearance
RÎRENS	arrearance
VÎRENS	perseverance

ĪRENT

(See ĪRANT)

ÎRENT

HÎRENT	adherent, inadherent, incoherent, inherent, coherent
JÎRENT	gerent, vicegerent
KWÎRENT	querent
VÎRENT	perseverant

ĪRER

(See ĪR, add *-er* where appropriate.)

ÎRER

(See ÎR, add *-er* where appropriate.)

ÎRES

PÎRES	peeress
SÎRES	seeress

ÎRĒZ

DÎRĒZ	dearies
DRÎRĒZ	dundrearies
HÎRĒZ	heres
KWÎRWĒZ	queries
SÎRĒZ	Ceres, mini-series, series, World Series
WÎRĒZ	wearies

ĪRFUL

ĪRFUL	ireful
DĪRFUL	direful
ZĪRFUL	desireful

ÎRFUL

ÎRFUL	earful
CHÎRFUL	cheerful, uncheerful
FÎRFUL	fearful, unfearful
SNÎRFUL	sneerful
TÎRFUL	tearful

ĪRID

ĪRID	irid
MĪRID	mormyrid
VĪRID	sempervirid, virid
ZĪRID	xyrid

ÎRĪD

BLÎRĪD	blear-eyed
KLÎRĪD	clear-eyed
TÎRĪD	tear-eyed

IRID

IRID	irid
VIRID	virid

ÎRIJ

KLÎRIJ	clearage
PÎRIJ	peerage, pierage
RÎRIJ	arrearage
STÎRIJ	steerage

ĪRIK

NĪRIK	oneiric
PĪRIK	epeiric

IRIK

JIRIK	argyric, photogyric, gyric, panegyric
LIRIK	lyric
PIRIK	empiric, Pyrrhic, vampiric
TIRIK	butyric, satiric, satyric

IRIL

(See IREL)

ĪRING

(See ĪR, add -ing where appropriate.)

ĪRING

BĪRING	Bering

(See ĪR, add -ing where appropriate.)

ĪRIS

ĪRIS	iris
SĪRIS	Osiris, Cyrus

ĪRISH

ĪRISH	Irish
SKWĪRISH	squirish

ĪRIST

ĪRIST	irised
JĪRIST	gyrist
LĪRIST	lyrist

IRIST

JIRIST	panegyrist
LIRIST	lyrist

ON THE HERMIT CRAB

The hermit crab lives safely curled
Inside the shell that is his world.
If you expose him to the sky,
He moans, "I faint!"; he groans, "I die!"

Next day you'll find him doing well
Inside some other hermit shell.
(Come back, dear; I am frailer absolutely than the hermit crab.)

ĪRLĒ

DĪRLĒ	direly
SKWĪRLĒ	squirely
TĪRLĒ	entirely

ÎRLĒ

CHÎRLĒ	cheerly
DÎRLĒ	dearly
DRÎRLĒ	drearly
KLÎRLĒ	clearly
KWÎRLĒ	queerly
LÎRLĒ	cavalierly
MÎRLĒ	merely
NÎRLĒ	nearly

SÎRLĒ	insincerely, sincerely
TÎRLĒ	austerely
VÎRLĒ	severely
YÎRLĒ	yearly

ĪRLES

(See ĪR, add -less where appropriate.)

ÎRLES

(See ÎR, add -less where appropriate.)

ĪRLING

HĪRLING	hireling
SKWĪRLING	squireling

ÎRLING

SHÎRLING	shearling
STÎRLING	steerling
YÎRLING	yearling

ĪRMAN

FĪRMAN	fireman
NĪRMAN	venireman

ĪRMENT

KWĪRMENT	acquirement, requirement
MĪRMENT	bemirement
TĪRMENT	attirement, retirement

ÎRMENT

DÎRMENT	endearment
SÎRMENT	cerement

ĪRNES

DĪRNES	direness
TĪRNES	entireness

ÎRNES

DÎRNES	dearness
KLÎRNES	clearness
KWÎRNES	queerness
NÎRNES	nearness
SÎRNES	sincereness
TÎRNES	austereness
VÎRNES	severeness

ĪRŌ

JĪRŌ	giro, gyro, autogyro
KĪRŌ	Cairo, chirho
PĪRŌ	pyro
TĪRŌ	tyro

ÎRŌ

HÎRŌ	anti-hero, hero, superhero
KÎRŌ	chirho
LÎRŌ	lillibullero
NÎRŌ	Nero, Pinero, Rio de Janeiro
RÎRŌ	riroriro
SÎRŌ	cero
ZÎRŌ	absolute zero, above zero, below zero, subzero, zero

ĪRŌD

BĪRŌD	byroad
HĪRŌD	highroad

ÎROID

SFÎROID	spheroid
THÎROID	theroid
TÎROID	pteroid

IRŌS

JĪRŌS	gyrose
VĪRŌS	virose

ÎRSER

FÎRSER	fiercer
PÎRSER	ear-piercer, piercer

ĪRSUM

ĪRSUM	iresome
TĪRSUM	tiresome
ZĪRSUM	desiresome

ĪRUN

ĪRUN	iron
BĪRUN	Byron
KĪRUN	Chiron
SĪRUN	lepidosiren, siren
VĪRUN	environ, viron

IRUP

CHIRUP	chirrup
SIRUP	syrup
STIRUP	stirrup

ĪRUS

JĪRUS	gyrus
PĪRUS	apyrous, Epirus, papyrus
SĪRUS	Cyrus
SPĪRUS	spirous
VĪRUS	ultravirus, virous, virus

ÎRUS

SÎRUS	serous
SKLÎRUS	sclerous

IRUS

BIRUS	byrrus
SIRUS	cirrhous, cirrus
SKIRUS	scirrhus

ÎRWERKS

FÎRWERKS	fireworks
WÎRWERKS	wireworks

ÎRZMAN

STÎRZMAN	steersman
TÎRZMAN	frontiersman, privateersman

ĪSA

BĪSA	beisa
DĪSA	dhaisa
MĪSA	Meissa

ISA

BRISA	vibrissa
MISA	Missa
RISA	paterissa
SISA	abscissa
TISA	mantissa

ĪSAL

SKĪSAL	skysail
TRĪSAL	trysail

(See also ĪSL)

ĪSĒ

ĪSĒ	icy
DĪSĒ	dicey, dicy
NĪSĒ	Nisei, nisi
PRĪSĒ	pricey
RĪSĒ	ricy
SPĪSĒ	spicy
VĪSĒ	vice

ISĒ

HISĒ	hissy
KISĒ	kissy
MISĒ	missi, missy
NISĒ	nisse
PRISĒ	prissy
SISĒ	sissy

ISEN

(See ISN)

ISENS

HISENS	dehiscence, indehiscence
NISENS	reminiscence
PISENS	resipiscence
TISENS	fatiscence
VISENS	obliviscence, reviviscence

ISENT

HISENT	dehiscent, indehiscent
NISENT	reminiscent
PISENT	resipiscent
TISENT	fatiscent
VISENT	obliviscent, reviviscent

ĪSER

ĪSER	deicer, icer
DĪSER	dicer
FĪSER	sacrificer, self-sacrificer
GĪSER	geyser
NĪSER	nicer

PRĪSER	pricer
RĪSER	ricer
SĪSER	conciser, preciser, cicer, Cicer
SLĪSER	meat-slicer, potato-slicer, vegetable-slicer, slicer
SPĪSER	spicer
SPLĪSER	resplicer, splicer
TĪSER	enticer

ISER

HISER	dehiscer, hisser
KISER	kissar, kisser
MISER	dismisser, misser, remisser
NISER	reminiscer
PISER	pisser

ISEZ

MISEZ	misses, missus, Mrs.

(See **IS**, add -s or -es where appropriate.)

ĪSFUL

LĪSFUL	lice-full
TĪSFUL	enticeful
RĪSFUL	rice-full
VĪSFUL	deviceful

ISFUL

BLISFUL	blissful, unblissful
MISFUL	remissful

ISHA

LISHA	militia, euphelicia
MISHA	comitia
STISHA	interstitia

ISHAL

DISHAL	extrajudicial, judicial, nonjudicial, prejudicial, unjudicial
FISHAL	artificial, beneficial, edificial, official, sacrificial, superficial, unartificial, unofficial, veneficial
LISHAL	gentilitial, natalitial, policial

MISHAL	comitial, postcomitial
NISHAL	initial, tribunicial
STISHAL	interstitial, solstitial
TISHAL	accrementitial, recrementitial, justicial
TRISHAL	altricial
VISHAL	novitial
ZISHAL	exitial

ISHAN

(See **ISHUN**)

ISHĒ

DISHĒ	dishy
FISHĒ	fishy
RISHĒ	maharishi, rishi
SKWISHĒ	squishy
SWISHĒ	swishy
VISHĒ	vichy, Vichy

ISHENS

FISHENS	deficience, efficience, insufficience, maleficience, proficience, self-sufficience
NISHENS	omniscience
SPISHENS	perspicience, prospicience

ISHENT

FISHENT	B beneficient, D deficient, E efficient, I indeficient, inefficient, insufficient, K calorificient, coefficient, M maleficient, P perficient, PR proficient, S self-sufficient, sufficient
JISHENT	objicient
LISHENT	volitient
NISHENT	omniscient
VISHENT	parviscient

ISHER

DISHER	disher
FISHER	fisher, fissure, kingfisher
SWISHER	swisher
WISHER	ill-wisher, well-wisher, wisher

ISHFUL

DISHFUL	dishful
WISHFUL	wishful

ISHING

DISHING	dishing
FISHING	fishing
HWISHING	whishing
SKWISHING	squishing
SWISHING	swishing
WISHING	ill-wishing, well-wishing, wishing

ISHOO

ISHOO	issue
FISHOO	fichu
TISHOO	tissue

ISHUN

ISHUN	exspuition, fruition, intuition, coition, circuition, tuition
BISHUN	adhibition, ambition, exhibition, imbibition, inhibition, prohibition, ratihabition, redhibition
BRISHUN	Hebrician, rubrician
DISHUN	A addition, D dedition, deperdition, E edition, expedition, extradition, erudition, K condition, O audition, P perdition, PR precondition, R reddition, recondition, rendition, S sedition, subaudition, super-addition, TR tradition, V vendition
FISHUN	binary fission, fission, nuclear fission
JISHUN	logician, magician
LISHUN	abolition, demolition, ebullition, Galician, coalition, nolition, Paulician, rebullition, volition
MISHUN	A admission, academician, D demission, dismission, E expromission, emission, I immission, insubmission, intermission,

intromission,
irremission, *K*
commission, *M*
manumission,
mission, *O*
obdormition,
omission, *P*
permission, *R*
readmission,
remission, *S*
submission, *TR*
transmission, *V*
vomition

NISHUN *A* abannition,
admonition, affinition,
agglutinition,
ammunition, *D*
definition, *E*
exinanition, epinicion,
F Phoenician, *I*
ignition, illinition,
inanition, inition, *K*
cognition, *KL*
clinician, *M*
mechanician,
monition, munition, *N*
neoplatonician, *P*
pyrotechnician, *PR*
precognition,
premonition,
premunition, *R*
recognition, reunition,
S submonition, *T*
technician, *TR*
tribunitian

PISHUN suspicion
PRISHUN Priscian
RISHUN apparition, deperition,
futurition, ligurition,
micturition,
parturition, preterition,
rhetorician,
vomiturition
SISHUN abscission, scission,
transition
STISHUN superstition
TISHUN *A* aglutition,
accrementition,
acoustician,
arithmetician, *B* bi-
partition, beautician,
D dedentition,
deglutition, dentition,
departition,
diagnostician,
dialectition, dietitian,
E equipartition,
esthetician, *GL*
glutition, *H*
hydrostatician, *K*
competition,
cosmetician, *L*

logistician, *M*
magnetition,
mathematician,
mortician, *O* optician,
P partition, petition,
politician, *PR*
practition, *R*
repartition, repetition,
S sortition, *ST*
statistician, *T*
tactician, Titian, *TH*
theoretician, *TR*
tralalition, tripartition

TRISHUN attrition, detrition,
electrician,
geometrician,
geriatrician,
contrition,
malnutrition,
metrician, nutrition,
obstetrician, patrician,
pediatrician

ZISHUN *A* acquisition,
apposition, *D*
deacquisition,
decomposition,
deposition,
disposition,
disquisition, *E*
exposition, *F*
physician, *I*
imposition,
indisposition,
inquisition,
interposition, *J*
juxtaposition, *K*
composition,
contraposition, *M*
malposition,
metaphysician,
missionary position,
musician, *O*
opposition, *P* position,
PR predisposition,
preposition,
presupposition,
proposition, *R*
requisition, reposition,
S superposition,
supposition, *TR*
transposition,
transition

(See **IS'I.AN**)

ISHUNZ

TISHUNZ   antiscians

(See **ISHUN**, add *-s* where appropriate.)

ISHUS

BISHUS   ambitious
BRISHUS   lubricious
DISHUS   expeditious, indicious,
                  injudicious, judicious,
                  seditious, spadiceous
FISHUS   beneficious,
                  inofficious, officious,
                  veneficious
JISHUS   flagitious
LISHUS   delicious, gentilitious,
                  malicious, mollitious,
                  natalitious, pulicious,
                  satellitious, cilicious,
                  siliceous
MISHUS   pumiceous,
                  vermicious
NISHUS   pernicious, puniceous
PISHUS   inauspicious,
                  auspicious, propitious,
                  suspicious,
                  unpropitious,
                  unsuspicious
PLISHUS   multiplicious
PRISHUS   capricious
RISHUS   avaricious, lateritious,
                  Mauritius, piperitious,
                  sericeous
STISHUS   superstitious
TISHUS   *A* addititious,
                  adjectitious,
                  adscititious,
                  adventitious,
                  arreptitious,
                  ascititious,
                  ascriptitious, *D*
                  deglutitious, *E*
                  exititious, *F* factitious,
                  fictitious, *I*
                  irreptitious, *O*
                  obreptitious, *PR*
                  profectitious, *R*
                  repetitious, *S*
                  secretitious,
                  subdititious,
                  supposititious,
                  surreptitious, *ST*
                  stillatitious, *TR*
                  tralatitious
TRISHUS   meretricious,
                  nutritious,
                  obstetricious
VISHUS   novitious, vicious
ZISHUS   suppositious

ISIK

LISIK   silicic
NISIK   anisic
TISIK   masticic

ISIL

(See ISL)

ĪSIN

LĪSIN	lysin
MĪSIN	tetramycin

ĪSING

ĪSING	icing
DĪSING	dicing
FĪSING	sacrificing, self-sacrificing, sufficing
PRĪSING	pricing
RĪSING	ricing
SLĪSING	slicing
SPISĪNG	spicing
SPLĪSING	splicing
TĪSING	enticing, ticing
VĪSING	vising

ISING

DISING	prejudicing
HISING	dehiscing, hissing
KISING	kissing
MISING	dismissing, missing
NISING	reminiscing
PISING	pissing

ĪSIS

ĪSIS	Isis
DĪSIS	misapodysis
FĪSIS	physis
KRĪSIS	energy crisis, epicrisis, identity crisis, crisis, midlife crisis
LĪSIS	lysis
NĪSIS	Dionysus, nisus
TĪSIS	phthisis

ISIT

LISIT	elicit, illicit, licit, solicit
PLISIT	explicit, implicit, inexplicit

ĪSIV

LĪSIV	collisive
RĪSIV	derisive

SĪSIV	decisive, indecisive, incisive
TRĪSIV	cicatrisive
VĪSIV	divisive

ISIV

FISIV	fissive
MISIV	A admissive, D demissive, dismissive, E emissive, I intermissive, irremissive, K commissive, M missive, N non-submissive, O omissive, P permissive, PR promissive, R remissive, S submissive, TR transmissive, U unsubmissive

ISKAL

DISKAL	discal
FISKAL	fiscal
FRISKAL	friscal
LISKAL	obeliscal

ISKĀT

FISKĀT	confiscate
PISKĀT	expiscate
VISKĀT	inviscate

ISKĒ

FRISKĒ	frisky
HWISKĒ	Bourbon whiskey, grain whiskey, whiskey, whisky, Irish whiskey, Canadian whiskey, malt whiskey, rye whiskey, Scotch whiskey
PISKĒ	pisky
RISKĒ	risky

ISKER

BRISKER	brisker
FRISKER	frisker
HWISKER	bewhisker, whisker
RISKER	risker

ISKET

BISKET	biscuit, dog biscuit
BRISKET	brisket
FRISKET	frisket
TISKET	tisket
WISKET	wisket

ISKFUL

FRISKFUL	friskful
RISKFUL	riskful

ISKIN

GRISKIN	griskin
HWISKIN	whiskin
SISKIN	siskin

ISKING

BRISKING	brisking
FRISKING	frisking
HWISKING	whisking
RISKING	risking

ISKIT

(See ISKET)

ISKŌ

BISKŌ	Nabisco
DISKŌ	disco
FRISKŌ	frisco, Frisco
SISKŌ	San Francisco, cisco

ISKUS

BISKUS	hibiscus
DISKUS	discous, discus
FISKUS	fiscus
KISKUS	trochiscus
KWISKUS	quiscos, quisquous
NISKUS	lemniscus, meniscus
SISKUS	abaciscus
THISKUS	calathiscus
TISKUS	lentiscus
VISKUS	viscous, viscus

ĪSL

DĪSL	paradisal
SKĪSL	skys'l
TRĪSL	trys'l

(See ĪSĀL)

ISL

BISL	abyssal
BRISL	bristle
FISL	fissile
GRISL	gristle
HWISL	whistle, penny whistle, police whistle, wolf whistle
KISL	kissel
MISL	dismissal, heat-seeking missile, cacomistle, cruise missile, missal, missile, mistle
NISL	Nissl
PISL	epistle
RISL	rissel, rissle
SISL	dickcissle, scissel, scissile, sisal, sistle
THISL	thistle

ĪSLĒ

NĪSLĒ	nicely, overnicely
SĪSLĒ	concisely, precisely

ISLĒ

BRISLĒ	bristly
GRISLĒ	gristly
THISLĒ	thistly

ĪSLES

(See ĪS, add -less where appropriate.)

ISLING

BRISLING	brisling, bristling
HWISLING	whistling

ĪSMAN

ĪSMAN	iceman
DĪSMAN	diceman
VĪSMAN	viceman, viseman

ĪSMENT

FĪSMENT	self-sufficement, sufficement
TĪSMENT	enticement

ISMUS

ISMUS	isthmus
KRISMUS	Christmas
TRISMUS	trismus

ISN

GLISN	glisten
KRISN	christen
LISN	lissen, listen
TISN	datiscin
VISN	viscin

ĪSNES

NĪSNES	niceness, overniceness
SĪSNES	conciseness, preciseness

ISNES

MISNES	remissness
THISNES	thisness

ISNING

GLISNING	glistening
KRISNING	christening
LISNING	listening

ISNZ

LISNZ	lissens, listens

(See ISN, add -s where appropriate.)

ISOM

(See ISUM)

ĪSON

BĪSON	bison
GRĪSON	grison
HĪSON	hyson
VĪSON	vison

ISPĒ

KRISPĒ	crispy
LISPĒ	lispy
WISPĒ	wispy

ISPER

HWISPER	stage whisper, whisper
KRISPER	crisper
LISPER	lisper
RISPER	risper
WISPER	wisper

ISPING

(See ISP, add -ing where appropriate.)

ISTA

KRISTA	crista
LISTA	ballista
NISTA	genista
RISTA	arista
VISTA	Buena Vista, vista

ISTAL

DISTAL	distal
KRISTAL	crystal
LISTAL	listel
MISTAL	mistal
PISTAL	pistil, pistol, pocket pistol, water pistol
SISTAL	cystal
VISTAL	vistal

ISTANS

DISTANS	distance, equidistance, outdistance
SISTANS	assistance, assistants, inconsistence, insistence, consistence, persistence, subsistence
ZISTANS	desistance, existence, inexistence, coexistence, nonexistence, nonresistance, persistence, pre-existence, resistance, unresistance

ISTANT

DISTANT	distant, equidistant
SISTANT	assistant, inconsistent, insistent, consistent, persistent, subsistent
ZISTANT	existent, inexistent, coexistent,

nonexistent,
nonresistant,
persistent, pre-
existent, resistant,
unresistant

ISTED

FISTED   fisted, hard-fisted,
iron-fisted, close-
fisted, tight-fisted,
two-fisted

LISTED   blacklisted, enlisted,
white-listed, listed,
relisted, unlisted

MISTED   misted

RISTED   limp-wristed, strong-
wristed, wristed,
thick-wristed, thin-
wristed, weak-wristed

SISTED   assisted, encysted,
insisted, consisted,
cysted, subsisted,
unassisted

TRISTED   trysted

TWISTED   entwisted,
intertwisted, twisted,
untwisted

ZISTED   desisted, existed,
persisted, pre-existed,
resisted

ISTĒN

LISTĒN   Philistine

PRISTĒN   pristine

SISTĒN   Sistine

THISTĒN   amethystine

(Also **ISTĪN**)

ISTENS

(See **ISTANS**)

ISTENT

(See **ISTANT**)

ISTER

ISTER   Istar

BISTER   bister, bistre

BLISTER   blister, water blister

GLISTER   glister

JISTER   agistor, magister

KLISTER   clyster

LISTER   enlister, lister

MISTER   mister, Mr.

RISTER   limp-wrister

SISTER   assister, foster-sister,
half-sister, insister,
sister, sob-sister,
subsister

TWISTER   intertwister, tongue-
twister, twister,
untwister

ZISTER   exister, nonresister,
passive resister,
persister, resister,
xyster

ISTFUL

FISTFUL   fistful

LISTFUL   listful

MISTFUL   mistful

WISTFUL   wistful

ISTIK

ISTIK   *A* altruistic, atheistic,
D deistic, *E* egoistic,
epideistic, *H*
Hebraistic, *J*
jingoistic, Judaistic, *K*
casuistic, *M*
monotheistic, *P*
pantheistic,
polytheistic, *T*
Taoistic, *TH* theistic,
TR tritheistic

BRISTIK   hubristic

DISTIK   aphrodistic,
Buddhistic, distich,
methodistic, sadistic,
Talmudistic

FISTIK   philosophistic, fistic,
sophistic

GWISTIK   linguistic

HISTIK   Elohistic

JISTIK   *A* aphlogistic,
antiphlogistic, *B*
bibliopegistic, *D*
dialogistic,
dyslogistic, *E*
epilogistic, phlogistic,
L logistic, *N*
neologistic, *P*
paleologistic, *S*
syllogistic,
synergistic, *SFR*
sphragistic, *Y*
eulogistic

KISTIK   anarchistic, ekistic,
catechistic,
masochistic,
sadomasochistic

KRISTIK   paleocrystic

LISTIK   *A* annalistic,
anomalistic, *B*
ballistic,
bibliopolistic, *D*
dualistic, *E*
electroballistic,
evangelistic, *F*
familistic, fatalistic,
phenomenalistic,
formalistic,
feudalistic, *I* idealistic,
imperialistic,
individualistic, *J*
journalistic, *K*
cabalistic,
cameralistic,
cannibalistic,
capitalistic,
commercialistic,
communalistic,
curialistic, *L*
liberalistic, *M*
materialistic,
monopolistic,
moralistic, *N*
nationalistic,
naturalistic, nihilistic,
nominalistic,
novelistic, *P*
parallelistic, pugilistic,
R rationalistic,
realistic, ritualistic,
royalistic, *S*
sensationalistic,
sensualistic,
symbolistic, sciolistic,
socialistic,
somnambulistic,
surrealistic, *SP*
spiritualistic, *ST*
stylistic, *U*
universalistic, *V*
vitalistic

MISTIK   alchemistic, animistic,
hemistich, intermistic,
mystic, optimistic,
pessimistic,
euphemistic

NISTIK   *A* agonistic,
achronistic,
anachronistic,
antagonistic, *F*
feuillitonistic, *H*
hedonistic,
Hellenistic,
humanistic, *I*
illuministic,
impressionistic,
Impressionistic, *K*
Calvinistic, canonistic,
communistic, *L*
Latinistic, *M*

mechanistic,
modernistic, monistic,
P post-impressionistic,
R Romanistic, *S*
synchronistic, *SH*
chauvinistic, *Y*
eudemonistic, unionistic
PISTIK   philanthropistic,
papistic, pistic
PLISTIK   simplistic
RISTIK   *A* adiaphoristic,
aphoristic, allegoristic,
aoristic, behavioristic,
E eristic, *F*
formularistic,
futuristic, *FL* floristic,
H humoristic,
heuristic, *J* juristic, *K*
characteristic, *M*
meristic, *P* polaristic,
poristic, puristic, *S*
solaristic, *T* terroristic,
touristic, *V*
voyeuristic, *Y*
euhemeristic, eucharistic
SHISTIK   fetishistic, schistic
SISTIK   cystic, solecistic
TISTIK   *A* absolutistic,
anabaptistic, artistic, *B*
baptistic, *E* egotistic,
F filiopietistic, *H*
hypnotistic, *I*
inartistic, *KR*
chromatistic, *KW*
quietistic, *O* autistic,
P pietistic, *R*
romantistic, *ST*
statistic
TRISTIK   belletristic, patristic,
tristich
VISTIK   atavistic, Jehovistic,
relativistic

ISTIKS

JISTIKS	sphragistics
KISTIKS	ekistics

(See **ISTIK**, add -*s* where appropriate.)

ISTĪN

(See **ISTĒN**)

ISTL

(See **ISTAL**)

ISTLES

LISTLES	listless
MISTLES	mistless
TWISTLES	twistless
ZISTLES	resistless

ISTMENT

JISTMENT	agistment
LISTMENT	enlistment

ISTOID

HISTOID	histoid
SISTOID	cystoid

ISTOL

(See **ISTAL**)

ISTRAL

MISTRAL	mistral
NISTRAL	sinistral

ISTUS

HISTUS	anhistous
SHISTUS	schistous
SISTUS	rock-cistus, cistus
THISTUS	acathistus
ZISTUS	xystus

ISŪ

(See **ISHOO**)

ISUM

BLISUM	blissom
KRISUM	crissum
LISUM	alyssum, lissom, lissome
MISSUM	fideicommissum

ĪSUS

(See **ĪSIS**)

ISUS

BISUS	byssus
SISUS	narcissus

ĪTA

LĪTA	amalaita
RĪTA	baryta
VĪTA	vita

ITA

LITA	lytta
PITA	pitta
SHITA	shittah
VITA	vitta

ĪTAL

DĪTAL	dital
FĪTAL	microphytal
KWĪTAL	requital
SĪTAL	cital, parasital, recital
TĪTAL	disentitle, entitle, mistitle, subtitle, title
TRĪTAL	detrital
VĪTAL	vital

ITAL

(See **ITL**)

ITANS

KWITANS	acquittance, quittance
MITANS	admittance, omittance, permittance, remittance, transmittance
PITANS	pittance

ĪTĒ

BLĪTĒ	blighty
DĪTĒ	Aphrodite
FLĪTĒ	flighty
HWĪTĒ	whitey, whity
LĪTĒ	pendente lite
MĪTĒ	almighty, God almighty, mighty, mity
NĪTĒ	nightie, Venite
RĪTĒ	all righty
TRĪTĒ	Amphitrite
VĪTĒ	aqua vitae, arbor vitae, lignum vitae, vitae

ITĒ

BITĒ	ambitty, bitty, itty-bitty

CHĬTĒ	chitty
DĬTĒ	banditti, ditty, poditti
FLĬTĒ	flitty
GRĬTĒ	gritty, nitty-gritty
KĬTĒ	kitty
MĬTĒ	committee, subcommittee, Walter Mitty
NĬTĒ	nitty
PĬTĒ	pity, self-pity
PRĬTĒ	pretty
SHĬTĒ	shitty
SĬTĒ	inner city, intercity, city
SKĬTĒ	skitty
SLĬTĒ	slitty
SMRĬTĒ	smriti
TĬTĒ	titty
TWĬTĒ	twitty
WĬTĒ	wittee, witty

ĪTED

BĪTED	bighted
BLĪTED	blighted
DĪTED	bedighted, dighted, dited, indicted, indited, undighted
FLĪTED	eagle-flighted
FRĪTED	affrighted, frighted, unaffrighted, unfrighted
HWĪTED	whited
KĪTED	kited
KWĪTED	requited, unrequited
LĪTED	alighted, delighted, candlelighted, lighted, relighted, unlighted
MĪTED	dynamited
NĪTED	beknighted, benighted, ignited, knighted, nighted, reunited, unbenighted, unknighted, united
PLĪTED	plighted, troth-plighted, unplighted
RĪTED	copyrighted, righted, unrighted
SĪTED	E eagle-sighted, excited, F farsighted, foresighted, I incited, KL clear-sighted, KW quick-sighted, L long-sighted, N nearsighted, O overexcited, oversighted, R recited, S second-sighted, cited, sighted, sited, SH sharpsighted, short-sighted, U unsighted

SLĪTED	slighted, unslighted
SPĪTED	despited, spited
TRĪTED	attrited, detrited
VĪTED	invited, reinvited, uninvited

ĬTĒD

DĬTĒD	dittied
PĬTĒD	pitied
SĬTĒD	citied, uncitied

ĬTED

BĬTED	bitted, rebitted, unbitted
FĬTED	befitted, fitted, misfitted, counterfeited, outfitted, refitted, unfitted
FLĬTED	flitted, reflitted
GRĬTED	gritted, regritted
KWĬTED	acquitted, quitted, reacquitted, requitted, unacquitted
MĬTED	admitted, demitted, emitted, committed, compromitted, manumitted, omitted, permitted, recommitted, remitted, transmitted, submitted
NĬTED	interknitted, knitted, reknitted, unknitted
PĬTED	pitted
TWĬTED	twitted, retwitted
WĬTED	A after-witted, BL blunt-witted, D dimwitted, dullwitted, F fat-witted, H half-witted, KW quick-witted, L lean-witted, N nimble-witted, O outwitted, R ready-witted, S subtle-witted, SH sharp-witted, short-witted, U under-witted, W witted

ĪTEM

ĪTEM	item
BLĪTEM	Blitum
NĪTEM	ad infinitum
SĪTEM	quaesitum

ĪTEN

BRĪTEN	brighten, Brighton
FRĪTEN	frighten
HĪTEN	heighten
HWĪTEN	whiten
KĪTEN	chitin, chiton
KRĪTON	Admirable Crichton
LĪTEN	enlighten, lighten, reenlighten
RĪTEN	righten
SĪTEN	cyton
TĪTEN	tighten, Titan
TRĪTEN	triton, Triton

ĬTEN

BĬTEN	bitten, flea-bitten, fly-bitten, frostbitten, hunger-bitten, weather-bitten
BRĬTEN	Britain, Briton, Great Britain
KĬTEN	kitten, sex kitten
LĬTEN	litten
MĬTEN	mitten
RĬTEN	handwritten, written, typewritten, underwritten, unwritten
SMĬTEN	heart-smitten, conscience-smitten, smitten, sun-smitten, terror-smitten, unsmitten
WĬTAN	witan

ĪTER

ĪTER	iter
BĪTER	backbiter, biter
BLĪTER	blighter
FĪTER	bullfighter, fighter, gunfighter, prizefighter
KĪTER	check kiter, kiter
LĪTER	gaslighter, Gauleiter, lamplighter, lighter, moonlighter
MĪTER	bemitre, miter, mitre, unmiter, unmitre
NĪTER	igniter, niter, all-nighter
RĪTER	ghostwriter, copywriter, writer, scriptwriter, songwriter, telewriter, typewriter, underwriter
SĪTER	exciter, excitor, sighter
TĪTER	titer

ITER

BITER	bitter, embitter
CHITER	chitter
FITER	befitter, benefitter, fitter, counterfeiter, outfitter, pipe fitter, refitter
FLITER	flitter
FRITER	fritter
GITER	go-gitter
GLITER	glitter
HITER	base-hitter, hitter, pinch-hitter
HWITER	whitter
JITER	jitter
KRITER	critter
KWITER	acquitter, quitter, quittor
LITER	litter
MITER	admitter, emitter, committer, manumitter, omitter, permitter, recommitter, remitter, transmitter
NITER	knitter
PITER	pitter
RITER	ritter
SITER	baby-sitter, house-sitter, outsitter, sitter
SKITER	skitter
SLITER	slitter
SPITER	spitter
SPLITER	lip-splitter, rail-splitter, splitter
TITER	titter
TWITER	atwitter, twitter
WITER	outwitter

ITERN

BITERN	bittern
FLITERN	flittern
GITERN	gittern
SITERN	cittern

ĪTFUL

FRĪTFUL	frightful
LĪTFUL	delightful
MĪTFUL	mightful
RĪTFUL	rightful
SPĪTFUL	despiteful, spiteful
SPRĪTFUL	sprightful

ITFUL

FITFUL	fitful
WITFUL	witful

ĪTHĒ

(TH as in *then*)

LĪTHĒ	lithy
SLĪTHĒ	slithy

ITHĒ

(TH as in *thin*)

PITHĒ	pithy
PRITHĒ	prithee
SMITHĒ	smithy
STITHĒ	stithy
WITHĒ	twigwithy, withy, withy

ĪTHER

(TH as in *then*)

ĪTHER	either
BLĪTHER	blither
NĪTHER	neither
RĪTHER	writher
TĪTHER	tither

ITHER

(TH as in *then*)

BLITHER	blither
DITHER	dither
HITHER	behither, hither
HWITHER	anywhither, whither, nowhither, somewhither
LITHER	lither
NITHER	nither
SLITHER	slither
SWITHER	swither
THITHER	thither
TITHER	tither
WITHER	wither
ZITHER	zither

ITHERD

(See **ITHER,** add -*ed* where appropriate.)

ITHERZ

WITHERZ	withers

(See **ITHER,** add -*s* where appropriate.)

ĪTHFUL

(TH as in *thin*)

BLĪTHFUL	blitheful
LĪTHFUL	litheful

ITHIK

(TH as in *thin*)

LITHIK	archaeolithic, eolithic, lithic, megalithic, microlithic, monolithic, neolithic, Paleolithic, trilithic
MITHIK	mythic, polymythic
NITHIK	philornithic, ornithic

ĪTHING

(TH as in *then*)

NĪTHING	nithing
RĪTHING	writhing
SĪTHING	scything
TĪTHING	tithing
TRĪTHING	trithing

ĪTHLĒ

(TH as in *then*)

BLĪTHLĒ	blithely
LĪTHLĒ	lithely

ĪTHNES

(TH as in *then*)

BLĪTHNES	blitheness
LĪTHNES	litheness

ĪTHSUM

(TH as in *then*)

BLĪTHSUM	blithesome
LĪTHSUM	lithesome

ITIK

ITIK	Jesuitic, Sinaitic
BITIK	phlebitic, Jacobitic, cenobitic, trilobitic
DITIK	aphroditic, hermaphroditic, troglodytic
FITIK	anthropomorphitic, eophytic, epiphytic, graphitic, holophytic, mephitic, necrophytic, neophytic, xerophytic, zoophytic
FRITIK	nephritic

GRITIK	Negritic
JITIK	laryngitic, meningitic
KITIK	bronchitic, conchitic, rachitic, trachitic
KLITIK	anaclitic, enclitic, heteroclitic, proclitic, euclitic
KRITIK	diacritic, hypercritic, hypocritic, critic, oneirocritic
LITIK	*A* acrolitic, actinolitic, analytic, *B* bacteriolytic, biolytic, *D* dialytic, *E* electrolytic, *GR* granulitic, *H* hydrolytic, *I* Israelitic, *K* catalytic, *L* lytic, *N* nummulitic, *O* oolitic, *P* paralytic, *S* scialytic, syphilitic, sympatholytic, psychoanalytic, *SF* spherulitic, *T* tonsillitic, toxophillitic, *TH* theodolitic, thermolytic, *V* variolitic, *Z* zeolitic
MITIK	*A* Adamitic, anti-Semitic, *D* dynamitic, dolomitic, *E* eremitic, *H* Hamitic, *I* Islamitic, *P* palmitic, *PR* pre-Adamitic, protosemitic, *S* Semitic, *ST* stalagmitic
NITIK	aconitic, granitic, lenitic, lignitic, sagenitic, selenitic, syenitic, Sinitic, Titanitic, tympanitic, uranitic
RITIK	diphtheritic, phosphoritic, Cabiritic, margaritic, meteoritic, Nazaritic, neritic, pyritic, pleuritic, porphyritic, sybaritic

---

REQUIESCAT IN PACE

When reading the obits, I frequently say,
"Well, there is another one out of the way"—
Referring to one of those clods who refuse
To second my sociological views,
Or one of those bleary-eyed, dim-witted blokes
Who yawn in the midst of my favorite jokes,
Or who squeeze through the door first, when I was ahead;
The world is improved when such people are dead.
(I know, when *I'm* obited, some folks will say,
"Well, there is another one out of the way.")

SHITIK	Cushitic
SITIK	anthracitic, erythrocitic, lymphocytic, parasitic, semiparasitic
SKRITIK	Sanskritic
THRITIK	arthritic, osteoarthritic
TITIK	hematitic, stalactitic, steatitic, strontitic
TRITIK	dentritic
VITIK	gingivitic, Levitic

ĪTING

BĪTING	backbiting, biting
RĪTING	handwriting

(See ĪT, add *-ing* where appropriate.)

ITING

FITING	fitting, pipefitting, steamfitting
HITING	hard-hitting, pinch-hitting
MITING	remitting, unremitting
SPLITING	hair-splitting, rail-splitting, splitting
WITING	unwitting, witting

(See **IT**, add *-ing* where appropriate.)

ĪTIS

ĪTIS	fasciitis, ileitis, ophryitis, osteitis, uveitis
BĪTIS	phlebitis
DĪTIS	endocarditis, carditis, mastoiditis, pericarditis, thyroiditis
FĪTIS	mephitis, typhitis
FRĪTIS	nephritis
JĪTIS	pharyngitis, laryngitis, meningitis, salpingitis
KĪTIS	bronchitis, rachitis, trachitis
LĪTIS	*D* diverticulitis, *E* encephalitis, *H* hyalitis, *K* colitis, *My* myelitis, *O* osteomyelitis, *P* pyelitis, poliomyelitis, *S* cellulitis, *SP* spondylitis, *T* tonsillitis, *V* valvulitis, *Y* utriculitis, uvulitis
MĪTIS	mitis, ophthalmitis
NĪTIS	adenitis, colonitis, pneumonitis, peritonitis, rhinitis, splenitis, vaginitis
RĪTIS	arteritis, blepharitis, enteritis, gastroenteritis, iritis, neuritis, ovaritis, scleritis
SĪTIS	appendicitis, bursitis, fibrositis, glossitis, sinusitis
THRĪTIS	arthritis, osteoarthritis, urethritis
TĪTIS	dermatitis, hepatitis, keratitis, mastitis, otitis, parotitis, prostatitis, cystitis
TRĪTIS	gastritis, metritis
VĪTIS	gingivitis, conjunctivitis, synovitis, vulvitis (etc.)

ĪTISH

(See ĪT, add *-ish* where appropriate.)

ITISH

BRITISH	British
SKITISH	skittish

(See **IT**, add *-ish* where appropriate.)

ĪTIV

DĪTIV	expeditive
SĪTIV	excitive
TĪTIV	appetitive
TRĪTIV	attritive

ĪTL

(See ĪTAL)

ITL

ITL	it'll
BRITL	brittle, peanut brittle
GRITL	grittle
HWITL	whittle
KITL	kittle
KWITL	acquittal
LITL	belittle, Chicken Little, little
MITL	committal, noncommittal, remittal, transmittal
NITL	knittle

SKITL	skittle
SPITL	lickspittle, spital, spittle
TITL	tittle
VITL	victual
WITL	wittol

ĪTLĒ

BRĪTLĒ	brightly
DĪTLĒ	eruditely
HWĪTLĒ	whitely
LĪTLĒ	impolitely, lightly, politely
NĪTLĒ	fortnightly, knightly, nightly, unknightly
RĪTLĒ	forthrightly, rightly, uprightly
SĪTLĒ	sightly, unsightly
SLĪTLĒ	slightly
SPRĪTLĒ	sprightly
TĪTLĒ	tightly
TRĪTLĒ	contritely, tritely

ITLĒ

(See **IT**, add -ly where appropriate.)

ITLER

BRITLER	brittler
HITLER	Hitler
HWITLER	whittler
SKITLER	skitler
LITLER	belittler, littler
TITLER	tittler
VITLER	victualler

ĪTLES

(See **ĪT**, add -less where appropriate.)

ITLES

(See **IT**, add -less where appropriate.)

ITLING

CHITLING	chitling
HWITLING	whittling
KITLING	kitling
LITLING	belittling
TITLING	titling, tittling
VITLING	victualing
WITLING	witling

ITLZ

SKITLZ	skittles
VITLZ	victuals

(See **ITL**, add -s where appropriate.)

ĪTMAN

HWĪTMAN	Whitman
PITMAN	pitman, Pitman
TITMAN	titman

ĪTMENT

DĪTMENT	indictment, reindictment
FRĪTMENT	affrightment, frightment
SĪTMENT	excitement, incitement
VĪTMENT	invitement

ITMENT

FITMENT	fitment, refitment
KWITMENT	acquitment
MITMENT	commitment, remitment

ĪTN

(See **ĪTEN**)

ITN

(See **ITEN**)

ITNĒ

HWITNĒ	Mount Whitney
JITNĒ	jitney
WITNĒ	witney

ĪTNER

BRĪTNER	brightener
FRĪTNER	frightener
HĪTNER	heightener
HWĪTNER	whitener
LĪTNER	enlightener, lightener

ĪTNES

(See **ĪT**, add -ness where appropriate.)

ITNES

FITNES	fitness, unfitness
WITNES	eyewitness, witness

ĪTNING

LĪTNING	chain lightning, enlightening, white lightning, lightening, lightning, sheet lightning, streak lightning

(See **ĪTEN**, add -ing where appropriate.)

ITOL

(See **ITL**)

ĪTON

(See **ĪTEN**)

ĪTRĀT

NĪTRĀT	nitrate
TĪTRĀT	titrate

ITRIK

SITRIK	citric
VITRIK	vitric

ITSĒ

BITSĒ	itsy bitsy
GLITSĒ	glitsy
RITSĒ	ritzy
SKITSĒ	schizzy

ĪTUM

(See **ĪTEM**)

ITUP

SITUP	sit-up
TITUP	tittup

ĪTUS

JĪTUS	vagitus
KLĪTUS	Heraclitus, Polyclitus
LĪTUS	litus

NĬTUS	tinnitus
RĬTUS	pruritus, ritus
SĬTUS	situs
TRĪTUS	attritus, detritus
VĪTUS	St. Vitus

ĪUN

(See ĪAN)

ĪUP

FRĪUP	fry-up
TĪUP	tieup

ĪUS

(See ĪAS)

ĪVA

ĪVA	iva
DĪVA	daiva, Godiva
LĪVA	saliva
TĪVA	conjunctiva
VĪVA	viva

ĪVAL

JĪVAL	ogival
KĪVAL	archival
LĪVAL	salival
NĪVAL	nival
PRĪVAL	deprival
RĪVAL	arrival, corrival, nonarrival, outrival, rival, unrival
THĪVAL	thivel
TĪVAL	adjectival, aestival, estival, imperatival, genitival, conjunctival, nominatival, relatival
VĪVAL	revival, survival

ĪVANS

NĪVANS	connivance
RĪVANS	arrivance
TRĪVANS	contrivance
VĪVANS	survivance

ĪVANT

NĪVANT	connivant
RĪVANT	arrivant
TRĪVANT	contrivant
VĪVANT	survivant

ĪVĒ

ĪVĒ	ivy, poison ivy
JĪVĒ	jivy
SKĪVĒ	skivie
STĪVĒ	stivy

IVĒ

BIVĒ	bivvy
CHIVĒ	chivvy
DIVĒ	dividivi, divvy
GIVĒ	givey
LIVĒ	Livy
PRIVĒ	privy
SIVĒ	civvy
SKIVĒ	skivvy
TIVĒ	tantivy, tivy

IVĒD

CHIVĒD	chivvied
DIVĒD	divvied

IVEL

DRIVEL	drivel
FRIVEL	frivol
RIVEL	rivel
SHRIVEL	shrivel
SIVEL	civil, uncivil
SNIVEL	snivel
SWIVEL	swivel

ĪVEN

ĪVEN	Ivan
DĪVEN	divan
LĪVEN	enliven, liven

IVEN

DRIVEN	driven, overdriven, rain-driven, snow-driven, storm-driven, underdriven, weather-driven, wind-driven
GIVEN	forgiven, given, unforgiven
RIVEN	riven
SHRIVEN	shriven, unshriven
SKRIVEN	scriven
STRIVEN	striven
THRIVEN	thriven

ĪVER

DĪVER	deep-sea diver, diver, helldiver, pearl diver, scuba diver
DRĪVER	driver, co-driver, screwdriver, slave driver
FĪVER	fiver
HĪVER	hiver
JĪVER	jiver
LĪVER	aliver, liver, livor
NĪVER	conniver
PRĪVER	depriver
RĪVER	arriver, deriver, river
SHRĪVER	shriver
SKĪVER	skiver
SLĪVER	sliver
STĪVER	stiver
STRĪVER	striver
THRĪVER	thriver
TRĪVER	contriver
VĪVER	reviver, survivor

IVER

FLIVER	flivver
GIVER	forgiver, giver, Indian giver, life-giver, lawgiver, misgiver
KWIVER	quiver
LIVER	deliver, free-liver, liver, outliver
RIVER	river
SHIVER	shiver
SIVER	siever
SKIVER	skiver
SLIVER	sliver
STIVER	stiver
TIVER	tiver
YIVER	yiver

IVERD

FLIVERD	flivvered
KWIVERD	quivered
LIVERD	delivered, white-livered, lily-livered, livered, pale-livered, undelivered, yellow-livered
SHIVERD	shivered
SKIVERD	skivered
SLIVERD	slivered

IVET

DIVET	divot
GRIVET	grivet

PIVET	pivot
PRIVET	privet
RIVET	rivet, unrivet
SIVET	civet
TRIVET	trivet

ĪVID

| LIVID | livid |
| VIVID | vivid |

ĪVIL

(See **IVEL**)

ĪVING

(See **ĪV**, add *-ing* where appropriate.)

IVING

GIVING	forgiving, giving, life-giving, law-giving, misgiving, thanksgiving, Thanksgiving, unforgiving
LIVING	everliving, living, outliving, reliving, unliving
SIVING	sieving

ĪVL

(See **ĪVAL**)

IVLING

(See **IVEL,** add *-ing* where appropriate.)

ĪVMENT

| PRĪVMENT | deprivement |
| VĪVMENT | revivement |

IVOL

(See **IVEL**)

IVOT

(See **IVET**)

ĪVUS

| DĪVUS | divus |
| KLĪVUS | acclivous, declivous, clivus, proclivous |

| LĪVUS | salivous |
| VĪVUS | redivivus |

IVYAL

(See **IV'I.AL**)

ĪWĀ

BĪWĀ	byway
FLĪWĀ	flyway
HĪWĀ	highway
SKĪWĀ	skyway

ĪZA

BĪZA	beisa
LĪZA	Eliza, Liza
RĪZA	coryza

ĪZAL

(See **ĪZL**)

IZARD

IZARD	izard, izzard, A to izzard
BLIZARD	blizzard
GIZARD	gizzard
LIZARD	lizard, lounge lizard, sofa lizard
SIZARD	scissored, sizzard
VIZARD	visored, vizard
WIZARD	wizard

IZBĒ

| FRIZBĒ | Frisbee |
| THIZBĒ | Thisbe |

IZĒ

BIZĒ	busy
DIZĒ	dizzy
FIZĒ	fizzy
FRIZĒ	frizzy
KWIZĒ	quizzy
LIZĒ	busy Lizzie, Lizzie, tin lizzie
MIZĒ	mizzy
NIZĒ	nizy
TIZĒ	tizzy

IZĒD

| BIZĒD | busied, unbusied |
| DIZĒD | dizzied |

IZEM

(See **IZM**)

ĪZEN

(See **ĪZON**)

IZEN

DIZEN	bedizen, dizen
HIZEN	his'n
JIZEN	jizzen
MIZEN	mizzen
PRIZEN	imprison, prison, reimprison
RIZEN	arisen, re-arisen, risen, unrisen
TIZEN	ptisan
WIZEN	wizen

ĪZER

DĪZER	aggrandizer, gormandizer, liquidizer
GĪZER	geyser, disguiser
JĪZER	apologizer, eulogizer
KĪZER	catechiser, Kaiser
LĪZER	A analyzer, BR Breathalyzer, D demoralizer, dialyser, E equalizer, elisor, F fertilizer, I idolizer, J generalizer, M monopolizer, moralizer, N neutralizer, P papalizer, paralyzer, S symbolizer, civilizer, ST stabilizer, sterilizer, T tantalizer, totalizer, TR tranquilizer, V vitalizer, vocalizer
MĪZER	atomizer, economizer, epitomizer, miser, remiser, surmiser
NĪZER	FR fraternizer, H harmonizer, humanizer, K canonizer, L lionizer, M modernizer, moisturizer, O organizer, P patronizer, S sermonizer, synchronizer, solemnizer, SK scrutinizer, W womanizer

PRĪZER appriser, enterpriser, prizer, surpriser

RĪZER deodorizer, extemporizer, high-riser, cauterizer, mesmerizer, authorizer, pulverizer, riser, temporizer, terrorizer, theorizer

SĪZER assiser, exerciser, exorciser, incisor, capsizer, synthesizer, sizar, sizer

THĪZER nonsympathizer, sympathizer

TĪZER advertiser, appetizer, baptizer, chastiser, magnetizer

VĪZER advisor, devisor, divisor, supervisor, visor

IZER

FIZER fizzer
FRIZER befrizzer, frizzer
HWIZER whizzer
KWIZER quizzer
SIZER scissor
VIZER visor

IZERD

(See **IZARD**)

IZHUN

FRIZHUN Frisian
LIZHUN allision, elision, Elysian, illision, collision, prodelision
PRIZHUN misprision
RIZHUN derision, irrision, Parisian, subrision
SIZHUN *A* abscission, *D* decision, *E* excision, *I* imprecision, indecision, incision, *K* concision, *O* occision, *PR* precisian, precision, *R* recision, rescission, *S* circumcision, scission
VIZHUN *D* division, *E* envision, *O* audiovision, *PR* prevision, provision, *R* revision, *S* subdivision, supervision, *ST*

stereovision, *T* television, tunnel vision, *V* vision, *X* x-ray vision, *Y* Eurovision

(See **IZ'I.AN**)

IZIK

DIZIK paradisic
FIZIK biophysic, physic, hydrophysic, geophysic, metaphysic, zoophysic
JIZIK jizzick
TIZIK phthisic

IZIKS

FIZIKS physics, metaphysics, paraphysics

(See **IZIK,** add *-s* where appropriate.)

ĪZING

(See **ĪZ,** add *-ing* where appropriate.)

IZING

FRIZING frizzing
KWIZING quizzing
ZIZING zizzing

IZIT

KWIZIT exquisite
VIZIT revisit, visit

ĪZL

ĪZL izle
DĪZL paradisal
MĪZL surmisal
PRĪZAL apprisal, apprizal, comprisal, reprisal, surprisal
RĪZL arrhizal
SĪZL insizal, capsizal, sisal, sizal
VĪZL advisal, revisal

IZL

CHIZL chisel, enchisel
DRIZL drizzle

FIZL fizzle
FRIZL frizzle
GRIZL grizzle
KRIZL crizzle
MIZL mizzle
PIZL pizzle
SIZL sizzle
SWIZL rumswizzle, swizzle
TWIZL twizzle

IZLD

(See **IZL,** add *-d* or *ed* where appropriate.)

IZLĒ

CHIZLĒ chiselly
DRIZLĒ drizzly
FRIZLĒ frizzly
GRIZLĒ grisly, grizzly
MIZLĒ misly, mizzly
SIZLĒ sizzly

IZLER

CHIZLER chiseler
FRIZLER frizzler
GRIZLER grizzler

IZLING

KWIZLING quisling

(See **IZL,** add *-ing* where appropriate.)

IZMA

LIZMA melisma
RIZMA charisma

IZMAL

BIZMAL abysmal, Pepto-Bismol, strabysmal
DIZMAL dismal
KIZMAL catechismal
KLIZMAL cataclysmal
KRIZMAL chrismal
LIZMAL embolismal
PRIZMAL prismal
RIZMAL aneurismal
SIZMAL paroxysmal
TIZMAL baptismal, rheumatismal

ĪZMAN

| PRĬZMAN | prizeman |
| SĬZMAN | exciseman |

ĪZMENT

CHĬZMENT	*disenfranchisement, disfranchisement, enfranchisement, franchisement*
DĬZMENT	aggrandizement
PRĬZMENT	apprizement
SĬZMENT	assizement
TĬZMENT	advertisement, baptizement
VĬZMENT	advisement

IZMIK

KLIZMIK	cataclysmic, clysmic
LIZMIK	embolismic
RIZMIK	aphorismic, algorismic
SIZMIK	paroxysmic
TRIZMIK	trismic

IZMUS

BIZMUS	strabismus
NIZMUS	vaginismus
SIZMUS	accismus, hircismus
TIZMUS	tarantismus
TRIZMUS	trismus

ĪZŌ

| RĪZŌ | Valparaiso |
| VĪZŌ | aviso, improviso, proviso |

ĪZON

BĪZON	bison
DĪZON	bedizen, dizen
GRĪZON	greisen, grison
LĪZON	Kyrie eleison, spiegeleisen
PĪZON	pizen
RĪZON	horizon

ĪZOR

(See ĪZER)

ŌA

ŌA	*Iowa*
BŌA	balboa, Balboa, boa, jerboa
DŌA	Shenandoah
GŌA	goa, Goa
LŌA	aloha, loa, Kanaloa
MŌA	moa, Samoa
NŌA	anoa, *Genoa, quinoa,* Noah
PŌA	leipoa
PRŌA	proa
STŌA	stoa
TŌA	Krakatoa, toatoa
ZŌA	Anthozoa, entozoa, epizoa, Hydrozoa, Metazoa, microzoa, protozoa, spermatozoa, Sporozoa

ŌAJ

(See ŌIJ)

ŌAN

ŌAN	eoan
KŌAN	cowan
LŌAN	lowan
MŌAN	Samoan
NŌAN	*dipnoan*, Minoan
RŌAN	rowan
ZŌAN	bryozoan, hydrozoan, protozoan

ŌBA

DŌBA	*cordoba*
GŌBA	*dagoba*
HŌBA	jojoba, cohoba
KŌBA	koba
RŌBA	algarroba, araroba, arroba, bona-roba
TŌBA	Manitoba

ŌBAL

(See ŌBL)

ŌBĀT

GLŌBĀT	globate, conglobate
KRŌBĀT	crowbait
LŌBĀT	bilobate, lobate, trilobate
PRŌBĀT	probate

ŌBĒ

ŌBĒ	obi
DŌBĒ	adobe, dhobi, dobee, dobie
GLŌBĒ	globy
GŌBĒ	Gobi, goby
RŌBĒ	Nairobi
TŌBĒ	toby, Toby

ÔBĒ

BÔBĒ	bawbee
DÔBĒ	dauby
GÔBĒ	gauby

OBĒ

BLOBĒ	blobby
BOBĒ	bobby
DOBĒ	dobby
GLOBĒ	globby
GOBĒ	gobby
HOBĒ	hobby
KOBĒ	cobby
LOBĒ	lobby
MOBĒ	mobby
NOBĒ	knobby, nobby
POBĒ	pobby
SKOBĒ	scobby
SNOBĒ	snobby

ŌBER

LŌBER	lobar
MŌBER	amobyr
PRŌBER	prober
RŌBER	disrober, enrober, rober, robur
SŌBER	sober
TŌBER	October

ÔBER

| DÔBER | bedauber, dauber |
| KÔBER | Micawber |

OBER

BLOBER	blobber
JOBER	jobber, stockjobber
KLOBER	clobber
KOBER	cobber
LOBER	lobber
NOBER	knobber
ROBER	robber
SLOBER	beslobber, slobber

SNOBER   snobber
SOBER   sobber
SWOBER   swabber
THROBER   throbber

OBET

GOBET   gobbet
HOBET   hobbit

ŌBIK

ŌBIK   niobic
FŌBIK   aerophobic,
             agorophobic,
             acrophobic, phobic,
             phobophobic,
             photophobic,
             hydrophobic,
             claustrophobic,
             necrophobic,
             xenophobic (For more
             words ending in
             -phobic, see FŌ'BI.A
             and change -a to -ic.)
KRŌBIK   microbic
RŌBIK   aerobic
STRŌBIK   strobic

OBIK

OBIK   niobic
STROBIK   strobic

ŌBIKS

RŌBIKS   aerobics

(See ŌBIK, add -s where appropriate.)

ŌBIL

(See ŌBL)

OBIN

BOBIN   bobbin
DOBIN   dobbin
ROBIN   cock robin, ragged
             robin, robbin, robin,
             round robin, wake
             robin

ŌBING

GLŌBING   englobing, globing

RŌBING   disrobing, enrobing,
             robing, unrobing
PRŌBING   probing

OBING

BOBING   bobbing
JOBING   jobbing
KOBING   cobbing
LOBING   lobbing
MOBING   mobbing
NOBING   hobnobbing
ROBING   robbing
SNOBING   snobbing
SOBING   sobbing
THROBING   throbbing

OBISH

BOBISH   bobbish
MOBISH   mobbish
NOBISH   nobbish
SKWOBISH   squabbish
SNOBISH   snobbish

ŌBL

GLŌBL   global
KŌBL   coble
KRŌBL   microbal
LŌBL   lobal
MŌBL   mobile, upwardly
             mobile, upward-
             mobile
NŌBL   ennoble, Grenoble,
             ignoble, noble,
             unnoble
PRŌBL   probal
TŌBL   Cristobal

ÔBL

BÔBL   bauble

(See OBL)

OBL

GOBL   gobble
HOBL   hobble
KOBL   cobble, coble
NOBL   nobble
SKWOBL   squabble
WOBL   wabble, wobble

(See ÄBL)

OBLĒ

OBLĒ   obley
GOBLĒ   gobbly
HOBLĒ   hobbly
SKWOBLĒ   squabbly
WOBLĒ   wabbly, wobbly,
             Wobbly

OBLER

GOBLER   gobbler, turkey
             gobbler
KOBLER   blackberry cobbler,
             cobbler, peach
             cobbler

(See OBL, add -r where appropriate.)

OBLING

(See OBL, add -ing where appropriate.)

ŌBŌ

ŌBŌ   oboe
BŌBŌ   bobo
DŌBŌ   adobo
HŌBŌ   hobo
KŌBŌ   kobo
LŌBŌ   lobo
ZŌBŌ   zobo

ŌBOI

ŌBOI   hautboy
DŌBOI   doughboy
HŌBOI   hautboy

ÔBŌNZ

JÔBŌNZ   jawbones
SÔBŌNZ   sawbones

ŌBRA

DŌBRA   dobra
KŌBRA   cobra

OBSON

DOBSON   dobson
JOBSON   hobson-jobson

OBSTER

LOBSTER lobster
MOBSTER mobster

OBŪL

GLOBŪL globule
LOBŪL lobule

ŌBUS

ŌBUS obus
GLŌBUS globous
KŌBUS jacobus

ŌCHĒ

LŌCHĒ veloce
VŌCHĒ sotto voce, viva voce

OCHĒ

BLOCHĒ blotchy
BOCHĒ botchy
KROCHĒ crotchy
NOCHĒ notchy
SKOCHĒ Scotchy
SPLOCHĒ splotchy
VOCHĒ sotto voce, viva voce

ŌCHER

BRŌCHER broacher
KLŌCHER cloture
KŌCHER coacher, stage-coacher
KRŌCHER encroacher
PŌCHER poacher
PRŌCHER approacher, reproacher

ÔCHER

BÔCHER debaucher
WÔCHER night watcher, watcher

OCHER

BLOCHER blotcher
BOCHER botcher
NOCHER notcher, top-notcher
SKOCHER hopscotcher
SPLOCHER splotcher

SWOCHER swatcher
WOCHER bird-watcher, weight-watcher, watcher

OCHET

KLOCHET *clochette*
KROCHET crotchet
ROCHET rochet

ŌCHING

(See ŌCH, add -ing where appropriate.)

ÔCHING

BÔCHING debauching
WÔCHING watching

OCHING

BLOCHING blotching
BOCHING botching
HOCHING hotching
KROCHING crotching
NOCHING notching
POCHING hotchpotching

OCHMAN

SKOCHMAN Scotchman
WOCHMAN watchman

ŌCHMENT

KRŌCHMENT encroachment
PRÔCHMENT approachment

ŌDA

ŌDA oda
GŌDA pagoda
KŌDA coda
SŌDA baking soda, bourbon and soda, brandy and soda, whiskey and soda, ice-cream soda, scotch and soda (etc.), salsoda, soda

ŌDAL

(See ŌDL)

ÔDAL

(See ÔDL)

ODAL

(See ODL)

ŌDĒ

ŌDĒ O.D.
BŌDĒ bodhi
GŌDĒ wally-gowdy
LŌDĒ petalody
NŌDĒ staminody
PŌDĒ polypody
TŌDĒ toady, tody
WŌDĒ woady

ÔDĒ

BÔDĒ bawdy
DÔDĒ dawdy
GÔDĒ gaudy
LÔDĒ cum laude, Lawdy, magna cum laude, summa cum laude

ODĒ

BODĒ afterbody, antibody, body, busybody, disembody, dogsbody, embody, anybody, everybody, nobody, somebody, underbody, wide-body
DODĒ hoddy-doddy
HODĒ hoddy
KLODĒ cloddy
NODĒ noddy, tomnoddy
PODĒ poddy
RODĒ roddy
SHODĒ shoddy
SKWODĒ squaddy
SODĒ soddy
TODĒ toddy
WODĒ Irrawaddy, waddy, wadi

(See ÄDĒ)

ŌDED

(See ŌD, add -d or -ed where appropriate.)

ODĒD

BODĒD able-bodied, bodied, disembodied,

embodied, unbodied,
unembodied

TODĔD   toddied, well-toddied

ÔDED

FRÔDED   defrauded
LÔDED   belauded, lauded,
unlauded
PLÔDED   applauded,
unapplauded
RÔDED   marauded

ODED

(See **OD,** add -ed where appropriate.)

ŌDEL

(See **ŌDL**)

ŌDEN

ŌDEN   Odin
BŌDEN   boden, foreboden
WŌDEN   Wodin

ODEN

HODEN   hodden
SODEN   sodden, water-sodden
TRODEN   downtrodden,
trodden, untrodden

ŌDENT

PLŌDENT   explodent
RŌDENT   corrodent, erodent,
rodent

ŌDER

ŌDER   malodor, Oder, odor
BŌDER   boder, foreboder
GŌDER   goader
KŌDER   decoder, coder,
uncoder
LŌDER   loader, muzzle-
loader, reloader,
unloader
PLŌDER   exploder
RŌDER   eroder, corroder,
roader
WŌDER   woader

ÔDER

BRÔDER   broader
FRÔDER   defrauder
LÔDER   belauder, lauder
PLÔDER   applauder
RÔDER   marauder
SÔDER   sawder, soft sawder

ODER

ODER   odder
DODER   dodder
FODER   fodder, cannon fodder
KODER   Cape Codder, codder
NODER   nodder
PLODER   plodder
PODER   podder
PRODER   prodder
SODER   sodder, solder

ODERD

DODERD   doddard
FODERD   foddered
SODERD   soldered

ODES

BODES   bodice
GODES   demigoddess, goddess

ODEST

ODEST   oddest
BODEST   bodiced
MODEST   immodest, modest

ŌDIK

ŌDIK   odic
NŌDIK   palinodic

ODIK

ODIK   antiperiodic,
aperiodic, hydriodic,
iodic, geodic, odic,
periodic, euodic
KODIK   sarcodic
LODIK   melodic
MODIK   antispasmodic,
psalmodic, spasmodic
NODIK   anodic, hellanodic,
palinodic, synodic,
threnodic

PODIK   epodic
RODIK   parodic
SODIK   episodic, exodic,
kinesodic, rhapsodic
THODIK   methodic

ŌDING

(See **ŌD,** add -ing where appropriate.)

ÔDING

FRÔDING   defrauding
LÔDING   belauding, lauding,
relauding
PLÔDING   applauding,
reapplauding

ODING

NODING   nid-nodding, nodding
PLODING   plodding

ODIS

(See **ODES**)

ŌDISH

MŌDISH   modish
TŌDISH   toadish

ODISH

ODISH   oddish
GODISH   goddish
KLODISH   cloddish
KODISH   coddish
PODISH   poddish

ŌDIST

ŌDIST   odist
KŌDIST   codist
MŌDIST   modist
NŌDIST   palinodist

ÔDIT

ÔDIT   audit
PLÔDIT   plaudit

ŌDL

ŌDL   odal
MŌDL   modal

NŌDL

NŌDL	binodal, internodal, nodal, trinodal
YŌDL	yodel

ÔDL

DÔDL	dawdle
KÔDL	bicaudal, caudal, caudle, longicaudal

ODL

BRODL	broddle
DODL	doddle
KODL	coddle, mollycoddle
MODL	model, remodel, role model
NODL	niddle-noddle, noddle
TODL	toddle
WODL	waddle

(See ÄDL)

ODLĒ

ODLĒ	oddly
GODLĒ	godly, ungodly
TODLĒ	toddly, untoddly

(See ÄDLĒ)

ODLER

KODLER	coddler, mollycoddler
MODLER	modeler
TODLER	toddler

(See ÄDL, ODL, add -r where appropriate.)

ODLING

GODLING	godling
KODLING	coddling, codling, mollycoddling
TODLING	toddling

ODMAN

ODMAN	oddman
DODMAN	dodman
HODMAN	hodman

ŌDŌ

DŌDŌ	dodo
MŌDŌ	Quasimodo, quomodo

ŌDOR

(See ŌDER)

ŌDOUN

GŌDOUN	godown
HŌDOUN	hoedown
LŌDOUN	lowdown
SHŌDOUN	showdown
SLŌDOUN	slowdown
STŌDOUN	stowdown

ÔDRĒ

BÔDRĒ	bawdry
NÔDRĒ	minauderie
TÔDRĒ	tawdry

ŌDSTER

GŌDSTER	goadster
RŌDSTER	roadster

ŌDSTŌN

LŌDSTŌN	loadstone, lodestone
TŌDSTŌN	toadstone

ODŪL

MODŪL	module
NODŪL	nodule

ŌDUS

MŌDUS	modus
NŌDUS	nodous, nodus

ŌĒ

BLŌĒ	blowy
BŌĒ	bowie, Bowie

> **MOSES INFANTI**
>
> She took for him an ark of bulrushes, and daubed it with slime and with pitch, and put the child therein; and she laid it in the flags by the river's brink.
>
> —Exodus 2:3
>
> Among the flags did Moses lie,
> Cradled in akaakai,
> While a hippopotamus
> Made a borborygmic fuss.

DŌĒ	doughy
GLŌĒ	glowy
HŌĒ	pahoehoe
PŌĒ	poë, poi
RŌĒ	rowy
SHŌĒ	showy
SNŌĒ	snowy
TŌĒ	towy
VŌĒ	evoe, evohe

ÔĒ

FLÔĒ	flawy
JÔĒ	jawy
STRÔĒ	strawy
THÔĒ	thawy
YÔĒ	yawy

(See OI)

ŌEM

BŌEM	jeroboam
FLŌEM	phloem
PŌEM	mythopoem, poem
PRŌEM	proem

ŌER

ŌER	o'er, ower
BLŌER	blower, glass blower, whistle-blower, snow blower
GLŌER	glower
GŌER	churchgoer, foregoer, goer, concertgoer, moviegoer, outgoer, playgoer, racegoer, undergoer
GRŌER	flower grower, grower, wine grower (etc.)
HŌER	hoer
KRŌER	cockcrower, crower
LŌER	lower
MŌER	lawn mower, mower
NŌER	foreknower, knower
RŌER	rower
SHŌER	foreshower, shower
SLŌER	slower
SŌER	sewer, sower
STŌER	bestower, stower
THRŌER	overthrower, thrower
TŌER	tower

ÔER

ÔER	awer, overawer
DRÔER	drawer, wire drawer, withdrawer

FÔER	guffawer
JÔER	jawer
KLÔER	clawer
KÔER	cawer
NÔER	gnawer
PÔER	pawer
RÔER	rawer
SÔER	sawer
TÔER	tawer

ŌERD

FRŌERD	froward
LŌERD	lowered
TŌERD	toward, untoward

ÔFAL

(See ÔFL)

ŌFĒ

ŌFĒ	oafy
STRŌFĒ	monostrophe, strophe
TRŌFĒ	trophy

OFĒ

KOFĒ	coffee
SPOFĒ	spoffy
TOFĒ	toffee

OFEN

(See OFN)

ŌFER

ŌFER	Ophir
GŌFER	gaufre, gofer, gopher
LŌFER	loafer, penny-loafer
SHŌFER	chauffeur

OFER

OFER	offer
DOFER	doffer
GOFER	goffer
KOFER	coffer, cougher
PROFER	proffer
SKOFER	scoffer

OFET

PROFET	archprophet, profit, prophet, weather prophet
SOFET	soffit

OFIK

OFIK	ophic
SOFIK	philosophic, theophilosophic, theosophic
STROFIK	anostrophic, antistrophic, apostrophic, geostrophic, catastrophic, strophic
TROFIK	atrophic, hypertrophic, heterotrophic, oligotrophic, autotrophic, protrophic, trophic, eutrophic

ÔFIN

(See ÔFN)

OFING

OFING	offing
DOFING	doffing
GOFING	golfing
KOFING	coughing
SKOFING	scoffing

ŌFISH

ŌFISH	oafish
BLŌFISH	blowfish

ÔFISH

KRÔFISH	crawfish
SÔFISH	sawfish
SKWÔFISH	squawfish

OFISH

OFISH	offish, standoffish
SPOFISH	spoffish

OFIT

(See OFET)

ÔFL

ÔFL	awful, offal
LÔFL	lawful, unlawful

OFL

KOFL	coffle
TOFL	pantoffle
WOFL	waffle

(See ÄFL)

ÔFN

DÔFN	dauphin

(See OFN)

OFN

OFN	often
KOFN	encoffin, coffin
SOFN	soften

(See ÔFN)

OFNER

OFNER	oftener
SOFNER	softener

(See OF'EN.ER)

ŌFOOT

KRŌFOOT	crowfoot
SLŌFOOT	slow-foot

OFTĒ

LOFTĒ	lofty, toplofty
SOFTĒ	softy

OFTER

KROFTER	crofter
LOFTER	lofter
SOFTER	softer

ŌFUL

BLŌFUL	blowful
DŌFUL	doughful
RŌFUL	roeful
WŌFUL	woeful

ÔFUL

(See ÔFL)

ŌGA

ŌGA	Tioga
RŌGA	daroga, Ticonderoga
SNŌGA	snoga
TŌGA	conestoga, Saratoga, toga
YŌGA	yoga

ŌGAN

BRŌGAN	brogan
HŌGAN	hogan
LŌGAN	logan
MŌGAN	Hogen-Mogen
RŌGAN	rogan
SLŌGAN	slogan

OGAN

BOGAN	toboggan
GOGAN	goggan
LOGAN	loggin
MOGAN	moggan, pogamoggan
NOGAN	noggin

OGBOUND

FOGBOUND	fogbound
SMOGBOUND	smogbound

ŌGĒ

BŌGĒ	bogey, bogie
DŌGĒ	dogie, judogi
FŌGĒ	fogey, old fogey
HŌGĒ	hoagie, hoagy
LŌGĒ	killogie, logy
PŌGĒ	pogy
STŌGĒ	stogie, stogy
VŌGĒ	voguey
YŌGĒ	yogi

OGĒ

BOGĒ	boggy
DOGĒ	doggy
FOGĒ	foggy
FROGĒ	froggy
GOGĒ	demagogy, pedagogy
SOGĒ	soggy

(See OG, add -y where appropriate.)

OGEN

(See OGAN)

ŌGER

(See ŌGR)

ÔGER

ÔGER	auger, augur
MÔGER	mauger
NÔGER	inaugur
SÔGER	sauger

OGER

DOGER	dogger
FLOGER	flogger
FOGER	befogger, pettifogger
HOGER	hogger, whole-hogger, road-hogger
JOGER	jogger
KLOGER	clogger
KOGER	cogger
LOGER	dialoguer, epiloguer, cataloguer, logger, monologuer, epiloguer
SLOGER	slogger
TOGER	togger

OGIN

(See OGAN)

OGING

(See OG, add -ing where appropriate.)

ŌGISH

RŌGISH	roguish
VŌGISH	voguish

OGISH

DOGISH	doggish
FROGISH	froggish
HOGISH	hoggish
WOGISH	woggish

ŌGL

ŌGL	ogle
BŌGL	bogle
FŌGL	fogle
MŌGL	mogul

OGL

BOGL	boggle
DOGL	boondoggle
GOGL	goggle, jargoggle
JOGL	joggle
KOGL	coggle
SWOGL	hornswoggle
TOGL	toggle
WOGL	woggle

OGLER

BOGLER	boggler
DOGLER	boondoggler
GOGLER	goggler
JOGLER	joggler
SWOGLER	hornswoggler

OGLING

(See OGL, add -ing where appropriate.)

ŌGŌ

GŌGŌ	a-go-go, go-go
LŌGŌ	logo, Logo
MŌGŌ	mogo
NŌGŌ	no-go
PŌGŌ	pogo, Pogo
TŌGŌ	Togo
ZŌGŌ	zogo

ŌGR

ŌGR	ogre
DRŌGR	drogher

ŌGRAM

FŌGRAM	fogram
PRŌGRAM	deprogram, program

ŌGRES

ŌGRES	ogress
PRŌGRES	progress

OGTROT

DOGTROT	dogtrot
HOGTROT	hogtrot
JOGTROT	jogtrot

OGWOOD

BOGWOOD	bogwood
DOGWOOD	dogwood
LOGWOOD	logwood

ŌHŌ

ŌHŌ	oho
KŌHŌ	coho
MŌHŌ	moho, mojo
RŌHŌ	coroho
SŌHŌ	Soho

OIA

GOIA	Goya
HOIA	hoya
KWOIA	Sequoia
NOIA	dianoia, palinoia, paranoia
SOIA	soya

OIAL

LOIAL	disloyal, loyal
ROIAL	chapel royal, penny-royal, royal, surroyal, viceroyal

OIANS

BOIANS	buoyance, flamboyance
JOIANS	joyance
NOIANS	annoyance
TOIANS	chatoyance
VOIANS	clairvoyance, prevoyance

OIANT

OIANT	buoyant, flamboyant
DOIANT	ondoyant
MOIANT	larmoyant
NOIANT	annoyant
TOIANT	chatoyant
VOIANT	clairvoyant, prevoyant

OIDAL

(See **OID**, add *-al* where appropriate.)

OIDER

BROIDER	broider, embroider
MOIDER	moider
VOIDER	avoider, voider

OIDIK

PLOIDIK	diploidic
ROIDIK	spheroidic

OIEM

GOIEM	goyim
TNOIEM	tnoyim

OIER

OIER	oyer
BOIER	boyar, boyer
FOIER	foyer
JOIER	enjoyer
KOIER	decoyer, coir, coyer
LOIER	caloyer
NOIER	annoyer
PLOIER	deployer, employer, self-employer
STROIER	destroyer, self-destroyer
TOIER	toyer

(See **ÔYER**)

OIIJ

BOIIJ	buoyage
LOIIJ	alloyage
VOIIJ	voyage

ŌING

FRŌING	to-and-froing

(See **Ō**, add *-ing* where appropriate.)

OIING

BOIING	buoying
JOIING	joying, enjoying
KLOIING	cloying
KOIING	coying, decoying
LOIING	alloying

NOIING	annoying
PLOIING	deploying, employing, ploying, self-employing
STROIING	destroying
TOIING	toying
VOIING	envoying, convoying

OIISH

BOIISH	boyish
JOIISH	joyish
KOIISH	coyish
TOIISH	toyish

ŌIJ

FLŌIJ	flowage
STŌIJ	stowage
TŌIJ	towage

ŌIK

KŌIK	anechoic, echoic
KRŌIK	amphicroic, dichroic, melanochroic, pleochroic, xanthochroic
NŌIK	dipnoic
PLŌIK	diploic
RŌIK	heroic, mock-heroic, unheroic
STŌIK	stoic
TRŌIK	Troic
ZŌIK	*A* azoic, *B* benzoic, *E* entozoic, Eozoic, epizoic, *H* hylozoic, hypnozoic, holozoic, *KR* cryptozoic, *M* Mesozoic, *N* Neozoic, *P* Paleozoic, polyzoic, *PR* protozoic, *S* saprozoic, Cenozoic

ŌIKS

RŌIKS	heroics
ZŌIKS	phthisozoics

(See **ŌIK**, add *-s* where appropriate.)

OILĒ

OILĒ	oily
DOILĒ	doily
KOILĒ	coyly

OILER

NOILĒ	noily
ROILĒ	roily

OILER

OILER	oiler
BOILER	boiler
BROILER	broiler, embroiler
FOILER	foiler, tin-foiler
KOILER	coiler, recoiler, uncoiler
MOILER	moiler
ROILER	roiler
SOILER	soiler
SPOILER	despoiler, spoiler
TOILER	toiler

OILET

OILET	oillet
TOILET	toilet

OILING

(See **OIL**, add -ing where appropriate.)

OILMENT

BROILMENT	embroilment
KOILMENT	recoilment
SPOILMENT	despoilment
TOILMENT	entoilment

OILSUM

ROILSUM	roilsome
TOILSUM	toilsome

OIMAN

HOIMAN	hoyman
KOIMAN	decoyman
TOIMAN	toyman

OIMENT

JOIMENT	enjoyment
KLOIMENT	cloyment
PLOIMENT	deployment, employment, ployment, unemployment

OINDER

JOINDER	joinder, misjoinder, nonjoinder, rejoinder
POINDER	poinder

OINER

GOINER	zigeuner
JOINER	enjoiner, joiner, conjoiner, rejoiner
KOINER	coiner
LOINER	purloiner

ŌING

ŌING	ohing, owing
BLŌING	blowing, mind-blowing
GŌING	easygoing, going, sea-going, thoroughgoing

(See **Ō**, add -ing where appropriate.)

ÔING

SHÔING	wappenschawing

(See **Ô**, add -ing where appropriate.)

OINING

(See **OIN**, add -ing where appropriate.)

OINTED

(See **OINT**, add -ed where appropriate.)

OINTER

JOINTER	disjointer, jointer
NOINTER	anointer
POINTER	appointer, disappointer, pointer

OINTING

(See **OINT**, add -ing where appropriate.)

OINTLES

JOINTLES	jointless
POINTLES	pointless

OINTMENT

OINTMENT	ointment
JOINTMENT	disjointment
NOINTMENT	anointment
POINTMENT	appointment, disappointment, reappointment

OISER

CHOISER	choicer
JOISER	rejoicer
VOISER	invoicer, voicer

ŌISH

(See **Ō**, add -ish where appropriate.)

OISING

JOISING	rejoicing, unrejoicing
VOISING	invoicing, unvoicing, voicing

OISLES

(See **OIS**, add -less where appropriate.)

OISTĒ

FOISTĒ	foisty
MOISTĒ	moisty

OISTER

OISTER	oyster, pearl oyster
DOISTER	Ralph Roister Doister
FOISTER	foister
HOISTER	hoister
KLOISTER	encloister, cloister, uncloister
MOISTER	moister
ROISTER	roister

OISTING

FOISTING	foisting
HOISTING	hoisting
JOISTING	joisting

OISTREL

KOISTREL	coistrel, coystrel
KLOISTREL	cloistral

OISUM

KLOISUM	cloysome
NOISUM	noisome
TOISUM	toysome

ŌIT

| KŌIT | inchoate |
| PŌIT | poet |

OITĒ

| KOITĒ | dacoity |
| OITĒ | hoity-toity |

OITED

DOITED	doited
KWOITED	quoited
PLOITED	exploited, unexploited

OITER

DROITER	adroiter
GOITER	goiter
KWOITER	quoiter
LOITER	loiter
NOITER	reconnoiter, reconnoitre
PLOITER	exploiter

OITRER

| LOITRER | loiterer |
| NOITRER | reconnoitrer |

(See **OIT'ER.ER**)

OITRING

| LOITRING | loitering |
| NOITRING | reconnoitering |

(See **OIT'ER.ING**)

OIUS

| JOIUS | joyous |
| NOIUS | annoyous |

OIZER

HOIZER	Tannhäuser
NOIZER	noiser
POIZER	poiser

OIZING

| NOIZING | noising |
| POIZING | poising |

OIZUN

FOIZUN	foison
POIZUN	empoison, poison
TOIZUN	toison

ŌJĒ

ŌJĒ	ogee
GŌJĒ	agoge, anagoge, androgogy, apagoge, epagoge, isagoge, paragoge, pedagogy, xenagogy
SHŌJĒ	shoji

OJĒ

DOJĒ	dodgy
GOJĒ	androgogy, demagogy, pedagogy
POJĒ	podgy
STOJĒ	stodgy

OJER

BOJER	bodger
DOJER	dodger
KOJER	codger
LOJER	dislodger, lodger
POJER	podger
ROJER	roger, Roger
STOJER	stodger

ŌJEZ

(See **ŌJ**, add -es where appropriate.)

OJIK

| GOJIK | *A* agogic, anagogic, apagogic, *D* demagogic, *E* epagogic, *H* hypnagogic, *I* isagogic, *My* mystagogic, *P* paragogic, pedagogic, *S* sialagogic, psychagogic |
| LOJIK | *A* aerologic, agrologic, acrologic, anthropologic, archaeologic, astrologic, *CH* choplogic, dialogic, *E* entomologic, epilogic, ethnologic, ethologic, etymologic, *F* philologic, physiologic, phytologic, phonologic, photologic, *FR* phraseologic, *H* hagiologic, hydrologic, hierologic, hypnologic, histologic, homologic, horologic, *I* ideologic, icthyologic, *J* geologic, *K* catalogic, cosmologic, curiologic, *KR* chronologic, *L* lexicologic, lithologic, logic, *M* martyrologic, metalogic, meteorologic, mycologic, micrologic, mineralogic, myologic, mythologic, morphologic, *N* necrologic, neologic, gnomologic, *O* ophiologic, ontologic, *P* paralogic, pathologic, penologic, *S* sarcologic, psychologic, cytologic, sociologic, *T* toxicologic, tautologic, *TH* theologic, *TR* tropologic, *U* eulogic, *Z* zymologic, zoologic |

OJING

| DOJING | dodging |
| LOJING | dislodging, lodging |

ŌJŌ

DŌJŌ	do-jo
JŌJŌ	Jo-jo
MŌJŌ	mojo

ŌJOB

BLŌJOB	blow-job
SNŌJOB	snow-job

OJŌŌL

(See **ODŪL**)

ŌJUN

TRŌJUN	Trojan
YŌJUN	yojan

ŌKĀ

ŌKĀ	O. K., okay
KRŌKĀ	croquet
RŌKĀ	roquet
TŌKĀ	Tokay

ŌKA

ŌKA	oca, oka, Oka, carioca, tapioca
BŌKA	boca, curiboca
CHŌKA	choca
FŌKA	phoca
KŌKA	coca, jocoque
LŌKA	loka
MŌKA	mocha
PŌKA	polka, mishpocheh
SLŌKA	sloka
STŌKA	stocah
TRŌKA	troca, trocha

OKA

BOKA	bocca
CHOKA	choca
KWOKA	quokka
ROKA	rocca

ŌKĀK

HŌKĀK	hoecake
NŌKĀK	nocake

ŌKAL

LŌKAL	lo-cal
NŌKAL	no-cal

(See **ŌKL**)

ŌKĒ

ŌKĒ	oaky, Okie
CHŌKĒ	choky
DŌKĒ	okey-dokey
HŌKĒ	hokey
JŌKĒ	joky
KŌKĒ	jocoqui, coky
KRŌKĒ	croaky
LŌKĒ	Loki, loci
MŌKĒ	moki, Moki, moky, Moqui
PŌKĒ	hokey-pokey, poky, slowpoky
RŌKĒ	roky
SŌKĒ	soaky
TRŌKĒ	ditrochee, troche, trochee
SMŌKĒ	smoky
YŌKĒ	yoky, yolky

ÔKĒ

BÔKĒ	balky
CHÔKĒ	chalky
GÔKĒ	gawky
HÔKĒ	hawky
PÔKĒ	pawky
SKWÔKĒ	squawky
STÔKĒ	stalky
TÔKĒ	talkie, talky, walky-talky
WÔKĒ	Milwaukee, walkie

OKĒ

BLOKĒ	blocky
FLOKĒ	flocky
HOKĒ	field hockey, hockey, ice hockey
JOKĒ	disc jockey, jockey, outjockey
KOKĒ	cocky
KROKĒ	crocky
LOKĒ	lochy, locky
POKĒ	pocky
ROKĒ	rocky
SHLOKĒ	schlocky
STOKĒ	stocky
WOKĒ	Jabberwocky

(See **ÄKĒ**)

ŌKEN

ŌKEN	oaken, ryokan
BŌKEN	Hoboken
BRŌKEN	broken, heartbroken, housebroken, unbroken
SŌKEN	soaken
SPŌKEN	B bespoken, F fair-spoken, fine-spoken, forespoken, FR free-spoken, O outspoken, PL plainspoken, S soft-spoken, SH short-spoken, SM smooth-spoken, SP spoken, TR true-spoken, U unspoken, W well-spoken
TŌKEN	betoken, foretoken, token
WŌKEN	awoken, woken

ŌKER

ŌKER	mediocre, ochre
BRŌKER	broker, pawnbroker, power broker, stockbroker
CHŌKER	choker
HŌKER	hoker
JŌKER	joker
KLŌKER	cloaker, uncloaker
KŌKER	coker
KRŌKER	croaker
PŌKER	poker
RŌKER	roker
SMŌKER	nonsmoker, smoker
SŌKER	soaker
STŌKER	stoker
STRŌKER	stroker
VŌKER	evoker, invoker, convoker, provoker, revoker
YŌKER	yoker

ÔKER

BÔKER	balker
CHÔKER	chalker
GÔKER	gawker
HÔKER	hawker, jayhawker, tomahawker
KÔKER	calker, cawker, caulker
SKWÔKER	squawker
STÔKER	deer-stalker, stalker
TÔKER	talker
WÔKER	floorwalker, jaywalker, nightwalker, shopwalker, sleepwalker, streetwalker, walker

OKER

OKER	ocker
BLOKER	beta-blocker, blocker
CHOKER	chocker
DOKER	docker
FLOKER	flocker
FOKER	focker, Fokker
HOKER	hocker, hougher
JOKER	jocker
KLOKER	clocker
KOKER	cocker
LOKER	locker
MOKER	mocker
NOKER	knocker
ROKER	patent rocker, rocker
SHOKER	penny shocker, shilling shocker, shocker
SMOKER	smocker
SOKER	soccer, socker
STOKER	stocker

OKERZ

BOKERZ	knickerbockers

(See **OKER**, add -s where appropriate.)

OKET

BROKET	brocket
DOKET	docket
KOKET	cocket
KROKET	crocket, Davy Crockett
LOKET	locket
POKET	air pocket, hip-pocket, impocket, pickpocket, pocket, vest-pocket, watch-pocket
ROKET	retrorocket, rocket, skyrocket, space-rocket
SOKET	socket
SPROKET	sprocket

OKHED

BLOKHED	blockhead
SHOKHED	shockhead

ŌKIJ

BRŌKIJ	brokage
CHŌKIJ	chokage
KLŌKIJ	cloakage
SŌKIJ	soakage

OKIJ

DOKIJ	dockage
LOKIJ	lockage
SOKIJ	socage

ŌKING

(See **ŌK**, add -ing where appropriate.)

ÔKING

(See **ÔK**, add -ing where appropriate.)

OKING

BOKING	bocking
STOKING	bluestocking, stocking

(See **OK**, add -ing where appropriate.)

ÔKISH

BÔKISH	balkish
CHÔKISH	chalkish
HÔKISH	hawkish
MÔKISH	mawkish

OKISH

BLOKISH	blockish
KOKISH	cockish, peacockish
MOKISH	mockish
STOKISH	stockish

ŌKL

BŌKL	bocal
DŌKL	okle-dokle
FŌKL	bifocal, focal, phocal, hyperfocal
LŌKL	collocal, local, matrilocal, neolocal, patrilocal, uxorilocal
SŌKL	socle
TRŌKL	trochal
VŌKL	bivocal, equivocal, multivocal, vocal
YŌKL	jokul, yokel

OKL

BROKL	brockle
KOKL	cockle
SOKL	socle
STROKL	strockle

ŌKLES

(See **ŌK**, add -less where appropriate.)

OKLET

FLOKLET	flocklet
LOKLET	locklet
SOKLET	socklet

OKLING

FLOKLING	flockling
KOKLING	cockling
ROKLING	rockling

OKNĒ

KOKNĒ	cockney
LOKNĒ	lock-knee
PROKNĒ	Procne

ŌKŌ

ŌKŌ	con fuoco
FŌKŌ	loco-foco
GŌKŌ	ngoko
KŌKŌ	barococo, cocoa, cocoa, koko, rococo
LŌKŌ	loco, Popoloco
MŌKŌ	moko, moko-moko
NŌKŌ	Orinoco
PŌKŌ	poco, poco-a-poco
RŌKŌ	baroco
SMŌKŌ	smoko
SŌKŌ	soco
TŌKŌ	toco
TRŌKŌ	troco

OKŌ

JOKŌ	Jocko
ROKŌ	Morocco, sirocco
SOKŌ	socko
YOKŌ	yocco

OKOUT

LOKOUT	lockout
NOKOUT	knockout

OKSA

DOKSA	chionodoxa
KOKSA	coxa
MOKSA	moxa

| NOKSA | noxa |
| TOKSA | toxa |

OKSAL

DOKSAL	paradoxal
KOKSAL	coxal
NOKSAL	noxal

OKSĒ

BOKSĒ	boxy
DOKSĒ	doxy, heterodoxy, cacodoxy, orthodoxy, paradoxy
DROKSĒ	hydroxy
FOKSĒ	foxy
LOKSĒ	Biloxi
MOKSĒ	moxie, Moxie
POKSĒ	poxy
PROKSĒ	proxy
ROKSĒ	roxy, Roxy

OKSEN

(See **OKSN**)

ŌKSER

| HŌKSER | hoaxer |
| KŌKSER | coaxer |

OKSER

OKSER	oxer
BOKSER	boxer
DOKSER	philodoxer, paradoxer
FOKSER	foxer
SOKSER	bobbysoxer

OKSĪD

| OKSĪD | ox-eyed, oxide, peroxide |
| FOKSĪD | fox-eyed |

OKSIK

KOKSIK	streptococcic, gonococcic
POKSIK	hypoxic
TOKSIK	nontoxic, radiotoxic, toxic

OKSIKS

| KOKSIKS | coccix |
| TOKSIKS | antitoxics, toxics |

OKSIN

(See **OKSN**)

ŌKSING

| HŌKSING | hoaxing |
| KŌKSING | coaxing |

OKSING

| BOKSING | boxing, shadowboxing |
| FOKSING | foxing |

ŌKSMAN

| SPŌKSMAN | spokesman |
| STRŌKSMAN | strokesman |

OKSN

OKSN	oxen, dioxin, myoxine
KOKSN	coxswain
TOKSN	antitoxin, tocsin, toxin

ŌKSTER

| FŌKSTER | folkster |
| JŌKSTER | jokester |

OKTER

DOKTER	doctor
KOKTER	decocter, concocter
PROKTER	proctor

OKTIL

| OKTIL | trioctile |
| KOKTIL | coctile |

OKTIV

| OKTIV | octave |
| KOKTIV | decoctive, concoctive |

ŌKUM

ŌKUM	oakum
HŌKUM	hokum
LŌKUM	locum
KŌKUM	kokam, kokum
SLŌKUM	slowcome

OKUP

KOKUP	cockup
LOKUP	lockup
MOKUP	mock-up

ŌKUS

FŌKUS	focus, unfocus
HŌKUS	hocus, Hohokus
KRŌKUS	crocus
LŌKUS	locus
PŌKUS	hocus-pocus
TŌKUS	tokis, tokus

ÔKUS

BÔKUS	Baucis
GLÔKUS	glaucous
KÔKUS	caucus
RÔKUS	raucous

OKUS

FLOKUS	floccus
KOKUS	echinococcus, pneumococcus, staphylococcus, streptococcus
LOKUS	lochus

ŌKUST

FŌKUST	focussed, unfocussed
LŌKUST	honey locust, locust, seven-year locust, sweet locust
PŌKUST	hocus-pocussed

ŌLA

ŌLA	gayola, gladiola, crayola, payola, scagliola, viola
BŌLA	bola, bowla, carambola
DŌLA	gondola, mandola
FŌLA	boffola

GŌLA	Angola, drugola, gola, plugola
KŌLA	Coca-Cola, cola, Cola, kola, Pensacola, Pepsi-cola
MŌLA	Mola, pimola
NŌLA	granola, pianola
RŌLA	pyrola, Savonarola
SKŌLA	schola
SŌLA	sola
STŌLA	stola
TŌLA	ayatollah, tola
TRŌLA	Victrola
YŌLA	scagliola
ZŌLA	Gorgonzola, Mazola, shnozzola, Zola

OLA

OLA	olla
HOLA	holla
ROLA	corolla
TOLA	ayatollah
WOLA	chuckwalla, wallah, walla-walla, Walla Walla

ŌLAND

| LŌLAND | lowland |
| RŌLAND | Roland |

ŌLAR

(See ŌLER)

OLARD

BOLARD	bollard
HOLARD	hollered
KOLARD	collard, collared
LOLARD	Lollard
POLARD	pollard
SKOLARD	scholared

ÔLBOI

BÔLBOI	ballboy
HÔLBOI	hallboy
KÔLBOI	callboy
TÔLBOI	tallboy

ŌLDĒ

ŌLDĒ	oldy, golden-oldy
FŌLDĒ	foldy
GŌLDĒ	goldy
MŌLDĒ	moldy

ŌLDED

(See **OLD,** add *-ed* where appropriate.)

ŌLDEN

ŌLDEN	olden
BŌLDEN	embolden
GŌLDEN	golden
HŌLDEN	beholden, holden, misbeholden, withholden
SŌLDEN	soldan

ŌLDER

ŌLDER	older
BŌLDER	bolder, boulder
FŌLDER	bill folder, enfolder, folder, infolder, interfolder, manifolder, refolder, unfolder
HŌLDER	B beholder, bond-holder, bottle-holder, FR freeholder, G gas-holder, H hand-holder, holder, householder, K candleholder, copyholder, L landholder, leaseholder, SH shareholder, SL slaveholder, SM smallholder, ST stadholder, stockholder, T ticket holder, U upholder, W withholder
KŌLDER	colder
MŌLDER	molder, moulder
PŌLDER	polder
SHŌLDER	cold-shoulder, shoulder
SKŌLDER	scolder
SMŌLDER	smolder, smoulder

ÔLDER

ÔLDER	alder
BÔLDER	balder, Balder
SKÔLDER	scalder

ŌLDERD

| BŌLDERD | bouldered |
| MŌLDERD | moldered, mouldered |

| SHŌLDERD | broad-shouldered, narrow-shouldered, round-shouldered, square-shouldered, shouldered, stoop-shouldered, wide-shouldered |
| SMŌLDERD | smoldered, smouldered |

ŌLDING

FŌLDING	enfolding, folding, interfolding
HŌLDING	B beholding, bond-holding, bottle-holding, FR freeholding, H hand-holding, holding, L landholding, leaseholding, SH shareholding, SL slave-holding, ST stock-holding, U upholding, W withholding
MŌLDING	molding
SKŌLDING	scolding

ÔLDING

| BÔLDING | balding |
| SKÔLDING | scalding |

ŌLDISH

ŌLDISH	oldish
BŌLDISH	boldish
KŌLDISH	coldish
MŌLDISH	moldish

ŌLDLĒ

ŌLDLĒ	oldly
BŌLDLĒ	boldly
KŌLDLĒ	coldly

ŌLDMENT

| FŌLDMENT | enfoldment |
| HŌLDMENT | withholdment |

ŌLDNES

| BŌLDNES | boldness |
| KŌLDNESS | coldness, stone-coldness |

RÔLDNES — enrolledness, unenrolledness
SÕLDNES — low-souledness, high-souledness
TRÕLDNES — controlledness, uncontrolledness

ÔLDRUN

KÔLDRUN — cauldron
PÔLDRUN — pauldron

ŌLĒ

ŌLĒ — aioli, Ole, ravioli
BŌLĒ — Stromboli, bolly, bowly
DRŌLĒ — drolly
FŌLĒ — foaly
GŌLĒ — goalie
HŌLĒ — holey, holy, wholly, maholi, unholy
KŌLĒ — caracoli, choli, coaly, coley, coly
LŌLĒ — lowly
MŌLĒ — guacamole, molely, moly
NŌLĒ — anole, cannoli, knolly, pinole
PŌLĒ — poly, rolypoly
RŌLĒ — rolly
SHŌLĒ — shoaly, sho'ly
SKRŌLĒ — scrolly
SLŌLĒ — slowly
SŌLĒ — posole, rissole, solely, soli
STRŌLĒ — strolly

ÔLĒ

ÔLĒ — awly
DRÔLĒ — drawly
GÔLĒ — gally
HWÔLĒ — whally
KÔLĒ — Macaulay
KRÔLĒ — crawly
MÔLĒ — mauley
RÔLĒ — rawly
SKRÔLĒ — scrawly
SKWÔLĒ — squally
SPRÔLĒ — sprawly

OLĒ

BOLĒ — Bali
DOLĒ — Dali, dolly
FOLĒ — folly
GOLĒ — golly

HOLĒ — holly
JOLĒ — jolly
KOLĒ — collie, colly, melancholy
LOLĒ — loblolly, trollylolly
MOLĒ — molle
POLĒ — poly
ROLĒ — rolley
TROLĒ — Toonerville trolley, trolley
VOLĒ — volley

(See ÄLĒ)

OLĒD

DOLĒD — dollied
JOLĒD — jollied
KOLĒD — collied
VOLĒD — volleyed, vollied

ŌLEM

DŌLEM — idolum
GŌLEM — golem
SŌLEM — solum

OLEM

KOLEM — column
SOLEM — solemn

ŌLEN

DŌLEN — eidolon
KŌLEN — colon, semicolon
SŌLEN — solen, solon, Solon
STŌLEN — stolen, stollen, stolon
SWŌLEN — swollen, unswollen

ÔLEN

(See ÔLIN)

ŌLENT

ŌLENT — olent
DŌLENT — dolent, condolent
VŌLENT — non-volent, volent

ŌLER

ŌLER — olor
BŌLER — bolar, bowler
DŌLER — doler, dolor, condoler
DRŌLER — droller

FŌLER — foaler
GŌLER — goaler, two-goaler, one-goaler
HŌLER — holer, wholer, potholer
JŌLER — cajoler
KŌLER — coaler
MŌLER — molar, premolar
NŌLER — knoller
PŌLER — multipolar, polar, poler, poller, circumpolar, transpolar, unipolar
RŌLER — enroller, high-roller, Holy Roller, lush-roller, pill-roller, roadroller, roller, steamroller, unroller, uproller
SHŌLER — shoaler
SKRŌLER — scroller
SŌLER — consoler, lunisolar, solar, soler
STRŌLER — stroller
TŌLER — extoller, toller

IDYL FOR MY IDLE IDOL

My idol!—your idle
    Tears drown my poor heart;
Why bridle, when bridal
    Delights I'd impart?
Think not from your side'll
    I sidle, my pet;
This idyl that died'll
    Abide a bit yet.
All loving is tidal;
    The tide'll go slack—
Yet after you've cried, 'll
    Come billowing back.

TRŌLER — comptroller, controller, patroller, troller
VŌLER — volar

ÔLER

BÔLER — baseballer, basketballer, baller, bawler, footballer, highballer, volleyballer
BRÔLER — brawler
DRÔLER — drawler
FÔLER — faller
HÔLER — hauler, overhauler
KÔLER — hog caller, caller, train caller
KRÔLER — crawler, pub-crawler
MÔLER — bemauler, mauler

SKRÔLER	scrawler
SKWÔLER	squaller
SMÔLER	smaller
SPRÔLER	sprawler
STÔLER	forestaller, staller
THRÔLER	enthraller
TÔLER	taller
TRÔLER	trawler
WÔLER	caterwauler, potwaller
YÔLER	yawler

OLER

DOLER	dollar, dolor, petrodollar, rix-dollar, Eurodollar
HOLER	holler
KOLER	choler
LOLER	loller
SKOLER	scholar
SKWOLER	squalor
SOLER	soller
TOLER	extoller

OLERD

(See OLARD)

ÔLES

ÔLES	aweless
FLÔLES	flawless
JÔLES	jawless
KLÔLES	clawless
KÔLES	cawless
LÔLES	lawless
MÔLES	mawless
PÔLES	pawless
SÔLES	sawless
STRÔLES	strawless

OLET

KOLET	collet
SWOLET	swallet
WOLET	wallet

(See ÁLET)

OLĒZ

FOLĒZ	follies
JOLĒZ	jollies

(See OLĒ, change -y to -ies where appropriate.)

ŌLFUL

BŌLFUL	bowlful
DŌLFUL	doleful
SŌLFUL	soulful

ŌLHOUS

PŌLHOUS	pollhouse
TŌLHOUS	tollhouse

OLID

OLID	olid
SKWOLID	squalid
SOLID	semi-solid, solid
STOLID	stolid

ŌLĪF

LŌLĪF	low-life
PRŌLĪF	pro-life

ÔLIJ

HÔLIJ	hallage, haulage
NÔLIJ	naulage
STÔLIJ	stallage

OLIJ

KOLIJ	college, community college, state college
NOLIJ	acknowledge, foreknowledge, knowledge, self-knowledge

ÔLIK

ÔLIK	aulic, interaulic
DRÔLIK	hydraulic
GÔLIK	Gaulic

OLIK

OLIK	Aeolic, Eolic, variolic, vitriolic
BOLIK	anabolic, diabolic, embolic, hyperbolic, carbolic, catabolic, metabolic, parabolic, symbolic
FROLIK	frolic
GOLIK	hypergolic, Mongolic

HOLIK	alcoholic, workaholic
KOLIC	bucolic, echolic, colic, melancholic, retrocollic
POLIK	bibliopolic, epipolic
ROLIK	rollick
TOLIK	apostolic, diastolic, epistolic, systolic, vicar-apostolic
TROLIK	petrolic

ÔLIN

ÔLIN	all-in
FÔLIN	downfallen, fallen, crestfallen, fall-in
KÔLIN	cauline, call-in
PÔLIN	Pauline, tarpaulin

ŌLING

(See ŌL, add -ing where appropriate.)

ÔLING

(See ÔL, add -ing where appropriate.)

OLING

DOLING	baby-dolling
KOLING	caracolling, colling
LOLING	loblolling, lolling

OLIS

FOLIS	follis
KOLIS	torticollis
POLIS	polis
SOLIS	solace
WOLIS	Cornwallis

ŌLISH

DRŌLISH	drollish
PŌLISH	Polish
SŌLISH	soulish
TRŌLISH	trollish

ÔLISH

GÔLISH	Gaulish
SKWÔLISH	squallish
SMÔLISH	smallish
TÔLISH	tallish

OLISH

BOLISH	abolish
DOLISH	dollish
LOLISH	lollish
MOLISH	demolish, mollish
POLISH	polish

OLISHT

BOLISHT	abolished, reabolished, unabolished
MOLISHT	demolished, redemolished, undemolished
POLISHT	polished, repolished, silver-polished, unpolished

ÔLKAN

BÔLKAN	Balkan
FÔLKAN	falcon

ÔLLES

(See ÔL, add -less where appropriate.)

ŌLMAN

KŌLMAN	coalman
TŌLMAN	tollman

ŌLMENT

DŌLMENT	condolement
JŌLMENT	cajolement
RŌLMENT	enrollment
TRŌLMENT	controlment

ÔLMENT

PÔLMENT	appallment, epaulement
STÔLMENT	installment
THRÔLMENT	disenthrallment, enthrallment

ŌLNES

DRŌLNES	drollness
HŌLNES	wholeness
SŌLNES	soleness

ÔLNES

ÔLNES	allness
SMÔLNES	smallness
TÔLNES	tallness

ŌLŌ

ŌLŌ	criollo
BŌLŌ	bolo, bolo-bolo
CHŌLŌ	cholo
GŌLŌ	golo
KŌLŌ	kolo, yakolo
LŌLŌ	palolo
PŌLŌ	Marco Polo, polo
RŌLŌ	barolo
SŌLŌ	solo
STŌLŌ	stolo

OLŌ

FOLŌ	follow
HOLŌ	hollo, hollow
POLŌ	Apollo
SWOLŌ	swallow
WOLŌ	wallow, hogwallow

(See ÂLŌ)

ŌLOK

MŌLOK	Moloch
RŌLOK	rowlock

OLOK

(See OLUK)

ŌLON

(See ŌLEN)

OLOP

(See OLUP)

ŌLOR

(See ŌLER)

ÔLSER

FÔLSER	falser
WÔLSER	waltzer

ŌLSTER

BŌLSTER	bolster
HŌLSTER	holster, reholster, reupholster, unholster, upholster

ŌLSUM

DŌLSUM	dolesome
HŌLSUM	wholesome, unwholesome

ÔLTA

MÔLTA	Malta
VÔLTA	Volta
YÔLTA	Yalta

ÔLTĒ

FÔLTĒ	faulty
MÔLTĒ	malty
SÔLTĒ	salty
VÔLTĒ	vaulty

ŌLTED

(See ŌLT, add -ed where appropriate.)

ÔLTED

(See ÔLT, add -ed where appropriate.)

ŌLTER

BŌLTER	bolter, unbolter
JŌLTER	jolter
KŌLTER	colter
MŌLTER	molter
VŌLTER	revolter

ÔLTER

ÔLTER	altar, alter, unalter
BRÔLTER	Gibraltar
FÔLTER	defaulter, falter, faulter, foot-faulter
HÔLTER	halter, unhalter, waghalter
MÔLTER	malter
PÔLTER	palter
SMÔLTER	smalter
SÔLTER	assaulter, psalter, salter
VÔLTER	vaulter
ZÔLTER	exalter

ÔLTERN

ÔLTERN	altern, subaltern
SÔLTERN	saltern

ŌLTIJ

BŌLTIJ	boltage
VŌLTIJ	voltage

ÔLTIJ

FÔLTIJ	faultage
MÔLTIJ	maltage
VÔLTIJ	vaultage

ÔLTIK

BÔLTIK	Baltic, cobaltic
FÔLTIK	asphaltic
SÔLTIK	basaltic
STÔLTIK	peristaltic
TÔLTIK	cystaltic

ŌLTING

BŌLTING	bolting, unbolting
JŌLTING	jolting
KŌLTING	colting
MŌLTING	molting
VŌLTING	revolting

ÔLTING

FÔLTING	defaulting, faulting
HÔLTING	halting
MÔLTING	malting
SÔLTING	assaulting, salting
VÔLTING	vaulting
ZÔLTING	exalting

ŌLTISH

DŌLTISH	doltish
KŌLTISH	coltish

ÔLTLES

FÔLTLES	faultless
MÔLTLES	maltless
SÔLTLES	saltless

ÔLTSER

(See ÔLSER)

OLUK

LOLUK	lollock
POLUK	pollack, pollock

ŌLUM

(See ŌLEM)

OLUP

DOLUP	dollop
GOLUP	gollop
JOLUP	jollop
KOLUP	collop
LOLUP	lollop
SKOLUP	escallop, escalop, scallop, scollop
TROLUP	trollop
WOLUP	codswallop, wallop

OLUPT

(See OLUP, add -ed where appropriate.)

ŌLUS

ŌLUS	gladiolus
BŌLUS	bolus, holus-bolus
DŌLUS	dolous, dolus, *subdolous*
SŌLUS	solus

OLVENT

SOLVENT	insolvent, solvent, absolvent
VOLVENT	evolvent
ZOLVENT	dissolvent, resolvent

OLVER

SOLVER	absolver, solver
VOLVER	devolver, evolver, involver, revolver
ZOLVER	dissolver, resolver

OLVING

SOLVING	absolving, dissolving, resolving, solving
VOLVING	devolving, evolving, intervolving, involving, obvolving, revolving, circumvolving
ZOLVING	dissolving, exolving, resolving

ÔLWĀ

HÔLWĀ	hallway
KRÔLWĀ	crawlway

ÔLWĂZ

ÔLWĂZ	always
HÔLWĂZ	hallways
KRÔLWĂZ	crawlways

OLYUM

KOLYUM	colyum
VOLYUM	volume

ŌMA

ŌMA	angioma, glioma, myoma, osteoma
BŌMA	aboma
BRŌMA	broma, firbroma, theobroma
GŌMA	agoma, zygoma
HŌMA	Oklahoma
KŌMA	glaucoma, coma, sarcoma, Tacoma, trachoma
LŌMA	aloma, encephaloma, condyloma, loma, myeloma, papilloma, Point Loma, spiloma
NGOMA	ngoma
NŌMA	adenoma, carcinoma, noma
PLŌMA	diploma
PŌMA	lipoma
RŌMA	aroma, atheroma, Roma, scleroma
SŌMA	prosoma, soma
STŌMA	stoma
STRŌMA	stroma
THŌMA	xanthoma
TŌMA	phytoma, hematoma, scotoma
ZŌMA	rhizoma

ÔMA

KÔMA	cauma
TRÔMA	trauma

OMA

KOMA	comma
MOMA	mama, mamma, momma
SOMA	zyxomma

ŌMAL

BRŌMAL bromal
DŌMAL domal
SŌMAL prosomal, somal
STRŌMAL stromal

ŌMAN

BŌMAN bowman
FŌMAN foeman
RŌMAN Roman
SHŌMAN showman
YŌMAN yeoman

OMBĀ

BOMBĀ Bombay
POMBĀ pombe

OMBA

BOMBA zambomba
DOMBA domba
LOMBA calomba
POMBA pombe
TROMBA tromba

OMBAT

KOMBAT combat
WOMBAT wombat

OMBĒ

DOMBĒ Dombey
ZOMBĒ zombie

OMBER

OMBER omber, ombre
SKOMBER scomber
SOMBER somber

ŌMĒ

ŌMĒ Cleome
DŌMĒ domy
FŌMĒ foamy
HŌMĒ homey, homy
KRŌMĒ photochromy,
heliochromy,
metallochromy,
monochromy,
polychromy,
stereochromy

LŌMĒ loamy, lomi-lomi,
Salome
RŌMĒ roamy

OMĒ

KOMĒ Commie
MOMĒ mommy
POMĒ pommy
TOMĒ tommy

(See ÄMĒ)

OMEL

POMEL pommel
TROMEL trommel

ŌMEN

ŌMEN omen
BŌMEN bowmen
DŌMEN abdomen
FŌMEN foemen
LŌMEN lowmen
NŌMEN agnomen, cognomen,
gnomon, nomen,
praenomen
YŌMEN yeomen

ŌMENT

FŌMENT foment
LŌMENT loment
MŌMENT moment
STŌMENT bestowment

ŌMER

ŌMER Omar, omer
GŌMER gomer, Gomer
HŌMER homer, Homer
KŌMER beachcomber,
comber, wool comber
NŌMER misnomer
RŌMER roamer
VŌMER vomer

OMET

DOMET domett
GROMET grommet
HOMET Mahomet
KOMET comet
VOMET vomit

OMIJ

HOMIJ homage
POMIJ pommage

ŌMIK

ŌMIK ohmic
BRŌMIK bromic, hydrobromic,
theobromic
DŌMIK domic
KRŌMIK achromic,
bathochromic,
dichromic,
heliochromic,
hypsochromic,
chromic,
monochromic,
polychromic,
stereochromic
NŌMIK gnomic

OMIK

OMIK Suomic
BROMIK antibromic,
hydrobromic,
theobromic
DOMIK oecodomic
DROMIK dromic, exodromic,
hippodromic,
loxodromic,
orthodromic,
palindromic,
paradromic,
syndromic
KOMIK acersecomic,
encomic, heroicomic,
comic, quasi-comic,
seriocomic,
tragicomic
KROMIK achromic,
bathochromic,
dichromic,
heliochromic,
hypsochromic,
monochromic,
polychromic,
stereochromic,
xanthochromic
MOMIK cinnamomic
NOMIK *A* agronomic,
astronomic, *B*
bionomic, *D* dinomic,
Deuteronomic, *E*
economic, ennomic,
F physiognomic,
phoronomic, *G*
gastronomic, *I*
isonomic, *K*

chironomic, *M*
metronomic, *N*
gnomic, nomic, *O*
autonomic, *P*
pathognomic,
pyrognomic, *PL*
plutonomic, *S*
socioeconomic, *T*
taxonomic, *U*
uneconomic

PROMIK   promic
SOMIK   acersomic
TOMIK   *A* anatomic, atomic,
D dermatomic,
diatomic, dystomic, *E*
entomic, epitomic, *F*
phantomic, *I*
interatomic, intra-
atomic, *M* microtomic,
monatomic, *O*
orthatomic, *P*
pentomic, *S* subatomic,
ST stereotomic, *T*
tesseratomic, *TR*
triatomic

VOMIK   vomic

OMIKS

KOMIKS   comics
NOMIKS   agronomics,
bionomics,
economics,
Nixonomics,
Reaganomics

(See **OMIK**, add -*s* where appropriate.)

ŌMING

ŌMING   Wyoming
DŌMING   doming
FŌMING   foaming
GLŌMING   gloaming
HŌMING   homing
KŌMING   beachcombing,
haircombing,
honeycombing,
coxcombing,
coaming, combing,
wool combing
KRŌMING   chroming
LŌMING   loaming
RŌMING   roaming

OMIS

PROMIS   promise
TOMIS   doubting Thomas

ŌMISH

DŌMISH   domish
FŌMISH   foamish
LŌMISH   loamish
NŌMISH   gnomish
RŌMISH   Romish
TŌMISH   tomish

ŌMLES

(See **ŌM**, add -*less* where appropriate.)

ŌMLET

DŌMLET   domelet
HŌMLET   homelet
TŌMLET   tomelet

ŌMŌ

DŌMŌ   majordomo
DWŌMŌ   duomo
HŌMŌ   ecce homo, homo
KŌMŌ   Lake Como
KRŌMŌ   chromo
MŌMŌ   momo
PRŌMŌ   promo

OMPĒ

POMPĒ   Pompey
ROMPĒ   rompy
SKOMPĒ   scampi
SWOMPĒ   swampy

OMPISH

ROMPISH   rompish
SWOMPISH   swampish

OMPUS

POMPUS   pompous
WOMPUS   gallywampus,
catawampus, wampus

ŌMUS

DŌMUS   domus
KRŌMUS   chromous
MŌMUS   momus
SŌMUS   disomus

ŌNA

ŌNA   ona
BŌNA   bona, carbona
DRŌNA   madrona
JŌNA   Jonah
KŌNA   kona, cinchona
KRŌNA   krona
LŌNA   Barcelona, Bellona,
bologna
MŌNA   Desdemona, kimono,
mona, Pomona
NŌNA   annona
RŌNA   corona, Verona
SŌNA   persona
TŌNA   Daytona
TRŌNA   trona
ZŌNA   Arizona, canzona, zona

ÔNA

FÔNA   avifauna, fauna,
piscifauna
SÔNA   sauna

ŌNAD

GŌNAD   gonad
MŌNAD   monad

ŌNAL

BŌNAL   subumbonal
FŌNAL   phonal
KRŌNAL   chronal
RŌNAL   coronal
THRŌNAL   thronal
TŌNAL   atonal, tonal
ZŌNAL   polyzonal, zonal

ŌNANT

(See **ŌNENT**)

ŌNĀT

DŌNĀT   donate
FŌNĀT   phonate
PRŌNĀT   pronate
ZŌNĀT   zonate

ÔNCHĒ

HÔNCHĒ   haunchy
KRÔNCHĒ   craunchy
PÔNCHĒ   paunchy
RÔNCHĒ   raunchy

ÔNCHEZ

(See ÔNCH, add -es where appropriate.)

ÔNCHING

HÔNCHING	haunching
KRÔNCHING	craunching
LÔNCHING	launching
STÔNCHING	staunching

ONCHŌ

HONCHŌ	honcho
PONCHŌ	poncho

ONDA

FONDA	Fonda
HONDA	honda, Honda
KONDA	anaconda, *La Gioconda,* Golconda
NONDA	nonda
ZONDA	zonda

ONDED

BONDED	bonded, unbonded
SKONDED	absconded
SPONDED	desponded, corresponded, responded

ŌNDEF

STŌNDEF	stone-deaf
TŌNDEF	tone-deaf

ONDEL

(See ONDL)

ONDENS

SKONDENS	abscondence
SPONDENS	despondence, correspondence, respondence

ONDENT

FRONDENT	frondent
SPONDENT	despondent, corespondent, correspondent, respondent

ÔNDER

LÔNDER	launder
MÔNDER	maunder

ONDER

BLONDER	blonder
BONDER	bonder
FONDER	fonder
KONDER	hypochonder, condor
PONDER	ponder
SKONDER	absconder
SPONDER	desponder, coresponder, corresponder, responder
YONDER	yonder

(See ÄNDER)

ONDIJ

BONDIJ	bondage, vagabondage
FRONDIJ	frondage

ONDING

ONDING	onding
BONDING	bonding, female-bonding, male-bonding, pair-bonding
SKONDING	absconding
SPONDING	desponding, corresponding, responding

ONDL

FONDL	fondle
RONDL	rondel, rondle

ONDLĒ

BLONDLĒ	blondly
FONDLĒ	fondly, overfondly

ONDNES

BLONDNES	blondness, blondeness
FONDNES	fondness

ONDŌ

HONDŌ	Hondo
KONDŌ	condo
RONDŌ	rondeau, rondo
TONDŌ	tondo

ŌNĒ

BŌNĒ	bony
DŌNĒ	Bodoni, chalcedony
DRŌNĒ	drony, padrone
FŌNĒ	phony, lamprophony, *euphony*
GŌNĒ	gony, kongoni
KŌNĒ	cony, Marconi
KRŌNĒ	crony
LŌNĒ	abalone, baloney, bologna, globaloney, cannelloni, polony
MŌNĒ	agrimony, acrimony, alimony, antimony, querimony, matrimony, palimony, parsimony, patrimony, sanctimony, ceremony, spumone, testimony
PŌNĒ	compony, pony
RŌNĒ	chitarrone, lazzaroni, macaroni, cicerone
SHŌNĒ	Shoshone
STŌNĒ	stony
STRŌNĒ	minestrone
TŌNĒ	panettone, tony, tortoni
YŌNĒ	yoni, zabaglione
ZŌNĒ	calzone, canzone

ÔNĒ

ÔNĒ	awny
BRÔNĒ	brawny
DÔNĒ	dawny
FÔNĒ	fawny
LÔNĒ	lawny
PÔNĒ	pawnee
PRÔNĒ	prawny
SKRÔNĒ	scrawny
SÔNĒ	sawney
SWÔNĒ	Suwanee, Swanee
TÔNĒ	mulligatawny, orange-tawny, Punxsutawney, tawny
YÔNĒ	yawny

ONĒ

BONĒ	bonnie, bonny
GONĒ	paizogony

RONĒ	gironny, gyronny
SWONĒ	Swanee, swanny
WONĒ	Sewanee
YONĒ	yonnie
ZONĒ	mezonny

(See ÄNE)

ŌNENT

PŌNENT	deponent, exponent, imponent, interponent, component, opponent, ponent, proponent
SŌNENT	intersonant, rhonisonant, sonant, supersonant
TŌNENT	tonant

ŌNER

ŌNER	landowner, co-owner, non-owner, owner, part-owner, shipowner
BŌNER	boner
DŌNER	donor, condoner
DRŌNER	droner
FŌNER	phoner, telephoner
GRŌNER	groaner, grunt-and-groaner
HŌNER	honer
LŌNER	loaner, loner
MŌNER	bemoaner, moaner
PŌNER	postponer
STŌNER	stoner
THRŌNER	dethroner, enthroner
TŌNER	atoner, intoner, toner

ÔNER

ÔNER	awner
BRÔNER	brawner
FÔNER	fawner
GÔNER	goner
PÔNER	pawner
SPÔNER	spawner
YÔNER	yawner

ONER

ONER	dishonor, honor, Scout's honor, Your Honor
KONER	aleconner, conner

ONERD

ONERD	honored
DONERD	donnered

ŌNES

LŌNES	lowness
SLŌNES	slowness

ONET

BONET	bluebonnet, bonnet, graybonnet, unbonnet
SONET	sonnet

ONGER

LONGER	longer, prolonger
PRONGER	pronger
RONGER	wronger
STRONGER	stronger
TONGER	tonger

ONGFUL

RONGFUL	wrongful
SONGFUL	songful
THRONGFUL	throngful

ONGGA

BONGGA	bonga
DONGGA	donga
KONGGA	conga
TONGGA	Batonga, tonga, Tonga
WONGGA	wonga, wonga-wonga

ONGGER

KONGGER	conger
LONGGER	longer
STRONGGER	stronger

ONGING

DONGING	ding-donging, donging
FONGING	underfonging
LONGING	belonging, longing, prolonging
PONGING	ponging
RONGING	wronging
THRONGING	thronging

ONGISH

LONGISH	longish
RONGISH	wrongish
STRONGISH	strongish

ONGKĒ

DONGKĒ	donkey
HONGKĒ	honkie, honky
KONGKĒ	conky
TONGKĒ	honkytonky
WONGKĒ	wonky

ONGKER

HONGKER	honker
KONGKER	conker, conquer, reconquer

ONGKERS

BONGKERZ	bonkers
HONKERZ	honkers
YONKERZ	Yonkers

ONGKUS

BRONGKUS	bronchus
RONGKUS	rhonchus

ONGLĒ

LONGLĒ	longly
RONGLĒ	wrongly
STRONGLĒ	strongly

ONGNES

LONGNES	longness
RONGNES	wrongness

ŌNIJ

DRŌNIJ	dronage
NŌNIJ	nonage
RŌNIJ	chaperonage
TRŌNIJ	tronage

ONIK

ONIK	A amphictyonic, avionic, B bionic, E embryonic, F

	Pharaonic, *G*	**MONIK**	*A* ammonic,
	gallionic, ganglionic,		anharmonic, *B*
	H histrionic, *I*		daemonic, demonic,
	interganglionic, ionic,		*E* enharmonic,
	K chameleonic, *N*		etymonic, *F*
	Napoleonic,		philharmonic, *H*
	nucleonic, *O*		harmonic,
	Olympionic, *P*		hegemonic, *N*
	paeonic, pantheonic,		mnemonic,
	T talionic, *TH*		gnomonic,
	thermionic, thionic, *Z*		nonharmonic,
	zoonic		pneumonic, *P*
BONIK	bubonic, carbonic,		pathognomonic,
	Sorbonic		pulmonic, *S*
BRONIK	vibronic		sermonic,
DONIK	Adonic, algedonic,		cinnamonic,
	hedonic,		Solomonic, *U*
	Chalcedonic,		eudaemonic
	chelidonic, sardonic	**NONIK**	canonic, nonic
FONIK	*A* antiphonic,	**PONIK**	hydroponic, Japonic,
	aphonic, *B*		geoponic
	baryphonic, *D*	**RONIK**	Byronic, ironic,
	diaphonic,		macaronic, moronic,
	dodecaphonic, *F*		Neronic, Pyrrhonic,
	phonic, photophonic,		stentoronic
	H homophonic, *K*	**SONIK**	freemasonic, imsonic,
	cacophonic,		infrasonic, masonic,
	cataphonic,		parsonic, subsonic,
	colophonic, *KW*		supersonic, transonic,
	quadraphonic, *M*		ultrasonic
	megaphonic,	**THONIK**	benthonic, Brythonic,
	megalophonic,		gnathonic, pythonic,
	microphonic,		chthonic
	monophonic, *P*	**TONIK**	*A* architectonic,
	polyphonic, *R*		atonic, *D* diatonic, *E*
	radiophonic, *S*		electrotonic, epitonic,
	psaphonic,		*F* phototonic, *H*
	saxophonic, siphonic,		hematonic,
	symphonic, *ST*		hypertonic,
	stentorophonic,		hypotonic,
	stereophonic, *T*		Housatonic, *I*
	telephonic, typhonic,		isotonic, *KR* crotonic,
	U euphonic, *Z*		*M* Metonic, Miltonic,
	xylophonic		monotonic, *N*
GONIK	agonic, glottogonic,		neoplatonic,
	isogonic, jargonic,		neuratonic, *O*
	geogonic,		orthotonic, *P*
	cosmogonic,		paratonic, pentatonic,
	polygonic, theogonic,		polytonic, *PL*
	trigonic		planktonic, platonic,
KLONIK	anticyclonic,		plutonic, *PR* protonic,
	cyclonic, clonic		*S* semitonic, syntonic,
KONIK	aconic, aniconic,		subtonic, supertonic,
	draconic, iconic,		*STR* stratonic, *T*
	conic, laconic,		tectonic, tonic,
	obconic, polyconic,		Teutonic
	Tychonic, zirconic	**TRONIK**	electronic,
KRONIK	acronic, anachronic,		microelectronic,
	diachronic, chronic,		technetronic
	monochronic,	**VONIK**	Slavonic
	synchronic	**YONIK**	yonic
LONIK	Babylonic, colonic	**ZONIK**	ozonic, zonic

ONIKS

ONIKS	avionics, bionics, histrionics, cryonics, nucleonics, onyx, thermionics
DONIKS	hedonics, chalcedonyx, sardonyx
FONIKS	phonics, quadraphonics
KONIKS	conics
LONIKS	Megalonyx
MONIKS	harmonics, mnemonics, gnomonics, eudaemonics
PONIKS	hydroponics, geoponics
SONIKS	supersonics, ultrasonics
TONIKS	tectonics
TRONIKS	electronics, microelectronics

(See **ONIK**, add *-s* where appropriate.)

ŌNING

BŌNING	boning, jawboning

(See **ŌN**, add *-ing* where appropriate.)

ÔNING

ÔNING	awning
DÔNING	dawning
FÔNING	fawning
PÔNING	pawning
SPÔNING	spawning
YÔNING	yawning

ONING

DONING	donning
KONING	conning

ŌNISH

DRŌNISH	dronish
KŌNISH	conish
LŌNISH	Babylonish
STŌNISH	stonish

ONISH

DONISH	donnish
MONISH	admonish, monish, premonish

STONISH	stonish
TONISH	astonish, tonish, tonnish
WONISH	wannish

ONJĒ

KONJĒ	congee
PONJĒ	pongee

ŌNLĒ

ŌNLĒ	eyes-only, only, one-and-only
LŌNLĒ	alonely, lonely
PRŌNLĒ	pronely

ŌNLES

(See ŌN, add -less where appropriate.)

ŌNMENT

ŌNMENT	disownment
DŌNMENT	condonement
PŌNMENT	postponement
THRŌNMENT	dethronement, enthronement
TŌNMENT	atonement, intonement

ŌNNES

ŌNNES	ownness
LŌNNES	aloneness, loneness
NŌNNES	knownness, unknownness
PRŌNNES	proneness

ŌNŌ

FŌNŌ	fono, phono
MŌNŌ	kakemono, kimono, makimono
NŌNŌ	no-no

ONSL

KONSL	consul, proconsul, vice-consul
SPONSL	responsal, sponsal
TONSL	tonsil

ONSOR

SPONSOR	sponsor
TONSOR	chirotonsor, tonsor

ONTAL

ONTAL	ontal
DONTAL	periodontal
FONTAL	fontal
FRONTAL	frontal
KWONTAL	quantal
PONTAL	pontal
RONTAL	gerontal
ZONTAL	horizontal

ÔNTĒ

FLÔNTĒ	flaunty
HÔNTĒ	haunty
JÔNTĒ	jaunty
VÔNTĒ	vaunty

ÔNTED

DÔNTED	daunted, undaunted
FLÔNTED	flaunted
HÔNTED	haunted
JÔNTED	jaunted
TÔNTED	taunted
VÔNTED	vaunted
WÔNTED	help wanted, unwanted, wanted

ÔNTER

(See ÔNT, add -er where appropriate.)

ONTIF

PONTIF	pontiff
YONTIF	yontif

ONTIJ

PONTIJ	pontage
WONTIJ	wantage

ONTIK

ONTIK	Anacreontic
DONTIK	mastodontic, odontic, orthodontic, periodontic
KONTIK	archontic
KWONTIK	quantic
PONTIK	pontic
RONTIK	gerontic

ONTĪN

KONTĪN	dracontine

PONTĪN	Hellespontine, pontine, cispontine, transpontine

ONTIN

KONTIN	dracontine
PONTIN	Hellespontine, pontine, cispontine, transpontine
TONTIN	tontine

ÔNTING

DÔNTING	daunting, undaunting
FLÔNTING	flaunting
JÔNTING	jaunting
TÔNTING	taunting
VÔNTING	vaunting
WÔNTING	wanting

ÔNTLES

DÔNTLES	dauntless
WÔNTLES	wantless

ONTŌ

KONTŌ	conto
PRONTŌ	pronto
RONTŌ	Toronto
TONTŌ	Tonto

ONTON

FRONTON	fronton
WONTON	wanton, wonton

ONTUS

DONTUS	microdontous
HONTUS	Pocahontas

ŌNUS

ŌNUS	onus
BŌNUS	bonus
LŌNUS	colonus
KŌNUS	conus
TŌNUS	tonus

ONZŌ

BONZŌ	Bonzo
GONZŌ	gonzo

OOA

HOOA	lehua
LOOA	ulua

(See ŪA)

OOAL

(See OOEL, ŬAL)

OOAN

(See OOIN)

OOANS

CHOOANS	eschewance

(See ŬANS)

OOANT

(See OOENT)

OOBA

JOOBA	juba
POOBA	pooh-bah
ROOBA	Aruba, Simarouba
SKOOBA	scuba
SOOBA	subah, tsuba
TOOBA	saxtuba, tuba

(See ŪBA)

OOBÂL

SKROOBÂL	screwball

(See ŬBÂL)

OOBAL

JOOBAL	Jubal

(See ŬBAL)

OOBĒ

BOOBĒ	booby
DOOBĒ	do-bee
JOOBĒ	jube
LOOBĒ	looby
ROOBĒ	ruby

(See ŪBĒ)

OOBER

GOOBER	goober
KOOBER	Khubur
ZOOBER	zubr

(See ŪBER)

OOBĒZ

BOOBĒZ	boobies
LOOBĒZ	loobies
ROOBĒZ	rubies

(See ŪBĒZ)

OOBIK

ROOBIK	cherubic, Rubic

(See ŬBIK)

OOBING

LOOBING	lubing

(See ŪBING)

OOBIT

TOOBIT	two-bit

(See ŪBIT)

OOBL

JOOBL	Jubal
ROOBL	ruble
TOOBL	tubal

(See ŪBL)

OOBRIK

LOOBRIK	lubric
ROOBRIK	rubric

OOCHĒ

DOOCHĒ	Il Duce
KOOCHĒ	hootchy-kootchy
LOOCHĒ	Baluchi
MOOCHĒ	mamamouchi
NOOCHĒ	penuche, penuchi
POOCHĒ	poochy, Vespucci
SMOOCHĒ	smoochy

OOCHER

MOOCHER	moocher
SMOOCHER	smoocher
SPOOCHER	spoucher

(See ŬCHER)

OODA

BOODA	Buddha
JOODA	Judah
KOODA	barracuda, picuda
MOODA	remuda

(See ŬDA)

OODAL

(See OODL)

OODĒ

BOODĒ	boodie
BROODĒ	broody
GOODĒ	wally-goudy
HOODĒ	yehudi, Yehudi
MOODĒ	almude, moody

(See ŪDĒ)

OODĔ

GOODĔ	goody, goody-goody
HOODĔ	hoody
WOODĔ	woody

OODED

(See OOD, ŪD, add -ed where appropriate.)

OODĔD

HOODĔD	hooded
WOODĔD	dense-wooded, green-wooded, copse-wooded, red-wooded, thick-wooded, well-wooded (etc.), wooded

OODENS

PROODENS	jurisprudence, prudence

(See OODENT, ŬDENT, add -s or change -t to -ce where appropriate.)

OŌDENT

KLOŌDENT	concludent, occludent
PROŌDENT	imprudent, jurisprudent, prudent
STOŌDENT	student

(See ŪDENT)

OŌDER

BROŌDER	brooder
KLOŌDER	excluder, includer, concluder
KROŌDER	cruder
ROŌDER	ruder
SHROŌDER	shrewder
TOŌDER	two-door, Tudor
TROŌDER	detruder, extruder, intruder, protruder

OODER

| GOODER | do-gooder |
| HOODER | hooder |

OŌDIK

(See ŪDIK)

OŌDING

BROŌDING	brooding
KLOŌDING	excluding, including, concluding, occluding, precluding, secluding
LOŌDING	alluding, deluding, eluding, colluding
TROŌDING	detruding, extruding, intruding, protruding, retruding, subtruding
ZOŌDING	exuding

(See ŪDER)

OODING

GOODING	do-gooding
HOODING	hooding
POODING	Indian pudding, pudding

OŌDISH

MOŌDISH	moodish
PROŌDISH	prudish
ROŌDISH	rudish

(See ŪDISH)

OODISH

GOODISH	goodish
HOODISH	hoodish
WOODISH	woodish

OŌDIST

| BOŌDIST | Buddhist |
| PROŌDIST | prudist |

(See ŪDIST)

OŌDL

BOŌDL	boodle, caboodle
DOŌDL	doodle, flapdoodle, fopdoodle, whangdoodle, cadoodle, wingdoodle, Yankee Doodle
KOŌDL	coodle
KROŌDL	croodle
LOŌDL	paludal
NOŌDL	canoodle, noodle
POŌDL	poodle
ROŌDL	roodle
SOŌDL	soodle
STROŌDL	strudel

(See ŪDL)

OŌDLĒ

KROŌDLĒ	crudely
PROŌDLĒ	prudely
ROŌDLĒ	rudely
SHROŌDLĒ	shrewdly

(See ŪDLĒ)

OŌDLZ

| OŌDLZ | oodles |

(See OŌDL, add -s where appropriate.)

OODMAN

GOODMAN	goodman
HOODMAN	hoodman
WOODMAN	woodman

OŌDNES

KROŌDNES	crudeness
LOŌDNES	lewdness
ROŌDNES	rudeness
SHROŌDNES	shrewdness

(See ŪDNES)

OŌDŌ

BOŌDŌ	barbudo, budo
KOŌDŌ	picudo
SKOŌDŌ	escudo, scudo

(See ŪDŌ

OŌDOO

HOŌDOO	hoodoo
POŌDOO	pudu
TOŌDOO	to-do
VOŌDOO	voodoo

OŌĒ

BLOŌĒ	blooie, bluey
BOŌĒ	bambui, bowie, buoy, Drambuie
CHOŌĒ	chewy
FLOŌĒ	flooey, fluey
FOŌĒ	fooey, pfui, phooey
GLOŌĒ	gluey
GOŌĒ	gooey
HOŌĒ	hooey, hui
KOŌĒ	cooee
SKROŌĒ	screwy
SOŌĒ	chop suey
TOŌĒ	ratatouille, tattooey, tui

(See ŪĒ)

OŌEL

CHOŌEL	eschewal
DOŌEL	dual, duel
GROŌEL	gruel
JOŌEL	bejewel, jewel
KROŌEL	crewel, cruel
SHOŌEL	shewel

(See ŪAL)

OŌEN

(See OŌIN)

OŌENT

| FLOŌENT | fluent, confluent, perfluent |

LOO͞ENT   eluent
SOO͞ENT   pursuant, suant
TROO͞ENT   truant

OO͞ER

BLOO͞ER   bluer
BROO͞ER   brewer
CHOO͞ER   chewer, eschewer
DOO͞ER   doer, evildoer, misdoer, outdoer, overdoer, wrongdoer, undoer
GLOO͞ER   gluer, ungluer
KOO͞ER   cooer
KROO͞ER   cruer
NOO͞ER   canoer, revenuer
POO͞ER   pooh-pooher, shampooer
ROO͞ER   ruer
SHOO͞ER   shoer
SOO͞ER   pursuer, sewer, suer
SKROO͞ER   screwer
STROO͞ER   strewer
TOO͞ER   tattooer
TROO͞ER   truer
WOO͞ER   wooer

(See U͞ER)

OO͞ERD

LOO͞ERD   leeward

(See U͞ERD)

OO͞ET

BLOO͞ET   bluet
CHOO͞ET   chewet
KROO͞ET   cruet
MOO͞ET   Moet
SOO͞ET   suet
TOO͞ET   intuit

O͞OF

BLO͞OF   blow-off
FLO͞OF   flow-off
SHO͞OF   show-off

OO͞FA

BOO͞FA   buffa
CHOO͞FA   chufa
GOO͞FA   gufa
LOO͞FA   catalufa, loofa

STOO͞FA   stufa
TOO͞FA   tufa

OO͞FĒ

OO͞FĒ   oofy
GOO͞FĒ   goofy
ROO͞FĒ   roofy
SPOO͞FĒ   spoofy
WOO͞FĒ   woofy

OO͞FER

GOO͞FER   goofer
LOO͞FER   aloofer
ROO͞FER   roofer
SPOO͞FER   spoofer
TOO͞FER   twofer
WOO͞FER   woofer

OO͞FING

GOO͞FING   goofing
PROO͞FING   bulletproofing, waterproofing, weatherproofing
ROO͞FING   composition roofing, roofing, cedar roofing, shake roofing, shingle roofing
SPOO͞FING   spoofing
WOO͞FING   woofing

OO͞FLES

GOO͞FLES   goofless
HOO͞FLES   hoofless
PROO͞FLES   proofless
ROO͞FLES   roofless
SPOO͞FLES   spoofless
WOO͞FLES   woofless

OO͞FUS

GOO͞FUS   goofus
ROO͞FUS   hirsutorufous, rufous

OO͞GA

FOO͞GA   fuga
LOO͞GA   beluga
MOO͞GA   mooga
NOO͞GA   Chattanooga
ROO͞GA   ruga
YOO͞GA   yuga

OO͞GAL

(See OO͞GL)

OO͞GĒ

BOO͞GĒ   boogey
POO͞GĒ   poogye
WOO͞GĒ   boogie-woogie

OO͞GER

KOO͞GER   cougar
LOO͞GER   Luger
SNOO͞GER   snooger

OO͞GER

BOO͞GER   booger
SHOO͞GER   beet sugar, brown sugar, cane sugar, maple sugar, spun sugar, sugar

OO͞GL

FROO͞GL   frugal, unfrugal
GOO͞GL   Barney Google
JOO͞GL   jugal, *conjugal*

(See U͞GL)

OO͞ID

BLOO͞ID   blue-eyed
TROO͞ID   true-eyed

(See U͞ID)

OO͞ID

DROO͞ID   druid
FLOO͞ID   fluid, semifluid, superfluid

OO͞IJ

BROO͞IJ   brewage
SOO͞IJ   sewage

See U͞IJ)

OO͞IK

LOO͞IK   toluic

(See U͞IK)

OOIN

BROOIN	Bruin
LOOIN	punaluan
SOOIN	auruin, ruin
SOOIN	sewen

(See **OOAN**)

OOING

(See **OO**, **U**, add *-ing* where appropriate.)

OOISH

BLOOISH	blueish
GLOOISH	glueish
JOOISH	Jewish

> There is a Greek word *synathroesmus* which means ''the piling up of adjectives.'' This is the way it works:
>
> *THE SYNATHROESMIC CAT*
>
> O mangy cat, O scruffy cat,
> O one-eyed, bobtailed, toughy cat—
> You're fleas and meows from foot to head,
> You mouse-destructive quadruped!
>
> At times you are a lazy sort,
> A dozing, lackadaisy sort,
> A sleep-all-day-upon-the-bed—
> With-paws-upended quadruped;
>
> A give-the-sofa-leg-a-swipe,
> Rub-up-against-the-pantleg type;
> But still, dear cat, when all is said,
> A worth-the-bother quadruped.

SHROOISH	shrewish
TROOISH	trueish

(See **UISH**)

OOIST

NOOIST	canoeist

(See **UIST**)

OOJE

BOOJE	bougie
FOOJE	fugie, fuji, Mt. Fuji
ROOJE	rougy, rugae
SOOJE	suji

OOKA

BOOKA	cambuca, sambouka
FOOKA	Juan de Fuca
LOOKA	felucca, melaleuca, noctiluca, palooka
NOOKA	manuka, nucha
ROOKA	farruca, garookuh, verruca
TOOKA	festuca, fistuca, katuka
ZOOKA	bazooka

(See **UKA**)

OOKA

HOOKA	hookah
LOOKA	felucca

OOKAL

KOOKAL	coucal

(See **UKAL**)

OOKAN

TOOKAN	toucan

(See **UKAN**)

OOKE

BOOKE	kabuki
FLOOKE	fluky
KOOKE	kooky
ROOKE	rouky
SNOOKE	snooky
SOOKE	sookie
SPOOKE	spooky
ZOOKE	bouzouki

OOKE

BOOKE	bookie, booky
BROOKE	brooky
HOOKE	hookey, hooky
KOOKE	cookie, cooky, sugar cooky
LOOKE	looky
NOOKE	nooky
ROOKE	rookie, rooky

OOKER

FLOOKER	fluker
LOOKER	involucre, lucre
SNOOKER	snooker

(See **UKER**)

OOKER

BOOKER	booker
HOOKER	hooker
CHOOKER	chukar
KOOKER	electric cooker, fireless cooker, cooker, pressure cooker
LOOKER	bad-looker, good-looker, landlooker, looker, onlooker, overlooker
ROOKER	rooker
STOOKER	stooker

OOKING

BOOKING	booking, overbooking, rebooking, underbooking
BROOKING	brooking
HOOKING	hooking, unhooking
KOOKING	cooking, overcooking, undercooking
LOOKING	bad-looking, good-looking, ill-looking, looking, onlooking, overlooking, well-looking

OOKISH

BOOKISH	bookish
HOOKISH	hookish
KOOKISH	cookish
KROOKISH	crookish
NOOKISH	nookish
ROOKISH	rookish

OOKLET

BOOKLET	booklet
BROOKLET	brooklet
NOOKLET	nooklet

OOKOO

KOOKOO	kavakuku, coocoo, kuku
POOKOO	seppuku
TOOKOO	kotukuku

OOKUS

(See **UKUS**)

OOKT

(See **OOK,** add *-ed*)

OOLA

BOOLA	Ashtabula, bamboula, boola, boola-boola
BROOLA	zebrula
GOOLA	goolah
HOOLA	hula-hula
JOOLA	joola
KOOLA	Bellacoola
MOOLA	moola
SOOLA	Missoula

OOLĒ

OOLĒ	oolly
BLOOLĒ	bluely
BOOLĒ	booly
CHOOLĒ	patchouli
DROOLĒ	drooly
HOOLĒ	gilhooley
KOOLĒ	douroucouli, Grand Coolee, coulee, coolie, coolly
ROOLĒ	unruly
SKOOLĒ	high-schooly, schoolie, schooly
THOOLĒ	Thule
TOOLĒ	Thule
TROOLĒ	truly, untruly, yours truly
YOOLĒ	guayule

(See **ŪLĒ**)

OOLĒ

BOOLĒ	bully
CHOOLĒ	patchouli
FOOLĒ	fully
MOOLĒ	mulley
POOLĒ	puli, pulley
WOOLĒ	woolly

OOLĒD

BOOLĒD	bullied
POOLĒD	pullied

OOLER

DROOLER	drooler
FOOLER	fooler
KOOLER	cooler, water cooler, wine cooler
POOLER	pooler
ROOLER	ruler
SPOOLER	spooler
TOOLER	retooler, tooler

(See **ŪLER**)

OOLER

BOOLER	buller
FOOLER	fuller
POOLER	puller, wire puller

OOLES

JOOLES	Jewless
KLOOLES	clueless
SKROOLES	screwless

(See **Ū, OO,** add *-less* where appropriate.)

OOLET

BOOLET	bullet, magic bullet
KOOLET	culett
POOLET	pullet

OOLING

DROOLING	drooling
FOOLING	fooling
KOOLING	cooling, recooling
POOLING	pooling
ROOLING	misruling, overruling, ruling
SKOOLING	schooling
SPOOLING	spooling
STOOLING	stooling
TOOLING	retooling, tooling

(See **ŪLING**)

OOLING

BOOLING	bulling
POOLING	pulling, wire-pulling

OOLIP

JOOLIP	julep, mint julep
TOOLIP	tulip

(See **ŪLIP**)

OOLISH

FOOLISH	foolish, pound-foolish, tomfoolish
GOOLISH	ghoulish
KOOLISH	coolish
SKOOLISH	schoolish

(See **ŪLISH**)

OOLISH

BOOLISH	bullish
FOOLISH	fullish
WOOLISH	woolish

OOLLES

(See **OOL,** add *-less* where appropriate.)

OOLOO

OOLOO	ulu
HOOLOO	hulu

> **WHY THINKING IS ITS OWN WORST ENEMY**
>
> How dangerous it is to *think!*
> To think too much may make you *know;*
> To know too much may make you *drink;*
> To drink too much may make you *throw*
> *All thought of thinking down the sink.*
> How dangerous it is to think!

LOOLOO	Honolulu, Lulu, lulu
SOOLOO	Sulu
ZOOLOO	Zulu

OOMA

DOOMA	Duma
ROOMA	empyreuma
SOOMA	satsuma
ZOOMA	mazuma, Montezuma

(See **ŪMA**)

OOMAL

BROOMAL	brumal
TOOMAL	tombal

OOMĒ

BLOOMĒ	bloomy
BOOMĒ	boomy

BRO͞OMĒ	broomy
GLO͞OMĒ	gloomy
GRO͞OMĒ	groomy
PLO͞OMĒ	plumy
RO͞OMĒ	rheumy, roomy

(See ŪMĒ)

O͞OMEN

FLO͞OMEN	flumen
KRO͞OMEN	crewmen
NO͞OMEN	numen
RO͞OMEN	rumen, cerumen

(See ŪMEN)

O͞OMENT

BRO͞OMENT	imbruement
CHO͞OMENT	eschewment
KRO͞OMENT	accruement

(See ŪMENT)

O͞OMER

BLO͞OMER	bloomer, late-bloomer
BO͞OMER	baby-boomer, boomer, schuss-boomer
DO͞OMER	doomer
GRO͞OMER	animal groomer, dog groomer, groomer, hair groomer, cat groomer
PLO͞OMER	plumer
RO͞OMER	roomer, rumor
STO͞OMER	stumor
TO͞OMER	entomber, tumor

(See ŪMER)

O͞OMERD

BLO͞OMERD	bloomered
RO͞OMERD	rumored

(See ŪMERD)

O͞OMIJ

DO͞OMIJ	doomage
PLO͞OMIJ	plumage
RO͞OMIJ	roomage

(See ŪMIJ)

O͞OMIK

TO͞OMIK	tombic

(See ŪMIK)

O͞OMING

(See O͞OM, ŪM, add -ing where appropriate.)

O͞OMKĒ

KO͞OMKĒ	koomkie
RO͞OMKĒ	room key

O͞OMLES

(See O͞OM, ŪM, add -less where appropriate.)

O͞OMO͞O

O͞OMO͞O	umu
MO͞OMO͞O	muumuu, mumu

O͞OMUS

BRO͞OMUS	brumous
GRO͞OMUS	grumous
PLO͞OMUS	plumous

(See ŪMUS)

O͞OMZMAN

DO͞OMZMAN	doomsman
GRO͞OMZMAN	groomsman

O͞ONA

GO͞ONA	guna
HO͞ONA	kahuna
KO͞ONA	lacuna, vicuna
LO͞ONA	luna, Luna
PO͞ONA	puna
RO͞ONA	koruna
TO͞ONA	tuna

(See ŪNA)

O͞ONAL

GO͞ONAL	lagoonal

(See ŪNAL)

O͞ONĒ

KLO͞ONĒ	Cluny
LO͞ONĒ	loony
MO͞ONĒ	Moonie, moony, Sakyamuni
SPO͞ONĒ	spoony
SWO͞ONĒ	swoony
TO͞ONĒ	festoony

(See ŪNĒ)

O͞ONER

GO͞ONER	dragooner
KRO͞ONER	crooner
LO͞ONER	ballooner, extralunar, interlunar, lunar, novilunar, plenilunar, semilunar, circumlunar, cislunar, sublunar, translunar
MO͞ONER	honeymooner, mooner
PO͞ONER	harpooner, lampooner
PRO͞ONER	pruner
RO͞ONER	marooner, runer
SKO͞ONER	schooner
SO͞ONER	sooner
SPO͞ONER	spooner
SWO͞ONER	swooner

(See ŪNER)

O͞ONES

BLO͞ONES	blueness
TRO͞ONES	trueness

(See ŪNES)

O͞ONĒZ

BO͞ONĒZ	boonies
LO͞ONĒZ	loonies
MO͞ONĒZ	Moonies

O͞ONFUL

LO͞ONFUL	balloonful
RO͞ONFUL	runeful
SPO͞ONFUL	spoonful, tablespoonful, teaspoonful
TO͞ONFUL	tuneful

(See ŪNFUL)

OŌNIK

ROŌNIK	runic
TOŌNIK	tunic

(See ŪNIK)

OŌNING

KROŌNING	crooning
LOŌNING	ballooning
MOŌNING	mooning
NOŌNING	nooning
POŌNING	harpooning, lampooning
PROŌNING	pruning
SOŌNING	bassooning
SPOŌNING	spooning
SWOŌNING	swooning
TOŌNING	cartooning, tuning

(See ŪNING)

OŌNISH

(See OŌN, ŪN, add -ish where appropriate.)

OŌNIST

DOŌNIST	rigadoonist
JOŌNIST	jejunest
LOŌNIST	balloonist
POŌNIST	harpoonist
SOŌNIST	bassoonist
TOŌNIST	cartoonist, opportunist

(See ŪNIST)

OŌNIZM

FOŌNIZM	buffoonism
TROŌNIZM	poltroonism

(See ŪNIZM)

OŌNLES

BLOŌNLES	doubloonless
BOŌNLES	babyoonless, boonless
DOŌNLES	bridoonless, doonless, rigadoonless
DROŌNLES	gadroonless, quadroonless
FOŌNLES	buffoonless, typhoonless
GOŌNLES	dragoonless, goonless, lagoonless
JOŌNLES	Juneless
KOŌNLES	barracoonless, cacoonless, cocoonless, coonless, raccoonless, rockoonless, tycoonless
LOŌNLES	balloonless, galloonless, pantaloonless, saloonless, shalloonless, Walloonless
MOŌNLES	honeymoonless, moonless
NOŌNLES	noonless
POŌNLES	harpoonless, lampoonless, poonless
ROŌNLES	floroonless, macaroonless, octoroonless, runeless, seroonless, vinegarroonless
SHOŌNLES	shoonless
SKOŌNLES	scoonless
SOŌNLES	bassoonless, gossoonless, monsoonless
SPOŌNLES	spoonless, tablespoonless, teaspoonless
TOŌNLES	altunless, frigatoonless, cartoonless, coquetoonless, musketoonless, pontoonless, platoonless, ratoonless, spittoonless, spontoonless, toonless
TROŌNLES	quintroonless, patroonless, poltroonless

(See ŪNLES)

OŌNLĪT

MOŌNLĪT	moonlight
NOŌNLĪT	noonlight

OŌNLIT

MOŌNLIT	moonlit
NOŌNLIT	noonlit

OŌNNES

JOŌNNES	jejuneness, Juneness

(See ŪNNES)

OŌNŌ

OŌNŌ	Numero Uno, uno
JOŌNŌ	Juneau, Juno

(See ŪNŌ)

OŌNUM

OŌNUM	e pluribus unum
JOŌNUM	jejunum

OŌPA

ROŌPA	rupa, kamarupa
SOŌPA	supa
STOŌPA	stupa
TOŌPA	ketupa

(See ŪPA)

OŌPĒ

DROŌPĒ	droopy
GROŌPĒ	groupie
HWOŌPĒ	whoopy
KROŌPĒ	croupy
LOŌPĒ	Guadalupe
ROŌPĒ	rupee
SKOŌPĒ	scoopy
SNOŌPĒ	snoopy
SOŌPĒ	soupy
STOŌPĒ	stoopy
SWOŌPĒ	swoopy

(See ŪPĒ)

OŌPER

BLOŌPER	blooper
DOŌPER	super-duper
DROŌPER	drooper
GROŌPER	grouper
HOŌPER	hooper
HWOŌPER	whooper
KOŌPER	cooper, recouper
KROŌPER	crouper
LOŌPER	looper, loop-the-looper

SKOŌPER	pooper-scooper, scooper
SNOŌPER	snooper
SOŌPER	peasouper, souper, super
STOŌPER	stooper, stupor
SWOŌPER	swooper
TROŌPER	mosstrooper, paratrooper, stormtrooper, trooper, trouper

(See ŪPER)

OŌPING

(See OŌP, ŪP, add -ing where appropriate.)

OŌPISH

DROŌPISH	droopish
GROŌPISH	groupish
KROŌPISH	croupish
LOŌPISH	loopish
SKOŌPISH	scoopish
SNOŌPISH	snoopish
STOŌPISH	stoopish
SWOŌPISH	swoopish

OŌPL

DOŌPL	duple, subduple
DROŌPL	drupel, quadruple
SKROŌPL	scruple
TOŌPL	quintuple, octuple, centuple, septuple, sextuple

(See ŪPL)

OŌPLET

DROŌPLET	drupelet, quadruplet
HOŌPLET	hooplet
LOŌPLET	looplet
TOŌPLET	quintuplet, octuplet, septuplet, sextuplet

OŌPMENT

GROŌPMENT	aggroupment, groupment, regroupment
KOŌPMENT	recoupment

OŌPON

JOŌPON	jupon

KOŌPON	coupon
YOŌPON	yupon

(See ŪPON)

OŌRA

BOŌRA	tamboura
JOŌRA	jura
KOŌRA	cura
LOŌRA	lura
ROŌRA	tambaroora
SHOŌRA	fissura, flexura
TOŌRA	acciaccatura, appoggiatura, coloratura, scordatura, tarsiatura, territura, velatura, vettura, villegiatura

(See ŪRA)

OŌRA

DOŌRA	madura
JOŌRA	Jura
PLOŌRA	pleura
SOŌRA	asura, sura, surra, surrah

OŌRAL

JOŌRAL	jural
KROŌRAL	bicrural, crural
PLOŌRAL	pleural, plural
ROŌRAL	rural
SHOŌRAL	commisural

OŌRANS

(See ŪRANS)

OŌRAT

JOŌRAT	jurat
SOŌRAT	surat

OŌRĒ

BROŌRĒ	brewery
DOŌRĒ	tandoori
HOŌRĒ	houri
JOŌRĒ	Jewry
POŌRE	potpourri

(See ŪRĒ)

OŌRĒ

FLOŌRĒ	fleury, counterfleury
JOŌRĒ	de jure, grand jury, jury, petit jury
LOŌRĒ	lurry
MOŌRĒ	moory
POŌRĒ	potpourri
ZOŌRĒ	Missouri

(See URĒ)

OŌRENS

(See URENS)

OŌRENT

JOŌRENT	adjurant, jurant
SHOŌRENT	assurant, insurant, reassurant

(See URENT)

OŌRER

MOŌRER	moorer, unmoorer
POŌRER	poorer
TOŌRER	detourer, tourer

(See URER)

OŌREST

(See OŌRIST)

OŌRING

CHOŌRING	maturing
DOŌRING	enduring, perenduring, perduring
LOŌRING	alluring

(See ŪRING)

OŌRING

CHOŌRING	caricaturing, maturing
MOŌRING	mooring, unmooring
TOŌRING	detouring, maturing, touring

(See URING)

OŌRISH

CHOŌRISH	amateurish

(See ŪRISH)

OORISH

BOORISH	boorish
CHOORISH	maturish
DOORISH	dourish
MOORISH	Moorish

(See **URISH**)

OORISHT

(See **URISHT**)

OORIST

CHOORIST	caricaturist
DOORIST	dourest
JOORIST	jurist
POORIST	poorest
TOORIST	Intourist, tourist

(See **ŪRIST**)

OORLĒ

DOORLĒ	dourly
CHOORLĒ	maturely
POORLĒ	poorly
SHOORLĒ	surely

(See **URLĒ**)

OORMENT

JOORMENT	abjurement, conjurement
LOORMENT	allurement
NOORMENT	manurement

(See **URMENT**)

OORNES

DOORNES	dourness
POORNES	poorness
SHOORNES	cocksureness

OORŌ

DOORŌ	duro, maduro
SKOORŌ	chiaroscuro
TROORŌ	Truro

(See **URŌ**)

OORTĒ

SHOORTĒ	cocksurety, surety

(See **URTĒ**)

OORUP

(See **URUP**)

OORUS

KROORUS	macrurous

(See **URUS**)

OOSA

DOOSA	medusa, Medusa
LOOSA	lallapaloosa, Tuscaloosa
POOSA	Tallapoosa
ROOSA	babirusa
SOOSA	Sousa
THOOSA	arethusa, Arethusa
TOOSA	tuza

(See **ŪSA**)

OOSAL

KLOOSAL	occlusal
NOOSAL	hypotenusal

(See **ŪSL**)

OOSĒ

DOOSĒ	Duce, Il Duce
GOOSĒ	goosy
JOOSĒ	juicy
MOOSĒ	moosey
SLOOSĒ	sluicy

(See **ŪSĒ**)

OOSENS

(See **ŪSENS**)

OOSENT

(See **ŪSENT**)

OOSER

GOOSER	gooser
JOOSER	juicer
LOOSER	looser
SLOOSER	sluicer
SPROOSER	sprucer
STROOSER	abstruser

(See **ŪSER**)

OOSFUL

GOOSFUL	gooseful
JOOSFUL	juiceful
SNOOSFUL	snooseful

(See **ŪSFUL**)

OOSHAL

DOOSHAL	fiducial
KROOSHAL	crucial

(See **ŪSHAL**)

OOSHED

GOOSHED	goosehead
JOOSHED	juicehead
MOOSHED	moosehead

OOSHER

BOOSHER	busher
POOSHER	drug-pusher, pedal-pusher, pen-pusher, pusher

OOSHING

DOOSHING	douching
ROOSHING	rouching, ruching

OOSHUN

DOOSHUN	caducean
FOOSHUN	Confucian
KROOSHUN	crucian, Rosicrucian
LOOSHUN	*A* ablution, absolution, Aleutian, *D* devolution, dilution, dissolution, *E* evolution, *I* involution, irresolution, *K* convolution, counterrevolution, *O* obvolution, *P* pollution, *R* resolution, revolution,

S self-pollution, circumvolution, solution, *T* Tuscaloosian, *TH* thermopollution, *V* volution

ROŌSHUN   Rooshan
TOŌSHUN   destitution, institution, constitution, prostitution, restitution, substitution

(See ŪSHUN)

OŌSIK

GLOŌSIK   glucic

(See ŪSIK)

OŌSING

LOŌSING   loosing, unloosing
SPROŌSING   sprucing

(See ŪS, OŌS, add *-ing* where appropriate.)

OŌSIS

KROŌSIS   anacrusis

(See ŪSIS)

OŌSIV

KLOŌSIV   exclusive, inclusive, inconclusive, conclusive, reclusive, seclusive
LOŌSIV   allusive, delusive, elusive, illusive, collusive
TROŌSIV   inobtrusive, intrusive, obtrusive, unobtrusive

(See ŪSIV)

OŌSLĒ

LOŌSLĒ   loosely
STROŌSLĒ   abstrusely

(See ŪSLĒ)

OŌSLES

GOŌSLES   gooseless
JOŌSLES   juiceless
MOŌSLES   mooseless
SLOŌSLES   sluiceless

(See ŪSLES)

OŌSNES

KLOŌSNES   recluseness
LOŌSNES   looseness
SPROŌSNES   spruceness
STROŌSNES   abstruseness

(See ŪSNES)

OŌSŌ

HOŌSŌ   whoso
KROŌSŌ   Robinson Crusoe
ROŌSŌ   Caruso, Rousseau
TROŌSŌ   trousseau

OŌSTER

BOŌSTER   booster
BROŌSTER   brewster
JOŌSTER   jouster
ROŌSTER   rooster

OŌSUM

GROŌSUM   gruesome
TOŌSUM   twosome

OŌTA

KOŌTA   barracouta, macuta
LOŌTA   valuta
TOŌTA   battuta

(See ŪTA)

OŌTANT

LOŌTANT   pollutant

(See ŪTANT)

OŌTĒ

BOŌTĒ   bootee, booty, Djibouti, freebooty

FLOŌTĒ   fluty
FROŌTĒ   fruity, tutti-frutti
GOŌTĒ   agouti
KOŌTĒ   cootie
MOŌTĒ   gomuti
POŌTĒ   pampootee, putti
ROŌTĒ   rooty
SOŌTĒ   sooty
SNOŌTĒ   snooty
TOŌTĒ   sweet patootie, tutti

(See ŪTĒ)

OŌTED

BOŌTED   jackbooted

(See ŪT, OŌT, add *-ed* where appropriate.)

OŌTED

FOOTED   *B* barefooted, big-footed, *D* dog-footed, duck-footed, *F* footed, four-footed, *FL* flat-footed, *K* cat-footed, *KL* claw-footed, cloven-footed, club-footed, *L* lame-footed, left-footed, light-footed, *N* nimble-footed, *P* pussyfooted, *S* six-footed, *SH* sure-footed, *SPL* splay-footed, *SW* swift-footed, *T* two-footed, *W* web-footed, wing-footed, one-footed (etc.)
SOOTED   sooted

OŌTEN

(See OŌTN)

OŌTER

BOŌTER   booter, freebooter
BROŌTER   bruiter
FLOŌTER   fluter
FOŌTER   fouter, foutre
FROŌTER   fruiter
HOŌTER   hooter
JOŌTER   coadjutor
KOŌTER   accoutre, cooter
KROŌTER   recruiter
LOŌTER   diluter, looter, luter, polluter, saluter

MOOTER mooter
NOOTER neuter
ROOTER rooter, router, uprooter
SHOOTER beanshooter, deershooter, duckshooter, crapshooter, parachuter, peashooter, sharpshooter, shooter, chuter, skeetshooter, troubleshooter
SKOOTER scooter
SOOTER cloak-and-suiter, souter, suiter, suitor
TOOTER astutor, institutor, constitutor, prostitutor, protutor, restitutor, ring-tailed tooter, substitutor, tooter, tutor

(See ŬTER)

OOTER

FOOTER first-footer, footer, four-footer, pussyfooter, six-footer, two-footer, web-footer (etc.)
POOTER down-putter, putter, shotputter

OOTHER
(TH as in *then*)

SOOTHER soother
SMOOTHER smoother

OOTHER
(TH as in *thin*)

KOOTHER couther, uncouther
LOOTHER Luther

OOTHFUL
(TH as in *thin*)

ROOTHFUL ruthful
TOOTHFUL toothful
TROOTHFUL truthful, untruthful
YOOTHFUL youthful

OOTHING
(TH as in *then*)

SMOOTHING smoothing
SOOTHING soothing
TOOTHING toothing

OOTHLES
(TH as in *thin*)

ROOTHLES ruthless
SOOTHLES soothless
TOOTHLES toothless
TROOTHLES truthless
YOOTHLES youthless

OOTHSUM (TH as in *thin*)

TOOTHSUM toothsome
YOOTHSUM youthsome

OOTIJ

FROOTIJ fruitage
ROOTIJ rootage

(See ŪTIJ)

OOTIK

LOOTIK probouleutic
NOOTIK digoneutic, hermeneutic, ichneutic
ROOTIK toreutic

(See ŪTIK)

OOTING

LOOTING highfaluting

(See OOT, add -*ing* where appropriate.)

OOTING

FOOTING footing, pussyfooting
POOTING putting, shot-putting
SOOTING sooting

OOTISH

BROOTISH brutish
JOOTISH Jutish
SOOTISH sootish

OOTIST

FLOOTIST flutist
FROOTIST fruitist
LOOTIST absolutist, lutist
SHOOTIST parachutist
SOOTIST pharmaceutist

(See ŪTIST)

OOTIV

FROOTIV fruitive
JOOTIV coadjutive

(See ŪTIV)

OOTIZM

BROOTIZM brutism
LOOTIZM absolutism

(See ŪTIZM)

OOTL

BROOTL brutal
FOOTL footle
KROOTL recruital
ROOTL rootle, rutile
TOOTL tootle

(See ŪTL)

OOTLĒ

BROOTLĒ brutely
KOOTLĒ Xiuhtecutli
LOOTLĒ absolutely, dissolutely, convolutely, posilutely, resolutely

(See ŪTLĒ)

OOTLES

BOOTLES bootless
FROOTLES fruitless
ROOTLES rootless

(See ŪTLES)

OOTLING

FOOTLING footling
TOOTLING tootling

OOTMENT

BROOTMENT	imbrutement
KROOTMENT	recruitment

(See **UTMENT**)

OOTN

GLOOTN	gluten, glutin
LOOTN	highfalutin'
ROOTN	rutin
TOOTN	rootin'-tootin'

(See **UTN, OOTON**)

OOTNES

BROOTNES	bruteness
LOOTNES	absoluteness, dissoluteness

(See **UTNES**)

OOTO

OOTO	prosciutto
BOOTO	marabuto
LOOTO	assoluto, risoluto
NOOTO	ritenuto, sostenuto, tenuto
PLOOTO	Pluto
SKROOTO	scruto
TOOTO	tutto

OOTON

BOOTON	bouton
KROOTON	crouton
MOOTON	mouton

(See **OOTN, UTN**)

OOTSE

WOOTSE	tootsy-wootsy

(See **OOTSE**)

OOTSE

FOOTSE	footsie
WOOTSE	tootsie-wootsie

OOTUM

ROOTUM	verutum

(See **UTUM**)

OOTUP

SHOOTUP	shoot-up
SOOTUP	suit-up

OOTUS

BROOTUS	Brutus

(See **UTUS**)

OOVAL

MOOVAL	removal
PROOVAL	approval, disapproval, disproval, reproval

OOVE

GROOVE	groovy
MOOVE	movie

OOVEN

HOOVEN	hooven
PROOVEN	disproven, proven, unproven

OOVER

GROOVER	groover
HOOVER	Hoover, hoover
KOOVER	Vancouver
LOOVER	louver, louvre, Louvre
MOOVER	mover, people mover, remover
NOOVER	maneuver
PROOVER	approver, disapprover, disprover, improver, prover, reprover

OOVING

(See **OOV**, add -ing where appropriate.)

OOVMENT

MOOVMENT	movement, women's movement

PROOVMENT

PROOVMENT	approvement, disprovement, improvement

OOYA

HOOYA	Huia
LOOYA	alleluia, hallelujah

OOZA

LOOZA	lallapalooza
SOOZA	Sousa
THOOZA	arethusa
TOOZA	tuza

OOZE

OOZE	oozy
BLOOZE	bluesy
BOOZE	boozy, bousy
CHOOZE	choosy
DOOZE	doozy
DROOZE	drusy
FLOOZE	floozy
NOOZE	newsy
SNOOZE	snoozy
TOOZE	Watusi
WOOZE	woozy

OOZEL

(See **OOZL**)

OOZER

OOZER	oozer
BOOZER	boozer
BROOZER	bruiser
CHOOZER	chooser
KROOZER	cruiser
LOOZER	loser, palouser
SNOOZER	snoozer
ROOZER	peruser

(See **UZER**)

OOZHUN

KLOOZHUN	exclusion, inclusion, interclusion, conclusion, malocclusion, occlusion, preclusion, reinclusion, reclusion, reocclusion, seclusion
LOOZHUN	allusion, delusion,

	disillusion, elusion, illusion, collusion, prolusion, self-delusion
STRO͞OZHUN	abstrusion
THO͞OZHUN	Malthusian
TO͞OZHUN	pertusion
TRO͞OZHUN	detrusion, extrusion, intrusion, obtrusion, protrusion, retrusion, trusian

(See Ū̄ZHUN)

O͞OZL

O͞OZL	ouzel
BO͞OZL	bamboozle
FO͞OZL	foozle, gumfoozle
RO͞OZL	perusal

(See ŪZAL)

O͞OZLER

BO͞OZLER	bamboozler
FO͞OZLER	foozler
GO͞OZLER	gougoozler

O͞OZMAN

| TRO͞OZMAN | trewsman |

(See ŪZMAN)

ŌPA

ŌPA	opah
CHŌPA	chopa
DŌPA	L-dopa, Ropa Dopa, methyldopa
KŌPA	Bacopa, copa
RŌPA	Europa
SKŌPA	scopa

OPA

(See ÄPA)

ŌPAL

(See ŌPL)

ŌPĒ

| DŌPĒ | dopey |
| HŌPĒ | hopi |

KŌPĒ	pericope
MŌPĒ	mopy
RŌPĒ	ropy
SLŌPĒ	slopy
SŌPĒ	soapy
TŌPĒ	topee, topi

OPĒ

CHOPĒ	choppy
DROPĒ	droppy
FLOPĒ	flippety-floppy, flip-floppy, floppy
HOPĒ	hoppy
KLOPĒ	clip-cloppy, clippety-cloppy, cloppy
KOPĒ	copy, phenocopy, photocopy, microcopy, recopy
KROPĒ	croppy
LOPĒ	loppy, jalopy
MOPĒ	moppy
PLOPĒ	ploppy
POPĒ	poppy, prosopopy
SHOPĒ	shoppe, shoppy
SLOPĒ	sloppy
SOPĒ	soppy
STROPĒ	stroppy

ŌPER

DŌPER	doper
GRŌPER	groper
HŌPER	hoper
KŌPER	coper
LŌPER	eloper, interloper, landloper, loper
MŌPER	moper
RŌPER	jump-roper, roper
SLŌPER	sloper
SŌPER	soft-soaper, soaper, sopor
STŌPER	stoper
TŌPER	toper

ÔPER

PÔPER	pauper
SKÔPER	scauper
YÔPER	yawper

OPER

| BOPER | bopper, teeny-bopper, weeny-bopper |
| CHOPER | chopper, meat-chopper, vegetable chopper |

DOPER	dopper, Dopper
DROPER	dropper, eavesdropper, eye-dropper
FLOPER	flip-flopper, flippety-flopper, flopper
HOPER	froghopper, grasshopper, hedge-hopper, hopper, clodhopper, table-hopper, treehopper
HWOPER	whopper
KLOPER	clip-clopper, clippety-clopper, clopper
KOPER	copper
KROPER	come a cropper, cropper, sharecropper
LOPER	lopper
MOPER	mopper
PLOPER	plopper
POPER	finger-popper, corn-popper, popper
PROPER	improper, proper, propper
SHOPER	shopper, window-shopper
SLOPER	slopper
SOPER	sopper
STOPER	stopper
STROPER	stropper
SWOPER	swapper
TOPER	overtopper, tiptopper, topper

OPET

LOPET	loppet
MOPET	moppet
POPET	poppet

OPHED

| HOPHED | hophead |
| MOPHED | mophead |

OPIJ

MOPIJ	moppage
PROPIJ	proppage
STOPIJ	estoppage, stoppage

OPIK

OPIK	boöpic, Ethiopic, myopic, presbyopic
DROPIK	hydropic
KLOPIK	cyclopic
KOPIK	acopic, syncopic

LOPIK	nyctalopic
NOPIK	canopic, sinopic
SKOPIK	*A* aeroscopic, aposcopic, arthoscopic, *D* dichroscopic, deuteroscopic, *E* electroscopic, *F* photoscopic, *FL* fluoroscopic, *G* galvanoscopic, *H* hagioscopic, helioscopic, hydroscopic, hygroscopic, horoscopic, *J* geoscopic, gyroscopic, *K* kaleidoscopic, *L* laryngoscopic, lychnoscopic, *M* macroscopic, metoscopic, microscopic, *N* necroscopic, noöscopic, *O* orthoscopic, autoscopic, *P* pantascopic, periscopic, polyscopic, poroscopic, *R* rheoscopic, *SK* scopic, *SP* spectroscopic, *ST* stereoscopic, stethoscopic, *STR* stroboscopic, *T* telescopic, *TH* thermoscopic
SOPIK	Aesopic, dolichroprosopic, prosopic
THROPIK	anthropic, philanthropic, lycanthropic, misanthropic, neoanthropic, paleanthropic, psilanthropic, theanthropic, theophilanthropic, therianthropic
TOPIK	atopic, ectopic, entopic, heterotopic, isotopic, metopic, polytopic, radioisotopic, topic
TROPIK	*A* allotropic, aerotropic, atropic, *D* dexiotropic, diatropic, *E* exotropic, *F* phototropic, *H* heliotropic, heterotropic, hydrotropic, *I* idiotropic, inotropic, isentropic, isotropic, *J* geotropic, *M* monotropic, *N* nyctitropic, neurotropic, *O* orthotropic, autotropic, *P* polytropic, *S* syntropic, subtropic, *ST* stenotropic, *TH* thixotropic, *TR* tropic, *V* vagotropic, *Y* eurytropic

ŌPING

ŌPING	oping, reoping
DŌPING	doping
GRŌPING	groping
HŌPING	hoping
KŌPING	coping
LŌPING	eloping, interloping, loping
MŌPING	moping
PŌPING	dispoping, poping, unpoping
RŌPING	roping
SLŌPING	sloping
SŌPING	soft-soaping, soaping

OPING

(See **OP**, add *-ping* where appropriate.)

ŌPISH

MŌPISH	mopish
PŌPISH	popish
TŌPISH	taupish

OPISH

FOPISH	foppish
POPISH	poppish, soda poppish
SHOPISH	shoppish

ŌPL

ŌPL	opal, periople
KŌPL	copal
NŌPL	Adrianople, Constantinople, nopal, *sinople*

OPL

HOPL	hopple
KOPL	copple
POPL	popple
STOPL	estoppel, stopple
THROPL	thropple
TOPL	overtopple, topple

ŌPLES

(See **ŌP**, add *-less* where appropriate.)

OPLIN

JOPLIN	Joplin
POPLIN	poplin

OPLING

FOPLING	fopling
HOPLING	hoppling
STOPLING	stoppling
TOPLING	overtoppling, toppling

OPLĪT

HOPLĪT	hoplite
STOPLĪT	stop light

OPOUT

DROPOUT	dropout
KOPOUT	cop-out
POPOUT	pop-out

OPSĒ

DROPSĒ	dropsy
FLOPSĒ	Flopsy
LOPSĒ	lopsy
MOPSĒ	Mopsy
POPSĒ	popsy
TOPSĒ	Topsy

OPSHUN

OPSHUN	option
DOPSHUN	adoption, readoption

OPSIS

OPSIS	caryopsis, coreopsis, stereopsis
KOPSIS	lycopsis

LOPSIS ampelopsis
NOPSIS synopsis
TOPSIS thanatopsis

OPTED

OPTED co-opted, opted
DOPTED adopted, readopted, unadopted

OPTER

OPTER diopter, co-opter, opter
DOPTER adopter
KOPTER phenicopter, helicopter, copter
THOPTER ornithopter, orthopter

OPTIK

OPTIK optic
KOPTIK Coptic
NOPTIK synoptic
THOPTIK orthoptic
TOPTIK autoptic

OPTIV

OPTIV co-optive, optive
DOPTIV adoptive

ŌPUS

ŌPUS opus
GŌPUS lagopous, Lagopus
MŌPUS mopus
NŌPUS Canopus
RŌPUS pyropus

ŌRĀ

KŌRĀ kore
LŌRĀ con dolore
MŌRĀ con amore, Moray
NYŌRĀ signore
TORĀ improvisatore, cacciatore

ORĀ

FORĀ foray
MORĀ Moray

ŌRA

ŌRA ora
BŌRA bombora, bora, Bora Bora, rasbora
DŌRA Andorra, dumb Dora, fedora, Floradora, Pandora, rhodora
FLŌRA flora, Passiflora
GŌRA angora
HŌRA hora
KŌRA kora
MŌRA mora
NŌRA menorah
NYŌRA señora, signora
RŌRA aurora, Tuscarora
SŌRA Masora, sora
TŌRA tora, torah, totora
YŌRA señora, signora

ÔRA

ÔRA aura
SÔRA chamaesaura

ORA

ORA orra
DORA Andorra
GORA begorra
MORA Gomorra, gomorrah
SORA sorra

ŌRAKS

BŌRAKS borax
STŌRAKS storax
THŌRAKS thorax

ŌRAL

ŌRAL aboral, oral
FLŌRAL floral, trifloral
GŌRAL goral
HŌRAL horal
KLŌRAL chloral
KŌRAL choral, coral
PŌRAL poral
RŌRAL auroral, peroral, roral, sororal
THŌRAL thoral

ÔRAL

ÔRAL binaural, monaural, aural
LÔRAL laurel
SÔRAL saurel

ORAL

FORAL forel
KWORAL quarrel
MORAL amoral, Balmoral, immoral, moral, unmoral
SORAL sorrel

ORAN

LORAN loran
SPORAN sporran

(See **OREN**)

ŌRANT

SŌRANT soarant
VŌRANT devorant, vorant

ORANT

(See **ORENT**)

ŌRĀT

ŌRĀT orate
BŌRĀT borate
FLŌRĀT biflorate, deflorate, florate
FŌRĀT biforate
KLŌRĀT chlorate, perchlorate

ÔRĀT

ÔRĀT inaurate
STÔRĀT instaurate

ÔRBĒ

ÔRBĒ orby
KÔRBĒ corby

ÔRBEL

ÔRBEL orbell
KÔRBEL corbel

(See **ÔRBL**)

ÔRBING

ÔRBING orbing

SÔRBING absorbing, reabsorbing, resorbing

ÔRBL

WÔRBL warble

(See ÔRBEL)

ÔRCHER

SKÔRCHER scorcher
TÔRCHER torcher, torture

ÔRCHERD

ORCHERD orchard
TORCHERD tortured, retortured, untortured

ÔRCHING

SKÔRCHING scorching
TÔRCHING torching

ÔRCHUN

FÔRCHUN bad fortune, befortune, enfortune, fortune, good fortune, misfortune
PÔRCHUN importune

ÔRDAN

(See ÔRDEN)

ÔRDANT

KÔRDANT accordant, disaccordant, discordant, inaccordant, concordant
MÔRDANT mordant, mordent

ÔRDED

BÔRDED boarded
FÔRDED afforded, forded
HÔRDED hoarded
SÔRDED sworded

ÔRDED

KÔRDED accorded, chorded, corded, recorded, unrecorded
LÔRDED belorded, lorded, unlorded
SÔRDED sordid, sworded
SWÔRDED swarded
WÔRDED awarded, rewarded, unrewarded, warded

ÔRDEN

JÔRDEN Jordan
KÔRDEN cordon
WÔRDEN game warden, prison warden, warden

ÔRDENT

(See ÔRDANT)

ŌRDER

BÔRDER bed-and-boarder, boarder, star boarder
FÔRDER afforder, forder
HÔRDER hoarder
SÔRDER sworder

ÔRDER

ÔRDER disorder, law and order, money order, order, overorder, reorder, short order, suborder, tall order, underorder, unorder
BÔRDER border, emborder
KÔRDER accorder, chorder, corder, recorder
SÔRDER sordor
WÔRDER awarder, rewarder, warder

ÔRDERD

ÔRDERD ordered, overordered, reordered, short-ordered, unordered
BÔRDERD bordered, embordered

ÔRDFUL

KÔRDFUL discordful
WÔRDFUL awardful

ÔRDIJ

BÔRDIJ boardage, bordage
KÔRDIJ cordage
WÔRDIJ wardage

ŌRDING

BÔRDING beaver-boarding, boarding, weatherboarding
FÔRDING affording, fording
HÔRDING hoarding
SÔRDING swording

(See ÔRDING)

ÔRDING

KÔRDING according, cording, chording, recording
LÔRDING lording, milording, overlording
WÔRDING awarding, rewarding, unrewarding, warding

(See ŌRDING)

ÔRDSHIP

LÔRDSHIP lordship
WÔRDSHIP wardship

ŌRĒ

ŌRĒ a fortiori, a posteriori, a priori, maggiore, oary, ory
BŌRĒ mbori
DŌRĒ dory, hunky-dory
FLŌRĒ flory, counterflory
GLŌRĒ glory, Old Glory, vainglory
GŌRĒ allegory, amphigory, phantasmagory, gory, category, tautegory
HŌRĒ hoary, whory
KŌRĒ kore, kori
LŌRĒ lory, pilori
MŌRĒ con amore, memento mori, more, pro patria mori, viola d'amore
NYŌRĒ signore
PŌRĒ pory
RŌRĒ furore
SHŌRĒ shory
SNŌRĒ snory
SŌRĒ dimissory,

Montessori,
promissory

SPŌRĒ   apospory
STŌRĒ   basement story,
blindstory, clerestory,
multistory, short
story, sob story, story

TŌRĒ   *A* abbreviatory,
abjuratory,
absolutory, additory,
adhortatory,
adjuratory,
admonitory,
adulatory,
advocatory,
affirmatory,
acclamatory,
acceleratory,
accusatory, aleatory,
alleviatory, amatory,
ambagitory,
ambulatory,
amendatory,
annotatory,
annunciatory,
anticipatory,
appellatory,
applicatory,
appreciatory,
approbatory, aratory,
articulatory,
aspiratory,
asseveratory,
assimilatory, *B*
bibitory, *D*
damnatory,
deambulatory,
dedicatory,
defamatory,
dehortatory,
declamatory,
declaratory,
decretory, deletory,
delineatory,
demonstratory,
denunciatory,
depilatory,
depository,
deprecatory,
depreciatory,
depredatory,
derogatory,
desquatory, desultory,
designatory,
dictatory, dilatory,
disapprobatory,
discriminatory,
dispensatory,
distillatory,
divinatory, donatory,
dormitory, *E*
edificatory,

educatory,
exaggeratory,
exhibitory,
exhortatory,
ejaculatory,
execratory,
executory,
exclamatory,
excretory,
exculpatory,
excusatory, expiatory,
expiratory,
explanatory,
expletory,
explicatory,
exploratory,
expository,
expostulatory,
expurgatory,
excitatory,
extenuatory,
exterminatory,
equivocatory,
elucidatory,
emancipatory,
emasculatory,
emendatory,
emigratory,
emulatory,
enunciatory, *F*
feretory, flagellatory,
phonatory, feudatory,
fulminatory,
fumatory, fumitory,
funambulatory, *FR*
frigeratory, *G*
gustatory, *GL*
gladiatory, *GR*
gradatory, grallatory,
gratulatory, *H*
habilitory,
hallucinatory,
hortatory, *I*
Il Trovatore,
immigratory,
imperatory,
imprecatory,
improvisatory,
improvvisatore,
indicatory,
inflammatory,
informatory,
inhibitory, initiatory,
incantatory,
incriminatory,
incubatory,
inculpatory,
inspiratory,
interlocutory,
interrogatory,
inventory,
investigatory,

invitatory,
invocatory,
involutory, *J*
jaculatory, gestatory,
gesticulatory,
gyratory, judicatory,
juratory, *K*
cachinnatory,
calculatory,
calumniatory,
castigatory,
commandatory,
commendatory,
comminatory,
communicatory,
compellatory,
compensatory,
competitory,
compulsatory,
condemnatory,
condolatory,
confabulatory,
confirmatory,
confiscatory,
congratulatory,
consecratory,
conservatory,
conciliatory,
consolatory,
constellatory,
consultatory,
contributory,
corroboratory,
cosignatory,
cubatory, culpatory,
curatory, *KR*
crematory,
criminatory, crinitory,
chrismatory, *L*
laboratory,
lachrymatory,
lacrimatory, lavatory,
libatory, liberatory,
libratory, laudatory,
lucubratory, *M*
mandatory,
manducatory,
manipulatory,
masticatory,
mediatory, migratory,
minatory, monitory,
mundatory, mutatory,
N narratory, natatory,
negatory, negotiatory,
nugatory, *O*
objurgatory,
obligatory,
observatory, auditory,
offertory, auxiliatory,
olitory, oratory,
oscillatory,
osculatory,

auscultatory, *P*
palliatory, parlatory,
pacificatory, pellitory,
perambulatory,
peremptory,
perfumatory,
perspiratory,
piscatory,
postulatory, potatory,
pulsatory, punitory,
purgatory,
purificatory, *PL*
placatory, plauditory,
PR preambulatory,
predatory,
predicatory,
prefatory,
premonitory,
preparatory,
preservatory,
probatory,
profanatory,
prohibitory,
proclamatory,
procrastinatory,
procuratory,
promonitory,
pronunciatory,
propitiatory, *R*
radiatory, raspatory,
reformatory,
refrigeratory,
refutatory, regulatory,
regeneratory,
recognitory,
recommendatory,
reconciliatory,
recriminatory,
requisitory,
remuneratory,
remourtratory,
repertory, repository,
reprobatory,
reptatory,
reciprocatory,
respiratory,
restoratory,
retaliatory,
retardatory,
retributory,
revelatory,
reverberatory,
revocatory, rogatory,
rotatory, *S*
sacrificatory,
saltatory, salutatory,
salvatory, sanatory,
sensificatory,
certificatory,
sibility, signatory,
significatory,
simulatory,

circulatory,
circumambulatory,
circumgyratory,
circumlocutory,
circumrotatory,
citatory, sublimatory,
sudatory,
supererogatory,
suppletory,
supplicatory,
suppository,
sussultatory, *SP*
speculatory, *ST*
statutory,
sternutatory, storey,
story, *T* terminatory,
territory, tory, *TR*
transitory,
transmigratory,
transpiratory,
transudatory, *U*
undulatory,
usurpatory, *V*
vacillatory,
viaggiatory,
vehiculatory,
vesicatory, vibratory,
vindicatory, vomitory

YŌRĒ   signore
ZŌRĒ   zori

ÔRĒ

LÔRĒ   Annie Laurie,
          outlawry
SKÔRĒ   scaurie
SÔRĒ   saury
TÔRĒ   Alpha Centauri,
          centaury

ORĒ

KORĒ   corrie
KWORĒ   quarry
LORĒ   lorry
SORĒ   sorry

ÔREL

(See **ÔRAL**)

OREL

(See **ORAL**)

OREN

FLOREN   florin
FOREN   foreign

SPOREN   sporran
WOREN   rabbit warren, warren

ÔRENS

HÔRENS   abhorrence
LÔRENS   St. Lawrence

(See **ORENS**)

ORENS

FLORENS   Florence
TORENS   torrents
WORENS   warrants

(See **ÔRENS**)

ORENT

HORENT   abhorrent
TORENT   torrent
WORENT   death warrant, search
          warrant, warrantk

ŌRER

BŌRER   borer, woodborer
DŌRER   adorer
FLŌRER   floorer
GŌRER   gorer
HŌRER   horror
KŌRER   decorer, encorer,
          corer
NŌRER   ignorer
PLŌRER   deplorer, explorer,
          implorer
PŌRER   outpourer, porer,
          pourer
SHNŌRER   schnorrer
SHŌRER   shorer
SKŌRER   scorer
SNŌRER   snorer
SŌRER   outsoarer, soarer,
          sorer
STŌRER   restorer, storer

(See **ÔRER**)

ÔRER

HÔRER   abhorrer
WÔRER   warrer

(See **ŌRER**)

OREST

FOREST	afforest, deforest, enforest, forest
KOREST	chorused
SOREST	sorest

(See ŌR, add -est where appropriate.)

ŌRĒZ

| MŌRĒZ | mores |

(See ŌRĒ, add -s or change -y to -ies where appropriate.)

ÔRFIK

| ÔRFIK | Orphic |
| MÔRFIK | A allomorphic, amorphic, anthropomorphic, B biomorphic, D dimorphic, deuteromorphic, E ephemeromorphic, exomorphic, ectomorphic, endomorphic, H heteromorphic, holomorphic, I idiomorphic, ichthyomorphic, isomorphic, J geomorphic, M mesomorphic, metamorphic, mnemomorphic, monomorphic, morphic, O ophiomorphic, automorphic, P pantamorphic, paramorphic, polymorphic, PR protomorphic, S pseudomorphic, T tauromorphic, TH theomorphic, theriomorphic, theromorphic, TR trimorphic, Z zygomorphic, zoomorphic |

ÔRFING

| DWÔRFING | dwarfing |
| HWÔRFING | wharfing |

ÔRFIST

| HWÔRFIST | wharfist |
| MÔRFIST | anthropomorphist |

(Substitute -ist for concluding -ic in appropriate words under ÔRFIK.)

ÔRFIZM

(Substitute -ism for concluding -ic in appropriate words under ORFIK.)

ÔRGAN

ÔRGAN	barrel organ, biorgan, idorgan, organ
DÔRGAN	idorgan
GÔRGAN	Demogorgon, gorgon, Gorgon
MÔRGAN	morgan, morgen

ŌRHOUS

| HÔRHOUS | whorehouse |
| STÔRHOUS | storehouse |

ŌRĪD

BŌRĪD	boride
FŌRĪD	four-eyed
KLŌRĪD	bichloride, dichloride, hydrochloride, chloride, perchloride, tetrachloride, trichloride
SŌRĪD	sore-eyed

ÔRID

| SÔRID | labrosaurid, mosasaurid |
| TÔRID | centaurid, Taurid |

(See ORID)

ORID

FLORID	florid
FORID	forehead
HORID	horrid
TORID	torrid

(See ÔRID)

ŌRIJ

ŌRIJ	oarage
BŌRIJ	borage
FŌRIJ	forage
PŌRIJ	porridge
SHŌRIJ	shorage
STŌRIJ	storage

(See ORIJ)

ORIJ

| KORIJ | corrige |
| PORIJ | porridge |

(See ŌRIJ)

ÔRIK

| ÔRIK | auric |
| TÔRIK | androtauric, tauric |

ŌRIK

BŌRIK	boric
DŌRIK	elydoric
KLŌRIK	chloric
LŌRIK	folkloric, peloric
RŌRIK	roric

(See ORIK)

ORIK

ORIK	fluoric, meteoric, theoric
DORIK	Doric, elydoric, sudoric
FORIK	amphoric, epiphoric, phosphoric, camphoric, cataphoric, metaphoric, pyrophoric, prophoric, semaphoric, symphoric, euphoric, zoophoric
GORIK	allegoric, amphigoric, phantasmagoric, goric, categoric, paregoric, Pythagoric
KLORIK	chloric, hydrochloric, perchloric
KORIK	enchoric, choric
LORIK	caloric, peloric, pyloric

MORIK   Armoric, sophomoric
SPORIK   zoosporic
THORIK   plethoric, thelyphthoric
TORIK   aleatoric, diatoric, historic, oratoric, pictoric, prehistoric, *rhetoric*, toric, unhistoric
YORIK   Yorick

(See ŌRIK)

ŌRIKS

ŌRIKS   oryx

(See ŌRIK, add -*s* where appropriate.)

ORIKS

ORIKS   oryx

(See ORIK, add -*s* where appropriate.)

ORIN

(See OREN)

ŌRING

ŌRING   oaring
BŌRING   boring
DŌRING   adoring
FLŌRING   flooring
GŌRING   goring
HŌRING   whoring
KŌRING   decoring, encoring, coring
NŌRING   ignoring
PLŌRING   deploring, exploring, imploring
RŌRING   roaring
SHNŌRING   schnorring
SHŌRING   shoring
SKŌRING   scoring
SNŌRING   snoring
SŌRING   outsoaring, soaring
STŌRING   restoring, storing

ÔRING

HÔRING   abhorring
WÔRING   warring

ŌRIS

KLŌRIS   chloris

LŌRIS   loris
TŌRIS   cantoris

(See ORIS, ŌRUS, ÔRUS)

ORIS

ORIS   orris
DORIS   doch-an-dorris
HORIS   Horace

(See ŌRIS, ŌRUS, ÔRUS)

ORIST

FLORIST   florist
FORIST   afforest, deforest, disafforest, forest, reafforest, reinforest
KORIST   chorist

ÔRJAL

KÔRJAL   cordial

(See ÔR'DI.AL)

ÔRJĒ

ÔRJĒ   orgy
KÔRJĒ   corgi
PÔRJĒ   Georgy Porgy
STÔRJĒ   storge

ÔRJER

ÔRJER   ordure
FÔRJER   forger
GÔRJER   gorger, disgorger

ÔRJING

FÔRJING   forging
GÔRJING   gorging, disgorging

ÔRKĒ

(See ÔRK, add -*y* where appropriate.)

ÔRKER

ÔRKER   kwashiorkor
FÔRKER   forker
KÔRKER   corker
PÔRKER   porker
YÔRKER   New Yorker, yorker

ÔRKING

FÔRKING   forking
KÔRKING   corking, uncorking
YÔRKING   yorking

ÔRKUS

ÔRKUS   orchis
NÔRKUS   anorchous

ÔRLĒ

SHÔRLĒ   schorly
WÔRLĒ   warly

ÔRLES

(See ÔR, add -*less* where appropriate.)

ŌRLOK

ŌRLOK   oarlock
FŌRLOK   forelock

(See ÔRLOK)

ÔRLOK

WÔRLOK   warlock

(See ŌRLOK)

ÔRMAL

FÔRMAL   formal, informal, conformal, uniformal
KÔRMAL   cormel
NÔRMAL   abnormal, anormal, normal, paranormal, subnormal, supernormal

ŌRMAN

(See ŌRMEN)

ÔRMANS

(See ÔRMENS)

ÔRMANT

DÔRMANT   dormant

FÔRMANT   formant, informant,
              conformant,
              performant

(See ŌRMENT)

ŌRMAT

DŌRMAT   doormat
FLŌRMAT floormat

ÔRMAT

DÔRMAT   doormat
FLÔRMAT floormat
FÔRMAT   format

ÔRMĒ

DÔRMĒ   dormie, dormy
FÔRMĒ   forme, formy,
             conformy, uniformy
HÔRMĒ   horme
STÔRMĒ   stormy
SWÔRMĒ   swarmy
WÔRMĒ   warmy

ŌRMEN

DŌRMEN   doorman, doormen
FLŌRMEN floorman, floormen
FŌRMEN   foreman, foremen
KŌRMEN   corpsman, corpsmen
MŌRMEN   Mormon
SHŌRMEN longshoreman,
             longshoremen
STŌRMAN storeman, storemen

ÔRMENS

DÔRMENS dormance
FÔRMENS conformance,
             performance

ŌRMENT

DŌRMENT adorement
NŌRMENT ignorement
PLŌRMENT deplorement,
             explorement,
             implorement
STŌRMENT restorement

(See ÔRMANT)

ÔRMER

ÔRMER   ormer
WÔRMER   bedwarmer,
             benchwarmer,
             footwarmer, warmer

(See ÔRM, add -er where appropriate.)

ÔRMING

(See ÔRM, add -ing where appropriate.)

ÔRMIST

FÔRMIST conformist,
             nonconformist,
             reformist, uniformist
WÔRMIST lukewarmest,
             warmest

ÔRML

(See ÔRMAL)

ÔRMLĒ

FÔRMLĒ   uniformly
WÔRMLĒ   warmly

ÔRMLES

(See ÔRM, add -less where appropriate.)

ÔRMOUTH

SÔRMOUTH sore-mouth
WÔRMOUTH warmouth

ÔRMUS

FÔRMUS   multiformous
KÔRMUS   cormous, cormus
NÔRMUS   abnormous, enormous

ÔRNĒ

HÔRNĒ   horny
KÔRNĒ   corny
SKÔRNĒ   scorny
THÔRNĒ   thorny

ÔRNER

BÔRNER   suborner
DÔRNER   adorner

HÔRNER   horner, Little Jack
             Horner
KÔRNER   chimney corner,
             catercorner,
             cattycorner,
             kittycorner, corner
MÔRNER   mourner
SKÔRNER bescorner, scorner
SÔRNER   sorner
WÔRNER   forewarner, warner

ÔRNET

HÔRNET   hornet
KÔRNET   cornet

ÔRNFUL

MÔRNFUL mournful
SKÔRNFUL scornful

ÔRNING

BÔRNING aborning

(See ÔRN, add -ing where appropriate.)

ÔRNIS

ÔRNIS   Aepyornis,
             Archaeornis, ornis,
             Heliornis, Ichthyornis
KÔRNIS   cornice
NÔRNIS   Dinornis
TÔRNIS   Gastornis, Notornis

ÔRNISH

HÔRNISH hornish
KÔRNISH Cornish
THÔRNISH thornish

ÔRNLES

(See ÔRN, add -less where appropriate.)

ŌRŌ

ŌRŌ   oro
BŌRŌ   Boro
LŌRŌ   loro
MŌRŌ   moro, Moro
PŌRŌ   Poro
SŌRŌ   aposoro
TŌRŌ   toro, torotoro

ORŌ

BORŌ	borrow
MORŌ	amorrow, good morrow, morro, morrow, tomorrow
SORŌ	seeksorrow, sorrow, Zorro

ŌRON

BŌRON	boron
MŌRON	moron

ÔRŌS

PÔRŌS	porose
TÔRŌS	torose

ÔRPER

SKÔRPER	scorper
TÔRPER	torpor
WÔRPER	warper

ÔRSĒ

GÔRSĒ	gorsy
HÔRSĒ	horsy

ÔRSEL

(See ÔRSL)

ŌRSEN

HŌRSEN	hoarsen, whoreson
KŌRSEN	coarsen

ŌRSER

HŌRSER	hoarser
KŌRSER	coarser, courser, discourser

ÔRSER

DÔRSER	endorser
FÔRSER	enforcer, forcer, reinforcer
HÔRSER	horser, unhorser
VÔRSER	divorcer

ÔRSFUL

ZÔRSFUL	resourceful, unresourceful

(See ÔRSFUL)

ÔRSFUL

FÔRSFUL	forceful, unforceful
MÔRSFUL	remorseful, unremorseful

(See ÔRSFUL)

ÔRSHUN

BÔRSHUN	abortion, anti-abortion, pro-abortion
PÔRSHUN	apportion, disproportion, portion, proportion
SÔRSHUN	consortion
TÔRSHUN	contortion, detortion, distortion, extorsion, extortion, intorsion, retorsion, torsion

ÔRSING

(See ÔRS, add -ing where appropriate.)

ŌRSIV

KŌRSIV	discoursive

(See ÔRSIV)

ÔRSIV

FÔRSIV	enforcive
TÔRSIV	extorsive, contorsive, torsive

(See ÔRSIV)

HOW ABOUT YOU AND ME ALLITERATING?

"Alliteration's artful aid"—
That is what the poet said:
"Sing a song of silliness";
"King and queen and court caress";
"Babes blow bubbles in a box";
"Seagulls sing when sewing socks";
"Down the drain the donkeys dive";
"Lions leap on lambs alive."
See? You needn't be a great
Genius to alliterate.

ÔRSL

DÔRSL	dorsal
MÔRSL	morsel
NÔRSL	norsel
SÔRSL	ensorcell, ensorcel
TÔRSL	torcel, torsal
TRÔRSL	dextrorsal, sinistrorsal

ÔRSLĒ

HÔRSLĒ	hoarsely
KÔRSLĒ	coarsely

ÔRSLES

(See ÔRS, add -less where appropriate.)

ÔRSMAN

HÔRSMAN	horseman, light-horseman
NÔRSMAN	Norseman

ÔRSMENT

DÔRSMENT	endorsement
FÔRSMENT	deforcement, enforcement, forcement, reinforcement
VÔRSMENT	divorcement

ÔRSMĒT

FÔRSMĒT	forcemeat
HÔRSMĒT	horsemeat

ÔRSNES

HÔRSNES	hoarseness
KÔRSNES	coarseness

ÔRSŌ

DÔRSŌ	dorso
KÔRSŌ	corso
TÔRSŌ	torso

ŌRSUM

FÔRSUM	foursome

(See ÔRSUM)

ÔRSUM

DÔRSUM	dorsum

(See ÔRSUM)

ÔRTA

ÔRTA	aorta
KWÔRTA	sesquiquarta
TÔRTA	torta

ÔRTAL

(See ÔRTL)

ÔRTANS

(See ÔRTENS)

ÔRTĒ

DÔRTĒ	dorty
FÔRTĒ	forte, forty, pianoforte
PÔRTĒ	porty
SHÔRTĒ	shorty
SNÔRTĒ	snorty
SÔRTĒ	sortie, resorty
SPÔRTĒ	sporty
SWÔRTĒ	swarty
WÔRTĒ	warty

ÔRTED

(See ÔRT, add -ed)

ÔRTEKS

KÔRTEKS	cortex
VÔRTEKS	vortex

ÔRTEN

CHÔRTEN	chorten
KWÔRTEN	quartan
SHÔRTEN	foreshorten, shorten

ÔRTENS

PÔRTENS	importance, comportance, transportance, supportance
SÔRTENS	sortance

ÔRTER

BÔRTER	aborter
HÔRTER	dehorter
KÔRTER	escorter, courter
KWÔRTER	forequarter, hindquarter, quarter, last quarter, weather-quarter
MÔRTER	mortar
PÔRTER	disporter, exporter, importer, colporteur, porter, reporter, supporter, transporter
SHÔRTER	shorter
SNÔRTER	ripsnorter, snorter
SÔRTER	assorter, kicksorter, consorter, resorter, sorter, wool sorter (etc.)
SPÔRTER	sporter
SWÔRTER	swarter
THWÔRTER	thwarter
TÔRTER	detorter, distorter, extorter, contorter, retorter
ZÔRTER	exhorter

ÔRTERZ

KWÔRTERZ	fall quarters, headquarters, quarters, spring quarters, summer quarters, winter quarters

(See ÔRTER, add -s where appropriate.)

ŌRTGĪD

PŌRTGĪD	port guide

(See ÔRTGĪD)

ÔRTGĪD

KÔRTGĪD	court guide

(See ŌRTGĪD)

ŌRTIJ

PŌRTIJ	portage

(See ÔRTIJ)

ÔRTIJ

SHÔRTIJ	shortage

(See ŌRTIJ)

ÔRTING

(See ÔRT, add -ing where appropriate.)

ÔRTIS

FÔRTIS	fortis
MÔRTIS	mortice, mortise
TÔRTIS	tortoise

ÔRTIV

ÔRTIV	ortive
BÔRTIV	abortive
PÔRTIV	nonsupportive, supportive, transportive, unsupportive
SPÔRTIV	disportive, sportive, transportive
TÔRTIV	distortive, extortive, contortive, retortive, tortive

ÔRTL

ÔRTL	aortal
CHÔRTL	chortle
HWÔRTL	whortle
MÔRTL	immortal, mortal
PÔRTL	portal, transportal
SÔRTL	sortal

ŌRTLĒ

KŌRTLĒ	courtly, uncourtly
PŌRTLĒ	portly

(See ÔRTLĒ)

ÔRTLĒ

SHÔRTLĒ	shortly

(See ŌRTLĒ)

ÔRTLING

CHÔRTLING	chortling
MÔRTLING	mortling

ÔRTMENT

KÔRTMENT	escortment
PÔRTMENT	deportment, disportment, comportment, transportment
SÔRTMENT	assortment, consortment, sortment

ÔRTNES

| SWÔRTNES | swartness |
| THWÔRTNES | thwartness |

ÔRTRES

| FÔRTRES | fortress |
| MÔRTRES | mortress |

ÔRTŪRD

(See ÔRCHERD)

ŌRUM

ŌRUM	variorum
FŌRUM	forum
JŌRUM	jorum
KŌRUM	decorum, indecorum
KWŌRUM	quorum
LŌRUM	ad valorem, cockalorum
NŌRUM	pons asinorum
SNŌRUM	snipsnapsnorum
SPŌRUM	Pittosporum
TŌRUM	sanctum sanctorum, schola cantorum

ÔRUM

| ÔRUM | aurum |

(See ŌRUM)

ŌRUS

FLŌRUS	tubuliflorous
HŌRUS	Horus
KLŌRUS	chlorous
KŌRUS	decorous, indecorous, corous, chorus
LŌRUS	pelorus, pylorus
NŌRUS	canorous, sonorous
PŌRUS	imporous, porous
SŌRUS	sorus
TŌRUS	torus

(See ŌRIS, ORIS, ÔRUS)

ÔRUS

ÔRUS	aurous
LÔRUS	laurus
SKÔRUS	scaurous
SÔRUS	B Brontosaurus, D Dolichosaurus, H Hadrosaurus, I Ichthyosaurus, L Labrosaurus, M Megalosaurus, Mixosaurus, Mosasaurus, PL Plesiosaurus, PR protorosaurus, T Teleosaurus, Tyrannosaurus, TH thesaurus
TÔRUS	Centaurus, Taurus

(See ŌRIS, ORIS, ŌRUS)

ÔRWERD

| FÔRWERD | forward, henceforward, straightforward, thenceforward |
| NÔRWERD | nor'ward |

ŌSA

DŌSA	dosa
KŌSA	mucosa
MŌSA	Formosa, mimosa
PŌSA	mariposa
RŌSA	Via Dolorosa, serosa
VŌSA	anorexia nervosa

OSA

OSA	Ossa
FOSA	fossa
GLOSA	glossa
GOSA	Saragossa
ROSA	Barbarossa

OSAL

(See OSL)

OSBAK

HOSBAK	hossback
MOSBAK	mossback
TOSBAK	tossback

ÔSĒ

| GÔSĒ | gawsie |
| SÔSĒ | saucy |

OSĒ

BOSĒ	bossy
DROSĒ	drossy
FLOSĒ	flossy
GLOSĒ	glossy
LOSĒ	lossy
MOSĒ	mossie, mossy
POSĒ	in posse, posse
PROSĒ	prossie
TOSĒ	tossy

ŌSENT

| DŌSENT | docent |
| NŌSENT | nocent |

ŌSER

DŌSER	doser
GRŌSER	engrosser, greengrocer, grocer
KLŌSER	closer
KŌSER	jocoser
RŌSER	moroser

ÔSER

CHÔSER	Chaucer
HÔSER	hawser
SÔSER	saucer

(See OSER)

OSER

BOSER	bosser, embosser
DOSER	dosser
GLOSER	glosser
JOSER	josser
KROSER	crosser
ROSER	rosser
TOSER	tosser

(See ÔSER)

OSET

BOSET	bosset
KOSET	cosset
POSET	posset, sack posset
TOSET	tossut

ŌSHA

ŌSHA	Beotia, OSHA
SKŌSHA	Nova Scotia, Scotia

OSHĒ

JOSHĒ	joshy
SKWOSHĒ	squashy
SLOSHĒ	sloshy
SWOSHĒ	swashy
TOSHĒ	toshy
WOSHĒ	washy, wishy-washy

ŌSHER

GŌSHER	gaucher
KLŌSHER	clocher
KŌSHER	kosher

OSHER

BOSHER	bosher
JOSHER	josher
KOSHER	cosher
POSHER	posher
SKWOSHER	squasher
SLOSHER	slosher
SWOSHER	swasher
TOSHER	tosher
WOSHER	dishwasher, whitewasher, washer

OSHING

WOSHING	dishwashing, whitewashing, washing

(See **OSH,** add -ing where appropriate.)

ŌSHUN

ŌSHUN	Boeotion, ocean
DŌSHUN	braggadocian
GŌSHUN	Goshen
GRŌSHUN	groschen
KŌSHUN	nicotian
LŌSHUN	lotion
MŌSHUN	Brownian motion, demotion, emotion, commotion, locomotion, motion, promotion, remotion
NŌSHUN	notion, prenotion
PŌSHUN	potion
VŌSHUN	devotion, indevotion, self-devotion

ÔSHUN

KÔSHUN	caution

(See **OSHUN**)

OSHUN

FOSHUN	defossion

(See **ÔSHUN**)

ŌSHUS

DŌSHUS	supercalifragilistic-expialidocious
KŌSHUS	precocious
PŌSHUS	nepotious
RŌSHUS	ferocious
STŌSHUS	stotious
TRŌSHUS	atrocious

ÔSIJ

GÔSIJ	gaussage
SÔSIJ	sausage

(See **OSIJ**)

OSIJ

BOSIJ	bossage
FOSIJ	fossage

(See **ÔSIS**)

OSIK

FOSIK	fossick
GLOSIK	glossic
LOSIK	molossic

(See **ÔSIK**)

ÔSIK

NOSIK	banausic

(See **OSIK**)

OSIL

(See **OSL**)

ŌSING

DŌSING	dosing
GRŌSING	engrossing, grossing

OSING

KROSING	children crossing, deer crossing, grade crossing, cattle crossing, crossing, railroad crossing

(See **OS**, add -ing where appropriate.)

ŌSIS

ŌSIS	A abiosis, anabiosis, anastomosis, antibiosis, apotheosis, B biosis, E enantiosis, endometriosis, H heliosis, I ichthyosis, K coccideosis, M meiosis, miosis, mononucleosis, N pneumonoultra-microscopicsilico-volcanoconiosis, N necrobiosis, pneumoconiosis, O orthobiosis, P parabiosis, pyosis, poliosis, S semiosis, symbiosis, SK scoliosis
BŌSIS	thrombosis
DŌSIS	lordosis
DRŌSIS	ischidrosis, cacidrosis, kakidrosis, maschalephildrosis, podobromhydrosis
FŌSIS	anamorphosis, gomphosis, morphosis
FRŌSIS	nephrosis
GŌSIS	rhigosis, zygosis
KŌSIS	metempsychosis, narcosis, sarcosis, psittacosis, psychosis
KRŌSIS	phalacrosis, necrosis
LŌSIS	ankylosis, dacrygelosis, diverticulosis, furunculosis, helosis, melosis, pediculosis, psilosis, tuberculosis
MŌSIS	endosmosis, exosmosis, cagamosis, limosis,

NŌSIS osmosis, patharmosis, zymosis, *A* asteriognosis, avitaminosis, *D* diagnosis, *H* hallucinosis, hypervitaminosis, hypnosis, hyssinosis, *J* geognosis, *K* kenosis, *L* lagnosis, loganamnosis, *K* carcinosis, *P* pollinosis, *N* gnosis, *S* cyanosis, *ST* stenosis, stereognosis, *T* telegnosis, *TR* trichinosis

PLŌSIS anadiplosis, epanadiplosis

PŌSIS adiposis, hypotyposis

RŌSIS *A* amaurosis, arteriosclerosis, atherosclerosis, *FL* phlabosclerosis, *H* heterosis, *K* chorosis, *M* morosis, *N* neurosis, *P* pyrosis, *S* cirrhosis, scirrhosis, sorosis, *SK* sclerosis, *T* tephrosis, *Z* xerosis

THŌSIS diorthosis, epanorthosis

TŌSIS *D* dermatosis, *E* epidermophytosis, *H* halitosis, hematosis, *J* gestosis, *K* kinetosis, *M* metasomatosis, metemptosis, metensomatosis, myxomatosis, *O* otosis, *PR* proemptosis, *S* cittosis, *T* teratosis, ptosis

ŌSIV

PLŌSIV explosive, implosive, inexplosive, plosive

RŌSIV erosive, corrosive

OSL

OSL ossal
DOSL docile, dosel, dossal, dossil
FOSL fossil
GLOSL glossal, hypoglossal
JOSL jostle
LOSL colossal

POSL apostle
THROSL throstle
TOSL tossel
WOSL wassail

ŌSLĒ

BŌSLĒ verbosely
GRŌSLĒ grossly
KLŌSLĒ closely
KŌSLĒ bellicosely, jocosely
RŌSLĒ morosely

OSLER

OSLER ostler
HOSLER hostler
JOSLER jostler

ŌSNES

BŌSNES verboseness
GRŌSNES grossness
KLŌSNES closeness
KŌSNES bellicoseness, jocoseness
RŌSNES moroseness
TŌSNES ventoseness

ŌSŌ

ŌSŌ arioso, furioso, grandioso, gracioso, capriccioso, curioso, Mafioso, virtuoso
LŌSŌ tremoloso
MŌSŌ animoso, lacrimoso, mosso
PŌSŌ pomposo
RŌSŌ amoroso, doloroso, corozo, oloroso, penseroso
SŌSŌ soso, so-so
TŌSŌ maestoso, strepitoso
TRŌSŌ nitroso

OSTA

HOSTA Hosta
KOSTA costa, subcosta

ŌSTAL

KŌSTAL intercoastal, intracoastal, coastal
PŌSTAL postal

OSTAL

(See **OSTEL**)

OSTĀT

KOSTĀT costate, quadricostate, laticostate
POSTĀT apostate
PROSTĀT prostate

OSTĒ

FROSTĒ frosty
PROSTĒ prostie

ŌSTED

BŌSTED boasted
GŌSTED ghosted
HŌSTED hosted
KŌSTED coasted
PŌSTED *composted,* posted, riposted, unposted
RŌSTED roasted, unroasted
TŌSTED toasted, untoasted

ÔSTED

ZÔSTED exhausted

(See **OSTED**)

OSTED

FROSTED defrosted, frosted
KOSTED accosted

(See **ÔSTED**)

OSTEL

HOSTEL hostel, hostile
KOSTEL infracostal, intercostal, costal, Pentacostal, supracostal
POSTEL postil
ROSTEL rostel

OSTEN

BOSTEN Boston
KOSTEN costean

ŌSTER

BŌSTER	boaster
GŌSTER	ghoster
KŌSTER	coaster, roller coaster
PŌSTER	four-poster, poster, riposter, wall poster
RŌSTER	roaster
THRŌSTER	throwster
TŌSTER	toaster

ÔSTER

ZÔSTER	exhauster

(See **OSTER**)

OSTER

FOSTER	foster
FROSTER	defroster, froster
GLOSTER	Gloucester
GOSTER	snollygoster
KOSTER	accoster, coster, pentecoster
NOSTER	paternoster, Pater Noster
POSTER	imposter
ROSTER	roster
ZOSTER	zoster

(See **ÔSTER**)

OSTERD

FOSTERD	fostered
KOSTERD	costard

ŌSTHOUS

ŌSTHOUS	oasthouse
GŌSTHOUS	ghosthouse
PŌSTHOUS	posthouse

ÔSTIK

KÔSTIK	encaustic, diacaustic, catacaustic, caustic
LÔSTIK	apolaustic

OSTIK

OSTIK	eteostic
KOSTIK	pentacostic
KROSTIK	acrostic, paracrostic, pentacrostic

NOSTIK	agnostic, diagnostic, geognostic, metagnostic, gnostic, prognostic

OSTIL

(See **OSTEL**)

ŌSTING

BŌSTING	boasting
GŌSTING	ghosting
HŌSTING	hosting
KŌSTING	coasting
PŌSTING	posting, riposting
RŌSTING	roasting
TŌSTING	toasting

ÔSTING

ZÔSTING	exhausting

(See **OSTING**)

OSTING

FROSTING	defrosting, frosting
KOSTING	accosting, costing

(See **ÔSTING**)

ÔSTIV, OSTIV

KOSTIV	costive
ZÔSTIV	exhaustive, inexhaustive

ŌSTLĒ

GŌSTLĒ	ghostly
MŌSTLĒ	mostly

ÔSTRAL

ÔSTRAL	austral
KLÔSTRAL	claustral
PLÔSTRAL	plaustral

OSTRAL

KOSTRAL	costrel
NOSTRAL	nostril
ROSTRAL	lamellirostral, longirostral, rostral

OSTRĀT

PROSTRĀT	prostrate
ROSTRĀT	brevirostrate, erostrate, hemirostrate, rostrate

OSTRUM

LOSTRUM	colostrum
NOSTRUM	nostrum
ROSTRUM	rostrum

OSUM

BLOSUM	apple blossom, blossom, cherry blossom, emblossom, fruit blossom, quince blossom, orange blossom, peach blossom, pear blossom (etc.), reblossom
GLOSUM	odontoglossum
POSUM	opossum, possum, water opossum

OSUS

LOSUS	colossus, molossus
NOSUS	Knossos

(See **OS**, add -es for imperfect rhyme where appropriate.)

ŌTA

ŌTA	iota, biota
BŌTA	bota
FLŌTA	flota
KŌTA	Dakota, North Dakota, South Dakota
KWŌTA	quota, non-quota
LŌTA	lota, lotah, pelota
PŌTA	sapota
RŌTA	rota
SŌTA	Minnesota
TŌTA	tota

OTA

GOTA	gotta
KOTA	cotta, ricotta, terra-cotta
KROTA	chrotta
POTA	pottah

ŌTAL

(See ŌTL)

OTAL

(See OTL)

ŌTANT

FLŌTANT	flotant
PŌTANT	*impotent,* counterpotent, potent, prepotent

ŌTĀT

NŌTĀT	*annotate,* denotate, notate
RŌTĀT	rotate

ŌTĒ

ŌTĒ	oaty
BLŌTĒ	bloaty
DŌTĒ	dhoti, doty
FLŌTĒ	floaty
GŌTĒ	goaty
HŌTĒ	Don Quixote
LŌTĒ	melote
RŌTĒ	roti
THRŌTĒ	throaty
YŌTĒ	coyote, peyote

ÔTĒ

HÔTĒ	haughty
LÔTĒ	philauty
NÔTĒ	naughty

OTĒ

BLOTĒ	blotty
DOTĒ	dotty
GROTĒ	grotty
HOTĒ	hottie
KLOTĒ	clotty
KOTĒ	cotty, manicotti
NOTĒ	Menotti, knotty
PLOTĒ	plotty
POTĒ	potty
SHOTĒ	shotty
SKOTĒ	Scottie, Scotty
SNOTĒ	snotty
SPOTĒ	spotty
TOTĒ	totty
ZLOTĒ	zloty

(See ÄTĒ)

ŌTED

ŌTED	oated
BLŌTED	bloated
BŌTED	boated, sailboated, steamboated
DŌTED	doted, anecdoted
FLŌTED	floated, refloated
GLŌTED	gloated
GŌTED	goated
KŌTED	frock-coated, coated, morning-coated, party-coated, petticoated, sugar-coated
KWŌTED	quoted, misquoted
MŌTED	demoted, moated, moted, promoted
NŌTED	denoted, connoted, noted, unnoted
THRŌTED	deep-throated, dry-throated, full-throated, honey-throated, red-throated, ruby-throated, swan-throated, throated, yellow-throated
TŌTED	toted
VŌTED	devoted, self-devoted, undevoted, voted

ÔTED

NÔTED	juggernauted
THÔTED	merry-thoughted, sad-thoughted

OTED

OTED	cheviotted
BLOTED	blotted, reblotted, unblotted
DOTED	dotted, redotted, undotted
JOTED	jotted, rejotted, unjotted
KLOTED	clotted, reclotted, unclotted
LOTED	alotted, misalloted, realotted, unalotted
NOTED	knotted, reknotted, unknotted
PLOTED	plotted, replotted, unplotted
POTED	potted, repotted, unpotted
ROTED	carotid, parotid, rotted
SKWOTED	squatted, resquatted
SLOTED	slotted, reslotted, unslotted
SNOTED	resnotted, unsnotted
SOTED	besotted, sotted, unsotted
SPOTED	respotted, spotted, unspotted
STOTED	stotted
SWOTED	reswatted, swatted, unswatted
TOTED	retotted, totted, untotted
TROTED	dogtrotted, foxtrotted, jogtrotted, trotted, turkey-trotted
VOTED	gavotted
YOTED	yachted

ŌTEN

(See ŌTN)

OTEN

GOTEN	*B* begotten, *F* first-begotten, forgotten, *G* gotten, *H* hard-gotten, *I* ill-gotten, *M* misbegotten, misgotten, *U* unbegotten, unforgotten, ungotten
GROTEN	Groton
KOTEN	guncotton, cotton
ROTEN	rotten
SHOTEN	shotten

ŌTENT

(See ŌTANT)

ŌTER

MŌTER	*B* bimotor, *D* demoter, *H* hydromotor, *L* locomotor, *M* magnetomotor, motor, *P* pulmotor, *PR* promoter; *R* remoter, rotomotor, *TR* trimotor, *V* vasomotor
RŌTER	rotor

(See ŌT, add *-er* where appropriate.)

ÔTER

ÔTER	oughter
DÔTER	daughter, goddaughter, granddaughter, stepdaughter
KÔTER	cauter
SLÔTER	manslaughter, slaughter
WÔTER	backwater, breakwater, dishwater, firewater, fizzwater, fresh water, giggle water, limewater, milk-and-water, rosewater, soda water, salt water, shearwater, water, zimmenwater

OTER

OTER	otter
BLOTER	blotter
DOTER	dotter
HOTER	hotter
JOTER	jotter
KLOTER	clotter
KOTER	cotter
NOTER	knotter, unknotter
PLOTER	complotter, plotter, underplotter, unplotter
POTER	potter
ROTER	garotter, rotter
SHOTER	shotter
SKWOTER	squatter
SPOTER	spotter
STOTER	stotter
SWOTER	swatter
TOTER	totter
TROTER	bogtrotter, globetrotter, prom-trotter, trotter
YOTER	yachter

(See ÄTER)

ÔTERD

DÔTERD	dotard
GŌTERD	goatherd
MŌTERD	motored

ŌTEST

| MŌTEST | remotest |
| PRŌTEST | protest |

OTHĒ

(TH as in *thin*)

BOTHĒ	bothy
FROTHĒ	frothy
MOTHĒ	mothy
SWOTHĒ	swathy

ÔTHER

(TH as in *thin*)

| ÔTHER | author |

(See OTHER, TH as in *thin*)

OTHER

(TH as in *thin*)

| FROTHER | frother |
| MOTHER | mother |

(See ÔTHER, TH as in *thin*)

OTHER

(TH as in *then*)

BOTHER	bother
FOTHER	fother
POTHER	pother

(See ÄTHER)

ŌTHING

(TH as in *then*)

CLŌTHING	clothing
LŌTHING	loathing
TRŌTHING	betrothing

OTID

(See OTED)

ŌTIJ

BŌTIJ	boatage
DŌTIJ	anecdotage, dotage, sacerdotage
FLŌTIJ	floatage, flotage

OTIJ

KLOTIJ	clottage
KOTIJ	cottage
PLOTIJ	plottage

| POTIJ | pottage |
| WOTIJ | wattage |

ŌTIK

ŌTIK	otic
FŌTIK	aphotic, photic, dysphotic
LŌTIK	lotic
RŌTIK	parotic

ÔTIK

| NÔTIK | astronautic, cosmonautic |

(See OTIK)

OTIK

OTIK	*A* abiotic, alleotic, amphibiotic, amniotic, antibiotic, antipatriotic, *B* biotic, *E* enzootic, epizootic, *H* halobiotic, *I* idiotic, ichthyotic, iscariotic, *K* chaotic, catabiotic, *M* macrobiotic, microbiotic, meiotic, *N* nebulochaotic, *O* otic, *P* patriotic, periotic, *S* semiotic, symbiotic, *Z* zootic, zoosemiotic
BOTIK	robotic, sybotic, thrombotic
DOTIK	anecdotic, lordotic
DROTIK	hidrotic
FOTIK	kyphotic, morphotic
GLOTIK	diglottic, epiglottic, glottic, polyglottic
GOTIK	argotic, dizygotic, indigotic, legotic, zygotic
KOTIK	dichotic, helcotic, mycotic, narcotic, postpsychotic, prepsychotic, psychotic
KROTIK	acrotic, anacrotic, dicrotic, catacrotic, monocrotic, necrotic, polycrotic, tricrotic
KWOTIK	aquatic
LOTIK	ankylotic, epulotic, culottic, Nilotic, sans-culottic, psilottic

MOTIK	demotic, endosmotic, exosmotic, enzymotic, osmotic, thermotic, seismotic, zymotic
NOTIK	*A* agrypnotic, acapnotic, *B* binotic, *H* henotic, hypnotic, *K* kenotic, *M* melanotic, monotic, *N* neurohypnotic, *O* autohypnotic, *P* pycnotic, posthypnotic, *S* cyanotic, *ST* stenotic
POTIK	despotic, nepotic, thalpotic
ROTIK	*A* amphierotic, *E* erotic, *KL* chlorotic, *N* neurotic, *O* oneirotic, *P* parotic, pyrotic, porotic, *R* rhinocerotic, *S* cerotic, psychoneurotic, cirrhotic, *SK* sclerotic, *Z* xerotic
SOTIK	exotic, creosotic, quixotic, loxotic
THOTIK	orthotic, xanthotic
TOTIK	anaptotic, aptotic, asymptotic, entotic
ZOTIK	azotic, exotic, rhizotic

OTIKS

BOTIKS	robotics

(See **OTIK,** add *-s* where appropriate.)

ŌTING

BLŌTING	bloating
BŌTING	boating, sail-boating
DŌTING	doting
FLŌTING	floating, refloating
GLŌTING	gloating
KŌTING	coating, sugar-coating
KWŌTING	quoting, misquoting
MŌTING	demoting, promoting
NŌTING	denoting, connoting, noting
TŌTING	toting
VŌTING	devoting, voting

ŌTISH

ŌTISH	oatish

BŌTISH	boatish
DŌTISH	dotish
GŌTISH	goatish

OTISH

HOTISH	hottish
SHOTISH	schottische
SKOTISH	Scottish
SOTISH	sottish

ŌTIST

DŌTIST	anecdotist
NŌTIST	noticed, unnoticed
PRŌTIST	protist
SKŌTIST	Scotist
VŌTIST	votist

ŌTIV

FLŌTIV	floative
MŌTIV	electromotive, emotive, locomotive, motive, promotive
NŌTIV	denotive, connotive
VŌTIV	votive

ŌTL

DŌTL	anecdotal, antidotal, dotal, extradotal, sacerdotal
FŌTL	faustenil
NŌTL	notal
RŌTL	rotal, sclerotal
TŌTL	grand total, subtotal, sumtotal, teetotal, total

OTL

OTL	Quetzalcoatl
BOTL	bluebottle, bottle, greenbottle
DOTL	dottle
GLOTL	epiglottal, glottal
HWOTL	Nahuatl
KOTL	acocotl
KROTL	crottle
LOTL	axolotl
MOTL	mottle
POTL	pottle
ROTL	rotl
THROTL	throttle
TOTL	Aristotle, tottle
TWOTL	twattle
WOTL	wattle

OTLĒ

HOTLĒ	hotly
MOTLĒ	motley

OTLER

BOTLER	bottler
MOTLER	mottler
THROTLER	throttler
TOTLER	tottler
TWOTLER	twattler
WOTLER	wattler

ŌTLES

(See **ŌT,** add *-less* where appropriate.)

ÔTLES

NÔTLES	aeronautless, argonautless, astronautless, dreadnoughtless, hydronautless, juggernautless, cosmonautless
SLÔTLES	onslaughtless
THÔTLES	thoughtless

OTLES

(See **OT,** add *-less* where appropriate.)

OTLING

(See **OTL,** add *-ing* where appropriate.)

ŌTMAN

BŌTMAN	boatman
GŌTMAN	goatman

ŌTMENT

MŌTMENT	demotement, promotement
NŌTMENT	denotement
VŌTMENT	devotement

OTMENT

LOTMENT	allotment
SOTMENT	besotment

ŌTN

ŌTN	oaten
KRŌTN	crotin, croton
PRŌTN	proton

ŌTŌ

FŌTŌ	photo, telephoto
KŌTŌ	koto
MŌTŌ	con moto, Mr. Moto
RŌTŌ	roto
TŌTŌ	in toto
VŌTŌ	divoto, ex voto

OTŌ

OTŌ	otto, Otto
BLOTŌ	blotto
DOTŌ	ridotto
GOTŌ	fagotto
JOTŌ	jotto
KOTŌ	staccato
LOTŌ	lotto
MOTŌ	motto
POTŌ	potto
SOTŌ	risotto
WOTŌ	Watteau

(See **ÄTŌ**)

ŌTON

(See **ŌTN**)

OTSĒ

NOTSĒ	Nazi
ROTSĒ	paparazzi, ROTC
TOTSĒ	hotsy-totsy

OTSMAN

SKOTSMAN	Scotsman
YOTSMAN	yachtsman

ŌTUM

KWŌTUM	quotum
NŌTUM	notum, pronotum
SKRŌTUM	scrotum
TŌTUM	factotum, teetotum, totem, totum

ŌTUS

BRŌTUS	brotus
KRŌTUS	macrotous
LŌTUS	lotus
MŌTUS	amotus
NŌTUS	gymnotus, Notus
SKŌTUS	Duns Scotus

OUAN

GOUAN	gowan
ROUAN	rowan, rowen

OUANS

LOUANS	allowance, disallowance
VOUANS	avowance, disavowance

OUARD

KOUARD	coward

(See **OUER**, add *-ed* where appropriate.)

OUCHĒ

GROUCHĒ	grouchy
KROUCHĒ	crouchy
POUCHĒ	pouchy
SLOUCHĒ	slouchy

OUCHER

GROUCHER	groucher
KOUCHER	coucher
KROUCHER	croucher
POUCHER	poucher
SLOUCHER	sloucher
VOUCHER	avoucher, voucher

OUCHING

(See **OUCH**, add *-ing* where appropriate.)

OUDA

GOUDA	gouda
HOUDA	howdah

OUDĒ

DOUDĒ	apple-pan dowdy, dowdy, pandowdy, rowdy-dowdy
GOUDĒ	Goudy
HOUDĒ	howdie, howdy
KLOUDĒ	cloudy, uncloudy
KROUDĒ	crowdy
LOUDĒ	cum laude, magna cum laude, summa cum laude
PROUDĒ	proudy
ROUDĒ	rowdy
SHROUDĒ	shroudy
TOUDĒ	towdy

OUDED

KLOUDED	beclouded, enclouded, interclouded, clouded, overclouded, reclouded, thunderclouded, unclouded
KROUDED	crowded, overcrowded
SHROUDED	beshrouded, disenshrouded, enshrouded, reshrouded, shrouded, unshrouded

OUDER

CHOUDER	clam chowder, chowder
KROUDER	crowder
LOUDER	louder
POUDER	baking powder, bepowder, face powder, gunpowder, powder, Seidlitz powder
PROUDER	prouder

OUDING

KLOUDING	beclouding, clouding, unclouding
KROUDING	crowding, overcrowding
SHROUDING	enshrouding, shrouding
STROUDING	strouding

OUDISH

LOUDISH	loudish
PROUDISH	proudish

OUDLĒ

LOUDLĒ	loudly
PROUDLĒ	proudly

OUDNES

LOUDNES	loudness
PROUDNES	proudness

OUĒ

DOUĒ	dowie
KOUĒ	cowy
WOUĒ	wowie
ZOUĒ	zowy

OUEL

BOUEL	bowel, disembowel, embowel
DOUEL	dowel
HOUEL	howel
KOUEL	cowal
NOUEL	nowel
ROUEL	rowel
TOUEL	towel
TROUEL	trowel

MAY I INTRODUCE ALISTOR CHANCELLAIR?

When announcers announce
John Chancellor,
Why do they pronounce
The name they announce
As if it rhymed with *or?*
I'd think he'd prefer
Ur.

They don't rhyme Alistair
Cooke with *air.*
Alistair, sir,
They end with *ur,*
And I should say
He likes it that way.

Now if Chancellor
Were spelled Chancellair,
And if Alistair
Were spelled Alistor,
Which would rhyme with *ur,*
And which with *or?*
Or would one rhyme with *air?*
You say you don't care?

Well, just you try to stand up in a crowd
And say this verse right—off the cuff—out loud.

VOUEL	avowal, disavowal, semivowel, vowel

(See **OUL**)

OUER

BOUER	bower, embower, imbower
DOUER	dower, endower
FLOUER	*B* beflower, bloodflower, *D* dayflower, deflower, *E* enflower, *F* fameflower, fanflower, flower, *G* gillyflower, *GR* grapeflower, *K* cauliflower, coneflower, cornflower, lampflower, *M* Mayflower, mistflower, moonflower, *P* passion flower, *S* safflower, sunflower, *SH* shoeflower, *T* tongueflower, *W* wallflower, windflower (etc.)
GLOUER	glower
KOUER	cower
LOUER	allower, lower
PLOUER	plougher, plower
POUER	empower, electric power, flower power, horsepower, candlepower, manpower, overpower, power, steam power, student power, superpower, waterpower
ROUER	rower
SHOUER	shower, thundershower
TOUER	beacontower, churchtower, fire tower, overtower, tower, watchtower
VOUER	avower, disavower, vower
WOUER	wower

(See **OUR**)

OUHAND

KOUHAND	cowhand
PLOUHAND	plowhand

OUHOUS

BOUHOUS	Bauhaus
CHOUHOUS	chowhouse

OUING

WOUING	bowwowing
YOUING	meowing

(See **OU**, add *-ing* where appropriate.)

OULĒ

OULĒ	owly
GROULĒ	growly
HOULĒ	haole
SKOULĒ	scowly

OULER

OULER	owler
FOULER	fouler, fowler
GROULER	growler
HOULER	howler
PROULER	prowler
SKOULER	scowler
YOULER	yowler

OULET

OULET	owlet
HOULET	howlet
ROULET	rowlet

OULING

OULING	owling
FOULING	befouling, fouling, fowling
GROULING	growling
HOULING	howling
KOULING	cowling
PROULING	prowling
SKOULING	scowling

OULISH

OULISH	owlish
FOULISH	foulish
GROULISH	growlish

OUMENT

DOUMENT	endowment

| LOUMENT | allowment, disallowment |
| VOUMENT | avowment, disavowment |

OUNDED

(See **OUND**, add *-ed* where appropriate.)

OUNDER

BOUNDER	bounder, rebounder
FLOUNDER	flounder
FOUNDER	dumfounder, founder, iron founder, confounder, profounder, type founder
HOUNDER	hounder
POUNDER	expounder, four-pounder, hundred-pounder (etc.), impounder, compounder, pounder, propounder
ROUNDER	rounder, surrounder
SOUNDER	sounder
STOUNDER	astounder
ZOUNDER	resounder

OUNDIJ

GROUNDIJ	groundage
POUNDIJ	impoundage, poundage
SOUNDIJ	soundage

OUNDING

| BOUNDING | abounding, bounding |
| SOUNDING | big-sounding, deep-sounding, evil-sounding, high-sounding, low-sounding (etc.), sounding |

(See **OUND**, add *-ing* where appropriate.)

OUNDLĒ

FOUNDLĒ	profoundly
ROUNDLĒ	roundly
SOUNDLĒ	soundly, unsoundly

OUNDLES

| BOUNDLES | boundless |

| GROUNDLES | groundless |
| SOUNDLES | soundless |

OUNDLING

| FOUNDLING | foundling |
| GROUNDLING | groundling |

OUNDMĒL

| GROUNDMĒL | groundmeal |
| STOUNDMĒL | stoundmeal |

OUNDNES

FOUNDNES	profoundness
ROUNDNES	roundness
SOUNDNES	soundness, unsoundness

OUNĒ

BROUNĒ	brownie, browny
DOUNĒ	downy
FROUNĒ	frowny
KLOUNĒ	clowny
TOUNĒ	towny

OUNER

BROUNER	browner
DOUNER	downer, sundowner
DROUNER	drowner
FROUNER	frowner
KROUNER	crowner
TOUNER	downtowner, out-of-tower, towner, uptowner

OUNING

BROUNING	browning, Browning
DOUNING	downing
DROUNING	drowning
FROUNING	frowning
GOUNING	gowning
KLOUNING	clowning
KROUNING	crowning, encrowning

OUNISH

(See **OUN**, add *-ish* where appropriate.)

OUNJER

| LOUNJER | lounger |
| SKROUNJER | scrounger |

OUNJING

| LOUNJING | lounging |
| SKROUNJING | scrounging |

OUNLES

DOUNLES	downless
GOUNLES	gownless
KLOUNLES	clownless
KROUNLES	crownless
TOUNLES	townless

OUNSER

BOUNSER	bouncer
FLOUNSER	flouncer
NOUNSER	announcer, denouncer, pronouncer, renouncer
POUNSER	pouncer
TROUNSER	trouncer

OUNSING

(See **OUNS**, add *-ing* where appropriate.)

OUNTĒ

BOUNTĒ	bounty
KOUNTĒ	county, viscounty
MOUNTĒ	Mountie

OUNTED

(See **OUNT**, add *-ed* where appropriate.)

OUNTER

| KOUNTER | accounter, discounter, encounter, counter, reencounter, recounter |
| MOUNTER | mounter, remounter, surmounter |

OUNTIN

| FOUNTIN | fountain |
| MOUNTIN | catamountain, cat o' mountain, man-mountain, mountain |

OUNTING

KOUNTING	accounting, discounting, counting, miscounting, recounting
MOUNTING	amounting, dismounting, mounting, remounting, surmounting

OUNWERD

DOUNWERD	downward
TOUNWERD	townward

OUNZMAN

GOUNZMAN	gownsman
TOUNZMAN	townsman

OURĒ

CHOURĒ	chowry
DOURĒ	dowry
FLOURĒ	floury, flowery
HOURĒ	houri
KOURĒ	kauri, cowrie, cowry
LOURĒ	loury, lowery
MOURĒ	Maori
VOURĒ	avowry

OURER

FLOURER	deflowerer
LOURER	lourer, lowerer
SKOURER	scourer
SOURER	sourer
VOURER	devourer

(See OUER, add -er where appropriate.)

OURING

SKOURING	bescouring, off-scouring, scouring

(See OUR, OUER, add -ing where appropriate.)

OURLĒ

OURLĒ	half-hourly, quarter-hourly, hourly

DOURLĒ	dourly
SOURLĒ	sourly

OURNES

DOURNES	dourness
SOURNES	sourness

OUSBRĒCH

HOUSBRĒCH	housebreach
SPOUSBRĒCH	spousebreach

OUSING

BLOUSING	blousing
DOUSING	dousing
MOUSING	mousing
SOUSING	sousing

OUSTED

OUSTED	ousted
JOUSTED	jousted
ROUSTED	rousted

OUSTER

OUSTER	ouster
JOUSTER	jouster
ROUSTER	rouster

OUSTING

(See OUST, add -ing where appropriate.)

OUTĒ

DOUTĒ	doughty
DROUTĒ	droughty
GOUTĒ	gouty
GROUTĒ	grouty
LOUTĒ	louty
POUTĒ	pouty
SNOUTĒ	snouty
SPOUTĒ	spouty
TOUTĒ	touty
TROUTĒ	trouty

OUTED

DOUTED	doubted
FLOUTED	flouted
GROUTED	grouted
KLOUTED	clouted

NOUTED	knouted
POUTED	pouted
ROUTED	derouted, routed
SHOUTED	shouted
SKOUTED	scouted
SMOUTED	smouted
SNOUTED	snouted
SPOUTED	spouted
SPROUTED	resprouted, sprouted
TOUTED	touted

OUTER

OUTER	down-and-outer, far-outer, in-and-outer, out-and-outer, outer
BOUTER	bouter
DOUTER	doubter, nondoubter
FLOUTER	flouter
GROUTER	grouter
JOUTER	jowter
KLOUTER	clouter
KROUTER	sauerkrauter
NOUTER	knouter
POUTER	pouter
ROUTER	router
SHOUTER	shouter
SKOUTER	scouter
SPOUTER	spouter
SPROUTER	sprouter
STOUTER	stouter
TOUTER	touter
TROUTER	trouter
VOUTER	devouter

OUTING

(See OUT, add -ing where appropriate.)

OUTISH

OUTISH	outish
LOUTISH	loutish
STOUTISH	stoutish

OUTLĒ

STOUTLĒ	stoutly
VOUTLĒ	devoutly

OUTNES

STOUTNES	stoutness
VOUTNES	devoutness

OUWOU

BOUWOU	bowwow

POUWOU powwow
WOUWOU wou-wou, wow-wow

OUZAL
(See OUZL)

OUZĒ
BLOUZĒ blousy, blowzy
BOUZĒ bousy
DROUZĒ drowsy
FROUZĒ frowsy, frowzy
GROUZĒ grousy
HOUZĒ housy
LOUZĒ lousy
MOUZĒ mousy
SPOUZĒ spousy

OUZEL
(See OUZL)

OUZER
BOUZER bouser, bowser
BROUZER browser
DOUZER douser, dowser
HOUZER houser
MOUZER Mauser, mouser
POUZER espouser
ROUZER arouser, carouser, rouser
SHNOUZER schnauzer
TOUZER towser
TROUZER trouser
WOUZER wowser
YOUZER yowzer

OUZERZ
TROUZERZ trousers
(See OUZER, add -s where appropriate.)

OUZIJ
HOUZIJ housage
SPOUZIJ espousage, spousage

OUZING
(See OUZ, add -ing where appropriate.)

OUZL
OUZL ousel, ouzel
HOUZL housal, housel

POUZL espousal
SPOUZL spousal
ROUZL arousal, carousal
TOUZL tousle

OUZLD
HOUZLD houselled, unhouselled
TOUZLD tousled, untousled

ŌVA
ŌVA ova
HŌVA Jehovah
KŌVA Markova
LŌVA Pavlova
NŌVA ars nova, bossa nova, Casanova, nova, supernova, Villanova
RŌVA korova

ŌVĒ
CHŌVĒ anchovy
GRŌVĒ grovy

OVEL
GROVEL grovel
HOVEL hovel
NOVEL novel
(See UVEL)

ŌVEN
HŌVEN hoven
KLŌVEN cloven, uncloven
WŌVEN interwoven, inwoven, rewoven, woven

ŌVER
ŌVER CH changeover, FL flashover, flyover, flopover, H half-seas-over, hangover, KR crossover, L leftover, M moreover, O over, P Passover, pullover, pushover, R wrapover, runover, SL sleepover, slipover, ST stopover, T turnover, W walkover

DŌVER Andover, Dover
DRŌVER drover
KLŌVER four-leaf clover, in clover, clover, sweet clover
NŌVER Hanover
PLŌVER plover
RŌVER rover, sea rover
STŌVER stover
TRŌVER trover

ŌVERZ
TŌVERZ estovers, leftovers
(See ŌVER, add -s where appropriate.)

ŌVĪN
ŌVĪN ovine
BŌVĪN bovine

ŌVING
KŌVING coving
RŌVING roving
SHRŌVING shroving
STŌVING stoving

ŌVŌ
ŌVŌ ab ovo
NŌVŌ de novo
PRŌVŌ provost

ŌYER
ŌYER oyer
BŌYER bowyer

ÔYER
BÔYER buoyer
LÔYER lawyer, delawyer
SÔYER sawyer, topsawyer
(See OIER)

ŌZA
NŌZA Spinoza
PŌZA Mariposa

ŌZAL
(See ŌZEL)

ÔZAL

KLÔZAL	clausal
KÔZAL	causal
PÔZAL	pausal

ŌZAL

PŌZAL	deposal, disposal, interposal, opposal, presupposal, reposal, supposal, transposal
RŌZAL	rosal

ŌZĒ

DŌZĒ	dozy
FŌZĒ	fozy
KŌZĒ	egg cozy, cosy, cozy, tea cozy
MŌZĒ	mozey
NŌZĒ	nosy
PŌZĒ	posy
PRŌZĒ	prosy
RŌZĒ	rosy
TŌZĒ	tosy, tozee, tozie

ÔZĒ

GÔZĒ	gauzy
KÔZĒ	causey
LÔZĒ	lawsie

ŌZĒD

PŌZĒD	posied
RŌZĒD	rosied

ŌZEL

LŌZEL	losel
PŌZEL	deposal, disposal, opposal, proposal, supposal, transposal

ŌZEN

CHŌZEN	chosen, forechosen
FRŌZEN	frozen
HŌZEN	hosen
RŌZEN	rosen
SKWŌZEN	squozen

ŌZER

DŌZER	bulldozer, dozer
GLŌZER	glozer

HŌZER	hoser
KLŌZER	discloser, encloser, forecloser, incloser, closer, uncloser
NŌZER	noser
PŌZER	D decomposer, deposer, disposer, E exposer, I imposer, interposer, J juxtaposer, K composer, O opposer, P poser, PR predisposer, presupposer, proposer, R reimposer, reposer, S superimposer, supposer, TR transposer
PRŌZER	proser
RŌZER	roser

ÔZER

HÔZER	hawser
KÔZER	first causer, causer
PÔZER	pauser

OZET

(See OZIT)

ŌZHA

BRŌZHA	ambrosia
MŌZHA	afrormosia

ŌZHER

ŌZHER	osier
HŌZHER	hosier
KLŌZHER	disclosure, enclosure, foreclosure, inclosure, closure
KRŌZHER	crosier
PŌZHER	discomposure, disposure, exposure, composure, superimposure

(See Ō'ZI.ER)

ŌZHUN

KLŌZHUN	eclosion
KŌZHUN	icosian
PLŌZHUN	applosion, explosion, implosion, plosion
RŌZHUN	erosion, corrosion

ŌZING

(See ŌZ, add -ing where appropriate.)

ÔZING

KÔZING	causing
PÔZING	pausing

OZIT

KLOZIT	closet
POZIT	deposit, interposit, juxtaposit, composite, oviposit, posit, reposit

OZL

NOZL	nozzle
SHNOZL	schnozzle
SNOZL	snozzle
SOZL	sozzle

OZMIK

OZMIK	aosmic, osmic
DOZMIK	endosmic
KOZMIK	cosmic, macrocosmic, microcosmic, neocosmic

ŌZŪR

(See ŌZHER)

ŪA

SKŪA	skua
SŪA	Apologia Pro Vita Sua
TŪA	atua

(See OOA)

ŪAL

DŪAL	dual, duel, subdual
FŪAL	fuel, refuel, synfuel
HŪAL	hwyl
NŪAL	newel, renewal, urban renewal
SŪAL	pursual
TŪAL	tewel
VŪAL	reviewal

(See OOEL)

ŪANS

NŪANS	renewance, nuance
SŪANS	pursuance

(See OŌANS)

ŪANT

FLŪANT	fluent, perfluent
SŪANT	pursuant, suant

(See OŌENT)

ŪARD

(See ŪERD)

ŪBA

JŪBA	Juba, jubbah
KŪBA	Cuba
SŪBA	subah, tsuba
TŪBA	saxtuba, tuba

(See OŌBA)

ŪBÂL

KŪBÂL	cue-ball

(See OŌBÂL)

ŪBAL

KŪBAL	cubal
TŪBAL	tubal

(See OŌBAL)

ŪBĒ

KŪBĒ	cuby

(See OŌBĒ)

UBĒ

BUBĒ	bubby
CHUBĒ	chubby
FUBĒ	fubby
GRUBĒ	grubby
HUBĒ	hubby
KLUBĒ	clubby
KUBĒ	cubby
NUBĒ	knubby, nubby
RUBĒ	Rabi, Rubbee
SHRUBĒ	shrubby
SKRUBĒ	scrubby
SLUBĒ	slubby
STUBĒ	stubby
TUBĒ	tubby

ŪBER

KŪBER	Khubur, cuber
SŪBER	suber
TŪBER	tubar, tuber

(See OŌBER)

UBER

BLUBER	blubber
DRUBER	drubber
DUBER	dubber, redubber
FLUBER	flubber
GLUBER	glubber
GRUBER	grubber, money-grubber
HUBER	hubber
KLUBER	clubber
LUBER	*landlubber,* lubber
RUBER	India rubber, rubber
SKRUBER	scrubber
SLUBER	slubber
SNUBER	snubber
STUBER	stubber
TUBER	tubber

UBERD

BLUBERD	blubbered
HUBERD	Mother Hubbard
KUBERD	cupboard
RUBERD	rubbered

ŪBĒZ

PŪBĒZ	pubes

(See OŌBĒZ)

ŪBIJ

KŪBIJ	cubage
TŪBIJ	tubage

ŪBIK

KŪBIK	cubic
PŪBIK	pubic

(See OŌBIK)

UBIN

DUBIN	dubbin
NUBIN	nubbin

ŪBING

KŪBING	cubing
TŪBING	tubing

(See OŌBING)

UBING

(See UB, add *-ing* where appropriate.)

UBISH

GRUBISH	grubbish
KLUBISH	clubbish
KUBISH	cubbish
RUBISH	rubbish
SHRUBISH	shrubbish
SNUBISH	snubbish

ŪBIT

KŪBIT	cubit

(See OŌBIT)

ŪBL

KŪBL	cubal
TŪBL	tubal

(See OŌBL)

UBL

BUBL	bubble, hubble-bubble
DUBL	daily double, double, redouble, subdouble
HUBL	hubble
NUBL	nubble
RUBL	rubble
STUBL	stubble
TRUBL	trouble

UBLD

BUBLD	bubbled
DUBLD	doubled, redoubled
STUBLD	stubbled
TRUBLD	troubled

ŪBLĒ

BUBLĒ	bubbly
DUBLĒ	doubly
HUBLĒ	hubbly
NUBLĒ	knubbly, nubbly
RUBLĒ	rubbly
STRUBLĒ	strubbly
STUBLĒ	stubbly

ŪBLET

KŪBLET	cubelet
TŪBLET	tubelet

UBLER

RUBLER	rubbler

(See UBL, add -r where appropriate.)

UBLET

DUBLET	doublet
KUBLET	cublet
SUBLET	sublet

UBLING

(See UBL, add -ing where appropriate.)

UBLZ

FUBLZ	mubble-fubbles

(See UBL, add -s where appropriate.)

ŪBRIK

(See ŌŌBRIK)

UBSTĀK

GRUBSTĀK	grubstake
KLUBSTĀK	club steak

ŪCHĒ

(See ŌŌCHĒ)

UCHĒ

DUCHĒ	archduchy, duchy
KLUCHĒ	clutchy
SMUCHĒ	smutchy
TUCHĒ	touchy

ŪCHER

BLŪCHER	blucher
FŪCHER	future
PŪCHER	puture
SŪCHER	suture

(See ŌŌCHER)

UCHER

DUCHER	Dutcher
HUCHER	hutcher
KLUCHER	clutcher
RUCHER	rutcher
SKUCHER	scutcher
SMUCHER	smutcher
TUCHER	retoucher, toucher

UCHING

(See UCH, add -ing where appropriate.)

ŪDA

MŪDA	Bermuda

(See ŌŌDA)

ŪDAL

(See ŪDL, ŌŌDL)

ŪDĒ

FŪDĒ	feudee, feudy
MŪDĒ	almude
NŪDĒ	nudie

(See ŌŌDĒ)

UDĒ

BLUDĒ	bloody
BUDĒ	buddy, anybody, everybody, nobody, somebody
DUDĒ	fuddy-duddy
KRUDĒ	cruddy
KUDĒ	cuddy
MUDĒ	muddy
NUDĒ	nuddy
PUDĒ	puddy
RUDĒ	ruddy
SKUDĒ	scuddy
STUDĒ	brown study, microstudy, overstudy, studdy, study, understudy
SUDĒ	soapsuddy

ŪDED

(See ŪD, ŌŌD, add -d, -ed where appropriate.)

UDĒD

BLUDĒD	bloodied
MUDĒD	muddied
RUDĒD	ruddied
STUDĒD	overstudied, studied, understudied, unstudied

UDED

STUDED	star-studded

(See UD, add -ed where appropriate.)

ŪDENS

(See ŌŌDENS)

ŪDENT

STŪDENT	student

(See ŌŌDENT)

ŪDER

LŪDER	alluder, deluder, eluder, lewder
NŪDER	denuder, nuder
SŪDER	sudor
TŪDER	Tudor

(See ŌŌDER)

UDER

UDER	udder
CHUDER	chudder
DUDER	dudder
FLUDER	flooder
JUDER	judder
MUDER	mudder
PUDER	pudder
RUDER	rudder
SHUDER	shudder
SKUDER	scudder
SUDER	sudder

UDIJ

BUDIJ	buddage
FLUDIJ	floodage

ŪDIK

LŪDIK	paludic
PŬDIK	antipudic, pudic

ŪDING

FŪDING	feuding
NŪDING	denuding
SŪDING	exuding, transuding
ZŪDING	exuding

(See O͞OD, add -ing where appropriate.)

UDING

BLUDING	blooding
BUDING	budding
FLUDING	flooding
KUDING	cudding
MUDING	mudding
RUDING	rudding
SKUDING	scudding
SPUDING	spudding
STUDING	bestudding, studding, unstudding
SUDING	sudding
THUDING	thudding

ŪDISH

DŪDISH	dudish
NŪDISH	nudish

(See O͞ODISH)

ŪDIST

FŪDIST	feudist
NŪDIST	nudist

(See O͞ODIST)

ŪDL

ŪDL	udal, kiyoodle
FŪDL	feudal
LŪDL	paludal

(See O͞ODL)

UDL

BUDL	buddle
FUDL	befuddle, fuddle
HUDL	huddle
KUDL	cuddle
MUDL	bemuddle, muddle
NUDL	nuddle
PUDL	puddle
RUDL	ruddle
SKUDL	scuddle
STUDL	studdle

UDLD

(See UDL, add -ed where appropriate.)

ŪDLĒ

LŪDLĒ	lewdly
NŪDLĒ	nudely

(See O͞ODLĒ)

UDLĒ

FUDLĒ	fuddly
KUDLĒ	cuddly
PUDLĒ	puddly

UDLER

FUDLER	befuddler, fuddler
HUDLER	huddler
KUDLER	cuddler
MUDLER	muddler
PUDLER	puddler

UDLING

(See UDL, add -ing where appropriate.)

ŪDNES

LŪDNES	lewdness
NŪDNES	nudeness

(See O͞ODNES)

ŪDŌ

SŪDŌ	pseudo
TŪDŌ	testudo, consuetudo

(See O͞ODŌ)

ŪDO͞O

(See O͞ODO͞O)

UDUK

PUDUK	puddock
RUDUK	ruddock

ŪĒ

DŪĒ	bedewy, dewy, Dewey, mildewy
STŪĒ	stewy
THŪĒ	thewy

(See O͞OĒ)

ŪEL

(See ŪAL, O͞OEL)

ŪER

ŪER	ewer
DŪER	subduer
FŪER	fewer
HŪER	hewer
NŪER	newer, renewer
SŪER	ensuer, pursuer, sewer, suer
VŪER	interviewer, viewer

(See O͞OER)

ŪERD

SŪERD	sewered
SKŪERD	skewered
STŪERD	steward

(See O͞OERD)

ŪET

(See O͞OET)

ŪFA

(See O͞OFA)

ŪFĒ

(See O͞OFĒ)

UFĒ

BLUFĒ	bluffy
BUFĒ	buffy

CHUFĒ	chuffy
FLUFĒ	fluffy
FUFĒ	fuffy
GUFĒ	guffy
HUFĒ	huffy
KUFĒ	cuffy
PLUFĒ	pluffy
PUFĒ	puffy
RUFĒ	roughie, ruffy
SKRUFĒ	scruffy
SLUFĒ	sloughy
SNUFĒ	snuffy
STUFĒ	stuffy
TUFĒ	toughy

UFEN

(See UFIN)

ŪFER

(See ŌŌFER)

UFER

BLUFER	bluffer
BUFER	buffer
CHUFER	chuffer
DUFER	duffer
FLUFER	fluffer
GRUFER	gruffer
GUFER	guffer
HUFER	huffer
KUFER	cuffer
LUFER	luffer
MUFER	muffer
PLUFER	pluffer
PUFER	puffer
RUFER	rougher, ruffer
SKUFER	scuffer
SLUFER	slougher, sluffer
SNUFER	snuffer
STUFER	stocking-stuffer, stuffer
SUFER	suffer
TUFER	tougher

UFET

BUFET	buffet
FUFET	fuffit
MUFET	Little Miss Muffet
TUFET	tuffet

UFIN

BUFEN	buffin
GUFEN	guffin
MUFEN	muffin, ragamuffin

PUFEN	puffin
RUFEN	mumruffin, roughen
TUFEN	toughen

ŪFING

(See ŌŌFING)

UFING

(See UF, add -ing where appropriate.)

UFISH

(See UF, add -ish where appropriate.)

UFIT

(See UFET)

UFL

BUFL	buffle
DUFL	duffle
FUFL	fuffle, kerfuffle
HWUFL	whuffle
MUFL	bemuffle, muffle, unmuffle
RUFL	ruffle, unruffle
SHUFL	double shuffle, reshuffle, shuffle
SKUFL	scuffle
SNUFL	snuffle
TRUFL	truffle

UFLD

(See UFL, add -d where appropriate.)

UFLĒ

BLUFLĒ	bluffly
GRUFLĒ	gruffly
MUFLĒ	muffly
RUFLĒ	roughly, ruffly
SKUFLĒ	scuffly
SNUFLĒ	snuffly
TRUFLĒ	truffly
TUFLĒ	toughly

UFLER

MUFLER	muffler
RUFLER	ruffler
SHUFLER	shuffler
SKUFLER	scuffler
SNUFLER	snuffler

UFLING

(See UFL, add -ing where appropriate.)

UFNES

(See UF, add -ness where appropriate.)

UFTĒ

MUFTĒ	mufti
TUFTĒ	tufty

ŪFUS

(See ŌŌFUS)

ŪGA

(See ŌŌGA)

ŪGAL

(See ŪGL)

ŪGAR

(See ŌŌGER)

ŪGĒ

(See ŌŌGĒ)

UGĒ

BUGĒ	buggy
DRUGĒ	druggie
FUGĒ	fuggy
LUGĒ	luggie, luggy
MUGĒ	muggy
PLUGĒ	pluggy
PUGĒ	puggi, puggy
RUGĒ	ruggy
SHUGĒ	shuggy
SLUGĒ	sluggy
THUGĒ	thuggee
VUGĒ	vuggy

ŪGER

(See ŌŌGER)

UGER

BUGER	bugger
CHUGER	chugger
DRUGER	drugger
HUGER	hugger
LUGER	luggar, lugger

MUGER	huggermugger, cuggermugger, mugger
NUGER	nugger
PLUGER	plugger
PUGER	pugger
RUGER	rugger
SHRUGER	shrugger
SLUGER	slugger
SMUGER	smugger
SNUGER	snugger
TUGER	tugger

UGET

DRUGET	drugget
MUGET	mugget
NUGET	nugget

UGING

(See UG, add -ing where appropriate.)

UGISH

(See UG, add -ish where appropriate.)

ŪGL

| BŪGL | bugle |
| FŪGL | febrifugal, fugal, fugle, vermifugal |

(See OOGL)

UGL

GUGL	guggle
JUGL	juggle
PUGL	puggle
SMUGL	smuggle
SNUGL	snuggle
STRUGL	death struggle, struggle

UGLĒ

UGLĒ	plug-ugly, ugli, ugly
GUGLĒ	guggly
JUGLĒ	juggly
SMUGLĒ	smugly
SNUGLĒ	snugly
STRUGLĒ	struggly

ŪGLER

| BŪGLER | bugler |
| FŪGLER | fugler |

UGLER

JUGLER	juggler
SMUGLER	smuggler
SNUGLER	snuggler
STRUGLER	struggler

UGLING

(See UGL, add -ing where appropriate.)

UGNES

| SMUGNES | smugness |
| SNUGNES | snugness |

ŪĪD

| SKŪĪD | skew-eyed |

(See OOĪD)

ŪĪJ

| SŪĪJ | sewage |

(See OOĪJ)

ŪIK

| BŪIK | Buick |

(See OOIK)

ŪING

(See Ū, OO, add -ing where appropriate.)

ŪISH

| NŪISH | newish |

(See OOISH)

ŪIST

| VŪIST | revuist, reviewist |

(See OOIST)

ŪJĒ

(See OOJĒ)

UJĒ

FUJĒ	fudgy
PUJĒ	pudgy
SLUJĒ	sludgy
SMUJĒ	smudgy

UJER

BUJER	budger
DRUJER	drudger
FUJER	fudger
GRUJER	begrudger, grudger
JUJER	adjudger, forejudger, judger, misjudger, prejudger, rejudger
NUJER	nudger
SLUJER	sludger
SMUJER	smudger
TRUJER	trudger

UJING

(See UJ, add -ing where appropriate.)

UJUN

BLUJUN	bludgeon
DUJUN	dudgeon, humdudgeon
GUJUN	gudgeon
MUJUN	curmudgeon
TRUJUN	trudgeon

ŪKA

(See OOKA)

UKĀ

BUKA	bucca
LUKA	felucca
PUKA	pucka, pukka
YUKA	yuca, yucca

ŪKAL

DŪKAL	archducal, ducal
LŪKAL	noctilucal
NŪKAL	nucal, nuchal
TŪKAL	pentateuchal

(See OOKAL)

ŪKAN

| LŪKAN | antelucan |

(See OOKAN)

ŪKĒ

(See OŌKĒ)

UKĒ

BUKĒ	buckie, bucky
DUKĒ	ducky
KLUKĒ	clucky
LUKĒ	lucky, unlucky
MUKĒ	mucky
PLUKĒ	plucky
TRUKĒ	truckie
TUKĒ	Kentucky, tucky
YUKĒ	yucky

ŪKER

ŪKER	euchre
BŪKER	rebuker
PŪKER	puker

(See OŌKER)

UKER

BUKER	bucker
CHUKER	chucker, chukker
DUKER	ducker
KLUKER	clucker
MUKER	mucker
PLUKER	plucker
PUKER	pucker
SHUKER	clam-shucker, oyster-shucker, shucker
SUKER	bloodsucker, goatsucker, honeysucker, all-day sucker, sapsucker, seersucker, windsucker, succor, sucker
TRUKER	trucker
TUKER	tucker

UKET

BUKET	bucket, gutbucket, milk bucket, water bucket
MUKET	mucket
TUKET	Nantucket, Pawtucket, tucket

UKIJ

PLUKIJ	pluckage
SUKIJ	suckage
TRUKIJ	truckage

ŪKING

BŪKING	rebuking
PŪKING	puking

UKING

(See UK, add -ing where appropriate.)

UKISH

BUKISH	buckish
MUKISH	muckish
PUKISH	puckish

UKL

BRUKL	bruckle
BUKL	buccal, buckle, parbuckle, swashbuckle, turnbuckle, unbuckle
CHUKL	chuckle
HUKL	huckle
MUKL	muckle
NUKL	knuckle
SUKL	honeysuckle, suckle
TRUKL	truckle
YUKL	yukkel

HOBSON'S CHOICE

Feeling sick?
Take your pick:
Anemia—
Leukemia—
Toxemia—
Uremia—
All ways of dying
Worth trying.

UKLD

BUKLD	buckled, swashbuckled, unbuckled
CHUKLD	chuckled
KUKLD	cuckold
NUKLD	knuckled
SUKLD	suckled
TRUKLD	truckled

UKLER

BUKLER	buckler, swashbuckler
CHUKLER	chuckler
NUKLER	knuckler
SUKLER	suckler
TRUKLER	truckler

UKLES

(See UK, add -less)

UKLING

DUKLING	duckling, ugly duckling
SUKLING	suckling

(See UKL, change -e to -ing where appropriate.)

UKOLD

(See UKLD)

UKSĒ

DRUKSĒ	druxy
LUKSĒ	Biloxi
MUKSĒ	mucksy
PUKSĒ	pucksy, puxy

UKSHUN

DUKSHUN	*A* abduction, adduction, *D* deduction, duction, *E* eduction, eroduction, *I* induction, introduction, *K* conduction, *L* lavoduction, *M* manuduction, mass production, *N* nonconduction, *O* obduction, overproduction, *PR* production, *R* reduction, reproduction, *S* seduction, subduction, superinduction, *TR* traduction, transduction, *U* underproduction
FLUKSHUN	affluxion, defluxion, effluxion, fluxion, influxion, solifluction
RUKSHUN	ruction
STRUKSHUN	destruction, instruction, construction, misconstruction, obstruction, reconstruction, self-destruction, substruction, superstruction
SUKSHUN	suction

UKSUM

BUKSUM	buxom
LUKSUM	lucksome

UKTANS

DUKTANS	inductance, conductance
LUKTANS	reluctance

UKTER

DUKTER	abducter, adductor, ductor, eductor, inductor, introductor, conductor, manuductor, nonconductor, producer, semiconductor
STRUKTER	destructor, instructor, constructor, obstructor, reconstructor

UKTED

(See **UKT**, add -ed where appropriate.)

UKTING

(See **UKT**, add -ing where appropriate.)

UKTIV

DUKTIV	A adductive, D deductive, I inductive, introductive, K conductive, counterproductive, M manuductive, N nonconductive, O overproductive, PR productive, R reductive, reconductive, reproductive, S seductive, superinductive, TR traductive, U underproductive
STRUKTIV	destructive, instructive, constructive, obstructive, reconstructive, self-destructive, superstructive

UKTOR

(See **UKTER**)

UKTRES

DUKTRES	abductress, introductress, conductress, seductress
STRUKTRES	instructress

ŪKUS

DŪKUS	caducous
FŪKUS	fucous, fucus
LŪKUS	leucous, noctilucous
MŪKUS	mucous, mucus

UKUS

MUKUS	mukkus
RUKUS	ruckus
SUKUS	exsuccus, succus

ŪLA

ŪLA	ula
GŪLA	gula

(See **ŌŌLA**)

ULA

DULA	medulla
GULA	Gullah
KULA	cuculla
MULA	mullah
NULA	nullah, nullanulla
PULA	ampulla
SULA	sulla, Sulla

ULCHER

KULCHER	A agriculture, aquaculture, apiculture, arboriculture, aviculture, B boviculture, domiculture, FL floriculture, H horticulture, I inculture, K counterculture, culture, M mariculture, monoculture, P pisciculture, pomiculture, puericulture, S self-culture, sericulture, sylviculture, ST stirpiculture, T terraculture, V vegeculture, viniculture, viticulture
MULCHER	mulcher, multure
PULCHER	sepulture
VULCHER	vulture

ŪLĒ

DŪLĒ	duly, iconoduly, unduly
GŪLĒ	guly
MŪLĒ	muley
NŪLĒ	newly
THŪLĒ	Thule, Ultima Thule

(See **ŌŌLĒ**)

ULĒ

DULĒ	dully
GULĒ	gully, hully-gully
HULĒ	hully
KULĒ	cully
MULĒ	mulley
SKULĒ	skully
SULĒ	sully

ULĒD

GULĒD	gullied
SULĒD	sullied, unsullied

ULEN

MULEN	mullein, mullen
SULEN	sullen

ŪLER

KŪLER	ridiculer
MŪLER	mewler
PŪLER	puler

(See **ŌŌLER**)

ULER

DULER	duller, medullar
GULER	guller

HULER	dehuller, huller
KRULER	cruller
KULER	discolor, color, culler, miscolor, multicolor, recolor, rose-color, Technicolor, tricolor, versicolor, watercolor
LULER	luller
MULER	muller
NULER	annuller
PULER	ampuller
SKULER	sculler

ULERD

DULERD	dullard
KULERD	*D* discolored, *E* every-colored, *H* high-colored, *K* colored, *M* many-colored, multicolored, *O* overcolored, *P* particolored, party-colored, peach-colored, *R* recolored, rosy-colored, *SK* sky-colored, *U* uncolored, *W* wine-colored (etc.)

ŪLES

(See Ū, OO, ŪL, OOL, add -*less* where appropriate.)

ULET

GULET	gullet
KULET	cullet
MULET	mullet, surmullet

ULGAR

(See ULGER)

ULGĀT

ULGĀT	promulgate
VULGĀT	divulgate, evulgate, pervulgate, vulgate

ULGER

BULGER	Bulgar
FULGER	fulgor
VULGER	vulgar

ULIJ

ULIJ	ullage
GULIJ	gullage
KULIJ	cullage
SULIJ	sullage

ŪLING

FŪLING	fueling
KŪLING	ridiculing
MŪLING	mewling, muling
PŪLING	puling

(See OOLING)

ULING

(See **UL,** add -*ing* where appropriate.)

ŪLIP

TŪLIP	tulip

(See OOLIP)

ŪLISH

MŪLISH	mulish
PŪLISH	pulish

(See OOLISH)

ULISH

DULISH	dullish
GULISH	gullish

ULJENS

DULJENS	indulgence, self-indulgence
FULJENS	affulgence, effulgence, refulgence
VULJENS	divulgence

ULJENT

DULJENT	indulgent, self-indulgent
FULJENT	effulgent, fulgent, profulgent, refulgent, circumfulgent
MULJENT	emulgent

ULJER

BULJER	bulger
DULJER	indulger
MULJER	promulger
VULJER	divulger

ULJMENT

DULJMENT	indulgement
VULJMENT	divulgement

ULKĀT

KULKĀT	inculcate
SULKĀT	sulcate, trisulcate

ULKĒ

BULKĒ	bulky
HULKĒ	hulky
SKULKĒ	skulky
SULKĒ	sulky

ULKER

BULKER	bulker
HULKER	hulker
SKULKER	skulker
SULKER	sulker

ULKING

(See **ULK,** add -*ing* where appropriate.)

ULŌ

HULŌ	hullo
NULŌ	nullo

ULPĒ

GULPĒ	gulpy
PULPĒ	pulpy

ULPER

GULPER	gulper
PULPER	pulper
SKULPER	sculper

ULSER

ULSER	ulcer

PULSER expulser, pulsar, repulser

ULSHUN

ULSHUN	ultion
MULSHUN	demulsion, emulsion
PULSHUN	appulsion, expulsion, impulsion, compulsion, lateropulsion, propulsion, pulsion, repulsion
VULSHUN	avulsion, divulsion, evulsion, convulsion, revulsion

ULSING

PULSING	expulsing, pulsing, repulsing
VULSING	convulsing

ULSIV

MULSIV	emulsive
PULSIV	appulsive, expulsive, impulsive, compulsive, propulsive, pulsive, repulsive
VULSIV	divulsive, convulsive, revulsive

ULSTER

ULSTER	Ulster
HULSTER	hulster

ULTANT

SULTANT	insultant, consultant
ZULTANT	exultant, resultant

ULTED

KULTED	occulted
PULTED	catapulted
SULTED	insulted, consulted
ZULTED	exulted, resulted

ULTER

(See **ULT,** add -*er* where appropriate.)

ULTING

KULTING	occulting
PULTING	catapulting
SULTING	insulting, consulting
ZULTING	exulting, resulting

ULTIV

KULTIV	occultive
SULTIV	consultive
ZULTIV	exultive, resultive

ULTNES

DULTNES	adultness
KULTNES	occultness

ULTŪR

(See **ULCHER**)

ŪLŪ

(See $\overline{OO}L\overline{OO}$)

ULVER

HULVER	hulver
KULVER	culver

ULYUN

GULYUN	slubberdegullion, slumgullion
KULYUN	cullion
MULYUN	mullion
RULYUN	rullion
SKULYUN	scullion

ŪMA

ŪMA	Yuma
NŪMA	pneuma
PŪMA	puma

(See $\overline{OO}MA$)

ŪMAL

(See $\overline{OO}MAL$)

ŪMAN

(See **ŪMEN**)

ŪMĀT

HŪMĀT	exhumate, inhumate
PŪMĀT	despumate

UMBA

BLUMBA	blumba
DUMBA	dumba
LUMBA	calumba, Columba
RUMBA	rumba

UMBEL

(See **UMBL**)

UMBER

UMBER	umber
KLUMBER	clumber
KUMBER	disencumber, encumber, cucumber, cumber, unencumber
LUMBER	lumbar, lumber
NUMBER	number, outnumber, renumber
SLUMBER	slumber

UMBERD

(See **UMBER,** add -*ed* where appropriate.)

UMBIK

LUMBIK	columbic
PLUMBIK	plumbic

UMBL

UMBL	umbel, umble
BUMBL	bumble
DRUMBL	drumble
FUMBL	fumble
GRUMBL	grumble
HUMBL	humble
JUMBL	bejumble, jumble
KRUMBL	crumble
MUMBL	mumble
NUMBL	numble
RUMBL	rumble
SKUMBL	scumble
STUMBL	stumble
TUMBL	tumble

UMBLD

(See **UMBL,** add -*d* where appropriate.)

UMBLĒ

(See **UMBL**, change *-e* to *-y* where appropriate.)

UMBLER

(See **UMBL**, add *-r* where appropriate.)

UMBLING

BUMBLING	bumbling
DRUMBLING	drumbling
FUMBLING	fumbling
GRUMBLING	grumbling
HUMBLING	humbling
JUMBLING	jumbling
KRUMBLING	crumbling
MUMBLING	mumbling
RUMBLING	rumbling
SKUMBLING	scumbling
STUMBLING	stumbling
TUMBLING	tumbling

UMBLZ

UMBLZ	umbles
NUMBLZ	numbles

(See **UMBL**, add *-s* where appropriate.)

UMBŌ

DUMBŌ	Dumbo
GUMBŌ	gumbo
JUMBŌ	jumbo, Jumbo, mumbo-jumbo
LUMBŌ	columbo
PUMBŌ	pumbo

UMBRA

UMBRA	umbra
NUMBRA	penumbra

UMBRAL

UMBRAL	umbral
DUMBRAL	adumbral
NUMBRAL	penumbral
TUMBRAL	tumbrel

UMBRĀT

UMBRĀT	inumbrate, obumbrate
DUMBRĀT	adumbrate

UMBREL

UMBREL	umbral
DUMBREL	adumbral
NUMBREL	penumbral
TUMBREL	tumbrel

UMBRUS

UMBRUS	umbrous
KUMBRUS	cumbrous
NUMBRUS	penumbrous
SLUMBRUS	slumbrous

UMBUS

PLUMBUS	plumbous
LUMBUS	Columbus

ŪMĒ

FŪMĒ	fumy, perfumy
SPŪMĒ	spumy

(See **ŌŌMĒ**)

UMĒ

CHUMĒ	chummy
DUMĒ	double dummy, dummy
GLUMĒ	glummy
GUMĒ	gummy
KRUMĒ	crumby, crummie
LUMĒ	Lord lumme, lummy
MUMĒ	mummy
PLUMĒ	plummy
RUMĒ	auction rummy, English rummy, four-hand rummy, Java rummy, gin rummy, Michigan rummy, rummy, Word Rummy
SKRUMĒ	scrummy
SKUMĒ	scummy
SLUMĒ	slummy
THRUMĒ	thrummy
THUMĒ	thumby
TUMĒ	tummy
YUMĒ	yummy

UMEL

GRUMEL	grummel
HUMEL	hummel
PUMEL	bepummel, pommel, pummel
TRUMEL	trummel

ŪMEN

BŪMEN	albumen, albumin
GŪMEN	energumen, hegumen, legumen, legumin, *tegumen*
HŪMEN	human, inhuman, nonhuman, preterhuman, protohuman, superhuman, ultrahuman
KŪMEN	acumen, catechumen
NŪMEN	ichneumon, numen
TŪMEN	bitumen

(See **ŌŌMEN**)

ŪMENT

BŪMENT	imbuement
DŪMENT	induement, subduement
NŪMENT	renewment

(See **ŌŌMENT**)

ŪMER

FŪMER	fumer, perfumer
HŪMER	bad humor, black humor, good humor, humor, ill-humor, sick humor
LŪMER	illumer
SŪMER	assumer, consumer
TŪMER	costumer
ZŪMER	presumer, resumer

(See **ŌŌMER**)

UMER

BUMER	bummer
DRUMER	drummer
DUMER	dumber
GLUMER	glummer
GRUMER	grummer
GUMER	gummer
HUMER	hummer
KUMER	incomer, comer, cummer, late-comer, newcomer, succumber
MUMER	mummer

NUMER	number
PLUMER	plumber, plummer
RUMER	rummer
SKRUMER	scrummer
SKUMER	scummer
SLUMER	slummer
STRUMER	banjo-strummer, strummer
SUMER	midsummer, summer
THRUMER	thrummer
THUMER	thumber

ŪMERD

HŪMERD	bad-humored, foul-humored, good-humored, humored, ill-humored
TŪMERD	tumored

(See **ŌŌMERD**)

UMET

GRUMET	grummet
PLUMET	plummet
SUMET	consummate, summit

ŪMID

FŪMID	fumid
HŪMID	humid
TŪMID	tumid

ŪMIJ

FŪMIJ	fumage

(See **ŌŌMIJ**)

UMIJ

CHUMIJ	chummage
PLUMIJ	plumbage
RUMIJ	rummage
SKRUMIJ	scrummage
SUMIJ	summage

ŪMIK

HŪMIK	humic
KŪMIK	cumic
TŪMIK	costumic

(See **ŌŌMIK**)

UMING

FRUMING	to-and-froming

(See **UM,** add -ing where appropriate.)

UMKWÄT

KUMKWÄT	cumquat
PLUMKWÄT	plumquat

UMLĒ

CHUMLĒ	Cholmondesley
DUMLĒ	dumbly
GLUMLĒ	glumly
KUMLĒ	comely, uncomely
MUMLĒ	mumly
NUMLĒ	numbly
PLUMLĒ	plumbly
RUMLĒ	rumly
SUMLĒ	frolicsomely, humorsomely, cumbersomely, troublesomely

ŪMLES

FŪMLES	fumeless, perfumeless
GŪMLES	legumeless
NŪMLES	neumeless
SPŪMLES	spumeless

UMNAL

LUMNAL	columnal
TUMNAL	autumnal

UMNES

(See **UM,** add -ness where appropriate.)

UMOK

(See **UMUK**)

UMOKS

(See **UMUKS**)

ŪMOR

(See **ŪMER**)

UMPAS

(See **UMPUS**)

UMPĒ

BUMPĒ	bumpy
CHUMPĒ	chumpy
DUMPĒ	dumpy
FRUMPĒ	frumpy
GRUMPĒ	grumpy
HUMPĒ	humpy
JUMPĒ	jumpy
KLUMPĒ	clumpy
KRUMPĒ	crumpy
LUMPĒ	lumpy
MUMPĒ	mumpy
PLUMPĒ	plumpy
RUMPĒ	rumpy
SKRUMPĒ	scrumpy
SLUMPĒ	slumpy
STUMPĒ	stumpy
THUMPĒ	thumpy
YUMPĒ	Yumpy

UMPER

BUMPER	bumper
DUMPER	dumper
FLUMPER	flumper
FRUMPER	frumper
GLUMPER	glumper
GRUMPER	grumper
HUMPER	humper
JUMPER	broad-jumper, high-jumper, jumper, counter-jumper
KLUMPER	clumper
KRUMPER	crumper
LUMPER	lumper
MUMPER	mumper
PLUMPER	plumper
PUMPER	pumper
RUMPER	rumper, Rumper
SLUMPER	slumper
STUMPER	stumper
SUMPER	sumper
THUMPER	bethumper, Bible thumper, thumper, tub-thumper
TRUMPER	no-trumper, over-trumper, trumper
TUMPER	tumper

UMPERZ

PLUMPERZ	plumpers

(See **UMPER,** add -s where appropriate.)

UMPET

KRUMPET	crumpet

STRUMPET   strumpet
TRUMPET   trumpet

UMPIJ

PUMPIJ   pumpage
STUMPIJ   stumpage

UMPING

THUMPING   tub-thumping

(See UMP, add -ing)

UMPISH

(See UMP, add -ish where appropriate.)

UMPKIN

BUMPKIN   bumpkin
LUMPKIN   lumpkin
PUMPKIN   pumpkin

UMPL

KRUMPL   crumple
RUMPL   rumple, unrumple

UMPLING

DUMPLING   dumpling
KRUMPLING   crumpling
RUMPLING   rumpling, unrumpling

UMPSHUN

GUMPSHUN   gumption,
   rumgumption
SUMPSHUN   assumption,
   consumption,
   presumption,
   resumption,
   subsumption,
   transumption

UMPSHUS

BUMPSHUS   bumptious
GUMPSHUS   gumptious
SKRUMPSHUS   scrumptious

UMPTIV

SUMPTIV   assumptive,
   consumptive,
   subsumptive
ZUMPTIV   presumptive,
   resumptive

UMPUS

KUMPUS   astrocompass,
   encompass,
   gyrocompass,
   compass
RUMPUS   rumpus

UMUK

DRUMUK   drummock
HUMUK   hummock
STUMUK   stomach

UMUKS

FLUMUKS   flummox
GLUMUKS   glommox
HUMUKS   hummocks
LUMUKS   lummox
STUMUKS   stomachs

ŪMUS

DŪMUS   dumous
FŪMUS   fumous
HŪMUS   humous, humus,
   posthumous
SPŪMUS   spumous

(See ŌŌMUS)

UMZĒ

KLUMZĒ   clumsy
MUMZĒ   mummsy, mumsie

ŪNA

ŪNA   Una
KŪNA   lacuna
PŪNA   puna
TŪNA   Fortuna, tuna

(See ŌŌNA)

ŪNAL

BŪNAL   tribunal
DŪNAL   dunal
KŪNAL   lacunal
MŪNAL   communal

(See ŌŌNAL)

UNCHĒ

BUNCHĒ   bunchy
HUNCHĒ   hunchy
KRUNCHĒ   crunchy
MUNCHĒ   munchy
PUNCHĒ   punchy
SKRUNCHĒ   scrunchy

UNCHER

PUNCHER   cowpuncher, puncher

(See UNCH, add -er where appropriate.)

UNCHĒZ

KRUNCHĒZ   Crunchies
MUNCHĒZ   Munchies

UNCHING

BRUNCHING   brunching
BUNCHING   bunching
HUNCHING   hunching
KRUNCHING   crunching
LUNCHING   lunching
MUNCHING   munching
SKRUNCHING   scrunching

UNCHUN

BRUNCHUN   bruncheon
LUNCHUN   luncheon
NUNCHUN   nuncheon
PUNCHUN   puncheon
SKUNCHUN   scuncheon
TRUNCHUN   truncheon

UNDA

BUNDA   floribunda
MUNDA   barramunda, osmunda
TUNDA   rotunda

UNDANS

BUNDANS	abundance, overabundance, superabundance
DUNDANS	redundance

UNDANT

BUNDANT	abundant, overabundant, superabundant
DUNDANT	redundant

UNDĒ

UNDĒ	aliunde, undy
BUNDĒ	bundy
FUNDĒ	fundi, Fundy
GRUNDĒ	Mrs. Grundy
GUNDĒ	gundi, salmagundi, Salmagundi
MUNDĒ	Monday
RUNDĒ	jaguarundi
SUNDĒ	Whitsunday, Sunday

UNDED

UNDED	undead
BUNDED	bunded
FUNDED	funded, refunded
TUNDED	retunded, rotunded

UNDER

UNDER	down-under, hereunder, thereunder, under
BLUNDER	blunder
BUNDER	bunder
CHUNDER	chunder
DUNDER	dunder
FUNDER	funder, refunder
PLUNDER	plunder
SUNDER	asunder, sunder
THUNDER	enthunder, thunder
TUNDER	rotunder
WUNDER	wonder

UNDL

BUNDL	bundle, unbundle
MUNDL	mundil, mundle
RUNDL	rundle
TRUNDL	trundle

UNDLD

BUNDLD	bundled, unbundled
TRUNDLD	trundled

UNDLER

BUNDLER	bundler
TRUNDLER	trundler

UNDLING

BUNDLING	bundling, unbundling
TRUNDLING	trundling

UNDŌ

FUNDŌ	basso profundo
KUNDŌ	secundo

UNDRUS

THUNDRUS	thundrous
WUNDRUS	wondrous

ŪNĒ

ŪNĒ	uni
DŪNĒ	duny
PŪNĒ	puisne, puny
TŪNĒ	tuny

(See $\overline{OO}NĒ$)

UNĒ

BUNĒ	bunny
DUNĒ	dunny
FUNĒ	do-funny, funny
GUNĒ	gunny
HUNĒ	honey, wild honey
KUNĒ	cunny
MUNĒ	agrimony, acrimony, alimony, antimony, baldmoney, front money, matrimony, money, parsimony, patrimony, sanctimony, ceremony, testimony
PUNĒ	punny
RUNĒ	runny
SUNĒ	sonny, Sunni, sunny, unsunny
TUNĒ	tunny

UNĒD

HUNĒD	honeyed
MUNĒD	monied

UNEL

FUNEL	funnel
GUNEL	gun'l, gunnel, gunwale
RUNEL	runnel
TRUNEL	trunnel
TUNEL	tunnel

ŪNER

KŪNER	lacunar
MŪNER	communer, cassumunar
PŪNER	expugner, impugner
TŪNER	attuner, importuner, piano tuner, tuner

(See $\overline{OO}NER$)

UNER

DUNER	dunner
GUNER	gunner
KUNER	cunner
PUNER	punner
RUNER	forerunner, frontrunner, gunrunner, outrunner, overrunner, roadrunner, rumrunner, runner
SHUNER	shunner
SKUNER	scunner
STUNER	stunner
TUNER	tonner, tunner, two-tonner, one-tonner (etc.)
WUNER	oner

ŪNES

FŪNES	fewness
NŪNES	newness

(See $\overline{OO}NES$)

UNET

PUNET	punnet
RUNET	runnet

ŪNFUL

TŪNFUL	tuneful

(See OŌNFUL)

UNGER

BUNGER	bunger
LUNGER	lunger
TUNGER	tonguer

UNGGER

HUNGGER	enhunger, hunger
MUNGGER	B balladmonger, barbermonger, boroughmonger, F fashionmonger, fellmonger, fishmonger, G gossipmonger, H whoremonger, I ironmonger, K costermonger, M meritmonger, monger, SK scandalmonger, scaremonger, W witmonger, warmonger
YUNGGER	younger

UNGGL

BUNGGL	bungle
JUNGGL	jungle
PUNGGL	pungle

UNGGUS

DUNGGUS	mundungus
FUNGGUS	fungus, smellfungus
MUNGGUS	humongous

UNGKARD

(See UNGKERD)

UNGKĀT

RUNGKĀT	averruncate
TRUNGKĀT	detruncate, truncate

UNGKCHER

JUNKCHER	juncture, conjuncture

PUNKCHER	acupuncture, quackupuncture, puncture

UNGKĒ

CHUNGKĒ	chunky
FLUNGKĒ	flunky
FUNGKĒ	funky
HUNGKĒ	hunky
JUNGKĒ	junkie, junky
MUNGKĒ	grease monkey, monkey, powder monkey, spider monkey (etc.)
PUNGKĒ	morpunkee, punkie, punky
SKUNGKĒ	skunky
SPUNGKĒ	spunky

UNGKEN

DRUNGKEN	drunken
PUNGKEN	punkin
SHRUNGKEN	shrunken
SUNGKEN	sunken

UNGKER

BLUNGKER	blunker
BUNGKER	Archie Bunker, bunker, kennebunker, mossbunker
DRUNGKER	drunker
DUNGKER	dunker
FLUNGKER	flunker
FUNGKER	funker
HUNGKER	hunker
JUNGKER	junker
KLUNGKER	clunker
PUNGKER	punker
TUNGKER	tunker
YUNGKER	younker, Junker

UNGKERD

BLUNGKERD	blunkered
BUNGKERD	bunkered
DRUNGKERD	drunkard
DUNGKERD	Dunkard
HUNGKERD	hunkered

UNGKET

JUNGKET	junket
TUNGKET	tunket

UNGKISH

DRUNGKISH	drunkish
LUNGKISH	lunkish
MUNGKISH	monkish
PUNGKISH	punkish
SKUNGKISH	skunkish
SPUNGKISH	spunkish

UNGKL

UNGKL	septiuncle, uncle
BUNGKL	carbuncle
DUNGKL	peduncle
MUNGKL	homuncle, sermuncle
NUNGKL	nuncle
RUNGKL	furuncle, caruncle
TRUNGKL	truncal

UNGKŌ

UNGKŌ	unco
BUNGKŌ	bunko
JUNGKŌ	junko
PUNGKŌ	punko

UNGKUS

DUNGKUS	aduncous
HUNGKUS	dohunkus
JUNGKUS	juncous

UNGKSHUN

UNGKSHUN	extreme unction, inunction, unction
FUNGKSHUN	defunction, dysfunction, function, malfunction
JUNGKSHUN	adjunction, disjunction, injunction, interjunction, junction, conjunction, rejunction, sejunction, subjunction
PUNGKSHUN	expunction, interpunction, compunction, punction

UNGKSHUS

UNGKSHUS	unctious
BUNGKSHUS	rambunctious
PUNGKSHUS	compunctious

UNGKTIV

JUNGKTIV	abjunctive, adjunctive, disjunctive, conjunctive, subjunctive
PUNGKTIV	compunctive

UNGKTŪR

(See **UNGKCHER**)

UNGSTER

TUNGSTER	tonguester
YUNGSTER	youngster

UNIJ

DUNIJ	dunnage
GUNIJ	gunnage
PUNIJ	punnage
TUNIJ	tonnage

ŪNIK

MŪNIK	Munich
PŪNIK	Punic
TŪNIK	tunic

(See **ŌŌNIK**)

ŪNING

MŪNING	communing
TŪNING	attuning, importuning, retuning, tuning

(See **ŌŌNING**)

UNING

DUNING	dunning
FUNING	funning
GUNING	gunning
KUNING	cunning
PUNING	punning
RUNING	gunrunning, outrunning, overrunning, rumrunning, running
SHUNING	shunning
STUNING	stunning
SUNING	sunning
TUNING	tunning

UNISH

BUNISH	bunnish
HUNISH	hunnish, Hunnish
NUNISH	nunnish
PUNISH	punish, punnish

ŪNIST

TŪNIST	opportunist

(See **ŌŌNIST**)

ŪNIZM

TUNIZM	opportunism

(See **ŌŌNIZM**)

UNJĒ

GRUNJĒ	grungy
PLUNJĒ	plungy
SPUNJĒ	spongy

UNJER

BLUNJER	blunger
KUNJER	conjure
LUNJER	lunger
PLUNJER	plunger
SPUNJER	expunger, sponger

UNJING

BLUNJING	blunging
LUNJING	lunging
PLUNJING	plunging
SPUNJING	expunging, sponging

ŪNLES

TŪNLES	tuneless

(See **ŌŌNLES**)

UNLES

PUNLES	punless
RUNLES	runless
SUNLES	sonless, sunless

ŪNLĬT

(See **ŌŌNLĬT**)

ŪNLIT

(See **ŌŌNLIT**)

ŪNNES

TŪNNES	inopportuneness, opportuneness

(See **ŌŌNNES**)

ŪNŌ

ŪNŌ	unau, you-know, UNO

(See **ŌŌNŌ**)

UNSHAL

UNSHAL	uncial
NUNSHAL	internuncial, pronuncial

UNSTER

GUNSTER	gunster
PUNSTER	punster

UNTA

BUNTA	marabunta
JUNTA	junta
PUNTA	punta

UNTAL

(See **UNTL**)

UNTĒ

PUNTĒ	punty
RUNTĒ	runty
STUNTĒ	stunty
WUNTĒ	wuntee

UNTED

WUNTED	unwonted, wonted

(See **UNT**, add -ed where appropriate.)

UNTER

BLUNTER	blunter
BUNTER	bunter

FRUNTER   affronter, fronter, confronter
GRUNTER   grunter
HUNTER   fortune hunter, headhunter, hunter, lion hunter, scalp hunter (etc.)
PUNTER   punter
SHUNTER   shunter
STUNTER   stunter

UNTING

BLUNTING   blunting
BUNTING   bunting, red bunting, snow bunting, yellow bunting
FRUNTING   affronting, fronting, confronting
GRUNTING   grunting
HUNTING   brush-hunting, fortune hunting, head-hunting, hunting, lion-hunting, scalp-hunting
PUNTING   punting
SHUNTING   shunting
STUNTING   stunting

UNTL

BUNTL   balibuntal, buntal
FRUNTL   frontal, full-frontal, confrontal, prefrontal
GRUNTL   disgruntle, gruntle
PUNTL   contrapuntal, puntal

UNTLES

(See **UNT,** add -less where appropriate.)

ŪNUM

(See $\overline{OO}$NUM)

ŪNYUN

ŪNYUN   disunion, labor union, company union, nonunion, reunion, trade union, union
MŪNYUN   excommunion, intercommunion, communion

UNYUN

UNYUN   onion, wild onion
BUNYUN   bunion, John Bunyan

RUNYUN   ronion, ronyon
TRUNYUN   trunnion

ŪPA

PŪPA   pupa
STŪPA   stupa

(See $\overline{OO}$PA)

UPANS

UPANS   come-uppance
THRUPANS   thruppence

ŪPĒ

KŪPĒ   kewpy

(See $\overline{OO}$PĒ)

UPĒ

GUPĒ   guppy
KUPĒ   hiccoughy, hiccupy, cuppy
PUPĒ   bumblepuppy, hushpuppy, puppy
YUPĒ   Yuppy

ŪPER

DŪPER   duper, super-duper
STŪPER   stupor
SŪPER   super

(See $\overline{OO}$PER)

UPER

UPER   upper
KRUPER   crupper
KUPER   cupper, kupper
SKUPER   scupper
SUPER   supper

UPET

MUPET   muppet
PUPET   puppet
SKUPET   scuppet

ŪPID

KŪPID   cupid

LŪPID   Lupid
STŪPID   stupid

UPING

UPING   swan-upping
KUPING   hiccoughing, hiccuping, cupping
SUPPING   supping
TUPPING   tupping

ŪPISH

(See $\overline{OO}$PISH)

UPISH

UPISH   uppish
KUPISH   cuppish
PUPISH   puppish

ŪPL

KŪPL   cupel
PŪPL   pupil

(See $\overline{OO}$PL)

UPL

KUPL   decouple, couple, recouple, uncouple
SUPL   supple

UPLER

KUPLER   coupler, recoupler, uncoupler
SUPLER   suppler

UPLET

KUPLET   couplet, cuplet
RUPLET   quadruplet
TUPLET   quintuplet, sextuplet, septuplet

ŪPMENT

(See $\overline{OO}$PMENT)

ŪPON

ŪPON   yupon

(See $\overline{OO}$PON)

ŪRA

LŪRA	lura
SKŪRA	camera obscura
TŪRA	coloratura
VŪRA	bravura
ZŪRA	caesura

(See **ŌORA**)

ŪRAL

ŪRAL	Ural
DŪRAL	dural, subdural
KŪRAL	sinecural
LŪRAL	lural, tellural
MŪRAL	antemural, extramural, intermural, intramural, mural
NŪRAL	adneural, interneural, neural
PŪRAL	hypural
SŪRAL	sural

URAL

(See **OORAL**)

ŪRANS

ŪRANS	durance, endurance, perdurance
KŪRANS	procurance
LŪRANS	allurance

ŪRANT

DŪRANT	durant, endurant, perdurant
KŪRANT	procurant
LŪRANT	allurant
SKŪRANT	obscurant

URANT

(See **URENT**)

ŪRĀT

KŪRĀT	curate
PŪRĀT	*purpurate*

URBAL

(See **URBL**)

URBAN

(See **URBN**)

URBĀT

SURBĀT	acerbate
TURBĀT	*perturbate*

URBĒ

URBĒ	herby
BLURBĒ	blurby
DURBĒ	derby, Derby
HURBĒ	herby
VURBĒ	verby

URBER

BLURBER	blurber
BURBER	Berber
KURBER	curber
PURBER	superber
TURBER	disturber, perturber

URBET

BURBOT	burbot
SHURBOT	sherbet
TURBOT	turbit, turbot

URBING

URBING	herbing
BLURBING	blurbing
HURBING	herbing
KURBING	curbing
TURBING	disturbing
VURBING	verbing

URBIT

(See **URBET**)

URBL

URBL	herbal
BURBL	burble
HURBL	herbal
JURBL	gerbil, jirble
VURBL	biverbal, nonverbal, verbal

URBN

URBN	interurban, urban

BURBN	Bourbon, suburban
TURBN	turban, turbine

URBOT

(See **URBET**)

URCHANT

MURCHANT	merchant
PURCHANT	perchant

URCHĒ

BURCHĒ	birchy
CHURCHĒ	churchy
LURCHĒ	lurchy
SMURCHĒ	smirchy

URCHEN

URCHEN	urchin
BURCHEN	birchen

URCHER

BURCHER	bircher
CHURCHER	churcher
LURCHER	lurcher
NURCHER	nurture
PURCHER	percher
SMURCHER	besmircher, smircher
SURCHER	researcher, searcher

URCHING

(See **URCH**, add -*ing* where appropriate.)

URCHLES

(See **URCH**, add -*less* where appropriate.)

URDBOOK

BURDBOOK	bird book
HURDBOOK	herdbook
WURDBOOK	wordbook

URDĒ

BURDĒ	birdy
GURDĒ	hurdy-gurdy
KURDĒ	curdy
PURDĒ	purdy
STURDĒ	sturdy
WURDĒ	wordy

URDED

(See **URD,** add *-ed* where appropriate.)

URDEN

BURDEN	burden, disburden, overburden, reburden, unburden
GURDEN	guerdon
LURDEN	lurdan

URDER

BURDER	birder
GURDER	engirder, girder
HURDER	goat-herder, herder, sheep-herder
MURDER	murder, first-degree murder (etc.), self-murder
SURDER	absurder
THURDER	thirder
WURDER	worder

URDING

BURDING	birding
GURDING	engirding, girding
HURDING	herding
WURDING	miswording, rewording, wording

URDL

FURDL	furdel, furdle
GURDL	begirdle, engirdle, girdle
HURDL	hurdle
KURDL	curdle

URDLĒ

KURDLĒ	curdly
SURDLĒ	absurdly
THURDLĒ	thirdly

URDZMAN

HURDZMAN	herdsman
WURDZMAN	wordsman

ŪRĒ

FŪRĒ	fury
KŪRĒ	curie, Curie

(See **OŌRĒ**)

URĒ

BLURĒ	blurry
BURĒ	burry
DURĒ	durrie, durry
FLURĒ	flurry, snow flurry
FURĒ	firry, furry
GURĒ	ghurry, gurry
HURĒ	hurry
HWURĒ	whirry
KURĒ	curry
LURĒ	lurry
MURĒ	murrey
PURĒ	purry
SKURĒ	hurry-scurry, scurry
SLURĒ	slurry
SPURĒ	spurry
SURĒ	surrey
WURĒ	worry

(See **OŌRĒ**)

URĒD

FLURĒD	flurried, unflurried
HURĒD	hurried, unhurried
KURĒD	curried, uncurried
SKURĒD	scurried
WURĒD	unworried, worried

UREL

BUREL	burrel
FUREL	deferral, referral
MUREL	demurral
SKWUREL	squirrel
STUREL	bestirral

URENS

FURENS	transference
KURENS	incurrence, intercurrence, concurrence, nonconcurrence, occurrence, recurrence
SHURENS	assurance, health insurance, insurance, life insurance (etc.), reassurance, reinsurance
TURENS	deterrence, nondeterrence

URENT

KURENT	decurrent, intercurrent, concurrent, crosscurrent, currant, current, recurrent, undercurrent
MURENT	demurrent
SURENT	susurrant
TURENT	deterrent

ŪRER

ŪRER	inurer
DŪRER	Dürer, durer, endurer
FŪRER	Fuehrer, furor
KŪRER	curer
MŪRER	immurer
NŪRER	manurer
PŪRER	purer
SKŪRER	obscurer
TŪRER	immaturer, maturer

URER

BLURER	blurrer
FURER	deferrer, inferrer, conferrer, preferrer, transferrer
JURER	abjurer, adjurer, grand juror, juror, petty juror, trial juror
KURER	incurrer, concurrer
LURER	allurer, lurer
MURER	demurrer
PURER	purrer
SHURER	assurer, ensurer, insurer, reassurer, reinsurer, shirrer, surer
SLURER	slurrer
SPURER	spurrer
STURER	bestirrer, stirrer
TURER	deterrer, interrer
VURER	averrer

(See **OŌRER**)

URFĒ

MURFĒ	murphy
SKURFĒ	scurfy
SURFĒ	surfy

URFING

SKURFING	skurfing
SURFING	surfing, windsurfing

URGAL

(See **URGL**)

URGĀT

JURGĀT	objurgate
PURGĀT	expurgate
VURGĀT	virgate

URGL

URGL	ergal
BURGL	burgle
GURGL	gurgle
TURGL	tergal
VURGL	virgal

URGLER

BURGLER	burglar
GURGLER	gurgler

URGŌ

URGŌ	ergo
VURGŌ	Virgo

URGUS

URGUS	demiurgus
PURGUS	Walpurgis
TURGUS	thaumaturgus

URIJ

KURIJ	discourage, encourage, courage
MURIJ	demurrage
STURIJ	stirrage

ŪRIK

FŪRIK	hydrosulphuric, sulphuric
KŪRIK	mercuric
LŪRIK	hydrotelluric, telluric
NŪRIK	aneuric, neuric
PŪRIK	purpuric
SŪRIK	caesuric
ZŪRIK	caesuric

URIK

PLURIK	pleuric

(See ŪRIK)

ŪRIN

ŪRIN	urine
FŪRIN	furan
NŪRIN	neurine

ŪRING

ŪRING	inuring
DŪRING	during, enduring, perduring, perenduring
FŪRING	coiffuring
KŪRING	curing, manicuring, pedicuring, procuring, securing
LŪRING	alluring, luring
MŪRING	immuring, muring
NŪRING	manuring
SKŪRING	obscuring
TŪRING	caricaturing, maturing

(See ŌŌRING, OORING)

URING

BLURING	blurring
BURING	birring, burring
CHURING	chirring, churring
FURING	befurring, furring, inferring, conferring, preferring, referring, transferring
HWURING	whirring
JURING	abjuring, adjuring, conjuring
KURING	incurring, concurring, occurring, recurring, sepulchering
MURING	demurring
NURING	manuring
SHURING	assuring, insuring, reinsuring, shirring
SLURING	slurring
SMURING	smurring
SPURING	spurring
STURING	administering, bestirring, restirring, stirring, unstirring
SURING	sirring
TURING	deterring, disinterring, interring
VURING	averring

ŪRISH

MŪRISH	demurish
PŪRISH	purish
SKŪRISH	obscurish
TŪRISH	amateurish, maturish

(See ŌŌRISH)

URISH

BURISH	burrish
FLURISH	flourish
KURISH	currish
NURISH	nourish, overnourish, undernourish
PURISH	poorish, purrish
TURISH	amateurish, maturish

(See OORISH)

URISHT

FLURISHT	flourished
NURISHT	nourished, overnourished, undernourished

ŪRIST

KŪRIST	manicurist
PŪRIST	purist
TŪRIST	caricaturist

(See OORIST)

ŪRIZM

PŪRIZM	purism

(See URIZM)

URIZM

TURIZM	

(See ŪRIZM)

URJĒ

URJĒ	aciurgy, periergy, theurgy
DURJĒ	dirgie, dirgy
KLURJĒ	clergy
KRURJĒ	micrurgy
LURJĒ	metallurgy
MURJĒ	chemurgy, zymurgy
SURJĒ	surgy
TURJĒ	dramaturgy, thaumaturgy

URJENS

URJENS	urgence
MURJENS	emergence, mergence, submergence
SURJENS	insurgence, resurgence

TURJENS

TURJENS	detergence
VURJENS	divergence, convergence, vergence

URJENT

URJENT	urgent
MURJENT	emergent, mergent, submergent
SPLURJENT	splurgent
STURJENT	abstergent
SURJENT	assurgent, insurgent, resurgent
TURJENT	detergent
VURJENT	divergent, convergent, vergent

URJER

URJER	urger
BURJER	berger
MURJER	emerger, merger, submerger
PURJER	perjure, purger
SKURJER	scourger
SPLURJER	splurger
VURJER	diverger, converger, verdure, verger

URJIK

URJIK	demiurgic, exoergic, endoergic, theurgic
LURJIK	allergic, metallurgic
NURJIK	adrenurgic, anergic, cholinergic
RURJIK	chirurgic
SURJIK	lysurgic
TURJIK	dramaturgic, liturgic, thaumaturgic

URJING

(See URJ, add -ing where appropriate.)

URJIST

LURJIST	metallurgist
TURJIST	dramaturgist, thaumaturgist

URJMENT

MURJMENT	submergement
VURJMENT	divergement, convergement

URJUN

BURJUN	burgeon
GURJUN	gurjun
STURJUN	sturgeon
SURJUN	neurosurgeon, surgeon
VURJUN	virgin

URKA

BURKA	burka
CHURKA	charkha
FURKA	furca
GURKA	Gurkha
MURKA	amurca
SURKA	circa
ZURKA	mazurka

URKAL

(See URKL)

URKĒ

JURKĒ	jerky
KURKĒ	Albuquerque
KWURKĒ	quirky
LURKĒ	lurky, Turkey-lurkey
MURKĒ	murky
PURKĒ	perky
SHURKĒ	shirky
SMURKĒ	smirky
TURKĒ	turkey, Turkey

URKER

BURKER	burker
JURKER	jerker, jerquer, soda jerker, tearjerker
KURKER	kirker
LURKER	lurker
PURKER	coffee-perker, perker
SHURKER	shirker
SMURKER	smirker
WURKER	guessworker, hard worker, migrant worker, nonworker, outworker, pieceworker, wonder worker, worker

URKIN

FURKIN	firkin
GURKIN	gherkin
JURKIN	jerkin
MURKIN	merkin
PURKIN	perkin

URKING

WURKING	guessworking, hardworking, nonworking, pieceworking, wonder working, working

(See URK, add -ing)

URKISH

JURKISH	jerkish
KLURKISH	clerkish
KWURKISH	quirkish
PURKISH	perkish
TURKISH	Turkish

URKL

SURKL	encircle, excircle, heterocercal, homocercal, inner circle, semicircle, cercle, circle
TURKL	turkle
VURKL	novercal

URKLĒ

BURKLĒ	Berkeley
KLURKLĒ	clerkly
SURKLĒ	circly

URKMAN

TURKMAN	Turkman
WURKMAN	workman

URKSUM

URKSUM	irksome
KWURKSUM	quirksome
MURKSUM	murksome

URKUS

FURKUS	bifurcous
MURKUS	amurcous
SURKUS	circus

ŪRLĒ

KŪRLĒ	securely
MŪRLĒ	demurely

PŪRLĒ	impurely, purely
SKŪRLĒ	obscurely
TŪRLĒ	immaturely, maturely, prematurely

URLĒ

URLĒ	early
BURLĒ	burley, burly, hurly-burly
CHURLĒ	churly
DURLĒ	dourly
FURLĒ	ferly
GURLĒ	girlie, girly, gurly
HURLĒ	hurley
HWURLĒ	whirly
KURLĒ	curly
MURLĒ	murly
NURLĒ	knurly
PURLĒ	pearly, pirlie, poorly
SHURLĒ	surely
SURLĒ	surly
SWURLĒ	swirly
TWURLĒ	twirly
WURLĒ	wurley

(See OORLĒ)

URLER

BURLER	birler, burler
FURLER	furler
HURLER	hurler
HWURLER	whirler
KURLER	curler
PURLER	pearler, purler
SKURLER	skirler
SWURLER	swirler
TWURLER	twirler

URLET

BURLET	burlet
PURLET	pearlet
SPURLET	spurlet
STURLET	sterlet

URLIN

KURLIN	carline
MURLIN	merlin, Merlin, murlin
PURLIN	pearlin, purlin

URLING

BURLING	birling, burling
FURLING	furling
HWURLING	whirling
KURLING	hair-curling, curling
PURLING	pearling, purling
SKURLING	skirling
SPURLING	sperling
SWURLING	swirling
TWURLING	twirling

URLISH

CHURLISH	churlish
GURLISH	girlish
PURLISH	pearlish

URLOIN

| PURLOIN | purloin |
| SURLOIN | sirloin |

URLŪ

| KURLŪ | curlew |
| PURLŪ | purlieu |

URMA

BURMA	Burma
DURMA	derma, pachyderma, xeroderma
FURMA	terra firma
SURMA	syrma

URMAL

| DURMAL | dermal, epidermal, hypodermal, pachydermal, taxidermal |
| THURMAL | diathermal, hydrothermal, isogeothermal, isothermal, geothermal, synthermal, thermal |

URMAN

URMAN	ermine
FURMAN	firman
JURMAN	german, German, germon, cousin-german
MURMAN	merman, mermen
SURMAN	sermon
TURMAN	determine, redetermine, termen, termin, termon

URMĒ

DURMĒ	taxidermy
FURMĒ	Fermi
JURMĒ	germy
SKWURMĒ	squirmy
SPURMĒ	spermy
THURMĒ	aluminothermy, diathermy, radiothermy
WURMĒ	wormy

URMEN

(See URMAN)

ŪRMENT

ŪRMENT	inurement
KŪRMENT	procurement, securement
LŪRMENT	allurement
MŪRMENT	immurement
SKŪRMENT	obscurement

URMENT

RURMENT	affirmant, deferment, ferment, preferment, referment
TURMENT	determent, disinterment, interment
VURMENT	averment

(See OORMENT)

URMER

FURMER	affirmer, firmer, infirmer, confirmer
MURMER	bemurmur, murmur
SKWURMER	squirmer
TURMER	first-termer, second-termer (etc.), termer, termor
WURMER	wormer

URMĒZ

| HURMĒZ | Hermes |
| KURMĒZ | kermes |

URMIK

| DURMIK | dermic, endermic, epidermic, |

	hydrodermic, hypodermic, clerodermic, pachydermic, taxidermic
SPURMIK	spermic
THURMIK	adiathermic, diathermic, exothermic, endothermic, photothermic, isogeothermic, geothermic, thermic, euthermic

URMIN

(See **URMAN**)

URMIND

URMIND	ermined
TURMIND	determined, undetermined
VURMIND	vermined

URMING

FURMING	affirming, firming, confirming
JURMING	germing
SKWURMING	squirming
TURMING	terming
WURMING	worming

URMIS

(See **URMUS**)

URMISH

SKURMISH	skirmish
WURMISH	wormish

URMIT

HURMIT	hermit
PURMIT	permit

URMLĒ

FURMLĒ	firmly, infirmly
TURMLĒ	termly

URMON

(See **URMAN**)

URMUS

DURMUS	dermis, exodermis, endodermis, epidermis, hypodermis, malacodermous
HURMUS	hirmos
KURMUS	kermes, kermis
NURMUS	inermous
SPURMUS	spermous
THURMUS	thermos
VURMUS	vermis

URNA

BURNA	taberna
DURNA	Dharna
FURNA	parapherna
SMURNA	Smyrna
STURNA	Sterna

URNAL

URNAL	diurnal, hodiernal, semidiurnal, terdiurnal, urnal
BURNAL	hibernal
FURNAL	infernal, paraphernal
JURNAL	journal
KURNAL	colonel, kernel
PURNAL	supernal
STURNAL	asternal, sternal
THURNAL	cothurnal
TURNAL	*D* diuturnal, *E* eternal, external, *FR* fraternal, *H* hesternal, *I* internal, *K* coeternal, *M* maternal, *N* nocturnal, *P* paternal, *S* sempiternal
VURNAL	cavernal, vernal

URNĒ

URNĒ	enurny
BURNĒ	byrnie, burny, burny-burny
-**FURNĒ**	ferny
GURNĒ	gurney
JURNĒ	journey
PURNĒ	pirnie
TURNĒ	attorney, tourney

URNENT

SURNENT	secernent
TURNENT	alternant
VURNENT	vernant

URNER

URNER	earner
BURNER	back burner, bookburner, bra burner, burner, four-burner, front burner, gas-burner, hay-burner, oil-burner, two-burner
CHURNER	churner
JURNER	adjourner
LURNER	learner
PURNER	pirner
SPURNER	spurner
STURNER	sterner
SURNER	discerner
TURNER	overturner, returner, turner
YURNER	yearner
ZURNER	discerner

ŪRNES

KŪRNES	insecureness, secureness
MŪRNES	demureness
SKŪRNES	obscureness

URNES

CHURNES	matureness
FURNES	furnace
PURNES	poorness
SHURNES	cocksureness, sureness
THURNES	cothurnus

(See **URNNES**)

URNEST

URNEST	earnest

(See **URN,** add -*est*)

URNING

URNING	earning
LURNING	book-learning, learning

(See **URN,** add -*ing* where appropriate.)

URNISH

BURNISH	burnish, reburnish
FURNISH	furnish, refurnish

URNISHT

(See **URNISH**, add *-ed* where appropriate.)

URNIT

TURNIT	*alternate*, biternate, quaternate, *subalternate*, ternate
THURNIT	cothurnate

URNMENT

JURNMENT	adjournment, sojournment
SURNMENT	discernment, concernment, secernment
TURNMENT	attornment, internment
ZURNMENT	discernment

URNNES

STURNNES	sternness
TURNNES	taciturnness

(See **URNES**)

URNŌ

FURNŌ	inferno
JURNŌ	journo
LURNŌ	Salerno
PURNŌ	Pernod
STURNŌ	sterno, Sterno

URNUM

BURNUM	alburnum, laburnum, viburnum
STURNUM	episternum, sternum, xiphisternum

URNUS

THURNUS	cothurnus
VURNUS	Avernus

ŪRŌ

BŪRŌ	bureau, Politbureo
SKŪRO	chiarascuro

URŌ

BURŌ	borough, burro, interborough, rotten borough
FURŌ	furrow
THURŌ	thorough, unthorough

(See **OORŌ**)

UROR

(See **URER**)

URPĒ

URPĒ	irpe
BURPĒ	Burpee, burpy
CHURPĒ	chirpy
SLURPĒ	slurpy

URPER

BURPER	burper
CHURPER	chirper
PURPER	hyperper
SLURPER	slurper
SURPER	usurper
ZURPER	usurper

URPĒZ

BURPĒZ	Burpee's
HURPĒZ	herpes
STURPĒZ	per stirpes, stirpes

URPING

(See **URP**, add *-ing* where appropriate.)

URPL

HURPL	hirple
KURPL	curple
PURPL	purple

URSA

URSA	ursa
BURSA	bursa
JURSA	djersa
VURSA	vice-versa

URSAL

(See **URSL**)

URSANT

KURSANT	recursant
VURSANT	aversant, conversant, multiversant, versant

URSĒ

BURSĒ	bersy
HURSĒ	hirci
MURSĒ	gramercy, mercy
NURSĒ	nursy
PURSĒ	pursy
SURSĒ	Circe
VURSĒ	arsey-versey, controversy

URSER

URSER	coercer
BURSER	bursar, disburser, reimburser
HURSER	hearser, rehearser
KURSER	accurser, antecursor, curser, cursor, precursor
MURSER	amercer, immerser, commercer, mercer
NURSER	nurser
PURSER	disperser, purser
SPURSER	intersperser
VURSER	converser, perverser, reverser, traverser, verser, versor
WURSER	worser

"CLUCK, CLUCK!" SAID THE CHICKENS

Charles Dickens was caught by the Devil
  Stealing the Devil's chickens.
"What the dickens!" said the Devil.
  "What the Devil!" said Charles Dickens.

URSET

TURSET	tercet
VURSET	verset

URSHA

URSHA	inertia
PURSHA	Persia
TURSHA	sesquitertia, tertia

URSHAL

URSHAL	inertial
MURSHAL	commercial, noncommercial, uncommercial
TURSHAL	sesquitertial, tertial
VURSHAL	controversial

URSHUN

URSHUN	coercion
KURSHUN	discursion, excursion, incursion, recursion
MURSHUN	emersion, immersion, mersion, submersion
PURSHUN	apertion, aspersion, dispersion, Persian
SPURSHUN	aspersion, inspersion, interspersion
STURSHUN	abstertion
SURSHUN	assertion, disconcertion, insertion, intersertion, concertion, lacertian, self-assertion
TURSHUN	extersion, nasturtion, sesquitertian, Cistercian, tersion, tertian
VURSHUN	*A* animadversion, aversion, *B* bioconversion, *D* diversion, *E* extroversion, eversion, *I* introversion, inversion, *K* contraversion, controversion, conversion, *O* obversion, *P* perversion, *R* retroversion, reversion, *S* circumversion, subversion, *V* version
ZURSHUN	desertion, exertion

URSĪN

URSĪN	urçine
HURSĪN	hircine

URSING

(See **URS,** add -*ing* where appropriate.)

URSIV

URSIV	coercive
KURSIV	decursive, discursive, excursive, incursive, cursive, precursive, recursive
MURSIV	immersive
PURSIV	aspersive, dispersive
STURSIV	abstersive
VURSIV	aversive, perversive, subversive

URSL

URSL	ursal
BURSL	birsle, bursal
HURSL	hirsel, rehearsal
KURSL	cursal, succursal
MURSL	demersal
NURSL	nursle
PURSL	aspersal, dispersal
SPURSL	interspersal
TURSL	tercel
VURSL	quaquaversal, partiversal, reversal, transversal, versal, universal

URSLĒ

TURSLĒ	tersely
VURSLĒ	adversely, aversely, diversely, inversely, conversely, obversely, perversely, reversely, transversely

URSMENT

BURSMENT	disbursement, imbursement, reimbursement
MURSMENT	amercement

URSN

URSN	urson
PURSN	chairperson, mediaperson, nonperson, newsperson, person, spokesperson, unperson

URSNES

TURSNES	terseness

VURSNES	adverseness, averseness, diverseness, inverseness, converseness, obverseness, perverseness, transverseness

URSŌ

KURSŌ	concurso
VURSŌ	reverso, verso

URSON

(See **URSN**)

URSTED

BURSTED	bursted
THURSTED	thirsted
WURSTED	worsted

URSTER

BURSTER	burster
FURSTER	America Firster, firster
THURSTER	thirster
WURSTER	worster

URSTING

BURSTING	bursting
THURSTING	thirsting
WURSTING	worsting

URSUS

URSUS	ursus
KURSUS	excursus, concursus, cursus
LURSUS	melursus
THURSUS	thyrsus
VURSUS	adversus, conversus, transversus, versus

URTAL

(See **URTL**)

URTAN

(See **URTN**)

URTĒ

CHURTĒ	cherty
DURTĒ	dirty, down and dirty
FLURTĒ	flirty
MURTĒ	Trimurti
PURTĒ	purty
SHURTĒ	shirty
SKWURTĒ	squirty
SPURTĒ	spurty
SURTĒ	certie
THURTĒ	thirty

URTED

SHURTED	blackshirted, brownshirted, shirted, unshirted

(See **URT,** add *-ed* where appropriate.)

URTER

FLURTER	flirter
FURTER	frankfurter
HURTER	hurter
KURTER	curter
PURTER	perter
SHURTER	blackshirter, brownshirter (etc.)
SKURTER	skirter
SKWURTER	squirter
SPURTER	spurter
STURTER	stertor
SURTER	asserter, disconcerter, inserter, concerter, preconcerter
VURTER	adverter, animadverter, averter, diverter, everter, evertor, inverter, converter, perverter, reverter, subverter
ZURTER	deserter, exerter

URTHĒ

(TH as in *thin*)

URTHĒ	earthy
BURTHĒ	birthy

(See **URTHĒ, TH** as in then.)

URTHĒ

(TH as in *then*)

WURTHĒ	noteworthy, praiseworthy, seaworthy, trustworthy, worthy, unworthy

(See **URTHĒ, TH** as in thin.)

URTHEN

(TH as in *thin*)

URTHEN	earthen
BURTHEN	burthen, disburthen, unburthen

URTHFUL

(TH as in *thin*)

MURTHFUL	mirthful
WURTHFUL	worthful

URTHLES

URTHLES	earthless
BURTHLES	birthless
GURTHLES	girthless
MURTHLES	mirthless
WURTHLES	worthless

URTIN

(See **URTN**)

URTING

(See **URT,** add *-ing* where appropriate.)

URTIV

FURTIV	furtive
SURTIV	assertive, insertive, self-assertive
VURTIV	divertive, extrovertive, introvertive, invertive, convertive, revertive
ZURTIV	exertive

URTL

FURTL	fertile, infertile
HURTL	hurtle
HWURTL	whortle
KURTL	kirtle, curtal
MURTL	myrtle
SPURTL	spurtle
SURTL	consertal
TURTL	turtle

URTLĒ

URTLĒ	inertly
KURTLĒ	curtly
LURTLĒ	alertly
PURTLĒ	*expertly, inexpertly,* pertly
TURTLĒ	turtly

URTLES

SHURTLES	shirtless
SKURTLES	skirtless
SKWURTLES	squirtless
SPURTLES	spurtless

URTN

BURTN	burton
KURTN	encurtain, iron curtain, curtain
SURTN	certain, uncertain

URTNES

URTNES	inertness
KURTNES	curtness
LURTNES	alertness
PURTNES	*expertness, inexpertness,* peartness, pertness
PYURTNES	peartness

URTUM

FURTUM	furtum
SURTUM	assertum, sertum

URUP

CHURUP	chirrup
STURUP	stirrup
YURUP	Europe

(See **OORUP**)

URUS

CHURUS	churrus
DURUS	Honduras
KURUS	dolichurus, mercurous
NURUS	anurous, coenurus
SURUS	susurrous
TURUS	Arcturus
WURUS	wurrus
YURUS	anurous, urus

(See **OORUS**)

URVA

URVA	urva
FURVA	conferva
NURVA	Minerva, Nerva
YURVA	contrayerva

URVAL

(See **URVL**)

URVANT

(See **URVENT**)

URVĂT

KURVĂT	incurvate, curvate, curvet, recurvate
NURVĂT	enervate, innervate, trinervate
SURVĂT	acervate

URVĒ

KURVĒ	curvy
NURVĒ	nervy
SKURVĒ	scurvy
TURVĒ	topsy-turvy

URVENS

FURVENS	fervence
SURVENS	inobservance, observance, servants, unobservance

URVENT

FURVENT	fervent
KURVENT	curvant, recurvant
SURVENT	bondservant, conservant, maidservant, manservant, servant
ZURVENT	inobservant, observant, unobservant

URVER

FURVER	fervor
NURVER	nerver, unnerver
SURVER	conserver, server, time-server
SWURVER	swerver
ZURVER	deserver, game preserver, life preserver, observer, preserver, reserver

URVET

KURVET	curvet
VURVET	vervet

URVIL

(See **URVL**)

URVĪN

NURVĪN	nervine
SURVĪN	cervine

URVIN

NURVIN	nervine
SURVIN	cervine

URVING

KURVING	*incurving*, curving, *outcurving*
NURVING	nerving, unnerving
SURVING	conserving, serving, time-serving
SWURVING	swerving, unswerving
ZURVING	deserving, observing, preserving, reserving, undeserving, unobserving

URVL

CHURVL	chervil
FURVL	conferval
NURVL	adnerval, nerval
SURVL	acerval, serval, servile
VURVL	vervel

URVLES

DURVLES	hors d'oeuvreless
KURVLES	curveless
NURVLES	nerveless
VURVLES	verveless

URVUS

FURVUS	confervous
KURVUS	curvous, recurvous
NURVUS	nervous, unnervous

URZĒ

FURZĒ	furzy
JURZĒ	jersey, Jersey, New Jersey
KURZĒ	kersey

URZHUN

KURZHUN	discursion, excursion, incursion
PURZHUN	Persian
SPURZHUN	aspersion, interspersion, dispersion
TURZHUN	extersion
VURZHUN	*A* animadversion, aversion, *D* deorsumversion, diversion, *E* extroversion, eversion, *I* introversion, inversion, *K* conversion, *O* obversion, *P* perversion, *R* retroversion, *V* version

ŪSA

DŪSA	medusa, Medusa
FŪSA	subsemifusa
MŪSA	Musa

(See $\overline{OO}$SA)

ŪSAL

(See $\overline{OO}$SAL)

USCHUN

USCHUN	inustion, ustion
BUSCHUN	combustion, moxibustion
DUSCHUN	adustion
FUSCHUN	fustian

ŪSĒ

BŪSĒ	Debussy
DŪSĒ	acey-deucy

(See $\overline{OO}$SĒ)

USĒ

FUSĒ	fussy, overfussy
GUSĒ	gussie
HUSĒ	henhussy, hussy
MUSĒ	mussy
PUSĒ	pussy

ŪSENS

LŪSENS	lucence, noctilucence, tralucence, translucence
NŪSENS	nuisance

ŪSENT

DŪSENT	abducent, adducent, conducent, producent, reducent, traducent
LŪSENT	interlucent, lucent, noctilucent, nonlucent, radiolucent, relucent, tralucent, translucent, unlucent

ŪSER

DŪSER	adducer, deducer, inducer, introducer, conducer, producer, reducer, reproducer, seducer, traducer

(See ŌŌSER)

USER

BUSER	busser
FUSER	fusser
KUSER	cusser, discusser, percussor
MUSER	musser
PLUSER	nonplusser
TRUSER	trusser

USET

GUSET	gusset
RUSET	russet

ŪSFUL

ŪSFUL	unuseful, useful

(See ŌŌSFUL)

USHA

PRUSHA	Prussia
RUSHA	Russia

ŪSHAL

DŪSHAL	fiducial
NŪSHAL	minutial

(See ŌŌSHAL)

USHĒ

BLUSHĒ	blushy
BRUSHĒ	brushy
GUSHĒ	gushy
LUSHĒ	lushy
MUSHĒ	mushy
PLUSHĒ	plushy
RUSHĒ	rushy
SLUSHĒ	slushy
THRUSHĒ	thrushy
TUSHĒ	tushy

USHER

USHER	usher
BLUSHER	blusher
BRUSHER	brusher
FLUSHER	flusher, four-flusher
GUSHER	gusher
HUSHER	husher
KRUSHER	crusher
LUSHER	lusher
MUSHER	musher
PLUSHER	plusher
RUSHER	rusher
SHUSHER	shusher

USHING

FLUSHING	flushing, four-flushing
RUSHING	onrushing, rushing

(See USH, add -ing where appropriate.)

ŪSHUN

BŪSHUN	attribution, distribution, contribution, redistribution, retribution
FŪSHUN	Confucian
GŪSHUN	redargution
KŪSHUN	A allocution, E execution, electrocution, elocution, I insecution, interlocution, K collocution, L locution, P persecution, PR prosecution, S circumlocution, V ventrilocution
NŪSHUN	diminution, imminution, comminution
PŪSHUN	Lilliputian
TŪSHUN	destitution, institution, constitution, prostitution, restitution, substitution

(See ŌŌSHUN)

USHUN

HUSHUN	hushion
KUSHUN	discussion, incussion, concussion, percussion, recussion, repercussion, succusian
PRUSHUN	prushun, Prussian
RUSHUN	Russian

ŪSID

DŪSID	deuced
LŪSID	lucid, pellucid, translucid
MŪSID	mucid

ŪSIJ

ŪSIJ	disusage, misusage, usage
BŪSIJ	abusage

ŪSIK

FŪSIK	fucic
JŪSIK	ageusic, parageusic
KŪSIK	anacusic
MŪSIK	mucic

(See ŌŌSIK)

ŪSING

(See ŪS, OOS, add -ing where appropriate.)

USING

BUSING	busing, bussing
FUSING	fussing
KUSING	discussing, concussing, cussing, percussing
MUSING	mussing
PLUSING	nonplussing
TRUSING	trussing, untrussing

ŪSIS

NŪSIS	prosneusis
PŪSIS	therapeusis
TŪSIS	pertusis

(See OOSIS)

ŪSIV

BŪSIV	abusive
DŪSIV	deducive, educive, inconducive, inducive, conducive, seducive
FŪSIV	diffusive, effusive, infusive, confusive, perfusive, transfusive
LŪSIV	allusive, delusive, elusive, illusive, collusive
TŪSIV	contusive

(See OOSIV)

USIV

JUSIV	jussive
KUSIV	discussive, concussive, percussive, repercussive, succussive
TUSIV	antitussive, tussive

USKAN

BUSKAN	buskin
DUSKAN	dusken
LUSKAN	molluscan
RUSKAN	ruskin, Ruskin
TRUSKAN	Etruscan
TUSKAN	Tuscan

USKĀT

FUSKĀT	infuscate, obfuscate
RUSKĀT	coruscate

USKĒ

BUSKĒ	busky
DUSKĒ	dusky
HUSKĒ	husky
MUSKĒ	musky
RUSKĒ	rusky, Rusky

USKER

BUSKER	busker
HUSKER	husker, cornhusker
TUSKER	tusker

USKET

BUSKET	busket
MUSKET	musket

USKIN

(See USKAN)

USKING

BUSKING	busking
DUSKING	dusking
HUSKING	husking, cornhusking
TUSKING	tusking

USKŪL

JUSKŪL	majuscule
KUSKŪL	ulcuscule
NUSKŪL	minuscule
PUSKŪL	crepuscule, opuscule

USKUS

FUSKUS	fuscous
KUSKUS	khuskhus
MUSKUS	muscous

ŪSL

DŪSL	medusal
NŪSL	hypotenusal

(See OOSAL)

USL

BUSL	arbuscle, bustle
DUSL	duscle
HUSL	hustle
JUSL	jussel, justle
KUSL	ulcuscle
MUSL	muscle, mussel
PUSL	corpuscle, crepuscle, opuscle
RUSL	rustle
TRUSL	trussell
TUSL	pertussal, tussal, tussle

ŪSLĒ

FŪSLĒ	diffusely, profusely

(See OOSLĒ)

USLĒ

MUSLĒ	muscley
RUSLĒ	rustly
THUSLĒ	thusly

USLER

BUSLER	bustler
HUSLER	hustler
RUSLER	rustler
TUSLER	tussler

ŪSLES

ŪSLES	useless

(See OOSLES)

USLING

(See USL, add -ing where appropriate.)

ŪSNES

FŪSNES	diffuseness, profuseness
TŪSNES	obtuseness

(See OOSNES)

ŪSŌ

(See OOSŌ)

USTA

GUSTA	Augusta
HUSTA	hasta
KRUSTA	lincrusta

USTARD

(See USTERD)

USTĒ

BUSTĒ	busty
DUSTĒ	dusty
FUSTĒ	fusty
GUSTĒ	gusty
KRUSTĒ	crusty
LUSTĒ	lusty
MUSTĒ	mustee, musty
RUSTĒ	rusty
TRUSTĒ	trusty, trustee

USTED

BUSTED	busted, combusted
DUSTED	bedusted, dusted
GUSTED	disgusted, gusted
JUSTED	adjusted, coadjusted, misadjusted, readjusted
LUSTED	lusted
RUSTED	rusted
TRUSTED	distrusted, entrusted, mistrusted, trusted

USTER

BLUSTER	bluster
BUSTER	blockbuster, broncobuster, buster, filibuster, combustor, robuster, trustbuster
DUSTER	duster, knuckleduster
FLUSTER	fluster
JUSTER	adjuster, juster, coadjuster, readjuster
KLUSTER	cluster
LUSTER	lackluster, luster
MUSTER	muster
RUSTER	ruster, rustre
THRUSTER	thruster
TRUSTER	distruster, mistruster, truster

USTERD

BLUSTERD	blustered
BUSTERD	bustard
FLUSTERD	beflustered, flustered
KLUSTERD	clustered, unclustered
KUSTERD	custard
LUSTERD	lustered
MUSTERD	mustard, mustered
RUSTERD	rustred

USTFUL

GUSTFUL	disgustful, gustful
LUSTFUL	lustful
RUSTFUL	rustful
TRUSTFUL	distrustful, mistrustful, trustful

USTIK

BUSTIK	bustic
FUSTIK	fustic
KRUSTIK	anacrustic
RUSTIK	rustic

USTING

BUSTING	busting
DUSTING	dusting
GUSTING	disgusting, gusting
JUSTING	adjusting, coadjusting, maladjusting, readjusting
KRUSTING	encrusting, crusting
LUSTING	lusting
RUSTING	rusting
THRUSTING	thrusting
TRUSTING	distrusting, entrusting, mistrusting, trusting

USTINGZ

HUSTINGZ	hustings

(See USTING, add -s where appropriate.)

USTIS

GUSTIS	Augustus
JUSTIS	justice, Justus

USTIV

BUSTIV	combustive
JUSTIV	adjustive

USTLĒ

BUSTLĒ	robustly
GUSTLĒ	augustly
JUSTLĒ	justly

USTMENT

JUSTMENT	adjustment, maladjustment, readjustment
KRUSTMENT	encrustment
TRUSTMENT	entrustment

USTNES

BUSTNES	robustness
GUSTNES	augustness
JUSTNES	justness, unjustness

USTŌ

BUSTŌ	basso robusto, robusto
GUSTŌ	gusto

USTRAL

KUSTRAL	lacustral
LUSTRAL	lustral, palustral

USTRĀT

FRUSTRĀT	frustrate
LUSTRĀT	illustrate, lustrate, perlustrate

USTRIN

KUSTRIN	interlacustrine, lacustrine
LUSTRIN	palustrine

USTRUM

FLUSTRUM	flustrum
LUSTRUM	lustrum

USTRUS

BLUSTRUS	blustrous
LUSTRUS	illustrous, lacklustrous, lustrous

USTUS

(See USTIS)

ŪSUM

(See OOSUM)

ŪTA

LŪTA   aluta

(See OOTA)

UTA

GUTA   gutta
KUTA   Calcutta

ŪTANT

MŪTANT   commutant, mutant
NŪTANT   nutant
PŪTANT   disputant

(See OOTANT)

ŪTAL

(See ŪTL)

UTAL

(See UTL)

ŪTĀT

MŪTĀT   immutate, mutate
NŪTĀT   circumnutate, nutate
SKŪTĀT   scutate

ŪTĒ

BŪTĒ   beauty
DŪTĒ   duty
KŪTĒ   cutie

(See OOTĒ)

UTĒ

BUTĒ   butty
CHUTĒ   chuttie
GUTĒ   gutty
JUTĒ   jutty
KUTĒ   cutty

NUTĒ   nutty
PUTĒ   puttee, putty
RUTĒ   rutty
SKUTĒ   scutty
SMUTĒ   smutty
SUTĒ   suttee
TUTĒ   tutty
YUTĒ   yati

ŪTED

FŪTED   confuted, refuted
KŪTED   electrocuted,
                executed, persecuted,
                prosecuted
LŪTED   diluted, convoluted,
                polluted, revoluted,
                saluted, voluted
MŪTED   commuted, muted,
                permuted, transmuted
NŪTED   comminuted, cornuted
PŪTED   deputed, disputed,
                imputed, computed,
                putid, supputed

(See OOT, add -ed where appropriate.)

UTED

(See UT, add -ed or -ted where appropriate.)

ŪTEN

(See ŪTN)

UTEN

(See UTN)

ŪTER

FŪTER   confuter, refuter
KŪTER   acuter, executor,
                electrocuter,
                collucutor, cuter,
                persecutor, prosecutor
MŪTER   commuter, muter,
                permuter, transmuter
NŪTER   minuter, neuter
PŪTER   deputer, digital

computer, disputer,
imputer, computer,
microcomputer,
pewter

(See OOTER)

UTER

UTER   utter
BUTER   abutter, bread-and-
                butter, butter, peanut
                butter, rebutter,
                surrebutter
FLUTER   flutter
GLUTER   glutter
GUTER   gutter
HWUTER   whutter
KLUTER   clutter
KUTER   daisycutter, cutter,
                leafcutter, meatcutter,
                pilot cutter,
                stonecutter,
                woodcutter
MUTER   mutter
NUTER   nutter
PUTER   putter
RUTER   rutter, swartrutter
SHUTER   shutter
SKUTER   scutter
SPLUTER   splutter
SPUTER   sputter
STRUTER   strutter
STUTER   stutter
SUTER   sutter

ŪTERD

NŪTERD   neutered
TŪTERD   tutored

UTERD

(See UTER, add -ed where appropriate.)

ŪTHER

(See OOTHER)

UTHER

(TH as in then)

UTHER   other
BRUTHER   brother, charter
                brother, foster
                brother, half brother,
                lodge brother,
                stepbrother

ONLY ONE DRINK AT A TIME, PLEASE

A nimiety of gin
Sows ebriety and sin;
In respectable society
This is viewed as impropriety;
The man of sagacity
Refrains from bibacity.

MUTHER   den mother,
                foremother, foster
                mother, godmother,
                grandmother, mother,
                stepmother
NUTHER   another, one another
SMUTHER   smother
TUTHER   t'other
WUTHER   wuther

ŪTHERZ

DRUTHERZ   druthers

(See **UTHER**, add -s where appropriate.)

ŪTHFUL

(See OŌTHFUL)

ŪTHING

(See OŌTHING)

ŪTHLES

(See OŌTHLES)

ŪTHSUM

(See OŌTHSUM)

ŪTIJ

MŪTIJ   mutage
PŪTIJ   putage
SKŪTIJ   scutage

(See OŌTIJ)

ŪTIK

ŪTIK   halieutic, maieutic
BŪTIK   antiscorbutic,
                scorbutic
DŪTIK   paideutic,
                propaedeutic
LŪTIK   probouleutic
MŪTIK   mutic
NŪTIK   digoneutic,
                hermeneutic,
                ichneutic
PŪTIK   radiotherapeutic,
                therapeutic
SŪTIK   pharmaceutic
TŪTIK   emphyteutic
ZŪTIK   diazeutic

(See OŌTIK)

ŪTIKS

(See **ŪTIK**, add -s where appropriate.)

ŪTIL

(See ŪTL)

ŪTING

(See **ŪT**, OŌT, add -ing where appropriate.)

ŪTISH

(See OŌTISH)

UTISH

NUTISH   nuttish
RUTISH   ruttish
SLUTISH   sluttish

ŪTIST

NŪTIST   hermeneutist
PŪTIST   therapeutist
SŪTIST   pharmaceutist

(See OŌTIST)

ŪTIV

BŪTIV   *retributive*
KŪTIV   persecutive
LŪTIV   evolutive,
                convolutive,
                resolutive
TŪTIV   constitutive,
                restitutive,
                substitutive

(See OŌTIV)

ŪTIZM

MŪTIZM   mutism

(See OŌTIZM)

ŪTL

ŪTL   utile, inutile
FŪTL   futile, refutal
SŪTL   sutile

(See OŌTL)

UTL

BUTL   abuttal, buttle,
                rebuttal, surrebuttal
GUTL   guttle
KUTL   cuttle
RUTL   ruttle
SHUTL   shuttle, space shuttle
SKUTL   scuttle
SUTL   subtle, suttle, unsubtle

ŪTLĒ

KŪTLĒ   acutely, cutely
MŪTLĒ   mutely
NŪTLĒ   minutely
TŪTLĒ   astutely

(See OŌTLĒ)

UTLER

BUTLER   butler
KUTLER   cutler, cuttler
SKUTLER   scuttler
SUTLER   subtler, sutler

ŪTLES

PŪTLES   reputeless

(See OŌTLES)

UTLET

KUTLET   cutlet
NUTLET   nutlet

ŪTLING

(See OŌTLING)

UTLING

BUTLING   buttling
GUTLING   gutling, guttling
SKUTLING   scuttling
SUTLING   sutling

ŪTMENT

FŪTMENT   confutement

(See OŌTMENT)

ŪTN

KŪTN	cutin
TŪTN	Teuton

(See ŌŌTN, ŌŌTON)

UTN

UTN	ughten
BUTN	bachelor button, belly button, bluebutton, button, unbutton
GLUTN	glutton
MUTN	mutton

ŪTNES

KŪTNES	acuteness, cuteness
MŪTNES	muteness
NŪTNES	minuteness
SŪTNES	hirsuteness
TŪTNES	astuteness

(See ŌŌTNES)

UTNING

BUTNING	buttoning
HUTNING	huttoning

ŪTŌ

(See ŌŌTŌ)

ŪTRIKS

KŪTRIKS	persecutrix
TŪTRIKS	tutrix

ŪTSĒ

KŪTSĒ	cutesie

(See ŌŌTSĒ)

UTUK

BUTUK	buttock, quakebuttock
FUTUK	futtock

ŪTUM

SKŪTUM	scutum
SPŪTUM	sputum

(See ŌŌTUM)

ŪTŪR

(See ŪCHER)

ŪTUS

KŪTUS	gyascutus

(See ŌŌTUS)

ŪVAL

(See ŌŌVAL)

ŪVĒ

(See ŌŌVĒ)

UVĒ

DUVĒ	dovey, lovey-dovey
KUVĒ	covey
LUVĒ	lovey

UVEL

GRUVEL	grovel
HUVEL	hovel
SHUVEL	shovel
SKUVEL	scovel

(See OVEL)

ŪVEN

(See ŌŌVEN)

UVEN

UVEN	oven
KUVEN	coven
SLUVEN	sloven

ŪVER

(See ŌŌVER)

UVER

GLUVER	glover
HUVER	hover, windhover
KUVER	discover, cover, recover, rediscover, tablecover, undercover, uncover
LUVER	lover, animal lover (etc.)
PLUVER	plover
SHUVER	shover

ŪVING

(See ŌŌV, add -ing where appropriate.)

UVING

GLUVING	gloving, ungloving
LUVING	loving, animal loving (etc.)
SHUVING	shoving

ŪVMENT

(See ŌŌVMENT)

ŪYA

(See ŌŌYA)

ŪZA

MŪZA	musa
TŪZA	tuza

(See ŌŌZA)

ŪZAL

FŪZAL	fusel, refusal, rumtifusel
KŪZAL	accusal
MŪZAL	musal

(See ŌŌZL)

ŪZANS

ŪZANS	misusance, usance
KŪZANS	recusance

UZARD

UZARD	uzzard
BUZARD	buzzard
HUZARD	huzzard

ŪZĒ

(See ŌŌZĒ)

UZĒ

BUZĒ	buzzy
FUZĒ	fuzzy

GUZĒ	fuzzy-guzzy
HUZĒ	hussy
MUZĒ	muzzy, tuzzymuzzy
SKUZĒ	skuzzy
WUZĒ	fuzzy-wuzzy, Fuzzy-Wuzzy, wuzzy

UZEN

| DUZEN | dozen |
| KUZEN | cousin |

UZENS

| DUZENZ | dozens |
| KUZENZ | cousins |

ŪZER

ŪZER	misuser, nonuser, user
BŪZER	abuser
FŪZER	diffuser, fuser, infuser, interfuser, confuser, refuser, suffuser, transfuser
KŪZER	accuser, excuser
MŪZER	amuser, muser

(See OOZER)

UZER

BUZER	buzzer
FUZER	fuzzer
NUZER	nuzzer

ŪZHUN

| BŪZHUN | abusion |
| FŪZHUN | A affusion, D diffusion, E effusion, F fusion, I infusion, |

interfusion, K confusion, P perfusion, PR profusion, R refusion, S circumfusion, suffusion, TR transfusion

| TŪZHUN | extusion, contusion, pertusion |

(See OOZHUN)

ŪZING

(See ŪZ, OOZ, add -ing where appropriate.)

UZING

BUZING	buzzing
FUZING	fuzzing
MUZING	muzzing

ŪZIV

| KŪZIV | accusive |
| MŪZIV | amusive, unamusive |

ŪZL

(See OOZL, ŪZAL)

UZL

BUZL	buzzle
FUZL	fuzzle
GUZL	guzzle
MUZL	bemuzzle, muzzle, unmuzzle
NUZL	nuzzle
PUZL	Chinese puzzle, jigsaw puzzle, crossword puzzle, monkey puzzle, puzzle, word puzzle

UZLĒ

(See UZL, add -y where appropriate.)

ŪZLER

(See OOZLER)

UZLER

GUZLER	gas guzzler, guzzler
MUZLER	muzzler
NUZLER	nuzzler
PUZLER	puzzler, word puzzler

UZLING

(See UZL, add -ing where appropriate.)

ŪZMAN

| NŪZMAN | newsman |

(See OOZMAN)

ŪZMENT

| KŪZMENT | accusement |
| MŪZMENT | amusement |

UZN

| DUZN | dozen |
| KUZN | catercousin, quatercousin, cousin, cozen |

UZNT

| DUZNT | doesn't |
| WUZNT | wasn't |

TRIPLE RHYMES

(Words accented on the syllable before the next-to-the-last syllable, or, in a few cases, on one or more syllables before *that*. They are also called dactylic rhymes.)

Ā'A.BL

FRĀ'A.BL	defrayable
PĀ'A.BL	impayable, payable, prepayable, repayable, unpayable
PLĀ'A.BL	playable, unplayable
PRĀ'A.BL	prayable, unprayable
SĀ'A.BL	sayable, unsayable
SLĀ'A.BL	slayable
SPĀ'A.BL	spayable
SWĀ'A.BL	swayable, unswayable
TRĀ'A.BL	portrayable, unportrayable
VĀ'A.BL	conveyable, surveyable, unconveyable, unsurveyable
WĀ'A.BL	weighable, unweighable

AB'A.RET

KAB'A.RET	cabaret
TAB'A.RET	tabaret

AB'A.BL

GRAB'A.BL	grabbable
JAB'A.BL	jabbable
NAB'A.BL	nabbable
STAB'A.BL	stabbable
TAB'A.BL	tabbable

AB'A.SIS

NAB'A.SIS	anabasis
RAB'A.SIS	parabasis
TAB'A.SIS	catabasis, metabasis

Ā'BER.ING

LĀ'BER.ING	belaboring, laboring
NĀ'BER.ING	neighboring
TĀ'BER.ING	taboring

Ā'BER.ER

LĀ'BER.ER	laborer
TĀ'BER.ER	taberer

Ā'BI.A

LĀ'BI.A	labia
RĀ'BI.A	Arabia, Bessarabia

SWĀ'BI.A	Swabia
TRĀ'BI.A	trabea

Ā'BI.AN

FĀ'BI.AN	Fabian
GĀ'BI.AN	gabion
RĀ'BI.AN	Arabian, Sorabian
SĀ'BI.AN	Sabian
SWĀ'BI.AN	Swabian

AB'ID.NES

RAB'ID.NES	rabidness
TAB'ID.NES	tabidness

AB'I.ER

BLAB'I.ER	blabbier
FLAB'I.ER	flabbier
GAB'I.ER	gabbier
GRAB'I.ER	grabbier
KRAB'I.ER	crabbier
SHAB'I.ER	shabbier
SKAB'I.ER	scabbier

Ā'BI.ĒZ

Ā'BI.ĒZ	abies
RĀ'BI.ĒZ	rabies
SKĀ'BI.ĒZ	scabies

AB'I.FĪ

LAB'I.FĪ	dissyllabify, labefy, syllabify
TAB'I.FĪ	tabefy

AB'I.KAL

LAB'I.KAL	monosyllabical, multisyllabical, polysyllabical, syllabical
RAB'I.KAL	Arabical

AB'I.LĒ

BLAB'I.LĒ	blabbily
FLAB'I.LĒ	flabbily
GAB'I.LĒ	gabbily
KRAB'I.LĒ	crabbily
LAB'I.LĒ	ballabile
SKAB'I.LĒ	scabbily

AB'I.NES

(See **AB'Ē**, add -*ness* where appropriate.)

AB'IT.Ē

BAB'IT.Ē	babbitty
RAB'IT.Ē	rabbity

AB'IT.ING

BAB'IT.ING	babbitting
HAB'IT.ING	habiting, inhabiting, cohabiting
RAB'IT.ING	rabbiting

AB'I.TŬD

HAB'I.TŬD	habitude
TAB'I.TŬD	tabitude

AB'L.MENT

BAB'L.MENT	babblement
BRAB'L.MENT	brabblement
DAB'L.MENT	dabblement
DRAB'L.MENT	drabblement
GAB'L.MENT	gabblement
GRAB'L.MENT	grabblement
RAB'L.MENT	rabblement
SKAB'L.MENT	scabblement
SKRAB'L.MENT	scrabblement

Ā'BL.NES

Ā'BL.NES	ableness
SĀ'BL.NES	sableness
STĀ'BL.NES	stableness, unstableness

AB'LI.ER

(See **ABLĒ**, change -*y* and add -*er* where appropriate.)

AB'O.LA

RAB'O.LA	parabola, sporabala
TAB'O.LA	Metabola

AB'O.LĪZ

RAB'O.LĪZ	parabolize
TAB'O.LĪZ	metabolize

AB'O.LIZM

AB'O.LIZM	diabolism
NAB'O.LIZM	anabolism
TAB'O.LIZM	catabolism, metabolism

AB'Ū.LA

FAB'Ū.LA	fabula
NAB'Ū.LA	incunabula
TAB'Ū.LA	tabula

AB'Ū.LAR

FAB'Ū.LAR	fabular, confabular
NAB'Ū.LAR	incunabular, cunabular, tintinnabular
PAB'Ū.LAR	pabular
TAB'Ū.LAR	acetabular, tabular

AB'Ū.LĀT

FAB'Ū.LĀT	fabulate, confabulate
NAB'Ū.LĀT	tintinnabulate
TAB'Ū.LĀT	tabulate

AB'Ū.LIST

FAB'Ū.LIST	fabulist
KAB'Ū.LIST	vocabulist
NAB'Ū.LIST	incunabulist, tintinnabulist

AB'Ū.LUM

NAB'Ū.LUM	incunabulum, tintinnabulum
PAB'Ū.LUM	pabulum
TAB'Ū.LUM	acetabulum

AB'Ū.LUS

FAB'Ū.LUS	fabulous
NAB'Ū.LUS	tintinnabulous
PAB'Ū.LUS	pabulous
SAB'Ū.LUS	sabulous
TAB'Ū.LUS	fantabulous

ACH'A.BL

BACH'A.BL	batchable
HACH'A.BL	hatchable, crosshatchable, unhatchable
KACH'A.BL	catchable, uncatchable
LACH'A.BL	latchable, unlatchable
MACH'A.BL	immatchable, matchable, rematchable, unmatchable
PACH'A.BL	dispatchable, patchable, repatchable, unpatchable
SKRACH'A.BL	scratchable, unscratchable
SNACH'A.BL	snatchable, unsnatchable
THACH'A.BL	thatchable, unthatchable

ACH'E.LA

MACH'E.LA	comatula
SKACH'E.LA	scatula
SPACH'E.LA	spatula

ACH'ER.Ē

HACH'ER.Ē	hatchery
PACH'ER.Ē	patchery

ACH'I.NES

(See ACH, add *-iness* where appropriate.)

ACH'OO.LĀT

GRACH'OO.LĀT	gratulate, congratulate
SPACH'OO.LĀT	spatulate

ACH'OOR.ĀT

MACH'OOR.ĀT	maturate
SACH'OOR.ĀT	polyunsaturate, saturate, super-saturate

Ā'DA.BL

BRĀ'DA.BL	braidable, unbraidable, upbraidable
GRĀ'DA.BL	biodegradable, degradable, gradable, undegradable, ungradable
SHĀ'DA.BL	shadable, unshadable
SWĀ'DA.BL	dissuadable, persuadable, undissuadable, unpersuadable
TRĀ'DA.BL	retradable, tradable, untradable
VĀ'DA.BL	evadable, invadable
WĀ'DA.BL	unwadable, wadable

Ā'DED.LĒ

FĀ'DED.LĒ	fadedly
GRĀ'DED.LĒ	degradedly
JĀ'DED.LĒ	jadedly

Ā'DED.NES

(See ĀD, add *-edness* where appropriate.)

Ā'DI.A

KĀ'DI.A	Acadia, Arcadia
LĀ'DI.A	Palladia
STĀ'DI.A	stadia

Ā'DI.AL

RĀ'DI.AL	multiradial, radial, uniradial
STĀ'DI.AL	interstadial, stadial

Ā'DI.AN

BĀ'DI.AN	Barbadian
KĀ'DI.AN	Acadian, Arcadian, Orcadian, circadian
LĀ'DI.AN	palladian
MĀ'DI.AN	gammadion, nomadian
NĀ'DI.AN	Canadian, Grenadian
RĀ'DI.AN	radian, steradian

Ā'DI.ANT

GRĀ'DI.ANT	gradient
RĀ'DI.ANT	irradiant, radiant

Ā'DING.LĒ

FĀ'DING.LĒ	fadingly
GRĀ'DING.LĒ	degradingly
VĀ'DING.LĒ	pervadingly

AD'ISH.NES

BAD'ISH.NES	baddishness
FAD'ISH.NES	faddishness
KAD'ISH.NES	caddishness
MAD'ISH.NES	maddishness
SAD'ISH.NES	saddishness

AD'I.TIV

AD'I.TIV	additive
TRAD'I.TIV	traditive

Ā'DI.UM

LĀ'DI.UM	caladium, palladium
NĀ'DI.UM	vanadium
RĀ'DI.UM	radium
STĀ'DI.UM	stadium
VĀ'DI.UM	vadium

Ā'DI.US

GLĀ'DI.US	gladius
RĀ'DI.US	adradius, hyporadius, radius

AF'I.A

GRAF'I.A	agraphia, dysgraphia, mogigraphia, paragraphia, strephographia
MAF'I.A	maffia, mafia
RAF'I.A	raffia
SAF'I.A	asaphia
TAF'I.Ä	tafia

AF'I.KAL

GRAF'I.KAL	*A* anthropographical, *B* bibliographical, biographical, biogeographical, *D* diagraphical, *E* electrocardiographical, epigraphical, ethnographical, *F* physiographical, phytographical, photographical, *GL* glossographical, *GR* graphical, *J* geographical, *K* calligraphical, cartographical, cosmographical, *L* lexigraphical, lexicographical, *O* autobiographical, autographical, orthographical, *P* paleographical, paleontographical, paragraphical, pornographical, *T* pterylographical, telegraphical, typographical, topographical *Z* zoographical, zoogeographical
RAF'I.KAL	seraphical
TAF'I.KAL	epitaphical

AF'L.MENT

BAF'L.MENT	bafflement
RAF'L.MENT	rafflement
SKRAF'L.MENT	scrafflement
SNAF'L.MENT	snafflement

AFT'A.BL

(See **AFT,** add -*able* where appropriate.)

AF'TI.LĒ

DRAF'TI.LĒ	draftily, draughtily
KRAF'TI.LĒ	craftily

AFT'LES.LĒ

DRAFT'LES.LĒ	draftlessly
GRAFT'LES.LĒ	graftlessly
KRAFT'LES.LĒ	craftlessly
SHAFT'LES.LĒ	shaftlessly

AG'A.BL

BAG'A.BL	baggable
DRAG'A.BL	draggable
FLAG'A.BL	flaggable
FRAG'A.BL	irrefragable
GAG'A.BL	gaggable
JAG'A.BL	jaggable
NAG'A.BL	naggable
RAG'A.BL	raggable
SAG'A.BL	saggable
SHAG'A.BL	shaggable
SKAG'A.BL	scaggable
SNAG'A.BL	snaggable
TAG'A.BL	taggable
WAG'A.BL	waggable

AG'ED.LĒ

JAG'ED.LĒ	jaggedly
RAG'ED.LĒ	raggedly
SKRAG'ED.LĒ	scraggedly

AG'ED.NES

JAG'ED.NES	jaggedness
KRAG'ED.NES	craggedness
RAG'ED.NES	raggedness
SKRAG'ED.NES	scraggedness

AG'ER.Ē

FAG'ER.Ē	faggery
JAG'ER.Ē	jaggery
LAG'ER.Ē	inlagary
RAG'ER.Ē	raggery
STAG'ER.Ē	staggery
SWAG'ER.Ē	swaggery
WAG'ER.Ē	waggery
ZAG'ER.Ē	zig-zaggery

AG'ER.ER

STAG'ER.ER	staggerer
SWAG'ER.ER	swaggerer

AG'ER.ING

STAG'ER.ING	staggering
SWAG'ER.ING	swaggering

AG'I.LĒ

BAG'I.LĒ	baggily
KRAG'I.LĒ	craggily
NAG'I.LĒ	naggily
RAG'I.LĒ	raggily
SHAG'I.LĒ	shaggily
SKRAG'I.LĒ	scraggily

AG'I.NES

BAG'I.NES	bagginess
BRAG'I.NES	bragginess
FLAG'I.NES	flagginess
KRAG'I.NES	cragginess
NAG'I.NES	knagginess, nagginess
SHAG'I.NES	shagginess
SKRAG'I.NES	scragginess

AG′ISH.LĒ

BRAG′ISH.LĒ	braggishly
HAG′ISH.LĒ	haggishly
NAG′ISH.LĒ	naggishly
WAG′ISH.LĒ	waggishly

AG′ON.AL

AG′ON.AL	agonal, diagonal, preagonal, triagonal
SAG′ON.AL	hexagonal
TAG′ON.AL	heptagonal, octagonal, pentagonal
TRAG′ON.AL	tetragonal

AG′O.NIST

AG′O.NIST	agonist, deuteragonist
TAG′O.NIST	antagonist, protagonist, tritagonist

AG′O.NĪZ

AG′O.NĪZ	agonize
TAG′O.NĪZ	antagonize

AG′O.TĒ

FAG′O.TĒ	faggoty, fagoty
MAG′O.TĒ	maggoty

Ā′GRAN.SĒ

FLĀ′GRAN.SĒ	flagrancy
FRĀ′GRAN.SĒ	fragrancy
VĀ′GRAN.SĒ	vagrancy

Ā′I.KAL

BRĀ′I.KAL	algebraical, Hebraical
DĀ′I.KAL	Judaical
KĀ′I.KAL	alcaical, archaical, trochaical
LĀ′I.KAL	formulaical, laical
MĀ′I.KAL	Aramaical, Ptolemaical
PĀ′I.KAL	apotropaical
ZĀ′I.KAL	pharisaical, Mosaical, paradisaical

Ä′ING.LĒ

Ä′ING.LĒ	ahingly, oh-and-ahingly
BÄ′ING.LĒ	baaingly, bahingly
BLÄ′ING.LĒ	blahingly, blah-blahingly

Ā′I.TĒ

GĀ′I.TĒ	gaiety
LĀ′I.TĒ	laity

Ā′JA.BL

GĀ′JA.BL	engageable, gaugeable
STĀ′JA.BL	stageable, unstageable
SWĀ′JA.BL	assuageable

AJ′ER.Ē

NAJ′ER.Ē	menagerie
TAJ′ER.Ē	potagerie

Ā′JI.A

FĀ′JI.A	aphagia, aerophagia, dysphagia, gamophagia, kreatophagia, omophagia, autophagia, pagophagia, polyphagia, chthonophagia
HĀ′JI.A	hagia
NĀ′JI.A	Panagia
RĀ′JI.A	menorrhagia, metrorrhagia

Ā′JI.AN

LĀ′JI.AN	archipelagian, pelagian
MĀ′JI.AN	magian

AJ′I.KAL

MAJ′I.KAL	magical, theomagical
TRAJ′I.KAL	tragical

Ā′JI.LĒ

KĀ′JI.LĒ	cagily
STĀ′JI.LĒ	stagily

AJ′IL.NES

AJ′IL.NES	agileness
FRAJ′IL.NES	fragileness

AJ′I.NAL

MAJ′I.NAL	imaginal
PAJ′I.NAL	paginal
VAJ′I.NAL	vaginal

AJ′I.NĀT

MAJ′I.NĀT	imaginate
PAJ′I.NĀT	paginate
SAJ′I.NĀT	saginate
VAJ′I.NĀT	evaginate, invaginate, vaginate

AJ′I.NUS

AJ′I.NUS	oleaginous
BAJ′I.NUS	lumbaginous
LAJ′I.NUS	cartilaginous, mucilaginous
RAJ′I.NUS	farraginous, voraginous
VAJ′I.NUS	favaginous

AJ′I.Ō

AJ′I.Ō	agio
DAJ′I.Ō	adagio

AJ′I.TĀT

AJ′I.TĀT	agitate
SAJ′I.TĀT	sagittate

Ā′JUS.LĒ

BRĀ′JUS.LĒ	umbrageously
PĀ′JUS.LĒ	rampageously
RĀ′JUS.LĒ	courageously, outrageously
TĀ′JUS.LĒ	advantageously, disadvantageously, contagiously

Ā′KA.BL

Ā′KA.BL	acheable
BRĀ′KA.BL	breakable, unbreakable
PĀ′KA.BL	impacable, pacable

PLĀ'KA.BL implacable, placable
SHĀ'KA.BL shakable, unshakable
SLĀ'KA.BL slakable, unslakable
TĀ'KA.BL mistakable, takable,
  undertakable,
  unmistakable
WĀ'KA.BL awakable, wakable

AK'A.NAL

AK'A.NAL diaconal
BAK'A.NAL bacchanal

Ā'KĀ.TED

PLĀ'KĀ.TED placated, unplacated
VĀ'KĀ.TED revacated,
  unvacated, vacated

AK'A.TŌ.RĒ

NAK'A.TŌ.RĒ kincknackatory
PLAK'A.TŌ.RĒ placatory

Ā'KA.WĀ

BRĀ'KA.WĀ breakaway
TĀ'KA.WĀ takeaway

AK'CHER.ING

FAK'CHER.ING manufacturing
FRAK'CHER.ING fracturing,
  refracturing

AK'CHŌŌ.AL

AK'CHŌŌ.AL actual
FAK'CHŌŌ.AL factual
PAK'CHŌŌ.AL impactual
TAK'CHŌŌ.AL contactual, tactual
TRAK'CHŌŌ.AL contractual

AK'EN.ING

BLAK'EN.ING blackening
SLAK'EN.ING slackening

Ā'KER.Ē

BĀ'KER.Ē bakery
FĀ'KER.Ē fakery, fakiry
KWĀ'KER.Ē quakery, Quakery
RĀ'KER.Ē rakery

SNĀ'KER.Ē snakery
TĀ'KER.Ē undertakery

AK'ER.Ē

HAK'ER.Ē hackery
JAK'ER.Ē hijackery
KRAK'ER.Ē jimcrackery
KWAK'ER.Ē quackery
NAK'ER.Ē knackery, knick-
  knackery
SNAK'ER.Ē snackery
THAK'ER.Ē Thackeray

AK'ER.EL

KAK'ER.EL cackerel
MAK'ER.EL mackerel

Ā'KER.IZM

FĀ'KER.IZM fakirism
KWĀ'KER.IZM Quakerism
SHĀ'KER.IZM Shakerism

AK'ER.ŌŌ

JAK'ER.ŌŌ Jackaroo, jackeroo
SMAK'ER.ŌŌ smackeroo

AK'ET.ED

BRAK'ET.ED bracketed
JAK'ET.ED jacketed
PAK'ET.ED packeted
PLAK'ET.ED placketed
RAK'ET.ED racketed

AK'ET.ING

(See AKET, add -ing where appropriate.)

Ā'KI.A

MĀ'KI.A naumachia
TRĀ'KI.A Batrachia, trachea

Ā'KI.AL

BRĀ'KI.AL brachial
RĀ'KI.AL rachial
TRĀ'KI.AL trachial

Ā'KI.AN

Ā'KI.AN Noachian
LĀ'KI.AN selachian
MĀ'KI.AN tauromachian
STĀ'KI.AN eustachian
TRĀ'KI.AN batrachian, trachean

AK'I.NĀT

KAK'I.NĀT cacchinate
MAK'I.NĀT machinate

Ā'KI.NES

FĀ'KI.NES fakiness
FLĀ'KI.NES flakiness
KWĀ'KI.NES quakiness
SHĀ'KI.NES shakiness
SNĀ'KI.NES snakiness

AK'I.NES

HAK'I.NES hackiness
HWAK'I.NES whackiness
KRAK'I.NES gimcrackiness
TAK'I.NES tackiness
WAK'I.NES wackiness

IN CASE ANYONE SHOULD ESK YOU

A stomach pump's required to rescue
A sheep that's eaten too much fescue.

AK'ISH.NES

BLAK'ISH.NES blackishness
BRAK'ISH.NES brackishness
KWAK'ISH.NES quackishness
NAK'ISH.NES knackishness
SLAK'ISH.NES slackishness

AK'Ō.NĪT

AK'Ō.NĪT aconite
TAK'Ō.NĪT taconite

AK'RI.TĒ

AK'RI.TĒ acrity
LAK'RI.TĒ alacrity

AK'RŌ.DONT

AK'RŌ.DONT acrodont
MAK'RO.DONT macrodont

AK'RO.NIZM

NAK'RO.NIZM	anachronism
RAK'RO.NIZM	parachronism
TAK'RO.NIZM	metachronism

AK'SA.BL

LAK'SA.BL	relaxable, unrelaxable
TAK'SA.BL	taxable, untaxable

AK'SHUN.AL

(See AK'SHUN, add -al where appropriate.)

AK'SA.BL

AK'SA.BL	axable
TAK'SA.BL	taxable

AK'SHUS.NES

FAK'SHUS.NES	factiousness
FRAK'SHUS.NES	fractiousness

AK'SI.A

PRAK'SI.A	apraxia, echopraxia
RAK'SI.A	ataraxia
TAK'SI.A	ataxia

AK'SI.AL

AK'SI.AL	axial, biaxial, coaxial
BAK'SI.AL	abaxial

AK'TA.BL

AK'TA.BL	actable, enactable, reactable, transactable
DAK'TA.BL	redactable
FAK'TA.BL	olfactible
FRAK'TA.BL	infractible, irrefractable, refractable
PAK'TA.BL	impactable, compactible
STRAK'TA.BL	abstractable, distractible
TAK'TA.BL	intactable, contactable, tactable
TRAK'TA.BL	abstractable, attractable, detractible, distractible, extractible, intractable, contractable, protractable, retractable, tractable

AK'TED.NES

PAK'TED.NES	impactedness
STRAK'TED.NES	abstractedness
TRAK'TED.NES	distractedness, contractedness, protractedness

AK'TER.Ē

AK'TER.Ē	enactory
FAK'TER.Ē	benefactory, dissatisfactory, factory, calefactory, malefactory, manufactory, olfactory, satisfactory, unsatisfactory
FRAK'TER.Ē	refractory
LAK'TER.Ē	lactary, phylactery
TRAK'TER.Ē	detractory, tractory

AK'TI.AL

BRAK'TI.AL	bracteal
LAK'TI.AL	lacteal

AK'TI.KAL

DAK'TI.KAL	didactical
LAK'TI.KAL	stalactical
PRAK'TI.KAL	impractical, practical, unpractical
TAK'TI.KAL	syntactical, tactical

AK'TIV.NES

(See AK'TIV, add -ness.)

AK'TŪ.AL

(See AK'CHŌŌ.AL)

AK'TŪR.ING

(See AK'CHER.ING)

AK'Ū.ĀT

AK'Ū.ĀT	acuate
VAK'Ū.ĀT	evacuate

AK'Ū.LA

BAK'Ū.LA	bacula
DRAK'Ū.LA	Dracula
FAK'Ū.LA	facula
MAK'Ū.LA	macula
TAK'Ū.LA	tentacula

AK'Ū.LAR

AK'Ū.LAR	piacular
NAK'Ū.LAR	supernacular, tabernacular, vernacular
RAK'Ū.LAR	oracular
TAK'Ū.LAR	ante-jentacular, jentacular, post-jentacular, spectacular, sustentacular, tentacular

AK'Ū.LĀT

JAK'Ū.LĀT	ejaculate, interjaculate, jaculate
MAK'Ū.LĀT	bimaculate, immaculate, maculate
SAK'Ū.LĀT	sacculate
TAK'Ū.LĀT	tentaculate

AK'Ū.LUM

AK'Ū.LUM	biaculum
BAK'Ū.LUM	baculum
NAK'Ū.LUM	hibernaculum
TAK'Ū.LUM	tentaculum

AK'Ū.LUS

BAK'Ū.LUS	abaculus, baculus
NAK'Ū.LUS	vernaculous
RAK'Ū.LUS	meraculous, miraculous, oraculous
SAK'Ū.LUS	sacculus

AK'Ū.PUNGK'CHER

AK'Ū.PUNGK.CHER	*acupuncture*

KWAK'Ū.PUNGK.CHER
           quackupuncture

AK'WI.US

AK'WI.US	aqueous
BAK'WI.US	subaqueous
RAK'WI.US	terraqueous

Ā'LA.BL

BĀ'LA.BL	bailable
HĀ'LA.BL	exhalable, inhalable
JĀ'LA.BL	jailable, unjailable
MĀ'LA.BL	mailable, unmailable
NĀ'LA.BL	nailable, unnailable
SĀ'LA.BL	assailable, wholesalable, sailable, salable, unassailable, unsalable, unsailable
SKĀ'LA.BL	scaleable, unscaleable
TĀ'LA.BL	retailable
TRĀ'LA.BL	trailable, untrailable
VĀ'LA.BL	available, unavailable

Ā'LER.Ē

Ā'LER.Ē	alary, subalary
NĀ'LER.Ē	nailery
RĀ'LER.Ē	raillery

AL'ER.Ē

AL'ER.Ē	alary, subalary, subalary
GAL'ER.Ē	gallery
KAL'ER.Ē	intercalary, calorie, kilocalorie
SAL'ER.Ē	salary
VAL'ER.Ē	vallary

AL'ER.JĒ

AL'ER.JĒ	allergy
TAL'ER.JĒ	metallurgy

AL'ET.ED

BAL'ET.ED	balloted
VAL'ET.ED	valeted

Ā'LI.A

Ā'LI.A	marsupialia
DĀ'LI.A	dahlia, idalia, vedalia
FĀ'LI.A	Westphalia
GĀ'LI.A	galea, regalia
KĀ'LI.A	Lupercalia
LĀ'LI.A	echolalia, eschrolalia, glossolalia, copralalia, mogilalia, palilalia, paralalia, pseudolalia
MĀ'LI.A	mammalia
NĀ'LI.A	bacchanalia, marginalia, paraphernalia, saturnalia, terminalia
PĀ'LI.A	palea
RĀ'LI.A	Psoralea
SĀ'LI.A	sponsalia
SKĀ'LI.A	tragomaschalia
TĀ'LI.A	Arctalia, genitalia
TRĀ'LI.A	Australia, penetralia, Centralia
ZĀ'LI.A	azalea

(See ĀL'YA)

Ā'LI.AN

Ā'LI.AN	alien, marsupialian
DĀ'LI.AN	Daedalian, hippopotomonstro-sesquipedalian, sesquipedalian
GĀ'LI.AN	Phigalian, regalian
KĀ'LI.AN	Deucalion
MĀ'LI.AN	phantasmalian, mammalian, Pygmalion, tatterdemalion
NĀ'LI.AN	bacchanalian, saturnalian, tenaillon, tobacconalian
PĀ'LI.AN	episcopalian, Episcopalian, saranapalian
RĀ'LI.AN	paralian
SĀ'LI.AN	Messalian, universalian
TRĀ'LI.AN	Australian, Centralian

(See ĀL'YAN)

AL'I.ANS

DAL'I.ANS	dalliance
RAL'I.ANS	ralliance

VAL'I.ANS	valiance
ZAL'I.ANS	mesalliance

Ā'LI.AS

Ā'LI.AS	alias
BĀ'LI.AS	Sibelius

AL'IAS

GAL'IAS	galleass
PAL'IAS	palliasse

AL'I.ĀT

GAL'I.ĀT	galeate
MAL'I.ĀT	maleate, malleate
PAL'I.ĀT	palliate
TAL'I.ĀT	retaliate, talliate

AL'I.A.TŌ'RĒ

AL'I.A.TŌ'RĒ	aleatory
TAL'I.A.TŌ'RĒ	retaliatory

AL'ID.LĒ

KAL'ID.LĒ	callidly
PAL'ID.LĒ	pallidly
VAL'ID.LĒ	invalidly, validly

AL'ID.NES

KAL'ID.NES	callidness
PAL'ID.NES	impallidness, pallidness
VAL'ID.NES	invalidness, validness

AL'I.ER

DAL'I.ER	dallier
RAL'I.ER	rallier
SAL'I.ER	sallier
TAL'I.ER	tallier

AL'I.FĪ

KAL'I.FĪ	alkalify, calefy
SAL'I.FĪ	salify

AL'I.ING

DAL'I.ING	dallying
RAL'I.ING	rallying
SAL'I.ING	sallying
TAL'I.ING	tallying

AL'IK.LĒ

GAL'IK.LĒ	Gallicly
KAL'IK.LĒ	vocalicly
TAL'IK.LĒ	metallicly, smart-alecly

AL'I.MŌ.NĒ

| AL'I.MŌ.NĒ | alimony |
| PAL'I.MŌ.NĒ | palimony |

Ā'LI.NES

Ā'LI.NES	ailiness
DĀ'LI.NES	dailiness
SKĀ'LI.NES	scaliness
WĀ'LI.NES	wailiness

AL'I.PED

| AL'I.PED | aliped |
| TAL'I.PED | taliped |

AL'I.POT

| GAL'I.POT | galipot, gallipot |
| TAL'I.POT | talipot |

AL'I.SIS

AL'I.SIS	dialysis, electrodialysis, hemodialysis
NAL'I.SIS	analysis, electroanalysis, phyloanalysis, cryptanalysis, metanalysis, microanalysis, psychoanalysis, urinalysis
RAL'I.SIS	paralysis
TAL'I.SIS	catalysis

AL'I.SUN

| AL'I.SUN | alison |
| MAL'I.SUN | malison |

AL'I.TĒ

| AL'I.TĒ | A actuality, artificiality, B bestiality, D duality, E effectuality, exterritoriality, extraterritoriality, essentiality, ethereality, eventuality, F filiality, GR graduality, H heterosexuality, hypersexuality, hyposexuality, I ideality, immateriality, impartiality, individuality, ineffectuality, inconsequentiality, intellectuality, J geniality, joviality, K collegiality, colloquiality, commerciality, confidentiality, congeniality, connubiality, consequentiality, conceptuality, consubstantiality, conviviality, cordiality, corporeality, curiality, L lineality, M materiality, mutuality, O officiality, P parochiality, partiality, perenniality, potentiality, punctuality, PR primordiality, proverbiality, provinciality, prudentiality, R reality, S sexuality, sequentiality, sensuality, seriality, circumstantiality, sociality, substantiality, pseudomutuality, superficiality, SP spatiality, speciality, spirituality, T territoriality, TR triality, triviality, U unreality, unusuality, |

	V veniality, virtuality, visuality
BAL'I.TĒ	verbality
DAL'I.TĒ	àlàmodality, bipedality, feudality, modality, pedality, sesquipedality, sodality
GAL'I.TĒ	egality, frugality, illegality, conjugality, legality, prodigality, regality
GRAL'I.TĒ	integrality
KAL'I.TĒ	B Biblicality, F fantasticality, farcicality, HW whimsicality, I illogicality, impracticality, inimicality, intrinsicality, K comicality, cosmicality, KL classicality, clericality, L laicality, logicality, locality, N nonsensicality, PR pragmaticality, practicality, R radicality, rascality, reciprocality, T technicality, topicality, TH theatricality, theoreticality, V verticality, vocality
LAL'I.TĒ	molality
MAL'I.TĒ	abnormality, animality, formality, informality, normality, subnormality
NAL'I.TĒ	A atonality, B banality, D devotionality, E exceptionality, externality, F feminality, finality, I impersonality, intentionality, internality, irrationality, K carnality, commonality, conditionality, constitutionality, conventionality, KR criminality, M meridionality, mesnality, N nationality,

notionality, *O*
originality, *P*
penality, personality,
polytonality, *PR*
proportionality, *R*
rationality, *S*
sectionality,
septentrionality,
signality, *T* tonality,
TR traditionality, *U*
unconventionality, *V*
venality, vernality, *Z*
zonality

PAL′I.TĒ municipality,
principality

RAL′I.TĒ *A* amorality, *E*
ephemerality, *G*
gutturality, *I*
immorality, *J*
generality, *K*
collaterality,
conjecturality,
corporality, *L*
laterality, liberality,
literality, *M*
morality, *N*
naturality, *P*
pastorality, *PL*
plurality, *PR*
preternaturality, *R*
rurality, *S* severality,
supernaturality, *SP*
spirality, *T*
temporality

SAL′I.TĒ commensality,
orthodoxality,
universality

TAL′I.TĒ *A* accidentality, *BR*
brutality, *E*
elementality, *F*
fatality,
fundamentality, *FR*
frontality, *H*
horizontality,
hospitality, *I*
immortality,
inhospitality,
instrumentality, *M*
mentality, mortality,
N natality, *O*
occidentality,
orientality, *S*
sentimentality, *T*
totality, *TR*
transcendentality, *V*
vegetality, vitality

THAL′I.TĒ lethality
TRAL′I.TĒ dextrality, magistrality,
neutrality, centrality,
spectrality

VAL′I.TĒ coevality, rivality
ZAL′I.TĒ causality, nasality

Ā′LI.UM

GĀ′LI.UM	Galium
KĀ′LI.UM	kalium
TRĂ′LI.UM	penetralium

AL′I.UM

AL′I.UM	allium
BAL′I.UM	ecballium
GAL′I.UM	gallium
PAL′I.UM	pallium
THAL′I.UM	thallium
VAL′I.UM	valium

Ā′LI.US

(See **Ā′LI.AS**)

AL′JI.A

AL′JI.A	analgia, hemialgia, cardialgia, myalgia
FAL′JI.A	cephalgia
FRAL′JI.A	nephralgia
KAL′JI.A	psychalgia
LAL′JI.A	cephalalgia
RAL′JI.A	neuralgia
SAL′JI.A	coxalgia, ombrosalgia
TAL′JI.A	dentalgia, nostalgia, odontalgia, otalgia, proctalgia, rectalgia
THRAL′JI.A	arthralgia
TRAL′JI.A	gastralgia, metralgia
ZAL′JI.A	causalgia

AL′MI.A

KAL′MI.A	kalmia
THAL′MI.A	ophthalmia, xerothalmia

AL′O.ER

FAL′O.ER	fallower
HAL′O.ER	hallower
KAL′O.ER	callower
SHAL′O.ER	shallower
TAL′O.ER	tallower

ÄL′O.ER

SWÄL′O.ER	swallower
WÄL′O.ER	wallower

(See **OL′O.ER**)

AL′O.ING

(See **AL′Ō**, add *-ing* where appropriate.)

ÄL′O.ING

SWÄL′O.ING	swallowing
WÄL′O.ING	wallowing

(See **OL′O.ING**)

AL′O.ISH

FAL′O.ISH	fallowish
SAL′O.ISH	sallowish
SHAL′O.ISH	shallowish
TAL′O.ISH	tallowish

AL′O.JĒ

AL′O.JĒ	genealogy, genethlialogy, nealogy
BAL′O.JĒ	pyroballogy
DAL′O.JĒ	dontepedalogy
MAL′O.JĒ	mammalogy
NAL′O.JĒ	analogy
RAL′O.JĒ	mineralogy, oralogy, paralogy
TAL′O.JĒ	crustalogy
TRAL′O.JĒ	tetralogy

AL′O.JIST

AL′O.JIST	dialogist, genealogist
KAL′O.JIST	Decalogist
MAL′O.JIST	mammalogist
NAL′O.JIST	analogist
RAL′O.JIST	mineralogist, paralogist

ÄL′O.JĪZ

ÄL′O.JĪZ	dialogize, genealogize
NAL′O.JĪZ	analogize
RAL′O.JĪZ	mineralogize, paralogize

AL′O.JIZM

AL′O.JIZM	alogism, dialogism
NAL′O.JIZM	analogism
RAL′O.JIZM	paralogism

AL′O.NES

(See **AL′Ō**, add *-ness* where appropriate.)

AL'UP.ER

GAL'UP.ER	galloper
KAL'UP.ER	escalloper
SKAL'UP.ER	scalloper

ÄL'UP.ER

(See OLUP, add -er)

AL'UP.ING

GAL'UP.ING	galloping
KAL'UP.ING	escalloping
SKAL'UP.ING	scalloping

Ē'VAL'Ū.ĀT

Ē'VAL'Ū.ĀT	evaluate
DĒ'VAL'Ū.ĀT	devaluate
RĒ'VAL'Ū.ĀT	revaluate

ĀL'YEN.IZM

ĀL'YEN.IZM	alienism
DĀL'YEN.IZM	sesquipedalianism
NĀL'YEN.IZM	bacchanalianism, saturnalianism
PĀL'YEN.IZM	episcopalianism
SĀL'YEN.IZM	universalianism

AL'YUN.ISH

DAL'YUN.ISH	medallionish
SKAL'YUN.ISH	rapscallionish, scallionish
STAL'YUN.ISH	stallionish

Ā'MA.BL

BLĀ'MA.BL	blamable, unblamable
FRĀ'MA.BL	framable, unframable
KLĀ'MA.BL	claimable, irreclaimable, reclaimable, unreclaimable
NĀ'MA.BL	namable, unnamable
TĀ'MA.BL	tamable, untamable

AM'A.NĒ

| SKAM'A.NĒ | scammony |
| TAM'A.NĒ | Tammany |

AM'ER.Ē

GRAM'ER.Ē	gramarye
MAM'ER.Ē	mammary
YAM'ER.Ē	yammery

AM'A.TIST

| DRAM'A.TIST | dramatist, melodramatist |
| GRAM'A.TIST | anagrammatist, diagrammatist, epigrammatist, grammatist, hierogrammatist, lipogrammatist |

AM'A.TIV

| AM'A.TIV | amative |
| KLAM'A.TIV | exclamative |

AM'A.TĪZ

| DRAM'A.TĪZ | dramatize |
| GRAM'A.TĪZ | anagrammatize, diagrammatize, epigrammatize |

AM'A.TŌ'RĒ

AM'A.TŌ'RĒ	amatory
FAM'A.TŌ'RĒ	defamatory
FLAM'A.TŌ'RĒ	inflammatory
KLAM'A.TŌ'RĒ	declamatory, exclamatory, proclamatory

AM'BŪ.LANT

AM'BŪ.LANT	ambulant, deambulant, circumambulent
NAM'BŪ.LANT	funambulant, somnambulant
RAM'BŪ.LANT	perambulant
TAM'BŪ.LANT	noctambulant

AM'BŪ.LĀT

AM'BŪ.LĀT	ambulate, deambulate
MAM'BŪ.LĀT	circumambulate
NAM'BŪ.LĀT	funambulate, somnambulate
RAM'BŪ.LĀT	perambulate
TAM'BŪ.LĀT	noctambulate

AM'BŪ.LIST

AM'BŪ.LIST	ambulist, deambulist, circumambulist, perambulist
NAM'BŪ.LIST	funambulist, somnambulist
TAM'BŪ.LIST	noctambulist

AM'BŪ.LIZM

AM'BŪ.LIZM	ambulism, deambulism, perambulism, circumambulism
NAM'BŪ.LIZM	funambulism, somnambulism
TAM'BŪ.LIZM	noctambulism

AM'ER.AL

KAM'ER.AL	bicameral, decameral, cameral, unicameral
SAM'ER.AL	hexameral
TAM'ER.AL	pentameral

AM'ER.ER

HAM'ER.ER	hammerer
KLAM'ER.ER	clamorer
STAM'ER.ER	stammerer
YAM'ER.ER	yammerer

AM'ER.ING

(See AM'ER.ER, change -er to -ing.)

AM'ER.UN

KAM'ER.UN	decameron
SAM'ER.UN	hexameron
TAM'ER.UN	heptameron

AM'ER.US

AM'ER.US	amorous
GLAM'ER.US	glamorous, unglamorous
KAM'ER.US	decamerous
KLAM'ER.US	clamorous
MAM'ER.US	nummamorous
SAM'ER.US	hexamerous
TAM'ER.US	heptamerous
TRAM'ER.US	tetramerous

ĀM'FUL.NES

ĀM'FUL.NES	aimfulness
BLĀM'FUL.NES	blamefulness
GĀM'FUL.NES	gamefulness
SHĀM'FUL.NES	shamefulness

Ā'MI.A

DĀ'MI.A	macadamia
LĀ'MI.A	lamia
NĀ'MI.A	adynamia
TĀ'MI.A	Mesopotamia
ZĀ'MI.A	zamia, Zamia

AM'I.KAL

AM'I.KAL	amical
NAM'I.KAL	dynamical
SAM'I.KAL	balsamical

ÄM'I.LĒ

BÄM'I.LĒ	balmily
PÄM'I.LĒ	palmily

AM'I.NA

LAM'I.NA	lamina
RAM'I.NA	foramina
STAM'I.NA	stamina

AM'I.NĀT

AM'I.NĀT	aminate, deaminate
LAM'I.NĀT	delaminate, interlaminate, laminate
RAM'I.NĀT	foraminate
STAM'I.NĀT	staminate
TAM'I.NĀT	decontaminate, contaminate

AM'I.NES

HAM'I.NES	hamminess
JAM'I.NES	jamminess
KLAM'I.NES	clamminess

ÄM'ISH.LĒ

KÄM'ISH.LĒ	calmishly
KWÄM'ISH.LĒ	qualmishly

ÄM'IS.TRĒ

PÄM'IS.TRĒ	palmistry
SÄM'IS.TRĒ	psalmistry

AM'I.TĒ

AM'I.TĒ	amity
LAM'I.TĒ	calamity

AM'I.TER

AM'I.TER	diameter, pluviameter, viameter
NAM'I.TER	dynameter
RAM'I.TER	parameter, peirameter
SAM'I.TER	hexameter
TAM'I.TER	heptameter, octameter, pentameter, voltameter
TRAM'I.TER	tetrameter

ĀM'LES.NES

(See ĀM, add *-lessness* where appropriate.)

AM'O.NĒ

(See DM'A.NĒ)

AM'O.NIZM

MAM'O.NIZM	mammonism
SHAM'O.NIZM	shamanism

AM'OR.US

(See AM'ER.US)

AM'PER.ER

HAM'PER.ER	hamperer
PAM'PER.ER	pamperer
SKAM'PER.ER	scamperer
TAM'PER.ER	tamperer

AM'PER.ING

HAM'PER.ING	hampering
PAM'PER.ING	pampering
SKAM'PER.ING	scampering
TAM'PER.ING	tampering

AM'PI.LĒ

KRAM'PI.LĒ	crampily
VAM'PI.LĒ	vampily

AM'PI.UN

CHAM'PI.UN	champion
KAM'PI.UN	campion
LAM'PI.UN	lampion
TAM'PI.UN	tampion

AM'Ū.LUS

FAM'Ū.LUS	famulus
HAM'Ū.LUS	hamulus
RAM'Ū.LUS	ramulous, ramulus

Ā'NA.BL

(See ĀN, add *-able* where appropriate.)

Ā'NA.BLĒ

(See ĀN, add *-ably* where appropriate.)

AN'A.BL

BAN'A.BL	bannable
HAN'A.BL	Hannibal
KAN'A.BL	cannable, cannibal
MAN'A.BL	mannable
PAN'A.BL	pannable
SAN'A.BL	insanable, sanable
TAN'A.BL	tannable

AN'A.KL

(See AN'I.KL)

AN'A.LĪZ

AN'A.LĪZ	analyze
CHAN'A.LĪZ	channelize
KAN'A.LĪZ	canalize

AN'BER.Ē

BAN'BER.Ē	Banbury
KRAN'BER.Ē	cranberry

AN'DA.BL

MAN'DA.BL	mandible

(See AND, add *-able* where appropriate.)

AN'DA.LĪZ

SKAN'DA.LĪZ	scandalize
VAN'DA.LĪZ	vandalize

AN'DED.LĒ

HAN'DED.LĒ	backhandedly, highhandedly, openhandedly, underhandedly
KAN'DED.LĒ	candidly

AN'DED.NES

BAN'DED.NES	bandedness
BRAN'DED.NES	brandedness
HAN'DED.NES	left-handedness, off-handedness, right-handedness, underhandedness
KAN'DED.NES	candidness
LAN'DED.NES	landedness

AN'DER.ER

AN'DER.ER	meanderer
LAN'DER.ER	philanderer
PAN'DER.ER	panderer
SLAN'DER.ER	slanderer

ÄN'DER.ER

SKWÄN'DER.ER	squanderer
WÄN'DER.ER	wanderer

(See ON'DER.ER)

AN'DER.ING

AN'DER.ING	meandering
LAN'DER.ING	philandering
PAN'DER.ING	pandering
SLAN'DER.ING	slandering

ÄN'DER.ING

SKWÄN'DER.ING	squandering
WÄN'DER.ING	wandering

(See ON'DER.ING)

AN'DER.US

PAN'DER.US	panderous
SLAN'DER.US	slanderous

AN'DI.ER

BAN'DI.ER	bandier
DAN'DI.ER	dandier
HAN'DI.ER	handier, unhandier
RAN'DI.ER	randier
SAN'DI.ER	sandier

AN'DI.FĪ

DAN'DI.FĪ	dandify
KAN'DI.FĪ	candify

AN'DI.IZM

DAN'DI.IZM	dandyism
RAN'DI.IZM	randyism
SHAN'DI.IZM	Tristram Shandyism

AN'DI.LĒ

BAN'DI.LĒ	bandily
DAN'DI.LĒ	dandily
HAN'DI.LĒ	handily, unhandily
RAN'DI.LĒ	randily
SAN'DI.LĒ	sandily

AN'DI.NES

(See AN'DĒ, add -ness where appropriate.)

AN'DING.LĒ

MAN'DING.LĒ	demandingly, commandingly
STAN'DING.LĒ	outstandingly, understandingly

AN'DING.NES

MAN'DING.NES	demandingness, commandingness
STAN'DING.NES	outstandingness, understandingness

AN'DISH.ING

BLAN'DISH.ING	blandishing
BRAN'DISH.ING	brandishing

AN'DISH.MENT

BLAN'DISH.MENT	blandishment
BRAN'DISH.MENT	brandishment

AN'EL.ING

CHAN'EL.ING	channeling
FLAN'EL.ING	flanneling
PAN'EL.ING	paneling

AN'EL.ĪZ

(See AN'AL.ĪZ)

Ā'NER.Ē

GRĀ'NER.Ē	granary
KĀ'NER.Ē	chicanery

AN'ER.Ē

CHAN'ER.Ē	channery
GRAN'ER.Ē	granary
KAN'ER.Ē	cannery
PAN'ER.Ē	panary
STAN'ER.Ē	stannary
TAN'ER.Ē	charlatanery, tannery

AN'ER.ET

BAN'ER.ET	banneret
LAN'ER.ET	lanneret

AN'E.TER'Ē

(See AN'I.TER'Ē)

ĀN'FUL.Ē

BĀN'FUL.Ē	banefully
DĀN'FUL.Ē	disdainfully
GĀN'FUL.Ē	gainfully, ungainfully
PĀN'FUL.Ē	painfully

ĀN'FUL.NES

DĀN'FUL.NES	disdainfulness
GĀN'FUL.NES	gainfulness, ungainfulness
PĀN'FUL.NES	painfulness

ANG'GLING.LĒ

(See ANGGL, add -ingly where appropriate.)

ANG'GL.SUM

ANG'GL.SUM	anglesome
DANG'GL.SUM	danglesome

JANG′GL.SUM	janglesome
RANG′GL.SUM	wranglesome
TANG′GL.SUM	tanglesome

ANG′GŪ.LAR

ANG′GŪ.LAR	angular, triangular
RANG′GŪ.LAR	quadrangular
SLANG′GŪ.LAR	slangular
TANG′GŪ.LAR	octangular, pentangular, rectangular

ANG′GŪ.LĀT

| ANG′GŪ.LĀT | angulate, triangulate |
| STRANG′GŪ.LĀT | strangulate |

ANG′I.LĒ

BANG′I.LĒ	bangily
KLANG′I.LĒ	clangily
SLANG′I.LĒ	slangily
TANG′I.LĒ	tangily
TWANG′I.LĒ	twangily

ANG′ING.LĒ

(See **ANG,** add *-ingly* where appropriate.)

ANG′KER.ER

| ANG′KER.ER | anchorer, reanchorer |
| HANG′KER.ER | hankerer |

ANG′KER.ING

ANG′KER.ING	anchoring, reanchoring
HANG′KER.ING	hankering
KANG′KER.ING	cankering

ANG′KER.US

HANG′KER.US	hankerous
KANG′KER.US	cankerous
TANG′KER.US	cantankerous

Ā′NI.A

Ā′NI.A	Lithuania, euania
BĀ′NI.A	Albania
DĀ′NI.A	succedanea
FĀ′NI.A	menophania
KĀ′NI.A	misocainia

KRĀ′NI.A	Ukrainia
LĀ′NI.A	miscellanea
MĀ′NI.A	*A* ablutomania, amania, andromania,, Anglomania, *B* Beatlemania, bibliomania, *BR* bruxomania, *D* dacnomania, decalcomania, demomania, dinomania, dipsomania, discomania, doromania, *DR* drapetomania, dromomania, *E* egomania, ecomania, eleutheromania, empleomania, entheomania, erotographomania, erotomania, *F* phagomania, phaneromania, *FL* florimania, *FR* Francomania, *G* Gallomania, gamomania, *H* habromania, hydromania, hippomania, *I* Italomania, *J* Germanomania, *K* callomania, catapedamania, choreomania, *KL* kleptomania, clinomania, *L* logomania, *M* mania, megalomania, melomania, metromania, misomania, mythomania, monomania, *N* nymphomania, nosomania, nostomania, nothosomania, *O* oniomania, onomatomania, opsomania, orchestromania, *P* pyromania, potichomania, potomania, *PL* planomania, *R* Rumania, Russomania, *S* sebastomania,

sophomania, pseudomania, *T* Tasmania, tomomania, *TH* theomania, thanatomania, *TR* trichotillomania, *Z* xenomania

(See Appendix D for additional words ending in *-mania*.)

RĀ′NI.A	Pomerania, Urania
SĀ′NI.A	dysania
TĀ′NI.A	Aquitania, castanea, collectanea, Lusitania, Mauretania, Ruritania, Titania, Tripolitania
VĀ′NI.A	Pennsylvania, Sylvania, Transylvania

AN ACYROLOGIC TREATISE ON GRAMMAR

Don't tell *me* no grammatic rules:
  Hey, man, I get on good enough.
  I don't talk like no powder puff,
But ladies looks at me and drools,
And feels my chest in swimming pools—
  Talk ain't no match for he-man stuff.
Don't tell *me* no grammatic rules;
  Hey, man, I get on good enough.

Man, when did junk you learns in schools
  Help anyone when times gets tough?
  I thumbs my nose; I calls your bluff.
I leaves that sissy stuff to fools.
Don't tell *me* no grammatic rules.

Ā′NI.AL

KRĀ′NI.AL	acranial, intracranial, cranial
MĀ′NI.AL	domanial, demesnial
RĀ′NI.AL	geranial, subterraneal
TĀ′NI.AL	cutaneal, subcutaneal

Ā′NI.AN

Ā′NI.AN	Lithuanian, cyanean
BĀ′NI.AN	Albanian
DĀ′NI.AN	Jordanian
KĀ′NI.AN	volcanian, vulcanian
KRĀ′NI.AN	Ukrainian
MĀ′NI.AN	Alemanian, Panamanian, Rumanian, Tasmanian
RĀ′NI.AN	extemporanean, Iranian, contemporanean,

	Mediterranean, Pomeranian, circumforanean, subterranean, terranean, Turanian, Uranian
TĀ'NI.AN	castanean, castanian
VĀ'NI.AN	Pennsylvanian, Transylvanian

AN'I.EST

KAN'I.EST	canniest, uncanniest
KLAN'I.EST	clanniest

AN'I.FĪ

MAN'I.FĪ	humanify
SAN'I.FĪ	insanify, sanify

AN'I.KIN

KAN'I.KIN	cannikin
MAN'I.KIN	manikin, mannequin
PAN'I.KIN	pannikin

AN'I.KL

GAN'I.KL	organical
KAN'I.KL	mechanical
MAN'I.KL	Brahmanical, manacle
PAN'I.KL	panicle
RAN'I.KL	tyrannical
SAN'I.KL	sanicle
TAN'I.KL	botanical, charlatanical, puritanical
VAN'I.KL	galvanical

AN'I.MUS

AN'I.MUS	animus, exanimous, flexanimous
LAN'I.MUS	pusillanimous
NAN'I.MUS	magnanimous, unanimous
TAN'I.MUS	multanimous

Ā'NI.NES

BRĀ'NI.NES	braininess
GRĀ'NI.NES	graininess
RĀ'NI.NES	raininess
VĀ'NI.NES	veininess

AN'I.NES

KAN'I.NES	canniness
KLAN'I.NES	clanniness

Ā'NING.LĒ

PLĀ'NING.LĒ	complainingly, uncomplainingly
TĀ'NING.LĒ	entertainingly

AN'ISH.ING

BAN'ISH.ING	banishing
PLAN'ISH.ING	planishing
VAN'ISH.ING	vanishing

AN'ISH.MENT

BAN'ISH.MENT	banishment
VAN'ISH.MENT	evanishment, vanishment

AN'IS.TER

BAN'IS.TER	banister, bannister
GAN'IS.TER	ganister
KAN'IS.TER	canister

AN'I.TĒ

AN'I.TĒ	Christianity, inanity
BAN'I.TĒ	inurbanity, urbanity
DAN'I.TĒ	mundanity
FAN'I.TĒ	profanity
GAN'I.TĒ	inorganity, organity, paganity
KAN'I.TĒ	volcanity
MAN'I.TĒ	aldermanity, gigmanity, humanity, immanity, inhumanity, yahoomanity
RAN'I.TĒ	subterranity
SAN'I.TĒ	insanity, sanity
VAN'I.TĒ	vanity

AN'I.TER.Ē

PLAN'I.TER.Ē	planetary
SAN'I.TER.Ē	sanitary

Ā'NI.UM

DĀ'NI.UM	succedaneum, suppedaneum

KRĀ'NI.UM	endocranium, cranium, pericranium
LĀ'NI.UM	Herculaneum
MĀ'NI.UM	germanium
RĀ'NI.UM	actinouranium, geranium, uranium
TĀ'NI.UM	titanium

Ā'NI.US

Ā'NI.US	cyaneous
BRĀ'NI.US	membraneous
DĀ'NI.US	antecedaneous, succedaneous
KĀ'NI.US	calcaneus, siccaneous, supervacaneous
LĀ'NI.US	miscellaneous, porcellaneous, subtegulaneous
RĀ'NI.US	A araneous, E extemporaneous, exterraneous, extraforaneous, F foraneous, K contemporaneous, M Mediterraneous, S circumforaneous, subterraneous, T temporaneous, terraneous
TĀ'NI.US	D dissentaneous, I instantaneous, K castaneous, coetaneous, consectaneous, consentaneous, cutaneous, M momentaneous, P percutaneous, PR proletaneous, S simultaneous, subcutaneous, SP spontaneous
TRĀ'NI.US	extraneous, frustraneous

ĀN'JA.BL

CHĀN'JA.BL	changeable, exchangeable, interchangeable, unchangeable
RĀN'JA.BL	arrangeable, derangeable, rearrangeable

AN'JEN.SĒ

PLAN'JEN.SĒ	plangency
TAN'JEN.SĒ	tangency

AN'JI.A

DRAN'JI.A   hydrangea
KAN'JI.A   cangia
SPRAN'JI.A   sprangia

AN'JI.BL

FRAN'JI.BL   frangible, infrangible,
                 irrefrangible,
                 refrangible
TAN'JI.BL   intangible, tangible

ĀN'JI.NES

MĀN'JI.NES   manginess
RĀN'JI.NES   ranginess

AN'O.GRAF

AN'O.GRAF   pianograph
KAN'O.GRAF   mechanograph
VAN'O.GRAF   galvanograph

AN'O.SKŌP

FAN'O.SKŌP   diaphanoscope
VAN'O.SKŌP   galvanoscope

AN'SI.LĒ

CHAN'SI.LĒ   chancily
DAN'SI.LĒ   dancily
FAN'SI.LĒ   fancily
PRAN'SI.LĒ   prancily

AN'SING.LĒ

DAN'SING.LĒ   dancingly
GLAN'SING.LĒ   glancingly
PRAN'SING.LĒ   prancingly
TRAN'SING.LĒ   entrancingly,
                 trancingly

AN'SIV.NES

PAN'SIV.NES   expansiveness,
                 inexpansiveness
VAN'SIV.NES   advanciveness

AN'SUM.ER

HAN'SUM.ER   handsomer
RAN'SUM.ER   ransomer

AN'SUM.EST

HAN'SUM.EST   handsomest
RAN'SUM.EST   ransomest

ĀN'TA.BL

KWĀN'TA.BL   acquaintable
PĀN'TA.BL   paintable
TĀN'TA.BL   taintable

AN'TA.BL

CHAN'TA.BL   chantable,
                 disenchantable,
                 enchantable,
                 unchantable,
                 unenchantable
GRAN'TA.BL   grantable,
                 ungrantable
KAN'TA.BL   decantable, cantable,
                 recantable,
                 undecantable,
                 uncantable,
                 unrecantable
PLAN'TA.BL   implantable,
                 plantable,
                 supplantable,
                 transplantable,
                 unplantable,
                 untransplantable
SLAN'TA.BL   slantable, unslantable

AN'TE.LŌP

AN'TE.LŌP   antelope
KAN'TE.LŌP   cantaloupe

AN'TER.ER

BAN'TER.ER   banterer
KAN'TER.ER   canterer

AN'TER.ING

BAN'TER.ING   bantering
KAN'TER.ING   cantering

AN'THRO.PĒ

AN'THRO.PĒ   boanthropy,
                 physianthropy,
                 galeanthropy,
                 theanthropy,
                 zoanthropy
KAN'THRO.PĒ   lycanthropy

LAN'THRO.PĒ   aphilanthropy,
                 philanthropy,
                 psilanthropy,
                 theophilanthropy
PAN'THRO.PĒ   apanthropy
SAN'THRO.PĒ   misanthropy
ZAN'THRO.PĒ   misanthropy

AN'THRO.PIST

AN'THRO.PIST   theanthropist
LAN'THRO.PIST   philanthropist,
                 psilanthropist,
                 theophilanthropist
SAN'THRO.PIST   misanthropist
ZAN'THRO.PIST   misanthropist

(See AN'THRO.PĒ, change -y to -ist
where appropriate.)

AN'THRO.PIZM

AN'THRO.PIZM   physianthropism,
                 theantropism,
                 zoanthropism
KAN'THRO.PIZM   lycanthropism
LAN'THRO.PIZM   aphilanthropism,
                 philanthropism,
                 psilanthropism,
                 theophilanthropism
SAN'THRO.PIZM   misanthropism
ZAN'THRO.PIZM   misanthropism

AN'TIK.LĒ

AN'TIK.LĒ   anticly
DAN'TIK.LĒ   pedantically
FRAN'TIK.LĒ   frantically
GAN'TIK.LĒ   gigantically
MAN'TIK.LĒ   romanticly

AN'TIK.NES

AN'TIK.NES   anticness
DAN'TIK.NES   pedanticness
FRAN'TIK.NES   franticness
MAN'TIK.NES   romanticness

AN'TI.LĒ

BAN'TI.LĒ   bantily
RAN'TI.LĒ   rantily
SKAN'TI.LĒ   scantily
SLAN'TI.LĒ   slantily

AN'TING.LĒ

CHAN'TING.LĒ	enchantingly
KAN'TING.LĒ	cantingly
PAN'TING.LĒ	pantingly
RAN'TING.LĒ	rantingly
SLAN'TING.LĒ	slantingly

AN'TI.SĪD

FAN'TI.SĪD	infanticide
GAN'TI.SĪD	giganticide

AN'Ū.AL

AN'Ū.AL	annual, biannual, semiannual
MAN'Ū.AL	manual

AN'Ū.LA

GRAN'Ū.LA	granula
KAN'Ū.LA	cannula
PAN'Ū.LA	campanula
PLAN'Ū.LA	planula
RAN'Ū.LA	ranula

AN'Ū.LAR

AN'Ū.LAR	annular, penannular
GRAN'Ū.LAR	granular
KAN'Ū.LAR	cannular
PAN'Ū.LAR	campanular
RAN'Ū.LAR	ranular

AN'Ū.LĀT

AN'Ū.LĀT	annulate
GRAN'Ū.LĀT	granulate
KAN'Ū.LĀT	cannulate
PAN'Ū.LĀT	campanulate

AN'Ū.LET

AN'Ū.LET	annulet
GRAN'Ū.LET	granulet

Ā'PA.BL

DRĀ'PA.BL	drapable
KĀ'PA.BL	escapable, incapable, inescapable, capable, unescapable, uncapable
PĀ'PA.BL	papable

RĀ'PA.BL	rapable
SHĀ'PA.BL	reshapable, shapable
SKRĀ'PA.BL	scrapable
TĀ'PA.BL	tapable

AP'A.BL

FLAP'A.BL	flappable, unflappable
MAP'A.BL	mappable, unmappable
RAP'A.BL	rappable, wrappable, unrappable, unwrappable
SAP'A.BL	sappable, unsappable
SNAP'A.BL	snappable, unsnappable
STRAP'A.BL	strappable, unstrappable
TAP'A.BL	tappable, untappable
TRAP'A.BL	trappable, untrappable
ZAP'A.BL	zappable, unzappable

AP'A.THĒ

AP'A.THĒ	apathy
PRAP'A.THĒ	naprapathy

AP'CHER.ING

KAP'CHER.ING	capturing, recapturing
RAP'CHER.ING	enrapturing, rapturing

Ā'PER.Ē

Ā'PER.Ē	apery
DRĀ'PER.Ē	drapery
GRĀ'PER.Ē	grapery
JĀ'PER.Ē	japery
KĀ'PER.Ē	capery
NĀ'PER.Ē	napery
PĀ'PER.Ē	papery
VĀ'PER.Ē	vapory

Ā'PER.ER

KĀ'PER.ER	caperer
NĀ'PER.ER	naperer
PĀ'PER.ER	paperer
TĀ'PER.ER	taperer
VĀ'PER.ER	vaporer

Ā'PER.ING

KĀ'PER.ING	capering
PĀ'PER.ING	papering

TĀ'PER.ING	tapering
VĀ'PER.ING	vaporing

AP'ID.LĒ

RAP'ID.LĒ	rapidly
SAP'ID.LĒ	sapidly
VAP'ID.LĒ	vapidly

AP'ID.NES

RAP'ID.NES	rapidness
SAP'ID.NES	sapidness
VAP'ID.NES	vapidness

AP'I.DUS

AP'I.DUS	sciapodous
LAP'I.DUS	lapidous

Ā'PI.ER

NĀ'PI.ER	Napier
RĀ'PI.ER	rapier

AP'I.ER

GAP'I.ER	gappier
HAP'I.ER	happier, unhappier
KRAP'I.ER	crappier
NAP'I.ER	nappier
SAP'I.ER	sappier
SKRAP'I.ER	scrappier
SNAP'I.ER	snappier

AP'I.LĒ

GAP'I.LĒ	gappily
HAP'I.LĒ	happily
KRAP'I.LĒ	crappily
SAP'I.LĒ	sappily
SKRAP'I.LĒ	scrappily
SNAP'I.LĒ	snappily

AP'I.NES

(See APĒ, add -ness where appropriate.)

ÄP'I.TĒ

(See OP'I.TĒ)

AP'O.LIS

AP'O.LIS	Minneapolis

NAP'O.LIS	Annapolis, Indianapolis
TAP'O.LIS	pentapolis
TRAP'O.LIS	tetrapolis

ÂR'A.BL

ÂR'A.BL	airable, unairable
BÂR'A.BL	bearable, unbearable
DÂR'A.BL	darable, undarable
KLÂR'A.BL	declarable, undeclarable
PÂR'A.BL	pairable, repairable, unpairable, unparable, unrepairable
SHÂR'A.BL	sharable, unsharable
SKÂR'A.BL	scarable, unscarable
SKWÂR'A.BL	squarable, unsquarable
SPÂR'A.BL	sparable, unsparable
SWÂR'A.BL	swearable
TÂR'A.BL	tearable, untearable
WÂR'A.BL	unwearable, wearable

(See ER'I.BL)

AR'A.BL

AR'A.BL	arable
NAR'A.BL	inennarable
PAR'A.BL	parable
SPAR'A.BL	sparable

AR'A.GON

AR'A.GON	Aragon
PAR'A.GON	paragon
TAR'A.GON	tarragon

AR'A.GRAF

| BAR'A.GRAF | barograph |
| PAR'A.GRAF | paragraph |

AR'ANT.LĒ

| AR'ANT.LĒ | arrantly |
| PAR'ANT.LĒ | apparently, transparently |

AR'AS.ING

| BAR'AS.ING | disembarrassing, embarrassing |
| HAR'AS.ING | harassing |

AR'AS.MENT

| BAR'AS.MENT | embarrassment, disembarrassment |
| HAR'AS.MENT | harassment |

AR'A.TIV

KLAR'A.TIV	declarative
NAR'A.TIV	narrative
PAR'A.TIV	comparative, preparative, reparative

AR'A.TŌ.RĒ

| KLAR'A.TŌ.RĒ | declaratory |
| PAR'A.TŌ.RĒ | preparatory |

ÄR'BER.ING

| BÄR'BER.ING | barbering |
| HÄR'BER.ING | harboring |

ÄR'DEN.ING

GÄR'DEN.ING	gardening
HÄR'DEN.ING	hardening
PÄR'DEN.ING	pardoning

ÄR'DI.A

GÄR'DI.A	LaGuardia
KÄR'DI.A	bradycardia, megalocardia, tachycardia
LÄR'DI.A	gaillardia

ÄR'DI.AN

GÄR'DI.AN	guardian
KÄR'DI.AN	pericardian
WÄR'DI.AN	Edwardian

ÄR'DI.LĒ

| HÄR'DI.LĒ | foolhardily, hardily |
| TÄR'DI.LĒ | tardily |

ÄR'DI.NES

| HÄR'DI.NES | foolhardiness, hardiness |
| TÄR'DI.NES | tardiness |

AR'EL.ING

BAR'EL.ING	barreling, pork-barreling, caroling
KAR'EL.ING	caroling
PAR'EL.ING	appareling

AR'E.NĪT

| AR'E.NĪT | arenite |
| MAR'E.NĪT | Maronite |

AR'ENT.LĒ

(See AR'ANT.LĒ)

ÂR'FUL.Ē

DÂR'FUL.Ē	darefully
KÂR'FUL.Ē	carefully, uncarefully
SPÂR'FUL.Ē	despairfully
PRÂR'FUL.Ē	prayerfully, unprayerfully

ÂR'FUL.NES

KÂR'FUL.NES	carefulness, uncarefulness
PRÂR'FUL.NES	prayerfulness
SPÂR'FUL.NES	sparefulness
WÂR'FUL.NES	awarefulness, warefulness

ÂR'I.A

ÂR'I.A	area, aria, miliaria, topiaria
BÂR'I.A	herbaria
GÂR'I.A	Bulgaria
KÂR'I.A	araucaria, Icaria, persicaria, cercaria, urticaria
KWÂR'I.A	aquaria
LÂR'I.A	adularia, alfilaria, filaria, Hilaria, malaria, solaria, talaria
MÂR'I.A	Samaria
NÂR'I.A	laminaria, ranaria, sanguinaria
PÂR'I.A	pariah
RÂR'I.A	honoraria, cineraria
SÂR'I.A	adversaria
TÂR'I.A	dataria, digitaria, cataria, planetaria, wistaria
VÂR'I.A	Bavaria, varia

ÂR'I.AL

ÂR'I.AL	actuarial, aerial, areal, Ariel, diarial, estuarial
DÂR'I.AL	calendarial
KÂR'I.AL	vicarial
LÂR'I.AL	antimalarial, malarial
NÂR'I.AL	narial
PÂR'I.AL	puparial, riparial
SÂR'I.AL	adversarial, bursarial, glossarial, commissarial
TÂR'I.AL	nectarial, notarial, secretarial, sectarial
VÂR'I.AL	ovarial

ÂR'I.AN

ÂR'I.AN	apiarian, Arian, Aryan, Briarean, diarian, estuarian, sententiarian
BÂR'I.AN	barbarian
BRÂR'I.AN	librarian
DÂR'I.AN	abecedarian, Abecedarian, Darien, lapidarian, cnidarian, stipendarian, ultracrepidarian
FÂR'I.AN	Rastafarian
GÂR'I.AN	Bulgarian, gregarian, Hungarian, vulgarian
GRÂR'I.AN	agrarian
KÂR'I.AN	Icarian, sicarian, suburbicarian
KWÂR'I.AN	antiquarian, aquarian, ubiquarian
LÂR'I.AN	atrabilarian, aularian, sertularian, telarian
MÂR'I.AN	grammarian
NÂR'I.AN	A adessenarian, altitudinarian, Apollinarian, attitudinarian, D disciplinarian, doctrinarian, KW quadragenarian, quinquagenarian, L latitudinarian, lunarian, lupanarian, M millenarian, miscellenarian, N nonagenarian, O octogenarian, P pornogenarian, PL planarian, platitudinarian, plenitudinarian, PR predestinarian, S seminarian, centenarian, sexagenarian, septimanarian, septuagenarian, superseptuagenarian, V valetudinarian, veterinarian
PÂR'I.AN	Parian, riparian
RÂR'I.AN	orarian
SÂR'I.AN	infralapsarian, necessarian, janissarian, supralapsarian
TÂR'I.AN	A alphabetarian, anecdotarian, antidisestablishmentarian, antisabbitarian, antitrinitarian, D dietarian, E egalitarian, experimentarian, equalitarian, F futilitarian, FR fruitarian, H humanitarian, K communitarian, L libertarian, limitarian, N necessitarian, nectarian, noli-mi-tangerietarian, nonsectarian, O authoritarian, P parliamentarian, PR proletarian, R Rotarian, S sabbatarian, sacramentarian, sanitarian, sectarian, societarian, T totalitarian, TR tractarian, trinitarian, V vegetarian, Y ubiquitarian, unitarian, utilitarian
VÂR'I.AN	Bavarian, ovarian
ZÂR'I.AN	janizarian, rosarian, Caesarian

ÂR'I.ANT

(See ÂR'I.ENT)

ÂR'I.ĀT

KÂR'I.ĀT	vicariate
VÂR'I.ĀT	variate

ÂR'I.AT

CHÂR'I.AT	chariot
KÂR'I.AT	Iscariot
LÂR'I.AT	lariat, salariat
SÂR'I.AT	commissariat
TÂR'I.AT	proletariat, prothonotariat, secretariat

ÂR'I.ENT

PÂR'I.ENT	omniparient
TRÂR'I.ENT	contrarient
VÂR'I.ENT	bivariant, invariant, covariant, variant

ÂR'I.ER

ÂR'I.ER	airier
CHÂR'I.ER	charier
GLÂR'I.ER	glarier
HÂR'I.ER	hairier
SKÂR'I.ER	scarier
VÂR'I.ER	varier
WÂR'I.ER	warier

AR'I.ER

BAR'I.ER	barrier
FAR'I.ER	farrier
HAR'I.ER	harrier
KAR'I.ER	carrier, miscarrier
MAR'I.ER	intermarrier, marrier, remarrier
PAR'I.ER	parrier
TAR'I.ER	tarrier

ÂR'I.EST

(See ÂRĒ, change -y to -iest where appropriate.)

ÂR'I.ĒZ

ÂR'I.ĒZ	Aries
KÂR'I.ĒZ	caries
PÂR'I.ĒZ	paries

ÂR'I.FĪ

ÂR'I.FĪ	aerify

(See ER'I.FĪ)

AR'I.FĪ

KAR'I.FĪ	saccharify
KLAR'I.FĪ	clarify
SKAR'I.FĪ	scarify

ÂR'I.FÔRM

ÂR'I.FÔRM	aeriform, scalariform
NÂR'I.FÔRM	nariform
VÂR'I.FÔRM	variform

AR'I.ING

HAR'I.ING	harrying
KAR'I.ING	carrying, miscarrying
MAR'I.ING	intermarrying, marrying
PAR'I.ING	parrying
TAR'I.ING	tarrying

ÂR'I.LĒ

ÂR'I.LĒ	airily
CHÂR'I.LĒ	charily
HÂR'I.LĒ	hairily
NÂR'I.LĒ	sanguinarily
RÂR'I.LĒ	temporarily
SKÂR'I.LĒ	scarily
STÂR'I.LĒ	starily
TÂR'I.LĒ	momentarily, salutarily, sedentarily, solitarily, voluntarily
WÂR'I.LĒ	warily

(See ER'I.LĒ)

AR'I.NĀT

KAR'I.NĀT	carinate
MAR'I.NĀT	marinate

ÂR'I.NES

ÂR'I.NES	airiness, tumultuariness
CHÂR'I.NES	chariness
GLÂR'I.NES	glariness
HÂR'I.NES	hairiness
NÂR'I.NES	sanguinariness
RÂR'I.NES	temporariness
TÂR'I.NES	momentariness, salutariness, sedentariness, solitariness, ubiquitariness, voluntariness
TRÂR'I.NES	arbitrariness, contrariness
WÂR'I.NES	wariness

ÄR'I.NES

STÄR'I.NES	starriness
TÄR'I.NES	tarriness

ÂR'ING.LĒ

BÂR'ING.LĒ	forbearingly
BLÂR'ING.LĒ	blaringly
DÂR'ING.LĒ	daringly
FLÂR'ING.LĒ	flaringly
GLÂR'ING.LĒ	glaringly
KÂR'ING.LĒ	caringly
SPÂR'ING.LĒ	sparingly
STÂR'ING.LĒ	staringly
TÂR'ING.LĒ	tearingly
WÂR'ING.LĒ	wearingly

ÂR'I.Ō

NÂR'I.Ō	scenario
SÂR'I.Ō	impresario
THÂR'I.Ō	lothario, Lothario

ÂR'I.ON

FÂR'I.ON	orpharion
MÂR'I.ON	Marion

AR'I.ON

KAR'I.ON	carrion
KLAR'I.ON	clarion
MAR'I.ON	Marion

ÂR'I.OT

(See ÂR'I.AT)

ÂR'ISH.LĒ

BÂR'ISH.LĒ	bearishly
GÂR'ISH.LĒ	garishly

ÂR'ISH.NES

BÂR'ISH.NES	bearishness
GÂR'ISH.NES	garishness

AR'I.SUN

GAR'I.SUN	garrison
PAR'I.SUN	caparison, comparison, parison
WAR'I.SUN	warison

ÂR'I.TĒ

NÂR'I.TĒ	debonairity
RÂR'I.TĒ	rarity

(See ER'I.TĒ)

AR'I.TĒ

AR'I.TĒ	familiarity, curvilinearity, multicollinearity, peculiarity, rectilinearity, unfamiliarity
BAR'I.TĒ	barbarity
CHAR'I.TĒ	charity, uncharity
DAR'I.TĒ	solidarity
GAR'I.TĒ	vagarity, vulgarity
KLAR'I.TĒ	clarity
LAR'I.TĒ	A angularity, D dissimilarity, GL glandularity, globularity, GR granularity, H hilarity, I insularity, irregularity, J jocularity, K capillarity, consularity, L lunularity, M modularity, molarity, molecularity, muscularity, N nodularity, O orbicularity, P particularity, perpendicularity, piacularity, polarity, popularity, pupilarity, R regularity, rectangularity, S secularity, similarity, singularity, circularity, SP spatularity, ST stellularity, T titularity, TR triangularity, U unpopularity, V vascularity, vernacularity
PAR'I.TĒ	disparity, fissiparity, imparity, gemniparity, multiparity, omniparity, oviparity, parity, viviparity
PLAR'I.TĒ	exemplarity

(See ER'I.TĒ)

AR'I.TŌ.RĒ

KLAR'I.TŌ.RĒ	declaratory
PAR'I.TŌ.RĒ	preparatory

ÂR'I.UM

ÂR'I.UM	glaciarium, polyzoarium
BÂR'I.UM	barium, herbarium, columbarium, verbarium
DÂR'I.UM	caldarium, sudarium, tepidarium, viridarium
KRÂR'I.UM	sacrarium
KWÂR'I.UM	aquarium
LÂR'I.UM	solarium, velarium
MÂR'I.UM	fumarium, samarium
NÂR'I.UM	oceanarium, ranarium, sabbulonarium
PÂR'I.UM	puparium
RÂR'I.UM	honorarium, cinerarium, terrarium
SÂR'I.UM	leprosarium
TÂR'I.UM	armamentarium, insectarium, cometarium, lactarium, planetarium, sanitarium, termitarium
VÂR'I.UM	aquivarium, vivarium
ZÂR'I.UM	rosarium

AR'I.UN

(See AR'I.ON)

ÂR'I.US

ÂR'I.US	Briareus
BÂR'I.US	cibarious
FÂR'I.US	bifarious, multifarious, nefarious, omnifarious
GÂR'I.US	gregarious, vagarious
KÂR'I.US	Icarius, calcareous, carious, precarious, sicarious, vicarious
KWÂR'I.US	Aquarius
LÂR'I.US	atribilarious, hilarious, malarious
MÂR'I.US	Marius
NÂR'I.US	arenarious, denarius, quadragenarious, senarius, testudinarious, valetudinarious
PÂR'I.US	riparious, viparious
RÂR'I.US	honorarious, temerarious
SÂR'I.US	confessarius

SKÂR'I.US	scarious
TÂR'I.US	acetarious, fimetarious, frumentarious, lutarious, nectarious, octarius, Sagittarius, setarious, tartareous
TRÂR'I.US	arbitrarious, contrarious
VÂR'I.US	various, Stradivarius

ÄR'KĀ.IST

ÄR'KĀ.IST	archaist
PÄR'KĀ.IST	parquatist

ÄR'KET.RĒ

MÄR'KET.RĒ	marketry
PÄR'KET.RĒ	parquetry

ÄR'KI.AN

RÄR'KI.AN	Petrarchian
TÄR'KI.AN	aristarchian

ÄR'KI.KAL

ÄR'KI.KAL	anarchical, archical
NÄR'KI.KAL	monarchical
RÄR'KI.KAL	hierarchical, tetrarchical

ÄR'LA.TAN

SHÄR'LA.TAN	charlatan
TÄR'LA.TAN	tarlatan

ÄR'MA.BL

ÄR'MA.BL	armable, forearmable, disarmable, rearmable, unarmable
CHÄR'MA.BL	charmable, uncharmable
FÄR'MA.BL	farmable, unfarmable
HÄR'MA.BL	harmable, unharmable
LÄR'MA.BL	alarmable, unalarmable

ÄR'MER.Ē

ÄR'MER.Ē	armory
DÄR'MER.Ē	gendarmerie

ÄR'MING.LĒ

ÄR'MING.LĒ	disarmingly
CHÄR'MING.LĒ	charmingly
HÄR'MING.LĒ	harmingly
LÄR'MING.LĒ	alarmingly

ÄR'MOR.Ē

(See ÄR'MER.Ē)

ÄR'NISH.ER

GÄR'NISH.ER	garnisher
TÄR'NISH.ER	tarnisher
VÄR'NISH.ER	varnisher

ÄR'NISH.ING

GÄR'NISH.ING	garnishing
TÄR'NISH.ING	tarnishing
VÄR'NISH.ING	varnishing

AR'O.Ē

AR'O.Ē	arrowy
BAR'O.Ē	barrowy
MAR'O.Ē	marrowy
SPAR'O.Ē	sparrowy
YAR'O.Ē	yarrowy

AR'O.ER

BAR'O.ER	barrower, wheelbarrower
FAR'O.ER	farrower
HAR'O.ER	harrower
NAR'O.ER	narrower

AR'O.GRAF

(See AR'A.GRAF)

AR'O.ING

AR'O.ING	arrowing
BAR'O.ING	barrowing, wheelbarrowing
FAR'O.ING	farrowing
HAR'O.ING	harrowing
NAR'O.ING	narrowing

AR'O.NĪT

(See AR'E.NĪT)

AR'OT.ING

GAR'OT.ING	garroting
PAR'OT.ING	parroting

ÄR'SE.NĒ

LÄR'SE.NĒ	larceny
PÄR'SE.NĒ	coparceny

ÄR'SE.NER

LÄR'SE.NER	larcener
PÄR'SE.NER	coparcener, parcener

ÄR'SHAL.IZM

MÄR'SHAL.IZM	martialism
PÄR'SHAL.IZM	partialism

ÄR'TED.NES

HÄR'TED.NES	BL blackheartedness, F falseheartedness, fickle-heartedness, frank-heartedness, free-heartedness, H hard-heartedness, K kind-heartedness, L light-heartedness, O open-heartedness, S soft-heartedness, T tender-heartedness, W warm-heartedness
PÄR'TED.NES	departedness, partedness

ÄR'TER.Ē

ÄR'TER.Ē	artery
BÄR'TER.Ē	bartery
MÄR'TER.Ē	martyry

ÄR'TER.ER

BÄR'TER.ER	barterer
CHÄR'TER.ER	charterer

ÄR'TER.ING

BÄR'TER.ING	bartering
CHÄR'TER.ING	chartering
GÄR'TER.ING	garter-ring
MÄR'TER.ING	martyring

ÄR'TI.KL

ÄR'TI.KL	article
PÄR'TI.KL	particle

ÄR'TI.ZAN

ÄR'TI.ZAN	artisan
BÄR'TI.ZAN	bartizan
PÄR'TI.ZAN	bipartisan, partisan

ÄRT'LES.LĒ

ÄRT'LES.LĒ	artlessly
HÄRT'LES.LĒ	heartlessly

ÄRT'LES.NES

ÄRT'LES.NES	artlessness
HÄRT'LES.NES	heartlessness

ĀS'A.BL

BĀS'A.BL	abasable, basable, debasable
CHĀS'A.BL	chasable
FĀS'A.BL	defaceable, effaceable, faceable, ineffaceable
GRĀS'A.BL	disgraceable
LĀS'A.BL	enlaceable, laceable
PĀS'A.BL	paceable
PLĀS'A.BL	displaceable, emplaceable, irreplaceable, misplaceable, placeable, replaceable
RĀS'A.BL	erasable, unerasable
SPĀS'A.BL	spaceable
SWĀS'A.BL	persuasible, suasible, unpersuasible
TRĀS'A.BL	retraceable, traceable, untraceable
VĀS'A.BL	evasible

AS'A.BL

KLAS'A.BL	declassable, classable, outclassable
MAS'A.BL	amassable, massable
NAS'A.BL	innascible, renascible
PAS'A.BL	bypassable, impassable, passable, passible, surpassable, unsurpassable
RAS'A.BL	irascible
SAS'A.BL	sassable, unsassable

AS'A.BLĒ

KLAS'A.BLĒ	classably, unclassably
PAS'A.BLĒ	passably, impassably, surpassably, unpassably, unsurpassably
RAS'A.BLĒ	irascibly

AS'E.LĀT

SFAS'E.LĀT	sphacelate
VAS'E.LĀT	vacillate

Ā'SEN.SĒ

JĀ'SEN.SĒ	adjacency, interjacency
PLĀ'SEN.SĒ	complacency

AS'E.RĀT

AS'E.RĀT	acerate
LAS'E.RĀT	lacerate
MAS'E.RĀT	emacerate, macerate

Ā'SE.RĒ

BRĀ'SE.RĒ	bracery, embracery
TRĀ'SE.RĒ	tracery

Ā'SHAL.Ē

FĀ'SHAL.Ē	facially
GLĀ'SHAL.Ē	glacially
RĀ'SHAL.Ē	racially

ASH'E.RĒ

ASH'E.RĒ	ashery
DASH'E.RĒ	haberdashery
FASH'E.RĒ	fashery
HASH'E.RĒ	hashery
SASH'E.RĒ	sashery
TRASH'E.RĒ	trashery

Ā'SHI.A

Ā'SHI.A	Asia
BĀ'SHI.A	sabbatia
GRĀ'SHI.A	ex gratia
KĀ'SHI.A	acacia
LĀ'SHI.A	Galatia, osteomalacia, solatia
MĀ'SHI.A	Dalmatia
RĀ'SHI.A	Eurasia, Laurasia
SĀ'SHI.A	Alsatia
TĀ'SHI.A	cetacea, crustacea

(See Ā'SHA, Ā'ZHA)

ASH'I.A

FASH'I.A	fascia
KASH'I.A	cassia, Circassia
NAS'I.A	Parnassia

Ā'SHI.AL

BĀ'SHI.AL	abbatial
FĀ'SHI.AL	facial
GLĀ'SHI.AL	glacial, postglacial, preglacial, subglacial
LĀ'SHI.AL	palatial
MĀ'SHI.AL	primatial
RĀ'SHI.AL	multiracial, racial
SPĀ'SHI.AL	interspatial, spatial
TĀ'SHI.AL	mystacial

(See Ā'SHAL)

Ā'SHI.AN

Ā'SHI.AN	Asian, Australasian
HĀ'SHI.AN	Haitian
LĀ'SHI.AN	Galatian
NĀ'SHI.AN	Athanasian
RĀ'SHI.AN	Eurasian
SĀ'SHI.AN	Alsatian
STĀ'SHI.AN	Eustachian
THRĀ'SHI.AN	Thracian

(See Ā'ZI.AN, also Ā'SHUN, Ā'ZHUN)

ASH'I.AN

KASH'I.AN	Circassian
NASH'I.AN	Parnassian

(See ASH'UN)

Ā'SHI.ĀT

GĀ'SHI.ĀT	sagatiate
GLĀ'SHI.ĀT	glaciate
GRĀ'SHI.ĀT	ingratiate
MĀ'SHI.ĀT	emaciate
PĀ'SHI.ĀT	expatiate
SĀ'SHI.ĀT	insatiate, satiate
SPĀ'SHI.ĀT	spaciate

(See Ā'SI.ĀT)

ASH'I.ER

ASH'I.ER	ashier
DASH'I.ER	dashier
FLASH'I.ER	flashier
HASH'I.ER	hashier
PLASH'I.ER	plashier
SPLASH'I.ER	splashier
TRASH'I.ER	trashier

Ā'SHI.Ō

LĀ'SHI.Ō	fellatio, Nova Constellatio
RĀ'SHI.Ō	Horatio, ratio

Ā'SHUN.AL

Ā'SHUN.AL	associational, aviational, ideational, creational, mediational, radiational, recreational, transubstantiational, variational
BĀ'SHUN.AL	incubational, probational
BRĀ'SHUN.AL	vibrational
DĀ'SHUN.AL	gradational
GĀ'SHUN.AL	interrogational, congregational, conjugational
GRĀ'SHUN.AL	emigrational, immigrational
KĀ'SHUN.AL	educational, convocational, vocational
KWĀ'SHUN.AL	equational
LĀ'SHUN.AL	relational, revelational, translational
MĀ'SHUN.AL	informational
NĀ'SHUN.AL	denominational, inclinational, combinational, terminational
PĀ'SHUN.AL	occupational
RĀ'SHUN.AL	inspirational, gyrational, commemorational, operational, respirational
SĀ'SHUN.AL	compensational, condensational, conversational, sensational
STĀ'SHUN.AL	stational
TĀ'SHUN.AL	deputational, dissertational, gravitational, imitational, quotational, presentational, representational, rotational, salutational
VĀ'SHUN.AL	amotivational, derivational, conservational, motivational, observational

(See ĀSHUN, add -al where appropriate.)

ASH'UN.AL

NASH'UN.AL	international, multinational, national, supranational
PASH'UN.AL	passional
RASH'UN.AL	irrational, rational

ASH'UN.AL.IST

NASH'UN.AL.IST	nationalist
RASH'UN.AL.IST	rationalist

ASH'UN.AL.ĪZ

NASH'UN.AL.ĪZ	denationalize, internationalize, nationalize
RASH'UN.AL.ĪZ	rationalize

Ā'SHUN.ER

BĀ'SHUN.ER	probationer, reprobationer
DĀ'SHUN.ER	foundationer
KĀ'SHUN.ER	summer vacationer, vacationer, winter vacationer
LĀ'SHUN.ER	oblationer
RĀ'SHUN.ER	rationer, restorationer
STĀ'SHUN.ER	stationer

Ā'SHUN.ING

(See ĀSHUN, add -ing where appropriate.)

ASH'UN.ING

FASH'UN.ING	fashioning, refashioning
PASH'UN.ING	compassioning

Ā'SHUN.IST

Ā'SHUN.IST	irradiationist, creationist, rationist, re-creationist, repudiationist
DĀ'SHUN.IST	foundationist
FLĀ'SHUN.IST	deflationist, inflationist
GRĀ'SHUN.IST	emigrationist, immigrationist
KĀ'SHUN.IST	educationist, convocationist, vacationist
LĀ'SHUN.IST	annihilationist, isolationist, neoisolationist
MĀ'SHUN.IST	cremationist
PĀ'SHUN.IST	emancipationist
RĀ'SHUN.IST	degenerationist, federationist, inspirationist, moderationist, reparationist, restorationist, tolerationist
SĀ'SHUN.IST	annexationist, conversationist
TĀ'SHUN.IST	annotationist, imitationist, transmutationist
VĀ'SHUN.IST	innovationist, salvationist
ZĀ'SHUN.IST	causationist, colonizationist

(See Ā'SHUN, add -ist where appropriate.)

Ā'SHUN.LES

(See Ā'SHUN, add -less where appropriate.)

Ā'SHUS.LĒ

DĀ'SHUS.LĒ	audaciously, edaciously, mendaciously, mordaciously, predaciously
GĀ'SHUS.LĒ	fugaciously, sagaciously
GRĀ'SHUS.LĒ	graciously, ungraciously
KĀ'SHUS.LĒ	efficaciously, inefficaciously, perspicaciously
KWĀ'SHUS.LĒ	loquaciously
LĀ'SHUS.LĒ	fallaciously, salaciously
MĀ'SHUS.LĒ	contumaciously
NĀ'SHUS.LĒ	minaciously, pertinaciously, pugnaciously, tenaciously
PĀ'SHUS.LĒ	capaciously, rapaciously
RĀ'SHUS.LĒ	veraciously, voraciously
SĀ'SHUS.LĒ	vexatiously
SPĀ'SHUS.LĒ	spaciously
TĀ'SHUS.LĒ	disputatiously, flirtatiously, ostentatiously
VĀ'SHUS.LĒ	curvaceously, vivaciously

(See ĀSHUS, add -ly where appropriate.)

Ā'SHUS.NES

(See Ā'SHUS, add -ness where appropriate.)

Ā'SI.ĀT

KĀ'SI.ĀT	caseate

(See Ā'SHI.ĀT)

AS'I.FĪ

GAS'I.FĪ	gasify
KLAS'I.FĪ	declassify, classify, reclassify
PAS'I.FĪ	pacify, repacify

AS'I.KL

FAS'I.KL	fascicle
KLAS'I.KL	classical, neoclassical, nonclassical

AS'I.LĀT

(See AS'E.LĀT)

AS'I.NĀT

BAS'I.NĀT	abacinate
FAS'I.NĀT	fascinate
RAS'I.NĀT	deracinate
SAS'I.NĀT	assassinate

Ā'SI.NES

LĀ'SI.NES	laciness
RĀ'SI.NES	raciness
SPĀ'SI.NES	spaciness

AS'I.NES

BRAS'I.NES	brassiness
GAS'I.NES	gassiness
GLAS'I.NES	glassiness
GRAS'I.NES	grassiness
KLAS'I.NES	classiness
MAS'I.NES	massiness
SAS'I.NES	sassiness

AS'I.TĒ

BAS'I.TĒ	bibacity, urbacity
DAS'I.TĒ	audacity, edacity, mendacity, mordacity
GAS'I.TĒ	fugacity, sagacity
KAS'I.TĒ	dicacity, perspicacity, pervicacity, procacity
KWAS'I.TĒ	loquacity, sequacity
LAS'I.TĒ	bellacity, salacity
MAS'I.TĒ	emacity, contumacity
NAS'I.TĒ	minacity, pertinacity, pugnacity, saponacity, tenacity
PAS'I.TĒ	incapacity, capacity, opacity, rapacity
RAS'I.TĒ	feracity, veracity, voracity
VAS'I.TĒ	vivacity

AS'I.TUS

AS'I.TUS	acetus
TAS'I.TUS	Tacitus

AS'IV.LĒ

MAS'IV.LĒ	massively
PAS'IV.LĒ	impassively, passively

Ā'SIV.NES

BRĀ'SIV.NES	abrasiveness
SWĂ'SIV.NES	assuasiveness, dissuasiveness, persuasiveness, suasiveness
VĂ'SIV.NES	evasiveness, invasiveness, pervasiveness

AS'IV.NES

MAS'IV.NES	massiveness
PAS'IV.NES	impassiveness, passiveness

AS'PE.RĀT

AS'PE.RĀT	asperate, aspirate
ZAS'PE.RĀT	exasperate

AS'PING.LĒ

GAS'PING.LĒ	gaspingly
GRAS'PING.LĒ	graspingly
RAS'PING.LĒ	raspingly

AS'TAR.DĒ

BAS'TAR.DĒ	bastardy
DAS'TAR.DĒ	dastardy

AS'TA.SIS

AS'TA.SIS	diastasis
TAS'TA.SIS	metastasis

AS'TER.Ē

KAS'TER.Ē	dicastery
MAS'TER.Ē	mastery, self-mastery

AS'TER.ING

FAS'TER.ING	philophastering
MAS'TER.ING	mastering, overmastering
PAS'TER.ING	pastoring
PLAS'TER.ING	beplastering, plastering
TAS'TER.ING	poetastering

AS'TER.SHIP

MAS'TER.SHIP	mastership
PAS'TER.SHIP	pastorship

ĀST'FUL.Ē

TĀST'FUL.Ē	distastefully, tastefully
WĀST'FUL.Ē	wastefully

AS'TI.GĀT

FAS'TI.GĀT	fastigate
KAS'TI.GĀT	castigate

AS'TI.KAL

AS'TI.KAL	ecclesiastical, encomiastical, enthusiastical
LAS'TI.KAL	elastical
NAS'TI.KAL	gymnastical, monastical
TAS'TI.KAL	fantastical

AS'TI.KĀT

LAS'TI.KĀT	elasticate, scholasticate
MAS'TI.KĀT	masticate

AS'TIK.LĒ

AS'TIK.LĒ	ecclesiastic'ly, encomiastic'ly, enthusiastic'ly
BAS'TIK.LĒ	bombastic'ly
DRAS'TIK.LĒ	drastic'ly
KAS'TIK.LĒ	sarcastic'ly
LAS'TIK.LĒ	elastic'ly, scholastic'ly
NAS'TIK.LĒ	gymnastic'ly, monastic'ly
PLAS'TIK.LĒ	plasticly
TAS'TIK.LĒ	fantasticly

ĀS'TI.LĒ

HĀS'TI.LĒ	hastily
PĀS'TI.LĒ	pastily
TĀS'TI.LĒ	tastily

AS'TI.LĒ

GAS'TI.LĒ	ghastily
NAS'TI.LĒ	nastily

AS'TI.SIZM

AS'TI.SIZM	ecclesiasticism, orgiasticism
BRAS'TI.SIZM	Hudibrasticism
KLAS'TI.SIZM	iconoclasticism
LAS'TI.SIZM	scholasticism
NAS'TI.SIZM	monasticism
PLAS'TI.SIZM	plasticism
TAS'TI.SIZM	fantasticism

AS'TRI.AN

AS'TRI.AN	Zoroastrian
BAS'TRI.AN	alabastrian

AS'TRO.FĒ

AS'TRO.FĒ	diastrophe
NAS'TRO.FĒ	anastrophe, epanastrophe
TAS'TRO.FĒ	catastrophe

Ā'TA.BL

Ā'TA.BL	abbreviatable

(See ĀT, add -able where appropriate.)

AT'A.BL

AT'A.BL	get-at-able, come-at-able, unget-at-able, uncome-at-able
BAT'A.BL	battable, combatable, unbattable, uncombatable

FOR PLANETS FORSAKEN

For planets forsaken;
  For galaxies lorn;
For youth from me taken—
  Forever I mourn.

For sin unforgiven;
  For passion forborne;
For heart from me riven—
  Forever I mourn.

For life without leaven;
  For duty forsworn;
For forfeiting heaven—
  Forever I mourn.

HAT'A.BL	hattable, unhattable	CHAT'ER.ER	chatterer	BLATH'ER.ING	blathering
MAT'A.BL	mattable, unmattable	FLAT'ER.ER	flatterer	GATH'ER.ING	forgathering, gathering, ingathering, woolgathering
PAT'A.BL	biocompatible, impatible, incompatible, compatible, patible, pattable, unpattable	KLAT'ER.ER	clatterer		
		PAT'ER.ER	patterer		
		SHAT'ER.ER	shatterer	LATH'ER.ING	lathering
		SKAT'ER.ER	scatterer	SLATH'ER.ING	slathering
RAT'A.BL	rattable	SMAT'ER.ER	smatterer		
VAT'A.BL	vattable	SPAT'ER.ER	bespatterer, spatterer		
		SPLAT'ER.ER	splatterer		

Ā'TAL.Ē

ATH'E.SIS

(TH as in *thin*)

FĀ'TAL.Ē	fatally
NĀ'TAL.Ē	natally, postnatally, prenatally

AT'ER.ĒZ

FRAT'ER.ĒZ	fraberies

ATH'E.SIS	diathesis
RATH'E.SIS	parathesis
TATH'E.SIS	metathesis

(See **AT'ER.Ē**, change -*y* to -*ies* where appropriate.)

ATH'I.KAL

(TH as in *thin*)

AT'E.LĪT

MAT'E.LĪT	stromatalite
SAT'E.LĪT	satellite

Ā'TER.FA.MĒL.YUS

MĀ'TER.FA.MĒL.YUS	*materfamilias*
PĀ'TER.FA.MĒL.YUS	*paterfamilias*

MATH'I.KAL	philomathical, chrestomathical
PATH'I.KAL	anthropopathical, idiopathical

AT'EN.ING

BAT'EN.ING	battening
FAT'EN.ING	fattening, unfattening
FLAT'EN.ING	flattening

AT'ER.ING

(See **AT'ER**, add -*ing* where appropriate.)

AT'I.BL

(See **AT'A.BL**)

KAT'E.NĀT

(See **KAT'I.NĀT**)

AT'FOOT.ED

ÄT'I.ER

FAT'FOOT.ED	fat-footed
FLAT'FOOT.ED	flat-footed
KAT'FOOT.ED	cat-footed
RAT'FOOT.ED	rat-footed

SKWÄT'I.ER	squattier
SWÄT'I.ER	swattier
YÄT'I.ER	yachtier

(See **OT'I.ER**)

Ā'TEN.SĒ

LĀ'TEN.SĒ	latency
PĀ'TEN.SĒ	patency

ĀT'FUL.Ē

AT'I.FĪ

FĀT'FUL.Ē	fatefully
GRĀT'FUL.Ē	gratefully, ungratefully
HĀT'FUL.Ē	hatefully

AT'I.FĪ	beatify
GRAT'I.FĪ	gratify
RAT'I.FĪ	ratify
STRAT'I.FĪ	interstratify, stratify

AT'ER.AN

KAT'ER.AN	cateran
LAT'ER.AN	Lateran

ATH'ER.ER

(TH as in *then*)

AT'I.KA

AT'I.KA	Attica, sciatica
JAT'I.KA	Jataka
MAT'I.KA	dalmatica
PAT'I.KA	hepatica

AT'E.RĒ

BLATH'ER.ER	blatherer
GATH'ER.ER	forgatherer, gatherer, ingatherer, tax gatherer, toll gatherer, upgatherer, woolgatherer
LATH'ER.ER	lather
SLATH'ER.ER	slatherer

BAT'E.RĒ	battery
CHAT'E.RĒ	chattery
FLAT'E.RĒ	flattery
HAT'E.RĒ	hattery
KAT'E.RĒ	cattery
SHAT'E.RĒ	shattery
SKAT'E.RĒ	scattery
SLAT'E.RĒ	slattery
TAT'E.RĒ	tattery

(See **ÄTIKA**)

Ä'TI.KA

JÄ'TI.KA	Jatika

ATH'ER.ING

(TH as in *then*)

AT'ER.ER

BAT'ER.ER	batterer
BLAT'ER.ER	blatterer

(See **AT'I.KA**)

AT'I.KAL

AT'I.KAL	sciatical
BAT'I.KAL	abbatical, acrobatical, sabbatical
FAT'I.KAL	emphatical
KRAT'I.KAL	aristocratical, bureaucratical, democratical, idiosyncratical, autocratical, Socratical
KWAT'I.KAL	aquatical, semiaquatical, subaquatical
MAT'I.KAL	*A* acroamatical, axiomatical, anagrammatical, anathematical, anidiomatical, apophthegmatical, asthmatical, *D* diplomatical, dogmatical, *DR* dramatical, *E* emblematical, enigmatical, epigrammatical, *F* phantasmatical, *GR* grammatical, *H* hebdomatical, *I* idiomatical, *KL* climatical, *M* mathematical, *N* numismatical, *O* automatical, *PR* pragmatical, primatical, prismatical, problematical, *S* schismatical, symptomatical, systematical, somatical, *SP* spasmatical, *U* ungrammatical, unsystematical
NAT'I.KAL	fanatical
RAT'I.KAL	erratical, hieratical, leviratical, operatical, piratical, separatical
STAT'I.KAL	aerostatical, apostatical, ecstatical, hydrostatical, hypostatical, statical
VAT'I.KAL	vatical

(See **AT'IK,** add *-al* where appropriate.)

AT'I.NA

PAT'I.NA	patina
PLAT'I.NA	platina

AT'I.NĀT

KAT'I.NĀT	catenate, concatenate
LAT'I.NĀT	gelatinate, Latinate, Palatinate
PAT'I.NĀT	patinate

Ā'TI.NES

SLĀ'TI.NES	slatiness
WĀ'TI.NES	weightiness

AT'I.NES

BAT'I.NES	battiness
CHAT'I.NES	chattiness
FAT'I.NES	fattiness
KAT'I.NES	cattiness
NAT'I.NES	nattiness
RAT'I.NES	rattiness

ÄT'I.NES

SKWÄT'I.NES	squattiness
SWÄT'I.NES	swattiness
YÄT'I.NES	yachtiness

(See **OT'I.NES**)

Ā'TING.LĒ

(See **ĀT,** add *-ingly* where appropriate.)

AT'IN.ĪZ

LAT'IN.ĪZ	gelatinize, Latinize
PLAT'IN.ĪZ	platinize
RAT'IN.ĪZ	keratinize

AT'I.NUS

LAT'I.NUS	gelatinous
PLAT'I.NUS	platinous

AT'I.SĪZ

AT'I.SĪZ	Atticize
MAT'I.SĪZ	emblematicize, grammaticize
NAT'I.SĪZ	fanaticize

AT'I.SIZM

AT'I.SIZM	Asiaticism
MAT'I.SIZM	grammaticism, pragmaticism
NAT'I.SIZM	fanaticism

AT'I.TŪD

AT'I.TŪD	attitude, beatitude
GRAT'I.TŪD	gratitude, ingratitude
LAT'I.TŪD	latitude
PLAT'I.TŪD	platitude

AT'I.TŪ'DI.NĪZ

AT'I.TŪ'DI.NĪZ	attitudinize
PLAT'I.TŪ'DI.NĪZ	platitudinize

Ā'TIV.LĒ

Ā'TIV.LĒ	insinuatively, creatively, uncreatively
KĀ'TIV.LĒ	implicatively, incommunicatively, multiplicatively, predicatively, significatively
LĀ'TIV.LĒ	accumulatively, emulatively, gesticulatively, cumulatively, legislatively, manipulatively
NĀ'TIV.LĒ	determinatively, imaginatively, germinatively, natively, opinionatively, terminatively
PĀ'TIV.LĒ	anticipatively, participatively
RĀ'TIV.LĒ	alliteratively, decoratively, invigoratively, commemoratively, commiseratively, cooperatively, corroboratively, operatively, reiteratively, vituperatively
TĀ'TIV.LĒ	dubitatively, hesitatively, imitatively, indubitatively,

cogitatively,
qualitatively,
quantitatively,
meditatively,
authoritatively
TRĀ'TIV.LĒ   administratively

(See **ĀTIV**, add -*ly* where appropriate.)

Ā'TIV.NES

(See **Ā'TIV**, add -*ness* where appropriate.)

AT'L.MENT

BAT'L.MENT	battlement, embattlement
PRAT'L.MENT	prattlement
TAT'L.MENT	tattlement

AT'O.MĒ

AT'O.MĒ	atomy
NAT'O.MĒ	anatomy
RAT'O.MĒ	tesseratomy

AT'O.MIST

AT'O.MIST	atomist, diatomist
NAT'O.MIST	anatomist

AT'O.MĬZ

AT'O.MĬZ	atomize
NAT'O.MĬZ	anatomize

AT'O.MIZM

AT'O.MIZM	atomism
NAT'O.MIZM	anatomism

AT'O.MUS

AT'O.MUS	diatomous
RAT'O.MUS	paratomous

Ā'TO.RĒ

KRĀ'TO.RĒ	obsecratory
LĀ'TO.RĒ	*recapitulatory*
NĀ'TO.RĒ	*ratiocinatory*

Ā'TRI.AL

Ā'TRI.AL	atrial
PĀ'TRI.AL	patrial

AT'RI.KAL

AT'RI.KAL	iatrical, psychiatrical, theatrical
LAT'RI.KAL	idolatrical
MAT'RI.KAL	matrical

AT'RI.MŌ.NĒ

MAT'RI.MŌ.NĒ	matrimony
PAT'RI.MŌ.NĒ	patrimony

AT'RI.SĬD

FRAT'RI.SĬD	fratricide
MAT'RI.SĬD	matricide
PAT'RI.SĬD	patricide

Ā'TRON.AL

MĀ'TRON.AL	matronal
PĀ'TRON.AL	patronal

Ā'TRON.IJ

MĀ'TRON.IJ	matronage
PĀ'TRON.IJ	patronage

Ā'TRO.NĬZ

MĀ'TRO.NĬZ	matronize
PĀ'TRO.NĬZ	patronize

AT'Ū.LĀT

(See **ACH'OO.LĀT**)

AT'Ū.RĀT

(See **ACH'OO.RĀT**)

Ā'VA.BL

LĀ'VA.BL	lavable
PĀ'VA.BL	pavable, repavable, unpavable
SĀ'VA.BL	savable, unsavable
SHĀ'VA.BL	shavable, unshavable

WĀ'VA.BL	unwaivable, unwavable, waivable, wavable

AV'A.JER

(See **AV'I.JER**)

AV'EL.ER

GAV'EL.ER	gaveler
GRAV'EL.ER	graveler
KAV'EL.ER	caviler
RAV'EL.ER	raveler, unraveler
TRAV'EL.ER	traveler

AV'E.LIN

JAV'E.LIN	javelin
RAV'E.LIN	ravelin

AV'EL.ING

(See **AVEL**, add -*ing* where appropriate.)

AV'E.LINZ

NAV'E.LINZ	manavelins

(See **AV'E.LIN**, add -*s* where appropriate.)

AV'EN.DER

CHAV'EN.DER	chavender
LAV'EN.DER	lavender

Ā'VE.RĒ

BRĀ'VE.RĒ	bravery
FLĀ'VE.RĒ	flavory
GRĀ'VE.RĒ	gravery
KWĀ'VE.RĒ	quavery
NĀ'VE.RĒ	knavery
SĀ'VE.RĒ	savory, unsavory
SLĀ'VE.RĒ	anti-slavery, pro-slavery, slavery
WĀ'VE.RĒ	wavery

Ā'VER.ER

FĀ'VER.ER	favorer
FLĀ'VER.ER	flavorer
HĀ'VER.ER	haverer
KWĀ'VER.ER	quaverer
LĀ'VER.ER	laverer

SĀ'VER.ER — savorer
WĀ'VER.ER — waverer

Ā'VER.ING

(See Ā'VER.ER, change -er to -ing.)

AV'ER.ING

HAV'ER.ING — havering
KLAV'ER.ING — clavering
LAV'ER.ING — palavering

Ā'VER.US

FĀ'VER.US — favorous
FLĀ'VER.US — flavorous
KWĀ'VER.US — quaverous
SĀ'VER.US — savorous

AV'ER.US

DAV'ER.US — cadaverous
PAV'ER.US — papaverous

Ā'VI.A

GRĀ'VI.A — Belgravia
NĀ'VI.A — ignavia, Scandinavia
RĀ'VI.A — Moravia
TĀ'VI.A — Batavia, Octavia

Ā'VI.AL

GĀ'VI.AL — gavial
KLĀ'VI.AL — clavial

Ā'VI.AN

Ā'VI.AN — avian
GRĀ'VI.AN — Belgravian
KLĀ'VI.AN — subclavian
NĀ'VI.AN — Scandinavian
RĀ'VI.AN — Moravian
SHĀ'VI.AN — Shavian
TĀ'VI.AN — Batavian, Octavian

Ā'VI.ER

KLĀ'VI.ER — clavier
WĀ'VI.ER — wavier

AV'I.JER

KLAV'I.JER — claviger
RAV'I.JER — ravager

SAV'I.JER — savager
SKAV'I.JER — scavager

AV'IJ.ING

RAV'IJ.ING — ravaging
SAV'IJ.ING — savaging
SKAV'IJ.ING — scavaging

AV'ISH.ER

LAV'ISH.ER — lavisher
RAV'ISH.ER — enravisher, ravisher

AV'ISH.ING

LAV'ISH.ING — lavishing
RAV'ISH.ING — enravishing, ravishing

AV'ISH.MENT

LAV'ISH.MENT — lavishment
RAV'ISH.MENT — enravishment, ravishment

Ā'VISH.NES

NĀ'VISH.NES — knavishness
SLĀ'VISH.NES — slavishness

AV'ISH.NES

LAV'ISH.NES — lavishness
SLAV'ISH.NES — Slavishness

AV'I.TĒ

GRAV'I.TĒ — gravity
KAV'I.TĒ — cavity, concavity
PRAV'I.TĒ — depravity, pravity
SWAV'I.TĒ — suavity

Ā'ZA.BL

FRĀ'ZA.BL — phrasable, unphrasable
GRĀ'ZA.BL — grazable, ungrazable
PRĀ'ZA.BL — appraisable, praisable, unappraisable, unpraisable
RĀ'ZA.BL — raisable, unraisable
SWĀ'ZA.BL — persuasible, suasible, unpersuasible

AZ'A.RĒN

MAZ'A.RĒN — mazarine
NAZ'A.RĒN — Nazarene

Ā'ZI.A

Ā'ZI.A — Asia
BĀ'ZI.A — abasia
FĀ'ZI.A — aphasia, paraphasia
FRĀ'ZI.A — paraphrasia, tachyphrasia
GĀ'ZI.A — ergasia
KĀ'ZI.A — Caucasia, sicchasia
KRĀ'ZI.A — dyscrasia
LĀ'ZI.A — onlochalasia, Australasia
MĀ'ZI.A — paronomasia, prosonomasia
NĀ'ZI.A — athanasia, gymnasia, euthanasia
PĀ'ZI.A — Aspasia
PLĀ'ZI.A — aplasia
RĀ'ZI.A — Laurasia, Eurasia
STĀ'ZI.A — Anastasia, astasia, hemostasia
TĀ'ZI.A — fantasia

(See ĀSHA, ĀZHA)

Ā'ZI.AL

BĀ'ZI.AL — basial
NĀ'ZI.AL — gymnasial

Ā'ZI.AN

Ā'ZI.AN — Asian
KĀ'ZI.AN — Caucasian
LĀ'ZI.AN — Australasian, Rabelasian
NĀ'ZI.AN — Athanasian
RĀ'ZI.AN — Eurasian

(See Ā'SHUN, Ā'ZHUN, Ā'SHI.AN)

Ā'ZI.LĒ

HĀ'ZI.LĒ — hazily
KRĀ'ZI.LĒ — crazily
LĀ'ZI.LĒ — lazily

Ā'ZI.NES

HĀ'ZI.NES — haziness
KRĀ'ZI.NES — craziness
LĀ'ZI.NES — laziness
MĀ'ZI.NES — maziness

Ā'ZING.LĒ

BLĀ'ZING.LĒ	blazingly
DĀ'ZING.LĒ	dazingly
GĀ'ZING.LĒ	gazingly
MĀ'ZING.LĒ	amazingly

AZ'L.MENT

DAZ'L.MENT	bedazzlement, dazzlement
FRAZ'L.MENT	frazzlement

AZ'Ū.RĪT

AZ'Ū.RĪT	azurite
LAZ'Ū.RĪT	lazurite

Ē'A.BL

FĒ'A.BL	feeable
FLĒ'A.BL	fleeable
FRĒ'A.BL	freeable
GRĒ'A.BL	agreeable, disagreeable
KRĒ'A.BL	decreeable, undecreeable
MĒ'A.BL	irremeable, meable, remeable
RĒ'A.BL	reable
SĒ'A.BL	seeable, unseeable
SKĒ'A.BL	skiable, unskiable
TRĒ'A.BL	treeable

Ē'A.LĒ

DĒ'A.LĒ	ideally
LĒ'A.LĒ	leally
RĒ'A.LĒ	really

Ē'A.LIST

DĒ'A.LIST	idealist
RĒ'A.LIST	realist, surrealist

Ē'A.LĪZ

DĒ'A.LĪZ	idealize
RĒ'A.LĪZ	realize

Ē'A.LIZM

DĒ'A.LIZM	idealism
RĒ'A.LIZM	realism, surrealism

Ē'AL.TĒ

FĒ'AL.TĒ	fealty
LĒ'AL.TĒ	lealty
RĒ'AL.TĒ	realty

Ē'A.NIZM

BĒ'A.NIZM	plebeianism
KĒ'A.NIZM	Manicheanism
PĒ'A.NIZM	paeanism
RĒ'A.NIZM	epicureanism, Pythagoreanism
SĒ'A.NIZM	Laodiceanism

EB'I.ER

BLEB'I.ER	blebbier
NEB'I.ER	nebbier
WEB'I.ER	cobwebbier, webbier

EB'I.EST

BLEB'I.EST	blebbiest
NEB'I.EST	nebbiest
WEB'I.EST	cobwebbiest, webbiest

EB'RI.TĒ

EB'RI.TĒ	muliebrity
LEB'RI.TĒ	celebrity
NEB'RI.TĒ	tenebrity

Ē'BRI.US

Ē'BRI.US	ebrious, inebrious
NĒ'BRI.US	funebrious, tenebrious

Ē'CHA.BL

BLĒ'CHA.BL	bleachable
PĒ'CHA.BL	impeachable, unimpeachable
PRĒ'CHA.BL	preachable, unpreachable
RĒ'CHA.BL	reachable, unreachable
TĒ'CHA.BL	teachable, unteachable

ECH'A.BL

ECH'A.BL	etchable, unetchable

FECH'A.BL	fetchable, unfetchable
SKECH'A.BL	sketchable, unsketchable
STRECH'A.BL	stretchable, unstretchable

ECH'E.RĒ

LECH'E.RĒ	lechery
TRECH'E.RĒ	treachery

ECH'ER.US

LECH'ER.US	lecherous
TRECH'ER.US	treacherous

ĒCH'I.FĪ

PRĒCH'I.FĪ	preachify
SPĒCH'I.FĪ	speechify

Ē'CHI.NES

PĒ'CHI.NES	peachiness
PRĒ'CHI.NES	preachiness
SKRĒ'CHI.NES	screechiness

ECH'I.NES

SKECH'I.NES	sketchiness
STRECH'I.NES	stretchiness
TECH'I.NES	tetchiness

Ē'DA.BL

DĒ'DA.BL	deedable
FĒ'DA.BL	feedable
HĒ'DA.BL	heedable
LĒ'DA.BL	leadable, unleadable
NĒ'DA.BL	kneadable, unkneadable
PĒ'DA.BL	impedible
PLĒ'DA.BL	pleadable, unpleadable
RĒ'DA.BL	readable, unreadable
SĒ'DA.BL	exceedable, seedable, supersedable, unexceedable, unseedable
WĒ'DA.BL	unweedable, weedable

ED'A.BL

(See ED'I.BL)

ED'A.LĒ

(See ED'I.LĒ)

ED'EN.ING

DED'EN.ING	deadening
LED'EN.ING	leadening
RED'EN.ING	reddening

Ē'DER.SHIP

LĒ'DER.SHIP	leadership
RĒ'DER.SHIP	readership

ĒD'FUL.Ē

HĒD'FUL.Ē	heedfully, unheedfully
NĒD'FUL.Ē	needfully, unneedfully

ĒD'FUL.NES

HĒD'FUL.NES	heedfulness, unheedfulness
NĒD'FUL.NES	needfulness, unneedfulness

Ē'DI.A

MĒ'DI.A	intermedia, comedia, media, print media, multimedia
PĒ'DI.A	encyclopedia, pharmacopedia, fissipedia, hypnopedia, lassipedia, misopedia, cyclopedia
SĒ'DI.A	acedia, epicedia

Ē'DI.AL

MĒ'DI.AL	admedial, intermedial, irremedial, comedial, medial, remedial
PĒ'DI.AL	pedial
PRĒ'DI.AL	praedial
SĒ'DI.AL	epicedial

Ē'DI.AN

JĒ'DI.AN	tragedian
MĒ'DI.AN	Archimedean, comedian, median, picedian
SĒ'DI.AN	
PĒ'DI.AN	encyclopedian

Ē'DI.A

MĒ'DI.A	media, multimedia
PĒ'DI.A	encyclopedia, hypnopedia, cyclopedia
SĒ'DI.A	acedia

ED'I.BL

ED'I.BL	edible, inedible
BED'I.BL	beddable, unbeddable
DRED'I.BL	dreadable
KRED'I.BL	incredible, credible
PED'I.BL	impedible

Ē'DI.ENS

BĒ'DI.ENS	disobedience, obedience
GRĒ'DI.ENS	ingredients
PĒ'DI.ENS	expedience, expedients, inexpedience

Ē'DI.ENT

BĒ'DI.ENT	disobedient, obedient
GRĒ'DI.ENT	digredient, ingredient
MĒ'DI.ENT	mediant, submediant
PĒ'DI.ENT	expedient, impedient, inexpedient

Ē'DI.ER

BĒ'DI.ER	beadier
GRĒ'DI.ER	greedier
NĒ'DI.ER	needier
RĒ'DI.ER	reedier
SĒ'DI.ER	seedier
SPĒ'DI.ER	speedier
WĒ'DI.ER	weedier

ED'I.ER

BRED'I.ER	breadier
HED'I.ER	headier
RED'I.ER	readier, unreadier
SHRED'I.ER	shreddier
SPRED'I.ER	spreadier
STED'I.ER	steadier, unsteadier
THRED'I.ER	threadier

ED'I.ING

ED'I.ING	eddying
RED'I.ING	readying
STED'I.ING	steadying

ED'I.KAL

(See ED'I.KL)

ED'I.KANT

DED'I.KANT	dedicant
MED'I.KANT	medicant
PRED'I.KANT	predicant

ED'I.KĀT

DED'I.KĀT	dedicate, rededicate
MED'I.KĀT	medicate, remedicate
PRED'I.KĀT	predicate, depredicate

ED'I.KL

MED'I.KL	medical, pre-medical
PED'I.KL	pedicle

Ē'DI.LĒ

BĒ'DI.LĒ	beadily
GRĒ'DI.LĒ	greedily
NĒ'DI.LĒ	needily
RĒ'DI.LĒ	reedily
SĒ'DI.LĒ	seedily
SPĒ'DI.LĒ	speedily
WĒ'DI.LĒ	weedily

ED'I.LĒ

DED'I.LĒ	logodaedaly
HED'I.LĒ	headily
RED'I.LĒ	readily, unreadily
STED'I.LĒ	steadily, unsteadily

ED'I.MENT

PED'I.MENT   impediment,
                  pediment
SED'I.MENT   sediment

Ē'DI.NES

(See ÊDĒ, add -ness where appropriate.)

ED'I.NES

SED'I.NES   mucediness

(See EDĒ, add -ness where appropriate.)

Ē'DING.LĒ

HĒ'DING.LĒ   heedingly,
                  unheedingly
LĒ'DING.LĒ   leadingly,
                  misleadingly
PLĒ'DING.LĒ   pleadingly
SĒ'DING.LĒ   exceedingly

ED'I.NUS

BED'I.NUS   rubedinous
GWED'I.NUS   pinguedinous
SED'I.NUS   mucediness
TRED'I.NUS   putredinous

ED'I.TĒ

BED'I.TĒ   rubedity
RED'I.TĒ   heredity

ED'I.TED

ED'I.TED   edited, unedited
KRED'I.TED   accredited,
                  discredited,
                  credited,
                  miscredited,
                  unaccredited,
                  undiscredited

ED'I.TER

ED'I.TER   editor, executive
                  editor, managing
                  editor, city editor,
                  subeditor (etc.)
KRED'I.TER   creditor

ED'I.TING

ED'I.TING   editing
KRED'I.TING   accrediting,
                  discrediting,
                  crediting,
                  miscrediting

ED'I.TIV

KRED'I.TIV   creditive
PED'I.TIV   impeditive
RED'I.TIV   redditive
SED'I.TIV   sedative

ED'I.TOR

(See ED'I.TER)

Ē'DI.UM

MĒ'DI.UM   intermedium,
                  medium
PĒ'DI.UM   cypripedium,
                  Cypripedium
RĒ'DI.UM   soredium, uredium
SĒ'DI.UM   epicedium
TĒ'DI.UM   tedium

Ē'DI.US

MĒ'DI.US   gluteus medius,
                  intermedious,
                  medious
TĒ'DI.US   tedious

ĒD'LES.LĒ

HĒD'LES.LĒ   heedlessly
NĒD'LES.LĒ   needlessly

ĒD'LES.NES

HĒD'LES.NES   heedlessness
NĒD'LES.NES   needlessness

ED'Ū.LUS

KRED'Ū.LUS   incredulous,
                  credulous
SED'Ū.LUS   sedulous,
                  unsedulous

EF'ER.ENS

DEF'ER.ENS   deference
PREF'ER.ENS   preference
REF'ER.ENS   cross-reference,
                  reference

EF'ER.ENT

EF'ER.ENT   efferent
DEF'ER.ENT   deferent
PREF'ER.ENT   preferent
REF'ER.ENT   referent

Ē'FI.NES

BĒ'FI.NES   beefiness
LĒ'FI.NES   leafiness
RĒ'FI.NES   reefiness

EF'I.SENS

LEF'I.SENS   maleficence
NEF'I.SENS   beneficence

EF'I.SENT

LEF'I.SENT   maleficent
NEF'I.SENT   beneficent

EG'A.BL

BEG'A.BL   beggable
PEG'A.BL   peggable

Ē'GAL.Ē

LĒ'GAL.Ē   illegally, legally
RĒ'GAL.Ē   regally

EG'A.LITH

MEG'A.LITH   megalith
REG'A.LITH   regolith

Ē'GA.LIZM

LĒ'GA.LIZM   legalism
RĒ'GA.LIZM   regalism

Ē'GAL.NES

LĒ'GAL.NES   legalness, illegalness
RĒ'GAL.NES   regalness

EG'E.RĒ

EG'E.RĒ	eggery
BEG'E.RĒ	beggary

Ē'GER.LĒ

Ē'GER.LĒ	eagerly, overeagerly, uneagerly
MĒ'GER.LĒ	meagerly

Ē'GER.NES

Ē'GER.NES	eagerness, overeagerness, uneagerness
MĒ'GER.NES	meagerness

EG'I.NES

EG'I.NES	egginess
DREG'I.NES	dregginess
LEG'I.NES	legginess

EG'NAN.SĒ

PREG'NAN.SĒ	pregnancy
REG'NAN.SĒ	regnancy

EG'Ū.LAR

REG'Ū.LAR	irregular, regular
TEG'Ū.LAR	tegular

Ē'I.FĪ

DĒ'I.FĪ	deify
RĒ'I.FĪ	reify

Ē'I.TĒ

BĒ'I.TĒ	plebeity
BLĒ'I.TĒ	tableity
DĒ'I.TĒ	deity, hermaphrodeity
LĒ'I.TĒ	velleity
NĒ'I.TĒ	D diathermaneity, E extraneity, erogeneity, F femininity, H

	heterogeneity, homogeneity, I instantaneity, K contemporaneity, M momentaneity, O omneity, P personeity, S simultaneity, SP spontaneity
RĒ'I.TĒ	incorporeity, corporeity
SĒ'I.TĒ	aseity, gaseity, haecceity, ipseity, perseity, seity
TĒ'I.TĒ	multeity

EJ'A.BL

EJ'A.BL	edgeable, unedgeable
DREJ'A.BL	dredgeable, undredgeable
HEJ'A.BL	hedgeable, unhedgeable
KEJ'A.BL	kedgeable, unkedgeable
LEJ'A.BL	allegeable, illegible, legible
PLEJ'A.BL	pledgeable, unpledgeable
WEJ'A.BL	unwedgeable, wedgeable

Ē'JI.A

LĒ'JI.A	aquilegia
PLĒ'JI.A	diplegia, hemiplegia, quadriplegia, cycloplegia
RĒ'JI.A	aqua regia

Ē'JI.AN

FWĒ'JI.AN	Fuegian
LĒ'JI.AN	collegian
WĒ'JI.AN	Norwegian, sou'wegian

(See EJUN)

EJ'I.O

FEJ'I.O	solfeggio
PEJ'I.O	arpeggio

Ē'JUS.LĒ

GRĒ'JUS.LĒ	egregiously
LĒ'JUS.LĒ	sacrilegiously

Ē'JUS.NES

GRĒ'JUS.NES	egregiousness
LĒ'JUS.NES	sacrilegiousness

Ē'KA.BL

LĒ'KA.BL	leakable, unleakable
SPĒ'KA.BL	speakable, unspeakable

EK'A.BL

CHEK'A.BL	checkable, uncheckable
PEK'A.BL	impeccable, peccable
SEK'A.BL	inseccable

EK'A.NAL

DEK'A.NAL	decanal
SEK'A.NAL	Seconal

EK'CHER.AL

JEK'CHER.AL	conjectural
TEK'CHER.AL	architectural

EK'CHER.ER

JEK'CHER.ER	conjecturer
LEK'CHER.ER	lecturer

EK'CHOO.AL

FEK'CHOO.AL	effectual, ineffectual, prefectual
LEK'CHOO.AL	anti-intellectual, intellectual, lectual, nonintellectual, unintellectual
PEK'CHOO.AL	aspectual

Ē'KI.LĒ

BĒ'KI.LĒ	beakily
CHĒ'KI.LĒ	cheekily
KRĒ'KI.LĒ	creakily
LĒ'KI.LĒ	leakily
SKWĒ'KI.LĒ	squeakily
SLĒ'KI.LĒ	sleekily
SNĒ'KI.LĒ	sneakily

Ē'KI.NES

(See ĒKĒ, add -ness where appropriate.)

Ē'KISH.NES

FRĒ'KISH.NES	freakishness
SNĒ'KISH.NES	sneakishness

(See ĒK, add -ishness where appropriate.)

EK'LI.NĀT

DEK'LI.NĀT	declinate
REK'LI.NĀT	reclinate

EK'OND.LĒ

(See EK'UND.LĒ)

EK'ON.ING

(See EK'UN.ING)

EK'RE.MENT

DEK'RE.MENT	decrement
REK'RE.MENT	recrement

EK'SA.BL

(See EK'SI.BL)

EK'SA.GON

FLEK'SA.GON	flexagon
HEK'SA.GON	hexagon

EK'SED.LĒ

PLEK'SED.LĒ	perplexedly
VEK'SED.LĒ	convexedly, vexedly

EK'SHUN.AL

FEK'SHUN.AL	affectional
FLEK'SHUN.AL	flectional, inflectional, reflectional, reflexional
JEK'SHUN.AL	interjectional, objectional, projectional
LEK'SHUN.AL	collectional
NEK'SHUN.AL	connectional
PLEK'SHUN.AL	complexional
REK'SHUN.AL	directional, insurrectional, correctional, resurrectional
SEK'SHUN.AL	bisectional, dissectional, intersectional, resectional, sectional, vivisectional
TEK'SHUN.AL	protectional
VEK'SHUN.AL	convectional

EK'SHUN.ER

FEK'SHUN.ER	confectioner, perfectioner
JEK'SHUN.ER	interjectioner, objectioner, projectioner
REK'SHUN.ER	correctioner

EK'SHUN.IST

FEK'SHUN.IST	perfectionist
JEK'SHUN.IST	projectionist
REK'SHUN.IST	insurrectionist, resurrectionist
SEK'SHUN.IST	antivivisectionist, vivisectionist
TEK'SHUN.IST	antiprotectionist, protectionist

EK'SHU.NĪZ

REK'SHU.NĪZ	insurrectionize, resurrectionize
SEK'SHU.NĪZ	sectionize

EK'SI.A

KEK'SI.A	cachexia
LEK'SI.A	alexia
NEK'SI.A	pleonexia
REK'SI.A	anorexia, parorexia
SEK'SI.A	aprosexia

EK'SI.BL

FLEK'SI.BL	flexible, inflexible, reflexible
NEK'SI.BL	annexable
VEK'SI.BL	vexable

EK'SI.KAL

DEK'SI.KAL	indexical
LEK'SI.KAL	lexical
REK'SI.KAL	pyrexical

EK'SI.TĒ

FLEK'SI.TĒ	reflexity
PLEK'SI.TĒ	duplexity, intercomplexity, complexity, perplexity
VEK'SI.TĒ	convexity

EK'SIV.NES

FLEK'SIV.NES	reflexiveness
PLEK'SIV.NES	perplexiveness

EK'TA.BL

(See EK'TI.BL)

EK'TA.SIS

EK'TA.SIS	bronchiectasis
LEK'TA.SIS	atalectasis

EK'TED.LĒ

FEK'TED.LĒ	affectedly, disaffectedly, infectedly, unaffectedly
FLEK'TED.LĒ	reflectedly
GLEK'TED.LĒ	neglectedly
LEK'TED.LĒ	electedly, collectedly, recollectedly, selectedly
NEK'TED.LĒ	disconnectedly, connectedly
SPEK'TED.LĒ	expectedly, respectedly, suspectedly, unexpectedly, unsuspectedly
TEK'TED.LĒ	protectedly, unprotectedly

EK'TED.NES

(See EKT, add -edness where appropriate.)

EK'TE.RAL

FEK'TE.RAL	prefectoral
LEK'TE.RAL	electoral
PEK'TE.RAL	pectoral
REK'TE.RAL	directoral, rectoral
SEK'TE.RAL	sectoral
SPEK'TE.RAL	inspectoral
TEK'TE.RAL	protectoral

EK'TER.ĀT

PEK'TER.ĀT	expectorate

(See EK'TER.IT)

EK'TE.RĒ

FEK'TE.RĒ	refectory, confectory
JEK'TE.RĒ	interjectory, trajectory
NEK'TE.RĒ	nectary
REK'TE.RĒ	directory, correctory, rectory
SEK'TE.RĒ	sectary
TEK'TE.RĒ	protectory

EK'TER.IT

LEK'TER.IT	electorate
REK'TER.IT	directorate, rectorate
SPEK'TER.IT	inspectorate
TEK'TER.IT	protectorate

(See EK'TER.ĀT)

EKT'FUL.Ē

GLEKT'FUL.Ē	neglectfully
SPEKT'FUL.Ē	disrespectfully, respectfully, unrespectfully

EKT'FUL.NES

GLEKT'FUL.NES	neglectfulness
SPEKT'FUL.NES	disrespectfulness, respectfulness, suspectfulness, unrespectfulness, unsuspectfulness

EK'TI.BL

FEK'TI.BL	affectible, defectible, effectible, indefectible, infectible, perfectible, unaffectible
FLEK'TI.BL	deflectible, reflectible
JEK'TI.BL	objectable, rejectable, subjectable, unrejectable
LEK'TI.BL	delectable, indelectable, collectable, uncollectable
NEK'TI.BL	connectible, unconnectible
SPEK'TI.BL	expectable, respectable, suspectible, unrespectable, unsusceptible
SEK'TI.BL	dissectible, undissectible
TEK'TI.BL	detectable, undetectable

EK'TI.FĪ

JEK'TI.FĪ	objectify, subjectify
REK'TI.FĪ	rectify

EK'TI.KL

LEK'TI.KL	dialectical
PLEK'TI.KL	apoplectical
SPEK'TI.KL	spectacle

EK'TING.LĒ

FEK'TING.LĒ	affectingly
FLEK'TING.LĒ	reflectingly
JEK'TING.LĒ	objectingly

EK'TI.TŌŌD

NEK'TI.TŌŌD	senectitude
REK'TI.TŌŌD	rectitude

EK'TI.VIST

JEK'TI.VIST	objectivist
LEK'TI.VIST	collectivist

EK'TIV.LĒ

(See **EKTIV**, add -ly where appropriate.)

EK'TIV.NES

(See **EKTIV**, add -ness where appropriate.)

EK'TO.MĒ

DEK'TO.MĒ	appendectomy, omphalectomy, orchidectomy
LEK'TO.MĒ	tonsillectomy, umbilectomy
PEK'TO.MĒ	lipectomy, lumpectomy
REK'TO.MĒ	hysterectomy, laparohysteroal-pingooophorectomy
SEK'TO.MĒ	vasectomy
TEK'TO.MĒ	mastectomy

EK'TO.RĒ

(See EK'TE.RĒ)

EK'TŪ.AL

(See EK'CHŌŌ.AL)

EK'TUR.ER

(See EK'CHER.ER)

EK'Ū.LAR

LEK'Ū.LAR	molecular, vallecular
PEK'Ū.LAR	vulpecular
SEK'Ū.LAR	secular
SPEK'Ū.LAR	specular

EK'Ū.LĀT

PEK'Ū.LĀT	peculate
SPEK'Ū.LĀT	speculate

EK'Ū.LUM

SEK'Ū.LUM	seculum
SPEK'Ū.LUM	speculum

EK'UND.LĒ

FEK'UND.LĒ	fecundly
SEK'UND.LĒ	secondly

EK'UN.ING

BEK'UN.ING	beckoning
REK'UN.ING	dead-reckoning, reckoning

EK'Ū.TIV

SEK'Ū.TIV	consecutive, subsecutive, unconsecutive
ZEK'Ū.TIV	executive

Ē'KWEN.SĒ

FRĒ'KWEN.SĒ	frequency, infrequency
SĒ'KWEN.SĒ	sequency

ĒL'A.BL

DĒL'A.BL	dealable, undealable
FĒL'A.BL	feelable, unfeelable
HĒL'A.BL	healable, unhealable
JĒL'A.BL	congealable, uncongealable
NĒL'A.BL	annealable
PĒL'A.BL	appealable, pealable, peelable, repealable, unpeelable, unrepealable
RĒL'A.BL	reelable
SĒL'A.BL	concealable, sealable, unconcealable, unsealable

EL'A.BL

BEL'A.BL	bellable
DEL'A.BL	delible, indelible
FEL'A.BL	fellable
JEL'A.BL	ingelable, gelable, jellable, unjellable
KWEL'A.BL	quellable, unquellable
PEL'A.BL	expellable, compellable
SPEL'A.BL	spellable, unspellable
TEL'A.BL	foretellable, tellable, untellable

EL'AN.US

FEL'A.NUS	felonous

MEL'A.NUS	leucomelanous, melanous, xanthomelanous

EL'A.TIN

JEL'A.TIN	gelatin
SKEL'A.TIN	skeleton

EL'A.TIV

PEL'A.TIV	appellative, compellative
REL'A.TIV	irrelative, correlative, relative

EL'E.GĀT

DEL'E.GĀT	delegate
REL'E.GĀT	relegate, religate

ĒL'ER.Ē

SĒL'ER.Ē	sealery
TWĒ'LER.Ē	Tuileries

EL'ER.Ē

HEL'ER.Ē	hellery
SEL'ER.Ē	celery, cellary
STEL'ER.Ē	stellary

EL'ET.Ē

DEL'ET.Ē	fidelity, infidelity
PEL'ET.Ē	pellety

EL'FISH.LĒ

EL'FISH.LĒ	elfishly
SEL'FISH.LĒ	selfishly, unselfishly

EL'FISH.NES

EL'FISH.NES	elfishness
SEL'FISH.NES	selfishness, unselfishness

Ē'LI.A

Ē'LI.A	syringomyelia
BĒ'LI.A	lobelia
DĒ'LI.A	grindelia, Cordelia

MĒ'LI.A	phocomelia, camellia

(See ĒLYA)

Ē'LI.AN

Ē'LI.AN	Ismailian
DĒ'LI.AN	Delian
FĒ'LI.AN	aphelion, Mephistophelian
HĒ'LI.AN	anthelion, parhelion, perihelion
MĒ'LI.AN	chameleon
NĒ'LI.AN	carnelian
PĒ'LI.AN	Pelion
SĒ'LI.AN	Caelian
TĒ'LI.AN	Aristotelian
THĒ'LI.AN	anthelion

EL'I.AN

EL'I.AN	Pantagruelian, pantagruelion
JEL'I.AN	evangelian
SKEL'I.AN	tetraskelion
VEL'I.AN	Machiavelian, Machiavellian
WEL'I.AN	Boswellian, Cromwellian

(See ELYUN)

EL'I.BL

(See EL'A.BL)

EL'I.FÔRM

KEL'I.FÔRM	cheliform
STEL'I.FÔRM	stelliform

EL'I.ING

BEL'I.ING	bellying
JEL'I.ING	jellying

EL'I.KAL

BEL'I.KAL	bellical
HEL'I.KAL	helical
JEL'I.KAL	angelical, evangelical
PEL'I.KAL	pellicle

EL'ING.LĒ

KWEL'ING.LĒ	quellingly
PEL'ING.LĒ	compellingly

TEL'ING.LĒ   tellingly
WEL'ING.LĒ   wellingly

EL'ISH.ING

BEL'ISH.ING   embellishing
REL'ISH.ING   relishing

EL'ISH.MENT

BEL'ISH.MENT   embellishment
REL'ISH.MENT   relishment

Ē'LI.US

BĒ'LI.US   Sibelius
HĒ'LI.US   Helios
MĒ'LI.US   contumelious
RĒ'LI.US   Aurelius

EL'O.DĒ

JEL'O.DĒ   hypogelody
MEL'O.DĒ   melody

EL'O.Ē

BEL'O.Ē   bellowy
MEL'O.Ē   mellowy
YEL'O.Ē   yellowy

EL'O.ER

BEL'O.ER   bellower
CHEL'O.ER   celloer
MEL'O.ER   mellower
YEL'O.ER   yellower

EL'O.ING

(See **ELŌ**, add *-ing* where appropriate.)

EL'O.NĒ

FEL'O.NĒ   felony
MEL'O.NĒ   melony

EL'O.NUS

FEL'O.NUS   felonous
MEL'O.NUS   leucomelanous, melanous, xanthomelanous

EL'TER.Ē

SHEL'TER.Ē   sheltery
SMEL'TER.Ē   smeltery
SWEL'TER.Ē   sweltery

EL'TER.ER

SHEL'TER.ER   shelterer
SMEL'TER.ER   smelterer
SWEL'TER.ER   swelterer
WEL'TER.ER   welterer

EL'TER.ING

SHEL'TER.ING   sheltering
SWEL'TER.ING   sweltering
WEL'TER.ING   weltering

EL'THI.ER

HEL'THI.ER   healthier
STEL'THI.ER   stealthier
WEL'THI.ER   wealthier

EL'THI.EST

HEL'THI.EST   healthiest
STEL'THI.EST   stealthiest
WEL'THI.EST   wealthiest

EL'THI.LĒ

HEL'THI.LĒ   healthily
STEL'THI.LĒ   stealthily
WEL'THI.LĒ   wealthily

EL'Ū.LAR

SEL'Ū.LAR   intercellular, cellular, unicellular
STEL'Ū.LAR   interstellular, stellular

EL'US.LĒ

JEL'US.LĒ   jealously, unjealously

ZEL'US.LĒ   overzealously, unzealously, zealously

Ē'MA.BL

(See **ĒM**, add *-able* where appropriate.)

EM'A.NĒ

(See **EM'O.NĒ**)

Ē'MA.TIST

SKĒ'MA.TIST   schematist
THĒ'MA.TIST   thematist

EM'A.TIST

BLEM'A.TIST   emblematist
REM'A.TIST   theorematist

EM'BER.ISH

EM'BER.ISH   emberish
SEM'BER.ISH   Decemberish
TEM'BER.ISH   Septemberish
VEM'BER.ISH   Novemberish

EM'ER.A

FEM'ER.A   ephemera
REM'ER.A   remora

EM'ER.AL

FEM'ER.AL   ephemeral, femerell, femoral
HEM'ER.AL   hemeral, trihemeral
NEM'ER.AL   nemoral

ĒM'ER.E

DRĒM'ER.Ē   dreamery
KRĒM'ER.Ē   creamery

EM'ER.Ē

EM'ER.Ē   emery
JEM'ER.Ē   gemmery
MEM'ER.Ē   memory

EM'E.SIS

EM'E.SIS	emesis
NEM'E.SIS	nemesis

Ē'MI.A

Ē'MI.A	pyemia
DĒ'MI.A	academia
HĒ'MI.A	Bohemia
FĒ'MI.A	coprophemia
KĒ'MI.A	ischemia, leukemia
LĒ'MI.A	paraphilemia
NĒ'MI.A	anemia
PRĒ'MI.A	sapremia
RĒ'MI.A	bacteremia, diarhemia, paroemia, uremia
SĒ'MI.A	anoxemia, hyperglycemia, hypoglycemia, septicemia, toxemia
THĒ'MI.A	schizothemia

Ē'MI.AL

Ē'MI.AL	proemial
DĒ'MI.AL	academial, endemial, vindemial
GRĒ'MI.AL	gremial
NĒ'MI.AL	cnemial
PRĒ'MI.AL	premial
RĒ'MI.AL	paroemial, uremial

Ē'MI.AN

DĒ'MI.AN	academian
HĒ'MI.AN	Bohemian

Ē'MI.ER

BĒ'MI.ER	beamier
DRĒ'MI.ER	dreamier
GLĒ'MI.ER	gleamier
KRĒ'MI.ER	creamier
PRĒ'MI.ER	premier
STĒ'MI.ER	steamier

EM'I.KAL

DEM'I.KAL	academical, endemical, epidemical, pandemical
KEM'I.KAL	alchemical, electrochemical, photochemical, chemical
LEM'I.KAL	polemical

Ē'MI.LĒ

BĒ'MI.LĒ	beamily
DRĒ'MI.LĒ	dreamily
GLĒ'MI.LĒ	gleamily
KRĒ'MI.LĒ	creamily
STĒ'MI.LĒ	steamily

EM'I.NAL

FEM'I.NAL	feminal
JEM'I.NAL	bigeminal, geminal, tergeminal
SEM'I.NAL	seminal

EM'I.NĀT

FEM'I.NĀT	effeminate, feminate
JEM'I.NĀT	ingeminate, geminate, tergeminate
SEM'I.NĀT	disseminate, inseminate, seminate

Ē'MI.NES

(See ĒMĒ, add -ness where appropriate.)

Ē'MING.LĒ

(See ĒM, add -ingly where appropriate.)

EM'I.PED

REM'I.PED	remiped
SEM'I.PED	semiped

EM'I.TĒ

SEM'I.TĒ	Yosemite
TREM'I.TĒ	extremity

Ē'MI.UM

PRĒ'MI.UM	premium, proemium
SĒ'MI.UM	gelsemium

EM'NI.FĪ

DEM'NI.FĪ	indemnify
LEM'NI.FĪ	solemnify

EM'NI.TĒ

DEM'NI.TĒ	indemnity
LEM'NI.TĒ	solemnity

EM'O.NĒ

JEM'O.NĒ	hegemony
LEM'O.NĒ	lemony
NEM'O.NĒ	anemone, pantanemone
SEM'O.NĒ	Gethsemane

EM'ON.STRĀT

DEM'ON.STRĀT	demonstrate
REM'ON.STRĀT	remonstrate

EM'PE.RĒ

EM'PE.RĒ	empery
STEM'PE.RĒ	extempore
TEM'PE.RĒ	tempery, tempore

EM'PER.ER

EM'PER.ER	emperor
TEM'PER.ER	temperer

EMP'TE.RĒ

DEMP'TE.RĒ	redemptory
REMP'TE.RĒ	peremptory

EM'Ū.LENT

EM'Ū.LENT	emulant
TEM'Ū.LENT	temulent
TREM'Ū.LENT	tremulant, tremulent

EM'Ū.LUS

EM'Ū.LUS	emulous
TREM'Ū.LUS	tremulous

Ē'NA.BL

GLĒ'NA.BL	gleanable, ungleanable
LĒ'NA.BL	leanable
MĒ'NA.BL	amenable, meanable, unamenable
VĒ'NA.BL	convenable, unconvenable

EN'A.BL

MEN'A.BL	amenable
PEN'A.BL	pennable

REN'A.BL   renable
TEN'A.BL   tenable, untenable

EN'A.RĒ

(See EN'E.RĒ)

EN'A.TER

JEN'A.TER   genitor, primogenitor, progenitor
SEN'A.TER   senator

EN'CHER.Ē

(See EN'SHER.Ē)

EN'CHOO.AL

SEN'CHOO.AL   accentual, percentual
VEN'CHOO.AL   adventual, eventual, conventual

EN'CHOO.ĀT

SEN'CHOO.ĀT   accentuate
VEN'CHOO.ĀT   eventuate

EN'DA.BL

EN'DA.BL   endable
BEN'DA.BL   bendable, unbendable
FEN'DA.BL   defendable, undefendable
HEN'DA.BL   comprehendible
LEN'DA.BL   lendable, unlendable
MEN'DA.BL   amendable, emendable, commendable, mendable, recommendable, unamendable, unemendable, uncommendable, unmendable, unrecommendable
PEN'DA.BL   appendable, dependable, impendable, pendable, suspendable
REN'DA.BL   rendable
SEN'DA.BL   accendible, ascendible
TEN'DA.BL   extendable
VEN'DA.BL   vendible, invendible

EN'DEN.SĒ

PEN'DEN.SĒ   appendency, dependency, impendency, independency, interdependency, pendency
SEN'DEN.SĒ   ascendancy, transcendency
SPLEN'DEN.SĒ   resplendency, splendency
TEN'DEN.SĒ   ambitendency, attendency, intendency, countertendency, superintendency, tendency

EN'DER.ER

JEN'DER.ER   engenderer, genderer
REN'DER.ER   renderer, surrenderer
SLEN'DER.ER   slenderer
TEN'DER.ER   tenderer

EN'DER.EST

SLEN'DER.EST   slenderest
TEN'DER.EST   tenderest

EN'DER.ING

JEN'DER.ING   engendering, gendering
REN'DER.ING   rendering, surrendering

EN'DER.LĒ

SLEN'DER.LĒ   slenderly
TEN'DER.LĒ   tenderly

EN'DER.NES

SLEN'DER.NES   slenderness
TEN'DER.NES   tenderness

EN'DI.US

PEN'DI.US   dispendious, compendious
SEN'DI.US   incendious

END'LES.LĒ

END'LES.LĒ   endlessly
BEND'LES.LĒ   bendlessly
BLEND'LES.LĒ   blendlessly
FREND'LES.LĒ   friendlessly

END'LES.NES

(See END, add -lessness where appropriate.)

EN'DUS.LĒ

MEN'DUS.LĒ   tremendously
PEN'DUS.LĒ   stupendously
REN'DUS.LĒ   horrendously

EN'DUS.NES

MEN'DUS.NES   tremendousness
PEN'DUS.NES   stupendousness
REN'DUS.NES   horrendousness

EN'ER.Ā.SHUN

JEN'ER.Ā.SHUN   ingeneration, generation, progeneration, regeneration
TEN'ER.Ā.SHUN   inteneration
VEN'ER.Ā.SHUN   veneration

EN'E.RĀT

JEN'E.RĀT   degenerate, ingenerate, generate, progenerate, regenerate
TEN'E.RĀT   intenerate
VEN'E.RĀT   venerate

Ē'NE.RĒ

BĒ'NE.RĒ   beanery
DĒ'NE.RĒ   deanery, denary, duodenary
GRĒ'NE.RĒ   greenery
PLĒ'NE.RĒ   plenary
SĒ'NE.RĒ   scenery, senary
SHĒ'NE.RĒ   machinery
TĒ'NE.RĒ   bicentenary, quatercentenary, quincentenary, centenary

EN'ER.Ē

DEN'ER.Ē   denary
HEN'ER.Ē   hennery

PLEN'ER.Ē   plenary
SEN'ER.Ē   decenary,
                  decennary, senery
TEN'ER.Ē   quatercentenary,
                  centenary,
                  septennary
VEN'ER.Ē   venery

EN'ER.IS

JEN'ER.IS   sui generis
VEN'ER.IS   mons veneris

EN'E.SIS

JEN'E.SIS   *A* abiogenesis,
                   agenesis,
                   anthropogenesis, *B*
                   biogenesis, *E*
                   ectogenesis,
                   epigenesis, *F*
                   phylogenesis,
                   photogenesis, *H*
                   hematogenesis,
                   heterogenesis,
                   hylogenesis,
                   histogenesis,
                   homogenesis, *I*
                   iatrogenesis, *J*
                   genesis, *K*
                   catagenesis, *M*
                   metagenesis,
                   monogenesis,
                   morphogenesis, *N*
                   neogenesis, *O*
                   ontogenesis,
                   oogenesis,
                   organogenesis,
                   osteogenesis, *P*
                   palingenesis,
                   pangenesis,
                   paragenesis,
                   parthenogenesis,
                   pathogenesis,
                   pyrogenesis,
                   polygenesis, *R*
                   regenesis, *S*
                   psychogenesis, *SP*
                   spermatogenesis,
                   sporogenesis, *Y*
                   eugenesis, *Z*
                   xenogenesis,
                   zoogenesis
REN'E.SIS   parenesis

EN'E.TING

JEN'E.TING   jenneting
REN'E.TING   renneting

ENG'THEN.ING

LENG'THEN.ING   lengthening
STRENG'THEN.ING   strengthening

Ē'NI.A

DĒ'NI.A   gardenia
DRĒ'NI.A   hypoadrenia
FRĒ'NI.A   *A* aphilophrenia,
                  azygophrenia, *H*
                  hebephrenia, *K*
                  castrophrenia, *L*
                  lypophrenia, *M*
                  malneirophrenia, *N*
                  nosocomephrenia, *O*
                  oligophrenia, *PR*
                  presbyophrenia, *SK*
                  schizophrenia, *ST*
                  strataphrenia, *Y*
                  euniophrenia
MĒ'NI.A   Armenia, catamenia,
                  neomenia
PĒ'NI.A   leucopenia
SĒ'NI.A   sarracenia
STHĒ'NI.A   sthenia
TĒ'NI.A   taenia
THĒ'NI.A   asthenia,
                  phonasthenia,
                  myasthenia,
                  neurasthenia,
                  Parthenia,
                  psychasthenia
VĒ'NI.A   Slovenia
ZĒ'NI.A   xenia

EN'I.A

DREN'I.A   quadrennia
LEN'I.A   millennia
SEN'I.A   decennia

Ē'NI.AL

JĒ'NI.AL   homogeneal, genial,
                  congenial,
                  primigenial,
                  primogenial,
                  uncongenial
MĒ'NI.AL   demesnial, menial
SPLĒ'NI.AL   splenial
TĒ'NI.AL   taenial
VĒ'NI.AL   venial
ZĒ'NI.AL   xenial

(See ĒNYAL)

EN'I.AL

EN'I.AL   biennial, triennial
KWEN'I.AL   quinquennial
LEN'I.AL   millennial
REN'I.AL   perennial,
                  plurennial,
                  quadrennial
SEN'I.AL   decennial,
                  duodecennial,
                  quindecennial,
                  tricennial, vicennial
TEN'I.AL   bicentennial,
                  quincentennial,
                  quotennial,
                  octennial,
                  centennial,
                  septennial,
                  tercentennial,
                  tricentennial
VEN'I.AL   novennial

(See ENYAL)

Ē'NI.AN

FĒ'NI.AN   Fenian
LĒ'NI.AN   Hellenian, selenian
MĒ'NI.AN   Armenian,
                  neomenian
RĒ'NI.AN   sirenian, Cyrenian
THĒ'NI.AN   Athenian, Ruthenian

Ē'NI.ENS

LĒ'NI.ENS   lenience
VĒ'NI.ENS   advenience,
                  inconvenience,
                  intervenience,
                  introvenience,
                  convenience,
                  prevenience,
                  supervenience

(See ĒNYENS)

Ē'NI.ENT

LĒ'NI.ENT   lenient, unlenient
VĒ'NI.ENT   advenient,
                  inconvenient,
                  intervenient,
                  introvenient,
                  convenient,
                  prevenient

(See ĒNYENT)

Ē'NI.ER

PLĒ'NI.ER	plenier
SHĒ'NI.ER	sheenier
SPLĒ'NI.ER	spleenier
TĒ'NI.ER	teenier
WĒ'NI.ER	teeny-weenier, weenier

(See ĒN'YER)

EN'I.FORM

| PEN'I.FORM | bipenniform, penniform |
| TEN'I.FORM | antenniform |

EN'I.KAL

EN'I.KAL	hygienical
LEN'I.KAL	galenical
MEN'I.KAL	ecumenical, catechumenical
REN'I.KAL	sirenical
SEN'I.KAL	arsenical, scenical

EN'I.TĒ

LEN'I.TĒ	lenity
MEN'I.TĒ	amenity
REN'I.TĒ	serenity, terrenity
SEN'I.TĒ	obscenity

EN'I.TEN.SĒ

| PEN'I.TEN.SĒ | penitency |
| REN'I.TEN.SĒ | renitency |

EN'I.TENT

| PEN'I.TENT | penitent |
| REN'I.TENT | renitent |

EN'I.TIV

JEN'I.TIV	genitive, primogenitive, progenitive
LEN'I.TIV	lenitive
SPLEN'I.TIV	splenitive

EN'I.TŪD

LEN'I.TŪD	lenitude
PLEN'I.TŪD	plenitude
REN'I.TŪD	serenitude

Ē'NI.UM

LĒ'NI.UM	selenium, solenium
MĒ'NI.UM	hymenium
RĒ'NI.UM	rhenium
SĒ'NI.UM	postscenium, proscenium
THĒ'NI.UM	calisthenium, ruthenium
ZĒ'NI.UM	xenium

EN'I.UM

EN'I.UM	biennium, triennium
KWEN'I.UM	quinquennium
LEN'I.UM	millennium
REN'I.UM	quadrennium
SEN'I.UM	decennium, sexennium
TEN'I.UM	septennium

Ē'NI.US

Ē'NI.US	aeneous
JĒ'NI.US	extrageneous, heterogeneous, homogeneous, genius, nitrogeneous, primigeneous
LĒ'NI.US	selenious
MĒ'NI.US	pergameneous
SĒ'NI.US	arsenious
SPLĒ'NI.US	splenius

(See ĒNYUS)

EN'I.ZEN

BEN'I.ZEN	benison
DEN'I.ZEN	denizen, endenizen
VEN'I.ZEN	venison

Ē'NO.KRIST

| FĒ'NO.KRIST | phenocryst |
| ZĒ'NO.KRIST | xenocryst |

Ē'NO.TĪP

| FĒ'NO.TĪP | phenotype |
| JĒ'NO.TĪP | genotype |

EN'SA.BL

DEN'SA.BL	incondensable, condensable
FEN'SA.BL	defensible, indefensible
HEN'SA.BL	apprehensible, deprehensible, incomprehensible, irreprehensible, comprehensible, reprehensible
PEN'SA.BL	dispensable, indispensable, suspensible
SEN'SA.BL	insensible, sensible, subsensible
TEN'SA.BL	distensible, extensible, inostensible, ostensible, tensible

EN'SA.TIV

(See EN'SI.TIV)

EN'SE.RĒ

DEN'SE.RĒ	condensery
FEN'SE.RĒ	defensory
HEN'SE.RĒ	prehensory, reprehensory
PEN'SE.RĒ	dispensary, suspensory
SEN'SE.RĒ	extrasensory, incensory, sensory, somatosensory
TEN'SE.RĒ	ostensory

EN'SHE.RĒ

EN'SHE.RĒ	obedientiary
DEN'SHE.RĒ	redentiary, residentiary
LEN'SHE.RĒ	silentiary
TEN'SHE.RĒ	penitentiary, plenipotentiary, sententiary

(See ÂRĒ)

EN'SHI.ĀT

REN'SHI.ĀT	differentiate
SEN'SHI.ĀT	essentiate, licentiate
TEN'SHI.ĀT	potentiate

EN'SHOO.AL

MEN'SHOO.AL	mensual, trimensual
SEN'SHOO.AL	consensual, censual, sensual

EN'SHUN.A.BL

MEN'SHUN.A.BL	mentionable, unmentionalbe
PEN'SHUN.A.BL	pensionable, unpensionable

EN'SHUN.AL

MEN'SHUN.AL	dimensional, hypertridimensional
SEN'SHUN.AL	ascensional, descensional
STEN'SHUN.AL	extensional
TEN'SHUN.AL	attentional, intentional, contentional, unintentional
VEN'SHUN.AL	conventional, preventional, unconventional

EN'SHUN.ER

MEN'SHUN.ER	mentioner
PEN'SHUN.ER	pensioner
VEN'SHUN.ER	conventioner

EN'SHUN.ING

MEN'SHUN.ING	mentioning
PEN'SHUN.ING	pensioning
TEN'SHUN.ING	tensioning

EN'SHUN.IST

SEN'SHUN.IST	ascenscionist, descenscionist, recensionist
TEN'SHUN.IST	extensionist
VEN'SHUN.IST	conventionist, preventionist

EN'SHUS.NES

(See ENSHUS, add -ness.)

EN'SI.BL

(See EN'SA.BL)

EN'SI.BLĒ

FEN'SI.BLĒ	defensibly
HEN'SI.BLĒ	incomprehensibly, comprehensibly, reprehensibly
SEN'SI.BLĒ	insensibly, sensibly
STEN'SI.BLĒ	ostensibly

EN'SI.FĪ

DEN'SI.FĪ	densify
SEN'SI.FĪ	sensify
TEN'SI.FĪ	intensify

EN'SI.KAL

REN'SI.KAL	forensical
SEN'SI.KAL	nonsensical

EN'SI.TĒ

DEN'SI.TĒ	density, condensity
MEN'SI.TĒ	immensity
PEN'SI.TĒ	propensity
TEN'SI.TĒ	attensity, intensity, tensity

EN'SI.TIV

DEN'SI.TIV	condensative
PEN'SI.TIV	dispensative, compensative, pensative
SEN'SI.TIV	photosensitive, hypersensitive, insensitive, radiosensitive, sensitive
TEN'SI.TIV	intensative

EN'SIV.LĒ

(See ENSIV, add -ly.)

EN'SIV.NES

(See ENSIV, add -ness.)

ENS'LES.LĒ

FENS'LES.LĒ	defenselessly, indefenselessly, inoffenselessly, offenselessly
SENS'LES.LĒ	senselessly
TENS'LES.LĒ	tenselessly

ENS'LES.NES

(See ENSLES, add -ness.)

EN'SO.RĒ

(See EN'SE.RĒ)

EN'TA.BL

KWEN'TA.BL	frequentable
MEN'TA.BL	fermentable, *lamentable*
PEN'TA.BL	repentable
REN'TA.BL	rentable
TEN'TA.BL	contentable, tentable
VEN'TA.BL	inventible, preventable, unpreventable
ZEN'TA.BL	presentable, representable, unpresentable

EN'TA.BLĒ

(See EN'TA.BL, change -e to -y.)

EN'TA.KL

DEN'TA.KL	dentical, denticle, identical
PEN'TA.KL	pentacle
TEN'TA.KL	tentacle
THEN'TA.KL	authentical
VEN'TA.KL	conventical, conventicle

EN'TAL.Ē

EN'TAL.Ē	orientally
DEN'TAL.Ē	accidentally, incidentally, occidentally, transcendentally
MEN'TAL.Ē	A alimentally, D detrimentally, developmentally, E experimentally, elementally, F fundamentally, FR fragmentally, G governmentally, I instrumentally, K complimentally, M mentally, momentally, monumentally, O ornamentally, P pigmentally, R

regimentally, *D*
segmentally,
sentimentally,
supplementally, *T*
temperamentally

NEN'TAL.Ē   continentally
REN'TAL.Ē   parentally

EN'TAL.IST

EN'TAL.IST	Orientalist
DEN'TAL.IST	Occidentalist, transcendentalist
MEN'TAL.IST	experimentalist, environmentalist, fundamentalist, instrumentalist, mentalist, sentimentalist

EN'TAL.ĪZ

EN'TAL.ĪZ	orientalize
DEN'TAL.ĪZ	occidentalize
MEN'TAL.ĪZ	departmentalize, compartmentalize, experimentalize, mentalize, sentimentalize
NEN'TAL.ĪZ	continentalize

EN'TAL.IZM

EN'TAL.IZM	Orientalism
DEN'TAL.IZM	accidentalism, Occidentalism, transcendentalism
MEN'TAL.IZM	elementalism, environmentalism, fundamentalism, mentalism, sentimentalism

EN'TAL.NES

(See **ENTAL,** add -*ness* where appropriate.)

EN'TA.TIV

(See **ENT,** add -*ative* where appropriate.)

EN'TED.LĒ

DEN'TED.LĒ	unprecedentedly
KWEN'TED.LĒ	frequentedly, unfrequentedly

MEN'TED.LĒ   dementedly, lamentedly, tormentedly, unlamentedly

EN'TED.NES

(See **ENT,** add -*edness* where appropriate.)

EN'TER.ĀT

LEN'TER.ĀT	coelenterate
TEN'TER.ĀT	extenterate

EN'TER.ING

EN'TER.ING	entering, re-entering
SEN'TER.ING	centering, recentering, self-centering

EN'TER.Ē

DEN'TER.Ē	accidentary, dentary
MEN'TER.Ē	*A* alimentary, *D* documentary, *E* elementary, emolumentary, *F* filamentary, *FR* fragmentary, *I* instrumentary, integumentary, *K* complementary, complimentary, *P* parliamentary, pigmentary, *R* rudimentary, *S* sacramentary, sedimentary, segmentary, supplementary, *T* tegumentary, testamentary, *U* uncomplimentary, unparliamentary
SEN'TER.Ē	placentary

EN'TER.ON

EN'TER.ON	enteron
SEN'TER.ON	mesenteron

ENT'FUL.Ē

VENT'FUL.Ē	eventfully, inventfully, uneventfully

ZENT'FUL.Ē   resentfully, unresentfully

ENT'FUL.NES

(See **ENTFUL,** add -*ness*)

EN'THE.SIS

PEN'THE.SIS	epenthesis
REN'THE.SIS	parenthesis

EN'TI.KL

(See **EN'TA.KL**)

EN'TI.KŪL

DEN'TI.KŪL	denticule
LEN'TI.KŪL	lenticule

EN'TI.MENT

SEN'TI.MENT	sentiment
ZEN'TI.MENT	presentiment

EN'TI.NAL

DEN'TI.NAL	dentinal
SEN'TI.NAL	sentinel

EN'TING.LĒ

LEN'TING.LĒ	relentingly, unrelentingly
MEN'TING.LĒ	augmentingly, tormentingly
PEN'TING.LĒ	repentingly, unrepentingly
SEN'TING.LĒ	assentingly, dissentingly, consentingly

EN'TI.TĒ

EN'TI.TĒ	entity, nonentity
DEN'TI.TĒ	identity

EN'TIV.LĒ

TEN'TIV.LĒ	attentively, retentively
VEN'TIV.LĒ	inventively, preventively
ZEN'TIV.LĒ	presentively

EN'TIV.NES

(See **ENTIV,** add *-ness* where appropriate.)

EN'TL.NES

(See **ENTAL,** add *-ness* where appropriate.)

EN'TRAL.Ē

SEN'TRAL.Ē   centrally, subcentrally
VEN'TRAL.Ē   dorsoventrally, ventrally

EN'TRI.KL

SEN'TRI.KL   eccentrical, concentrical, centrical
VEN'TRI.KL   ventricle

EN'TŪ.AL

(See **EN'CHOO.AL**)

EN'TŪ.ĀT

(See **EN'CHOO.ĀT**)

EN'TUS.LĒ

MEN'TUS.LĒ   momentously
TEN'TUS.LĒ   portentously

EN'TUS.NES

MEN'TUS.NES   momentousness
TEN'TUS.NES   portentousness

Ē'NUN.SI.ĀT

Ē'NUN.SI.ĀT   *enunciate*
DĒ'NUN.SI.ĀT   *denunciate*

EN'Ū.US

JEN'Ū.US   disingenuous, ingenuous
STREN'Ū.US   strenuous
TEN'Ū.US   tenuous

ĒN'YEN.SĒ

LĒN'YEN.SĒ   leniency
VĒN'YEN.SĒ   adveniency, inconveniency, interveniency, introveniency, conveniency, superveniency

ĒN'YENT.LĒ

(See **ĒNYENT,** add *-ly* where appropriate.)

Ē'O.FĪT

JĒ'O.FĪT   geophyte
NĒ'O.FĪT   neophyte

Ē'O.KRAT

RĒ'O.KRAT   rheocrat
THĒ'O.KRAT   theocrat

Ē'O.LA

BĒ'O.LA   rubeola
RĒ'O.LA   areola
VĒ'O.LA   alveola, foveola
ZĒ'O.LA   roseola

Ē'O.LUS

LĒ'O.LUS   malleolus, nucleolus
VĒ'O.LUS   alveolus

EP'A.RĀT

REP'A.RĀT   reparate
SEP'A.RĀT   separate

EP'ER.US

LEP'ER.US   leperous
STREP'ER.US   obstreperous, streperous

EP'I.DŌT

EP'I.DŌT   epidote
LEP'I.DŌT   lepidote

Ē'PI.LĒ

KRĒ'PI.LĒ   creepily
SLĒ'PI.LĒ   sleepily
WĒ'PI.LĒ   weepily

Ē'PI.NES

KRĒ'PI.NES   creepiness
SLĒ'PI.NES   sleepiness
WĒ'PI.NESS   weepiness

EP'I.TANT

KREP'I.TANT   crepitant
STREP'I.TANT   strepitant

EP'SI.A

BLEP'SI.A   ablepsia, chionablepsia, monoblepsia, opsablepsia
PEP'SI.A   apepsia, dyspepsia, eupepsia

EP'TI.KL

LEP'TI.KL   sylleptical
SEP'TI.KL   antiseptical, aseptical, conceptacle, receptacle, septical
SKEP'TI.KL   skeptical, unskeptical

ER'A.FIM

SER'A.FIM   seraphim
TER'A.FIM   teraphim

ER'A.KLĒZ

ER'A.KLĒZ   Heracles
PER'A.KLĒZ   Pericles

ER'AN.SĒ

ER'AN.SĒ   errancy, inerrancy
BER'AN.SĒ   aberrancy

ER'E.MŌ.NĒ

KWER'E.MŌ.NĒ   querimony
SER'E.MŌ.NĒ   ceremony

ER'ET.ED

FER'ET.ED	ferreted
HER'ET.ED	disherited, disinherited, inherited, uninherited
HWER'ET.ED	wherreted
MER'ET.ED	demerited, emerited, merited

ER'ET.ER

(See ERET, add -er where appropriate.)

ER'ET.ING

(See ERET, add -ing where appropriate.)

ĒR'I.A

(See ÎR'I.A)

ER'I.A

| NER'I.A | spaneria |
| STER'I.A | hysteria |

ĒR'I.AD

(See ÎR'I.AD)

ĒR'I.AL

(See ÎR'I.AL)

ĒR'I.A.LIST

(See ÎR'I.A.LIST)

ĒR'I.A.LIZM

(See ÎR'I.A.LIZM)

ĒR'I.AN

(See ÎR'I.AN)

ER'I.BL

| ER'I.BL | errable, inerrable |
| TER'I.BL | terrible |

(See ÂR'A.BL)

ĒR'I.ER

(See ÎR'I.ER)

ER'I.ER

BER'I.ER	berrier, burier
FER'I.ER	ferrier
MER'I.ER	merrier
TER'I.ER	terrier

ER'I.FĪ

SFER'I.FĪ	spherify
TER'I.FĪ	esterify, terrify
VER'I.FĪ	verify

(See ÂR'I.FĪ)

ER'I.ING

BER'I.ING	berrying, burying, blackberrying, blueberrying, huckleberrying, cranberrying, strawberrying (etc.)
FER'I.ING	ferrying
HWER'I.ING	wherrying
SER'I.ING	serrying

ER'I.KA

| ER'I.KA | erica |
| MER'I.KA | America |

ER'I.KAL

FER'I.KAL	atmospherical
KLER'I.KAL	anticlerical, clerical, pro-clerical
MER'I.KAL	Homerical, chimerical, mesmerical, numerical
NER'I.KAL	generical
SER'I.KAL	rhinocerical
SFER'I.KAL	heliospherical, hemispherical, spherical, sphericle
TER'I.KAL	exoterical, esoterical, phylacterical, hysterical, climacterical

ER'I.KAN

| JER'I.KAN | jerrican |
| MER'I.KAN | American |

ĒR'I.LĒ

(See ÎR'I.LĒ)

ER'I.LĒ

| MER'I.LĒ | merrily |
| VER'I.LĒ | verily |

(See ÂR'I.LĒ)

ER'I.MAN

FER'I.MAN	ferryman
HWER'I.MAN	wherryman
MER'I.MAN	merryman

ER'I.MENT

| MER'I.MENT | merriment |
| PER'I.MENT | experiment |

ĒR'I.NES

(See ÎRĒ, add -ness where appropriate.)

ĒR'ING.LĒ

(See ÎR'ING.LĒ)

ĒR'I.Ō

(See ÎR'I.Ō)

ER'ISH.ING

| CHER'ISH.ING | cherishing |
| PER'ISH.ING | perishing, unperishing |

ER'I.TA.BL

| HER'I.TA.BL | heritable, inheritable |
| VER'I.TA.BL | veritable |

ER'I.TĒ

FER'I.TĒ	ferity
JER'I.TĒ	legerity
LER'I.TĒ	celerity
MER'I.TĒ	temerity
PER'I.TĒ	asperity, prosperity
SER'I.TĒ	insincerity, procerity, sincerity
TER'I.TĒ	alterity, ambidexterity,

VER'I.TĒ	dexterity, indexterity, austerity, posterity severity, verity

(See ÂR'I.TĒ)

ER'IT.ED

(See ER'ET.ED)

ER'I.TIV

PER'I.TIV	aperitive, imperative
TER'I.TIV	preteritive

ER'I.TŌ.RĒ

FER'I.TŌR.Ē	feretory
TER'I.TŌR.Ē	territory

ĒR'I.UM

(See ÎR'I.UM)

ĒR'I.US

(See ÎR'I.US)

ĒR'LES.NES

(See ÎR'LES.NES)

ER'O.GĀT

DER'O.GĀT	derogate
RER'O.GĀT	supererogate
TER'O.GĀT	interrogate

ER'O.POD

TER'O.POD	pteropod
THER'O.POD	theropod

ER'UP.ON

HWER'UP.ON	whereupon
THER'UP.ON	thereupon

Ē'SA.BL

(See ĒS, add -able where appropriate.)

ES'A.BL

(See ES'I.BL)

ES'CHER.AL

JES'CHER.AL	gestural
VES'CHER.AL	vestural

ES'CHOO.US

ES'CHOO.US	estuous
PES'CHOO.US	tempestuous
SES'CHOO.US	incestuous

Ē'SEN.SĒ

DĒ'SEN.SĒ	decency, indecency
RĒ'SEN.SĒ	recency

ES'EN.SĒ

ES'EN.SĒ	acquiescency, quiescency
BES'EN.SĒ	erubescency, pubescency
DES'EN.SĒ	incandescency, recrudescency
JES'EN.SĒ	turgescency
KRES'EN.SĒ	excrescency
KWES'EN.SĒ	liquescency
LES'EN.SĒ	adolescency, alkalescency, incalescency, convalescency
RES'EN.SĒ	efflorescency
SES'EN.SĒ	acescency
TES'EN.SĒ	delitescency
VES'EN.SĒ	defervescency, effervescency

Ē'SENT.LĒ

DĒ'SENT.LĒ	decently, indecently
RĒ'SENT.LĒ	recently

ES'ER.Ē

FES'ER.Ē	confessary, professory
PES'ER.Ē	pessary
SES'ER.Ē	accessory, intercessory, concessory, successary
ZES'ER.Ē	possessory

ES'FUL.Ē

BLES'FUL.Ē	blessfully

STRES'FUL.Ē	distressfully, stressfully
SES'FUL.Ē	successfully, unsuccessfully

ESH'EN.ER

FRESH'EN.ER	freshener
SESH'EN.ER	accessioner

Ē'SHI.A

LĒ'SHI.A	silesia, Silesia, kerdomeletia
NĒ'SHI.A	magnesia, Polynesia
PĒ'SHI.A	alopecia
VĒ'SHI.A	Helvetia

(See ĒSHA, ĒZHA)

Ē'SHI.AN

GRĒ'SHI.AN	Grecian
LĒ'SHI.AN	Silesian
NĒ'SHI.AN	internecian, Pelopennesian, Venetian
TĒ'SHI.AN	Epictetian
VĒ'SHI.AN	Helvetian

(See ĒSHUN)

ESH'I.ENS

(See ESHENS)

ESH'I.ENT

NESH'I.ENT	nescient
PRESH'I.ENT	prescient

(See ESHENT)

ESH'I.NES

FLESH'I.NES	fleshiness
MESH'I.NES	meshiness

Ē'SHI.UM

DRĒ'SHI.UM	androecium
NĒ'SHI.UM	gynoecium, technetium
TĒ'SHI.UM	lutecium, lutetium

ESH'UN.AL

FESH'UN.AL	confessional, professional, semiprofessional, unprofessional
GRESH'UN.AL	digressional, congressional, progressional, transgressional
KRESH'UN.AL	discretional
PRESH'UN.AL	expressional, impressional, compressional
SESH'UN.AL	accessional, intercessional, processional, recessional, retrocessional, sessional, successional
ZESH'UN.AL	possessional

ESH'UN.IST

FESH'UN.IST	confessionist
GRESH'UN.IST	progressionist, retrogressionist
PRESH'UN.IST	expressionist, impressionist, Impressionist
SESH'UN.IST	concessionist, processionist, retrocessionist, secessionist
ZESH'UN.IST	possessionist

Ē'SHUS.NES

SĒ'SHUS.NES	facetiousness
SPĒ'SHUS.NES	speciousness

ES'I.BL

DES'I.BL	decibel
DRES'I.BL	dressable, redressible, undressable, unredressible
GES'I.BL	guessable, unguessable
GRES'I.BL	gressible, transgressible
KRES'I.BL	concrescible
PRES'I.BL	*D* depressible, *E* expressible, *I* impressible, incompressible, inexpressible,

insuppressible, irrepressible, *K* compressible, *PR* pressable, *R* repressable, *S* suppressible

SES'I.BL	accessible, assessable, immarcescible, inaccessible, incessable, concessible, marcescible, unassessable
TES'I.BL **TRES'I.BL**	fermentescible imputrescible, putrescible, vitrescible
VES'I.BL	effervescible, ineffervescible
ZES'I.BL	possessable, unpossessable

(See **ES**, add *-able* or *-ible* where appropriate.)

ES'I.BLĒ

(See **ES'I.BL**, replace *-e* with *-y; see* **ES**, add *-ably* or *-ibly* where appropriate.)

Ē'SI.ER

FLĒ'SI.ER	fleecier
GRĒ'SI.ER	greasier
KRĒ'SI.ER	creasier

ES'I.KA

JES'I.KA	Jessica
VES'I.KA	vesica

ES'I.KANT

DES'I.KANT	desiccant
VES'I.KANT	vesicant

ES'I.KĀT

DES'I.KĀT	desiccate
VES'I.KĀT	vesicate

ES'I.MAL

DES'I.MAL	decimal, duodecimal, hexadecimal

JES'I.MAL	quadragesimal, quinquagesimal, nonagesimal, septuagesimal, sexagesimal, trigesimal, vigesimal
LES'I.MAL	millesimal
TES'I.MAL	infinitesimal, centesimal

ES'I.MEN

DES'I.MEN	quartodeciman
SPES'I.MEN	specimen

Ē'SING.LĒ

KRĒ'SING.LĒ	decreasingly, increasingly
SĒ'SING.LĒ	unceasingly

ES'ING.LĒ

PRES'ING.LĒ	depressingly, pressingly
RES'ING.LĒ	caressingly
TRES'ING.LĒ	distressingly
ZES'ING.LĒ	prepossessingly

ES'I.TĒ

BES'I.TĒ	obesity
SES'I.TĒ	necessity, cecity

ES'IV.LĒ

GRES'IV.LĒ	aggressively, digressively, progressively, regressively, transgressively
PRES'IV.LĒ	depressively, expressively, impressively, oppressively, repressively
SES'IV.LĒ	excessively, successively
ZES'IV.LĒ	possessively

ES'IV.NES

(See **ESIV**, add *-ness* where appropriate.)

ES'TA.BL

(See **ES'TI.BL**)

ES'TA.MENT

TES'TA.MENT	testament
VES'TA.MENT	vestiment

ES'TER.ING

FES'TER.ING	festering
KWES'TER.ING	sequestering
PES'TER.ING	pestering
WES'TER.ING	westering

EST'FUL.Ē

KWEST'FUL.Ē	questfully
REST'FUL.Ē	restfully
ZEST'FUL.Ē	zestfully

ES'TI.AL

(See **ESCHAL**)

ES'TI.BL

JES'TI.BL	digestible, indigestible, congestible, suggestible
MES'TI.BL	comestible
TES'TI.BL	detestable, incontestable, intestable, contestable, testable, untestable
VES'TI.BL	divestible

ES'TI.KL

JES'TI.KL	majestical
KRES'TI.KL	catachrestical
PES'TI.KL	anapestical
TES'TI.KL	testicle

ES'TI.MĀT

ES'TI.MĀT	estimate, overestimate, underestimate
GES'TI.MĀT	guesstimate

ES'TI.NAL

DES'TI.NAL	destinal, predestinal
TES'TI.NAL	intestinal

ES'TI.NĀT

DES'TI.NĀT	predestinate
FES'TI.NĀT	festinate

ĒS'TI.NES

RĒS'TI.NES	reastiness
YĒS'TI.NES	yeastiness

ES'TI.NES

RES'TI.NES	restiness
TES'TI.NES	testiness

ES'TING.LĒ

JES'TING.LĒ	jestingly
RES'TING.LĒ	interestingly, uninterestingly
TES'TING.LĒ	protestingly, testingly

ES'TIV.LĒ

FES'TIV.LĒ	festively
JES'TIV.LĒ	suggestively
RES'TIV.LĒ	restively

ES'TIV.NES

FES'TIV.NES	festiveness
JES'TIV.NES	suggestiveness
RES'TIV.NES	restiveness

ĒST'LI.NES

BĒST'LI.NES	beastliness
PRĒST'LI.NES	priestliness

EST'Ō.VERZ

EST'Ō.VERZ	estovers
REST'Ō.VERZ	rest-overs

ES'TRI.AL

DES'TRI.AL	pedestrial
MES'TRI.AL	bimestrial, decimestrial, trimestrial
RES'TRI.AL	extraterrestrial, superterrestrial, terrestrial

ES'TRI.AN

DES'TRI.AN	pedestrian
KWES'TRI.AN	equestrian
LES'TRI.AN	palestrian
PES'TRI.AN	campestrian, rupestrian
VES'TRI.AN	sylvestrian

ES'TRI.US

DES'TRI.US	pedestrious
RES'TRI.US	terrestrious

ES'TŪ.RAL

(See **ES'CHER.AL**)

ES'TŪ.US

(See **ES'CHOO.US**)

ĒT'A.BL

ĒT'A.BL	eatable, uneatable
BĒT'A.BL	beatable, unbeatable
CHĒT'A.BL	cheatable, escheatable, uncheatable
FĒT'A.BL	defeatable, undefeatable
HĒT'A.BL	heatable, preheatable, reheatable, unheatable
LĒT'A.BL	deletable, undeletable
PĒT'A.BL	repeatable, unrepeatable
SĒT'A.BL	seatable, unseatable
TRĒT'A.BL	entreatable, treatable, unentreatable, untreatable

ET'A.BL

GET'A.BL	begettable, forgettable, gettable, unforgettable, ungettable
HWET'A.BL	whettable
LET'A.BL	lettable
NET'A.BL	bayonettable, nettable
PET'A.BL	pettable
SET'A.BL	settable, unsettable, unupsettable, upsettable

ET'A.BLĒ

GET'A.BLĒ	forgettably, unforgettably
GRET'A.BLĒ	regrettably

ET'A.LĪN

(also -LIN)

MET'A.LĪN	metalline
PET'A.LĪN	petaline

ET'AL.IZM

MET'AL.IZM	bimetallism, monometallism
PET'AL.IZM	petalism

ET'A.LOID

MET'A.LOID	metalloid
PET'A.LOID	petaloid

ET'A.NĒ

BET'A.NĒ	betony
TET'A.NĒ	tetany

ĒT'ED.LE

FĒT'ED.LĒ	defeatedly, undefeatedly
HĒT'ED.LĒ	heatedly
PĒT'ED.LĒ	repeatedly

ET'ER.Ē

KRET'ER.Ē	secretory
PLET'ER.Ē	depletory, completory, repletory

Ē'TER.ING

MĒ'TER.ING	metering
PĒ'TER.ING	petering

ET'ER.ING

BET'ER.ING	bettering
FET'ER.ING	fettering
LET'ER.ING	lettering

ET'ER.IT

PRET'ER.IT	preterit, preterite
VET'ER.IT	inveterate

ET'FUL.Ē

FRET'FUL.Ē	fretfully
GET'FUL.Ē	forgetfully
GRET'FUL.Ē	regretfully

ET'FUL.NES

FRET'FUL.NES	fretfulness
GET'FUL.NES	forgetfulness
GRET'FUL.NES	regretfulness

ETH'A.NOL

ETH'A.NOL	ethanol
METH'A.NOL	methanol

ETH'ER.Ē

(TH as in then)

FETH'ER.Ē	feathery
HETH'ER.Ē	heathery
LETH'ER.Ē	leathery
TETH'ER.Ē	tethery
WETH'ER.Ē	weathery

ETH'ER.ING

(TH as in then)

FETH'ER.ING	feathering
LETH'ER.ING	leathering
TETH'ER.ING	tethering, untethering
WETH'ER.ING	weathering

ETH'I.KAL

ETH'I.KAL	ethical, non-ethical, unethical
LETH'I.KAL	alethical

ETH'I.LĀT

ETH'I.LĀT	ethylate
METH'I.LĀT	methylate

ETH'LES.LĒ

(TH as in thin)

BRETH'LES.LĒ	breathlessly
DETH'LES.LĒ	deathlessly

ETH'LES.NES

(TH as in thin)

BRETH'LES.NES	breathlessness
DETH'LES.NES	deathlessness

ET'I.KAL

ET'I.KAL	dianoetical, noetical, poetical, unpoetical
BET'I.KAL	alphabetical, analphabetical, diabetical
DET'I.KAL	syndetical
FET'I.KAL	prophetical
JET'I.KAL	apologetical, exegetical, energetical
KET'I.KAL	catachetical
KRET'I.KAL	syncretical
LET'I.KAL	athletical, homiletical
MET'I.KAL	arithmetical, emetical, hermetical, cosmetical, mismetical
NET'I.KAL	antimagnetical, isomagnetical, genetical, magnetical, planetical, thermomagnetical, threnetical
RET'I.KAL	anchoretical, diaphoretical, diuretical, emporetical, heretical, theoretical
SET'I.KAL	ascetical
TET'I.KAL	dietetical, peripatetical
THET'I.KAL	A antipathetical, antithetical, apathetical, E aesthetical, epithetical, F photosynthetical, H hyperthetical, hypothetical, M metathetical, N nomothetical, P parenthetical, pathetical, polysynthetical, S synthetical, TH thetical

ET'I.KŪL

ET'I.KŪL	poeticule
RET'I.KŪL	reticule

ĒT'I.NES

MĒT'I.NES	meatiness
PĒT'I.NES	peatiness
SLĒT'I.NES	sleetiness

ET'I.NES

JET'I.NES	jettiness
PET'I.NES	pettiness
SWET'I.NES	sweatiness

ET'IN.Ū

| DET'IN.Ū | detinue |
| RET'IN.Ū | retinue |

ET'ISH.LĒ

| KET'ISH.LĒ | coquettishly |
| PET'ISH.LĒ | pettishly |

ET'ISH.NES

| KET'ISH.NES | coquettishness |
| PET'ISH.NES | pettishness |

ET'I.SIZM

LET'I.SIZM	athleticism
NET'I.SIZM	phoneticism
SET'I.SIZM	asceticism
TET'I.SIZM	peripateticism
THET'I.SIZM	aestheticism

ET'I.TIV

| PET'I.TIV | competitive, noncompetitive, repetitive, uncompetitive |
| VET'I.TIV | vetitive |

ET'L.SUM

| MET'L.SUM | mettlesome |
| NET'L.SUM | nettlesome |

ET'RI.FĪ

| MET'RI.FĪ | metrify |
| PET'RI.FĪ | petrify |

ET'RI.KAL

| MET'RI.KAL | *A* alkalimetrical, asymmetrical, *B* barometrical, bisymmetrical, *D* diametrical, dynametrical, *GR* graphometrical, *H* hexametrical, heptometrical, horometrical, *I* isometrical, isoperimetrical, *J* geometrical, *K* kilometrical, *KL* clinometrical, *KR* craniometrical, chronometrical, *M* metrical, *P* pedometrical, perimetrical, *PL* planimetrical, pluviometrical, *S* symmetrical, *ST* stichometrical, *TR* trigonometrical, *U* unsymmetrical |
| STET'RI.KAL | obstetrical |

ĒV'A.BL

CHĒV'A.BL	achievable, unachievable
GRĒV'A.BL	grievable
HĒV'A.BL	heavable, unheavable
KLĒV'A.BL	cleavable, uncleavable
LĒV'A.BL	believable, relievable, unbelievable, unrelievable
SĒV'A.BL	deceivable, imperceivable, inconceivable, conceivable, perceivable, receivable, undeceivable

ĒV'A.BLĒ

(See ĒV'A.BL, add -y where appropriate.)

EV'A.LIN

| EV'A.LIN | Evalyn |
| SHEV'A.LIN | chevaline |

EV'EL.ER

BEV'EL.ER	beveler
DEV'EL.ER	bedeviler, deviler
LEV'EL.ER	leveler
REV'EL.ER	reveler
SHEV'EL.ER	disheveler, sheveler

EV'EL.ING

(See EVEL, add -ing where appropriate.)

EV'EL.IZM

| DEV'EL.IZM | devilism |
| LEV'EL.IZM | levelism |

EV'EL.MENT

DEV'EL.MENT	bedevilment, devilment
SHEV'EL.MENT	dishevelment, shevelment
REV'EL.MENT	revelment

EV'EL.RĒ

| DEV'EL.RĒ | devilry |
| REV'EL.RĒ | revelry |

EV'ER.ĀT

| LEV'ER.ĀT | levirate |
| SEV'ER.ĀT | asseverate |

EV'ER.Ē

| EV'ER.Ē | every |
| REV'ER.Ē | reverie |

EV'ER.ENS

| REV'ER.ENS | irreverence, reverence |
| SEV'ER.ENS | disseverance, severance |

EV'ER.ER

DEV'ER.ER	endeavorer
KLEV'ER.ER	cleverer
LEV'ER.ER	leverer
SEV'ER.ER	severer

EV'ER.EST

EV'ER.EST	Everest
KLEV'ER.EST	cleverest

(See **EVER,** add *-est* where appropriate for archaic verbs.)

EV'ER.IJ

BEV'ER.IJ	beverage
LEV'ER.IJ	leverage

EV'ER.ING

DEV'ER.ING	endeavoring
LEV'ER.ING	levering
SEV'ER.ING	severing

EV'ER.MŌR

EV'ER.MŌR	evermore
NEV'ER.MŌR	nevermore

Ē'VI.ĀT

BRĒ'VI.ĀT	abbreviate
DĒ'VI.ĀT	deviate
LĒ'VI.ĀT	alleviate

Ē'VISH.LĒ

PĒ'VISH.LĒ	peevishly
THĒ'VISH.LĒ	thievishly

Ē'VISH.NES

PĒ'VISH.NES	peevishness
THĒ'VISH.NES	thievishness

EV'I.TĒ

BREV'I.TĒ	brevity
JEV'I.TĒ	longevity
LEV'I.TĒ	levity

Ē'VI.US

DĒ'VI.US	devious
PRĒ'VI.US	previous

EV'O.LENS

LEV'O.LENS	malevolence
NEV'O.LENS	benevolence
PREV'O.LENS	prevalence

EV'O.LENT

LEV'O.LENT	malevolent
NEV'O.LENT	benevolent
PREV'O.LENT	prevalent

EV'O.LUS

LEV'O.LUS	malevolous
NEV'O.LUS	benevolous

EV'O.LŪT

EV'O.LŪT	evolute
DEV'O.LŪT	devolute
REV'O.LŪT	revolute

Ē'ZA.BL

FĒ'ZA.BL	defeasible, feasible, indefeasible, infeasible
FRĒ'ZA.BL	freezable
HĒ'ZA.BL	cohesible
PĒ'ZA.BL	appeasible, inappeasable, unappeasable
SĒ'ZA.BL	seizable
SKWĒ'ZA.BL	squeezable

EZ'AN.TRĒ

FEZ'AN.TRĒ	pheasantry
PEZ'AN.TRĒ	peasantry
PLEZ'AN.TRĒ	pleasantry

EZH'ER.ER

MEZH'ER.ER	measurer
PLEZH'ER.ER	pleasurer
TREZH'ER.ER	treasurer

EZH'ER.ING

MEZH'ER.ING	measuring
PLEZH'ER.ING	pleasuring
TREZH'ER.ING	treasuring

EZH'ER.LES

MEZH'ER.LES	measureless

PLEZH'ER.LES	pleasureless
TREZH'ER.LES	treasureless

Ē'ZHI.A

(See Ē'ZI.A)

Ē'ZHI.AN

(See ĒZHUN)

Ē'ZI.A

BĒ'ZI.A	framboesia, Zambesia
DĒ'ZI.A	Rhodesia
FRĒ'ZI.A	freesia, oxyosphresia
JĒ'ZI.A	analgesia, hyperthermalgesia
KLĒ'ZI.A	ecclesia
LĒ'ZI.A	silesia, Silesia
MĒ'ZI.A	iatromisia
NĒ'ZI.A	amnesia, hyperkinesia, hypermnesia, Indonesia, magnesia, neomnesia, paleomnesia, paramnesia, pseudomnesia, Tunisia
PĒ'ZI.A	trapezia
RĒ'ZI.A	parrhesia
THĒ'ZI.A	anesthesia, esthesia, hyperesthesia, hypesthesia, kinesthesia, cryptesthesia, oxyesthesia, radiesthesia, synesthesia, telesthesia, thermanesthesia, thermesthesia, zonesthesia

(See ĒZHA)

Ē'ZI.AN

FĒ'ZI.AN	Ephesian
KLĒ'ZI.AN	ecclesian
PĒ'ZI.AN	trapezian
TĒ'ZI.AN	Artesian, etesian, Cartesian

(See ĒZHUN)

Ē′ZI.BL

(See Ē′ZA.BL)

EZ′I.DENT

PREZ′I.DENT	president, vice-president
REZ′I.DENT	resident, non-resident

Ē′ZI.ER

Ē′ZI.ER	easier, uneasier
BRĒ′ZI.ER	breezier
CHĒ′ZI.ER	cheesier
GRĒ′ZI.ER	greasier
HWĒ′ZI.ER	wheezier
KWĒ′ZI.ER	queasier
SLĒ′ZI.ER	sleazier
SNĒ′ZI.ER	sneezier

Ē′ZI.LĒ

Ē′ZI.LĒ	easily, uneasily
BRĒ′ZI.LĒ	breezily
CHĒ′ZI.LĒ	cheesily
GRĒ′ZI.LĒ	greasily
HWĒ′ZI.LĒ	wheezily
KWĒ′ZI.LĒ	queasily
SLĒ′ZI.LĒ	sleazily
SNĒ′ZI.LĒ	sneezily

Ē′ZI.NES

(See ĒZĒ, add -ness where appropriate.)

ĒZ′ING.LĒ

FRĒZ′ING.LĒ	freezingly
HWĒZ′ING.LĒ	wheezingly
PĒZ′ING.LĒ	appeasingly
PLĒZ′ING.LĒ	displeasingly, pleasingly
SNĒZ′ING.LĒ	sneezingly
TĒZ′ING.LĒ	teasingly

Ē′ZUN.A.BL

RĒ′ZUN.A.BL	reasonable, unreasonable
SĒ′ZUN.A.BL	seasonable, unseasonable
TRĒ′ZUN.A.BL	treasonable, untreasonable

Ē′ZUN.ER

RĒ′ZUN.ER	reasoner
SĒ′ZUN.ER	seasoner

Ē′ZUN.ING

RĒ′ZUN.ING	reasoning, unreasoning
SĒ′ZUN.ING	seasoning

Ī′A.BL

Ī′A.BL	eyeable
FĪ′A.BL	A acidifiable, D diversifiable, E electrifiable, exemplifiable, F falsifiable, fortifiable, I identifiable, J justifiable, KL classifiable, KW qualifiable, L liquefiable, M magnifiable, modifiable, P pacifiable, petrifiable, R rarefiable, rectifiable, S sanctifiable, saponifiable, satisfiable, solidifiable, U unidentifiable, unjustifiable, V verifiable, vitrifiable
FRĪ′A.BL	friable
LĪ′A.BL	liable, reliable, unreliable
NĪ′A.BL	deniable, undeniable
PLĪ′A.BL	appliable, impliable, compliable, multipliable, pliable
TRĪ′A.BL	triable
VĪ′A.BL	viable

Ī′A.BLĒ

FĪ′A.BLĒ	justifiably, unjustifiably
LĪ′A.BLĒ	liably, reliably, unreliably
NĪ′A.BLĒ	deniably, undeniably
PLĪ′A.BLĒ	appliably, compliably, pliably

Ī′A.DĒZ

DRĪ′A.DĒZ	dryades, hamadryades
HĪ′A.DĒZ	Hyades
NĪ′A.DĒZ	naiades
PLĪ′A.DĒZ	Pleiades

Ī′A.GRAM

DĪ′A.GRAM	diagram
SKĪ′A.GRAM	skiagram
VĪ′A.GRAM	viagram

Ī′A.KAL

DĪ′A.KAL	dandiacal, encyclopediacal, cardiacal, prosodiacal, zodiacal
DRĪ′A.KAL	hypochondriacal
JĪ′A.KAL	elegiacal
LĪ′A.KAL	heliacal
NĪ′A.KAL	bibliomaniacal, demoniacal, dipsomaniacal, kleptomaniacal, maniacal, pyromaniacal, simoniacal
RĪ′A.KAL	theriacal
ZĪ′A.KAL	paradisiacal

Ī′A.LIN

HĪ′A.LIN	hyaline
TĪ′A.LIN	ptyalin
VĪ′A.LIN	violin

Ī′A.LĪT

HĪ′A.LĪT	hyalite
KRĪ′A.LĪT	cryolite
RĪ′A.LĪT	rhyolite

Ī′A.LIZM

MĪ′A.LIZM	myalism
TĪ′A.LIZM	ptyalism

Ī′A.LOID

HĪ′A.LOID	hyaloid
STĪ′A.LOID	styaloid

Ī'AN.SĒ

KLĪ'AN.SĒ	cliency
PLĪ'AN.SĒ	compliancy, pliancy
RĪ'AN.SĒ	riancy

Ī'ANT.LĒ

FĪ'ANT.LĒ	defiantly
LĪ'ANT.LĒ	reliantly
PLĪ'ANT.LĒ	compliantly, pliantly, uncompliantly

Ī'A.RĒ

(See Ī'E.RĒ)

Ī'A.RIST

DĪ'A.RIST	diarist
PĪ'A.RIST	Piarist

Ī'ÄR.KĒ

DĪ'ÄR.KĒ	diarchy
JĪ'ÄR.KĒ	hagiarchy
TRĪ'ÄR.KĒ	triarchy

Ī'A.SIS

BĪ'A.SIS	amoebiasis
DĪ'A.SIS	archdiocese, diocese
DRĪ'A.SIS	hypochondriasis, mydriasis
FĪ'A.SIS	gomphiasis
KĪ'A.SIS	psychiasis, trichiasis
MĪ'A.SIS	myasis, schistosomiasis, trypanosomiasis
NĪ'A.SIS	leishmaniasis, pogoniasis, teniasis
RĪ'A.SIS	acariasis, ascariasis, filariasis, satyriasis, psoriasis
THĪ'A.SIS	lithiasis
TĪ'A.SIS	elephantiasis, odontiasis
ZĪ'A.SIS	bilharziasis

Ī'A.SIZM

DRĪ'A.SIZM	hypochondriacism
NĪ'A.SIZM	demoniacism

Ī'A.SKŌP

BĪ'A.SKŌP	bioscope
DĪ'A.SKŌP	diascope, apidiascope
SKĪ'A.SKŌP	skiascope

Ī'A.TER

KĪ'A.TER	archiater, psychiater
PĪ'A.TER	hippiater

Ī'A.TRĒ

DĪ'A.TRĒ	podiatry
KĪ'A.TRĒ	antipsychiatry, neuropsychiatry, psychiatry
NĪ'A.TRĒ	phoniatry
PĪ'A.TRĒ	hippiatry

Ī'A.TRIST

DĪ'A.TRIST	podiatrist
KĪ'A.TRIST	psychiatrist
PĪ'A.TRIST	hippiatrist

ĪB'A.BL

BRĪB'A.BL	bribable, unbribable
SKRĪB'A.BL	A ascribable, D describable, I indescribable, inscribable, P postscribable, PR prescribable, S circumscribable, subscribable, SK scribable, U undescribable, uninscribable, unscribable

IB'ET.ED

(See IBET, add -ed where appropriate.)

IB'ET.ING

(See IBET, add -ing where appropriate.)

IB'ET.IV

(See IBET, add -ive where appropriate.)

IB'I.A

FIB'I.A	amphibia
TIB'I.A	tibia

(See IBYA)

IB'I.AL

FIB'I.AL	amphibial
STIB'I.AL	stibial
TIB'I.AL	tibial

IB'I.AN

FIB'I.AN	amphibian
LIB'I.AN	Lybian
THIB'I.AN	bathybian

IB'ING.LĒ

BIB'ING.LĒ	bibbingly
FIB'ING.LĒ	fibbingly
JIB'ING.LĒ	jibbingly
KRIB'ING.LĒ	cribbingly
LIB'ING.LĒ	ad libbingly
RIB'ING.LĒ	ribbingly
SKWIB'ING.LĒ	squibbingly

IB'IT.ER

HIB'IT.ER	inhibiter, inhibitor, cohibitor, noninhibitor, prohibiter, prohibitor
ZIB'IT.ER	exhibitor, nonexhibitor

IB'I.US

FIB'I.US	amphibious, triphibious
LIB'I.US	Polybius
STIB'I.US	stibious
THIB'I.US	bathybius

IB'Ū.LAR

DIB'Ū.LAR	infundibular, mandibular
FIB'Ū.LAR	fibular
STIB'Ū.LAR	vestibular

ICH'E.RĀT

BICH'E.RĀT	barbiturate
LICH'E.RĀT	liturate
TRICH'E.RĀT	triturate

ICH'E.RĒ

BICH'E.RĒ	bitchery
FICH'E.RĒ	fitchery
MICH'E.RĒ	michery
PICH'ER.Ē	pituri
STICH'E.RĒ	stitchery
WICH'E.RĒ	bewitchery, witchery

ICH'E.TĒ

TWICH'E.TĒ	twitchety
WICH'E.TĒ	witchetty

ICH'ING.LĒ

ICH'ING.LĒ	itchingly
PICH'ING.LĒ	pitchingly
RICH'ING.LĒ	enrichingly
SWICH'ING.LĒ	switchingly
TWICH'ING.LĒ	twitchingly
WICH'ING.LĒ	bewitchingly, witchingly

ICH'I.NES

(See ICHĒ, add -ness)

ICH'OO.AL

BICH'OO.AL	habitual, obitual, unhabitual
RICH'OO.AL	ritual
SICH'OO.AL	situal

ICH'OO.ĀT

BICH'OO.ĀT	habituate
SICH'OO.ĀT	situate

ICH'OO.LER

PICH'OO.LER	capitular
MICH'OO.LER	amitular
TICH'OO.LER	titular

ĪD'A.BL

GĪD'A.BL	guidable, unguidable
HĪD'A.BL	hidable
LĪD'A.BL	elidable
RĪD'A.BL	ridable, unridable
SĪD'A.BL	decidable, undecidable
STRĪD'A.BL	bestridable
VĪD'A.BL	dividable, providable, undividable, unprovidable

ID'A.BL

BID'A.BL	biddable, forbiddable, rebiddable, unbiddable, unforbiddable
KID'A.BL	kiddable, unkiddable

Ī'DED.LĒ

(See ĪD, add -edly where appropriate.)

ID'EN.NES

BID'EN.NES	forbiddenness
HID'EN.NES	hiddenness

ID'I.AL

SID'I.AL	presidial
TID'I.AL	noctidial

ID'I.AN

FID'I.AN	nullifidian, ophidian, solifidian, ultrafidian
GID'I.AN	Gideon
KID'I.AN	rachidian
KLID'I.AN	Euclidean
LID'I.AN	Lydian
MID'I.AN	Numidian
NID'I.AN	anidian
PID'I.AN	taxaspidean
RID'I.AN	antemeridian, enchiridion, meridian, post-meridian, viridian
SID'I.AN	ascidian, obsidian, proboscidean
TID'I.AN	quotidian
VID'I.AN	Dravidian, Ovidian

ID'I.ĀT

MID'I.ĀT	dimidiate
SID'I.ĀT	insidiate

ID'I.FĪ

ID'I.FĪ	fluidify
JID'I.FĪ	rigidify
LID'I.FĪ	solidify
MID'I.FĪ	humidify, dehumidify
NID'I.FĪ	nidify
PID'I.FĪ	lapidify
SID'I.FĪ	acidify, rancidify

ID'I.KAL

ID'I.KAL	druidical
MID'I.KAL	pyramidical
RID'I.KAL	juridical, veridical
SID'I.KAL	spurcidical
ZID'I.KAL	causidical

ĪD'ING.LĒ

BĪD'ING.LĒ	abidingly
CHĪD'ING.LĒ	chidingly, unchidingly
FĪD'ING.LĒ	confidingly
GĪD'ING.LĒ	guidingly, misguidingly
GLĪD'ING.LĒ	glidingly
HĪD'ING.LĒ	hidingly, unhidingly
SĪD'ING.LĒ	sidingly
SLĪD'ING.LĒ	slidingly
STRĪD'ING.LĒ	stridingly

ID'I.NUS

BID'I.NUS	libidinous
GWID'I.NUS	pinguidinous

ID'I.OM

(See ID'I.UM)

ID'I.TĒ

ID'I.TĒ	fluidity, superfluidity
BID'I.TĒ	morbidity, rabidity, turbidity
BRID'I.TĒ	hybridity
GWID'I.TĒ	pinguidity
JID'I.TĒ	algidity, frigidity, rigidity, turgidity

KRID'I.TĒ acridity
KWID'I.TĒ quiddity, liquidity
LID'I.TĒ insolidity,
invalidity, gelidity,
calidity, pallidity,
solidity, squalidity,
stolidity, validity
MID'I.TĒ humidity, timidity,
tumidity
PID'I.TĒ *H* hispidity, *I*
insipidity,
intrepidity, *K*
cupidity, *L*
limpidity, *R*
rapidity, *S* sapidity,
ST stupidity, *T*
tepidity, torpidity,
TR trepidity, *V*
vapidity
RID'I.TĒ aridity, floridity,
torridity, viridity
SID'I.TĒ acidity, flaccidity,
hyperacidity,
hypoacidity,
lucidity, marcidity,
pellucidity,
placidity, rancidity,
translucidity, viscidity
TID'I.TĒ putidity
TRID'I.TĒ putridity
VID'I.TĒ avidity, gravidity,
lividity, pavidity,
vividity

ID'I.UM

ID'I.UM idiom, oïdium,
Oïdium
BID'I.UM rubidium
FRID'I.UM nephridium
KID'I.UM glochidium
NID'I.UM gonidium,
conidium, ctenidium
RID'I.UM ante meridiem,
antheridium,
hesperidium,
iridium, osmiridium,
peridium, post
meridiem
SID'I.UM basidium,
miracidium,
presidium, psidium,
cecidium
TRID'I.UM clostridium

ID'I.US

DID'I.US splendidious
FID'I.US ophidious,
perfidious, Phidias

HID'I.US hideous
MID'I.US chlamydeous
PID'I.US lapideous
SID'I.US insidious,
parricidious,
stillicidious
TID'I.US fastidious
VID'I.US invidious

ID'Ū.AL

(See IJ'ŌŌ.AL)

ID'Ū.ĀT

(See IJ'ŌŌ.ĀT)

ID'Ū.LĀT

(See IJ'ŌŌ.LĀT)

ID'Ū.LUS

(See IJ'ŌŌ.LUS)

ID'U.US

(See IJ'ŌŌ.US)

Ī'EN.SĒ

(See Ī'AN.SĒ)

Ī'E.RĒ

BRĪ'E.RĒ briary, briery
DĪ'E.RĒ diary
FĪ'E.RĒ fiery
FRĪ'E.RĒ friary
LĪ'E.RĒ lyery
PRĪ'E.RĒ priory

(See ĪRĒ)

Ī'E.TAL

DĪ'E.TAL dietal
HĪ'E.TAL hyetal, isohyetal
RĪ'E.TAL parietal, varietal
SĪ'E.TAL societal

Ī'E.TĒ

BĪ'E.TĒ dubiety, nullibiety,
ubiety
BRĪ'E.TĒ ebriety, inebriety,
insobriety, sobriety
DĪ'E.TĒ mediety
LĪ'E.TĒ filiety
MĪ'E.TĒ nimiety

NĪ'E.TĒ omniety
PĪ'E.TĒ impiety, piety
PRĪ'E.TĒ impropriety,
propriety
RĪ'E.TĒ contrariety,
luxuriety, notoriety,
variety
SĪ'E.TĒ society
TĪ'E.TĒ satiety
ZĪ'E.TĒ anxiety

Ī'ET.ED

DĪ'ET.ED dieted
KWĪ'ET.ED disquieted, quieted,
unquieted
RĪ'ET.ED rioted

Ī'ET.ER

DĪ'ET.ER dieter
KWĪ'ET.ER disquieter, quieter
PRĪ'ET.ER proprietor
RĪ'ET.ER rioter

Ī'ET.ING

DĪ'ET.ING dieting
KWĪ'ET.ING disquieting, quieting
RĪ'ET.ING rioting

Ī'E.TIST

PĪ'E.TIST pietist
PRĪ'E.TIST proprietist
RĪ'E.TIST varietist
ZĪ'E.TIST anxietist

Ī'E.TIZM

KWĪ'E.TIZM quietism
PĪ'E.TIZM pietism
RĪ'E.TIZM varietism

Ī'FE.NĀT

HĪ'FE.NĀT hyphenate
SĪ'FE.NĀT siphonate

IF'E.NĒ

LIF'E.NĒ polyphony
PIF'E.NĒ epiphany
SIF'E.NĒ oxyphony

TIF'E.NĒ   antiphony, tiffany,
                  Tiffany
TRIF'E.NĒ   triphony

IF'ER.ĀT

LIF'ER.ĀT   proliferate
SIF'ER.ĀT   vociferate

IF'ER.US

IF'ER.US   oleiferous
BIF'ER.US   bulbiferous,
                  herbiferous,
                  limbiferous,
                  morbiferous,
                  nimbiferous,
                  nubiferous,
                  plumbiferous
BRIF'ER.US   umbriferous
DIF'ER.US   acidiferous,
                  diamondiferous,
                  frondiferous,
                  glandiferous,
                  geodiferous,
                  splendiferous
GWIF'ER.US   sanguiferous
JIF'ER.US   frugiferous,
                  tergiferous
KIF'ER.US   branchiferous,
                  conchiferous,
                  zinciferous
KRIF'ER.US   lucriferous
KWIF'ER.US   aquiferous
LIF'ER.US   *A* aliferous, *F*
                  favilliferous,
                  filiferous, foliferous,
                  fossiliferous, *GL*
                  glanduliferous, *GR*
                  granuliferous, *K*
                  cheliferous,
                  cauliferous,
                  coraliferous, *L*
                  lameliferous, *M*
                  maculiferous,
                  maliferous,
                  mammaliferous,
                  melliferous,
                  metalliferous, *N*
                  nickeliferous, *P*
                  papilliferous,
                  papuliferous,
                  petroliferous,
                  piliferous,
                  pistilliferous, *PR*
                  proliferous, *R*
                  ramuliferous, *S*
                  saliferous,
                  celliferous,
                  soboliferous, *ST*

MIF'ER.US   stelliferous, *T*
                  tentaculiferous, *U*
                  umbelliferous,
                  umbraculiferous, *V*
                  vasculiferous,
                  veliferous
                  A armiferous,
                  atomiferous, *B*
                  balsamiferous, *F*
                  fumiferous, *FL*
                  flammiferous, *J*
                  gemmiferous, *K*
                  coniferous, *M*
                  mammiferous, *P*
                  palmiferous,
                  pomiferous, *R*
                  ramiferous,
                  racemiferous
NIF'ER.US   *A* aluminiferous,
                  antenniferous, *B*
                  balaniferous, *GR*
                  graniferous, *I*
                  igniferous, *K*
                  carboniferous,
                  coniferous, *L*
                  laniferous,
                  ligniferous,
                  luminiferous, *M*
                  membraniferous, *O*
                  omniferous,
                  ozoniferous, *P*
                  penniferous,
                  pulmoniferous, *PL*
                  platiniferous, *PR*
                  pruniferous, *R*
                  resiniferous, *S*
                  saliniferous,
                  somniferous,
                  soniferous, *ST*
                  stanniferous,
                  stoloniferous, *V*
                  veneniferous
                  polypiferous,
                  scopiferous
PIF'ER.US

RIF'ER.US   *D* doloriferous, *F*
                  ferriferous, *FL*
                  floriferous, *H*
                  hederiferous, *K*
                  calcariferous,
                  cupriferous, *L*
                  lauriferous, *N*
                  nectariferous, *O*
                  odoriferous,
                  auriferous, *P*
                  poriferous, *R*
                  roriferous, *S*
                  sacchariferous,
                  ceriferous,
                  cirriferous,
                  soporiferous,
                  sudoriferous, *T*
                  tuberiferous, *TH*

                  thuriferous, *V*
                  vaporiferous
SIF'ER.US   *B* bacciferous,
                  boraciferous, *F*
                  furciferous, *J*
                  gypsiferous, *K*
                  calciferous,
                  calyciferous,
                  corticiferous, *KR*
                  cruciferous, *KW*
                  quartziferous, *L*
                  lanciferous,
                  laticiferous,
                  luciferous, *M*
                  muciferous, *N*
                  nuciferous, *O*
                  ossiferous, *S*
                  sensiferous,
                  siliciferous,
                  succiferous, *SP*
                  spiciferous, *V*
                  vociferous, *Z*
                  zucciferous
STRIF'ER.US   monstriferous,
                  rostriferous
THIF'ER.US   lethiferous
TIF'ER.US   *A* ammonitiferous,
                  argentiferous, *D*
                  diamantiferous, *E*
                  estiferous, *F*
                  fatiferous, *FL*
                  fluctiferous, *FR*
                  fructiferous, *K*
                  chaetiferous, *L*
                  lactiferous,
                  lignitiferous,
                  luctiferous, *M*
                  magnetiferous,
                  margaritiferous,
                  mortiferous,
                  multiferous, *N*
                  noctiferous, *O*
                  oölitiferous, *P*
                  pestiferous, *S*
                  salutiferous,
                  setiferous, *SK*
                  scutiferous
TRIF'ER.US   astriferous,
                  nitriferous,
                  ostriferous
VIF'ER.US   oviferous,
                  valviferous

IF'I.KAL

NIF'I.KAL   magnifical
RIF'I.KAL   mirifical, saporifical
SIF'I.KAL   pacifical, specifical
TIF'I.KAL   beatifical, lactifical,
                  pontifical
VIF'I.KAL   vivifical

IF'I.KANT

DIF'I.KANT	mundificant, nidificant
NIF'I.KANT	insignificant, significant
RIF'I.KANT	sacrificant

IF'I.KĀT

DIF'I.KĀT	nidificate
LIF'I.KĀT	improlificate, prolificate
SIF'I.KĀT	pacificate
TIF'I.KĀT	pontificate, certificate
TRIF'I.KĀT	nostrificate

ĬF'LING.LĒ

| TRĬF'LING.LĒ | triflingly |
| STĬF'LING.LĒ | stiflingly |

IF'LOO.US

| GWIF'LOO.US | sanguifluous |
| LIF'LOO.US | fellifluous, mellifluous |

IF'O.NĒ

(See IF'A.NĒ)

IFT'A.BL

LIFT'A.BL	liftable
SHIFT'A.BL	shiftable
SIFT'A.BL	siftable

IF'TI.LĒ

NIF'TI.LĒ	niftily
SHIF'TI.LĒ	shiftily
THRIF'TI.LĒ	thriftily

IF'TI.NES

NIF'TI.NES	niftiness
SHIF'TI.NES	shiftiness
THRIF'TI.NES	thriftiness

IFT'LES.LĒ

SHIFT'LES.LĒ	shiftlessly
SHRIFT'LES.LĒ	shriftlessly
THRIFT'LES.LĒ	thriftlessly

IF'Ū.GAL

BRIF'Ū.GAL	febrifugal
MIF'Ū.GAL	vermifugal
TRIF'Ū.GAL	centrifugal

IF'Ū.GUS

DIF'Ū.GUS	nidifugous
MIF'Ū.GUS	vermifugous
NIF'Ū.GUS	somnifugous
SIF'Ū.GUS	lucifugous

IG'A.MĒ

BIG'A.MĒ	bigamy
DIG'A.MĒ	digamy
LIG'A.MĒ	polygamy
SIG'A.MĒ	opsigamy
TRIG'A.MĒ	trigamy

IG'A.MIST

BIG'A.MIST	bigamist
DIG'A.MIST	digamist
LIG'A.MIST	polygamist
RIG'A.MIST	quadrigamist
TRIG'A.MIST	trigamist

IG'A.MUS

BIG'A.MUS	bigamous
DIG'A.MUS	digamous, myriadigamous
LIG'A.MUS	polygamous
TRIG'A.MUS	trigamous

IG'ER.Ē

HWIG'ER.Ē	whiggery, Whiggery
PIG'ER.Ē	piggery
TRIG'ER.Ē	triggery
WIG'ER.Ē	wiggery

IG'ER.US

| RIG'ER.US | rigorous |
| VIG'ER.US | vigorous |

IG'ET.Ē

| BIG'ET.Ē | biggety |
| SPIG'ET.Ē | spigotty |

IG'HED'ED.NES

| BIG'HED'ED.NES | bigheadedness |
| PIG'HED'ED.NES | pigheadedness |

IG'MA.TIST

| NIG'MA.TIST | enigmatist |
| STIG'MA.TIST | stigmatist |

IG'MA.TĪZ

DIG'MA.TĪZ	paradigmatize
NIG'MA.TĪZ	enigmatize
STIG'MA.TĪZ	stigmatize

IG'NAN.SĒ

DIG'NAN.SĒ	indignancy
LIG'NAN.SĒ	malignancy
NIG'NAN.SĒ	benignancy

IG'NANT.LĒ

DIG'NANT.LĒ	indignantly
LIG'NANT.LĒ	malignantly
NIG'NANT.LĒ	benignantly

IG'NI.FĪ

IG'NI.FĪ	ignify
DIG'NI.FĪ	dignify, condignify, undignify
LIG'NI.FĪ	lignify, malignify
SIG'NI.FĪ	presignify, signify

IG'NI.TĒ

DIG'NI.TĒ	dignity, indignity, condignity
LIG'NI.TĒ	malignity
NIG'NI.TĒ	benignity

IG'NI.US

IG'NI.US	igneous
LIG'NI.US	ligneous, pyroligneous
SIG'NI.US	cygneous

IG'O.NAL

| LIG'O.NAL | polygonal |
| TRIG'O.NAL | ditrigonal, trigonal |

IG'OR.US

(See IG'ER.US)

IG'RA.FĒ

KIG'RA.FĒ	tachygraphy
LIG'RA.FĒ	calligraphy, polygraphy
PIG'RA.FĒ	epigraphy, pseudepigraphy
SIG'RA.FĒ	lexigraphy, pasigraphy
TIG'RA.FĒ	stratigraphy

IG'Ū.LĀT

FIG'Ū.LĀT	figulate
LIG'Ū.LĀT	ligulate

IG'Ū.US

BIG'Ū.US	ambiguous
RIG'Ū.US	irriguous
TIG'Ū.US	contiguous
ZIG'Ū.US	exiguous

Ī'ING.LĒ

Ī'ING.LĒ	eyeingly
FĪ'ING.LĒ	defyingly, gratifyingly, mystifyingly, satisfyingly
FLĪ'ING.LĒ	flyingly
LĪ'ING.LĒ	lyingly
PRĪ'ING.LĒ	pryingly
SĪ'ING.LĒ	sighingly
VĪ'ING.LĒ	vyingly

IJ'E.NUS

BIJ'E.NUS	ambigenous, nubigenous, rubigenous
DIJ'E.NUS	digenous, indigenous
GWIJ'E.NUS	sanguigenous
LIJ'E.NUS	alkaligenous, fuliginous, caliginous, cauligenous, coralligenous, melligenous, nepheligenous, polygenous, uliginous
NIJ'E.NUS	ignigenous, omnigenous, unigenous
PIJ'E.NUS	epigenous
RIJ'E.NUS	marigenous, pruriginous, rurigenous, terrigenous
SIJ'E.NUS	oxygenous
TIJ'E.NUS	gelatigenous, lentigenous, montigenous, tentiginous, vertigenous, vortigenous

IJ'E.RĀT

BIJ'E.RĀT	verbigerate
FRIJ'E.RĀT	refrigerate
LIJ'E.RĀT	belligerate
RIJ'E.RĀT	hederigerate

IJ'ER.ENT

FRIJ'ER.ENT	refrigerant
LIJ'ER.ENT	belligerent
RIJ'ER.ENT	hederigerent

IJ'ER.US

DIJ'ER.US	pedigerous
LIJ'ER.US	aligerous, belligerous, coraligerous, peligerous, veligerous
MIJ'ER.US	armigerous, plumigerous
NIJ'ER.US	cornigerous, lanigerous, linigerous, pennigerous, spinigerous
PIJ'ER.US	palpigerous
RIJ'ER.US	immorigerous, morigerous, cirrigerous
SIJ'ER.US	discigerous, crucigerous
TIJ'ER.US	dentigerous, setigerous
VIJ'ER.US	navigerous, ovigerous

IJ'I.A

BRIJ'I.A	Cantabrigia
FLIJ'I.A	oenophilygia
FRIJ'I.A	Phrygia
JIJ'I.A	Ogygia
PIJ'I.A	pygia, steatopygia
TIJ'I.A	fastigia

IJ'I.AN

BRIJ'I.AN	Cantabrigian
FRIJ'I.AN	Phrygian
JIJ'I.AN	Ogygian
PIJ'I.AN	Callipygian, steatopygian
RIJ'I.AN	acanthopterygian, crossopterygian, malacopterygian
STIJ'I.AN	Stygian
TIJ'I.AN	vestigian

IJ'ID.LĒ

FRIJ'ID.LĒ	frigidly
RIJ'ID.LĒ	rigidly

IJ'ID.NES

FRIJ'ID.NES	frigidness
RIJ'ID.NES	rigidness

IJ'I.TĒ

DIJ'I.TĒ	digiti
FIJ'I.TĒ	fidgety
MIJ'I.TĒ	midgety

IJ'IT.ER

FIJ'IT.ER	fidgeter
LIJ'I.TER	subintelligitur

IJ'I.UM

FRIJ'I.UM	phrygium
PIJ'I.UM	uropygium
RIJ'I.UM	pterygium
TIJ'I.UM	fastigium
ZIJ'I.UM	syzygium

IJ'OO.AL

VIJ'OO.AL	individual, dividual
ZIJ'OO.AL	residual

IJ'OO.ĀT

| SIJ'OO.ĀT | assiduate |
| VIJ'OO.ĀT | individuate |

IJ'OO.LĀT

NIJ'OO.LĀT	nidulate
SIJ'OO.LĀT	acidulate
STRIJ'OO.LĀT	stridulate

IJ'OO.LUS

| SIJ'OO.LUS | acidulous |
| STRIJ'OO.LUS | stridulous |

IJ'OO.US

IJ'OO.US	druiduous
BIJ'OO.US	biduous
SIJ'OO.US	assiduous, deciduous, occiduous, prociduous, succiduous
VIJ'OO.US	viduous
ZIJ'OO.US	residuous

IJ'US.LĒ

DIJ'US.LĒ	prodigiously
LIJ'US.LĒ	irreligiously, religiously
TIJ'US.LĒ	litigiously

IJ'US.NES

DIJ'US.NES	prodigiousness
LIJ'US.NES	religiousness
TIJ'US.NES	litigiousness, prestigiousness

ĬK'A.BL

| LĬK'A.BL | dislikable, likable, unlikable |
| SPĬK'A.BL | spikable, unspikable |

ED'IK'A.MENT

| MED'IK'A.MENT | *medicament* |
| PRED'IK'A.MENT | *predicament* |

IK'A.TIV

DIK'A.TIV	abdicative, *applicative*, indicative, *judicative*, predicative, vindicative
FRIK'A.TIV	affricative, fricative
NIK'A.TIV	*communicative*
PLIK'A.TIV	explicative, *multiplicative*, plicative
SIK'A.TIV	desiccative, exsiccative, siccative

IK'A.TRIS

| FRIK'A.TRIS | fricatrice |
| SIK'A.TRIS | cicatrice |

IK'EN.ER

| KWIK'EN.ER | quickener |
| THIK'EN.ER | thickener |

IK'EN.ING

KWIK'EN.ING	quickening
SIK'EN.ING	sickening
THIK'EN.ING	thickening

IK'ER.Ē

IK'ER.Ē	ikary
CHIK'E.RĒ	chicory
HIK'E.RĒ	hickory
LIK'E.RĒ	lickery, liquory
MIK'E.RĒ	mickery
SIK'E.RĒ	terpsichore
TRIK'E.RĒ	trickery

IK'ER.ING

BIK'ER.ING	bickering
DIK'ER.ING	dickering
FLIK'ER.ING	flickering
SNIK'ER.ING	snickering

IK'ET.Ē

KRIK'ET.Ē	crickety
NIK'ET.Ē	pernickety
RIK'ET.Ē	rickety
SNIK'ET.Ē	persnickety
THIK'ET.Ē	thickety

IK'ET.ER

KRIK'ET.ER	cricketer
PIK'ET.ER	picketer, picqueter
TIK'ET.ER	ticketer

IK'ET.ING

KRIK'ET.ING	cricketing
PIK'ET.ING	picketing
TIK'ET.ING	ticketing

IK'I.LĒ

| STIK'I.LĒ | stickily |
| TRIK'I.LĒ | trickily |

IK'I.NES

| STIK'I.NES | stickiness |
| TRIK'I.NES | trickiness |

IK'LI.NES

| PRIK'LI.NES | prickliness |
| SIK'LI.NES | sickliness |

IK'O.LIST

BIK'O.LIST	plebicolist
NIK'O.LIST	ignicolist
RIK'O.LIST	agricolist

IK'O.LUS

BIK'O.LUS	plebicolous, urbicolous
DIK'O.LUS	nidicolous
MIK'O.LUS	fimicolous, limicolous
NIK'O.LUS	arenicolous, Father Nicholas, sphagnicolous, stagnicolous
PIK'O.LUS	sepicolous
RIK'O.LUS	agricolous, maricolous, stercoricolous, terricolous
SIK'O.LUS	saxicolous
VIK'O.LUS	silvicolous

IK'O.MUS

| RIK'O.MUS | auricomous |
| VIK'O.MUS | flavicomous |

IK'O.PĒ

| RIK'O.PĒ | pericope |
| WIK'O.PĒ | wicopy |

IK'O.RĒ

(See IK'ER.Ē)

Ī'KRO.MAT.IK

| BĪ'KRO.MAT.IK | *bichromatic* |
| DĪ'KRO.MAT.IK | *dichromatic* |

IK'SA.BL

| FIK'SA.BL | fixable, unfixable |
| MIK'SA.BL | immixable, mixable, unmixable |

IK'SED.LĒ

| FIK'SED.LĒ | fixedly |
| MIK'SED.LĒ | mixedly |

IK'SHUN.AL

DIK'SHUN.AL	benedictional, jurisdictional, contradictional, maledictional
FIK'SHUN.AL	fictional, nonfictional
FRIK'SHUN.AL	frictional
VIK'SHUN.AL	convictional

IK'SI.TĒ

FIK'SI.TĒ	fixity
LIK'SI.TĒ	prolixity
NIK'SI.TĒ	phoenixity
SIK'SI.TĒ	siccity

IK'TA.BL

DIK'TA.BL	contradictable, predictable, unpredictable
STRIK'TA.BL	restrictable, unrestrictable
VIK'TA.BL	convictable, unconvictable

IK'TIV.LĒ

DIK'TIV.LĒ	predictively, vindictively
FIK'TIV.LĒ	fictively
FLIK'TIV.LĒ	conflictively
STRIK'TIV.LĒ	constrictively, nonrestrictively, restrictively

IK'TIV.NES

DIK'TIV.NES	predictiveness, vindictiveness
FIK'TIV.NES	fictiveness
FLIK'TIV.NES	conflictiveness
STRIK'TIV.NES	constrictiveness, nonrestrictiveness, restrictiveness

IK'TER.Ē

DIK'TER.Ē	benedictory, interdictory, contradictory, maledictory, valedictory
RIK'TER.Ē	serictery
VIK'TER.Ē	victory

IK'Ū.LA

BIK'Ū.LA	corbicula
DIK'Ū.LA	fidicula
NIK'Ū.LA	canicula, cunicula
RIK'Ū.LA	curricula, auricula
SIK'Ū.LA	acicula
TIK'Ū.LA	cuticula, reticula, zeticula

IK'Ū.LANT

| TIK'Ū.LANT | articulant |
| TRIK'Ū.LANT | matriculant |

IK'Ū.LAR

BIK'Ū.LAR	cubicular, orbicular, scobicular
DIK'Ū.LAR	appendicular, pedicular, perpendicular, radicular
HIK'Ū.LAR	extravehicular, vehicular
LIK'Ū.LAR	follicular, calycular, pellicular
MIK'Ū.LAR	vermicular
NIK'Ū.LAR	adminicular, funicular, canicular, cunicular
PIK'Ū.LAR	apicular
RIK'Ū.LAR	extracurricular, curricular, auricular
SIK'Ū.LAR	acicular, fascicular, versicular, vesicular
SPIK'Ū.LAR	spicular
TIK'Ū.LAR	articular, denticular, cuticular, quinquarticular, lenticular, particular, reticular, subcuticular
TRIK'Ū.LAR	matricular, ventricular
VIK'Ū.LAR	clavicular, navicular, ovicular

IK'Ū.LĀT

BIK'Ū.LĀT	orbiculate, scrobiculate
DIK'Ū.LĀT	pediculate
GWIK'Ū.LĀT	unguiculate
MIK'Ū.LĀT	vermiculate
NIK'Ū.LĀT	geniculate, corniculate, paniculate
RIK'Ū.LĀT	auriculate
SIK'Ū.LĀT	aciculate, fasciculate, vesiculate
SPIK'Ū.LĀT	spiculate
TIK'Ū.LĀT	articulate, disarticulate, gesticulate, particulate, reticulate
TRIK'Ū.LĀT	matriculate

IK'Ū.LIT

BIK'Ū.LIT	orbiculate, scrobiculate
DIK'Ū.LIT	appendiculate, pediculate
FIK'Ū.LIT	forficualte
GWIK'Ū.LIT	unguiculate
LIK'Ū.LIT	folliculate, canaliculate
MIK'Ū.LIT	vermiculate
NIK'Ū.LIT	funiculate, geniculate, corniculate, paniculate
PIK'Ū.LIT	apiculate
RIK'Ū.LIT	auriculate, turriculate

SIK'Ū.LIT aciculate, fasciculate, vesicualte
SPIK'Ū.LIT spiculate
TIK'Ū.LIT articualte, denticulate, inarticulate, monticulate, particulate, reticulate, straticulate

IK'Ū.LUM

BIK'Ū.LUM cubiculum
NIK'Ū.LUM Janiculum, geniculum
RIK'Ū.LUM curriculum, periculum
SIK'Ū.LUM aciculum
SPIK'Ū.LUM spiculum
TIK'Ū.LUM reticulum

IK'Ū.LUS

DIK'Ū.LUS pediculous, pediculus, ridiculous
DRIK'Ū.LUS dendriculous
LIK'Ū.LUS folliculous, calyculous, canaliculus, cauliculous
MIK'Ū.LUS vermiculous
NIK'Ū.LUS funiculus, cuniculous, panniculous
SIK'Ū.LUS fasciculus, vesiculous
TIK'Ū.LUS denticulous, meticulous
TRIK'Ū.LUS ventriculous

IK'Ū.US

IK'Ū.US proficuous
SPIK'Ū.US inconspicuous, conspicuous, perspicuous, transpicuous

IK'WI.TĒ

BIK'WI.TĒ ubiquity
LIK'WI.TĒ obliquity
NIK'WI.TĒ iniquity
TIK'WI.TĒ antiquity

IK'WI.TUS

BIK'WI.TUS ubiquitous
LIK'WI.TUS obliquitous
NIK'WI.TUS iniquitous

ĪL'A.BL

FĪL'A.BL defilable, filable
GĪL'A.BL beguilable
HĪL'A.BL heilable
NĪL'A.BL enislable
PĪL'A.BL compilable, pilable, recompilable, repilable, unpilable
RĪL'A.BL rilable
SĪL'A.BL domicilable, ensilable, exilable, reconcilable, irreconcilable
SPĪL'A.BL spilable
STĪL'A.BL stylable
TĪL'A.BL tilable
VĪL'A.BL revilable
ZĪL'A.BL exilable

IL'A.BL

SIL'A.BL henedecasyllable, monosyllable, multisyllable, polysyllable, syllable

(See **IL**, add -*able* where appropriate.)

IL'A.BUB

SIL'A.BUB sillabub
TRIL'A.BUB trillibub

IL'A.JER

(See **IL'I.JER**)

Ī'LAN.DER

Ī'LAN.DER islander
HĪ'LAN.DER highlander
SKĪ'LAN.DER skylander
TĪ'LAN.DER Thailander

Ī'LAT.ER.AL

BĪ'LAT.ER.AL *bilateral*
TRĪ'LAT.ER.AL *trilateral*

IL'A.TŌ.RĒ

DIL'A.TŌ.RĒ dilatory
PIL'A.TŌ.RĒ depilatory

IL'E.GRAM

KIL'E.GRAM kilogram
MIL'E.GRAM milligram
TIL'E.GRAM dactylogram

IL'E.JENT

(See **IL'I.JENT**)

Ī'LER.Ē

GĪL'ER.Ē guilery
PĪ'LER.Ē pilary
TĪ'LER.Ē tilery

IL'ER.Ē

FIL'ER.Ē phyllary
FRIL'ER.Ē frillery
MIL'ER.Ē armillary
PIL'ER.Ē capillary, pillery, pillory
SIL'ER.Ē ancillary, axillary, codicillary, cilery, submaxillary
TIL'ER.Ē artillery, distillery, fritillary

IL'ET.ED

BIL'ET.ED billeted, unbilleted
FIL'ET.ED filleted, unfilleted

IL'ET.ING

BIL'ET.ING billeting
FIL'ET.ING filleting

ĪL'FUL.Ē

GĪL'FUL.Ē beguilefully, guilefully
WĪL'FUL.Ē wilefully

IL'FUL.Ē

SKIL'FUL.Ē skilfully, unskilfully
WIL'FUL.Ē wilfully, unwilfully

ĪL'FUL.NES

GĪL'FUL.NES	guilefulness
WĪL'FUL.NES	wilefulness

IL'FUL.NES

SKIL'FUL.NES	skillfulness, unskillfulness
WIL'FUL.NES	willfulness

IL'I.A

IL'I.A	ilia
BIL'I.A	imponderabilia, memorabilia, mirabilia, notabilia, sensibilia
DIL'I.A	sedilia
FIL'I.A	*A* ailurophilia, alcoholophilia, androphilia, Anglophilia, anophilia, *B* bibliophilia, *F* phallophilia, *FR* Francophilia, *G* gamophilia, *H* hemophilia, *J* Germanophilia, *K* coprophilia, *L* lygophilia, *M* melcryptovestiment-aphilia, *N* necrophilia, *O* osphresiophilia, *P* pedophilia, *R* Russophilia, *SP* spasmophilia, *T* taphophilia, *U* urinophilia, *V* vulvophilia, *Z* zoophilia (etc.)
MIL'I.A	familia
NIL'I.A	juvenilia
SIL'I.A	Brasilia, cilia
TIL'I.A	adactylia, dactylia

IL'I.AD

IL'I.AD	Iliad
GIL'I.AD	Gilead
KIL'I.AD	chiliad
MIL'I.AD	milliad

IL'I.AL

IL'I.AL	ilial

FIL'I.AL	filial, grandfilial, unfilial
MIL'I.AL	familial

IL'I.AN

BIL'I.AN	perfectabilian
CHIL'I.AN	Chilean
DIL'I.AN	crocodilian
JIL'I.AN	Virgilian
MIL'I.AN	Maximilian
PIL'I.AN	epyllion
SIL'I.AN	caecilian, Sicilian
SKIL'I.AN	skillion
TIL'I.AN	Castilian, lacertilian, reptilian, vespertilian
VIL'I.AN	civilian
ZIL'I.AN	Brazilian

(See **ILYUN**)

IL'I.AR

BIL'I.AR	atrabiliar
MIL'I.AR	familiar, unfamiliar
SIL'I.AR	domiciliar, conciliar
ZIL'I.AR	auxiliar

(See **ILYAR**)

IL'I.ARDZ

(See **ILYARDZ**)

IL'I.ER.Ē

(See **IL'YER.Ē**)

IL'I.ĀT

FIL'I.ĀT	affiliate, disaffiliate, filiate
MIL'I.ĀT	forisfamiliate, humiliate
PIL'I.ĀT	pileate
SIL'I.ĀT	comiciliate, conciliate, reconciliate, ciliate

IL'I.ENS

BRIL'I.ENS	brilliance
SIL'I.ENS	dissilience, consilience, transilience
ZIL'I.ENS	resilience

(See **ILYENS**)

IL'I.ENT

BRIL'I.ENT	brilliant
SIL'I.ENT	dissilient, intersillient, consilient, transilient
ZIL'I.ENT	resilient

(See **ILYENT**)

IL'I.ER

CHIL'I.ER	chillier
FRIL'I.ER	frillier
HIL'I.ER	hillier
KWIL'I.ER	quillier
RIL'I.ER	rillier
SIL'I.ER	sillier
STIL'I.ER	stillier
THRIL'I.ER	thrillier
TIL'I.ER	tillier
TRIL'I.ER	trillier
TWIL'I.ER	twillier

(See **IL'YAR**)

IL'I.EST

(See **IL'I.ER**; change -*r* to -*st*.)

IL'I.FĪ

BIL'I.FĪ	nobilify, stabilify
HIL'I.FĪ	nihilify
SIL'I.FĪ	fossilify
VIL'I.FĪ	vilify

IL'I.FÔRM

FIL'I.FÔRM	filiform, phylliform
LIL'I.FÔRM	liliform
NIL'I.FÔRM	moniliform
PIL'I.FÔRM	papilliform
SIL'I.FÔRM	ypsiliform
STIL'I.FÔRM	stilliform

IL'I.JENT

DIL'I.JENT	diligent
NIL'I.JENT	omniligent

IL'I.JER

PIL'I.JER	pillager
VIL'I.JER	villager

IL′I.KAL

BIL′I.KAL umbilical
FIL′I.KAL filical
SIL′I.KAL basilical, silicle

IL′I.KIN

BIL′I.KIN billikin
SIL′I.KIN basilican
SPIL′I.KIN spilikin, spillikin

IL′I.NES

CHIL′I.NES chilliness
FIL′I.NES dilliness
HIL′I.NES hilliness
SIL′I.NES silliness

Ī′LING.LĒ

GĪ′LING.LĒ beguilingly
SMĪ′LING.LĒ smilingly,
unsmilingly

IL′ING.LĒ

CHIL′ING.LĒ chillingly
FIL′ING.LĒ fillingly
KIL′ING.LĒ killingly
THRIL′ING.LĒ thrillingly
TRIL′ING.LĒ trillingly
WIL′ING.LĒ unwillingly,
willingly

IL′I.Ō

BIL′I.Ō billyo
TIL′I.Ō punctilio
VIL′I.Ō pulvilio

IL′I.SĪD

SIL′I.SĪD silicide
STIL′I.SĪD stillicide

IL′I.TĀT

BIL′I.TĀT abilitate, debilitate,
habilitate,
impossibilitate,
nobilitate,
rehabilitate,
stabilitate
MIL′I.TĀT militate

SIL′I.TĀT facilitate,
imbecilitate

IL′I.TĒ

BIL′I.TĒ *A* ability,
absorbability,
adaptability,
addability,
adjustability,
admirability,
admissibility,
adoptability,
adorability,
advisability,
affectibility,
agreeability,
accendibility,
acceptability,
accessibility,
accountability,
acquirability,
alienability,
amability,
amenability,
amiability,
amicability,
admissibility,
answerability,
appetibility,
applicability,
approachability,
ascendability,
assimilability,
associability,
attainability,
attemptability,
attractability,
availability,
avoidability, *B*
biodegradability, *BR*
bribability, *CH*
changeability,
chargeability, *D*
damnability,
debility,
deceptibility,
deductibility,
defectibility,
defensibility,
defeatibility,
delectability,
demisability,
demonstrability,
deplorability,
descendibility,
describability,
despicability,
destructibility,
determinability,
detestability,

desirability,
diffusibility,
digestibility,
dilatability,
dirigibility,
disability,
dispensability,
dissolubility,
dissolvability,
disputability,
distensibility,
divisibility,
docibility,
durability, *E*
edibility,
educability,
effectibility,
effervescibility,
exchangeability,
excitability,
exhaustibility,
existibility,
exorability,
expansibility,
expressibility,
extensibility,
equability,
eligibility,
endurability,
enunciability,
errability, *F*
fallibility,
feasibility,
fermentability,
formidability,
fusibility, *FL*
flammability,
flexibility,
fluxibility,
fluctuability, *FR*
frangibility,
friability, *G*
gullibility,
governability, *H*
habitability,
hereditability,
hyperirritability, *I*
ignobility, illability,
illegibility,
illimitability,
imitability,
immeability,
immeasurability,
immiscibility,
immobility,
immovability,
immutability,
impalpability,
impartibility,
impassibility,
impeccability,
impenetrability,

imperdibility,
imperfectibility,
imperishability,
impermeability,
imperceptibility,
imperturbability,
imperviability,
implacability,
imponderability,
impossibility,
impracticability,
impregnability,
impressibility,
impressionability,
imprescriptibility,
improbability,
improvability,
imputability,
inability,
inadmissibility,
inaccessibility,
indefatigability,
indefeasibility,
indefectibility,
indefensibility,
indelibility,
indemonstrability,
indescribability,
indestructibility,
indigestibility,
indiscernibility,
indiscerptibility,
indescribability,
indispensability,
indissolubility,
indisputability,
indestructability,
indivisibility,
indocibility,
inducibility,
inedibility,
ineffability,
ineffervescibility,
inexcusability,
inexhaustibility,
inexorability,
inexplicability,
inexpressibility,
ineligibility,
ineradicability,
inerrability,
inevitability,
infallibility,
infeasibility,
inflexibility,
influencibility,
infrangibility,
infusibility,
inhability,
inhabitability,
inheritability,
inimitability,

incalculability,
incapability,
incognitability,
incognizability,
incognoscibility,
incogitability,
incombustibility,
incommensurability,
incommeasurability,
incommunicability,
incommutability,
incomparability,
incompatibility,
incomprehensibility,
incompressibility,
incondensability,
inconceivability,
incontestability,
incontrovertibility,
inconvertibility,
incorrigibility,
incorruptibility,
incredibility,
inoperability,
innumerability,
inaudibility,
insanability,
insatiability,
insensibility,
inseparability,
insurability,
inscrutability,
insolubility,
insociability,
instability,
insuperability,
insurmountability,
insusceptibility,
intangibility,
intelligibility,
interchangeability,
intractability,
invariability,
invendibility,
invincibility,
inviolability,
invisibility,
invulnerability,
irascibility,
irredeemability,
irredressibility,
irreducibility,
irreducibility,
irreformability,
irrefragability,
irrefutability,
irremissibility,
irremovability,
irreparability,
irrepressibility,
irreproachability,
irresponsibility,

irretrievability,
irreversibility,
irrevocability,
irritability,
irresistibility,
irresolvability, *J*
generability,
justifiability, *K*
calculability,
capability,
coagulability,
cognizability,
cognoscibility,
cohesibility,
collapsibility,
combustibility,
commensurability,
communicability,
commutability,
comparability,
compatibility,
comprehensibility,
compressibility,
computability,
condensability,
conductability,
conformability,
confusability,
conceivability,
contemptibility,
contractibility,
convertibility,
convincibility,
corrigibility,
corrodibility,
corrosibility,
corruptibility,
culpability,
curability, *KR*
credibility,
creditability, *KW*
questionability,
quotability, *L*
lability,
laminability,
legibility, liability,
laudability, *M*
malleability,
manageability,
manipulability,
marketability,
masticability,
meliorability,
memorability,
mensurability,
mentionability,
measurability,
miscibility,
mobility,
modifiability,
modificability,
movability,

mutability, *N*
namability,
navigability,
negotiability,
nobility, notability,
knowability,
nubility, nullibility,
O audibility,
alterability,
opposability,
organizability,
ostensibility, *P*
palpability,
partibility,
passibility,
peccability,
penetrability,
perdurability,
perfectibility,
perishability,
permeability,
permissibility,
perceptibility,
persuasibility,
perturbability,
ponderability,
portability,
possibility,
potability,
punishability, *PR*
practicability,
predictability,
preferability,
precipitability,
prescriptibility,
preventability,
probability,
producibility,
provability, *R*
ratability,
readability,
redeemability,
redressibility,
reductibility,
reducibility,
reflectibility,
reformability,
refragability,
refrangibility,
refutability,
recognizability,
reconcilability,
relatability,
reliability,
remissibility,
removability,
remunerability,
renewability,
reparability,
repealability,
receivability,
receptibility,

responsibility,
retractability,
retrievability,
reversibility,
revocability,
resistibility,
resolvability,
writability, risibility,
S salability,
salvability,
sanability,
seducibility,
secability,
sensibility,
censurability,
separability,
solubility,
solvability,
sociability,
suability,
suggestibility,
susceptibility,
suspensibility,
suitability, *SKW*
squeezability, *SP*
sportability, *ST*
stability, *SW*
swayability, *T*
taxability,
tamability,
tangibility,
temptability,
tenability,
tensibility,
tolerability,
torsibility, *TR*
tractability,
transferability,
translatability,
transmissibility,
transmutability,
transportability,
traceability, *U*
unaccountability,
unbelievability,
undesirability,
unreliability,
unsuitability,
untranslatability,
unutterability,
utterability, *V*
vaporability,
variability,
vegetability,
vendibility,
venerability,
versability, viability,
vindicability,
vincibility,
violability,
visibility, vocability,
volubility,

vulnerability, *W*
wearability,
workability

BRIL'I.TĒ febrility
DIL'I.TĒ crocodility
HIL'I.TĒ nihility
JIL'I.TĒ agility, fragility
KWIL'I.TĒ tranquillity
MIL'I.TĒ humility,
verisimility
NIL'I.TĒ anility, femininity,
juvenility, senility,
vernility
RIL'I.TĒ febrility, neurility,
puerility, scurrility,
sterility, virility
SIL'I.TĒ *D* docility, *E* exility,
F facility, fossility,
FL flexility, *GR*
gracility, *I*
imbecility,
indocility, *P*
pensility, *PR*
prehensility, *T*
tensility
TIL'I.TĒ *B* beautility, *D*
ductility, *F* fertility,
fictility, futility, *H*
hostility, *I*
inductility,
infantility,
infertility, inutility,
J gentility, *K*
contractility, *M*
motility, *R*
retractility, *T*
tactility, tortility, *TR*
tractility, *V*
versatility,
vibratility, volatility,
Y utility
VIL'I.TĒ incivility, servility,
civility

IL'I.UM

IL'I.UM ileum, ilium, Ilium,
illium
LIL'I.UM Liliom, Lilium
MIL'I.UM millium
PIL'I.UM pileum
RIL'I.UM beryllium
SIL'I.UM concilium,
penicillium, cillium
TRIL'I.UM trillium
ZIL'I.UM auxilium

IL'I.US

BIL'I.US atrabilious, bilious

SIL'I.US supercilious
TIL'I.US punctilious

IL'KI.ER

MIL'KI.ER milkier
SIL'KI.ER silkier

IL'KI.EST

MIL'KI.EST milkiest
SIL'KI.EST silkiest

Ĭ'LO.BĀT

STĬ'LO.BĀT stylobate
TRĬ'LO.BĀT trilobate

IL'O.Ē

BIL'O.Ē billowy
PIL'O.Ē pillowy
WIL'O.Ē willowy

Ĭ'LO.GRAF

STĬ'LO.GRAF stilograph
ZĬ'LO.GRAF xylograph

IL'O.ING

BIL'O.ING billowing
PIL'O.ING pillowing
WIL'O.ING willowing

IL'O.JĒ

DIL'O.JĒ dilogy
KIL'O.JĒ brachylogy
LIL'O.JĒ palilogy, polilogy
SIL'O.JĒ fossilogy, sylloge
TIL'O.JĒ antilogy, festilogy
TRIL'O.JĒ trilogy

IL'O.JĬZ

PIL'O.JĬZ epilogize
SIL'O.JĬZ syllogize

IL'O.JIZM

FIL'O.JIZM amphilogism
PIL'O.JIZM epilogism
SIL'O.JIZM episyllogism,
  pseudosyllogism,
  syllogism

IL'O.KWĒ

DIL'O.KWĒ blandiloquy,
  grandiloquy
JIL'O.KWĒ longiloquy
LIL'O.KWĒ melliloquy,
  soliloquy
NIL'O.KWĒ inaniloquy,
  magniloquy,
  pleniloquy,
  somniloquy,
  vaniloquy
RIL'O.KWĒ pectoriloquy,
  veriloquy
SIL'O.KWĒ dulciloquy,
  flexiloquy,
  mendaciloquy,
  pauciloquy
TIL'O.KWĒ antiloquy,
  dentiloquy,
  multiloquy,
  sanctiloquy,
  stultiloquy,
  tolutiloquy,
  tristiloquy
TRIL'O.KWĒ gastriloquy,
  ventriloquy
VIL'O.KWĒ breviloquy,
  suaviloquy

IL'O.KWENS

(See **IL'O.KWĒ**, change -y to -ence.)

IL'O.KWENT

(See **IL'O.KWĒ**, change -y to -ent.)

IL'O.KWIST

(See **IL'O.KWĒ**, change -y to -ist.)

IL'O.KWĪZ

(See **IL'O.KWĒ**, change -y to -ize.)

IL'O.KWIZM

(See **IL'O.KWĒ**, change -y to -ism.)

IL'O.KWUS

(See **IL'O.KWĒ**, change -y to -ous.)

IL'YEN.SĒ

BRIL'YEN.SĒ brilliancy
SIL'YEN.SĒ transiliency
ZIL'YEN.SĒ resiliency

IL'YER.Ē

BIL'YER.Ē atrabiliary, biliary,
  nobiliary
MIL'YER.Ē miliary
SIL'YER.Ē domiciliary,
  superciliary
ZIL'YER.Ē auxiliary

IM'A.NUS

DIM'A.NUS pedimanous
JIM'A.NUS longimanous

IM'A.THĒ

SIM'A.THĒ opsimathy
TIM'A.THĒ timothy, Timothy

IM'BRI.KĀT

IM'BRI.KĀT imbricate
FIM'BRI.KĀT fimbricate

Ī'ME.NĒ

KRĬ'ME.NĒ crimeny
SĬ'ME.NĒ simony

IM'E.NĒ

JIM'E.NĒ jiminy
SIM'E.NĒ simony
TIM'E.NĒ antimony

Ī'MER.Ē

PRĬ'MER.Ē primary
RĬ'MER.Ē rhymery

IM'ER.Ē

GLIM'ER.Ē	glimmery
SHIM'ER.Ē	shimmery
SIM'ER.Ē	simmery

IM'ER.ING

GLIM'ER.ING	glimmering
SHIM'ER.ING	shimmering
SIM'ER.ING	simmering

IM'ER.US

DIM'ER.US	dimerous
GLIM'ER.US	glimmerous
LIM'ER.US	polymerous
TRIM'ER.US	trimerous

IM'E.TER

DIM'E.TER	acidimeter, dimeter
LIM'E.TER	alkalimeter, delimiter, limiter, polymeter, salimeter planimeter
NIM'E.TER	calorimeter, colorimeter, perimeter, polarimeter, saccharimeter, solarimeter, vaporimeter
RIM'E.TER	dasymeter, dousimeter, dosimeter, focimeter, licimeter, pulsimeter, rhysimeter, scimitar, tasimeter, velocimeter, zymosimeter
SIM'E.TER	altimeter, *centimeter*, voltimeter
TIM'E.TER	trimeter
TRIM'E.TER	gravimeter, pelvimeter
VIM'E.TER	

IM'E.TRĒ

DIM'E.TRĒ	acidimetry, oxidimetry
LIM'E.TRĒ	alkalimetry
NIM'E.TRĒ	planimetry
RIM'E.TRĒ	dolorimetry, calorimetry, perimetry, polarimetry

SIM'E.TRĒ	asymmetry, dyssemetry, symmetry
THIM'E.TRĒ	bathymetry
TIM'E.TRĒ	altimetry

IM'I.A

LIM'I.A	bulimia
MIM'I.A	hypermimia, paramimia
SIM'I.A	Simia
THIM'I.A	parathymia, pikithymia

IM'I.AN

DIM'I.AN	Endymion
PIM'I.AN	opimian
SIM'I.AN	prosimian, simian

IM'I.KAL

KIM'I.KAL	alchymical
MIM'I.KAL	mimical, pantomimical
NIM'I.KAL	anonymical, homonymical, inimical, metonymical, patronymical, toponymical

IM'IK.RĒ

GIM'IK.RĒ	gimmickry
MIM'IK.RĒ	mimicry, theriomimicry

IM'I.NAL

BIM'I.NAL	bimanal
JIM'I.NAL	regiminal
KRIM'I.NAL	criminal
LIM'I.NAL	liminal, subliminal
VIM'I.NAL	viminal, Viminal

IM'I.NĀT

KRIM'I.NĀT	discriminate, incriminate, indiscriminate, criminate, recriminate
LIM'I.NĀT	eliminate

IM'I.NĒ

BIM'I.NĒ	Bimini
JIM'I.NĒ	jiminy
KRIM'I.NĒ	criminy
LIM'I.NĒ	postliminy
PIM'I.NĒ	nimini-pimini

Ī'MI.NES

GRĪ'MI.NES	griminess
LĪ'MI.NES	liminess
RĪ'MI.NES	riminess
SLĪ'MI.NES	sliminess

IM'I.NUS

KRIM'I.NUS	criminous
LIM'I.NUS	moliminous

IM'I.ON

(See **IM'I.AN**)

IM'I.TĀT

IM'I.TĀT	imitate
LIM'I.TĀT	delimitate, limitate

IM'I.TĒ

DIM'I.TĒ	dimity
LIM'I.TĒ	limity, ophelimity, sublimity
NIM'I.TĒ	anonymity, equanimity, longanimity, magnanimity, parvanimity, pusillanimity, sanctanimity, pseudonymity, synonymity, unanimity
SIM'I.TĒ	proximity, simity

IM'I.TER

(See **IM'E.TER**)

IM'I.TRĒ

(See **IM'E.TRĒ**)

IM'PER.ER

HWIM'PER.ER	whimperer
SIM'PER.ER	simperer

IM′PER.ING

HWIM′PER.ING	whimpering
SIM′PER.ING	simpering

IM′Ū.LANT

SIM′Ū.LANT	simulant
STIM′Ū.LANT	stimulant

IM′Ū.LĀT

SIM′Ū.LĀT	assimulate, dissimulate, simulate
STIM′Ū.LĀT	stimulate, restimulate

IM′Ū.LUS

LIM′Ū.LUS	limulus
STIM′Ū.LUS	stimulus

ĪN′A.BL

BĪN′A.BL	combinable, uncombinable
FĪN′A.BL	definable, finable, indefinable, refinable, unfinable, unrefinable
KLĪN′A.BL	declinable, inclinable, indeclinable
LĪN′A.BL	linable
MĪN′A.BL	minable, unminable
PĪN′A.BL	opinable
SĪN′A.BL	assignable, consignable, signable
TWĪN′A.BL	intertwinable, twinable, untwinable
VĪN′A.BL	divinable, undivinable
ZĪN′A.BL	designable

IN′A.BL

HIN′A.BL	hinnible
PIN′A.BL	pinnable
SKIN′A.BL	skinnable
WIN′A.BL	winnable

ĪN′A.BLĒ

KLĪN′A.BLĒ	declinably
FĪN′A.BLĒ	definably, undefinably

SĪN′A.BLĒ	assignably, unassignably

IN′A.KL

BIN′A.KL	binnacle, binocle, rabbinical
FIN′A.KL	finical
KLIN′A.KL	clinical, synclinical
MIN′A.KL	adminicle, Brahmnical, dominical, cominical, flaminical
PIN′A.KL	pinnacle
SIN′A.KL	Sinical, cynical

Ī′NA.LĒ

FĪ′NA.LĒ	finally
SPĪ′NA.LĒ	spinally

Ī′NA.RĒ

(See Ī′NE.RĒ)

IN′A.TIV

(See IN′I.TIV)

IN′CHING.LĒ

(See INCH, add -ingly where appropriate.)

ĪN′DE.RĒ

BĪN′DE.RĒ	bindery
GRĪN′DE.RĒ	grindery

IN′DER.Ē

SIN′DER.Ē	cindery
TIN′DER.Ē	tindery

IN′DI.KĀT

IN′DI.KĀT	indicate, contraindicate
SIN′DI.KĀT	syndicate
VIN′DI.KĀT	vindicate

IN′E.MA

(See IN′I.MA)

IN′E.RĀT

SIN′E.RĀT	incinerate
TIN′E.RĀT	itinerate

Ī′NE.RĒ

BĪ′NE.RĒ	binary
FĪ′NE.RĒ	finery, refinery
KWĪ′NE.RĒ	quinary
MĬ′NE.RĒ	minery
PĪ′NE.RĒ	alpinery, pinery
SWĬ′NE.RĒ	swinery
VĪ′NE.RĒ	vinery
WĬ′NE.RĒ	winery

ING′GER.ER

FING′GER.ER	fingerer
LING′GER.ER	lingerer, malingerer

ING′GER.ING

FING′GER.ING	fingering
LING′GER.ING	lingering, malingering

ING′GŪ.LĀT

LING′GŪ.LĀT	lingulate
SING′GŪ.LĀT	cingulate

INGK′A.BL

DRINGK′A.BL	drinkable, undrinkable
LINGK′A.BL	linkable, unlinkable
SHRINGK′A.BL	shrinkable, unshrinkable
SINGK′A.BL	sinkable, unsinkable
THINGK′A.BL	thinkable, unthinkable
WINGK′A.BL	winkable

INGK′I.NES

INGK′I.NES	inkiness
KINGK′I.NES	kinkiness
PINGK′I.NES	pinkiness
SLINGK′I.NES	slinkiness

INGK′ING.LĒ

(See INGK, add -ingly where appropriate.)

INGK'WI.TĒ

JINGK'WI.TĒ	longinquity
PINGK'WI.TĒ	propinquity

IN'I.A

IN'I.A	inia
BIN'I.A	robinia
DIN'I.A	anodynia, oneirodynia, pleurodynia, Sardinia
HIN'I.A	bauhinia
JIN'I.A	albuginea, discalloginia, Virginia
LIN'I.A	linea
SIN'I.A	Abyssinia, dosinia, Dulcinia, gloxinia, lacinia, vaccinia
TIN'I.A	actinia, Nemertinea, tinea
VIN'I.A	vinea
ZIN'I.A	zinnia

IN'I.AL

IN'I.AL	inial
FIN'I.AL	finial
GWIN'I.AL	consanguineal, sanguineal
LIN'I.AL	interlineal, lineal, matrilineal, patrilineal
MIN'I.AL	dominial, gramineal, stamineal
PIN'I.AL	pineal
TIN'I.AL	pectineal, tineal
VIN'I.AL	vineal

IN'I.AN

DIN'I.AN	Sardinian
FIN'I.AN	Delphinian
JIN'I.AN	anthropophaginian, Carthaginian, viraginian, Virginian
LIN'I.AN	Carolinian, sterquilinian
MIN'I.AN	Arminian, Flaminian
RIN'I.AN	leptorrhinian, czarinian
SIN'I.AN	Abyssinian
TIN'I.AN	Augustinian, Justinian, Palestinean, serpentinean
WIN'I.AN	Darwinian

(See INYUN)

IN'I.ĀT

LIN'I.ĀT	delineate, lineate
MIN'I.ĀT	miniate
SIN'I.ĀT	laciniate

Ī'NI.ER

BRĪ'NI.ER	brinier
SHĬ'NI.ER	shinier
SPĬ'NI.ER	spinier
TĬ'NI.ER	tinier
WĬ'NI.ER	winier

IN'I.ER

DRIN'I.ER	Fourdrinier
FIN'I.ER	finnier
LIN'I.ER	colinear, bilinear, interlinear, curvilinear, linear, rectilinear, trilinear
SKIN'I.ER	skinnier
TIN'I.ER	tinnier

IN'I.FÔRM

MIN'I.FÔRM	aluminiform
SIN'I.FÔRM	laciniform
TIN'I.FÔRM	actiniform

IN'I.KIN

FIN'I.KIN	finikin
MIN'I.KIN	minikin

IN'I.KL

(See IN'A.KL)

IN'I.MA

MIN'I.MA	minima
SIN'I.MA	cinema

IN'I.MENT

LIN'I.MENT	liniment
MIN'I.MENT	miniment

IN'ISH.ER

FIN'ISH.ER	finisher
MIN'ISH.ER	diminisher

IN'ISH.ING

FIN'ISH.ING	finishing, refinishing
MIN'ISH.ING	diminishing, undiminishing

IN'IS.TER

MIN'IS.TER	administer, minister
SIN'IS.TER	ambisinister, sinister

IN'IS.TRAL

MIN'IS.TRAL	ministral
SIN'IS.TRAL	dextrosinistral, sinistral

IN'I.TĒ

FIN'I.TĒ	affinity, diffinity, finity, infinity, confinity
GRIN'I.TĒ	peregrinity
GWIN'I.TĒ	exsanguinity, consanguinity, sanguinity
JIN'I.TĒ	viraginity, virginity
LIN'I.TĒ	alkalinity, felinity, masculinity, salinity
NIN'I.TĒ	asininity, caninity, femininity
SIN'I.TĒ	inconcinnity, concinnity, vicinity
TIN'I.TĒ	Latinity, satinity
TRIN'I.TĒ	trinity
VIN'I.TĒ	divinity, patavinity

IN'I.TIV

BIN'I.TIV	combinative
FIN'I.TIV	affinitive, definitive, finitive, infinitive
MIN'I.TIV	carminitive

JOGGER, JOG!

Jogger, jog, and runner, run!
How I envy you your fun!
Agony distorts your face;
Yet I know some hidden grace—
Some ebullient, inner leaven—
Raises you to joggers' heaven.

Jogger, gasping by the road,
Easing lungs of overload,
May I have your name, old scout?
If the leaven should run out—
If you jog off to your Maker—
I will call the undertaker.

IN'I.UM

FIN'I.UM	delphinium
JIN'I.UM	virginium
KLIN'I.UM	androclinium, triclinium
LIN'I.UM	gadolinium, illinium
MIN'I.UM	aluminium, dominium, condominium, minium, postliminium
RIN'I.UM	perineum
SIN'I.UM	tirocinium
TIN'I.UM	actinium, protactinium

IN'I.US

BIN'I.US	rubineous
DIN'I.US	testudineous
GWIN'I.US	consanguineous, sanguineous
JIN'I.US	cartilagineous
MIN'I.US	flamineous, fulmineous, gramineous, ignominious, stamineous, stramineous, vimineous

IN'JEN.SĒ

FRIN'JEN.SĒ	refringency
STRIN'JEN.SĒ	astringency, constringency, stringency
TIN'JEN.SĒ	contingency

IN'JI.LĒ

DIN'JI.LĒ	dingily
STIN'JI.LĒ	stingily

IN'JI.NES

DIN'JI.NES	dinginess
STIN'JI.NES	stinginess

IN'LAN.DER

IN'LAN.DER	inlander
FIN'LAN.DER	Finlander

IN'O.LIN

KRIN'O.LIN	crinoline
KWIN'O.LIN	quinoline

Ī'NŌ.MI.AL

BĪ'NŌ.MI.AL	binomial
TRI'NŌ.MI.AL	trinomial

IN'SING.LĒ

MIN'SING.LĒ	mincingly
VIN'SING.LĒ	convincingly

IN'TE.GRĀT

IN'TE.GRĀT	integrate, reintegrate
DIN'TE.GRĀT	redintegrate
SIN'TE.GRĀT	disintegrate

IN'TER.Ē

PRIN'TER.Ē	printery
SPLIN'TER.Ē	splintery
WIN'TER.Ē	wintery

(See INTRĒ)

IN'TER.ING

SPLIN'TER.ING	splintering
WIN'TER.ING	wintering

IN'THI.AN

RIN'THI.AN	Corinthian, labyrinthian
SIN'THI.AN	absinthian, hyacinthian

IN'Ū.ĀT

SIN'Ū.ĀT	insinuate, sinuate
TIN'Ū.ĀT	continuate

IN'Ū.IT

IN'Ū.IT	Innuit
SIN'Ū.IT	sinuate

IN'Ū.US

SIN'Ū.US	sinuous

TIN'Ū.US	discontinuous, continuous

Ī'O.FĪT

BRĪ'O.FĪT	bryophite
KRĪ'O.FĪT	cryophite

Ī'O.JEN

BĪ'O.JEN	biogen
KRĪ'O.JEN	cryogen

Ī'O.LA

RĪ'O.LA	variola
VĪ'O.LA	*viola*, Viola

Ī'O.LET

STRĪ'O.LET	striolet
TRĪ'O.LET	triolet
VĪ'O.LET	violet

Ī'O.LIN

(See Ī'A.LIN)

Ī'O.LIST

SĪ'O.LIST	sciolist
VĪ'O.LIST	violist

Ī'O.LĬT

(See Ī'A.LĬT)

Ī'O.LUS

DĪ'O.LUS	gladiolus, modiolus, Modiolus
RĪ'O.LUS	variolous
SĪ'O.LUS	sciolous

Ī'O.NĪZ

Ī'O.NĪZ	ionize
KĪ'O.NĪZ	kyanize
LĪ'O.NĪZ	lionize

Ī'O.PĒ

BĪ'O.PĒ	presbyopy
LĪ'O.PĒ	calliope
MĪ'O.PĒ	myopy

Ī′O.SĒN

MĬ′O.SĒN	Miocene, post-Miocene
PLĬ′O.SĒN	Pliocene, post-Pliocene

Ī′O.SIS

(See Ĭ′A.SIS)

I′O.SKŌP

(See I′A.SKŌP)

IP′A.BL

CHIP′A.BL	chippable
DIP′A.BL	dippable
KLIP′A.BL	clippable
NIP′A.BL	nippable
PIP′A.BL	pippable
RIP′A.BL	rippable
SHIP′A.BL	shippable
TIP′A.BL	tippable

IP′A.RA

(See IP′A.RUS, change -ous to -a.)

Ī′PÄR′TĪT

BĪ′PÄR′TĪT	bipartite
TRĬ′PÄR′TĪT	tripartite

IP′AR.US

IP′AR.US	deiparous
BIP′AR.US	ambiparous, biparous
DIP′AR.US	frondiparous
LIP′AR.US	gemelliparous, nulliparous, polyparous
MIP′AR.US	gemmiparous, primiparous, vermiparous
NIP′AR.US	criniparous, omniparous, uniparous
PIP′AR.US	opiparous
RIP′AR.US	floriparous, pluriparous, sudoriparous
SIP′AR.US	fissiparous
TIP′AR.US	dentiparous, fructiparous, multiparous, sextiparous

VIP′AR.US	larviparous, oviparous, ovoviparous, viviparous

IP′A.THĒ

NIP′A.THĒ	somnipathy
TIP′A.THĒ	antipathy

IP′A.THIST

NIP′A.THIST	somnipathist
TIP′A.THIST	antipathist

IP′ER.Ē

FLIP′ER.Ē	flippery
FRIP′ER.Ē	frippery
SLIP′ER.Ē	slippery

IP′E.TAL

(See IP′I.TAL)

IP′I.ENT

PIP′I.ENT	pipient
SIP′I.ENT	appercipient, desipient, incipient, insipient, percipient, recipient

IP′I.NES

(See IPĒ, add -ness)

ĪP′ING.LĒ

GRĬP′ING.LĒ	gripingly
PĪP′ING.LĒ	pipingly

IP′I.TAL

SIP′I.TAL	ancipital, bicipital, occipital
TRIP′I.TAL	centripetal

IP′I.TUS

DIP′I.TUS	serendipitous
KRIP′I.TUS	lucripetous
SIP′I.TUS	precipitous

IP′LI.KĀT

KWIP′LI.KĀT	sesquiplicate
TRIP′LI.KĀT	triplicate

IP′I.TAL

SIP′I.TAL	ancipetal, basipetal, bicipital, occipital, sincipital
TRIP′I.TAL	centripetal

IP′O.DĒ

DIP′O.DĒ	dipody
TRIP′O.DĒ	tripody

IP′O.DĒZ

DIP′O.DĒZ	dipodies, Pheidippides
RIP′O.DĒZ	Euripides
TIP′O.DĒZ	antipodes

IP′O.LĒ

LIP′O.LĒ	Gallipoli
TRIP′O.LĒ	Tripoli

IP′O.TENS

MIP′O.TENS	armipotence
NIP′O.TENS	ignipotence, omnipotence, plenipotence

IP′O.TENT

IP′O.TENT	deipotent
LIP′O.TENT	bellipotent
MIP′O.TENT	armipotent
NIP′O.TENT	ignipotent, omnipotent, plenipotent
RIP′O.TENT	viripotent
TIP′O.TENT	cunctipotent, multipotent, noctipotent
TRIP′O.TENT	ventripotent

IP′TER.AL

DIP′TER.AL	dipteral
MIP′TER.AL	hemipteral
RIP′TER.AL	peripteral

IP'TER.US

DIP'TER.US	dipterous
RIP'TER.US	peripterous
TRIP'TER.US	tripterous

IP'TI.KAL

GLIP'TI.KAL	glyptical
KLIP'TI.KAL	ecliptical
KRIP'TI.KAL	cryptical, procryptical
LIP'TI.KAL	apocalyptical, elliptical

IP'Ū.LAR

| NIP'Ū.LAR | manipular |
| STIP'Ū.LAR | stipular |

IP'Ū.LĀT

DIP'Ū.LĀT	pedipulate
NIP'Ū.LĀT	manipulate
STIP'Ū.LĀT	astipulate, stipulate

ÎR'A.BL

(See ÎR, add -able where appropriate.)

IR'A.KL

(See IR'I.KL)

Ī'RA.SĒ

| PĪ'RA.SĒ | piracy |
| TĪ'RA.SĒ | retiracy |

IR'A.SĒ

| LIR'A.SĒ | deliracy |
| SPIR'A.SĒ | conspiracy |

Ī'RĀT.ED

| JĪ'RĀT.ED | gyrated |
| SPĪ'RĀT.ED | spirated |

ÎR'FUL.Ē

CHÎR'FUL.Ē	cheerfully
FÎR'FUL.Ē	fearfully
TÎR'FUL.Ē	tearfully

ÎR'FUL.NES

ÎR'FUL.NES	irefulness
DĪR'FUL.NES	direfulness
ZĪR'FUL.NES	desirefulness

ÎR'FUL.NES

(See ÎRFUL, add -ness where appropriate.)

ÎR'I.A

ÎR'I.A	eria
BÎR'I.A	Iberia, Liberia, Siberia
FÎR'I.A	feria
JÎR'I.A	Algeria, Egeria, Nigeria
MÎR'I.A	krameria, cryptomeria, latimeria
PÎR'I.A	Hesperia
SÎR'I.A	ceria
SKLÎR'I.A	scleria
THÎR'I.A	diphtheria, gaulthiria
TÎR'I.A	acroteria, asteria, bacteria, hysteria, cafeteria, criteria, nitrobacteria, wisteria, washateria
VÎR'I.A	echeveria, sanseveria

(See IR'I.A)

IR'I.A

FIR'I.A	porphyria
KIR'I.A	Valkyria
LIR'I.A	Elyria, Illyria
SIR'I.A	Assyria, Syria
STIR'I.A	Styria

(See ÎR'I.A)

ÎR'I.AD

| PÎR'I.AD | period |
| TÎR'I.AD | anteriad, posteriad |

(See IR'I.AD)

IR'I.AD

| MIR'I.AD | myriad |

(See ÎR'I.AD)

ÎR'I.AL

ÎR'I.AL	aerial
DÎR'I.AL	intersiderial, siderial
FÎR'I.AL	ferial
JÎR'I.AL	managerial
NÎR'I.AL	funereal, manereal, venereal
PÎR'I.AL	imperial
SÎR'I.AL	biserial, rhinocerial, cereal, serial
THÎR'I.AL	diphtherial, ethereal, therial
TÎR'I.AL	arterial, asterial, bacterial, immaterial, magisterial, material, ministerial, monasterial, presbyterial
ZÎR'I.AL	vizerial

ÎR'I.A.LIST

PÎR'I.A.LIST	imperialist
THÎR'I.A.LIST	etherealist
TÎR'I.A.LIST	immaterialist, materialist

ÎR'I.A.LĪZ

SÎR'I.A.LĪZ	serialize
TÎR'I.A.LĪZ	arterialize, dematerialize, immaterialize, materialize
THÎR'I.A.LĪZ	etherealize

ÎR'I.A.LIZM

PÎR'I.A.LIZM	imperialism
THÎR'I.A.LIZM	etherealism
TÎR'I.A.LIZM	immaterialism, materialism

ÎR'I.AN

ÎR'I.AN	aerian, Erian, Pierian
BÎR'I.AN	Iberian, Liberian, Siberian
FÎR'I.AN	Luciferian
JÎR'I.AN	Algerian
LÎR'I.AN	allerion, Keplerian, valerian
MÎR'I.AN	Cimmerian, Sumerian
NÎR'I.AN	Wagnerian

PÎR'I.AN	Hesperian, Hyperion, Shakespearean
SÎR'I.AN	Chaucerian, Spencerian, Spenserian, tricerion
STÎR'I.AN	phalansterian
TÎR'I.AN	criterion, Presbyterian, psalterian
THÎR'I.AN	philotherian, metatherian, protetherian, eutherian
VÎR'I.AN	Hanoverian
ZÎR'I.AN	mezereon

(See IR'I.AN)

IR'I.AN

| KIR'I.AN | Valkyrian |
| SIR'I.AN | Assyrian, Syrian |

(See ÎR'I.AN)

ÎR'I.ER

ÎR'I.ER	eerier
BÎR'I.ER	beerier
BLÎR'I.ER	blearier
CHÎR'I.ER	cheerier
DRÎR'I.ER	drearier
FÎR'I.ER	inferior
PÎR'I.ER	superior
TÎR'I.ER	anterior, exterior, interior, posterior, tearier, ulterior
WÎR'I.ER	wearier

ÎR'I.FÔRM

PÎR'I.FÔRM	viperiform
SFÎR'I.FÔRM	spheriform
SÎR'I.FÔRM	seriform

IR'I.KL

JIR'I.KL	panegyrical
LIR'I.KL	lyrical
MIR'I.KL	miracle
PIR'I.KL	empirical, metempirical
SPIR'I.KL	spiracle
TIR'I.KL	satirical, satyrical

ÎR'I.LĒ

ÎR'I.LĒ	eerily
BÎR'I.LĒ	beerily
BLÎR'I.LĒ	blearily
CHÎR'I.LĒ	cheerily
DRÎR'I.LĒ	drearily
TÎR'I.LĒ	tearily
WÎR'I.LĒ	wearily

ÎR'I.NES

(See ÎRĒ, change -y to -iness where appropriate.)

ĬR'ING.LĒ

KWĬR'ING.LĒ	inquiringly
MĬR'ING.LĒ	admiringly
SPĬR'ING.LĒ	aspiringly, inspiringly, conspiringly
TĬR'ING.LĒ	retiringly, tiringly
ZĬR'ING.LĒ	desiringly

ÎR'ING.LĒ

CHÎR'ING.LĒ	cheeringly
DÎR'ING.LĒ	endearingly
FÎR'ING.LĒ	fearingly, unfearingly
JÎR'ING.LĒ	jeeringly
NÎR'ING.LĒ	domineeringly
PÎR'ING.LĒ	peeringly

ÎR'I.Ō

CHÎR'I.Ō	cheerio
DÎR'I.Ō	deario
SÎR'I.Ō	serio

ÎR'I.OR

(See ÎR'I.ER)

IR'I.SIST

| LIR'I.SIST | lyricist |
| PIR'I.SIST | empiricist |

IR'I.SIZM

| LIR'I.SIZM | lyricism |
| PIR'I.SIZM | empiricism |

ÎR'I.UM

DÎR'I.UM	desiderium
FÎR'I.UM	atmospherium
PÎR'I.UM	imperium, puerperium
SÎR'I.UM	cerium
TÎR'I.UM	acroterium, apodyterium, bacterium, deuterium, elaterium, magisterium, ministerium, psalterium
THÎR'I.UM	Dinotherium, Megatherium, Notetherium, Paleotherium, Titanotherium
ZÎR'I.UM	mezereum

(See IR'I.UM)

IR'I.UM

| LIR'I.UM | delirium, collyrium |

(See ÎR'I.UM)

ÎR'I.US

BÎR'I.US	Tiberius
DÎR'I.US	siderious
NÎR'I.US	cinerious
PÎR'I.US	imperious, suspirious
SÎR'I.US	jocoserious, ludicroserious, cereous, cereus, serious
STÎR'I.US	stirious
THÎR'I.US	ethereous
TÎR'I.US	deleterious, mysterious

(See IR'I.US)

IR'I.US

| LIR'I.US | delirious |
| SIR'I.US | Sirius |

(See ÎR'I.US)

ÎR'LES.NES

| BÎR'LES.NES | beerlessness |
| CHÎR'LES.NES | cheerlessness |

FÎR'LES.NES fearlessness
PÎR'LES.NES peerlessness

Ī'RO.NĒ

Ī'RO.NĒ irony
JĪ'RO.NĒ gyrony
SĪ'RO.NĒ sireny

ĪS'A.BL

PRĪS'A.BL priceable, unpriceable
SLĪS'A.BL sliceable, unsliceable
SPĪS'A.BL spiceable, unspiceable
RĪS'A.BL riceable, unriceable
TĪS'A.BL enticeable, unenticeable

IS'A.BL

(See IS'I.BL)

IS'A.BLĒ

(See IS'I.BLĒ)

IS'CHOO.LA

FIS'CHOO.LA fistula
VIS'CHOO.LA Vistula

IS'EN.ER

KRIS'EN.ER christener
LIS'EN.ER listener

IS'EN.ING

GLIS'EN.ING glistening
KRIS'EN.ING christening
LIS'EN.ING listening

IS'ER.ĀT

VIS'ER.ĀT eviscerate, viscerate

(See IS'ER.IT)

IS'ER.IT

LIS'ER.IT chelicerate

(See IS'ER.ĀT)

Ī'SE.RĒ

RĪ'SE.RĒ derisory, irrisory
SĪ'SE.RĒ decisory, incisory
SPĪ'SE.RĒ spicery

(See Ī'ZER.Ē)

IS'ER.Ē

MIS'ER.Ē admissory, dimissory, dismissory, emissory, remissory
SIS'ER.Ē rescissory

ISH'AL.Ē

(See ISHAL, add -ly.)

ISH'AL.IZM

DISH'AL.IZM judicialism
FISH'AL.IZM officialism

ISH'EN.SĒ

FISH'EN.SĒ beneficiency, deficiency, efficiency, inefficiency, insufficiency, proficiency, self-sufficiency, sufficiency
LISH'EN.SĒ alliciency

ISH'ENT.LĒ

(See ISHENT, add -ly where appropriate.)

ISH'ER.Ē

DISH'ER.Ē judiciary
FISH'ER.Ē beneficiary, officiary
TISH'ER.Ē justiciary

ISH'I.A

DISH'I.A indicia
LISH'I.A Galicia
MISH'I.A comitia
NISH'I.A Phoenicia, Tunisia
SISH'I.A apositia, asitia, syssitia
TISH'I.A adventitia, noticia

ISH'I.ĀT

FISH'I.ĀT maleficiate, officiate
NISH'I.ĀT initiate
PISH'I.ĀT propitiate

(See ISH'I.IT)

ISH'I.ENS

(See ISHENS)

ISH'I.ENT

(See ISHENT)

ISH'I.IT

NISH'I.IT initiate
TRISH'I.IT patriciate
VISH'I.IT novitiate, vitiate

(See ISH'I.ĀT)

ISH'UN.AL

ISH'UN.AL intuitional, tuitional
BISH'UN.AL exhibitional
DISH'UN.AL additional, conditional, preconditional, traditional, unconditional
LISH'UN.AL salicional, volitional
MISH'UN.AL commissional, missional
NISH'UN.AL definitional, recognitional
SISH'UN.AL transitional
TISH'UN.AL petitional, repetitional
TRISH'UN.AL nutritional
ZISH'UN.AL D depositional, disquisitional, dispositional, E expositional, I impositional, inquisitional, K compositional, P positional, PR prepositional, propositional, S suppositional, TR transitional, transpositional

ISH'UN.ER

BISH'UN.ER exhibitioner
DISH'UN.ER conditioner, traditioner

LISH'UN.ER	coalitioner	transmissible, *U*	**PIS'I.NAL**	piscinal
MISH'UN.ER	commissioner, missioner	unpermissable, untransmissible	**TIS'I.NAL**	vaticinal
			VIS'I.NAL	vicinal

NISH'UN.ER	admonitioner
RISH'UN.ER	parishioner
TISH'UN.ER	partitioner, petitioner, practitioner

SIS'I.BL	scissible
VIS'I.BL	obliviscible

ISH'UN.ING

DISH'UN.ING	conditioning, auditioning, reconditioning, traditioning
FISH'UN.ING	fissioning, refissioning
MISH'UN.ING	commissioning, missioning
PISH'UN.ING	suspicioning
TISH'UN.ING	partitioning, petitioning, repetitioning
ZISH'UN.ING	positioning, repositioning

ISH'UN.IST

BISH'UN.IST	exhibitionist, prohibitionist
DISH'UN.IST	traditionist
LISH'UN.IST	abolitionist, coalitionist
ZISH'UN.IST	oppositionist, requisitionist

ISH'US.LĒ

(See **ISHUS**, add *-ly* where appropriate.)

ISH'US.NES

(See **ISHUS**, add *-ness* where appropriate.)

IS'I.BL

KIS'I.BL	kissable, unkissable
MIS'I.BL	*A* admissible, amissible, *D* dismissible, *I* immiscible, incommiscible, irremissable, *M* miscible, missable, *O* omissible, *P* permiscible, permissable, *R* remissable, *TR*

IS'I.BLĒ

KIS'I.BLĒ	kissably
MIS'I.BLĒ	admissibly, permissibly
SIS'I.BLĒ	scissibly
VIS'I.BLĒ	obliviscibly

Ī'SI.ER

Ī'SI.ER	icier
SPĪ'SI.ER	spicier

IS'I.ER

KIS'I.ER	kissier
PRIS'I.ER	prissier
SIS'I.ER	sissier

Ī'SI.KL

Ī'SI.KL	icicle
BĪ'SI.KL	bicycle
TRĪ'SI.KL	tricycle

Ī'SI.LĒ

Ī'SI.LĒ	icily
SPĪ'SI.LĒ	spicily

IS'I.LĒ

PRIS'I.LĒ	prissily
SIS'I.LĒ	Sicily, sissily

IS'I.MŌ

CHIS'I.MŌ	dolcissimo
LIS'I.MŌ	generalissimo
NIS'I.MŌ	pianissimo
TIS'I.MŌ	altissimo, fortissimo, prestissimo
VIS'I.MŌ	bravissimo

IS'I.NAL

DIS'I.NAL	fidicinal, medicinal
FIS'I.NAL	officinal

Ī'SI.NES

Ī'SI.NES	iciness
RĪ'SI.NES	riceyness
SPĪ'SI.NES	spiciness

IS'I.PĀT

DIS'I.PĀT	dissipate
TIS'I.PĀT	anticipate, participate

IS'I.TĒ

IS'I.TĒ	stoicity
BIS'I.TĒ	cubicity, nullibicity
BRIS'I.TĒ	lubricity, rubricity
DIS'I.TĒ	benedicity, immundicity, impudicity, mendicity, periodicity, pudicity, spheroidicity
LIS'I.TĒ	alcoholicity, evangelicity, felicity, helicity, infelicity, catholicity, Catholicity, publicity, triplicity
MIS'I.TĒ	atomicity, endemicity
NIS'I.TĒ	atonicity, electronicity, canonicity, conicity, tonicity, volcanicity, vulcanicity, unicity
PIS'I.TĒ	hygroscopicity
PLIS'I.TĒ	accomplicity, duplicity, complicity, quadruplicity, multiplicity, simplicity, triplicity
RIS'I.TĒ	historicity, caloricity, sphericity
SIS'I.TĒ	basicity, toxicity
TIS'I.TĒ	*A* achromaticity, *D* domesticity, *E* elasticity, ellipticity, ensynopticity, *H* heteroscedasticity, homoscedasticity, *I* inelasticity, *K*

causticity, *KR*
chromaticity, *M*
mysticity, *O*
authenticity,
autopticity, *P*
pepticity, *PL*
plasticity, *R*
rusticity, *S* septicity,
SP spasticity, *ST*
stypticity, *V*
verticity, vorticity, *Y*
eupepticity
TRIS'I.TĒ   egocentricity,
eccentricity,
electricity,
photoelectricity,
hydroelectricity,
concentricity,
centricity, tetricity,
thermoelectricity

IS'IT.LĒ

LIS'IT.LĒ   illicitly, licitly
PLIS'IT.LĒ   explicitly, implicitly

IS'IT.NES

LIS'IT.NES   illicitness, licitness
PLIS'IT.NES   explicitness,
implicitness

IS'I.TŪD

LIS'I.TŪD   solicitude
SIS'I.TŪD   vicissitude
SPIS'I.TŪD   spissitude

Ī'SIV.LĒ

RĪ'SIV.LĒ   derisively
SĪ'SIV.LĒ   decisively,
incisively,
indecisively

Ī'SIV.NES

RĪ'SIV.NES   derisiveness
SĪ'SIV.NES   decisiveness,
indecisiveness,
incisiveness

IS'KI.ER

FRIS'KI.ER   friskier
RIS'KI.ER   riskier

ISK'I.LĒ

FRISK'I.LĒ   friskily
RISK'I.LĒ   riskily

IS'Ō.NUS

NIS'Ō.NUS   unisonous
TIS'Ō.NUS   fluctisonous

IS'OR.Ē

(See IS'ER.Ē)

IS'TEN.SĒ

DIS'TEN.SĒ   distancy
SIS'TEN.SĒ   inconsistency,
insistency,
consistency,
persistency,
subsistency
ZIS'TEN.SĒ   existency,
pre-existency

IS'TENT.LĒ

DIS'TENT.LĒ   distantly
SIS'TENT.LĒ   inconsistently,
insistently, consistently,
persistently,
subsistently
ZIS'TENT.LĒ   existently,
pre-existently

IS'TER.Ē

BIS'TER.Ē   bistoury
BLIS'TER.Ē   blistery
DIS'TER.Ē   faldistory
HIS'TER.Ē   history, prehistory,
protohistory,
psychohistory
MIS'TER.Ē   mystery
SIS'TER.Ē   consistory
TIS'TER.Ē   baptistery

IST'FUL.Ē

LIST'FUL.Ē   listfully
WIST'FUL.Ē   wistfully

IS'TI.KAL

IS'TI.KAL   atheistical, deistical,
egoistical,
casuistical,
pantheistical,
theistical,
euphuistical
DIS'TI.KAL   methodistical
FIS'TI.KAL   paragraphistical,
sophistical,
theosophistical
GWIS'TI.KAL   linguistical
JIS'TI.KAL   dialogistical,
logistical,
synergistical,
eulogistical
KIS'TI.KAL   anarchistical,
antanarchistical,
catechistical
LIS'TI.KAL   anomalistical,
cabalistical
MIS'TI.KAL   alchemistical,
hemistichal,
chemistical,
mystical,
euphemistical
NIS'TI.KAL   agonistical,
antagonistical,
Calvinistical,
canonistical,
synchronistical
PIS'TI.KAL   papistical
RIS'TI.KAL   aoristical,
aphoristical,
eristical,
hypocoristical,
juristical,
characteristical,
puristical,
eucharistical
TIS'TI.KAL   artistical, egotistical,
pietistical,
statistical,
syncretistical
THIS'TI.KAL   apathistical
TRIS'TI.KAL   patristical

IS'TI.KĀT

FIS'TI.KĀT   sophisticate
JIS'TI.KĀT   dephlogisticate,
phlogisticate

IS'TI.KUS

DIS'TI.KUS   distichous
TRIS'TI.KUS   tristichous

IST'LES.NES

LIST'LES.NES   listlessness
ZIST'LES.NES   resistlessness

IS'TOR.Ē

(See IS'TER.Ē)

IS'ŢU.LA

(See IS'CHŌŌ.LA)

Ī'SUL.FĪD

BĪ'SUL.FĪD	*bisulphide*
DĪ'SUL.FĪD	*disulfide*

ĪT'A.BL

DĪT'A.BL	extraditable, indictable, inditable, unindictable, uninditable
KWĪT'A.BL	requitable, unrequitable
LĪT'A.BL	lightable, unlightable
NĪT'A.BL	ignitable, reunitable, unignitable, unitable, ununitable
RĪT'A.BL	writable, unwritable
SĪT'A.BL	excitable, incitable, recitable, citable, sightable, unexcitable, unincitable, uncitable, unsightable

IT'A.BL

FIT'A.BL	fittable, unfittable
HIT'A.BL	hittable, Mehitable, unhittable
KWIT'A.BL	acquittable, quittable, unacquittable
MIT'A.BL	admittable, committable, omittable, permittable, submittable, transmittable, unadmittable, unremittable, unsubmittable
NIT'A.BL	knittable, unknittable
PIT'A.BL	pittable

Ī'TA.BLĒ

DĪ'TA.BLĒ	indictably

NĪ'TA.BLĒ	unitably
SĪ'TA.BLĒ	excitably, unexcitably

IT'A.LĒ

(See IT'I.LĒ)

IT'AN.Ē

BRIT'AN.Ē	Brittany
DIT'AN.Ē	dittany
KIT'AN.Ē	kitteny
LIT'AN.Ē	litany

Ī'TA.TIV

KWĪ'TA.TIV	requitative
RĪ'TA.TIV	writative
SĪ'TA.TIV	excitative, incitative, recitative

IT'EN.ER

BRIT'EN.ER	brightener
FRIT'EN.ER	frightener
HĪT'EN.ER	heightener
HWĪT'EN.ER	whitener
LĪT'EN.ER	enlightener, lightener

(See ĪTNER)

Ī'TEN.ING

(See ĪTEN, add *-ing* where appropriate.)

IT'ER.AL

BIT'ER.AL	presbyteral
LIT'ER.AL	adlittoral, alliteral, biliteral, illiteral, literal, littoral, triliteral

IT'ER.ĀT

IT'ER.ĀT	iterate, reiterate
LIT'ER.ĀT	alliterate, obliterate, transliterate

(See IT'ER.IT)

IT'ER.Ē

GLIT'ER.Ē	glittery
JIT'ER.Ē	jittery

LIT'ER.Ē	littery
TIT'ER.Ē	tittery
TWIT'ER.Ē	twittery

IT'ER.ER

(See ITER, add *-er* where appropriate.)

IT'ER.ING

(See ITER, add *-ing* where appropriate.)

IT'ER.IT

BIT'ER.IT	Presbyterate
LIT'ER.IT	illiterate, literate

(See IT'ER.ĀT)

ĪT'FUL.Ē

FRĪT'FUL.Ē	frightfully
LĪT'FUL.Ē	delightfully
RĪT'FUL.Ē	rightfully
SPĪT'FUL.Ē	spitefully
SPRĪT'FUL.Ē	sprightfully

ITH'ER.Ē

DITH'ER.Ē	dithery
SMITH'ER.Ē	smithery
WITH'ER.Ē	withery

ITH'ER.ING

BLITH'ER.ING	blithering
DITH'ER.ING	dithering
WITH'ER.ING	withering

ITH'I.A

LITH'I.A	lithia
SITH'I.A	forsythia
TITH'I.A	hamartithia

ITH'I.SIS

PITH'I.SIS	epithesis
TITH'I.SIS	antithesis

ĪTH'SUM.LĒ

(TH as in *then*)

BLĪTH'SUM.LĒ	blithesomely
LĪTH'SUM.LĒ	lithesomely

ĪTH′SUM.NES

(**TH** as in *them*)

BLĪTH′SUM.NES   blithesomeness
LĪTH′SUM.NES   lithesomeness

Ī′TI.ER

FLĪ′TI.ER   flightier
MĪ′TI.ER   almightier, mightier

IT′I.ER

FLIT′I.ER   flittier
GRIT′I.ER   grittier
HWIT′I.ER   Whittier
PRIT′I.ER   prettier
WIT′I.ER   wittier

IT′I.GĀT

LIT′I.GĀT   litigate, vitilitigate
MIT′I.GĀT   mitigate

IT′I.KAL

IT′I.KAL   Jesuitical
KRIT′I.KAL   acritical, diacritical,
hypercritical,
hypocritical, critical,
oneirocritical
LIT′I.KAL   analytical,
apolitical,
cosmopolitical,
metropolitical,
political
MIT′I.KAL   eremitical, hermitical,
stalagmitical
RIT′I.KAL   soritical
SIT′I.KAL   parasitical,
thersitical
TIT′I.KAL   stalactitical
TRIT′I.KAL   tritical
VIT′I.KAL   Levitical

Ī′TI.LĒ

FLĪ′TI.LĒ   flightily
MĪ′TI.LĒ   almightily, mightily
SPRĪ′TI.LĒ   sprightily

IT′I.LĒ

IT′I.LĒ   Italy
GRIT′I.LĒ   grittily

PRIT′I.LĒ   prettily
WIT′I.LĒ   wittily

ĪT′I.NES

(See ĪTĒ, add -ness)

IT′I.NES

(See ITĒ, add -ness)

ĪT′ING.LĒ

BĪT′ING.LĒ   bitingly
BLĪT′ING.LĒ   blightingly
SĪT′ING.LĒ   sightingly
SLĪT′ING.LĒ   slightingly
VĪT′ING.LĒ   invitingly

IT′ING.LĒ

(See IT; ITING; add -ingly or -ly where
appropriate.)

IT′I.SĪD

MIT′I.SĪD   miticide
RIT′I.SĪD   pariticide

IT′I.SĪZ

KRIT′I.SĪZ   criticize
LIT′I.SĪZ   depoliticize,
politicize

IT′I.SIZM

BRIT′I.SIZM   Briticism
KRIT′I.SIZM   criticism
WIT′I.SIZM   witticism

ĪT′LI.NES

NĪT′LI.NES   knightliness
SĪT′LI.NES   sightliness
SPRĪT′LI.NES   sprightliness

IT′L.NES

BRIT′L.NES   brittleness
LIT′L.NES   littleness

IT′RI.FĪ

NIT′RI.FĪ   nitrify
VIT′RI.FĪ   vitrify

IT′RI.KA

FIT′RI.KA   amphitrica
RIT′RI.KA   peritricha

IT′Ū.AL

(See ICH′OO.AL)

IT′Ū.LER

(See ICH′OO.LER)

IT′Ū.RĀT

(See ICH′E.RĀT)

ĪV′A.BL

DRĪV′A.BL   drivable, undrivable
PRĪV′A.BL   deprivable
RĪV′A.BL   derivable,
underivable
TRĪV′A.BL   contrivable,
uncontrivable
VĪV′A.BL   revivable,
survivable,
unrevivable,
unsurvivable

IV′A.BL

GIV′A.BL   forgivable, givable,
unforgivable,
ungivable
LIV′A.BL   livable, unlivable

IV′A.LENT

BIV′A.LENT   ambivalent, bivalent
DIV′A.LENT   divalent
KWIV′A.LENT   equivalent,
quinquivalent
LIV′A.LENT   polyvalent
NIV′A.LENT   omnivalent,
univalent
SIV′A.LENT   diversivolent
TIV′A.LENT   multivalent,
multivolent
TRIV′A.LENT   trivalent

ĪV′AN.SĒ

NĪV′AN.SĒ   connivancy
TRĪV′AN.SĒ   contrivancy
VĪV′AN.SĒ   survivancy

IV'A.TIV

PRIV'A.TIV	deprivative, privative
RIV'A.TIV	derivative

IV'EL.ER

DRIV'EL.ER	driveller
SIV'EL.ER	civiller
SNIV'EL.ER	sniveller

Ī'VE.RĒ

Ī'VE.RĒ	ivory
VĪ'VE.RĒ	vivary

IV'ER.Ē

KWIV'ER.Ē	quivery
LIV'ER.Ē	delivery, livery
RIV'ER.Ē	rivery
SHIV'ER.Ē	shivery
SLIV'ER.Ē	slivery

IV'ER.ER

LIV'ER.ER	deliverer
KWIV'ER.ER	quiverer
SHIV'ER.ER	shiverer
SLIV'ER.ER	sliverer

IV'ER.ING

(See **IVER**, add -ing where appropriate.)

IV'ER.US

BIV'ER.US	herbivorous
DIV'ER.US	frondivorous
FIV'ER.US	amphivorous
GWIV'ER.US	sanguivorous
JIV'ER.US	frugivorous
KWIV'ER.US	equivorous
LIV'ER.US	mellivorous
MIV'ER.US	limivorous, pomivorous, vermivorous
NIV'ER.US	graminivorous, granivorous, carnivorous, omnivorous, panivorous, ranivorous, sanguinivorous
PIV'ER.US	apivorous, cepivorous
SIV'ER.US	baccivorous, fucivorous, mucivorous, nucivorous, ossivorous, piscivorous, succivorous
TIV'ER.US	fructivorous, phytivorous, photivorous, insectivorous, vegetivorous
VIV'ER.US	ovivorous
ZIV'ER.US	oryzivorous

IV'I.A

LIV'I.A	Bolivia, Olivia
TRIV'I.A	trivia

IV'I.AL

DRIV'I.AL	quadrivial
LIV'I.AL	oblivial
SIV'I.AL	lixivial
TRIV'I.AL	trivial
VIV'I.AL	convivial

IV'ID.LĒ

LIV'ID.LĒ	lividly
VIV'ID.LĒ	vividly

IV'ID.NES

LIV'ID.NES	lividness
VIV'ID.NES	vividness

IV'IL.Ē

SIV'IL.Ē	civilly, uncivilly
SNIV'IL.Ē	snivelly

ĪV'ING.LĒ

(See **ĪV**, add -ingly where appropriate.)

IV'ING.LĒ

(See **IVING**, add -ly where appropriate.)

IV'I.TĒ

KLIV'I.TĒ	acclivity, declivity, proclivity
PRIV'I.TĒ	privity

SIV'I.TĒ	expressivity, emissivity, impassivity, compassivity, passivity
TIV'I.TĒ	*A* absorptivity, activity, *F* festivity, hyperactivity, *I* inactivity, inductivity, incogitativity, instinctivity, *K* captivity, cogitativity, collectivity, conductivity, connectivity, correlativity, causativity, *KR* creativity, *M* motivity, *N* nativity, negativity, *O* objectivity, alternativity, *P* permittivity, perceptivity, positivity, *PR* productivity, *R* radioactivity, reactivity, reflectivity, relativity, reproductivity, receptivity, retroactivity, resistivity *S* selectivity, sensitivity, subjectivity, susceptivity

IV'I.UM

DRIV'I.UM	quadrivium
SIV'I.UM	lixivium
TRIV'I.UM	trivium

IV'I.US

BIV'I.US	bivious
BLIV'I.US	oblivious
NIV'I.US	niveous
SIV'I.US	lascivious, lixivious
TIV'I.US	multivious

IV'O.KAL

KWIV'O.KAL	equivocal, unequivocal
NIV'O.KAL	univocal

IV'O.LĒ

RIV'O.LĒ	Rivoli
TIV'O.LĒ	Tivoli

Ĭ'VO.RĒ

(See Ĭ'VE.RĒ)

IV'OR.US

(See IV'ER.US)

ĪZ'A.BL

NĪZ'A.BL	cognizable

(See ĪZ, add -ABL)

IZ'A.BL

KWIZ'A.BL	acquisible, quizzable, unquizzable
RIZ'A.BL	derisible, risible
VIZ'A.BL	divisible, indivisible, invisible, undivisible, visible

ĪZ'A.BLĒ

SĪZ'A.BLĒ	sizably
VĪZ'A.BLĒ	advisably, inadvisably

ĪZ'ED.LĒ

MĪZ'ED.LĒ	surmisedly
VĪZ'ED.LĒ	advisedly, improvisedly, provisedly, unadvisedly

Ĭ'ZER.Ē

RĬ'ZER.Ē	derisory, irrisory
VĬ'ZER.Ē	advisory, provisory, revisory, supervisory

IZ'ER.Ē

KWIZ'ER.Ē	quizzery
MIZ'ER.Ē	misery

IZH'UN.AL

SIZH'UN.AL	transitional, precisional
VIZH'UN.AL	divisional, previsional, provisional, revisional, visional

IZ'I.AK

DIZ'I.AK	aphrodisiac
NIZ'I.AK	Dionysiac

IZ'I.AN

DIZ'I.AN	aphrodisian, paradisian
FRIZ'I.AN	Frisian
LIZ'I.AN	Elysian
RIZ'I.AN	Parisian

(See IZHUN)

IZ'I.BL

(See IZ'A.BL)

IZ'I.ER

BIZ'I.ER	busier
DIZ'I.ER	dizzier
FIZ'I.ER	fizzier
FRIZ'I.ER	frizzier

IZ'I.EST

(See IZĒ, change -y to -iest.)

IZ'I.KAL

DIZ'I.KAL	paradisical
FIZ'I.KAL	biophysical, physical, geophysical, cataphysical, metaphysical, psychophysical, zoophysical
KWIZ'I.KAL	quizzical
TIZ'I.KAL	phthisical

IZ'I.LĒ

BIZ'I.LĒ	busily
DIZ'I.LĒ	dizzily
FIZ'I.LĒ	fizzily

IZ'I.NES

BIZ'I.NES	busyness
DIZ'I.NES	dizziness
FIZ'I.NES	fizziness

ĪZ'ING.LĒ

LĪZ'ING.LĒ	tantalizingly
NĪZ'ING.LĒ	agonizingly, scrutinizingly
PRĪZ'ING.LĒ	apprisingly, enterprisingly, surprisingly, unsurprisingly
SPĪZ'ING.LĒ	despisingly
TĪZ'ING.LĒ	appetizingly

IZ'ING.LĒ

HWIZ'ING.LĒ	whizzingly
KWIZ'ING.LĒ	quizzingly

IZ'I.TOR

KWIZ'I.TOR	acquisitor, disquisitor, inquisitor, requisitor
VIZ'I.TOR	visitor

Ĭ'ZO.RĒ

(See Ĭ'ZE.RĒ)

Ō'A.BL

Ō'A.BL	owable
BLŌ'A.BL	blowable
MŌ'A.BL	mowable
NŌ'A.BL	knowable, unknowable
RŌ'A.BL	rowable
SHŌ'A.BL	showable
SLŌ'A.BL	slowable
SŌ'A.BL	sewable, sowable, unsewable, unsowable
STŌ'A.BL	bestowable, stowable
THRŌ'A.BL	overthrowable, throwable
TRŌ'A.BL	trowable, untrowable

OB'A.BL

PROB'A.BL	improbable, probable

ROB'A.BL   robbable,
unrobbable

Ō'BER.Ē

KRŌ'BER.Ē   crowberry
SNŌ'BER.Ē   snowberry

ÔB'ER.Ē

DÔB'ER.Ē   dauberie
STRÔB'ER.Ē   strawberry

OB'ER.Ē

BOB'ER.Ē   bobbery
JOB'ER.Ē   jobbery,
stock-jobbery
KLOB'ER.Ē   clobbery
NOB'ER.Ē   hobnobbery
ROB'ER.Ē   corroboree, robbery
SLOB'ER.Ē   slobbery
SNOB'ER.Ē   snobbery

OB'ER.ING

KLOB'ER.ING   clobbering
SLOB'ER.ING   slobbering

Ō'BI.A

Ō'BI.A   obeah
FŌ'BI.A   *A* aerophobia,
agoraphobia,
airphobia,
acarophobia,
acousticophobia,
acrophobia,
algophobia,
amathophobia,
amaxophobia,
androphobia,
Anglophobia,
anthropophobia,
anuptaphobia,
arachibutyrophobia,
astrophobia,
atychiphobia, *B*
bacteriophobia,
ballistrophobia,
basophobia,
batophobia,
batrachophobia,
blennophobia, *BR*
bromidrosiphobia,
brontophobia, *D*
dextrophobia,

demonphobia,
dermatophobia,
dikephobia,
dysmorphobia,
dystychiphobia,
domatophobia,
doraphobia, *DR*
dromophobia, *E*
ecophobia,
enissophobia,
enosiophobia,
eosophobia,
eremophobia,
ergasophobia,
ergophobia,
erythrophobia,
erotophobia, *F*
pharmacophobia,
fibriphobia,
philophobia, phobia,
phobophobia,
phonophobia,
photophobia, *FR*
Francophobia, *G*
Galliphobia,
gamophobia, *H*
hagiophobia,
hamartiophobia,
harpaxophobia,
helminthophobia,
heresyphobia,
hydrophobia,
hydrophobophobia,
hygrophobia,
hyophobia,
hypengyophobia,
hypnophobia,
hodophobia,
homichlophobia,
homophobia, *I*
iatrophobia,
ichthyophobia, *J*
gephyrophobia,
geniophobia,
jentaculophobia,
gerascophobia,
gymnophobia,
gynekophobia, *K*
kakorrhaphiophobia,
catageophobia,
kathisophobia,
kenophobia,
cherophobia,
kinesophobia,
kokophobia, *KL*
climacophobia,
clinophobia,
claustrophobia, *KR*
chrematophobia,
cremnophobia,
chronophobia, *L*
lallophobia,

levophobia,
lygophobia,
lilapsophobia,
linonophobia,
lyssophobia, *M*
maieusiophobia,
macrophobia,
maniaphobia,
mastigophobia,
mechanophobia,
megalophobia,
melissophobia,
melophobia,
metrophobia,
myophobia,
mysophobia,
mytrophobia,
molysmophobia,
monophobia,
muriphobia, *N*
nebulaphobia,
negrophobia,
nyctophobia,
nosophobia,
noysnophobia,
novercaphobia,
numerophobia, *O*
odynophobia,
ophidiophobia,
ophthalmophobia,
ochlophobia,
ombrophobia,
onomatophobia,
optophobia,
osmophobia, *P*
paralilipophobia,
parthenophobia,
pathophobia,
pediculophobia,
paedophobia,
pediophobia,
peccatiphobia,
peniaphobia,
pentheraphobia,
pyrophobia,
pogonophobia,
ponophobia,
porphyrophobia,
pornophobia, *PL*
placophobia,
pluviophobia *PR*
prosophobia, *R*
rhabdophobia,
rhyophobia,
rhytiphobia,
Russophobia, *S*
selenophobia,
cenophobia,
sciaphobia,
cibophobia,
siderodromophobia,
syphiliphobia,

syngenosophobia,
cynophobia,
sitophobia,
soceraphobia,
sociophobia, *SK*
scoleciphobia,
scopophobia,
Scotophobia, *SP*
spectrophobia, *ST*
stasibasiphobia,
stasiphobia,
stenophobia,
stygiophobia,
staurophobia, *T*
taphephobia,
tapinophobia,
technophobia,
teleophobia,
teratophobia,
tobaccophobia,
tocophobia,
tonitrophobia,
topophobia,
teutophobia, *TH*
thalassophobia,
thanatophobia,
theophobia,
phthiriophobia, *TR*
traumatophobia,
triskaidekaphobia,
tropophobia, *V*
verbophobia,
verminophobia, *Y*
euphobia,
uranophobia,
urethrophobia, *Z*
xanthophobia,
zelophobia,
xenophobia,
zoophobia*

KŌ'BI.A	cobia

Ō'BI.AN

GRŌ'BI.AN	grobian
KRŌ'BI.AN	macrobian, microbian
NŌ'BI.AN	cenobean

OB'I.NET

BOB'I.NET	bobbinet
ROB'I.NET	robinet

(*For still more phobias, see Appendix D. How many phobias we do have—and to rhyme with them all, just two little words: *obeah*, "a religious belief of African origin involving witchcraft"; and *cobia*—the sergeant fish!)

Ō'BI.UM

Ō'BI.UM	niobium
RŌ'BI.UM	aerobium
ZŌ'BI.UM	rhizobium

OB'O.LUS

OB'O.LUS	obolus
KOB'O.LUS	discobolus

OB'Ū.LAR

GLOB'Ū.LAR	globular
LOB'Ū.LAR	lobular

ŌCH'A.BL

PŌCH'A.BL	poachable
PRŌCH'A.BL	approachable, irreproachable, reproachable, unapproachable

Ô'DA.BL

Ô'DA.BL	audible, inaudible
LÔ'DA.BL	laudable, unlaudable
PLÔ'DA.BL	applaudable, plaudable

Ō'DA.LER

Ō'DA.LER	odaller
YŌ'DA'.LER	yodeler

OD'ER.ER

DOD'ER.ER	dodderer
FOD'ER.ER	fodderer
SOD'ER.ER	solderer

OD'ER.ING

DOD'ER.ING	doddering
FOD'ER.ING	foddering
SOD'ER.ING	soldering

Ō'DI.AK

KŌ'DI.AK	Kodiak
NŌ'DI.AK	nodiak
ZŌ'DI.AK	zodiac

Ō'DI.AL

LŌ'DI.AL	allodial
NŌ'DI.AL	palinodial, threnodial
PŌ'DI.AL	podial
SŌ'DI.AL	episodial, prosodial
TŌ'DI.AL	custodial

Ō'DI.AN

Ō'DI.AN	triodion
BŌ'DI.AN	Cambodian
LŌ'DI.AN	collodion, melodeon, nickelodeon
RŌ'DI.AN	Rhodian
SŌ'DI.AN	prosodian
TŌ'DI.AN	custodian

Ô'DI.BL

(See Ô'DA.BL)

OD'I.FĪ

KOD'I.FĪ	codify
MOD'I.FĪ	modify

OD'I.KAL

OD'I.KAL	periodical
KOD'I.KAL	codical
MOD'I.KAL	spasmodical
NOD'I.KAL	monodical, nodical, synodical
SOD'I.KAL	episodical, prosodical, rhapsodical
THOD'I.KAL	methodical, unmethodical

Ô'DI.NES

BÔD'I.NES	bawdiness
GÔD'I.NES	gaudiness

Ō'DI.ON

(See Ō'DI.AN)

OD'I.TĒ

OD'I.TĒ	oddity
KWOD'I.TĒ	quoddity
MOD'I.TĒ	discommodity, incommodity, commodity

Ô'DI.TER

Ô'DI.TER	auditor
PLÔ'DI.TER	plauditor

Ō'DI.UM

Ō'DI.UM	odeum, odium, triodium
LŌ'DI.UM	allodium
MŌ'DI.UM	plasmodium
PŌ'DI.UM	lycopodium, monopodium, parapodium, podium, sympodium
RŌ'DI.UM	rhodium
SŌ'DI.UM	sodium, taxodium

Ō'DI.US

Ō'DI.US	odious
LŌ'DI.US	melodious, unmelodious
MŌ'DI.US	Asmodeus, discommodious, incommodious, commodious, uncommodious

OD'Ū.LAR

MOD'Ū.LAR	modular
NOD'Ū.LAR	nodular

OF'A.GA

OF'A.GA	zoöphaga
KOF'A.GA	sarcophaga

OF'A.GAL

OF'A.GAL	zoöphagal
KOF'A.GAL	sarcophagal

OF'A.GAN

OF'A.GAN	ichthyophagan, geophagan, ophiophagan, theophagan, zoophagan
DROF'A.GAN	androphagan
KOF'A.GAN	batrachophagan, sarcophagan
KROF'A.GAN	necrophagan

LOF'A.GAN	hylophagan, xylophagan
POF'A.GAN	hippophagan
PROF'A.GAN	saprophagan
THOF'A.GAN	lithophagan
THROF'A.GAN	anthrophagan

OF'A.GUS

OF'A.GUS	ichthyophagous, geophagous, creophagous, ophiophagous, theophagous, zoophagous
DROF'A.GUS	androphagous
GOF'A.GUS	oligophagous
KOF'A.GUS	batrachophagous, sarcophagous, sarcophagus, scolecophagous
KROF'A.GUS	necrophagous
LOF'A.GUS	hylophagous, xylophagous
POF'A.GUS	hippophagous
PROF'A.GUS	saprophagous
SOF'A.GUS	esophagus
THOF'A.GUS	lithophagous
THROF'A.GUS	anthrophagous
TOF'A.GUS	phytophagous, galactophygous, harpactophagous, pantophagous, scatophagous

OF'A.JĒ

OF'A.JĒ	ichthyophagy, geophagy, ophiophagy, ostreophagy, theophagy, zoophagy
DOF'A.JĒ	cardophagy
DROF'A.JĒ	androphagy
KOF'A.JĒ	batrachophagy, mycophagy, onychophagy, sarcophagy
KROF'A.JĒ	necrophagy
LOF'A.JĒ	hylophagy, xylophagy
MOF'A.JĒ	omophagy, psomophagy
POF'A.JĒ	anthropophagy, hippophagy
PROF'A.JĒ	saprophagy
ROF'A.JĒ	Heterophagi, xerophagy
SOF'A.JĒ	exophagy, opsophagy

THOF'A.JĒ	lithophagy
TOF'A.JĒ	phytophagy, galactophagy, Lotophagi, pantophagy, poltophagy

OF'A.JIK

(See **OF'A.JĒ**, replace -y with -ic)

OF'A.JIST

(See **OF'A.JĒ**, replace -y with -ist)

O'FA.NĒ

(See **O'FO.NĒ**)

OF'EN.ER

OF'EN.ER	oftener
KOF'EN.ER	encoffiner, coffiner
SOF'EN.ER	softener

(See **OF'TEN.ER**)

OF'ER.ER

OF'ER.ER	offerer
GOF'ER.ER	gofferer
KOF'ER.ER	cofferer
PROF'ER.ER	profferer

OF'ER.ING

OF'ER.ING	burnt offering, offering, peace offering
GOF'ER.ING	goffering
KOF'ER.ING	coffering
PROF'ER.ING	proffering

OF'E.RUS

OF'E.RUS	zoophorous, zoophorus
GOF'E.RUS	mastigophorous
LOF'E.RUS	phyllophorous
NOF'E.RUS	adenophorous
ROF'E.RUS	pyrophorous
SOF'E.RUS	isophorous
TOF'E.RUS	galactophorous, chaetophorous
TROF'E.RUS	electrophorous, loutrophoros

OF'I.KAL

SOF'I.KAL	philosophical, sophical, theosophical
TROF'I.KAL	trophical

OF'I.LIST

OF'I.LIST	bibliophilist, zoophilist
KOF'I.LIST	Francophilist
NOF'I.LIST	oenophilist
ROF'I.LIST	peristerophilist

OF'I.LIZM

OF'I.LIZM	bibliophilism, biophilism
KOF'I.LIZM	Francophilism
KROF'I.LIZM	necrophilism

OF'I.LUS

OF'I.LUS	heliophilous, Theophilus, zoophilous
BROF'I.LUS	ombrophilous
DOF'I.LUS	acidophilus
DROF'I.LUS	dendrophilous, hydrophilous
GROF'I.LUS	hygrophelous
KOF'I.LUS	sarcophilous
LOF'I.LUS	xylophilous
MOF'I.LUS	anemophilous, chasmophilous, nemophilous, potamophilous
NOF'I.LUS	limnophilous
POF'I.LUS	tropophilous
PROF'I.LUS	coprophilous, saprophilous
ROF'I.LUS	xerophilous
THOF'I.LUS	ornithophilous
ZOF'I.LUS	mazophilous

OF'O.LIST

NOF'O.LIST	cacophonophilist, canopholist
SOF'O.LIST	chrysopholist

OF'O.NĒ

OF'O.NĒ	radiophany, stereophany, theophany
JOF'O.NĒ	laryngophony
KOF'O.NĒ	cacophony
KROF'O.NĒ	microphony
LOF'O.NĒ	colophony, xylophony
MOF'O.NĒ	homophony
NOF'O.NĒ	monophany, satanophany
PROF'O.NĒ	lamprophony
ROF'O.NĒ	heterophony
THOF'O.NĒ	orthophony
TOF'O.NĒ	photophony, Christophony, tautophony

OF'O.NIST

(See **OF'O.NĒ**, change -y to -ist where appropriate.)

OF'O.NUS

DROF'O.NUS	hydrophanous
GROF'O.NUS	hygrophanous
KOF'O.NUS	cacophonous
LOF'O.NUS	megalophonous
MOF'O.NUS	homophonous
NOF'O.NUS	monophonous
ROF'O.NUS	pyrophanous, pyrophonous, stentorophonous

OF'O.RUS

(See **OF'ER.US**)

OF'TEN.ER

OF'TEN.ER	oftener
SOF'TEN.ER	softener

(See **OF'EN.ER**)

Ô'FUL.Ē

Ô'FUL.Ē	awfully
LÔ'FUL.Ē	lawfully, unlawfully

Ô'FUL.NES

Ô'FUL.NES	awfulness
LÔ'FUL.NES	lawfulness, unlawfulness

OG'A.MĒ

OG'A.MĒ	oögamy
DOG'A.MĒ	endogamy
FOG'A.MĒ	adelphogamy
KOG'A.MĒ	dichogamy
MOG'A.MĒ	homogamy
NOG'A.MĒ	monogamy
ROG'A.MĒ	deuterogamy, heterogamy
SOG'A.MĒ	anisogamy, exogamy, isogamy, mixogamy, misogamy
TOG'A.MĒ	autogamy

OG'A.MIST

DOG'A.MIST	endogamist
NOG'A.MIST	monogamist
ROG'A.MIST	deuterogamist
SOG'A.MIST	exogamist, misogamist
TOG'A.MIST	cryptogamist

OG'A.MUS

DOG'A.MUS	endogamous
MOG'A.MUS	homogamous
NOG'A.MUS	monogamous
ROG'A.MUS	phanerogamous, heterogamus
SOG'A.MUS	exogamous
TOG'A.MUS	cryptogamous

OG'ER.Ē

DOG'ER.Ē	doggery
FOG'ER.Ē	pettifoggery
FROG'ER.Ē	froggery
GOG'ER.Ē	demagoguery
GROG'ER.Ē	groggery
HOG'ER.Ē	hoggery
TOG'ER.Ē	toggery

OG'ER.EL

DOG'ER.EL	doggerel
HOG'ER.EL	hoggerel

Ō'GI.IZM

BŌ'GI.IZM	bogeyism
FŌ'GI.IZM	fogeyism

OG'NO.MĒ

OG'NO.MĒ	physiognomy, craniognomy
ROG'NO.MĒ	chirognomy
THOG'NO.MĒ	pathognomy

OG'NO.SĒ

OG'NO.SĒ	geognosy
KOG'NO.SĒ	pharmacognosy

OG'O.NĒ

OG'O.NĒ	bibliogony, physiogony, heroögony, geogony, theogony
HOG'O.NĒ	mahogany
MOG'O.NĒ	homogony, cosmogony
NOG'O.NĒ	monogony
ROG'O.NĒ	heterogony
THOG'O.NĒ	mythogony, pathogony

OG'O.NIST

OG'O.NIST	theogonist
MOG'O.NIST	cosmogonist

OG'RA.FĒ

OG'RA.FĒ	*A* areography, archaeography, *B* balneography, bibliography, biography, biogeography, *BR* brachyography, *D* dactyliography, *E* ecclesiography, electrocardiography, *F* phythogeography, physiography, *H* hagiography, haliography, heliography, heresiography, historiography, horography, horologiography, *I* ideography *J* geography, *K* cacography, cardiography, choreography, *M* myography, *N* neography, *O* ophiography, oreography, osteography, autobiography, *P* paleography, paramiography, *R* radiography, *S*

DOG'RA.FĒ	semeiography, symbolaeography, sciography, *ST* stereography, *T* tacheography, *Z* zoogeography, zoography celidography, pseudography
DROG'RA.FĒ	dendrography, hydrography
FOG'RA.FĒ	glyphography, morphography
GOG'RA.FĒ	logography
KOG'RA.FĒ	discography, pharmacography, phycography, cacography, calcography, chalcography, lexicography, zincography
KROG'RA.FĒ	macrography, micrography
LOG'RA.FĒ	*D* dactylography, *E* encephalography, epistolography, *H* haplography, hyalography, holography, *KR* crystallography, chromoxylography, *M* metallography, *P* pyelography, *S* sigillography, sillography, *ST* stelography, stylography, *T* pterylography, *Z* xylography
MOG'RA.FĒ	*A* anemography, *D* demography, *F* phantasmography, filmography, *H* homography, *K* cosmography, *M* mammography, microcosmography, mimography, *N* nomography, pneumography, *S* psalmography, seismography, *T* tomography, *TH* thermography
NOG'RA.FĒ	*E* ethnography, *F* phonography, *G* galvanography, *H* hymnography, *I* ichnography, iconography, *KR* Christianography,

	chronography, *L* lichenography, lipsanography, *M* mechanography, monography, *O* organography, oceanography, *P* paleethnography, pornography, *PL* planography, *S* scenography, *SF* sphenography, *ST* stenography, *T* technography, *Y* uranography, *Z* zenography
POG'RA.FĒ	anthropography, phototypography, lipography, prosopography, stereotypography, topography, typography
PROG'RA.FĒ	reprography
ROG'RA.FĒ	*H* heterography, hierography, horography, *K* chirography, chorography, *M* macrography, *N* neurography, *O* orography, *P* papyrography, petrography, pyrography, *R* rhyparography, *S* cerography, siderography, *T* pterography, xerography, xylopyrography
SOG'RA.FĒ	doxography, hypsography, isography, gypsography, nosography, thalassography
THOG'RA.FĒ	anthography, ethography, photolithography, chromolithography, lithography, mythography, orthography
TOG'RA.FĒ	*A* astrophotography, *D* dittography, *F* phantasmatography, phytography, photography, *GL* glyptography, *H* hematography, hyetography,

histography, *K*
cartography,
chartography,
cometography, *KL*
climatography, *KR*
cryptography,
chromatography,
chromophotography,
N numismatography,
pneumatography, *O*
odontography,
ontography,
autography, *P*
paleontography,
pantography,
perspectography, *PL*
plastography, *S*
sematography,
cinematography, *SK*
skeletography,
scotography, *STR*
stratography, *T*
telephotography,
toreumatography,
TH thanatography

TROG'RA.FĒ petrography

OG'RA.FER

(See **OG'RA.FĒ,** change -*y* to -*er* where appropriate.)

OG'RA.FIST

(See **OG'RA.FĒ,** change -*y* to -*ist* where appropriate.)

OI'A.BL

BOI'A.BL	buoyable
JOI'A.BL	enjoyable
KLOI'A.BL	cloyable
KOI'A.BL	decoyable
PLOI'A.BL	deployable, employable
TOI'A.BL	toyable
VOI'A.BL	convoyable

OI'AL.Ē

LOI'AL.Ē	disloyally, loyally
ROI'AL.Ē	royally

OI'A.LIST

LOI'A.LIST	loyalist
ROI'A.LIST	royalist

OI'A.LIZM

LOI'A.LIZM	loyalism
ROI'A.LIZM	royalism

OI'AL.TĒ

LOI'AL.TĒ	disloyalty, loyalty
ROI'AL.TĒ	royalty, vice-royalty

OI'AN.SĒ

BOI'AN.SĒ	buoyancy, flamboyancy
TOI'AN.SĒ	chatoyancy
VOI'AN.SĒ	clairvoyancy

OI'ANT.LĒ

BOI'ANT.LĒ	buoyantly, flamboyantly
VOI'ANT.LĒ	clairvoyantly

OI'ING.LĒ

KLOI'ING.LĒ	cloyingly
NOI'ING.LĒ	annoyingly
TOI'ING.LĒ	toyingly

Ō'I.KAL

GŌ'I.KAL	egoical
RŌ'I.KAL	heroical
STŌ'I.KAL	stoical

Ō'IL.Ē

BLŌ'IL.Ē	blowily
SHŌ'IL.Ē	showily
SNŌ'IL.Ē	snowily

OIL'ING.LĒ

(See **OIL,** add -*ingly* where appropriate.)

OIN'A.BL

JOIN'A.BL	disjoinable, joinable
KOIN'A.BL	coinable, uncoinable

Ō'ING.LE

FLŌ'ING.LĒ	flowingly
GLŌ'ING.LĒ	glowingly

KRŌ'ING.LĒ	crowingly
NŌ'ING.LĒ	knowingly, unknowingly

OIN'TED.LĒ

JOIN'TED.LĒ	disjointedly, jointedly
POIN'TED.LĒ	pointedly

OIS'TER.ER

KLOIS'TER.ER	cloisterer
ROIS'TER.ER	roisterer

OIS'TER.ING

KLOIS'TER.ING	cloistering
ROIS'TER.ING	roistering

OIS'TER.US

BOIS'TER.US	boisterous
ROIS'TER.US	roisterous

OI'SUM.LĒ

KLOI'SUM.LĒ	cloysomely
NOI'SUM.LĒ	noisomely
TOI'SUM.LĒ	toysomely

OI'TER.ER

LOI'TER.ER	loiterer
NOI'TER.ER	reconnoiterer

(See **OITRER**)

OI'TER.ING

LOI'TER.ING	loitering
NOI'TER.ING	reconnoitering

(See **OITRING**)

OJ'E.NĒ

OJ'E.NĒ	abiogeny, biogeny, embryogeny, geogeny, cryogeny, ontogeny, oögeny, ostogeny, zoögeny
DOJ'E.NĒ	pseudogyny
DROJ'E.NĒ	androgeny, androgyny

LOJ'E.NĒ	philogeny, philogyny, metallogeny
MOJ'E.NĒ	homogeny, nomogeny
NOJ'E.NĒ	ethnogeny, hymenogeny, monogeny, monogyny, spanogyny
POJ'E.NĒ	anthropogeny
PROJ'E.NĒ	progeny
ROJ'E.NĒ	epeirogeny, erogeny, heterogeny, orogeny
SOJ'E.NĒ	misogyny
THOJ'E.NĒ	pathogeny
TOJ'E.NĒ	autogeny, photogeny, histogeny, odontogeny, ontogeny, autogeny, protogyny

OJ'E.NIST

OJ'E.NIST	abiogenist, biogenist
LOJ'E.NIST	philogynist
NOJ'E.NIST	monogenist, monogynist
ROJ'E.NIST	heterogynist
SOJ'E.NIST	misogynist

OJ'E.NĪZ

MOJ'E.NĪZ	homogenize
TROJ'E.NĪZ	nitrogenize

(See **OJ'E.NĒ**, change *-y* to *-ize* where appropriate.)

OJ'E.NUS

OJ'E.NUS	biogenous, ideogenous, idiogenous, geogenous
DOJ'E.NUS	endogenous, kedogenous, spodogenous
DROJ'E.NUS	androgenous, androgynous, hydrogenous
LOJ'E.NUS	philogynous
MOJ'E.NUS	homogenous, primogenous, thermogenous
NOJ'E.NUS	monogenous, monogynous

POJ'E.NUS	hypogenous
ROJ'E.NUS	heterogenous, pyrogenous
SOJ'E.NUS	exogenous, isogenous, misogynous
THOJ'E.NUS	lithogenous
TROJ'E.NUS	nitrogenous

Ō'JI.A

BŌ'JI.A	cambogia
LŌ'JI.A	apologia

Ō'JI.AN

BŌ'JI.AN	gambogian
LŌ'JI.AN	archaelogian, astrologian, philologian, geologian, mythologian, neologian, theologian

OJ'I.KAL

GOJ'I.KAL	anagogical, apagogical, demagogical, synagogical

(See **OL'O.JĒ**, change *-y* to *-ical* where appropriate; see **OJIK**, add *-al* where appropriate.)

OJ'I.NĒ
(See **OJ'E.NĒ**)

OJ'I.NUS
(See **OJ'E.NUS**)

Ō'KA.BL

PŌ'KA.BL	pokable
SMŌ'KA.BL	smokable, unsmokable
VŌ'KA.BL	invocable, revokable, vocable
YŌ'KA.BL	unyokable, yokable

Ō'KAL.Ē

FŌ'KAL.Ē	focally
LŌ'KAL.Ē	locally
VŌ'KAL.Ē	vocally

Ō'KA.LIST

LŌ'KA.LIST	philocalist, localist
VŌ'KA.LIST	vocalist

Ō'KA.LĪZ

FŌ'KA.LĪZ	focalize
LŌ'KA.LĪZ	localize
VŌ'KA.LĪZ	vocalize

Ō'KA.LIZM

LŌ'KA.LIZM	localism
VŌ'KA.LIZM	vocalism

ÔK'A.TIV

TÔK'A.TIV	talkative

(See OK'A.TIV)

OK'A.TIV

LOK'A.TIV	locative
VOK'A.TIV	invocative, provocative, vocative

(See ÔK'A.TIV)

Ō'KEN.LĒ

BRŌ'KEN.LĒ	brokenly
SPŌ'KEN.LĒ	outspokenly

OK'ER.Ē

KROK'ER.Ē	crockery
MOK'ER.Ē	mockery
ROK'ER.Ē	rockery
STOK'ER.Ē	Comstockery

Ō'KI.ER

Ō'KI.ER	oakier
CHŌ'KI.ER	chokier
KRŌ'KI.ER	croakier
PŌ'KI.ER	pokier
SMŌ'KI.ER	smokier
SŌ'KI.ER	soakier
YŌ'KI.ER	yolkier

OK'I.LĒ

| KOK'I.LĒ | cockily |
| STOK'I.LĒ | stockily |

ÔK'I.LĒ

CHÔK'I.LĒ	chalkily
GÔK'I.LĒ	gawkily
PÔK'I.LĒ	pawkily
SKWÔK'I.LĒ	squawkily
STÔK'I.LĒ	stalkily

Ō'KI.NES

(See ŌKĒ, add -ness where appropriate.)

ÔK'I.NES

CHÔK'I.NES	chalkiness
GÔK'I.NES	gawkiness
PÔK'I.NES	pawkiness
SKWÔK'I.NES	squawkiness
STÔK'I.NES	stalkiness
TÔK'I.NES	talkiness

(See OK'I.NES)

OK'I.NES

KOK'I.NES	cockiness
ROK'I.NES	rockiness
STOK'I.NES	stockiness

(See ÔK'I.NES)

Ō'KING.LĒ

CHŌ'KING.LĒ	chokingly
JŌ'KING.LĒ	jokingly
KRŌ'KING.LĒ	croakingly
STRŌ'KING.LĒ	strokingly
VŌ'KING.LĒ	provokingly, unprovokingly

ÔK'ING.LĒ

| MOK'ING.LĒ | mockingly |
| SHOK'ING.LĒ | shockingly |

OK'LI.A

| KOK'LI.A | cochlea |
| TROK'LI.A | trochlea |

OK'RA.SĒ

OK'RA.SĒ	hagiocracy, idiocracy, neocracy, plousiocracy, theocracy, theocrasy
BOK'RA.SĒ	mobocracy, snobocracy
DOK'RA.SĒ	landocracy
DROK'RA.SĒ	androcracy
GOK'RA.SĒ	logocracy
HOK'RA.SĒ	adhocracy
KLOK'RA.SĒ	ochlocracy
KOK'RA.SĒ	gynecocracy, ptococracy
LOK'RA.SĒ	doulocracy, ochlocracy
MOK'RA.SĒ	arithmocracy, democracy, cosmocracy, nomocracy, timocracy
NOK'RA.SĒ	ethnocracy, juvenocracy, cottonocracy, millionocracy, monocracy, pornocracy, technocracy
POK'RA.SĒ	hypocrisy, shopocrasy
ROK'RA.SĒ	bureaucracy, hierocracy
SOK'RA.SĒ	isocracy, chrysocracy, pantisocracy, thalassocracy
TOK'RA.SĒ	*A* aristocracy, *D* despotocracy, *E* ergatocracy, *J* gerontocracy, *K* kakistocracy, *KL* kleptocracy, *M* meritocracy, *O* autocracy, *P* pedantocracy, *PL* plantocracy, plutocracy, *SKW* squattocracy, *STR* stratocracy, *T* ptochocracy
VOK'RA.SĒ	slavocracy

OK'RA.TIZM

OK'RA.TIZM	theocratism
MOK'RA.TIZM	democratism
ROK'RA.TIZM	bureaucratism
SOK'RA.TIZM	Socratism

(See **OK'RA.SĒ,** change -cy to -tism where appropriate.)

OK'RO.NUS

NOK'RO.NUS	monochronous
SOK'RO.NUS	isochronous
TOK'RO.NUS	tautochronous

OK'SI.KAL

DOK'SI.KAL	orthodoxical, paradoxical
POK'SI.KAL	hypoxical
TOK'SI.KAL	radiotoxical, toxical

ŌK'SING.LĒ

| HŌK'SING.LĒ | hoaxingly |
| KŌK'SING.LĒ | coaxingly |

OK'TOR.SHIP

| DOK'TOR.SHIP | doctorship |
| PROK'TOR.SHIP | proctorship |

OK'Ū.LAR

OK'Ū.LAR	ocular
JOK'Ū.LAR	jocular
LOK'Ū.LAR	locular
NOK'Ū.LAR	binocular, monocular, senocular
VOK'Ū.LAR	vocular

OK'Ū.LĀT

OK'Ū.LĀT	exoculate, oculate
FLOK'Ū.LĀT	flocculate
NOK'Ū.LĀT	binoculate, inoculate

OK'Ū.LUS

OK'Ū.LUS	oculus
FLOK'Ū.LUS	flocculus
LOK'Ū.LUS	loculus
NOK'Ū.LUS	monoculous, monoculus

Ō'KUS.ING

| FŌ'KUS.ING | focusing, focussing |
| HŌ'KUS.ING | hocusing, hocussing |

ŌL'A.BL

BŌL'A.BL	bowlable, unbowlable
GŌL'A.BL	goalable
HŌL'A.BL	holable, unholable
JŌL'A.BL	cajolable, uncajolable
PŌL'A.BL	pollable, unpollable
RŌL'A.BL	enrollable, rollable, unenrollable, unrollable
SŌL'A.BL	inconsolable, consolable, unconsolable
TŌL'A.BL	extollable, tollable
TRŌL'A.BL	controllable, uncontrollable

ÔL'A.BL

KÔL'A.BL	callable, recallable, uncallable, unrecallable
THRÔL'A.BL	enthrallable, unenthrallable

ŌL'A.BLĒ

(See ŌL'A.BL, add -y where appropriate.)

ŌL'AR.Ē

(See ŌL'ER.Ē)

Ō'LA.RĪZ

PŌ'LA.RĪZ	depolarize, polarize
SŌ'LA.RĪZ	solarize

OL'A.TER

(See OL'A.TRĒ, change concluding -ry to -er where appropriate.)

OL'A.TRĒ

OL'A.TRĒ	A angeolatry, archaeolatry, B babyolatry, bibliolatry, E ecclesiolatry, F physiolatry, H hagiolatry, heliolatry, hygiolatry, I idiolatry, ichthyolatry, J

geolatry, geniolatry, gynaeolatry, M Mariolatry, O orphiolatry, P patriolatry, TH theolatry, Z zoolatry

BOL'A.TRĒ	mobolatry
DOL'A.TRĒ	bardolatry, idolatry, lordolatry
KROL'A.TRĒ	necrolatry
LOL'A.TRĒ	angelolatry, symbololatry
MOL'A.TRĒ	cosmolatry
NOL'A.TRĒ	demonolatry, iconolatry, monolatry, onolatry, parthenolatry, cynolatry, thenolatry, uranolatry
POL'A.TRĒ	anthropolatry, topolatry
ROL'A.TRĒ	arborolatry, hierolatry, pyrolatry, staurolatry
THOL'A.TRĒ	litholatry
TOL'A.TRĒ	grammatolatry, Christolatry, autolatry, plutolatry, thaumatolatry
TROL'A.TRĒ	astrolatry

OL'A.TRUS

(See OL'A-TRĒ, change concluding -y to -ous where appropriate.)

ŌL'DA.BL

FŌL'DA.BL	foldable, unfoldable
MŌL'DA.BL	moldable, unmoldable
SKÔL'DA.BL	scoldable, unscoldable

ŌL'ER.E

BŌL'ER.Ē	bolary
DRŌL'ER.Ē	drollery
JŌL'ER.Ē	cajolery
MŌL'ER.Ē	molary
PŌL'ER.Ē	polary
RŌL'ER.Ē	rigamarolery
SŌL'ER.Ē	solary
VŌL'ER.Ē	volary

ŌL'FUL.Ē

DŌL'FUL.Ē	dolefully
SŌL'FUL.Ē	soulfully

Ō'LI.A

BŌ'LI.A	strephyosymbolia
GŌ'LI.A	Mongolia
KŌ'LI.A	melancholia
NŌ'LI.A	magnolia
SKŌ'LI.A	scholia
TŌ'LI.A	Aetolia, Anatolia

Ō'LI.AN

Ō'LI.AN	Aeolian, Creolian
BŌ'LI.AN	metabolian
GŌ'LI.AN	Mongolian
KŌ'LI.AN	melancholian
MŌ'LI.AN	simoleon
PŌ'LI.AN	Napoleon
TŌ'LI.AN	Aetolian, Anatolian, capitolian

Ō'LI.Ā'SHUN

FŌ'LI.Ā'SHUN	defoliation, foliation
SPŌ' Ā'SHUN	despolition, spoliation

Ō'LI.ĀT

Ō'LI.ĀT	oleate
FŌ'LI.ĀT	bifoliate, defoliate, exfoliate, foliate, infoliate
SPŌ'LI.ĀT	spoliate

OL'ID.LĒ

SKWOL'ID.LĒ	squalidly
SOL'ID.LĒ	solidly
STOL'ID.LĒ	stolidly

OL'ID.NES

SKWOL'ID.NES	squalidness
SOL'ID.NES	solidness
STOL'ID.NES	stolidness

OL'I.DUS

OL'I.DUS	olidous
SOL'I.DUS	solidous

Ō'LI.ER

FŌ'LI.ER	foliar
GRŌ'LI.ER	Grolier

HŌ'LI.ER   holier, unholier
LŌ'LI.ER   lowlier

OL'I.FĪ

DOL'I.FĪ   idolify
JOL'I.FĪ   jollify
KWOL'I.FĪ   disqualify, qualify,
                unqualify
MOL'I.FĪ   mollify

OL'I.FĪD

(See OL'I.FĪ, change -y to -ied)

ÔL'I.FÔRM

KÔL'I.FÔRM   cauliform

(See OL'I.FÔRM)

OL'I.FÔRM

BOL'I.FÔRM   emboliform
KOL'I.FÔRM   colliform

(See ÔL'I.FÔRM)

Ô'LI.KL

KÔ'LI.KL   caulicle

(See OL'I.KL)

OL'I.KL

BOL'I.KL   diabolical,
                hyperbolical,
                parabolical, symbolical
FOL'I.KL   follicle
POL'I.KL   bibliopolical
STOL'I.KL   apostolical,
                diastolical, systolical
THOL'I.KL   catholical

(See Ô'LI.KL)

OL'IK.SUM

FROL'IK.SUM   frolicsome
ROL'IK.SUM   rollicksome

Ō'LI.NES

HŌ'LI.NES   holiness, unholiness
LŌ'LI.NES   lowliness
SHŌ'LI.NES   shoaliness

ŌL'ING.LĒ

DÔL'ING.LĒ   condolingly
JÔL'ING.LĒ   cajolingly
SÔL'ING.LĒ   consolingly
TÔL'ING.LĒ   extollingly

ÔL'ING.LĒ

DRÔL'ING.LĒ   drawlingly
KRÔL'ING.LĒ   crawlingly
PÔL'ING.LĒ   appallingly
THRÔL'ING.LĒ   enthrallingly

Ō'LI.Ō

Ō'LI.Ō   oleo, olio
BRŌ'LI.Ō   imbroglio
FŌ'LI.Ō   folio, portfolio
PŌ'LI.Ō   polio
RŌ'LI.Ō   roleo
VŌ'LI.Ō   Malvolio

OL'ISH.ER

BOL'ISH.ER   abolisher
MOL'ISH.ER   demolisher
POL'ISH.ER   polisher

OL'ISH.ING

BOL'ISH.ING   abolishing
MOL'ISH.ING   demolishing
POL'ISH.ING   polishing

OL'I.SIS

OL'I.SIS   bacteriolysis,
                biolysis
DROL'I.SIS   hydrolysis
KOL'I.SIS   glycolysis
MOL'I.SIS   hemolysis,
                thermolysis
ROL'I.SIS   catarolysis,
                neurolysis
TOL'I.SIS   autolysis, histolysis,
                pneumatolysis,
                cytolysis
TROL'I.SIS   electrolysis

OL'I.TĒ

JOL'I.TĒ   jollity
KWOL'I.TĒ   equality, inequality,
                coequality, quality

POL'I.TĒ   interpolity,
                isopolity, polity
VOL'I.TĒ   frivolity

Ō'LI.UM

Ō'LI.UM   oleum
FŌ'LI.UM   folium, trifolium
NŌ'LI.UM   linoleum
SKŌ'LI.UM   scholium
TŌ'LI.UM   crystoleum
TRŌ'LI.UM   petroleum

OL'I.WOG

GOL'I.WOG   golliwog
POL'I.WOG   polliwog

ÔL'KA.NĪZ

BÔL'KA.NĪZ   Balkanize

(See OL'KA.NĪZ)

OL'KA.NĪZ

VOL'KA.NĪZ   volcanize

(See ÔL'KA.NĪZ)

OL'O.ER

FOL'O.ER   follower
HOL'O.ER   holloer, hollower

(See ÄL'D.ER)

OL'O.GUS

MOL'O.GUS   homologous
ROL'O.GUS   heterologous
SOL'O.GUS   isologous
TOL'O.GUS   tautologous

OL'Ō.ING

FOL'Ō.ING   following
HOL'Ō.ING   holloing, hollowing

(See ÄL'O.ING)

Ō'LO.IST

PŌ'LO.IST   poloist
SŌ'LO.IST   soloist

OL'O.JĒ

OL'O.JĒ   *A* abiology,
agriology,
agrobiology,
acryology, axiology,
alethiology,
algriology,
amphibiology,
areology,
archaeology,
arteriology,
astrogeology,
astrotheology,
atheology, *B*
bacteriology,
balneology,
bibliology, biology,
BR bryology,
bromatology, *D*
dactyliology,
deltiology,
dicaeology,
dysteleology, *E*
ecclesiology,
exobiology,
electrobiology,
electrophysiology,
embryology,
endemiology,
entozoology,
epidemiology,
aesthiology,
etiology, *F*
phytophysiology,
phytosociology,
physiology, *FR*
phraseology, *GL*
glaciology, *H*
hagiology,
hamartiology,
heliology,
heresiology,
heroöology,
hygiology,
historiology, *I*
ideology,
ichthyology, *J*
geology, *K*
caliology, chaology,
cardiology,
conchiology,
koniology,
choreology, *KR*
craniology,
cryobiology, *L*
liturgiology, *M*
Mariology,
microbiology,
microgeology,
myology,
mommiology,

museology, *N*
naology, neology,
noölogy,
gnosiology, *O*
audiology,
ophiology, ology,
oölogy, osteology, *P*
palaeology,
palaetiology,
palaeozoology,
pantheology,
paroemiology, *PR*
praxiology,
protozoology, *R*
radiobiology,
radiology, rheology,
S semasiology,
semeiology,
semiology,
psychobiology,
sophiology,
sociobiology,
sociology,
soteriology, *SP*
speleology, *ST*
stoichiology,
storiology, *T*
teleology,
testaceology, *TH*
theology,
thereology, *TS*
tsiology, *V*
venereology,
vermeology, *Z*
zoölogy

BOL'O.JĒ   amphibology,
phlebology,
symbology

BROL'O.JĒ   ambrology,
ombrology,
timbrology

DOL'O.JĒ   acidology,
methodology,
monadology,
odology,
orchidology,
paedology,
pedology,
periodology,
podology,
pseudology,
pteridology, tidology

DROL'O.JĒ   dendrology,

FOL'O.JĒ   hydrology
edaphology,
graphology,
geomorphology,
metamorphology,
morphology,
nephology,
psephology,
trophology, ufology

FROL'O.JĒ   nephrology
GOL'O.JĒ   algology, bugology,
ergology,
pharyngology,
fungology,
laryngology,
logology,
otolaryngology,
spongology

GROL'O.JĒ   agrology, hygrology
KOL'O.JĒ   *A* acology,
archology, *E*
ecology, *F*
pharmacology,
phycology,
filicology, *I*
idiopsychology, *J*
gynecology, *K*
cacology,
codicology,
conchology, *L*
lexicology, *M*
malacology,
metapsychology,
mycology,
myrmecology,
muscology,
musicology, *O*
oikology, oncology,
autecology, *P*
paleopsychology,
parapsychology, *S*
sarcology,
psychology,
synecology, *T*
ptochology,
tocology,
toxicology, *TR*
trichology, *Y*
euchology

KROL'O.JĒ   macrology,
micrology,
necrology

LOL'O.JĒ   *A* angelology, *D*
dactylology,
diabolology, *F*
philology, *H*
haplology, hylology,
hoplology, *K*
callology, kalology,
P pelology, *S*
syphilology,
psylology, *T*
typhlology, *V*
vexilology, *Z*
xylology

MOL'O.JĒ   *A* anemology,
atomology, *D*
desmology,
docimology, *E*
entomology,
enzymology,

epistemology,
etymology, *H*
hebephalmology,
homology, *J*
gemmology, *K*
cosmology, *KR*
chresmology, *M*
miasmology, *N*
gnomology,
nomology,
pneumology, *O*
ophthalmology,
orismology, *P*
paromology,
polemology,
pomology,
potamology, *S*
syndesmology,
seismology, *SF*
sphygmology, *SP*
spasmology,
spermology, *TH*
thermology, *Z*
zymology

NOL'O.JĒ   *A* aphnology,
agnology,
actinology,
arachnology,
asthenology, *B*
biocenology,
botanology, *D*
demonology,
dendrochronology,
E eccrinology,
emmenology,
endochrinology,
enology, oenology,
ethnology, *F*
phenology,
phenomenology,
phonology, *FR*
phrenology, *G*
galvanology, *H*
hymenology,
hymnology,
hypnology, *I*
ichnolithnology,
ichnology,
iconology,
immunology, *J*
geochronology, *K*
campanology,
carpology,
carcinology,
kinology, *KR*
criminology,
chronology, *KW*
quinology, *L*
lichenology,
limnology, *M*
maternology,
mechanology,

meconology,
menology,
menonology,
monology, *N*
gnomonology,
noseconology,
neurypnology, *O*
organology,
oceanology, *P*
palaeoethnology,
palynology,
parthenology,
penology,
pogonology,
punnology, *R*
rhinology,
roentgenology,
runology, *S*
selenology,
synchronology,
Sinology, cynology,
SPL splanchnology,
splenology, *T*
technology,
terminology,
termonology,
tonology, *V*
volcanology
vulcanology, *Y*
uranology,
urinology

POL'O.JĒ   antapology,
anthropology,
apology,
escapology,
hippology,
carpology,
kompology,
paleanthropology,
typology, topology,
tropology

ROL'O.JĒ   *A* aerology,
acarology,
arthrology,
acyrology,
astrometeorology, *B*
barology, *D*
dolorology, *E*
enterology, *F*
pharology,
futurology, *G*
gastroenterology, *H*
heterology,
hierology,
hysterology,
horology, *I*
ichorology, *K*
chirology,
coprology,
chorology, *M*
martyrology,
meteorology,

morology, *N*
necrology,
numerology,
neurology, *O*
oneirology, orology,
P papyrology,
pyrology,
ponerology, *S*
serology, *T*
pterology, *TH*
therology, *V*
virology, *Y* urology

SOL'O.JĒ   *D* doxology,
dosology, *GL*
glossology, *J*
gypsology, *KR*
chrysology, *M*
misology, *N*
neossology,
nosology, *O*
auxology,
osmonosology, *P*
paradoxology,
parisology,
posology, *S*
sexology,
psychonosology, *T*
taxology, *THR*
threpsology, *Y*
universology

STROL'O.JĒ   astrology,
gastrology

THOL'O.JĒ   *A* agathology,
anthology, *E*
ethology, *F*
phytolithology,
phytopathology,
helminthology, *L*
lithology, *M*
mythology, *N*
neuropathology, *O*
ornithology,
orthology, *P*
pathology, *S*
sexology,
psychopathology,
TH theomythology

THROL'O.JĒ   arthrology

TOL'O.JĒ   *A* agmatology,
agrostology,
aretology,
aristology, *B*
battology, *BR*
bromatology,
brontology, *CH*
chartology, *D*
deontology,
dermatology,
dialectology,
dittology, *E*
Egyptology,
emblematology,

emetology,
enigmatology,
environmentology,
erotology,
eschatology,
aesthematology,
esthetology, *F*
fetology,
philematology,
phytology,
photology, *GL*
glottology, *GR*
grammatology, *H*
heartology,
hematology,
herpetology,
hyetology,
histology, *I*
insectology, *J*
geratology,
gerontology,
gigantology, *K*
cartology,
kymatology, *KL*
climatology, *KR*
cryptology,
Christology,
chromatology, *L*
leptology, *M*
mantology,
melittology,
microclimatology,
micropalaeontology,
N neontology,
nostology,
pneumatology,
numismatology, *O*
odontology,
olfactology,
onomatology,
ontology,
oryctology, otology,
P palaeophytology,
palaeoclimatology,
palaeontology,
pantology,
parasitology,
patronomatology,
pestology,
pyritology,
pistology, *PL*
planktology,
plutology, *PR*
primatology,
proctology,
protophytology, *R*
rhematology,
rheumatology, *S*
semantology,
sematology,
cetology,
scientology,

psicatology,
symptomatology,
systematology,
cytology, sitology,
somatology,
Sovietology, *SK*
scatology,
skeletology, *SP*
spermatology, *ST*
statistology,
stomatology, *STR*
stromatology, *T*
tantology,
telematology,
teratology,
ctetology, typtology,
tautology, *TH*
thanatology,
thermatology,
thaumatology, *THR*
thremmatology, *Z*
zoophytology
arthrology

THROL'O.JĒ   astrology,
TROL'O.JĒ   electrology,
gastrology,
iatrology,
metrology,
patrology, petrology

OL'O.JER

DOL'O.JER   sockdolager

(See **OL'O.JĒ**; drop -*y*, add -*er* where appropriate.)

OL'O.JIST

ROL'O.JIST   moirologist

(See **OL'O.JĒ**; drop -*y*, add -*ist* where appropriate.)

OL'O.JĪZ

THOL'O.JĪZ   demythologize

(See **OL'O.JĒ**; drop -*y*, add *ize* where appropriate.)

OL'OP.ER

(See **OLUP**, add -*er* where appropriate.)

OL'OP.ING

(See **OLUP**, add -*ing* where appropriate.)

OL'O.TĪP

HOL'O.TĪP	holotype
KOL'O.TĪP	collotype

ŌL'STER.ER

BŌL'STER.ER	bolsterer
HŌL'STER.ER	upholsterer

ÔL'TER.ER

ÔL'TER.ER	alterer
FÔL'TER.ER	falterer
HÔL'TER.ER	halterer, unhalterer
PÔL'TER.ER	palterer
SÔL'TER.ER	psalterer

ÔL'TER.ING

ÔL'TER.ING	altering, unaltering
FÔL'TER.ING	faltering, unfaltering
HÔL'TER.ING	haltering, unhaltering
PÔL'TERING	paltering

ÔL'TI.NES

FÔL'TI.NES	faultiness
MÔL'TI.NES	maltiness
SÔL'TI.NES	saltiness

OL'Ū.BL

SOL'Ū.BL	indissoluble, insoluble, soluble
VOL'Ū.BL	voluble

OL'Ū.BLĒ

SOL'Ū.BLĒ	indissolubly, insolubly, solubly
VOL'Ū.BLĒ	volubly

OL'Ū.TIV

SOL'Ū.TIV	solutive
VOL'Ū.TIV	supervolutive, volutive

OL'VA.BL

SOL'VA.BL	absolvable, insolvable, solvable

ZOL'VA.BL	dissolvable, indissolvable, resolvable, unresolvable

OL'VEN.SĒ

SOL'VEN.SĒ	insolvency, solvency
VOL'VEN.SĒ	revolvency

OM'A.KĒ

OM'A.KĒ	alectryomachy, batrachomyomachy, duomachy, hieromachy, sciomachy, theomachy
GOM'A.KĒ	logomachy
KOM'A.KĒ	psychomachy
NOM'A.KĒ	iconomachy, monomachy, naumachy
ROM'A.KĒ	pyromachy, centauromachy, tauromachy
TOM'A.KĒ	giantomachy
WOM'A.KĒ	wommacky

OM'A.THĒ

KOM'A.THĒ	pharmacomathy
LOM'A.THĒ	philomathy
SOM'A.THĒ	misomathy
TOM'A.THĒ	chrestomathy

Ō'MA.TIZM

KRŌ'MA.TIZM	achromatism, chromatism
PLŌ'MA.TIZM	diplomatism

OM'E.NA

GOM'E.NA	antilegomena, prolegomena
NOM'E.NA	phenomena
POM'E.NA	paralipomena

OM'E.NAL

(See **OM'I.NAL**)

OM'E.NON

(See **OM'I.NUN**)

OM'E.TER

OM'E.TER	*A* absorptiometer, aerometer, areometer, *B* biometer, *FL* fluviometer, *G* goniometer, *H* heliometer, *J* geometer, *K* cardiometer, *KR* craniometer, cryometer, *M* mileometer, *O* audiometer, oleometer, oömeter, *P* potentiometer, *PL* pluviometer, *R* radiometer, *ST* stereometer, *SW* swingometer, *T* tacheometer, tensionometer, *V* variometer, *Y* eudiometer
BOM'E.TER	tribometer
BROM'E.TER	ombrometer, vibrometer
DOM'E.TER	odometer, pedometer, speedometer, udometer
DROM'E.TER	dendrometer, hydrometer
FOM'E.TER	graphometer
GOM'E.TER	algometer, ergometer, logometer
GROM'E.TER	hygrometer
KLOM'E.TER	cyclometer
KOM'E.TER	echometer, oncometer, psychometer, tachometer, trochometer, viscometer
KROM'E.TER	macrometer, micrometer, psychrometer
LOM'E.TER	alcoholometer, bolometer, kilometer, coulometer, oscillometer, cephalometer, sillometer, silometer, scintillometer, psycholometer, stylometer
MOM'E.TER	*A* anemometer, arithmometer, atmometer, *D* dermometer, dynamometer, *E* endosmometer, *J* geothermometer, *KR* chromometer, *O* osmometer, *P* pulmometer, *S* cymometer, seismometer, *TH* thermometer, *TR* tromometer, *V* volumometer, *Z* zymometer
NOM'E.TER	*A* actionometer, actinometer, *D* declinometer, diaphanometer, *F* phonometer, *G* galvanometer, *H* harmonometer, horizonometer, *I* inclinometer, *KL* clinometer, *KR* chronometer, *M* manometer, micronometer, monometer, *N* nanometer, *O* ozonometer, *P* passionometer, pycnometer, *PL* planometer, *S* salinometer, sonometer, *SF* sphygmomanometer, *T* tannometer, tonometer, *TR* trigonometer, *V* vinometer, volumenometer
POM'E.TER	hippometer, nauropometer, tropometer
ROM'E.TER	*A* accelerometer, aerometer, *B* barometer, *FL* fluorometer, *H* horometer, *I* interferometer, *O* orometer, *P* pyrometer, *R* respirometer, *S* saccharometer, *SF* spherometer, *SKL* sclerometer, *SP* spirometer, *T* tellurometer
SOM'E.TER	drosometer, gasometer, hypsometer, opisometer,

passometer,
pulsometer,
thalassometer

THOM'E.TER bathometer,
stethometer

TOM'E.TER *A* altometer, *CH*
chartometer, *F*
photometer, *H*
haptometer,
hectometer, *K*
chartometer,
comptometer, *KL*
climatometer, *KR*
chromatometer, *L*
lactometer,
leptometer, *M*
magnetometer, *N*
pneumatometer, *O*
olfactometer,
optometer, *P*
pantometer, *PL*
platometer, *R*
refractometer, *S*
sensitometer,
cyrtometer, *ST*
stactometer, *STR*
stratometer, *TH*
thanatometer

TROM'E.TER astrometer,
electrometer,
nitrometer,
spectrometer

ZOM'E.TER applauseometer,
horizometer,
piezometer

OM'E.TRĒ

OM'E.TRĒ biometry,
historiometry,
geometry, craniometry,
osteometry,
sociometry,
stereometry,
stoichiometry,
tacheometry,
zoometry

DOM'E.TRĒ iodometry
FOM'E.TRĒ morphometry
HOM'E.TRĒ Mahometry
KOM'E.TRĒ psychometry,
stichometry
LOM'E.TRĒ allometry, colometry
MOM'E.TRĒ anemometry,
anthropomometry,
dynamometry,
pneumometry
NOM'E.TRĒ chronometry,
ozonometry,
trigonometry,
uranometry

POM'E.TRĒ anthropometry,
typometry
ROM'E.TRĒ gyrometry,
chorometry
SOM'E.TRĒ hypsometry,
isometry
THOM'E.TRĒ orthometry
TOM'E.TRĒ photometry,
optometry
TROM'E.TRĒ astrometry

(See **OM'E.TER**, change *-er* to *-ry*
where appropriate.)

Ō'MI.A

KŌ'MI.A acomia, encomia
NŌ'MI.A lethonomia
TŌ'MI.A ozostomia

Ō'MI.AL

NŌ'MI.AL binomial,
monomial, nomial
TŌ'MI.AL tomial

Ō'MI.ER

DŌ'MI.ER domier
FŌ'MI.ER foamier
HŌ'MI.ER homier
KRŌ'MI.ER chromier
LŌ'MI.ER loamier

OM'I.KAL

DOM'I.KAL domical
KOM'I.KAL comical,
coxcombical,
tragicomical
NOM'I.KAL agronomical,
astronomical,
economical,
gastronomical,
iconomachal,
metronomical,
uneconomical
TOM'I.KAL anatomical,
atomical,
phantomical,
zoötomical

OM'I.NAL

DOM'I.NAL abdominal
NOM'I.NAL adnominal,
binominal,

phenomenal,
cognominal,
nominal, prenominal,
pronominal,
surnominal

OM'I.NANS

DOM'I.NANS dominance,
predominance,
subdominance
PROM'I.NANS prominence

OM'I.NANT

DOM'I.NANT dominant,
predominant,
subdominant,
superdominant
PROM'I.NANT prominent

OM'I.NĀT

OM'I.NĀT preominate
BOM'I.NĀT abominate
DOM'I.NĀT dominate,
predominate
KOM'I.NĀT comminate
NOM'I.NĀT agnominate,
denominate,
nominate,
prenominate,
renominate

OM'I.NĒ

DOM'I.NĒ dominie
HOM'I.NĒ Chicahominy,
hominy
NOM'I.NĒ nominee, nominy
ROM'I.NĒ Romany

Ō'MI.NES

DŌ'MI.NES dominess
FŌ'MI.NES foaminess
HŌ'MI.NES hominess
KRŌ'MI.NES chrominess
LŌ'MI.NES loaminess

ŌM'ING.LĒ

FŌM'ING.LĒ foamingly
GLŌM'ING.LĒ gloamingly
HŌ'MING.LĒ homingly
RŌ'MING.LĒ roamingly

OM'I.NA

(See OM'E.NA)

OM'I.NAL

DOM'I.NAL	abdominal
GOM'I.NAL	antilegomenal, prolegomenal
NOM'I.NAL	adnominal, binominal, phenomenal, nominal, prenominal
POM'I.NAL	paralipomenal

OM'I.NĀ'SHUN

BOM'I.NĀ'SHUN	abomination
DOM'I.NĀ'SHUN	domination, predomination
KOM'I.NĀ'SHUN	commination
NOM'I.NĀ'SHUN	denomination, nomination

OM'I.NUN

GOM'I.NUN	antilegomenon, prolegomenon
NOM'I.NUN	phenomenon
POM'I.NUN	paralipomenon

OM'I.NUS

OM'I.NUS	ominous
DOM'I.NUS	abdominous, Dominus
GOM'I.NUS	prolegomenous
NOM'I.NUS	binominous

Ō'MI.UM

KŌ'MI.UM	encomium, gerontocomium, nosocomium
KRŌ'MI.UM	ferrochromium, chromium
TŌ'MI.UM	prostomium, tomium

ŌN'A.BL

ŌN'A.BL	ownable
BŌN'A.BL	bonable
DŌN'A.BL	condonable
FŌN'A.BL	phonable
HŌN'A.BL	honable, unhonable
LŌN'A.BL	loanable, unloanable
PŌN'A.BL	exponible, unexponable
TŌN'A.BL	atonable, tonable, unatonable
ZŌN'A.BL	unzonable, zonable

ON'A.KAL

(See ON'I.KAL)

ÔN'DER.ER

LÔN'DER.ER	launderer
MÔN'DER.ER	maunderer

ON'DER.ER

PON'DER.ER	ponderer

(See ÄN'DER.ER)

ÔN'DER.ING

LÔN'DER.ING	laundering
MÔN'DER.ING	maundering

ON'DER.ING

PON'DER.ING	pondering

(See ÄN'DER.ING)

ON'ER.US

ON'ER.US	onerous
SON'ER.US	sonorous

Ō'NI.A

Ō'NI.A	bryonia, Ionia
DŌ'NI.A	anhedonia, hyperhedonia, Caledonia, Macedonia, nikhedonia
FŌ'NI.A	aphonia, dysphonia, heraphonia, rhinophonia
GŌ'NI.A	begonia, Patagonia, pogonia, tecnogonia
HŌ'NI.A	mahonia
KŌ'NI.A	aniseikonia, Laconia, zirconia
LŌ'NI.A	Babylonia, escalonia, Catalonia, paulownia, cephalonia, valonia
MŌ'NI.A	ammonia, bronchopneumonia, harmonia, pleuropneumonia, pneumonia, eudemonia
NŌ'NI.A	bignonia
RŌ'NI.A	boronia
SŌ'NI.A	asonia
TŌ'NI.A	boltonia, houstonia, catatonia, claytonia, myotonia
VŌ'NI.A	Livonia, Slavonia

Ō'NI.AL

KŌ'NI.AL	aconeal
LŌ'NI.AL	colonial, intercolonial
MŌ'NI.AL	demonial, harmonial, matrimonial, monial, patrimonial, sanctimonial, testimonial
RŌ'NI.AL	baronial

Ō'NI.AN

Ō'NI.AN	aeonian, eonian, halcyonian, Ionian
DŌ'NI.AN	Aberdonian, Caledonian, Macedonian, Myrmidonian
FŌ'NI.AN	colophonian
GŌ'NI.AN	gonion, gorgonian, Oregonian, Patagonian
KŌ'NI.AN	Baconian, draconian, Franconian, Laconian, shaconian
LŌ'NI.AN	Apollonian, Babylonian, Catalonian, chelonian, Thessalonian
MŌ'NI.AN	demonian, Lacedaemonian
PŌ'NI.AN	Lapponian
RŌ'NI.AN	Pyrrhonian, Ciceronian
SHŌ'NI.AN	Shoshonean
SŌ'NI.AN	Jeffersonian, Johnsonian, Oxonian, Smithsonian
THŌ'NI.AN	chthonian

TŌ′NI.AN

	Estonian, Etonian, Hambletonian, catachtonian, Miltonian, Newtonian, Plutonian, Washingtonian
VŌ′NI.AN	Devonian, favonian, pavonian, Slavonian
ZŌ′NI.AN	Amazonian, bezonian

Ō′NI.ER

BŌ′NI.ER	bonier
DRŌ′NI.ER	dronier
PHŌ′NI.ER	phonier
STŌ′NI.ER	stonier
TŌ′NI.ER	tonier

ÔN′I.ER

BRÔN′I.ER	brawnier
TÔN′I.ER	tawnier

ÔN′I.EST

BRÔN′I.EST	brawniest
TÔN′I.EST	tawniest

ON′I.FĪ

BON′I.FĪ	bonify
PON′I.FĪ	saponify
SON′I.FĪ	personify
ZON′I.FĪ	ozonify

ON′I.KA

MON′I.KA	harmonica, Santa Monica
PON′I.KA	japonica
RON′I.KA	veronica
TON′I.KA	santonica

ON′I.KAL

ON′I.KAL	histrionical
BON′I.KAL	Sorbonical
FON′I.KAL	antiphonical, diaphonical, tautophonical, euphonical
GON′I.KAL	cosmogonical
KON′I.KAL	aconical, conical, iconical

KRON′I.KAL	acronical, acronycal, antichronical, diachronical, chronicle, synchronical
LON′I.KAL	Babylonical
MON′I.KAL	harmonical, monachal, monocle, mnemonical
NON′I.KAL	canonical, uncanonical
PON′I.KAL	geoponical
RON′I.KAL	ironical
SON′I.KAL	thrasonical
TON′I.KAL	architectonical, tonical

(See **ONIK**, add *-al* where appropriate.)

ON′I.KON

KRON′I.KON	chronicon
MON′I.KON	harmonicon

ON′I.MĒ

LON′I.MĒ	poecilonymy
MON′I.MĒ	homonymy
NON′I.MĒ	synonymy, teknonymy
PON′I.MĒ	eponymy, toponymy
TON′I.MĒ	metonymy
TRON′I.MĒ	patronymy

(See **ON′O.MĒ**)

ON′I.MIST

(See **ON′O.MIST**)

ON′I.KL

(See **ON′I.KAL**)

ON′I.MUS

ON′I.MUS	onymous, polyonymous, euonymous
DON′I.MUS	pseudonymous
LON′I.MUS	allonymous
MON′I.MUS	homonymous
NON′I.MUS	anonymous, synonymous
PON′I.MUS	eponymous
RON′I.MUS	heteronymous, Hieronymus, paronymous
TON′I.MUS	autonymous

(See **ON′O.MUS**)

ÔN′ING.LĒ

FÔN′ING.LĒ	fawningly
YÔN′ING.LĒ	yawningly

ON′ISH.ING

MON′ISH.ING	admonishing, monishing, premonishing
STON′ISH.ING	astonishing

ON′ISH.MENT

MON′ISH.MENT	admonishment, premonishment
STON′ISH.MENT	astonishment

ON′I.SIZM

ON′I.SIZM	histrionicism
DON′I.SIZM	sardonicism
KON′I.SIZM	laconicism
TON′I.SIZM	Teutonicism

Ō′NI.UM

FŌ′NI.UM	euphonium
GŌ′NI.UM	agonium, ascogonium, carpogonium, pelargonium, spermogonium, sporogonium
KŌ′NI.UM	conium, meconium, synconium, zirconium
LŌ′NI.UM	polonium
MŌ′NI.UM	ammonium, harmonium, pandemonium, stramonium, testimonium
SŌ′NI.UM	opsonium
TŌ′NI.UM	plutonium
TRŌ′NI.UM	positronium

Ō′NI.US

DŌ′NI.US	ideoneous
FŌ′NI.US	symphonious, euphonious
LŌ′NI.US	felonious, Polonius
MŌ′NI.US	*A* acrimonious, alimonious, *H* harmonious, *I* inharmonious, *KW*

querimonious, *M*
matrimonious, *P*
parsimonious, *S*
sanctimonious,
ceremonious, *U*
unceremonious,
unsanctimonious

| RŌ'NI.US | erroneous |
| TRŌ'NI.US | Petronius, ultroneous |

ŌN'O.GRAF

FŌN'O.GRAF	phonograph
RŌN'O.GRAF	coronograph
TŌN'O.GRAF	tonograph

ON'O.GRAF

KRON'O.GRAF	chronograph
MON'O.GRAF	monograph
TON'O.GRAF	tonograf

Ō'NO.GRAM

| FŌ'NO.GRAM | phonogram |
| TŌ'NO.GRAM | tonogram |

ON'O.GRAM

KRON'O.GRAM	chronogram
MON'O.GRAM	monogram
SON'O.GRAM	sonogram
TON'O.GRAM	tonogram

ON'O.MĒ

ON'O.MĒ	polyonomy, theonomy
BON'O.MĒ	bonhommie
FON'O.MĒ	morphonomy
GRON'O.MĒ	agronomy
KON'O.MĒ	economy
LON'O.MĒ	dactylonomy
MON'O.MĒ	homonomy
NON'O.MĒ	synonomy
PON'O.MĒ	antroponomy
RON'O.MĒ	aeronomy, Deuteronomy
SON'O.MĒ	isonomy, nosonomy, cytotaxonomy, taxonomy
TON'O.MĒ	autonomy
TRON'O.MĒ	astronomy, gastronomy, metronomy

(See ON'I.MĒ)

ON'O.MER

MON'O.MER	monomer
STRON'O.MER	astronomer
TRON'O.MER	gastronomer

ON'O.MIST

ON'O.MIST	polyonomist
GRON'O.MIST	agronomist
KON'O.MIST	economist
NON'O.MIST	synonymist
PON'O.MIST	eponymist
TON'O.MIST	autonomist, plutonomist
TRON'O.MIST	gastronomist

ON'O.MĪZ

KON'O.MĪZ	economize
STRON'O.MĪZ	astronomize
TON'O.MĪZ	autonomize
TRON'O.MĪZ	gastronomize

ON'O.MUS

ON'O.MUS	polyonomous
RON'O.MUS	heteronomous
SON'O.MUS	isonomous, taxonomous
TON'O.MUS	autonomous
TRON'O.MUS	gastronomous

(See ON'I.MUS)

ÔNT'ING.LĒ

DÔNT'ING.LĒ	dauntingly
HÔNT'ING.LĒ	hauntingly
TÔNT'ING.LĒ	tauntingly
VÔNT'ING.LĒ	vauntingly
WÔNT'ING.LĒ	wantingly

ŌN'WOR.THĒ

GRŌN'WUR.THĒ	groanworthy
LŌN'WUR.THĒ	loanworthy
MŌN'WUR.THĒ	moanworthy

OO'A.BL

DOO'A.BL	doable, subduable, undoable
NOO'A.BL	renewable, unrenewable
SHOO'A.BL	shoeable, shooable, unshoeable, unshooable
SOO'A.BL	pursuable, suable, unpursuable, unsuable
STOO'A.BL	stewable, unstewable
STROO'A.BL	construable, strewable, unconstruable, unstrewable

(See Ū'A.BL)

OO'ANT.LĒ

FLOO'ANT.LĒ	fluently, confluently
SOO'ANT.LĒ	pursuantly
TROO'ANT.LĒ	truantly

OO'BER.ANS

| TOO'BER.ANS | protuberance |
| ZOO'BER.ANS | exuberance |

OO'BER.ANT

| TOO'BER.ANT | protuberant |
| ZOO'BER.ANT | exuberant |

OO'BER.Ē

| BLOO'BER.Ē blueberry |

(See Ū'BER.Ē)

OO'BER.US

| TOO'BER.US | protuberous, tuberous |
| ZOO'BER.US | exuberous |

(See Ū'BER.US)

OO'BI.A

| NOO'BI.A | Nubia |
| ROO'BI.A | rubia |

OO'BI.KL

| ROO'BI.KL | cherubical |

(See Ū'BI.KL)

$\overline{OO}$'BI.LĀT

JOO'BI.LĀT   jubilate

(See Ū'BI.LĀT)

$\overline{OO}$'BI.US

DOO'BI.US   dubious
ROO'BI.US   rubious

(See Ū'BI.US)

$\overline{OO}$'BRI.KĀT

LOO'BRI.KĀT   lubricate
ROO'BRI.KĀT   rubricate

$\overline{OO}$'BRI.US

GOO'BRI.US   lugubrious
LOO'BRI.US   insalubrious,
                 salubrious

(See Ū'BRI.US)

$\overline{OO}$D'A.BL

KLOOD'A.BL   includable,
                 includible,
                 concludable,
                 precludable
LOOD'A.BL   eludible, ineludible

$\overline{OO}$'DEN.SĒ

KLOO'DEN.SĒ   concludency
KROO'DEN.SĒ   recrudency

(See Ū'DEN.SĒ)

$\overline{OO}$'DI.A

(See Ū'DI.A)

$\overline{OO}$'DI.NAL

LOO'DI.NAL   paludinal
TOO'DI.NAL   altitudinal,
                 aptitudinal,
                 attitudinal,
                 desuetudinal,
                 consuetudinal,
                 latitudinal,
                 longitudinal,
                 testitudinal

(See ŪDI.NAL)

$\overline{OO}$'DI.NES

BROO'DI.NES   broodiness
MOO'DI.NES   moodiness

OOD'I.NES

GOOD'I.NES   goodiness, goody-
                 goodiness
WOOD'I.NES   woodiness

AT'I.TOO'DI.NĪZ

AT'I.TOO'DI.NĪZ   *attitudinize*
PLAT'I.TOO'DI.NIZ
                 platitudinize

$\overline{OO}$'DI.NUS

LOO'DI.NUS   paludinous
TOO'DI.NUS   fortitudinous,
                 latitudinous,
                 longitudinous,
                 multitudinous,
                 platitudinous,
                 solicitudinous,
                 vicissitudinous

(See Ū'DI.NUS)

$\overline{OO}$'DI.Ō

LOO'DI.Ō   preludio
STOO'DI.Ō   studio

(See Ū'DI.Ō)

$\overline{OO}$'DI.TĒ

KROO'DI.TĒ   crudity
NOO'DI.TĒ   nudity
ROO'DI.TĒ   rudity

(See Ū'DI.TĒ)

$\overline{OO}$'DI.UM

LOO'DI.UM   postludium,
                 preludium
STOO'DI.UM   studium

(See Ū'DI.UM)

$\overline{OO}$'DI.US

LOO'DI.US   preludious
STOO'DI.US   studious

$\overline{OO}$'EL.ER

DOO'EL.ER   dueler
GROO'EL.ER   grueler
JOO'EL.ER   jeweler
KROO'EL.ER   creweler, crueler

(See Ū'EL.ER)

$\overline{OO}$'EL.ING

DOO'EL.ING   dueling
GROO'EL.ING   grueling
JOO'EL.ING   bejewelling,
                 jewelling

(See Ū'EL.ING)

$\overline{OO}$'EL.IST

DOO'EL.IST   duelist
KROO'EL.IST   crewelist, cruelest

$\overline{OO}$'EN.SĒ

FLOO'EN.SĒ   fluency
TROO'EN.SĒ   truancy

$\overline{OO}$'ER.Ē

BROO'ER.E   brewery

(See Ū'ER.Ē)

$\overline{OO}$'I.NES

DOO'I.NES   dewiness
GLOO'I.NES   glueyness
GOO'I.NES   gooiness
SKROO'I.NES   screwiness

$\overline{OO}$'I.NUS

BROO'I.NUS   bruinous
PROO'I.NUS   pruinous
ROO'I.NUS   ruinous

$\overline{OO}$'ISH.NES

JOO'ISH.NES   Jewishness

$\overline{NOO}'$ISH.NES

NOO'ISH.NES — newishness
SHROO'ISH.NES — shrewishness

$\overline{OO}'$I.TĒ

DOO'I.TĒ — assiduity
FLOO'I.TĒ — superfluity
GROO'I.TĒ — incongruity, congruity
KROO'I.TĒ — cruety
NOO'I.TĒ — annuity, discontinuity, ingenuity, continuity, tenuity
SOO'I.TĒ — suety
TOO'I.TĒ — fatuity, fortuity, gratuity, perpetuity

(See Ū'I.TĒ)

$\overline{OO}'$I.TIV

FROO'I.TIV — fruitive

(See Ū'I.TIV)

$\overline{OO}'$I.TUS

(See Ū'I.TUS)

$\overline{OO}'$JI.NUS

NOO'JI.NUS — lanuginous
ROO'JI.NUS — aeruginous, ferruginous
SOO'JI.NUS — salsuginous

$\overline{OO}'$KER.Ē

DOO'KER.Ē — ducery, caducary
JOO'KER.Ē — jookerie
SPOO'KER.Ē — spookery

OOK'ER.Ē

BOOK'ER.Ē — bookery
KOOK'ER.Ē — cookery
NOOK'ER.Ē — nookery
ROOK'ER.Ē — rookery

$\overline{OO}'$LI.A

BOO'LI.A — abulia, dysbulia, hyperbulia, parabulia, sthenobulia
THOO'LI.A — thulia

$\overline{OO}'$LI.AN

JOO'LI.AN — joulean, Julian
ROO'LI.AN — cerulean

(See Ū'LI.AN)

$\overline{OO}'$LI.FÔRM

(See Ū'LI.FÔRM)

OOL'I.NES

BOOL'I.NES — bulliness
WOOL'I.NES — wooliness

$\overline{OO}'$LISH.LĒ

FOO'LISH.LĒ — foolishly
GOO'LISH.LĒ — ghoulishly
KOO'LISH.LĒ — coolishly

(See Ū'LISH.LĒ)

$\overline{OO}'$LISH.NES

FOO'LISH.NES — foolishness
GOO'LISH.NES — ghoulishness
KOO'LISH.NES — coolishness

(See Ū'LISH.NES)

OOL'ISH.NES

BOOL'ISH.NES — bullishness
FOOL'ISH.NES — fullishness
WOOL'ISH.NES — woolishness

Ō'Ö.LĪT

Ō'Ö.LĪT — oölite
ZŌ'Ö.LĪT — zoölite

$\overline{OO}'$LI.TĒ

DOO'LI.TĒ — incredulity, credulity, sedulity
ROO'LI.TĒ — garrulity

$\overline{OO}$M'A.BL

(See $\overline{OO}$M, add -able where appropriate.)

$\overline{OO}'$ME.NAL

(See $\overline{OO}'$MI.NAL)

$\overline{OO}'$MER.AL

NOO'MER.AL — numeral

(See Ū'MER.AL)

$\overline{OO}'$MERD.LĒ

ROO'MERD.LĒ — rumoredly

(See Ū'MERD.LĒ)

OO'MER.Ē

BLOO'MER.Ē — bloomery
PLOO'MER.Ē — plumery
TOO'MER.Ē — costumery

(See Ū'MER.Ē)

$\overline{OO}'$MER.US

NOOMER.US — numerous, innumerous
ROO'MER.US — rumorous
TOO'MER.US — tumerous

(See Ū'MER.US)

$\overline{OO}'$MI.LĒ

BOO'MI.LĒ — boomily
GLOO'MI.LĒ — gloomily
ROO'MI.LĒ — rheumily, roomily

(See Ū'MI.LĒ)

$\overline{OO}'$MI.NA

LOO'MI.NA — alumina, lumina
NOO'MI.NA — numina

$\overline{OO}'$MI.NAL

LOO'MI.NAL — luminal, voluminal
NOO'MI.NAL — noumenal
ROO'MI.NAL — ruminal

(See Ū'MI.NAL)

$\overline{OO}'$MI.NANT

LOO'MI.NANT — illuminant, luminant
ROO'MI.NANT — nonruminant, ruminant

$\overline{OO}$'MI.NĀ'SHUN

L$\overline{OO}$MI.NĀ'SHUN illumination
R$\overline{OO}$'MI.NĀ'SHUN
            rumination

$\overline{OO}$'MI.NĂT

L$\overline{OO}$'MI.NĂT illuminate, luminate
R$\overline{OO}$'MI.NĂT ferruminate,
            ruminate

(See Ū'MI.NĂT)

$\overline{OO}$'MI.NES

BL$\overline{OO}$'MI.NES bloominess
GL$\overline{OO}$'MI.NES gloominess
PL$\overline{OO}$'MI.NES pluminess
R$\overline{OO}$'MI.NES rheuminess,
            roominess

(See Ū'MI.NES)

$\overline{OO}$'MING.LĒ

(See $\overline{OO}$M, ŬM, add -ingly where appropriate.)

$\overline{OO}$'MI.NĬZ

L$\overline{OO}$'MĬ.NĬZ aluminize
T$\overline{OO}$'MI.NĬZ bituminize

(See U'MI.NĬZ)

$\overline{OO}$'MI.NUS

B$\overline{OO}$'MI.NUS albuminous
FL$\overline{OO}$'MI.NUS fluminous
G$\overline{OO}$'MI.NUS leguminous
L$\overline{OO}$'MI.NUS aluminous,
            luminous,
            voluminous
N$\overline{OO}$'MI.NUS numinous
T$\overline{OO}$'MI.NUS bituminous

(See Ū'MI.NUS)

$\overline{OO}$'MŪ.LĀT

T$\overline{OO}$'MŪ.LĀT intumulate, tumulate

(See Ū'MŪ.LĀT)

$\overline{OO}$N'ER.Ē

F$\overline{OO}$N'ER.Ē buffoonery
K$\overline{OO}$N'ER.Ē cocoonery
L$\overline{OO}$N'ER.Ē lunary,
            pantalooneery,
            plenilunary,
            sublunary
T$\overline{OO}$N'ER.Ē festoonery
TR$\overline{OO}$N'ER.Ē poltroonery

$\overline{OO}$'NI.FORM

L$\overline{OO}$'NI.FORM luniform
R$\overline{OO}$'NI.FORM runiform

(See Ū'NI.FORM)

$\overline{OO}$'NI.KL

(See Ū'NI.KL)

$\overline{OO}$'NI.LĒ

L$\overline{OO}$'NI.LĒ loonily
M$\overline{OO}$'NI.LĒ moonily
SP$\overline{OO}$'NI.LĒ spoonily
SW$\overline{OO}$'NI.LĒ swoonily

$\overline{OO}$'NISH.LĒ

F$\overline{OO}$'NISH.LĒ buffoonishly
TR$\overline{OO}$'NISH.LĒ poltroonishly

$\overline{OO}$'NI.TĒ

J$\overline{OO}$'NI.TĒ jejunity

(See Ū'NI.TĒ)

$\overline{OO}$'PA.BL

K$\overline{OO}$'PA.BL recoupable,
            unrecoupable

(See Ū'PA.BL)

$\overline{OO}$'PE.RĀT

K$\overline{OO}$'PE.RĀT recuperate
T$\overline{OO}$'PE.RĀT vituperate

$\overline{OO}$'PER.Ē

D$\overline{OO}$'PER.Ē dupery
K$\overline{OO}$'PER.Ē coopery

$\overline{OO}$'PI.AL

R$\overline{OO}$'PI.AL rupial
S$\overline{OO}$'PI.AL marsupial
TR$\overline{OO}$'PI.AL troopial, troupial

$\overline{OO}$'PI.ER

DR$\overline{OO}$'PI.ER droopier
KR$\overline{OO}$'PI.ER croupier
L$\overline{OO}$'PI.ER loopier
S$\overline{OO}$'PI.ER soupier

$\overline{OO}$P'ING.LĒ

DR$\overline{OO}$P'ING.LĒ droopingly
HW$\overline{OO}$P'ING.LĒ whoopingly
L$\overline{OO}$P'ING.LĒ loopingly
SK$\overline{OO}$P'ING.LĒ scoopingly
SN$\overline{OO}$P'ING.LĒ snoopingly
ST$\overline{OO}$P'ING.LĒ stoopingly
SW$\overline{OO}$P'ING.LĒ swoopingly
TR$\overline{OO}$P'ING.LĒ troopingly

$\overline{OO}$P'LI.KĀT

D$\overline{OO}$P'LI.KĀT duplicate,
            reduplicate
DR$\overline{OO}$P'LI.KĀT quadruplicate
T$\overline{OO}$P'LI.KĀT contortuplicate,
            centuplicate

(See Ū'PLI.KĀT)

$\overline{OO}$'PŪ.LUS

L$\overline{OO}$'PŪ.LUS lupulus
SKR$\overline{OO}$'PŪ.LUS scrupulous,
            unscrupulous

OOR'A.BLĒ

DOOR'A.BLĒ durably, endurably,
            unendurably

(See UR'A.BLĒ)

OOR'A.LĒ

PLOOR'A.LĒ plurally
MYOOR'A.LĒ murally
ROOR'A.LĒ rurally

OOR'A.LIST

PLOOR'A.LIST   pluralist
ROOR'A.LIST   ruralist

(See Ū'RA.LIST)

OOR'A.LĬZ

PLOOR'A.LĬZ   pluralize
ROOR'A.LĬZ   ruralize

OOR'A.LIZM

PLOOR'A.LIZM   pluralism
ROOR'A.LIZM   ruralism

OOR'A.TIV

DOOR'A.TIV   durative, indurative
TOOR'A.TIV   maturative

(See ŪR'A.TIV)

OOR'I.A

CHOOR'I.A   Manchuria
NOOR'I.A   anuria
TROOR'I.A   Etruria

OOR'I.AL

OOR'I.AL   oorial, urial

(See Ū'RI.AL)

OOR'I.AN

CHOOR'I.AN   Manchurian
DOOR'I.AN   Durian
GOOR'I.AN   Ben-Gurion, pagurian
KOOR'I.AN   decurion
LOOR'I.AN   Silurian, tellurian, tellurion
MOOR'I.AN   lemurian
THOOR'I.AN   Arthurian, holothurian
TOOR'I.AN   centurion, turion
TROOR'I.AN   Etrurian
ZOOR'I.AN   Missourian

OOR'I.ĀT

(See UR'I.ĀT)

OOR'I.ENS

(See UR'I.ENS)

OOR'I.ENT

(See UR'I.ENT)

OOR'ING.LĒ

LOOR'ING.LĒ   alluringly

(See UR'ING.LĒ)

OOR'I.TĒ

SHOOR'I.TĒ   cocksurety, surety

(See Ū'RI.TĒ)

OOR'I.US

JOOR'I.US   injurious, perjurious
ZHOOR'I.US   luxurious, usurious

(See Ū'RI.US)

OOS'A.BL

DOOS'A.BL   adducible, deducible, educible, inducible, irreducible, conducible, produceable, seducible, traducible, unproduceable, unseducible, untraducible
KROOS'A.BL   crucible
LOOS'A.BL   loosable, unloosable

OO'SE.RĒ

KLOO'SE.RĒ   exclusory, conclusory, reclusory
LOO'SE.RĒ   delusory, elusory, illusory, collusory, lusory, prelusory, prolusory
TROO'SE.RĒ   extrusory

(See Ū'SER.Ē)

OO'SHI.A

FOO'SHI.A   fuchsia
NOO'SHI.A   minutia

OO'SHI.AL

(See OOSHAL)

OO'SHUN.AL

LOO'SHUN.AL   evolutional, revolutional
TOO'SHUN.AL   institutional, constitutional, substitutional

(See Ū'SHUN.AL)

OO'SHUN.ER

LOO'SHUN.ER   ablutioner, resolutioner, revolutioner

(See Ū'SHUN.ER)

OO'SHUN.IST

LOO'SHUN.IST   evolutionist, revolutionist, resolutionist
TOO'SHUN.IST   constitutionist

(See Ū'SHUN.IST)

OO'SI.AN

(See OOSHUN, ŪSHUN)

OO'SI.BL

(See OO'SA.BL)

OO'SID.LĒ

DOO'SID.LĒ   deucedly
LOO'SID.LĒ   lucidly, pellucidly

(See Ū'SID.LĒ)

OO'SI.FER

KROO'SI.FER   crucifer
LOO'SI.FER   Lucifer

OO'SI.FÔRM

KROO'SI.FÔRM	cruciform
LOO'SI.FÔRM	luciform
NOO'SI.FÔRM	nuciform

OO'SIV.LĒ

KLOO'SIV.LĒ	exclusively, inclusively, inconclusively, conclusively
LOO'SIV.LĒ	allusively, delusively, elusively, illusively, collusively
TROO'SIV.LĒ	inobtrusively, intrusively, obtrusively, protrusively

(See Ū'SIV.LĒ)

OO'SIV.NES

DOO'SIV.NES	conduciveness
KLOO'SIV.NES	exclusiveness, inclusiveness, inconclusiveness, conclusiveness
LOO'SIV.NES	allusiveness, delusiveness, elusiveness, illusiveness, collusiveness
TROO'SIV.NES	inobtrusiveness, intrusiveness, obtrusiveness, protrusiveness

(See Ū'SIV.NES)

OO'SO.RĒ

(See OO'SE.RĒ)

OO'TA.BL

LOO'TA.BL	lootable, unlootable
MOO'TA.BL	mootable
SOO'TA.BL	suitable, unsuitable
SKROO'TA.BL	inscrutable, scrutable
TOO'TA.BL	tootable

(See Ū'TA.BL)

OO'TA.BLĒ

(See OO'TA.BL, Ū'TA.BL, change -e to -y where appropriate.)

OO'TER.Ē

BOO'TER.Ē	bootery, free-bootery
FROO'TER.Ē	fruitery
ROO'TER.Ē	rootery
ZHOO'TER.Ē	bijouterie

(See Ū'TER.Ē)

OOTH'FUL.Ē

ROOTH'FUL.Ē	ruthfully
TROOTH'FUL.Ē	truthfully

(See ŪTH'FUL.Ē)

OOTH'FUL.NES

ROOTH'FUL.NES	ruthfulness
TROOTH'FUL.NES	truthfulness

(See ŪTH'FUL.NES)

OO'TI.AL

GLOO'TI.AL	gluteal
LOO'TI.AL	luteal

(See Ū'TI.AL)

OO'TI.FĪ

BROO'TI.FĪ	brutify

(See Ū'TI.FĪ)

OO'TI.FUL

DOO'TI.FUL	dutiful, undutiful

(See Ū'TI.FUL)

OO'TI.KL

SOO'TI.KL	pharmaceutical
TROO'TI.KL	latreutical

(See Ū'TI.KL)

OO'TI.LĪZ

BROO'TI.LĪZ	brutalize

(See Ū'TI.LĪZ)

OO'TI.NĀT

GLOO'TI.NĀT	agglutinate
SKROO'TI.NĀT	scrutinate
TROO'TI.NĀT	trutinate

OO'TI.NĒ

SKROO'TI.NĒ	scrutiny

(See Ū'TI.NĒ)

OO'TI.NES

FROO'TI.NES	fruitiness
SNOO'TI.NES	snootiness
SOO'TI.NES	sootiness

OO'TI.NÎR

BOO'TI.NÎR	boutonniere
SKROO'TI.NÎR	scrutineer

(See Ū'TI.NÎR)

OO'TI.NUS

GLOO'TI.NUS	glutinous
LOO'TI.NUS	velutinous
SKROO'TI.NUS	scrutinous

(See Ū'TI.NUS)

OO'TI.US

DOO'TI.US	duteous
GLOO'TI.US	gluteous
LOO'TI.US	luteous

(See Ū'TI.US)

OO'VA.BL

MOO'VA.BL	immovable, irremovable, movable, removable

526

PRŌO'VA.BL
approvable, improvable, provable, reprovable, unprovable, unimprovable

OŌ'VI.AL
FLŌO'VI.AL	effluvial, fluvial
LŌO'VI.AL	alluvial, antediluvial, diluvial, colluvial, post-diluvial
PLŌO'VI.AL	pluvial
ZŌO'VI.AL	exuvial

(See Ū'VI.AL)

OŌ'VI.AN
HŌO'VI.AN	Scandihoovian
LŌO'VI.AN	alluvian, antediluvian, diluvian, post-diluvian
RŌO'VI.AN	Peruvian
SŌO'VI.AN	Vesuvian

OŌ'VI.ĀT
LŌO'VI.ĀT	alluviate
SŌO'VI.ĀT	exuviate

OŌ'VING.LE
MŌO'VING.LĒ	movingly
PRŌO'VING.LĒ	approvingly, reprovingly

OŌ'VI.UM
FLŌO'VI.UM	effluvium
LŌO'VI.UM	alluvium, diluvium, eluvium, colluvium, pediluvium
PLŌO'VI.UM	impluvium, compluvium

OŌ'VI.US
GLŌO'VI.US	ingluvious
PLŌO'VI.US	Jupiter Pluvius, pluvious
SŌO'VI.US	Vesuvius

OŌ'ZA.BL
LŌO'ZA.BL	losable, unlosable
RŌO'ZA.BL	perusable
TRŌO'ZA.BL	protrusible

(See Ū'ZA.BL)

OŌ'ZHUN.IST
LŌO'ZHUN.IST	delusionist, illusionist
KLŌO'ZHUN.IST	exclusionist

OP'A.THĒ
OP'A.THĒ	homeopathy, ideopathy, osteopathy, theopathy
DROP'A.THĒ	hydropathy
KOP'A.THĒ	psychopathy
LOP'A.THĒ	allopathy
NOP'A.THĒ	somnopathy
ROP'A.THĒ	deuteropathy, heteropathy, naturopathy, neuropathy
SOP'A.THĒ	isopathy
TOP'A.THĒ	autopathy

OP'A.THIST
OP'A.THIST	homeopathist, osteopathist
DROP'A.THIST	hydropathist
KOP'A.THIST	psychopathist
LOP'A.THIST	allopathist, hylopathist
NOP'A.THIST	somnopathist
ROP'A.THIST	neuropathist

Ō'PE.RĒ
DŌ'PE.RĒ	dopery
MŌ'PE.RĒ	mopery
PŌ'PE.RĒ	popery
RŌ'PE.RĒ	ropery

OP'ER.Ē
OP'ER.Ē	opery, zoöpery
FOP'ER.Ē	foppery
KOP'ER.Ē	coppery

OP'E.TĒ
HOP'E.TĒ	hippety-hoppety, hoppety
KLOP'E.TĒ	clippety-cloppety, cloppety
WOP'E.TĒ	wapiti

Ō'PI.A
Ō'PI.A	amblyopia, Ethiopia, myopia, presbyopia
KŌ'PI.A	cornucopia
LŌ'PI.A	hemeralopia, nyctalopia
NŌ'PI.A	asthenopia, protanopia, tritanopia
PLŌ'PI.A	diplopia
SKŌ'PI.A	keraunoscopia, rhytiscopia
TŌ'PI.A	dystopia, ectopia, photopia, heterotopia, scotopia, topia, Utopia

Ō'PI.AN
Ō'PI.AN	Ethiopian
KŌ'PI.AN	cornucopian
LŌ'PI.AN	Fallopian
SŌ'PI.AN	Aesopian
TŌ'PI.AN	Utopian

Ō'PI.ER
DŌ'PI.ER	dopier
MŌ'PI.ER	mopier
SLŌ'PI.ER	slopier
SŌ'PI.ER	soapier

OP'I.ER
CHOP'I.ER	choppier
FLOP'I.ER	floppier
HOP'I.ER	hoppier
KOP'I.ER	copier
SLOP'I.ER	sloppier
SOP'I.ER	soppier

OP'I.KAL
SKOP'I.KAL	metoscopical, microscopical

THROP′I.KAL	philanthropical, misanthropical
TOP′I.KAL	topical
TROP′I.KAL	allotropical, subtropical, tropical

Ō′PI.NES

DŌ′PI.NES	dopiness
MŌ′PI.NES	mopiness
RŌ′PI.NES	ropiness
SLŌ′PI.NES	slopiness
SŌ′PI.NES	soapiness

Ō′PISH.NES

DŌ′PISH.NES	dopishness
MŌ′PISH.NES	mopishness
PŌ′PISH.NES	popishness

OP′I.TĒ

(See OP′E.TĒ)

OP′O.LIS

OP′O.LIS	Heliopolis
BOP′O.LIS	booboopolis
KROP′O.LIS	acropolis, necropolis
LOP′O.LIS	megalopolis
MOP′O.LIS	cosmopolis
PROP′O.LIS	propolis
TROP′O.LIS	metropolis

OP′O.LIST

OP′O.LIST	bibliopolist
KOP′O.LIST	pharmacopolist
NOP′O.LIST	monopolist

OP′O.LĬT

| MOP′O.LĬT | cosmopolite |
| TROP′O.LĬT | metropolite |

OP′SI.KL

DROP′SI.KL	dropsical
MOP′SI.KL	mopsical
POP′SI.KL	popsicle
TOP′SI.KL	nimptopsical

OP′TER.AN

| ROP′TER.AN | chiropteran |
| THOP′TER.AN | orthopteran |

OP′TER.US

DOP′TER.US	lepidopterous
KROP′TER.US	macropterous
THOP′TER.US	orthopterous

OP′TI.KAL

OP′TI.KAL	optical
NOP′TI.KAL	synoptical
TOP′TI.KAL	autoptical

OP′Ū.LĀT

| KOP′Ū.LĀT | copulate |
| POP′Ū.LĀT | depopulate, populate |

OP′Ū.LUS

| OP′Ū.LUS | opulous |
| POP′Ū.LUS | populous, unpopulous |

ÔR′A.BL

DÔR′A.BL	adorable
HÔR′A.BL	abhorrable, horrible
PLÔR′A.BL	deplorable, explorable, unexplorable
SÔR′A.BL	soarable
STÔR′A.BL	restorable, storable, unrestorable, unstorable

ÔR′A.BLĒ

DÔR′A.BLĒ	adorably
HÔR′A.BLĒ	abhorrably, horribly
PLÔR′A.BLĒ	deplorably

ÔR′A.KL

ÔR′A.KL	meteorical, auricle, oracle
FÔR′A.KL	anaphorical, metaphorical
GÔR′A.KL	allegorical, categorical, tautegorical
KÔR′A.KL	coracle
TÔR′A.KL	historical, mythihistorical, oratorical, pictorical, rhetorical

Ō′RAL.Ē

Ō′RAL.Ē	orally
GÔR′A.LE	gorily
FLŌ′RAL.Ē	florally
MŌ′RAL.Ē	morally

Ō′RAL.IST

| Ō′RAL.IST | oralist |
| MŌ′RAL.IST | moralist |

Ō′RAL.ĪZ

| FLŌ′RAL.ĪZ | floralize |
| MŌ′RAL.ĪZ | moralize |

OR′A.TŌ.RĒ

OR′A.TŌ.RĒ	oratory
BOR′A.TŌ.RĒ	laboratory
PLOR′A.TŌ.RĒ	exploratory

ÔR′A.TIV

JÔR′A.TIV	pejorative
PLÔR′A.TIV	explorative
STÔR′A.TIV	restorative
VÔR′A.TIV	devorative

ÔR′CHE.NIT

| FÔR′CHE.NIT | fortunate |
| PÔR′CHE.NIT | importunate |

ÔR′DER.ING

| ÔR′DER.ING | ordering |
| BÔR′DER.ING | bordering, embordering |

ÔR′DI.AL

| MÔR′DI.AL | primordial |
| SÔR′DI.AL | exordial |

(See ÔR′JAL)

ÔR′DI.AN

GÔR′DI.AN	Gordian
KÔR′DI.AN	accordion
WÔR′DI.AN	Edwardian

ÔR'DI.NĀT

ÔR'DI.NĀT	foreordinate, coordinate, ordinate
BÔR'DI.NĀT	subordinate

ÔR'DI.NIT

ÔR'DI.NIT	inordinate, coordinate, ordinate, uncoordinate
BÔR'DI.NIT	insubordinate, subordinate

ÔR'DI.ON

(See ÔR'DI.AN)

ÔR'FIZ.M

(Subsitute -*ism* for concluding -*ic* in words under ÔRFIK.)

ÔR'GA.NĪZ

ÔR'GA.NĪZ	disorganize, organize, reorganize
GÔR'GA.NĪZ	gorgonize
MÔR'GA.NĪZ	morganize

ÔR'I.A

Ō'RI.A	Peoria, theoria
FŌ'RI.A	dysphoria, • haptodysphoria, euphoria
GLŌ'RI.A	Gloria
GŌ'RI.A	phantasmagoria, oligoria
LŌ'RI.A	peloria
MŌ'RI.A	memoria
NŌ'RI.A	noria
PŌ'RI.A	aporia, emporia
SKŌ'RI.A	scoria
SŌ'RI.A	infusoria
STŌ'RI.A	Astoria, Waldorf Astoria, Castoria
THŌ'RI.A	thoria
TŌ'RI.A	littoria, moratoria, Pretoria, Victoria

Ō'RI.AL

Ō'RI.AL	oriel
BŌ'RI.AL	arboreal, boreal, subboreal
DŌ'RI.AL	ambassadorial

FŌ'RI.AL	phosphoreal
GŌ'RI.AL	phantasmagorial
KŌ'RI.AL	enchorial, correal
KWŌ'RI.AL	aequorial
MŌ'RI.AL	armorial, immemorial, marmoreal, memorial
NŌ'RI.AL	manorial, seignorial
PŌ'RI.AL	corporeal, emporial, incorporeal
SKŌ'RI.AL	Escorial
SŌ'RI.AL	A accessorial, assessorial, D dismissorial, F fossorial, GR gressorial, I infusorial, insessorial, intercessorial, K compromissorial, cursorial, PR professorial, R rasorial, responsorial, risorial, S censorial, sensorial, SK scansorial, SP sponsorial, T tonsorial, U uxorial
THŌ'RI.AL	authorial
TŌ'RI.AL	A adaptorial, admonitorial, accusatorial, amatorial, ancestorial, assertorial, D dedicatorial, dictatorial, directorial, disquisitorial, doctorial, E editorial, executorial, expurgatorial, exterritorial, extraterritorial, equatorial, electorial, F factorial, G gubernatorial, GL gladiatorial, GR grallatorial, I inquisitorial, J gestatorial, K cantorial, commentatorial, compurgatorial, consistorial, conspiratorial, curatorial, KL clamatorial, L

	legislatorial, M mediatorial, mentorial, monitorial, motorial, multifactorial, N natatorial, O observatorial, auditorial, auctorial, oratorial, P pictorial, piscatorial, purgatorial, PR praetorial, prefatorial, prefectorial, preceptorial, proctorial, procuratorial, proprietorial, protectorial, R raptorial, rectorial, repertorial, reportorial, reptatorial, S salatorial, sartorial, sectorial, senatorial, suctorial, sutorial, SK scriptorial, SP spectatorial, speculatorial, T tectorial, textorial, territorial, tinctorial, tutorial, V vectorial, victorial, visitatorial
ZŌ'RI.AL	rasorial, rosorial

ÔR'I.A.LĪZ

MÔR'I.LĪZ	memorialize
TÔR'I.A.LÎZ	editorialize, territorialize

Ō'RI.AN

BŌ'RI.AN	brimborion, hyperborean, roborean
DŌ'RI.AN	Dorian
GŌ'RI.AN	Gregorian
MŌ'RI.AN	marmorean
RŌ'RI.AN	aurorean
SŌ'RI.AN	censorian

(See Ô'RI.AN)

TŌRI.AN

TÔR'I.AN	A amatorian, D dictatorian, GL gladiatorian, H

historian, *K*
consistorian, *N*
Nestorian, *O*
oratorian, *P*
purgatorian, *PR*
praetorian, *S*
salutatorian,
senatorian, *ST*
stentorian, *V*
valedictorian,
Victorian

Ô'RI.AN

SÔ'RI.AN   dinosaurian,
         morosaurian, saurian
TÔ'RI.AN   centaurian, taurian

(See Ō'RI.AN)

Ō'RI.AT

FLŌ'RI.ĂT   floriate
KŌ'RI.ĂT   excoriate
SŌ'RI.ĂT   professoriate
STŌ'RI.ĂT   storiate

ÔR'I.BL

(See ÔR'A.BL)

OR'ID.LĒ

FLOR'ID.LĒ   floridly
HOR'ID.LĒ   horridly
TOR'ID.LĒ   torridly

ÔR'I.ENT

ÔR'I.ENT   orient
MÔR'I.ENT   commorient

ÔR'I.ER

KWÔR'I.ER   quarrier
SÔR'I.ER   sorrier
WÔR'I.ER   warrior

(See OR'I.ER)

Ō'RI.FĪ

GLŌ'RI.FĪ   glorify
LŌ'RI.FĪ   calorify
SKŌ'RI.FĪ   scorify
STŌ'RI.FĪ   historify, storify

(See OR'I.FĪ)

OR'I.FĪ

HOR'I.FĪ   horrify
TOR'I.FĪ   torrefy

(See Ō'RI.FĪ)

Ō'RI.FÔRM

PŌ'RI.FORM   poriform

(See OR'I.FORM)

OR'I.FÔRM

BOR'I.FÔRM   arboriform
FLOR'I.FÔRM   floriform
MOR'I.FÔRM   moriform

ÔR'I.IT

ÔR'I.IT   aureate
LÔR'I.IT   baccalaureate,
         laureate, poet
         laureate

ÔR'I.KL

(See ÔR'A.KL)

Ō'RI.NES

GŌ'RI.NES   goriness
HŌ'RI.NES   hoariness, whoriness
PŌ'RI.NES   poriness
TŌ'RI.NES   desultoriness,
         dilatoriness,
         peremptoriness

Ō'RI.ŌL

Ō'RI.ŌL   oriole
GLŌ'RI.ŌL   gloriole

ÔR'I.ŌL

ÔR'I.ŌL   aureole, oriole
LÔR'I.ŌL   laureole

OR'I.TĒ

OR'I.TĒ   anteriority,
         deteriority,
         exteriority,
         inferiority,
         interiority, meliority,
         posteriority,
         priority, superiority
JOR'I.TĒ   majority
NOR'I.TĒ   minority, sonority
ROR'I.TĒ   sorority
THOR'I.TĒ   authority
YOR'I.TĒ   juniority, seniority

Ō'RI.UM

BŌ'RI.UM   ciborium
FŌ'RI.UM   triforium
KŌ'RI.UM   corium
MŌ'RI.UM   in memoriam
NŌ'RI.UM   anticlinorium,
         synclinorium
PŌ'RI.UM   emporium
SŌ'RI.UM   aspersorium,
         sensorium, uxorium
THŌ'RI.UM   thorium
TŌ'RI.UM   *D* digitorium, *F*
         fumatorium, *H*
         haustorium, *I*
         inclinatorium, *KR*
         crematorium, *M*
         moratorium, *N*
         natatorium, *O*
         auditorium, *P*
         pastorium, *PR*
         praetorium,
         prospectorium, *S*
         sanatorium,
         sudatorium, *SK*
         scriptorium, *Y*
         eupatorium

Ō'RI.US

BŌ'RI.US   arboreous, Boreas,
         laborious
GLŌ'RI.US   glorious, inglorious,
         vainglorious
RŌ'RI.US   uproarious
SKŌ'RI.US   scorious
SŌ'RI.US   accessorious,
         censorious,
         subderisorious,
         uxorious
TŌ'RI.US   notatorious,
         notorious,
         proditorious,
         sartorius

Ô'RI.US

Ô'RI.US   aureous

(See Ō'RI.US)

Ō.RI.US.LĒ

BŌ.RI.US.LĒ	laboriously
GLŌ'RI.US.LĒ	gloriously, ingloriously, vaingloriously
RŌ'RI.US.LĒ	uproariously
SŌ'RI.US.LĒ	censoriously, uxoriously
TŌ'RI.US.LĒ	meritoriously, notoriously, stentoriously, stertoriously, victoriously

ÔR'MA.BL

FÔR'MA.BL	formable, informable, conformable, performable, transformable
STÔR'MA.BL	stormable
WÔR'MA.BL	warmable

ÔR'MA.LĬZ

FÔR'MA.LĬZ	formalize, informalize
NÔR'MA.LĬZ	normalize

ÔR'MA.TIV

DÔR'MA.TIV	dormative
FÔR'MA.TIV	afformative, deformative, formative, informative, reformative, transformative

ÔR'MI.TĒ

FÔR'MI.TĒ	deformity, inconformity, conformity, multiformity, nonconformity, uniformity
NÔR'MI.TĒ	abnormity, enormity

ÔR'NI.A

FÔR'NI.A	California
KÔR'NI.A	cornea, salicornia

OR'O.ER

BOR'O.ER	borrower
SOR'O.ER	sorrower

OR'O.ING

BOR'O.ING	borrowing
MOR'O.ING	morrowing, tomorrowing
SOR'O.ING	sorrowing

Ô'RO.SKŌP

HOR'O.SKŌP	horoscope
STÔ'RO.SKŌP	stauroscope

ÔRS'A.BL

DÔRS'A.BL	endorsable
FÔRS'A.BL	enforceable, forcible
VÔRS'A.BL	divorceable

ÔR'SHUN.AL

BÔR'SHUN.AL	abortional
TÔR'SHUN.AL	distortional, contortional, torsional

ÔR'SHUN.IST

BÔR'SHUN.IST	abortionist, antiabortionist, pro-abortionist
TÔR'SHUN.IST	extortionist, contortionist

ÔRT'A.BL

KÔRT'A.BL	courtable, uncourtable
PÔRT'A.BL	deportable, exportable, importable, insupportable, portable, reportable, transportable
SÔR'TA.BL	sortable, unsortable
TÔR'TA.BL	distortable

ÔR'TA.TIV

HÔR'TA.TIV	hortative
POR'TA.TIV	portative
ZÔR'TA.TIV	exhortative

ÔR'TER.IJ

KWÔR'TER.IJ	quarterage
PÔR'TER.IJ	porterage

ÔR'TI.FĪ

FÔR'TI.FĪ	fortify
MÔR'TI.FĪ	mortify

ÔR'TI.KL

KÔR'TI.KL	cortical
VÔR'TI.KL	vortical

ÔRT'LI.NES

KŌRT'LI.NES	courtliness
PŌRT'LI.NES	portliness

Ō'RUS.LĒ

KŌ'RUS.LĒ	decorously
NŌ'RUS.LĒ	sonorously
PŌ'RUS.LĒ	porously

OS'FO.RUS

BOS'FO.RUS	Bosphorus
FOS'FO.RUS	phosphorous, phosphorus

Ō'SHA.BL

GŌ'SHA.BL	negotiable, non-negotiable, unnegotiable
SŌ'SHA.BL	dissociable, sociable, unsociable

Ō'SHI.A

KŌ'SHI.A	nicotia
KRŌ'SHI.A	macrotia, microtia
NŌ'SHI.A	anotia
RŌ'SHI.A	miserotia

Ō'SHI.AN

(See ŌSHUN)

Ō'SHI.ANT

Ō'SHI.ANT	otiant
GŌ'SHI.ANT	negotiant
SŌ'SHI.ANT	dissociant

Ō'SHI.ĀT

| GŌ'SHI.ĀT | negotiate |
| SŌ'SHI.ĀT | associate, dissociate, consociate |

Ō'SHUN.AL

MŌ'SHUN.AL	emotional, commotional, motional, promotional, unemotional
NŌ'SHUN.AL	notional
VŌ'SHUN.AL	devotional

Ō'SHUS.LĒ

KŌ'SHUS.LĒ	precociously
RŌ'SHUS.LĒ	ferociously
TRŌ'SHUS.LĒ	atrociously

Ō'SHUS.NES

KŌ'SHUS.NES	precociousness
RŌ'SHUS.NES	ferociousness
TRŌ'SHUS.NES	atrociousness

Ō'SI.ĀT

(See Ō'SHI.ĀT)

OS'I.BL

| DOS'I.BL | docible, indocible |
| POS'I.BL | impossible, possible |

OS'I.NĀT

| OS'I.NĀT | ratiocinate |
| TROS'I.NĀT | patrocinate |

ÔS'I.ER

BÔS'I.ER	bossier
FLÔS'I.ER	flossier
GLÔS'I.ER	glossier
MÔS'I.ER	mossier
SÔS'I.ER	saucier

ÔS'I.NES

BÔS'I.NES	bossiness
DRÔS'I.NES	drossiness
FLÔS'I.NES	flossiness
GLÔS'I.NES	glossiness
MÔS'I.NES	mossiness
SÔS'I.NES	sauciness

ÔS'I.TĒ

| PÔS'I.TĒ | paucity |
| RÔS'I.TĒ | raucity |

(See OS'I.TĒ)

OS'I.TĒ

OS'I.TĒ	*A* actuosity, anfractuosity, *D* dubiosity, *E* ebriosity, *F* foliosity, furiosity, *FL* flexuosity, *FR* fructuosity, *GR* grandiosity, graciosity, *H* hideosity, *I* impecuniosity, impetuosity, *I* infractuosity, ingeniosity, incuriosity, *K* curiosity, *O* otiosity, *PR* preciosity, *R* religiosity, *S* sensuosity, seriosity, sinuosity, *SP* speciosity, *ST* strenuosity, *T* tortuosity, *U* unctuosity, *V* viciosity, virtuosity, vitiosity, vitreosity
BOS'I.TĒ	gibbosity, globosity, verbosity
BROS'I.TĒ	tenebrosity
DOS'I.TĒ	docity, nodosity
GOS'I.TĒ	fungosity, rugosity
KOS'I.TĒ	bellicosity, hircosity, jocosity, mucosity, uscosity, precocity, spicosity, varicosity, viscosity
KWOS'I.TĒ	aquosity
LOS'I.TĒ	*A* ampollosity, angulosity, *F* fabulosity, filosity, *G* gulosity, *GL* glandulosity, *K* callosity, *M* meticulosity, musculosity, *N* nebulosity, *P* pilosity, *R* ridiculosity, rugulosity, *S* sabulosity, *SKR* scrupulosity, *T* tumulosity, *V* velocity, villosity
MOS'I.TĒ	animosity, anonymosity, fumosity, gemmosity, gummosity, plumosity, rimosity
NOS'I.TĒ	*A* arenosity, *F* fuliginosity, *GL* glutinosity, *K* caliginosity, carnosity, *L* libidinosity, luminosity, *SP* spinosity, *V* venosity, vinosity, voluminosity
POS'I.TĒ	pomposity
PROS'I.TĒ	reciprocity
ROS'I.TĒ	*F* ferocity, *J* generosity, *N* neurocity, *P* ponderosity, porosity, *S* saporosity, scirrhosity, serosity, *T* torosity, tuberosity, *V* vaporosity, vociferosity
STROS'I.TĒ	monstrosity
TOS'I.TĒ	schistosity
TROS'I.TĒ	atrocity
VOS'I.TĒ	nervosity, nivosity

(See ÔS'I.TĒ)

Ō'SIV.LĒ

| PLŌ'SIV.LĒ | explosively, implosively |
| RŌ'SIV.LĒ | erosively, corrosively |

Ō'SIV.NES

| PLŌ'SIV.NES | explosiveness, implosiveness |
| RŌ'SIV.NES | erosiveness, corrosiveness |

ÔS'KO.PĒ

NÔS'KO.PĒ   nauscopy

(See OS'KO.PĒ)

OS'KO.PĒ

OS'KO.PĒ	bioscopy, geoscopy, cranioscopy, cryoscopy, radioscopy, stereoscopy
DOS'KO.PĒ	endoscopy
KROS'KO.PĒ	microscopy, necroscopy
LOS'KO.PĒ	dactyloscopy, geloscopy
MOS'KO.PĒ	ophthalmoscopy
NOS'KO.PĒ	lecanoscopy, organoscopy, retinoscopy, rhinoscopy, ceraunoscopy, uranoscopy
POS'KO.PĒ	metoposcopy
ROS'KO.PĒ	deuteroscopy, fluoroscopy, hieroscopy, horoscopy, meteoroscopy, uroscopy
SOS'KO.PĒ	mixoscopy, misoscopy
THOS'KO.PĒ	ornithoscopy, stethoscopy
TOS'KO.PĒ	autoscopy, brontoscopy, omoplatoscopy, teratoscopy
TROS'KO.PĒ	gastroscopy, spectroscopy

(See ÔS'KO.PĒ)

OS'KO.PIST

(See OS'KO.PĒ, drop concluding -y and add -ist where appropriate.)

OS'O.FĒ

OS'O.FĒ	theosophy
LOS'O.FĒ	philosophy, psilosophy
NOS'O.FĒ	gymnosophy
POS'O.FĒ	anthroposophy
ROS'O.FĒ	chirosophy
SOS'O.FĒ	misosophy

OS'O.FER

OS'O.FER	theosopher
LOS'O.FER	philosopher, psilosopher
SOS'O.FER	misosopher

OS'O.FIST

OS'O.FIST	theosophist
LOS'O.FIST	philosophist
NOS'O.FIST	deipnosophist, gymnosophist
POS'O.FIST	anthroposophist
ROS'O.FIST	chirosophist
SOS'O.FIST	misosophist

OS'O.FĪZ

OS'O.FĪZ	theosophize
LOS'O.FĪZ	philosophize

OS'TA.SĒ

POS'TA.SĒ	apostosy
SOS'TA.SĒ	isostasy

OS'TER.OL

OS'TER.OL	zoösterol
GOS'TER.OL	ergosterol
TOS'TER.OL	sitosterol

OS'TE.RŌN

DOS'TE.RŌN	aldosterone
DROS'TE.RŌN	androsterone
STOS'TER.ŌN	testosterone

OS'TI.KAL

KROS'TI.KAL	acrostical
NOS'TI.KAL	agnostical, gnostical

ŌS'TING.LĒ

BŌS'TING.LĒ	boastingly
KŌS'TING.LĒ	coastingly
RŌS'TING.LĒ	roastingly
TŌS'TING.LĒ	toastingly

OS'TI.SIZM

KROS'TI.SIZM	acrosticism

NOS'TI.SIZM	agnosticism, Gnosticism

ŌST'LI.NES

GŌST'LI.NES	ghostliness
HŌST'LI.NES	hostliness

OS'TRO.FĒ

NOS'TRO.FĒ	monostrophe
POS'TRO.FĒ	apostrophe

Ō'TA.BL

FLŌ'TA.BL	floatable
KWŌ'TA.BL	quotable, unquotable
NŌ'TA.BL	denotable, notable, unnotable
PŌ'TA.BL	potable, unpotable
VŌ'TA.BL	votable, unvotable

Ō'TA.BLĒ

KWŌ'TA.BLĒ	quotably
NŌ'TA.BLĒ	notably

Ō'TA.LIZM

DŌ'TA.LIZM	sacerdotalism
TŌ'TA.LIZM	teetotalism

OT'A.NĒ

(See OT'O.NĒ)

Ō'TA.RĒ

KŌ'TA.RĒ	coterie
NŌ'TA.RĒ	notary
RŌ'TA.RĒ	rotary
VŌ'TA.RĒ	votary

Ō'TA.TIV

FLŌ'TA.TIV	flotative
NŌ'TA.TIV	connotative, denotative
RŌ'TA.TIV	rotative

Ō'TED.LĒ

BLŌ'TED.LĒ	bloatedly
NŌ'TED.LĒ	notedly

THRŌT'ED.LĒ	deep-throatedly, sweet-throatedly
VŌ'TED.LĒ	devotedly

Ō'TE.RĒ

(See **Ō'TA.RĒ**)

ÔT'E.RĒ

KÔT'ER.Ē	cautery
WÔT'ER.E	watery

OT'E.RĒ

LOT'ER.Ē	lottery
POT'ER.Ē	pottery
TOT'ER.Ē	tottery

ÔT'ER.ER

SLÔT'ER.ER	slaughterer
WÔT'ER.ER	waterer

OT'ER.ER

POT'ER.ER	potterer
TOT'ER.ER	totterer

ÔT'ER.ING

SLÔT'ER.ING	slaughtering
WÔT'ER.ING	watering

OT'ER.ING

POT'ER.ING	pottering
TOT'ER.ING	tottering

Ō'TER.ĪZ

MŌ'TER.ĪZ	motorize
NŌ'TER.ĪZ	notarize

Ô'TER.MAN

SLÔ'TER.MAN	slaughterman
WÔ'TER.MAN	waterman

OTH'E.SIS

POTH'E.SIS	apothesis, hypothesis
PROTH'E.SIS	prothesis

ÔT'I.ER

HÔT'I.ER	haughtier
NÔT'I.ER	naughtier

OT'I.ER

BLOT'I.ER	blottier
DOT'I.ER	dottier
KLOT'I.ER	clottier
POT'I.ER	pottier
SKWOT'I.ER	squattier
SPOT'I.ER	spottier

(See **ÄT'I.ER**)

OT'I.KA

ROT'I.KA	erotica
ZOT'I.KA	exotica

OT'I.KAL

OT'I.KAL	biotical, idiotical
DOT'I.KAL	anecdotical
GOT'I.KAL	bigotical
LOT'I.KAL	zealotical
POT'I.KAL	despotical
ROT'I.KAL	erotical
ZOT'I.KAL	exotical

OT'I.LĒ

DOT'I.LĒ	dottily
SNOT'I.LĒ	snottily
SPOT'I.LĒ	spottily

ÔT'I.LĒ

HÔT'I.LĒ	haughtily
NÔT'I.LĒ	naughtily

ÔT'I.LUS

KÔT'I.LUS	cautilous
NÔT'I.LUS	nautilus

ÔT'I.NES

HÔT'I.NES	haughtiness
NÔT'I.NES	naughtiness

OT'I.NES

DOT'I.NES	dottiness
NOT'I.NES	knottiness
SKWOT'I.NES	squattiness
SNOT'I.NES	snottiness
SPOT'I.NES	spottiness

(See **ÄT'I.NES**)

Ō'TING.LĒ

BLŌ'TING.LĒ	bloatingly
DŌ'TING.LĒ	dotingly
GLŌ'TING.LĒ	gloatingly
KWŌ'TING.LĒ	quotingly

OT'I.SIZM

ROT'I.SIZM	eroticism, neuroticism
ZOT'I.SIZM	exoticism

Ō'TIV.LĒ

MŌ'TIV.LĒ	emotively
VŌ'TIV.LĒ	votively

OT'O.MĒ

OT'O.MĒ	episiotomy, herniotomy, ichthyotomy, cardiotomy, craniotomy, osteotomy, Otomi, ovariotomy, peotomy, stereotomy, tracheotomy, zootomy
BOT'O.MĒ	bottomy, phlebotomy, lobotomy, strabotomy
FROT'O.MĒ	nephrotomy
GOT'O.MĒ	pharyngotomy, laryngotomy
KLOT'O.MĒ	cyclotomy
KOT'O.MĒ	bronchotomy, dichotomy, leucotomy, thoracotomy, trichotomy, varicotomy
KROT'O.MĒ	microtomy, necrotomy

LOT'O.MĒ	encephalotomy, helotomy, colotomy, tonsillotomy	**DOU'A.BL**	endowable	**FLOU'ER.LES**	flowerless, flourless
MOT'O.MĒ	dermotomy	**LOU'A.BL**	allowable, disallowable	**POU'ER.LES**	powerless
NOT'O.MĒ	pogonotomy, tenotomy	**VOU'A.BL**	avowable, unavowable, vowable		
PLOT'O.MĒ	aplotomy				
POT'O.MĒ	anthropotomy, apotome, hippopotamy				

OUL'ER.Ē

OUL'ER.Ē	owlery
FOUL'ER.Ē	fowlery
PROUL'ER.Ē	prowlery

OU'A.BLĒ

LOU'A.BLĒ	allowably, unallowably
VOU'A.BLĒ	avowably

ROT'O.MĒ — enterotomy, hysterotomy, laparotomy, neurotomy, Caesarotomy, sclerotomy

SKOT'O.MĒ — scotomy
SOT'O.MĒ — loxotomy
THOT'O.MĒ — lithotomy
TOT'O.MĒ — phytotomy, autotomy, cystotomy
TROT'O.MĒ — gastrotomy

OUN'DA.BL

BOUN'DA.BL	boundable, unboundable
FOUN'DA.BL	dumfoundable, confoundable, unconfoundable
GROUN'DA.BL	groundable
POUN'DA.BL	impoundable, compoundable
ROUN'DA.BL	roundable
SOUN'DA.BL	resoundable, soundable, unsoundable
STOUN'DA.BL	astoundable
ZOUN'DA.BL	resoundable

OUD'ED.NES

KLOUD'ED.NES	becloudedness, cloudedness
KROUD'ED.NES	crowdedness, overcrowdedness, uncrowdedness

OT'O.MIST

(See **OT'O.MĒ,** change -y to -ist where appropriate.)

OT'O.MĪZ

(See **OT'O.MĒ,** change -y to -ize where appropriate.)

OU'DI.IZM

DOU'DI.IZM	dowdyism
ROU'DI.IZM	rowdyism

OUN'DED.LĒ

BOUN'DED.LĒ	unboundedly
FOUN'DED.LĒ	dumbfoundedly, confoundedly, unconfoundedly
TOUN'DED.LĒ	astoundedly

OT'O.NĒ

OT'O.NĒ	neoteny
BOT'O.NĒ	astrobotany, botany, paleobotany
KOT'O.NĒ	cottony
MOT'O.NĒ	homotony
NOT'O.NĒ	monotony
ROT'O.NĒ	chirotony

OU'DI.LĒ

DOU'DI.LĒ	dowdily
KLOU'DI.LĒ	cloudily
ROU'DI.LĒ	rowdily

OUN'DED.NES

(See **OUND,** add -edness where appropriate.)

OU'DI.NES

DOU'DI.NES	dowdiness
KLOU'DI.NES	cloudiness
ROU'DI.NES	rowdiness

OUN'DING.LĒ

(See **OUND,** add -ingly where appropriate.)

Ō'TO.TĪP

FŌ'TO.TĪP	phototype
PRŌ'TO.TĪP	prototype

OU'ER.Ē

BOU'ER.Ē	bowery
DOU'ER.Ē	dowery
FLOU'ER.Ē	flowery
GLOU'ER.Ē	glowery
LOU'ER.Ē	lowery
SHOU'ER.Ē	showery
TOU'ER.Ē	towery

OUND'LES.LĒ

BOUND'LES.LĒ	boundlessly
GROUND'LES.LĒ	groundlessly
SOUND'LES.LĒ	soundlessly

OT'RI.KUS

OT'RIK.KUS	leiotrichous
LOT'RI.KUS	ulotrichous
SOT'RI.KUS	lissotrichous

OU'ER.ING

(See **OUER,** add -ing where appropriate.)

OUN'TA.BL

KOUN'TA.BL	accountable, discountable, countable, unaccountable, uncountable

OU'A.BL

PLOU'A.BL	plowable, unplowable

OU'ER.LES

DOU'ER.LES	dowerless

MOUN'TA.BL

MOUN'TA.BL	insurmountable, mountable, surmountable, unmountable

OUN'TA.BLĒ

KOUN'TA.BLĒ	accountably, unaccountably
MOUN'TA.BLĒ	insurmountably

OU'TI.NES

DOU'TI.NES	doughtiness
DROU'TI.NES	droughtiness
GOU'TI.NES	goutiness
SPOU'TI.NES	spoutiness

OU'ZI.LĒ

DROU'ZI.LĒ	drowsily
FROU'ZI.LĒ	frowsily

OU'ZI.NES

DROU'ZI.NES	drowsiness
FROU'ZI.NES	frowsiness
LOU'ZI.NES	lousiness

OU'ZING.LĒ

BROU'ZING.LĒ	browsingly
ROU'ZING.LĒ	carousingly, rousingly

OV'EL.ER

GROV'EL.ER	groveler
HOV'EL.ER	hoveler

OV'EL.ING

GROV'EL.ING	groveling
HOV'EL.ING	hoveling

Ō'VEN.LĒ

KLŌ'VEN.LĒ	clovenly
WŌ'VEN.LĒ	interwovenly, wovenly

Ō'VI.A

FŌ'VI.A	fovea

GŌ'VI.A	Segovia
NŌ'VI.A	synovia
RŌ'VI.A	Monrovia

Ō'VI.AL

FŌ'VI.AL	foveal
JŌ'VI.AL	jovial
NŌ'VI.AL	synovial

Ō'ZA.BL

KLŌ'ZA.BL	closable, reclosable, unclosable
PŌ'ZA.BL	decomposable, deposable, disposable, imposable, indisposable, opposable, supposable, transposable, undisposable, untransposable

ÔZ'A.BL

KÔZ'A.BL	causable
PLÔZ'A.BL	implausible, plausible

Ō'ZE.RĒ

DŌ'ZER.Ē	dozery
PŌ'ZER.Ē	composery
RŌ'ZER.Ē	rosary

Ō'ZHE.RĒ

Ō'ZHE.RĒ	osiery
HŌ'ZHE.RĒ	hosiery

Ō'ZI.A

BRŌ'ZI.A	ambrosia
PŌ'ZI.A	symposia

Ō'ZI.AL

BRŌ'ZI.AL	ambrosial
RŌ'ZI.AL	roseal

Ō'ZI.ER

KŌ'ZI.ER	cozier
MŌ'ZI.ER	moseyer

NŌ'ZI.ER	nosier
PRŌ'ZI.ER	prosier
RŌ'ZI.ER	rosier

(See ŌZHER)

Ō'ZI.LĒ

KŌ'ZI.LĒ	cozily
NŌ'ZI.LĒ	nosily
PRŌ'ZI.LĒ	prosily
RŌ'ZI.LĒ	rosily

Ō'ZI.NES

DŌ'ZI.NES	doziness
FŌ'ZI.NES	foziness
KŌ'ZI.NES	coziness
NŌ'ZI.NES	nosiness
PRŌ'ZI.NES	prosiness
RŌ'ZI.NES	rosiness

ÔZ'I.TIV

KÔZ'I.TIV	causative

(See OZ'I.TIV)

OZ'I.TIV

POZ'I.TIV	appositive, depositive, expositive, compositive, positive, prepositive, postpositive, suppositive, transpositive

(See ÔZ'I.TIV)

Ū'A.BL

NŪ'A.BL	renewable, unrenewable
STŪ'A.BL	stewable, unstewable
VŪ'A.BL	reviewable, unreviewable, unviewable, viewable

(See OO'A.BL)

Ū'ANT.LĒ

(See OO'ANT.LĒ)

UB'A.BL

KLUB'A.BL	clubbable
RUB'A.BL	rubbable
SKRUB'A.BL	scrubbable
TUB'A.BL	tubbable

Ū'BER.ANS

TŪ'BER.ANS	protuberance

(See $\overline{OO}$'BER.ANS)

Ū'BER.ANT

TŪ'BER.ANT	protuberant

(See $\overline{OO}$'BER.ANT)

Ū'BER.Ē

NŪ'BER.Ē	Newbury

(See $\overline{OO}$'BER.Ē)

UB'ER.Ē

BLUB'ER.Ē	blubbery
RUB'ER.Ē	rubbery
SHRUB'ER.Ē	shrubbery
SKRUB'ER.Ē	scrubbery

Ū'BER.TĒ

Ū.BER.TĒ	uberty
PŪ'BER.TĒ	puberty

Ū'BER.US

Ū'BER.US	uberous
SŪ'BER.US	suberous
TŪ'BER.US	protuberous, tuberous

(See $\overline{OO}$'BER.US)

Ū'BI.A

(See $\overline{OO}$'BI.A)

UB'I.ER

CHUB'I.ER	chubbier
GRUB'I.ER	grubbier
SHRUB'I.ER	shrubbier
SKRUB'I.ER	scrubbier
TUB'I.ER	tubbier

Ū'BI.KL

BŪ'BI.KL	bubukle
KŪ'BI.KL	cubicle

(See $\overline{OO}$'BI.KL)

Ū'BI.LĀT

LŪ'BI.LĀT	volubilate
NŪ'BI.LĀT	nubilate, obnubilate

(See $\overline{OO}$'BI.LĀT)

UB'I.LĒ

CHUB'I.LĒ	chubbily
GRUB'I.LĒ	grubbily
SHRUB'I.LĒ	shrubbily
SKRUB'I.LĒ	scrubbily
STUB'I.LĒ	stubbily
TUB'I.LĒ	tubbily

UB'I.NES

(See **UBĒ**, add -*ness* where appropriate.)

Ū'BI.US

DŪ'BI.US	dubious

(See $\overline{OO}$'BI.US)

Ū'BRI.KĀT

(See $\overline{OO}$'BRI.KĀT)

Ū'BRI.US

(See $\overline{OO}$'BRI.US)

Ū'DA.BL

(See $\overline{OO}$'DA.BL)

Ū'DEN.SĒ

PŪ'DEN.SĒ	pudency

(See $\overline{OO}$'DEN.SĒ)

UD'ER.Ē

UD'ER.Ē	uddery
DUD'ER.Ē	duddery
SHUD'ER.Ē	shuddery
STUD'ER.Ē	studdery

Ū'DI.A

NŪ'DI.A	iatronudia
STŪ'DI.A	studia

UD'I.ER

BLUD'I.ER	bloodier
MUD'I.ER	muddier
RUD'I.ER	ruddier

UD'I.LĒ

BLUD'I.LĒ	bloodily
DUD'I.LĒ	fuddy-duddily
MUD'I.LĒ	muddily
RUD'I.LĒ	ruddily

Ū'DI.NAL

TŪ'DI.NAL	altitudinal, aptitudinal, attitudinal, desuetudinal, consuetudinal, latitudinal, longitudinal, testitudinal

(See $\overline{OO}$'DI.NAL)

Ū'DI.NES

(See $\overline{OO}$'DI.NES)

UD'I.NES

BLUD'I.NES	bloodiness
MUD'I.NES	muddiness
RUD'I.NES	ruddiness

Ū'DI.NUS

TŪ'DI.NUS	fortitudinous, latitudinous, longitudinous, multitudinous, solicitudinous,

testudinous,
vicissitudinous

(See OO'DI.NUS)

Ū'DI.Ō

LŪ'DI.Ō   preludio
STŪ'DI.Ō   studio

(See OO'DI.Ō)

Ū'DI.TĒ

NŪ'DI.TĒ   nudity, seminudity

(See OO'DI.TĒ)

Ū'DI.UM

LŪ'DI.UM   postludium,
                 preludium
STŪ'DI.UM   studium

(See OO'DI.UM)

Ū'DI.US

LŪ'DI.US   preludious
STŪ'DI.US   studious

(See OO'DI.US)

Ū'EL.ER

DŪ'EL.ER   dueler, dueller
FŪ'EL.ER   fueler, fueller

(See OO'EL.ER)

Ū'EL.ING

DŪ'EL.ING   dueling, duelling
FŪ'EL.ING   fueling, fuelling,
                 refueling, refuelling

(See OO'EL.ING)

Ū'ER.Ē

Ū'ER.Ē   ewery

(See OO'ER.Ē)

UF'A.BL

BLUF'A.BL   bluffable
BUF'A.BL   buffable
RUF'A.BL   ruffable, unruffable

UF'I.ER

FLUF'I.ER   fluffier
HUF'I.ER   huffier
PUF'I.ER   puffier
SNUF'I.ER   snuffier
STUF'I.ER   stuffier

UF'I.LĒ

FLUF'I.LĒ   fluffily
HUF'I.LĒ   huffily
PUF'I.LĒ   puffily
SNUF'I.LĒ   snuffily
STUF'I.LĒ   stuffily

UF'I.NES

(See UFĒ, add -ness where appropriate.)

UF'ING.LĒ

(See UF, add -ingly where appropriate.)

UG'A.BL

HUG'A.BL   huggable
PLUG'A.BL   pluggable

UG'ER.Ē

BUG'ER.Ē   buggery
DRUG'ER.Ē   druggery
DUG'ER.Ē   skullduggery
PUG'ER.Ē   puggaree
SNUG'ER.Ē   snuggery
THUG'ER.Ē   thuggery

UG'ER.MUG'ER

HUG'ER.MUG'ER   huggermugger
KUG'ER.MUG'ER   cuggermugger

UG'I.NES

BUG'I.NES   bugginess
HUG'I.NES   hugginess
MUG'I.NES   mugginess
PUG'I.NES   pugginess
SLUG'I.NES   slugginess

Ū'GL.MAN

BŪ'GL.MAN   bugleman
EŪ'GL.MAN   fugleman

Ū'I.NES

DŪ'I.NES   dewiness

(See OO'I.NES)

Ū'I.NUS

(See OO'I.NUS)

Ū'ISH.NES

(See OO'ISH.NES)

Ū'I.TĒ

DŪ'I.TĒ   assiduity
GŪ'I.TĒ   ambiguity, exiguity,
                 contiguity
KŪ'I.TĒ   acuity, innocuity,
                 conspicuity,
                 perspicuity,
                 promiscuity,
                 circuity, vacuity
NŪ'I.TĒ   annuity,
                 discontinuity,
                 ingenuity,
                 continuity, tenuity
SŪ'I.TĒ   suety
TŪ'I.TĒ   fatuity, fortuity,
                 gratuity, perpetuity

(See OO'I.TĒ)

Ū'I.TIV

TŪ'I.TIV   intuitive, tuitive

(See OO'I.TIV)

Ū'I.TUS

KŪ'I.TUS   circuitous
TŪ'I.TUS   fatuitous, fortuitous,
                 gratuitous, pituitous

UJ'ER.Ē

BUJ'ER.Ē   budgeree
DRUJ'ER.Ē   drudgery
GRUJ'ER.Ē   grudgery

Ū'JI.NUS

(See OO'JI.NUS)

Ū'KER.Ē

(See OO'KER.Ē)

UK'ER.ING

PUK'ER.ING	puckering
SUK'ER.ING	succoring, suckering

UK'I.LĒ

LUK'I.LĒ	luckily
PLUK'I.LĒ	pluckily

ŪK'I.NES

Ū'KI.NES	yeukiness
PŪ'KI.NES	pukiness

UK'SHUN.AL

DUK'SHUN.AL	deductional, inductional, conductional, productional, reductional
FLUK'SHUN.AL	fluxional
SUK'SHUN.AL	suctional
STRUK'SHUN.AL	destructional, instructional, constructional, obstructional

UK'SHUN.IST

(See UKSHUN, add -ist)

UK'TI.BL

DUK'TI.BL	abductible, deductible, inductible, conductible, productible, seductible, reductible, unproductible
LUK'TI.BL	eluctable, ineluctable
STRUK'TI.BL	destructible, indestructible, instructible, constructible, obstructible, reconstructible, unreconstructible

UK'TIV.LĒ

(See UKTIV, add -ly where appropriate.)

UK'TIV.NES

(See UKTIV, add -ness where appropriate.)

UK'Ū.LENS

SUK'Ū.LENS	succulence
TRUK'Ū.LENS	truculence

Ū'KŪ.LENT

LŪ'KŪ.LENT	luculent
MŪ'KŪ.LENT	muculent

UK'Ū.LENT

SUK'Ū.LENT	succulent
TRUK'Ū.LENT	truculent

UL'CHER.AL

KUL'CHER.AL	agricultural, apicultural, floricultural, horticultural, cultural
VUL'CHER.AL	vultural

UL'CHER.IZM

KUL'CHER.IZM	agriculturism
VUL'CHER.IZM	vulturism

UL'ER.Ē

DUL'ER.Ē	medullery
GUL'ER.Ē	gullery
KUL'ER.Ē	colory
SKUL'ER.Ē	scullery, skullery
TRUL'ER.Ē	trullery

Ū'LI.A

(See OO'LI.A)

Ū'LI.AN

KŪ'LI.AN	Herculean

(See OO'LI.AN)

Ū'LI.FÔRM

KŪ'LI.FÔRM	baculiform, cuculiform
MŪ'LI.FÔRM	cumuliform

Ū'LING.LĒ

KŪ'LING.LĒ	ridiculingly
MŪ'LING.LĒ	mewlingly
PŪ'LING.LĒ	pulingly

(See OOL, ŪL add -ingly where appropriate.)

Ū'LISH.LĒ

MŪ'LISH.LĒ	mulishly

(See OO'LISH.LĒ)

Ū'LISH.NES

MŪ'LISH.NES	mulishness

(See OO'LISH.NES)

UL'ISH.NES

DUL'ISH.NES	dullishness
GUL'ISH.NES	gullishness

Ū'LI.TĒ

(See OO'LI.TĒ)

Ū'LI.UM

BŪ'LI.UM	nebulium
KŪ'LI.UM	peculium
THŪ'LI.UM	thulium

UL'KI.NES

BUL'KI.NES	bulkiness
HUL'KI.NES	hulkiness
SUL'KI.NES	sulkiness

UL'MI.NANT

FUL'MI.NANT	fulminant
KUL'MI.NANT	culminant

UL'MI.NĀT

FUL'MI.NĀT	fulminate
KUL'MI.NĀT	culminate

UL'PA.BL

GUL'PA.BL	gulpable
KUL'PA.BL	inculpable, culpable

UL'SI.FĪ

DUL'SI.FĪ	dulcify
MUL'SI.FĪ	demulsify, emulsify

UL'SIV.LĒ

PUL'SIV.LĒ	impulsively, compulsively, repulsively
VUL'SIV.LĒ	convulsively, revulsively

UL'SIV.NES

PUL'SIV.NES	impulsiveness, compulsiveness, repulsiveness
VUL'SIV.NES	convulsiveness, revulsiveness

UL'TER.Ē

DUL'TER.Ē	adultery
SUL'TER.Ē	consultary

UL'TI.MIT

UL'TI.MIT	ultimate
NUL'TI.MIT	penultimate

UL'TING.LĒ

SUL'TING.LĒ	insultingly
ZUL'TING.LĒ	exultingly, resultingly

UL'TŪR.IZM

(See UL'CHER.IZM)

UL'VER.IN

KUL'VER.IN	culverin
PUL'VER.IN	pulverin

Ū'MA.BL

(See O͞OM, ŪM, add -able where appropriate.)

UM'A.JER

RUM'A.JER	rummager
SKRUM'A.JER	scrummager

UM'BER.Ē

UM'BER.Ē	umbery
SLUM'BER.Ē	slumbery

UM'BER.ER

(See UMBER, add -er where appropriate.)

UM'BER.ING

KUM'BER.ING	disencumbering, encumbering, cumbering
LUM'BER.ING	lumbering
NUM'BER.ING	numbering, outnumbering
SLUM'BER.ING	slumbering

UM'BER.US

NUM'BER.US	numberous
SLUM'BER.US	slumberous

UM'BLING.LĒ

RUM'BLING.LĒ	rumblingly
STUM'BLING.LĒ	stumblingly
TUM'BLING.LĒ	tumblingly

Ū'ME.NAL

KŪ'ME.NAL	cacuminal, catechumenal

(See O͞O'MI.NAL)

Ū'MER.AL

HŪ'MER.AL	humeral
NŪ'MER.AL	numeral

(See O͞O'MER.AL)

Ū'MERD.LĒ

HŪ'MERD.LĒ	bad-humoredly, good-humoredly, ill-humoredly

(See O͞O'MERD.LĒ)

Ū'MER.Ē

FŪ'MER.Ē	perfumery
TŪ'MER.Ē	costumery

(See O͞O'MER.Ē)

UM'ER.Ē

CHUM'ER.Ē	chummery
FLUM'ER.Ē	flummery
MUM'ER.Ē	mummery
NUM'ER.Ē	nummary
PLUM'ER.Ē	plumbery
SUM'ER.Ē	summary, summery

Ū'MER.US

HŪ'MER.US	humerus, humorous, unhumorous
TŪ'MER.US	tumerous

(See O͞O'MER.US)

Ū'MI.FĪ

HŪ'MI.FĪ	humify
TŪ'MI.FĪ	tumefy

Ū'MI.LĒ

FŪ'MI.LĒ	fumily

(See O͞O'MI.LĒ)

Ū'MI.NAL

KŪ'MI.NAL	cacuminal, catechumenal

(See O͞O'MI.NAL)

Ū′MI.NANT

(See $\overline{OO}$′MI.NANT)

Ū′MI.NĀ.SHUN

(See $\overline{OO}$′MI.NĀ.SHUN)

Ū′MI.NĀT

KŪ′MI.NĀT acuminate,
       cacuminate,
       catechumenate

(See $\overline{OO}$′MI.NĀT)

Ū′MI.NES

FŪ′MI.NES   fuminess

(See $\overline{OO}$′MI.NES)

Ū′MING.LĒ

FŪ′MING.LĒ fumingly

(See $\overline{OOM}$, add *-ingly* where appropriate.)

UM′ING.LĒ

HUM′ING.LĒ hummingly
KUM′ING.LĒ becomingly,
       unbecomingly
NUM′ING.LĒ benumbingly,
       numbingly
STRUM′ING.LĒ strummingly

Ū′MI.NĪZ

HŪ′MI.NĪZ   dehumanize,
       humanize

(See $\overline{OO}$′MI.NĪZ)

Ū′MI.NUS

BŪ′MI.NUS   albuminous
GŪ′MI.NUS   leguminous
KŪ′MI.NUS   acuminous
NŪ′MI.NUS   numinous

UMP′CH$\overline{OO}$.US

SUMP′CH$\overline{OO}$.US sumptuous
ZUMP′CH$\overline{OO}$.US presumptuous

UMP′ER.Ē

FRUMP′ER.Ē frumpery
TRUMP′ER.Ē trumpery

UM′PI.NES

DUM′PI.NES dumpiness
FRUM′PI.NES frumpiness
HUM′PI.NES humpiness
GRUM′PI.NES grumpiness
JUM′PI.NES jumpiness
LUM′PI.NES lumpiness
STUM′PI.NES stumpiness

UM′PISH.NES

(See **UMP**, add *-ishness* where appropriate.)

UMP′SHUS.LĒ

BUMP′SHUS.LĒ bumptiously
SKRUMP′SHUS.LĒ
       scrumptiously

UMP′SI.MUS

MUMP′SI.MUS mumpsimus
SUMP′SI.MUS sumpsimus

UMP′TŪ.US

(See **UMP′CH$\overline{OO}$.US**)

Ū′MŪ.LĀT

KŪ′MŪ.LĀT accumulate,
       cumulate

(See $\overline{OOM}$′Ū.LĀT)

Ū′MŪ.LUS

KŪ′MŪ.LUS cumulus
TŪ′MŪ.LUS tumulus

UN′A.BL

PUN′A.BL   punnable
RUN′A.BL   runnable
SHUN′A.BL shunnable

UNCH′A.BL

(See **UNCH**, add *-able* where appropriate.)

UN′DANT.LĒ

BUN′DANT.LĒ abundantly,
       superabundantly
DUN′DANT.LĒ redundantly

UN′DER.ER

BLUN′DER.ER blunderer
PLUN′DER.ER plunderer
SUN′DER.ER sunderer
THUN′DER.ER thunderer
WUN′DER.ER wonderer

UN′DER.ING

BLUN′DER.ING blundering
PLUN′DER.ING plundering
SUN′DER.ING sundering
THUN′DER.ING thundering
WUN′DER.ING wondering

UN′DER.US

BLUN′DER.US blunderous
CHUN′DER.US chunderous
PLUN′DER.US plunderous
THUN′DER.US thunderous
WUN′DER.US wonderous

(See **UN′DRUS**)

UN′DI.TĒ

BUN′DI.TĒ   moribundity
FUN′DI.TĒ   profundity
KUN′DI.TĒ   fecundity,
       infecundity,
       jocundity, jucundity,
       rubicundity
MUN′DI.TĒ immundity
TUN′DI.TĒ   obtundity,
       orotundity, rotundity

Ū′NER.Ē

(See $\overline{OO}$N′ER.Ē)

UN′ER.Ē

GUN′ER.Ē   gunnery
NUN′ER.Ē   nunnery

UNG′GER.ING

HUNG′GER.ING hungering

MUNG'GER.ING   fishmongering,
whoremongering,
ironmongering,
costermongering,
mongering,
newsmongering,
scandalmongering,
scaremongering,
warmongering,
wordmongering

UNGK'SHUN.AL

UNGK'SHUN.AL   unctional
FUNGK'SHUN.AL
         functional
JUNGK'SHUN.AL   junctional,
conjunctional

UNGK'TER.Ē

FUNGK'TER.Ē   perfunctory
MUNGK'TER.Ē   emunctory

UNG'KŪ.LAR

UNG'KŪ.LAR   uncular
BUNG'KŪ.LAR   carbuncular
DUNG'KŪ.LAR   peduncular
RUNG'KŪ.LAR   caruncular
VUNG'KŪ.LAR   avuncular

UNG'KŪ.LĀT

DUNG'KU.LĀT   pedunculate
VUNG'KŪ.LĀT   avunculate

UNG'KŪ.LUS

MUNG'KŪ.LUS   homunculus
RUNG'KŪ.LUS   ranunculus

Ū'NI.FÔRM

Ū'NI.FÔRM   uniform
FŪ'NI.FÔRM   funiform
KŪ'NI.FÔRM   cuneiform

(See O͞O'NI.FÔRM)

Ū'NI.KĀT

MŪ'NI.KĀT   excommunicate,
communicate
TŪ'NI.KĀT   tunicate

Ū'NI.KL

FŪ'NI.KL   funicle
TŪ'NI.KL   tunicle

UN'I.LĒ

FUN'I.LĒ   funnily
SUN'I.LĒ   sunnily

Ū'NING.LĒ

TŪ'NING.LĒ   tuningly

(See O͞ONING, ŪNING, add -ly where appropriate.)

Ū'NI.TĒ

Ū'NI.TĒ   unity, triunity
MŪ'NI.TĒ   immunity,
intercommunity,
community, munity
PŪ'NI.TĒ   impunity
TŪ'NI.TĒ   importunity,
inopportunity,
opportunity

(See O͞O'NI.TĒ)

Ū'NI.TIV

Ū'NI.TIV   unitive
MŪ'NI.TIV   communitive
PŪ'NI.TIV   punitive

UN'JI.BL

FUN'JI.BL   fungible
PUN'JI.BL   expungible,
inexpungible

UN'SI.NĀT

UN'SI.NĀT   uncinate
RUN'SI.NĀT   runcinate

UN'SI.Ō

MUN'SI.Ō   homuncio
NUN'SI.Ō   nuncio

UN'STA.BL

DUN'STA.BL   Dunstable
KUN'STA.BL   constable

UN'TED.LĒ

FRUN'TED.LĒ   affrontedly
HUN'TED.LĒ   huntedly
STUN'TED.LĒ   stuntedly
WUN'TED.LĒ   unwontedly,
wontedly

UN'TI.NES

RUN'TI.NES   runtiness
STUN'TI.NES   stuntiness

UN'TING.LĒ

BUN'TING.LĒ   buntingly
GRUN'TING.LĒ   gruntingly
HUN'TING.LĒ   huntingly
STUN'TING.LĒ   stuntingly

ŪN'YUN.IST

ŪN'YUN.IST   nonunionist,
reunionist, unionist
MŪN'YUN.IST   communionist

Ū'PA.BL

DŪ'PA.BL   dupable, undupable
(See O͞O'PA.BL)

Ū'PE.RĀT

(See O͞O'PE.RĀT)

Ū'PER.Ē

(See O͞O'PER.Ē)

Ū'PI.AL

(See O͞O'PI.AL)

Ū'PING.LĒ

(See O͞OP'ING.LĒ)

Ū'PLI.KĀT

(See O͞OP'LI.KĀT)

Ū'PŪ.LUS

(See OO'PŪ.LUS)

Ū'RA.BL

DŪ'RA.BL   durable, endurable,
                 undurable,
                 unendurable
KŪ'RA.BL   incurable, curable,
                 procurable,
                 securable

UR'A.BL

FUR'A.BL   inferable,
                 conferable,
                 referable,
                 transferable
MUR'A.BL   demurrable
SHUR'A.BL   assurable, insurable,
                 unassurable,
                 uninsurable
STUR'A.BL   stirrable

Ū'RA.BLĒ

DŪ'RA.BLĒ   durably, endurably,
                 unendurably
KŪ'RA.BLĒ   curably, incurably

Ū'RA.LIST

MŪ'RA.LIST   muralist

(See OOR'A.LIST)

Ū'RA.LIZM

(See OOR'A.LIZM)

Ū'RA.TIV

DŪR'A.TIV   durative, indurative
KŪR'A.TIV   curative
PŪR'A.TIV   depurative
TŪR'A.TIV   maturative

UR'BA.BL

BLUR'BA.BL   blurbable
KUR'BA.BL   curbable, uncurbable
TUR'BA.BL   disturbable,
                 imperturbable,
                 perturbable,
                 undisturbable

UR'BAL.IST

UR'BAL.IST   herbalist
HUR'BAL.IST   herbalist
VUR'BAL.IST   verbalist

UR'BA.LĪZ

PUR'BA.LĪZ   hyperbolize
VUR'BA.LĪZ   verbalize

UR'BAL.IZM

HUR'BAL.IZM   herbalism
VUR'BAL.IZM   verbalism

UR'BI.A

BUR'BI.A   suburbia
SUR'BI.A   Serbia
TUR'BI.A   ytterbia

UR'BI.AL

BUR'BI.AL   suburbial
VUR'BI.AL   adverbial, proverbial

UR'BI.SĪD

HUR'BI.SĪD   herbicide
VUR'BI.SĪD   verbicide

UR'BI.UM

UR'BI.UM   erbium
TUR'BI.UM   terbium

UR'BŪ.LENT

HUR'BŪ.LENT   herbulent
TUR'BŪ.LENT   turbulent

UR'DER.ER

MUR'DER.ER   murderer
VUR'DER.ER   verderer

UR'DI.LĒ

STUR'DI.LĒ   sturdily
WUR'DI.LĒ   wordily

UR'DI.NES

KUR'DI.NES   curdiness
STUR'DI.NES   sturdiness
WUR'DI.NES   wordiness

UR'EN.SĒ

FUR'EN.SĒ   conferrency,
                 transferency
KUR'EN.SĒ   concurrency,
                 currency, recurrency

UR'FLOO.US

PUR'FLOO.US   superfluous
TUR'FLOO.US   subterfluous

Ū'RI.A

Ū'RI.A   polyuria, thiourea,
                 urea
KŪ'RI.A   decuria, curia
NŪ'RI.A   albuminuria, anuria,
                 phenylketonuria,
                 hemoglobinuria,
                 ketonuria
SŪ'RI.A   glycosuria
TŪ'RI.A   hematuria

(See OOR'I.A)

UR'I.A

(See OOR'I.A)

Ū'RI.AL

GŪ'RI.AL   augurial, figurial
KŪ'RI.AL   curial, mercurial
NŪ'RI.AL   seigneurial
PŪ'RI.AL   purpureal
TŪ'RI.AL   centureal

(See OO'RI.AL)

UR'I.AN

(See OOR'I.AN)

Ū'RI.ĀT

FŪ'RI.ĀT   infuriate
MŪ'RI.ĀT   muriate
TŪ'RI.ĀT   centuriate, parturiate
ZHŪ'RI.ĀT   luxuriate

UR'ID.LĒ

FLUR'ID.LĒ	flurriedly
HUR'ID.LĒ	hurriedly
WUR'ID.LĒ	worriedly

UR'I.ENS

PRUR'I.ENS	prurience
SUR'I.ENS	esurience
TUR'I.ENS	parturience, scripturience
ZHUR'I.ENS	luxuriance

UR'I.ENT

PRUR'I.ENT	prurient
SUR'I.ENT	esurient
TUR'I.ENT	parturient, scaturient, scripturient
ZHUR'I.ENT	luxuriant

UR'I.ER

BUR'I.ER	burrier
FLUR'I.ER	flurrier
FUR'I.ER	furrier
HUR'I.ER	hurrier
KUR'I.ER	courier, currier, vancourier
PUR'I.ER	purrier
SKUR'I.ER	scurrier
SPUR'I.ER	spurrier
WUR'I.ER	worrier

UR'I.ER.Ē

FUR'I.ER.Ē	furriery
KUR'I.ER.Ē	curriery

Ū'RI.FĪ

PŪ'RI.FĪ	purify
THŪ'RI.FĪ	thurify

UR'I.ING

FLUR'I.ING	flurrying
HUR'I.ING	hurrying
KUR'I.ING	currying

Ū'RI.KĀT

MŪ'RI.KĀT	muricate
SŪ'RI.KĀT	suricate

UR'I.MENT

FLUR'I.MENT	flurriment
WUR'I.MENT	worriment

UR'ING.LĒ

UR'ING.LĒ	erringly, inerringly
BLUR'ING.LĒ	blurringly
DUR'ING.LĒ	enduringly
FUR'ING.LĒ	deferringly, inferringly, conferringly
HWUR'ING.LĒ	whirringly
LUR'ING.LE	alluringly
MUR'ING.LĒ	demurringly
KUR'ING.LĒ	concurringly, nonconcurringly, recurringly
SHUR'ING.LĒ	assuringly, reassuringly
PUR'ING.LĒ	purringly
SLUR'ING.LĒ	slurringly
STUR'ING.LĒ	stirringly
VUR'ING.LĒ	averringly

Ū'RI.Ō

DŪ'RI.Ō	durio
KŪ'RI.Ō	curio

UR'ISH.ING

FLUR'ISH.ING	flourishing
NUR'ISH.ING	nourishing

UR'ISH.LĒ

BUR'ISH.LĒ	boorishly
KUR'ISH.LĒ	currishly
PUR'ISH.LĒ	poorishly
TUR'ISH.LĒ	amateurishly

Ū'RI.TĒ

KŪ'RI.TĒ	insecurity, security, Social Security
MŪ'RI.TĒ	demurity
PŪ'RI.TĒ	impurity, purity
SKŪ'RI.TĒ	obscurity

TŪ'RI.TĒ	futurity, immaturity, maturity, prematurity

(See **OOR'I.TĒ**)

ŪRI.US

FŪRI.US	furious, sulphureous
GŪRI.US	strangurious
KŪRI.US	incurious, curious
NŪRI.US	penurious
SPŪRI.US	spurious

UR'JEN.SĒ

UR'JEN.SĒ	urgency
MUR'JEN.SĒ	emergency
SUR'JEN.SĒ	assurgency, insurgency, resurgency
TUR'JEN.SĒ	detergency
VUR'JEN.SĒ	divergency, convergency, vergency

UR'JER.Ē

PUR'JER.Ē	perjury, purgery
RUR'JER.Ē	chirurgery
SUR'JER.Ē	electrosurgery, cryosurgery, neurosurgery, psychosurgery, surgery
VUR'JER.Ē	vergery

UR'JI.KAL

UR'JI.KAL	demiurgical, theurgical
KLUR'JI.KAL	clergical
LUR'JI.KAL	metallurgical
NUR'JI.KAL	energical, synergical
RUR'JI.KAL	chirurgical
SUR'JI.KAL	electrosurgical, cryosurgical, neurosurgical, psychosurgical, surgical
TUR'JI.KAL	dramaturgical, liturgical, thaumaturgical

UR'KA.LĀT

PUR'KA.LĀT	percolate
TUR'KA.LĀT	intercalate

UR'KI.LĒ

JUR'KI.LĒ	jerkily
MUR'KI.LĒ	murkily
PUR'KI.LĒ	perkily

UR'KŪ.LAR

BUR'KŪ.LAR	tubercular
FUR'KŪ.LAR	furcular
PUR'KŪ.LAR	opercular
SUR'KŪ.LAR	semicircular, circular

UR'KŪ.LĀT

BUR'KŪ.LĀT	tuberculate
PUR'KŪ.LĀT	operculate
SUR'KŪ.LĀT	recirculate, circulate

UR'KŪ.LUM

BUR'KŪ.LUM	tuberculum
FUR'KŪ.LUM	furculum
PUR'KŪ.LUM	operculum

UR'KŪ.LUS

BUR'KŪ.LUS	tuberculous
SUR'KŪ.LUS	surculous, surculus

UR'LI.ER

UR'LI.ER	earlier
BUR'LI.ER	burlier
CHUR'LI.ER	churlier
KUR'LI.ER	curlier
PUR'LI.ER	pearlier
SUR'LI.ER	surlier

UR'LI.NES

(See **URLĒ**, add *-ness* where appropriate.)

UR'LISH.LĒ

CHUR'LISH.LĒ	churlishly
GUR'LISH.LĒ	girlishly

UR'LISH.NES

CHUR'LISH.NES	churlishness
GUR'LISH.NES	girlishness

UR'MA.NĒ

JUR'MA.NĒ	Germany
VUR'MA.NĒ	verminy

UR'MA.NĪZ

JUR'MA.NĪZ	Germanize
SUR'MA.NĪZ	sermonize

UR'MA.RĒ

FUR'MA.RĒ	infirmary
SPUR'MA.RĒ	spermary

UR'MI.NAL

JUR'MI.NAL	germinal
TUR'MI.NAL	adterminal, conterminal, terminal

UR'MI.NANT

JUR'MI.NANT	germinant
TUR'MI.NANT	determinant, interminant, terminant

UR'MI.NĀT

JUR'MI.NĀT	germinate
TUR'MI.NĀT	determinate, exterminate, indeterminate, interminate, predeterminate, terminate

UR'MI.NUS

TUR'MI.NUS	coterminous, terminous
VUR'MI.NUS	verminous

UR'MI.SĪD

JUR'MI.SĪD	germicide
SPUR'MI.SĪD	spermicide
VUR'MI.SĪD	vermicide

UR'MO.FĪL

SPUR'MO.FĪL	spermophile
THUR'MO.FĪL	thermophile

UR'NA.BL

BUR'NA.BL	burnable, unburnable
LUR'NA.BL	learnable, unlearnable
SUR'NA.BL	discernible, indiscernible
TUR'NA.BL	nonreturnable, overturnable, returnable, turnable, unreturnable, unturnable

UR'NA.LĒ

FUR'NA.LĒ	infernally
TUR'NA.LĒ	externally, eternally, internally
VUR'NA.LĒ	vernally

UR'NA.LIST

JUR'NA.LIST	journalist
TUR'NA.LIST	eternalist, externalist, internalist

UR'NA.LĪZ

JUR'NA.LĪZ	journalize
FUR'NA.LĪZ	infernalize
TUR'NA.LĪZ	externalize, eternalize, internalize
VUR'NA.LĪZ	vernalize

UR'NA.LIZM

FUR'NA.LIZM	infernalism
JUR'NA.LIZM	journalism
TUR'NA.LIZM	externalism, eternalism

UR'NED.LĒ

LUR'NED.LĒ	learnedly
SUR'NED.LĒ	concernedly, unconcernedly

UR'NER.Ē

FUR'NER.Ē	fernery
TUR'NER.Ē	ternery, turnery

UR'NI.A

BUR'NI.Ă	Hibernia
HUR'NI.A	hernia
TUR'NI.A	Saturnia
VUR'NI.A	evernia

UR'NI.AN

BUR'NI.AN	eburnean, Hibernian
TUR'NI.AN	quaternion, Saturnian
VUR'NI.AN	Avernian

UR'NI.CHER

FUR'NI.CHER	furniture
SUR'NI.CHER	cerniture

UR'NISH.ER

BUR'NISH.ER	burnisher
FUR'NISH.ER	furnisher, refurnisher

UR'NISH.ING

BUR'NISH.ING	burnishing
FUR'NISH.ING	furnishing, refurnishing

UR'NI.TĒ

DUR'NI.TĒ	modernity
TUR'NI.TĒ	alternity, diuturnity, eternity, fraternity, coeternity, maternity, paternity, sempiternity, taciturnity

UR'NI.TŪR

(See UR'NI.CHER)

UR'O.ER

BUR'O.ER	burrower
FUR'O.ER	furrower

UR'PEN.TĬN

SUR'PEN.TĬN	serpentine
TUR'PEN.TĬN	turpentine

UR'PI.ER

BUR'PI.ER	burpier
CHUR'PI.ER	chirpier
SLUR'PI.ER	slurpier

UR'PI.LĒ

BUR'PI.LĒ	burpily
CHUR'PI.LĒ	chirpily
SLUR'PI.LĒ	slurpily

UR'PI.NES

(See URPĒ, add -ness where appropriate.)

UR'SA.BL

(See UR'SI.BL)

UR'SA.RĒ

BUR'SA.RĒ	bursary
KUR'SA.RĒ	discursory, cursory, precursory
NUR'SA.RĒ	nursery
SPUR'SA.RĒ	aspersory
VUR'SA.RĒ	anniversary, controversary

UR'SHI.A

(See URSHA)

UR'SHI.AL

(See URSHAL)

UR'SHI.AN

(See URSHUN)

UR'SHI.UM

KWUR'SHI.UM	quinquertium
TUR'SHI.UM	nasturtium

UR'SI.BL

UR'SI.BL	coercible, incoercible
BUR'SI.BL	reimbursable
MUR'SI.BL	amerceable, immersible, submersible
VUR'SI.BL	introversible, irreversible, conversable, reversible, traversable

UR'SI.FÔRM

UR'SI.FÔRM	ursiform
BUR'SI.FÔRM	bursiform
FUR'SI.FÔRM	furciform
VUR'SI.FÔRM	diversiform, versiform

UR'SIV.LĒ

UR'SIV.LĒ	coercively, uncoercively
KUR'SIV.LĒ	decursively, discursively, excursively
SPUR'SIV.LĒ	aspersively, dispersively
TUR'SIV.LĒ	detersively

UR'SIV.NES

UR'SIV.NES	coerciveness
KUR'SIV.NES	decursiveness, discursiveness, excursiveness
SPUR'SIV.NES	aspersiveness, dispersiveness

URTH'LES.NES

MURTH'LES.NES	mirthlessness
WURTH'LES.NES	worthlessness

UR'TI.BL

HUR'TI.BL	hurtable
SUR'TI.BL	insertable
VUR'TI.BL	avertible, divertible, incontrovertible, inconvertible, invertible, controvertible, convertible

UR'TI.TŪD

UR'TI.TŪD	inertitude
SUR'TI.TŪD	incertitude, certitude

UR'VA.BL

KUR'VA.BL	curvable

SUR'VA.BL   conservable, observable, preservable, reservable, servable

SWUR'VA.BL   swervable, unswervable

ZUR'VA.BL   reservable

UR'VA.TIV

KUR'VA.TIV   curvative
NUR'VA.TIV   enervative
SUR'VA.TIV   conservative, neoconservative
ZUR'VA.TIV   observative, preservative, reservative

UR'VED.LĒ

FUR'VED.LĒ   fervidly
ZUR'VED.LĒ   deservedly, observedly, reservedly, undeservedly, unreservedly

UR'VEN.SĒ

FUR'VEN.SĒ   fervency
SUR'VEN.SĒ   conservancy
ZUR'VEN.SĒ   observancy

UR'VI.LĒ

KUR'VI.LĒ   curvily
NUR'VI.LĒ   nervily
SWUR'VI.LĒ   swervily
TUR'VI.LĒ   topsy-turvily

UR'ZHUN.AL

KUR'ZHUN.AL   excursional
VUR'ZHUN.AL   aversional, conversional, reversional, versional

UR'ZHUN.IST

KUR'ZHUN.IST   excursionist
MUR'ZHUN.IST   immersionist, total-immersionist
VUR'ZHUN.IST   aversionist, conversionist, reversionist, versionist

ŪS'A.BL

(See O̅O̅S'A.BL)

US'A.BL

BUS'A.BL   busable, bussable
KUS'A.BL   discussable, cussable, undiscussable, uncussable
MUS'A.BL   mussable, unmussable

UR'NER.Ē

FUR'NER.Ē   fernery
TUR'NER.Ē   quaternary, ternary, turnery

UR'ZHI.AN

(See URZHUN)

US'CHO̅O̅.LIT

US'CHO̅O̅.LIT   ustulate
PUS'CHO̅O̅.LIT   pustulate

Ū'SED.LĒ

(See Ū.SID.LĒ)

Ū'SE.LIS

(See Ū'SI.LIS)

Ū'SER.Ē

Ū'SER.Ē   usury
(See OO'SE.RĒ)

USH'A.BL

BRUSH'A.BL   brushable
FLUSH'A.BL   flushable
HUSH'A.BL   hushable
KRUSH'A.BL   crushable, uncrushable

Ū'SHI.A

(See OO'SHI.A)

Ū'SHI.AL

DŪ'SHI.AL   fiducial
(See OO'SHI.AL)

USH'I.LĒ

GUSH'I.LĒ   gushily
MUSH'I.LĒ   mushily

USH'ING.LĒ

BLUSH'ING.LĒ   blushingly
GUSH'ING.LĒ   gushingly
KRUSH'ING.LĒ   crushingly
RUSH'ING.LĒ   rushingly

Ū'SHUN.AL

KŪ'SHUN.AL   elocutional, circumlocutional

(See OO'SHUN.AL)

Ū'SHUN.ER

KŪ'SHUN.ER   executioner, elocutioner

(See OO'SHUN.ER)

Ū'SHUN.IST

KŪ'SHUN.IST   elocutionist, executionist, perpilocutionist

(See OO'SHUN.IST)

Ū'SI.AN

(See OOSHUN, ŪSHUN)

Ū'SI.BL

(See OO'SA.BL)

Ū'SID.LĒ

DŪ'SID.LĒ   deucedly
LŪ'SID.LĒ   lucidly, pellucidly, translucidly
MŪ'SID.LĒ   mucidly

(See OO'SID.LĒ)

Ū'SI.FER

(See OO'SI.FER)

Ū′SI.FÔRM

LŪ′SI.FÔRM	luciform
NŪ′SI.FÔRM	nuciform

(See $\overline{OO}$′SI.FÔRM)

Ū′SI.LIJ

FŪ′SI.LIG	fuselage
MŪ′SI.LIJ	mucilage
PŪSI.LIJ	pucelage

Ū′SIV.LĒ

BŪ′SIV.LĒ	abusively
DŪ′SIV.LĒ	conducively
FŪ′SIV.LĒ	diffusively, effusively

(See $\overline{OO}$′SIV.LĒ)

Ū′SIV.NES

BŪ′SIV.NES	abusiveness
DŪ′SIV.NES	conduciveness
FŪ′SIV.NES	diffusiveness, effusiveness

(See $\overline{OO}$′SIV.NES)

US′KI.LĒ

DUS′KI.LĒ	duskily
HUS′KI.LĒ	huskily
MUS′KI.LĒ	muskily

US′KI.NES

DUS′KI.NES	duskiness
HUS′KI.NES	huskiness
MUS′KI.NES	muskiness
TUS′KI.NES	tuskiness

US′KŪ.LAR

JUS′KŪ.LAR	majuscular
KUS′KŪ.LAR	lacuscular
MUS′KŪ.LAR	bimuscular, muscular, neuromuscular, unmuscular
NUS′KŪ.LAR	minuscular

PUS′KŪ.LAR	corpuscular, crepuscular, opuscular

US′KŪ.LUS

MUS′KŪ.LUS	musculus
PUS′KŪ.LUS	corpusculous, crepusculous

US′TA.BL

BUS′TA.BL	bustable, incombustible, combustible
DUS′TA.BL	dustable
GUS′TA.BL	gustable, ingustable
JUS′TA.BL	adjustable, inadjustable
RUS′TA.BL	rustable
THRUS′TA.BL	thrustable
TRUS′TA.BL	trustable

US′TER.Ē

BLUS′TER.Ē	blustery
FLUS′TER.Ē	flustery
KLUS′TER.Ē	clustery

US′TER.ER

BLUS′TER.ER	blusterer
FLUS′TER.ER	flusterer
KLUS′TER.ER	clusterer
MUS′TER.ER	musterer

US′TER.ING

(See USTER, add -ing where appropriate.)

UST′FUL.Ē

GUST′FUL.Ē	disgustfully, gustfully
LUST′FUL.Ē	lustfully
TRUST′FUL.Ē	distrustfully, mistrustfully, trustfully

US′TI.BL

(See US′TA.BL)

US′TI.ER

DUS′TI.ER	dustier
FUS′TI.ER	fustier
GUS′TI.ER	gustier
KRUS′TI.ER	crustier
LUS′TI.ER	lustier
MUS′TI.ER	mustier
RUS′TI.ER	rustier
TRUS′TI.ER	trustier

US′TI.LĒ

(See USTĒ, add -ly where appropriate.)

US′TI.NES

(See USTĒ, add -ness where appropriate.)

US′TRI.US

DUS′TRI.US	industrious
LUS′TRI.US	illustrious

ŪT′A.BL

FŪT′A.BL	irrefutable, confutable, refutable, unconfutable
KŪT′A.BL	executable, prosecutable
MŪT′A.BL	immutable, incommutable, commutable, mutable, permutable, transmutable
PŪT′A.BL	disputable, imputable, indisputable, computable, uncomputable
SŪT′A.BL	suitable, unsuitable

(See $\overline{OO}$T′A.BL)

Ū′TA.BLĒ

(See Ū′TA.BL, $\overline{OO}$′TA.BL, change -e to -y where appropriate.)

Ū′TA.TIV

FŪ′TA.TIV	confutative, refutative
MŪ′TA.TIV	commutative, mutative, transmutative

NŪ'TA.TIV   sternutative
PŪ'TA.TIV   disputative,
    imputative, putative,
    reputative

Ū'TED.LĒ

MŪ'TED.LĒ   mutedly
PŪ'TED.LĒ   reputedly

Ū'TER.Ē

PŪ'TER.Ē   pewtery

(See ŌŌ'TER.Ē)

UT'ER.Ē

BUT'ER.Ē   buttery
FLUT'ER.Ē   fluttery
GUT'ER.Ē   guttery
MUT'ER.Ē   muttery
PUT'ER.Ē   puttery
SPLUT'ER.Ē   spluttery
SPUT'ER.Ē   sputtery
STUT'ER.Ē   stuttery

UT'ER.ER

(See UTER, add -er where appropriate.)

UT'ER.ING

(See UTER, add -ing where appropriate.)

UTH'ER.Ē

(TH as in then)

MUTH'ER.Ē   mothery
SMUTH'ER.Ē   smothery

UTH'ER.ER

(TH as in then)
BRUTH'ER.ER   brotherer
MUTH'ER.ER   motherer
SMUTH'ER.ER   smotherer

UTH'ER.ING

(TH as in then)
BRUTH'ER.ING   brothering
MUTH'ER.ING   mothering
SMUTH'ER.ING   smothering
SUTH'ER.ING   southering
WUTH'ER.ING   wuthering

UTH'ER.LĒ

(TH as in then)
BRUTH'ER.LĒ   brotherly,
    unbrotherly
MUTH'ER.LĒ   motherly,
    unmotherly
SUTH'ER.LĒ   southerly

ŪTH'FUL.Ē

(TH as in thin)
ŪTH'FUL.Ē   youthfully

(See ŌŌTH'FUL.Ē)

ŪTH'FUL.NES

(TH as in thin)
ŪTH'FUL.NES   youthfulness

(See ŌŌTH'FUL.NES)

Ū'TI.AL

PŪ'TI.AL   puteal

(See ŌŌ'TI.AL)

Ū'TI.FĪ

BŪ'TI.FĪ   beautify

(See ŌŌ'TI.FĪ)

Ū'TI.FUL

BŪ'TI.FUL   beautiful
DŪ'TI.FUL   dutiful, undutiful

Ū'TI.KL

BŪ'TI.KAL   antiscorbutical,
    scorbutical
DŪ'TI.KAL   propaedeutical
KŪ'TI.KL   cuticle
NŪ'TI.KL   hermaneutical
PŪ'TI.KL   therapeutical

(See ŌŌ'TI.KL)

Ū'TI.LĪZ

Ū'TI.LĪZ   utilize

(See ŌŌ'TI.LĪZ)

Ū'TI.NĒ

MŪ'TI.NĒ   mutiny

(See ŌŌ'TI.NĒ)

UT'ING.LĒ

JUT'ING.LĒ   juttingly
KUT'ING.LĒ   cuttingly
STRUT'ING.LĒ   struttingly

Ū'TI.NÎR

MŪ'TI.NÎR   mutineer

(See ŌŌ'TI.NÎR)

Ū'TI.NUS

MŪ'TI.NUS   mutinous

(See ŌŌ'TI.NUS)

Ū'TI.US

BŪ'TI.US   beauteous
DŪ'TI.US   duteous

(See ŌŌ'TI.US)

UT'LER.Ē

BUT'LER.Ē   butlery
KUT'LER.Ē   cutlery
SUT'LER.Ē   sutlery

UT'ON.Ē

BUT'ON.Ē   buttony
GLUT'ON.Ē   gluttony
MUT'ON.Ē   muttony

Ū'VA.BL

(See ŌŌ'VA.BL)

UV'A.BL

LUV'A.BL   lovable, unlovable
SHUV'A.BL   shovable

UV'EL.ER

HUV'EL.ER   hoveler
SHUV'EL.ER   shoveler

UV'ER.Ē

KUV'ER.Ē	discovery, recovery
PLUV'ER.Ē	plovery

UV'ER.ER

HUV'ER.ER	hoverer
KUV'ER.ER	discoverer, coverer, recoverer, uncoverer

UV'ER.ING

HUV'ER.ING	hovering
KUV'ER.ING	discovering, covering, recovering, uncovering

UV'ER.LĒ

KUV'ER.LĒ	deCoverley
LUV'ER.LĒ	loverly

Ū'VI.AL

Ū'VI.AL	uveal

(See $\overline{OO}$'VI.AL)

Ū'VI.AN

(See $\overline{OO}$'VI.AN)

Ū'VING.LĒ

(See $\overline{OO}$'VING.LĒ)

Ū'VI.UM

(See $\overline{OO}$'VI.UM)

Ū'VI.US

(See $\overline{OO}$'VI.US)

ŪZ'A.BL

ŪZ'A.BL	usable

FŪZ'A.BL

FŪZ'A.BL	diffusible, fusible, infusible, confusible, transfusible

(See $\overline{OO}$'ZA.BL)

Ū'ZHUN.IST

(See $\overline{OO}$'ZHUN.IST)

UZ'I.LĒ

FUZ'I.LĒ	fuzzily
MUZ'I.LĒ	muzzily
WUZ'I.LĒ	wuzzily

UZ'I.NES

BUZ'I.NES	buzziness
FUZ'I.NES	fuzziness
MUZ'I.NES	muzziness
WUZ'I.NES	wuzziness

THE GLOSSARY

CAUTION Of the manifold defects of commisson and omission in this glossary, two humble me particularly.

First, I became so entranced by odd meanings that I quite *forgot to check whether all the words rhymed.* By the time the oversight occurred to me, the section was already in page proofs. I have thrown out the interlopers I could find in haste; but I am by no means sure that I found them all. It is some small comfort that if non-rhyming words do remain, they should not bother you much, since you will generally be going from the rhyming list to the glossary, not the other way around.

Second, my original purpose was to define all the rhyming words I had that do not appear in most college-level dictionaries. But after I had adopted or adapted dictionary definitions for perhaps 9,000 of these—all there was room for—others continued to appear; I would guess that the rhyming list contains at least 25,000 such uncommon words, of which 16,000 remain undefined.

Oh well—some day the publisher may let me publish the missing meanings in a companion volume. And even now, you do have a fighting chance—say one in three—of finding the definition you want. You don't get as good odds as that with a lottery ticket.

W.R.E.

How Dreka's Blotting-Case Fathered a Glossary

About seventy-five years ago a young man named Cecil Jefferson Espy, soon to become my uncle, either bought, borrowed, found, or was given—I am sure he did not steal—a Dreka's Blotting-Case. This was, as the name indicates, a container for blotters, and a handsome one, bound in genuine simulated leather.

Uncle Cecil, not being one to let a good thing slip away from him, still had Dreka's Blotting-Case in his desk drawer when he died not long ago at the age of ninety-three; and his daughter Barbara kindly gave it to me as a keepsake. Besides several ink-smudged blotters, the case contains a twenty-four-page word list, printed in type too small to be read without a magnifying glass.

Mr. Dreka introduced the list with these remarks:

"This word book, being an addition to the ordinary Blotting-Case, renders it of the greatest assistance to the letter-writer, with but a trifling addition to its bulk or cost, and comprehending the whole of the English language in general use. The absence of definitions will not diminish its utility to the letter-writer, for whom alone it is intended; it is not he, but the *reader* (Mr. Dreka's italics) who seeks them."

Mr. Dreka's definition of the purpose of his word list could not have been more fitting for my own project of the moment—this book.

Or, indeed, for any current rhyming dictionary of my acquaintance. Their authors seem to be in agreement that poets—as Mr. Dreka said about letter writers—need not bother to understand (much less explain) the words in their verses—let the readers worry about the meanings. Rhyming dictionaries and Mr. Dreka's word book have at least this in common: they both dispense with definitions.

So I decided to call my book not a dictionary but simply *Words to Rhyme With*.

But if only for my own satisfaction I did want to know the meanings of the words I was listing. If I could not find them in a college, unabridged, or specialized dictionary, I left them out. If they were not in a college-level dictionary but were in one of the others, I recorded the words with their definitions on filing cards.

The time came when my file defined 9,000 unfamiliar words, and I faced the fact that it would be unfair not to share their meanings with my readers. Dreka's Blotting-Case had fathered a glossary.

Not a comprehensive one, to be sure, as you are aware from the cautionary note a few pages back. But enough is enough; I am through. ·

I am through rechecking the rhyming list as well. With each new look another word pops up, waving its letters about as an octopus waves its arms, and insisting that it too deserves a place in the glossary. I would have caught more of them, and corrected more errors, too, were it not that I tend to doze off while reviewing word lists, particularly when in the midst of interminable rhyme categories like ĀSHUN and OLOJĒ. If you find misspellings, or words that show up neither in your desk dictionary nor in my glossary, or that show up in both places, I apologize.

To be eligible for the glossary, a word had not only to rhyme, but to be too rarefied for most college-level dictionaries. Countless words that tickled my fancy could not be defined here because they did not meet one or the other requirement. Take, for instance, the variety of lovely names of just one field flower, names that nod their sun-colored heads in this anthological quatrain:

INSTRUCTIONS FOR MY FLORIST

Send my dear a cowslip; send my dear an oxlip.
　　Send my dear a cuckooflower; a stitchwort send her.
Send my dear a crowfoot, ragged robin, paigle,
　　Wood sorrel, primrose . . . tender for the tender.

Of all those delightful names, only *paigle*—defined in Webster's Second and so here as ''The cowslip, or the oxlip; the cuckooflower; the stitchwort; any of several crowfoots''—is entered in the following pages. *Cowslip* and *oxlip* are out because they have no rhyming matches.* The others do (though you have to puff a little on the last syllable of *stitchwort* and *crowfoot* to blow them into the ring)—but they are ineligible for the glossary because they appear in most college dictionaries.

A number of words that deal with acids, chemicals, minerals, and the like did make the glossary. I could work up little interest in them. But who knows? For you they may be just what the muse ordered.

Some words improve on acquaintance. There may seem little, for instance, to be made in rhyme of geometrical terms such as *rhombicosidecahedron* or *pseudorhombicuboc-*

---

*This is not quite correct. They would have plenty of matches if I listed them in italics to indicate they were to be accented (illegitimately) on the last syllable. But I did not.

tahedronal; but they are willing to cooperate—certainly for jingles, or nominies, or amphigories, if not for Poetry. Jingles and nominies have their place in the tolerant world of rhyme; if I did not believe so, I would not be rhyming. Alexander the Great was permitted to slice the Gordian knot in two with his sword; surely one may be permitted to slice a knotty word like *rhombicosidecahedron* into manageable sections:

ANN, BECKY, AND CLEO:
TRAGEDY OF A CRYSTAL, A PRISM, AND A SOLID

A Crystal and a Prism
Spoke nasty criticism
  Of the profile of a Solid in the street.
This resulted in a squalid
Altercation; for the Solid
  Considered her appearance rather neat.

  So Ann, Beck, and Cleo
  Debated, *con brio*
    And static,
  Which one of the trio
  Was really most Pleo-
  chromatic.

A honey was Rebecca!—
A Rhombicosideca-
  hedron, and sexangled to attract!
Ann's lure was more back-homey—
A little Pseudorhombi-
  cuboctrahedronal, in point of fact.

And Cleo!—her Hexagonal
Was *blatantly* Sexagonal!
  She barely tried to hide her Dodecants.
In angles as in features
All three were charming creatures,
  Configured for Euclidean romance.

They vied for top position
In a beauty competition,
  Each feeling prettiest of all the pretty.
But a Parallelepiped
Is a Prism, not a biped;
  They weren't considered at Atlantic City.

  A tragical blow!
  No way to show
    They were pretty!
  Poor, rhombidec
  Ann, Cleo, Beck!
    What a pity!
    What a pity!

Easy-come-easy-go verses, no better and no worse than the foregoing, are scattered throughout the glossary to show unfamiliar words at play.

If the glossary had been around in Mr. Dreka's time, he might have used it to prepare the Dreka word list. But of course he would have left out the definitions.

To Use the Glossary Effectively, Remember That . . .

• The pronunciation guide below explains the symbols used to show the pronunciation of words.

• Appendix A explains the numerals that accompany some definitions. The number 9, for instance, stands for *archaic;* 44D for *Scotland and dialectal;* 58 for *humorous.*

• Appendices B, C, and D define, respectively, words ending in -mancy, -mania, and -phobia that are not included in the rhyming list.

*Words forming triple rhymes may be used to match single rhymes by adding stress to the last syllable. Double rhymes may sometimes be made into single rhymes in the same way, though the result is likely to be awkward.

KEY TO PRONUNCIATIONS IN THE GLOSSARY

This key explains the system used in the glossary to approximate the pronunciation of the words defined. There are differences between the scheme used here and the one for identifying rhyme categories in the list of rhymes. Here, for instance, the sound of long e followed by r in a stressed syllable is shown as ĒR: **fearful:** (fēr′ful). In the rhyming list, the same sound is given as ÎR: **FÎRFUL** (fearful). The sound of a long unstressed e making up the last syllable of a word is shown in the glossary as i: **only** (ōn′li), but in the rhyming list as Ē: **ŌNLĒ.**

A′ following a syllable indicates stress:

ectal (ek′tal):

A. following a syllable indicates lack of stress:

mistetch (mis.tech′):

A syllable with little or no stress at the end of a word has no accent mark:

poimenics (poi.men′iks)
abaculus (a.bak′ū.lus)
pretty (prit′i)

If a word of several syllables has one major stress and one or more minor stresses, the minor stresses are occasionally but not always shown:

chimopelagic (kī′mo.pi.laj′ik)
chimopelagic (kī.mo.pi.laj′ik)

Phonetic marking		*Sounds as in*
ā	in stressed syllables	**weight** (wāt)
		retainer (ri.tā′ner)
		matelassé (mat′la.sā)
	in unstressed syllables	**chaotic** (kā.ot′ik)
âr	only in stressed syllables	**air** (âr)
		octarius (ok.târ′i.us)

a	in stressed syllables	**battery** (bat′er.i)
	in unstressed and indeterminate syllables	**phalacrosis** (fal′a.krō′sis) **tetrao** (tet′ra.ō)
ä	only in stressed syllables	**alala** (ä′la.lä) **majagua** (ma.hä′gwa) **father** (fä′ther) **Lakme** (läk′mi)
är	in both stressed and unstressed syllables	**archaist** (är′kā.ist) **archiater** (är.kī′a.ter)
ar	in stressed syllables	**carriage** (kar′ij)
ē	only in stressed syllables	**compete** (kum.pēt) **feeling** (fē′ling)
e	in stressed syllables	**bet** (bet) **bellow** (bel′ō)
e	in unstressed syllables	**escudo** (es.kū′do, -kōō′dō)
er	in stressed syllables	**berry** (ber′i)
	in unstressed syllables	**quaver** (kwā′ver) **pervade** (per.vād′) **circuitous** (ser.kū′i.tus)
ī	in stressed syllables	**fiery** (fī′er.i) **alight** (a.līt′)
	in unstressed syllables	**iambic** (ī.am′bik)
i	in stressed syllables in unstressed syllables, the sound of long unstressed e or of -y	**middle** (mid′l) **depart** (di.pärt′) **lonely** (lōn′li) **archaeology** (är′ki.ol′o.ji)
	in unstressed -ate or -age ending a word, the sound of i in it; or ij	**intemperate** (in.tem′per.it) **immaculate** (i.mak′u.lit) **courage** (kur′ij) **carnage** (kär′nij)
ō	in stressed syllables	**goat** (gōt) **revolt** (ri.vōlt′)
	in unstressed syllables, at the end of a word	**hollow** (hol′ō) **faro** (fâr′ō)
ô	in stressed or unstressed syllables	**exaugurate** (eg.zôg′ū.rāt) **gorbelly** (gôr′bel.i) **musquashroot** (mus′kwôsh.rōōt)

o	in stressed syllables	**got** (got)
		bottle (bot′l)
		Hottentot (hot′n.tot)
	in unstressed syllables (when not the last sound in the word)	**orthodoxy** (ôr′tho.dok′si)
		plutocrat (plo͞o′to.krat)
o͞o	in stressed and unstressed syllables	**canoodle** (ka.no͞o′dl)
		catalufa (kat′a.lo͞o′fa)
oo	in stressed and unstressed syllables	**foot** (foot)
		carucage (kar′oo.kij)
ou	in stressed syllables	**allowed** (a.loud′)
ū	in stressed syllables	**acute** (a.kūt′)
		pituitary (pi.tū′i.ter′i)
	in unstressed syllables	**utility** (ū.til′i.ti)
		diminuendo (di.min′ū.en′dō)
u	in stressed and unstressed syllables	**butter** (but′er)
		datum (dā′tum)
		compare (kum.pâr)
ur	in stressed and some unstressed syllables	**courage** (kur′ij)
		courageous (ku.rā′jus)

There are no phonetic keys for the pronunciation of consonants, except in two cases:

- N indicates the French nasal sound.
          malentendu: mal′äN.täN.dū
- K indicates the sound of -ch in Scottish *loch* or German *ich*.

loch: loK
ich: iK

KEY TO ABBREVIATIONS IN THE GLOSSARY

cap.	capitalized		**n. pl.**	noun plural
dial.	dialectal		**obs.**	obsolete
eccl.	ecclesiastical		**orig.**	originally
Eng.	English		**part.**	particularly
equiv.	equivalent		**pert.**	pertaining
esp.	especially		**pl.**	plural
fem.	feminine		**prob.**	probably
fig.	figuratively		**specif.**	specifically
hist.	historically		**usu.**	usually
incl., inc.	including		**v.**	verb
n.	noun		**var.**	variant

A

aar (är): in South Africa, an underground stream.

abacinate (a.bas′i.nāt): to blind by means of a red-hot metal plate held before the eyes. 52.

abaciscus (ab′a.sis′kus): an abaculus.

abactor (ab.ak′ter): one that steals cattle.

abaculus (a.bak′ū.lus): a mosaic tile; a tessera.

abalienation (ab.āl′yen.ā′shun): the transference of a legal title.

aband (a.band′): forsake, abandon. 1.

abannition (ab′a.nish′un): a curse.

abasia (a.bā′zhi.a): inability to coordinate muscular actions properly in walking.

abatis (ab′a.tis, a.bat′i): a defensive obstacle of felled trees, with their butts toward the place defended and their sharpened points toward the enemy.

abatize (ab′a.tīz): to make an abatis.

abaton (ab′a.ton): among the ancient Greeks, a sacred place forbidden to unauthorized visitors.

abducent (ab.dū′sent): carrying or drawing away; abducting.

abecedism (ā′bi.si.dizm): a word created from the initials of a word in a phrase; an acronym.

aberdevine (ab′er.di.vīn): the European siskin, a kind of finch.

abiotic (ā′bī.ot′ik): characterized by the absence of life.

abishag (ab′i.shag): per Mrs. Byrne, the child of a woman and a married man not her husband.

ablactate (ab.lak′tāt): to wean.

ablegate (ab′li.gāt): a papal envoy on a special mission.

ablepsia (ab.lep′si.a): blindness.

ablutomania (a.bloo′to.mā′ni.a): a mania for washing oneself.

abnormous (ab.nôr′mus): abnormal, irregular. 9.

aboma (a.bō′ma): any of several large South American constrictor snakes.

abra (ä′bra): a narrow pass or defile. 35A.

abraxis (a.brak′sis): a word that creates a powerful charm if carved into wood or stone.

abreaction (ab.ri.ak′shun): the release of repressed ideas or emotions during psychoanalysis.

Abrus (ābrus): a genus of tropical vines incl. the Indian licorice.

abscinder (ab.sind′er): one that cuts (something) off.

absinthiate (ab.sin′thi.āt): to impregnate with wormwood.

absinthium (ab.sin′thi.um): the common wormwood, or its dried leaves and tops, used as a bitter stomachic and tonic.

abstergent (ab.stur′jent): a substance used in cleansing; a detergent.

abstersion (ab.stur′shun): the process of cleansing, esp. by wiping.

abstersive (ab.stur′siv): abstergent. 1.

acanaceous (ak′a.nā′shus): prickly.

acanthine (a.kan′thīn, -thin): pert. to or resembling the acanthus plant or its leaves.

acara (a.kä′ra): a South American fish that builds nests and guards its young.

acapnotic (a.kap.not′ik): a nonsmoker.

acarophobia (ak′a.ro.fō′bi.a): fear of itching, or of insects causing itching.

acarpous (a.kär′pus): fruitless, sterile.

acataleptic (a.kat.a.lep′tik): one who suspends judgment, believing certainty is impossible.

acathistus (ak.a.this′tus): a Lenten hymn of the Eastern Orthodox Church.

acceptilation (ak.sep′ti.lā′shun): the settlement of a debt without payment.

accidentary (ak.si.den′ta.ri): fortuitous; also, nonessential. 1.

accidentiary (ak.si.den′shi.âr.i): pert. to the accidence, an elementary book of (esp. Latin) grammar; hence, rudiments.

accipient (ak.sip′i.ent): one who receives. 1.

accipitrine (ak.sip′i.trīn): hawklike, raptorial.

accismus (ak.siz′mus): in rhetoric, a feigned refusal.

accite (ak.sīt): to cite; summon. 1.

accolent (ak′o.lent): neighboring.

accresce (a.kres′): to accrue. 1.

accrescence (a.kres′ens): continuous growth; accretion.

accubitum (a.kū′bi.tum): a Roman couch of crescent shape, accommodating five persons at a meal.

acersecomic (a.ser.si.com′ic): one whose hair has never been cut.

acervuline (a.sur′vū.-līn, -lin): resembling small heaps.

acescency (a.ses′en.si): the condition of turning sour.

achaetous (a.kē′tus): hairless.

aciniform (a.sin′i.form): shaped like a grape cluster.

aciurgy (as′i.ur.ji): operative surgery.

aclinal (a.klī′nal): not sloping; horizontal.

acocotl (ak′o.kot′l): the clarin, a trumpetlike wind instrument used by the aborigines in Mexico.

acomia (a.kō′mi.a): baldness; *alopecia*.

acopic (a.kop′ik): in medicine, relieving weariness.

acousticophobia (a.koos′ti.ko.fō′bi.a): fear of noise.

acquent (a.kwent′): acquainted. 11.

acquest (a.kwest′): acquisition. 9. (cap) Property acquired through means other than inheritance.

acrity (ak′ri.ti): sharpness, keenness. 1.

acrolith (ak′ro.lith): a statue with a trunk of wood, usu. covered with metal or drapery, and with extremities of stone.

acronic (a.kron′ik), acronyctous (a.kro.nik′tus): occurring at nightfall, or sunset—said of the rising or setting of a star.

acronyx (ak′ro.niks): in medicine, an ingrowing nail.

acroterium (ak.ro.tē′ri.um): on a classical building, one of the angles of a pediment. A statue or ornament placed at one of these angles.

acrotic (a.krot′ik): in medicine, pert. to or affecting the surface.

actinograph (ak.tin′o.graf): an instrument for calculating exposure time in photography.

actinolitic (ak′tin.o.lit′ik): pert. to actinolite, a bright green or grayish green variety of amphibole.

actuosity(ak′tū.os′i.ti): great activity.1.

actus (ak′tus): an act or thing done, specif. a mental or spiritual act.

acutate (a.kū′tāt): in botany, slightly sharpened.

acutiator (a.kū′shi.ā′ter): in medieval times, a sharpener of weapons.

acyesis (as′i.ē′sis): female sterility.

acyrology (as.i.rol′o.ji): poor diction.

adactyl (a.dak′til): congenitally lacking fingers or toes.

adactylia (a.dak.til′i.a): congenital lack of fingers and toes.

adapic (ad′a.pik), adapid (ad′a.pid): pert. to a genus of crested fossil lemurs from the Eocene of Europe.

adda (ad′a): the common Egyptian skink.

adelophogamy (ad.el.o.fog′a.mi): marriage in which brothers share wives.

Adessenarian (ad.es′i.nâr′i.an): one believing in the real presence of Christ's body in the Eucharist, but not by transsubstantiation.

adhamant (ad.hā′mant): clinging as if by hooks—used esp. of the feet of certain birds, as the swift.

adharma (a.där′ma): in Hindu religion, unrighteousness—opposed to *dharma*, religious law or gospel.

adhibit (ad.hib′it): to let in (as a person), bring in. To affix (a label). To use, administer.

adiantum (ad′i.an′tum): a genus of plants comprising the maidenhair fern.

adiaphoristic (ad′i.af′o.ris′tik), adiaphorous (ad′i.af′o.rus): indifferent concerning religious or theological matters.

adipate (ad′i.pāt): a salt of edipic acid.

adipogenesis (ad′i.po.jen′e.sis): the formation of fat or fatty tissue.

aditus (ad′i.tus): a passage or opening for entrance.

adjag (aj′ag): a wild dog found in Java.

adject (a.jekt′): to add or annex; to join.

adlittoral (ad.lit′o.ral): pert. to the shallow water near the shore.

admedial (ad.mē′di.al): in biology, near the median plane.

adminicle (ad.min′i.kl): in law, a help or support; an auxiliary. Corroborative or explanatory proof.

adminiculary (ad.mi.nik′ū.lar.i): one who supplies help.

adnerval (ad.nur′val): in physiology, toward a nerve—said of electrical impulses passing toward the nerve through a muscle fiber.

adneural (ad.nū′ral): adjacent to a nerve.

adonean (ad′o.nē′an): pert. to Adonis.

adosculation (ad.os′kū.lā′shun): fertilization by external contact only.

adradius (ad.rā′di.us): in corals, sea anemones, jellyfishes, etc., one of the imaginary radial lines dividing the body into similar parts.

adrogation (ad′ro.gā′shun): adoption of a boy under 14 or a girl under 12.

adterminal (ad.tur′mi.nal): passing toward the end of a muscle—said in physiology of electrical impulses.

adulterine (a.dul′ter.īn): an illegitimate child.

aduncous (a.dung′kus): curved inward; hooked.

adustion (a.dus′chun): a burning or parching.

advenience (ad.vēn′yens): result of outward causes.

adversus (ad.vur′sus): against; toward in a hostile sense.

advesperate (ad.ves′pe.rāt): to draw toward evening.

advowee (ad′vou.ē′): one with the right of presenting a nominee to a vacant ecclesiastical benefice.

adynamia (a.dī.nā′mi.a): in medicine, lack or loss of the vital powers, caused by disease.

Aello (a.el′ō): a harpy.

aelurophile (i.lōō′ro.fīl): a cat lover.

aeneous (a.ē′ni.us): brassy; brasslike.

Aepyornis (ē′pi.ôr′nis): a genus of gigantic ratite birds known from remains found in Madagascar and believed to be the source of legends about the roc. They laid eggs fourteen inches long.

aequorial (i.kwôr′i.al): marine; oceanic. 52.

aeration (ā′er.ā′shun): aerating; exposure to air. Also, a process for eliminating undesirable flavors in milk or cream.

aerolite (ā.er.o.līt), aerolith (ā′er.o.lith): a stony meteorite.

aerophane (ā′er.o.fān): a thin, transparent crepe material.

aerophobia (ā′er.o.fō′bi.a): abnormal fear of flying.

aerotropic (ā′er.o.trop′ik): in plants, responding by changes in direction of growth of roots to changes in oxygen tension.

aesthematology, esthematology (es.-thē′ma.tol.o.ji): formerly, the science of the senses and the sense organs.

aesthesiology, esthesiology (es.thē′zi.ol.o.ji): the science of sensations.

Aetolian (i.tō′li.an): pert. to Aetolia, a district of Greece, or its inhabitants.

affiche (a.fēsh′): a placard posted in a public place.

affidavy (af′i.dā′vi): affidavit.

afflatus (a.flā′tus): an artistic inspiration.

aftaba (af.tä′ba): in Persia, a metal water vessel with a handle and long spout.

agacella (ag.a.sel′a): in heraldry, an antelope somewhat resembling a tiger, but with horns and hoofs.

agal (a.gal′, äg′al): a cord of goats' hair, worn by Bedouins to hold down the neckerchief.

agalma (a.gal′ma): a memorial; specif., a primitive Greek statue of a god.

> *ABERDEVINE*
>
> This yellow bird, who loves to frisk in
>   The umbrage of the pine,
> Describes himself as Piny Siskin,
>   Or else Aberdevine.
> But caught off guard, or in a pinch,
> He's just an ordinary Finch.

Agapemone (ag′a.pem′o.ni): a communistic establishment, founded about 1849 at Spaxton, England, that had a reputation for immoral behavior; hence any institution practicing free love.

agathism (ag′a.thizm): the concept that all is for the better.

agathokakological (ag′a.tho.kak′o.-loj′i.kal): composed of both good and evil.

agathology (ag′a.thol.o.ji): the science or doctrine of the good.

agee (a.jē′): off the straight line; awry. 11.

agerasia (aj′e.rā′zi.a): youthful appearance in an older person.

ageusic (a.gū′sik): in medicine, relating to the absence or impairment of the sense of taste.

agger (aj′er): a double tide; high, with two maxima, and low, with two minima. Also, a Roman earthwork or road.

aggeration (aj.er.ā′shun): an accumulation.

aggerose (aj′er.ōs): in heaps; filled with heaps.

agistment (a.jist′ment): the taking in of livestock for feeding at a specified rate; the opening of a forest to livestock for a specified period; prices paid in these connections.

agmatology (ag′ma.tol′o.ji): the branch of surgery that treats of fractures.

agnathic (ag.nath′ik): jawless.

agnogenic (ag.no.jen′ik): of unknown cause.

agnology (ag.nol′o.ji): the study of ignorance.

agon (ag′ōn, -on): a struggle or contest in ancient Greece, as in sports, literature, or music, or the dramatic conflict between the chief characters in a play.

agonistic (ag′o.nis′tik): combative.

agonium (a.gō′ni.um): any of the four Roman festivals celebrated yearly on January 9, March 17, May 21, and December 11.

agricere (ag′ri.sēr): a waxy coating on soil particles.

agroof (a.grōōf′): flat on one's face. 44.

agrypnotic (a.grip.not′ik): anything that induces wakefulness, as strong tea or coffee.

agyrate (a.jī′rāt): in botany, without whorls.

ahemeral (a.hem′er.al): not constituting a full day.

aikido (a.kī′dō): a Japanese method of self-defense involving powerful concentration and harmonious movements.

ailette (e.let′): in medieval armor, a plate of forged iron or steel worn over the coat of mail to protect the shoulder.

aischrolatreia (īs′kro.la.trī′a): the worship of filth.

ait (āt): an islet.

alabastrum (al′a.bas′trum): an ancient Greek or Roman jar for oils, ointments, or perfumes.

alala (ä′la.lä): a war cry of the ancient Greeks.

albarello (al′ba.rel′ō): a majolica jar with concave sides, used esp. to contain drugs.

albata (al.bä′ta): a kind of German silver.

albicant (al′bi.kant): becoming white.

Alceste (al.sest′): the hero of Molière's *Le Misanthrope,* a man outraged by the duplicity of society.

alchimic, alchymic (al.kim′ik): var. of alchemic.

aleconner (āl′kon′er): an English town official formerly charged with tasting and testing beer and ale.

alectryomancy (a.lek′tri.o.man′si): divination by means of a cock encircled by grains of corn placed on letters of the alphabet, which are then put together in the order in which the cock ate the grain.

alef, aleph (ā′lef, ä′lef): the first letter of the Hebrew alphabet, or the corresponding letter of other Semitic alphabets.

alethical (a.leth′i.kal): pert. to truth.

alette (a.let′): the pilasterlike abutment of an arch.

aleuromancy (a.lōō′ro.man′si): divination by means of flour.

alexia (a.lek′si.a): inability to read.

alexiteric (a.lek′si.ter′ik): resisting poison. An antidote against poison.

algedonic (al.je.don′ik): pert. to pain, esp. as associated with pleasure.

algesis (al.jē′sis): sensitiveness to pain.

algetic (al.jet′ik): sensitive to pain.

algophobia (al′go.fō′bi.a): fear of pain.

algriology (al.gri.ol′o.ji): the study of the customs of savages.

aliferous (a.lif′er.us), **aligerous** (a.lij′er.us): winged.

aliped (al′i.ped): wing-footed, as the bat.

alk (alk): resin of Chian turpentine.

alkahest (al′ka.hest): the universal solvent vainly sought by alchemists.

alla (äl′la): according to; in the manner or style of (as Italians say it).

Allemanian (al′e.mā′ni.an): the group of dialects of German spoken in Alsace, Switzerland, and southwestern Germany.

allerion (a.lēr′i.on): in heraldry, an eagle without beak or feet, and with extended wings.

allice (al′is): a European shad of the Severn and other rivers.

alliciency (a.lish′en.si): attractiveness.

alligation (al.i.gā′shun): the act of attaching or the state of being attached.

allineation (a.lin′i.ā′shun): alignment.

allochiral (al′o.kī′ral): symmetrically alike, but reversed in arrangement as to right and left, as one's hands.

allocochick (al′o.ko.chik): Indian shell money of northern California.

allogenic (al.o.jen′ik): genetically different.

allograft (al′o.graft): a tissue graft from the body of another person.

allograph (al′o.graf): a signature made for someone else.

allonymous (a.lon′i.mus): ghosted; ghostwritten.

allotheism (al′o.thē.izm): worship of strange gods.

allotriphagy (al′o.trif′a.ji): a craving for unlikely food.

allumette (a.lü.met′): a match for lighting.

almagest (al′ma.jest): a treatise on astronomy.

almirah (al.mī′ra): an Anglo-Indian cabinet, wardrobe.

almoign, almoin (al.moin′, al′moin): alms; an alms chest. *Frankalmoign.* 1.

almud, almude (al.mōōd′, -mōō′di): any of various old Portuguese and Spanish units of measure.

alogism (al′o.jizm): something contrary to or regardless of logic; an irrational statement or piece of reasoning.

aloma (a.lō′ma): light brown to yellowish brown.

alopecia (al′o.pē′shi.a): baldness.

alopecoid (a.lop.e.koid): foxlike, foxy.

alose (a.lōs): any fish of the genus Alosa, esp. the common European shad. To praise; commend. 1.

alpeen (al.pēn′): a cudgel. 50.

alphenic (al.fen′ik): the crystallized juice of the sugar cane; sugar candy.

alphitomancy (al.fit′o.man′si): divination by means of barley flour and honey loaves. 1.

alpigene (al′pi.jēn): growing in alpine regions.

altaian, altaic (al.tā′an, al.tā′ik): pert. to the Altai mountains of central Asia, or to the Altai people or language family (Turkic, Tungusic, and Mongolic).

alterity (al.ter′i.ti): otherness.

altrigenderism (al′tri.jen′der.izm): the point of development at which one becomes attracted to persons of the opposite sex.

altun (al.tōōn′): gold. Specif., a gold piece first issued by Mohammed II in the 15th century.

aluta (a.lōō′ta): a soft tanned leather.

aly (āl′i): of or like ale.

amalaita (ä′ma.lī′ta): in South Africa, native criminals or hooligans.

amalgamize (a.mal′ga.mīz): to amalgamate.

amania (a.mā′ni.a): a gold coin of Afghanistan.

amaranthine (am′a.ran′thīn): everlasting, unfading. Reddish purple in color.

amasesis (am′a.sē′sis): the inability to chew.

amathophobia (a.math′o.fō′bi.a): fear of dust.

amaxophobia (a.mak′so.fō′bi.a): fear of riding in an automobile.

ambagitory (am.baj′i.tō′ri): circumlocutory; circuitous.

ambassade (am′ba.sād): embassy.

ambigenous (am.bij′i.nus): of two kinds. Among plants, having the outer series of floral leaves differing from the inner.

ambiparous (am.bip′a.rus): pert. to buds that contain both flowers and leaves.

ambrology (am.brol′o.ji): the natural history of amber.

ambrosialize (am.brō′zhi.a.līz): to turn into ambrosia.

ambulophobia (am′bū.lo.fō′bi.a): fear of walking.

ambuscado (am′bus.kā′do): ambuscade. 9.

ameen, amin (a.mēn): in India, a confidential agent.

amelia (a.mēl′ya): a limbless monster. Congenital absence of the arms or legs.

amercement (a.murs′ment): the infliction of a penalty at the discretion of the court.

ametropic (am′i.trop′ik): pert. to an abnormal condition of the eye in which visual images do not come to a focus.

amidin (am′i.din): a hydrochloride.

amissible (a.mis′i.bl): liable to be lost. 52.

amma (am′a): an abbess or spiritual mother.

amobyr (a.mō′ber): in Welsh law, a fee formerly payable for a woman to the lord of the manor upon her marriage.

amoebaeum (am′i.bē′um): a kind of poem by Vergil involving alternate speakers. Also, a member of an order of rhyopods, incl. the common soil and water amoebas.

amort (a.môrt′): in Shakespeare, as if dead; spiritless.

amotus (a.mō′tus): not touching the ground; elevated—said of the hind toe of some birds. 52.

amourette (am′oor.et): a trifling love affair.

ampelite (am′pe.līt): a black earth abounding in pyrites, used by the ancients to kill insects on vines.

amphiblastic (am′fi.blas′tik): in embryology, segmenting unequally—said of certain eggs.

amphierotic (am′fi.e.rot′ik): capable of erotic reaction toward either sex.

amphigaean, amphigean (am.fi.jē′an): occurring in both hemispheres.

amphigory (am′fi.gō′ri): nonsense verse or composition.

amphilogism (am.fil′o.jizm): ambiguity of speech; equivocation.

amphivorous (am.fiv′o.rus): eating both animal and vegetable food.

amplectant, amplectic (am.plek′tant, -tik): pert. to the mating embrace of the frog or toad, during which eggs are shed into the water and there fertilized.

ampliate (am′pli.āt): with a prominent outer edge, as the wings of certain insects.

ampollosity (am′po.los′i.ti): bombast.

amsel (am′sel): the ring ouzel. The European blackbird.

amurca (a.mur′ka): lees of olive oil.

amurcous (a.mur′kus): full of dregs; foul. 52.

amyctic (a.mik′tik): irritating; abrasive.

amyous (a.mī'us): without strength.

anacardic (an'a.kär'dik): relating to the cashew and other tropical American trees having kidney-shaped fruit.

anaclastic (an'a.klas'tik): capable of springing back.

"ABATIS: A DEFENSIVE OBSTACLE OF FELLED TREES"

I felled my words as trees fall . . . fanned their stout
Rough trunks before me in an abatis,
The butt ends in, the sharp ends pointing out,
Pretending to defend against your kiss.
(Of course you knew I really had in mind
Piling a screen of words to kiss behind.)

---

anacrotic (an'a.krot'ik): pert. to an abnormality of the blood circulation shown by a sphygmographic tracing.

anacrusis (an'a.krōō'sis): in music, an upbeat.

anacusic (an'a.kū'sik): pert. to absolute deafness.

anaglyphy (a.nag'li.fi): the art of carving, chasing, or embossing in relief.

anagnost (an'ag.nost): a cleric in the first of the minor orders of the Eastern church.

analect (an'a.lekt): a literary fragment, short saying.

analeptic (an'a.lep'tik): a restorative; tonic.

analgic (an.al'jik): analgesic.

analysand (a.nal'i.zand): a person undergoing analysis, esp. psychoanalysis.

ananas (a.nä'nas): a pineapple or pinguin.

ananym (an'a.nim): a name written backward.

anapanapa (a.nä'pa.nä'pa): a widely distributed tropical shrub. The bark is used as soap. 38.

anapodeictic (an.ap'o.dīk'tik): undemonstrable.

anaptotic (an'ap.tot'ik): of a language, characterized by deterioration and deficiency of declensional forms, as English.

anaqua (a.nä'kwa): a shade tree of southern Texas and Mexico.

anarchal (an.ärk'al): pert. to or tending toward anarchy.

anastatic (an'a.stat'ik): pert. to a process of printing from a zinc plate that leaves a transferred design in relief.

anastrophic (an'a.strof'ik): pert. to the inversion of the usual syntactical order of words for rhetorical effect.

anatheme (an'a.thēm): anathema. Also, a votive offering.

anatine (an'a.tīn): ducklike.

anatron (an'a.tron): native soda carbonate; nitron.

ancile (an.sī'li): any of the 12 sacred shields of the ancient Romans that were thought to guarantee the preservation of the city.

ancipital (an.sip'i.tal): having two edges.

anconeal (an.kō'ni.al): pert. to the elbow.

androcentrism (an'dro.sen'trizm): emphasis on maleness.

androcratic (an'dro.krat'ik): pert. to the political and social supremacy of men—contrasted with *gynecocratic*.

androgeny (an.droj'i.ni): a condition in which the chromosomes of the embryo come only from the father.

androgyny (an.droj'i.ni): effeminacy; hermaphroditism.

andromania (an.dro.mā'ni.a): nymphomania.

androphagan, androphagic, androphagous (an.drof'a.gan, -a.jik, -a.gus): man-eating.

androphobia (an.dro.fō'bi.a): dread of men; repugnance to the male sex.

anenst (a.nenst'): anent. 1.

angekok (ang'ge.kok): an Eskimo medicine man.

angor (ang'gor): great anxiety accompanied by painful constriction at the upper part of the belly.

angster (ang'ster): a Swiss minor coin of copper coined from the 15th to the 19th centuries.

angulous (ang'gū.lus): angular.

angusticlave (ang.gus'ti.klāv): a narrow purple stripe worn on each side of the head as a mark of rank by minor Roman aristocrats.

anhedonia (an'hi.dō'ni.a): the inability to be happy.

anhistous (an.his'tus): not differentiated into tissues; noncellular.

anidian (a.nid'i.an): shapeless.

anility (a.nil'i.ti): state of being an old woman.

animastic (an'i.mas'tik): spiritual.

animetta (an'i.met'a): the cover for the cloth in the Eucharist.

animoso (an'i.mō'sō): animated—a direction in music.

anisomeric (an'i.so.mer'ik): tending to become differentiated; not having the same elements in the same proportions; not isomeric.

ankee (ang'ki): barn grass. The Mohaves grind its seed into flour.

annectant, annectent (a.nek'tent): connecting, linking. Used esp. of a species or group having characters intermediate between those of two other species or groups.

annona (a.nō'na): in ancient Rome, the agricultural product of a year. (cap) A genus of trees and shrubs with leathery leaves, solitary nodding flowers, and compound fruit, incl. the custard apple and the soursop.

annulose (an'ū.lōs): ringed, as the *Annulosa,* a genus of worms with a body composed of ringlike segments.

annumerate (a.nū'mer.āt): to add on; count in.

anoetic (an'o.et'ik): unthinkable. 52.

anomoean (an'o.mē'an): one who believes that since the son of God is a created being, he is unlike God in essence.

anorchous (an.ôr'kus): without testicles.

anoretic (an'o.ret'ik), anorexic (an.o.rek'sik): suffering lack of appetite, esp. from emotional distress.

anotia (a.nō'shi.a): absence of the ears.

anserous (an'ser.us): gooselike; stupid.

antaean (an.tē'an): pert. to Antaeus, a legendary wrestler who was invincible as long as he was touching the earth.

antapology (an'ta.pol'o.ji): an answer to an apology.

antecedaneous (an'ti.si.dā'ni.us): antecedent; preceding in time.

antecessor (an'ti.ses'er): a previous incumbent or owner; predecessor.

antecibal (an'ti.sī'bal): happening before meals.

antecursor (an'ti.kur'ser): forerunner; preceder. 1.

antelucan (an'ti.lōō'kan): before dawn. 9.

antenati (an'ti.nä'ti): persons born before a certain date or event, esp. with regard to political rights.

antepaschal (an'ti.pas'kal): before Passover or Easter.

anteriad (an.tēr'i.ad): toward the front part of the body.

anthine (an'thīn, an'thin): belonging to a genus of singing birds, the typical pipits.

anthracomancy (an'thra.ko.man'si): divination using burning coal.

anthropographical (an'thro.po.graf'i.kal): pert. to the branch of anthropology that treats of the human race in its different divisions.

anthropolith (an'thro.po.lith): a petrified human body.

anthroponymy (an'thro.pon'i.mi): the science of the study of personal names.

anthropophagan (an.thro.pof'a.gan): anthropophagous.

anthropophobia (an'thro.po.fō'bi.a): fear of meeting strangers.

antibacchius (an'ti.ba.kī'us): in prosody, a metrical foot of three syllables of differing stresses.

antibromic (an'ti.brō'mik): a deodorant.

antichresis (an'ti.krē'sis): a mortgage contract by which the mortgagee takes possession of the property and has its fruits or profits in lieu of interest.

anticlinal (an'ti.klī'nal): inclining in opposite directions.

anticous (an.tī'kus): in botany, turned away from the axis, facing anteriorly.

anticus (an.tī'kus): anterior.

antilegomena (an'ti.li.gom'e.na): those books of the New Testament whose canonicity was for a time in dispute.

antilogy (an.til'o.ji): a contradiction in terms of ideas.

antiloquy (an.til'o.kwi): contradiction. 1.

antinomian (an'ti.nō'mi.an): one who holds that faith alone is sufficient for salvation.

antipathic (an'ti.path'ik), antipathous (an.tip'a.thus): antipathetic; contrarious. 1.

antiperiodic (an'ti.pēr'i.od'ik): preventing periodic returns of paroxysms or exacerbations of disease. An antiperiodic remedy.

antiphrastic (an'ti.fras'tik): referring to the use of words in senses opposite to the generally accepted meanings, usu. for humorous or ironic purposes.

antipudic (an'ti.pū'dik): worn to conceal the genitals.

antiscians (an.tish'anz): people living on the same meridian, but on different sides of the equator, so that at noon they cast shadows in opposite directions.

antispast (an'ti.spast): in prosody, a foot of four syllables.

Antum (an'tum): in the Babylonian religion, the consort of Anu, the god of heaven.

anuptaphobia (a.nup'ta.fō'bi.a): fear of remaining single.

ao (ä'ō): among the Maoris and Polynesians, the personification of light and of the upper world of the living.

aosmic (a.oz'mik): odorless.

apa (ä'pa): the wallaba tree.

apadana (a'pa.dä'na): the great hall in ancient Persian palaces.

apagoge (a'pa.gō'ji): abduction. Also, argument by the reductio ad absurdum.

apagogic (ap'a.goj'ik): in rhetoric, proceeding by the method of disproving the proposition that contradicts the one to be established.

apar, apara (a.pär', -pä'ra): the three-banded armadillo of South America.

apanthropy (a.pan'thro.pi): love of solitude.

apastron (ap.ast'ron): the point in the orbit of one star of a binary when it is farthest from the other.

apathic (a.path'ik): having no sensation.

apathistical (a.pa.this'ti.kal): devoid of feeling or emotion.

apepsy (a.pep'si): var. of apepsia, indigestion.

apeptic (a.pep'tik): suffering from indigestion.

aphilanthropy (af'i.lan'thro.pi): distaste for social intercourse.

aphilophrenia (a.fil'o.frē'ni.a): a feeling that one is unloved or unwanted.

aphlogistic (a'flo.jis'tik): flameless.

aphnology (af.nol'o.ji): the science of wealth.

apiole, apiol (ā'pi.ōl, ap'i.ōl, -ol): a colorless crystalline ether.

aplotomy (a.plot'o.mi): in surgery, a simple incision.

apocarteresis (ap'o.kär'te.rē'sis): suicide by starvation.

apodictic (ap'o.dik'tik): clearly true.

apodysophilia (ap'o.dis'o.fil'ya): a feverish desire to undress.

apodyterium (ap'o.di.tē'ri.um): an undressing room in an ancient Greek or Roman bath or gymnasium.

apojove (ap'o.jōv): that point farthest from the planet Jupiter of each of its satellites.

apolaustic (ap'o.lôs'tik): fond of pleasure; self-indulgent.

apologue (ap'o.log): a fable with a moral.

apopemptoclinic (a.po.pemp'to.klin'ik): inclined toward divorce.

apositia (a.po.sish'i.a): aversion to food.

aposoro (ap'o.sō'ro): one of the African lemurs, esp. the potto of West Africa, which resembles the loris in its nocturnal, arboreal, and slow-moving habits.

apothesis (a.poth'i.sis): in early churches, a place on the south side of the chancel for books, vestments, etc. A dressing room at a public bath. The setting of a fractured or dislocated limb.

apotome (a.pot'o.mi): an interval in Greek music. A variety of the mineral celestite.

apotropaic (ap'o.tro.pā'ik): designed to avert or turn aside evil.

appeach (a.pēch'): to impeach; accuse. To cast aspersions on. 1.

appentice (a.pen'tis): a penthouse. 1.

appetant (ap'e.tant): pert. to desire. In phonetics, a gliding sound.

applosion (a.plō'zhun): in phonetics, the interruption and compression of a breath.

appulsion (a.pul'shun): the act of striking against. A bringing to land. 1. The near approach of one celestial body to another. In civil law, the process by which land is visibly torn away from one part of the banks of a stream and added to another part.

apricate (ap'ri.kāt): to bask in or expose to the sun.

aprosexia (ap'ro.sek'si.a): inability to concentrate.

aptote (ap'tōt): an indeclinable noun.

aptotic (ap.tot'ik): (of a language) lack-

ing denominational inflections, as Chinese.

apyrous (a.pī'rus): noncombustible.

aracari (är'a.sä'ri): any of several brilliantly colored South American toucans.

arachibutyrophobia (a.rak'i.bū.tī'ro.fō'bi.a): fear of peanut butter sticking to the roof of the mouth.

arachidic (ar'a.kid'ik): caused by or pert. to peanuts.

araneous (a.rā'ni.us): arachnoid.

arara (a.rä'ra): a macaw. The palm cockatoo of Australia. (cap) An Indian of a Cariban tribe in Brazil.

aratory (ar'a.tō'ri): contributing to tillage. 52.

arbuscle (är'bus'l): a dwarf tree or tree-like shrub.

archaist (är'kā.ist): an antiquary. One who uses archaisms.

archiater (är.kī'a.ter): a chief physician of the court of a Hellenistic king or a Roman emperor. Later, a leading local physician, publicly employed.

archical (är'ki.kl): governmental; primary, primordial. 1.

archimagus (är'ki.mā'gus): a great wizard, magician, or enchanter.

archology (är.kol'o.ji): the doctrine of origins. The science of government.

archtoid (ärk'toid): like a bear.

Arctalia (ärk.tāl'ya): a marine realm including all northern seas as far south as floating ice occurs.

arefy (ar'e.fī): to dry. 1.

arenosity (ar'i.nos'i.ti): sandiness.

areometer (ar'i.om'e.ter): a hydrometer.

aretaics (ar'i.tā'iks): the study of virtue.

arethusa (ar'i.thoo'za): any of several orchids having a solitary rose-purple flower fringed with yellow. (cap) In mythology, a wood nymph who, pursued by the river god Alpheus, was changed by Artemis into a stream.

aretological (ar'i.to.loj'i.kal): pert. to moral philosophy. 1.

argh (ärg): timid, cowardly. 2.

argillaceous (ar'ji.lā'shus): clayey; containing clay.

argute (är.gūt'): sharp, shrill; acute, sagacious.

arigato (ar'i.gä'to): "thank you" in Japanese.

ariole (ar'i.ōl): a soothsayer. 1.

Aristaeus (ar'is.tē'us): in Greek mythology, a beneficent hero, usu. said to have been the son of Apollo and the nymph Cyrene.

armilla (är.mil'a): the annular ligament of the wrist. Also, a stole like the ecclesiastical stole used in the British coronation ceremony.

armitage (är′mi.tij): hermitage. 1.

armscye (ärm′sī): the armhole or opening in a garment for the attaching of a sleeve.

arna (är′na): a wild water buffalo.

arrect (a.rekt′): to make erect. To direct. 1. Erect; attentive.

arreptitious (ar.ep.tish′us): snatched away; possessed, as a demoniac; raving; mad. 1.

Arretine (ar′e.tīn): pert. to ancient Arretium, now Arezzo, Italy, where the red terracotta ware called Arretine was made in ancient times.

arrhizal (a.rī′zal): destitute of a true root, as a parasitic plant.

arride (a.rīd′): to smile or laugh at. To please, delight. 1.

arriviste (a′ri′vēst): an opportunist; one who uses any means to attain success.

arter (är′ter): var. of *after*.

arthrology (är.throl′o.ji): the science that treats of joints.

arva (är′va): mistaken spelling of *'ava* (kava) in Herman Melville's *Typee*.

arval (är′val): a funeral feast. (cap) Relating to a body of ancient Roman priests who presided over an annual May fertility rite.

arvicole (är′vi.kōl): a water vole.

ary (âr′i): any. 11.

aryballos, aryballus (ar′i.bal′os, -us): a short-necked flask or bottle having a single handle, small orifice, and globular body, used for holding oils or ointments.

asaphia (a.sā′fi.a): indistinct utterance, as that due to cleft palate.

ascesis (a.sē′sis): rigorous training, self-discipline, or self-restraint.

ascian (ash′i.an, ash′un): one without a shadow, as an inhabitant of the torrid zone, where for a few days each year the sun is vertical at noon.

aseity (a.sē′i.ti): the quality or state of being self-derived or self-originated; God in his eternal and independent being.

asherah (a.shē′ra): a sacred wooden post that stood near the altar in Canaanite high places and symbolized the goddess Asherah.

asitia (a.sish′i.a): want of appetite; loathing of food.

asonia (a.sō′ni.a): deafness to certain tones or pitches.

aspectant (as.pek′tant): looking at; beholding. 1.

asperge (as.purj′): to sprinkle.

assart (a.särt′): act of grubbing, as bushes; land so cleared.

assertum (a.sur′tum): something that is asserted.

assidean (a.si.dē′an), hasidean (ha.si.dē′an): pert. to the Hasidim, a Jewish sect devoted to mysticism and strict ritual observance.

assiduate (a.sid′ū.it): assiduous; diligent. 1.

assis (a.sē′, as′is): sitting down; used of animals in heraldry.

assise (a.sēz′): a succession of paleontological zones bearing fossils of the same genera.

assoluto (äs′so.loo′tō): in music, absolute; one voice alone.

assuetude (as′wi.tood): custom; habit. In medicine, accustomedness to disturbing influences. 1.

astasia (as.tā′zhi.a): inability to sit or stand erect.

asteism (as′ti.izm): genteel irony; polite and ingenious derision.

astereognosis (as.tēr′i.og.nō′sis): loss of ability to recognize the shapes of objects by touch.

asteria (as.tē′ri.a): in Greek antiquity, a gem reflecting light in six rays, suggesting a star—perhaps the star sapphire.

asthenia (as.thē′ni.a): loss of strength.

asthenology (as′thi.nol′o.ji): the scientific study of disease due to debility.

astorgia (a.stôr′ji.a): lack of interest in one's children.

astragalomancy (as.trag′a.lo.man′si): divination by means of small bones or dice.

astrologaster (as.trol′o.gas′ter): a charlatan astrologer.

Astrophel (as′tro.fel): the name used for himself by Sir Philip Sidney in his sonnet sequence *Astrophel and Stella* (1591).

astrophobia (as′tro.fō′bi.a): fear of outer space.

asura (a.soo′ra): in the oldest parts of the Rig-Veda, a god or spirit; later, a demon; an enemy of the gods.

ataunt (a.tônt): of a sailing vessel, fully rigged; shipshape.

atavus (at′a.vus): an ancestor or ancestral type, from which a character is assumed to be inherited. Spec., a grandfather.

ate (ā′ti): blind impulse, reckless ambition, or excessive folly that drives men to ruin. (cap) A Greek goddess of infatuation.

Aten (ä′ten, at′en): the sun as god, which Amenhotep of Egypt (d. about 1358 B.C.) sought to make the supreme cult of the people.

athanasia (ath′a.nā′zhi.a): deathlessness; immortality.

athetize (ath′i.tīz): to spurn, reject.

atis (a.tēs′): a poisonous herb of the monkshood family, found in the Himalayas.

atle (at′li): the tamarask salt tree of western Asia and India.

atmospherium (at.mos.fē′ri.um): a room for simulating atmospheric or meteorological phenomena.

atocia (a.tō′shi.a): female sterility.

atopic (a.top′ik): not in the usual place—said by physicians of an organ in the body.

atrabilarian (at′ra.bi.lâr′i.an): a hypochondriac.

atrabile (at′ra.bīl): black bile; melancholy. 1.

atrichia (a.trik′i.a): baldness.

atropic (a.trop′ik): pert. to atropine, a bitter, poisonous alkaloid.

atry (a.trī′): (a ship) kept bow to the sea by a balance of sails.

Atta (at′a): a New World genus of leaf-eating, chiefly tropical ants, often very destructive to plants. (not cap) In India, the sweetsop tree; also, unsorted wheaten flour or meal.

attensity (a.ten′si.ti): sensory clearness; differentiation between a sensation that is the focus of attention and one that is not.

attent (a.tent′): attentive; heedful.

attingent (a.tin′jent): touching; in contact. 1.

attornment (a.turn′ment): an assignment. In law, the acknowledgment by a tenant that he holds his property on behalf of a new landlord.

attrahent (at′ra.hent): an attractant, as a magnet.

attrectation (a.trek.tā′shun): handling or touching. 1.

atua (a.too′a): in Polynesia and esp. among the Maoris, a supernatural being; a god or demon.

atychiphobia (a.tik′i.fō′bi.a): fear of failure.

aube (ōb): archaic form of *alb, albe*, a liturgical vestment.

aubergiste (ō′ber.zhēst): an innkeeper.

auctorial (ôk.tō′ri.al): like an author.

aularian (ô.lâr′i.an): pert. to a hall.

aum (ôm): alum. 44.

auricomous (ô.rik′o.mus): golden-haired.

auricularis (ô.rik′ū.lā′ris): any of three muscles attached to the cartilage of the external ear.

aurify (ô′ri.fī): to turn into gold.

auriscalp (ô.ri.skalp): an earpick.

auscultate (ôs′kul.tāt): to examine by listening, as with a stethoscope.

austral (ôs′tral): southern.

autodidact (ô′to.di.dakt): one self-taught.

autogeny (ô.toj′e.ni): self-generation.

autognosis (ô.tog.nō′sis): self-awareness.

automysophobia (ô′to.mī′so.fōbi.a): fear of being dirty.

autophagia (ô.to.fā′ji.a): the feeding of the body by the consumption of its own tissues, as in fasting. Also, biting oneself.

autoptic (ô.top′tik): based on personal observation.

autoschediastic (ô.to.skē′di.as.tik): impromptu.

autotomy (ô.tot′o.mi): self-mutilation.

autotype (ô′to.tīp): a picture made by a carbon process.

auxilium (ôg.zil′i.um): a military ambulance wagon. In old English law, an extraordinary yearly tax.

Avena (a.vē′na): a genus of widely distributed grasses, incl. the oats.

averruncate (av′e.rung′kāt): to avert; ward off; also, erroneously, ro root up.

aviatic (ā′vi.at′ik): pert. to flight.

avizandum (av′i.zan′dum): in Scots law, private consideration.

awk (ôk): done in the wrong way; clumsy. 1.

awless (ô′les): var. of aweless.

awn (ôn): in grasses, one of the slender bristles that terminate the scales of the spikelet. Among reptiles, one of the barbs on the hemipenis.

axinomancy (ak.sin′o.man′si): divination by means of an ax placed on a post.

azarole (az′a.rōl): a shrub of southern Europe, or its edible and pleasant-flavored fruit.

azurine (az′ū.rīn, -rin): azure.

B

babby (bab′i): dial. var. of *baby.*

babyolatry (bā′bi.ol′a.tri): baby worship.

bacca (bak′a): tobacco. 21.

bacchius (ba.kī′us): in prosody, a metrical foot of three syllables of varying stresses.

bacillary (bas′i.ler′i): rod-shaped. Pert. to bacilli.

Bacopa (ba.kō′pa): a genus of chiefly tropical herbs, inc. the water hyssop, with opposite leaves and small solitary flowers.

bacula (bak′ū.la): in astronomy, strips or streamers of nebulous matter.

baculus (bak′ū.lus): a staff or rod, esp. one symbolizing authority, as the pastoral staff of a bishop.

badderlocks (bad′er.loks): a large black seaweed often eaten as a vegetable in Europe.

baddock (bad′uk): the pollack, or coalfish. 44.

badia (ba.dē′a): in Italy, a monastery or abbey.

baffy (baf′i): a short wooden golf club with a deeply lofted face.

baggitt (bag′it): a recently spawned salmon, or a female just before or after spawning. 41.

baira, beira (bī′ra): a small gazelle-like antelope of Somaliland that is purplish black and brightly marked with yellowish fawn.

bal (bal): a mine. 41A.

balaniferous (bal′a.nif′er.us): bearing acorns.

balanoid (bal′a.noid): acorn-shaped.

balatron (bal′a.tron): a buffoon.

baldicoot (bôl′di.kŌŌt): the bald coot. A monk.

Bali (bä′li): a king of the monkeys in the Sanskrit epic *Ramayana.*

balisaur (bal′i.sôr): the hog-nosed badger of India.

ballabile (ba′lä′bi.lā): in classical ballet, a dance performed by the corps de ballet with or without the principal dancers.

ballistrophobia (ba.lis′tro.fō′bi.a): fear of missiles, or of being shot.

bamboula (bam.bŌŌ′la): a primitive drum used in voodoo ceremonies and incantations, or the dance performed to its beat.

bambuk (bam.bŌŌk′), bambui (bam.bŌŌ′i): butter from the seeds of the shea, an African tree.

Bana (bä′na): in Hindu mythology, a thousand-armed giant.

banausic (ba.nô′sik): smacking of the workshop.

bandoline (ban′do.lin): a glutinous pomade for dressing the hair.

banig (ba.nēg′): in the Philippines, a mat or matting made of dried palm leaves or grass.

banket (bang′ket): the auriferous conglomerate rock of the Transvaal.

A PERPLEXITY OF PISCINITY

It's written in each piscine part, it's stamped upon
  the whole fish:
A pollack is a baddock, and a baddock is a coalfish.
Yet coalfish-pollack-baddock isn't haddock—which
  is odd,
Since coalfish-pollack-baddock
Is just the same as haddock
In being quite inferior-tasting cod.

Baphometic (baf′o.met′ik): pert. to Baphomet, an idol that the Templars were accused of using in their mysterious rites.

barbaralalia (bär′ber.a.lāl′ya): a speech impairment manifested when speaking a foreign language.

barble (bär′bl): barbarian.

bardel, bardell (bär.del′): a packsaddle. 1.

bardolatry (bär.dol′a.tri): Shakespeare-worship.

bareca, bareka (ba.rä′ka): on ships, a small cask; a breaker.

baric (bar′ik): pert. to barium.

baris (bar′is): a Balinese spear dance or warriors' dance depicting a sham battle. A flat-bottomed rowboat used for freight on the Nile.

barken (bär′ken): made of bark.

barkle (bär′kl): to encrust, cake. 13.

barley-bree, barley-broo (bär′li.bri, bär′li.brŌŌ): liquor made from barley. Whiskey; also, strong ale. 44.

barmecide (bär′mi.sīd): a false benefactor.

barolo (ba.rō′lō): a red wine of Piedmont, Italy.

barracan (bar′a.kan): a fabric of the Levant. A mantle or wrap of such fabric.

barracouta (bar′a.kŌŌ′ta): a large food fish found along the coasts of Australia, New Zealand, and southern Africa; barracuda.

barras (bar′as): galpot, a crude turpentine formed from the pine tree. Also, a kind of coarse linen.

barricado (bar′i.kä′dō): barricade.

barton (bär′ton): a large farm. A farmyard or the outbuildings behind a farmhouse. A poultry yard or hen coop. 13.

barvel, barvell (bär′vel): a fisherman's large leather apron. 28A.

barylalia (bar′i.lāl′ya): indistinctly articulated speech.

baryphonic (bar′i.fon′ik): pert. to difficulty of speech.

baryta (ba.rī′ta): any of several compounds of barium; esp., barium monoxide.

basial (bā′zi.al): kissing; osculatory.

basiate (bā′zi-āt): to kiss. 52.

basihyal (bā′si.hī′al): pert. to a bone at the ventral point of the arch that forms the hyoid bone at the base of the human tongue.

basilect (bas′i.lekt): to speakers of a language, the variety or dialect with least prestige.

basilicon (ba.sil′i.kon): an ointment composed of rosin, yellow wax, and lard.

basophobia (bā′so.fō′bi.a): inability to stand caused by fear of falling.

basta (bas′ta): the third-highest trump (queen of spades) in omber, solo, and other card games.

batata (ba.tä′ta): sweet potato.

batch (bach): a bachelor. 26.

batcher (bach′er): one who operates the machine that weighs the material for batches of concrete; the machine itself.

bathetic (ba.thet′ik): falsely sentimental.

bathic (bath′ik): pert. to depth, esp. the depth of the sea.

bathybian (ba.thib′i.an): pert. to or living in the deepest parts of the sea.

batino (ba.tē′nō): a Philippine tree that yields a moderately valuable timber.

batophobia (bat′o.fō.bi.a): fear of being close to high buildings.

batrachomyomachy (bat′ra.ko.mi.om′-a.ki): the battle between the frogs and the mice—a Greek parody of the *Iliad*.

batrachophobia (bat′ra.ko.fō′bi.a): terror of frogs and toads.

batta (bat′a): in India, subsistence money (as for a witness or prisoner); maintenance or traveling expenses of an employee. Also, extra pay.

battologize (ba.tol′o.jīz): to repeat needlessly; to iterate.

battue (ba.tōō′): a hunt where the game is driven into the arms of the hunters; the game so driven; any mass slaughter of the unresisting.

battuta (bat.tōōt′a): the beat of a musical composition. A measure.

bawbee (bô′bi): an old Scottish coin. An English halfpenny.

beal (bēl): a mouth or narrow pass, as of a river or valley. 44. To bellow; roar. 1. To come to a head, as a pimple. 2.

beatus (bi.ā′tus): in the Roman Catholic Church, a man or boy who has been beatified.

bedaggle (bi.dag′l): daggle. To clog with mud and mire. 1.

beele (bēl): the crossbar of a yoke. 1. A pickax with both ends sharp, used to pick out ore from rocks. 2.

beeve (bēv): beef; a ''beef creature,'' per Washington Irving.

beezer (bē′zer): nose. 21.

beisa (bī′sa): an antelope found in northeastern Africa.

beken (bi.ken′): to make known; deliver; commend; entreat. 1.

bekko (bek′ō): in Japan, articles made from tortoise shell.

belah (bē′la): a beefwood of Australia. A tall forest tree of Queensland.

Bellatrix (be.lāt′riks): a bright star in Orion.

belletristic (bel′le.tris′tik): pert. to belles lettres.

bellic (bel′ik): martial. 1.

bellipotent (be.lip′o.tent): strong in war.

belomancy (bel′o.man′si): divination by drawing arrows at random from a container.

belton (bel′tun): a combination of blue and lemon colors, as in the coats of certain collies and setters. A dog with a coat of these two tones.

benda (ben′da): a measure of weight in Guinea.

beneceptor (ben′i.sep′ter): any sense organ that is responsive to beneficial stimulus.

beneficious (ben′i.fish′us): pert. to a benefice.

benet (bi.net′): to catch with a net; to ensnare.

benn (ben): a colored silk sash. 44.

bennel (ben′el): the ditch reed. 13.

benthonic (ben.thon′ik): occurring on the bottom underlying a body of water.

benthopelagic (ben.thop′i.laj′ik): inhabiting the depths of the ocean.

beray (bi.rā′): to make foul; to soil.

Berean (bi.rē′an): a native or inhabitant of the ancient city Beroea, in either Macedonia or Syria.

bever (bē′ver): a drink, a between-meals snack. 1. To tremble. 13.

bhang (bang): an intoxicant made from Indian hemp; hashish, cannabis.

bheestie, bheesty (bēs′ti): in India, a water carrier of a household or regiment.

bibacious (bī.bā′shus, bi-): addicted to drinking; bibulous.

bibasic (bī.bā′sik): in chemistry, containing two replaceable hydrogen atoms; dibasic.

bibble (bib′l): to drink often, much, or noisily. 11.

bibbons (bib′uns): a nonsense word used and prob. coined by Edward Lear to supplement *ribbons* in his poem *The Quangle Wangle's Hat.*

biblioclasm (bib′li.o.klazm): destruction of the Bible, or of books generally.

bibliognost (bib′li.og.nost): one knowledgeable about books and bibliography.

bibliomancy (bib′li.o.man′si): divination by picking Bible passages at random.

bibliopegic (bib′li.o.pej′ik), bibliopegistic (bib′li.o.pe.jis′tik): pert. to bookbinding.

bibliotaph (bib′li.o.taf): one who hoards or hides books.

bicaudal (bī.kô′dal): having or terminating in two tails.

bicephalous (bī.sef′a.lus): two-headed.

bicrural (bī.kroor′al): having two legs.

biduous (bid′ū.us): lasting, or remaining open, two days, as some flowers.

bifer (bī′fer): a plant that bears fruit twice a year.

biflex (bī′fleks): bent in two directions.

bifronted (bī.frun′ted): having two fronts.

biga (bī′ga): a two-horse chariot of ancient Mediterranean countries.

bigential (bī.jen′shal): including two tribes or races.

biggin (big′in): house, outbuilding. 13. A coffee percolator used early in the 19th century. A child's cap; nightcap.

Billiken (bil′i.ken): a squat, smiling, comic figure used as a mascot.

billikin (bil′i.kin): a billy or billycan. 53.

billingsgate (bil′ingz.gāt): coarse or abusive talk.

billman (bil′man): a soldier or watchman armed with a bill (a kind of pike).

billot (bil′ut): firewood. 1. Bullion, in the bar or mass.

bim (bim): a woman, esp. one of loose morals. 21. Nickname for an inhabitant of Barbados.

bimaculate (bī.mak′ū.lit): marked with two blotches.

bimanal (bim′a.nal, bī.mā′nal), bimanous (bim′a.nus): having two hands.

bimbil (bim′bil): the Australian eucalypt, whose flowers yield a good honey.

bimester (bī.mes′ter): two months.

binghi (bing.gi): aborigine. 23A.

binna (bin′a): unless; be not. 44.

binocle (bin′o.kl): a binocular telescope, field glass, or opera glass.

binotic (bī.not′ik): pert. to both ears.

binous (bī′nus): double; binate.

bint (bint): a daughter; girl; woman. 53.

biocompatible (bī′o.kom.pat′i.bl): not causing rejection—said of certain transplanted tissues.

biome (bī.ōm′): a community of living organisms of a single major ecological region.

bion (bi′on): in biology, the physiological individual, as opposed to the morphological, or structural individual.

biophilism (bī.of′i.lizm): the belief that animals have rights that humans should respect.

bioplasmic (bī′o.plaz′mik): *bioplastic.*

bioplastic (bī′o.plas′tik): pert. to the bioplast, or cell.

biorgan (bī′ôr′gan): a physiological organ—distinguished from *idorgan.*

bioscopy (bī.os′ko.pi): examination of a body to discover whether life is present.

biotaxy (bī′o.tak′si): taxonomy.

bipenniform (bī.pen′i.fôrm): resembling a feather barbed on both sides—said of certain muscles.

biretta (bi.ret′a): the hat of a Catholic priest (black), bishop (purple), or cardinal (red).

birse (burs): a bristle or bristles. Temper or irritation. To scorch or toast; to broil. 43.

bise (bīz): a cold, dry north wind of southern France, Switzerland, and Italy. Hence, any cold wind; fig., winter.

bisectric (bī.sek′trik): having a straight line that bisects an angle or a line segment.

bisectrix (bī.sek′triks): a line bisecting the angle between the optic axes of a biaxial crystal.

biserial (bī.sēr′i.al): arranged in two rows or series.

bismarine (bis′ma.rēn′): between two seas.

bissextile (bi.seks′til): leap year.

biternate (bī.tur′nit): double trifoliate, as when each division of a three-part leaf is also tripartite.

bivector (bī.vek′ter): a quantity in mathematics.

biverbal (bī.vur′bal): pert. to two words; punning.

bixin (bik′sin): a dark-red crystalline compound, the chief coloring principle of the dyestuff annatto.

blad (blad): a slap; also, a blotting pad. 44.

blandiloquence (blan.dil′o.kwens): smooth speech; flattering talk. 52.

blas (blas): an emanation from the stars. 1.

bleb (bleb): a blister or bubble, as in water or glass; to bubble, cover with bubbles.

bleery (blēr′i): a firebrand. 44. A kind of thin gruel. 11.

blennophobia (blen′o.fō′bi.a): horror of slime.

bleo (blā′o): a tropical American shrubby cactus used for hedges; also, its edible fruit.

blepharospasm (blef′a.ro.spazm): uncontrollable winking.

blet (blet): internal decay in fruit.

blinger (bling′er): a superlative example of its kind. 21.

blissom (blis′um): in heat. To copulate with a ewe.

Blitum (blī′tum): a genus of two species of herbs of the goosefoot family, the blites.

blottesque (blot.esk′): painted with heavy touches or blotlike brushwork.

bluet (blōō′et): a delicate plant of the U.S. with four-parted bluish flowers and tufted stems; called also *innocence*, *quaker-ladies*. A small Texas plant with a single blue flower. A light to moderate blue.

blumba (blum′ba): a certifying tag attached to kosher meat.

blunge (blunj): to amalgamate and blend; to beat up or mix (as clay) in water. *(Plunge + blend.)*

bly (blī): look, aspect; species, character. 2.

blype (blīp): a piece or shred, as of skin. 44.

SONG FOR A SLOW DANCE

Swing and sway with me, my dear,
In our band of biosphere.
As we circle we shall pass
Other clumps of biomass,
All biota, each with home
In some suitable biome,
Heeling, toeing, to the fiddle
Of a biologic riddle.

---

boanthropy (bo.an′thro.pi): a type of insanity in which one thinks oneself an ox.

boation (bo.ā′shun): a loud noise; bellowing, roaring. 1.

bobo (bō′bō): the owala tree. Also, a mullet of the rivers and cataracts of Mexico and Central America.

boca (bō′ka): a river mouth; a harbor entrance (as of a South American seaport).

bocal (bō′kal): the mouthpiece of a brass wind instrument.

bocardo (bo.kär′dō): a prison—originally, that in the north gate in Oxford. In logic, a figure: "some M is not P; all M is S; hence some S is not P."

bocca (bok′a): the mouth of a glass furnace. A vent on the side or near the base of an active volcano from which lava issues.

boce (bōs): a brightly colored European fish of the Spiradae family.

bocking (bok′ing): the red herring.

bodega (bo.dē′ga): a small grocery or liquor store.

boden (bō′den): equipped, provided. 44A.

bodger (boj′er): one who botches (something). 11. A woodcarver or woodturner, esp. a turner of beechwood chairs.

bodhi (bō′di): in Buddhism, the state of enlightenment attained by one who has practiced the Eight-fold Path and achieved salvation.

bodikin (bod′i.kin): a tiny body; an atom. 1.

bogle (bō′gl): a Scottish bogy, or boggart. Hide-and-seek. 44A.

bogue (bōg): in sailing, to fall away to leeward. Also, a creek. 40.

bolar, bolary (bō′ler, -ler.i): pert. to bole or clay; clayey.

bolo-bolo (bō′lo.bō′lō): a West African tree and its fiber, resembling jute.

bombilation (bom′bi.lā′shun): a buzzing, droning sound.

bona (bō′na): property—used in Roman and civil law of real and personal property.

bonga (bong′ga): in the Philippines, the betel palm; the betel nut.

bonhomie (bon′o.mi): cheerfulness.

bonify (bon′i.fī): to convert into, or render, good.

bonnibel (bon′i.bel): a handsome girl. 9.

boobopolis (bōō.bop′o.lis): an imaginary hick town.

boodie (bōō′di): hobgoblin. 44.

boof (bōōf): a scare. 28. Peach brandy. 39.

booger (bōōg′er): boogerman. 12. A piece of dried nasal mucus. 11. A head

---

louse. 41B. To take fright, shy. To startle (an animal).

booly (bōō′li): a temporary enclosure for the shelter of cattle or their keepers. A company of herdsmen wandering with their cattle. 50.

boondaggling (boon′dag.ling): var. of *boondoggling*.

boöpis (bo.op′is): ox-eyed; applied to certain Greek goddesses.

borachio (bo.rä′ki.ō): a large leather bottle for holding liquor; hence, a drunkard. (cap) A drunken follower of Don John in Shakespeare's *Much Ado About Nothing*.

boracite (bō′ra.sīt): a mineral, pyroelectric borate and chloride of magnesium.

borassic (bo.ras′ik): pert. to the Borassus, a genus of sugar palms of Africa naturalized throughout the tropics.

borborygm (bôr.bô.rim′), **borborygmy** (bor.bô.rig.mi): the noise made by gas in the bowels, or leaving them; a fart. 1.

boro (bō′rō): in India, rice harvested in the spring. (cap) A people of southeastern Colombia, northeastern Peru, and adjacent areas in Brazil.

bosch, bosh (bosh): butterine. 41.

bosset (bos′et): the rudimentary antler of a young male red deer.

bot, bott (bot): the larva of the botfly, esp. the species infesting the horse.

botargo (bo.tär′gō): a relish of salted mullet or tunny roes.

bothy (both′i): a rude dwelling. A hut, as a shepherd's shelter or quarters for unmarried laborers. 44A.

bourn, bourne (bōrn, bôrn): boundary; domain. To limit or bound. 52.

bousy (bōō′zi, bou′zi): drunken; sotted; boozy.

bovarysm (bō′va.rizm): one's romantic conception of oneself.

bovver (bov′er): street fighting. 23.

bowla (bō′la): a tart of sugar, apple, and bread. 41.

boyar (bo.yär′, boi′er): a member of a Russian aristocratic order that was next in rank to the ruling princes.

boyer (boi′er): a small Flemish sailing boat.

brab (brab): the palmyra palm.

brabblement (brab′l.ment): quarreling; the noise of discord. 2.

brabypeptic (brab′i.pep′tik): slow in digestion; sluggish in temperament.

brach, brachet (brach, brak, brach′et): a bitch hound.

brachiation (brā′ki.ā′shun, brak′i.ā′shun): locomotion by swinging from hold to hold by the arms.

brachistocephalic (bra.kis′to.si.fal′ik): in craniology, short-headed or broadheaded with a cephalic index of over 85.

brachycataletic (brak′i.kat′a.let′ik): in prosody, characterized by the omission of two syllables at the end of a verse.

brachyography (brak′i.og′raf.i): stenography

bradypeptic (brad′i.pep′tik): *brabypeptic.*

braggard (brag′ard): var. of *braggart.*

brancard (brang′kerd): a horse litter.

brangle (brang′gl): a squabble, wrangle, set-to. 13.

brank (brangk): a sort of bridle with wooden sidepieces.

branks (brangks): an iron frame used for correcting a scolding woman, surrounding the head and having a triangular piece entering the mouth. Also, the mumps. 44.

brassage (bras′ij): a charge made to an individual under a system of free coinage for the minting of any gold or silver brought to the mint.

brasset (bras′et): archaic var. of *brassard, brassart*—armor for the upper arm.

brawner (brôn′er): a boar killed for the table.

braxy (brak′si): a malignant edema of sheep. A sheep dead from natural causes; also, mutton from its carcass.

bree (brē): an eyelid, eyelash, eyebrow. 1. Liquor or broth. 44. To scare. 1.

brek (brek): outcry. 1.

bret (bret): a kind of flatfish, the brill. Also, the turbot.

bretelle (bre.tel′): an ornamental shoulder strap like a suspender.

breviloquence (bre.vil′o.kwens): brevity of speech.

breviped (brev′i.ped): having short legs. A short-legged bird.

brevipennate (brev′i.pen′āt): short-winged—said of birds having such short wings that they cannot fly.

brevirostrate (brev′i.ros′trāt): having a short nose.

bricole (bri.kōl′): a catapult. Also, an apparatus with hooks and rings to drag guns. In court tennis, the rebound of a ball from the wall. In billiards, a shot in which the cue ball strikes the cushion after hitting the object ball and before hitting the carom ball.

brigue (brēg): a cabal, intrigue, quarrel. To beguile; to intrigue. 1.

brimborion (brim.bō′ri.on): a charm—used derisively. Something nonsensical or useless.

brinded (brin′ded): brindled. 9.

britch (brich): breech. 1.

brockle (brok′l): of weather, variable; of cattle, apt to break fence. Rubbish; fragments. 2.

broderie (brôd.rē′): a style of pottery decoration resembling embroidery.

brog (brog): a pointed instrument, as an awl; a branch or stick, as a pole or goad. 17.

broma (brō′ma): aliment; food. Also, a form of cocoa from which the oil has been thoroughly extracted.

bromal (brō′mal): an oily, colorless fluid related to bromoform as chloral is to chloroform.

bromatology (brō′ma.tol′o.ji): the science of nutrition.

bromidrosiphobia (brō′mi.dro.si.fō′bi.a): fear of body odors.

bromopnea (brō′mop.nē′a): bad breath.

brontophobia (bron′to.fō′bi.a): fear of thunderstorms.

broo (brōō): broth; juice; water. Good opinion; inclination. 45.

brool (brōōl): a low roar; a deep murmur or humming.

brose (brōz): a dish made by pouring boiling liquid on meal (esp. oatmeal). 44.

brotus (brō′tus): an extra measure without charge, as a baker's dozen.

browst (broust, brōōst): a brewing, as of malt; hence, the consequences of one's conduct. 43.

---

*THEY WOULD HAVE CALLED HIM
BILLY HIRPLE IF HE'D LIMPED*

The Scots may have some moral taint,
But sycophants is what they ain't.
I prove this by the dreadful things
They used to call their English kings.

Take one whom they detested lots
(Though he had only slain some Scots).
He had a flower named for him.
The Scottish view of this was dim.

Sweet William was its English name;
The Scots forgathered to proclaim
This inappropriate and silly,
And called the blossom Stinky Billy.

Though William grew up in the purple,
Those vulgar Scots, alas,
Remember him as Billy Curple
(That's "Billy, horse's ass.")

---

bruckle (bruk′l): to dirty, begrime. 1. Breakable, brittle. 44C.

brumous (brōō′mus): foggy.

bruxomania (bruk′so.mā′ni.a): the habit of unconsciously grinding one's teeth.

bubukle (bū′buk.l): a red pimple.

bucca (buk′a): in insects, the cheek or part of the head next to the mouth.

buccinator (buk′si.nā′ter): a thin broad muscle forming the wall of the cheek.

bucentaur (bū.sen′tôr): a fabulous monster, half man, half ox; a centaur with a bull's body. Also, the state barge of Venice, used by the doge in the ceremony of the marriage of the Adriatic.

buckeen (buk.ēn′): in Ireland, a young man of the poorer gentry, aping the style of the rich; a shabby genteel idler. 51. In Guiana, an Indian woman.

budgeree (buj′er.i): good; fine; handsome or pretty—a bush word. 54.

budgereegah (buj′er.i.gä′): the zebra parakeet. 53.

buffa (bōōf′fa): a woman singer of comic roles in opera.

buffin (buf′in): a coarse woolen fabric used for clothing in England during the 16th and 17th centuries. 1.

buffle (buf′l): a buffalo. A fool; a bufflehead. 1.

bulse (buls): a purse or bag in which to carry or measure valuables. Broadly, a packet of jewels.

Bumbledom (bum′bl.dum): the pomposity of petty officials; beadledom—after Bumble, a parish beadle in *Oliver Twist.*

bummalo (bum′a.lō): a small Asiatic fish, the Bombay duck.

bunce (buns): money; a bonus. 21.

bunder (bun′der): a Netherlands measure of land area equal to about 2½ acres. In the East, a landing place; pier.

bundy (bun′di): a timeclock. 53.

burletta (bur.let′a): a kind of musical comic opera popular in England in the latter half of the 18th century.

burrasca (bur.as′ka): a musical passage that imitates a storm.

burrel (bur′el): a sort of pear.

busket (bus′ket): a small bush. 1.

bustic (bus′tik): a hardwood tree of Florida and the West Indies having shining lanceolate leaves and white flowers.

butterine (but′er.ēn): artificial butter or oleomargarine, esp. if made with the addition of butter.

buzzle (buz′l): a buzzing sound.

bwana (bwä′na): in Africa, master, boss.

byrrus (bir′us): a heavy woolen cape worn by the ancient Romans, and in the Middle Ages by the lower orders.

byte (bīt): a group of adjacent binary digits processed as a unit by a computer.

C

caama (käm′a): a South American fox. In Africa, a hartebeest.

caballetta (kab′a.let′a): a melody imitating a horse's gallop; the last, fast strains of an aria.

caballine (kab′a.līn): pert. to horses; equine.

cabane (ka.ban′): a framework supporting the wings of an airplane at the fuselage.

cabble (kab′l): to break up, as from bars or slabs, into pieces suitable for forming fagots.

Cabiritic (kab′i.rit′ik): pert. to the Cabiri, ancient Greek deities whose cult was connected with the mysteries of Samothrace.

caboceer (kab′o.sēr): a west African native chief.

Cacalia (ka.kāl′i.a): any plant of the genus *Emilia*, as the tassel flower.

cacation (ka.kā′shun): excretion.

cacestogenous (kak′es.toj′e.nus): caused by unfavorable home environment.

cacidrosis (kak′i.drō′sis): smelly sweat.

cackerel (kak′er.el): a small Mediterranean fish.

cacodoxy (kak.o.dok′si): departure from orthodoxy; heterodoxy.

cacology (ka.kol′o.ji): poor pronunciation or diction.

cacophemism (ka.kof′i.mizm): an unfairly harsh word or description.

cacophrenic (kak′o.fren′ik): pert. to an inferior intellect.

cacozeal (kak′o.zēl): faulty imitation or affectation in literary composition. Perverted or misdirected zeal. 1.

cactolith (kak′to.lith): according to the *Glossary of Geology and Related Sciences*, a quasi-horizontal chonolith composed of anastomising ductoliths, whose distal ends curl like a harpolith, thin like a sphenolith, or bulge discordantly like an akmolith or ethmolith.

cadi (kä.di, kā′di): a low-ranking magistrate or judge among the Mohammedans.

caducary (ka.dū′ka.ri): in law, pert. to, or transferred by, escheat, lapse, or forfeiture.

caecal, cecal (sē′kal): pert. to the *caecum*.

caecum, cecum (sē′kum): a bodily cavity open at one end; esp. the blind gut of the large intestine.

cag (kag): offend, insult. 2.

cagamosis (kag′a.mō′sis): an unhappy marriage.

calaber (kal.a.ber): in commerce, the gray fur of a Siberian squirrel.

calamary (kal′a.mer′i): a squid.

calcite (kal′sīt): calcium carbonate crystallized in hexagonal form.

calcographer (kal.kog′ra.fer): one who draws with chalks or pastels.

calcuminate (kal.kū′min.āt): to make sharp or pointed.

calecannon (kāl.kan′on): var. of *colcannon*.

calefactory (kal′i.fak′to.ri): producing or communicating heat.

calefy (kal′i.fī): to warm; to become warm.

calescence (ka.les′ens): heat.

calid (kal′id): warm; hot; burning.

caliology (kal′i.ol′o.ji): the study of birds' nests.

calistheneum (kal′is.thē′ni.um): a gymnasium for calisthenics.

callet (kal′et): a prostitute; scold; virago. To rail, scold, gossip. 2.

callidly (kal′id.li): cunningly; craftily. 52.

callisteia (kal′is.tē′a): prizes for beauty, awarded in competition among the ancient Greeks.

callomania (kal′o.mā′ni.a): the delusion that one is beautiful.

calology (ca.lol′o.ji): the study of beauty.

calomba (ka.lom′ba): an Australian cloverlike plant with yellow flowers and fragrant foliage, valued as forage.

calor (kal′er, kal′ôr): heat. 1.

calumba (ka.lum′ba), columba (ko.lum′ba): the root of an African plant. It contains the bitter principle columbin, and is used as a tonic.

calx (kalks): the friable residue of a burned or calcinated metal.

cambuca (kam.bōō′ka): a bishop's staff or crook.

camino (ka.mē′nō): a road.

cammock (kam′uk): a curved or crooked stick, esp. a field hockey stick. 5. A European woody herb (restharrow) with pink flowers; also, loosely, tansy ragwort, etc.

campeachy, campeche (kam.pē′chi): logwood.

canaster (ka.nas′ter): a kind of tobacco, formerly imported from South America in rush baskets.

cancelli (kan.sel′i): latticework; a latticed wall or screen, as between the chancel and nave of a church. In anatomy, the intersecting plates and bars of which spongy bone is composed.

canella (ka.nel′a): the cinnamon, or any of several related trees. Its highly aromatic inner bark.

canelo (ka.nā′lo): the Winter's bark of Chile. (cap) An Indian people of central Ecuador.

cangia (kan′ji.a): a kind of long light sailboat used on the Nile.

cannabic (ka.nab′ik, kan′a.bik): pert. to hemp; derived from hemp.

cannet (kan′et): in heraldry, a representation of a duck without feet or bill.

canoodle (ka.nōōd′l): to caress. 21.

canopholist (ka.nof′o.list): a dog lover.

cantatrice (kan′ta.trē′chi): a woman singer, esp. an opera singer.

cantilena (kan′ti.lē′na): in music, graceful; legato.

cantlet (kant′let): a small cantle; a piece; a fragment.

cantoris (kan.tō′ris): relating to the north side of the choir of a cathedral or church; cantorial. Also, pert. to a cantor.

capa (kä′pa): a mantle or cloak.

capel (kā′pel): a rock composed of quartz, tourmaline, and hornblende, occurring in the walls of some tin and copper lodes. 41A.

capillose (kap′i.lōs): hairy.

capitatum (kap′i.tā′tum): the largest bone of the wrist.

capnomancy (kap′no.man′si): divination by smoke.

capple (kap′l): having a white face with reddish or brown spots, said of a cow. Of a person, pale and sickly looking. 13.

capripede (kap′ri.pēd): a satyr.

caprylic (ka.pril′ik): pert. to the strong smell of an animal, esp. a goat.

captation (kap.tā′shun): a reaching after something, as favor or applause, esp. by flattery.

cara (kä′ra): dear. (cap) An Indian of an extinct Barbacoan tribe, traditionally from Ecuador.

caracoli (kar′a.kō′li): an alloy of gold, silver, and copper, used in making jewelry. A timber tree of northern South America used for dugout canoes.

carambola (kar′am.bō′la): an East Indian tree. Its green to yellow, usu. acid fruit is much used in Chinese cooking.

carambole (kar′am.bōl): a carom. Also, a shot in billiards in which the cue ball strikes more than one cushion before completing the carom. 1.

carbona (kär.bō′na): in mining, an irregular deposit of tin ore consisting of a network of veinlets; a stockwork. 41A.

carcel (kär′sel): a light standard much used in France, with illuminating power from 8.9 to 9.6 British standard candles.

carcer (kär′ser): a prison. Also, one of the stalls at the starting point of the race course of a Roman circus.

carcinomorphic (kär′si.no.môr′fik): crablike.

cardophagy (kär.dof′a.ji): the eating of thistles.

carinate (kar′i.nāt): shaped like the keel or bow of a ship. Also, one of the carinates, an old classification for the principal group of birds.

carker (kär′ker): one who loads or burdens (others), as with a worry. One who is anxious, troubled. 1.

carky (kär′ki): troubled, anxious.

carlin (kär′lin): a small silver coin first struck by Charles II, king of Naples and Sicily at the end of the 13th century.

carline (kär′lin, kur′lin): a woman, esp. an old one; often used contemptuously, as of a witch. 44A. A variety of pool, called also *Russian pool*. 47 E.

carmagnole (kär′ma.nyōl): a lively song popular during the French Revolution. A street dance to the tune of this song.

carnificial (kär′ni.fish′al): pert. to a public executioner or a butcher.

carrow (kar′ō): an itinerant gambler. 50.

carval (kär′val): a hymn formerly sung in church on Christmas Eve. 55.

casal (kā′sal): in grammar, pert. to case. Also, a hamlet, as in Italy or Malta.

casco (kas′kō): a ship's hull. A barge or lighter, sometimes with sails, used in the Philippines.

caseic (ka.sē′ik): cheeselike.

casquer (kas′ker): one who provides or wears a casque.

casquet (kas′ket): a helmet-shaped hat; a light, open headpiece. Also, var. of casket.

casquette (kas.ket′): a cap with a visor.

cassabanana (kas.a.ba.nä′na): an ornamental tropical vine, called also musk cucumber.

cassena (ka.sē′na): a species of holly, the *yaupon*.

cassolette (kas′o.let): a box or vase in which perfumes may be kept or burned.

cassonade (kas.on.ād′): unrefined or raw sugar.

cassumunar (kas′oo.mū′ner): the pungent root of an East Indian plant, resembling ginger.

Castalia (kas.tā′li.a): a spring sacred to the Muses at Delphi; hence, a source of poetic inspiration.

castanean, castanian (kas.tā′ni.an): of or belonging to the genus *Castanea*, the chestnuts.

castaneous (kas.tā′ni.us): of chestnut color.

castoreum (kas′tō.ri.um): castor.

castral (kas′tral): pert. to a camp.

castrametation (kas.tra.mi.tā′shun): the act or art of military encampment.

castrophrenia (kas′tro.frē′ni.a): the belief that one's thoughts are being stolen by enemies.

castrum (kas′trum), pl. castra (kas′tra): a Roman encampment.

catabasis (ka.tab′a.sis): the stage of decline of a disease.

catabatic (kat′a.bat′ik): declining by degrees, as a fever.

catabiotic (kat′a.bī.ot′ik): pert. to the degenerative changes accompanying cellular senescence.

catachthonian (kat′ak.thō′ni.an): underground.

cataclastic (kat′a.klas′tik): pert. to a granular fragmental texture induced in rocks by mechanical crushing.

catacrotic (kat′a.krot′ik): in physiology, pert. to a particular form of pulse tracing.

catagenesis (kat′a.jen′e.sis): retrogressive evolution.

catageophobia (kat′a.jē′o.fō′bi.a): fear of being ridiculed.

catalexis (kat′a.lek′sis): in prosody, incompleteness of the last foot of a verse, or, loosely, any foot.

catallactic (kat′a.lak′tik): pert. to exchange.

catallum (ka.tal′um): in law, orig., capital wealth, property of all kinds; in the feudal system, movable property; a chattel.

catalufa (kat′a.lōō′fa): any of various brightly colored marine percoid fishes of tropical seas.

catamenia (kat′a.mē′ni.a): menstruation.

catapedamania (kat′a.pē′da.mā′ni.a): an impulse to jump from high places.

cataplexy (kat′a.plek′si): the motionless, rigid, and supposedly insensible condition of an animal feigning death; catalepsy.

catarolysis (kat′a.rol′i.sis): the relief of one's emotions by cursing.

catasta (ka.tas′ta): a scaffold or stage, as where slaves were sold or criminals tortured. The stocks. 1.

catasterism (ka.tas′ter.izm): the use of mythological names for constellations.

catathymic (kat′a.thī′mik): resulting from an emotional complex.

catechetical (kat′a.ket′i.kal): consisting of questions and answers.

catenoid (kat′i.noid): chain-shaped, referring esp. to the colonies of certain protozoans.

cateran (kat′er.an): an irregular soldier or marauder of the Scottish Highlands. A freebooter; brigand.

catercousin (kā′ter.kuz′n, kat′er.kuz′n): a distant relative, esp. a cousin. An intimate friend.

cathisophobia (kath′is.o.fō′bi.a): fear of sitting.

catoptromancy (ka.top′tro.man′si): the use of mirrors for divination.

catter (kat′er): one who flogs with a cat-o′-nine-tails. To fish for catfish. 27. To vomit. 23.

cauline (kô.līn, -lin): belonging to or growing on the upper part of a stem.

cauma (kô′ma): great heat, as in fever.

cauponize (kô′po.nīz): to mix and adulterate for profit.

cautelous (kô′te.lus): crafty; wily; cautious.

cauter (kô′ter): an iron for cauterizing.

cavaliere (ka′va.lyâr′i): a cavalier; knight; cavalier servente, a gallant attentive to a married lady.

cavatina (käv′a.tē′na): orig. a melody of simpler form than the aria; now, almost any kind of musical composition.

cawk (kôk): to utter a cawk, as a crow.

caxon (kak′sun): a wig, esp. one much worn. 1.

caza (kä.za): in Turkey, a subdivision of a vilayet, or administrative district.

cebil (sā.bēl′): a South American tree that yields angico gum, used in tanning.

cecidium (si.si′di.um): a gall or swelling of plant tissue due to parasites.

cecity (ses′i.ti): blindness.

cedron (sē′drun): the fruit of a tropical American tree, used against snakebite and hydrophobia.

celarent (si.lâr′ent): in logic, the proposition "No M is P; all S is M; hence, no S is P."

celidography (sel′i.dog′ra.fi): the description of the markings on the disk of the sun or on the planets.

cellate (sel′āt): in zoology, formed as, divided into, or furnished with a cell or cells. Cellated.

cellidh (kā′li): a visit; a private conversation; an evening's musical entertainment. 44, 51.

cenobian (si.nō′bi.an): pert. to a cenoby, a religious community. Monkish, monastic.

cenophobia (sen′o.fō′bi.a): fear of empty spaces.

centesis (sen.tē′sis): in surgery, a puncture, as of a cavity or tumor.

centillion (sen.til′yun): the number denoted by a unit with 303 zeros annexed (in French and American notation) or with 600 (in British and German).

cepaceous (si.pā′shus): like an onion.

cephalocide (sef′al.o.sīd): the murder of intellectuals as a group.

cephaloid (sef′a.loid): in botany, abruptly enlarged; headshaped. Capitate.

cephalonamancy (sef′a.lo.na.man′si): divination by boiling an ass's head.

cepivorous (si.piv′o.rus): onion-eating. 60.

ceraunograph (si.rô′no.graf): an instrument that records thunder and lightning.

ceraunoscopy (ser′ô.nos′ko.pi): the observance of thunder as an omen.

cereous (sēr′i.us): waxen.

ceriferous (si.rif′er.us): producing wax.

cerniture (sur′ni.cher): in Roman law, a formal acceptance of an inheritance.

cerography (si.rog′ra.fi): the art of making designs in wax.

ceromancy (sēr′o.man′si): the use of melted wax, dropped in water, for divination.

cerulean (si.rōō′li.an): azure; sky blue.

cervicide (sur′vi.sīd): deer-killing.

cessavit (se.sā′vit): a writ given by Edward I to recover lands upon the tenants' failure to meet the conditions of tenure.

cessed (sest): assessed; taxed. 41.

cesser (ses′er): in law, failure of a tenant to perform due services. Also, a ceasing of liability.

chaetiferous (ki.tif′er.us): having bristles.

chamade (sha.mäd): the drumbeat or trumpet blast announcing a surrender.

Chamaesaura (kam´i.sô´ra): a genus of African snakelike lizards, limbless or with scaly vestigial limbs.

chamma (cham´ma): the chief garment of the Abyssinians, a wide cotton scarf wrapped around the body leaving one arm free.

chandoo (chan.dōō´): a preparation of opium smoked in China.

chank (changk): a large spiral shell found near the coasts of the East Indies.

chaology (kā.ol´o.ji): the study of chaos.

chapatty (cha.pat´i): a thin griddlecake of unleavened bread, used in northern India.

charbon (shär´bon): a small black spot remaining in the cavity of the corner tooth of a horse after the large spot has been obliterated.

charientism (kar´i.en.tizm): a gracefully veiled insult.

chartomancy (kär´to.man´si): divination by maps.

charuk (cha.rōōk): a sandal with upturned tips, used in Anatolia from remote antiquity.

chasmophilous (kaz.mof´i.lus): fond of nooks, crannies, chasms.

chatoyant (sha.toi´ant): having a changeable luster marked by an undulating narrow band of white light, as a cat's eye in the dark.

chavender (chav´en.der): the chevin (the chub fish).

cheechako (chi.chä´kō): a tenderfoot.

cheet (chēt): to cheep. 11. To call a cat. 44.

cheimaphilic (kī´ma.fil´ik): fond of cold.

chelidonic (kē´li.don.ik): a kind of crystalline acid.

cheliferous (ki.lif´er.us): bearing a pincerlike organ or claw.

Chen (chen): the genus of the snow goose.

cherophobia (kēr´o.fō´bi.a): fear of gaiety.

chessel (ches´el): a cheese vat.

chetty (chet´i): a caste of Tamil merchants in southern India and Ceylon.

chevaline (shev´a.lin): horselike. Horseflesh.

cheve (shēv): to turn out (*well, ill,* etc.); hence, to prosper. 1.

chevrette (shev.ret´): a thin kind of goatskin.

chewet (chōō´et): a small European bird of the crow family; a chough; hence a chatterer. A pie of minced meat or fish, with fruits, spices, etc. 1.

chia (chē´a): a tea-like beverage. 1. Any of several species of the herb Salvia of Mexico and the southwestern U.S.; its seeds make a beverage or oil.

chicago (shi.kä´gō): in Algonquian, fields of wild onions—of a particularly odoriferous sort, according to John Chancellor. (cap) The largest city in the Middle West.

chichevache (shēsh´vash): a fabulous monster that ate only patient (some say faithful) wives, and was therefore very lean.

Chickahominy (chik.a.hom´i.ni): an Indian of an Algonquin tribe in eastern Virginia.

chiel (chēl): fellow, lad, child. 44A.

chil (chil): a small hawk of India. The chir pine.

chimb (chim): (var. of *chime*) to ring chimes with bells.

chimopelagic (kī.mop.i.laj´ik): pert. to certain deep-sea organisms that surface only in winter.

chinquapin (ching´ka.pin): the dwarf chestnut of the U.S. or related trees. The sweet edible nut of this tree.

chinse (chins): to calk temporarily, as a boat.

chionablepsia (kī.o.no.blep´si.a): snow blindness.

chiragric (kī.rag´rik): affected with gout in the hand.

chiral (kī´ral): pert. to the hand.

chirognomy (kī.rog´no.mi): palmistry.

chirology (kī.rol´o.ji): study of the hands.

chiropraxis (kī´ro.prak´sis): chiropractic.

chirospasm (kī´ro.spazm): writer's cramp.

chirotony (kī.rot´o.ni): an election or appointment by show of hands. Ecclesiastically, the extension of hands in blessing, etc.

chitarra (ki.tär´a): a guitar in Italy.

chittak (chi.täk´): in India, a measure of weight ranging from about half an ounce to about three ounces.

chloralism (klō´ral.izm): a morbid condition resulting from habitual use of chloral.

chloralum (klôr.al´um): an aqueous solution of aluminum chloride, used as an antiseptic.

Chloris (klō´ris): a genus of grass including finger grass and crabgrass.

choca (chok´a): a beverage of coffee and chocolate.

choliamb (kō´li.amb), choliambic (kō´li.am´bik): in prosody, an iambic trimeter having a spondee or trochee in the last foot.

Cholo (chō´lō): in Spanish America, a civilized Indian. (not cap) A lower-class Mexican or person of Mexican ancestry—often used disparagingly. A person of mixed Spanish and Indian blood.

chopa (chō´pa): any of several rudderfishes, said to accompany ships.

choralcelo (kō´ral.sel´ō): an electric piano.

choreomania (kō´ri.o.mā´ni.a): mania for dancing, sometimes occurring in epidemics.

choreus (ko.rē´us): a trochee.

chorten (chôr´ten): a Lamaist shrine or monument.

chouse (chous): a chiaus—a Turkish messenger. A cheat, swindler. One easily cheated; a gull, dupe. 1. A trick, sham, imposition.

chowry (chou´ri): an East Indian fly swatter made from a yak's tail.

chrematophobia (kri.mat.o.fō´bi.a): fear of money.

chresmology (kres.mol.o.ji): in ancient Greek religion, the utterance of oracular prophecies.

chria (krī´a): in rhetoric, a quotation or aphoristic saying developed according to a prescribed scheme into a short essay.

Christophany (kris.tof´a.ni): an appearance of Christ after resurrection, esp. as recorded in the Gospels.

chromophobia (krō´mo.fō´bi.a): fear of colors.

chromoxylography (krō´mo.zī.log´ra.fi): printing in colors from wooden blocks.

chronicon (kron´i.kon): a chronicle or chronology. 6.

chronogram (kron´o.gram): an inscription in which certain letters taken in order express a particular date or epoch.

chronophobia (kron´o.fō´bi.a): fear of the passage of time.

chrotta (krot´a): a *crwth* or *crowd,* an ancient Celtic musical instrument. A small medieval harp.

chrysopholist (kri´sof´o.list): a lover of gold.

chthonic (thon´ik): designating gods or spirits of the underworld.

chthonophagia (thon´o.fā´ji.a): the eating of dirt.

chummage (chum´ij): a fee demanded from a new prisoner by old prisoners. 25. The quartering of persons together as chums.

churrus (chur.us): in India, a device for drawing water from deep wells, consisting of a leather bag hung on a rope running over a pulley and drawn by oxen. Var. of *charas,* a narcotic and intoxicating resin that exudes from hemp; a smoking mixture containing it.

cibarious (si.bâr´i.us): pert. to food; edible.

cibation (si.bā´shun): in alchemy, the process of feeding the crucible with fresh material. The act of taking food. 1.

cibol (sib´ul): the Welsh onion. A shallot.

cibophobia (sī´bo.fō´bi.a): fear of food.

cicer (sī´ser): the chick-pea. 1. (cap) A genus of herbs of the pea family.

ciconine (sik′o.nīn, -nin): storklike.

cilery (sil′er.i): in architecture, the carved foliage, etc., ornamenting the head of a column; a volute. 9.

cilicious (si.lish′us): made of haircloth. 1.

cimelia (si.mē′lya): treasure; esp. in the 17th and 18th centuries, heirlooms or church treasures.

cincinnate (sin′si.nāt): curled in ringlets.

cineplasty (sin′i.plas′ti): surgical fitting of a muscle to a prosthetic device to be operated by muscle contractions.

cinerescent (sin′er.es′ent): ashen, grayish.

circumduct (sur′kum.dukt): to turn about an axis; revolve. In law, to put a limit or end to; to abrogate, annul.

circumforaneous (sur′kum.fo.rā′ni.us): wandering from market to market, or place to place.

circumfulgent (sur′kum.ful′jent): shining around or about.

circumincession (sur′kum.in.sesh′un): the doctrine of the reciprocal existence in each other of the three persons of the Trinity.

cirrigerous (si.rij′er.us): forming curls or ringlets.

cismarine (sis′ma.rēn): on the near side of the sea.

Cistus (sis′tus): a genus of shrubs, the rockroses.

cital (sī′tal): citation. 1.

citole (sit′ōl, si.tōl′): a small flat-backed lute of medieval times.

cittosis (si.tō′sis): abnormal desire for strange foods.

cladus (klā′dus): a branch of one of the branching spicules that support the soft tissues of sponges and some other invertebrates.

clapperclaw (klap′er.klô), clappermaclaw (klap′er.ma.klô): to claw and scratch; to scold. 10.

claribel (klar′i.bel): brightly fair.

clart (klärt): a clot or daub of mud or other sticky substance. 11.

clavial (klā′vi.al): an upright piano of the sostinenta pianoforte type.

clavicin (klav.i.sin): the harpsichord. Also, the keys by which a bell ringer plays a carillon.

clavicymbal (klav′i.sim′bl): an old name of the harpsichord.

clavicytherium (klav′i.si.thēr′i.um): a harpsichord-like musical instrument.

claviger (klav′i.jer): one who keeps the keys; a custodian, warden.

clavis (klā′vus): a key; a glossary to aid interpretation.

cleck (klek): to hatch. 44A.

cledge (klej): clay or clayey soil.

cledonism (klē′do.nizm): the use of euphemisms to avert misfortune.

clem (klem): to suffer or cause to suffer from hunger, thirst, or cold. 2. A fight or brawl between circus or carnival workers and the local townspeople. 21.

DIRGE IN C

When my craft first set to sea,
Never chopa swam by me,
Showing me the way to go.
    No;
I was frequently adrift,
    Squiffed,
Or at tropic isle ashore;
    For
Capripede I made my role—
Chose to dance the carmignole;
With the great-eyed maidens croodled,
Sighed and trembled and canoodled.
Now, where once sang gay conquedle,
Digs the sexton, prays the beadle;
Now, where hair sprang fair and flaxen,
Sits askew the stringy caxon;
Cheek, once redder than an apple,
    Now capple;
Eyes, once eager, twinkly-sparky,
    Carky;
Voice, once honey in its talk,
    Cawk.
Grudgingly I face my culp,
    And gulp.

---

clematite (klem′a.tīt): the European birthwort.

cletch (klech): a brood or hatching; a clutch. Contemptuously, a family or clique. 13.

cleve (klēv): a cliff; also, a brae. 2.

clevy (klev′i): var. of *clevis*, a U-shaped device used on the end of the tongue of a wagon, etc., to attach it to the whiffletree, etc.

clifty (klif′ti): clifty.

climacophobia (klī.ma.ko.fō.bi.a): fear of falling downstairs.

climacter (klī.mak′ter): a climacteric period. 1.

clinamen (klī.nā′men): a turn; bias; twist.

clinomania (klī′no.mā.ni.a): excessive desire to stay in bed.

clinophobia (klī′no.fōbi.a): fear of going to bed.

clishmaclaver (klish′ma.klav′er): foolish gossip. 43.

clive (klīv): a plant of the genus *Agrimonia*, inc. the common burdock. 13.

clocher (klō′sher): a bell tower.

clochette (klo.shet′): in the arts, any small bell-shaped ornament; also, a bell-shaped cover, as for dishes.

cloff (klof): a cleft or fork, as of legs, branches, or hills. 43. An allowance formerly given on certain goods to cover small losses in retailing.

clonic (klon′ik): spastic.

cloop (klo͞op): the sound made when a cork is drawn from a bottle, or any such sound.

cloot (klo͞ot): a cleft hoof, or one of its divisions, as in the ox. (usu. cap & pl.) A devil. 44A.

Clootie (klo͞ot′i): cloot.

clough (kluf): gully.

clunch (klunch): a clump or lump. A lout. Lumpy, stiff, as clay. 2.

cnemial (nē′mi.al): pert. to the shin or shinbone.

coak (kōk): a projection connecting the notched face of a timber with the similarly notched face of another timber. A dowel set into timbers to unite them or keep them from slipping. To join by the aid of coaks.

coaptation (ko.ap.tā′shun): the mutual adaptation of broken parts to each other, as the edges of a wound.

coarb (ko′ärb): in early Irish and Scottish churches, the incumbent of an abbey or bishopric as successor to the patron saint.

cobby (kob′i): hearty, lively. Headstrong. 13. Like a cob horse in shape, with a deep strong body and relatively short sturdy legs.

cobra de capello (kō′bra dē ka.pel′ō): a variety of venomous Asiatic and African snakes.

cockawee (kok′a.wi): the old-squaw, a common sea duck of the far northern latitudes—called also *old injun, oldwife.*

coctile (kok′tīl, -til): made by baking or exposure to heat (as a brick).

codetta (ko.det′a.): in music, a short coda.

codilla (ko.dil′a): the shorter fibers produced in scutching flax.

coemption (ko.emp′shun): purchase of the whole supply of commodities in the market, as for purposes of monopoly.

coggle (kog′l): to repair roughly, cobble (used with *up*). 11. A ceramics tool used to make indentations or grooves in the outer edges of plates.

cogman (kog′man): one who erects mine cogs; a cogger. A roller in charge of the first set of rolls in a steelworks.

cohibit (ko.hib′it): to restrain or restrict.

cohoba (ko.hō′ba): a narcotic snuff made from the leaves of a tropical American tree, *Piptadena peregrinia.*

coign (koin), quoin (kwoin): an angle; corner. A wedge.

coistrel, coystrel (kois′trel): a groom employed to care for a knight's horses. A mean fellow.

Colada (ko.lä′da): the gold-hilted sword which the Cid took from Ramon Berenger.

colcannon (kol.kan′un, kol′kan.un): a

stew made mostly from potatoes and greens. 50.

colletic (ko.let'ik): made of glue.

colliculation (ko.lik'ū.lā'shun): a low hill.

collieshangie (kol'i.shang'i): a noisy or confused fight. 44.

colliform (kol'i.fôrm): neckshaped.

colling (kol'ing): embracing, petting. 13.

collocution (kol'o.kū'shun): a speaking together.

colobin (kol'o.bin): a long-tailed African monkey.

colometry (ko.lom'i.tri): in prosody, measurement of verses by cola, which are smaller and less independent than a sentence but larger and less dependent than a phrase.

colonus (ko.lō'nus): a freeborn serf or tenant farmer in the later Roman empire.

colossean (kol'o.sē'an): colossal.

columbic (ko.lum'bik): pert. to or containing columbium.

columbo (ko.lum'bō): var. of *columba*, a root used in medicine as a stomachic and tonic.

comino (ko.mē'nō): a path or trail; also, a journey.

comitatus (kom'i.tā'tus): a body of wellborn men attached to a king or chieftain by the duty of military service.

commandry (kom.man'dri): var. of *commandery*.

commasculation (ko.mas'kū.lā'shun): sexuality between men.

commatic (ko.mat'ik): divided into short clauses or verses, as a hymn. Pert. to a minute difference in pitch.

commentitious (kom'en.tish'us): imaginary.

commorient (ko.mō'ri.ent): dying together.

comoid (kō'moid): resembling a tress or tuft of hair.

comosce (kō'mōs): hairy, tufted.

compend (kom.pend'): a compendium, epitome.

compere (kom.pēr'): a master of ceremonies, esp. on radio or television. To act as a compere.

compesce (kom.pes'): to restrain.

comploration (kom.plôr.ā'shun): wailing and weeping together.

complot (kom'plot): a plot, conspiracy. To plot together, conspire. 9.

comprecation (kom'pri.kā'shun): a prayer meeting.

compt (kompt): neat; spruce; polished. 1.

compursion (kom.pur'shun): the wrinkling of one's face.

concameration (kon.kam'er.ā'shun): vaulting; a vaulted roof or ceiling.

concent (kon.sent'): a concert of voices,

concord of sounds. Accordance; consistency. 9.

concetto (kon.chet'tō) pl. **concetti** (kon.chet.i): a witty turn of thought or expression; quip, conceit.

conchitic (kong.kit'ik): composed of shells.

concilium (kon.sil'i.um): council.

concitation (kon.si.tā'shun): the act of exciting or stirring up.

concursus (kon.kur'sus): influence of divine causation upon secondary causes; esp. the doctrine that before the fall man was preserved from sin by the aid of God.

condensary (kon.den'sa.ri): a factory for condensing, as of milk.

condylure (kon'di.loor): the star-nosed mole.

confarreation (kon.far.i.ā'shun): in Roman law, a ceremony of patrician marriage that conferred upon the husband absolute control of the wife.

confirmand (kon'fer.mand): a candidate for ecclesiastical confirmation.

confix (kon.fiks'): to fasten together.

confrater (kon.frā'ter): an honorary guest member of a monastery.

conglaciate (kon.glā'shi.āt): to freeze.

conglobulation (kon.glob'ū.lā'shun): the act or result of gathering (something) into a global mass.

congreet (kon.grēt'): to greet mutually.

congroid (kon'groid): pert. to the conger eels.

coniaker (ko.nī'a.ker): a coin counterfeiter.

conject (kon.jekt'): to prognosticate. To throw, or throw together. Connection; plan, plot. 1.

connascence (ko.nas'ens): the state of being born together, united at birth. 52.

connex (ko.neks'): a bond, tie. A connected incident or property. A conditional proposition in logic. 1.

conoid (kō'noid): shaped like a cone.

conquedle (kon.kwē'dl): the bobolink. 12.

consarcination (kon.sär.si.nā'shun): the act of patching.

conscribe (kon.skrīb'): to limit, circumscribe. To enlist by force; conscript.

consectaneous (kon.sek.tā'ni.us): relating to a logical consequence.

consertal (kon.sur'tal): designating texture of igneous rocks in which the irregularly shaped crystals interlock.

consilience (kon.sil'i.ens): concurrence in inferential results.

consortion (kon.sôr'shun): association, alliance.

conspissation (kon'spi.sā'shun): thickness; the act of thickening. 1.

conspue (kon.spū'): to spurn contemptuously.

conspurcate (kon'sper.kāt): to pollute, defile.

constuprate (kon'stū.prāt): to violate, debauch.

contabescence (kon'ta.bes'ens): a wasting away.

contect (kon.tekt'): to cover or cover up.

contesseration (kon.tes'er.ā'shun): the act of making friends. 1.

contortuplicate (kon'tor.toop'li.kāt): twisted back upon itself.

contrada (kon.trä'da): a street or way; also, a quarter or ward.

contrahent (kon'tra.hent): a contracting party. Entering into a contract.

contraplex (kon'tra.pleks): capable of sending two telegraphed messages in opposite directions at the same time.

contrectation (kon.trek.tā'shun): touching, handling. In psychology, the first of two stages of the sexual act.

contumulation (con.tū.mū.lā'shun): burial in the same tomb with another.

Conus (kō'nus): a genus of tropical marine snails comprising the cones and incl., among many beautiful and harmless forms, some that inject a paralytic venom.

conversus (kon.vur'sus): a lay brother—orig. applied to one who entered a monastery to do penance. An administrator of episcopal or monastic property.

convive (kon.vīv'): a comrade at table. To feast together. 1.

coodle (koo'dl): a terrapin. 35.

coomb (koom): four bushels.

copa (kō'pa): a gum-yielding tree of Panama, called also *yaya*.

copple (kop'l): a crest on a bird's head; also, a hill or knoll of land. 2.

coprolalia (kop'ro.lāl'ya): the use of words relating to dirt and excrement.

coprophemia (kop'ro.fē'mi.a): obscene language.

corallite (kôr'a.līt): the skeleton formed by a single coral polyp.

corb (kôrb), **corf** (kôrf): a truck, tub, or basket used in a mine.

corbie, corby (kôr'bi): the raven; the carrion crow.

cordel (kôr.del'): name of certain old coins of Cuba, Paraguay, and Spain.

corella (ko.rel'a): a parrot of the genus *Trichoglossus*, as the Australian crested parakeet; also, any of certain cockatoos.

corge (kôrj): a score; twenty. 51A.

corke, corcir (kôrk, -kir): any of the colors imparted by the dye archil, varying from moderate red to dark purplish red.

corm (kôrm): a short, bulblike, fleshy stem, bearing buds at the summit, as in the corcus and gladiolus.

cormel (kôr'mel): a small or secondary corm produced by an old corm.

cormus (kôr'mus): the plant body in the higher plants, with segmentation into stem and leaf units. The entire body or colony of a compound animal.

cornific (kôr.nif′ik): producing horns; forming horn.

coronach (kôr′o.nak): a dirge played on bagpipes.

coronoid (kôr′o.noid): resembling the beak of a crow.

corozo (ko.rō′sō): any of several American palms, incl. the ivory palm and the cohune palm.

correal (kor′i.al): pert. in civil law to a joint obligation or right that may be enforced against any one of several joint debtors or by any one of several joint creditors against a single debtor.

correption (ko.rep′shun): a shortening in pronunciation. Also, chiding; reproof; reproach. 1.

cosmopathic (koz′mo.path′ik): receiving impressions from the universe by other means than through the senses.

cosmorama (koz′mo.rä′ma): an exhibition of views made to appear natural by mirrors, lenses, illumination, etc.

cosmorganic (koz′môr.gan′ik): pert. to an organic cosmos.

cosmothetic (koz′mo.thet′ik): pert. to a doctrine that affirms the real existence of the external world.

costean (kos.tēn′, kos′ten): to dig trenches or pits into rock so as to determine the course of a mineral deposit.

coucal (kōō′kal): any of various large long-tailed, brown-and-black cuckoos of Africa, southern Asia, and Australia, pheasant-like in plumage, pattern, and habits.

couchee (kōō′shā, kōō.shā′): bedtime; a bedtime visitor; hist., a reception held at the time of going to bed.

coumb (kōōm): a comb. 1.

coutil (kōō.til′): a close-woven cotton fabric used for mattresses, corsets, etc.

cowal (kou′al): a depression or channel, similar to a billabong. 31A.

cowan (kou′an): one who is not a Freemason; esp., one who would pretend to Freemasonry or intrude upon its secrets. Also, a dry-stone diker; one not a regular mason.

cowle (koul): in India, an engagement in writing, esp. of safe conduct or amnesty.

cowy (kou′i): suggestive of a cow.

coze (kōz): friendly chat.

cran (kran): the common swift. Also, a measure for quantity of fresh herring, amounting to 45 gallons. 41.

craniofacial (krā′ni.o.fā′shal): both cranial and facial.

crannage (kran′ij): in herring fishing, the total catch in *crans*.

crapaudine (krap′o.dēn): swinging on top and bottom pivots like a door. The socket for such a pivot.

crassitude (kras′i.tūd): thickness, as of a solid body. 1. Grossness, or an instance of it.

cratch (krach): a crib or rack, esp. for fodder. 11.

craunch (krônch, kränch): crunch. 26.

creatic (kri.at′ik): pert. to, or caused by, flesh or animal food.

cremnophobia (krem′no.fō′bi.a): fear of cliffs.

crenelle (kre.nel′): an indentation in a parapet from which projectiles are launched upon the enemy.

creophagous (kri.of′a.gus): carnivorous.

crescive (kres′iv): increasing; growing.

cribble (krib′l): in engraving, to make a pattern of small round punctures in a block or plate. A sieve. Coarse flour or meal. To sift. 1.

criblé (krē′blā): in engraving, having a background of small white dots produced by cribbling the plate.

crig (krig): a bruising blow.

crimply (krim′pli): curly, wavy.

crin (krin): a heavy silk.

crinal (krī′nal): pert. to the hair.

crine (krīn): hair; head of hair. To shrink; shrivel. 44.

criniparous (krin.ip′er.us): producing hair.

crith (krith): the weight of a liter of hydrogen at 0°C and 760 mm pressure.

crithomancy (krith′o.man′si): divination by the dough in the cakes offered in ancient sacrifices.

cro (krō): among the ancient Celts, the compensation made for the slaying of a man, according to his rank.

croche (krōch): a little knob at the top of a deer's antler. A pastoral staff; a crozier. 1.

cronk (krongk): the croak of a raven or honk of a wild goose. Discordant, harsh. Sick or unsound, physically or financially. 23B.

croodle (krōō′dl): to cling to; to nestle together.

crore (krōr): a sum of money equal to 10 million rupees, or 100 lacs. Ten million.

crossette (kros.et′): a projection at the corner of an arch or a door or window casing.

crotaline (krot.a.līn, -lin; krō′ta.līn, -lin): pert. to rattlesnakes.

crotin (krō′tin): a mixture of poisonous proteins found in the seeds of a small Asiatic tree related to the spurges.

crottle (krot′l): any of several lichens from which dyes are made.

croupade (krōō.pād′): a curvet (of a horse) with the hind legs well under the belly.

cruor (krōō′ôr): clotted blood.

crurophilous (kroo.rof′il.us): liking legs.

crustation (krus.tā′shun): an incrustation.

crwth (krōōth): an ancient Celtic musical instrument with a shallow body and a varying number of strings. (Called also *chrotta, crowd*.)

cryobiology (krī′o.bī.ol′o.ji): the study of the effects of freezing on living things.

cryptarchy (krip′tär.ki): rule by a secret authority.

ctetology (ti.tol′o.ji): the study of acquired characteristics.

cuarta (kwär′ta): a measure of quantity or of distance in Brazil, Paraguay, Spain, and Guatemala.

cubatory (kū′ba.tō′ri): reclining; resting.

cuck (kuk): to void. To be punished by the cucking stool, in which an offender was fastened, to be pelted and hooted at by the mob. 1. To utter the call of the cuckoo. 13.

cuculine, cuculoid (kū′kū.lin, -lin, -loid): pert. to the cuckoos.

cuculla (kū.kul′a): a loose sleeveless garment put on over the head and used esp. to protect other garments; specif., the sleeveless outer part of a monk's habit.

cueca (kwā′ka): a dance of Peruvian origin, popular in South American countries.

cuggermugger (kug′er.mug′er): whispered gossip. 50.

cullion (kul′yun): a testicle.

culottic (kū.lot′ik): wearing breeches; respectable.

culp (kulp): sin; guilt. 1.

cumic (kū′mik): pert. to or designating a certain white crystalline acid.

cummer (kum′er): a godmother; a midwife; also, a witch. An intimate female companion. A woman or girl; a lass. 44A.

cunabula (kū.nab′ū.la): cradle; earliest abode.

cunctipotent (kungk′tip′o.tent): omnipotent.

cuniculus (kū.nik′ū.lus): an underground passage, as a mine or rabbit burrow.

cunny (kun′i): the cony.

cuproid (kū′proid): a solid related to a tetrahedron and having 12 equal triangular faces.

cupronickel (kū′pro.nik′el): an alloy of copper and nickel.

curiboca (kōō′ri.bō′ka): a dark-complexioned Brazilian of mixed white and Indian or Indian and black blood.

curple (kur′pl): the cruppers, rump, posterior. 44.

cursal (kur′sal): pert. to a course or series of studies.

cursus (kur′sus): a course, as for racing. A course of study. Movement or flow (of style).

Curtana (ker.tä′na): the pointless sword carried by British monarchs at their coronation, and emblematically considered the sword of mercy.

cush (kush): in India, sorghum. (cap) In the Bible, the eldest son of Ham. Bread or crackers boiled and seasoned. 35. A cow. 11. Money. 22.

cushlamochree (koosh′la.ma.kri): darling. 50.

custodee (kus′to.di): one to whom custody is given.

cuticula (kū.tik′ū.la): cuticle; specif., the outer body wall of an insect, secreted by the hypodermis.

cuttle (kut′l): a swaggerer or ruffian; a cuttler. 1.

cyanean (sī′a.nē′an): of a genus of jellyfish; also, the dark blue color of certain jellyfish.

cycloplegic (sī′klo.plej′ik): producing paralysis of the ciliary muscle of the eye.

cyclotomy (sī.klot′o.mi): in mathematics, the theory of the division of the circle into equal parts. In surgery, an incision or division of the ciliary body of the eyeball.

cyanthropy (sī.an′thro.pi): insanity in which one fancies oneself a dog.

cyniatrics (sin′i.at′riks): that branch of veterinary medicine that treats of diseases of the dog.

cynoid (sī′noid, sin-): doglike. Pert. to the dog family.

cynolatry (sī.nol′a.tri, sin.ol′-): dog worship.

cynophobia (sī′no.fō′bi.a): fear of dogs.

cyrtometer (ser.tom′i.ter): in medicine, an instrument for determining the dimensions and movements of curved surfaces, esp. of the chest.

cyton (sī′ton): a cell, esp. a nerve cell.

D

dacnomania (dak′no.mā′ni.a): a mania for killing.

dacrygelosis (dak′ri.ji.lō′sis): the condition of alternately laughing and crying.

dactyliography (dak.til′i.og′ra.fi): the history or art of gem engraving. 52.

dactylion (dak.til′i.on): the tip of the middle finger. Also, an obsolete device for developing the fingers of a piano player.

dactylology (dak′ti.lol′o.ji): the art of communicating ideas by signs made with the fingers, as in the manual alphabets of deaf-mutes.

dactyloscopy (dak′ti.los′ko.pi): identification by or classification of fingerprints.

dadder (dad′er): to shiver, tremble. 4.

daff (daf): a numbskull; a coward. 2. To act foolishly. 42. To thrust aside. 1.

daffle (daf′l): to be mentally senile. 13.

daggle (dag′l): to clog or befoul with mud or mire. To draggle.

daggly (dag′li): wet; drizzly. 11.

daggy (dag′i): having daglocks—said of sheep. Drizzling; misty. 15A.

Dagon (dā′gon): the principal deity of the Philistines, first a fish god, later a god of agriculture. (not cap) A piece, as of a blanket. 1.

dahabeah (dä′ha.bē′a): a long, light-draft houseboat, lateen-rigged but often propelled by engines, used on the Nile.

Daikoku (dī.kō′koo): in Japanese mythology, one of the seven gods of happiness.

daimen (dā′min): occasional. 44A.

daint (dānt): dainty.

daira (da.ē′ra): formerly, any of several valuable estates of the Egyptian khedive or his family.

dak (dak): in India, transport by relay of men or horses; hence, post; mail.

dal (däl): a kind of yellow split pea.

daler (dä′ler): obs. var. of *dollar*. Also, a Spanish or Swedish dollar.

Damara (da.mä′ra): a native of Damaraland, southwest Africa.

damascene (dam′a.sēn): damask. 1. Pert. to damask. The damson plum. The color damson. (cap) Pert. to Damascus.

damassin (dam′a.sin): a kind of damask or brocade made with gold and silver floral ornamentation.

damiana (dam′i.an.a): a dried leaf used as a tonic and aphrodisiac. Any other drug prepared from plants of the family Carduaceae.

dand (dand): a dandy.

dandiacal (dan.dī′a.kal): characterized by dandyism.

dao (dä′ō): a very large Philippine tree having edible fruit and fibrous bark used for cordage.

dapifer (dap′i.fer): one who brings meat to the table; hence, the steward of a king's or nobleman's household.

daroga (da.rō′ga): in India, a chief officer; partic. the head of a police, customs, or excise station.

darnel (där′nel, -nl): an annual grass found as a weed in cultivated grounds.

darrein (dar′ān): in old law, "last," as in "darrein resort."

dasymeter (da.sim′e.ter): formerly, a thin glass globe weighed in gases to measure their density.

dataria, datary (dä.tä′ri.a, dä′ta.ri): an office of the Roman Curia charged with investigating the fitness of candidates for benefices.

datil (dä′til): any of several plants and

their fibers from Mexico or Central or South America used for baskets or hats.

dauw (dou): the Burchell zebra, having a striped body and plain legs.

dawdy (dô′di): dowdy. 13.

dawk (dôk): var. of *dak*.

dealbation (dē′al.bā′shun): hair bleaching.

deambulant, deambulatory (di.am′bu.-lant, -bu.latō.ri): going about from place to place; wandering.

deasil, dessil (desh′l): right-handwise; clockwise; sunwise. Also, a charm performed by going three times about the object, following the course of the sun.

debarrass (di.bar′as): to disembarrass, relieve.

debellate (di.bel′āt): to conquer.

debitum (deb′i.tum): in law, a debt.

deblaterate (di.blat′er.āt): to babble.

debulliate (di.bul′i.āt): to boil over.

decadic (di.kad′ik): pert. to the decimal system of counting.

decaliter (dek′a.lē′ter): a metric measure of volume containing 10 liters.

Decalogist (de.kal′o.jist): an expounder of the Ten Commandments.

decameral (di.kam′er.al): in mathematics, divided into ten parts.

Decameron (di.kam′er.on): a collection of 100 stories written by Boccaccio in the 14th century.

decile (des′il): in statistics, any of 9 numbers in a series dividing the distribution of the individuals in the series into 10 groups of equal frequency. One of these groups.

declamando (dā′kla.män′do): in declamatory style.

decourt (di.kôrt): to banish from court. 1.

decurtate (di.kur′tat): curtailed. 1.

decurvation (dē′kur.vā′shun): the attribute of being curved or bent downward.

dedal, daedal (dē′dal): ingenious, highly skilled; intricate; varied.

dedendum (di.den′dum): in mechanics, the root of a gear tooth.

dedentition (dē′den.tish′un): the loss of teeth.

dedition (di.dish′un): surrender.

deesis (di.ē′sis): a tripartite icon of the Eastern Orthodox Church showing Christ usu. enthroned between the Virgin Mary and St. John the Baptist.

defeneration (di.fen′er.ā′shun): usury.

defervescency (dē′fer.ves′en.si): in medicine, a loss of heat; cooling. The subsidence of a fever.

deflex (di.fleks′): to bend or curve downward.

defluxion (di.fluk′shun): in medicine, a flowing down of fluid matter, as a copious discharge from the nose in catarrh.

Inflammation. Formerly, sudden loss of hair.

defoedation (dē.fi.dā′shun): the act of polluting.

defossion (di.fosh′un): live burial.

defunction (di.fungk′shun): death. 52.

dehort (di.hôrt′): to urge to abstain or refrain; to dissuade. 52.

deil (dēl): the Devil. 44.

deiparous (di.ip′a.rus): giving birth to a god—said of the Virgin Mary, hence called Deipara.

deipnosophist (dīp.nos′o.fist): one adept in table talk.

dejecture (di.jek′cher): excrement.

dekko (dek′ō): look, peep. 21.

delate (di.lāt): to make public, report.

delator (di.lā′ter): an accuser; esp. a common informer.

delectus (di.lek′tus): a book of selected passages, esp. for learners of Latin or Greek.

delenda (di.len′da): things to be deleted.

delf (delf): an excavation, usu. a mine or quarry. A pond; also, a drain, ditch. 13.

delictum (di.lik′tum): an offense or transgression against law; a delict.

deligation (del′i.gā′shun): bandaging.

deliquium (di.lik′wi.um): deliquescence. 1.

delitescent (del′i.tes′ent): lying hid; inactive.

delphin (del′fin): classics prepared for the use of the dauphin in the reign of King Louis XIV of France. A dolphin. 1.

delphine (del′fin, -fīn): pert. to the dolphins.

demal (dē′mal): in physical chemistry, having a concentration of one gram equivalent per cubic centimeter.

demersal (di.mur′sal): tending to sink, as certain fish eggs.

demesnial (di.mān′i.al, di.mēn′-): pert. to or belonging to a demesne.

demi (dem′i): a half. 1.

demijambe (dem′i.jam): a piece of armor for the front of the leg.

demiquaver (dem′i.kwā′ver): a semiquaver.

Demogorgon (dē′mo.gôr′gun): in mythology, a mysterious, terrible, and evil divinity, commanding the spirits of the lower world.

demology (di.mol′o.ji): the science of collective human activities.

demophil (dem′o.fil): a friend of the people.

dempster (demp′ster): in old Scots law, an officer whose duty it was to pronounce the doom of the court.

demulsion (di.mul′shun): the act of soothing. That which soothes.

NO RANKS OF INALIENABLE LAW FOR DEMOGORGON
(with the barest of nods to George Meredith)

Great Demogorgon[1], on a daggly[2] day,
Uprose diversivolent[3] to the light.
Dasypygal,[4] disomous[5] too he lay
Until a tender virgin hove in sight—
A dryad, toothsome and devorative[6],
Who, puzzled, paused and gave the fiend the eye.
''No roots . . . no leaves.'' She murmured, ''As I live,
Here is an object hard to classify.''

She was dendrophilous[7]—a lass who weened
All strangers to be variants of trees.
Some doty dotterel[8], she thought the fiend;
She figured she could chop him down with ease.

But he proceeded to dilaniate[9] her,
    And ate her.

[1] a terrible divinity, commanding the spirits of the lower world.
[2] drizzly, if you insist on plain speaking.
[3] looking for trouble.
[4] hairy-assed.
[5] having two joined bodies.
[6] he could swallow her in one bite.
[7] living in trees, and loving it.
[8] a decaying tree, or an old fool. The *doty* is redundant.
[9] rend to bits.

---

denary (den′a.ri): tenfold; based on tens. The number ten; a tithing; a group of ten. A gold coin of the ancient Romans—a denarius. 1.

denda (den′da): a measure of length in ancient India.

dendraxon (den.drak′son): in anatomy, a nerve cell whose axis cylinder divides into terminal filaments soon after leaving the cell.

dendrochronology (den′dro.kro.nol′o.ji): the computation of time by counting tree rings.

dendrophilous (den.drof′i.lus): tree-loving; living in or on trees.

dene (dēn): a sandy tract by the sea; a dune. 41.

dennet (den′et): a light, open, two-wheeled, one-horse carriage popular around 1825; a gig.

dentata (den.tā′ta): part of the second vertebra of the neck of higher vertebrates.

dentelle (den.tel′): lace; lacework. A lacy style of bookcover decoration.

dentiloquy (den.til′o.kwi): the practice of speaking through the teeth.

dentoplastic (den′to.plas′tik): a plastic used in dentistry.

den-tree (den′tri): the popular box, widely used for hedges, etc. 53.

Deo (dē′ō): God.

deodand (dē′o.dand): a thing forfeited or given to God because it was the immediate cause of a death.

---

deontology (dē′on.tol′o.ji): the study of morality or ethics.

deoppilation (di.op′i.lā′shun): the act of freeing from or removing obstruction.

deorsumversion (di.ôr′sum.vur′zhun): a turning downward.

deosculate (di.os′kū.lāt): to kiss affectionately. 1.

depeculation (di.pek′ū.lā′shun): the embezzlement of public funds.

deperition (dep′er.ish′un): a destructive process.

dephlogisticate (dē′flo.jis′ti.kāt): to make fireproof.

depone (di.pōn): to testify under oath. To depose.

depredicate (di.pred′i.kāt): to proclaim aloud; call out; celebrate.

deprehensible (dep′ri.hen′si.bl): able to be seized, detected, apprehended. 1.

depucelate (di.pū′si.lāt): to deflower. 1.

deraign (di.rān′): in old law, a combat to settle a claim or dispute. To fight for this purpose.

deric (der′ik): pert. to the skin.

derm (durm): skin; cuticle; dermis.

dermophyte (dur′mo.fīt): an organism living on or in the skin.

desecate (des′i.kāt): to cut off.

desiderium (des′i.dē′ri.um): an ardent desire or longing; a feeling of grievous loss.

desidious (di.sid′i.us): slothful.

desipient (di.sip′i.ent): foolish.

desmology (des.mol′o.ji): the science treating of the ligaments. The art of bandaging.

desparple (des.pär′pl): to scatter, become scattered.

despumate (des′pū.māt): to skim.

dess (des): a layer or pile, as of stones or hay. To arrange in layers. 43.

detenebrate (di.ten′i.brāt): to lighten.

detorter (di.tôr′ter): one that twists, detorts, perverts. 9.

detrition (di.trish′un): erosion by friction.

detruncate (di.trung′kāt): to shorten by cutting; lop off; decapitate.

deuteragonist (dū′ter.ag′o.nist): in Greek drama, an actor taking the parts of second importance.

deuterogamist (dū′ter.og′a.mist): a widower or widow who remarries.

deuteroscopy (dū′ter.os′ko.pi): hidden meaning or second sight.

devall (di.vôl′): cessation; pause. To leave off, cease. 44.

devast (di.vast′): to devastate.

devastavit (dev′as.tā′vit): a common-law writ against an executor or administrator for mismanagement. Such mismanagement.

devorative (di.vôr´a.tiv): capable of being swallowed whole.

dexiotropic (dek´si.o.trop´ik): turning to the right, dextral—said of certain shells.

dextrogyrate (dek´stro.jī´rāt): turning toward the right hand, or clockwise.

dextrophobia (dek´stro.fō´bi.a): fear of anything on the right.

dextrosinistral (dek´stro.sin´is.tral): in anatomy, extending in a right and left direction. Naturally left-handed but trained to use the right hand in writing.

dghaisa (dī´sa): in Malta, a small boat resembling a gondola.

dhabb (dab): the dried flesh of the skink, used as a medicine.

dharna (dur´na): in India, a way of collecting debts by sitting on the debtor's doorstep.

dhimmi (dim´i): a person living in a region overrun by Moslem conquest who was accorded a special status and allowed to retain his original faith.

dhobi, dobee, dobie (dō´bi): a member of a low caste in India once employed to wash; a washerman or washerwoman.

dhyana (dyä´na): in Hinduism and Buddhism, religious meditation.

dia (dī´a): a medical or pharmaceutical preparation. 1.

diacope (dī.ak´o.pi): the separation of a word by the insertion of another, as *dis-horrible-gusting;* tmesis. In surgery, a deep incised wound or cut.

diaglyphic (dī´a.glif´ik): pert. to sculpture, engraving, etc., formed by depressions in the surface, as in intaglio.

diagraphical (dī´a.graf´i.kal): pert. to graphic representation, esp. drawing. 52.

diapente (dī´a.pen´ti): in ancient music, the interval or consonance of the fifth. In pharmacy, a composition of five ingredients. 1.

diaphane (dī´a.fān): a diaphanous substance, as a woven silk scarf with transparent figures.

diaphanic (dī´a.fan´ik): diaphanous. 1.

diarhemia (dī´a.rē´mi.a): an abnormally watery state of the blood often occurring in animals heavily infested with parasites.

diarian (dī´âr´i.an): the writer of a diary; formerly, a journalist.

diastomatic (dī´as.to.mat´ik): through the pores. Also, gap-toothed.

diathesis (dī.ath´i.sis): an inherited tendency toward certain diseases.

diatoric (dī´a.tôr´ik): having a recess in the base for attachment to the dental plate—used of an artificial tooth.

diaxon (dī.ak´son): a nerve cell with two axons.

diazeuctic (dī´a.zōōk´tik), **diazeutic** (dī´a.zōō´tik): in ancient music, dis-jointed; applies to two tetrachords so placed as to have a tone between them, or to the resultant tone.

dibber (dib´er): a pointed gardening tool used to make holes; a dibble.

dicacity (di.kas´i.ti): raillery; sauciness. 1.

dicaeology (di´si.ol.o.ji): in rhetoric, defense by urging justification.

dichastasis (dī.kas´ta.sis): spontaneous subdivision.

dichroous (dī´kro.us): presenting different colors by transmitted light, when viewed in two different directions.

didactyl (dī.dak´til): said of animals having only two digits on each extremity.

diddy (did´i): nipple; teat; breast milk. 11.

didelf (dī´delf): one of a group of mammals comprising the marsupials, as the opossums, kangaroos, etc.

didgeridoo (dij´er.i.doo´): a large bamboo musical pipe of the Australian aborigines.

didodecahedral (dī´do.dek´a.hē´dral): pert. to a diploid, an isometric crystal form that has 24 similar quadrilateral faces arranged in pairs.

dieb (dēb): a jackal of North Africa.

diegesis (dī´i.jē´sis): a recitation or narration.

diffluent (dif´lōō.ent): readily dissolving; deliquescent.

diffugient (di.fū´ji.ent): scattering.

digamous (dig´a.mus): married a second time.

digenesis (di.jen´i.sis): reproduction that is alternately sexual and asexual.

digenous (dij´i.nus): bisexual.

Digitigrada (dij.i.ti.grā´da): a group of animals consisting of the digitigrade carnivora, in which only the digits bear on the ground.

digitorium (dij´i.tō´ri.um): a silent machine for piano practice.

diglot (dī´glot): bilingual. A diglot edition, as of a book.

diglyph (dī´glif): in a Doric frieze, a projecting face like the triglyph, but having only two grooves.

digoneutic (dig´o.nyū´tik): reproducing twice a year.

digredient (dī.grē´di.ent): in mathematics, subject to different linear transformations—opposed to *cogredient.*

dikephobia (dī´ke.fō´bi.a): fear of police, courts, and jails.

dikkop (dik´kop): in South Africa, the thick-knee; stone curlew.

dilaniate (di.lā´ni.āt): to rend or tear to pieces.

dilection (di.lek´shun): love; also, one's choice.

dilogical (dī.loj´i.kal): ambiguous; having more than one interpretation.

dilogy (dil´o.ji): an ambiguous speech or remark, as in the young couple's statement: ''We are telling people we are married.''

dimication (dim´i.kā´shun): a contest.

dimidiation (di.mid´i.ā´shun): the state of being halved; halving.

dimplement (dim´pl.ment): the state of being dimpled. 52.

dinge (dinj): a dent made by a blow; a surface depression. To bruise. To make dingy. Dinginess. A black—usu. used disparagingly. 21.

dingle (ding´gl): a dell, esp. a secluded ravine. A tinkle. Also, a storm door or weather shed at the entrance of a camp or house. A roofed-over passageway between the cooking and sleeping areas of a logging camp. 33A.

dinic (din´ik): pert. to dizziness.

dink (dingk): trim; neat. To dress elegantly. 44. A drop shot in tennis. A small boat, esp. one used in duck shooting. The beanie traditionally worn by college freshmen.

dinomania (din´o.mā´ni.a): a mania for dancing.

dinomic (dī.nom´ik): belonging to two divisions of the globe.

Dinornis (dī.nôr´nis): a genus of ratite birds inc. the extinct flightless moas of New Zealand, which reached 12 feet in height.

dinus (dī´nus): vertigo.

diorthosis (dī.ôr´tho.sis): a straightening out. The reshaping of deformed limbs.

dipleidoscope (dip.lī´do.skōp): an instrument for determining the time of apparent noon.

dipnoous (dip´no.us): having both lungs and gills.

dipsetic (dip´set´ik): a thirst-provoker. Thirst-provoking.

diptote (dip´tōt): a noun that has only two cases.

diremption (di.remp´shun): a tearing apart. Specif., the utter separation of a man and wife, as by death. 52.

direption (di.rep´shun): in history, sack or pillage.

dirgie, dirgy (dur´ji): a funeral feast. 44.

dis (dēs): in Norse mythology, a generic title for any of several kinds of superhuman female beings such as Valkyries and Norns. (cap) An underworld Roman god identical with the Greek Pluto.

disbocation (dis.bo.kā´shun): deforestation.

discal (dis´kal): like, or pert. to, a disk.

discalceate (dis.kal´si.āt): to take off one's shoes.

discalogynia (dis.cal.o.jīn′i.a): dislike of beautiful women.

discerp (di.surp′): to tear; to rend.

discinct (di.singkt): without a belt; ungirdled; loosely dressed.

disembogue (dis′em.bōg): to pass through the mouth of a stream in a sea; to flow into; to emerge.

disgregate (dis′gre.gāt): to separate; disperse.

disomus (dī.sō′mus): in zoology, a two-bodied monster.

Dis pater (dis pā′ter): (also Dis), an underworld god of the Romans, identical with the Greek Pluto.

dispondee (di.spon′di): in prosody, a foot having two long syllables.

dispope (dis.pōp′): to remove from popehood.

diss (dis): a reedlike Mediterranean grass, utilized in basketry and for making cordage, etc.

dissentaneous (dis′en.tā′ni.us): disagreeable; negative.

dissilient (di.sil′i.ent): bursting apart.

distent (dis.tent′): distended. Breadth, distention. 1.

dita (dē′ta): a forest tree of eastern Asia and the Philippines, called *devil's tree* in India. Also, its bark, used as a tonic and antiperiodic.

dital (dī′tal): a key by which the pitch is raised a half step in a harp guitar.

ditation (dī.tā′shun): the act of making rich. 1.

ditrigonal (dī.trig′o.nal): designating a six-sided crystal whose alternate interfacial angles only are equal.

ditrochean, ditrochic (dī.tro.kē′an, dī.trō′kik): in prosody, relating to a double trochee.

dittamy, dittany (dit′a.mi, dit′a.ni): an aromatic plant of Crete, once famous for its supposed medical virtues.

dittander (di.tan′der): a fern, the European pepperwort.

diuturnal (dī′ū.tur′nal): of long continuance; lasting.

div (div): to do. 43.

divel (di.vel′): to rend asunder. 9, 52.

divellent (di.vel′ent): drawing asunder. 52.

diversivolent (di.vur′si.vō′lent): looking for trouble.

dividual (di.vid′ū.al): separate, distinct. Fragmentary; divisible. Divided or shared.

divoto (di.vō′tō): with religious emotion—a direction in music.

divus (dī′vus): divine, or of godlike nature—an epithet applied by the Romans to deceased emperors.

dobby (dob′i): a silly person; dolt. A brownie or sprite. 13. A loom or loom attachment for weaving small figures; a fabric made with a *dobby.*

dobra (dō′bra): any of various former Portuguese coins.

doch-an-dorrach, doch-an-dorris (dok′an.dôr.ak, -is): a stirrup cup; a nightcap. 44.

docible (dos.i.bl): easily taught or managed. Impartable by teaching. 52.

docimastic (dos′i.mas′tik): relating to proof by experiments or tests. 9.

docity (dos′i.ti): teachability. 11.

doddard (dod′ard): a branchless tree stump. Also, a dotard. 1.

dodecant (dō′de.kant): any of the 12 parts about the center of a hexagonal crystal.

dodman (dod′man): a snail. 2.

doit (doit): a trifle. To go about stupidly; to confuse. 43.

doited (doit′ed): declining into dotage; confused. 44A.

dolabriform (do.lab′ri.fôrm): shaped like an ax head.

dolent (dō′lent): sad.

dolente (do.len′ti): in music, plaintive—a direction indicating mood.

dolichopodous (dol.i.kop′o.dus): having long feet.

dolichoprosopic (dol.i.ko.pro.sop′ik): having a disproportionately long face.

Dolichosaurus (dol.i.ko.sô′rus): a genus of small long-necked aquatic fossil lizards from the Upper Cretaceous of England.

dolichurus (dol′i.kōōr′us): in Greek and Latin prosody, a dactylic hexameter with an actual or apparent redundant syllable in the last foot.

dollyman (dol′i.man): a laborer who works with a dolly.

dolorifuge (do.lôr′i.fūj): something that relieves sadness or pain.

dolorology (dō′lo.rol′o.ji): the scientific study of pain. 32.

dolus (dō′lus): in Roman, civil, and Scots law, the doing of anything that is contrary to good conscience.

dom (dom): a member of one of the lowest castes of India.

domatophobia (dō′ma.to.fō′bi.a): loathing of housekeeping.

domba (dom′ba): the *poon.*

domet, domett (dom′et, -it): a cotton or wool flannel; outing flannel.

domiculture (dom′i.kul.cher): home economics.

domn (dom): lord. The official title of the ruler of Rumania, Prince Carol I, from 1866 to 1881, when he was proclaimed king.

domus (dō′mus): a dwelling of ancient Roman or medieval times.

doncella (don.sel′a): any of several wrasse-like fishes of the West Indies and Florida; specif., the *puddingwife,* slippery eel, and related species.

donnered (don′erd): stupefied; stunned; dazed. 43.

dontepedalogy (don′ti.pi.dal′o.ji): a propensity for putting one's foot in one's mouth.

doob (dōōb): the Bermuda grass of India.

doodlebug (dōō′dl.bug): the larva of the ant lion.

doodlesack (dōō′dl.sak): a bagpipe. 17A.

doon (dōōn): a large Ceylonese tree yielding durable wood and a colorless varnish resin.

dop (dop): a brandy of South Africa. Also, a cup in which a diamond is held while being cut. To dive; to duck or curtsey. 1.

doramania (dôr′a.mā′ni.a): a passion for the possession of furs.

doraphobia (dôr′a.fō′bi.a): dread of touching the fur or skin of an animal.

dorn (dôrn): the thornback ray. 30.

dorp (dôrp): a village, esp. in the Netherlands. 1. A village or township in South Africa.

dorsiflexor (dôr′si.flek′ser): a muscle causing flexion in a dorsal direction.

dorso (dôr′sō): an endorsement on the outside or reverse of a manuscript record.

dorsum (dôr′sum): the back part of the tongue.

dorty (dôr′ti): peevish; sulky. 44.

dosa (dō′sa): in Buddhism, a ceremonial ride by the sheik of the Sa′di dervishes over the prostrate bodies of his followers. Also, hatred.

Dosinia (do.sin′i.a): a genus of bivalve mollusks having a flattened round shell.

dossil (dos′il): a spigot. 4. In surgery, a small roll of lint, for keeping a sore, wound, etc., open.

dotation (do.tā′shun): an endowment or bestowal.

doty (dōt′i): of timber, affected by incipient or partial decay. Weak-minded; having the mentality impaired in old age. 35.

doulocracy (dōō.lok′ra.si), dulocracy (dū.lok′ra.si): government by slaves.

doum (dōōm): the doom palm, also called *dome palm.*

dowie, dowy (dou′i. dō′i): doleful; dispirited; dull and oppressive. 44A.

doxastic (dok.sas′tik): pert. to opinion.

doxography (dok.sog′ra.fi): a compilation of extracts from the ancient Greek philosophers.

drabbet (drab′et): a coarse drab linen fabric, or duck, used for smocks, etc. 41.

dracontine (dra.kon′tīn, -tin): dragonlike; belonging to a dragon.

draffy (draf′i): dreggy; waste; worthless.

dragade (dra.gād′): to break up (glass) by pouring (it) molten into water.

dragman (drag′man): one who drags something, as a fisherman who uses a dragnet.

dragonnade (drag′o.nād): the persecution of Protestants under Louis XIV by dragoons; hence, any rapid and devastating incursion.

drammock (dram′uk): a mixture, gen. raw, of meal and water. 45.

drap (drap): var. of *drop.* 15A.

drapetomania (drap′i.to.mā′ni.a): an overwhelming desire to run away from home.

dree (drē): suffering. To undergo, suffer. Tedious, dreary, stingy. 43A.

dreidel (drā′dl): a 4-sided toy that revolves like a top, used esp. during the Hanukkah festival. A game of chance played with the dreidel.

drek (drek): filth. 21.

dreng, drengh (dreng): a free tenant, esp. in pre-Norman Northumbria.

drepanoid (drep′a.noid): shaped like a scythe or sickle.

drias (drī′as): the deadly carrot, a large European herb with an emetic and cathartic root.

drillet (dril′et): a commercial product formed of the acorn cups of the valonia oak, used for tanning and dyeing.

drogh (drōg): a hooped canvas bag towed at the stern of a boat to prevent it from turning broadside to the waves. A contrivance attached to the end of a harpoon line to check the movements of a whale.

drogher (drō′ger): a sailing barge used in the West Indian trade. A clumsy cargo boat. A carrier, porter.

dromic (drō′mik): pert. to the shape of a racecourse. Having a long and narrow ground plan.

dromomania (drō′mo.mā′ni.a): a compulsion to travel.

dromophobia (drō′mo.fō′bi.a): fear of running.

drumble (drum′bl): a sluggish person or animal; to be sluggish or lazy; to be confused; to mumble. 2. To disturb; to render turbid. 43.

drummock (drum′uk): var. of *drammock.*

drury (drōō′ri): short for the Drury Lane theater.

druxy (druk′si): having decayed spots in the heartwood—applied to timber.

dryades (drī′a.dēz) (pl. of *dryas*): in Greek mythology, wood nymphs whose life is bound to that of their trees.

Duat (dōō′at): in Egyptian mythology, one of the abodes of the dead.

duction (duk′shun): the act of leading.

ductor (duk′ter): one that leads.

dudder (dud′er): to shiver; tremble. 2. To confuse with noise, bewilder. 44C.

duddyfunk (dud′i.fungk): a pie made of beef, lamb, or venison, and salt pork and ground cloves. 37A.

dulcamara (dul′ka.mā′ra): the bittersweet, or deadly nightshade, a sprawling, poisonous Old World plant that in America is a weed.

dulce (duls): sweet; sweetness; to sweeten. 1.

dulcifluous (dul.sif′lōō.us): sweet-flowing. 52.

dulciloquy (dul.sil′o.kwi): a soft manner of speaking. 1.

dulcorate (dul′ko.rāt): to sweeten. 1.

dulia (dū.li′a): lesser kind of veneration or worship, given to the angels and saints as the servants and friends of God.

dumba (dum′ba): a fat-tailed sheep of Bukhara and the Kirghiz steppe, which furnishes astrakhan.

dumbledor (dum′bl.dôr): a dorbeetle or bumblebee.

dumose, dumous (dū′mōs, -mus): bushy.

duomachy (dū.om′a.ki): single combat.

dup (dup): to open. 1.

duplify (dū′pli.fī): to make double.

dynamis (dī′na.mis): in Aristotelianism, a state not yet fully realized; potentiality.

dynamitard (dī′na.mi.tärd): a dynamiter.

Dyophysite (dī.of′i.sīt): one who maintains that Christ was at once fully divine and fully human.

dysania (di.sā′ni.a): difficulty in waking up.

dysbulia (dis.bōō′li.a): loss of willpower.

dysgenics (dis.jen′iks): the science dealing with hereditary deterioration.

PERHAPS HE PREFERS FISHES

A Fish dreamed the sea had turned dry as the shore,
And rendered his species extinct.
A Man dreamed he'd entered his office discinct,
And his trousers had dropped to the floor.

So they prayed. If one prays just as hard as one can,
God is certain to answer one's wish.
With lungs He augmented the gills of the Fish—
With suspenders, the belt of the Man.

Two splendid advances! Why then did He plan
Fame for one—and t'other one squish? . . .
For we all know the Fish is the Dipnoous Fish,
But who knows the name of the Man?

---

dyslogistic (dis′lo.jis′tik): unfavorable—opposed to *eulogistic.*

dysmorphophobia (dis′môr.fo.fō′bi.a): dread of misshapenness.

dyspathy (dis′pa.thi): the opposite of sympathy; antipathy.

dysphemism (dis′fi.mizm): the substitution of an offensive for an inoffensive word—opposed to *euphemism.*

dysthymic (dis.thim′ik): chronically sad or depressed.

dystomic (dis.tom′ik): difficult to split, as certain rocks.

dystopia (dis.tō′pi.a): the disagreeable opposite of utopia.

dystychiphobia (dis.tik.i.fō′bi.a): fear of accidents.

dzo (dzō): a hybrid between the yak and the domestic cow.

E

ean (ēn): to give birth; *yean.*

eanling (ēn′ling): a young lamb or kid.

ebenezer (eb.en.ē′zer): a memorial stone. A dissenting chapel.

eboe (ē′bō): a Central American tree, the roots of which yield eboe oil.

ebriection (eb′ri.ek′shun): a breakdown from overdrink.

ebrious (ē′bri.us): tending to overimbibe; slightly drunk.

ebullism (eb′ul.izm): the bubbling of body fluids, resulting from a sudden reduction of air pressure.

eburnean (i.bur′ni.an): resembling ivory in color.

ecbactic (ek.bak′tik): in grammar, denoting a mere result or consequence, as distinguished from *telic,* denoting intention or purpose.

ecballium (ek.bal′i.um): the squirting cucumber.

ecce (ek′si, ek′i): (Latin *see, behold*); used to call attention, often to one persecuted unjustly, as in *Ecce Homo.*

ecdemic (ek.dem′ik): not endemic; of a foreign cause.

echinidan (e.kin′i.dan): a sea urchin.

echopraxia (ek′o.prak′si.a): a habit of repeating the actions of other people.

ecmnesia (ek.nē′zhi.a): loss of the memory of a recent period, with retention of earlier memories.

ecofreak (ē′ko.frēk): a fervent conservationist or environmentalist. 21.

ecomania (ē′ko.mā′ni.a): humility toward superiors combined with arrogance toward one's own family.

ecophobia (ē′ko.fō′bi.a): fear of home.

ectal (ek′tal): exterior; outer.

ectoentad (ek′to.en′tad): from without inward.

ectogenesis (ek′to.jen′i.sis): development outside the body, esp. of a mammalian embryo in an artificial environment.

ectophyte (ek′to.fīt): a vegetable parasite that lives on the exterior of animals.

edaphology (ed′a.fol′o.ji): the science of soils.

Eddaic, Eddic (e.dā′ik, ed′ik): referring to the Old Norse Edda, a 13th century collection of mythology and heroic and gnomic songs.

eddish (ed′ish): aftermath, stubble. 13.

edea (e.dē′a): the external genitals.

edentulous (i.den′tū.lus): toothless.

edipol (ed′i.pōl): a mild oath; any common asseveration.

educt (ē′dukt): something which is educed, as by analysis. In chemistry, a substance separated from material in which it has already existed.

edulcoration (i.dul′ko.rā′shun): the act of sweetening.

efflation (e.flā′shun): an emanation; a puff; blowing or puffing. 52.

effleurage (ef′ler.äzh): a gentle stroking movement used in massage and lovemaking.

effulge (e.fulj′): to shine forth, radiate.

egotheism (ē′go.thi.izm): self-deification.

egredouce (eg′re.d͞oos): a sweet-and-sour sauce. Formerly, a rabbit curry.

eidograph (ī′do.graf): a kind of pantograph.

eigne (ān): the firstborn, eldest, heir-apparent.

Eir (âr): in Norse religion, the goddess of healing.

eirenicon (ī.ren′i.kon): *irenicon.*

eisegesis (ī′se.jē′sis): misinterpretation of a text by reading into it one's own ideas.

ejoo (i.j͞oo′): the Malay *gomuti,* also a feather palm; also its wiry fiber.

ejulation (ej.ū.lā′shun): lamentation. 1.

ejuration (ej.ū.rā′shun): renunciation, repudiation.

ekka (ek′a): in India, a native one-horse carriage.

elapid, elapine (el′a.pid, el′a.pīn, -pin): pert. to a family of front-fanged venomous snakes inc. the cobras, mambas, and coral snakes.

elaterium (el′a.tēr′i.um): a purgative substance precipitated as a fine powder from the juice of the squirting cucumber.

eld (eld): age; old age. Old times; antiquity; an old person. 9.

electicism (e.lek′ti.sizm): eclecticism. 52.

electropathic (i.lek′tro.path′ik): electrotherapeutic.

elegiambic (el′e.ji.am′bik): pert. to a type of verse in classical Greek and Latin poetry.

eleutheromania (i.lū′ther.o.mā′ni.a): frantic zeal for freedom.

ellagic (e.laj′ik): pert. to or designating a crystallinic acid found in beozar stones, oak galls, etc.

elogy (el′o.ji): an inscription, esp. on a tombstone; a funeral oration. 1. A characterization or biographical sketch, esp. in praise. 9.

elusory (i.l͞oo′so.ri): pert. to an attempt to elude.

elute (i.lūt): to wash out.

elydoric (el′i.dō′rik): pert. to painting that combines oil and watercolor.

embolalia (em′bo.lā′li.a): habitual utterance of nonsense.

embracery (em.brās′er.i): in law, an attempt to influence a court, jury, etc., corruptly, by promises, money, threats, entertainments, etc.

eme (ēm): an uncle. Also, a friend; a gossip. 11.

emerods (em′er.odz): hemorrhoids. 9.

emgalla (em.gal′a): the South American warthog.

emmenology (em′i.nol′o.ji): the branch of medical science that deals with menstruation.

empasm (em.pazm′): deodorant powder.

emphractic (em.frak′tik): closing the pores of the skin. In medicine, an emphractic agent.

emphyteutic (em′fi.tū′tik): in civil law, relating to a land grant made subject to keeping up the land, paying annual rent, or other conditions.

emplastic (em.plas′tik): adhesive; also, costive.

empleomania (em.plē′o.mā′ni.a): a violent desire to hold public office.

emporetical (em′po.ret′i.kal): pert. to trade or merchandise; emporeutic. Also, merchandise.

emporeutic (em′po.r͞oo′tik): pert. to trade or merchandising.

emption (emp′shun): in law, a buying; purchase.

emptor (emp′tôr): a purchaser or buyer.

empyreumatic (em′pi.r͞oo.mat′ik): having the peculiar smell of organic substances burned in close vessels.

emuscation (i.mus.kā′shun): the act of freeing from moss. 1.

enantiosis (en.an′ti.ō′sis): in rhetoric, a negative statement of what is to be understood affirmatively, or vice versa.

enatation (en′a.tā′shun): escape by swimming.

enation (i.nā′shun): kinship on the mother's side.

encephaloid (en.sef′a.loid): like the brain in form or structure. An encephaloid cancer.

encrinic (en.krin′ik): pert. to, or made up of enclinites, as certain limestones; encrinal.

endocoele (en′do.sēl): the primitive digestive sac of certain embryos.

endogamy (en.dog′a.mi): marriage within the tribe, caste, or social group; inbreeding.

endogen (en′do.jen): a plant that grows from the inside out.

endometric (en′do.met′rik): pert. to the measurement of the interior of a cavity.

endothecal (en′do.thē′kal): pert. to the interior tissue of the interseptal chambers of most stony corals.

enew (e.nū′): to plunge (a fowl) into water. 1.

engastration (en.gas.trā′shun): the art of stuffing one fowl inside another.

> *VIRTUE TRIUMPHS AGAIN*
>
> A fair entellus in a banyan swung,
> By tail secured, and by her faith in Brahma.
> (Entellesus are sacred beasts among
> The simple folk out there in Sutra Khama.)
> That she was lissom, virtuous, and young
> Made her estiverous for blissom male
> Entelluses who ogled as she hung,
> And called her to descend, to no avail.
>
> Those rammish males, their dreams epithymastic,
> Their hips extorsive, pranced, and cried "Evoe!"
> Till, whelmed by exundation orgiastic,
> They fell afaint beneath the banyan tree,
> And lay unmoving after all that ruckus—
> If not exanimous, at least exsuccous.

---

engastrimyth (en.gas′tri.mith): a ventriloquist. 1.

enissophobia (en.is′o.fō′bi.a): fear of being reproached.

enneaeteric (en.i.a.ter′ik): occurring every eighth or ninth year, depending on how you count.

enneatic (en′i.at′ik): occurring once in every nine times; every ninth.

ennomic (en.nom′ik): lawful.

enoptromancy (en.op′tro.man′si): divination by means of a mirror.

enosiophobia (en.o′si.o.fō′bi.a): fear of having committed an unpardonable sin.

enquete (en.ket′): in France, an inquiry, investigation.

ens, ense (ens): else. 44.

ensky (en.skī′): to make immortal.

ensynopticity (en′sin.op.tis.i.ti): the capacity to take a general view.

entad (en′tad): inward; toward the center.

ental (en′tal): inner; opposed to *ectal.*

entellus (en.tel′us): an East Indian long-tailed monkey regarded as sacred by the natives.

enteropathogenic (en′ter.o.path′o.jen.-ik): producing intestinal disease.

entheomania (en′thi.o.mā′ni.a): the unfounded conviction that one is divinely inspired.

entomoid (en′to.moid): resembling an insect. 52.

entomolite (en.tom′o.līt): a fossil insect-like animal.

entopic (en.top′ik): in anatomy, occurring in the usual place.

entortillation (en.tôr′ti.lā′shun): turning in a circle.

entotic (en.tō′tik): pert. to the interior of the ear.

enurny (en.ur′ni): in heraldry, a bordure charged with beasts.

eoan (i.ō′an): pert. to the dawn or the east.

eonism (ē′on.izm): the tendency to adopt the mental attitudes, habits, and costume of the other sex.

eosophobia (i.os′o.fō′bi.a): the fear of dawn.

Eozoic (ē′o.zō′ik): in geology, pre-Cambrian, Proterozoic, or Algonkin.

epagoge (ep′a.gog): logical induction from all the particulars implied under the inferred generalization. Induction by simple enumeration.

epanadiplosis (ep.an′a.di.plō′sis): in rhetoric, use of a word both at the beginning and the end of a sentence.

epanalepsis (ep.an′a.lep′sis): in rhetoric, a repetition; echo.

epanorthosis (ep.an′ôr.thō′sis): the substitution of a more emphatic word or phrase for one just preceding it.

epanthous (ep.an′thus): growing on flowers; said of certain fungi.

ephectic (ef.ek′tik): given to suspension of judgment.

ephemeromorph (i.fem′er.o.môrf): a low form of life intermediate between an animal and a plant.

epiblema (ep′i.blē′ma): among the ancient Greeks, an outer garment; shawl.

epicede (ep′i.sēd): a funeral song or ode. A dirge; elegy.

epideictic (ep′i.dīk′tik): designed primarily for rhetorical effect.

epidermophytosis (ep′i.dur′mo.fī.tō′sis): athlete's foot.

epigamic (ep′i.gam′ik): tending to attract the opposite sex during the breeding season, as the *epigamic* coloration of a bird.

epigean (ep′i.jē′an): living close to the ground, as some insects.

epilate (ep′i.lāt): to remove hair.

epimyth (ep′i.mith): the moral of a story.

epinaos (ep′i.nā′os): a room or vestibule in the rear of a Greek temple.

epinician (ep′i.nish′un): celebrating victory; as, an *epinician* ode.

epiphoric (ep′i.fôr′ik): relating to the watering of the eyes.

epiphytic (ep′i.fit′ik): pert. to or like an epiphyte, a plant that grows upon others, but is not parasitic.

epiplexis (ep′i.plek′sis): in rhetoric, an upbraiding.

epipolic (ep′i.pol′ik): in optics, fluorescent.

episematic (ep′i.se.mat′ik): designating certain markings that assist individ-

uals of the same species in recognizing each other.

epistemophilia (i.pis′ti.mo.fil′i.a): obsession with knowledge.

epitaxis, epitaxy (ep′i.tak′sis, -si): the oriented growth of one crystalline substance on a substrate of a different crystalline substance.

epithymetic (ep′i.thi.met′ik): pert. to desire; sensual.

epitonic (ep′i.ton′ik): overstrained.

epulotic (ep′ū.lot′ik): having healing power.

epuration (ep′ū.rā′shun): the act of purifying.

equaeval (i.kwē′val): of equal age.

equipendent (ek′wi.pen′dent): hanging in equipoise. 1.

equivorous (i.kwiv′o.rus): eating horseflesh.

eral (ēr′al): pert. to an era. 52.

eremic (i.rē′mik): pert. to desert or sandy regions.

eremophobia (er′e.mo.fō′bi.a): fear of loneliness.

ereption (i.rep′shun): a snatching away.

ergal (ur′gal): in physics, potential energy.

ergasiophobia (er.gas′i.o.fō′bi.a): fear of work; ergophobia.

ergatocracy (ur′ga.tok′ra.si): government by workers.

ergophile (ur′go.fīl): one who loves work.

ergophobia (ur′go.fō′bi.a): a strong aversion to work. *Ergasiophobia.*

eria (ā′ri.a, ē′ri.a): the Assam silkworm, which feeds on the castor-oil plant.

eric (er′ik): in old Irish law, a blood fine.

Erica (er′i.ka): a genus of low evergreen shrubs, the true heaths. (not cap) A plant of this genus.

erinaceous (er′i.nā′shus): pert. to the hedgehog.

erminois (ur′mi.noiz): in heraldry, spots of black ermine fur on a golden field.

eroduction (ē′ro.duk′shun): a pornographic motion picture.

erostrate (i.ros′trāt): beakless.

eroteme (er′o.tēm): a mark indicating a question, as (?).

erotesis (er′o.tē′sis): interrogation for rhetorical effect.

erotographomania (i.rō′to.graf′o.mā′ni.a): an irresistible impulse to write love letters.

erotology (ē′ro.tol′o.ji): the study of love.

errabund (er′a.bund): wandering; erratic.

erugate (er′ū.gāt): without wrinkles; smooth.

Eryngium (i.rin′ji.um): a genus of

coarse bristly herbs having white or blue flowers in dense heads.

erythrophobia (i.rith′ro.fō′bi.a): fear of redness or blushing.

eschrolalia (es′kro.lā′li.a): dirty language.

esclandre (es.klän′dr): notoriety; a disgraceful occurrence or scene.

esclavage (es′kla.väzh): a necklace resembling 18th-century slave chains.

escribe (i.skrīb′, es.krīb′): to copy out. 1. To draw (a circle) touching one side of a triangle externally and the other two sides internally.

escrime (es.krēm): fencing.

escudero (es′kōō.thä′rō): a shield-bearer.

esemplastic (es′em.plas′tik): unifying.

esquamate (es.kwā′māt): having no scales.

esquisse (es.kēs′): a preliminary sketch or model.

essling (es′ling): a young salmon. 13.

essoin (e.soin′): an excuse for not appearing in court. To excuse (one) for nonappearance.

esssse (esh′i): ashes. 1.

estafette (es′ta.fet): a mounted courier.

estiferous (es.tif′er.us): producing heat.

estive (es′tiv): pert. to summer; hot. 1.

estoile (es.toil′, -twäl): a star conventionally represented in heraldry, usu. with six wavy points.

estrade (es.träd′, -träd′): a dais.

estrapade (es′tra.pād): the attempt of a horse to get rid of its rider by rearing, plunging, etc.

estuous (es′tū.us): excited, passionate, agitated.

et (et): dial. past tense and past participle of *eat*.

eteostic (et′i.os′tik): a chronogram. 1.

ethal (eth′al, ē′thal): cetyl alcohol.

ethel (eth′el): ancestral land. 6. The *atle.*

ettle (et′l): to plan, try, design. 11. Nettle. 11. An intent; chance. 44.

euania (ū.ā′ni.a): ease of waking up in the morning.

eugenesis (ū.jen′i.sis): fertility between hybrids.

euhemeristic (ū.hem′er.is′tik): pert. to the interpretation of myths as traditional accounts of historical personages and events.

eumorphous (u.môr′fus): well-formed.

euneirophrenia (ū.nī′ro.frē′ni.a): peace of mind after a pleasant dream.

euodic (ū.od′ik): aromatic.

euphelicia (ū.fe.lis′i.a): well-being resulting from having all one's wishes granted.

euphobia (ū.fō′bi.a): fear and hatred of what is good.

euphon (ū′fon): euphonic.

euphone (ū′fōn): a free-reed organ stop, giving a soft expressive tone.

eurethrophobia (ū.rē′thro.fō′bi.a): fear of blushing.

euripize (ū.ri.pīz): to fluctuate.

Euroclydon (ū.rok′li.don): a strong cold northeast wind of the Mediterranean.

eurycephalic (ū′ri.si.fal′ik): brachycephalic with a cephalic index from .80 to .84.

euthermic (ū.thur′mik): inducing warmth.

eutrophied (ū′tro.fid): polluted.

evagation (ē′va.ga′shun, ev′a.-): mental wandering; digression.

evasé (ā′va.zā): enlarging gradually, as a chimney, funnel, etc.

Evernia (i.vur′ni.a): a genus of lichens. (not cap) Any lichen of this genus.

evertor (i.vur′ter): a muscle that rotates a part outward.

eviration (ē′vi.rā′shun): castration. 1.

evoe (e.vē′, i.vē′): an exclamation expressing exhilaration; the cry of bacchanals.

evolation (ev.o.lā′shun): a flying out or up. 1.

evulgate (i.vul′gāt): to publish, divulge.

ewery (ū.er.i): a room for pitchers, basins, towels, etc.

exagitation (ek.saj′i.tā′shun): a stirring up; agitation; harassment. 1.

exanimous (eg.zan′i.mus): lifeless.

exaugurate (eg.zôg′ū.rāt): to unhallow; desecrate.

excalceate (eks.kal′si.āt): to unshoe. 52.

excerebrose (ek.ser′i.brōs): brainless.

excide (ek′sīd′): to cut out, excise.

excircle (eks.sur′kl): in mathematics, an enscribed circle.

excogitation (eks.koj′i.tā′shun): a contrivance; the act of inventing or contriving.

excursus (eks.kur′sus): an appendix to a work, containing a more extended exposition of some point or topic. A digression; an incidental discussion.

excuss (eks.kus′): to shake off or out; discard. To investigate. 1. In civil law, to proceed against (a principal debtor) before falling back on a surety.

exergue (eg.zurg′, ek′surg): on a coin or medal, the segment beneath the base line of the subject, often with the date, place, or engraver's name.

exfodiate (eks.fō′di.āt): to dig out.

exheredate (eks.her′i.dāt): to disinherit.

exinanition (eg.zin′a.nish′un): an emptying, enfeeblement, humiliation, abasement.

exobiology (ek′so.bī.ol′o.ji): the study of life outside the earth.

exoculate (eg.zok′ū.lāt): to blind; to deprive of eyes.

exodic (eg.zod′ik): in physiology, conveying outward, or discharging; efferent.

exodromic (ek′so.drom′ik): relating to the movement of exchange between two countries designed to stabilize or fix the rates.

exogen (ek′so.jen): a plant that grows from the outside in.

exolve (eg.zolv): to slacken, diminish. 1.

exophagy (eg.zof′a.ji): cannibalism outside the tribe.

exorganic (eks′ôr.gan′ik): having lost organic character.

exornation (ek′sôr.nā′shun): an ornament, decoration.

exotropic (ek′so.trop′ik): curved away from the main axis.

expergefaction (eks.pur′ji.fak′shun): an awakening; the state of being awakened.

experientialism (eks.pēr′i.en′shal.izm): the doctrine that experience is the source of all knowledge.

expiscate (eks.pis′kāt): to search out; to investigate skillfully.

expromission (eks′pro.mish′un): in law, the act of binding oneself for another's debt.

expurger (eks.pur′jer): one that expurges; expurgater.

exsect (ek.sekt′): to cut out.

exsiccant (ek′si.kant): drying up; causing to dry up.

exspuition (eks′pū.ish′un): the act of spitting. 52.

exsuccous (eks.suk′us): dry, sapless.

extersion (eks.tur′shun): the act of wiping or rubbing out. 1.

extorsion (eks.tôr′shun): outward rotation (as of a body part) about an axis or fixed part.

extraforaneous (eks′tra.fo.rā′ni.us): outdoor.

extravagate (eks.trav′a.gāt): to rove; to exceed normal limits; to elaborate.

extusion (eks.tū′zhun): the act of beating or forcing (something) out. 52.

exuberous (eg.zū′ber.us): exuberant.

exundation (eks′un.dā′shun): an overflowing. 52.

eyot (ī′ut, āt): an islet.

F

faba (fā′ba): a genus of leguminous plants comprising the broad bean.

fabaceous (fa.bā′shus): of the nature of, or like, a bean.

fabular (fab′ū.lar): pert. to a fable.

fabulate (fab′ū.lāt): to fable. 1.

facette (fa.set′): facetious; witty. 9. Polished; elegant. 1.

facient (fā′shent): one that does something; a doer, agent.

factive (fak′tiv): making; having power to make. 1.

factum (fak′tum): in law, a man's own act and deed. The due execution of a will; a fact; event.

facundity (fa.kun′di.ti): eloquence.

fadge (faj): wheaten or barley flat cake. 45. A round thick loaf of bread. 44A. Potato cake or bread. 50A. A heavy package of wool. 53.

fadger (faj′er): one who or that which thrives or succeeds by fitting to surroundings. 9.

faff (faf): to blow in puffs. 44.

faffle (faf′l): to stammer; to mumble; to saunter; to fumble; (of a sail) to flap lazily. 2.

faffy (faf′i): blowing in puffs; puffy. 43.

fagin (fā′gin): a teacher of crime.

fagotto (fa.got′ō): a bassoon. An eight-foot pipe-organ stop of the same general quality as a bassoon.

faham (fä′am, fā′am): the leaves of an orchid used (in France) as a substitute for Chinese tea; also, the plant.

fainague, finagle (fi.nāg′, fi.nā′gl): to revoke at cards; hence, to shrink, to cheat.

falcade (fal.kād′): in equitation, the action of a horse in throwing itself on its haunches two or three times, bending in quick curvets.

faldistory (fal.dis′tō.ri): the throne or seat of a bishop within the chancel.

fallowchat (fal′o.chat): a wheatear.

falx (falks): a fold of the inner surface enveloping the brain.

Fama (fā′ma): rumor, personified.

famble (fam′bl): to stutter. 2.

familistere (fa.mē′li.stâr): a house for communal living.

famulus (fam′ū.lus): the servant of a medieval scholar or magician.

fangle (fang′gl): a silly or foolish contrivance; a gewgaw. 1.

fanion (fan′yun): a small flag orig. used by horse brigades, now by soldiers and surveyors to mark positions.

fantoccini (fan′to.chē′ni): puppets moved by machinery, or the shows in which they are used.

fantocine (fan′to.sēn): a puppet.

fard (färd): paint; to paint, as with cosmetics. Also, a kind of date tree.

fardh (färd): a commercial variety of date.

farkleberry (fär′kl.ber′i): a multi-seeded blackberry bush.

farraginous (fa.raj′i.nus): formed of various materials; mixed; hotchpotch. 52.

farruca (fa.rōōk′a): a Spanish gypsy dance having sudden changes of mood and tempo.

fascine (fa.sēn′): a long bundle of sticks, used for filling ditches, etc. To cover or strengthen with fascines.

fascis (fas′is): a bundle.

fash (fash): to vex; annoy. 43A.

fasset (fas′et): in glass manufacturing, a tool used to carry bottles to the annealing furnace.

fastigate (fas′ti.gāt): pointed.

fastigium (fas.tij′i.um): apex; summit; specif., the ridge of a house.

fatiferous (fa.tif′er.us): destructive; deadly.

fatiscent (fa.tis′ent): chinky. 52.

favaginous (fa.vaj′i.nus): like a honeycomb.

favilliferous (fav′il.if′er.us): producing lava.

favillous (fa.vil′us): of or resembling ashes.

feak (fēk): a lock of hair. 1. To twitch, fidget. 11. In falconry, to wipe (the hawk's beak) after feeding.

feal (fēl): faithful; loyal. 9.

februation (feb′rōō.ā′shun): exorcism; religious purification.

feck (fek): efficacy; force; value. 43. Amount; quantity. 44D.

feeze (fēz): to drive, impel, drive away, put to flight; to disturb, worry; to beat; rush; rub; a short run before a jump. 2. Fretful excitement or alarm. 27. To turn, as a screw. 44C. A heavy impact. 57.

feil (fēl): neat and cozy; comfortable. 44A.

feldspathic, felspathic (feld.spath′ik, fel.spath′ik): containing feldspar.

fellic (fel′ik): pert. to a crystalline acid present in human bile.

fellifluous (fe.lif′lōō.us): flowing with gall. 52.

fellness (fel′nes): destructive cruelty.

felloe, felly (fel′ō, -i): the exterior rim of a wheel, or part of it.

femcee (fem.sē′): a female emcee.

femerell (fem′er.el): a small open structure on a roof (as of a medieval kitchen) for ventilation or escape of smoke. 9.

feminate (fem′i.nāt): feminine; effeminate. 1.

fendy (fen′di): clever in providing; thrifty. 11.

feneration (fen′er.ā′shun): lending on interest. 1.

fenestella (fen′es.tel′a): a small window.

fenestral (fi.nes′tral): a window sash closed with cloth or translucent paper instead of glass. 9. Windowlike.

fent (fent): a remnant of cloth; an imperfect piece of goods. A slit or opening in a garment, esp. a neck opening. 13.

fenting (fen′ting): a type of Chinese porcelain with a soft-looking white glaze.

feracious (fi.rā′shus): fruitful; fertile.

feratory (fer′a.tō′ri): a bier. 52. A generally ornate bier for the relics of saints.

ferd (furd): an army; a large number; fear. 1.

fere (fēr): a mate, companion. 10. A peer. 1. To accompany; mate. 1. Sympathetic; companionable. 11. Able; healthy. 5.

feriation (fēr′i.ā′shun): the keeping of a holiday, esp. by not working.

ferly (fur′li): a sudden, surprising, or unusual sight; a marvel; an eccentricity, foible. 2. To amaze; wonder. 2.

fermentor (fer.men′ter): an apparatus for fermenting.

ferrumination (fe.rōō′mi.nā′shun): the act of soldering or uniting, as metals.

ferulaceous (fer′ōō.lā′shus): reedlike.

fervescent (fer.ves′ent): growing hot or feverish.

festilogy (fes.til′o.ji): historically, a treatise on church festivals.

festinate (fes′ti.nāt): to hasten. In a hurry. 52.

festine, festino (fes.tēn′, -tē′nō): a feast; entertainment.

festspiel (fest′shpēl): a festival play.

festuca (fes.tōō′ka): a large genus of grasses, the fescues. Among the Franks, a rod or staff given as a symbol to bind a contract.

fet (fet): to fetch. 11.

feu (fū): in Scots law, a fee; a tenure where the return is made in grain or money. Land so held. To grant (land) upon feu.

feudee (fū.dē′): a feudal tenant. 52.

fibble-fabble, fibble-fable (fib′l.fab′l, -fā′bl): nonsense. 11.

fibriphobia (fib′ri.fō′bi.a): fear of fever.

ficelle (fi.sel′): a device, trick. 21. Thread-colored. 2.

fiche (fēsh): a card; ticket; label.

fico (fē′kō): a fig. Also, a sign of contempt made by the fingers, signifying "a fig for you." 1.

fictor (fik′ter. -tor): one who fashions or shapes, esp. an artist. 1.

fiddleback (fid′l.bak): anything conceived of as shaped like a fiddle.

fideicommissum (fī′di.ko.mis′um): a bequest in which a decedent asks his heir to turn over a portion of the estate to another.

fidge (fij): an uneasy or restless motion or person. 44B. To fidget, esp. in eagerness or anxiety. 11.

fidicinal (fi.dis′i.nal): pert. to stringed instruments.

fidicula (fi.dik′ū.la): a small lyre-like stringed instrument; a lute.

fifinella (fif.i.nel′a): a female gremlin.

figulate (fig′ū.lat): made or molded of potter's clay. 52.

fike (fīk): to fidget; fuss; flirt. 45. To trouble; vex. 44. A whimsey; trifle. 43.

filaceous (fi.lā′shus): composed of threads. 52.

filicology (fil.i.kol′o.ji): *pteriodology*.

filiopietistic (fil′i.o.pī′e.tis′tik): pert. to ancestor worship.

filippo (fi.lip′po): a silver scudo struck at Milan by the Spanish under Philips II, III, and IV (1556–1665).

fillock (fil′uk): a wanton girl. 1.

fimble (fim′bl): the male hemp plant; its fiber. Also, to feel with the fingers moving lightly over (anything). 11.

fimbricate (fim′bri.kāt): fringed.

fimetarious (fim′i.târ′i.us): growing or living in excrement.

finewed (fin′ūd): moldy.

fingent (fin′jent): fashioning; molding.

finick (fin′ik): to mince; put on airs; dawdle.

finific (fi.nif′ik): to Coleridge, a limiting element or quality.

finitive (fin′i.tiv): in grammar, terminative.

fioritura (fyō.ri.tōō′ra): in music, an embellishment (usu. in pl., *fioriture*).

firk (furk): a freak; trick; a smart stroke, lash; to help, drive; to hasten, be frisky. 1. To beat; conquer. 9. To move jerkily; fidget. 14.

fiscus (fis′kus): the public treasury of Rome; esp. the branch that was most under imperial control.

fishgarth (fish′gärth): a dam or weir for keeping or taking fish.

Fissipedia (fis′i.pē′di.a): a suborder of Carnivora, including the land carnivores, as the dogs, cats, and bears.

fistiana (fis′ti.an′a): pugilistic anecdotes, records, etc.

fistuca (fis.too̅′ka): an instrument used by the ancients in driving piles.

fitchery (fich′er.i): (in mining) obstructive; containing an obstacle, or itself constituting one—said of ground in which a drill sticks.

fitchet (fich′et): the polecat of Europe.

flabrum (flā′brum): a fan; flabellum.

flacket (flak′et): a barrel-shaped bottle; flagon. 5.

flaminical (fla.min′i.kal): in Roman religion, pert. to a flamen—a priest devoted to the service of a particular god.

flammifer (flam′i.fer): something producing flame.

flammulated (flam′ū.lāt.ed): rusty, reddish.

flanch (flanch): a flange, esp. of a wheel. 41.

flanconnade (flang′ko.nȧd): in fencing, a maneuver ending in a thrust under the adversary's arm.

flatulopetic (flat′ū.lo.pet′ik): pert. to flatulence.

flaught (flôt): a flake; a flash of fire; a bit of wool or hair; turf. 44D. Flight; flutter; lying flat, with outstretched arms, eagerly. 44.

flavicomous (fla.vik′o.mus): having yellow hair.

fleam (flēm): a sharp lancet used for bloodletting. A stream, esp. a millstream.

---

*FLAVICOMOUS, AURICOMOUS
BY ANY OTHER NAME . . .*

Her lambent gaze came up, a full moon rising;
  And venturing the path of light it shed,
He touched and held her. (This is not surprising—
  Less moon drew Oceanus from his bed.)

Yet not of love triumphant is my story;
  I speak that other lovers may beware
Of giving to a woman's crowning glory
  A name that she has never heard for hair.

I know 'twas but the color he referred to,
  The while his fingers ran in worship through it;
But I suspect he really used the word to
  Impress her by displaying that he knew it.

He whispered that her tresser were *flavicomous* . . .
  She shuddered, and the moon grew sick and wan.
Then tenderly he labelled them *auricomous* . . .
  Down went the moon. She ordered him begone.

The moral of this sad account, young fellow,
  Is, *women like to ken what they are told.*
Why didn't he just say her hair was *yellow?*—
  Or (oh, she would have loved to hear it) *gold?*

---

flect (flekt): in heraldry, short for *flected,* bent-bowed.

fleech (flēch): coaxing; flattery. 44.

fleed, flead (flēd): the inside fat of a hog before it is melted into lard.

flench, flense (flench, flens): to strip the skin or blubber from (as a whale or seal).

flender (flen′der): to go fast. 35.

flerry (fler′i): to split—said of slate.

flet (flet): made from skimmed milk. 13. A plaited straw mat to protect the back of a packhorse. 44.

fleur (flur): the fleur-de-lys. An ornamental flower. A patterned woolen stuff like a Brussels carpet.

flexanimous (fleks.an′i.mus): mentally flexible.

flexiloquy (fleks.il′o.kwi): ambiguity of speech.

flittern (flit′ern): a young oak. 11.

floccilation (flok′si.lā′shun): an aimless semiconscious plucking at the bedclothes.

floccose (flok′ōs, flō.kōs′): woolly, flocculent. Of plants, having tufts of soft, woolly, often deciduous hairs.

flong (flong): a sheet of specially prepared paper used for making a matrix or mold.

flōta (flō′ta): a fleet of Spanish ships that sailed every year from Cadiz to Vera Cruz in Mexico to obtain the products of the Spanish colonies for Spain.

fluminous (floo̅′mi.nus): pert. to rivers; also, abounding in rivers and streams.

flump (flump): to set, move, or fall suddenly and heavily.

flustrum (flus′trum): fluster. 52.

flutina (floo̅.tē′na): a small musical instrument resembling the accordion.

fnast (fnast): breath; to pant. 1.

fnese (fnēz): to breathe heavily, snore. 1.

fogle (fō′gl): a silk handkerchief or neckerchief.

foliole (fō′li.ōl): a plant leaflet. In zoology, a small leaf-shaped organ or part.

follis (fol′is): a silver-coated Roman coin of the late Empire. A large bronze Byzantine coin of the 6th century.

fomento (fo.men′tō): patronage; encouragement.

fono (fō′nō): a Samoan council, the central political structure of a village, district, or island.

foozle (foo̅′zl): a bungler. To bungle, as a golf shot. 26.

fopdoodle (fop′doo̅.dl): a fool, an insignificant wretch. 1.

foraminous (fo.ram′i.nus): having small openings; porous.

foraneous (fo.rā′ni.us): pert. to a law court or a market.

forel, forrel (for′el): a sheath, a case. 4. A book jacket.

forisfamiliate (fō′ris.fa.mil′i.āt): to disinherit; to shed parental authority.

forlie (for.lī′): to deflower, to commit fornication or adultery. 1.

forme (fôr′me): first; former. 1. A form of heraldic crown.

formeret (fôr′mer.et): a wall rib in a roof vaulted with ribs.

fornent, fornenst (fôr.nent′, -nenst′): in front of; opposite. Near to; alongside. 11A.

forset (for.set′): to beset; invest; waylay. 2.

forslack (for.slak′): to hinder or delay by laziness; to be remiss. 1.

forslug (for.slug′): to lose by sluggishness. 1.

fortalice (fôr′ta.lis): a small fort, or an outwork of a fortification.

fossette (fo.set′): a little hollow; a dimple.

fou (foo): var. of *foul, full.* 15A. A bushel. 44.

foud (foud): a magistrate, sheriff, or bailie in the Orkney, Shetland, and Faroe islands.

fouter, foutre (foo̅′ter): a fig (a word of contempt). Something of little value. 9. A chap, fellow; an objectionable or tedious person; a worthless or bungling person. 44A.

foveola (fo.vē′o.la): a very small pit. In botany and embryology, a small depression.

fozy (fō′zi): of a vegetable, overgrown. Of a person, obese; also, fatheaded. 44A.

foziness (fō′zi.nes): sponginess; flabbiness; fat-wittedness; mugginess (of weather). 44D.

frab (frab): to scold, nag. 13.

fractile (frak′tīl, -til): fragile; also, of or pert. to fracture.

francisc (fran.sisk′): a battle-ax or hatchet used by the Franks, often as a missile.

franion (fran′yun): a paramour; a gay, idle fellow; a loose woman. 1.

frankalmoign (frangk′al.moin): a tenure in which a religious organization holds land on condition of praying for the souls of the donors.

frateries (frā′ter.iz): dining halls in monasteries.

frazil (fra.zil′, fraz′l, frā′zl): ice crystals within a body of water.

fream (frēm): to roar, as a boar in rut.

fremd (fremd): alien, strange, unfriendly. 2.

fremescence (fri.mes′ens): the state of being murmurous, or noisy. 52.

frescade (fres.kād′, -käd): a cool or shady place.

frett (fret): to prepare (materials for glass) by heat; to fuse partially.

frette (fret): a hoop of wrought iron or

steel, shrunk on a cast-iron gun to strengthen it.

fretum (frē'tum): a narrow waterway or canal.

friation (frī.ā'shun): act of breaking up or pulverizing.

fribby (frib'i): small; short—said of locks of wool.

fricandel (frik'an.del): a fried or boiled ball of minced meat mixed with bread crumbs, seasoning, and egg.

fricatrice (frik'a.tris): a lewd woman; a harlot. 52.

friggle (frig'l): to fuss. 13.

frim (frim): flourishing; thriving; juicy. 2.

fringent (frin'jent): (of uncertain meaning, used by Emerson in "a shower of meteors—lit by *fringent* air." Perh., as O.E.D. interprets, "exercising friction.")

fripper (frip'er): one who deals in frippery or old clothes. 1.

frist (frist): a delay. To grant a delay; to postpone. 1.

froise (froiz): a large, thick pancake, often with bacon in it. 2.

frondesce (fron.des'): to unfold leaves.

fronton (fron.ton'): a court or building for the game of jai alai or pelota.

frounce (frouns): curl, frizzle. 9. A disease of hawks, in which white spittle gathers about the bill. A disease of horses, marked by small warts on the palate.

fructescent (fruk.tes'ent): beginning to bear fruit. 52.

frugivore (fōō'ji.vôr): an animal, esp. a primate, that feeds on fruits.

frush (frush): the frog of a horse's hoof; the discharge from it. Thrush. Decayed to the point of brittleness; of soil, friable and mellow. 13. A din; a clash of weapons. 5. To rush. 1.

frustraneous (frus'trā'ni.us): vain, useless. 1.

fub (fub): a plump child. (var. of *fob*), to cheat. 1.

fubby, fubsy (fub'i, -si): plump; chubby: short and stuffy; as a *fubsy* sofa. 25A.

fucic (fū'sik): a gelatinous acid found in the fucoids and other algae.

fucivorous (fū.siv'o.rus): eating seaweeds.

fucous (fū'kus): pert. to the fucoids, a kind of seaweed.

fud (fud, food): the buttocks; the tail of a hare, rabbit, etc; woolen waste, for mixing with mungo and shoddy. 43.

fuff (fuf): puff; whiff; sputter. 43.

fuffit (fuf'it): the long-tailed titmouse.

fuffle (fuf'l): to be, or put, in disorder. 44.

fug (fug): reek. 21.

fugara (fōō.gä'ra): in music, a labial

organ stop of 8-foot or 4-foot pitch and of string quality.

fulgor (ful'ger): dazzling brightness; splendor.

fuligo (fū.lī'go): soot. Also, a widely distributed genus of slime molds.

fumacious (fū.mā'shus): smoky; hence, fond of smoking or addicted to tobacco.

fumado (fū.mä'dō): a salted and smoked pilchard.

fumage (fū'mij): hearth money. 6.

fumet, fumette (fū'met, fū.met'): a concentrated essence of game or fish, herbs, and spices used in flavoring a sauce.

fumid (fū'mid): smoky; vaporous. 1.

fumiduct (fū'mi.dukt): an outlet for smoke.

funambulist (fū.nam'bū.list): a tight-rope walker.

fundatrix (fun.dāt'riks): a female aphid that founds a new colony.

fundi (fun'di): a tropical African grass cultivated for its millet-like seed.

AN INGLE IS AN INSIDE ANGLE

Seek out the Elbow Ingle,
Ye bride and benedick;
Ye lovers, wed or single,
Seek out the Elbow Ingle,
The tender of the Tingle,
The turner of the Wick—
The ready Elbow Ingle,
Where nerve and vein commingle . . .
Seek out the Elbow Ingle—
A touch will do the trick.

---

funebrious, funebrous (fū.nē'bri.us, -nē'brus): funereal. 1.

funest (fū.nest'): portending death or evil; fatal, dire, doleful.

funiform (fū'ni.fôrm): resembling a cord or rope.

furacious (fū.rā'shus): thievish.

furca (fur'ka): a fork; yoke; instrument of torture. Any forked structure in an insect.

furibund (fū'ri.bund): furious, frenzied.

furole (fū.rōl'): St. Elmo's fire. 52. Also, furfural, a colorless oily liquid.

furtum (fur'tum): in Latin, theft.

fusarole (fū'za.rōl): a rounded molding placed beneath the capital of a Doric, Ionic, or Corinthian column.

fusc (fusk): of dusky or somber hue. 52.

fust (fust): mustiness; to taste or smell moldy or stale. 13. The shaft of a column or pilaster. A wine cask. 1. Dial. var. of *first*.

fustanella (fus'ta.nel'a): a short full skirt of stiffened white linen or cotton worn by men in some Balkan countries.

fyrd (furd, fērd): prior to the Norman conquest, the English armed forces; the duty of serving in them.

G

ga (gä): Scottish var. of *gall*. Also, an obsolete system of denoting the tones of a musical scale.

gabelle (ga.bel'): a tax. Specif., an impost on salt, levied in France for several centuries prior to the French Revolution.

gaddi (gad'i): in India, a cushion, esp. for a throne; hence, a throne. (cap) One of a low-caste people of Kashmir, mostly shepherds.

gaffle (gaf'l): a steel lever to bend a crossbow. A musket fork or rest. 6.

gair (gâr): a corner section of unplowed ground. Sharp, eager, greedy. 43.

galactophogy (gal'ak.tof'o.ji): milk-drinking.

galactophygous (gal.'ak.tof'i.gus): arresting the secretion of milk.

Galanthus (ga.lan'thus): a small genus of European bulbous herbs, the snow-drops.

galapago (ga.lä'pa.gō): one of the huge land tortoises of the Galapagos islands. Also a short cape.

galba (gal'ba): corruption of *calaba*, an evergreen tropical American tree.

galea (gā'li.a): in ancient Rome, a helmet. In zoology, a helmetlike structure of certain birds; part of the membrane enveloping a fetus, etc. In botany, any helmet-shaped part of a calyx or corolla.

galeanthropy (gal'i.an'thro.pi): the delusion that one has become a cat.

galee (gal'i): in India, abuse.

galeeny (ga.lē'ni): a guinea fowl. 13.

galenic (ga.len'ik): pert. to galena, or lead sulphide. (cap) Pert. to Galen, a noted physician of ancient Rome.

galera (ga.lē'ra): the tayra, a long-tailed mammal of South and Central America, related to the weasel.

galericulate (gal.er.ik'u.lāt): covered, as with a hat or cap.

galette (ga.let'): a flat, round pastry, usu. sweet. Also, a sea biscuit.

galipot (gal'i.pot): a crude turpentine formed by exudation upon the bark of the cluster pine in southern Europe.

Galium (gā'li.um): a genus of usu. trailing herbs, such as cleavers and wild licorice.

gallet (gal'et): a chip of stone; a spall. To fill in the fresh mortar joints of (rubble masonry) with gallets.

galliambic (gal'i.am'bik): in prosody, consisting of two iambic dimeters cataletic of which the last lacks the final syllable.

galliardise (gal´yer.diz): great merriment.

gallionic (gal´i.on´ik): indifferent; careless; irresponsible.

gallium (gal´i.um): a rare bluish white metallic element, obtained usu. as a byproduct in the extraction of aluminum from bauxite or of zinc from zinc ores.

gally (gôl´i): like gall; bitter as gall.

galp (gälp): a gaping. To yawn; to gape; to belch. 1.

galvanoplastic (gal´van.o.plas´tik, gal. van´o.-): employing the science of electroforming; something so formed.

gamashes (ga.mash´ez, gam´ash.-): leggings worn for protection by horsemen.

gambade (gam.bād´): a spring of a horse.

gamdeboo (gam´de.boo): a South African tree having tough wood.

gambist (gam´bist): a performer on the viola da gamba.

gambrinous (gam.brī´nus): full of beer.

gambroon (ga..n.broon´): a twilled cloth of linen, of linen and wool, or wool alone.

gammacism (gam´a.sizm): difficulty in pronouncing gutturals *(g, k)*. Childish talk.

gammadion (ga.mā´di.on): a cross resembling the swastika, made of four capital gammas.

gamophagia (gam´o.fā´ji.a): the destruction of one gamete by the other during fertilization.

gamophobia (gam´o.fō´bi.a): fear of sexual union.

ganancial (ga.nan´shal): relating to the Spanish system of law, which controls the title and disposition of property acquired during marriage by the husband or wife.

ganch (ganch): to execute by impaling on stakes or hooks.

gange (ganj): to fasten a fishhook to a line; to protect the line nearest the fishhook by winding it with fine wire.

ganza (gan´za): one of the birds that (in a romance by Bp. F. Godwin) bore Domingo Gonsales to the moon. 52.

ganzie (gan´zi): waste cotton cloth used as a wiping material around machinery or as rags for making paper.

gapo (ga.pō´): a forest that borders a river and is inundated in rainy seasons.

garce (gärs): a measure of capacity or weight in India.

garden (gär.dēn´): guardian. 1.

gardyloo (gär´di.loo): a warning cry used in Scotland when it was customary to throw household slops from upstairs windows.

gare (gär): coarse wool on the legs of a sheep. A depot. Beware!—take care! Violent excitement. 1. Keen, esp. covetous. 44.

garookuh (ga.roo´ku): a shallow-keeled fishing boat used in the Persian Gulf.

garum (gā´rum, gâr´um): a fish sauce of the ancient Greeks, prob. a sort of caviar.

gasogene, gazogene (gas´o.jēn, gaz-): an apparatus that produces a combustible gas for motor fuel by burning charcoal or wood.

gaster (gas´ter): in ants, the enlarged part of the abdomen behind the pedicel.

Gastornis (gas.tôr´nis): a genus of large extinct birds from the Eocene formations of the Paris basin, perhaps allied to the goose.

gastralgia (gas.tral´ji.a): pain in the stomach or epigastrium, esp. of a neuralgic type.

gastriloquy (gas.tril´o.kwi): ventriloquy.

gastromancy (gas´tro.man´si): divination by ventriloquism or crystal gazing.

gastropholite (gas.trof´o.līt): one fond of pampering the stomach. 52.

gateau (ga.tō´): cake, esp. a rich or fancy cake.

gaub (gôb): an East Indian persimmon tree; its fruit, which has strong astringent qualities.

gaud (gôd): a trick or fraud; a trinket; to make merry. 1.

gault (gôlt): a heavy clay; to cover (soil) with clay from the subsoil. 13. (cap) a series of Lower Cretaceous beds of clay and marl in southern England.

gavelock (gav´e.lok): a spear or dart; an iron crowbar or lever. 10.

gaw (gô): a drain; trench. 44A. To gape. 1. Var. of *gall*. 44C.

gawsie (gô´si): large and jolly; lusty. 43.

gazel, ghazel (gā´zel): a type of Arabic lyric, usu. erotic. An Arabian melody characterized by the frequent recurrence of a short refrain.

geck (gek): a dupe, object of scorn. 5. To scorn, cheat, trick. 45.

geegee (jē´ji): a horse. 26.

geest (gēst): alluvial matter of considerable age on the surface of the land. Loose earth or soil formed by decay of rocks.

gelastic (ji.las´tik): disposed to laugh.

gelogenic (jel´o.jen´ik): laughter-provoking.

geloscopy (ji.los´ko.pi): divination by interpretation of laughter.

Gelsemium (jel.sē´mi.um): a genus of woody vines incl. the yellow jasmine.

gemellipara (jem´e.lip´a.ra): a woman who has given birth to twins.

gena (jē´na): the cheek or lateral part of the head.

genappe (ji.nap´): a yarn used with silk in braids, fringes, etc.

genethlialogy (je.neth´li.al´o.ji): the art of casting nativities in astrology. Also, a theory of the lineage of the gods.

geniculum (ji.nik´ū.lum): a small knee-shaped anatomical structure.

geniophobia (jen´i.o.fō´bi.a): fear of chins.

genioplasty (jen´i.o.plas´ti): plastic surgery of the chin.

Genista (ji.nis´ta): an Old World genus of often spiny shrubs of the pea family, inc. the woodwaxen. (not cap) Any plant of this genus. The Canary broom.

gentianella (jen´shan.el´la): a blue color. Any of several large gentians having large blue flowers.

TEMPEST IN A FUFFIT NEST

There's scandal out in Birdland. One morning Mr. Fuffit

Was overseen delivering a mighty fuffit buffet

On little Mrs. Fuffit; he declared that she was dottle

For always building birdnests in the fashion of a bottle.

He faffed and drabbed and friggled, and he called her wicked words;

He said that she was fuffled, and her nests were for the birds.

A fallowchat said, "Dearie, what your husband really means

Is, you are on the wait-list for a two-room nest in Queens."

The bird was right, and (I suspect this won't be news to you)

The two-room nest in Queens is shaped much like a bottle too.

The Fuffits, though, are happy there, and gaily gibble-gabble;

They'll hear no talk of quarrels—they would call it fibble-fabble.

---

gentilitial (jen´ti.lish´al): pert. to a family or a people; national. Of gentle birth.

genuflex (jen´ū.fleks): to genuflect. 52.

geodic (ji.od´ik): pert. to a geode, a nodule of stone having a cavity lined with crystals or mineral matter.

geogenous (ji.oj´e.nus): growing in or on the ground.

geognost (jē´og.nost): one knowledgeable about the materials of the earth and its general exterior and interior constitution.

geogony (ji.og´o.ni): the science of the formation of the earth.

georama (jē´o.ram´a): a hollow globe on the inner surface of which is a map of the world, to be examined by one inside.

geoselenic (jē´o.si.len´ik): pert. to earth and moon.

geostatic (jē´o.stat´ik): in civil engineering, pert. to pressure exerted by the earth.

geotaxis, geotaxy (jē′o.tak′sis, -tak′si): a response to a stimulation in which the force of gravitation is the directive factor.

gephyrophobia (ji.fī′ro.fō′bi.a): fear of crossing bridges.

gerascophobia (jer.as′ko.fō′bi.a): fear of growing old.

geratic (je.rat′ik): pert. to old age; geriatric.

gerb. gerbe (jurb): a sheaf, as of wheat. A firework throwing a shower of sparks.

germon (jur′mun): albacore.

geromorphism (jer′o.môr′fizm): the condition of appearing older than one is.

gerontocomium (ji.ron′to.kō′mi.um): an institution for the care of the aged.

geysir (gī′ser): var. of *geyser*.

ghafir (ga.fēr′): in Egypt, a native guard or watchman.

gharri, gharry (gar′i): in India, a wheeled cart or carriage, often one for hire.

ghawazi (ga.wä′zi): Egyptian female dancers, who call themselves *Baramika* and do not marry outside of their tribe.

ghoom (goom): to hunt in the dark, in India.

ghurry (gur′i): a waterclock or other timepiece of India. A period of twenty-four minutes among Hindus; among Anglo-Indians, an hour.

giardinetto (ji.är′di.net′ō): precious stones arranged into a spray of flowers for a ring or brooch.

gibbed (jibd): castrated, as a cat.

gibby (gib′i): a walking stick with a crook; a similar stick of candy. 30.

gibel (gib′l): the crucian carp of Europe.

giglet (gig′let): a wanton; a lascivious woman. 9.

gigmanity (gig.man′i.ti): the worship of smug respectability as the great object in life; philistinism.

gillaroo (gil′a.roo): an Irish trout with thickened gizzard-like inner walls for crushing the shells of freshwater mollusks.

gilliver (jil′i.ver): the common wallflower of Europe.

gillygaloo (gil′i.ga.loo): a mythical bird that lays square eggs. 21.

gilravage (gil.rav′ij): a noisy celebration. To frolic in a disorderly fashion.

gimble (gim′bl): to make a wry face, grimace. 11.

gime (gīm): a hole made when water pours through a leak in an embankment.

gimmal (gim′l): joined work (as clockwork) whose parts move within each other. Made or consisting of gimmals.

gipon (ji.pon′, jip′on): a tight-fitting garment like a shirt often worn under medieval armor; a jupon.

gippo (jip′ō): a short tunic or cassock; also, a scullion, varlet. 1.

Gir (jir): a breed of medium-sized Indian cattle of dairy type, having a distinctive dull red or brown speckling on a white background. An animal of this breed.

girn (gurn): to snarl, whine, bare the teeth in rage. 2, 44C.

gish (gish): in Moroccan public domain, land subject to usufructuary rights.

gittern (git′ern): a medieval wire-strung musical instrument like a guitar, played with a plectrum.

givy (givy): relaxed. 32.

gizz (giz): a wig. 43.

gladius (glā′di.us): the internal shell of a cuttlefish or squid.

glandaceous (glan.dā′shus): acorn-colored.

Glaswegian (glas.wē′jan): a native or inhabitant of Glasgow, Scotland; pert. to Glasgow.

glaucescent (glô.ses′ent): having a somewhat glaucous appearance; becoming glaucous.

glebous (glē′bus): full of clods; like a clod; earthy. 52.

gleek (glēk): a gibe, jest, practical joke; a flirtatious glance. 2. To gain an advantage (as by trickery). 9. An old three-handed card game.

glenoid (glē′noid): in anatomy, having the form of a smooth shallow depression, as the cavity of the scapula.

gliff (glif): a fleeting glance, faint sound, brief moment, or sudden shock. To frighten. 5A.

glin (glin): haze on the horizon at sea, signaling an approaching storm.

glink (glingk): to look at slyly, sideways. 43.

glist (glist): mica. A gleam. To glisten. 1.

globaloney (glōb′a.lō′ni): softheaded world politics, as described by Clare Booth Luce.

gloff (glof): a shock; a scare. To feel a shock. 44.

glom (glom): to take, steal, swipe. 21.

glome (glōm): a ball or clue, as of thread. 1.

glommox (glom′uks): a conglomeration; muss. 12.

glose (glōz): var. of *gloze*.

glot (glot): Alistair Reid's word for a person who cannot bear to waste anything.

glottonogonic (glo.ton′o.gon′ik): pert. to the origin of language.

glucic (gloo′sik): referring to an acid obtained as a viscid syrup by the action of lime or baryta on glucose.

glucina (gloo.sī′na): beryllia.

gluck, gluck-gluck (gluk, gluk′gluk): a gulping sound.

glutenous (gloo′ti.nus): resembling or containing gluten.

glutition (gloo.tish′un): the act of swallowing.

glycolimia (glī′ko.lim′i.a): a craving for sweets.

glyphography (glī.fog′ra.fi): a process for making relief printing plates, first engraving the design on a wax-covered matrix.

Glyptodon (glip′to.don): a genus of large extinct mammals related to the armadillos.

glyptotheca (glip.to.thē′ka): a building or room devoted to works of sculpture.

gnathonic, gnathonical (na.thon′ik, -ik.al): flattering, deceitful.

gnoff (nof): a lout, boor. 1.

gnomonics (no.mon′iks): the art or science of constructing dials, esp. sundials.

gnosiology (nō′si.ol′o.ji): the theory of the origin, nature, and validity of knowledge; epistemology.

goaf (gōf): a mow or rick of grain or hay, stored in a born; a bay of a barn. 13.

gobby (gob′i): rough or uneven; lumpy; in gobs; also, viscous. 11A.

gobemouche (gōb′moosh′): a gullible person; lit., a fly-swallower.

goff (gof): a silly clown; a foolish fellow. 11.

goggan (gog′an): a small wooden or metal dish or noggin; a game played with such vessels. 13.

gola (gō′la): a warehouse for grain in India. (cap.) An Indian caste, chiefly engaged in preparing rice and salt.

Golo (gō′lō): one of a Nilotic tribe in eastern Sudan.

gombeen (gom.bēn′): usury. 50.

gombroon (gom.broon′): a kind of white semiporcelain.

gomer (gō′mer): a conical chamber at the breech of the bore in old smoothbore ordnance. (cap) A northern people from the Armenian highlands; also, wife of the prophet Hosea.

gomphiasis (gom.fī′a.sis): looseness of the teeth.

gomuti (go.moo′ti): a Malayan feather palm, yielding sweet sap from which palm wine is made.

gonemous (gō′ni.mus): bearing many children.

gonfalon, gonfanon (gon′fa.lon, -non): the small pennant attached to a knight's lance. A lance that flies a pennant.

gony, goney (gō′ni): a booby; dunce. 2. Any of several large seabirds, esp. the black-footed albatross and the young of the black-tailed albatross.

gool (gōol): a ditch or sluice. A breach in a bank or seawall; a fissure. 13.

goolah (gōo′la): in India, an earthen water vessel.

goozle (gōo′zl): guzzle. 11.

goracco (go.rak′ō): a tobacco paste smoked in hookahs.

gorbelly (gôr′bel.i): a prominent belly; a big-bellied person. 2.

goric (gor′ik): in Breton folklore, one of a class of malevolent spirits supposed to dance about monoliths.

gork (gôrk): one who has lost mental function from senility, stroke, etc.

gorp (gôrp): a mixture of dried fruits and nuts, seeds, and the like. 32.

gotch (goch): a bulging jug or pitcher. 13.

gradatim (grā.dā′tim): step by step; gradually.

graffer (graf.er): a notary or scrivener. 1.

graip (grāp): a pitchfork or dungfork. 45.

graith (grāth): readiness. 1. Furniture, apparel. 5. Material, also soapy water. 44A. Ready; prepared. 1. To build. 1. To furnish, adorn. 44C.

grallatorial, grallatory (gral′a.tō′ri.al, -tō′ri): pert. to the Grallatores, or wading birds.

grallic (gral′ik): grallatorial.

grammaticaster (gra.mat′i.kas′ter): a petty grammarian; a grammatical pedant.

grammatolatry (gra.ma.tol′a.tri): the worship of letters or words.

granadillo (gran′a.dil′ō): the granadilla tree. Any of various tropical American passion flowers, or their oblong fruit.

grandgousier (grän′gōo.zyā): a glutton.

granza (gran′za): mercury ore in pieces over an inch in diameter.

graphospasm (graf′o.spazm): writer's cramp.

gratten (grat′en): stubble. 11.

gravedo (gra.vē′dō): a head cold.

gravic (grav′ik): pert. to gravitation. 52.

gravimeter (gra.vim′i.ter): an instrument to measure weight or density.

grece (grēs): a flight of steps; also, a step in a flight. 2.

greenth (grēnth): green growth; verdure.

greffier (gref′i.er): a register or recorder.

gregal (grē′gal): pert. to a flock. 9. Gregarious. 1.

gregale (grā.gä′le): a dry, cold northeast wind over Malta.

grege, greige (grāzh): a textile in an early stage of preparation.

grego (grē′gō, grä′gō): a short hooded jacket or cloak of thick, coarse cloth, worn in the Levant and formerly by seamen.

gremial (grē′mi.al): pert. to the lap or bosom; specif., eccl., pert. to an apron used by a bishop when seated at Mass or when anointing during ordination ceremonies. The apron itself. Intimate, "bosom"; hence, in history, having a full or resident membership in a society or university. 6. A bosom friend. 1.

grenado (gri.nā′dō): a grenade. 9.

gressible (gres′i.bl): able to walk.

grice (grīs): a young pig. 9, 17A.

griffe (grif): the offspring of a black and a mulatto. A person of mixed black and American Indian blood (also *griff*). In architecture, an ornament resembling a claw that projects from the round base of a column.

griffonage (grif.o.näzh): careless handwriting; an illegible scribble.

grike (grīk): a crevice; chink; ravine. 13. A narrow opening in a fence that allows people but not farm animals to get through.

grimme (grim): a small West African antelope, colored deep bay.

griph (grif): a puzzle; enigma. A vulture. 1.

gripple (grip′l): a drain; ditch. 10.

grisamber (grēs′am′ber): ambergris. 1.

griskin (gris′kin): the spine of a hog; the lean part of a pork loin; a small piece of meat for roasting. 41.

grivoiserie (gri.vwä′zer.i): a lewd act; lewd and lascivious behavior.

grobianism (grō′bi.a.nizm): rudeness; boorishness.

gromatics (gro.mat′iks): the science of surveying. 1.

grues (grōoz): Robert Louis Stevenson's word for Little Willies and other such gruesome rhymes.

grummel (grum′el): sediment; dregs. 2.

grumph (grumf): grunt. 44.

Grundyism (grun′di.izm): prudish conventionalism.

grunge (grunj): something bad, inferior, ugly, or boring.

grylli (gril′i), (pl. of *gryllos*): a comic combination of animals or of animal and human forms in Greco-Roman glyptic arts, esp. in intaglios.

Gryllus (gril′us): a genus of Old World crickets.

guarana (gwä′ra.nä): a Brazilian climbing shrub yielding caffeine from leaves and bark; a paste made from it; an astringent drink from the paste.

gufa (gōo′fa): a round boat made of wickerwork used in ancient Mesopotamia.

guffer (guf′er): the eelpout. 44.

guffin (guf′in): an awkward person. 21A. (pl.) Very large feet. 35.

guggle (gug′l): the windpipe. 21A. A sound of guggling, a gurgle. 25.

THE FABULOUS HUNT OF THE JACKAROO

Do you recall the jackaroo
  Who left his sheep at home
To hunt the wily kangaroo
  That skulks through frosty Nome?

(Would he have went had he but knew,
  As many might explain,
That *several* sorts of kangaroo
  Bound on the bounding main?—
The walleroo—the poteroo—
  The kangaroo again?)

He sat in shade of gamdeboo
  To rest him from his search.
Although the tree wore gingham blue
  In readiness for church,
She stayed at home; 'twould never do
  To leave him in the lurch.

He shook his jug of hoochinoo,
  And offered her a quaff,
And sang, and played the digerydoo
  To make the good tree laugh.

Then up there swam a gillaroo,
  And much that trout did please them;
They fed it bones of cockatoo
  So its insides could squeeze them.

A square-egg-laying gillygaloo
  Refused in manner curt
To lay a square egg for the two—
  She said that it would hurt.

A wolf leaped out with tingling cry—
  A fearful kabaru!
The jackaroo prepared to die,
  And uttered pililoo.

Up jumped a sleepy kinkajou,
  And bit that wolf in twain,
And gently kicked the jackaroo,
  And went to sleep again.

The jackaroo when home he came
  Brought nary a kangaroo.
His sheep baaed welcome all the same
  With lullilulliloo.

---

guignol (gi.nyol′): puppet; a puppet show. (cap) The main character in a French puppet show.

guitguit (gwēt′gwit): any of several small tropical American honey creepers.

gula (gū′la): the upper front of the neck, next to the chin; the gullet. In some insects, a plate forming the lower surface of the head. In architecture, one or more moldings having a large hollow; also, an ogee, or S-shaped curve.

gulosity (gū.los′i.ti): greed; gluttony.

gummastic (gum.mas′tik): an aromatic resinous sap obtained from mastic trees; mastic.

gunation (goo.nā′shun): in Sanskrit grammar, a strengthening of the simple vowels by prefixing an *a* element to each.

gundi (gun′di): a short-tailed rodent, about 8 inches long, related to the porcupines, cavies, chinchillas, etc.

gup (gup): an exclamation of reproof, derision, or remonstrance. 1. In India, gossip.

gurk (gurk): a fat person. 44.

gurl (gurl): to growl; howl. 44A.

gurly (gur′li): rough; boisterous; also, surly. 44A.

gurt (gurt): a trench; drain. Also, dial. Eng. var. of *great.*

guss (gus): in mining, a dragrope. 41.

gussie (gus′i): swine; pig. 43.

gutling (gut′ling): a glutton. 2.

guttatim (gu.tā′tim): drop by drop (used in prescriptions).

guttle (gut′l): to gormandize.

gyascutus (jī′as.kū′tus): an imaginary beast with legs longer on one side than the other, so that it walks easily, but in only one direction, on steep hillsides.

gyle (gīl): a brewing. The beer produced at one brewing. Malt in the process of fermentation added to stout or ale.

gymnophobia (jim′no.fō′bi.a): fear of nudity.

Gymnotus (jim.nō′tus): a genus of South American cyprinoid fishes that sometimes includes the electric eel.

gynecocentric (jī′ni.ko.sen′trik): centering on or in the female, as a *gynecocentric* society.

gynecophobia (jī′ni.ko.fō′bi.a, jin′i-): morbid fear of women.

gyneolatry (jī′ni.ol′a.tri, jin′i-): worship of women.

gynesic (ji.nes′ik): pert. to femaleness.

gynocratic (jī′no.krat′ik, jin′o-): pert. to government by women.

gynotikolobomassophile (jī.not′i.ko.lō′-bo.mas′o.fīl, jin′ot-, -fil): one who likes to nibble on women's earlobes.

gyromancy (jī.ro.man′si, jir′o.-): divination by walking in a circle until falling from dizziness, the place of the fall determining one's fortune.

gyropigeon (jī′ro.pijun): a clay pigeon or similar target.

gyrovagues (jī′ro.vāgz): monks who wander from monastery to monastery.

H

haboob (ha.boob′): a violent dust storm or sandstorm of northern Africa or India.

habromania (hab′ro.mā′ni.a): extreme euphoria.

Hadrosaurus (had′ro.sô′rus): a genus of heavy herbivorous dinosaurs found in the Cretaceous of North America that attained a length of over thirty feet.

haecceity (hek.sē′i.ti): thisness; specificity. The character of being here and now.

Haemanthus (hi.man′this): a genus of African herbs often called *blood lilies* or *blood-flowers.*

haffle (haf′l): to stammer; also, to quibble. 13.

hafter (haf′ter): one who makes or fits hafts or handles.

hagia (hā′ji.a): holy things; specif. (cap), the consecrated bread and wine in the Eucharist.

hagiolatry (hag′i.ol′a.tri): the worship of saints.

hagiophobia (hag′i.o.fō′bi.a): morbid dread of holy things.

haikai (hī′kī): an often playful type of Japanese verse or prose cultivated in the later feudal ages.

hairif (här′if, har′if): goose grass or other kinds of cleavers. 13.

Hakka (häk′kä): a distinct strain of the Chinese people in southeastern China.

hala (hä′la): a common Pacific-island screw pine whose fiber is woven into coarse mats.

halieutics (hal′i.ū′tiks): fishing.

haliography (hal′i.og′ra.fi): description of the sea.

halituous (ha.lit′ū.us): related to breath, vapor, exhalation.

hallelujatic (hal′i.loo.yat′ik): pert. to or containing hallelujahs.

halma (hal′ma): in ancient Greece, the long jump with weights in the hands—the first exercise of the pentathlon.

halobiotic (hal′o.bī.ot′ik): relating to the total oceanic flora and fauna.

halomancy (hal′o.man′si): divination by salt.

halophile (hal′o.fīl, -fil): an organism flourishing in saltwater.

hals, halse (hals): the neck, throat, windpipe. A pass or defile. 13.

hamartiology (ha.mär′ti.ol′o.ji): that part of theology which treats of sin.

hamartithia (ham.är.tith′i.a): proneness to mistakes.

hamartiophobia (ha.mär′ti.o.fō′bi.a): fear of sin or sinning.

hamble (ham′bl): to cut off the balls of dogs' feet to make them useless for hunting. To limp. 1.

hamiform (hā′mi.fôrm): hook-shaped.

hamirostrate (hā′mi.ros′trāt): having a hooked beak.

hamman (ham′an): a building or room for bathing; a Turkish bath.

hamus (hā′mus): in biology, a hook or curved process.

hanif (ha.nēf′): a pre-Islamic hermit of Arabia who lived a wandering ascetic life and professed a vague form of monotheism.

hankle (hang′kl): to fasten; entangle; twist. 13.

haole (hä′o.lā): a white or a foreigner in Hawaii.

Hapi (hä′pi): in Egyptian religion, one of the four genii of Amenti, the region of the dead. Also, Apis, a sacred bull believed to be the embodiment of Ptah, father of gods and men. Also, the Nile, represented as a fat man, flower-crowned, and wearing a loincloth.

haplography (hap.log′ra.fi): the inadvertent omission in writing of adjacent and similar letters, syllables, and words, as *intususception* for *intussusception.*

haptodysphoria (hap′to.dis.fôr′i.a): the unpleasant sensation some feel when touching peaches, cotton, or such surfaces.

harageous (ha.rā′jus): rough and bold; stern, cruel. 1.

haramaitism (har′a.mā′i.tizm): the Hindu practice of child marriage.

hardock (här′dok): the burdock.

harengiform (ha.ren′ji.fôrm): herring-shaped.

hariolation (har′i.o.lā′shun): the act or practice of deduction; guesswork. Ventriloquism.

harlock (här.lok): burdock; prob. corruption of *charlock* or *hardock.*

harmine (här′min): a white crystalline alkaloid found in harmel seeds.

harmonicon (här.mon′i.kon): a harmonica. An orchestrion.

harmoniphon (här.mon′i.fon): an obsolete wind instrument with a tone resembling that of the oboe.

harpactophagous (här.pak.tof′a.gus): predatory—used esp. of insects.

harpaxophobia (här.pak′so.fō′bi.a): fear of robbers or of being robbed.

harpocratic (här′po.krat′ik): pert. to silence.

harquebusade (här′kwi.bus.ād′): a discharge of fire from one or more harquebuses.

hassar (has′er): any of several catfishes of the Orinoco and its tributaries, remarkable for their nest-building habits and their ability to travel some distance on land.

hasta (hus′ta): symbolic positions of the fingers and hands employed in iconography and in dramatic dancing.

hatchel (hach′el): an instrument with long iron teeth, set in a board, for cleansing flax or hemp.

haustrum (hôs′trum): a recess in the colon.

haver (hav′er): an oat; esp., volunteer or uncultivated oats. Tall oat grass. (hā′ver): To hem and haw. 40A. A comrade or associate. In Scots law, the holder of a deed.

havier (hāv′yer): a castrated deer.

havior (hāv′yer): property. 1. Behavior; demeanor. 10.

haya (hā′a, hā′ya): an arrow poison used by natives on the west coast of Africa, said to be derived from sassy bark.

haybote (hā′bōt): in English law, wood or thorns allowed a tenant for repair of hedges or fences; the right to take such material.

haznadar (haz.na.där): in Turkey, a treasurer.

heald (hēld): in weaving, a harness or heddle.

hebetant (heb′i.tant): making dull, as blunting the cutting edge of a knife.

hederaceous (hed′er.ā′shus): growing ivy.

hederate (hed′er.āt): to decorate with ivy.

hederiferous (hed′er.if′er.us): *hederaceous.*

hederigerate (hed′er.ij′er.āt): pert. to ivy; ivy-covered.

heeze (hēz): hoist, exalt. 14.

heinie (hī′ni): the buttocks. 21. (cap) A German, German soldier, German airplane, or the like. 22A.

helcotic (hel.kot′ik): ulcerated.

helicity (hi.lis′i.ti): in nuclear physics, the direction of the spin of an elementary particle.

heliochrome (hē′li.o.krōm): a photograph in natural colors.

heliolater (hē′li.ol′a.ter): a sun worshiper.

heliophilous (hē′li.of′o.lus): attracted by sunlight.

Heliornis (hē′li.ôr′nus): a genus of finfoots consisting of a single species, the sun-grebe.

heliosis (hē′li.ō′sis): sunstroke.

helispheric, helispherical (hel′i.sfer′ik, -i.kal): winding, like a spiral, on a sphere.

hellanodic (hel′a.nod′ik): an official at an Ancient Greek game or combat, serving as a herald or judge.

hellhag (hel′hag): an evil old woman; a hellcat.

hellkite (hel′kīt): a fierce bird of prey; an extremely cruel person.

helminthology (hel′min.thol′o.ji): the study of worms, esp. parasitic worms.

helminthophobia (hel.min′tho.fō′bi.a): fear of worms.

helosis (hi.lō′sis): the condition of having corns.

helotomy (hi.lot′o.mi): the cutting of corns.

hemeral (hem′er.al): in geology, pert. to the time range of a particular fossil species. Pert. to a period of time during which a race of organisms is at the apex of its evolution.

hemeralopia (hem′er.a.lō′pi.a): a condition in which one can see well only at night.

hemeraphonia (hem′er.a.fō′ni.a): a condition in which one can hear or speak only at night.

hemipenis (hem′i.pē′nis): one of the paired sex organs of lizards and snakes.

henhussy (hen′hus.i): a man who does housework.

henotic (he.not′ik): harmonizing, pacific.

HASSAR: A CATFISH THAT BUILDS NESTS AND WALKS ON LAND

I met a dear old catfish as I walked the road to Vassar;

She dropped a humble curtsey, and said, "Sir, I am a hassar;

And begging of your pardon, sir, I've trudged a weary way,

And sun is hard on catfish in the middle of the day;

So would you be so kind, sir, as to help me build a nest

Where I can stretch my aching fins and take a fishy rest?"

"With pleasure, Madam," I replied; and as I laid a heap

Of straw she knelt, and prayed, "Dear Lord, I lay me down to sleep."

And as she slept I lit the straw, and soon I had her basted.

As sweet a piece of catfish as a fellow ever tasted.

---

hent (hent): to seize, lay hold of, carry off. 9, 11.

heptaglot (hep′ta.glot): using seven languages. A book in seven languages.

Heptameron (hep.tam′er.on): a French collection of tales, modeled upon Boccaccio's *Decameron.*

herbulent (hur′bū.lent): containing herbs.

heraism (hē′ra.izm): faithfulness in marriage.

heresiography (her′i.si.og′ra.fi): a treatise on heresy.

heresyphobia (her′i.si.fō.bi.a): hatred of heresy.

herl (hurl): a barb of a feather used in dressing artificial flies. A fly so dressed.

herle (hurl): a heron. 44.

hern, herne (hurn): a corner, a nook. 11.

heroogony (hē′ro.og′o.ni): a genealogy of heroes.

herpetoid (hur′pi.toid): like a reptile. 52.

herse (hurs): a harrow. 2. A harrow-like battle formation. A frame for drying skins. A spiked portcullis; a hearse. 2. (cap) A Greek goddess of the dew.

hestern (hes′tern), hesternal (hes.-tur′nal): pert. to yesterday. 1.

hesychastic (hes′i.kas′tik): soothing, calming—said of a style of ancient Greek music. Also, pert. to the 14th-century *Hesychasts,* who believed they could see a divine light by gazing at their navels.

het (het): dial. past and past participle of *heat.*

heterize (het′er.īz): to transform.

hetero (het′er.ō): attracted to members of the opposite sex; not homosexual.

heteroclite (het′er.o.klīt): deviating from ordinary forms or rules; irregular, anomalous, abnormal. One that deviates in this fashion. In grammar, a word of irregular inflection.

heterogene (het′er.o.jén): heterogeneous.

heterogony (het′er.og′o.ni): in botany, the state of having two or more hermaphrodite or perfect flowers. In biology, the alternation of generations between the sexual and the asexual.

heteropathic (het′er.o.path′ik): morbidly or abnormally sensitive to stimuli.

Heterophagi (het′er.of′a.jī): the altrices, birds having their young hatched in a very helpless condition, so as to require care for some time.

heterophobia (het′er.o.fō′bi.a): fear of or aversion to those of the opposite sex.

heterotaxis (het′er.o.tak′sis), heterotaxy (het′er.o.tak′si): abnormal arrangements, as of organs of the body, geological strata, etc.

heterotelic (het′er.o.tel′ik): existing for something else; having an extraneous end or purpose—contrasted with *autotelic.*

heterotopic (het′er.o.top′ik): in medicine, relating to a shift in position, as of an organ or growth.

heterotropic (het′er.o.trop′ik): in physics, showing different properties in different directions—not isotropic.

heuretic (hoo.ret′ik): the logic of discovery.

hexaglot (hek′sa.glot): using six languages. A book in six languages.

hexameron (heks.am′er.on): the six days of creation.

hexamerous (heks.am′er.us): in botany and geology, having six parts.

hia (hē′a): the hawk parrot.

hiant (hī′ant): gaping.

Hibernicism (hī.bur′ni.sizm): Irishness; an Irish trait.

hidrotic (hī.drot′ik): causing sweating. A medicine that causes sweating.

hield (hēld): a slope or incline. 1. To incline, tilt, be favorable. 2. To decline, droop. 4. To yield, turn away. 1.

hierography (hī′er.og′ra.fi): descriptive writing on sacred subjects.

hieromachy (hī′er.om′a.ki): a dispute between ecclesiastics.

hieromancy (hī′er.o.man′si): divination by interpreting sacrifices.

Hilaria (hi.lā′ri.a): a genus of grasses of the southwestern United States and Mexico, incl. the curly mesquite grass of Texas.

hilding (hil′ding): a base wretch or jade; mean, cowardly. 9.

hilum, hilus (hī′lum, -lus): in botany, a scar on a seed (as a bean) where an ovule is attached to the stalk. In anatomy, a notch in a bodily part suggestive of a hilum.

hindermate (hin′der.māt): a mate who is a hindrance rather than a help.

hinnible (hin′i.bl): able to whinny. 52.

hipe (hīp): a throw in which a wrestler lifts his opponent from the ground and throws him on his back. To throw by means of a hipe.

hippiater (hip′i.ā′ter): a horse doctor.

hippiatric (hip′i.at′rik): pert. to the diagnosis and treatment of diseases of the horse.

hippocaust (hip′o.côst): the burning of a horse in sacrifice.

hippocerf (hip′o.surf): a monster combining horse and stag.

hippocrepiform (hip′o.krep′i.fôrm): horseshoe-shaped.

hippomania (hip′o.mā′ni.a): a passion for horses.

hippometer (hi.pom′e.ter): an upright with a movable arm to measure the height of a horse.

hippophagan, hippophagous (hi.pof′-a.gan, -gus): eating horseflesh.

hippophile (hip′o.fīl): a lover of horses.

hippopotomonstrosesquipedalian (hip′-o.pot′o.mon′stro.ses′kwi.pi.dā′-li.an): pert. to a longer than sesquipedalian word.

hipsy (hip′si): a drink made of wine, water, and brandy.

hirci (hur′si): armpit hair.

hircinous (hur′si.nus): having a goaty smell.

hircismus (her.siz′mus): a smell as of a goat.

hirmos, hirmus (hur′mos, -mus): in the Eastern Church, a verse used as a standard rhythmic and melodic pattern for troparions, hymns, or canticles.

hirondelle (hir′on.del): a swallow.

hirple (hur′pl): a limp. To hobble, walk with a limp. 44A.

hirsel, hirsle (hur′sl): a herd, flock, pasture ground; a large number or quantity; to arrange as in flocks. 44A. To hitch along; slither; move with a rustle or restlessly. 44.

hirsutorufous (her.sū′to.rōō′fus): red-haired.

historionomer (his.tôr′i.on′o.mer): one versed in the laws or principles governing historical phenomena.

histrio (his′tri.ō): a stage player or dancer. 1.

hobbadehoy, hobbledehoy (hob′a.di.hoi, hob′l-): a youth entering manhood.

hoddypeak (hod′i.pēk): a fool. 1.

hodiernal (hō′di.ur′nal): of this day.

hodman (hod′man): a hod carrier; a hack; assistant.

hodophobia (hod′o.fō′bi.a): fear of road travel.

hoggerel (hog′er.el): a boar of the second year; a yearling sheep in its first fleece; a yearling colt. 2.

hoitzitzillin (hoit.zit.zil′en): a showy American bird.

hoker (hō′ker): scorn; derision. To scorn, mock. 1.

holagogue (hol′a.gog): a medication that removes all trace of a disease.

holarctic (hol.ärk′tik, hōl.-): pert. to the Arctic regions collectively.

holluschick (hol′us.chik): a young male fur seal; a bachelor.

holmgang (hōm′gang): a duel, esp. one fought on an island.

holocryptic (hol′o.krip′tik): wholly concealing; incapable of being deciphered without a key.

holodactylic (hol′o.dak.til′ik): in classical prosody, having all its feet (except the last) dactyls; said of a hexameter.

holomorphic (hol′o.môr′fik): in mathematics, designating a certain function of a complex variable. Of crystals, symmetrical in form as regards the two ends.

holophrasis (ho.lof′ra.sis): a whole phrase or idea expressed in one word.

holus-bolus (hō′lus.bō′lus): all at once; altogether.

homichlophobia (hō′mi.klo.fō′bi.a): fear of fog.

homilophobia (hom′i.lo.fō′bi.a): fear of sermons.

homodox (hom′o.doks): having the same opinion. 1.

homogeny (ho.moj′e.ni): in biology, correspondence between parts or organs due to descent from the same ancestral type.

homogony (ho.mog′o.ni): of a plant, the state of having one kind of flower, with stamen and pistil of equal length, as distinguished from heterogony.

homophobia (hō′mo.fō′bi.a): fear of sameness or monotony.

homotaxis, homotaxy (hō′mo.tak′sis, -si): similarity in arrangement. In geology, similarity in order of arrangement of stratified deposits.

homuncle (ho.mung′kl): a homunculus.

hondo (hon′dō): a broad, deep gully or dry gulch.

hoochinoo (hōō′chi.nōō): an alcoholic beverage distilled from boiled farina and flour by the Hoochinoo Indians of Alaska.

hordaceous (hor.dā′shus): pert. to barley.

horme (hôr′mi): vital energy as an urge to purposeful activity.

horography (ho.rog′ra.fi): the making of clocks, watches, sundials, etc.

horral (hôr′al): a kind of small wheel or caster. 44.

horreum (hôr′i.um): in antiquity, a building for storage, esp. of grain.

horrisonant (ho.ris′o.nant): horrible-sounding.

hortensian (hor.ten′shi.an, -shun): grown in a garden.

hospodar (hos′po.där): a governor of Moldavia and Walachia under Turkish rule.

hougher (hok′er): one that hamstrings cattle; specif., one of a band of 18th-century lawbreakers in Ireland.

housal (houz′al): pert. to the house; domestic. 1.

housebreak (hous′brāk): housebreaking. 1.

housel (hou′zl): the Eucharist or the act of administering or receiving it. To administer the Eucharist to. 9.

hoveler (hov′el.er, huv-): a coast boatman who does odd jobs in assisting ships. His boat. 41.

hoven (hō′ven): of an animal, afflicted with bloat; to bloat.

howadji (hou.aj′i): in the East, formerly, a traveler or merchant, merchants being the chief travelers there.

howel (hou′el): a cooper's plane for smoothing the insides of casks. A rounded cut above and below the croze in a barrel stave.

hoyman (hoi′man): one who owns or navigates a hoy, or small coastal vessel.

huck (huk): short for *huckabuck,* a kind of textured weave. Dial. English for *hook.* The hip, haunch. 11. To higgle; bargain. 2.

huckle (huk′l): to haggle. 1. To bend. 13. The hip, haunch.

hui (hōō′i): a firm or partnership. 38. An assembly united for a common purpose. 38A.

hulster (hul′ster): a lurking place. 11.

hulu (hōō′lōō): a tuft of brilliant yellow feathers from the o-o, a bird of Hawaii.

humdudgeon (hum.duj′un): an imaginary illness or pain; a complaint about nothing. 25A.

humicubation (hū.mik′ū.bā′shun): the act of lying on the ground, esp. in penitence.

hummel (hum′l): hornless—of cattle; awnless—of grain; to separate from the awns—of barley. 17A.

hup (hup): a word used to urge on a horse, or to command it to turn to the right. 44A.

hurlbat (hurl'bat): an ancient weapon that was whirled to increase the force of a blow. 1.

hurley-hacket (hur'li.hak'et): a wobbly horse-drawn carriage; downhill sledding. 7A.

hurst (hurst): a grove or sandbank (often used in place names).

hushion (hush'un): a stocking without a foot; hence, a useless creature. 44.

huttoning (hut'n.ing): the manipulation of a dislocated or stiff joint.

huzzard (huz'erd): a yellow fly used in angling.

hwyl (hū'el): fervor, excitement. 41C.

hyalescence (hī'a.les'ens): the state of becoming or appearing hyaline, or glassy.

hyalography (hī'a.log'ra.fi): the art of writing or engraving on glass.

hyblaean (hī.blē'an): honeyed; mellifluous.

hydragogue (hī'dra.gog): a cathartic that causes a copious watery discharge from the bowels.

hydrogel (hī'dro.jel): a gel in which the liquid is water.

HOW THEIR NEIGHBORS ENVIED THEM!

Because of chronic *hemeraphonia*,
  Jack Spratt could hear in darkness only*—
Which in his view made matrimony a
  Quite tolerable state, though lonely.

His wife sang all day long off-key;
  He might have wished the woman dead,
But when he could have heard her, she
  Was silently asleep in bed.

And she, because of *hemeralopia*,
  Could never see a thing till night,
Yet found her handicap Utopia—
  For Jack was not a pleasant sight.

On scale of one to twenty, he
  Might rate a two, if lights were dim;
But by the time that she could see,
  He had the covers over him.

He heard no plaints *ad hominem;*
  She saw no scowl or sullen mien,
And so between the two of them
  They licked the marriage platter clean.

*Some say that hemeraphonia is the ability to *speak* only at night—but that would spoil my story.

---

hydromica (hī'dro.mī'ka): any of several varieties of muscovite that are less elastic and more unctuous than mica.

hydrophobophobia (hī'dro.fō'bo.fō'bi.a): fear of hydrophobia.

hydropic (hī.drop'ik): characterized by swelling and imbibation of fluid. Eden.ic. Dropsical.

hydrotelluric (hī'dro.te.lōō'rik): the acid hydrogen telluride.

hyetography (hī'i.tog'ra.fi): the scientific description of the geographical distribution of rain.

hygiolatry (hī'ji.ol'a.tri): fanaticism about health.

hygiology (hī'ji.ol'o.ji): the science of hygiene.

hygrology (hī.grol'o.ji): the branch of physics that deals with humidity.

hygrophobia (hī'gro.fō'bi.a): fear of liquids.

hylactic (hī.lak'tik): pert. to barking. 52.

hyle (hī'li): in philosophy, matter, or whatever receives its form or determination from outside itself. (cap) The name given by the Manicheans to the Regent of the World of Darkness.

hylogenesis (hī'lo.jen'i.sis): the beginning of matter.

hylophagan (hi.lof'a.gan): wood-eating.

hylotheist (hī'lo.thē'ist): one who believes that matter is God.

hymenogeny (hī'mi.noj'i.ni): the production of artificial membranes by contact of two fluids.

hymnography (him.nog'ra.fi): the composition and writing of hymns.

hypaethral (hī.pē'thral, hi-): open to the sky.

hypantrum (hī.pan'trum): a notch on the neural arch at the anterior ends of the vertebrae of certain reptiles.

hypengyophobia (hī.pen'ji.o.fō'bi.a): fear of responsibility.

hyperbatic (hī'per.bat'ik): pert. to transposed word order (as "tolled the bell" for "the bell tolled").

hyperdulia (hī'per.dōō'li.a): veneration of the Virgin Mary as the holiest of mere creatures.

hyperesthesia, hyperesthesis (hī'per.-es.thē'zhi.a, -zi.a, -zha; -thē'sis): a state of exalted or morbidly increased sensitivity.

hyperhedonia (hī'per.hi.dō'ni.a): abnormal pleasure from any sensory perception.

hypermimia (hī'per.mim'i.a): excessive gesticulation while talking.

hyperthermalgesia (hī'per.thur'mal.jē'-zhi.a, -zi.a): abnormal sensivity to heat.

hyperthetical (hī'per.thet'i.kal): in classical prosody, pert. to an interchange of position between a successive long and short syllable in a verse of mixed rhythm. In philology, pert. to transposition of a sound or letter from one syllable to an adjoining syllable.

hypertridimensional (hī'per.trī'di.men'shun.al): having more than three dimensions.

hypnoetic (hip'no.et'ik): pert. to mental processes of a logical form or nature, but not involving consciousness of logic nor effort to think logically.

hypnopedia (hip'no.pē'di.a): sleep-learning, sleep-teaching.

hypnophobia (hip'no.fō'bi.a): morbid fear of sleep.

hypobulia (hī'po.bū'li.a): difficulty in making decisions.

hypochonder (hī'po.kon'der, hip'o-): the abdomen just below the rib cartilages; the hypochondrium. 1.

hypogeal (hī'po.jē'al, hip'o-): subterranean, as *hypogeal* ants or beetles.

hypogelody (hī'po.jel'o.di, hip'o-): underground surveying, as of mines.

hypomnematic (hī'pom.ni.mat'ik, hip'om-): consisting of notes or memoranda.

hypophobia (hī'po.fō'bi.a, hip'o-): fearlessness.

hyporadius (hī'po.rā'di.us, hip'o-): in zoology, a barbule on the feather shaft.

hyporchema, hyporcheme (hī'pôr.kē'ma, -kēm, hip'ôr-): an ancient Greek choral song and dance usu. in honor of Apollo or Dionysus.

hyporchesis (hī'pôr.kē'sis, hip'ôr-): among the ancient Greeks, the choric dance to which the hyporchema was sung.

hypostigma (hī'po.stig'ma, hip'o-): a point in punctuation, orig. used with the value of a comma.

hypostyptic (hī'po.stip'tik, hip'o-): moderately styptic, or contraction-producing; a mild styptic.

hypothymic (hī'po.thī'mik, hip'o-): low in thymic functions such as immunological responses.

hypotyposis (hī'po.tī.pō'sis, hip'o-): vivid, picturesque description.

hypsiloid (hip'sī.loid, hip.sī'loid): resembling in form the Greek letter Y, upsilon.

hypural (hī.pū'ral): pert. to or designating the bony structure that supports the fin ray in the ordinary fishes.

hysteranthous (his'ter.an'thus): of a plant, developing leaves after the flowers have expanded.

hystricine (his'tri.sīn, -sin): pert. to porcupines.

I

iambographer (ī.am.bog.ra'fer): a writer of iambic verse. 52.

iatraliptic (ī.at'ra.lip'tik): treating disease by anointing and friction.

iatramelia (ī.at'ra.mēl'ya): medical negligence.

iatrogenesis (ī.at'ro.jen'i.sis): the occurrence of a disease through the medical activity of the physician.

iatrology (ī.a.trol'o.ji): the science of healing; a treatise on it.

iatromisia (ī.at'ro.mis'i.a): dislike of doctors.

iatrophobia (ī.at'ro.fō'bi.a): fear of going to the doctor.

iba (ē'ba): a medium-sized Philippine tree, prized for its roundish greenish-white fruit.

Ibo (Ē'bō): a Negro people of the lower Niger.

icaco (i.kak'ō): the coco plum.

Iceni (ī.sē'ni): a tribe of Britons that, under its queen Boadicea, revolted against the Romans in the 1st century A.D.

ichneutic (ik.nū'tik): pert. to tracking or trailing. 52.

ichnogram (ik'no.gram): a footprint.

ichnolatry (ik.nol'a.tri): the worship of idols.

ichnolite (ik'no.līt): a fossil footprint.

ichnology (ik.nol'o.ji): the study of (generally fossilized) footprints.

ichthyomancy (ik.thi.o.man'si): divination with fish offal.

ichthyophobia (ik.thi.o.fō'bi.a): fear of fish.

icker (ik'er): an ear of corn. 44.

iconoduly (ī.kon'o.dū.li): veneration of images.

iconomatic (ī.kon'o.mat'ik): pert. to the stage of writing between picture writing and phonetic writing.

icosian (ī.kō'si.an): relating to twenty.

ictic (ik'tik): caused by a blow; abrupt. Also, pert. to medical stress.

idalia (ī.dā'li.a): a large red-and-black butterfly of the eastern United States. Its caterpillar feeds on violets.

iddat (i.dät'): a period of several months in which a Moslem widow or divorcée may not remarry.

ideaist (ī.dē'a.ist): an idealist; a Platonist.

ideate (id'i.āt): to form an idea; to have or work through ideas.

idiogamist (id.i.og'a.mist): one capable of coitus only with his wife.

ideogenous (id'i.oj'i.nus): mental in origin.

idiograph (id'i.o.graf): a trademark.

idiolalia (id'i.o.lāl'ya): a mental state characterized by the use of invented language.

ideopraxis (id'i.o.prak'sis): the putting of ideas into effect.

idiostatic (id'i.o.stat'ik): pert. to a method of measurement of electricity without employing auxiliary electrification.

Ido (ē'do): an artificial language, devised in 1907; a modified form of Esperanto.

idoneous (i.dō'ni.us): apt; suitable.

idorgan (id'ôr.gan): a morphological unit consisting of a group of cells composing an organ, but without possessing the characteristics of an individual or colony.

ignavia (ig.nā'vi.a): idleness; laziness.

ignescent (ig.nes'ent): emitting sparks of fire when struck by steel; scintillating; becoming inflamed; inflammatory.

ignify (ig'ni.fī): to set on fire; to burn.

ignigenous (ig.nij'i.nus): producing or yielding fire.

ignipotent (ig.nip'o.tent): having power over fire.

ignoscency (ig.nos'en.si): forgiveness; a forgiving nature.

iiwi (i.ē'wi): a Hawaiian bird with brilliant red feathers, once used for regal capes.

illability (il.a.bil'i.ti): infallibility.

illaqueation (i.lak'wi.ā'shun): the act of ensnaring, entrapping, catching. 52.

illation (i.lā'shun): an inference or conclusion.

illicitator (il.lis'i.tā.ter): an auctioneer's shill. 22.

illinition (il'i.nish'un): a smearing or rubbing in or on; inunction.

illinium (i.lin'i.um): an element of the rare-earth group.

illision (i.lizh'un): a striking against something.

illium (il'i.um): an alloy of nickel, chromium, copper, manganese, silicon, and tungsten, used esp. for laboratory ware.

illth (ilth): the condition of being poor and miserable. The opposite of wealth.

illutation (il'ū.tā'shun): a mud bath.

imaginate (i.maj'i.nat): to imagine. 52. Imaginary. 1. To change (an insect) to an imago. 52.

imbibition (im.bi.bish'un): absorption, saturation, steeping.

imbosk (im.bosk'): to hide, conceal.

immanity (i.man'i.ti): monstrosity. 1.

immarcescible (im'är.ses'i.bl): indestructible, imperishable. 52.

immeability (im'i.a.bil'i.ti): want of power to pass or flow; impassableness.

immer (im'er): ever (German).

immerd (i.murd'): to cover with ordure.

immie (im'i): a marble, esp. one streaked with color.

imminution (im'i.nū'shun): diminution.

immorigerous (im'ôr.ij'e.rus): rude, boorish.

immund (i.mund'): unclean; filthy.

immundicity, immundity (i.mun.dis'i.ti, -mun'di.ti): uncleanliness, filth. 1.

impacable (im.pā'ka.bl): not to be pacified; implacable.

impanate (im.pā'nāt): containing (as Eucharistic bread and wine) the body of Christ without change in any substance.

imparl (im.pärl'): to consult; discuss. 1.

impatible (im.pat'i.bl): that cannot suffer or be suffered. 1.

impavid (im.pav'id): fearless.

impeccant (im.pek'ant): sinless.

impedient (im.pē'di.ent): (one) that impedes.

impeditive (im.ped'i.tiv): tending to impede; obstructive.

impertinacy (im.pur'ti.na.si): erroneous for *impertinency.*

impetulant (im.pech'ōō.lant): not petulant.

impi (im'pi): a body of Kaffir warriors or native armed men.

impletion (im.plē'shun): state of being full; that which fills, a filling. Fulfillment, as of prophecy. 1.

implex (im'pleks): involved, intricate, complex.

imprese (im.prēz'): historically, a device or emblem; the sentence usu. accompanying it; a motto, proverb, or maxim. 1.

improlificate (im.pro.lif'i.kāt): to impregnate.

INIA, MINIA: A COUNTING SONG

Inia, minia, one two three,—
Inia, minia, out blows he—
Seven-foot whale with a long long snout,
First he is Inia, then he's out.

Inia, minia, one three two,
Inia, minia, out goes who?
Seven-foot whale with a seven-foot spout,
First he is Inia, then blows out.

---

impropriate (im.prō'pri.āt): in English law, to transfer monastic properties to lay control.

impropriatrix (im.prō'pri.āt'riks): a female impropriator (one that takes over an ecclesiastical property).

improvvisatore (im.prov.vē'za.tō'ri): one who recites his own improvised poetry.

impudicity (im.pū.dis'i.ti): immodesty.

imsonic (im.son'ik): onomatopoeic.

imu (i.mōō): in Hawaii, a baking pit dug in the sand.

inaniloquy (in.a.nil'o.kwi): an idle and garrulous bit of chatter.

inaugur (in.ô'ger): to inaugurate. 52.

inauration (in.ô.rā'shun): the act of gilding.

inby (in'bī): inwardly, within; nearby, beside. An inner room. 44.

incalescent (in.ka.les'ent): growing warm or ardent.

incameration (in.kam'er.ā'shun): an addition to papal property.

incarn (in.kärn'): to become covered with flesh; to heal over.

incastellate (in.kas′te.lāt): to change into, or make like, a castle. 1.

incatenate (in.kat′i.nāt): to fetter; to restrain with chains.

incoalescent (in.ko.a.les′ent): not coalescing. 52.

incommiscible (in.ko.mis′a.bl): incapable of mixing or blending; immiscible.

inconnicity (in.ko.nis′i.ti): unsuitableness; ineptitude.

incrassate (in.kras′āt): in plants or animals, thickened and swollen. To thicken, inspissate. 1.

increpation (in.kri.pā′shun): criticism; censure.

incruental (in.kr͞oo.en.tal): bloodless.

incuss (in.kus′): to impress, inspire. 1.

indican (in′di.kan): a colorless glucoside, the source of natural indigo.

indicatrix (in′di.kā′triks): indicator; specif. *Dupin's indicatrix,* a limiting form in mathematics.

indicavit (in.di.kā′vit): in English law, a writ of prohibition for removal of certain cases affecting tithes from the ecclesiastical to the common-law courts.

indiscerptibility (in.di.surp′ti.bil′i.ti): the state of not being subject to dissolution.

indocible (in.dos′i.bl): unteachable.

inearth (in.urth′): to inter.

inenarrable (in′e.nar′a.bl): indescribable, ineffable.

inequable (in.ek′wa.bl): not uniform, even, tranquil; not equable.

inermous (in.ur′mus): without thorns or prickles, as some leaves.

infaust (in.fôst′): unlucky. 52.

infibulation (in.fib′ū.lā′shun): the sewing up of the genitals to prevent sexual intercourse.

OR PERHAPS A PELTOGRAM

Do you recall that florid, convoluting,
Declamatory old professor
Who spent a fustian lifetime substituting
The greater lexeme for the lesser?

    (When others spoke of ''idle chatter,'' he
    Said, ''More precisely, *inaniloquy.''*)

That hippopotomonstrosesquipedal
Altiloquenter? For the birds!—
(And yet he won the William Morris Medal
By never using little words.)

    (He reached his peak in verbal self-indulgence
    When milking cows—which he called
    ''*vaccimulgence.''*)

At last those Golden Stairs he had to climb.
    He capered up in dithyramb.
And left behind him on the sands of time
    Not footprints, but an ichnogram.

---

inficete (in′fi.sēt): dull; unfunny; humorless; deadly serious. 52.

infracostal (in′fra.kos′tal): below the ribs.

infrapose (in′fra.pōz): to place beneath.

infucation (in.fū.kā′shun): the putting on of makeup.

infumate (in′fū.māt): to smoke, as a fish.

infuscate (in.fus′kāt): obscured; specif., darkened with a brownish tinge—said of the wings of insects.

ing (ing): a low-lying pasture. 42A.

ingannation (in.ga.nā′shun): deception; fraud.

ingestar (in.jes′tar): a large 17th-century decanter.

ingle (ing′gl): a fire; a fireplace. An angle, a corner. 52. To cajole, wheedle. A catamite. 1.

ingluvious (in.gl͞oo′vi.us): gluttonous.

ingustable (in.gus′ta.bl): tasteless.

inhearse (in.hurs′): to put in a hearse or coffin. 52.

Inia (in′i.a): a genus of dolphin-like cetaceans of the Amazon and its tributaries, with but one species, seven feet long and having a long snout.

inition (in.ish′un): initiation; beginning. 1.

inkle (ing′kl): a kind of linen tape or braid; also, the thread or yarn from which it is made. To have an inkling of. 13.

inlagary (in.lā′ga.ri): the legal restoration of the rights of criminals. 1.

innascible (in.nas′i.bl): without a beginning.

in petto (in pet′tō): in the breast; not yet made public.

insanable (in.san′a.bl): incurable.

insecable (in.sek′a.bl): indivisible.

insecution (in.si.kū′shun): a following after; close pursuit. 1.

inshallah (in.shal′a): in Arabic, ''God willing.''

insuetude (in′swi.tūd): unaccustomedness. A state of disuse. 52.

insulse (in.suls′): tasteless, flat, insipid.

insussuration (in.sus′e.rä′shun): a whispering in the ear; insinuation. 1.

intactable (in.tak′ta.bl): imperceptible to the touch.

intempestive (in.tem.pes′tiv): untimely; inopportune.

interaulic (in′ter.ôl′ik): existing only between two royal households.

intercrop (in′ter.krop): to grow two or more crops simultaneously in the same ground.

interdigitate (in′ter.dij′i.tāt): to interlace the fingers.

interfenestration (in′ter.fen′es.trä′shun): the space between windows. The placing of windows.

interfret (in′ter.fret): the interaction between two wind currents, frequently producing such effects as a mackerel sky.

intergern (in′ter.gurn): to snarl back. 1.

interjaculate (in′ter.jak′ū.lāt): to ejaculate parenthetically, interject.

interlacustrine (in′ter.la.kus′trin): between lakes.

interlucation (in′ter.lū.kā′shun): the thinning out of trees in a forest to let in light.

intermundane (in′ter.mun′dān): existing between stars or planets.

internecion (in′ter.nē′shun): mutual destruction; massacre. 52.

interneural (in′ter.nū′ral): in anatomy, between the neural arches or neural spines.

interpilaster (in′ter.pi.las′ter): in architecture, the space between two pilasters.

interpunction (in′ter.pungk′shun): act of interpointing; punctuation.

intersert (in′ter.surt): to interpolate, insert.

intersidereal (in′ter.sī.dēr′i.al): interstellar.

intersilient (in′ter.sil′yent): emerging suddenly in the midst of something. 1.

interstadial (in′ter.stā′di.al): a halt, with minor oscillations, in the advance or retreat of an ice sheet.

interstrial (in′ter.strī′al): between striae—grooves, strips, or lines.

intertessellation (in′ter.tes′i.lā′shun): an intricate design, as mosaic.

intertill (in′ter.til): to till between the rows of a crop.

intervallic (in′ter.val′ik): pert. to an interval.

intervert (in′ter.vurt): to turn to an improper course; misuse, esp. embezzle. To change, invert.

intorsion (in.tôr′shun): a winding, bending, or twisting, as of the stem of a plant.

intrapial (in′tra.pī′al): in anatomy, within the pia mater, which connects the brain and spinal cord.

intrathecal (in′tra.thē′kal): in anatomy, within a sheath. Under the membranes covering the brain or spinal cord.

intropression (in′tro.presh′un): pressure acting within. 52.

introsusception, intussusception (in′tro.su.sep′shun, in′tus.-): the reception of one part within another. Invagination.

introvenience (in′tro.vēn′yens): the act of coming in; entering.

intumulate (in′tū′mū.lāt): to bury.

inturgescence (in′ter.jes′ens): a swelling.

inumbrate (in.um′brāt): to shade. 52.

inusitate (in.ūz′i.tāt): obsolete.

inustion (in.us′chun): burning; cauterization.

invalescence (in.va.les′ens): the state of being an invalid.

inviscate (in.vis′kāt): to make viscid; to entangle, as an insect, in a sticky substance.

invultuation (in.vul′chōō.ā′shun): witchcraft in which a wax image is melted or stuck with pins to cause death or injury to the intended victim.

ipsedixitism (ip′se.dik′sit.izm): dogmatism.

ipseity (ip.sē′i.ti): self-identity; selfhood.

irade (i.rä′de): a decree of a Mohammedan ruler, as formerly of the Sultan.

irenark (ī′re.närk): a Roman official corresponding to a justice of the peace.

irenicon (ī.ren′i.kon): a statement that attempts to harmonize conflicting doctrines, as in theology.

iridize (ir′i.dīz): to point or tip with iridium, as a gold pen.

irpe (urp): a grimace or bodily contortion (as used by Ben Jonson).

irreptitious (ir.rep.tish′us): creeping stealthily.

irriguous (i.rig′ū.us): irrigated; watered. 9. Serving to irrigate, water, moisten.

irrisory (i.rī′so.ri): derisive.

irrorate (ir′o.rāt): to bedew, moisten. 1. In zoology, covered with minute grains, appearing like sand, or with small specks of color.

irrugate (ir′u.gāt): to wrinkle. 1.

irrumation (ir.ōō.mā′shun): oral stimulation of the penis; fellatio.

isagoge (ī′sa.gō′ji): a scholarly introduction to a branch of research.

iscariotic (is.kar′i.ot′ik): traitorous.

ischiatic (is.ki.at′ik): pert. to the region of the ischium, or seat bone; ischial. Affected with sciatica. 1.

ischidrosis (is′ki.drō′sis): suppression of the secretion of sweat.

isocheimal, eisocheimic (ī′so.ki′mal, -mik): pert. to an imaginary line connecting places having the same mean winter temperature.

isocracy (ī.sok′ra.si): a system of government in which all have equal political power.

isocrymal (ī′so.krī′mal): isocheimal.

isodiabatic (ī′so.dī′a.bat′ik): pert. to the equal transmission of heat to or from a substance.

isogenous (ī.soj′e.nus): having a common origin.

isonomic (ī′so.nom′ik): pert. to equality of law or rights.

isopectic (ī′so.pek′tik): an equiglacial line drawn through points where ice begins to form at the beginning of winter.

isoperimetrical (ī′so.per′i.met′ri.kal): in geometry, having equal perimeters.

isophorous (ī.sof′er.us): in medicine, having the visual axes of the two eyes in the same horizontal plane.

isopsephic (ī′sop.sef′ik): equal in numerical value. Also, one of two or more isopsephic verses.

isopycnic (ī′so.pik′nik): of equal density; passing through points at which the density is equal.

iter (ī′ter): an eyre, or circuit, orig. of certain justices in England; the record of the proceedings during an eyre. 6. In Roman law, the right to pass over another's property by foot or horseback. In anatomy, a passage.

izle (ī′zl) (usu. pl.): a speck of soot; a spark. 43.

J

jacchus (jak′us): a kind of marmoset.

jacent (jā′sent): recumbent.

jackaroo, jackeroo (jak′a.rōō, jak′e-): in Australia, a green hand on a sheep ranch; in the western U.S., a cowboy.

jacoby (jak′o.bi): the purple ragwort.

jactancy (jak′tan.si): boasting, bragging.

jadu (jä′dōō): conjuring; magic; fortune-telling.

jager (yā′ger): a hunter; a huntsman. (cap) A German or Austrian rifleman.

jaggish (jag′ish): tiddly.

jagua (häg′wa): the inaja, a tall Brazilian palm having immense spathes used for baskets, tubs, etc. In the Caribbean, the genipap tree or its orange-sized fruit.

jako (jak′ō): the gray parrot.

jama (jä′ma): a long Indian cotton gown.

jambee (jam.bē′): an East Indian rattan cane; the tree from which it is made.

jamdani (jam.dä′ni): a flower-patterned muslin.

jami (jä′mi): in Turkey, a principal or central mosque.

jampan (jam′pan): in the hill country of India, a sedan chair carried by four men.

janiceps (jan′i.seps): a two-headed monster facing opposite ways.

Janiculum (ja.nik′ū.lum): a hill on the west bank of the Tiber, opposite the seven hills of Rome.

jannock (jan′uk): leavened oatmeal bread. 13. Candid, pleasant, liberal. 11.

jarbird (jär′burd): the nuthatch.

jarble (jär′bl): to wet; bemire. 13.

jargogle (jär.gog′l): to befuddle. 1.

jargonelle (jär′go.nel): an early variety of pear.

jarl (järl): to quarrel. Historically, a Danish or Norse chieftain below the king.

jasey (jā′zi): a wig of jersey or of a similar yarn. 13.

Jataka (jä′ta.ka): stories about incarnations of Buddha.

jauk (jôk): to trifle or toy with. 44.

jawab (ja.wäb′, -wôb): in India, an answer or reply. Also, a building corresponding to another.

jazerant (jaz′er.ant): armor made of overlapping metal pieces, like fish scales.

jeel (jēl): jelly. 44. Damage, mischief. 55. var. of *jheel*.

jejunator (jej′ōō.nā′ter): one who fasts. 52.

jelab (je.läb′): a hooded jacket of North Africa.

jemadar (jem′a.där): an officer in the army of India equivalent to a lieutenant in the English army.

jenna (jen′a): Paradise, in the Mohammedan religion.

jennerize (jen′er.īz): to vaccinate; immunize.

jentacular (jen.tak′ū.lar): pert. to breakfast.

jeopard (jep′erd): to put in jeopardy.

jereed (je.rēd′): a blunt javelin used in military games in Muslim countries; also, a game played with it.

jerque (jurk): to search (a vessel) for unauthorized goods, etc. 41.

jerrican (jer′i.kan): a five-gallon jug. 13.

jessamy (jes′a.mi): jasmine. 2. A dandy, fop.

jheel (jēl): in India, a pool or marsh left after inundation; a rain puddle. Jelly. 44.

jhool (jōōl): in India, trappings for a horse, elephant, etc.

jhow (jou): a tamarisk of India, used for basket making.

jibble-jabble (jib′l.jab′l): nonsense chatter.

jigamaree (jig′ma.ri): something fanciful or ridiculous.

jimp (jimp): slender; trim; also, scant. Barely; scarcely. 15A. To cut short; skimp. 13.

jingal (jin′gal): a long, heavy musket, or rude cannon, fired from a rest, often with a swivel, formerly used in central Asia.

jingbang (jing′bang): a crowd; shebang (only in "the whole *jingbang*"). 21.

jirble (jur′bl): to spill (a liquid) by jolting or shaking; hence, to pour from one vessel to another. 44.

jism (jizm): semen. Pep; vigor. 21.

jiti (jē′ti): a woody Asian vine, the Rajmahal creeper, which yields hemp.

jiva (jē′va): in Hinduism, the life energy, vital principle; individual soul.

jixie (jik′si): a two-seated cab. 23.

jobation (jo.bā′shun): a scolding; a long, tedious reproof. 26.

jocker (jok′er): a tramp who takes with him a boy to beg and steal. 32A.

jocoque, jocoqui (ho.kō′kā, -ki): a preparation of sour milk; buttermilk. 35A.

jocoserious (jok′o.sē′ri.us): mingling mirth and seriousness.

jojoba (ho.hō′ba): a small tree of southwestern North America, with oil-bearing, edible seeds. 35A.

jokul (yō′kool): in Iceland, a mountain covered with snow and ice.

jollop (jol′up): a fowl's dewlap, or wattle.

jookerie (jook′er′i): trickery; swindling. 44.

joola (joo′la): a Himalayan rope suspension bridge.

joom (joom): in Bengal, the cultivation of forest land by burning and then sowing it with mixed crops.

jornada (hor.nä′tha, -näda): a full day's travel with no stops. In Mexico, as a land measure, as much land as can be plowed in a day. 35A.

jorum (jō′rum): a large wine jug or bowl. 26.

josser (jos′er): a fool, simpleton. 23.

jotation (yo.tä′shun): palatalization.

jouk (jouk): an obeisance; a trick; a shelter. To roost; sleep; dodge; hide. 44A.

jowter (jou′ter): a peddler or hawker, esp. of fish. 13.

Ju (joo): blue or white porcelain of the Sung dynasty.

Jubal (Joo′bal): in the Bible, a son of Lamech. He is called the father of those who play the harp or organ.

jubbah (joob′ba): a long garment worn in Mohammedan countries by both sexes.

jube (joob): a screen separating the chancel of a church from the nave; also called *rood screen*. A lozenge like the jujube.

jucundity (joo.kun′di.ti): pleasantness. 1. Jocundity. 52.

jumart (joo′mart): the fabled offspring of a bull mating a mare or jenny, or of a horse or ass mating a cow.

jumelle (joo.mel′): paired; jugate.

jumentous (joo.men′tus): having a strong animal smell, as that of horse urine.

juncous (jung′kus): full of, or resembling, rushes.

jupe (joop): a man's shirt or jacket; a woman's blouse or skirt. 44.

jupon (joo′pon): a tight-fitting garment like a shirt, often paddled and quilted and worn under medieval armor. Also, a late medieval jacket similar to the surcoat.

jussel (jus′el): in cookery, a hodge-podge. 1.

justaucorps (zhoos′to.kôr): a fitted coat or jacket; specif., a man's knee-length coat with flaring and stiffened skirts worn in the late 17th and early 18th centuries.

juvenate (joo′ve.nāt): in the Society of Jesus, a two-year course of instruction for junior members.

juzgado (hoos.gä′do, -thō): hoosegow; jail. 35A.

THE JAKO, THE JARBIRD, AND THE JUMARTS

A jako and a jarbird were appalled one day to see
A pair of jumarts jouking in a jacaranda tree.
One jumart was the offspring of a bull upon a mare;
The other had a cow for ma, a Percheron for père.

The jako and the jarbird were not snobbish in the least,
Nor cared about the parentage of any bird or beast,
But feared the branches were too frail to hold such massive things.
Besides, a jumart shouldn't fly—it hasn't any wings.

Those jumarts got the jako and the jarbird so jargogled,
They thought and *thought* and THOUGHT, and still their intellects were boggled.
They jawed, they jibble-jabbled, and they even jarled a wee,
But could not solve the problem of that jumart jigamaree.

So jocoseriously they decided to get soused,
In hopes they'd sleep the whole thing off before the time they roused.
And sure enough, when they had slept, and woke at break of dawn,
They checked and found they were correct; the jumarts both were gone.

K

ka (kä): the Scottish jackdaw. In ancient Egypt, the immortal soul.

kaama (kä′ma): a hartebeest.

kabaya (ka.bä′ya): a loose cotton Malayan tunic.

kaberu (ka.bä′roo): the Abyssinian mountain wolf.

kachina (ka.chē′na): the spirit of a departed Hopi Indian, or some representation of it.

kadein (ka.dīn′): a member of the imperial Turkish harem.

kadoodle (ka.doo′dl): to romp; cavort.

Kaf, Qaf (käf): in Moslem cosmology, a mountain range supposedly encircling the earth, home of a bird of great wisdom.

kaffiyeh (ka.fē′ye): a Bedouin headdress consisting of a square kerchief bound around the head with a cord.

kaha (kä′ha): the proboscis monkey.

kahuna (ka.hoo′na): in Hawaii, a medicine man or high priest; also a master artisan.

kai (kä′i): to the Maoris, food. 56.

kai-kai (kä′i.kä.i): among the Maoris, feasting; to feast. 56.

kaikara (kī.kä′ra): the demoiselle crane.

kailyard (kāl′yärd): a school of writing characterized by sentimental description of Scots life and much use of Scottish dialect.

kaivakuku (kä′i.va.koo′koo): Papuan police hired to protect the crops. 56.

kaki (kä′ki): the Japanese persimmon. The New Zealand stilt-bird.

kakidrosis (kak.i.drō′sis): disagreeable body smell.

kakistocracy (kak.i.stok′ra.si): government by the worst elements of society.

kakkak (kak′kak): in Guam, a small bittern.

kakorrhaphiophobia (kak′or.a.fē′o.fō′bi.a): fear of failure.

kala (kä′la): a black bulbul of India, often kept as a cage bird.

kali (kä′li): the glasswort. Alkali; potash. 1. A carpet of extra length used in the center of Persian rooms. (cap) In the Hindu poem *Nala and Damayani*, an evil genius who causes Nala to gamble his kingdom away. (cap) In Vedic myth, one of the tongues of the fire-god Agni.

kalium (kä′li.um, kal-): potassium.

kalogram (kal′o.gram): a monogram using one's name rather than initials.

kalon (kal′on): the beautiful—frequently with an implication of moral as well as aesthetic beauty.

kamala (ka.mä′la, kam′e.la): an East Indian tree. The orange-red powder from its capsules, used as a vermifuge.

kamalayka (kam.a.lä′ka): a waterproof shirt made from seal guts.

kameel (ka.mēl): an African giraffe.

kamerad (kä′mer.ad): to surrender. 26. (cap) Comrade—used as an appeal for quarter by German soldiers in the First World War.

kamichi (ka.mē′shi): the horned screamer, a South American bird with a hornlike projection on its forehead.

Kanaloa (kan.a.lō′a): one of the principal gods of the Hawaiian pantheon.

kankedort (kang′ke.dôrt): in Chaucer's works, a critical state or affair. 1.

kantele (kan′te.lā): an ancient five-stringed Finnish harp.

kapa (kä′pa): tapa, the bark of the paper mulberry; hence, tapa cloth. Cloth or clothes in general. 38.

karao (ka.rä′o): in Hindu law, a widow's marriage to her brother-in-law. Concubinage.

karimata (kä.ri.mä′ta): a whistling, two-headed Japanese arrow.

kaross (ka.ros′): a simple square garment or rug of animal skins used by native tribesmen of southern Africa.

kasida (ka.sē′da): in Arabic, Persian, and related Oriental literature, a poem of a laudatory, elegiac, or satiric character.

katabasis, catabasis (ka.tab′a.sis): a going or marching down or back; a military retreat.

katar (ka.tär′): in India, a short dagger with a handle of two parallel bars and a cross grip.

kathenotheism (ka.then′o.thi.izm): polytheism with one ruling god.

kathisophobia (kath′i.so.fō′bi.a): fear of sitting down.

katun (ka.tōōn): among the Mayans, twenty years.

kava (kä′va): an Australian pepper used to make an intoxicating drink. The drink so made.

Kavi, Kawa (kä′vi): the ancient language of Java, parent of Javanese.

keb (keb): a ewe that has lost her lamb. To bear a stillborn lamb. Also, a sheep tick, *ked.* 43.

ked (ked): a sheep tick.

kedogenous (ke.doj′i.nus): produced by worry.

keek (kēk): an industrial spy. A peeping Tom. 21.

keelivine (kē′li.vīn): a pencil having black lead. 43.

keest (kēst): sap; substance; marrow. 44.

keet (kēt): a guinea fowl; esp., a young guinea fowl.

keeve, kieve (kēv): a vat or tub, as a brewer's mash tub. (Also *kiver, keever.*) A rock basin hollowed out by water. 41.

kef (kef): tranquility induced by drugs. Indian hemp.

---

*WARNING AGAINST
AN EARLY-GROWING PEAR*

Seek not, seek not, lest mind and life you
    jeopard—
  Seek not, I say, to pluck the jargonelle.
It grows in jungles where the feral leopard,
  The jackal, and the naked savage dwell.

And if you needs must brave those floors of
    marble,
  Those dusty deserts, and those huddled rocks,
Wear rubbers—else your Sunday boots you'll
    jarble;
  And take a jerrican to hold your sox.

The houris touch it to their tongues in jenna;
  The blessed angels wear it in their hair.
Why's Satan still in exile in Gehenna?
  Because he sold his soul to bite that pear.

No letter of this warning dare you garble;
  Recall it as you stand there in the stocks;
Wear rubbers—else your Sunday boots you'll
    jarble;
  And take a jerrican to hold your sox.

Kefti (kef′ti): pert. to ancient Crete; an ancient Cretan; a Keftian.

keiri (kē′ri): the wallflower. 1.

keld (keld): a spring or fountain; the still part of a body of water. 13.

kell (kel): a caul; specif., a net cap worn by women. 13.

kellion (kel′yun): a monastery housing not more than three monks and three lay persons.

kelly (kel′i): ver. of *killie, killy.* A stiff hat, esp. a derby. 22. The topsoil removed in order to secure clay for brickmaking. A kind of green associated with the Irish.

kemb (kemb): comb. 11.

kemp (kemp): a coarse hair. 1. A champion; a warrior or athlete. 43. A harvesting contest; to compete in harvesting. 44.

kempt (kemt): neatly kept; trim.

kench (kench): a bin where fish or skins are salted. To install a kench. 32.

kennebunker (ken′i.bung′ker): a kind of large suitcase. 36A.

kenophobia (ken′o.fō′bi.a): fear of empty or open spaces.

kenspeckle (ken.spek′l): conspicuous. 44.

kerana (ke.rä′na): a kind of long Persian trumpet.

kerasine (ker′a.sin): horny; corneous.

keraunoscopia (ke.rô.no.skō′pi.a): divination by thunder.

kerdomeletia (kur′do.me.lē′shi.a): excessive attention to wealth.

kerygma (ke.rig′ma): preaching; the proclamation of the gospel.

ket (ket): filth, rubbish. A good-for-nothing person. 13.

keta (kē′ta): the dog salmon.

ketupa (ke.tōōpa): a fish owl.

kex (keks): the dry, usually hollow stem of cow parsnip, wild chervil, and the like.

khet (ket): in Egyptian religion, the mortal, corruptible body, in contrast to the *sahu,* or spirit body.

Khubur (koo′bōōr): in Babylonian religion, a river that had to be crossed to reach the underworld.

khuskhus (kus′kus): the sweet-scented root of an Indian grass used in the manufacture of mats or screens.

kibbling (kib′ling): cut-up fish used as bait in Newfoundland.

kibe (kīb): as used by Shakespeare, a crack in the flesh caused by cold; to affect with kibes.

kife (kīf): prostitutes; male homosexuals. To rob. 21.

killie, killy (kil′i): the killifish, often used as bait.

killow (kil′ō): graphite. 1.

kinch (kinch): a noose or twist in a cord. To fasten a noose on the tongue of (a horse). 17A.

kinclunk (kin.klungk′): per Alistair Reid, the sound of a car going over a manhole cover.

kinesiatrics (kin′i.si.at′riks): a mode of treating disease by appropriate muscular movements.

kinesodic (kin′i.sod′ik): in physiology, conveying motion or motor impulses—applied esp. to the spinal cord.

kinesophobia (kin′i.so.fō′bi.a): fear of movement.

kingling (king′ling): a small or petty king.

kinic, quinic (kin′ik, kwin-): pert. to cinchona bark.

kinology (ki.nol′o.ji): the physics of motion. 52.

kip (kip): half a ton—1,000 pounds.

kipe (kīp): an osier basket for catching fish.

kippage (kip′ij): commotion, confusion, excitement. 44.

kiri (kē′ri): a *knobkerrie.*

kissar (kis′ar): the five-stringed Abyssinian lyre.

kitsch (kich): a rather second-hand, synthetic, and self-conscious emotion; anything (as certain art, literature, etc.) that gives rise to such emotion.

kitling (kit′ling): one of the young of an animal; a whelp. 1. Kittenish; petty; inexperienced. A young cat or kittenish person. 17A.

kittereen (kit′er.én): a two-wheeled one-horse carriage with a movable top.

kitthoge (ki.thōg′): a lefty. Left-handed; awkward. 51, 32.

kiva (kē′va): in Pueblo architecture, an underground ceremonial chamber.

kivu (kē′vōō): the tsetse fly.

kleagle (klē′gl): a high-ranking official in the Ku Klux Klan.

Klepht (kleft): one of the Greeks who formed communities of brigands after their country was conquered by the Turks in the 15th century.

kleptic (klep′tik): thievish.

kleptocracy (klep.tok′ra.si): rule by thieves.

klippe (klip′i): a coin struck with a square-shaped or lozenge-shaped rim.

klipspringer (klip′spring′er): a small African antelope with big ears.

knag (nag): a knot in wood; a wooden peg; a short spur from a tree trunk.

knaggy (nag′i): knotty, rough.

knapple (nap′l): clapboard. 18A.

knez (knez): a Slavic prince or duke.

knibber (nib′er): a male deer beginning its first antlers.

knickknackatory (nik′nak′a.tō′ri): a collection or storehouse of knickknacks.

knissomancy (nis′o.man′si): divination by incense burning.

knittle (nit′l): var. of *nettle.* A string or cord for tying or fastening. 1.

knobkerrie (nob′ker′i): a short club with a knobbed end used as a missile weapon by the aborigines of South Africa.

knop, knosp (nop, nosp): an ornamental knob, as on the stem of a goblet or the shaft of a candlestick; a boss. An ornamental ball or tuft of contrasting color on yarn, thread, or cloth. A projection up or out; a hill. 44C.

knub, nub (nub): a knob; to thump, nudge. 11. Waste silk produced in winding threads from a cocoon.

knubby, knubbly (nub′i, -li): abounding in, or covered by, knubs.

ko (kō): a Chinese liquid measure. (cap) A dark clay Chinese porcelain produced in the 12th century.

kob, koba (kob, kōb, -a): an African antelope related to the water buck.

kobo (kō′bō): a Nigerian penny.

kobold (kō′bold, -bōld): in Germany, a mischievous domestic spirit. A gnome living underground.

koi (koi, ko′i): in Japan, the carp.

koimesis (koi.mē′sis): in the Eastern church, a commemoration of the death and assumption of the Virgin Mary.

kokam (ko.käm′): the slow loris of the Philippines.

koko (kō′kō): any of several araceous plants inc. the taro, cultivated in tropical West Africa for their starchy, edible roots.

kokomo (kō′ko.mō): a drug addict, esp. of cocaine. 21.

kokophobia (kō′ko.fō′bi.a): fear of exhaustion.

kokum (kō′kum): pretended sympathy. 23.

kompology (kom.pol′o.ji): boastful speech.

kona (kō′na): a storm of southerly or southwesterly winds and heavy rains in Hawaii.

konimeter (ko.nim′e.ter): an instrument for measuring dust in the air.

koochahbee (koo′cha.bi): a California Indian dish made from fly larvae.

koomkie (koom′ki): a female elephant that has been trained to decoy wild males.

koph, qoph (kōf): the 19th letter of the Hebrew alphabet, representing the sound of English *k,* or *q* in *qu.*

kora (kō′ra): the water cock, a large gallinule bird of southeastern Asia and the East Indies. (cap) An almost extinct Hottentot dialect.

kore (kō′rā): in Maori mythology, the primordial void or first cause of the universe. 56. (cap) In Greek mythology, Persephone, daughter of Demeter.

korova (ko.rō′va): calfskin.

koto (kō′to): a long Japanese zither having 13 silk strings.

kotukutuku (ko.too′koo.too′koo): the New Zealand fuchsia.

Krama (krä′ma): the aristocratic or courtly form of Javanese speech. (not

cap.) The wine mingled with water used in Eastern Orthodox churches in celebrating the Eucharist.

krasis (krā′sis, krä′sis): dilution of the Eucharist wine.

kratogen (krat′o.jen): a dormant area next to one beset by earthquakes.

kreatophagia (krē′a.to.fā′ji.a): the eating of raw meat.

krieker (krē′ker): the pectoral sandpiper.

krypsis (krip′sis): the secret exercise by Christ as a man of his divine powers.

kuku (koo′koo): the New Zealand fruit pigeon.

kurveyor (ker′vā′er): in South Africa, a traveling salesman who carts his goods.

kyack (kī′ak): a packsack to be swung on either side of a packsaddle. 35C.

kyacting (ki.ak′ting): clowning while at work. 21.

kylie (kī′li): a boomerang having one side flat and the other convex. 53.

kymatology (kī′ma.tol′o.ji): the science of waves and wave motion.

kyphotic (ki.fot′ik): hump-backed.

Kyrie (kir′i.e, kē-): short for *Kyrie eleison,* ''Lord have mercy on us,'' used in various offices of the Eastern and Western churches.

kyrine (kī′rén): any of a class of basic peton-like substances, obtained by hydrolysis of gelatin, casein, etc.

L

laaba (lä′ba): a storage platform high enough to be beyond the reach of animals. 37B.

labefy (la′be.fī): to weaken or impair. 52.

labia (lā′bi.a): pl. of *labium,* lip.

Labrosaurus (lab′ro.sô′rus): a genus of dinosaurs, related to *Megalosaurus,* from the Colorado Jurassic.

lacca (lak′a): a resinous substance from a scale insect esp. cultivated in northern India, used in the making of shellac, etc.

lacertian, lacertilian (la.sur′shun, -ser.til′yun): lizard-like.

lacrimando (lak.ri.män′dō): in music, lamenting; plaintive—used as a direction.

lactary (lak′ter.i): a dairy house. 52.

lactescent (lak.tes′ent): of plants, having a milky look; becoming milky. Secreting milk. Yielding latex.

lactivorous (lak.tiv′or.us): living on milk.

ladrone (la.drōn′): a rogue; blackguard; slattern. 44A. In Spanish-speaking countries, a thief, highwayman.

lagarto (la.gär′tō): an alligator.

lagnosis (lag.nō′sis): satyriasis.

lagopous (la.gō′pus): in plants, having hairy rhizomes suggestive of the foot of a hare.

Lagopus (la.gō′pus): a genus of northern game birds comprising the ptarmigans and the red grouse.

lagostic (la.gos′tik): having rabbitlike ears.

laine (lān): an open tract of arable land at the foot of the Downs, in Sussex.

lairwife (lâr′wīf): in old English law, a fine against a married woman for adultery.

lairy (lâr′i): earthy; filthy. 1. Miry. 43.

Lais (lä.ēs′): a hetaera who lived during the Peloponnesian War and was regarded as the most beautiful woman of her age.

Lakme (läk′mi): an Anglo-Indian opera (1885) by Delibes.

lallophobia (lal′o.fō′bi.a): fear of speaking.

lalo (lal′ō): the powdered leaves of the baobab tree, used in Africa in soups.

lamellirostral (la.mel′i.ros′tral): having a bill with transverse toothlike ridges inside the edges, as a duck.

lametta (la.met′a): foil or wire of gold, silver, or brass.

lamin (lam′in): a thin plate or scale. An astrologer's charm consisting of such a plate.

lampadomancy (lam′pad.o.man′si): divination by means of the flickering flame of a torch.

lampas (lam′pas): an ornamental textile fabric with a somewhat elaborate pattern, used chiefly for upholstery.

---

*HOW TO TELL THE SCOTTISH
FROM THE EGYPTIAN KA*

The ka, deemed deathless on the teeming Nile,
   In Scotland moulders in but little while.
Come, rain down tears for that poor Scottish ka—
   He caws his little caw, and gangs awa′;
Though sometimes rather he may gang awô,
   And not awä, when he has cawed his caw.

The Scottish ka's a jackdaw. Don't forget
   That jackdaws are entirely formed of *khet,*
The ''part corruptible,'' Egyptians say.
   That is, the Scottish ka is mortal clay
(Or mortal clô, or maybe mortal clä;
   In any case, it's bad news for the ka).

Not so the ka of Egypt; through and through
   The lucky creature's essence of *sahu.*
The flesh has fled, and spirit is the whole.
   (Egyptians say *sahu,* and mean the soul.)
Souls have no gang awäing, gang awôing;
   They hang around the place, and keep on
      cawing.

I find that travel fuddles. When I stay
   In Scotland, and espy a ka, I pray.
Were I in Egypt, and a ka I saw,
   I'd try to pray, but probably I'd caw.

lamprophony (lam′pro.fō′ni, lam.-prof′o.ni): loud, ringing speech.

lancepesade (lans′pi.zäd, -pe.zäd): a lance corporal. 7.

lancinate (lan′si.nāt): to tear, stab, lacerate.

landlooker (land′look′er): a timber surveyor. 32.

landloper (land′lō′per): one who runs about the land; a vagabond; a renegade.

languescent (lan.gwes′ent): becoming languid or fatigued. 52.

laniation (lā′ni.ā′shun): the act of tearing in pieces. 52.

THE ZAMBIAN KWACHA'S WORTH 100
NGWEES (PRONOUNCED NGWAYS)

O you kwacha!
Once I've gotcha
I'll have a hundred ngwees!
A kwacha's smaller
Than a Yankee dollar . . .
But it ain't hay these days.

---

lant (lant): urine, esp. stale urine used in manufacturing. 1.

lanx (langks): in ancient Rome, a large metal platter.

laparohysterosalpingoooophorectomy (lap′a.ro.his′ter.o.sal′ping.o.o.e.fo.-rek′to.mi): surgical removal of the female reproductive organs.

laparoscope (la′pa.ro.skōp): an instrument inserted through the intestinal wall for direct medical examination.

lapicide (lap′i.sīd): a stonecutter.

lapidify (la.pid′i.fī): to turn into stone.

lapling (lap′ling): one who particularly enjoys reclining on women's laps.

lappaceous (la.pā′shus): in botany, resembling a burdock burr; echinate.

lappage (lap′ij): the amount that surfaces or layers overlap.

lari (lā′ri): money consisting of silver wire doubled, either twisted into the form of fishhooks or straight. Hook money. (cap) A suborder of Charadiformes, including the gulls, terns, jaegers, and skimmers.

larigot (lar′i.got): a shepherd's pipe or flageolet.

larmoyant (lär.moi′ant): tearful.

laroid (lar′oid, lā′roid): pert. to gulls.

larve (lärv): larva.

laryngophony (la′ring.gof′o.ni): the sound of the voice as heard through a stethoscope placed upon the larynx.

lasket (las′ket): on ships, an eye formed on a headrope for attaching a piece of canvas to the foot of a sail. A latching.

lassipedia (las′i.pē′di.a): a case of tired feet.

lat (lat): a pillar in some Indian Buddhist buildings; also, a gold coin of Latvia.

latericeous, lateritious (lat′er.ish′us): brick-red; resembling brick.

lateropulsion (lat.er.o.pul′shun): a sidewise way of walking, as from Parkinson's disease.

latescent (lā.tes′ent): becoming, or being, hidden from view, as a *latescent* meaning.

latibulize (la.tib′ū.līz): to hibernate.

laticostate (lat′i.kos′tāt): broad-ribbed.

Latinitaster (la.tin′i.tas′ter): one who has a smattering of Latin.

latipennate (lat′i.pen′āt): broad-winged.

latria (la.trī′a): the highest kind of worship, given to God only.

latrobe (la.trōb′): a kind of stove that heats the room above too.

latus (lā′tus): side.

lau-lau (lou′lou): meat and fish wrapped in leaves and baked or steamed. 38.

laureole (lô′ri.ōl): spurge-laurel. 1.

Laurus (lô′rus): a genus of trees comprising the laurel, bay laurel, bay tree, etc.

lavolt, lavolta (la.vōlt′, -a): an old dance for two persons, consisting largely of making high springs. 1.

lav (lav): short for lavatory.

lavor (lav′er): basin, laver.

lawk, lawks (lôk, -s): minced form of *Lord*, used esp. in surprise. 11.

layboy (lā′boi): a papermaking-machine attachment that delivers sheets in piles.

leal (lēl): faithful; loyal; true. Genuine, correct. 5.

leam (lēm): a gleam of light, radiance. To shine forth; gleam. 44A. A drain in a fen. 13. To remove (nuts) from the husk.

leat (lēt): an artificial trench for water, esp. one leading to or from a mill. 13.

lecanomancy, lecanoscopy (lek.a.no.-man′si, -nos′ko.pi): divination by gazing fixedly at water in a basin.

lech (lech): a prehistoric monumental stone. A lecher. 21.

lectual (lek′chōō.al): bedridden.

Ledum (lē′dum): a small genus of shrubs of cold regions, as the Labrador tea and the marsh tea. (not cap) A plant of this genus.

leeangle, liangle (lē′ang′gl): a heavy weapon of the Australian aborigines having a sharp-pointed end bent at right angles to the shank.

legulian (leg′ū.lē′an): a lawyer, pettifogger. Lawyerlike (used pejoratively).

legumen (li.gū′men): a legume.

legumin (li.gū′min): vegetable cassein.

Leipoa (lī.pō′a): a genus of Australian mound-building birds of mixed white, brown, black, and gray plumage. The adults are about two feet long.

lelotrichous (le.lot′ri.kus): smooth-haired.

lemel (lē′mel): metal filings.

lenify (len′i.fi, lēn-): to assuage; soften. 52.

lenitic (li.nit′ik): living in quiet waters.

lenitude (len′i.tūd): the quality of being lenient. A lenient action.

lentando (len.tän′dō): in music, becoming slower; retarding—used as a direction.

lentiginous (len.tij.i.nus): freckly.

lentiscus (len.tis′kus): the mastic tree. A preparation of its leaves, used as an adulterant of sumac.

lentitude (len′ti.tūd): slowness; sluggishness; languor.

lentoid (len′toid): lens-shaped.

lentor (len′tôr): tenacity; also, sluggishness.

lenvoy (len.voi′): to bid farewell.

lepid (lep′id): pleasant; jocose; charming. 52.

lepidosiren (lep′i.do.sī′ren): a dipnoan eel-shaped fish inhabitating the swamps and tributaries of the Amazon and La Plata.

leptorrhinian (lep′to.rin′i.an): having a long thin nose.

lerret (ler′et): a powerful sea boat with sails and oars, used in the English Channel.

lesed (lēst): damaged; injured. 18A.

lethiferous (le.thif′er.us): deadly; destructive.

leucomelanous (lū.ko.mel′a.nus): pert. to a light complexion with dark hair and eyes.

leucous (lū′kus): white, blond—applied esp. to albinos.

levoduction (lev′o.duk′shun): a leftward movement, esp. of the eye.

lexiphanic (lek′si.fan′ik): interlarded with pretentious words; bombastic.

li (lē): in China, as a measure of weight, a decigram; as a measure of distance, a millimeter, kilometer, or centiare. In Chinese philosophy, correct behavior as the expression of inner harmony.

Liassic (li.as′ik): in geology, pert. to the Lias, the oldest division of the European Jurassic system.

liberticidal (li′bur′ti.sī′dal): destroying or tending to destroy liberty.

licca (lik′a): a West Indian tree.

lich (lich): a body; esp., a dead body, a corpse. 17A.

licitation (lis′i.tā′shun): the act of selling or bidding at auction.

lieve (lēv): lief.

ligger (lig′er): a counterpane, coverlet; a float that usu. consists of a bundle of reeds with baited line attached for pike fishing; a footpath (as a plank) across a ditch or drain. 13.

liguration (lig′ū.rā′shun): a greedy licking or devouring. 52.

ligyrophobia (lij′i.ro.fō′bi.a): fear of loud noises.

lilaceous (lī.lā′shus): like the color lilac.

lilapsophobia (lī.lap′so.fō′bi.a): fear of tornadoes.

liliaceous (lil′i.ā′shus): like or pert. to lilies.

lill (lil): in music, one of the holes of a pipe or other wind instrument. 44. A very small pin. To loll; said of the tongue. 11.

limaceous, limacine (lī.mā′shus, līm′a.sin): pert. to slugs.

Limax (lī′maks): the genus containing the typical slugs.

limberham (lim′ber.ham): a supple-jointed person; one who is obsequious. 1.

limbous (lim′bus): with slightly overlapping borders—said of a suture.

limen (lī′men): the borderline of awareness.

limicolous (lī.mik′o.lus): living in mud.

limitrophe (lim′i.trōf): adjacent; on the frontier.

limity (lim′i.ti): a limit. 1.

limivorous (li.miv′o.rus): swallowing mud for the organic matter contained in it.

limnophilous (lim.nof′i.lus): living in freshwater ponds.

limosis (lī.mō′sis): a morbid desire to eat chalk. Any insatiable craving for food.

Limulus (lim′ū.lus): the commonly used generic name of the king or horseshoe crab.

lin (lin): the linden. Flax; linen; to stop; desist. 11. In Chinese mythology, a female unicorn.

lincture (lingk′cher): a thick cough syrup to be licked or sucked.

lind, lynde (lind): the linden.

lindo (lin′dō): any of several bright-colored South American tanagers.

lingel, lingle (ling′gl): a shoemaker's thread; a little thong of leather. 44.

linguacious (lin.gwā′shus): loquacious.

linonophobia (lin′on.o.fō′bi.a): fear of string.

linous (lī′nus): pert. to, or in, a line. 52.

liparoid (lip′a.roid): fatty.

lipectomy (li.pek′to.mi): the surgical removal of fat.

lipogram (lip′o.gram): a written passage in which specified letters of the alphabet are avoided.

lipography (li.pog′ra.fi): the inadvertent omission of a letter, syllable, etc. in writing.

lipper (lip′er): ripply waves; light sea spray. In whaling, a piece of blubber used for wiping the deck. A tool for forming the lip on glass containers. To wipe with a lipper. 13.

THE LIRIPOOP AND HIS LIRIPIPE

A liripoop (read *nincompoop*)
  Affected silly clothing,
Quite unaware folks called him "stupe,"
  And looked on him with loathing.

One day he donned a liripipe,
  And rudely he was baited
When strolling in his hood and stripe,
  Liripipionated.

Some kids, cheered on by kin and kith,
  Soon had his life at risk.
They pummeled him in every lith,
  They kicked him in the lisk.

And when he sought to loppet off,
  They threw him in a ditch,
Where still his hood he would not doff,
  Though beaten to a lich.

They laid him in a litten dim,
  Nor guessed, those guttersnipes,
The saints in heaven welcomed him
  All wearing liripipes.

---

lippitude (lip′i.tūd): soreness or bleariness of the eyes.

lipsanography (lip′sa.nog′ra.fi): the study of relics.

lipsanotheca (lip′sa.no.thē′ka): a shrine or container for relics.

liration (lī.rā′shun): a ridge (as on some shells) resembling a fine thread or hair.

lirella (li.rel′a): an elongated spore structure in lichens that has a furrow along the middle.

liripipe (lir′i.pīp): a medieval hood, esp. one worn by academics. 6.

liripoop (lir′i.pōop): a trick. A silly ass. Also, a liripipe. 6.

lirp (lurp): a snap of the fingers; to snap them. 1.

lis (lēs): in heraldry, a fleur-de-lis.

lish (lish): active; agile; quick. 43.

lisk (lisk): the groin. 11.

lissen (lis′en): a cleft dividing the seam of a rock. A support for a beehive. A strand of rope. 11.

lissotrichous (lis′o.trik′us): having straight hair.

literatim (lit′er.ā′tim): letter for letter; literally.

lith (lith): a joint or limb; a bodily member. A division or segment, as of an orange. 44A.

lithoglyph (lith′o.glif): an engraving on stone, esp. on a gem; an engraved stone.

lithoid (lith′oid): like a stone.

lithomancy (lith.o.man′si): divination by stones or stone charms.

lithophagan, lithophagous (li.thof′a.gan, -gus): swallowing stones or gravel. Burrowing in rock.

lithophane (lith′o.fān): porcelain impressed with figures that are made distinct by transmitted light, as in a lampshade.

---

lithotripter (lith′o.trip′ter): a medical device that shatters stones in the kidney by shock waves without injuring surrounding tissue.

litten (lit′en): a churchyard or cemetery. 2.

littlin (lit′lin): a young or small child or animal. 43.

liturate (lich′er.āt): spotted. To blot out, erase. 1.

litus (lī′tus): in Frankish and some German medieval law, one of a class between the free man and the slave or serf.

llanero (lya.ner′ō): a cowboy or herdsman in South America.

loa (lō′a): a kind of African filiarial worm infecting humans, and transmitted by the bite of a fly.

lochus (lō′kus): a small division of an ancient Greek army, of about 100 to 200 men.

logan, login (lō′gen): a stretch of still water in a river or bay. 28.

loganamnosis (lō′ga.nam.nō′sis): preoccupation with trying to recall forgotten words.

loggin (log′in): a bundle, as of straw.

logodaedaly (lō′go.ded′a.li): verbal legerdemain; wordplay. 52.

logolept (lō′go.lept): a word freak.

logology (lo.gol′o.ji): the science of words. 52.

logomachy (lo.gom′a.ki): contention about or by means of words.

loka (lō′ka): in Hindu mythology, a world; sphere; universe.

loke (lōk): var. of *lawk.* A private road; a lane; a blind alley. 13.

lollock (lol′uk): per Mrs. Byrne, a large lump.

lollop (lol′up): to loll, lounge, slouch about. To proceed with a bouncing or bobbing motion. 13.

Loma (lō′ma): a people of the border regions of Liberia, Sierra Leone, and the Republic of Guinea. (not cap) A broad-topped hill. 35A.

lomi-lomi (lō′mi.lō′mi): a vigorous massage used by Hawaiians to relieve pain and fatigue.

---

*YOUNG MAN'S PLEA OF NOT GUILTY
TO A VERY LONG WORD*

What—did I trap her? No.
What—have I kissed her? No.
What—were we palping? No.
All was correct with me.
  She'll say the same.

She's had a *laparo-*
       hystero-
    salpingo-
      o-o-forectomy?
I'm not to blame.

longe (lunj): var. of *lunge*. A long rope used to lead a horse in training. A place, usu. a ring, for training horses. The *namaycush*.

longicaudal (lon′ji.kô′dal): long-tailed.

longiloquy (lon.jil′o.kwi): long-windedness.

longimanous (lon.jim′a.nus): long-handed.

longinquity (lon.jin′kwi.ti): remoteness. 52.

longipennate (lon.ji.pen′āt): long-winged.

longirostral (lon′ji.ros′tral): having a long jaw.

loob (lōōb): the slimy dregs of tin ore; the trough containing them.

loof (lōōf): the palm of the hand; the inside of a cat's paw. 43A.

lopper (lop′er): curdled milk; a blood clot; slush; curdled. 5. To curdle. 12, 13.

loppet (lop′et): to walk or run awkwardly. 13.

lorikeet (lor′i.kēt): a small brightly colored parrot of the Malay archipelago.

lorimer (lor′i.mer): a maker of bits, spurs, and metal mountings for bridles and saddles.

loro (lō′rō): the monk parrot. The parrot fish.

lotic (lō′tik): pert. to or living in actively moving water.

Lotophagi (lo.tof′a.jī, -ji): in the *Odyssey*, a people who subsisted on the lotus and lived in the dreamy indolence it induced.

lotophagous (lo.tof′a.gus): lotus-eating.

louche (lōōsh): squinting. Oblique, devious, sinister.

loury (lou′ri): var. of *lowery*, overcast.

loutrophoros (loo.trof′er.os): in ancient Greece, a vase used for transporting ceremonial bathwater for the bride and groom.

lovertine (luv′er.tēn): one addicted to lovemaking. 1.

lowmen (lō′men): dice loaded to turn up low numbers.

loxotic (lok.sot′ik): in medicine, slanting, distorted.

loxotomy (lok.sot′o.mi): in amputation, an oblique section.

loy (loi): a long narrow spade used in Ireland. A tool for digging postholes. 32.

lubric (lōō′brik): lubricious. 52.

luce (lōōs): a pike, esp. when full grown. In heraldry, a fleur-de-lis. A lynx. 1.

luciferous (lōō.sif′er.us): affording physical or mental illumination.

lucifugous (loo.sif′u.gus): avoiding light.

lucivee (lōō′si.vi): a lynx (corruption of *loup-cervier*).

lucriferous (loo.krif′er.us): profitable; lucrative.

luctation (luk.tā′shun): a struggle; endeavor. 1.

luctiferous (luk.tif′er.us): mournful; sorry. 52.

lud (lud): var. of *lord*. (cap) A legendary king of Britain.

ludicropathetic, ludicroserious (lōō-′di.kro.pa.thet′ik, -sēr′i.us): ludicrous and either pathetic or serious at once.

ludification (lōō′di.fi.kā′shun): the act of deriding.

luggar (lug′er): any of several large Asiatic falcons of dull-brown color.

luggy (lug′i): a small wooden pail or dish with a handle. 44A.

lulliloo (lul.i.lōō): to welcome with cries of joy.

lum (lum): a chimney; a sink; pool; pond. 11. An area of softness in a coal seam. 30.

lunt (lunt): smoke, esp. of a pipe; a torch; to kindle, light. 44A.

lupanarian (lōō′pa.nâr′i.an): pert. to brothels.

lupulus (lōō′pū.lus): the hop plant.

lura (lōō′ra): in anatomy, the orifice of the infundibulum of the brain.

lurry (lur′i): something, as a formula or a canting speech, repeated by rote; a confused throng or aggregation; a jumble of sounds, tumult. 10. To drag; worry; hurry. 11. Var. of *lorry*.

lusk (lusk): lazy; a lazy person. 11. To loaf; idle; skulk. 1.

lusory (lū′zer.i): sportive; playful; composed in a playful style.

lutarious (lōō.târ.i.us): living in mud.

lutescent (lōō.tes′ent): yellowish.

lutulence (lōō′tū.lens): muddiness, turbidity.

lychnoscopic (lik′no.skop′ik): pert. to a low side window of medieval churches.

lycopode (lī′ko.pōd): powder of lycopodium, the club moss known also as ground pine, ground fir, etc.

Lycopsis (lī.kop′sis): a genus of bristly herbs, inc. the wild bugloss.

lygophilia (lī′go.fēl′ya): love of darkness.

lygophobia (lī′go.fō′bi.a): fear of darkness.

lymacatexis (lī′ma.ka.tek′sis): preoccupation with dirt.

lypophrenia (lī′po.frē′ni.a): sadness for no known reason.

lyssophobia (lis′o.fō′bi.a): morbid dread of hydrophobia.

M

mab (mab): to dress sloppily; a slattern. 1.

Macaca (ma.kä′ka): a genus of Old World monkeys, the macaques.

macaco (ma.kä′kō): any of several lemurs, as the black lemur and the ring-tailed lemur.

macarize (mak.a.rīz): to laud; declare happy or blessed.

machi (mä′chi): in Japan, a town or commercial center.

machinal (ma.shē′nal): pert. to machines.

mackalow (mak.a.lō): goods held in trust by a foster parent for the child. 7A.

macrobian (ma.krō′bi.an): long-lived.

macrodactylic (ma′kro.dak.til′ik): long-fingered.

macrology (ma.krol′o.ji): redundancy.

macromastic (ma′kro.mas′tik): having excessively developed mammary glands.

macrophobia (ma′cro.fō′bi.a): a fear of long waits.

macrosmatic (mak′rz.mat′ik): having a supersensitive nose.

macrotome (ma′kro.tōm): an instrument for making large sections of anatomical specimens.

macrotous (ma.krō′tus): having large ears.

mactation (mak.tā′shun): sacrificial murder.

OR AT LEAST MAKE UP AFTERWARDS

Since women take *mariticide*
  In stride
(I understand the merest bride
  Can do it):
While husbands hear that word and flinch,
For their own wives might in a pinch
  Go to it;

Since women, though, cannot abide
  Uxoricide,
Whence certain of their sex have died
  Unknowing—
Have vanished from the ones they love,
Nor stood upon the order of
  Their going;

Since dead by either word is just
  As dust;—
Let me suggest, to be discussed,
  A moral:
Can't men be more *uxorious*,
And wives more *maritorious*?
To drive uxoricide away,
To keep mariticide at bay—
  Don't quarrel.

---

macuta (ma.kōō′ta): an old west African coin or unit of value.

madefaction (mad′i.fak′shun): wetting.

madrasah (ma.dras′a): in India, a Mohammedan university.

maffle (maf′l): to stammer; blunder. To confuse. 2.

mafflin (maf′lin): a simpleton. 13.

mafoo, mafu (ma.fōō′): in China, a groom or stable boy.

magadis (mag′a.dis): a Greek dulcimer. A Lydian flute on which octaves could be played.

magger (mag′er): var. of *mauger*. 9.

magian (mā′ji.an): magical. (cap) One of the Magi, a priestly order of ancient Medea and Persia.

magiric (ma.ji′rik): pert. to the art of cookery. 52.

magister (maj′is.ter): a medieval title given to a person in authority or to a licensed teacher.

magnetopause (mag.net′o.pôz): the boundary between the terrestrial and the interplanetary magnetic field.

maha (mä′ha): the Ceylonese langur, a long-tailed monkey. Also, the sambar deer.

Mahadeva (mä′ha.dē′va): Siva.

maholi (ma.hō′li): a long-eared African lemur.

maieusiophobia (mä.ū′si.o.fō′bi.a): fear of childbirth.

mainour (mā′ner): in old English law, stolen goods found on the thief.

maja (mä′ha): a Spanish belle of the lower classes.

majagua (ma.hä′gwa): a small tropical tree yielding a durable fiber.

majestatic (maj′es.tat′ik): majestic. 1.

maki (mak′i): a lemur.

makimono (mäk.i.mō′nō): in Japan, a picture, picture story, or writing mounted on paper and usu. rolled in a scroll.

mako, makomako (mä′kō, mä′ko.-mä′kō): a New Zealand tree.

malacissation (mal′a.si.sā′shun): the act of making something soft or pliable.

malacodermous (mal′a.ko.dur′mus): soft-skinned.

malactic (ma.lak′tik): emollient; tending to soften.

malaxator (mal.ak.sā′ter): a machine for grinding, kneading, or stirring into a pasty or doughy mass.

malentendu (mal′än′tän.dū): misunderstood; a misunderstanding.

maliferous (ma.lif′er.us): harmful; unhealthy, as certain climates.

malik (mal′ik): in Hindu law, an owner, a proprietor.

malleate (mal′i.āt): to hammer; to beat into a plate, sheet, or leaf, as a metal. 52.

malleolus (ma.lē′ō.lus): the rounded lateral projection on the bone of the leg at the ankle.

malmaison (mal′mä′zen′): any of various tender greenhouse carnations with large, fully double, usu. pink flowers.

malmy (mä′mi): clayey, chalky soil. Soft; warm and sticky, as weather. 44C.

malneirophrenia (mal.nī′ro.frē′ni.a): depression following a nightmare.

malo (mal′ō): in Hawaii, a loincloth worn by men. An ornamental royal girdle.

malum (mā′lum): pl. *mala*. An offense against right or law; evil, wrong.

mamamouchi (mä.ma.mōō′chi): in Molière's *Le Bourgeois Gentilhomme*, a bogus Turkish title. One with such a title.

mameliere (mam.el.yâr): in medieval armor, one of two round plates, or a single plate, covering the breasts.

mamelon (mam′i.lon): a low, rounded hill.

mameluco (mam′i.lōō′kō): in Brazil, a mestizo.

mammock (mam′uk): a shapeless piece; a scrap. 11.

mammonism (mam′un.izm): devotion to wealth; worldliness.

mammothrept (mam′o.thrept): a spoiled child; lit., a child brought up by its grandmother.

manal (man′al): pert. to the hand.

manavelins (ma.nav′el.inz): leftovers; odds and ends. 59.

manbote (man′bōt): in Anglo-Saxon and old English law, compensation paid to a lord for the killing of his man.

manchet (man′chet): a wheaten bread of the highest quality. 9. A spindle-shaped roll of manchet. A piece of white bread. 11A.

mancinism (man′si.nizm): left-handedness.

mancipate (man′si.pāt): enslaved. To enslave or restrict. 1.

mandillion (man.dil′yun): a loose outer garment of the 16th and 17th centuries, as a soldier's sleeved cloak or a servant's sleeveless garment.

mandola (man.dō′la): a 16th- and 17th-century lute with a pear-shaped body, the ancestor of today's smaller mandolin.

mandom (man′dum): a word used by Browning for *mankind*.

mandra (man′dra): in the Eastern church, a monastery.

manducatory (man′dū.ka.tôr′i): related to or adapted for chewing.

manerial (ma.nē′ri.al): manorial. 52.

mang (mang): to lead or go astray. 43.

mangonize (mang′go.nīz): to traffic in slaves. 52. To furbish up for sale. 1.

maniaphobia (mä′ni.a.fō′bi.a): fear of insanity.

manipulandum (ma.nip′ū.lan′dum): in psychology, something to be manipulated.

manit (man′it): the amount of work done by one worker in one minute; a man-minute.

mannie (man′i): a little man; in affectionate use, a boy or lad. 44A.

mansuete (man.swēt′, man′swēt): tame; gentle; kind.

manteel (man.tēl′): a cloak or cape; a mantle. 1.

mantology (man.tol′o.ji): divination. 52.

manucaption (man.ū.kap′shun): a former system of law serving a purpose similar to bail, or writ for the production in court of an alleged felon.

manucaptor (man′ū.kap′ter): one who takes responsibility for the appearance of an accused in court and for defending him.

manuduction (man′ū.duk′shun): guidance as by the hand; direction. A guide; an introduction.

manuductor (man′ū.duk′ter): director, esp. of a band or choir.

manurement (ma.nūr′ment): cultivation. 1.

manustupration (man′ū.stū.prä′shun): masturbation.

maquillage (ma′ki.yäzh): makeup.

Mara (mä′ra): in Teutonic folklore, nightmare taken as a demon, usu. female. In Buddhist mythology, the spirit of evil and enemy of the Buddha. In the Bible, the name claimed by Naomi, meaning bitter. Also (not cap.) a rodent of Patagonia related to the cavies.

marcato (mär.kä′to): in music, marked, emphatic; accented.

marcescible (mär.ses′i.bl): liable to wither or fade.

marcidity (mär.sid′i.ti): state of witheredness, decay, exhaustion. 1.

maremma (ma.rem′a): in Italy, low marshy maritime country, which in summer is so unhealthy as to be uninhabitable. The miasma of such a region.

margaritaceous (mär′ga.ri.tä′shus): pearly.

margent (mär′jent): a margin; border; brink; edge. 9.

margosa (mär.gō′sa): a large East Indian tree having a bitter bark used as a tonic.

maricolous (ma.rik′o.lus): inhabiting the sea.

marigenous (ma.rij′i.nus): produced in or by the sea.

marikina (mar′i.kē′na): the silky tamarind.

mariticide (ma.rit′i.sīd): murder of a husband by his wife; a wife who kills her husband.

maritodespotism (mar′i.to.des′po.tizm): domination by the husband.

maritorious (mar′i.tôr′i.us): excessively fond of one's husband; female equivalent of *uxorious*.

markhor (mär′kôr): a wild goat of mountainous regions from Afghanistan to India.

markka (märk′ka): the gold monetary unit of Finland.

marlet (mär′let): a martin or a swift. 1.

marlock (mär′lok): to frolic; sport; a frolic. 13.

marmarize (mär′ma.rīz): to convert (limestone) into marble.

marouflage (ma′rōō.fläzh): the process of painting on canvas and then gluing the picture to the wall.

marrano (ma.rä′nō): a Jew or Moor in medieval Spain who professed Christianity to escape prosecution.

martyrium (mär.tir′i.um): a building or chamber used by early Christians as a burial place. A place where the relics of martyrs are stored.

marum (mar′um): cat thyme. Also, var. of *marram*, beach grass.

marver (mär′ver): a flat slab (as of metal, stone, or wood) on which a gather of glass is rolled, shaped, and cooled.

maschaliphidrōsis (mas.kal.i.fi.drō′sis): heavy sweating of the armpits.

mascle (mas′kl): male. 1. A steel plate, esp. of lozenge shape, used in series on 13th-century armor.

mashallah (mash.al′a): an Arabic exclamation, signifying "What wonders has God wrought!"

mashugga (ma.shoog′a): crazy.

maskoid (mas′koid): like a mask. A masklike carving on ancient Mexican and Peruvian buildings.

masticic (mas.tis′ik): pert. to mastic.

mastigophobia (mas′ti.go.fō′bi.a): fear of punishment.

mataco (ma.tä′kō): a three-banded armadillo, the apar. (cap) A people of Bolivia, Paraguay, and Argentina.

matamata (mä′ta.mä′ta): a turtle of the rivers of Guiana and northern Brazil, reaching a length of three feet, with rough shell and long neck. Also, any of several South American trees.

matanza (ma.tan′za): a slaughterhouse. 35C.

matchy (mach′i): fit for matching or mating.

matelassé (mat′la.sā): decorated with markings like quilting; a fabric so decorated.

matelotage (mat′lo.täzh): the hire of a boat. The communal living of West Indian buccaneers in the 18th century.

mathesis (ma.thē′sis): learning; mental discipline, esp. in mathematics.

matico (ma.tē′kō): a shrubby tropical American wild pepper. Also, its leaves, used formerly as a stimulant and hemostatic.

matra (mä′tra): in Sanskrit and other Indian languages, a unit of metrical quantity.

matric (mā′trik): pert. to a matrix.

matripotestal (mā′tri.po.tes′tal): pert. to maternal control.

matronize (mā′tro.nīz): to make into or like a matron. To chaperone.

mauger, maugre (mô′gr): in spite of, notwithstanding. 9. Ill will; spite—often used as a mild imprecation. 1.

maugh (môg): a brother-in-law; a son-in-law; a companion. 13.

maut (môt): var. of *malt*. 44A.

maxilliped (mak.sil′i.ped): one of the mouth appendages of crustaceans.

mazological (mā′zo.loj′i.kal): pert. to mammiferous animals.

mazomancy (mā′zo.man′si): divination by interpretation of a baby's nursing.

mazophilous (ma.zof′i.lus): mad about breasts.

mbori (em.bôr′i): a fever and hemhorragic disease, a mild form of surra, affecting camels.

meable (mē′a.bl): readily penetrable.

meacock (mē′kok): an uxorious, effeminate, or spiritless man. 1.

meak (mēk): a long-handled hook or scythe. 13.

mease (mēz): to pacify, calm. 44A. A measure for counting herrings, varying in different localities. 14.

mechanograph (mi.kan′o.graf): a copy of an artwork, produced by mechanical means.

mechanomorphism (mi.ka′no.môr′fizm): the belief that the universe can be explained mechanically.

mechanophobia (mek′a.no.fō′bi.a): fear of machines.

meconology (mek′o.nol′o.ji): the study of opium.

meconophagism (mek′o.nof′a.jizm): addiction to opium.

meda (mē′dä): var. of *mide, midewiwin*.

medalet (med′l.et): a small medal.

medicaster (med′i.kas′ter): a medical charlatan or quack.

mediety (mi.dī′i.ti): the half; moiety. 6A. Middle or intermediate part. 1. Moderation, temperance.

meech, miche (mēch, mich): to move in a furtive or cringing manner; to skulk, sneak; to complain, whine. 11.

meechy (mēch′i): sneaky, dishonorable.

megalonisis (meg′a.lō′ni.sis): a tendency to exaggerate.

Megalonyx (meg′a.lon′iks): a genus of large extinct Pliocene and Pleistocene toothless mammals of North America.

megalophobia (meg.a.lo.fō′bi.a): fear of anything large.

megalophonous (meg.a.lof′a.nus): having a loud voice.

megatype (meg′a.tīp): an enlarged copy of a picture or negative.

mehari (me.hä.ri): a kind of swift dromedary once used by the French army in Algeria.

meinie (mān′i): a family, household; a herd. 1.

meizoseismal (mī′zo.sīz′mal): pert. to the maximum destructive force of an earthquake.

mel (mel): honey. Also, a subjective unit of tone pitch.

melangeur (me.län.zhur′): a machine for making chocolate syrup.

melanochroic (mel.an.o.krō′ik): pert. to Caucasians having dark hair and pale complexions.

melanous (mel′a.nus): having dark skin and black hair.

melcryptovestimentaphilia (mel.krip′to.ves′ti.men′ta.fil′i.a): a fondness for women's black underwear.

melic (mel′ik): of or pert. to song.

meline (mē′līn, -lin): canary yellow. Also, made up of or resembling badgers.

melisophobia (mel′is.o.fō′bi.a): fear of bees.

melittology (mel.i.tol′o.ji): the scientific study of bees.

mell (mel): the last cut of grain in the harvest; a feast at the close of harvest; a hammer or mallet made of wood; a booby prize; to join; to join in combat (usu. with *with*). 13.

melliloquy (mel.lil′o.kwi): sweet speech.

melodion (mi.lō′di.on): a keyboard musical instrument of graduated metal rods, sounded by a revolving metal cylinder.

melogram (mel′o.gram): a graphic record showing the tones of successive syllables, words, phrases, sentences, etc.

melograph (mel′o.graf): a contrivance for recording the order and length of musical notes by recording the action of the keys of a keyboard.

melolog (mel′o.log): a declamation with musical accompaniment.

melomania (mel′o.mā′ni.a): inordinate passion for music.

melophobia (mel′o.fō′bi.a): hatred of music.

melopeia (mel′o.pē′a): the art of inventing melody; melodics; melody.

melote (mi.lō′ti): a monk's hair coat. 1.

Melursus (mel.ur′sus): the genus consisting of the sloth bear.

menacme (mi.nak′mi): the part of her life in which a woman menstruates.

mendaciloquy (men′da.sil′o.kwi): lying as a fine art.

mendicity (men.dis′i.ti): begging; mendicancy.

menilite (men′i.līt): an impure opal of a dull brown to gray color.

mennom (men′um): a minnow. 44A.

menology (mi.nol′o.ji): an ecclesiastical calendar of festivals honoring saints and martyrs. A register of saints.

menophania (men′o.fā′ni.a): false menstruation.

menticide (men′ti.sīd): brainwashing.

mentimutation (men′ti.mū.tā′shun): a change of mind.

mentulate (men′tū.lāt): having a large penis.

meracious (mi.rā′shus): unadulterated; pure.

meraculous (mi.rak′ū.lus): slightly dirty.

mercative (mur′ka.tiv): pert. to trade or commerce.

merdaille (mer.dīl′): the rabble.

merdivorous (mer.div′o.rus): dung-eating.

merenda (mi.ren′da): a snack between meals.

meritmonger (mer′it.mung′ger): one who expects salvation as a reward for good works.

merkin (mur′kin): the female pubis; a wig for it. 3A.

merorganization (mer.ôr′gan.i.zā′shun): a partial organization. 52.

merse (murs): land near water. 43. To immerse. 52.

mersion (mur′zhun): immersion. 1.

merulator (mer′ū.lā′ter): a wine bibber.

merycism (mer′i.sizm): the chewing of regurgitated food, or of the cud.

mesophilic (mez′o.fil′ik): thriving or growing best in medium temperatures.

mesothetic (mez′o.thet′ik): intermediate.

Messalian (mi.sāl′yun): a Euchite, one of an ecstatic, mendicant, vagrant Christian sect of the 4th to 8th century, which believed man's congenital devil could be expelled only by unremitting prayer.

mestee (mes.tē′): strictly, an octoroon; loosely, a half-caste.

metabasis (mi.tab′a.sis): in rhetoric, a transition from one subject or point to another. In medicine, a change in a disease, its symptoms, or treatment.

metabatic (met′a.bat′ik): pert. to the transfer of heat or any form of energy.

Metabola (mi.tab′o.la): a division of the insects that undergo a metamorphosis.

metad (me.täd′): a small field rat.

metagnostic (met′ag.nos′tik): unknowable.

metagrabolize (met.a.grab′o.līz): to mystify. 58.

metalepsis (met′a.lep′sis): in rhetoric, substitution by metonymy of one figurative sense for another.

metaleptic (met.a.lep′tik): pert. to a metalepsis. Also, designating a muscle having synergetic action with another muscle.

metallochrome (mi.tal′o.krōm): a coloring or ring produced on metal by the electrolytic decomposition of copper, lead peroxide, etc.

metallogeny (met′l.oj′e.ni): the branch of geology dealing with the origin of ore deposits.

metanalysis (met.a.nal′i.sis): the evolution of words into new elements (*a napron* into *an apron*) or their misdivision (*selfish* into *sell fish*).

metaplast (met′a.plast): a form made by a change in the letters or syllables of a word.

metayer (met′a.yā): a sharecropper.

metempirical (met′em.pir′i.kal): pert. to concepts outside human experience.

metempsychosis (met′em.sī.kō′sis): the transmigration of souls.

metemptosis (met′emp.tō′sis): the suppression of a day in the calendar to prevent the date of the new moon being set a day too late. The suppression of the bissextile day once in 134 years.

metensomatosis (met′en.sō′ma.tō′sis): the migration into one body of different souls.

meteoromancy (mē′ti.er.o.man′si): divination through thunder and lightning.

meterstick (mē′ter.stik): a device for leveling or measuring cargo.

metic (met′ik): in ancient Greece, a settler; immigrant; at Athens, an alien resident who had some civil privileges.

metical (met′i.kal): a coin of Mozambique.

metopomancy (met′o.po.man′si): divination by examination of the face.

metoposcopy (met′o.pos′ko.pi): the art of discovering character from the markings of the forehead.

metrician (mi.trish′un): a writer or student of verse.

metromania (met′ro.mā′ni.a): a mania for writing verse.

metrophobia (met′ro.fō.bi.a): hostility toward poetry.

meum (mē′um): mine, as in *meum and tuum*, "mine and yours." (cap) A genus of European herbs of the carrot family.

meuse (mūz): a gap or hole, as in a hedge or wall, through which a wild animal is accustomed to pass. A loophole.

meute (mūt): a mew or cage for hawks.

mezonny (mi.zon′i): money spent on drugs. 21.

miche (mich): a loaf of bread. 1. To pilfer. 1. To lurk; grumble secretly; play truant. 11.

michery (mich′er.i): theft; cheating. 1.

mico (mē′kō): a marmoset, esp. the black-tailed marmoset of parts of tropical South America.

microbiotic (mī′kro.bī.ot′ik): of a seed, surviving dormant for not more than three

years. Also, pert. to the microscopical flora and fauna of a region.

microlipet (mī′kro.lip′et): one upset by trifles.

microlithic (mī′kro.lith′ik): pert. to a tiny blade tool used in the paleolithic culture.

micromastic (mī′kro.mas′tik): having abnormally small breasts.

microstudy (mī′kro.stud′i): a study of a minute, specific, or minor part of a subject.

microtia (mī.krō′sha): smallness of the ear.

microtome (mī′kro.tōm): in biology, an instrument for cutting sections, as of organic tissues, for microscopic examination.

mide, midewiwin (mē′di, mi.di′wi.win): a once-powerful secret religious organization among the Ojibway Indians. A member of this organization.

milder (mil′der): to molder, decay. 13.

militaster (mil′i.tas′ter): an insignificant military man. 1.

mim (mim): affectedly shy. To act in a mim fashion. 11.

mimographer (mi.mog′ra.fer): a writer of mimes, in which scenes from life were represented in a ridiculous manner.

mimography (mi.mog′ra.fi): the art of reducing gestures or sign language to writing by means of symbols.

mimp (mimp): a pursing of the mouth or lips; to speak or act affectedly or mincingly. 44B.

mimsey (mim′zi): prim; prudish. 11.

minargent (mi.när′jent): a white alloy of copper, nickel, tungsten, and aluminum.

minauderie (mi.nôd′ri): (usu. pl.) Coquetry.

mingy (min′ji): stingy; mean. 26.

miniate (min′i.āt): pert. to the color of minium; to paint red.

minimifidianism (min′i.mi.fid′i.an.izm): the condition of having a minimal amount of faith.

minionette (min′yun.et): small, delicate. 1. In printing, a type size.

minium (min′i.um): red lead.

mino (mī′nō): in Japan, a cape or overcoat of straw, rushes, or the like, worn by peasants.

miny (mī′ni): pert. to a mine.

minyan (min′yun): in Jewish religion, a quorum, or number necessary for conducting public worship, consisting of not less than 10 males above the age of 13. (cap) Pert. to a prehistoric Greek civilization noted for its pottery.

Mirabel (mir′a.bel): a witty gentleman in Congreve's *Way of the World*. (not cap) A kind of plum.

mirabilia (mir′a.bil.i.a): wonders; miracles.

mirador (mir′a.dôr): a watchtower; a turret or window with an extensive outlook. The color reddish-orange.

mird (murd): to meddle; toy amorously; try. 44.

mirific, mirifical (mi.rif′ik, -rif′i.kal): working wonders; wonderful.

misapodisis (mis′a.pō′di.sis): a dislike of undressing in front of others.

miserotia (mis′er.ot′i.a): aversion to sex.

misocainia (mis′o.kī′ni.a): hatred of anything new or strange.

misogallic (mis′o.gal′ik): hating the French.

misomania (mis′o.mā′ni.a): hatred of everything.

misopedia (mis′o.pē′di.a): hatred of children, esp. one's own.

misophy (mis′o.fi): hatred of wisdom.

misopolemic (mis′o.po.lem′ik): hating war.

misoscopy (mi.sos′ko.pi): hatred of beauty or sights in general.

misotheism (mis′o.thē′izm): hatred of gods.

misotramontanism (mis′o.tra.mon′ta.-izm): hatred of the unknown.

missa (mis′a): (Latin): Mass, as *Missa bassa*, Low Mass, etc.

missionate (mish′u.nāt): to proselytize.

missis, missus (mis′iz, -uz): a married woman. Informally, one's wife.

mistetch (mis.tech′): a bad habit. To teach bad habits to. 13.

mistle (mis′l): mistletoe. 52.

mitrophobia (mī′tro.fō′bi.a): fear of hate.

mixogamy (mik.sog′a.mi): a surplus of male fish at spawning time.

Mixosaurus (mik′so.sôr′us): a genus of swimming reptiles of the Triassic Age similar to *Ichthyosaurus* but with less fully developed paddles.

mixoscopy (mik.sos′ko.pi): peeking at sexual intercourse from hiding.

mizzy (miz′i): a bog or quagmire. 11.

mneme (nē′mi): the persistent or recurrent effect of past experience of the individual or of the race.

mnesic (nē′sik): pert. to *mneme*.

mobby (mob′i): an alcoholic drink made from sweet potatoes in the West Indies. Fruit juice for distilling brandy; the brandy.

moch (mok, mōk): a moth. 44.

mogadore (mog′a.dôr): a ribbed silk or rayon fabric, used esp. for neckties.

moggan (mog′un): stocking; esp. a long stocking without a foot. 44.

mogigraphia (moj′i.graf′i.a): writer's cramp.

mogilalia (moj′i.lā′li.a, -lāl′ya): painful speech; stuttering.

mogo (mō′gō): an aboriginal stone hatchet.

moho (mō′hō): a Hawaiian honey eater having yellow breast feathers. (cap) A point at a depth ranging from about 3 miles beneath the ocean floor to about 25 miles beneath the continental surface where the earth's materials change from the crust to the mantle.

mohr (mōr): a gazelle of northern Africa with 11 or 12 prominent rings on its horns.

moider (moi′der): to throw into an unsettled state; perplex, bewilder, distract; to talk incoherently; to wander about in a confused manner. 13.

moiré (mô.rā, mwä′rā): a watered, clouded, or frosted appearance of silk, paper, rocks, or metals. To give such an appearance to (a surface).

moirologist (mwä.rol′o.jist): in Greece, a hired mourner.

moit (moit): var. of *mote*; usu. pl. A piece of stick or other matter found in wool.

OF MUGGETS AND MIRRORS

When muggets aren't the entrails of a calf or of a sheep,
They're lilies of the valley (you'll admit that's quite a leap).
Yet when I see the stranger in the mirror on the wall,
The difference in muggets seems no difference at all.

---

mojo (mō′jō): the *majagua*. A voodoo charm or amulet. 35A. (cap) An Arawakan people of northern Bolivia.

moki (mō.ki): the bastard trumpeter fish. A native raft made of bundles of rushes, flags, or dried flower stalks of flax. 56. (cap) Var. of *Moqui*, a branch of or another name for the Hopi Indians.

moko (mō′kō): the Maori system of tattooing. Also, a Maori tattoo of spiral grooves rubbed into the skin with a small instrument resembling an adz.

moko-moko (mō′ko.mō′kō): a common small lizard of New Zealand.

moky (mō′ki): foggy; misty. 11.

Mola (mō′la): the genus consisting of the sunfish.

molendinaceous (mo.len′di.nā′shus): resembling a windmill, as certain vegetable fruits or seeds.

moliminous (mo.lim′in.us): massive; momentous; also, laborious. 1.

mollescence (mo.les′ens): the state of softening, or tending to soften.

mollitious (mo.lish′us): softening; luxurious; sensuous.

mollitude (mol′i.tūd): softness. 52.

molossic, molossus (mo.los′ik, -us): in classical prosody, a foot of 3 long syllables. (cap) A genus of mastiff bats.

molybdomancy (mo.lib.do.man′si): divination by dropping molten lead on water.

molysmophobia (mol′is.mo.fō′bi.a): fear of dirt or contamination.

mome (mōm): a blockhead. 9. A cavilling critic. 1. A buffoon. 60.

mommiology (mom′i.ol′o.ji): the science of mummies. 52.

momo (mō′mō): the short-eared owl of Guam.

monachal (mon′a.kal): monastic.

monachist (mon′a.kist): monkish.

monadology (mō′na.dol′o.ji): the theory that the universe is composed of monads, or individual units. Monadism.

monepic (mo.nep′ik): consisting of one word or of sentences of one word.

monial (mō′ni.al): a nun.

monoblepsia (mon′o.blep′si.a): vision normal when but one eye is used, but indistinct with two. Also, color blindness for all but one color.

monocrotic (mon′o.krot′ik): of the pulse, having a simple beat and forming a smooth, single-crested curve on a sphygmogram.

monoculous (mo.nok′ū.lus): one-eyed.

monodelphic (mon′o.del′fik): pert. to the placental mammals.

monoglot (mon′o.glot): familiar with but a single language.

monogony (mo.nog′o.ni): asexual reproduction.

monokini (mon.o.kē′ni): a bikini without the top.

monolatry (mo.nol′a.tri): the worship of but one among several gods.

monophasic (mon′o.fā′zik): of electricity, single-phase; of an animal, having a single period of activity followed by a period of rest in each 24 hours.

monophobia (mon′o.fō′bi.a): fear of being alone.

monophylite (mo.nof′i.līt): one who believes that mankind developed from a single parent form.

monophysite (mo.nof′i.sīt): one who maintains that there was but a single nature in Christ, or that the human and divine in Him constituted but one composite nature.

monostrophe (mon′o.strōf′i): a poem in which all the stanzas are of the same metric form.

monotic (mo.not′ik): affecting a single ear, as a sound.

monotriglyph (mon′o.trī′glif): in architecture, intercolumniation with only one triglyph over the space between two columns.

monotropic (mon′o.trop′ik): visiting only a single kind of flower for nectar.

monstration (mon.strā′shun): demonstration. 1.

monstricide (mon′stri.sīd): the slaying of a monster.

monteith (mon.tēth′): an 18th-century silver punch bowl. A kind of polka dot handkerchief.

montigenous (mon.tij′e.nus): produced on a mountain.

Montjoy (mont.joi′): a medieval French battle cry. 1.

mool (mōol): mold; dry earth. (often pl.) a grave or its earth; to crumple; bury. 44C.

mopsical (mop′si.kal): like a spoiled child; pettish. 1.

mopus (mō′pus): a small coin. 23. (usu. pl) Money. 13.

mora (mō′ra): in Roman and civil law, a culpable delay. In Sparta, an army division. Also, a poisonous tree of the Amazon valley.

morcellate (môr′si.lāt): to divide into small pieces.

moreta (mo.ret′a): a salad with garlic.

morganize (môr′ga.nīz): to kidnap as insurance against a security leak.

moriform (môr.i.fôrm): shaped like a mulberry.

morigerous (mo.rij′er.us): obsequious.

mormaor (môr.mā′er): the ruler of one of the seven provinces into which medieval Scotland was divided. 44.

Moro (mō′rō, mo′rō): any of several Muslim peoples of the southern Philippines, or their languages.

morology (mo.rol′o.ji): nonsense; foolishness.

morosaurian (môr′o.sô′ri.an): one of a genus of large dinosaurs found in Jurassic strata in Colorado and Wyoming.

morosis (mo.rō.sis): moronity.

morph (môrf): a sound unit in language.

morphous (môr′fus): having a definite form.

morpunkee (môr.pung′ki): in India, a long, paddle-powered pleasure barge.

morro (môr′ō): a round hill or point of land; hence, *morro castle*, a castle on a hill.

morth (môrth): in Teutonic tribal law, murder (as by poison or witchcraft) that cannot be extenuated.

mortling (môrt′ling): wool taken from a dead sheep. 9.

mortress (môr′tres): a kind of soup or pottage, made of either bread and milk or various kinds of meat. 1.

Mosaism (mō′zā.izm): the religious and legal system attributed to Moses. Attachment to the Mosaic system.

mosasaurus (mō.sa.sôr′us): a genus of large, extinct, aquatic, Cretaceous fish-eating lizards.

motatorious (mō′ta.tôr′i.us): constantly active.

moted (mō′ted): filled with motes.

motet (mo.tet′): a polyphonic choral composition on a sacred text.

motitation (mō′ti.tā′shun): a quivering movement. 52.

moulleen (mōo.lēn′): a hornless cow; a muley.

moxibustion (mok′si.bus′chun): cauterization by moxa, the downy covering of a kind of dried leaf.

moyle (moil): a kind of shoe or slipper. In mining, a kind of wedge or drill.

mpret (em.pret′): title of the ruler of Albania, 1913–1914.

mubble-fubbles (mub′l.fub′ls): a fit of depression. 1.

mucedinous (mū.sed′i.nus): pert. to mold or mildew.

mucid (mū′sid): musty; slimy; mucous.

mucket (muk′et): any of several freshwater mussels esp. used in button manufacture.

muckmidden (muk′mid′en): a dunghill.

muculent (mū′kū.lent): slimy; moist and viscous; full of mucus.

mudge (muj): budge; move. 44.

muffineer (muf′i.nēr): a dish for keeping muffins hot.

mufflin (muf′lin): the long-tailed titmouse.

muga (mōo′ga): a kind of silk made from the cocoons of an Indian moth. The caterpillar producing this silk.

mugget (mug′et): entrails of a sheep or calf. 2. The woodruff; the lily of the valley. 13.

mukkus (muk′us): a dull, stupid person. 21.

mulada (mū.lä′da): a drove of mules. 35A.

mulierose (mū′li.er.ōs): woman-crazy.

mulita (mōo.lē′ta): the mule armadillo.

mulk (mulk): in Turkey, land that is the absolute property of its owner.

mullein, mullen (mul′en): any herb of the genus *Verbascum*, incl. the common mullein and the moth mullein.

mulley (mool′i, mōol′i): var. of *muley*, hornless.

mulm (mulm): organic sediment that accumulates in an aquarium.

mulse (muls): wine boiled and mixed with honey.

multanimous (mul.tan′i.mus): mentally multifaceted.

multiloquy (mul.til′o.kwi): talkativeness.

multiversant (mul′ti.vur′sant): protean; assuming many forms. 52.

multure (mul′cher): a toll or fee for the grinding of grain at a mill. 10.

mumblecrust (mum′bl.krust): a toothless person; a beggar.

mumpish (mump′ish): sullen; sulky.

mumpsimus (mump′si.mus): a bigoted adherent to exposed error. A fixed prejudice. 9.

mumruffin (mum′ruf′in): the long-tailed titmouse. 30.

mumu, muumu (mōo′mōo): a woman's loose-fitting dress, usu. brightly colored and patterned, adapted by the Hawaiians from the "Mother Hubbard" dress provided by the missionaries.

Munchausenism (mun-chouz′n.izm): the habit of telling extravagant fictions as truth.

mund (mund): in early English law, the right of protection or guardianship, as over a widow or orphan.

mundatory (mun′da.tôr.i): a towel or cloth used to cleanse ecclesiastical vessels used in Holy Communion.

mundify (mun′di.fī): to cleanse; deterge.

mundil (mun′dil): a turban ornamented with an imitation of gold or silver embroidery.

mundle (mun′dl): a stick for stirring. 2.

mundungus (mun.dung′gus): vile-smelling tobacco. 9. Waste, trash. 1.

munity (mū′ni.ti): a granted right or privilege. 52.

munjeet (mun.jēt′): Indian madder, a herb used in dyeing.

muriphobia (mū′ri.fō′bi.a): fear of mice.

murlin (mur′lin): *badderlocks*. 50. A round basket with a narrow opening. 44.

murly (mur′li): crumbly—used esp. of soil. 11.

Musa (mū′sa): a genus of perennial herbs, incl. the common banana.

muscoid (mus′koid): mosslike.

musculus (mus′kū.lus): a muscle.

museographist (mū.zi.og′ra.fist): one who writes about or classifies objects in a museum.

muskimoot (mus′ki.mōot): among certain Indians, a sack for holding pelts.

musquashroot (mus′kwôsh.rōot): the water hemlock. The musquash weed. The fall meadow rue. 32.

mussitation (mus′i.tā′shun): a muttering.

mustee (mus.tē′): *mestee*.

mutch (much): a head covering. 17A.

mutescent (mū.tes′ent): becoming mute or silent, as a final syllable.

mutuum (mū′chōo.um): a loan of things to be restored in kind. A contract for such a loan.

mux (muks): mess; botch. 11.

myall (mī′ôl): any of various Australian acacias having hard, fragrant wood. An uncivilized native of Australia. Wild, uncultivated.

mycoid (mī′koid): fungoid.

mycophagy (mī.kof′a.ji): the eating of fungi, as mushrooms.

mycterism (mik′ter.izm): in rhetoric, sneering derision.

mymy (mī′mī): an aboriginal hut; a bed. 53.

myophobia (mī′o.fō′bi.a): fear of mice.

SOME OF MY BEST FRIENDS ARE MULES

I don't deny I'm mulierose,
But this is also true:
Though mules and I are very close,
I'm fond of women too.

---

myoxine (mī.ok′sīn, -sin): pert. to dormice.

myriadigamous (mir′i.a.dig′a.mus): many times marrying or married.

myriologue (mir′i.o.log): in Greece, an extemporaneous funeral song composed and sung by a woman on the death of a close friend.

myriorama (mir′i.o.rama, -rä′ma): a picture made up of several smaller pictures combinable in many different ways.

myriotheism (mir′i.o.thi.izm): polytheism.

mysophobia (mī′so.fō′bi.a): fear of dirt; molymsophobia.

mystacial (mis.tā′shal): mustachial; pert. to a mustache.

mystagogic (mis.ta.goj′ik): pert. to one who initiates or interprets mysteries (as the Eleusinian mysteries), or to the practice of interpretation of mysteries.

mytacism (mī′ta.sizm): excessive or incorrect use of the letter *m* or its sound.

mythogony (mi.thog′o.ni): the study of the origin of myths.

mythogreen (mith′o.grin): a yellowish-green color of low saturation and high brilliance.

mythopoetic (mith′o.po.et′ik): making or giving rise to myths; mythopoeic.

N

nagaika (na.gī′ka): a thick, tightly twisted whip, used by Cossacks.

nagana (na.gä′na): in South Africa, a disease of livestock transmitted by the tsetse fly.

nagsman (nagz′man): a man who rides horses in a sales ring.

Naia (nā′a): var. of *Naja*.

nais (nā′is): a naiad; river nymph.

naissant (nā′snt): newly born or about to come into being; nascent.

Naja (nā′ja): a genus of elapine serpents containing the cobras.

namaqua (na.mäk′wa): a long-tailed African dove. (cap) One of a Hottentot people in southwest Africa.

namaycush (nam′ā.kush): a large trout, reaching 20 pounds, of the lakes of northern Africa. 37.

nanoid (nā′noid): having an abnormally small body; dwarfish.

nanosecond (nan.o.sek′und, -unt): one billionth of a second.

nanpie (nan′pī): the magpie. 30.

naology (nā.ol′o.ji): the study of holy buildings.

naos (nā′os): a temple or shrine. (cap) A star in the constellation Argus Navus.

naperer (nā′per.er): an officer of a royal household in charge of table linen.

napoo (na.pōō′): in British soldiers' slang, no more; all finished; dead. To be done for; die. To put an end to; kill.

naprapathy (na.prap′a.thi): a medical treatment by manipulation of strained ligaments.

naras, narras (nar′as): a South African desert shrub with melonlike fruit of a pleasant flavor.

narr (när): to growl or snarl, as a dog. 2. A legal declaration. 1, 28.

narra (nä′ra): a timber tree of the genus Lingoum; also, its hard wood, which takes a fine polish.

nasillate (nä′zi.lāt): to speak or sing through the nose.

nast (nast): filth; dirt. 13.

natalitial, natalitious (nā′ta.lish′al, -us): natal. 1.

natterjack (nat′er.jak): the common toad of western Europe.

natuary (nā′chōō.er′i): a ward or division of a hospital, set off for women in childbirth.

naulage (nô′lij): payment for sea freight.

naumochy (nô′mo.ki): in ancient Rome, a mock sea battle, or the theater in which it takes place.

nauropometer (nô′ro.pom′e.ter): an instrument for measuring a ship's heeling at sea. 52.

nauscopy (nôs′ko.pi): the pretended power of discovering ships or land at a great distance.

navicella (nav′i.sel′a): any vessel-shaped ornamental object, as one for holding incense.

navicert (nā′vi.surt): a certificate exempting a noncontraband shipment from search or seizure by British patrols.

nealogy (ni.al′o.ji): the study of young animals.

neanic (ni.an′ik): youthful. Specif., constituting the pupal stage of insect development.

nebby (neb′i): given to impertinent interference; spiteful. 45.

nebneb (neb′neb): acacia bark used in tanning.

Nebo (nē′bō): in the Babylonian religion, god of wisdom and agriculture. In the Bible, the mountain in Moab from which Moses saw the land of Canaan.

nebulaphobia (neb′ū.la.fō′bi.a): fear of fog.

nebulium (ne.bū′li.um): a hypothetical chemical element formerly inferred from certain lines in the spectra of nebulae.

nebulochaotic (neb′ū.lo.kā.ot′ik): hazily confused. 60.

necation (ni.kā′shun): a killing. 1.

necrologue (nek′ro.log): an obituary.

necromimesis (nek′ro.mi.mē′sis): the pretence or delusion of being dead.

necroponent (nek′ro.pō′nent): one temporarily in charge of a household after a death.

necyomancy (nes′i.o.man′si): divination through the summoning of Satan.

nedder (ned′er): an adder. 2.

neddy (ned′i): a donkey. A life preserver. 21.

neele (nēl): darnel, an annual grass found as weeds in cornfields and other cultivated grounds. 29. An eel. 1.

neem (nēm): the *margosa*.

neep (nēp): a turnip. 11A.

neer (nēr): a kidney. 11.

neese, neeze (nēz): to sneeze. 43.

nef (nef): a 16th-century clock in the form of a ship, having mechanical devices to simulate astronomical movements. A table utensil for napkins, salt, etc., in the shape of a ship. 6. The nave of a church. 1.

negritude (nē′gri.tūd): the distinctive qualities or characteristics of blacks.

neif (nēf): in law, one born a serf; a native. Also, var. of *nieve*.

nelipot (nel′i.pot): barefoot.

nema (nē′ma): a roundworm, eelworm, nematode.

nematocide (ni.mat′o.sīd): a chemical used to destroy roundworms.

Nemertinea (nem′er.tin′i.a): a class of carnivorous, mostly marine worms ranging in length from a fraction of an inch to many yards.

nemo (nē′mō): a radio or television broadcast that originates outside the studio.

nemophilous (ni.mof′i.lus): forest-loving.

nemoral (nem′o.ral): pert. to a wood or grove.

nenta (nen′ta): a chronic nervous disease of grazing animals in South Africa, similar to loco disease.

neocracy (ni.ok′ra.si): government by inexperienced people. 52.

neography (ni.og′ra.fi): any new system of writing. 52.

neolith (nē′o.lith): a neolithic stone instrument.

neolocal (nē′o.lō′kal): living away from the families of either spouse.

neomenia (nē′o.mē′ni.a): the time of the new moon; also, the festival of the new moon. (cap) A genus of marine mollusks having a thick, turgid body, and the foot represented by a narrow groove.

neomnesia (nē′om.nē′zha): a clear memory of recent events.

Neophron (nē′o.fron): a genus of Old World vultures, named for a legendary Greek who has turned into one.

neoplasm (nē′o.plazm): in medicine, any abnormal new formation or morbid growth.

neoplastic (nē′o.plas′tik): pert. to a *neoplasm*, or to *neoplasty*.

neoplasty (nē′o.plas′ti): in surgery, restoration of a part by a plastic operation.

neorama (nē′o.rä′ma): a panorama of the interior of a building, seen from within.

neossology (nē′o.sol′o.ji): the study of young birds.

neoteinic (nē′o.tī′nik): pert. to prolonged adolescence.

nephalism (nef′a.lizm): total abstinence from spirituous liquor.

nepheligenous (nef′i.lij′i.nus): emitting clouds, esp. of tobacco smoke.

nephology (ni.fol′o.ji): the study of clouds.

nephroid (nef′roid): kidney-shaped.

nephrosis (ni.frō′sis): a degenerative condition of the kidneys.

nepotation (nep′o.tā′shun): living high. 1.

nepotic (ni.pot′ik): pert. to a nephew or nepotism.

nerval (nur′val): a salve for the sinews. Pert. to the nerves; neural.

nervine (nur′vīn, -vin): having the quality of affecting the nerves; soothing nervous excitement. A nerve tonic. An orchid of the genus *Cypripedium*.

nes, nese (nes, nēz): nose. 5.

nesh (nesh): soft; tender. Timid; delicate; weak. Dainty; fastidious. To make or become soft. 1. To act timidly (with *it*). 13.

nesiote (nē′si.ōt): inhabiting an island.

neskhi (nes′ki): cursive Arabic script used in writing scientific and esp. religious books.

neurocoele (nū.ro.sēl): the cavity or series of cavities in the interior of the central nervous system.

neuromimesis (nū′ro.mī.mē′sis, -mi.-mē′sis): neurotic simulation of organic disease.

neurotropic (nū′ro.trop′ik): having an affinity for nerve tissues, as a drug or poison.

neurypnology (nū′rip.nol′o.ji): the branch of science that treats of sleep, partic. hypnotic sleep; hypnology.

nevel, nevell (nev′el): a fisticuff. To beat with the fists. 43.

ngoko (en.gō′kō): a dialect used by Javanese when speaking to social inferiors.

ngwee (en.gwā′): a Zambian coin equal to 1/100 of a kwacha.

nibber (nib′er): one who or that which puts a nib on, as on a pen. A tool for nibbing a pen.

nibby-jibby (nib′i.jib′i): a narrow margin, as in making a train.

nicker (nik′er): one of the 18th-century London brawlers noted for breaking windows with halfpence. A fabulous water monster; a nix. To snigger; to neigh. 43B.

nickle (nik′l): the green woodpecker. 30.

nicotian (ni.kō′shan): a user of tobacco.

niddle-noddle (nid′l.nod′l): having an unstable nodding head; nodding; to nod or wobble.

nidge (nij): var. of nig. Also, to shake, quiver. 52.

nidget (nij′et): idiot; fool. 9. A kind of horse-drawn cultivator. To till (soil) or to mix (manure, etc., with soil) with a nidget. 30.

nidicolous (ni.dik′o.lus): reared in a nest.

nidifugous (ni.dif′ū.gus): leaving the nest soon after birth.

nidulate (nid′u.lāt): to make a nest.

niente (ni.en′ti): nothing (Italian).

nieve (nēv): the fist; hand. 10. Also, a female *neif*.

nievie-nievie-nick-nack (nē′vi.nē′vi.-nik′nak): a children's choosing game. 45.

niffle (nif′l): a trivial or worthless person or thing. To steal in small quantities. 11A.

nific (nī′fic): pert. to *nife*, the hypothetical core material of the earth, supposed to be nickel and iron.

nig (nig): short for *nigger, renege*. To dress (stone) with a sharp-pointed hammer.

nikhedonia (nik′i.dō′ni.a): pleasure derived from the anticipation of success.

nikin (nik′in): a very soft creature. 1.

nim (nim): to filch, steal. 9.

nimb (nim, nimb): a nimbus or halo.

nimious (nim′i.us): in Scots law, excessive; extravagant.

nimmer (nim′er): a thief, pilferer.

nimtopsical (nim.top′si.kal): one of Benjamin Franklin's 228 words for "drunk."

nipperkin (nip′er.kin): a quantity of liquor of not more than a half pint. 9.

nisse (nis′e): in Scandinavian folklore, a friendly goblin or brownie that frequents farm buildings, similar to the German *kobold*.

nither (nith′er): to humiliate, debase. To shiver, tremble as with cold. 17. Var. of *neither, nether*. 11.

nithing (nith′ing): a coward; niggard; dastard. 9.

nobilitation (no.bil′i.tā′shun): the act of ennobling. Ennoblement.

nocake (nō′kāk): Indian corn pounded into a powder.

noctivagation (nok.tiv′a.gā′shun): night wandering.

noctuary (nok′chōō.er′i): a diary of nighttime activities.

nodose (no.dōs′, nō′dōs): knotty; knobbed.

nodulous, nodulose (nod′ū.lus, -lōs): having nodules.

noematachograph (no.ē′ma.tak′o.graf): an instrument for measuring complex reaction time.

noematic, noetic (nō′i.mat′ik, no.et′ik): apprehended only by the intellect; given to purely intellectual reason.

noemics (no.ē′miks): the science of understanding.

noily (noil′i): pert. to short fiber removed during the combing of a textile fiber and spun into yarn for cloth.

noli-mi-tangeretarian (nō′li.mi.tan′je.-ri.tā′ri.an): a rigid, unbending person.

nolition (no.lish′un): adverse action of will; unwillingness.

nomancy (nō′man.si): divination by letters of the alphabet.

nomic (nom′ik, nō′mik): in spelling, traditional as opposed to phonetic. Customary; conventional.

nominy (nom′i.ni): rhyming doggerel. A rigmarole; a wordy tale. 13.

nomology (no.mol′o.ji): the science of the laws of the mind.

nomothetic (nom′o.thet′ik): giving or enacting laws; legislative.

nonda (non′da): a kind of Australian tree, or its edible, plumlike fruit.

none (nōn): by ancient Roman and Eastern canonical reckoning, the ninth hour of the day. A religious office recited in the Roman Catholic Church.

nonic (nō′nik): in mathematics, a curve or quantic of the ninth degree.

noology (no.ol′o.ji): the study or science of intuition.

noop (nōōp): a rounded prominence, as the point of the elbow. 44. The fruit of the cloudberry. 13.

nooscopic (nō′o.skop′ik): pert. to the examination of the mind.

nordcaper (nôrd′kā′per): a right whale.

norsel (nôr′sel): a short line for fastening fishnets or fishhooks.

norward (nôr′ward): northward.

nosocomephrenia (nos.o.kō′mi.frē′-ni.a): depression from a prolonged stay in the hospital.

nosocomium (nos'o.kō'mi.um): a hospital.

nosoconology (nos'o.ko.nol'o.ji): the study of hospital administration.

nosophobia (nos'o.fō'bi.a): abnormal fear of disease.

nostology (nos.tol'o.ji): the study of senility.

nostomania (nos'to.mā'ni.a): overwhelming homesickness.

nostrificate (nos.trif'i.kāt): to accept as one's own.

notaeum (no.tē'um): the upper surface of a bird's body.

notandum (no.tan'dum): a thing to be noted, or an entry of it; a note; memorandum.

nothosomia (noth'o.sō'mi.a): the act of calling someone a bastard.

novendrial (no.ven'dri.al): lasting nine days; a nine-day festival.

novercaphobia (nō'ver.ka.fō'bi.a): fear of a stepmother.

novilunar (nō'vi.lōō'nar): pert. to the new moon.

novitial (no.vish'al): pert. to a novice. 52.

novitious (no.vish'us): recently invented.

nowel (no.el', nou.el'): Noel. 9. The inner part of a mold for casting a large hollow object.

Nox (noks): Roman goddess of the night.

noxa (nok'sa): in medicine, something that exerts a harmful effect on the body.

noyade (nwa.yäd'): drowning, usu. of many persons at once. To put to death by drowning.

nubiferous (nū.bif'er.us): producing or bringing clouds.

nubigenous (nū.bij'e.nus): produced by clouds.

nubilate (nū'bi.lāt): to cloud; obscure.

nucal (nū'kal): pert. to a nut.

nucha (nū'ka): in anatomy, the spinal cord; the nape of the neck. 1. In insects, the hind part of the thorax.

nuciverous (nū.siv'er.us): nut-eating.

nucleomitaphobia (nū'kli.o.mit'a.fō'bi.a): fear of death by nuclear weapons.

nuddle (nud'l): to thrust with the nose, as in suckling; to press close, nuzzle. 11.

nudiped (nū'di.ped): having feet without a natural covering (as of hair or feathers).

nudiustertian (nū'di.ū.stur'shun): pert. to the day before yesterday.

nugacity (nū.gas'i.ti): triviality; futility.

nullibicity, nullibiety (nul'i.bis'i.ti, -bī'e.ti): the state of being nowhere. 52.

nullifidian (nul'i.fid'i.an): a skeptic; an unbeliever. Skeptical.

nulliparous (nu.lip'a.rus): pert. to a woman who has never borne a child.

nullo (nul'ō): a game in which the player undertakes not to take a trick.

numble (num'bl): pert. to the numbles, edible entrails of deer. 9.

numerophobia (nū'mer.o.fō'bi.a): fear of numbers.

nummamorous (num.mam'er.us): money-loving.

nummary (num'er.i): pert. to coins or money.

nunch, nuncheon (nunch, nun'chun): a light midmorning or midafternoon refreshment, as of bread, cheese, and beer. 2.

nundine (nun'dīn, -din): a market day held every ninth day according to ancient Roman reckoning.

nuptaphobia (nup'ta.fō'bi.a): fear of marriage or weddings.

nursle (nur'sl): to rear, bring up.

nutricism (nū'tri.sizm): symbiosis in which one organism nourishes or protects another with no apparent reciprocal benefit.

nuzzer (nuz'er): in India, a ceremonial gift to a superior.

nyanza (nyan'za): in Central Africa, any large body of water; a lake or river.

nychthemeron (nik.thē'mer.on): a period of 24 hours.

nyctalopia (nik'ta.lō'pi.a): night blindness.

nyctophobia (nik.to.fō'bi.a): dread of the night or darkness.

Nymphea (nim.fē'a): the true water lily; synonymous with *Castalia*.

Nyx (niks): Greek goddess of the night.

O

oam (ōm): steam, warm air. 44A.

obambulate (o.bam'bū.lāt): to walk about, wander. 52.

obdormition (ob.dôr.mish'un): numbness and anesthesia caused by a pressure on a nerve; the condition of a limb when it is "asleep."

obduce, obduct (ob.dūs', -dukt'): to cover with, cover over. 1. To conduct an autopsy.

obequitation (o.bek'wi.tā'shun): the act of riding about on a horse. 1.

oblati (ob.lā'ti): those (esp. in the Middle Ages) who have offered themselves and their property to the church.

oblatration (ob.la.trā'shun): railing, reviling, scolding. 1.

obley (ob'li): a small flat cake or wafer, esp. of altar bread.

obliviscent (ob'li.vis'ent): forgetful.

obmutescent (ob'mū.tes'ent): becoming or staying silent.

obnubilate (ob.nū'bi.lāt): to cloud; obscure. 52.

obolary (ob'o.ler'i): very poor; having only small coins. 60.

obreption (ob.rep'shun): act of creeping upon with secrecy or by surprise. 1. The fraudulent obtainment or attempt to obtain a dispensation (from ecclesiastical authorities) or a gift (from the sovereign).

obreptitious (ob'rep.tish'us): obtained by trickery or by concealing the truth. 1.

obrogate (ob'ro.gāt): to supersede one law by another.

obrotund (ob'ro.tund): nearly spherical, but with one diameter slightly exceeding the other.

observandum (ob'ser.van'dum): a thing to be observed. (pl. *observanda*.)

obsidional (ob.sid'i.on.al): pert. to a siege; besetting.

obsignation (ob'sig.nā'shun): formal ratification. 52.

obstipation (ob'sti.pā'shun): extreme constipation. 1.

obstringe (ob.strinj'): to constrain or bind. To put under obligation. 52.

obstupefy (ob.stū'pi.fī): to stupefy.

obumbrate (o.bum'brāt): to shade; darken; cloud. 52. To adumbrate. 1. Darkened, as by shadow; also, concealed beneath a protecting part, as the antennae of certain insects.

obus (ō'bus): an artillery shell.

obvallate (ob.val'āt): walled in or around.

obvention (ob.ven'shun): an incidental or occasional gift or offering.

obvolve (ob.volv'): to enwrap. 52.

occecation (ok'se.kā'shun): blindness; going blind.

occiduous (ok.sid'ū.us): going down, as the setting of a heavenly body. 52.

occision (ok.sizh'un): slaughter.

ochlesis (ok.lē'sis): medically, a morbid condition induced by the crowding together of many persons, esp. sick persons.

ochone (o.kōn'): alas—an Irish and Scottish exclamation of lamentation.

ochroid (ok'roid): like ocher, esp. yellow ocher, in color.

octarius (ok.târ.i.us): one-eighth of a gallon; a pint.

octogild (ōk.to.gild): in Anglo-Saxon law, a pecuniary compensation for an injury, coming to eight times the determined value of the injury.

od (od): a minced form of *God*. Also, a force once believed by some to underlie hypnotism, magnetism, etc.

oda (ō'da): a room in a harem.

odaler, odaller (ō'dal.er): among early Teutonic peoples, one who owns heritable land.

oddman (od′man): an arbiter having the deciding vote; umpire. Also, *oddsman.*

oddsman (odz′man): an umpire, arbiter.

odontalgy, odontalgia (od.on. tal′ji, -ji.a): toothache.

odonterism (o.don′ter.izm): the chattering of teeth.

odontic (o.don′tik): pert. to the teeth.

Odontoglossum (o.don′to.glos′um): a genus of showy American orchids, incl. the baby orchid of Guatemala. A plant of this genus.

ON THE IMMEMORIAL WORSHIP OF ASSES: A KYRIELLE

Now hangs occiduous the sun;
All things must end that have begun—
Save this, that sounds eternally:
Ass-worshipping onolatry.

I hear the mourners wail ''Ochone''
Who soon are one with them they moan.
Macrotous Spirit, hear the plea
They utter in onolatry!

From shade of atom bomb and missile
They pray to You Who champ the thistle.
As ass to Ass they bend the knee
In asinine onolatry.

---

odorivector (o.dor′i.vek′ter): a substance that gives off a smell.

ods bobs (odz bobz): a minced form of the oath ''God's blood.'' 10.

odylic (o.dil′ik): pert. to *od.*

odynophobia (o.din′o.fō′bi.a): fear of pain.

oecodomic (i.ko.dō′mik): architectural.

oeillade (oo.yäd): a flirtatious glance; an ogle.

oenanthic, enanthic (i.nan′thik, en.an′-): pert. to a certain acid found in wine.

oenomancy (ē′no.man′si): divination by the color or other peculiarities of wine.

oenophilist (i.nof′il.ist): a lover of wine.

ogdoad (og′do.ad): the number eight; a group or set of eight.

Ogygia (o.jij′i.a): the island on which the sea nymph Calypso kept Odysseus for seven years.

Ogygian (o.jij′i.an): pert. to Ogyges, first king of Thebes, or to a flood said to have occurred during his reign. Extremely ancient.

ohia (o.hē′a): any of several myrtles of the genus *Metrosideros,* such as the lehua and the Malay apple.

oikology (oi.kol′o.ji): the science of housekeeping; household economics.

oikophobia (oi.ko.fō′bi.a): fear of one's own home.

oillet (oi′let): an eyelet. 9.

oke, oka (ōk, -a): Turkish and Egyptian measures of weight.

olamic (o.lam′ik): eternal; infinite.

oldwench (ōld′wench): the triggerfish of the Atlantic and Indian oceans.

oleiferous (ō.li.if′er.us): producing oil.

olent (ō′lent): fragrant.

olid (ō′lid): smelly.

olidous (ō′li.dus): olid, smelly. 52.

oligogenics (ō′li.go.jen′iks): birth control.

oligophagous (ō.li.gof′a.gus): eating only a few specific kinds of foods.

oligophrenia (ō′li.go.frē′ni.a): mental deficiency.

oligoria (ō′li.gôr′i.a): cessation of interest in former associations.

oligotokous (ō′li.got′o.kus): laying fewer than four eggs.

olitory (ō′li.tôr′i): a kitchen garden. 9.

olivet (ol′i.vet): an olive grove. 1. A bogus pearl.

om (ôm): a mantra used in the mystical contemplation of the cosmos.

omadhaun (om′a.thôn): a fool; simpleton; idiot. 51.

ombrology (om.brol′o.ji): the branch of meteorology that deals with rain. 52.

ombrometer (om.brom′i.ter): a rain gauge.

ombrophilous (om.brof′i.lus): thriving in the rain, as some plants in humid tropics.

ombrophobia (om.bro.fō′bi.a): fear of rain.

ombrosalgia (om′bro.sal′ji.a): pain or discomfort connected with rain.

omneity (om.nē′i.ti): allness.

omnigenous (om.nij′i.nus): of all types and kinds.

omniligent (om.nil′i.jent): reading constantly and indiscriminately.

omniparient (om′ni.par′i.ent): the source or origin of all. 52.

omnitude (om′ni.tūd): universality; allness.

omnivalent (om.niv′a.lent): in chemistry, capable of combining with any atom of another element.

omophagic (ō′mō.faj′ik): pert. to the eating of raw flesh.

omoplatoscopy (ō′mo.pla.tos′ko.pi): divination by study of a cracked shoulder blade.

omphacine (om′fa.sēn): pert. to unripe fruit.

omphaloid (om′fa.loid): resembling a navel.

omphalomancy (om′fa.lo.man′si): prediction of the number of children a woman will have by the number of knots in the umbilical cord of her first. **omphalopsychite (om.fa.lop′si.kīt):** a *Hesychast.*

omphaloskepsis (om′fa.lo.skep′sis): meditation while gazing at the navel.

Ona (ō′na): one of a Chonan people of Tierra del Fuego off the southern tip of South America.

ondoyant (on.doi′ant): wavy.

oneirocritic (o.nī′ro.krit′ik): an interpreter of dreams.

oneirodynia (o.nī′ro.din′i.a): a nightmare.

oneirotaxia (o.nī′ro.tak′si.a): confusion between fantasy and reality.

oneirotic (o.nī′rot′ik): pert. to dreams.

oniomania (ō′ni.o.mā′ni.a): a mania for buying things.

onlocholasia (on.lok′o.lā.zhi.a): shopping as a means of relaxation.

onolatry (o.nol′a.tri): the worship of asses.

onomantic (on′o.man′tik): pert. to divination by means of names.

onomasticon (on′o.mas′ti.kon): a vocabulary or collection of names or nouns.

onomatomania (on′o.mat′o.mā′ni.a): preoccupation with words and names.

onomatophobia (on′o.mat′o.fō′bi.a): fear of hearing a special name.

ontal (on′tal): in philosophy, pert. to real, as opposed to phenomenal existence or being; noumenal.

onychomancy, onymancy (on′i.ko.man′si, -i.man′si): divination by means of the fingernails.

onychophagy (on′i.kof′a.ji): fingernail-biting.

onymatic (on′i.mat′ik): pert. to nomenclature.

oolly (ool′i): in India, a lump or loop of iron, when taken as a pasty mass from the crucible.

ooid, ooidal (o′oid, -al): egg-shaped.

oom (ōōm): in South Africa, an uncle.

opacate (o.pā′kāt): to make opaque, darken.

ophelia (o.fēl′ya): a hybrid tea rose with salmon-yellow flowers. A reddish purple color. (cap) A genus of small burrowing worms. (cap) The daughter of Polonius in *Hamlet.*

ophelimity (ō′fi.lim′i.ti): satisfaction; the ability to provide it.

ophic (of′ik): of or relating to snakes.

ophicleide (of′i.klīd): a deep-toned brass wind instrument replaced by the tuba about 1850.

ophidiophobia (o.fid′i.o.fō′bi.a): fear of snakes.

ophioid (of′i.oid): pert. to snakes.

ophiomancy (of′i.o.man′si): divination by means of snakes.

ophiophagan, ophiophagous (of′i.of′-a.gan, -gus): feeding on snakes; one that feeds on snakes.

ophryitis (of′ri.ī′tis): inflammation of the eyebrow.

ophthalmophobia (of′thal.mo.fō′bi.a): fear of being stared at.

opianic (ō′pi.an′ik): pert. to a certain bitter, crystalline, aldehyde acid.

opimian (o.pim′i.an): pert. to a famous Roman wine of 121 B.C., when *Opimius* was consul.

opiparous (o.pip′ar.us): sumptuous. 9.

opisthograph (o.pis′tho.graf): a manuscript written on both sides.

opisthoporeia (o.pis.tho.pôr′i.a): involuntary walking backward.

oppidan (op′i.dan): pert. to town as opposed to country. A townsman. At Eton, a student who boards in town. 1.

oppidum (op′i.dum): in the Roman Empire, a provincial town, not self-governing, as London when under Roman rule.

oppignorate (o.pig′nor.āt): to pawn.

oppilation (op′i.lā′shun): the state of being stopped up. An obstruction.

opsablepsia (op′sa.blep′si.a): inability to look another in the eye.

opsigamy (op.sig′a.mi): a late marriage.

opsimathy (op.sim′a.thi): education late in life.

opsonium (op.sō′ni.um): food used as a relish. 52.

optophobia (op′to.fō′bi.a): fear of opening one's eyes.

opsophagist (of.sof′a.jist): a fastidious eater; an epicure.

opuscule, opuscle (o.pus′kūl, -pus′l): a small or petty work.

oquassa (o.kwas′a): a small, rather slender trout found in Maine.

oragious (o.rā′jus): stormy. 52.

oralogy (o.ral′o.ji): the science of the mouth and its diseases.

orarian (o.râr′i.an): pert. to the seashore; a coast dweller. (cap) An Eskimo or Aleut of the Bering Sea coastal region.

orbation (ôr.bā′shun): lack of parents or children; bereavement.

orbell (ôr′bel): a small circular place. 1.

orbific (ôr.bif′ik): pert. to the creation of the world.

orchesis (ôr.kē′sis): the art of dancing, as in the ancient Greek chorus.

orchestic (ôr.kes′tik): pert. to dancing.

orchestrion (ôr.kes′tri.on): a device with stops capable of imitating a variety of musical instruments.

orchestromania (ôr.kes′tro.mā′ni.a): a passion for dancing.

orchidectomy (ôr′ki.dek′to.mi): castration.

orectic (o.rek′tik): pert. to the desires; hence, impelling to gratification, appetitive.

oreillet (ôr′e.let): a covering for the ear.

oreography, orography (ôr′i.og′ra.fi, o.rog′ra.fi): the branch of geography that deals with mountains; orology.

orexigenic (o.rek′si.jen′ik): whetting the appetite.

orexis (o.rek′sis): desire, appetite. The feeling and striving aspect of the mind as compared with the intellectual.

orgia (ôr′ji.a): orgies.

orgillous (ôr.gil′us): var. of *orgulous*.

orgue (ôrg): in military history, one of the long, thick timbers behind the gateway of a fortress or castle, to be let down in case of attack. Also, an old-time piece of ordnance having a number of barrels arranged side by side.

orgulous (ôr′gū.lus): proud, haughty. Hence, showy; splendid.

orignal (o.rēn′yal): the American moose.

orismology (ôr′is.mol′o.ji): the science of defining technical terms.

orle (ôrl): in heraldry, a band following the outline of the shield inside the edge. The metal rim of a shield.

ornis (ôr′nis): the bird life of a region.

ornithoid (ôr′ni.thoid): birdlike.

ornithon (ôr′ni.thon): an aviary.

ornithophilous (ôr.ni.thof′i.lus): bird-loving; said specif. of plants pollinated through the agency of birds.

ornithorhynchous (ôr′ni.tho.ring′kus): having a beak like a bird.

ornithorhynchus (ôr′ni.tho.ring′kus): a creditor—i.e., ''a beast with a bill.'' 23A (cap) A genus of egg-laying mammals incl. only the platypus.

oro (ôr′ō): gold; sometimes, in Spanish American countries, specif. U.S. money. (cap) In Polynesian religion, the god of fertility, procreation, and war.

orra (ôr.a): odd; not matched; good-for-nothing. 44.

orthobiosis (ôr′tho.bi.ō′sis): normal life; life according to accepted hygienic and moral principles.

orthodromics (ôr′tho.drō′miks): the act or art of sailing by the great-circle route.

orthology (ôr.thol′o.ji): the art of using words correctly.

orthophobia (ôr′tho.fō′bi.a): a distaste for propriety.

orthophony (ôr.thof′o.ni): voice training.

orthopter (ôr.thop′ter): a flying machine with flapping wings.

orthoptic (ôr.thop′tik): pert. to the treatment of defective vision or bad visual habits.

orthotectic (ôr′tho.tek′tik): in geology, pert. to the results of directly magmatic processes, as the segregation of an ore body from molten material.

orthotetrakaldekahedron (ôr′tho.tet′ra.kal.dek′a.hē′dron): the truncated octahedron.

orthotic (ôr.thot′ik): pert. to erect posture; standing upright.

orthotomic (ôr′tho.tom′ik): in geometry, cutting at right angles.

ortive (ôr′tiv): pert. to the time of rising; eastern. 52.

oryctology (o′rik.tol′o.ji): the science of things dug from the earth. 1.

oryzivorous (ôr′i.ziv′o.rus): rice-eating.

osela (o.sel′a): a silver or gold medal representing a bird, presented each New Year's Day by the 16th-century doges of Venice to the Venetian noble families.

---

*IT ALL DEPENDS
ON THE SUFFIX*

Beth emerged from bath of bubble.
Sweet of scent and tempting trouble.
From the pigpen Hank, her neighbor,
Rushed still reeking from his labor.
Beth would not be kissed by Hank;
She informed him that he stank.
Hank to pen retreated dolent:
He was olid, she was olent.

---

osmagogue (oz′ma.gog): stimulating to the sense of smell.

osmonsology (oz′mon.sol′o.ji): the study of the sense of smell.

osmophobia (oz′mo.fō′bi.a): fear of smells.

osphresiophilia (os.frē′zi.o.fil′i.a): love of smells.

ossature (os′a.cher): the skeleton. 52. In architecture, the framework.

osso buco (os′ō bōō′kō): marrow bone of veal. A Milanese dish consisting of leg of veal with rice cooked in saffron sauce.

ostent (os′tent, os.tent′): a significant sign; portent. A manifestation. Ostentatious display.

ostreophagy (os′tri.of′a.ji): the eating of oysters.

othergates (uth′er.gāts): in another manner. 4.

otiant (ō′shi.ant): unemployed, idle. 52.

otiation (ō′shi.a′shun): leisure, idleness. 1.

otosis (o.tō′sis): inability to hear correctly.

ouakari (wa.kä′ri): a South American monkey with silky hair and a short tail like a baboon's.

ouf (ouf): a dog's bark; woof. An exclamation of impatience.

ouph, ouphe (ouf): an elf or goblin.

outfangthief (out′fang.thēf): in medieval English law, the right of a lord to try one of his vassals for thievery, even if caught outside his manor.

outgang (out′gang): departure; also, a road out. 43.

outgrabe (out.grāb′): squeaked.

outrance (ōō.träns′): the utmost or last extremity.

outrecuidance (ōō′tre.kwē′dens): extreme self-conceit; presumption.

outrooper (out′rōōper): an auctioneer. 1.

overslaugh (ō′ver.slô): in England, exemption from one military duty by being assigned a more important one. In the U.S., a sandbar. Also, to hinder, obstruct, pass over for appointment. 41.

ovivorous (o.viv′e.rus): egg-eating.

owala (o.wä′la): a tropical African tree with seeds yielding a lubricant.

ower (ō′wer): dial. version of *over*.

owler (ou′ler): someone who hoots like an owl; a prowler. 2.

owling (ou′ling): formerly, in England, the smuggling of wool or sheep from the country.

oxgang (oks′gang): an English unit of land measure. 1.

oxycanthous (ok′si.kan′thus): having sharp spines or thorns.

oxyesthesia (ok′si.es.thē′zi.a): extreme sensitivity to touch.

oxyosphresia (ok′si.os.frē′zi.a): extreme sensitivity to smell.

oxyphony (ok.sif′o.ni): in medicine, shrillness of voice.

oxyrhynch (ok′si.ringk): a crab having a pointed rostrum.

oxyrhynchous (ok.si.ring′kus): pert. to a large superfamily of crabs, incl. the spider crabs. Sharp-snouted; sharp-billed.

oyer (oi′er): in law, a criminal trial conducted by a particularly authorized judge. The hearing of a document read in court. A copy of the instrument given rather than read to the petitioning party.

ozostomia (ō′zo.stō′mi.a): bad breath.

P

pabular, pabulous (pab′ū.lär, -lus): pert. to pabulum. 52.

pabulation (pab′ū.lā′shun): food; fodder; the providing of them.

pacable (pā′ka.bl): pacable.

pacate (pā′kāt): appeased; pacified. 1.

pachinko (pa.ching′kō): a Japanese slot machine.

pachycephalic (pak′i.si.fal′ik): thick-skulled.

paco (pä′kō): an earthy-looking ore, consisting of brown oxide of iron with minute particles of native silver.

paction (pak′shun): an agreement; a compact; a bargain. 44A.

padella (pa.del′a): in Italy, a shallow dish used for fat or oil, in which a wick is placed for burning.

padmasana (pad.mä′sa.na): statue base shaped like a lotus flower.

paedophobia (pē′do.fō′bi.a): fear of dolls.

paeanism (pe′a.nizm): the singing or chanting of paeans.

paggle (pag′l): to hang loosely, sag.

pagophagia (pag′o.fā′ji.a): a program of eating ice to help offset iron deficiency.

pahmi (pä′mi): the bobac (a marmot of eastern Europe and Asia), or its fur.

pahoehoe (pa.hō′i.hō′i): in Hawaii, lava that has cooled in ropy forms.

paideutic, paideutics (pā′dū′tik, -s): pedagogy.

paigle (pā′gl): the cowslip, or oxlip. The cuckooflower. The stitchwort. Any of several crowfoots. 13.

paillette (pal.yet′): spangle.

paizogony (pī′zo.gon′i): love play—*paraphilemia, sarmassation*.

paktong (pak.tong′): a Chinese alloy of nickel, zinc, and copper, resembling German silver.

paladin (pal′a.din): one of the twelve peers of Charlemagne's court. Hence, a knight of the Round Table; a knight errant.

palafitte (pal′a.fit): a pile-built structure used by neolithic lake dwellers.

palama (pal′a.ma): the webbing on the feet of aquatic birds.

palame (pa.lä′me): a Greek measure of length, 3.937 inches.

paleanthropic (pal′i.an′throp′ik): pert. to a genus of homonids often incl. the Neanderthals.

paleocrystic (pal′i.o.kris′tik): pert. to ice of ancient origin.

paleogenetic, palaeogenetic (pal′i.o.ji.-net′ik): originating in the past.

paleomnesia (pal′i.om.nē′zhi.a): a sharp memory for the far past.

Paleotherium (pal′i.o′thē′ri.um): a genus of extinct tapir-like mammals, of which one species was as large as a rhinoceros.

paletiology (pal′i.ti.ol′o.ji): the explanation of past events by the laws of causation, as in geology.

paletot (pal′ō.tō): a man's or woman's loose overcoat.

palfrenier (pal′fre.nēr): a groom. 9.

palification (pal′i.fi.kā′shun): the driving of piles or posts into the ground to make it firm. 52.

palilalia (pal′i.lāl′ya): the ailment of helplessly repeating a phrase faster and faster.

palilogy (pa.lil′o.ji): in rhetoric, the repetition of words for emphasis.

palinoia (pal′i.noi′a): the compulsive repetition of an act until it is perfect.

palla (pal′a): among the Romans, a loose outer garment for women formed by wrapping or draping a large square of cloth.

pallah (pal′a): the impala.

palmigrade (pal′mi.grād): plantigrade.

palmiped (pal′mi.ped): web-footed. A web-footed animal.

palo (pä′lō): a pole, stick; in Spanish America, used in the names of trees. 35B.

palpebrate (pal′pi.brāt): to wink.

paludamentum (pa.lōō′da.men′tum): a military cloak worn by a Roman general; also, the imperial cloak.

palustral (pa.lus′tral): living in marshy places; marshy; pert. to marshes. Malarial. Paludal.

palycrotic (pal′i.krot′ik): of the pulse, having a complex or multiple beat and forming a curve with several crests on a sphygmogram.

pament, pamment (pam′ent): in brewing, the tile or brick used for paving malting floors.

pampootee (pam.pōō′ti): an Irish moccasin of untanned cowhide.

pampre (pam′per): in sculpture, ornamentation of vine leaves and grapes.

panade (pa.näd′): a large knife or dagger. 1.

Panagia (pa.nä′ji.a): literally, the All Holy—the most common epithet of the Virgin Mary. A ceremony observed in honor of her assumption. (not cap) A medallion of the Virgin Mary, worn by bishops.

pancheon (pan′chun): a large flaring shallow vessel variously used, as to set milk for cream. 41.

pancratic (pan.krat′ik): pert. to a pancratium, an ancient Greek athletic contest. Having all or many degrees of power (said esp. of an adjustable eyepiece for a microscope).

pandal (pan′dal): in India and Ceylon, a shed, esp. a temporary one; a booth; bower; arbor.

Pandean (pan.dē.an): pert. to the god Pan.

pandiculation (pan.dik′ū.lā′shun): a stretching and stiffening, esp. of one's trunk and extremities (as when fatigued or drowsy).

pandita (pan.dē′ta): a priest of the Philippine Moros.

pandle (pan′dl): a shrimp. 30.

panduriform (pan.dū′ri.fôrm): having an indentation on both sides, like a violin.

pandy (pan′di): a hit on the palm, as with a cane. 45.

panela (pa.nel′a): low-grade brown sugar.

panivorous (pa.niv′o.rus): bread-eat-ing.

pannage (pan′ij): in English law, the feeding of, or right to feed, swine in a wood; also, the fee for it. Food (as chestnuts, etc.) for swine in a wood or forest.

panstereorama (pan.stēr′i.o.rämä): a relief map of a town or country.

Pantagruelian (pan′ta.grōō.ēl′yan): ribaldly satirical, with great exaggeration.

pantanemone (pan′ta.nem′o.ni): a windmill with two semicircular vanes.

pantarbe (pan.tärb′): a precious stone supposed to shine like the sun and act as a magnet on gold. 52.

panthophobia, pantophobia (pan′tho.-fō′bi.a, pan′to-): fear of suffering and disease.

pantisocracy (pan′ti.sok′ra.si): a Utopian community (imagined by Coleridge, Southey, etc., in their youth), in which all rule equally.

pantler (pant′ler): in a great household, the servant in charge of the bread and the pantry. 9.

panto (pan′tō): short for *pantomime*. 26A.

pantological (pan′to.loj′i.kal): pert. to a systematic view of all knowledge.

pantophagous (pan.tof′a.gus): omnivorous.

panurgy (pan′er.ji): universal skill or craft.

papaphobia (pā′pa.fō′bi.a): dread of the pope or of popery.

papaverous (pa.pav′er.us): pert. to the poppy.

papilionaceous (pa.pil′i.o.nā′shus): butterfly-like.

papiopio (pä′pyō.pyō): the young of the ulua, a Hawaiian fish.

papyrography (pa′pi.rog′ra.fi): a process of multiplying copies of writings, etc., by use of a paper stencil and corrosive ink.

parabolanus (par.a.bo.lā′nus): in the early church, a monk who treated contagious diseases.

parabolize (pa.rab′o.līz): to speak in parables. Also, to make parabolic, as a mirror for a telescope.

Parabrahm, Parabrahman (par′a.bräm, -brä′man): in the Hindu religion, the supreme, absolute, nameless, impersonal principle.

paracenastic (par′a.si.nas′tik): relating to one of the two projecting wings of the skene of a Greek theater.

paracentesis (par′a.sen.tē′sis): in surgery, the puncture of a cavity of the body with an instrument, to draw off effused fluid; tapping.

paracentral (par′a.sen′tral): lying near a center or central part.

TONGUE-TIED LOVER

The jackal on the prowl cries, ''Pheal!''
  A-hunt for dearer prey,
The boar in rutting time cries ''Fream!''
  The stag on oestral day
Cries ''Troat!'' . . .
        Would I, dear, so could squeal!—
Would I could scream!—
  But pheal, and fream, and troat
  Lock in my throat.

---

parachronism (pa.rak′ro.nizm): a chronological error, esp. one in which a date is set late.

paraclete (par′a.klēt): an aide, legal helper. (cap) The Holy Spirit as intercessor.

paracoita (par′a.ko.ē′ta): a female sexual partner.

paracoitus (par′a.ko.ē′tus): a male sexual partner.

paracrostic (par′a.kros′tik): a poetical composition in which the first verse contains, in order, the first letters of the following verses.

paradiddle (par′a.did′l): a certain roll of the snare drum.

paradromic (par′a.drō′mik, -drom′ik): running side by side; following a parallel course.

parageusic (par′a.jōō′sik): relating to abnormality of the sense of taste.

paragoge (par′a.gō′je): the addition of a sound or syllable to the end of a word.

paragram (par′a.gram): a pun, esp. one made by changing the first letter of a word.

paragraphia (par.a.graf′i.a): aphasia in which the patient writes unintended words or letters.

paralalia (par′a.lāl′ya): a speech disorder marked by distortion of sound.

paralepsis (par′a.lep′sis): in rhetoric, a passing over with brief mention so as to emphasize the suggestiveness of what is omitted.

paralian (pa.rāl′yan): a dweller by the sea. 1.

paralipomena (par′a.li.pom′e.na): passages that are deleted, but added as a supplement.

paralipophobia (par′a.li.po.fō′bi.a): fear of responsibility.

parallelepiped (par′a.lel′i.pī′ped): a six-sided prism with parallelogram faces.

paralogic (par′a.loj′ik): illogic.

paralogist (pa.ral′o.jist): one who uses reasoning that begs the question.

paramimia (par′a.mim′i.a): a pathological misuse of gestures.

paramimiographer (par′a.mim′i.og′ra.fer): a collector or writer of proverbs.

paranymph (par′a.nimf): a best man; bridesmaid; advocate.

paraphasia (par.a.fā′zhi.a): aphasia in which the patient talks volubly but misuses words.

paraphilemia (par′a.fi.lē′mi.a): love play; paizogony.

paraphrast (par.a.frast): a paraphraser.

paraphrenic (par′a.frē′nik, fren′ik): pert. to any of the paranoid disorders, but usu. excluding paranoid schizophrenia.

parapraxia (par′a.prak′si.a): faulty or blundering action.

---

paratamous (pa.rat′a.mus): pert. to a bird's upper jaw.

parathesis (pa.ra′thi.sis): in grammar, the setting of a second word beside the first as an adjunct term (''Jesus *Savior*''); apposition. A parenthesis. 1.

parathetic (par′a.thet′ik): parenthetic. 1.

paratonic (par′a.ton′ik): retarding movement or growth.

parenesis (pa.ren′i.sis): advice; counsel; an exhortatory composition.

parenetic (par.i.net′ik): advisory, consulting.

parentate (pa.ren′tāt): to perform funeral rites, esp. for a relative. 1.

parepithymia (par.ep.i.thīm′i.a): distorted cravings due to mental illness.

paretic (pa.ret′ik): pert. to paresis, or paralysis. One who is paretic.

pargasite (pär′ga.sīt): the mineral hornblende.

pari (par′i): in textiles, the weight of raw silk before it is degummed.

parisology (par′i.sol′o.ji): intentional ambiguity.

parison (par′i.son): a gob of partially shaped molten glass. A receptacle in a bottle-making machine that releases the exact amount of metal needed for making a bottle. In rhetoric, an even balance between the members of a sentence.

Pariti (pa.rī′tī): a small genus of tropical trees with entire cordate leaves and yellow flowers, as the *majagua*.

paroemia (pa.rē′mi.a): a proverb.

parorexia (par.o.rek′si.a): perverted appetite, demanding strange foods.

parral, parrel (par′al, -el): in ships, the rope loop or sliding collar by which a yard or spar is held to the mast in such a way that it may be hoisted or lowered. To fasten by means of a parrel.

parrhesia (pa.rē′zhi.a): in rhetoric, boldness or freedom of speech.

parten (pär′ten): to impart; partake. 1.

parthenic (pär.then′ik): pert. to a virgin or virginity.

parthenolatry (pär′thi.nol′a.tri): the worship of virgins.

parthenology (pär′thi.nol′o.ji): the study of virgins and virginity.

Parthenopean (pär′thi.no.pē′an): pert. to Parthenope, a Siren who threw herself into the sea after failing to beguile Odysseus by her songs. Also, pert. to a large genus of spider crabs.

parthenophobia (pär′thi.no.fō′bi.a): fear of virgins.

partimen (pär.ti.men): a disputatious lyrical poem composed by Provençal troubadors.

partiversal (pär.ti.vur′sal): in geology, dipping in different directions, as at each end of an anticlinal axis.

parturifacient (pär.tū.ri.fā′shent): inducing childbirth. A medicine to induce childbirth.

parvanimity (pär.va.nim′i.ti): pettiness; meanness; a petty or mean person.

parviscient (pär.vish′ent): uninformed.

pash (pash): to throw violently, crush; a crushing blow; a heavy fall of rain or snow. 11A.

pasigraphy (pa.sig.ra.fi): any system of writing using signs to represent ideas rather than words. Loosely, any artificial language designed for universal use.

pasilaly (pa′si.lā′li): a universal language. 52.

passade (pa.sād′): a turn of a horse backward or forward on the same spot.

Passiflora (pas′i.flôr′a): a genus of mainly tropical and mostly tendril-bearing American vines with showy red, white, or purple flowers, incl. the passion flower. (not cap) A plant of this genus.

patache (pa.tash′): a tender to a fleet of sailing vessels.

patata (pa.tä′ta): the potato. The sweet potato.

patavinity (pat′a.vin′i.ti): local or provincial words, pronunciations, or expressions, and their use.

paterissa (pat′e.ris′a): a crosier surmounted by a small cross from whose base issue two serpents.

patesi (pa.tā′zi): in Babylon, a ruler of a Sumerian city-state who combined the religious and the secular chieftaincies; a priest-king.

patharmosis (path′är.mō′sis): mental adjustment to one's disease.

pathematic (path′i.mat′ik): pert. to emotion; emotive. 52. Pert. to disease.

pathic (path′ik): passive; suffering; also, a passive participant; a catamite. 52.

pathognomic, pathognomonic (path′og.nom′ik, -no.mon′ik): characteristic of a particular disease (as a symptom).

pathognomy (pa.thog′no.mi): the study of the signs of human passions. Medically, the science of diagnosis.

pathomimesis (path′o.mi.mē′sis): the act of malingering.

pathophobia (path.o.fō′bi.a): fear of disease or germs.

patible (pat′i.bl): the transom of a cross; the cross itself. Sufferable; tolerable. 52. Capable of suffering; capable of being acted on. 1.

patibulary (pa.tib′u.ler′i): pert. to the gallows or hanging.

patinate (pat′i.nāt): to coat or become coated with a patina.

patripotestal (pa.tri.po.tes′tal): pert. to paternal authority.

patrix (pā′triks): a pattern or die to form matrixes.

patrocinate (pa.tros′i.nāt): to patronize.

patroclinous (pa.tro.klī′nus): having characteristics inherited from the father.

patrology (pa.trol′o.ji): the branch of historical theology treating of the teachings of the Fathers of the Christian church.

patronate (pā′tro.nāt): the right, duty, and jurisdiction of a patron; patronage.

patronomatology (pat′ro.nō′ma.tol′o.ji): the study of patronymics.

patronymic (pat′ro.nim′ik): strictly, a name formed from that of the father; generally, a surname handed down in the paternal line.

pauciloquy (pô.sil′o.kwi): brevity in speech.

pauldron (pôl′drun): a piece of armor covering the shoulder where the body piece and arm piece join.

pavid (pav′id): timid; fearful. 52.

pawk (pôk): a clever device; a trick or wile. 44. Impertinence; an impertinent person. 42.

peage (pā′ij): a toll. 2.

pean (pēn): a kind of heraldic fur. Var. of *peen*.

pearlin, pearling (pur′lin, -ling): a kind of silk or thread; pl., trimmings of this; also, clothes trimmed with it. 44A.

peart (pērt, pyurt): dial. var. of *pert*. Brisk; active; flourishing.

peba (pē′ba): a small armadillo, ranging from Texas to Paraguay and having nine movable bands of scutes.

peccatiphobia, peccatophobia (pe.ka.ti.fō′bi.a, -to.fō′bi.a): fear of committing or having committed a crime.

peckerwood (pek′er.wood): a woodpecker. In parts of the south, a poor white.

pectoriloquy (pek.to.ril′o.kwi): the distinct sound of a patient's voice heard in auscultation, usu. indicating a morbid change in the lungs.

pectous (pek′tus): pert. to pectin.

pectus (pek′tus): the breast of a bird. The lower surface of the thorax of an insect.

peculium (pe.kū′li.um): in Roman law, property held by a subject at the pleasure of the male head of a household.

pedalier (ped′a.lēr): the pedal keyboard of an organ, harpsichord, pianoforte, or piano.

pedality (pe.dal′i.ti): a measuring by paces; a going on foot. 52.

pedantocracy (ped′an.tok′ra.si): government by pedants.

pedetentious (ped′i.ten′shus): proceeding gradually or cautiously. 52.

pedial (ped′i.al): asymmetric.

pediculophobia (pi.dik′ū.lo.fō′bi.a): fear of lice.

Pediculus (pi.dik′ū.lus): a genus of true lice, incl. the common forms infesting man.

pedigerous (pi.dij′er.us): having feet.

pediluvium (ped′i.loo′vi.um): a foot bath.

pedimanous (pe.dim′a.nus): having feet like hands.

pediophobia (pē′di.o.fō′bi.a): fear of dummies, dolls, puppets, mannequins, etc.

pedology (pi.dol′o.ji): the study of soil.

peele (pēl): the rhebock, a South American antelope.

peelee (pē′li): in croquet, a ball which is peeled.

peen (pēn): the sharp end of the head of a hammer or sledge opposite the face.

peesweep (pē′swēp): the lapwing; the greenfinch. 30.

peever (pē′ver): a stone used in hopscotch; the game hopscotch. 44.

peirameter (pī.ram′i.ter): an apparatus for measuring the amount of power necessary to haul a truck or carriage over a given way.

peirastic (pī.ras′tik): fitted for trial; experimental; tentative.

peisage, pesage (pā′sij, pes′ij): formerly, in English law, a toll charge for weighing avoirdupois goods, except for wool; also, the right to impose such a toll. 1.

pelargic (pi.lär′jik): pert. to storks; storklike.

pelfed (pelft): robbed; pilfered; despoiled. 1.

pell (pel): pelt; to pelt; also, a garment lined with skins or fur. 1. A roll or record of parchment. 6.To hasten; hurry.2.

pellas (pel′as): the small cheese-shaped fruit of the dwarf mallow.

pellate (pel′āt): to tend to separate, to repel mutually.

pelmatic (pel.mat′ik): pert. to the sole of the foot.

pelmatogram (pel.mat′o.gram): a footprint.

pelology (pi.lol′o.ji): the study of mud and its therapeutic applications.

pelta (pel′ta): in Greek antiquity, a small light shield.

peltast (pel′tast): a soldier of ancient Greece armed with a pelta.

pelvimeter (pel.vim′i.ter): an instrument for measuring the dimensions of the pelvis.

penduline (pen′dū.līn, -lin): pendulous—applied to birds that build hanging nests.

penelopize (pe.nel′o.pīz): to undo and redo to gain time.

penetralium (pen′i.trāl′yum): the most secret or hidden part.

peniaphobia (pē′ni.a.fō′bi.a): fear of poverty.

peninsulate (pen.in′sū.lāt): to form into a peninsula.

pennanular (pi.nan′ū.lar): nearly ring-shaped.

penniform (pen′i.fôrm): feather-shaped.

penotherapy (pē′no.ther′a.pi): the regulation of prostitutes to control venereal disease.

pensum (pen′sum): a task, esp. one set as punishment in school.

pentacrostic (pen′ta.kros′tik): a set of verses containing five acrostics of a name, one in each of five divisions.

pentaglot (pen′ta.glot): using five different languages. A pentaglot book.

pentalpha (pen.tal′fa): a five-pointed star.

pentapolis (pen.tap′o.lis): a union, confederacy, or group of five cities.

Pentelic (pen.tel′ik): pert. to Mount Pentelicus, near Athens, where the fine white marble of the Parthenon was quarried.

penteteric (pen′ti.ter′ik): recurring every five years.

pentheraphobia (pen′ther.a.fō′bi.a): fear of one's mother-in-law.

pentice (pen′tis): a penthouse. 9.

peotomy (pi.ot′o.mi): amputation of the penis.

peperino (pep′er.ē′nō): dark-colored volcanic detritus containing crystals of minerals and fragments of rock.

percussor (per.kus′er): a doctor's hammer, used in examining patients.

perduellion (pur′dū.el′yun): in Roman law, treason.

perdure, perendure (per.dūr, pur′-en.dūr): to last, continue to exist.

perdurant (per.dū.rant): very long lasting.

perendinate (pe.ren′di.nāt): to postpone until the next day, or indefinitely.

perennate (per′en.āt): in botany, to be perennial.

perflation (per.flā′shun): the act of blowing through; ventilation.

perfluant (per.flōō′ant): flowing; flowing through; as, a *perfluent* battery.

perfrication (pur′fri.kā′shun): a thorough rubbing; the rubbing in of ointment.

perfuse (per.fūz): to suffuse or sprinkle with, or as with, a liquid.

pergameneous (pur′ga.mē′ni.us): like parchment.

perhiemate (per.hī′e.māt): to spend the winter. 1.

peri (per′i): in Persian mythology, an imaginary being like an elf or fairy. A very beautiful person.

periastrum (per′i.as′trum): that point in the real orbit of a binary at which the stars are nearest together.

perichareia (per′i.ka.rē′a): violent rejoicing.

perichoresis (per′i.ko.rē′sis): in theology, the reciprocal existence in each other of the three persons of the Trinity, or the human and divine natures of Christ. *Circumincession.*

periclitation (per′i.kli.tā′shun): the act of exposing to danger.

periculous (pe.rik′ū.lus): perilous. 1.

periegesis (per.i.i.jē′sis): a description of an area.

periergy (per′i.ur′ji): excessive care. 1.

perigon (per′i.gon): a round angle.

perigraph (per′i.graf): an inexact description or drawing. An instrument for drawing outlines of bones.

perijove (per′i.jōv): the point in the orbit of a Jovian satellite nearest the center of the planet.

periople (per′i.ō′pl): the thin waxy outer layer of a hoof.

periplus (per′i.plus): a voyage or trip around, as an island or coast. An account of such a journey.

perispheric (per′i.sfer′ik): exactly spherical; globular.

perissological (per′is.o.loj′i.kal): relating, in old rhetoric, to a superfluity of words.

peristerophilist (pi.ris′ter.of′i.list): a pigeon fancier.

peristrephic (per′is.tref′ik): turning around; rotatory.

perkin (pur′kin): a kind of weak cider.

perlaceous (per.lā′shus): pearly; resembling pearl.

perlustration (pur′lus.trā′shun): a thorough survey or examination, as of a museum or set of documents.

permiscible (per.mis′i.bl): capable of being mixed.

pernancy (pur′nan.si): in law, the receiving of rent or profit.

pernoctation (pur′nok.tā′shun): an all-night vigil.

peroral (per′or.al): via the mouth.

perpilocutionist (pur′pi.lo.kū′shun.ist): one who talks through his hat.

perqueer (per.kwēr′): by heart, perfectly; perfect, accurate. 7A.

perruquier (pe.rōō′ki.er): a wigmaker or dealer in wigs.

perscrutation (pur′skrōō.tā′shun): subjection to scrutiny or close examination.

perseity (per.sē′i.ti): self-sufficiency.

persicary (pur′si.kâr′i): a herb of the genus *Persicaria*—sometimes called *lady's thumb.*

persico, persicot (pur′si.kō): a liqueur made from brandy flavored with the kernels of peaches, apricots, etc.

persienne (per.zi.en′): a kind of painted or printed cotton or silk, orig. from Persia.

persifleur (pur′si.floor): one given to persiflage or banter, esp. about matters usu. considered as serious.

perstringe (per.strinj′): to find fault with; criticize. To touch upon lightly or in passing. 9. To dull the vision of. 1.

pertusion (per.tū′zhun): a perforation; the act of punching or piercing.

perula, perule (per′ū.la, -ōō.la, per′ōōl): one of the scales of a leaf bud. A basal projection in certain orchid flowers.

pervicacity (pur′vi.kas′i.ti): extreme obstinacy; wilfulness. 52.

pervulgate (per.vul′gāt): to publish. 52.

petalism (pet′a.lizm): in ancient Syracuse, banishment for five years. Ostracism.

petardeer, petardier (pet.ar.dēr′): a soldier who manages a petard. 6.

petronel (pet′ro.nel): a large carbine or pistol used in the 16th century and early 17th century by horse soldiers.

pettichaps (pet′i.chaps): a European warbler.

pettitoes (pet′i.tōz): the feet of a pig, often used as a food; toes or feet, esp. those of a child. An insignificant person or thing. 1.

peyton (pā′ton): a smokeless gunpowder containing nitroglycerin and guncotton.

phagomania (fag′o.mā′ni.a): madness marked by insatiable hunger.

phalacrosis (fal′a.krō′sis): baldness.

Phalaris (fal′a.ris): a small genus of American and European grasses with rather broad flat leaves and a dense head of flowers, incl. canary grass and ribbon grass.

phaneromania (fan′er.o.mā′ni.a): a morbid compulsion to pick at a skin growth, bite the nails, etc.

phanic (fan′ik): manifest; apparent.

pharmacophobia (fär′ma.ko.fō′bi.a): fear of drugs or medicine.

pharmic (fär′mik): pert. to drugs or pharmacy. A student of pharmacy. 48.

pharology (fa.rol′o.ji): the art or science of lighthouses or signal lights.

pharyngology (far′ing.gol′o.ji): the science of the pharynx and its diseases.

phasic (fā′zik): pert. to a phase or phases.

phasis (fā′sis): phase. The first appearance of the new moon. An aspect; a mode or manner of being.

phasm (fazm): an appearance, as a meteor or an apparition. 8A.

Phasma (faz′ma): the type genus of Phasmatidae, a family of running insects incl. the stick insects and the leaf insects.

pheal (fēl): the cry of the jackal on the hunt.

phelloplastic (fel′o.plas′tik): a figure or model in cork.

phemic (fē′mik): pert. to or like speech.

phenakistoscope (fen′a.kis′to.skōp): an optical toy resembling the *zoetrope*.

phenicopter (fen′i.kop.ter): a flamingo.

Pherecratic (fer′i.krat′ik): in prosody, a logaoedic tripody acatalectic, of a dactyl and two trochees. Get it?

Phigalian (fi.gāl′yun): pert. to Phigalia, a city in the Peloponnesus; as the *Phigalian* sculptures of the 5th century B.C., now in the British Museum.

philalethe (fil′a.lēth′i): one who enjoys forgetting.

philauty (fi.lôt′i): self-love; selfishness. 1.

philematology (fil′i.ma.tol′o.ji): the art of kissing.

philhellene (fil′he.lēn′): a friend of Greece or of the Greeks.

philiater (fil′i.ā′ter): one interested in medical science.

philocalist (fi.lō′ka.list): a lover of beauty.

philodox, philodoxer (fil′o.doks, -er): one who loves his own opinions; a dogmatist.

philogynist (fi.loj.i.nist): a lover of women and womankind.

philomathic (fil′o.math′ik): loving learning. 52.

philopena (fil.o.pē′na): a game in which a man and a woman each try to claim a forfeit from the other by fulfilling certain conditions, as being the first to cry ''philopena.''

philophobia (fil′o.fō′bi.a): fear of loving or being loved.

philopolemic (fil′o.po.lem′ik): loving argument or controversy.

philornithic (fil′ôr.nith′ik): bird-loving. 52.

philosity (fi.los′i.ti): the degree of body hair.

philosophastering (fi.los′o.fas′ter.ing): pseudo-philosophizing.

philosophicopsychological (fil.o.sof′i. ko.sī′ko.loj′i.kal): philosophical and psychological in one.

philotherian (fil′o.thēr′i.an): fond of animals.

phit (fit): a sound suggesting that of a rifle bullet.

phlebotomize (fli.bot′o.mīz): to let blood by opening a vein; to bleed (one).

phlegmagogue (fleg′ma.gog): a medicine for expelling phlegm.

phlogogenetic (flō′go.ji.net′ik): causing inflammation.

phobophobia (fō′bo.fō′bi.a): fear of fear.

Phoca (fō′ka): a genus of seals now restricted to the harbor seal and a few closely related forms.

phocine (fō′sēn): pert. to the seals.

phoenixity (fi.nik′si.ti): the state of being a paragon, a model of one's kind.

phon (fon): a unit for measuring sound.

phonasthenia (fō′nas.thē′ni.a): hoarseness.

phoniatrics, phonistry (fō′ni.at′riks, -nis.tri): the scientific study and treatment of voice defects.

phonogram (fō.no.gram): a character or symbol representing a word, syllable, or single speech sound.

phonophobia (fō′no.fō′bi.a): fear of noise or of speaking aloud.

phoronomic (fôr.o.nom′ik): pert. to kinematics, the science of the motions or elements of bodies.

photology (fo.tol′o.ji): photics, the science of light.

photophobia (fō′to.fō′bi.a): fear of light.

photophony (fo.tof′o.ni): the transmission of sounds by the modulation of light beams and their reconversion into sound.

phrenesiac (fre.nē′zi.ak): subject to delirium or brain fever.

phronesis (fro.nē′sis): practical wisdom, prudence.

phrontistery (fron.tis′ter.i): a place for study and contemplation.

phrygium (frij′i.um): a helmet-like white cap, worn in the early Middle Ages by the popes at nonliturgical ceremonies.

phthiriophobia (thir.i.o.fō′bi.a): fear of lice.

phthisozoics (tiz′o.zō′iks): the art of destroying noxious animals.

phycography (fī.kog′ra.fi): description of algae or seaweeds.

phylacter (fi.lak′ter): phylactery. 1.

phylarch (fī′lärk): in ancient Greece, the chief ruler of a phyle, or tribe. The commander of the cavalry furnished by each tribe. In the Asiatic provinces of the Roman Empire, the accepted head of a tribal division.

phyllary (fil′a.ri): one of the involuted bracts in a cluster of sessile flowers.

phylliform (fil′i.fôrm): leaf-shaped.

phyllomancy (fil′o.man′si): divination with leaves.

phyllophorous (fi.lof′o.rus): leaf-bearing.

phyloanalysis (fī′lo.a.nal′i.sis): a study of the psychology of society.

phylon (fī′lon): a tribe or race; a genetically related group.

phyma (fī′ma): in medicine, an external nodule; a skin tumor.

physagogue (fiz′a.gog): a medicine to induce expulsion of gas from the bowels.

physianthropy (fiz′i.an′thro.pi): the study of the constitution and diseases of man, and their remedies. 52.

physiogony (fiz′i.og′o.ni): the theory of the origin of nature.

physiolatry (fiz′i.ol′a.tri): nature worship.

physis (fī′sis): nature; that which grows or becomes.

physitheism (fī′zi.thē′izm): the belief that God has a physical form.

phytivorous (fī.tiv′o.rus): feeding on plants; herbivorous.

phytolithology (fī′to.li.thol′o.ji): the paleontology of plants; paleobotany.

phytoma (fī.tō′ma): the vegetative substance of plants.

phytophagous (fī.tof′a.gus): *phytivorous*.

phytophil (fī.to.fil): one fond of plants, or feeding on plants.

pia (pē′a): a perennial herb of East India, Australasia, and Polynesia, cultivated for its large, starch-yielding root.

piacle (pī′a.kl): a heinous offense; a crime; sin; guilt. Also, a sacrificial rite; an expiatory offering. 1.

pial (pī′al): pert. to the pia mater, the connective tissue investing the brain and spinal cord.

pianino (pē′a.nē′nō): pianette.

pianteric (pī.an.ter′ik): fattening food.

Piarist (pī′a.rist): a clerk of the Scuole Pie (religious schools) founded at Rome early in the 17th century.

piation (pī.ā′shun): the act of atoning, expiating. 52.

piatti (pi.ät′i): cymbals.

piccadill (pik′a.dil): a flaring collar worn at the back of decolleté gowns in the 17th century.

pickedevant (pik′de.vänt): a Vandyke beard. 1.

picosecond (pī′ko.sek.unt, -und): one thousandth of a nanosecond; one trillionth of a second.

picqueter (pik′e.ter): one who bunches artificial flowers.

pictorical (pik.tôr′i.kal): pictorial. 52.

picuda (pi.kōō′da): the great barracuda.

pidan (pi.dän′): Chinese duck eggs aged in brine.

piet, piot (pī′et): the magpie; like a magpie—piebald, chattering. A piebald horse. A chatterbox; a saucy person. The water ouzel. 44.

piff (pif): an exclamation.

pightle (pī′tl): a small field or enclosure. 30.

pignorative (pig′no.rā′tiv): pledging; pawning. 52.

pika (pī′ka, pē′ka): any small gnawing mammal of the family Ochotonidae inhabiting high mountains in Asia and western North America, related to rabbits, but having small ears, rudimentary tail, and relatively short hind legs.

pikel, pikle (pik′l): hayfork; *pightle*. 13B.

pilaf, pilaff (pi.läf′, pi.laf′): a Turkish dish of rice combined with meat and other vegetables and seasoned with herbs.

pilar, pilary (pī′lar, pī′lar.i): pert. to hair; hairy.

pilau, pilaw (pi.lô): var. of pilaf, pilaff.

pilch (pilch): an outer garment made orig. of skin and fur and later of leather or wool. An infant's diaper cover. A light child's saddle. A saddle cover. 1. To pilfer; filch. 2.

pilcher (pil′cher): an Elizabethan term of contempt. 1.

pilgarlic (pil.gär′lik): formerly, a bald-headed man; now, a poor sort of fellow.

pili (pē′li): the edible nut of a Philippine tree, *Canarium ovatum,* or the tree itself. In Hawaii, twisted beard grass. Also, pl. of *pilus,* a hair or hairlike structure in botany and zoology.

pilikea (pē.li.kē′a): trouble, in Hawaii.

pililoo (pil′i.l͞oo): in hunting, a cry of distress.

pillet (pil′et): a pellet; a small pill.

pilliwinks (pil′i.wingks): an instrument of torture for the thumbs and fingers. 6.

piloerection (pī′lo.i.rek′shun): the standing of hair on end.

pilwillet (pil.wil′et): the American oyster catcher. 28.

Pimenta (pi.men′ta): a small genus of tropical American aromatic trees of the myrtle family, incl. the allspice tree. Pimento. The black pepper.

pimola (pi.mō′la): an olive stuffed with pimiento.

Pimpinella (pim′pi.nel′a): a large genus of herbs of the carrot family, incl. the anise and the burnet saxifrage.

pinacoid (pin′a.koid): a crystal form with two faces parallel to two axes.

pinacotheca (pin′a.ko.thē′ka): a picture gallery.

pincette (pin.set′): a small pair of pincers, tweezers, or forceps used in surgery.

pincpinc (pingk′pingk): an African warbler.

pindy (pin′di): gone bad; tainted. 13.

pingle (ping′gl): to strive or struggle, esp. for a living; to trifle, esp. with one's food; a struggle; effort. 17A. A small piece of enclosed ground. 2.

pinguefy (ping′gwi.fī): to fatten; to make fat or greasy; to enrich (the soil). 52.

pinguidness, pinguitude (ping′gwid.nes, -gwi.tūd): fatness; obesity; oiliness.

pinic (pī′nik): pert. to or obtained from the pine.

pinnet (pin′et): a pinnacle; a pennant. 44. A pin; a pint. 13.

Pinus (pī′nus): the largest and most important genus of coniferous trees.

pipa (pē′pa): the Surinam toad.

piperacious (pip′er.ā′shus): pert. to the *Piperaciae,* a family of tropical plants having aromatic herbage.

pipistrel, pipistrelle (pip′is.trel): the brown bat of Europe.

pipple (pip′l): to murmur, as the wind or rippling water. 1.

pir (pir): a Mohammedan saint or his tomb.

pirl (purl): var. of *purl.*

pirlie (pur′li): anything small, esp. the little finger (also *pirlie-pig*); a money box. 44.

pirn (purn): any of various devices resembling a reel. 44A. A twitch or nose ring for a refractory animal. 11.

pirner (pur′ner): one who winds thread or yarn on pirns.

pirnie, pirny (pur′ni): a little *pirn,* or bobbin. 44.

pishaug (pish′ôg): a female or young sea duck—surf scoter. 36.

pishogue (pi.shōg′): sorcery; witchcraft. 50.

pisk (pisk): the common American nighthawk.

pisky (pis′ki): var. of *pixy.* Also, a moth.

pissabed (pis′a.bed): any of various wild plants, as the dandelion, with diuretic properties.

pistic (pis′tik): pure; genuine.

pistolade (pis′to.lād): a pistol shot or wound. To fire on with pistols. 1.

pistology (pis.tol′o.ji): the study of faith.

pithecological (pi.thē′ko.loj.i.kal): pert. to the study of apes. 52.

pithiatism (pith′i.a.tizm): a forceful suggestion.

pitpit (pit′pit): a *guitguit.* Also, having a rapid succession of slight sounds of unvarying quality and stress.

Pittosporum (pit′o.spôr′um): a genus of evergreen trees and shrubs of Asia, Africa, and Australasia, often having fragrant white or yellow flowers succeeded by berries, as the laurel. (not cap) A plant of this species.

pituitous (pi.tū′i.tus): consisting of, resembling, or discharging mucus.

pixillation (pik′si.lā′shun): stop-motion photography that gives live actors the appearance of jerky movement associated with cartoon characters.

placet (plā′set): an expression of approval or vote of assent.

placophobia (pla′ko.fō′bi.a): fear of tombstones.

plafond (pla.fond′): in architecture, a ceiling formed by the underside of a floor. Also, contract bridge.

plaga (plā′ga): in animals, a stripe of color.

plancier (plan.sēr′): in architecture, the underside of a cornice; a soffitt.

planeta (pla.net′a): among Romans, a cloak that enveloped the person, leaving the face free.

planiloquent (pla.nil′o.kwent): straightforward in speech.

planiped (plā′ni.ped): barefoot; a barefoot person.

planomania (plā′no.mā′ni.a): a passion for the bohemian life.

planta (plan′ta): the sole of the foot. The back side of the shank of a bird's leg. The first joint of the tarsus of an insect. An anal clasping leg of a caterpillar.

plantigrade (plan′ti.grād): walking on the sole with the heels touching the ground, as bears and people.

plantocracy (plan.tok′ra.si): government by planters.

plaquette (pla.ket′): a small plaque. In anatomy, a blood platelet.

plastron, plastrum (plas′trun, -um): a metal breastplate. A protection for the breast of a fencer. A trimming for the front of a woman's dress. The starched front of a man's shirt.

plateresque (plat′er.esk): pert. to a 16th-century Spanish architectural style with rich ornamentation suggestive of silver plate.

platic (plat′ik): not exact; imperfect—said in astrology of the imperfect conjunction of two planets.

platinize (plat′i.nīz): to cover, treat, or combine with platinum.

platitudinarian (plat′i.tū.di.nâr′i.an): full of platitudes.

platonize (plā′to.nīz): to conform to Platonic principles. To render Platonic; idealize.

platycephalic (plat′i.si′fal′ik): tending toward flatness of the crown of the head.

plaustral (plôs′tral): of or relating to a wagon or cart.

plebicolous (pli.bik′o.lus): courting the favor of the common people. 52.

plegometer (pli.gom′e.ter): an instrument to measure and record the force of blows.

pleionosis (plī′o.nō′sis): exaggeration of one's own importance.

pleniloquence (pli.nil′o.kwens): talking to excess.

plenipotence (pli.nip′o.tens): the quality of being invested with authority to transact business. 52.

plenist (plē′nist): pert. to the theory that every part of space is full of matter. One who believes in this theory.

pleochromatic (plē′o.kro.mat′ik): pert. to the property of some crystals of showing different colors when viewed in the direction of different axes.

pleon (plē′on): a crustacean's abdomen. The terminal segment of a king crab.

pleonaxia (plē′o.nak′si.a): avarice.

Plesiosaurus (plē′si.o.sôr′os): a genus of marine reptiles of the Mesozoic, having a very long neck, a small head, and all four limbs developed as paddles for swimming.

pleurodynia (plur′o.dī′ni.a): a sharp pain in the side, usu. located in the rib muscles.

plex (pleks): to form a plexus or network; to make plexiform.

plexure (plek'sher): a weaving together; that which is woven together.

plicative (plik'a.tiv): capable of being folded.

plimp (plimp): to take part in an event so as to write about it, as George Plimpton does—a *Time* magazine coinage.

plock (plok): an imitative word.

plonk (plongk): cheap table wine.

plouk, plook (plo͞ok): a pimple. 44A.

plousiocracy (plo͞o'si.ok'ra.si): plutocracy.

ployment (ploi'ment): the act of forming a column from a line, in the military.

pluffer (pluf'er): a shooter; marksman. A popgun. 43.

pluffy (pluf'i): puffy; fat; fluffy. 17A.

plumassier (plū.ma.syā'): a dealer in ornamental plumes or feathers.

plumbeous (plum'bi.us): consisting of, or resembling, lead; leaden; the color of lead.

plumbic (plum'bik): pert. to, or containing lead.

plumcot (plum'kot): a hybrid between the plum and the apricot.

plumigerous (plo͞o.mij'er.us): feathered.

plumiped (plo͞o'mi.ped): having feather-covered feet. A plumiped bird.

plummer (plum'er): a pillow block or bearing block. Var. of *plumber*. 1.

plumper (plum'per): something held in the mouth to fill out the cheeks; also, a false bosom. A heavy blow. 21.

plurennial (ploo.ren'ial): lasting for many years. A long-lived plant.

plushette (plush.et'): an inferior kind of plush.

plutomania (ploo'to.mā'ni.a): madness for money.

pluviograph (ploo'vi.o.graf): a rain gauge.

pluviophobia (ploo'vi.o.fō'bi.a): fear of rain.

pneumonoultramicroscopicsilicovolcanoconiosis (nū.mon'ool.tra.mī'kro.-skop'ik.sil'i.ko.vol.kan'o.kō'ni.ō.sis): a lung disease caused by inhaling fine particles of silicon dust.

pnigophobia (nī'go.fō'bi.a): fear of choking, as during sleep.

po (pō): in English folklore, an impish spirit. 1. In Polynesian mythology, the realm of darkness and the dead.

pobby (pob'i): puffed up; swollen. 13.

pochette (po.shet'): a handbag. A small envelope of transparent paper for holding stamps.

poculation (pok.ū.lā'shun): the drinking of wine, spirits, etc.

poculiform (pok'ū.li.fôrm): cup-shaped.

podger (poj'er): a small taper rod used to align rivet holes.

podgy (poj'i): softly fat; pudgy.

poditti (po.dit'i): an Australian kingfisher.

podobromhidrosis (pō'do.brom'hī.drō'-sis): sweatiness and smelliness of the feet.

poe (pō'i): the parson bird of Tahiti, which has two tufts of white on its throat.

poecilonymy (pē'si.lon'i.mi): the use of several names for one thing.

poeticule (po.et'i.kūl): a poetaster.

pogamoggan (pog'a.mog'an): a club used as a weapon or ceremonial object by various American Indian peoples.

pogoniasis (pō'go.nī'a.sis): excessive growth of beard in a man, or any such growth in a woman.

pogonology (pō'go.nol'o.ji): a treatise on beards.

pogonophobia (po.gō'no.fō'bi.a): fear of beards.

pogonotomy (pō'go.not'o.mi): shaving.

poikilothymia (poi.kil'o.thim'i.a): extreme fluctuations of mood.

poimenics (poi.men'iks): pastoral theology.

polacca (po.lak'a): the polonaise, a stately Polish dance developed from the promenade.

polacre (po.lä'ker): a vessel with two or three masts, having sails usu. in one piece and square, but occas. lateen, used in the Mediterranean.

polder (pol'der): land reclaimed from the sea.

polemology (pol'i.mol'o.ji): the study of war.

polemoscope (po.lem'o.skōp'): an opera or field glass arranged for seeing objects not directly before the eye.

polenta (po.len'ta): in Italy, a thick porridge of corn meal, semolina, barley, or chestnut meal.

poliosis (pō'li.ō'sis): premature graying of the hair.

pollicitation (po.lis'i.tā'shun): a promise. 52. In civil law, an unaccepted promise or offer.

pollincture (po.lingk'cher): preparation of a corpse for interment or cremation. 1.

polony (po.lō'ni): a polonaise.

poltina (pol.tē'na): a Russian silver coin equivalent to 50 kopecks or half a ruble.

poltophagy (pol'tof'a.ji): the prolonged chewing of food, reducing it to a semiliquid state.

polychrestic (pol'i.kres'tik): having many uses.

polyemia (pol'i.ē'mi.a): a condition marked by an excessive amount of blood in the system—plethora.

polygenic (pol'i.jen'ik): pert. to a group of genes that collectively control aspects of inheritance.

polygenous (po.lij'i.nus): containing many kinds, as of elements or rocks—a *polygenous* mountain.

polygonous (po.lig'o.nus): having many angles and sides; polygonal.

polygyral (pol'i.jī'ral): having, or pert. to, many cycles, rounds, or whorls.

polyhemic (pol'i.hēm'ik): pert. to *polyemia*.

polylemma (pol'i.lem'a): a dilemma with several solutions, all undesirable.

polylogy (po.lil'o.ji): verbosity.

polymeric (pol'i.mer'ik): in chemistry, consisting of the same elements in the same proportions by weight, but differing in molecular weight.

polymicrian (pol'i.mik'ri.an): compact.

polymythic (pol'i.mith'ik): having to do with the inclusion of many or several stories or plots in one narrative or dramatic work.

polynesic (pol'i.nē'zik): in medicine, occurring in different spots or in sporadic patches like islands.

polyonomous (pol'i.on'o.mus): synonymous. Also, having many names.

polyorama (pol'i.o.rä'ma, -ram'a): a view of many objects; also, a kind of panorama with a dissolving view.

polyphagous (po.lif'a.gus): subsisting on a moderate variety of foods.

polypharmic (pol'i.fär'mik): containing many drugs.

polytopic (pol'i.top'ik): occurring in many places.

polytropic (pol'i.trop'ik): visiting many kinds of flowers for nectar—used of an insect.

pomato (po.mā'tō): a fragrant, succulent, tomato-like fruit, produced by grafting tomato scions on potato plants.

pomatum (po.mā'tum): a perfumed unguent, esp. for the hair; pomade. To dress (as hair) with pomatum.

pombe (pom'be): in Africa, a kind of beer made from grain, usu. from millet. Also, a Tibetan chief.

pombo (pum'bō): a chief or headman in Tibet.

pommage (pom'ij): the substance of apples crushed by grinding as in making cider. Cider. 1.

ponent (pō'nent): western; occidental.

ponerology (pō'ne.rol'o.ji): a branch of theology dealing with the doctrine of evil.

pong (pong): a hollow ringing sound. On the British stage, to improvise to cover up a fluff.

ponophobia (pō'no.fō'bi.a): fear of overwork.

pontage (pon'tij): a bridge toll.

pont-levis (pont.lev′is): a drawbridge.

poogye (poo′gi): the Hindu nose flute.

poon (poon): an East Indian tree that yields hard, light wood used for masts, spars, etc.

poorwill (poor′wil): a bird of the western United States and Mexico, like but smaller than the whippoorwill.

popinary (pop.i.nâr.i): a short-order cook.

popination (pop′i.nā′shun): the frequenting of bars or taverns.

popoloco (pō′po.lō′kō): to the Nahuatl Indians, one who speaks a barbarous or foreign language. (cap) A people of southern Pueblo, Mexico.

porcelanic (pôr′se.lan′ik): resembling porcelain; said of certain rocks.

poriomania (pôr′i.o.mā′ni.a): wanderlust.

porismatic (po.riz.mat′ik): in geometry, pert. to a proposition that affirms the possibility of finding conditions that will render a certain problem either indeterminate or capable of innumerable solutions.

pornerastic (pôr′ne.ras′tik): licentious.

pornocracy (pôr.nok′ra.si): government by whores.

pornogenarian (pôr.no.je.nâr.i.an): a dirty old man.

pornophobia (pôr′no.fō′bi.a): fear of prostitutes.

Poro (pō′rō): a native secret society in Sierra Leone, having only men as members.

porotic (po.rot′ik): promoting the formation of a callus.

porphyrogene (pôr′fir.o.jēn): born to the purple; royal born.

porphyrophobia (pôr′fi.ro.fō′bi.a): fear of purple.

porraceous (po.rā′shus): resembling the leek in color; leek-green.

porrect (po.rekt′): extended horizontally, stretched out. To extend in this fashion.

portglave (pôrt′glāv): one of a Livonian religious order of knights in the first half of the 13th century.

portlast (pôrt′last): the porpoise. 52. The upper edge of a gunwale. 1.

portmantologism (pôrt′man.tol′o.jizm): a blending of two or more words into one.

portreeve (pôrt′rēv): in early England, the official charged with keeping the peace in a port or market town.

porwigle (pôr′wig′l): a tadpole, pollywog. 1.

posada (po.sä′da): in Spain, a hotel or inn.

posole (pō′sōl): in Spanish America, a dish or thick soup composed of meat, hominy, garlic, and chili.

posology (po.sol′o.ji): in medicine, the science of doses. In mathematics, the doctrine of pure quantity.

postcibal (pōst′sī′bal): after dinner.

posteriad (pos.tēr′i.ad): posteriorly, in anatomy and zoology.

posticous (pos′ti.kus): posterior. In botany, situated on the outer side of a filament—said of an extrorse anther.

postil (pos′til): a marginal note or comment, specif. of the Bible. To make marginal notes.

postillate (pos′ti.lāt): to postil. To preach by expounding Scripture verse by verse, in regular order. 52.

postliminium (pōst.li.min′i.um): the law under which things taken by the enemy in war are returned afterward to the previous ownership.

postscenium (pōst.sē′ni.um): the back part of the stage of a theater; the part behind the scenes.

potagerie (po.taj′e.ri): garden vegetables and herbs; a kitchen garden.

potamic (po.tam′ik): pert. to rivers.

potamophilous (pō′ta.mof′i.lus): riverloving.

potassic (po.tas′ik): a combining form of potassium.

pote (pōt): a stick or rod for poking or stirring; a poker; a kick or push with the foot. 21.

potichomania (pō′ti.sho.mā′ni.a,po′ti.ko-): a craze for imitating painted porcelain ware by coating the inside of glass vessels.

potomania (pō′to.mā′ni.a): dipsomania. Delirium tremens.

potoroo (pot′o.roo): a rat kangaroo.

pott (pot): a size of paper—$12\frac{1}{2} \times 15''$ for writing paper, $13 \times 16''$ for printing paper.

pottah (pot′a): in India, a certificate of tenure; title deed; lease.

potvalor (pot′val′er): boldness or courage resulting from alcoholic drink.

potwaller, potwalloper (pot′wôl′er, -wol′up.er): prior to the Reform Act of 1832, an Englishman whose qualification for voting was that he boiled (walloped) his own pot—i.e., was a householder.

pouze (pooz): refuse from cider-making.

pozzy-wallah (poz′i.wol′a): a jam lover. 23.

practic (prak′tik): *practice* in various senses. 9. Practical. Practiced; also, cunning, shrewd. Requiring skill or experience. A practical man, as opposed to a student or theorist.

prana (prä′na): in the Vedic and later Hindu religion, life breath; the life principle.

pranayama (prä′na.yä′ma): certain Yoga exercises.

pratal (prä′tal): pert. to, growing in, or living in, meadows.

pratiloma (prat′i.lō′ma): contrary to custom—said in India of a marriage in which the man is of a lower class than the woman.

pratityasamutpada (prä′ti.tya.sa.mut.pä′da): in Hindu philosophy, the chain of causation.

pravity (prav.i.ti): depravity. Badness or foulness; physical deformity. 9.

praya (prä′ya): beach; strand; specif. (cap), in Hong Kong, a road bordering the shore.

preagonal (pri.ag′o.nal): just before death.

preantepenultimate (pri.an′ti.pi.nul′ti.mit): fourth from the last.

precentral (pri.sen′tral): in anatomy and zoology, situated in front of the central furrow of the brain.

preception (pri.sep′shun): a preconception; presumption; a precept; command. 1. Instruction by a preceptor. 52. In Roman law, the taking, as of a legacy, before the distribution of the estate of the testator.

precibal (pri.cī′bal): before dinner.

preconize (prē′ko.nīz): to proclaim; publish; commend publicly; summon publicly.

predacean (pri.dā′shun): a carnivorous animal.

predal (prē′dal): predatory; plundering.

predella (pri.del′a): a step on which an altar is placed; a painting or sculpture on the face of a predella; a portable altar of marble, etc.

predicant (pred′i.kant): one who preaches; a preacher; specif., a preaching friar; a Dominican. Preaching; addicted to preaching.

preferent (pref′e.rent): exhibiting or enjoying preference.

premial (prē′mi.al): of the nature of a reward. 52.

premorse (pri.môrs′): ended abruptly, as if bitten off.

premundane (pri.mun′dān): antedating the creation of the world.

prender (pren′der): in law, the right to take something without its being offered.

preominate (pri.om′i.nāt): to forecast by omens.

prepend (pri.pend′): to consider, premeditate. 1.

presbyophrenia (prez′bi.o.frē′ni.a, pres-): female senility attended espec. by loss of memory.

prester (pres′ter): a priest or presbyter. (1, except for *Prester John,* a legendary Christian priest and king in the Middle Ages).

preterhuman (prē′ter.hū′man): beyond human, more than human.

prevene (pri.vēn′): to come before, precede. 52. To forestall, prevent. 1.

prickmadam (prik′mad′am): the stonecrop, a mosslike herb used in gardens.

prickmedainty (prik′mi.dān′ti): affectedly nice; a goody-goody. 44A.

pridian (prid′i.an): pert. to the day before yesterday. 52.

prill (pril): a stream, rill. In mining, an ore selected for excellence. To turn sour; to get drunk. 41A.

primigenous, primigenial (prī.mij′i.nus, prī′mi.jē′ni.al): first created or formed; original; primary, primal. 52.

pringle (pring′gl): to tingle annoyingly; to cause a tingle.

Priscian (prish′i.an): a grammarian; a grammar.

priss (pris): to act or dress in a prissy or fussy manner—usu. with up. 27.

proa (prō′a): a Malaysian sailing outrigger.

probal (prō′bal): approved, probable. 52.

probouleutic (prō′boo.loo′tik): pert. to previous deliberation.

procacious (pro.kā′shus): pert; petulant; insolent.

proceleusmatic (prō′se.looz.mat′ik): inciting; animating; encouraging (esp. applied to a song). In prosody, a foot of 4 short syllables; pert. to such a foot.

procellas (pro.sel′as): a tool for imparting a characteristic shape to the neck of a forming bottle or other object as the work is rotated.

procellous (pro.sel′us): stormy.

procerity (pro.ser′i.ti): tallness; height. 52.

prochronism (prō′kro.nizm): the referring of an event to an earlier date than the true one.

prociduous (pro.sid′ū.us): in medicine, prolapsed.

proctalgia (prok.tal′ji.a): a pain in the rear; pygia.

prodelision (prō′di.lizh′un): elision of the initial vowel of a verse.

proditorious (prō′di.tôr′i.us): traitorous. Apt to betray secret thoughts.

proemptosis (prō′emp.tō′sis): the addition of a day to the lunar calendar at intervals of about 310 years.

profectitious (prō′fek.tish′us): derived; in Roman law, pert. to inherited property.

proficuous (pro.fik′ū.us): profitable; useful. 52.

profulgent (pro.ful′jent): in poetic use, shining forth; effulgent.

progenerate (pro.jen′er.āt): to beget.

progeria (pro.jēr′i.a): premature senility.

projicient (pro.jish′ent): serving to bring an organism into relation with the environment.

prolegeron (pro.lej′e.ron): the period of life in which a woman can bear children.

prolegomena (prō′li.gom′i.na): preliminary remarks.

prolepsis (pro.lep′sis): anticipation.

proletaneous (prō′li.tā′ni.us): having many children.

prolecide (pro′li.sīd′): the killing of offspring.

promic (prom′ik): in the theory of numbers, designating a number of the *form* $x + x^n$ where x and n are positive integers.

promulge (pro.mulj′): to promulgate, publish, make known.

pronaos (pro.nā′os): the outer part of an ancient Greek temple forming a portico or vestibule, immediately in front of the cella or *naos*.

pronovalence (prō′no.vā′lens): inability to have sexual intercourse except lying down.

propale (pro.pāl′): to divulge. 9.

propense (pro.pens′): leaning or inclining toward; favorably disposed; favorable, partial. 9.

prophoric (pro.fôr′ik): enunciative. 52.

propination (prō′pi.nā′shun): the act of drinking to someone's health.

proplastic (pro.plas′tik): the art of making molds for castings; pert. to this art.

propugnator (prō′pug.nā′ter): a defender; vindicator.

prorhinal (pro.rī′nal): in front of the nasal cavities.

prosaist (pro.zā′ist): a writer of prose. A prosaic person.

prosneusis (pros.nū′sis): in a nuclear eclipse, the angle of position of the part of the moon first obscured.

prosoma (pro.sō′ma): in zoology, the anterior division of the body, esp. of a mollusk.

prosonomasia (pros′o.no.mā′zhi.a): a nicknaming by punning on the real name.

prosophobia (prō′so.fō′bi.a): fear of progress.

prosopic (pro.sop′ik): pert. to the face.

prosopography (pros′o.pog′ra.fi): description of the face or personal appearance.

prosopolepsy (pros′o.po.lep′si): acceptance of persons, esp. prematurely, from their appearance. 1.

prosopolethy (pros′o.po.lē′thi): inability to remember faces.

protactic, protatic (pro.tak′tik, -tat′ik): telling or explaining beforehand, as the plot of a play; introductory.

protagon (prō′ta.gon): a powder mixture of lipides from the brain.

protophytology (prō.to.fī.tol′o.ji): the study of unicellular plants.

Protorosaurus (prō′to.ro.sôr′us): a genus of upper Permian reptiles resembling lizards and attaining a length of several yards.

protreptic (pro.trep′tik): an exhortation. 52. Persuasive; doctrinal.

protutor (pro′tū′tor): in civil law, one who acts as tutor or guardian without legal appointment.

provection (pro.vek′shun): advancing; advancement. 1. In philology, the carrying forward of a final sound or letter to a following word, as *a nickname* for *an ekename*.

provine (pro.vīn′): to layer.

proxenete (prok′si.nēt): a marriage broker; a procurer.

prud′homme (proo′dum′): orig., a wise or prudent man. Now, specif., a member of a French industrial arbitration board, or Conseil des Prud′hommes.

pruriginous (proo.rij′i.nus): tending to, or caused by, prurigo, a chronic inflammatory skin disease.

prytaneum (prit.a.nē′um): in ancient Greece, a public building consecrated to Hestia, goddess of the hearth, in which the chief officials met and dined, and where official hospitality was extended.

psaphonic (sa.fon′ik): planning one's rise to fame.

psellismophobia (sel′is.mo.fō′bi.a): fear of stuttering.

HOGAMUS, HIGAMUS

When Churchill told us that democracy
  Is an infernal bother—
Of governments, the worst that there could be
  (Except for any other)—

He might have had *monogamy* in mind.
  What man would stay on track
Except that, having left it, he might find
  That there was no way back?

Show me a man who's not philogynous,
  And I will show again
A mewling meacock any prudent puss
  Would leave out in the rain.

An eye should wander; that's the way of laughter,
  And speeds slow-beating hearts;
It's when the rest gets up and wanders after
  That all the trouble starts.

Though womankind must surely feel more cheery
  To know men prize them,
Use *one* for practice, and the rest for theory:
  Idealize them.

Mazophilous, crurophilous are fine
  To stir temptation;
But skip the human—stick to the divine;
  Try sublimation.

(The author was moved to add the following postscriptum):

Misogynists wish Eve were still a rib;
Philogynists love even Women's Lib.

psephology (si.fol´o.ji): the study of elections.

psephomancy (sef´o.man´si): divination by pebbles.

pseudandry (sūd´an.dri): female use of a male pseudonym.

pseudautochiria (su.dô.to.kī´ri.a): murder disguised as suicide.

pseudepisematic (sū´di.pis´i.mat´ik): an animal colored like its prey or its surroundings.

pseudoantidisestablishmentarianism (sū´do.an´ti.dis´e.stab´lish.men. târ´- i.a.nizm): pretended opposition to the withdrawal of state support from an established church.

pseudocyesis (sū´do.sī.ē´sis): false pregnancy.

pseudography (sū.dog´ra.fi): incorrect writing, printing, or spelling.

pseudogyny (su.doj´i.ni): male use of a female name, as taking it at marriage.

pseudolalia (sū´do.lāl´ya): nonsense talk; the uttering of meaningless speech sounds.

pseudomancy (sū´do.man´si): intentionally fraudulent divination.

pseudomania (sū´do.mā´ni.a): the neurotic assumption of guilt by one who is innocent.

pseudomnesia (sū´dom.nē´zhi.a): memory for things that never happened.

pseudophonia (sū´do.fō´ni.a): a suicide disguised as murder.

pseudorhombicuboctahedron (sū´do. rom´bi.kū´bok.ta.hē´dron): an Archimedean solid with 26 faces.

Psidium (sid.i.um): a genus of tropical American trees of the myrtle family, incl. the common guava.

psilanthropy (si.lan´thro´pi): the doctrine of the merely human existence of Christ.

psilology (sī.lol´o.ji): empty talk.

psilosophy (sī.los´o.fi): superficial or fake philosophy.

psilotic (sī.lot´ik): pert. to the falling out of hair.

psithurism (sith´ū.rizm): a whispering sound, as of wind among leaves.

psittaceous (si.tā´shus): parrotlike.

psomophagy (so.mof´a.ji): the swallowing of food without thorough chewing.

Psoralea (so.rā´li.a): a genus of herbs and shrubs of the pea family common in the western United States, incl. the breadroot.

psychagogic (sī´ka.goj´ik): attractive, persuasive, inspiring. Having to do with psychagogy, a method of influencing behavior by suggesting desirable life goals.

psychalgia (sī.kal´ji.a): mental anguish.

psychasthenia (sī.kas.thē´ni.a): a neurosis involving indecision, doubts, and phobias.

psychiasis (sī.kī´a.sis): spiritual healing; religious healing for the soul.

psychiater (sī.kī´a.ter): a psychiatrist.

psychonosology (sī.ko.no.sol´o.ji): the study or science of psychogenic ailments.

psychrophile (sī´kro.fīl): an organism thriving at a relatively low temperature.

psychrotherapy (sī´kro.ther´a.pi): the use of cold water in medical treatment.

psychurgy (sī´kur.ji): mental energy.

ptarmic (tär´mik): provoking sneezing; sternutative.

pteric (ter´ik): pert. to or like a wing.

pteriodology (ter´i.o.dol´o.ji): the study of ferns; *filicology.*

pteroid (ter´oid): fernlike. Winglike.

pteronophobia (ter´o.no.fō´bi.a): fear of being tickled by feathers.

pterygium (ti´rij´i.um): a film on the eye.

ptochocracy (to.kok´ra.si): rule by the poor.

ptochogony (to.kog´o.ni): the production of poverty.

ptochology (to.kol´o.ji): the study of poverty.

pucelage (pū´sel.ij): virginity. 1.

pucelle (pū.sel´): maid; damsel; virgin. (1, exc. as an appellation for Joan of Arc.) Prostitute. 1.

pud (pud): Forefoot; paw; hand. Vulgar slang for penis.

puddee, puddy (pud´i): a measure of capacity in Madras.

pudder (pud´er): pother. 11.

puddingwife (pood´ing.wīf): a large, handsomely colored, wrasselike fish of Florida, Bermuda, and the West Indies. A woman skilled in making puddings, or sausages. 11.

puddock (pud´uk): dial. var. of *paddock,* toad.

pudge (puj): a puddle. A pudgy person or thing. 26.

pudiano (poo´dyä´nō): the *puddingwife.*

pudu (poo´doo): a small reddish deer of the Chilean Andes having simple antlers resembling spikes, and standing only 12 or 13 inches high.

puericulture (pū´er.i.kul´cher): the science of bringing up children. Prenatal care.

pugger (pug´er): a worker who mixes and stirs wet material to make brick, enamel, etc.

puggi (pug´i): in India, a tracker, esp. one of a caste trained to track criminals.

puggle (pug´l): to poke a rod through or into; to clear out or stir up by poking.

puist (pwist): in comfortable circumstances. 43.

pulicious (pū.lish´us): pert. to or abounding with fleas.

pulsion (pul´shun): a pulsing. 1. The act of driving forward; propulsion—opposed to *suction* or *traction.*

pultaceous (pul.tā´shus): of porridge-like consistency; pulpy.

pulvil (pul´vil): cosmetic or perfumed powder. 9.

pulvinar (pul.vī´ner): cushion-like. A cushioned seat at a public spectacle.

puna (poo´na): a bleak, desolate region. In South America, the higher Andes; also, mountain sickness. In Peru, a cold mountain wind.

punaluan (poo´na.loo´an): pert. to a marriage of several brothers to several sisters.

punction (pungk´shun): a pricking; a puncture. 1.

pundonor (pun´do.nôr): a point of honor.

pungle (pung´gl): to pay up, pony up, contribute—usu. with *up.*

puniceous (pū.nish´us): bright-red or purplish-red.

punnet (pun´et): a shallow basket for displaying fruit or flowers, esp. strawberries.

punquetto (pun.ket´ō): a young punk. 1.

punta (pun´ta): in fencing, a point; a pass.

puparial (pū.pā´ri.al): pert. to the outer shell of a pupa.

pupilarity (pū´pi.lar´i.ti): the years before puberty.

purana (poo.rä´na): in Hinduism, astronomical knowledge—third of the four shastras, or categories, of sacred knowledge. The other three are the cosmogonic, theological, and physical.

purdy (pur´di): disagreeably self-important; surly. 11.

purl (purl): to twist, twine. 9. To spin, revolve. 44A.

purlicue (pur´li.kū): a peroration; to perorate. 44A. The space between the thumb and forefinger extended. A curlicue at the end of a word.

purpurate (pur´pū.rāt): purple-colored; royal. To empurple. A salt of purpuric acid.

purpureal, purpureous (per.pū´ri.al, -us): purple.

purpuric (per.pū´rik): pert. to a nitrogenous acid related to uric acid and obtained as an orange-red powder.

purseproud (purs´proud): haughtily proud of one's wealth.

puteal (pū´ti.al): in ancient Rome, a well curb. 1.

putid (pū´tid): rotten; fetid; worthless.

putredinous (pū.tred′i.nus): proceeding from putrefaction; stinking; rotten.

putti (pōō′ti): cupids in sculpture and painting.

puture (pū′cher): food for men or for animals; hence, in old English law, the customary right of keepers of forests, and some others, to take food from the land of certain tenants.

putz (puts): among the Pennsylvania Dutch, a crèche.

puxy (puk′si): a quagmire; swampy ground. Hence, a difficult situation; a quandary. Swampy; miry. 13. Ill-tempered; snappish; puckish. 32.

pycnotic (pik.not′ik): pert. to pycnosis, a degenerative condition of a cell nucleus.

pygal (pī′gal): pert. to the region of the rump.

pygia (pij′i.a): a pain in the rear; *proctalgia.*

pyknic (pik′nik): stout; fat-bellied; round; squat. A pyknic person.

pyroballogy (pī′ro.bal′o.ji): the art of throwing fire; the science of ballistics. 1.

Pyrola (pir′o.la): a genus of short-stemmed herbs, called *wintergreen* in England and *false wintergreen* or *shinleaf* in the United States.

pyromantic (pī′ro.man′tik): pert. to divination by means of fire or flames.

pyrophanous (pī.rof′a.nus): becoming translucent or transparent when heated.

pyrophobia (pī′ro.fō′bi.a): fear of fire.

pyrophone (pī′ro.fōn): a musical instrument in which the tones are produced by flames of gas.

pyrophonous (pī.rof′o.nus): pert. to the pyrophone.

pyrotic (pī.rot′ik): pert. to heartburn.

Pyrrhonic (pi.ron′ik): pert. to the doctrines of Pyrrho, a skeptic philosopher of ancient Greece.

pyrrhotism (pir.o.tizm): the characteristic of having red hair.

pysmatic (piz.mat′ik): interrogatory.

Pythiambic (pith′i.am′bik): Pythian verse (dactylic hexameter) followed by an iambic dimeter or trimeter.

pythogenic (pī′tho.jen′ik): producing, or originating in, decomposition and filth.

Q

qabbalah (kä′ba.la, ka.bä′la): cabala—secret or occult doctrine; a system based on Búber doctrine.

qadi (kä′di): cadi.

qoph (kōf): the 19th letter of the Hebrew alphabet.

qua (kwä): as, in the role of. Also, the night heron. 30.

qua, quaa (kwä): a quagmire.

quab (kwäb): one of several small fishes, incl. the eelpout and gudgeon. Something immature or unfinished. 1.

quackle (kwak′l): to quack.

quaddle (kwä′dl): to grumble; a grumbler. 13.

quadragene (kwä′dra.jēn): a person of forty, or in their forties.

quadragesimal (kwa′dra.jes′i.mal): consisting of 40. A 40-day fast. Pert. to Lent.

quadratrix (kwad.rā′triks): in geometry, a curve used in determining the area of other curves.

quadratum (kwad.rā′tum): in medieval music, a natural. A breve.

quadratus (kwad.rā′tus): any of several muscles, used for rotating the thigh outward, pulling the lower lip down or laterally, etc.

quadrifurcation (kwäd.ri.fer.kā′shun): a branching into four parts.

quadriga (kwad.rī′ga): a Roman chariot drawn by four horses abreast, together with the horses. The four horses alone; less often, the chariot alone.

quadrigamist (kwad.rig′a.mist): one who has married four times, or who has four spouses concurrently.

quadrigenarious (kwäd′ri.je.nāri.i.us): consisting of four hundred.

quadripennate (kwäd.ri.pen′āt): four-winged.

quadrumana (kwa′drōō′ma.na): a group of mammals comprising the monkeys, lemurs, baboons, and apes.

quaesitum (kwi.sī′tum): something sought or desired. In mathematics, the true value.

quaestuary, questuary (kwes′choo.âr′i): undertaken for money. One whose first consideration is profit.

quag (kwäg): a quagmire. To quake or quiver. To sink (someone or something) in a quag. 2.

quakebuttock (kwāk′but′ok): a coward. 2.

qualtagh (kwäl′täk): the first person one sees on waking or leaving home on a special day. 55.

quandong (kwän′dong): an Australian tree; also its edible fruit or nut.

quannet (kwan′et): a flat file with a handle at one side, used for making combs.

quant (kwant, kwänt): a pole for propelling a punt. To punt with such a pole.

quap (kwap): to heave; throb; palpitate. A throb, palpitation. 13.

quaquaversal (kwä′kwa.vur′sal): turning or dipping in every direction; specif., in geology, dipping from a center toward all points of the compass, as in a dome. A quaquaversal dome or ridge.

quar (kwär): to fill; choke; block. 2. To curdle. 4.

quardeel (kär′dāl) a cardel, or cask, used by Dutch sailors.

quarenden (kwôr′en.den): in England, a deep-red, early apple.

quarentene (kwor′en.tēn): a furlong; a rood. 6.

quarl (kwôrl): a large brick or tile, esp. one used to support melting pots for zinc. A jellyfish. 52. To curdle. 1.

quarternight (kwôr′ter.nīt): halfway between sundown and midnight.

quarterpace (kwôr′ter.pās): a staircase platform where the stair turns at a right angle.

quartodeciman (kwôr′to.des′i.man): one of a sect of early Christians who celebrated the Pascual on the date of the Jewish Passover.

quassation (kwa.sä′shun): a shaking; a beating. 52.

quatercentenary (kwä′ter.sen.ten′a.ri, kwä′-): a 400th anniversary. 52.

quatercousin (kwä′ter.kuz′in, kwä′-): *catercousin.* 1.

quaternary, quaternate (kwa.tur′nā.ri, kwä′ter.nāt): arranged in sets of four, as *quaternate* leaves.

quatorzain (kat′er.zān): a poem of 14 lines, such as the sonnet. (The verse below is *not* a quatorzain.)

WEDE IS MY NICKNAME, AND YOU CAN GUESS WHO QUEDE IS

Now quap and quop, my heart! The east
  Again to quarternight gyres 'round.
Stilled is the ever-moaning queest;
  The quiller sleeps without a sound.
The quackle of the duck has ceased;
  The quis dreams, nesting on the ground.

So queme!—but ah, what quags beneath?
  What quelches through the queachy glede
And quiffs and quetches—seeks to quethe?
  Must my next qualtagh be dread Quede?
(The Qs, you see, bring quaving teeth
  To quaggly old quakebuttocks Wede.)

---

quatre (katr, kä′ter): a card, die, or domino having four spots, or pips.

quatuorvirate (kwä′tōō.ôr′vi.rāt): an association of four men. 52.

quawk (kwôk): caw, screech. 11. A night heron. 32.

queach (kwēch): thicket. 13B.

queachy (kwē′chi): boggy, marshy. 13B. Forming a dense growth; bushy. 4.

quede (kwēd): evil; also, an evil person. Specif., (cap), the Devil. 1.

queechy (kwē′chi): sickly, puny. 13.

queest (kwēst): a ringdove, wood pigeon.

queesting (kwēs'ting): bundling—said of sweethearts who occupy the same bed without undressing.

queet (kwēt): ankle. 44.

queeve (kwēv): a twist or turn, as in a road. To twist or turn. 13A.

queezmadam (kwēz'ma'dam): an early variety of pear. 11.

quelch (kwelch): to make a sucking or gulping sound; to squelch. 11A.

quelquechose (kel'ke.shōz): a mere trifle; a nothing.

quemado (ki.mä'dō): a district that has been burned. 34B.

queme (kwēm): pleasant, agreeable. 2. To suit, satisfy. 1.

quercitannic (kwur'si.tan.ik): relating to the tannin of oak bark.

querimonious (kwer'i.mō'ni.us): querulous.

querl (kwurl): twirl; coil. 28.

quern (kwurn): a small handmill for grinding spice.

quetch (kwech): to break silence; utter a sound. 11A.

quethe (kwēth): to speak, tell. (1, except in past tense *quoth*). Clamor, cry; a will, testament.

quiapo (ki.ä'po): a water lettuce of the Philippines.

quia-quia (kē'a.kē'a): the cigarfish.

quica (kē'ka): a small South American opossum.

quiff (kwif): a puff; whiff. For some in Britain, a prominent forelock. A girl. 21.

quiller (kwil'er): a fledgling. 1. A machine for transferring yarn from spools to quills; the operator of such a machine.

quincentenary (kwin'sen.ten'a.ri): a 500th anniversary.

quincentennial (kwin'sen.ten'i.al): pert. to 500 years. A quincentenary.

quinic (kwin'ik): pert. to or obtained from cinchona bark.

quinoa (ki.nō'a): a pigweed of the high Andes or its seeds, ground for food and widely used as a cereal in Peru.

quinology (kwi.nol'o.ji): the science of the cultivation of the cinchona tree, and the chemistry and medical use of its bark.

quinquarticular (kwin'kwär.tik'u.lär): relating to five articles or points, particl. (in religion) those in dispute between Arminians and Calvinists.

quinquertium (kwin.kwur'ti.um): an athletic meet in which each contestant participates in five different events; a pentathlon. 1.

quinse (kwins): to carve. 1.

quintessentialize (kwin'ti.sen'sha.liz): to extract the quintessence of.

quintroon (kwin.trōōn): a person 1/16 black—the offspring of an octaroon and a white.

quirl (kwurl): a curl. To bend; coil; twist.

quis (kwis): the European woodcock.

quisquillious (kwis.kwil'i.us): trashy; rubbishy. 52.

quisquose (kwis'kwōs, -kōs): perplexing. 44.

quizzacious (kwi.zā'shus): bantering; given to quizzing. 52.

quo (kwō): something received in an exchange.

quoddity (kwod'i.ti): quiddity—used derisively. 52.

quodlibetic (kwod.li.bet'ik): consisting of or like quodlibets—purely academic. Given to quodlibets, or academic discussion.

quop (kwop): to throb. 2.

quotennial (kwo.ten'i.al): annual. 52.

quoz (kwoz): something queer or absurd. 1.

R

rab (rab): master, teacher—a Jewish title of respect.

rabiator (rab'i.ä.tor): a violent man. 44 (52).

rabic (rab'ik): pert. to rabies.

raca (rä'ka): a term of reproach used by the Jews of the time of Christ, meaning ''fool.''

rach (rach): a hunting dog. 10.

rackett (rak'et): an old wind instrument of the bassoon kind, having a double-reed mouthpiece and a wooden tube, bent upon itself, with ventages but no keys.

radicant (rad'i.kant): rooting from the stem, as common ivy.

radicate (rad'i.kāt): to plant firmly; to establish solidly. 52.

radiesthesia (rä'di.es.thē'zi.a): the claimed ability to detect underground water by means of a divining rod; dowsing.

radiolucent (rä'di.o.lōō'sent): permeable to radiation.

radiopraxis (rä'di.o.prak'sis): the use of ultraviolet rays or x-rays in medicine.

rafale (ra.fal'): a rapid burst of artillery fire, consisting of several rounds.

raff (raf): riffraff. Rubbish. 11.

rafty (raf'ti): rancid; stale or musty. 4.

ragarock (rag'a.rok): a kind of rock 'n' roll using an Indian melodic form.

raggee (rä'gi): an East Indian cereal grass whose ground seeds make a somewhat bitter flour.

raggle (rag'l): a groove cut in masonry, esp. one to receive the upper edge of a flashing above a roof. To cut such a groove. A rag; shred. 52.

rais (rīs): a Muslim ship's captain. A Muslim chief. (cap, n. pl.) A Mongoloid people of Nepal.

raisonné (rā'zo.nā): logical; arranged systematically.

raith (rāth): a quarter of a year. 44.

ramage (ram'ij): the boughs or branches of a tree. 9. Wildness, courage. Wild, shy. 1.

A QRIOUS COLLECTION, BUT KIND OF QT

A Q in most words should be followed by U,
But once in awhile it is not.
To find Q without U, simply follow my Q—
I'll show you a few of the lot.

There's *Qabbala*—mystical meanings attached
To Scripture by certain old Jews;
And *Qadarites*—sheiks whom the Moslems dispatched
For having claimed freedom to choose.

There's *Qadi*—a judge who apportions a loaf
By guessing Mahomet's intention.
There's one little letter (ק) that answers to *Qoph*—
Another old Hebrew invention.

There's *Q-boat*—a warship disguised as a botch;
And *Qantas*, an airline to watch.
New York has a mayor, I think, name of *Qoch*,
Though maybe the spelling is *Kwôch*.

*ק. The nineteenth letter of the Hebrew alphabet, sounding like our *k* or *qu*.

---

ramarama (rä'ma.rä'ma): a New Zealand myrtle sometimes cultivated for its curiously wrinkled leaves and pale pink flowers.

rambooze (ram.bōōz'): wine and sugar mixed (in winter) with ale and eggs, or (in summer) with milk and rose water. 52.

ramentum (ra.men'tum): something scraped off; a shaving. One of the thin, brownish, chaffy scales borne upon the leaves or young shoots of many ferns.

ramfeezled (ram.fē'zld): worn out; exhausted. 44.

ramiferous (ra.mif'e.rus): bearing branches.

rammish (ram'ish): lustful; lewd. Rank in smell or taste. 11. Violent; untamed. 43. To rush about as if frenzied. 43.

rampacious, rampagious (ram.pā'shus, -pā'jus): rampageous; given to displays of recklessness; wild, unruly.

ramus (rā'mus): (pl. *rami*). A branch. In biology, one of several bones, incl. the posterior part of the lower jaw and a branch of the pubis. Also, a branch of a nerve, a barb of a feather, etc.

rana (rä'na): prince—a title of some of the native rulers of India. (cap) A large genus of tailless leaping amphibians, incl. the frogs.

ranaria (pl. of *ranarium*) (ra.när'i.a): places for keeping or rearing frogs.

rance (rans): a dull red Belgian marble with blue-and-white markings. A prop or support; to prop. 44A.

rancer (ran′ser): a tool that enlarges or shapes holes or smooths bores; a worker who uses such a tool; a reamer.

rangatira (rang.a.tē′ra): a Maori chief; a leading citizen. 56.

ranic, ranine (rā′nik, -nīn): pert. to frogs.

ranivorous (ra.niv′o.rus): frog-eating.

rantipole (ran′ti.pōl): a reckless, sometimes quarrelsome person. Wild; unruly. To behave in a wild fashion. 52.

rantism (ran′tizm): ranting. 1.

ranula (ran′ū.la): a cyst formed under the tongue by the obstruction of a gland duct.

rastik, rastick (ras′tik): any of various hair dyes.

ratafee, ratafia (rat′a.fi, -fē′a): a fruit-flavored liqueur, gen. with a taste of bitter almond.

ratal (rā′tal): the amount at which a person is rated with reference to tax assessment.

ratamacue (rat′a.ma.kū): in drumming, a figure more difficult than the paradiddle.

rataplan (rat′a.plan): the sound of rhythmic beating, as a drum or a galloping horse. To make such a sound.

ratch (rach): a notched bar with which a pawl or click works to prevent reversal of motion. A blaze on an animal's face. In sailing, to reach. 1.

ratchel (rach′el): stone in small fragments; gravel; gravelly subsoil. 11A.

ratihabition (rat′i.ha.bish′un): ratification, sanction.

ratten (rat′en): to steal tools from an employer as a way of enforcing trade union demands. 40A.

rawn (rôn): roe; spawn. Also, a female fish, esp. a herring or salmon.

raya (rā′a): the East Indian broadbill, a sluggish duck with a rather wide flat bill. Also, a subject Christian peasant under the Ottoman Empire.

razee (ra.zē′): a wooden ship reduced in class by having her upper deck cut away, as a seventy-four cut down to a frigate. A razeed chest, book, or the like. To razee.

razoo (ra.zōō′): a razzing; a racket. 22.

rea (rē′a): a female defendant in a court trial (fem. of *reus*).

reable (ri.ā′bl): to rehabilitate. 40A.

reasty, reasy (rēs′ti, rē′zi): rancid. 2.

reaver, riever (rē′ver): one that takes away by stealth or force.

rebia (rē′bi.a): a gold coin of the Ottoman Empire in the 19th century. A Turkish silver coin.

reboantic (reb′o.an′tik): reverberating.

rebullition (reb.ul.lish′un): a boiling up again. 1.

recadency (ri.kā′den.si): a relapse. 52.

RUMBELOW, RUMBELOW

Oh, did you know the rumbelow,
Rumbelow, rumbelow—
Oh, did you know the rumbelow
Who lived in Drury Lane?

She'd chug-a-lug her ratafee,
Ratafee, ratafee,
She'd chug-a-lug her ratafee,
And chug-a-lug again.

Rambooz to her was mother's milk,
Mother's milk, mother's milk,
Rambooz to her was mother's milk,
And never weaned was she;

Rumgumption was her middle name,
Middle name, middle name,
Rumgumption was her middle name,
A shilling was her fee.

Once in there came a rantipole,
Rantipole, rantipole,
Once in there came a rantipole,
And ordered her to bed;

"I give to you the old razoo,
The old razoo, the old razoo;
I give to you the old razoo,
For sir, we are not wed."

A round ribroasting gave her he,
Gave her he, gave her he,
A round ribroasting gave her he,
And of it she did die;

Ramfeezled by her weary life,
Weary life, weary life,
Ramfeezled by her weary life,
She rose up to the sky.

And oh, how happy we should be,
We should be, we should be,
And oh, how happy we should be
Were she but redivivus;

We'll no more know a rumbelow,
Rumbelow, rumbelow,
We'll no more know a rumbelow
So excellent to swive us.

---

recalesce (rē′ka.les): to release heat, as a metal when cooling.

recaptor (ri.kap′tor): one who recaptures; one who takes a prize that had been previously taken.

recension (ri.sen′shun): a scholarly editorial revision.

receptary (ri.sep′ta.ri): accepted as fact but unproved; a postulate. A collection of recipes.

recheat (ri.chēt′): a blast on the horn to call the hunting hounds. 9.

reclivate (rek′li.vāt): s-shaped; sigmoid.

recoct (ri.kokt): to recook; to redo.

rectalgia (rek′tal′ji.a): proctalgia.

rectigrade (rek′ti.grād): moving in a straight line.

rection (rek′shun): in grammar, the influence of a word that requires another word to be placed in a certain case or mood.

---

rectopathic (rek′to.path′ik): easily hurt emotionally.

recubation (rek′u.bā′shun): recumbency. 1.

reculade (rek′ū.läd): a retreat.

recussion (ri.kush′un): repercussive action.

redan (ri.dan′): a fortification having two faces that form a salient angle.

redargution (red′är.gū′shun): orig., reproof; later, refutation. 52.

reddition (re.dish′un): restoration; restitution; surrender. Formal restitution by judicial confession.

redditive (red′i.tiv): in grammar, corresponding; correlative.

redhibition (red′hi.bish′un): the return of defective merchandise to the seller.

redintegrate (re.din′ti.grāt): to renew. To be restored to a previous condition.

redition (ri.dish′un): returning, return. 1.

redivivus (red′i.vī′vus): revived; living again.

redubber (ri.dub′er): in history, one who buys, alters, and resells stolen cloth.

reduct (ri.dukt′): to reduce. 1. To deduct. 11.

redux (rē′duks): indicating return to a healthy state.

reechy (rē′chi): rancid. 2.

reeden (rē′den): of or like a reed. 52. Reedy. 1.

reem (rēm): the wild ox mentioned in the Old Testament. To cry, shout. 1.

reese, reeze (rēs, rēz): to become rancid. 2. To scorch. 1.

refocillation (ri.fos′i.lā′shun): revival; refreshment. 52.

refrangible (ri.fran′ji.bl): capable of being refracted, as rays of light.

refrangent (ri.fran′jent): refrangible.

regalian (ri.gāl′yan): pert. to regalia; regal.

reif (rēf): robbery; plunder. 44A.

reiver (rē′ver): a raider. 44.

rejessed (ri.jest′): reattached jesses to (a hawk).

rejunction (ri.jungk′shun): a reuniting. 52.

relata (ri.lā′ta): a group of related things.

religate (rel′i.gāt): to tie together. 52.

remanet (rem′a.net): in law, the postponement of a case. In the British Parliament, a bill carried over to another session.

remeant (rē′mi.ent): returning. 52.

remiped (rem′i.ped): having feet or legs used as oars, as certain crustaceans and insects. A remiped animal.

remontado (ri.mon.tä′dō): a Filipino who has renounced civilization and "fled to the mountains."

renable (ren′a.bl): fluent; eloquent; glib. 2.

renascible (ri.nas´i.bl): capable of rebirth. 52.

renidification (ri.nid´i.fi.kā´shun): the building of another nest.

renifleur (ren´i.floor): one who derives sexual pleasure from body odors.

rennet (ren´et): an old form of apple. 41.

reparationist (rep´a.rā´shun.ist): one who believed in reparation to ex-slaves.

repartimiento (rā.par´ti.mi.en´tō): in the Spanish colonies of America, a grant, esp. of Indian forced labor.

repertorium (rep.er.tôr´i.um): an index, catalogue, or collection. A storehouse, repository.

repristinate (ri.pris´ti.nāt): to revive; to restore.

reptatorial (rep´ta.tôr´i.al): creeping, as a reptile.

repullulate (ri.pool´yōō.lāt): to bud or sprout again; to recur, as a disease. 52.

resiccant (res´i.kant): drying up; causing to dry up. 1.

resiccate (res.´i.kāt): to make dry again. 1.

resile (ri.zīl´): to draw back, recoil; retract.

resipiscent (res´i.pis´ent): changing the mind and heart; reforming; returning to a sane, sound, or correct view.

restis (res´tis): a pair of nerve fibers on the dorsal surface of the medulla oblongata.

restringent (ri.strin´jent): binding; astringent; styptic. 52. A restrictive word. 1. In medicine, an astringent or styptic.

retorsion (ri.tôr´shun): var. of *extortion.*

retrad (rē´trad): backward or posteriorly.

retrochoir (ret´ro.kwīr): the space in a church behind the high altar or choir enclosure.

retrocollic (ret´ro.kol´ik): pert. to the back of the neck.

retrocopulation (ret´ro.kop´u.lā´shun): copulation from the rear.

retromancy (ret´ro.man´si): divination by looking back over the shoulder.

retromingent (ret´ro.min´jent): urinating to the rear; an animal that does so.

retter (ret´er): one who soaks or exposes to moisture (as flax, hemp, timber). 52.

retunded (ri.tun´ded): beaten or driven back; rendered impotent, weak, or useless. 1.

reus (rē´us): a male defendant in a court trial.

revalescent (rev´a.les´ent): convalescing.

revalorize (ri.val´o.rīz): to restore the value of a monetary unit.

reve (rēv): to muse in revery. 52.

revehent (ri.vē´hent, rev´i.hent): carrying back.

revellent (ri.vel´ent): causing revulsion; revulsive.

reverso (ri.vur´sō): the reverse, or left-hand page of a book or folded sheet of paper; a verso. The reverse, as that which appears when something is seen from opposite to the usual direction.

rhabdophobia (rab´do.fō´bi.a): fear of being punished or severely criticized.

rhapsodomancy (rap.so.do.man´si): divination by poetry.

rhema (rē´ma): a verb; word; term.

rheme (rēm): any semantic unit or element of a speech.

rheocrat (rē´o.krat): a kind of speed controller for an electric motor.

rheophile (rē´o.fīl): living in rivers or streams.

rheotan (rē´o.tan): an alloy of copper, zinc, nickel, and iron.

Rhiannon (ri.an´on): the Great Queen or Mother Goddess of Welsh mythology, whose three birds could sing the dead to life or the living to death.

rhigosis (ri.gō´sis): a sensation of cold.

rhinocerical (rī´no.ser´i.kal): gorged with money, rich. 9.

rhinocerotic (rī´no.si.rot´ik): pert. to or resembling a rhinoceros.

rhinophonia (rī´no.fō´ni.a): marked nasal resonance in speech.

rhinoplasty (rī´no.plas´ti): a nose job; nasoplasty.

rhipidate (rip´i.dāt): fan-shaped.

Rhodian (rō´di.an): a native or inhabitant of Rhodes. Pert. to Rhodes, or to the Knights of Rhodes (Hospitallers).

rhombicosidodecahedron (rom´bi.kos´i.do.dek´a.hē´dron): an Archimedean solid with 62 faces.

rhonchisonant (rong´ki.sō´nant): snorting; snoring.

rhopalism (rō´pa.lizm): a rhopalic.

rhyophobia (rī´o.fō´bi.a): fear of filth.

rhyparography (rī.pa.rog´ra.fi): the painting or literary depiction of mean or sordid subjects.

rhysimeter (rī.sim´e.ter): an instrument for measuring the velocity of a fluid, current, a ship's speed, etc.

rhytiphobia (rī´ti.fō´bi.a): fear of getting wrinkles.

rhytiscopia (rī´ti.skō´pi.a): neurotic preoccupation with facial wrinkles.

riancy (rī´an.si): state of one laughing, smiling; gaiety; brightness.

ribble (rib´l): to remove seed from (flax) by combing before the flax is retted.

ribroasting (rib´rōs´ting): a sound beating; a thrashing.

ricercare (rē´cher.kä´rā): a fugue-like composition; an elaborate fugue.

rident (rī´dent): laughing or broadly smiling; riant. 52.

ridotto (ri.dot´ō): a public entertain-ment consisting of music and dancing, often in masquerade, introduced from Italy and very popular in England in the 18th century. An arrangement or abridgement of a musical composition from the full score.

riem (rēm): in South Africa, a thong; a strap. A pliable strip of rawhide, used for twisting into ropes, etc.

rifacimento (ri.fach´i.men´tō): a remaking or recasting; an adaptation, esp. of a literary or musical composition.

rigation (ri.gā´shun): the act of wetting.

rigescent (ri.jes´ent): growing stiff or numb.

riggot (rig´ot): a half-castrated male animal, esp. a horse. 11. A gutter. 13.

rignum (rig´num): the horsemint *Monarda punctata.*

rincon (ring.kōn´): a small circular valley, usu. one containing a house. 35A.

rindle (rin´dl): a rivulet; brook, runnel. 11.

ripa (rī´pa): a bank of a river, beyond which the waters do not normally flow. A ptarmigan. 52.

ripal (rī´pal): riparian. 52.

ripieno (rip´yā´no): in music, a supplementary instrument or performer.

riroriro (rē´ro.rē´rō): the gray warbler of New Zealand.

rishi (rish´i): a Hindu mystic or mystical poet.

risoluto (rē´so.lōō´tō): resolutely and with marked accent—a direction in music.

risorial (ri.sō´ri.al): pert. to or producing laughter.

risp (risp): the stem of such plants as peas and strawberries. A coarse kind of grass. 43. A sound of risping; a carpenter's file; a tirling pin; to rasp; turl; a metal bar on a house door, rubbed with an attached ring to draw attention. 44.

risper (ris´per): in South Africa, a caterpillar.

rissel (ris´el): the common red currant.

rissle (ris´l): a stick, staff, or pole. 17A.

rist (rist): to engrave, scratch, or wound; insurrection; also, resurrection; an ascent (of ground) or increase (of price). 1.

ritornel, ritornelle (rit´ôr.nel): a short instrumental passage in a vocal composition, often a refrain. Also, an instrumental interlude between the parts of an opera or a tutti passage in a concerto.

rix (riks): dial. var. of *rush;* a reed.

rixation (rik.sā´shun): a quarrel. 52.

rixatrix (riks.ā´triks): a termagant, scold. 1.

roborean (ro.bō´ri.an): oaken; stout; strong. 1.

robur (rō´ber): the British oak.

rocambole (rok′am.bōl): a European leek or wild garlic, cultivated as a flavoring ingredient.

rocca (rok′a): a fortress, hold, donjon, keep.

rochet (roch′et): a medieval outer garment, usu. short-skirted, worn by men or women. A loose cloak; a frock. 49. A close-fitting ecclesiastical vestment, worn by bishops in certain ceremonies; hence, a bishop. 1. The red gurnard, a fish with fanlike pectoral fins.

rock-cistus (rok.sis′tus): the rockrose.

rockoon (ro.kōōn′): a small rocket fired from a balloon.

rogan (rō′gan): a kind of wooden bowl or receptacle, as for holding maple sap. 12.

roid (roid): rough; unmanageable. 11. Riotous; frolicsome. 44.

rokelay (rok′e.lā): a knee-length coat, buttoned in front, worn after 1700. 44A.

roky (rō′ki): foggy, misty. 13B.

roleo (rō′li.ō): a contest at birling logs.

rolley (rol′i): a lorry. 41. Formerly, any of various vehicles drawn by horses or by hand. 53A.

Rom (rom): a male gypsy.

rondache (ron.dash′): a round shield carried by medieval foot soldiers.

rondle (ron′dl): a rung of a ladder. 1. In metallurgy, the crust on molten metal in the crucible.

rone (rōn): a clump of briars or bushes. 2. A rainspout. A small patch of ice. 44.

ronyon (ron′yun): a mangy or scabby creature. 1.

roodle (rōō′dl): in poker, one of a round of hands played after a player has won a round with an esp. high hand. The pot limit is usu. doubled.

rootle (rōō′tl): to root, as a pig. 52.

roral, roric, rorulent (rō′ral, -ik, -ū.lent): dewy.

THE MISTAKEN GRATITUDE OF THE
GODDESS RHIANNON'S BIRDS
(WHO CAN SING THE DEAD TO LIFE,
OR THE LIVING TO DEATH)

Three birds flew down, and perched among the
　　ramages
　　Extending in the greenwood from a robur.
They sat there calculating legal damages.
　　(I listened from below, and I was sober.)

It seems the Mother Goddess, great Rhiannon,
　　Had sent them on a mission to a Scot.
But he had died while eating cold colcannon;
　　So, sensibly, they finished off the lot.

They found that spud-and-cabbage mix so tasty
　　That though they'd come to sing the man to
　　　death
Rhiannon's order now seemed over-hasty;
　　And so instead they sang him back to breath.

For dereliction in their duty to her,
　　The goddess fired them; and they plan to sue her.

---

rosal (rō′zal): rosy. 1. Belonging to the Rosales, an order of 25 plant families incl. those of the plum, pea, saxifrage, and stonecrop.

rosella (ro.zel′a): a vividly colored Australian parakeet. A European who works bared to the waist (from the scarlet color of his skin). 53. A sheep that has shed a portion of its wool. 20.

rosen (rō′zen): consisting of, or resembling, roses; rosy. 1.

roser (rō′zer): a rosebush. 1.

rosinante (rō′zi.nan′ti): a broken-down horse, nag—called after Don Quixote's bony horse.

rosmarine (ros.ma.rēn′): sea dew. Also, a sea animal fabled to climb rocks by its teeth to feed on the dew. A walrus. 1.

rosorial (ro.zō′ri.al): pert. to the rodents; gnawing.

ross (ros): rubbish; waste. 1. The rough exterior of bark. To strip the bark.

rosser (ros′er): a logger who smooths the wood on one side of logs so they can be dragged more easily, or who peels bark from pulpwood by hand to avoid waste. An attachment for a circular saw to remove scaly and gritty bark.

rostel (ros′tel), rostellum (ros.tel′um): a small beak. In orchids, a small projection beneath the retinacula. The sucking beak of lice; more rarely, the beak of true bugs. In certain parasitic worms, a forward extension of the head bearing hooks.

rostral (ros′tral): pert. to a rostrum.

rotch (roch): the dovekie, a small, short-billed auk of the Arctic.

rotchet (roch′et): a vestment.

rouky (rōō′ki): foggy, misty. 44A.

rounce (rouns): the apparatus that moves the bed of a hand printing press under the platen; the handle of this apparatus. To flounce about, fuss. A card game in which jacks are trumps.

rowlet (rou′let): a little roller. 52.

rowlyrag (rou′li.rag): a dark gray stone.

rowy (rō′i): of uneven texture or appearance; streaked.

rox (roks): to decay, rot. 13.

roxy (rok′si): decayed; softened. 13.

ruana (rōō.ä′na): a viol instrument used in India.

rubai (rōō.bä′i): a Persian quatrain.

rubedinous (rōō.bed′i.nus): reddish.

rubific (rōō.bif′ik): causing redness, as of the skin; rubefacient.

rubiginous (rōō.bij′i.nus): rust-colored; rusty.

rubineous (rōō.bin′i.us): ruby-red, rubious.

ructation (ruk.tā′shun): the act of belching. 52.

rudenture (rōō.den′cher): in architecture, a cabling.

rudge (ruj): dial. var. of *ridge*.

ruelle (rōō.el′): the space between the bed and the wall. 1. In 17th- and 18th-century France, a morning reception held in the bedroom; hence, a select gathering.

rugulose (roo′gū.lōs): finely wrinkled.

rukh (rōōk): in Kipling, a forest, jungle.

rumbelow (rum′bi.lō): a refrain in old songs, esp. sea songs. 52. A prostitute. 1.

rumgumption (rum′gump′shun): keenness; shrewdness. 43.

rumtifusel (rum.ti.fū′sel): a supposed beast, flat as a laprobe, which attracts human prey by its resemblance to a rich fur coat, and in a trice sucks out their flesh.

runcation (rung.kā′shun): the removal of weeds. 1.

runch (runch): charlock; jointed charlock or wild radish. 43.

rundle (run′dl): a step of a ladder; a rung. Something that rotates about an axis, as a wheel. One of the pins of a lantern pinion. The drum of a windlass or capstan.

runnet (run′et): the contents of the stomach of an unweaned calf or other animal, used for curdling milk. Also, obs. form of *rennet*.

runnion (run′yun): a scurvy wench.

rupestrian (rōō.pes′tri.an): composed of rock; inscribed on rocks.

ruptuary (rup′chōō.âr′i): a plebean; a commoner. 52.

rurigenous (rōō.rij′i.nus): born in the country. 52.

ruskin (rus′kin): a receptacle, as for butter, made of bark; also, butter kept in a ruskin. 13.

rustre (rus′ter): in medieval armor, a metal scale of oval or lozenge shape.

rutaceous (rōō.tā′shus): pert. to Rutaceae, a family of herbs, shrubs, and trees, often glandular and strong-scented.

rutcher (ruch′er): something that moves with a crunching or shuffling noise. 52.

rutin (rōō′tin): a yellow crystalline glycoside found in various leaves and flower buds. It is used in medicine to strengthen capillary blood vessels.

ruttle (rut′l): a rattle; a gurgle, as the breath of one dying.

S

sabbatia (sa.bā′shi.a): the sabbat—in medieval demonology a midnight assembly in which demons, sorcerers, and witches celebrated their orgies. (cap) A genus of smooth, slender North American herbs incl. the marsh or sea pinks.

sabbulonarium (sab′ū.lo.nâr′i.um): a gravel pit. The digging of gravel, or a wage paid for such digging.

sabeca (sa.bek′a): an ancient instrument, prob. a kind of harp, mentioned in the Bible.

sabretache (sā′ber.tash, sab′er-): a leather case or pocket sometimes worn, suspended on the left from the saber belt, by cavalry.

saburration (sab′e.rā′shun): application of sand to the body as therapy; arenation.

saccade (sa.kād′): a quick, violent check of a horse by a single twitch of the reins. A sudden strong pressure of a violin bow, causing strings to sound simultaneously.

saccadic (sa.kad′ik): jerky, twisting.

sacellum (sa.sel′um): in ancient Rome, an unroofed space consecrated to a divinity. A small monumental chapel in a church.

Sacheverell (sa.shev′er.el): a kind of blower once used on stoves.

sacket (sak′et): a small sack or wallet; also, a small, stupid, or rascally person. 44.

sacrificant (sak.rif′i.kant): one who offers up a sacrifice.

Sacripant (sak′ri.pant): a boastful coward, from the name of a king of Circassia (in Boiardo's *Orlando Innamorato*) whose charger was stolen from between his legs without his knowing it. 52.

sadda (sad′a): a book of Zoroastrian writings.

Sadducaic (sad′ū.kā′ik): pert. to the Sadducees, a priestly sect of the Jews that flourished from the 2nd century B.C. to the latter part of the 1st century A.D.

sadr (säd′r): the lotus tree. (cap) A star in the constellation Cygni.

saeculum, seculum (sek′ū.lum): a long time. A generation.

saeter (sē′ter): a meadow or a mountain pasture. 61.

saeterious (si.tēr′i.us): pert. to a *saeter*. 61.

saffian (saf′i.an): a kind of leather made of goatskins or sheepskins tanned with sumac and dyed with bright colors.

sagaciate (sa.gā′shi.āt): to get along; thrive. 34A.

sagene (sa.jēn): a network. 52. A fishing net.

saginate (saj′i.nāt): to pamper; fatten.

sahu (sā′hōō): in Egyptian religion, the spirit body, in contrast to the *khet*.

sai (sä′i): the capuchin monkey.

said (sa.ēd): a kind of ketch common in the Levant.

sain (sān): to cross (oneself); to consecrate. To save from evil by invocation or blessing. 10. Poetically, to heal.

saj (säj): an East Indian tree. Its wood, widely used for construction.

sakeen (sa.kēn′): an ibex of the Himalayas.

sakkara (sa.kä′ra): the color mouse gray.

salago (sa.lä′gō): any of several Philippine shrubs of the genus Wikstroemia; also, their bast fiber, used for making bank-note paper and other strong papers.

salatorial (sal′a.tôr′i.al): pert. to a ritual prayer of Muslims.

salimeter (sa.lim′e.ter): an instrument for measuring the amount of salt in a solution; a *salinometer*.

salinometer (sal′i.nom′e.ter): *salimeter*.

salnatron (sal.nā′tron): crude sodium carbonate.

salsuginous (sal.sū′ji.nus): growing naturally in soil impregnated with salts.

saltimbanco (sal′tim.bang′ko): a mountebank; a quack. 9.

saltimbocca (sal′tim.bok′a): scallops of veal rolled up with ham, cheese, etc.

salvific (sal.vif′ik): tending to save or to secure safety.

saman (sä′man): the rain tree. In India, furniture; stores; equipage; baggage.

sambo (sam′bō): an Indian or mulatto and black half-breed. (cap) A black, often used disparagingly.

sambouka (sam.bōō′ka): var. of *sambuk*.

sambuk (sam′book): a small Arabian dhow.

sambuke (sam′būk): an ancient shrill-toned harp. A bagpipe. A hurdygurdy.

sammy (sam′i): damp, clammy. 11A. A ninny; simpleton. 13. (cap) A U.S. soldier. 21.

Samsam (sam′sam): a Malayan-Siamese people on the west coast of the Malay peninsula.

san (san): a sibilant letter (ꟊ) of the primitive Greek alphabet. By shortening, sanatorium. A plant similar to hemp, also called sunn.

sanable (san′a.bl): capable of being healed or cured.

sanative (san′a.tiv): having the power to cure or heal; curative.

sanctanimity (sangk′ta.nim′i.ti): holiness of mind. 52.

sandek, sandik (san′dek, -dik): one who holds the Jewish infant during circumcision.

sandever, sandiver (san′di.ver): scum cast up in glassmaking—glass gall.

sanglot (sän.glō′): in singing, a sobbing grace note.

sanguify (sang′gwi.fī): to produce blood; to change into blood. 1.

sanguinivorous, sanguivorous (sang′-gwi.niv′o.rus, -gwiv′o.rus): feeding on blood.

sans-culottic (sanz′kū.lot′ik): radical; Jacobinic; uncouth for lack of breeches.

santon (san′ton): a Muslim saint; a dervish or hermit regarded as a saint.

sapan (sa.pan′): the heartwood of the sappanwood tree, formerly used as an astringent.

saponacity (sa′po.nas′i.ti): soapiness. 58.

sapphism (saf′izm): lesbianism.

saprophilous (sa.prof′i.lus): thriving in decaying matter, as certain bacteria.

saraad (sa.räd′): in early Welsh law, a fine for injury, payable in cattle.

sarcel (sär.sel′): a pinion feather of a hawk's wing.

sarcelle (sär.sel′): a teal. 39A.

sarcle (sär′kl): a hoe. To weed. 1.

sarcodic (sär.kod′ik): pert. to or resembling protoplasm.

sarcophagic, sarcophagous (sär′ko.faj′ik, -kof′a.gus): feeding on flesh.

sarcophilous (sär.kof′i.lus): fond of flesh.

sardanapalian (sär′da.na.pāl′yun): having a luxurious, effeminate nature.

sardel, sardelle (sär.del′): a sardine.

sark (särk): a shirt; a body garment for either sex. To cover with sarking. 11.

sarmassation (sär′ma.sā′shun): love play, *paizogony*.

sarmassophobe (sär.mas′o.fōb): one who dreads love play.

sarment, sarmentum (sär′ment, -.men′tum): in botany, a cutting; a scion; a slender, prostrate, running shoot.

sarna (sär′na): among the Kols of India, a sacred grove.

Sarsar (sär′ser): in Muslim countries, a whistling, violently cold, deadly wind.

sart (särt): the town dwellers of a native race in Turkestan. Also, var. of *soft*. 11.

sasin (sä′sin): the black buck, or Indian antelope.

sasine (sä′sīn, -sin): in Scots law, seizin, or possession of feudal property; also, the formality by which it is acquired.

satanophany (sä′ta.nof′a.ni): possession by the devil.

sati (sut′i): var. of suttee, the former practice of a Hindu widow cremating herself on her husband's funeral pyre. The cremated widow. (cap) In Egyptian religion, the queen of the gods, depicted with cow's horns.

sation (sā′shun): a sowing or planting. 1.

satisdiction (sat′is.dik′shun): the condition of having said enough. 59.

satispassion (sat′is.pash′un): in theology, a satisfactory level or amount of suffering.

satrapess (să′tra.pes): a female sa-trap—a petty ruler or subordinate official in ancient Persia. Hence, a woman in a responsible administrative or executive position.

savate (sa.vat′): a form of boxing in which blows may be delivered with the feet.

sawder, soft sawder (sô′der): to flatter. Flattery. 26.

sawney (sô′ni): a fool; simpleton; naively foolish; silly; to talk blandishingly. 26A.

saxcornet (saks′kôr.net): a small sax-horn.

saxify (sak′si.fī): to petrify, turn into stone.

saya (sä.ya): in the Philippines, a woman's outer skirt, tied at the waist with a tape and extending to the ankles.

scacchic (skak′ik): pert. to or like chess.

scaddle (skad′l): noxious; cruel; timid; skittish; mischievous; thievish. To run off in fright. 11. Injury; mischief; confusion. 2.

scaldabanco (skal′da.bang′ko): a fervent debater or preacher. 1.

scall (skôl): a scabby disease, esp. of the scalp.

scamander (ska.man′der): to wind, meander, as the Scamander river in Asia Minor.

scamell, scammel (skam′l): the bar-tailed godwit.

scaphism (skaf′izm): in ancient Persia, execution by exposure to the sun, head and limbs being smeared with honey to attract insects.

scapple (skap′l): var. of *scabble.*

scapulimancy (skap′ū.li.man′si): divination by the study of a shoulder blade, usu. as blotched from the fire.

scarabee (skar.a.bi): a scarab, or dung beetle.

scarebabe (skâr′bāb): a thing to scare a baby; a bogy.

scarious (skâr′i.us): in botany, thin and membraneous in texture, as a bract.

scarrow (skar′ō): a faint light or shadow; to shine faintly. 44.

scatch (skach): a stilt; a crutch. 1. A kind of oval bit for a bridle.

scatomancy (skat′o.man′si): divination by the study of feces.

scat-singing (skat′sing′ing): the improvising or repeating of meaningless syllables to a melody.

scatula (skach′e.la): in pharmacy, a flat rectangular box used for dispensing powder and pills.

scaturient (ska.choor′i.ent): gushing forth; full to overflowing; effusive.

scauper, scorper (skô′per, skôr′per): one of various tools used in wood engraving, line engraving, jewel chiseling, etc.

scaurie (skô′ri, skä′ri): a young gull; esp., a young herring gull. 44.

scaurous (skô′rus): thick-ankled.

scavage, scavenge (skav′ij, -inj): the act of scavenging. In old English law, a toll duty exacted of merchant strangers by mayors, sheriffs, etc. for goods shown or offered for sale.

scavager (skav′a.jer): scavenger.

scaw (skô): var. of *scall.* 43.

scena (sē′na): *skene.*

scenography (si.nog′ra.fi): the art of perspective.

schesis (skē′sis): the general disposition of the body or mind; habitude. 1. In rhetoric, the citing of an opponent's mental set as tending to invalidate his arguments.

scete (skēt): *skete.*

schizothemia (skiz′o.thē′mi.a, skit′so-): digression by a long reminiscence.

BUT COWS ARE ''KINE'' IN ENGLAND?

A picnic is a pasture feast,
    A pyknic is a fat-stuff;
But nothing care we two, at least,
    That *this* stuff leads to *that* stuff.

So we shall splore among the cows,
    And on the grass sit stodging;
If lambs come bounding as we smouse,
    Let others do the dodging.

Let others jog, their waists to shear—
    Slipe lipids off by diet;
We'll lean against some Jersey's rear,
    And sloam in God's own quiet.

Let others scuddle; let them strain,
    And fitness pamphlets study;
Though we grow squaddy, we'll remain
    As seely as a scuddy.

While they do push-ups on the lea,
    And play the cockalorum,
Our briskest exercise will be
    A hand of snipsnapsnorum.

---

schlenter (schlen′ter): in South Africa, an imitation, as an imitation diamond.

schnitz (shnits): sliced dried fruit, esp. apples.

schoenobatist (ski.nob′a.tist): a tight-rope walker.

schola (skō′la): in ancient Rome, a school or meetingplace for associations.

schola cantorum (skō′la kan.tō′rum): a singing school; specif., the choir or choir school of a monastery or a cathedral. The part of an ecclesiastical edifice reserved for the choir.

scholia (skō′li.a): scholarly notes, specif. insertions by the editors in Euclid's *Elements.*

schorl , shorl (shôrl): tourmaline, esp. of a common black iron-rich variety. Any of several dark-colored minerals other than tourmaline. 9.

schorly, shorly (shôr′li): containing or mingled with schorl, or with black tourmaline, a gemstone.

schrik (shrik): in South Africa, a sudden fright; panic.

scialytic (sī′a.lit′ik): shadow-dispersing.

sciaphobia (sī′a.fō′bi.a): fear of shadows.

sciapodous (sī.ap′o.dus): having very large feet, as the Sciapods, a fabulous Libyan people who used their feet as sunshades and umbrellas.

sciatheric (sī′a.ther′ik): pert. to a sundial.

scincous (sing′kus): like or pert. to skinks; scincoid.

scintle (sin′tl): to stack (molded brick) with spaces between to allow ventilation for drying. To set (brick) in a wall so as to produce a rough quality. Brick so stacked or set.

sciography (sī.og′ra.fi): a superficial study.

sciophyte (sī′o.fīt): a plant that endures the shade or thrives in it.

sciopticon (sī.op′ti.kon): a magic lantern.

Sciot (sī′ot): pert. to the isle of Chios. A native or inhabitant of Chios.

sciotheism (sī′o.thē′izm): belief in disembodied spirits as effective agents in human affairs.

sclerema (skli.rē′ma): hardening of bodily tissue, esp. the subcutaneous tissue.

Scleria (sklē′ri.a): a genus of sedges. The American species is often called nut grass.

scob (skob): a rod or splint of wood, esp. a thatch peg. 41.

scobby (skob′i): the chaffinch. 13.

scobicular (sko.bik′ū.lar): sawdust-like.

scobs (skobs): raspings of ivory, hartshorn, metal, or other hard substances.

scoleciphobia (skol′es.i.fō′bi.a): fear of worms.

scolecophagous (skol′i.kof′a.gus): worm-eating.

Scomber (skom′ber): the genus containing the common Atlantic mackerel.

sconcheon, scuncheon (skon′chun, skun′chun): in architecture, the part of an opening from the back of the reveal to the inside face of the wall.

scoon (skoon): to skip a flat rock across water. 11.

scopa (skō′pa): an arrangement of short stiff hairs on an insect that functions like a brush in collecting something (as pollen).

scopiferous (sko.pif′er.us): furnished with one or more dense brushes of hair.

scopophobia (skop′o.fō′bi.a): fear of being seen.

scordatura (skôr′da.too′ra): an unusual tuning of a stringed instrument for some special effect.

scortation (skôr.tā′shun): fornication.

scote (skōt): a prop; chock. To prop. 13.

scotography (sko.tog′ra.fi): the process of producing a picture in the dark; radiography.

scotoma (sko.tō′ma): in medicine, a blind or dark spot in the visual field.

scotomy (skot′o.mi): dizziness with dimness of sight. 1.

scotophobia (skot′o.fō′bi.a): fear of darkness.

scovel (skuv′el): a mop for sweeping ovens. 13.

scraffle (skraf′l): scramble; struggle, wrangle. 13B.

scranch (skranch): to crunch. 11A.

scrannel (skran′el): slight; thin; lean; weak; poor. 9A. Harsh; unmelodious.

scrappet (skrap′et): dim. of *scrap*.

scray (skrā): a frame to hold textiles, as for drying. A bush. The common tern. 29A.

screeve (skrēv): to write (as begging letters); to draw on a sidewalk, in order to attract passers and elicit charity. 21.

scride (skrīd): to creep; to crawl on all fours. 11.

scringe (skrinj): to cringe; flinch. To flog the water in fishing. 11. To squeeze or rub with force; to pry, search. 13.

scriniary (skrin′i.er.i): a keeper of archives.

scripee (skrip.ē′): one to whom land scrip is issued.

scriptor (skrip′ter): one who writes; a scribe.

scripturient (skrip.choor′i.ent): having a desire to write or a passion for writing.

scritch (skrich): screech. 10.

scrivello (skri.vel′o): an elephant's tusk, esp. one weighing less than 20 pounds.

scrog (skrog): scrubby land—used usu. in pl.; the blackthorn; any stunted shrub or bush. 49. The crab apple.

scroop (skro͞op): to creak, grate; to sound like silk; the rustle of silk. 13A.

scrotiform (skrō′ti.fôrm): pouch-shaped.

scrouge (skrouj, skro͞oj): to squeeze together; crowd, press. 26.

scrow (skrou): a cutting from a skin, used for making glue. A schedule or list; a scroll (pl.) Writings. 1.

scrump (skrump): something shriveled or undersized; to shrivel. 13A.

scrutineer (skro͞o′ti.nēr): an examiner, as of votes at an election.

scruto (skro͞o′tō): a kind of trapdoor in a theater stage.

scry (skrī): outcry; shout. 11. To descry; to practice crystal gazing. 9. A kind of sieve; to sift. 2.

scuddle (skud′l): hurry, scuttle. 11.

scuddy (skud′i): naked; a naked child. 44.

scuft (skuft): cuff; buffet. 13.

sculp (skulp): An engraving; a piece of sculpture; to engrave. 1. To sculpture. 58. (var. of *scalp*) To break (slate) into slabs. The skin or pelt of a seal, esp. a young seal. To remove this (skin).

scuppet (skup′et): a small spade or shovel. 13.

scutiferous (skū.tif′er.us): shield-carrying. Bearing scutes or scales, as reptiles.

scutum (skū′tum): among the Romans, an oblong, leather-covered shield, esp. for heavily armed infantry. A bony, horny, or chitinous plate of an insect. One of the two lower valves of the movable shell plate of a barnacle.

scybalum (sib′a.lum): a hardened fecal mass.

scye (sī): *armscye*.

seave (sēv): a rush; a rushlight. 42.

sebago (si.bā′go): the landlocked salmon.

sebastomania (si.bas′to.mā′ni.a): religious mania.

secability (sek′a.bil′i.ti): divisibility. 52.

secernent (si.sur′nent): separating; secreting. Something that secretes or promotes secretion.

secernment (si.surn′ment): the act of separating, distinguishing, discriminating. The act of secreting, as mucus.

secesh (si.sesh′): secessionist. Secessionists collectively. 23.

sectary (sek′ta.ri): a zealous adherent of a sect. (often cap) A nonconformist.

sectiuncle (sek′ti.ung′kl): an insignificant sect. 52.

sective (sek′tiv): capable of being cut; sectile.

secundation (sek′un.dā′shun): the act of making (one) lucky or prosperous.

secundo (se.kun′dō): secondly; in the second (year).

secundogeniture (se.kun′do.jen′i.cher): the state of being second-born, esp. among sons. The inheritance of a second son.

sedile (si.dī′li): a seat in the chancel near the altar for the officiating clergy during intervals of the service.

sedilia (si.dil′ya): pl. of *sedile*.

seeksorrow (sēk′sor′ō): one who finds pleasure in sadness or pain.

seely (sē′li): blessed, happy: good, kind: innocent, harmless; weak, poor, wretched; simple, timid, foolish, silly. 10.

seesee (sē′si): a small Asiatic sand partridge.

seg (seg): an animal castrated when full grown. 14. Sedge; the iris. 11A.

segger (seg′er): a boaster, braggart. 1.

seghol, segol (se.gōl′): in Hebrew grammar, a vowel sign (··) written below its consonant and nearly equivalent to English *e* as in *set*.

seinsemblers (saɴ′säɴ.blā): falsies.

seity (sē′i.ti): a quality peculiar to oneself; selfhood; individuality.

sejoin (si.join′): to separate. 52.

sejugate (sej′o͞o.gāt): to sunder.

sejunction (si.jungk′shun): separation. 1.

selcouth (sel′ko͞oth): marvelous; wonderful. 9. A marvel; a wonder. 1.

selenian (si.lē′ni.an): pert. to the moon.

selenophobia (si.lē′no.fō′bi.a): fear of the moon.

selion (sel′yun): in early England, one of the strips or ridges in which land was plowed in the open-field system.

sella (sel′a): in Roman antiquity, a seat, saddle. In anatomy, a saddle-shaped portion of the sphenoid, a compound bone at the base of the cranium.

sellar (sel′er): pert. to a depression in the middle line of the bone at the base of the cranium, lodging the pituitary body.

sematology (sem′a.tol′o.ji): the study of the relation of signs, or words, to thought. 52.

semeiological, semiological (sē′mi.o.loj′i.kal): pert. to the study of signs.

semese (se.mēs′): half-eaten. 52.

semic (sem′ik, sē′mik): pert. to a sign.

semiped (sem′i.ped): in prosody, a half foot.

semiustulate (sem′i.us′cho͞o.lāt): half burned.

semordnilap (se.môrd′ni.lap): a word that spells another word in reverse; "palindromes" spelled backward.

sempervirent (sem′per.vī′rent): evergreen. 52.

sempster (semp′ster): var. of *seamster*, tailor.

sendal (sen′dal): a thin silk fabric used in the Middle Ages.

sennight (sen′īt): the space of seven nights and days; a week. 9.

senocular (sen.ok′ū.lar): having six eyes.

sensific, sensificatory (sen.sif′ik, -a.tō′ri): producing sensation.

sensor (sen′ser): sensory.

sensum (sen′sum): in philosophy, an object of sense, or content of sense perception; a sense datum.

sententiarian (sen.ten′shi.er′i.un): an aphorist. A discourse full of meaning or wisdom.

sepicolous (si.pik′o.lus): inhabiting hedges or hedgerows.

seppuku (sep.po͞o′ko͞o): in Japan, suicide by disembowelment; hara-kiri.

septangle (sep′tang′gl): a heptagon.

septemplicate (sep.tem′pli.kāt): one of seven copies.

septenate (sep'ti.nāt): divided into seven parts—said of leaves.

septentrionate (sep.ten'tri.o.nāt): to point north. 52.

septile (sep'tīl, -til): pert. to a septum, or partition—in anatomy, to the partition between the nostrils.

septimanal (sep.tim'a.nal): weekly.

septimanarian (sep'ti.ma.nâr'i.an): in a monastery, a monk who served in certain capacities for a week.

septimole (sep'ti.mōl): in music, a group of seven notes to be played in the time of four or six of the same value. Septuplet.

septophobia (sep'to.fō'bi.a): fear of decaying matter.

septulum (sep'tū.lum): a small septum—partition, membrane.

serang (se.rang'): the boatswain of an East Indian crew; also, the skipper of a small native boat.

serenitude (si.ren'i.tūd): serenity. 1.

sereno (si.rā'nō, -rē'nō): in Spain, serene. Also, a night watchman.

seri (sē'ri): var. of *siri*. (cap) An Indian people of the state of Sonora, Mexico.

serictery (si.rik'ter.i): the silk-producing gland of a caterpillar or other insect larva.

sermocination (ser.mos'i.nā'shun): a form of rhetoric in which one immediately answers one's own question. 52.

sermuncle (sur'mung'kl): a short sermon.

serriped (ser'i.ped): having serrated feet.

serrurerie (se.rur'e.ri): highly finished work in wrought iron.

sertulum (sur'tū.lum): in botany, a collection of scientifically studied plants. Having the flower cluster arising from a common point; an umbel.

sertum (sur'tum): a scientific treatise upon a collection of plants.

seruke (si.rook): a bloodsucking fly of Nubia and the Sudan, remarkable for its long sucking organ.

servation (ser.vā'shun): preservation. 52.

sesquitricentennial (ses'kwi.trī'sen.ten'i.al): a four hundred and fiftieth anniversary.

sestole (ses'tōl): a group of six equal musical notes performed in the time ordinarily given to four of the same value, and written in three groups of two. A sextuplet.

setal (sē'tal): in zoology and botany, pert. to any slender, typically rigid or bristly and springy organs or parts of animals or plants.

setarious (si.târ'i.us): resembling a bristle.

seth (seth): in India, a merchant or banker.

seton (sē'tn): in medicine and veterinary medicine, one or more threads or horsehairs or a strip of linen introduced beneath the skin by a knife or needle to form an issue; also, the issue.

set, sett (set): in Scots law, the constitution of a burgh. A spot in a river where nets are set. A tartan pattern.—44A.

sevocation (sev'o.kā'shun): the act of calling apart or aside. 52.

sewen (sū'en): a British trout regarded as a subspecies of the sea trout.

sexangle (seks'ang'gl): a hexagon.

sfumato (sfoo.mä'tō): of a painting, having hazy outlines, shades, and colors.

sgabello (zga.bel'ō): an octagonal Italian Renaissance chair.

shaconian (shā.kō'ni.an): one who believes Bacon wrote Shakespeare's plays.

shadoof (sha.doof'): a counterpoised sweep used in Egypt and nearby countries for raising water.

shaftsbury (shafts'ber'i): a gallon jug of wine.

shaganappy (shag'a.nap'i): a thread, cord, or thong of rawhide.

shahzadah (sha.zä'da): son of a shah.

shamal (sha.mäl'): a northwesterly wind over Mesopotamia and the Persian Gulf.

shamateur (sham'a.ter): one pretending to be an amateur.

shandry (shan'dri): short for *shandrydan*, an old-fashioned chaise or gig. A rickety vehicle.

shandy (shan'di): wild in mirth or fancy; boisterous; visionary. 13. To discourse in the manner of Sterne's Tristram Shandy.

shanker (shang'ker): one whose work consists of making or fastening on shanks.

shapoo (sha.poo'): a wild mountain sheep of Kashmir and Tibet.

shardborn (shärd'bôrn): born in dung.

shastra (shas'tra): in Hinduism, the four classes of scriptures known as *sruti, smriti, purana,* and *tantra.* Also, technical treatises on religious or other subjects.

sheal (shēl): a shelter; to shelter. 17A.

shebeen (she.bēn'): an illegal drinking establishment; a speakeasy; to keep a shebeen. 47A.

shee, sidhe (shē): an underground fort or palace of the fairies in Gaelic folklore. A general name for the fairyfolk of Ireland.

sheel (shēl): shovel. 44.

shelta (shel'ta): a secret jargon of tinkers and kindred classes, still to be found in Britain and Ireland.

Shen (shen): the name of the Christian God as adopted by some Chinese Protestants.

shend (shend): to protect or defend. To punish, revile, put to shame and confusion; to injure, ruin. 10. To worst, as in battle. 1.

sheng (sheng): in China, a province divided into districts. A Chinese wind instrument, with music produced both by exhaling and inhaling. A Chinese measure.

shep (shep): short for shepherd. 2.

shereef, sharif (she.rēf'): an Arab prince or chief.

sherryvallies (sher'i.val'iz): chaps, leggings. 52A.

shet (shet): dial. var. of shut.

sheugh (shūk): to make ditches or drains; to cover over. A ditch; gully. 44A.

shevel (shev'el): to distort or be distorted; to walk waveringly. 43.

shewel (shoo'el): a scarecrow, esp. one made of feathers tied to a string. 11.

shicker (shik'er): a drunk; a drunkard. 21.

shikasta (shi.kas'ta): a Persian hand in which correspondence and sometimes manuscripts are written.

shillaber (shil'a.ber): a shill, a decoy. 22.

shillibeer (shil'i.bēr): a horse-drawn omnibus. A hearse, with seats for mourners.

shilpit (shil'pit): feeble, puny, worthless, stupid. 44.

shintiyan (shin'ti.yan): wide loose trousers worn by Muslim women.

shinty (shin'ti): shinny. 43A.

shippo (ship'ō): in Japanese art, cloisonné enamel on a background of metal or porcelain.

shippon (ship'un): a cow barn. 14.

shish (shish): a prolonged sibilant sound. To shish, esp. for the purpose of quieting.

shitepoke (shīt'pōk): any of various herons, esp. the green heron or night heron.

shoad (shōd): in mining, a fragment of vein material removed by natural agencies from the outcrop, and lying in the surface soil.

shode (shōd): the top of the head; the parting of the hair there. 1.

shog (shog): to shake, jog, jolt; a shake, jog, jerk. 10.

shole (shōl): a plank or plate placed beneath an object to give increased bearing surface or to act as a protection.

shoneen (shō'nēn, sho.nēn'): a would-be gentleman who puts on superior airs; a snob; a toady. 51.

shott (shot): a shallow salty lake in one of the closed basins of northern Africa.

shram (shram): to shrink or shrivel with cold; to be numb. 13.

shroff (shrof): in the Far East, a money changer or banker. To inspect coins.

shtreimal (shtrī′mal): a tall round fur cap.

shud (shud): a shed. 4.

sialogogic (sī′a.lo.goj′ik): promoting the flow of saliva.

sicarian (si.kâr′i.an): an assassin.

sicarious (si.kâr′i.us): murderous.

sicca (sik′a): a coining die. A newly coined rupee; hence, any silver (coin) in excellent condition.

siccaneous (si.kā′ni.us): of soil, dry, unwatered. 52.

siccar (sik′er): dial. form of *sicker*.

sicchasia (si.kā′zhi.a, -zi.a): nausea.

sice (sīs): the number six on a die; the throw of six. 9. A sixpence. 23.

sicker (sik′er): secure; trustworthy; firm and well established. Securely; safely. 44A. Trickle, ooze. 11A. To assure, secure, pledge. 9.

sicsac (sik′sak): the crocodile bird of Egypt.

sideration (sid′er.ā′shun): a sudden attack of disease for no known cause; erysipelas. 1. The use of green manure in agriculture.

siderodromophobia (sid′er.o.drō′mo.-fō′bi.a): fear of train travel.

siderographist (sid′er.og′ra.fist): one who engraves steel.

sideromancy (sid′er.o.man′si): divination by regarding stars or watching burning straw.

sidi (sē′di): a title of respect given to an African Mohammedan, usu. to one in authority.

sidy (sī′di): pretentious. 26.

Sif (sif): in Norse mythology, the wife of Thor and the guardian of the home.

sifaka (si.fak′a): any of several diurnal lemurs of Malagasy that have a long tail and silky fur and are of a usu. black and white color.

siffilate (sif′i.lāt): to whisper.

sigillate (sij′i.lāt): decorated with seal-like markings. To seal.

sigillography (sij′i.log′ra.fi): the study of seals.

signaletics (sig′na.let′iks): the science of making or using signalments.

sika (sē′ka): the Japanese deer, or any closely allied deer of the eastern Asiatic mainland. (cap) A subgenus of the genus *Cervus,* comprising these deer.

sike (sīk): a small stream, esp. one that dries up in summer; a ditch; trench; drain; a gully; ravine. 43A. A sigh. 2.

Sikinnis (si.kin′is): in Greek antiquity, an orgiastic dance of satyrs.

sile (sīl): to drop, drip; to subside. 2. To strain, filter; a strainer. 2.

silentiary (si.len′shi.er′i): one appointed to keep order and silence.

sillar (sēl.yär′): building material, chiefly Mexican, consisting of blocks of clay cut from a natural clay deposit and differing from adobe in not being pugged or molded.

siller (sil′er): var. of silver. 43.

sillock (sil′uk): a young coalfish. 44.

silphium (sil′fi.um): an extinct plant, perhaps the laserwort, used medicinally by the ancient Greeks. (cap) A large genus of North American herbs having coarse heads and yellow flowers.

simba (sim′ba): to the Bantus, a lion.

simbil (sim′bil): an African stork with bronzy back and white underparts.

simblot (sim′blot): in weaving, the harness of a drawloom.

sime (sīm): a monkey. A rope or frame of straw. 42.

Simia (sim′i.a): a genus orig. incl. most apes and monkeys, but now confined to the Barbary ape.

simity (sim′i.ti): pug-nosedness.

simous (sī′mus): snub-nosed. Concave; snub. 1.

sinapis (si.nap′is): a white mustard, charlock, or other weedy herb of the subgenus Sinapis.

sinapize (sin′a.pīz): to powder or sprinkle.

sinarchism (sin′är.kizm): a Mexican counterrevolutionary movement seeking a return to early Christian principles, and opposing communism.

sind (sind): to rinse; wash out; quench; drench. 4A. A rinsing; a drink to wash down solid food. 43.

sinistrogyrate (sin′is.tro.jī′rat): inclined or moving toward the left.

sinople (sin′o.pl): ferruginous quartz of a blood-red or brownish-red color, sometimes with a tinge of yellow.

sinsyne (sin′sīn): since that time; ago. 44A.

siphonage (sī′fon.ij): the action or use of a siphon.

sipid (sip′id): tasty, flavorful.

sipple (sip′l): tipple. 44A.

sircar (ser.kär′, sur′kär): in India, the government, the supreme authority. Also, a house servant.

sirenic (si.ren′ik): siren-like; fascinating, melodious; deceptive.

sirgang (sur′gang): an Asiatic, long-crested jay, called also the Chinese roller.

siri (si′ri): betel.

siserara (sis′er.âr′a): a severe blow; a violent scolding. 11.

sist (sist): a stay of legal proceedings, or an order for such a stay. To bring into court; summon. 44A.

sistle (sis′l): to whistle with a hissing sound.

sithe (sīth): dial. var. of sigh. A journey; conduct; course of life; chance, mishap; time. 1.

sitophobia (sī′to.fō′bi.a): fear of eating.

situal (sich′oo.el): positional.

sizar (sī′zer): a student (as in the universities of Cambridge and Dublin) who receives an allowance, formerly for serving other students.

sizarship (sī′zer.ship): the position or standing of a sizar.

sizz (siz): a hissing sound. To hiss.

sizzard (siz′erd): heat with high humidity. 27.

sizzen (siz′en): childbed. 7A.

skaddle (skad′l): short for skedaddle. 32. Var. of *scaddle.*

skag (skag): a low-decked boat for duck shooting. To shoot from a skag. A cigarette. 21.

skedge (skej): the common privet.

skeeg (skēg): lash; flog; slap. 44.

skeel (skēl): a pail, bucket, or tub. 2.

skegger (skeg′er): a young salmon in the stage when it has dark transverse bands on its sides; a parr.

skelder (skel′der): to cheat, panhandle. A cheat, panhandler. 60.

skelb (skelb): a splinter; slice. 44.

skelp (skelp): a strip of wrought iron for making a hollow piece or tube. To form into skelp. A splinter, scratch. To strike, drive with blows; to perform in a lively fashion; to beat, as a clock. 49.

sken (sken): squint, stare. 13.

skene (skē′ni): in the ancient Greek theater, the structure behind the orchestra, facing the theatron.

skep (skep): a kind of farm basket, or the quantity it holds; a bowl-shaped ladle; a coal scuttle. 42.

skerry (sker′i): a rocky isle; an insulated rock or reef. 44A. A kind of potato. 45. A punt seating two. 1.

skete (skēt): any settlement of Eastern Orthodox monks, called *sketiotai,* who form a loosely knit religious community, living outside their monastery in cottages.

skillagalee (skil′a.ga.li): a worthless coin; a thin broth or porridge. 13C.

skilly (skil′i): skilfull; skilled. 43. Skillagalee.

skilpot (skil′pot): the red-bellied terrapin.

skimmington (skim′ing.tun): one publicly impersonating and ridiculing a henpecked or disgraced husband or his shrewish or unfaithful wife. A boisterous procession intended to ridicule such a husband or wife. 13.

skinker (sking′ker): one who serves liquor; a tapster. 9. A drinking vessel. 1.

skite (skīt): a sudden glancing blow; a trick, a prank; an offensive person; to move hurriedly. 11. To strike an object with a glancing blow; ricochet, skip. 44. Boast, brag. 53.

skittler (skit′ler): one who plays skittles.

skivered (skiv′erd): skewered; impaled. 44A.

skivie (skiv′i): silly 44.

sklent (sklent): to slant, cast aspersions, fib, balance sidewise; a slant, untruth, side glance. 43.

slade (slād): a hillside; a cave; a flat piece of bogland. 11A. A sledge. 11. To slide; glide. 13. The sole of a plow.

slaister (slās′ter): to smear; bedaub; to do dirty or sloppy work; to do anything clumsily or untidily or carelessly; to idle. 43A. A mess. 43. To beat; flog. 13.

slampamp (slam′pamp): a medley; rigamarole; trick. 1.

sleech (slēch): silt, slime, or ooze from rivers or the sea, esp. as used for manure. 11A.

sleechy (slēch′i): oozy, slimy. 11A.

slipe (slīp): a thin, narrow strip, esp. of land. Wool removed from skins by using lime. A sleigh, a sled. 13. To peel, pare, strip. 44D. To glide or slip away. 44C.

slish (slish): in Shakespeare, a cut, slash. To slish.

slobber-chops (slob′er.chops): a slobberer.

sloka (slō′ka): a distich having two lines of 16 syllables each or four octosyllabic hemstichs—the chief verse form of the Sanskrit epics.

sloke (slōk): any of var. edible marine algae, as sea lettuce and Irish moss. 50. Slime or scum in water. To sneak away. 11.

sloom, sloam (slōōm, slōm): to slumber, doze; become weak and flaccid; decay; swoon; move slowly and silently; drift. 2.

slougher, sluffer (sluf′er): in medicine, that which becomes encrusted with a slough. A sloughing agent.

slote, sloat (slōt): a former device for moving persons or scenery above or below a theater stage.

slowcome (slō′kum): a lazy person. 21.

sloyd (sloid): skilled mechanical work, as in carving; specif., a system of manual training based on one in Sweden.

slub (slub): a mess, a mire. 11A. To muddy, mire. 11. A slubbed roll of cotton, wool, or silk.

slubber (slub′er): to darken, obscure, skim cursorily; mire, slime. 11A.

slubby (slub′i): muddy. 11A.

sluit (slōōt): in South Africa, a ditch or gully, usu. dry, produced when heavy rains form a crack in sun-baked soil.

smabbled (smab′ld): killed in action. 21.

smatch (smach): to smack. 1.

smatchet (smach′et): a small, contemptible fellow; also, an unmannerly child. 44.

smearcase (smēr′kās): cottage cheese. 32.

smee (smē): a pintail duck. 32. A smew. 41. A widgeon; pochard.

smeeth (smēth): mist, haze; to screen with mist. 13.

smeu, smeuth (smū, smūth): the willow warbler. 44.

smew (smū): a merganser of northern Europe and Asia, smallest of the mergansers and one of the most expert divers of all ducks. A widgeon, pollard, pintail duck.

smich (smich): the stonechat. 31.

smicker (smik′er): to smile amorously; smirk. 5.

smilet (smīl′et): a little smile.

smolt (smōlt): smooth; calm; clear; bright. 4A.

smoot (smōōt): a narrow passageway; to move stealthily. 42A.

smouse (smouz): to eat with gusto; to feast. In South Africa, an itinerant peddler.

smout (smōōt): to work at odd jobs in a printing establishment. One who smouts. Also, var. of *smolt*.

smur, smurr (smur): a mist or cloud. Drizzle, mist. 11.

snarleyyow (snär′li.you): a dog. 21.

snash (snash): insolence; gibing. 44A. To talk insolently. 44.

snast, snaste (snast, snāst): a candlewick. 2.

snath (snath): the handle of a scythe.

snathe (snāth): var. of *snath*. To lop; prune. 5A.

snead (snēd): a scythe handle or shaft; a snath. 11.

sneap (snēp): to chide, chasten; spy; sneak. 11. To blast or blight with cold; nip. 9.

sneath (snēth): dial. var. of *snath*.

sneesh (snēsh): snuff; a pinch of snuff. To take snuff. 49.

sneest (snēst): taunt; sneer.

sneg (sneg): cut. 44.

snig (snig): a small eel. 13. To chop off; jerk; to drag on a rope or chain, as a log. 11. To sneak; pilfer. 21.

snipsnapsnorum (snip′snap′snō′rum): a card game with this name.

snoach (snōch): to snuffle. 11.

snod (snod): trim, smooth, neat; to make so. 43A.

snoga (snō′ga): a Sephardic synagogue.

snollygaster, snollygoster (snol′i.gas′ter, -gos′ter): per Sen. Charles Mathias, a monster that sought to prevent Maryland blacks from voting after the Civil War. Used by President Truman for a politician with no principles.

snooger (snōō′ger): in marbles, a close miss.

snum (snum): vow; declare; "vum." 12.

snurge (snurj): to avoid an unpopular job. 23.

sny (snī): the upward curve of a plank, esp. toward the bow or stern of a ship; to bend upward. To cut. 1.

S STANDS FOR SCOBBY, SEESEE, SHITEPOKE, SQUACCO . . .

Of certain birds that start with *s* I'll sing a pretty song,

And you are welcome, if you wish, to sit and sing along.

The first is shorter than a span, but longer than a half-inch;

The British call it *scobby,* but it's better known as chaffinch.

The second lives in Inja. If you take a gun and cartridges,

Perhaps you'll bag some *seesees,* which your friends will swear are partridges.

The *shitepoke* is a heron that's embarrassed as the deuce

Because its name includes a word that's not in decent use.

Another heron spreads its wings from Shanghai to Monaco,

And since it's always squacking, the Italians named it *squacco.*

Brazilians have a heron too, of curvature rococo,

That bites if called a bittern, but will bow if called a *soco.*

In Asia there's a crested jay that, moulting, changes color;

When green it is a *sirgang,* and when blue a Chinese roller.

Our widgeon, pollard, pintail duck, exposed to English view,

Will drop those silly Yankee names, and call itself a *smew,*

Or else a *smee.* (The Scots have got a warbler known as *smeu.*)

Another *smew's* a diving bird—a jolly good one, too.)

I overheard a Brit and Scot who thought they were alone chat

About a *smich,* and that was rich—I knew they meant a *stonechat.*

The saddest of the *s*'es is the bird that ends this ditty,

The *squonk.* It's always full of warts, and weeping from self-pity.

---

snye (snī): a natural channel that bypasses rapids or a waterfall.

soboliferous (sō′bo.lif′er.us): producing shoots or suckers.

socage (sok′ij): a form of land tenure in medieval England, obtained by service, such as military service.

soce (sōs, sos): comrades, friends—used as a form of address. 9.

soceraphobia (so′ser.a.fō′bi.a): fear of parents-in-law.

Socinianism (sō.sin′i.an.izm): a 16th-century doctrine of Faustus Socinus, who denied the Trinity, the divinity of Christ, and the personality of the Devil.

sociophobia (sō′si.o.fō′bi.a): fear of friendship or society.

socle (sok′l, sō′kl): in architecture, a molded projection at the foot of a wall or beneath the base of a column or pedestal. In cooking, a rice or bread base that allows elaborate garnishing of a dish.

soco (sō′kō): any of several Brazilian herons, esp. certain night herons and bitterns.

sodaic (so.dā′ik): pert. to or containing soda.

sodder (sod′er): dial. var. of solder.

sog (sog): boggy ground; to soak, saturate. 11A. To drowse. 11.

solano (so.lä′nō): a hot, oppressive east wind of the Mediterranean, esp. on the eastern coast of Spain; also, such a wind bringing rain.

Solanum (so.lä′num): a large genus of herbs, shrubs, or trees, incl. the potato, the eggplant, the Jerusalem cherry, and the horse nettle.

soldatesque (sôl′da.tesk): soldierlike; marauding.

Solen (sō′len): a genus of razor clams. (not cap) A clam of that genus.

solenium (so.lē′ni.um): in zoology, a *stolon*.

soli (sō′li): having only one performer in each part—a direction in choral and orchestral music.

Solidago (sō′li.dā′go): a large genus of chiefly North American herbs, the goldenrods.

solidum (sol′i.dum): the dado of a pedestal. A whole; an entire sum.

solidus (sol′i.dus): the oblique stroke (/) sometimes used in fractions (5/8), in expressing sums of money £4/12/6), and in and/or (either *and* or *or*). A gold coin of Roman antiquity. A medieval money of account.

soliped (sō′li.ped): having a single hoof on each foot, as a horse.

sollar, soller (sol′er): in mining, a platform in a shaft, esp. between a series of ladders. To install such a platform.

somnifugous (som.nif′ū.gus): driving out sleep.

somniloquacious (som′ni.lo.kwā′shus): given to talking in one's sleep. 52.

somnipathy (som′nip′a.thi): hypnotic sleep.

somnolism (som′no.lizm): hypnotic drowsiness.

sonorescent (son′o.res′ent): capable of emitting sound when acted upon by light.

soodle (soo′dl): to saunter; stroll. 13.

sook (sook, sook): Scot. & dial. var. of *suck*. A call for cattle and hogs. In the Muslim East, a booth or market.

sookie (soo′ki): a call to cattle. 11.

sooterkin (soo′ter.kin): a kind of false birth, which Dutch women are fabled to produce by sitting over their stoves; fig., an abortion, an abortive scheme.

sophister (sof′is.ter): a sophist. In Oxford and Cambridge, a student in his second or third year.

sophistic (so.fis′tik): sophistical. The art, method, or doctrine of a sophist or Sophist. Sometimes, sophistry.

sophomania (sof′o.mā′ni.a): a delusion of being exceptionally intelligent.

sophophobia (sof′o.fō′bi.a): fear of learning.

Sordello (sôr.del′ō): the title and chief figure of a philosophical and narrative poem by Browning.

sordor (sôr′der): refuse, dregs; also, sordidness.

sorema (so.rē′ma): in flowers, a mass of imbricated carpels forming a compound pistil, as in the magnolia.

sorner (sôr′ner): a sponger. 44A.

sorra (sor′a): A blessing; bad cess; sorrow. 47.

sortance (sôr′tans): agreement. 1.

sortita (sôr′tē′ta): an issuing forth; a coming or going out. In opera, an entrance aria. A postlude.

sorus (sō′rus): in ferns, one of the clusters of sporangia forming so-called fruit dots on the fertile fronds. In parasitic fungi, any mass of spores bursting through the epidermis of a host plant. In lichens, a heap of brood buds on the thallus.

sosh (sosh): drunk; intoxicated. A jag; as, to have a *sosh* on. A small quantity; a dash. 11.

soss (sos): a call to food addressed to dogs or swine. 11. Slop, swill; also, to lap. 44C. Heavily; also, to plunge, thump. 17B.

sotadic (so.tad′ik): a scurrilous, often lewd, satire, usu. in verse, named for the Greek poet Sotades. Also, palindromic verse.

sottise (so.tēz): stupidity.

soum, sum (soom, sum): the area of pastureland that will support a fixed number of stock; the number of cattle that can be pastured in a given area. 47B.

sous-entendu (soo′zän′tän.dü): something hinted at but not openly expressed.

souter, soutar (soo′ter): shoemaker, cobbler. 43.

souterrain (soo′te.rän): an underground passage or chamber.

spadassin (spad′a.sin): a swordsman; duelist; bravo.

spadille (spa.dil′): the ace of spades.

spadonism (spā′do.nizm): eunuchry. 52.

spadroon (spa.droon′): a sword lighter than the broadsword. 9. Cut-and-thrust swordplay.

spale (spāl): a splinter or chip of wood. 13.

spalpeen (spal.pēn′, spal′pin): a scamp; a rascal (often used playfully); a boy, a mere lad. 51.

spalt (spalt, spält): to split off; chip. Liable to split; brittle. 11.

spaneria (spa.nēr′i.a): a scarcity of men.

spanogyny (spa.noj′i.ni): a scarcity of women.

spasmatomancy (spaz′ma.to.man′si): divination by watching the twitching of a body.

spatchcock (spach′kok): a fowl split and grilled immediately after being killed. So to prepare a fowl.

spatiate (spā′shi.āt): to stroll, ramble.

spatilomancy (spat′i.lo.man′si): divination by observation of the droppings of animals.

spatrify (spat′ri.fī): to besmirch; sully.

spatulamancy (spat′ū.la.man′si): divination by examining the shoulder blade of a sheep.

spawl (spôl): spittle; to spit. 9. Var. of *spall*, a chip or flake from a piece of stone or ore.

speckioneer (spek′i.o.nēr): in whaling, the inspectioneer, or chief harpooner.

spectroheliokinematograph (spek′tro.-hē′li.o.kin.e.mat′o.graf): a camera for taking motion pictures of the sun.

spectrophobia (spek′tro.fō′bi.a): fear of looking in a mirror.

speel (spēl): to climb, mount; the act of climbing or mounting. 44.

sperling (spur′ling): a smelt; a sparling. 13. A young herring. 28.

spermology (sper.mol′o.ji): the branch of botany dealing with seeds.

sphacelate (sfas′e.lāt): to become gangrenous.

sphagnicolous (sfag.nik′o.lus): growing in peat moss.

sphenography (sfi.nog′ra.fi): the art of writing in or deciphering cuneiform characters.

spial (spī′al): espial; watch. 1. A spy, a scout. 9.

spiegelschrift (spē′gel.shrift): mirror-writing.

spiff (spif): spiffy; to spruce (up). 21. Push money, paid to a salesman to push certain goods. 23.

spiflicated (spif′li.kā′ted): intoxicated. 11.

spiflication (spif′li.kā′shun): the act of astonishing, bewildering, confounding. 58.

spig (spig): short for *spigotty*.

spigotty (spig.o.ti): a Spanish American, esp. a Mexican—usu. taken to be offensive. 21.

spik (spik): *spigotty*. 21.

spiloma (spi.lō′ma): a birthmark.

spindrift (spin′drift): sea spray.

spink (spingk): the chaffinch. 31. The common primrose; cuckoo flower; maiden pink. 44C.

spintry (spin′tri): a male whore.

spinulescent (spin′ū.les′ent): in botany, having small spines; somewhat spiny.

spirated (spī′rāt.ed): corkscrew-shaped.

spissitude (spis′i.tūd): density; viscosity.

spitchcock (spich′kok): var. of *spatchcock*. Also, to treat summarily; to handle roughly.

splanchnology (splangk.nol′o.ji): study of the viscera.

splenial (splē′ni.al): pert. to the splenium or the splenius muscle. Also, pert. to a thin splint-like bone of the mandible of many submammalian vertebrates.

splodge (sploj): var. of *splotch*.

splore (splōr): a carouse, merrymaking; to carouse; to brag. 44.

spodogenous (spo.doj′i.nus): pert. to or due to waste matter.

spodomancy (spō′do.man′si): divination by ashes.

spoffish (spof′ish): fussbudgety. 21.

spoffokins (spof.o.kinz): a prostitute pretending to be a wife.

spongology (spon.gol′o.ji): the study of sponges.

sponsal (spon′sal): spousal.

sponsalia (spon.sā′li.a): a formal betrothal.

spoom (spo͞om): of a boat, to run before the sea or wind; to scud. 1.

sporabola (spo.rab′o.la): the trajectory of a falling spore.

sporange (spo.ranj′): a plant's sporecase, within which asexual spores are produced.

Sporozoa (spō′ro.zō′a): a large class of parasitic protozoans with a life cycle usu. involving alternation of sexual and asexual generation, incl. many causing diseases such as malaria.

spoucher (spo͞och′er): a utensil for bailing water; a bailer. 44A.

spousal (spous′al): marriage, nuptials. 1. Relating to or celebrating marriage.

spousebreach (spous′brēch): adultery. 1.

spraints (sprānts): otter dung. 41.

sprangle (sprang′gl): to struggle. 7A. To sprawl; spread out; straggle; a strangling mass, as a *sprangle* of mistletoe. 11. To cause to sprangle or straggle. 11A.

sprent (sprent): to run, leap; spring, sprint, catch; a hasp; a prune. 43A.

sprew (spro͞o): a South African starling of glossy plummage. In medicine, thrush; sprue.

springal (spring′al): a medieval engine for hurling missiles. 6.

sprunt (sprunt): a spasmodic movement; a spring, leap; active, brisk, spruce. 1.

spumescent (spū.mes′ent): like foam; foaming.

spurcidical (sper.sid′i.kal): foulmouthed.

spurgall (spur′gôl): a gall or wound from a spur.

spurtle (spur′tl): a spurt; a trickle; to flow in jets, trickle. A stick for stirring porridge and the like; a sword. 44A.

sputation (spū.tā′shun): spitting.

squabash (skwa.bash′): to crush, esp. by criticism; a crushing blow. 26B.

squabbish (skwä′bish): thick, fat, heavy.

squacco (skwak′ō): a small crested heron that breeds in parts of Asia, Africa, and southern Europe.

squaddy (skwäd′i): squat; fat and heavy. 11A.

squail (skwāl): a counter that is snapped at a mark in the center of a board in the game of squails.

squaliform (skwäl′i.fôrm): sharkshaped.

squaloid (skwä′loid): sharklike.

squarson (skwär′sun): formerly, a landed proprietor who was also a clergyman of the Church of England—used in ridicule. *(Squire + parson.)*

squelette (ske.let′): a thin wood veneer used in making match boxes; a skillet.

squench (skwench): to quench. 11.

squidge (skwij): a squelching sound.

squidgereen (skwij′e.rēn): a short, insignificant person. 21.

squinny (skwin′i): squint; peep. 4. Squinting, peering. Slender; thin; long and narrow. To weep or fret.

squireen (skwīr.ēn′): a petty squire; a gentleman in a small way.

squonk (skwongk): an imaginary, wartcovered bird that weeps in self-pity.

sraddha (srad′da, shrad′da): in Hinduism, a rite or ceremony in which balls of rice are offered to ancestors, as after a birth.

sri (shrē): in India, fortunate, glorious, holy, as a king or divinity.

stablestand (stā′bl.stand): in old English law, the fixed position of one about to shoot his bow or slip his dogs in deer hunting.

stactometer (stak.tom′e.ter): a pipette of small bore for counting drops.

staddle (stad′l): a small tree or sapling, esp. a forest tree. The lower part of a stack, as of hay; the supporting framework or base of a stack; to form into staddles. A support, staff, crutch. 1. A stain. 13.

stadial (stā′di.al): pert. to a stadium or a stadia.

stagflation (stag.flā′shun): persistent inflation combined with stagnant consumer demand and relatively high unemployment.

staggard, staggart (stag′erd, -ert): the male red deer in its fourth year.

stagiary (stā′ji.er.i): a resident canon; a law student.

stagnicolous (stag.nik′o.lus): inhabiting stagnant water.

staith (stāth): a landing stage or wharf for transshipment. 42.

stamin (stam′in): a coarse woolen cloth usu. dyed red and used for undergarments. An undergarment for penitents made of harsh stamin.

standage (stan′dij): privilege of or room for standing, as of cattle, or a fee paid for it.

stanniferous (sta.nif′er.us): containing tin.

starken (stär′ken): to make stiff or inflexible.

stasibasiphobia (stas.i.bas.i.fō′bi.a): fear of standing or walking.

stasiphobia (stas′i.fō′bi.a): fear of standing upright.

stasivalence (stas′i.vā′lens): inability to have sexual intercourse except when standing.

statal (stā′tal): pert. to a state.

stathmograph (stath′mo.graf): an instrument for measuring the speed of trains or projectiles.

staurolatry (stô.rol′a.tri): worship of a cross or crucifix.

staurophobia (stô′ro.fō′bi.a): dread of a crucifix.

staxis (stak′sis): in medicine, a dripping; specif., hemorrhage.

stean, steen (stēn): a stone. 44C. A vessel of stone. 11A. To line (as a well or cistern) with stone, brick, or the like.

steganographist (steg′a.nog′ra.fist): a cryptographer.

stelar (stē′ler): resembling or pert. to a stele, or pillar.

stellification (stel′i.fi.kā′shun): glorification.

stellionate (stel′yun.āt): in Roman and civil law, any fraud not set apart by a special name.

stemple, stempel (stem′pl): in mining, a crossbar of wood in a shaft serving as a step, or as a support for a platform or roof. A strut, as a spur timber. 41.

stend (stend): a spring, bound, stride, rearing-up; a stick to distend a carcass. To stend. 44A.

stenopaic (sten′o.pā′ik): having a narrow opening—applied specif. to certain optical devices. Also, using such devices.

stenophobia (sten′o.fō′bi.a): a fear of narrow things.

stenosis (ste.nō′sis): a narrowing of bodily tubes, cavities, or orifices.

stent (stent): extent; bound; to extend, stretch; outstretched, tight. 44A. A compound for holding a surgical graft in place. Dial. var. of stint; also, past and past participle of *stend*.

stentorophonous (sten′to.rof′o.nus): very loud-voiced.

stephane (stef′a.ni): a headband, narrowing toward the temples, in statues of the divinities.

stercoricolous (stur′ko.rik′o.lus): living in dung.

stereognosis (ster′i.og.nō′sis): the art of learning the weight of a solid by handling it.

sterquilian (ster.kil′yun): pert. to a dunghill; filthy.

sthenia (sthi.nī′a, sthē′ni.a): strength, vigor.

sthenic (sthen′ik): in medicine, strong, active, as a *sthenic* fever. In psychology, indicative of strength and vigor; as the *sthenic* emotions.

sthenobulia (sthen′o.bū′li.a): strength of willpower.

stibbler (stib′ler): a horse grazing on stubble. A gleaner. A probationer. 44.

stibium (stib′i.um): antimony.

siccado (sti.kä′dō): a kind of xylophone.

stichomancy (stik′o.man′si): divination based on passages from books.

stigonomancy (stig′o.no.man′si): divination by writing on tree bark.

stillatitious (stil′a.tish′us): falling in drops; drawn by a still. 52.

stillicidious (stil′i.sid′i.us): constantly dripping.

stillion (stil′yun): a cradle for vats in a brewery.

stimulose (stim′ū.lōs): having stinging hairs.

stingo (sting′gō): sharp or strong liquor, esp. ale or beer; stinging quality; zest; zip. 21.

Stipa (stī′pa): a widely distributed genus of grasses incl. feather grass, bunch grass, silky grass, porcupine grass, etc.

stirious (stir′i.us): icicle-like.

stirpiculture (stur′pi.kul.cher): the breeding of special stocks; animal eugenics.

stive (stīv): dust; smoke; the floating dust in flour mills caused by grinding. 13. A stew. 52. To keep close and warm; stifle. 2.

stob (stob): a stake or post; a gibbet; to pierce, stab. 11.

stocah (sthō′ka): an idle fellow; a menial attendant. 51.

stoccado (sto.kä.dō): a stab; a thrust with a rapier or in fencing. 9.

stochiology (stok′i.ol′o.ji): the art of conjecture or guesswork.

stodge (stoj): to stuff full, as with food. To mix or stir up together. To tramp clumsily. A thick, filling food (as oatmeal or stew). A dull, stupid person, idea, or literary work.

stodger (stoj′er): a large, heavy person or thing. 11. An old fogy. 26.

stola (stō′la): a long robe worn by women of ancient Rome.

stolo (stō′lō): a runner; a shoot; a branch growing at or near the base of the parent plant; a *stolon*.

stolon (stō′lon): in botany, a *stolo*. In zoology, an extension of the body wall, from which buds of new zooids develop.

stook (stook): a shock of corn. 37A. A shock of small grains, beans, etc. 41B. A pillar of coal standing as a support in a coal mine. 41. A handkerchief. 23.

stooker (stoo′ker): one who works at arranging (as grain or hay) in shocks. 40A.

stoop-gallant (stoop′gal′ant): humbling; that which humbles. 1.

storge (stor′je): parental affection; the instinctive affection that animals have for their young.

storify (stō′ri.fī): to narrate or describe in story. To arrange in stories, as beehives.

storiology (stō′ri.ol′o.ji): the study of folklore.

stot (stot): a young horse. 1. A young bull or ox, esp. one that is three years old; a castrated bull. 5A. To bounce, rebound, jump; stammer; stagger; lurch. Also, a leap in dancing. 43. Swing, rhythm. 44.

stote (stōt): var. of *stoat*.

stoundmeal (stound′mēl′): gradually; from time to time; now and then. 1.

stramineous (stra.min′i.us): like straw; valueless.

stratephrenia (strat′i.frē′ni.a): neurosis associated with military service.

strathspey (strath′spā): a Scottish dance, lively but slower than a reel; its music.

stratonic (stra.ton′ik): pert. to an army. 52. (cap) Pert. to the 3rd century B.C. Greek Strato or his naturalistic philosophy.

stremma (strem′a): in Greece, two measures of land quantity, each less than an acre.

strephographia (stref′o.graf′i.a): mirror-writing; *spiegelschrift*.

strephonade (stref′on.ād): a love song.

strephosymbolia (stref′o.sim.bō′li.a): a perceptual disorder in which objects appear reversed.

strepitant (strep′i.tant): noisy; clamorous.

strepitoso (strep′i.tō′sō): noisy, impetuous—a direction in music.

strepor (strep′ôr): strident or clanging sound; noise.

stria (strī′a): a faint or minute groove or channel; a minute band, as of color.

striga (strī′ga): a striation. In architecture, a flute in a column. In botany, a pointed, rigid, hairlike scale or bristle.

(cap) A genus of seed plants living as root parasites.

striggle (strig′l): a trail—"the hurt mouse left a *striggle* of blood."

Strine (strīn): an Australian way of slurring words, as "air fridge" for "average" and "fraffly" for "frightfully."

strinkle (string′kl): to sprinkle. 5A.

striola, striolet (strī.ō′la, strī′o.let): *stria*.

strobic (strō′bik): spinning, as a top.

strockle (strok′l): a shovel with a turned-up edge used by glassworkers.

stroil (stroil): couchgrass, or certain other weeds with creeping rootstock.

stromatology (strō′ma.tol′o.ji): the study of stratified rock formation.

stromb (strom, stromb): a mollusk or shell of the genus Strombus, as the king conch.

stromboid (strom′boid): pert. to the genus Strombus.

strow (strō, stroo): disturbance; turmoil. 44D. To strew. 9.

stroy (stroi): destroy. 1.

strubbly (strub′li): untidy; unkempt. 12.

strue (stroo): to construe.

studdle (stud′l): to stir up so as to muddy. 13. A prop in or about a loom. 1. A prop or stud used in timbering a mine shaft.

studia (stū′di.a): schools. (pl. of *studium*.)

studium (stū′di.um): an institute where people from all parts of the world come to study any subject, as a medieval university.

stufa (stoo′fa): a jet of steam issuing from a fissure in the earth.

stulm (stulm): an approximately horizontal passageway in a mine; an adit, *aditus*.

stultiloquy (stul.til′o.kwi): foolish talk; babble. 52.

stumpage (stum′pij): uncut timber; its value; the right to cut it.

stupration (stū.prā′shun): violation of chastity; rape. 1.

stupulose (stū′pū.lōs): covered with fine short hairs.

stuss (stus): a gambling game like faro, in which the banker wins on splits.

styan (stī′an, stīn): a stye on the eye. 5A.

stygiophobia (stij′i.o.fō′bi.a): fear of hell.

stylagalmaic (stī′la.gal.mā′ik): resembling caryatids, ancient Greek columns in the shape of women.

Stylaster (stī.las′ter): a genus of delicate, usu. pink, hydroid corals. (not cap) Any coral of this genus.

styryl (stī′ril): the univalent radical found in certain derivatives of styrene, etc.

suability (sū′a.bil′i.ti): capacity to be sued.

suant (sū′ant): smooth; regular; placid; grave; demure. 11.

suasible (swä′si.bl, -zi.bl): capable of being persuaded; easily persuaded.

suaviation (swä′vi.ā′shun, swā-): a love kiss.

suaviloquy (swa.vil′o.kwi): soothing, agreeable speech.

subacid (sub.as′id): slightly tart.

subah (sōō′ba): a province or division of the Mogul Empire, or its government. The ruler of such a province—short for *subahdar*.

subahdar (sōō′ba.där): in India, a viceroy. Also, the chief native officer of a native company in the former British Indian army.

subalary (sub.ā′la.ri): under the wings.

subarrhation (sub′a.rā′shun): betrothal by the bestowal, on the part of the man, of marriage gifts or tokens upon the woman.

subboreal (sub.bō′ri.al): cold, just short of freezing.

subderisorious (sub′di.rī.sō′ri.us): mildly ridiculing.

subdititious (sub′di.tish′us): (something) put secretly in the place of something else.

subdolous (sub′do.lus): somewhat crafty or sly.

subduct (sub.dukt′): subtract, deduct, remove.

subduple (sub′dū.pl): in mathematics, subdouble, in the ratio of 1 to 2.

suber (sū′ber): in botany, cork tissue; also, the outer bark of the cork oak.

subfusc (sub.fusk′): lacking brightness or appeal. Somewhat dusky. Drab, dingy.

subhastation (sub′has.tā′shun): a public sale or auction. 52.

subingression (sub′in.gresh′un): a hidden entrance. 52.

subintelligitur (sub′in.te.lij′i.ter): a meaning implied but not specifically stated. 52.

subrision (sub.rizh′un): the act of smiling. 52.

subsannation (sub′sa.nā′shun): derision. 1.

subsemifusa (sub′sem.i.fū′sa): in medieval music, a thirty-second note.

substaquilate (sub.stak′wi.lāt): to defeat, overwhelm.

substruct (sub.strukt′): to build or lay beneath.

subtegulaneous (sub′teg.ū.lā′ni.us): indoor. 52.

subterfluous (sub.tur′flōō.us): flowing or running under or beneath.

subumbonal (sub′um.bō′nal): situated beneath or forward of the umbones of a bivalve shell.

subverse (sub.vurs′): to subvert. 52.

succedaneous (suk′si.dā′ni.us): pert. to

one who serves as a substitute. Substituted; supplementary.

succentor (suk.sen′ter): one who sings the close or second part of (a verse), as in responsive singing. A precentor's assistant, esp. in some monasteries and cathedrals.

succiduous (suk.sid′ū.us): ready to fall; falling.

succiferous (suk.sif′er.us): feeding on plant juices. 52.

succursal (su.kur′sal): subsidiary; auxiliary, as a *succursal* church, a *succursal* bank.

succus (suk′us): juice; specif., in pharmacy, the expressed juice of fresh drugs for medicinal use.

succuss (su.kus′): to shake violently. In medicine, to perform succussion upon (a patient).

sudarium (sū.dâr′i.um): a sweat cloth or handkerchief, specif. the one with which St. Veronica wiped the brow of the dying Christ. 1.

sudder (sud′er): in India, chief—applied to several government departments and chiefs. The headquarters of the provincial or rural districts. (cap) The Indian Supreme Court.

sudor (sū′dôr): sweat; perspiration; exudation.

Suevi (swē′vi): the Suevians, or Swabians, inhabitants of part of Bavaria, Germany. Also, the Germanic horde from east of the Rhine that overran France and Spain early in the 5th century.

suffrago (su.frā′gō): the tarsal joint—sometimes called the knee—of a bird.

suggilate (sug′ji.lāt): to beat black and blue; to defame.

suilline (sū′i.līn): piglike.

suji (sōō′ji): in India, wheat granulated but not pulverized.

sull (sul): a plow; to plow. 2. To sulk. 35.

sulla (sul′a): a European herb valued for forage, and cultivated for its pink flowers under the name French honeysuckle.

sumbooruk (sum′boor.uk): a small swivel-cannon carried on the back of a camel.

summage (sum.ij): a former toll on goods carried on horseback.

sumpitan (sum′pi.tan): in Borneo, a blowgun for poison darts.

sumpsimus (sump′si.mus): a strictly correct grammatical usage replacing an error.

supellectile (sū′pe.lek′til): pert. to furniture.

superalimentation (sū′per.al′i.men.tā′shun): overfeeding, once prescribed for certain diseases.

superbiate (sū.pur′bi.āt): to make arrogant, haughty.

supercalifragilisticexpialidocious (sū′per.kal.i.fraj.i.lis′tik.eks′pi.al′i.dō′shus): a nonsense term that might be rendered as "highly educable in atoning for great and delicate beauty."

supercrescence (sū′per.kres′ens): a parasitic organism.

superlation (sū′per.lā′shun): glorification, stellification.

supernacular (sū′per.nak′u.lar): first-rate; as, a *supernacular* wine. 52.

superseptuagenarian (sū′per.sep′tu.aj′e.nâr′i.an): one who is over seventy.

superstruct (sū′per.strukt): to build over or on; to erect on a foundation.

supervacaneous (sū′per.va.kā′ni.us): needlessly added; redundant.

supinovalent (sū′pi.no.vā′lent): unable to perform sexual intercourse except when supine.

suppulpation (sup′ul.pā′shun): the act of winning affection by caressing.

supputate, suppute (sup′ū.tāt, -pūt): to reckon, compute. 1.

supracostal (sū′pra.kos′tal): above the ribs.

sural (sū′ral): pert. to the calf of the leg.

surbated (ser.bāt′ed): bruised, made sore—said esp. of overworked feet.

surculation (sur′kū.lā′shun): the act of cutting off suckers; pruning.

surculus (sur′kū.lus): a shoot from the roots or the lower stem of a plant; a sucker.

surdity (sur′di.ti): deafness.

surnap (sur′nap): a cloth with towels spread, for use in washing at formal banquets.

surra, surrah (sōōr′a, sur′a): a severe Old World disease of domestic animals, marked by edema and anemia, transmitted by the bite of certain insects.

surrejoin (sur′ri.join): in law, to reply as a plaintiff to a defendant's rejoinder.

surreption (su.rep′shun): fraudulent means; underhanded methods; a surreptitious getting; a coming unperceived. 1.

suspercollate (sus′per.kol′āt): to hang by the neck. 58.

suspirious (sus.pir′i.us): breathing heavily; sighing.

sussultatory (su.sul′ta.tō.ri): of an earthquake, characterized by up-and-down vibrations of large magnitude.

susu (sōō′sōō): a blind dolphin-like cetacean, about eight feet long, inhabiting the larger rivers of India.

susulike (sōō′sōō.līk): resembling the susu.

susurrous (sū.sur′us): rustling; full of whispering sounds.

sutile (sū′til): done by stitching. 52.

sutteeism (su.tē′izm): suttee. (See *sati*.)

sutter (sut′er): var. of *souter*.

suttle (sut'l): to act as a sutler. 10. In commerce, light—designating the weight of packed goods when the weight of the container has been deducted.

swallet (swol'it): an underground stream; also, an opening through which a stream disappears underground.

swan-upping (swän-up-ing): nicking of the beaks of the swans on the Thames to show ownership by the Crown or certain corporations.

swape (swāp): a pole or bar used as a lever or swivel. A long steering oar used by keelmen on the Tyne.

swaraj (swa.räj'): in India, political independence; national self-government.

swarth (swôrth): skin; rind; sward; turf; a crop of grass or hay. 11. To produce greensward. 11A. Apparition; wraith. 13. Swarthy; swarthiness.

swartrutter (swôrt'rut'er): a trooper of one of the bands in blackface and black garb that harassed the Netherlands in the 16th and 17th centuries.

sweal (swēl): to burn; singe; scorch. 11.

swelp (swelp): corruption of "*so help me* God."

sweven (swev'en): sleep; a vision seen in sleep; a dream. 9.

swillbowl (swil'bōl): a drunkard.

swingle (swing'gl): a wooden instrument like a large knife, about two feet long, used for beating and cleaning flax. A scutcher; the *swiple* of a flail; a flail-like cudgel; a spoke-like lever used for turning the barrel in wire drawing, etc.; to clean with a swingle. Swing, to swing. 11A.

swink (swingk): labor, drudgery; to labor, toil, slave. 10.

swiple, swipple (swip'l): the part of a flail that strikes the grain in threshing; a *swingle.*

swipper (swip'er): nimble; quick. 2.

swither (swith'er): to doubt, waver, hesitate. Hesitation; quandary; agitation. 44A. A faint. 13. A rush. To whiz; to rush; also, to fall down. 17A. To scorch. 44D.

swow (swou): to swoon, faint. 1. To swear, as "I swow." 28B. Sough. 11.

syagush (syä.gōōsh'): the caracal, a lynx of Africa and southern Asia.

sybotic (sī.bot'ik): pert. to a swineherd or his employment.

syce (sīs): in India, a groom or attendant.

sycomancy (sik'o.man'si): divination by figs.

sylloge (sil'o.ji): a collection; a compendium.

sylvestrian (sil.ves'tri.an): sylvan. 52.

symbolaeography (sim'bo.li.og'ra.fi): the art of drawing up legal documents.

symbolography (sim'bo.log'ra.fi): symbolic writing or designs.

symbolum (sim'bo.lum): a symbol; a creed. The Apostles' Creed.

symphoric (sim.fôr'ik): accident-prone.

synactic (si.nak'tik): acting together; cumulative in effect.

synallagmatic (sin'a.lag.mat'ik): imposing reciprocal obligations in civil law; bilateral.

synanthous (si.nan'thus): bearing flowers and leaves that appear at the same time.

synartetic (sin'är.tet'ik): in Greek prosody, metrically continuous.

synaxis (si.nak'sis): an assembly met for worship, esp. in the early church. A congregation gathered for a liturgical service. An early part of the divine liturgy of the Eastern Church.

syncretical (sin.kret'i.kal): pert. to the reconciliation of conflicting beliefs, esp. religious beliefs; also, to egregious compromise. Pert. to any grammatical case that has absorbed the function of others, as the Greek genitive or the Latin ablative.

synderesis, synteresis (sin'der.ē'sis, -ter-): inborn knowledge of the primary principles of moral action.

syndesmology (sin'des.mol'o.ji): the anatomy of ligaments.

syne (sīn): next; then; later; since. 44A.

synectic (si.nek'tik): joining; connecting; (of a cause) immediate. 52. In mathematics, *holomorphic.*

syngenesophobia (sin'ji.nes'o.fō'bi.a): fear of relatives.

synodite (sin'o.dīt): a friend or companion.

synonymicon (sin'o.nim'i.kon): a dictionary of synonyms.

synomosy (si.nom'o.si): a political association.

synovia (si.nō'vi.a): in anatomy, a transparent, viscal lubricating fluid secreted by membranes of bursae, articulations, and tendon sheaths.

synsacrum (sin.sā'krum): in birds, dinosaurs, and pterosaurs, a solidly fused series of vertebrae in the pelvic region.

syntality (sin.tal'i.ti): the inferred behavioral tendencies of a group, acting as a group, which correspond to personality in an individual.

syntectic (sin.tek'tik): wasting; melting away.

synthermal (sin.thur'mal): having the same degree of heat.

syntomy (sin'to.mi): brevity.

syntropic (sin.trop'ik): repeated symmetrically without being reversed, as the ribs of one side.

syrma (sur'ma): in the classical theater, a trailing robe, worn esp. by tragic actors. (cap) A star in the constellation Virginis.

syrt (surt): a quicksand; bog. 52.

syssitia (si.sish'i.a): the practice among the Spartans and Cretans of eating the one chief meal of the day at a public mess to promote discipline and good habits.

T

tabardillo (tab'är.dēl'yō): a form of typhus fever occurring esp. in Mexico.

tabasheer, tabashir (tab'a.shēr): a siliceous mass in the joints of the bamboo, valued in the East Indies as a medicine—called also *sugar of bamboo.*

tabefy (tab'i.fī): to waste away gradually. 52.

tabella (ta.bel'a): a medicated lozenge or tablet.

tabetic (ta.bet'ik): pert. to, or affected with tabes.

tabi (tä'bi): a cotton sock, usu. white, having a thick sole and a separate part for the big toe, once commonly worn by the Japanese. (also pl.)

tabific (ta.bif'ik): producing tabes; wasting.

tabinet, tabbinet (tab'i.net): a poplin made chiefly in Ireland. A dress of this material.

tableity (tab.lē'i.ti): the abstract concept of which a table is the concrete.

tache (tach): a spot, stain. 1. A fault. 9. A characteristic. 11. To attach. 2. Var. of *teach.* 2. One of the evaporating pans in sugar making.

tacheography (tak'i.og'ra.fi): speedwriting.

tachydidaxy (tak'i.di.dak'si): quick teaching.

tachylalia (tak'i.lāl'ya): rapid speech.

A ROSE BY ANY OTHER NAME

L.P. Beria*
Could not have hysteria,
And Jackie Onassis
Cannot have tarassis—
The words disagree
Genderally.

That's been the idea
Since the tritavia
Of my tritavia;
Been drilled in us
Since the tritavus
Of my tritavus.

Different name—
Symptoms the same.

*Lavrenti Pavlovich Beria ran the OGPU for Stalin.

---

tachyphrasia (tak'i.frā'zhi.a, -zi.a): extremely voluble speech, sometimes resulting from emotional disturbances.

tacket (tak′et): a nail or tack. 1. A hobnail; also, a hobnailed shoe; to strengthen or fasten with tackets. 17A.

tactor (tak′ter): in zoology, a tactile organ; specif., a feeler or antenna or a tactile corpuscle.

tactus (tak′tus): sense of touch; touch.

taenifuge (tē′ni.fūj): a medicine for getting rid of tapeworms.

taffle (taf′l): tangle. 17A.

taha (tä′ha): a South American weaverbird with black and yellow plumage in the male.

tahali (ta.hä′li): to Arabs, an adornment to be worn.

Tai (tī): a family of languages in Southeast Asia, incl. Thai, Lao, and Shan. A group of tribes in Burma and Thailand. (not cap) Any of several brilliant crimson Japanese porgies.

taiaha (tä′i.a.hä): a long light staff or club adorned with red feathers or dog's hair, carried by Maori chiefs as a sign of authority and used as a two-handed striking weapon. 56.

t′ai chi ch′uan (tä′i.chē′choo.än): a Chinese system of physical exercises similar to shadow boxing.

talao (ta.lä′o): in Kipling, a low flat ground; a plain.

tali (tä′li): in India, a gold piece tied about a bride's neck by the groom and worn by her during his lifetime.

taligrade (tal′i.grād): walking on the outer side of the foot, as the great anteater.

tallet (tal′et): a hayloft; attic. 2.

talliate (tal′i.āt): to impose a tax.

talo (tal′ō): a starchy tuber of the Pacific islands; taro.

tambaroora (tam′ba.roo̅′ra): a dice game in which equal amounts are subscribed to a pool, the winner paying for drinks for all the others. 53.

tamis (tam′is): tammy.

tammy (tam′i): a kind of woolen or woolen and cotton cloth, often highly glazed, used for gowns, linings, curtains, etc. A strainer, or sieve, made of this material; a tamis. To strain through a tammy. A tam-o′-shanter.

tampan (tam′pan): a venomous South American tick.

Taniwha (tan′i.hwä): a lizard-like monster of Maori legend. 56.

tankle (tang′kl): a sound louder and less acute than that represented by "tinkle."

tanling (tan′ling): one tanned by the sun. 52.

tannate (tan′āt): a salt or ester of tannin.

tannometer (tan.om′e.ter): a device for determining the strength of a tanning liquor by drawing it through hide.

tao (tou, dou): in China, a road, way; fig., the absolute; truth; right conduct. In the Philippines, a peasant.

tapen (tāp′en): of tape. 52.

taphephobia (taf′i.fō′bi.a): fear of being buried alive, or of cemeteries.

taphephilia (taf′i.fil′i.a): fondness for funerals.

tapinophobia (tap′i.no.fō′bi.a): fear of being contagious.

tarassis (ta.ras′is): the male equivalent of hysteria.

Tarpeia (tär.pē′a): in Roman legend, a maiden who betrayed the citadel to the Sabines for the promise of "what they wore on their arms," meaning their gold bracelets. They threw a shield on her and killed her.

tarsiatura (tär′si.a.tū′ra): a kind of mosaic woodwork.

tascal (tas′kal): formerly, a reward for information about stolen cattle. 44.

tasco (tas′kō): a kind of clay for melting pots.

tash (tash): stain; soil; also, fatigue; disgrace. 44A. An East Indian fabric containing much gold and silver thread.

tasher (tash′er): one who stains, soils, disgraces. 44A.

taskit (tas′kit): fatigued; fagged. 44.

tasimeter (ta.sim′iter): an instrument for measuring minute extensions or movements of solid bodies by the changes of pressure produced.

taslet, tasse, tasset (tas′let, tas, tas′et): in a body of armor, one of a series of overlapping metal plates that form a short skirt.

tassie (tas′i): a small cup. 44A.

tath (tath): the dung of sheep and cattle; the coarse grass growing near manure; to manure by pasturing sheep and cattle. 2.

tauromorphic (tô′ro.môr′fik): shaped in the form of a bull—said of vases found in several early Mediterranean cultures.

tautegory (tô′te.gō′ri, -ger-i): expression of the same thing with different words.

tautoousious (tô′to.us.i.us): exactly the same.

tautophony (tô.tof′o.ni): repetition of sound.

tavell (tav′el): a bobbin on which silk is wound.

Taxodium (tak.sō′di.um): a genus of tall, deciduous trees, incl. the common bald cypress of the southern United States.

tchin (jin): in pre-communist Russia, rank; persons of rank. Var. of chin, a Chinese weight.

tead (tēd): var. of toad. 43.

teagle (tē′gl): dial. var. of tackle.

teap (tēp): a ram. 11.

technicon (tek′ni.kon): a gymnastic device for developing the hands for piano or organ playing.

technophobia (tek′no.fō′bi.a): fear of technology.

teck (tek): a ready-made cravat imitating a four-in-hand. Var. of teak, also of tec, short for detective.

tecnogonia (tek′no.gō′ni.a): childbearing.

tectal (tek′tal): pert. to the dorsal part of the midbrain, the tectum.

tectiform (tek′ti.fôrm): roof-shaped, tent-shaped.

tectorial (tek.tō′ri.al): in anatomy, forming a covering; resembling a roof.

ted (ted): a toad. 44. To put a serrated edge on, as on a scythe. 30. To dung, manure; to spread out.

Tedeschi (te.des′ki): in Italy, Germans.

tedesco (te.des′kō): in music, "the German style."

teenage (tēn′ij): brushwood used for fences and hedges. 13.

teer (tēr): to plaster; daub. To stir up colors. 44.

teetertail (tē′ter.tāl): the spotted sandpiper.

teg (teg): a sheep in its second year, or its fleece (var. of tag). Formerly, a doe in its second year; also, a woman.

tegmental (teg.men′tal): pert. to a tegument; covering.

tegumen (teg′ū.men): in zoology and botany, a tegmen or integument, such as the tough, leathery forewing of certain insects or the inner coat of a seed.

teil (tēl): a European linden, or lime tree.

teknonymy (tek.non′i.mi): the custom in certain savage tribes of naming the parent after the child.

telamnesia (tel′am.nē′zhi.a, -zi.a): loss of memory for long past events.

telarian (te.lâr′i.an): web-spinning. A web-spinning spider.

telegnosis (tel′eg.nō′sis): supposed occult knowledge of distant events.

telenergy (tel.en′er.ji): a display of force or energy without contact—applied to mediumistic phenomena.

teleophobia (tel′i.o.fō′bi.a): fear of definite plans, or of religious ceremony.

Teleosaurus (tel′i.o.sô′rus): a genus of crocodilian reptiles of the Jurassic having a long and slender snout and platycelous vertabrae.

telepheme (tel′i.fēm): a telephone message. 52.

telephote (tel′e.fōt): an apparatus for producing photographic images of distant objects.

telestic (ti.les′tik): mystical.

telestich (ti.les′tik, tel′i.stik): a poem in which the consecutive letters of the lines spell a name; a form of acrostic.

Tellima (te.li′ma): a genus of herbs, incl. the false alumroot.

Telina (te.lī′na): a genus of marine bi-valves, often handsomely covered.

tellural (te.lū′ral): pert. to the earth. 52.

tellurate (tel′ū.rāt): a salt of telluric acid.

telurgy (tel′ur.ji): the hypothetical action of one's thought upon another person by means of some unknown form of energy.

temeration (tem′er.ā′shun): violation, desecration. 1.

tempean (tem.pē′an): beautiful and charming.

temporaneous (tem′po.rā′ni.us): temporary. Temporal. 52.

temse, tems (tems, -z): a sieve. To sift. 11.

temulence (tem′ū.lens): drunkenness.

temulous (tem′ū.lus): intoxicated. 52.

tenaille (te.nāl′): in fortifications, an outwork in the main ditch between two bastions.

tenaillon (te.nāl′yun): a work constructed on each side of a ravelin in a fortification.

tendance (ten′dans): bestowal of attention; ministration; watchful care. Also, service done to gain favor.

tenent (ten′ent): a tenet. 1. In zoology, adapted for clinging. 52. Var. of tenon, tendon.

tenney (ten′i): var. of tenné, an orange or bright brown color in heraldry.

tentable (ten′ta.bl): temptable.

tentacula (ten.tak′ū.la): tentacles (pl. of *tentaculum*).

tenterbelly (ten′ter.bel′i): one whose gluttony distends his belly. 1.

tentiginous (ten.tij′i.nus): sensuous, lascivious. Also, stiff or strained.

tentigo (ten.tī′go): priapism; also, satyriasis.

tenture (ten′cher): wall decoration, esp. paper. 52.

tephramancy (tef′ra.man′si): divination by studying ashes from an altar.

tephrosis (ti.frō′sis): incineration.

tepidarium (tep.i.dâr′i.um): a warm room for a bath.

tepor (tē′per): gentle heat; tepidness.

teratophobia (ter′a.to.fō′bi.a): fear of having a deformed child.

teratoscopy (ter′a.tos′ko.pi): divination by watching monsters.

terdiurnal (ter′dī.ur′nal): thrice daily.

terebinthine (ter′e.bin′thin): turpentine. 1. Pert. to turpentine, or the terebinth tree, which yields it.

Terebra (ter′i.bra): a genus of marine gastropods, incl. the auger shells.

terebration (ter′i.brā′shun): a boring or drilling; a perforation; a pain. 52.

terek (ter′ek): a sandpiper, breeding in the far north of eastern Europe and Asia and migrating to South Africa and Australia.

tergeminal (ter.jem′i.nal): thrice twin; in botany, forking with three pairs of leaflets.

termen (tur′men): the outer margin of a triangularly shaped wing of an insect.

termin (tur′men): an Algerian measure of length, varying approx. from 2 to 4 inches.

Terminalia (tur′mi.nāl′ya): a Roman festival held on Feb. 23 in honor of Terminus, god of landmarks. A genus of tropical trees and shrubs with entire leaves clustered at the end of the branches, as the Malabar almond. (not cap.) The final segments of the insect abdomen modified to form the external genitalia.

termitarium (tur′mi.târ′i.um): a termites' nest.

termon (tur′men): land belonging to a religious house in Ireland; church land, exempt from secular imposition.

terp (turp): a large artificial mound in the Netherlands providing a refuge for a prehistoric people in a seasonally flooded area.

terriginous (te′rij′i.nus): earthborn; produced by the earth.

tersion (tur′shun): the act of cleaning by rubbing. 52.

tertian (tur′shun): occurring every third day.

tertiate (tur′shi.āt): to examine the thickness of the metal of a piece of ordnance in three places. To do or perform for the third time. 1.

tessaraglot (tes′er.a.glot): one who speaks four languages. Speaking in, written in, or versed in four languages.

testamur (tes.tā′mer): in English universities, a certificate of proficiency.

testar (tes′ter): a West Indian clingfish.

testatum (tes.tā′tum): in law, that portion of the purchase deed which contains the statement of the consideration, covenants for title, and the operative words.

teste (tes′ti): in law, the witnessing or concluding clause of a writ or other precept. Also, a statement used to indicate that what immediately follows is the authority for what precedes.

testudinarious (tes.tū′di.nâr′i.us): like a tortoise shell; arched; vaulted.

testudineous (tes′tū.din′i.us): slow, like a tortoise.

tetradrachma (tet′ra.drak′ma): in ancient Greece, a silver coin of the value of four drachmas. A weight equiv. to 265 grams.

tetralemma (tet′ra.lem′a): an argument analogous to a dilemma but presenting four alternatives in the premise.

Tetrao (tet′ra.ō): a genus of grouse now restricted to the capercaillie (cock of the wood) and closely related forms.

tetrapolis (tet.rap′o.lis): a group or confederation of four cities or towns.

tetraskelion (tet′ra.skēl′yun): a figure having four arms or rays, as the swastika.

tetricity (tet.ris′i.ti): austerity; harshness; gloom. 52.

teutophobia (tū′to.fō′bi.a): fear of Germans or things German.

tew (tū): a state of worried agitation; a stew. To fuss, worry; to work hard. 11A. To beat, belabor; pull, haul. 2.

tewel (tū′el): a hole; a bore; a vent; esp. a pipe, funnel, or chimney, as for smoke. 1.

textorial, textrine (teks. tō′ri.al, teks′-trin): pert. to weaving. 52.

thalassochemistry (tha.las′o.kem′is.tri): the chemistry of the sea.

thalassophobia (tha.las′o.fō′bi.a): fear of the sea.

thalassotherapy (tha.las′o.ther′a.pi): treatment of disease by sea baths, sea air, etc.

thalian (tha.lī′an): pert. to comedy; comic.

thalpotic (thal.pot′ik): pert. to the sensation of warmth.

thanatoid (than′a.toid): deathly; resembling death. Deadly, as a poisonous snake.

thanatology (than′a.tol′o.ji): the study of the effects and treatment of approaching death.

thanatomania (than′a.to.mā′ni.a): suicidal mania. Also, death by autosuggestion.

thanatophobia (than′a.to.fō′bi.a): dread of death.

tharm (thärm): an intestine; the belly. Twisted gut; catgut. 2.

thasophobia (thas′o.fō′bi.a): fear of being seated.

theantropism, theantropy (thi.an′tro.-pizm, thi.an′tro.pi): the state of being both god and man. Also, the ascription of human attributes to the Deity.

thelyotokous (thel′i.ot′o.kus): producing only female offspring.

thelymachy (thi.lim′a.ki): war by or among women.

thelyphthoric (thel′if.thôr′ik): corrupting to women.

theocrasy (thi.ok′ra.si): a fusion of the divinities of different religions in the minds of worshipers.

theody (thē′o.di): a hymn praising God.

theogony (thi.og′o.ni): the generations or genealogy of the gods.

theologicophobia (thē′o.loj′iko.fō′bi.a): fear of theology.

theomagical (thē′o.maj′i.kal): pert. to divine wisdom, esp. to miracles claimed to be performed by divine help.

theomancy (thē′o.man′si): divination by the responses of oracles supposed to be divinely inspired.

theomicrist (thi.om′i.krist): one who makes light of God or of divinity.

theopathetic, theopathic (thē′o.pa.thet′ik, -path-ik): pert. to the experience of the divine illumination.

theophagic, theophagous (thē′o.faj′ik, thi.of′a.gus): practicing theophagy—the sacramental eating of a god, often in the form of an animal.

theophanic (thē′o.fan′ik): pert. to a physical manifestation of a god to man, esp. by incarnation in a human body or appearance in a human form.

theophobia (thē′o.fō′bi.a): phobia against God, or gods.

thereanent (ther′a.nent): with reference to a certain matter.

theriacal, theri.al (thi.rī′a.kal, thēr′i.al): medicinal.

therianthropic (thēr′i.an.throp′ik): combining animal and human form, as the centaur.

theriomancy (thēr′i.o.man′si): divination by observing wild animals.

theriomimicry (thēr′i.o.mim′ik.ri): imitation of animal behavior.

thermotic (ther.mot′ik): pert. to or caused by heat.

theroid (thēr′oid): resembling a beast in nature or habit.

therology (thi.rol′o.ji): the study of mammals; mammalogy.

theromorphic (thēr′o.môr′fik): pert. to an order of primitive reptiles, Pelycosaura, resembling mammals and often having a sail-like crest along the spine.

thersitical (ther.sit′i.kal): loudmouthed, scurrilous.

thesmothete (thes′mo.thēt): a lawgiver, legislator.

thestreen (thes′trēn): last night. 44.

thig (thig): to beg, borrow. 44A.

thiller (thil′er): the horse that goes between the thills of a vehicle and supports them; also, the last horse in a team, called thill horse.

thirl (thurl): a hole, as for a window. To perforate, drill. 2. To pierce, as with emotion. To subject to *thirlage*. 62.

thirlage (thur′lij): A requirement that certain tenants carry their grain to a particular mill and pay for the grinding. 62.

thoke (thōk): to lie abed; to idle. 13.

thoral (thō′ral): pert. to a bed; hence, nuptial. 52.

thrack (thrak): to burden; to pack full. 4.

thrail (thrāl): flail. 13.

thrapple (thrap′l): var. of *thropple*.

thrave (thrāv): a bundle; a quantity; a crowd. 11. A measure for unthreshed grain. 41.

thraw (thrô): throe, agony; a twist or wrench; ill-humor, anger; to be in pain. 44, 44A, 44B, 44C.

Thrax (thraks): in ancient Rome, a Thracian; hence, a gladiator armed like a Thracian.

threap, threep (thrēp): to scold; chide; to affirm, urge acceptance of; to wrangle, haggle; to complain, insist; the act of threaping. 44C.

threed (thrēd): var. of thread. 2.

threne (thrēn): lamentation; threnody; dirge. 1.

threpsology (threp.sol′o.ji): the science of nutrition.

threpterophilia (threp′ter.o.fil′i.a): fondness for nurses.

threptic (threp′tik): pert. to the feeding of insect offspring, esp. among social insects, as ants.

thribble (thrib′l): triple; threefold.

thrid (thrid): var. of thread, esp. the verb. 5.

thrimble (thrim′bl): to handle, esp. to test for quality, or with hesitation; to fumble; to squeeze; to wrestle. 43A.

Thrinax (thrī′naks): a genus of North American fan palms incl. the thatch palm. The leaves are used for thatches, fans, etc.

thrion (thrī′on): the fig-leaf garb of Adam and Eve.

thrip (thrip): a threepenny piece. 26A. To snap (one's fingers) softly. To twitch slightly. Var. of thrips.

thropple (throp′l): the throat, windpipe—esp. used of a horse. 11A.

thurl, thurle (thurl): var. of *thirl*. 4.

thwaite (thwāt): forest land cleared and converted to tillage, or used as a meadow (chiefly used in place names of England).

thylacine (thī′la.sīn, -sin): a flesh-eating marsupial of Tasmania, slightly larger than a fox and looking like a dog.

tiarella (tī′a.rel′a): a little tiara. (cap) A small genus of chiefly North American herbs having a slender raceme of delicate white flowers, as the false bitterwort.

ticca (tik′a): in India, for hire, as a *ticca* carriage.

tice (tīs): an enticement. In cricket, a kind of pitched ball. To entice. 2.

tid (tid): the right time or season; mood, humor; ill-temper; to time. 44A. Fond; tender. 13.

tidology (tīd.ol′o.ji): the science of tides.

tift (tift): a puff or gust of wind; a whiff, a sniff; hurry, breathlessness; a state, condition, or mood. 43. To put in order. 2. To pant. 13.

tignum (tig′num): a building material.

tikka (tik′a): in India, a leaf spot of the peanut caused by a fungus.

tikker, ticker (tik′er): a form of interrupter of electric current used in the early days of radio as a detector of continuous waves.

tikolosh (tik′o.losh): a South African water spirit in the form of a little man, friendly to children.

tillot (til′ut): a cloth for wrapping fabric.

tilly (til′i): composed of, or pert. to, till, or clay. Something added for good measure. 51.

timbrology (tim.brol′o.ji): the study of postage stamps.

timon (tī′mon): helm; rudder. 1. (cap) The hero of Shakespeare's *Timon of Athens;* hence, a misanthrope.

timoneer (tī′mon.ēr): a helmsman. 52.

timothy (tim′o.thi): short for timothy grass.

tinamou (tin′a.mōō): a bird of southern Brazil and Argentina similar to the partridge.

tingent (tin′jent): having the power to tinge. 1.

tink (tingk): a tinkle; to tinkle. To tinker. 5.

tintamarre (tin′ta.mär): a confused uproar; din. 9.

tirl (turl): a bout or turn, as at drinking; something that revolves, as a turnstile or wheel; to strip the covering from, divest, unroof; to make a rattling sound with a door latch; to twirl. 44A.

tirocinium (tir′o.sin′i.um): apprenticeship. A band of raw recruits.

tither (tīth′er): one who collects, pays, or advocates the payment of tithes.

tiver (tiv′er): ‵red ocher. 4.

tjaele (chä′li): permafrost.

tmema (tmē′ma): a segment; a section. 52.

tnoyim (tnoi.im): a Jewish engagement party, or a marital agreement made at such a party.

toatoa (tō′a.tō′a): a striking New Zealand evergreen tree with whorled branches, often cultivated for ornament.

tock (tok): an African hornbill.

toco, toko (tō′kō): a flogging, thrashing; sometimes a tongue-lashing. 23. A large South American toucan.

tocophobia (tō′kō.fō′bi.a): fear of pregnancy or childbirth.

toddick (tod′ik): a very small quantity.

toison (twa.zoN′): a sheep's fleece.

toke (tōk): a puff on a cigarette, espec. a marijuana cigarette. 22.

toko (tō′kō): in the Dutch East Indies, a shop or store, usu. one kept by Chinese.

tolpatch (tol′pach): in Carlyle's works, a foot soldier.

toluic (to.lū′ik, tol′ū.ik): pert. to four isomeric acids.

tolutiloquy (tol′ū.til′o.kwi): a voluble speech.

tombolo (tom′bo.lō): a bar or reef of sand or gravel connecting an island to the mainland.

tomium (tō′mi.um): the cutting edge of the bill of a bird.

tomnoddy (tom′nod′i): a simpleton. A kind of puffin. 44A.

tomomania (tō′mo.mā′ni.a): a mania for surgery.

tonant (tō′nant): making a thundering noise.

tondino (ton.dē′no): a metal disk for striking a coin. A small *tondo*.

tondo (ton′dō): a circular painting. A sculpture medallion.

tonga (tong′ga): a light two-wheeled carriage in India, drawn by one horse. A creeper living on the surface of other plants, used in Malaysian folk medicine. Formerly, a pharmaceutical drug containing tonga. (cap) Any of several Bantu-speaking peoples in parts of East Africa.

tonish, tonnish (ton′ish): stylish, chic.

tonitruophobia (to.nit′roo.o.fō′bi.a): fear of thunder.

toom (tōom): empty. 45. Lank; lean; lacking wit; empty-sounding; a dumping ground. 44. To empty, pour. 43. Leisure; spare time. 1.

tootlish (tōot′lish): childish; muttering, as an aged person. 11.

topia (tō′pi.a): a mural of Roman times representing fanciful landscapes.

toph (tōf): tufa; travertine; porous rock. A Hebrew musical instrument resembling a timbrel.

tophaceous (to.fā′shus): gritty, sandy, rough, stony.

topolatry (to.pol′a.tri): worship of a place, or excessive reverence for it. 52.

topomancy (tō′po.man′si): divination by land contours.

topophobia (tō′po.fō′bi.a): a morbid fear of certain places.

topopolitan (tō.po.pol′i.tan): limited to a certain area (as opposed to cosmopolitan).

torcel (tôr′sel): the larva of the South American botfly, living beneath the human skin.

torcular (tôr′kū.lar): a wine press. 1. A surgeon's tourniquet.

toreumatography (to.roo′ma.tog′ra.fi): a description of work wrought in metal by embossing, chasing, etc.

torfaceous (tôr.fā′shus): turflike. 52.

toril (to.rēl′): in bullfighting, a corral from which the bull enters the ring.

torminous (tôr′mi.nus): afflicted with the gripes.

toro (tō′rō): a bull. A cowfish. A food fish of the tropical American coasts, the cavalla. A New Zealand tree with reddish wood used for inlaying.

torotoro (tō′ro.to′rō): a kingfisher of New Guinea, having an orange beak.

torp (tôrp): a croft; a small leased farm. Short for torpedo, torpedoman.

torpescent (tôr.pes′ent): becoming torrid.

torpify (tôr′pi.fī): to make torpid; stupefy.

torpillage (tôr′pi.yäzh): electric shock treatment.

torrefy (tôr′i.fī): to heat; to dry or roast by a fire; scorch.

torrentine (tôr′en.tin, to.ren′tin, -in): torrential. 52.

torse (tôrs): a torso. Twisted spirally.

torta (tôr′ta): a flat heap of moist, crushed silver ore ready for further processing.

tortility (tôr.til′i.ti): the state of being twisted, coiled, or twistable.

tosh (tosh): bosh; sheer nonsense. Tidy; neat. To make tidy. 44.

tossel (tos′el): var. of tassel. 2.

tossut (tos′ut): the tunnel of an igloo.

tosy (tō′zi): slightly intoxicated; also, snug; comforting. 44.

tota (tō′ta): the grivet monkey.

totora (to.tō′ra): a tall South American cattail having shoots edible when new, and reedy stems yielding fiber useful for making fences, boats, etc.

tottle (tot′l): dial. var. of toddle; to walk with short tottering steps, as a child.

touse, towse (touz): a noisy disturbance; ado, fuss; to pull or handle roughly; to dishevel. 11.

towdie (tou′di): a young hen that has not yet laid; a young unmarried girl. 44.

toxicoid (tok′si.koid): like poison.

toxophily (tok.sof′i.li): love of archery.

toze (tōz): to tease, comb; to pull about, esp. in disentangling. 9.

tozee (tōz′i): in the Scottish game of curling, the mark aimed at by players who hurl heavy stones along a smooth stretch of ice.

trabea (trā′bi.a): a type of Roman toga with a border of colored stripes.

tractoration (trak′to.rā′shun): a former process of drawing two small rods of different metals over an affected part of the body to reduce pain or local inflammation.

tradal (trād′al): commercial.

traditive (trad′i.tiv): pert. to tradition; transmitted or transmissible by tradition.

traduction (tra.duk′shun): defamation; slander. Also, the repetition of a word or term with a change in sense for rhetorical effect. Something transmitted; esp., a tradition.

tragacanthin (trag′a.kan′thin): in chemistry, a substance obtained from certain gums that swell to form a gel.

tragicomipastoral (traj′i.kom′i.pas′-tor.al): pert. to or combining tragic, comic, and pastoral poetry. 52.

traik (trāk): to waste away, break down. To stroll, lounge, follow; a plague, pest;

a fatiguing journey; flesh of a sheep that died by accident or disease; a fatiguing tramp or journey. 44A. Fatigue, misfortune. 1.

traiky (trā′ki): exhausted; wasted away. 44A.

traiteur (tre.tur′): a restaurateur.

tralatitious (tra.la.tish′us): metaphorical; figurative; as the primary and *tralatitious* meanings of a word. Also, passed along; handed down from generation to generation; traditional.

tralucent (tra.lū′sent): translucent. 1.

trampot (tram′pot): in milling, the step supporting the lower end of a millstone spindle.

trank (trangk): an oblong piece of skin from which glove shapes are cut.

tranky (trang′ki): a small undecked sailing vessel used in the Persian Gulf.

transfuge (trans′fūj): a deserter; an apostate. 52.

transilience (tran.sil′yens): the quality of passing, as by a leap, from one thing to another, marked by abrupt change or variation.

translucid (trans.lū′sid): translucent.

translunar (trans.loo′ner): in or toward the direction of the moon.

transpontine (trans.pon′tīn, -tin): on the other side of the bridge; specif. in London, south of the Thames. Resembling cheap melodramas once popular there.

THESTREEN

"Pray tell me why women
Are like a persimmon?"
A lad thestreen did pipe.
And I answered thestreen,
"They're astringent when green,
But remarkably sweet when ripe."

---

transshape (trans.shāp′): to transform.

transumption (tran.sump′shun): a transference; a metaphor. 1.

transvase (trans.vās′): to pour out of one vessel into another.

transversus (trans.vur′sus): in anatomy, any of several small transverse muscles.

transvert (trans.vurt′): to change or turn about; transform. 1.

trape (trāp): traipse. 2.

trappoid, trappous (trap′oid, -us): pert. to traprock.

traulism (trô′lizm): a stammering or stuttering.

traumatophobia (trô′mat.o.fō′bi.a): fear of injury.

travale (tra.val′, tra.val′i): a vibrant sound produced by rubbing the head of a tambourine with a wet finger or thumb.

tremellose (trem′e.lōs): gelatinous.

tremolant (trem′o.lant): having a vibrant, tremolo note, as certain organ pipes. Such a pipe.

trenchermate (tren′cher.măt): a mess-mate, eating companion.

trendle (tren′dl): a circular object, as a wheel, hoop, or spindle; a trundle. 52. A large, round, shallow tub, trough, or vessel. 13.

trental (tren′tal): in the Roman Catholic Church, a series of thirty masses for the dead, celebrated one daily, or formerly sometimes all in one day.

trepidity (tre.pid′i.ti): a state of alarm or trembling agitation; trepidation.

tresaiel, tresayle (tres.āl′, tres′īl): a grandfather's grandfather. 6.

tressure (tresh′er): a headdress, as a caul or ribbon; an arrangement of hair; coiffure. 1. A double-orle design within the border of a heraldic bearing. An additional border or ornamental enclosure in numismatology.

tret (tret): at one time, a weight allowance to purchasers for waste or refuse.

trewsman (trōōz′man): a Highlander. 44.

trialogue (trī′a.log): a colloquy between three persons.

tribometer (trī.bom′e.ter): an instrument for measuring sliding friction.

tricerion (trī.sē′ri.on): a three-branched candlestick symbolizing the Trinity.

trichology (tri.kol′o.ji): the science treating of the hair.

trichotillomania (trik.o.til′o.mā′ni.a): insane desire to pull out one's hair.

trigamy (trig′a.mi): bigamy plus one.

trigintal (trī.jin′tal): trental.

trigonal (trig′o.nal): triangular.

trigrammatic, trigrammic (trī′gra.mat.ik, trī.gram′ik): pert. to a three-letter inscription or a three-line figure.

trihemeral (trī.hem′er.al): lasting three days. 52.

trilith, trilithon (trī′lith, tril′i.thon): a monument consisting of two upright megaliths carrying a third as a lintel.

trillet (tril′et): a slight trill.

trillibub (tril′i.bub): tripe; a trifle. 2.

Trillium (tril′i.um): a genus of herbs with short rootstocks and an erect stem, chiefly North American, incl. the wakerobin.

trimenon (trī′me.non): a three-month period.

trinervate (trī.nur′vāt): trineural; three-nerved.

tringle (tring′gl): in architecture, a narrow straight molding, usu. of square section; a fillet. A low guardrail on a gun platform to keep the trucks of the gun carriage from running off.

tringoid (tring′goid): pert. to the sandpipers.

trink (tringk): a kind of fishing net. 1. A trench; channel. 44.

Trinkgeld (tringk′gelt): a gratuity, pourboire, tip.

trioctile (trī.ok′til): the aspect of two planets with regard to the earth when three octants (135°) apart.

triodion, triodium (trī.ō′di.on, -um): in the Eastern church, a liturgical book containing the offices from the fourth Sunday before Lent to Easter eve.

trior (trī′er): a person appointed by law to try challenges of jurors; (var. of trier).

tripennate (trī.pen′āt): having three sets of leaves on each side of a common leafstalk; tripinnate.

triphibious (trī.fib′i.us): at home in the sea, on the land, or in the air.

triphony (trif′o.ni): in medieval music, diaphony for three voice parts.

triplasian (trī.plā′zhun): threefold. 52.

tripody (trip′o.di): in prosody, a unit of three feet.

trippant (trip′ant): of a heraldic lion or other beast, walking with the farther forepaw raised; passant.

tripsis (trip′sis): the act of giving a shampoo or a massage. Also, in medicine, the act of rubbing or grinding to a very fine powder; trituration.

tripterous (trip′ter.us): three-winged, as certain fruits or seeds.

triptote (trip′tōt): a noun having only three cases.

tripudiation (trī.pū′di.ā′shun): dancing, rejoicing. 52.

trisection (trī.sek′shun): the division of a thing into three parts.

trisectrix (trī.sek′triks): in geometry, a curve that trisects an arbitrary angle.

triskaidekaphobia (tris′kī.dek′a.fō′bi.a): morbid fear of the number 13.

trispast, trispaston, trispaston (trī′spast, tri.spas′ton): an ancient machine with three pulleys acting together to raise great weights.

tristiloquy (tris.til′o.kwi): a dull, gloomy speech or way of speaking.

trisulcate (trī.sul′kāt): having three furrows, forks, prongs, or the like.

tritagonist (trī.tag′o.nist): in ancient Greek plays, the third-ranked actor.

tritavia (trit′a.vē′a): a great-grandmother's great-grandmother. 6.

tritavus (trit′a.vus): a great-grandfather's great-grandfather. 6.

trithing (trī′thing): one of the three administrative jurisdictions into which the county of York, in England, is divided; a riding. The name was also given to divisions in colonial Pennsylvania and Long Island.

troat (trōt): the cry of a buck in rutting time. To troat.

troca (trō′ka): a top shell used to make pearl buttons.

trochilic (tro.kil′ik): the science of rotary motion. 1. Pert. to rotary motion.

trochiscus (tro.kis′kus): a kind of tablet or lozenge.

trochomancy (trō′ko.man′si): divination by studying wheel tracks.

troco (trō′kō): an old English game played on a lawn, using wooden balls and cues; also called lawn billiards.

trogue (trōg): in mining, a wooden trough, forming a drain (var. of trough). 30.

troilism (troi′lizm): three-way sex.

troke (trōk): to barter or negotiate; a barter; trash. 44.

trollylolly (trol′i.lol′i): a song refrain, suggesting careless gaiety. Coarse lace.

tromba (trom′ba): a trumpet, or an organ stop imitating the tone quality of a trumpet.

trophaeum (tro.fē′um): a Greek or Roman monument commemorating a victory.

tropophobia (trō′po.fō′bi.a): fear of change.

tropophilous (tro.pof′i.lus): thriving under seasonal changes, as of temperature or humidity.

trucidation (trōō′si.dā′shun): slaughter.

trummel (trum′l): a round tin box for cake or bread. 28.

trusion (trōō′zhun): act of pushing or shoving. 52.

trussell (trus′el): the upper or reverse die used in coining. 1.

trutinate (trōō′ti.nāt): to weigh; balance; consider.

truttaceous (tru.tā′shus): pert. to or like a trout.

tsine (tsīn): the banteng, a wild ox of the Malay peninsula and archipelago.

tsiology (tsi.ol′o.ji): a dissertation on tea.

tsuba (tsōō′ba): the metal guard of a Japanese sword, often elaborately decorated.

tubar (tū′ber): tubular.

tubicinate (tū.bis′i.nāt): to blow a trumpet.

tucky (tuk′i): the common spatterdock, or yellow water lily, of North America.

tui (tōō′i): a New Zealand honey eater, predominantly glossy black with white markings. It is a notable mimic and often kept as a cage bird. Also called parson bird.

tumeric (tū.mer′ik): var. of turmeric.

tump (tump): a small rise of ground; a mound, molehill, etc.; a clump of vegetation, esp. one making a dry spot in a swamp. 30.

tumulate (tū′mū.lāt): to entomb.

tunk (tungk): rap; thump. 11.

tupman (tup′man): a man who breeds or deals in rams. 13.

turbitteen (tur′bi.tēn): a type of Oriental frilled pigeon.

turfite (turf′īt): a horse-racing addict. 26.

turkle (tur′kl): turtle. 11.

turmeric (ter.mer′ik): an East Indian herb; its aromatic rootstock, used in powdered form as a condiment, esp. in curry powder.

turncock (turn′kok): a stopcock with a plug that is turned in opening and closing.

turp (turp): to rub with turpentine. 21.

turriculate (tu.rik′ū.lāt): having, or formed like, a turret.

tussal (tus′el): pert. to a cough.

tussive (tus′iv): *tussal.*

tute (tūt): to tutor. 58.

tutrix (tū′triks): tutoress. 52.

tuza (tōō′sa, tū′za): a pocket gopher, common in Mexico.

tuzzymuzzy (tuz′i.muz′i): a garland of flowers, nosegay. 9.

twangle (twang′gl): to twang. 52.

twank (twangk): to sound like a twang sharply cut off; to slap smartly.

twattle (twät′l): to talk idly; chatter, prate, twaddle. 13.

tweel (twēl): a clay covering for the mouth of a glass furnace. Also, Scot. var. of *twill.*

twiddlepoop (twid′l.pōōp): an effeminate-appearing man.

twink (twingk): the chaffinch. 31. A wink, a twinkling; to wink, to twinkle; to punish, thrash. 13.

twinter (twin′ter): a sheep two years old; also applied to cattle and horses. 44C.

tychism (tī′kizm): a theory of evolution which holds that variation may be purely fortuitous.

Tychonic (tī.kon′ik): pert. to the 17th-century Danish astronomer Tycho Brahe or his system of astronomy.

tyg (tig): a ceramic drinking cup with two or more handles.

tymbal (tim′bal): var. of timbal.

tymp (timp): the mouth of a blast-furnace hearth.

typhonic (tī.fon′ik): pert. to a typhoon.

typtology (tip.tol′o.ji): the theory or lore of spirit rappings.

tyromancy (tī′ro.man′si): divination by watching the coagulation of cheese.

U

uakari (wa.kä′ri): *ouakari.*

uayeb (wa.yeb′): in the Mayan calendar, the five days added at the end of each year to complete 365 days.

uberty (ū′ber.ti): fruitfulness; plenty.

ubiety (ū.bī′e.ti): the quality or state of being in a place. Location. The abstract quality of whereness.

ubiquarian, ubiquitarian (u′bi.kwâr′i.an, -bik′wi.târ′i.an): ubiquitous. 52. (cap) One of a school of Lutheran divines which held that, Christ being omnipresent, his body is everywhere, esp. in the Eucharist.

ucalegon (ū.kal′e.gon): a neighbor whose house is on fire.

udometer (ū.dom′e.ter): a rain gauge.

ufologist (u.fol′o.jist): a student of flying saucers.

ughten (ut′en): morning twilight. 1.

uitlander (oit′lan′der, ut-): formerly, in South Africa, a foreigner, esp. a Briton residing in the Transvaal or the Orange Free State.

ula (ū′la): the gums.

ulcuscle, ulcuscule (ul′kus′l, ul.kus′kūl): a little ulcer. 52.

uliginose, uliginous (ū.lij′i.nōs, -nus): muddy; oozy; swampy. Also, growing in many places.

ultion (ul′shun): revenge. 1.

ultraantidisestablishmentarianism (ul′-tra.an′ti.dis′es.tab′lish.men.târ′i.a.-nizm): Gladstone's reported term for extreme opposition to sundering the relationship between state and established church.

ultracrepidarian (ul′.tra.krep′i.dâr′i.an): presumptuous.

ultrafidian (ul′.tra.fid′i.an): gullible.

ultroneous (ul.trō′ni.us): spontaneous; voluntary.

ulu (ōō′lōō): an Eskimo woman's knife resembling a food-chopper with a crescent blade. An Indian grass used for forage.

ulua (ōō.lōō′a): any of several large fishes of Hawaiian waters highly prized for food and sport.

umble (um′bl): singular form of *umbles* (var. of *numbles*).

umbrette (um.bret′): an African wading bird allied to the storks and herons.

umbriferous (um.brif′er.us): casting a shade; umbrageous.

umu (ōō′mōō): in Polynesia, a native earth oven or baking pit for cooking food wrapped in leaves.

Una (ōō′na): a lovely lady in Spenser's *Faerie Queene* intended as a personification of Truth.

unau (ū′nō, ōō′nou): the two-toed sloth.

uncular (ūng′kū.lar): avuncular. 52.

underfong (un′der.fong): to undertake; receive; sustain. 1. In Spenser, to entrap.

undernim (un′der.nim): to perceive; understand; undertake; rebuke; seize. 1. In Spenser, to ensnare; circumvent; trap.

underspurleather (un′der.spur′leth′er): a humble attendant or underling. 9.

undinism (un′din.izm): the arousal of erotic thoughts by the sight, sound, or touch of water.

unicity (ū.nis′i.ti): uniqueness.

unicum (ū′ni.kum): a thing unique in its kind; esp. a sole existing exemplar (as of writing).

unigenous (ū.nij′i.nus): in biology, being of one and the same kind.

unthrid (un.thrid′): unthread. 9A.

untrowable (un.trō′a.bl): incredible. 1.

upasian (ū.pā′zhun): deadly, as the sap of the upas tree of Java.

upbreak (up.brāk′): to break up or open. To force a way up or to the surface.

URVAS ARE CRABBY ABOUT AMBROSIA

In ancient days the Asian mongoose Urva
 Climbed high Olympus on a quest for crab,
His food of choice. He came across Minerva,
 And asked her if she'd rustle up a dab.
But stay-at-home Minerva thought he meant
Ambrosia, which delights immortal gods.
She brought a bowlful, to his discontent;
 They parted angry, and are still at odds.
Ambrosia? Pooh! For Urva, uberty
Means *crab;* and I wholeheartedly agree.

---

upeygan (ōō.pā′gan): the black rhinoceros.

uranism (ū′ra.nizm): male homosexuality.

uranography (ū.ra.nog′ra.fi): a description of heaven; the science of describing the heavens and the heavenly bodies.

uranophobia (ū.ra.no.fō′bi.a): fear of heaven or the sky.

urbacity (er.bas′i.ti): excess of pride in one's city.

urbicolous (er.bik′o.lus): living in a city.

urethrophobia (ū.rē′thro.fō′bi.a): aversion to the urethra.

urimancy (ū′ri.man′si): divination by the examination of urine.

urning (ur′ning): a male homosexual.

Uro (ōō′rō): an Indian of a tribe of primitive culture, living in western Bolivia.

ursal (ur′sal): churlish; bearish in disposition. 52.

ursoid (ur′soid): bearlike.

urson (ur′son): the Canada porcupine.

Ursus (ur′sus): a genus now commonly restricted to the European brown bear and its allies, incl. the American grizzly bear.

urubu (ōō′rōō.bōō): the black vulture.

urus (ū′rus): a large, long-horned wild ox of the German forests, now extinct, believed to be the ancestor of the domestic ox.

urva (ur′va): the crab-eating mongoose of southeastern Asia. It has black fur with white at the tip of each hair, and a white streak extends from the mouth to the shoulder.

ustion (us′chun): cauterization. 52.

V

vaccary (vak′a.ri): a cow or dairy building; a cow pasture. 2.

vaccimulgence (vak.si.mul′jens): the milking of cows.

vacuist (vak′ū.ist): one who maintains that nature has vacuums.

vade (vād): to go away, leave. (52, except as Latin imperative—*go hence! Depart!*)

vagitus (va.jī′tus): the cry of the just-born.

vairé, vaireé (vā.rā′): pert. to a fur (prob. squirrel) much used in medieval times to line and trim robes. Also, pert. to a heraldic representation of fur.

valence, valency (vā′lens, vā′len.si): power; importance; value. In chemistry and physics, the degree of combining power of an element or radical.

valeta (va.lā′ta, -lē′ta): a dance in slow waltz time.

vali (val′i): a governor general of a vilayet, an administrative division of Turkey. (cap) In Norse mythology, the son of Odin and avenger of Balder. Var. of *Bali*.

vallary (val′a.ri): designating a palisade crown of gold bestowed by the Romans on the soldier who first surmounted the rampart and broke into the enemy's camp. Such a crown in heraldry.

vallum (val′um): a Roman rampart, esp. one set with a palisade or stakes. Also, the combination of earthworks and ditch that follows the line of Hadrian's Wall in Britain.

vancourier (van′kōō.rēr): an advance man. 9.

Vanda (van′da): a genus of Indo-Malayan orchids. (not cap) A plant of this genus. A pale purple to pale reddish-purple color.

vanfoss (van′fos): in fortifications, a ditch for defense usu. filled with water.

vanillism (va.nil′izm): a morbid skin condition caused by handling vanilla.

vaniloquy (va.nil′o.kwi): a vain and foolish speech.

vannet (van′et): in heraldry, an open scallop shell.

vapulation (vap′ū.lā′shun): the act of beating or flogging.

vare (vār): a weasel. A staff, a wand. 1.

varicelloid (vâr′i.sel′oid): resembling chicken pox.

varietist (va.rī′e.tist): one who varies from the norm in attitudes, habits, desires, etc.

variole (vâr′i.ōl): something resembling a smallpox marking; a small pit.

varsal (vär′sal): dial. corruption of *universal*.

varsovienne (vär′so.vyen): a dance similar to the polka or mazurka, popular in the 19th century.

vasal (vā′sal): pert. to an anatomical vessel, as a vein or artery.

vastation (vas.tā′shun): devastation. 1. Purification through fire.

vates (vā′tis): among the Gauls, a learned class of soothsayers, prophets, and seers.

vaticide (vat′i.sīd): the murder of a prophet.

vaultage (vôl′tij): a vaulted place; an arched cellar.

Vayu (va.yōō′): in Vedic mythology, the wind-god. In the Sanskrit epic Ramayana, the father of Hanuman, the monkey god.

vectitation (vek′ti.tā′shun): the act of carrying or being carried. 52.

vega (vā′ga): in Spanish America and the Philippines, a fertile meadow.

Vega (vē′ga): a brilliant star in the constellation Lyra.

vegete (vi.jet′): lively, healthy; flourishing. 52.

velarian (vi.lâr′i.an): in ancient Rome, the awning of an amphitheater.

veliferous (vi.lif′er.us): carrying or bearing sails.

veligerous (vi.lij′er.us): pert. to a larval mollusk in the stage where it has developed its velum, a swimming organ.

---

*A WORD OF APPRECIATION
FROM AN AMATEUR OF THE CLASSIC
TONGUES*

There's something fine in Latin. Something—oh,
How should I say it? Something like . . . you
　　know . . .
Well, *fine!* Like, I could call a man
(A sucker, say)—an *ultrafidian!*

And Greek's great too. They've even got a noun
For "neighbor with a house that's burning down"!
I kid you not. They turn the firehose on,
And shout across, "Hi there, *ucalegon!*"

I'm for the classics. Like . . . you'll think I'm
　　loony . . .
But honey, just you listen. You're my *uni-
cumissimus*—my very most unique!
Hey, Latin's good for grammar. So is Greek.

---

velitation (vel′i.tā′shun): a minor battle; a skirmish.

vellicative (vel′i.kā′tiv): in medicine, causing to twitch.

velocimeter (vel′o.sim′e.ter): an apparatus for measuring speed, as of machinery or vessels, or esp. of projectiles.

venditation (ven′di.tā′shun): a display as if for sale. 52.

veneficious (ven′i.fish′us): acting by poison; used in poisoning or in sorcery. 52.

venenation (ven′i.nā′shun): the act of poisoning. The condition of being poisoned.

veneniferous (ven′i.nif′er.us): bearing or transporting poison.

venin (ven′in): poison. 1. Any of a class of toxic substances in snake venom.

venireman (ve.nī′re.man): a juror.

ventoseness (ven.tōs′nes): flatulence, windiness. 52.

ventripotent (ven.trip′o.tent): fat-bellied; also, gluttonous.

venust (vi.nust′): beautiful; elegant; Venus-like. 1.

verbasco (ver.bas′kō): the *mullein*.

verbicide (vur′bi.sīd): the mangling of words.

verbigerate (ver.bij′er.āt): to talk; chat. 1. To be unable to stop repeating words.

verbophobia (vur′bo.fō′bi.a): fear of words.

verd (vurd): green, greenness, freshness. 9.

verecund (ver′i.kund): bashful, modest.

veridical (vi.rid′i.kal): truthful, veracious, genuine.

veriloquy (vi.ril′o.kwi): truthful speech.

vermeology (vur′mi.ol′o.ji): the study of worms. 52.

verminophobia (vur.min.o.fō′bi.a): fear of vermin.

vernality (ver.nal′i.ti): the state of being springlike. 52.

vernant (vur′nant): flourishing, as in spring; vernal. 52.

verset (ver′set): a short verse, esp. one from the Bible, the Koran, or some other book regarded as holy.

versor (vur′sor): in geometry, the turning factor of a quaternion (if, unlike me, you know what *that* means).

verutum (vi.rōō′tum): a short spear or dart carried by the Roman light infantry.

vervel (vur′vel): a ring attached to a bird's leg for securing the bird to its perch.

vespertilian (ves′per.til′yun): batlike.

vespertine (ves′per.tīn, -tin): pert. to the evening.

vespoid (ves′poid): pert. to the wasps.

vetitive (vet′i.tiv): prohibiting; having or pert. to the power of vetoing.

vettura (vet.tōō′ra): an Italian four-wheeled carriage; a hackney coach.

vetturino (vet′tōō.rē′nō): one who drives a vettura or has one for hire.

vetust (vi.tust′): venerable from antiquity; ancient; old. 52.

viaggiatory (vi.aj′i.a.tō′ri): traveling; restlessly moving around. 52.

viagram (vī′a.gram): a chart produced by a *viagraph*.

viagraph (vī′a.graf): an instrument on wheels used to determine the relative smoothness or roughness of pavement surfaces.

viameter (vī.am′e.ter): an odometer to measure distance on roads.

viator (vī.ā′tor): a traveler.

vibex (vī′beks): a linear bruise.

vibratiunculation (vi.brāt′i.ung′kū.lā′shun): a slight vibration. 52.

viduous (vid′ū.us): widowed; bereaved. 52.

vigesimation (vī.jes′i.mā′shun): the act of killing every twentieth man. 52.

vihara (vi.hä′ra): in ancient India, a pleasure garden, esp. the precincts of temples and monasteries; hence, a Buddhist monastery or temple.

vill (vil): in the feudal system, a township, or division of a hundred. Hence, a village. A villa. 1.

villanella (vil′a.nel′a): an old rustic dance; its music. An Italian rustic song, precursor to the stricter canzonet and madrigal.

villanette (vil′a.net): a small villa. 52.

villeggiatura (vi.lej′i.a.tōō′ra): a stay at a villa; occasionally, the villa itself.

vimineous (vi.min′i.us): pert. to twigs; woven of twigs. Producing long slender twigs or shoots.

vinal (vī′nal): of or from wine; vinous.

vindemial (vin.dē′mi.al): pert. to a vintage.

vindemiation (vin.dē′mi.ā′shun): a gathering of grapes for wine, or a harvesting of fruit.

vinea (vin′i.a): in Roman warfare, a shedlike structure serving as protection to besiegers.

vinification (vin′i.fi.kā′shun): the conversion of fruit juice into alcohol by fermentation.

vinny (vin′i): moldy. 53.

vinquish (ving′kwish): dial. var. of vanquish, a wasting disease in sheep, attributed to feeding on certain plants. 44.

vint (vint): a card game similar to auction bridge.

vintry (vin′tri): a place where wine is sold or stored.

violescent (vī′o.les′ent): tending to a violet color.

viparious (vī′pâr′i.us): a mistaken form of vivacious in the sense of "tenacious of life." 52.

viperine (vī′per.īn, -in): pert. to a viper; venomous.

vire (vīr): an arrow feathered so as to acquire a rotary motion.

virent (vī′rent): green; not withered. 52.

viridarium (vir′i.dâr′i.um): a garden in an ancient Roman villa.

virilescence (vir′i.les′ens): among certain animals, the acquiring of characteristics more or less like those of the male, often observed in barren or old females.

viripotent (vir′i.pō′tent): of a man, sexually mature.

virole (vi.rōl′): in heraldry, a ring surrounding a bugle or hunting horn.

viron (vī′ron): a circuit; to environ, encircle. 1.

virose (vī′ros, vī.rōs′): virulent; poisonous.

vis (vis): a brief visit. 1. Vis-a-vis. 52. Force, vigor.

viscin (vis′in): a clear, sticky, tasteless substance from the sap of the mistletoe or holly.

visne (vēn, vē′ni): vicinage; in law, venue.

vison (vī′sun): the American mink.

vitilitigate (vit′i.lit′i.gāt): to wrangle. 1.

vitiosity (vish′i.os′i.ti): viciousness; depravity.

vitricophobia (vit′ri.ko.fō′bi.a): fear of one's stepfather.

vituline (vit′ū.līn, -lin): pert. to a calf, or veal.

vivandier (ve′van′dyā): in continental armies, esp. the French, a sutler.

vivandière (vi.van′dyâr): a female sutler.

viviparous (vī.vip′a.rus): producing living young.

vivisepulture (viv′i.sep′ul.cher): the practice of burying people alive.

vocabulation (vo.kab′ū.lā′shun): selection or use of words. 52.

Volapuk (vō′la.puk): an international language, based on English, developed in the 19th century.

volery (vol′er′i): a large birdcage; an aviary; the birds in an aviary; a flight or flock of birds.

volitient (vo.lish′ent): exercising free will.

voltigeur (vôl′ti.zhur): a sharpshooter in the French military. 1. A tumbler, leaper, vaulter.

volucrine (vol′ū.krīn, -krin): pert. to birds.

volumnist (vol′um.nist): one who writes a volume.

voortrekker (fōr′trek′er): in South Africa, a pioneer; esp. (cap) a Boer who trekked from the Cape Colony to the Transvaal in 1834–37.

voraginous (vo.raj′i.nus): pert. to a gulf; hence, devouring. 52.

vorago (vo.rā′gō): a gulf; an abyss.

vorant (vō′rant): in heraldry, (a creature) shown in the act of devouring.

vorticism (vôr′ti.sizm): in post-Impressionist art, emphasis on the complexity of modern civilization, incl. machines.

vortiginous (vôr.tij′i.nus): moving rapidly around a center; vortical; whirling.

votaress, votress (vō′ta.res, vō′tres): a female votary. A woman voter. 52.

vouchee (vouch′i): one called into court to warrant or defend a title. One cited as an authority or sponsor.

vouge (vōōzh): a long-handled, halberd-like weapon of the later Middle Ages.

vraisemblance (vrā′sän′bläns): the appearance of truth; verisimilitude.

vrille (vril): in aviation, a deliberate spinning nose dive.

vuggy (vug′i): pert. to vugs, small unfilled cavities in a lode or in the rock around it.

vulnerative, vulnific (vul′ner.ā′tiv, vul.nif′ik): causing wounds.

vulpecular (vul.pek′ū.lar): pert. to a fox, esp. a young one; vulpine.

W

wabby (wä′bi): the red-throated loon.

wabe, (wä′bi): the huisache, a shrub of the southern U.S. and tropical regions, bearing fragrant flowers used for making perfume.

wabeno (wô.bē′nō): a magician; specif., one of a class of shamans among the Ojibway Indians.

wack (wak): damp; clammy. 44.

Waco (wā′kō): an Indian of a small tribe of the Wichita confederacy in Texas.

wadget (waj′et): a little bundle. 11.

waggel (wag′el): a black-backed gull in immature plumage. 30.

waghalter (wag′hôl′ter): a rogue, rascal; one likely to be hanged. 1.

wagwag (wag′wag): a polishing device used by watchmakers.

walla-walla (wôl′a.wôl′a): an unintelligible sound produced by many people talking at once. (cap) An Indian people of the Pacific Northwest; a city of Washington state.

wallydrag (wăl′i.drag, wol-): the youngest of the litter; the runt. 44.

wally-gowdy (wăl′i.gō′di, gōōd′i): in endearment, a precious jewel or ornament. 44.

walm (wälm): to well up, gush forth. 9.

wamefoo, wamefu (wăm′fōō): a bellyful. 43.

wampee (wăm′pi): the pickerelweed. 35.

wampus (wăm′pus): a heavy, stupid, sluggish person; sometimes, a person objectionable for any reason. 21.

Wanderjahr (vän′der.yär, wän′der.yär): a year of traveling before settling down.

waniand (wā′ni.and): the waning moon, regarded as unlucky. 1.

wankapin (wăng′ka.pin): an American lotus, the water chinquapin. Its edible nutlike seed.

wantwit (wănt′wit, wônt′wit): a fool; foolish, idiotic.

wappenschaw (wap′en.shaw): a rifle-shooting contest. 44.

wappenschawing (wap′en.shô′ing): a military muster or review. 44.

wapperjawed (wăp′er.jôd): having crooked jaws, or sometimes an undershot jaw. 28.

waringin (wor′in.jin): a common fig tree of India, with inedible fruit.

warmouth (wôr′mouth): a freshwater sunfish of the eastern United States.

wase (wāz): a wisp or bundle of hay or straw; a pad, as of straw to support a burden on the head. 2. A torch. 1.

waterchat (wâ′ter.chat): any of numerous South American flycatchers. A forktail.

wayman (wā′man): a shipwright who prepares and lays launching ways. A laborer who lays tracks or keeps them in repair.

wayzgoose (wāz′gōōs): in Britain, a printers' annual holiday or entertainment.

weanel (wēn′el): weanling. 2.

weatherfend (weth′er.fend): in Shakespeare, to defend from the weather; to shelter.

wede (wēd): shrivelled. 11. To be or become mad; to be wild with anger or desire; to rage. 1.

weet (wēt): the call of any of several birds, as the European sandpiper; also, the bird itself. A sound imitative of the cry of a small bird. To weet.

weeze (wēz): to ooze. 44C.

wegotism (wē′got.izm): excessive use of the editorial we. 58.

wem (wem): a spot, stain, flaw. 10.

wergild (wur′gild): in Anglo-Saxon and Germanic law, the price paid by a killer's family to the family of the victim to prevent a blood feud.

wey (wā): any of several local British measures of weight. Also, to move; agitate. 1.

whabby (hwä′bi): *wabby*.

whally (hwä′li): having a light-colored iris. 52.

whangdoodle (hwang′dōō′dl): an imaginary creature of undefined character. 58A.

whata (hwä′ta): a storehouse, usu. thatch-roofed, built on posts capped with inverted cones to prevent rats from getting in. 56.

wheeple (hwē′pl): the drawn-out shrill cry of certain birds, as the curlew or plover. To utter such a cry.

wheetle (hwē′tl): to chirp or whistle shrilly. 44A.

wheft (hweft): a nautical pennant.

wherret (hwer′et): hit, box, slap. 11. Var. of *worrit*.

whid (hwid): a word. 3A. Lie, fib. 44A. A silent, rapid motion; to move silently. 47.

whigmaleery (hwig′ma.lē′ri): a knickknack; whim; vagary. 44A.

whinchacker (hwin′chak′er): a small European singing bird that frequents grassy meadows; the whinchat.

whipjack (hwip′jak): a beggar pretending to have been shipwrecked; a vagabond.

whiskerino (hwis′ker.ē′no): a whisker-growing contest. 21.

whiskin (hwis′kin): a shallow drinking bowl. 1.

whisp (hwisp): a low sound as of puffing, rustling, or sprinkling; to whisp. Also, var. of *wisp*. 11A.

whisterpoop (hwis′ter.pōōp): a blow, buffet. 11.

whuff, whuffle (hwuf, hwuf′l): to emit whuffs or whiffs; of a dog or horse, to breathe with noisy whiffs.

widdifow (wid′i.fōō): a rogue, *waghalter*. 1.

wiff (wif): wife. 1.

windhover (wind′huv′er): the kestrel. 30.

wingmanship (wing′man.ship): skill in flying. 52.

winklehawk (wing′kl.hôk): a rectangular rent in cloth. 28.

winze (winz): a vertical or steeply inclined passageway connecting one mine working place with another at a different level.

wisket (wis′ket): a basket; esp. a straw provender basket. 13.

witchety (wich′e.ti): a grub—the chief food of the marsupial mole. 53.

witney (wit′ni): a heavy, woolen fabric, napped and shrunk, used for coats and blankets.

wittee (wit′i): a wife who is encouraged in unfaithfulness by her husband. 60.

wittol (wit′ul): a man who encourages his wife's infidelity. 9.

witzchoura (wi.chōō′ra): a woman's mantle with large sleeves and deep falling collar, fashionable in the reign of George IV.

witzelsucht (vit′sel.sookt): an emotional state involving futile attempts at humor.

woader (wō′der): one who employs the blue dye woad; a woadman.

wobbegong (wob′i.gong): in New South Wales, the carpet shark.

wod (wod): dial. var. of *would;* obs. past tense of *wade*.

wonga, wonga-wonga (wong′ga, wong′ga.wong′ga): a woody vine with loose panicles of yellowish white flowers; a narrow-leaved cattail; a large pigeon with very white flesh. 53.

wonk (wongk): one who studies excessively (perhaps *know* spelled backwards). 21.

wooer-bab (wōō′er.bab): a garter tied below the knee as a love knot. 44.

woom (wōōm): to the Cantonese, beaver fur.

wootz (wōōtz): a steel made anciently in India in small crucibles; the oldest known process for making fused steel.

worricow (wur′i.kōō): a bugaboo, hobgoblin; esp. (cap) the Devil. 44A.

worrit (wur′it): worrier; worry; to worry. 11.

wou-wou (wou′wou′): the silver gibbon, an ashy-gray species of Java. The agile gibbon, a dark-brown species of Sumatra.

WANDERJAHR

Young I began my Wanderjahr;
    A gibbous moon was climbing.
I blew it smoke from my cigar,
    And set about my rhyming.

I rhymed in country and in town,
    In bed and in the loo;
I rhymed for princess and for clown,
    I rhymed for Worricow.

But words to them were walla-walla;
    They cried, "Your rhymes are whacko;
Besides, you bring into the hall a
    Miasma of tobacco."

Old I returned from Wanderjahr;
    The moon hung waniand;
Dead as the butt of my cigar
    The rhymes were in my hand.

The moon will wax and climb encore;
    Yet here, until they end me,
I'll puff my rhymes out, grateful for
    A hut to weatherfend me.

wowf (woōf): wild; crazed. 44.

wowser (wou′zer): one who is censoriously hostile to minor vices. 26.

wrasse (ras): any of numerous edible, marine, usu. brilliantly colored, spiny-finned fishes of the family Labridae, allied to the parrot fish.

wrig (rig): the feeblest member of a brood or litter; a puny child, or the youngest child of a family. 44. To wriggle. 2.

wull (wul): dial. var. of will.

wuntee (wun′ti): a lone ole buffalo bull.

wurrus (wur′rus): the *kamala*.

wuther (wuth′er): var. of whither, n. & v. 13. A sharp blow; flurry. To hurry; rush; bluster; to tremble; totter. 44. To hurl; shake. 44C.

wuzzy (wuz′i, wooz′i): var. of woozy.

wyliecoat (wī′li.kōt): an undervest or petticoat; a nightdress. 44A.

wype (wīp): the lapwing. 4.

X

Xanthippe (zan′tip′i): the shrewish wife of Socrates.

xanthoderm (zan′tho.durm): a member of a yellow-skinned race.

xanthodont (zan′tho.dont): one with yellowish teeth.

xanthomelanous (zan.tho.mel′a.nus): pert. to races having an olive or yellow complexion and black hair.

xanthophobia (zan′tho.fō′bi.a): fear of the color yellow.

xanthoproteic (zan′tho.pro.tē′ik): relating to xanthoprotein, a yellow substance formed by action of hot nitric acid on albuminous or protein matter.

xanthyocyanopsia (zan′thi.o.sī.a.nop′-si.a): a form of color blindness in which one sees only yellows and browns.

xat (zat): a carved post in front of certain Indian houses.

xenagogue (zen′a.gog): a guide. 52.

xenagogy (zen′a.gō′ji): a guidebook. 52.

xenial (zē′ni.al): pert. to hospitality, or relations between guest and host.

xenium (zē′ni.um): a present given among the ancient Greeks and Romans to a guest or stranger.

xenodochium (zen′o.do.kī′um): in the Middle Ages, a home for the disabled and friendless.

xenodochy (zen.o′do.ki): hospitality.

xenoepist (zen′i.pist): one who speaks with a foreign accent.

xenomancy (zen′o.man′si): divination by study of the first stranger to appear.

xenomania (zen′o.mā′ni.a): a mania for things foreign.

xenophobia (zen′o.fō′bi.a): fear of strangers or foreigners.

xeromyron (zi.rom′i.ron): a dry or stiff ointment.

xeronisus (zi.ron′i.sis): inability to achieve orgasm.

xerophagy (zi.rof′a.ji): the strictest Christian fast, in which only bread, salt, water, and vegetables may be eaten; observed chiefly in the Eastern churches during Lent or esp. Holy Week.

xerophobous (zi.rof′o.bus): of plants, easily succumbing to drought.

xibalba (hi.bäl′ba): in the Mayan religion, the underworld; the abode of the dead.

xiphopagus (zi.fop′a.gus): a monster consisting of twins joined at the abdomen.

Xiuhtecutli (he′oo.ta.koo′tli): the Aztec fire god.

xoanon (zō′a.non): in ancient Greece, a primitive image of carved wood.

xylite, xylitol (zī′lit, zī′li.tol): an alcohol obtained as a sirupy liquid by reduction of xylose.

xylographer (zī.log′ra.fer): one who makes prints from the natural wood grain.

xylology (zī.lol′o.ji): the part of the study of trees that treats of the gross and the minute structure of wood.

xylomancy (zī′lo.man′si): divination by pieces of wood.

xylophobia (zī′lo.fō′bi.a): fear of wood or of forests.

xylopolist (zī.lop′o.list): one who deals in wooden objects.

xylopyrography (zī′lo.pī.rog′ra.fi): the art of producing pictures or designs by burning or scorching wood with hot instruments.

xyresic (zī.res′ik): sharp as a razor.

xystus (zis′tus): in Greek and Roman architecture, a long open portico, used in winter or in stormy weather for athletic exercises. Incorrectly, a walk lined with trees.

THEY WERE BOTH XANTHODONTIC, TOO

In a xystus, shrew Xanthippe
Fell in love with Socrates.
Nag in love with aging hippy—
Hippy hipped on shrew Xanthippe—
In the name of all that's dippy,
   What are we to make of these?
In a xystus, shrew Xanthippe
Fell in love with Socrates!

Y

yabber (yab′er): talk; jabber; language; esp., the broken English of the Australian aborigines. 53.

yabbi (yab′i): the *thylacine*.

yabbie, yabby (yab′i): a small burrowing crayfish found in creeks and water holes in Australia.

yaboo, yabu (ya.boo′): a strong, hardy pony bred in the mountains of Afghanistan.

yaff (yaf): to bark; yelp; scold. 44.

yaffle (yaf′l): To yaff. 44. An armful, handful; the green woodpecker. 11.

yagua (yä′gwa): a Puerto Rican palm resembling the royal palm. Also, its thick woody leaf. (cap) A Peban Indian dwelling along the Amazon in northeastern Peru.

yahoomanity (ya.hoo.man′i.ti): the supposedly boorish mass of humanity.

Yahwism (yä′wizm): the worship of Yahweh (Jehovah). The use of Yahweh as a name for God.

yair (yār, yâr): an enclosure for catching salmon. 43.

yapok (ya.pok′): the water opossum.

yapp (yap): a style of bookbinding in which a limp cover is bent over the edge without being cut at the corners.

yarb (yärb): herb. 11.

yardang (yär′dang): a sharp-crested ridge carved by wind erosion.

yardwand (yärd′wänd): a yardstick.

yark (yärk): var. of *yerk*. 2.

yarwhelp (yär′hwelp): the bar-tailed godwit. 31B.

yati (yat′i, yut′i): a Hindu ascetic; a devotee.

yatter (yat′er): chatter, clamor. 44A.

yaud (yôd, yäd): a workhorse, esp. a mare; also, a jade. 43.

yauld (yôd, yäd, yäld): alert, able-bodied; also, sharp, as weather. 43.

yaya (ya.yä′): any of several tropical trees, inc. the gum-yielding copa of Panama, the lancewood of Puerto Rico, and the chaparro of Belize.

ydromancy (id.ro.man′si): divination using water.

yed (yed): fib; wrangle. 44.

yede (yēd): to go, proceed. 10A.

yehudi (ye.hoo′di): a British gremlin, so-named because it is always fiddling around.

yeld (yeld): (of a cow or ewe) barren; having slipped her young; not old enough to bear; giving no milk. 44D.

yeme (yēm): to take care of; heed; observe. Solicitude. 1.

yerk (yurk): to make ready; prepare. 2.

yestern (yes′tern): yester. 9.

yette (yet′i): to grant; concede. 1.

yeuk, yewk, yuke (yook): itch. 43.

yex (yeks): sob. 1. Hiccup; cough. 11.

yez (yēz, yiz): you (pl.). 51.

yirn (yurn): whine; grimace. 47.

yiver (yī′ver): eager; greedy. 1.

ylahayll (il′a.hāl): bad luck to you. 1.

ylespil (il'es.pel): the hedgehog. 1.

ynambu (ē'nam. bōō): a large kind of *tinamou.*

yocco (yok'ō): a Colombian plant allied to the *guarana,* and, like it, yielding caffeine from the bark and leaves.

yojan (yō'jan): a Hindu unit of distance equal to about 5 miles.

yperite (ē'per.īt): mustard gas.

ypsiliform (ip.sil'i.fôrm): Y-shaped.

ythe (ēth): a wave of the sea. 1.

yuca (yōō'ka): cassava.

yukkel (yuk'el): the green woodpecker. 30A. The flicker. 28.

yupon (yōō'pon): var. of yaupon, a species of holly native to the southern United States.

Z

zaman (sä'man): the rain tree.

zambo (zam'bō): *sambo.*

zambomba (tham.bom'ba): a crude musical instrument made by inserting a stick through parchment stretched over a widemouthed earthen jar, and sounded by rubbing the stick.

Zan (zan): an old Doric name for Zeus.

zander (zan'der): a pike perch of central Europe, allied to the walleyed pike.

zante (zan'ti): the smoke tree, or fustet; its wood.

zapateado (thap'a.ti.ä'dō): a Spanish tap dance.

zaptiah (zap.tē'a): a Turkish policeman.

zarzuela (thär.thwā'la): a 17th-century Spanish variety of operetta or vaudeville, mixing songs and dialogue.

zati (zä'ti): the bonnet monkey.

Zea (zē'a): a genus of large grasses, incl. Indian corn. (not cap) Formerly, a diuretic made from elements of Indian corn.

zebrula (zē'broo.la, zeb'roo.la): a cross between a male zebra and a female horse.

zedland (zed'land): the English countries of Devonshire, Dorsetshire, and Somersetshire, where Z replaces S in colloquial speech.

zedonk (zi.dongk): the offspring of a male zebra and a female donkey.

zeist (zē'ist): in medicine, one who supports the theory that pellagra is the result of a diet of corn.

zelophobia (zel'o.fō'bi.a): fear of jealousy.

zemi (sā'mi): among the extinct Taino Indians of the Greater Antilles and the Bahamas, a spirit or supernatural being. Also, an object believed to be the dwelling of a spirit and hence to possess magic potency.

zemmi (zem'i): the great mole rat.

zenography (zi.nog'ra.fi): the study or description of the surface of the planet Jupiter.

zester (zes'ter): a small rake-like tool used to shave the top layer from an orange or lemon.

zetetic (zi'tet'ik): seeking; proceeding by inquiry.

zeticula (zi.tik'ū.la): a small withdrawing room.

ziara, ziarat (zi.ä'ra, zē'a.rät): a tomb of Muslim saint; hence, a shrine.

zibetum (zib'i.tum): civet from the zibet, a civet cat of India.

zieger (zē'ger): a cheese made from whey, consisting principally of albumin.

Zigeuner (tsi.goi'ner): a gypsy.

zimb (zimb, zim): a large two-winged fly of Abyssinia, resembling the tsetse, and very destructive to cattle.

zimentwater (zim'ent.wô'ter): a kind of water found in copper mines; water impregnated with copper. 52.

zimme (sim'i): a gem.

zimmi, zimmy (zim'i): a *dhimmi.*

zizz (ziz): an imitative syllable.

zoanthropy (zo.an'thro.pi): a monomania in which one believes oneself changed into an animal and acts accordingly.

zobo (zō'bō): a kind of Asian cattle, supposedly a cross between the zebu and the yak, used for its flesh and milk.

zoetic (zo.et'ik): pert. to life; living; vital.

zoetrope (zō'i.trōp): a toy in which figures on the inside of a revolving cylinder are viewed through slits, and appear to be a single animated figure.

zogo (zō'gō): among the Miriam-speaking people of the Torres Strait, a sacred object of magic potency.

zoiatrics (zō'i.at'riks): veterinary medicine.

Zoilean (zo.il'i.an): having the characteristics of Zoilus, a bitter, envious, unjust Greek critic who lived in the 4th century B.C.

Zoilism (zō'i.lizm): carping criticism.

zomotherapy (zō'mo.ther'a.pi): a raw meat diet as a treatment for tuberculosis.

zona (zō'na): a zone or band. A girdle; a layer.

zonda (zon'da): a hot wind of the Argentine pampas.

zonesthesia (zōn'es.thē'zhi.a, -zha): a feeling of restriction about the waist.

zonulet (zō'nu.let): a little girdle; a zonule.

zoodynamics (zō'o.dī.nam'iks): the science that treats of the vital powers of animals.

zooid (zō'oid): in zoology, an entity that resembles but is not wholly the same as an individual organism, as a phagocyte or sperm cell having locomotion.

zoolite (zō'o.līt): a fossil animal.

zoopery (zo.op'er.i): experimentation on the lower animals.

zoophobia (zō'o.fō'bi.a): fear of animals.

zoophorous (zo.of'er.us): in classical architecture, a frieze having continuous relief sculptures of men or animals or both.

zoopraxiscope (zō.o.prak'si.skōp): an early form of motion-picture projector.

zoopsychologist (zō'o.sī.kol'o.jist): a student of animal psychology.

zoosemiotics (zō'o.sem'i.ot'iks): the study of communication between animals.

zoozoo (zōō'zōō): the ringdove. 30.

zorillo (zo.ril'o, so.rē'ō): a tropical American shrub or small tree with a skunk-like odor.

zortzico (zôr.sē'kō): a song or dance in quintuple or sextuple time, common among the Basques.

Zu (zōō): in Babylonian mythology, an evil storm-god in the form of a black bird.

zubr (zōō'br): the European bison or aurochs.

zuche (zōōch): a tree stump. 1.

Zugzwang (zoogz'väng): a chess dilemma where any move will weaken the player's position.

zuureveldt (zur'velt): in South Africa, a tract of land covered with coarse grass.

zygal (zī'gal): H-shaped.

zygomancy (zī'go.man'si): divination by weights.

zymometer, zymosimeter (zī'mom'i.ter, zī'mo.sim'i.ter): an instrument measuring fermentation.

zypthepsary (zip.thep'sa.ri): a brewery.

zyxomma (zik.som'a): an Indian dragonfly. Also, the last word in several dictionaries.

Zyzzogeton (ziz.o.jē'ton): a genus of large South American leaf hoppers. The last word in this glossary.

Appendix A: Meaning of the Number Keys

1.	Obsolete.	21A.	Dialectal and slang.	40A.	Chiefly England.
2.	Obsolete except dialectal.	22.	United States slang.	41.	England.
2A.	Chiefly obsolete except dialectal.	22A.	United States and Canadian slang.	41A.	Cornwall.
3.	Obsolete or dialectal.	23.	English slang.	41B.	England and Cornwall.
3A.	Obsolete slang.	23A.	Australian slang.	41C.	Wales.
4.	Obsolete except dialectal, England.	23B.	Australian slang and dialectal.	42.	North of England.
4A.	Obsolete except the north of England.	24.	School slang.	42A.	Chiefly north of England.
		24A.	Scottish slang.	43.	North of England and Scotland.
4B.	Obsolete except Scotland and the north of England.	25.	English prison slang.	43A.	Chiefly north of England and Scotland.
5.	Obsolete except Scotland.	26.	Colloquial.		
5A.	Obsolete except Scotland and dialectal, England.	26A.	Colloquial, England.	43B.	North of England; Scotland, dialectal.
		26B.	Colloquial, Scotland.	44.	Scotland.
6.	Obsolete except historic.	27.	Colloquial, United States.	44A.	Chiefly Scotland.
6A.	Obsolete except in law.	28.	Local, United States.	44B.	Chiefly Scotland and dialectal, England.
7.	Obsolete except military.	28A.	Local, chiefly United States.		
7A.	Obsolete, Scotland.	28B.	Chiefly local, United States.	44C.	Scotland and dialectal, England.
8.	Obsolete except heraldry.	29.	Local, United States and Canada.	44D.	Scotland and dialectal.
8A.	Obsolete or archaic.	29A.	Local or dialectal, England.	45.	North of England, Scotland, and Ireland.
9.	Archaic.	30.	Local, England.		
9A.	Archaic and dialectal, England.	30A.	Local, Scotland.	46.	England, Scotland, and Ireland.
10.	Archaic and dialectal.	31.	Local, England and Scotland.	47.	Scotland and Ireland.
10A.	Pseudoarchaic.	31A.	Local, Australia.	47A.	Chiefly Scotland and Ireland.
11.	Dialectal.	31B.	Local, England and Ireland.	47B.	Scotland and northern Ireland.
11A.	Chiefly dialectal.	32.	United States.	48.	College slang.
12.	Dialectal, United States.	32A.	Thieves' language, United States.	49.	Scotland and Ireland; dialectal, England.
13.	Dialectal, England.	33.	United States and Scotland.		
13A.	Dialectal, Sussex.	33A.	Northern United States.	50.	Ireland.
13B.	Chiefly dialectal, England.	34.	Northern United States and Canada.	50A.	Chiefly Ireland.
13C.	Dialectal, England, and slang.			51.	Anglo-Irish.
14.	Dialectal, England and Scotland.	34A.	Chiefly southern United States.	51A.	Anglo-Indian.
15.	Dialectal, north of England and Scotland.	34B.	Texas.	52.	Rare.
		35.	Southern United States.	52A.	Rare, United States.
16.	Dialectal, north of England, Scotland, and Ireland.	35A.	Southwestern United States.	53.	Australia.
		35B.	Chiefly southwestern United States.	53A.	England and Australia.
16A.	Chiefly Scots dialectal.	35C.	Western United States.	54.	New South Wales.
17.	Dialectal, England, Scotland, and Ireland.	36.	Massachusetts.	55.	Isle of Man.
		36A.	Maine.	56.	New Zealand.
17A.	Scotland and dialectal, England.	37.	Vermont.	57.	Regional.
17B.	Chiefly Scotland and dialectal, England.	37A.	New England.	58.	Humorous.
		37B.	Alaska.	58A.	Humorous, chiefly United States.
18.	Dialectal except Scotland.	38.	Hawaii.	59.	Slang, chiefly nautical. Also, nonce.
18A.	Obsolete, Scotland.	38A.	Hawaii and New Zealand.	60.	Nonce. Also, old slang.
19.	Dialectal, Sussex.	39.	Pennsylvania.	61.	Shetland and Orkney Islands.
20.	Dialectal and slang, Australia.	39A.	Louisiana.	62.	Scots and Old English law.
21.	Slang.	40.	Alabama, Louisiana, and Mississippi.		

APPENDIX B: — -MANCY

To Webster's Second, -*mancy* (from Greek *mantis*, divination) is "a combining form denoting divination, esp. by means of a (specified) thing, as in aleuro*mancy*, chiro-*mancy*, necro*mancy*."

The rhyming list had been put to bed with ninety-one -*mancy* words in it—a very adequate supply, it seemed to me—when I came across one hundred and fifty in Paul Dickson's *Words*. There were fifty-eight that I did not have, and he let me use them. Here they are, listed alphabetically, with abbreviated definitions:

The word	*That is, divination by*
aichomancy (ā′ko.man.si)	sharp points.
alomancy (al′o.man′si)	salt.
amathomancy (a.math′o.man′si)	walking.
amniomancy (am′ni.o.man′si)	a newborn's caul.
anthomancy (an′tho.man′si)	flowers.
anthropomancy (an′thro.po.man′si)	human entrails.
apantomancy (a.pan′to.man′si)	objects appearing haphazardly.
arithmancy (ar′ith.man′si)	numbers.
aspidomancy (as′pid.o.man′si)	a trance while seated on a shield in a magic circle.
astromancy (as′tro.man′si)	the stars.
brontomancy (bron′to.man′si)	thunder.
cartomancy (kär′to.man′si)	dealing cards.
causimomancy (kô.sim.o.man′si)	flammability. (The longer some object takes to ignite, the better the outlook.)
chaomancy (kā′o.man′si)	clouds and airborne apparitions.
cheiromancy (kī′ro.man′si)	palmreading.
cledonomancy (kled′o.no.man′si)	interpreting mystical utterances.
conchomancy (kong′ko.man′si)	seashells.
cromniomancy (krom′ni.o.man′si)	onions on the Christmas altar.
cryptomancy (krip′to.man′si)	hidden signs.
cubomancy (kū′bo.man′si)	dice.
daphnomancy (daf′no.man′si)	the crackle of a laurel branch on a fire.
demonomancy (dē′mun.o.man′si)	the help of demons.
dririmancy (drir′i.man′si)	dripping blood.
elaeomancy (i.lē′o.man′si)	a liquid surface.
empyromancy (em.pir′o.man′si)	fire.
graphomancy (graf′o.man′si)	handwriting.
hippomancy (hip′o.man′si)	the neighing of horses.
hyomancy (hī′o.man′si)	the hyoid, or tongue bone.
iconomancy (ī.kon′o.man′si)	images.
idolomancy (ī.dol′o.man′si)	idols.
labiomancy (lā′bi.o.man′si)	lip-reading.
libanomancy (lib′a.no.man′si)	the smoke of incense.
logomancy (log′o.man′si)	magic words.
machairomancy (ma.kī′ro.man′si)	knives or swords.
macromancy (mak′ro.man′si)	the largest thing at hand.
maculomancy (mak′ū.lo.man′si)	splotches, stains, spots.
magastromancy (mag′as.tro.man′si)	astrological magic.
margaritomancy (mar′ga.rit′o.man′si)	pearls.
meconomancy (mek′o.no.man′si)	drug-induced visions.

The word	*That is, divination by*
micromancy (mī'kro.man'si)	the smallest thing available.
moromancy (mor'o.man'si)	nonsense.
nephelomancy (nef'el.o.man'si)	clouds.
nephromancy (nef'ro.man'si)	the kidneys.
nomancy (no'man.si)	the letters of a name—onomancy.
odontomancy (o.don'to.man'si)	the condition of the teeth.
ololygmancy (ō'lo.lig.man'si)	the howling of dogs.
omphalomancy (om'fal.o.man'si)	the navel.
ornomancy (ôr'no.man'si)	the flight of birds.
osteomancy (os'ti.o.man'si)	bones.
pegomancy (peg'o.man'si)	fountains.
pessomancy (pess'o.man'si)	clothes-brushing.
phyllorhodomancy (fil'o.rō'do.man'si)	rose leaves.
pneumancy (nū'man.si)	blowing.
sphondulomancy (sfon'dū.lo.man'si)	spindles.
stercomancy (stur'ko.man'si)	the seeds in dung.
stolcheomancy (stol'ki.o.man'si)	a random pick from a book of poetry.
stolisomancy (stō'lis.o.man'si)	one's manner of dressing.
topomancy (top'o.man'si)	the terrain.
tyromancy (tī'ro.man'si)	cheese.

A Note about Appendices C and D

After the body of this book was finished, Paul Dickson mentioned to me that a man named Rudy Ondrijka had assembled a tremendous collection of words ending in -*mania* and -*phobia*. I wrote to Mr. Ondrijka, and he sent me his manuscript, defining more than 450 maniac and more than 850 phobic words. With the most uncalled-for and welcome generosity, he said that though the manuscript had been prepared for publication, I was welcome to use as many of his words in my book as I found convenient. I wish I could use them all. Since that is impossible, I have chosen, to save space, only those words that have definitions less than a line long.

APPENDIX C: — -MANIA

A mania is a morbid impulse or derangement concerning something, and when it is used as a suffix the something is defined by the root word to which the mania is appended. A mania may be a maniacal desire to *do* something—*nepiomania*, for instance, is an overwhelming desire to have a child—or an equally maniacal passion *for* something; *pizzamania* is an obsession with pizza. I do not know why manias are less abundant than phobias; theoretically, one would have the other as its opposite.

The following list represents a little more than a quarter of the manias that Rudy Ondrijka has assembled for his forthcoming book. (I refer to the book as Ondrijka's "Manias and Phobias," which may not be his final title.) None of the paltry seventy-one manias in my rhyming list is included here. In a few cases I have modified Mr. Ondrijka's definitions slightly to save space.

anagramania (an'a.gra.mā'ni.a): the anagram craze.

apimania (a'pi.mā'ni.a): obsession with bees.

autophonomania (o'to.fō'no.mā'ni.a): suicidal insanity.

balletomania (ba.let'o.mā'ni.a): passionate addiction to ballet.

brychomania, brycomania (brī'ko.mā'ni.a): the grinding of teeth in insanity.

cataromania (ka.ta'ro.mā'ni.a): an uncontrollable urge to curse.

copromania (kop'ro.mā'ni.a): an obsession with feces.

decubomania (di.kū'bo.mā'ni.a): an urgent desire to lie down.

desanimania (des'an.i.mā'ni.a): Amentia, or mindless insanity.

doromania (dôr'o.mā'ni.a): a morbid desire to give presents.

economania (i.kon'o.mā'ni.a): a mania for economy.

emetomania (i.met'o.mā'ni.a): a compulsive drive to vomit.

entomania (en'to.mā'ni.a): obsession with insects.

epairomania (i.pi'ro.mā'ni.a): insane elation.

eremiomania (er'i.mi.o.mā'ni.a): obsession with stillness.

erythromania (i.rith'ro.mā'ni.a): excessive and uncontrollable blushing.

grammania (gra.mā'ni.a): a mania for correct grammar.

guinnessmania (gin'es.mā'ni.a): the urge to set a world record.

hedonomania (hi.don'o.mā'ni.a): obsession with pleasure.

hieromania (hi'er.o.mā'ni.a): religious madness; sebastomania.

hippomania (hip'o.mā'ni.a): extreme fondness for horses.

hodomania (hō.do.mā'ni.a): abnormal desire to travel.

hymenomania (hī'men.o.mā'ni.a): an inordinate desire to deflower a virgin.

hypnomania (hip'no.mā'ni.a): a mania for sleep.

ichthyomania (ik'thi.o.mā'ni.a): an obsession with fish.

ideomania (id'i.o.mā'ni.a): an obsession with ideas.

jumbomania (jum'bo.mā'ni.a): fascination with mammoth dimensions.

lalomania (lal'o.mā'ni.a): obsession with speech.

malaxomania (mal'ak.so.mā'ni.a): a wild craving to knead the flesh of a woman.

mammathigmomania (mam'a.thig'mo.mā'ni.a): a compulsion to touch a woman's breasts.

nominomania (nom'in.o.mā'nia): a mania for naming.

nudomania (nū'do.mā'ni.a): morbid desire to go nude.

onychotillomania (on'i.ko.ti.'o.mā'ni.a): neurotic picking at the nails.

orchidomania (ôr'kid.o.mā'ni.a): a craze for orchids.

ornithomania (ôr'ni.tho.mā'ni.a): a craze for birds.

pareunomania (par'ū.no.mā'ni.a): a compelling need for sexual intercourse.

phrenomania (frē'no.mā'ni.a): acute mania; delirious mania; collapse, delirium.

phronemomania (frō'ni.mo.mā'ni.a): an obsession with thinking.

phytomania (fī'to.mā'ni.a): a mania for collecting plants.

polemomania (pō'li.mo.mā'ni.a): a rage for war.

polkamania (pōl'ko.mā'ni.a): a mania for dancing the polka.

pteridomania (ter'i.do.mā'ni.a): excessive enthusiasm for ferns.

resomania (rē'so.mā'ni.a): uncontrollable desire to gather things.

selenomania (si.lē'no.mā'ni.a): maniacal symptoms induced by moonlight.

studimania (stū'di.mā'ni.a): abnormal devotion to a hobby. Hedonism.

stupemania (stū'pi.mā'ni.a): insanity with symptoms of stupor.

succubamania (suk'ū.ba.mā'ni.a): intense desire by a woman to lie under a man.

titillomania (tit'i.lo.mā'ni.a): a morbid desire to scratch.

tomomania (tō'mo.mā'ni.a): a craze for needless surgical operations.

tristimania (tris'ti.mā'ni.a): melancholia.

uxoricidomania (uks.ôr'i.sī'do.mā'ni.a): obsession with killing one's wife.

uxoromania (uks.ôr'o.mā'ni.a): a strong desire to have a wife; desire for one's wife.

videomania (vid′i.o.mā′ni.a): infatuation with television.

yakomania (yak′o.mā′ni.a): a chattering of youngsters—and older people too.

zoomania (zo.o.mā′ni.a): a morbid love of animals.

APPENDIX D — -PHOBIA

In Greek, *phobia* means fear or dread that contains a strong element of loathing; in its present-day suffix form the loathing often has the upper hand. Strictly, like mania, it should be suffixed only to Greek roots; popularly, however, it is added freely to any substantive, and is frequently a tool of word play, as in "absenceophobia: fear of having the heart grow fonder," or "agateophobia: fear of losing one's marbles." Rudy Ondrejka's 850-word collection of phobias has many of the punning kind, and some are represented in my abbreviated selections below, but most are of the more conservative variety. You will see the others when Mr. Ondrejka's book appears—and it cannot be too soon.

agateophobia (ag′a.to.fō′bi.a): fear of insanity.

agonologophobia (a′go.no.log′o.fō′bi.a): fear of sports language.

agrizoophobia (ag′ri.zo′o.fō′bi.a): terror of wild animals.

aichurophobia (ī.ker.o.fō′bi.a): fear of points.

alektorophobia (a.lek′tôr.o.fō′bi.a): fear of chickens.

alphabetophobia (al′fa.bet′o.fō′bi.a): fear of things in alphabetical order.

amoebaphobia (a.mē′ba.fō′bi.a): fear of being infected with amoebae.

amnesiophobia (am.nē′zi.o.fō′bi.a): fear of amnesia.

anablepophobia (an′a.blep′o.fō′bi.a): fear of looking up at high places.

angelstreadophobia (ān′jelz.tred′o.fō′bi.a): fear of places where fools rush in.

angrophobia (ang′gro.fō′bi.a): fear of anger.

anophelophobia (a.nof′e.lo.fō′bi.a): fear of hurting the woman in sexual intercourse.

antlophobia (ant.lo.fō′bi.a): unwarranted fear of floods.

antrodermatophobia (an′tro.dur′ma.to.fō′bi.a): fear of acne.

anuptophobia (a.nup′ta.fō′bi.a): fear of being a spinster.

argumentophobia (är′gū.men′to.fō′bi.a): fear of arguments.

arsonophobia (är′son.o.fō′bi.a): fear of being set on fire.

astrologophobia (as′tro.log′o.fō′bi.a): fear of your birth sign.

astrophingophobia (as′tro.fing′go.fō′bi.a): fear of insecurity.

atelophobia (atel′o.fō′bi.a): fear of imperfection or incompletion.

auchmophobia (ôk′mo.fō′bi.a): fear of disorder, disarray, or confusion.

aurophobia (ô′ro.fō′bi.a): fear or dislike of gold.

auroraphobia (ô.rō′ra.fō′bi.a): fear of the northern lights.

autophobophobia (ô′to.fō′bo.fō′bi.a): fear of one's own fears.

bagophobia (bag′o.fō′bi.a): fear of wrinkled panty hose.

bathmophobia (bath′mo.fō′bi.a): fear of stairways or steep slopes.

blissophobia (blis′o.fō′bi.a): fear of ignorance.

botanophobia (bo.tan′o.fō′bi.a): intense dislike of plants and flowers.

boustrophobia (boo′stro.fō′bi.a): fear of cattle.

bozophobia (bō′zo.fō′bi.a): fear of blind dates.

cacistophobia (kak′is.to.fō′bi.a): fear of the worst.

callophobia (kal′o.fō′bi.a): fear or hatred of beauty.

calyprophobia (ka.lip′ro.fō′bi.a): fear of mystery, hidden or obscure meaning.

carnophobia (kär′no.fō′bi.a): abnormal aversion to a meat diet.

catapedaphobia (kat′a.pē′da.fō′bi.a): fear of jumping from even the slightest elevation.

cataphobia (kat′a.fō′bi.a): fear of falling.

chionomophobia (kī′o.no.mo.fō′bi.a): fear of snow.

chiraptophobia (ki.rap′to.fō′bi.a): fear of being touched by hands.

chirophobia (kī′ro.fō′bi.a): fear of hands.

chlorephobia (klor′i.fō′bi.a): fear of, or aversion to, the color green.

chronometrophobia (kron′o.met′ro.fō′bi.a): fear of clocks.

chrysophobia (kris′o.fō′bi.a): fear of gold or wealth.

cnidophobia (nī′do.fō′bi.a): fear of stings.

coimetrophobia (ko′i.met′ro.fō′bi.a): fear of cemeteries.

comapocophobia (kom′a.pok′o.fō′bi.a): fear of being shorn of hair.

cometaphobia (ko.met′a.fō′bi.a): fear of long hair.

conistraphobia (kon′is.tra.fō′bi.a): fear of slovenly places or untidiness.

cosmophobia (koz′mo.fō′bi.a): fear of cities.

crunchophobia (krunch′o.fō′bi.a): fear of shaking hands with weightlifters.

cryophobia (krī′o.fō′bi.a): fear of frost and ice.

cymophobia (sī′.mo.fō′bi.a): fear of sea swells or waves.

cyprinophobia (sīp′ri.no.fō′bi.a): fear of lewd women.

demophobia (dē′mo.fō′bi.a): dislike of crowds or people.

dendrophobia (den′dro.fō′bi.a): fear of big trees.

dentophobia (den′to.fō′bi.a): fear of dentistry.

diaperophobia (dī′a.per.o.fō′bi.a): fear of being alone with an infant.

didymophobia (did′i.mo.fō′bi.a): fear of twins.

dinophobia (din′o.fō′bi.a): fear of dizziness or of whirlpools.

dishpanophobia (dish′pan.o.fō′bi.a): fear of being caught red-handed.

doxophobia (dok′so.fō′bi.a): fear of expressing opinions or receiving praise.

dysphobia (dis.fō′bi.a): fear of knowing what to fear.

enetephobia (en′i.ti.fō′bi.a): fear of pins.

enterophobia (en′ter.o.fō′bi.a): fear of intestines, intestinal diseases.

epistagmophobia (ep′i.stag′mo.fō′bi.a): fear of nosebleeds.

equinophobia (i.kwī′no.fō′bi.a): fear of horses.

ergolatrophobia (ur′go.lat′tro.fō′bi.a): fear of overdevotion to work.

fechtenophobia (fek′ten.o.fō′bi.a): fear of fights.

feefifofumophobia (fē′fī′fō′fum′o.fō′bi.a): fear of giants on beanstalks.

friggaphobia (frig′a.fō′bi.a): fear of Fridays.

geniophobia (jē′ni.o.fō′bi.a): fear of chins.

genitophobia (jen′i.to.fō′bi.a): fear of the genitals.

genuphobia (jen′ū.fō′bi.a): fear of knees.

giraffaphobia (ji.raf′a.fō′bi.a): fear of sticking your neck out.

googoophobia (gōō′gōō.fō′bi.a): fear of baby talk.

groanophobia: (grōn′ō.fō′bi.a): aversion to puns.

gyrephobia (jīr′fō′bi.a): fear of being encircled, or enclosed, by other people.

halophobia (hal′o.fō′bi.a): fear of saltiness or salty flavors.

hedysophobia (hed′i.so.fō′bi.a): fear of sweetness or sweet flavors.

herpetophobia (hur′pi.to.fō′bi.a): dread of reptiles.

hormephobia (hôr′mi.fō′bi.a): fear of shock.

hybophobia (hī′bo.fō′bi.a): fear of hunchbacks.

hylophobia (hī′.lo.fō′bi.a): fear of forests.

hypertrichophobia (hī′per.trik′o.fō′bi.a): fear of hair on the body.

hypophobia (hī′po.fō′bi.a): lack of fear.

ichnophobia (ik.no.fō′bi.a): fear of footprints.

iconophobia (ī.kon′o.fō′bi.a): hatred of images.

isopterophobia (ī.sop′ter.o.fō′bi.a): fear of termites.

ithyphallophobia (ith′i.fal′o.fō′bi.a): female fear of the erected phallus.

Jonesophobia (jōnz.o.fō′bi.a): fear of not keeping up.

kyphophobia (kī′fo.fō′bi.a): fear of stooping.

lachanophobia (la.kan.o.fō′bi.a): fear of vegetables.

laliphobia (lal′i.fō′bi.a): in persons with a speech impediment, fear of speaking.

leucophobia (loō′ko.fō′bi.a): fear of white.

ligyrophobia (li′ji.ro.fō′bi.a): fear of loud noises.

limnophobia (lim′no.fō′bi.a): fear of lakes.

lipophobia (lip′o.fō′bi.a): fear of getting fat, or of fat people.

logophobia (log′o.fō′bi.a): fear of study, speech, words.

lycanthrophobia (li.kan′thro.fō′bi.a): fear of werewolves.

lycophobia (lī′ko.fō′bi.a): fear of wolves.

mageiricophobia (ma.jī′ri.ko.fō′bi.a): fear of having to cook.

melanophobia (mel′a.no.fō′bi.a): fear of the color black.

millstreamophobia (mil′strēm′o.fō′bi.a): fear of barbershop quartets.

mitrophobia (mī′tro.fō′bi.a): fear of hats or head coverings.

mnemophobia (nē′mo.fō′bi.a): fear of memories.

mycophobia (mī′ko.fō′bi.a): unreasoning fear of mushrooms.

myrmecophobia (mur′mi.ko.fō′bi.a): dread of ants.

nagophobia (nag′o.fō′bi.a): fear or hatred of backseat drivers.

nosocomephobia (nos′o.kō′mi.fō′bi.a): fear of hospitals.

nuciphobia (nū′si.fō′bi.a): dread of nuclear warfare.

obesophobia (o.bē′so.fō′bi.a): fear of gaining weight.

octophobia (ok′to.fō′bi.a): fear of the figure eight.

odontriatrophobia (o.don′tri.at.ro.fō′bi.a): fear of dentists.

ommatophobia (om′a.to.fō′bi.a): fear of eyes.

oneirophobia (o.nī′ro.fō′bi.a): fear of dreams.

oompahpahphobia (oōm′pa.pa.fō′bi.a): fear of German marching bands.

ophthalmophobia (of.thal′mo.fō′bi.a): aversion to being stared at.

ornithophobia (ôr′ni.tho.fō′bi.a): fear of birds.

osphresiophobia (os.frē′zi.o.fō′bi.a): a morbid aversion to odors.

ostraconophobia (os.tra′kon.o.fō′bi.a): fear of shellfish.

pantaphobia (pan′ta.fō′bi.a): absolute fearlessness.

penguinophobia (pen′gwin.o.fō′bi.a): fear of tuxedos.

phaphaphobia (faf′a.fa.fō′bi.a): fear of stutterers.

phasmophobia (faz′mo.fō′bi.a): fear of ghosts.

phemophobia (fē′mo.fō′bi.a): fear of voices.

philemaphobia (fil′i.ma.fō′bi.a): intense dislike of kissing.

philosophobia (fi.los′o.fō′bi.a): dread of philosophy or philosophers.

phyllophobia (fil′o.fō′bi.a): fear of leaves.

plastiphobia (plas′ti.fō′bi.a): fear of credit cards.

pnigerophobia (nī′jer.o.fō′bi.a): fear of smothering.

podophobia (pō′do.fō′bi.a): fear of feet.

poinephobia (poi′ni.fō′bi.a): fear of punishment.

prepuciophobia (pri.pū′si.o.fō′bi.a): fear of being circumcised.

primesodophobia (prī′mi.sod′o.fō′bi.a): the female's fear of first sexual intercourse.

psellismophobia (sel′iz.mo.fō′bi.a): fear of stammering or stuttering.

pteronophobia (ter′o.no.fō′bi.a): fear of feathers or being tickled by them.

pterygophobia (ter′i.go.fō′bi.a): fear of flying; also of airplanes.

qwertyuiophobia (kwur′tī.i.o.fō′bi.a): fear of touch typing.

rhacophobia (rak.o.fō′bi.a): fear of tattered garments.

runcophobia (rung′ko.fō′bi.a): fear of weeds.

satanophobia (sā′tan.o.fō′bi.a): dread of the devil.

saurophobia (sô′ro.fō′bi.a): fear of lizards.

scelerophobia (sel′er.o.fō′bi.a): fear of criminals.

selachophobia (si.lā′ko.fō′bi.a): fear of sharks.

semnologophobia (sem'no.log'o.fō'-bi.a): fear of moralizing.

senilisophobia (si.nil'i.so.fō'bi.a): fear of senility.

septophobia (sep.to.fō'bi.a): fear of decaying matter.

shushophobia (shush'o.fō'bi.a): fear of librarians.

sophobia (sof'o.fō'bi.a): fear of learning.

spheksophobia (sfek'so.fō'bi.a): fear of wasps.

synophobia (sin'o.fō'bi.a): fear of togetherness.

tachistothanatoophobia (ta.kis'to.than'-a.to.fō'bi.a): fear of head-on crashes.

taurophobia (tô.ro.fō'bi.a): fear of bulls.

threnotophobia (thren'o.to.fō'bi.a): fear of dirges or funerals.

tomophobia (tō'mo.fō'bi.a): fear of surgical operations.

tremophobia (trem'o.fō'bi.a): fear of trembling or shaking.

trypanophobia (trip.a.no.fō'bi.a): fear of inoculations or injections.

typhlophobia (tif'lo.fō'bi.a): fear of blindness, blind people, or going blind.

tyrannophobia (ti.ran'o.fō'bi.a): fear and hatred of tyrants.

undulaphobia (un'jōō.la.fō'bi.a): fear of water beds.

urophobia (ū'ro.fō'bi.a): fear of urination.

vestiophobia (ves'ti.o.fō'bi.a): fear and hatred of clothing.

villophobia (vil'o.fō'bi.a): fear of hairy people.

vitricophobia (vit'ri.ko.fō'bi.a): fear of or hatred for a stepfather.

xenoglossophobia (zen'o.glos'o.fō'bi.a): fear of foreign languages.

xyrophobia (zī'ro.fō'bi.a): fear of razors.

Index
First Lines of Verses

OVERLOOKED RHYMES

The rhyming words that follow, missed in the original manuscript of WORDS TO RHYME WITH, are listed in the same sequence as those in the foregoing rhyming list. Each is preceded by the appropriate subcategory heading, in capital letters: *MINYUN minion, PINYUN opinion, pinion,* etc. If there is no existing subcategory for the new word, the mother rhyme comes first, and then the subcategory heading, both in capitals: *UKTANT LUKTANT reluctant RUKTANT eructant,* etc.

Single Rhymes

KĀ embusqué PYĀ croupier, WĀ aweigh, outweigh, under weigh, weigh, YĀ ennuyé, couturier DÄ la-di-da NĀB nabe SNACH bandersnatch FĀJ bibliophage DAKT theodidact SKÄM scaum LÄNCH relaunch, unlaunch STÄNCHT staunched, unstaunched BANGKS banks MÂR bêche de mer YÄR debrouillard, grognard LÄRJD enlarged STÄRK aristarch, FÄRKT infarct FĀS pippinface MAST gynecomast BĀT hypnobate BLĀT blate PĀT apocopate RĀT subodorate TĀT parentate NÄZH cabotinage BRĒ abris KĒ quay PĒ metope SHĒ sidhe SPRĒ bel esprit, TĒ facticity, intrepidity TEK high-tec BEL Bel SKEL skell TEL boatel JĒN oncogene, MĒN amphetamine, methamphetamine, TĒN Philistine FET nymphet LĒTH (*th* as in *thin*) philalethe GREZ Éminence Grise PLĒZ pleas FĪ fishify SĪD facticide, hospiticide WIG wysiwyg FĪL heliophile, melcryptovestimentaphile, ctenophile, typhlophile KĪL chyle THĪM cyclothyme KLĪN cline LĪN aline PLÎR isoplere BRIS briss RIS clitoris ISH ish, orangeish KIST misarchist MĪT thelemite NĪT capet knight VĪT uvarovite LĪZ desacralize, sacralize SIZM lexiphanicism DŌ badaud BRÔD cackle-broad POD sacropod KLOF cloff SOF morosoph GOG grinagog, pintagogue, psychagogue POINT appoint HÔK chicken hawk NYOK paskudnak KOX box and cox SKÔM scaum JŌN Darby and Joan, Joan WOMP wamp SKRÔNCH scraunch BLOND dolichocephaleblong BŌNZ rackabones

BŌŌ àme de boue TŌŌ potoo GOOD unco' guid BRŌŌM new broom KŌŌN taikun TŌŌN importune NOOR flaneur, proneur, souteneur OOS POOS puss SHOOS schuss SHŌŌT shoot ŌP presbyope KŌP glaucope LŌP hemeralope NŌP cyanope SKŌP apadiascope, diascope, skiascope TŌP onomatatope NŌS venenose POT hydropot MYOU meow, miaow KŪB cube TUNG third tongue KŪR piqùre, BRUR beau sabreur KUR tiqueur TUR frotteur DURL dirl VURL virl BURM berm, berme DURM phaeoderm BŪS self-abuse TUSH gubbertush KŪT fefnicute.

Double Rhymes

KĀA keya ĀBAK PLĀBAK playback SWĀBAK swayback FĀBER homo faber FLACHET flatchet ACHWĀ HACHWĀ hatchway KACHWĀ catchway ĀDEL (see ĀDL) DĀDL daidle SPĀDŌ spado MĀEM mayhem TĀER metayer RÄGWA Nicaragua JAKARD jacquard LAKARD lacquered AKERD (see AKARD) ÄKL BÄKL debacle (see OKL) BAKŌ backhoe GALIK acromegalic GÄLĒ Svengali ĀLYA idalia KĀLYA lupercalia, tragomaschalia TĀLYA Arctalia TRAMEL untrammel JAMER katzenjammer AMŌ ammo HWAMŌ whammo GAMUK gammock YÄNA Siciliana NANDROID gynandroid KANĒ ca-canny HANGER crepehanger DĀNTĒ prickmedainty RAPEN rapine SNAPER wit-snapper ĀPL priapal ÂRĒ plenipotentiary, residentiary, sententiary, usufructuary NÂRĒ quatercentenary, quincentenary RÂRĒ raree ÄRGET argot TÄRGET target ÄRGN argon BÄRGN bargain JÄRGN jargon ÂRHED airhead BÂRHED barehead FÂRHED fairhead SKÂRHED scarehead BÂRING Bering ÄRKĒ polyarchy TĀSHUN subagitation, supputation RĀSHUS meracious NASTĒ beaunasty ĀTER creator, opiniator BĀTER surbater BRĀTER lucubrator GĀTER fustigator, compurgator LĀTER exosculator, sibilator NĀTER cachinnator, pronator KRATIK gynecocratic MATIK kerygmatic, sterigmatic RĀTIV maturative FATLĒ fatly PATLĒ patly LĀTŌ isolato MĀTŌ potomato MÄTŌ potomato LATRIK iconolatric STRATUM substratum, superstratum PLAZMUS metaplasmus RAZMUS Erasmus FĒA hanifiya KĒA keya SĒDNT sedent, sedent LĒDTĪM leadtime TRĒKŌ tricot LEKSIK dyslexic ELFISH ellfish FĒMIST heterophemist EMIST KEMIST chemist PREMIST premised ENDĒ duende ENDER bitter-ender ĒNES HĒNES he-ness SHĒNES she-ness WĒNES weeness, we-ness JENIK psychogenic THENIK psychasthenic FENSER spite fencer ENSHER SENSHER censure TENSHER tensure REPSHUN irreption ERANT errant BERANT aberrant ERĒ bestiary ĒRHOUND DĒRHOUND deerhound WĒRHOUND werehound HERIN heron PERIN perrin BĒRING Bering ERON (see ERIN) BESENS adlubescence GRESER egressor, ingressor ĒSES PRĒSES precess RĒSES recess NESHENS nescience PRESHENS prescience ĒSHĒZ MĒSHĒZ kamiches SPĒSHĒZ species ĒSIS Croesus ESPET DESPET despot RESPET respite ESPOT (see ESPET) ESTHOUS GESTHOUS guesthouse KWESTHOUS questhouse PESTHOUS pesthouse RESTHOUS resthouse ESTRAL oestral ĒTHEN (*th* as in *this*) HĒTHEN heathen RĒTHEN wreathen METIK pathomimetic ETUP GETUP get-up LETUP let-up SETUP setup FĒZER tort-feaser GRIBER grimgribber NIDER nidder SNIGLET sniglet GIGMAN gigman PIGMAN pigman PIJUN pouter pigeon WIJUN pigwidgeon, pigwidgin LIJUS irreligious PĪKER shunpiker ĪKON icon DĪKON daikon IKTIM DIKTIM dictum VIKTIM victim IKTUM (see IKTIM) SILA ancilla DILING dilling SILYUN Sicilian LIMIK bulimic DĪNAL paludinal SINIK philocynic INSKĒ buttinsky MINYUN minion PINYUN opinion, pinion STRIPLING stripling ÎRDNES SÎRDNES searedness WÎRDNES weirdness IREL SIREL Cyril SKWIREL squirrel JĪRIST magirist IRIT SPIRIT spirit TIRIT tirrit STÎROID steroid ĪRON iron* JĪRON gyron NISHUN unrecognition TISHUN an-

---

*Usually pronounced ĪERN, with no rhyme

tiscian SISHUS spurcitious BRISLER bristler HWISLER whistler SISLER sistler HĪS-
TER heister MĪSTER schlockmeister SHĪSTER shyster HISTER polyhistor LISTIK plu-
ralistic ĪTĒZ NĪTĒZ nighties RĪTĒZ sorites ĪWÔSH eyewash SĪWÔSH siwash, Siwash
GRIZERD grisard SHŌA Shoah RŌDĒ rhody, roadie GODERD goddard PODIK di-
podic, minopodic, podic, tripodic ÔDLIN MÔDLIN maudlin (see ODLIN) ŌEL GŌEL
goel NŌEL Noel OFTLĒ oftly SOFTLĒ softly FŌGŌ fogo OIZĒ BOIZĒ Boise NOIZĒ
noisy GŌJĒ mystagogy BROKĒ brocky KOKER alter kocker OKNĒ HOKNĒ Hockney
KOKNĒ cockney NOKNĒ knock-knee SOKSN mixoxene KÔLER choler ÔLWĀ alway
ÔLYŌ (see Ō'LI.Ō) PRŌMAN pro-man FŌNA baffona ONGHÔRN LONGHÔRN long-
horn PRONGHÔRN pronghorn DONIK boustrophedonic SONIK sonic PONTON ponton WONTON witwanton POODING jack-pudding O͞OEL accrual PO͞OKA pooka O͞OLAK
oolak KO͞OLAK Kulak GO͞OPĒ goopy LO͞OPĒ loopy BOORA kookaburra SHOORA
caesura WOORA wurra, wurra wurra ZOORA caesura ZYOORA caesura DO͞ORAS
Honduras CHO͞ORISH maturish KO͞OSIS presbycousis KLO͞OTĒ clootie TO͞OTSĒ tootsy
LO͞OZHUN prelusion ŌPEN open KŌPEN copen KÔRBEL corbeil ŌRĒ (see ÔRĒ,
ORĒ) ORĒ (see ŌRĒ, ÔRĒ) ÔRĒ (see ŌRĒ, ORĒ) ORKED orchid FORKED forkèd
ORKID (see ORKED) DÔRKUS Dorcas ÔRMENT TÔRMENT torment (see ŌR-
MENT) WÔRMER chairwarmer ÔRNMENT DÔRNMENT adornment HÔRNMENT
dehornment MŌRON oxymoron ŌRTENS portents (see ÔRTENS) PÔRTRES portress
ŌRTSMAN PŌRTSMAN portsman SPŌRTSMAN sportsman NŌSIS perigrinosis TŌ-
SIS proctoptosis ZOSTER herpes zoster ŌSTMARK ostmark PŌSTMARK postmark
LŌTA zopilote SKŌTER scoter ROTIK miserotic OUING meowing miauing (delete
YOUING meowing) ŌVERT overt KŌVERT covert PŌZHER reposure MOZL schli-
mazl STUDĒ quick study SPUDL spuddle SÜERD Seward SÜIST suist TUKER Old
Dan Tucker UKTANT LUKTANT reluctant RUKTANT eructant ULFER GULFER en-
gulfer SULFER sulphur MULJENS vaccimulgence MUNGGER airmonger MUNGKĒ
Pamunkey HUNTER tufthunter ŪPĪN LŪPĪN lupine SŪPĪN supine UREL BUREL burrel RUREL rural SKWUREL squirrel MURFĒ Murphy KŪRIST sinecurist VURNAL
avernal ŪRUS urus KŪRUS dolichurus, mercurous NŪRUS anurous, coenurus TŪRUS
Arcturus SURVENT eyeservant SWURVER bedswerver DUSTER bun-duster FŪTANT
confutant HUZĒ henhussy.

Triple Rhymes

FAB'Ū.LA lupus in fabula AJ'I.NÂR.Ē KWAJ'I.NÂR.Ē quinquagenary MAJ'I.NÂR.Ē
imaginary LAK-TI.KAL prophylactical NAK'Ū.LUS coenaculous GĀ'LI.A acrome-
galia KĀ'LI.A tragomaschalia LĀ'LI.A barbaralalia, barylalia, embolalia, idiolalia,
tachylalia TĀ'LI.A castalia MĀ'NI.A enosimania, klazomania AN'JE.LIST autoange-
list VAN'JE.LIST evangelist AN'THRO.PĒ cyanthropy AR'A.TER BAR'A.TER bar-
rator NAR'A.TER narrator ÂR'I.AN bestiarian LÂR'I.AN nihilarian NÂR'I.AN recti-
tudinarian, solitudinarian SÂR'I.AN postlapsarian, prelapsarian TÂR'I.AN quodlibetarian
ZÂR'I.AN rosarian PAT'I.KAL dapatical ÄT'I.Ō LÄT'I.Ō fellatio PÄT'I.Ō patio
LEK'SI.A dyslexia DĒ'LI.AN Mendelian HĒ'LI.AN Helion NĒ'LI.AN Cornelian
LĒ'MI.A bulimia TEN'ER.Ē bicentenary, quincentenary, sexcentenary TEN'TA.TIV
pretentative, sustentative NESH'I.ENS nescience PRESH'I.ENS prescience ET'I.KET
etiquette NET'I.KET Connecticut ET'I.KUT (see ET'I-KET) NĒ'ZI.A cryptomnesia,
psychokinesia LĒ'ZI.AN Milesian, Silesian KWĪ'E.TIST quietist SIG'A.MIST opsiga-
mist VIK'TA.BL evictable IL'A.JER (see IL'I.JER) TIM'ER.US timorous IM'I.NENT
imminent KRIM'I.NENT discriminant IN'I.ĀT opiniate BRĪ'NA.LĒ brinily HWĪ'NA.LĒ
whinily SHĪ'NA.LĒ TĪ'NA.LĒ tinily GWIN'I.U anguineous KWIN'I.TĒ equinity

IN′TE.GRĀT disintegrate IN′Ū.IT Innuit, Peter Minuet SIP′I.TAL basipetal, sincipetal IP′I.TĒ DIP′I.TĒ serendipity RIP′I.TĒ peripety IR′OO̅.ET PIR′OO̅.ET pirouette ZHIR′OO̅.ET girouette TIS′I.TĒ facticity IS′I.TUS LIS′I.TUS felicitous PLIS′I.TUS complicitous SIV′I.TĒ transmissivity NĪZ′A.BL recognizable, unrecognizable FŌ′BI.A aphephobia, anemophobia, asthenophobia, enidophobia, genophobia, kilobytophobia, narensophobia, musophobia, augophobia, peladophobia, spermophobia OD′ES.EZ BOD′ES.EZ bodices GOD′ES.EZ goddesses KOD′ES.EZ codices ROF′A.JĒ aeroph-agy MOF′I.LIST nemophilist KOG′RA.FĒ psychography LOJ′E.NIST philogenist NOK′RA.SĒ gynocracy POK′RA.SĒ corpocracy OL′A.TRĒ epeolatry GOL′A.TRĒ lo-golatry KOL′O.JĒ agathakakology NOM′I.NAL pronominal OM′I.NĒ epagomenae DOOR′A.BL durable, endurable, unendurable (see UR′A.BL) CHOOR′I.TĒ futurity, immaturity, maturity, prematurity TŌ′PI.A cacotopia KŌ′PI.US copious SKŌ′PI.US scopious KŌ′RA.LIST choralist KÔR′DI.AL cordial Ō′RI.US BŌ′RI.US laborious GLŌ′RI.US glorious, inglorious, vainglorious RŌ′RI.US uproarious SŌ′RI.US censo-rious, uxorious TŌ′RI.US maritorious, meritorious, notorious, stentorious ÔR′NI.Ō BÔR′NI.Ō Borneo FÔR′NI.O aldiborontiphoscophornio OS′I.ER BOS′I.ER bossier DOS′I.ER dossier FLOS′I.ER flossier GLOS′I.ER glossier MOS′I.ER mossier NOS′O.FĒ deipnosophy DŪ′BER.Ē dewberry NŪ′MER.US numerous KUR′A.BL incurrable, un-incurrable TUR′FLOO̅.US interfluous.